myeconlab

www.myeconlab.com

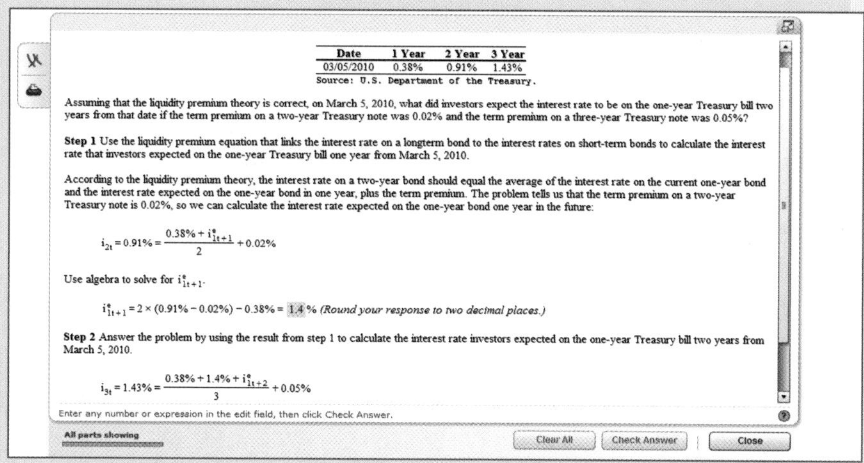

Date 1 Year 2 Year 3 Year
03/05/2010 0.38% 0.91% 1.43%
Source: U.S. Department of the Treasury.
Assuming that the liquidity premium theory is correct, on March 5, 2010, what did investors expect the interest rate to be on the one-year Treasury bill two years from that date if the term premium on a two-year Treasury note was 0.02% and the term premium on a three-year Treasury note was 0.05%?
Step 1 Use the liquidity premium equation that links the interest rate on a longterm bond to the interest rates on short-term bonds to calculate the interest rate that investors expected on the one-year Treasury bill one year from March 5, 2010.
According to the liquidity premium theory, the interest rate on a two-year bond should equal the average of the interest rate on the current one-year bond and the interest rate expected on the one-year bond in one year, plus the term premium. The problem tells us that the term premium on a two-year Treasury note is 0.02%, so we can calculate the interest rate expected on the one-year bond one year in the future:
$i_{2t} = 0.91\% = \frac{0.38\% + i^e_{1t+1}}{2} + 0.02\%$
Use algebra to solve for i^e_{1t+1}.
$i^e_{1t+1} = 2 \times (0.91\% - 0.02\%) - 0.38\% =$ 1.4 % (Round your response to two decimal places.)
Step 2 Answer the problem by using the result from step 1 to calculate the interest rate investors expected on the one-year Treasury bill two years from March 5, 2010.
$i_{3t} = 1.43\% = \frac{0.38\% + 1.4\% + i^e_{1t+2}}{3} + 0.05\%$
Enter any number or expression in the edit field, then click Check Answer.
All parts showing
Clear All
Check Answer
Close

Learning Resources. To further reinforce understanding, Study Plan and Homework problems link to additional learning resources:

- *A step-by-step Guided Solution* helps students break down a problem much the same way as an instructor would do during office hours.
- *The eText page* on which the topic of the exercise is explained promotes reading the text when further explanation is needed.
- *A graphing tool* encourages students to draw and manipulate graphs and deepen their understanding by illustrating economic relationships and ideas.

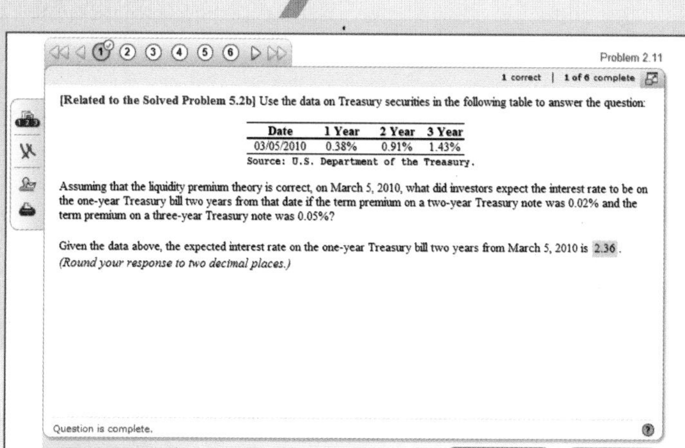

Problem 2.11
1 correct | 1 of 6 complete
[Related to the Solved Problem 5.2b] Use the data on Treasury securities in the following table to answer the question:
Date 1 Year 2 Year 3 Year
03/05/2010 0.38% 0.91% 1.43%
Source: U.S. Department of the Treasury.
Assuming that the liquidity premium theory is correct, on March 5, 2010, what did investors expect the interest rate to be on the one-year Treasury bill two years from that date if the term premium on a two-year Treasury note was 0.02% and the term premium on a three-year Treasury note was 0.05%?
Given the data above, the expected interest rate on the one-year Treasury bill two years from March 5, 2010 is 2.36 .
(Round your response to two decimal places.)
Question is complete.
All parts showing
Similar Exercise
Close

Unlimited Practice. Many Study Plan and Instructor-assigned exercises contain algorithms to ensure students get as much practice as they need.

As students work through Study Plan or Homework exercises, instant feedback and tutorial resources guide them towards understanding.

Macroeconomics

R. GLENN HUBBARD
COLUMBIA UNIVERSITY

ANTHONY PATRICK O'BRIEN
LEHIGH UNIVERSITY

MATTHEW RAFFERTY
QUINNIPIAC UNIVERSITY

PEARSON

Boston Columbus Indianapolis New York San Francisco Upper Saddle River
Amsterdam Cape Town Dubai London Madrid Milan Munich Paris Montreal Toronto
Delhi Mexico City São Paulo Sydney Hong Kong Seoul Singapore Taipei Tokyo

Dedication

For Constance, Raph, and Will
—R. Glenn Hubbard

For Lucy
—Anthony Patrick O'Brien

For Sacha
—Matthew Rafferty

Editorial Director: Sally Yagan
Editor in Chief: Donna Battista
Executive Editor: David Alexander
Executive Development Editor: Lena Buonanno
VP/Director of Development: Stephen Deitmer
Editorial Project Manager: Lindsey Sloan
Director of Marketing: Patrice Jones
Executive Marketing Manager: Lori DeShazo
Market Development Manager: Kathleen McLellan
Senior Managing Editor: Nancy Fenton
Production Project Manager: Carla Thompson
Manufacturing Director: Evelyn Beaton
Senior Manufacturing Buyer: Carol Melville
Creative Director: Christy Mahon
Senior Art Director: Jonathan Boylan
Cover Art: Shutterstock/cobalt88
Manager, Rights and Permissions: Michael Joyce
Text Permissions Editor: Jill Dougan
Media Producer: Melissa Honig
Associate Production Project Manager: Alison Eusden
Full-Service Project Management: PreMediaGlobal
Composition: PreMediaGlobal
Printer/Binder: R.R. Donnelley/Willard
Cover Printer: Lehigh-Phoenix Color/Hagerstown
Text Font: Minion

Credits and acknowledgments of material borrowed from other sources and reproduced, with permission, in this textbook appear on the pages with the respective material.

Cataloging-in-Publication Data is on file at the Library of Congress

10 9 8 7 6 5 4 3 2 1

ISBN 10: 0-13-211047-4
ISBN 13: 978-0-13-211047-1

About the Authors

Glenn Hubbard, Professor, Researcher, and Policymaker

R. Glenn Hubbard is the dean and Russell L. Carson Professor of Finance and Economics in the Graduate School of Business at Columbia University and professor of economics in Columbia's Faculty of Arts and Sciences. He is also a research associate of the National Bureau of Economic Research and a director of Automatic Data Processing, Black Rock Closed-End Funds, KKR Financial Corporation, and MetLife. Professor Hubbard received his Ph.D. in economics from Harvard University in 1983. From 2001 to 2003, he served as chairman of the White House Council of Economic Advisers and chairman of the OECD Economy Policy Committee, and from 1991 to 1993, he was deputy assistant secretary of the U.S. Treasury Department. He currently serves as co-chair of the nonpartisan Committee on Capital Markets Regulation and the Corporate Boards Study Group. Professor Hubbard is the author of more than 100 articles in leading journals, including *American Economic Review*; *Brookings Papers on Economic Activity*; *Journal of Finance*; *Journal of Financial Economics*; *Journal of Money, Credit, and Banking*; *Journal of Political Economy*; *Journal of Public Economics*; *Quarterly Journal of Economics; RAND Journal of Economics*; and *Review of Economics and Statistics.*

Tony O'Brien, Award-Winning Professor and Researcher

Anthony Patrick O'Brien is a professor of economics at Lehigh University. He received a Ph.D. from the University of California, Berkeley, in 1987. He has taught principles of economics, money and banking, and intermediate macroeconomics for more than 20 years, in both large sections and small honors classes. He received the Lehigh University Award for Distinguished Teaching. He was formerly the director of the Diamond Center for Economic Education and was named a Dana Foundation Faculty Fellow and Lehigh Class of 1961 Professor of Economics. He has been a visiting professor at the University of California, Santa Barbara, and Carnegie Mellon University. Professor O'Brien's research has dealt with such issues as the evolution of the U.S. automobile industry, sources of U.S. economic competitiveness, the development of U.S. trade policy, the causes of the Great Depression, and the causes of black–white income differences. His research has been published in leading journals, including *American Economic Review*; *Quarterly Journal of Economics*; *Journal of Money, Credit, and Banking*; *Industrial Relations*; *Journal of Economic History*; *Explorations in Economic History*; and *Journal of Policy History.*

Matthew Rafferty, Professor and Researcher

Matthew Christopher Rafferty is a professor of economics and department chairperson at Quinnipiac University. He has also been a visiting professor at Union College. He received a Ph.D. from the University of California, Davis, in 1997 and has taught intermediate macroeconomics for 15 years, in both large and small sections. Professor Rafferty's research has focused on university and firm-financed research and development activities. In particular, he is interested in understanding how corporate governance and equity compensation influence firm research and development. His research has been published in leading journals, including the *Journal of Financial and Quantitative Analysis, Journal of Corporate Finance, Research Policy,* and the *Southern Economic Journal.* He has worked as a consultant for the Connecticut Petroleum Council on issues before the Connecticut state legislature. He has also written op-ed pieces that have appeared in several newspapers, including the *New York Times.*

Brief Contents

Contents

Chapter 3 The Financial System 59

Chapter 14 Consumption and Investment 521

Chapter 15 The Balance of Payments, Exchange Rates, and Macroeconomic Policy 559

Preface

Why a New Intermediate Macroeconomics Text?

The students enrolled in today's intermediate macroeconomics courses are either undergraduates or master's students who are likely to become entrepreneurs, managers, bankers, stock brokers, accountants, lawyers, or government officials. Very few students will pursue a Ph.D. in economics. Given this student profile, we believe it is important for the course to move from emphasizing models for their own sake to using theory to understand real-world, relevant examples and current policies that are in today's news headlines.

We believe that short-run macroeconomic policy plays too small a role in current texts. There was a time when it seemed self-evident that policy should be the focus of a course in intermediate macroeconomics. The extraordinary macroeconomic events surrounding the Great Depression, World War II, and the immediate postwar era naturally focused the attention of economists on short-run policy measures. But by the 1970s, the conventional Keynesian–neoclassical synthesis of Samuelson, Hansen, and Hicks had come to seem inadequate to many economists. To summarize briefly, the complicated evolution of macroeconomic theory during those years, conventional macroeconomics was seen as being inadequately grounded in microeconomic foundations and as being too neglectful of long-run considerations.

Although macroeconomic theory evolved rapidly during the 1970s and 1980s, intermediate macroeconomic textbooks largely remained unchanged. Only in the 1990s did the first generation of modern intermediate textbooks appear. These new texts dramatically refocused the intermediate course. The result was a welcome emphasis on the long run and on microfoundations. The Solow growth model, rather than the Keynesian *IS–LM* model, became the lynchpin of these texts.

While in many ways we agree with the focus on the long run and on microfoundations, we have found ourselves in our own courses increasingly obliged to supplement existing texts with additional material.

Our Approach

It is important to note that our aim is certainly not to revolutionize the teaching of the intermediate macroeconomics course. Rather, we would like to shift its emphasis. We elaborate on our approach in the next sections.

A Modern Short-Run Model That Is Appropriate for the Intermediate Course (Chapters 9–11)

> "*After developing the theory (i.e., the* IS-LM-MP *model), they used the model to analyze the 2007–09 recession. . . . I really like this approach. And students? Well, they don't like it, they love it . . . when we apply theory to the checkerboard of real life.*"
>
> William Hart, Miami University

> "IS-MP *is a major innovation.*"
>
> James Butkiewicz, University of Delaware

> "*I absolutely love the* IS–MP *model, I think it is more realistic and has been a long time coming. Morphs the theory in well with the graphs that are shown. Clear, and I love the tables like Table 9.2.*"
>
> Nate Perry, Mesa State College

> "*The integration of current economic events with the theory in the chapter is a strength.*"
>
> Soma Ghosh, Albright College

In the texts of the 1980s and earlier, the *IS–LM* model held center stage. The *IS–LM* model provided a useful way for instructors to present the major points of the Keynesian model of how short-run GDP is determined. Investigating the slopes of the *IS* and *LM* curves gave students some insights into the policy debates of the 1960s and early 1970s. In 2011, the *IS–LM* model has two obvious pedagogical shortcomings:

- The Keynesians versus Monetarists debates, while substantively important, are now a part of the history of macroeconomics.
- The assumption of a constant money supply used in constructing the *LM* curve no longer correctly describes the policy approach of the Fed or the central banks of other developed countries. When central banks target interest rates rather than the money stock, the *LM* curve is no longer as useful as it once was in discussing monetary policy.

We do believe that the *IS* curve story provides a good account of the sources of fluctuations in real GDP in the short run when prices are fixed. But, because the Fed targets interest rates rather than the money stock, we substitute a monetary policy, *MP*, curve for the *LM* curve. The result is similar to the *IS–MP* model first suggested by David Romer. We cover the *IS–MP* model in Chapter 9, "*IS–MP:* A Short-Run Macroeconomic Model." We include a full appendix on the *IS–LM* model at the end of this chapter for those who wish to cover that model. We use the *IS–MP* model to analyze monetary policy in Chapter 10, "Monetary Policy in the Short Run," and fiscal policy in the short run in Chapter 11, "Fiscal Policy in the Short Run."

Significant Coverage of Financial Markets, Beginning with Chapter 3

> *"Integrating finance, as opposed to having only a separate chapter, is a strength."*
>
> John Dalton, Wake Forest University

> *"I'm really glad to see financial markets given more coverage in Chapter 3 and throughout the book—this is one of its best features."*
>
> David Gulley, Bentley College

> *"VERY relevant material and also missing from many other books (or at least the one I use)."*
>
> John Brock, University of Colorado

One of the most fundamental observations about conventional monetary policy is that, while the Fed has substantial influence over short-term nominal interest rates, long-term real interest rates have a much larger impact on the spending decisions of households and firms. To understand the link between nominal short-term rates and real long-term rates, students need to be introduced to the role of expectations and the term structure of interest rates. We provide a careful, but concise, discussion of the term structure in Chapter 3, "The Financial System," and follow up this discussion in Chapter 9, "*IS–MP*: A Short-Run Macroeconomic Model," and Chapter 10, "Monetary Policy in the Short Run," by analyzing why the Fed's interest rate targeting may sometimes fail to attain its goals.

The conventional story of central bank targeting of interest rates or monetary aggregates is told in terms of the commercial banking system, so an overview of commercial banks is included in all texts. The explosion in securitization in the past 20 years has caused tremendous changes in the financial system and, recently, in Fed policy. Although securitization has been an important part of the financial system for years, its significance for Fed policy only became clear with the problems in the markets for mortgage-backed securities that developed during 2007. We provide an overview of securitization in Chapter 3, including a discussion of the increased importance of investment banks. Interest rate targeting is simply no longer the be all and end all of Fed policy. The events of 2008 have made it clear that an exclusive focus on commercial banks provides too narrow an overview of the financial system.

Early Discussion of Long-Run Growth (Chapters 4 and 5)

> *"Excellent discussions of potential GDP and aggregate production function [in Chapter 4]."*
>
> Satyajit Ghosh, University of Scranton

> *"The authors are very methodical in their presentation of the model and derivation of the equations [Chapter 5]. Also, I feel the material is well explained. Other books I've read don't do a good job of contextualizing the importance of long-run growth and the relevance of the various determinants of growth. I think this chapter does a pretty remarkable job of that. Especially good is the progression through the various components of the Solow model before it finally arrives at technology—a fine job."*
>
> Douglas Campbell, University of Memphis

Students need to be able to distinguish the macroeconomic forest—long-run growth—from the macroeconomic trees—short-run fluctuations in real GDP, employment, and the rate of inflation. Because many macroeconomic principles texts put a heavy emphasis on the short run, many students enter the intermediate macro course thinking that macroeconomics is *exclusively* concerned with short-run fluctuations. The extraordinary success of the market system in raising the standard of living of the average person in the United States and the other currently developed economies comes as surprising news to many students. Students know where we are today, but the economic explanation of how we got here is unfamiliar to many of them.

In addition, it makes sense to us for students to first understand both a basic model of long-run growth and the determination of GDP in a flexible-price model before moving on to the discussion of short-run fluctuations and short-run policy. In Chapter 4, "Determining Aggregate Production," we show the determination of GDP in a classical model and also discuss the difference between flexible price models and fixed price models. We place this discussion in a broader context of the reallocation of resources. In other words, we emphasize that, for example, the decline in spending on residential construction during 2006–2009 affects short-run real GDP not just because prices are sticky but also because, in the short run, resources cannot be reallocated frictionlessly to new uses. Although economists think of this resource reallocation problem as being fundamentally a question of prices being inflexible in the short run and flexible in the long run, our experience is that students are confused if the dichotomy between the long run and the short run is told entirely in terms of price flexibility.

Modern Federal Reserve Policy and Its Broadened Emphasis Beyond Interest Rate Targeting

The developments of 2007–2009 have demonstrated that the Fed has moved beyond the focus on interest rate targeting that had dominated policy since the early 1980s. To understand the broader reach of Fed policy, students need to be introduced to material, in particular the increased importance of investment banking and role of securitization in modern financial markets, that is largely missing from competing texts. In addition, recent Fed policy initiatives require extended discussion of issues of moral hazard. While these discussions are common in money and banking texts, they have been largely ignored in intermediate macro texts. We cover these topics in Chapter 6, "Money and Inflation," Chapter 10, "Monetary Policy in the Short Run," and Chapter 12, "Aggregate Demand, Aggregate Supply, and Monetary Policy."

Integration of International Topics

When the crisis in subprime mortgages began, Federal Reserve Chairman Ben Bernanke famously observed that it was unlikely to cause much damage to the U.S. housing market, much less the wider economy. (Of course, Bernanke was hardly alone in making such statements.) As it turned out, the subprime crisis devastated not only the U.S. housing market but the U.S. financial system, the U.S. economy, and the economies of most of the developed world. That a problem in one part of one sector of one economy could cause a worldwide crisis is an indication that a textbook on macroeconomics must take seriously the linkages between the U.S. and other economies. We cover these linkages throughout the text. In discussing each topic, we provide data not just for the United States, but for many other countries. We also explore such issues as the European sovereign debt crisis and the increased coordination of monetary policy among central banks.

12 Core Chapters

> *"I like the long-run-first arrangement. I appreciate the "Extensions" at the end; do them as time permits in the term. The inclusion of* IS–LM *as an appendix alongside the more current* IS–MP *model is an excellent idea. I like the relatively limited number of chapters, it's less daunting to students."*
>
> Christopher Burkart, University of West Florida

> *"I like it. It is good to have the financial system early in the book. I always struggle teaching that section since I find it very important for the development of the course."*
>
> Luisa Blanco, Pepperdine University

This text consists of 12 core chapters and 3 "extension" chapters. Many instructors subscribe to the idea that fewer topics covered well is better than many topics covered superficially. However, it can be difficult to find a concise text. We achieve brevity in two ways: First, we ignore almost entirely the "dueling schools of thought" approach. We do this for several reasons: Although this approach at one time provided a useful way of organizing textbooks, it no longer represents well the actual views of the profession. Emphasizing differences among economists obscures for students the broad areas of macroeconomics on which a professional consensus exists. Finally, most students find detailed discussions of disagreements among economists to be dull and unhelpful in understanding today's policy issues.

Our second key to achieving brevity in the core presentation is to push all nonessential topics to a separate Part 4, "Extensions," at the end of the text. While many of the topics covered in the three chapters in Part 4—long-run fiscal challenges (Chapter 13, "Fiscal Policy and the Government Budget in the Long Run"), the microfoundations of consumption and investment decisions (Chapter 14, "Consumption and Investment"), and the balance of payments (Chapter 15, "Balance of Payments, Exchange Rates, and Macroeconomic Policy")—are important (and we typically cover many of them in our own courses), they are not *essential* to the basic macroeconomic story. In our view, it is better for instructors to present students with the key ideas in a relatively brief way with minimum distractions and then consider additional material during the last few weeks of the course when students have mastered the key ideas.

Flexible Chapter Organization

We have written the text to provide instructors with considerable flexibility. Instructors who wish to emphasize the short run can begin by covering Chapters 1–3 (Part 1, "Introduction"), and then jump to Chapters 8–12 (Part 3, "Macroeconomics in the Short Run: Theory and Policy"), before covering Chapters 4–7 (Part 2, "Macroeconomics in the Long Run: Economic Growth"). We have arranged content so that nothing in Chapters 8–12 requires knowledge of the discussion in Chapters 4–7.

Instructors wishing to omit the Solow model of long-run growth can skip Chapters 4, 5, and 13 without loss of continuity.

Special Features

We have developed a number of special features. Some are similar to the features that have proven popular and effective aids to learning in the Hubbard/O'Brien *Principles of Economics* textbook and the Hubbard/O'Brien *Money, Banking, and the Financial System* textbook, while others were developed specifically for this book.

Key Issue-and-Question Approach

To provide a roadmap for the book, we use an issue–question framework that shows why learning macroeconomics gives students the tools they need to analyze intelligently some of the important issues of our time. See pages 16–17 of Chapter 1, "The Long and Short of Macroeconomics," for a complete list of the 14 issues and questions. We start each subsequent chapter with a key issue and key question and end each of those chapters by using the concepts introduced in the chapter to answer the question.

Key Issue and Question

At the end of Chapter 1, we noted key issues and questions that serve as a framework for the book. Here are the key issue and question for this chapter:

Issue: Some countries have experienced rapid rates of long-run economic growth, while other countries have grown slowly, if at all.

Question: Why isn't the whole world rich?

Answered on page 173

Answering the Key Question

Continued from page 143

At the beginning of this chapter, we asked the question:

"Why isn't the whole world rich?"

Our discussion has shown that the growth rate of labor productivity is the key determinant of the growth rate of the standard of living. But what determines the growth rate of labor productivity? According to the Solow growth model, the growth rate of total factor productivity is *the* determinant of the growth rate of labor productivity. As a result, total factor productivity growth causes improvements in the standard of living and economic growth over the long run. We also saw that there is no single factor that causes total factor productivity to grow. The level of technology, the quality of the labor force, the quality of government and social institutions, geography, and the quality of financial institutions all play an important role in explaining differences in total factor productivity across countries. If a country fails to achieve sustained economic growth then, it is due to its failure in one or more of these areas. Therefore, while some countries are simply unlucky because of their geography, other countries are poor because of institutions that their governments are unable, or unwilling to reform.

Contemporary Opening Cases and *An Inside Look* News Articles

"[This book] is very closely related to the current issues and real world. Students should enjoy reading those examples and stories."

Liaoliao Li, Kutztown University

"Engages students in macroeconomics with interesting real-life examples and questions."

Fabio Mendez, University of Arkansas

"I like how they break down the article and guide the student into understanding what the article is pointing to. I do this in class sometimes, and I do find students sometimes don't know what they should be looking for."

Janice Yee, Worcester State University

"I really like the international applications, as I have many students who are coming from overseas."

Serife Nuray Akin, University of Miami

"Similar to the benefit of the solved problems, but with an emphasis on more relatable 'real world' issues. These are nice because they are not straightforward applications of the concepts, which force students to apply and link multiple concepts."

Guy Yamashiro, California State University, Long Beach

A common complaint among students is that economics is too dry and abstract. At the intermediate level, students will inevitably have to learn a greater amount of model building and algebra than they encountered in their principles course. Nevertheless, a real-world approach can keep students interested. We open each chapter with a real-world example—drawn from either policy issues in the news or the business world—to help students begin the chapter with a greater understanding that the material to be covered is directly relevant. We revisit the example within the chapter to reinforce the link between macroeconomics and the real world.

CHAPTER 9

IS–MP: A Short-Run Macroeconomic Model

LEARNING OBJECTIVES

After studying this chapter, you should be able to:

- **9.1** Explain how the *IS* curve represents the relationship between the real interest rate and aggregate expenditure (pages 304–312)
- **9.2** Use the monetary policy, *MP*, curve to show how the interest rate set by the central bank helps to determine the output gap (pages 312–319)
- **9.3** Use the *IS–MP* model to understand why real GDP fluctuates (pages 319–327)
- **9.4** Understand the role of the Phillips curve in the *IS–MP* model (pages 327–338)
- **9.5** Use the *IS–MP* model to understand the performance of the U.S. economy during the recession of 2007–2009 (pages 339–342)
- **9A** Use the *IS–LM* model to illustrate macroeconomic equilibrium (pages 353–362)

THE LEHMAN BROTHERS BANKRUPTCY AND THE GREAT RECESSION OF 2007–2009

In December 1930, the Bank of United States, a large private bank located in New York City, collapsed. The bank ran into trouble in part because an unusually high percentage of its loans were in real estate. By the fall of 1930, the prices of houses, as well as office buildings and other commercial real estate, were falling, and borrowers were defaulting on mortgages. The failure of the Bank of United States triggered a wave of banking failures that

Nearly 78 years later, the bankruptcy of Wall Street investment bank Lehman Brothers on Monday, September 15, 2008, helped turn a serious financial situation into a financial crisis that severely worsened the recession that had begun in December 2007. At the time, Lehman Brothers was the fourth-largest U.S. investment bank. The bankruptcy of Lehman Brothers was linked in part to its role in the market for mortgage-backed securities.

kets declined by almost $2.85 trillion, which represented about 6% of the value of these markets. The flow of funds through the financial system was disrupted, causing real GDP and employment in the United States to decline sharply. Some economists believe that the failure of Lehman Brothers was a symptom of the underlying problems in the financial system. These economists argue that even if Lehman Brothers had avoided bankruptcy, the results for the financial system and the economy would have been much the same. In any event, it is clear that the financial crisis and the economic recession became much more severe beginning about the time that Lehman Brothers failed.

ys an important role in the transfer of funds s to borrowers, who use the funds to buy con- and investment goods. More important than its ts, the Lehman Brothers bankruptcy generated ut the ability of other investment banks, as well as many commercial banks and other financial institutions to survive. As a result, it became very difficult for many financial institutions to borrow from each other or from investors, as lenders feared that borrowers would not pay them back. When financial institutions have difficulty borrowing, they reduce lending to households and firms, so consumption and investment expenditures decrease. The reduction in these expenditures deepened the global recession.

AN INSIDE LOOK AT POLICY on page 344 discusses the financial reform bill signed into law by President Obama in July 2010.

Sources: Bob Ivry, Christine Harper, and Mark Pittman, "Missing Lehman Lesson of Shakeout Means Too Big Banks May Fail," *Bloomberg.com*, September 7, 2009; "What If?" *Economist*, September 12, 2009; Chris Giles, "Bank Failure That Triggered the Panic," *Financial Times*, September 14, 2009; Gary Duncan, "Lehman Brothers Collapse Sends Shockwaves Round World," *Times Online*, September 16, 2008; and U.S. Bureau of Economic Analysis.

We close each chapter with *An Inside Look*, a two-page feature that shows students how to apply the concepts from the chapter to the analysis of a news article. This feature presents an excerpt from an article, an analysis of the article, one or more graphs, and critical thinking questions. Several articles deal with policy issues. Articles are from sources such as the *Wall Street Journal*, the *Economist*, and *Bloomberg BusinessWeek*.

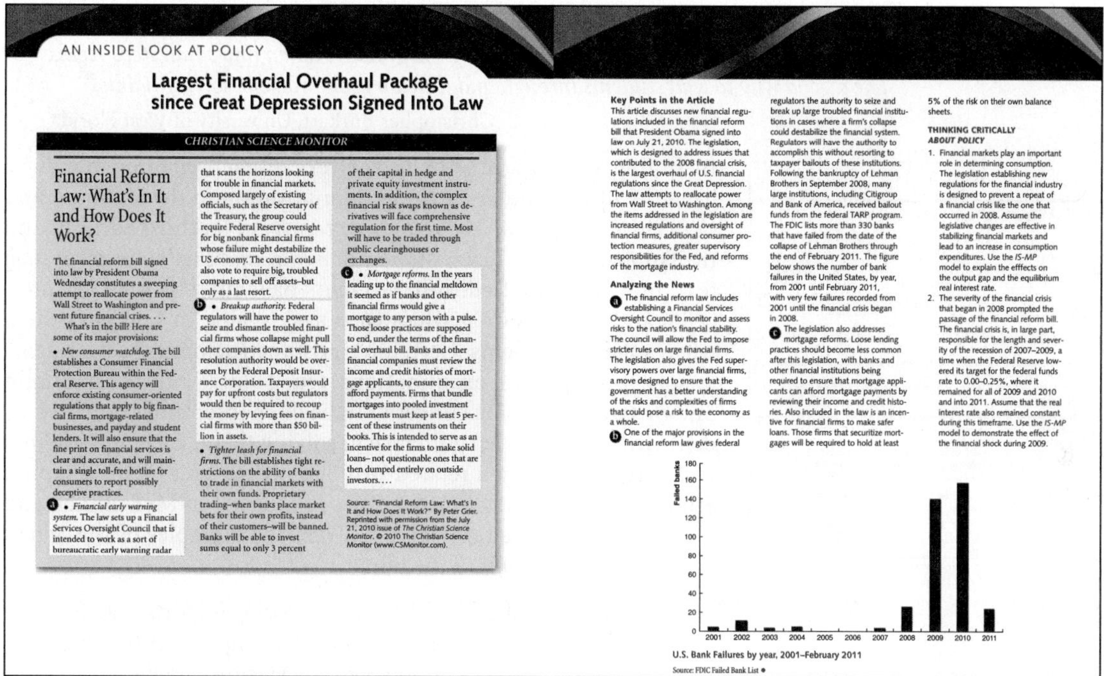

AN INSIDE LOOK AT POLICY

Largest Financial Overhaul Package since Great Depression Signed Into Law

CHRISTIAN SCIENCE MONITOR

Financial Reform Law: What's In It and How Does It Work?

The financial reform bill signed into law by President Obama Wednesday constitutes a sweeping attempt to reallocate power from Wall Street to Washington and prevent future financial crises. . . .

What's in the bill? Here are some of its major provisions:

• *New consumer watchdog.* The bill establishes a Consumer Financial Protection Bureau within the Federal Reserve. This agency will enforce existing consumer-oriented regulations that apply to big financial firms, mortgage-related businesses, and payday and student lenders. It will also ensure that the fine print on financial services is clear and accurate, and will maintain a single toll-free hotline for consumers to report possibly deceptive practices.

(a) • *Financial early warning system.* The law sets up a Financial Services Oversight Council that is intended to work as a sort of bureaucratic early warning radar that scans the horizons looking for trouble in financial markets. Composed largely of existing officials, such as the Secretary of the Treasury, the group could require Federal Reserve oversight for big nonbank financial firms whose failure might destabilize the US economy. The council could also vote to require big, troubled companies to sell off assets–but only as a last resort.

(b) • *Breakup authority.* Federal regulators will have the power to seize and dismantle troubled financial firms whose collapse might pull other companies down as well. This resolution authority would be overseen by the Federal Deposit Insurance Corporation. Taxpayers would pay for upfront costs but regulators would then be required to recoup the money by levying fees on financial firms with more than $50 billion in assets.

• *Tighter leash for financial firms.* The bill establishes tight restrictions on the ability of banks to trade in financial markets with their own funds. Proprietary trading–when banks place market bets for their own profits, instead of their customers–will be banned. Banks will be able to invest sums equal to only 3 percent of their capital in hedge and private equity investment instruments. In addition, the complex financial risk swaps known as derivatives will face comprehensive regulation for the first time. Most will have to be traded through public clearinghouses or exchanges.

(c) • *Mortgage reforms.* In the years leading up to the financial meltdown it seemed as if banks and other financial firms would give a mortgage to any person with a pulse. Those loose practices are supposed to end, under the terms of the financial overhaul bill. Banks and other financial companies must review the income and credit histories of mortgage applicants, to ensure they can afford payments. Firms that bundle mortgages into pooled investment instruments must keep at least 5 percent of these instruments on their books. This is intended to serve as an incentive for the firms to make solid loans– not questionable ones that are then dumped entirely on outside investors. . . .

Source: "Financial Reform Law: What's In It and How Does It Work?" By Peter Grier. Reprinted with permission from the July 21, 2010 issue of *The Christian Science Monitor*. © 2010 The Christian Science Monitor (www.CSMonitor.com).

Key Points in the Article

This article discusses new financial regulations included in the financial reform bill that President Obama signed into law on July 21, 2010. The legislation, which is designed to address issues that contributed to the 2008 financial crisis, is the largest overhaul of U.S. financial regulations since the Great Depression. The law attempts to reallocate power from Wall Street to Washington. Among the items addressed in the legislation are increased regulations and oversight of financial firms, additional consumer protection measures, greater supervisory responsibilities for the Fed, and reforms of the mortgage industry.

Analyzing the News

(a) The financial reform law includes establishing a Financial Services Oversight Council to monitor and assess risks to the nation's financial stability. The council will allow the Fed to impose stricter rules on large financial firms. The legislation also gives the Fed supervisory powers over large financial firms, a move designed to ensure that the government has a better understanding of the risks and complexities of firms that could pose a risk to the economy as a whole.

(b) One of the major provisions in the financial reform law gives federal regulators the authority to seize and break up large troubled financial institutions in cases where a firm's collapse could destabilize the financial system. Regulators will have the authority to accomplish this without resorting to taxpayer bailouts of these institutions. Following the bankruptcy of Lehman Brothers in September 2008, many large institutions, including Citigroup and Bank of America, received bailout funds from the federal TARP program. The FDIC lists more than 330 banks that have failed from the date of the collapse of Lehman Brothers through the end of February 2011. The figure below shows the number of bank failures in the United States, by year, from 2001 until February 2011, with very few failures recorded from 2001 until the financial crisis began in 2008.

(c) The legislation also addresses mortgage reforms. Loose lending practices should become less common after this legislation, with banks and other financial institutions being required to ensure that mortgage applicants can afford mortgage payments by reviewing their income and credit histories. Also included in the law is an incentive for financial firms to make safer loans. Those firms that securitize mortgages will be required to hold at least 5% of the risk on their own balance sheets.

THINKING CRITICALLY *ABOUT POLICY*

1. Financial markets play an important role in determining consumption. The legislation establishing new regulations for the financial industry is designed to prevent a repeat of a financial crisis like the one that occurred in 2008. Assume the legislative changes are effective in stabilizing financial markets and lead to an increase in consumption expenditures. Use the *IS-MP* model to explain the efffects on the output gap and the equilibrium real interest rate.
2. The severity of the financial crisis that began in 2008 prompted the passage of the financial reform bill. The financial crisis is, in large part, responsible for the length and severity of the recession of 2007–2009, a time when the Federal Reserve lowered its target for the federal funds rate to 0.00–0.25%, where it remained for all of 2009 and 2010 and into 2011. Assume that the real interest rate also remained constant during this timeframe. Use the *IS-MP* model to demonstrate the effect of the financial shock during 2009.

U.S. Bank Failures by year, 2001–February 2011

Source: FDIC Failed Bank List

The following are some examples:

Chapter 3, "The Financial System"

Opens with "The Wonderful World of Credit," a discussion of how consumer and small business access to bank loans contributed to the financial crisis.

Ends with "Credit Market Easing for Small Businesses," a news article and analysis about the improving credit market for small business and possible effects on employment.

Chapter 7, "The Labor Market"

Opens with "Ernst & Young and Pharmaceutical Firms Are Hiring, So What's the Problem?", a discussion of how some firms during the financial crisis continued to seek and hire skilled workers.

Ends with "Unemployment Rate Falls, yet Remains Significantly Lower than Underemployment Rate," a news article and analysis about unemployment measures.

Chapter 8, "Business Cycles"

Opens with "Ford Rides the Business Cycle Rollercoaster," a discussion of Ford sales during business cycles.

Ends with "New Vehicle Sales Increase by 11 Percent in 2010," a news article and analysis about positive sales results for the close of 2010 but a caution about how rising gas prices could affect future sales.

Chapter 9, "*IS–MP*: A Short-Run Macroeconomic Model"

Opens with "The Lehman Brothers Bankruptcy and the Great Recession of 2007–2009."

Ends with "Largest Financial Overhaul Package since Great Depression Signed into Law," a news article about the financial reform bill that President Obama signed into law in 2010.

Solved Problem Feature

"The step-by-step approach to the problem is very clear and makes the material digestible to the students by breaking it down. The tie-in to end-of-chapter exercises is excellent. The student can very quickly see where to go for more practice."

Francis Mummery, California State University Fullerton

"I appreciate the connection between the solved problem and one of the end-of-chapter problems—this is an excellent idea. Breaking the problem down into small steps seems like a good way to lead students through and develop good problem-solving habits."

Christopher Burkart, University of West Florida

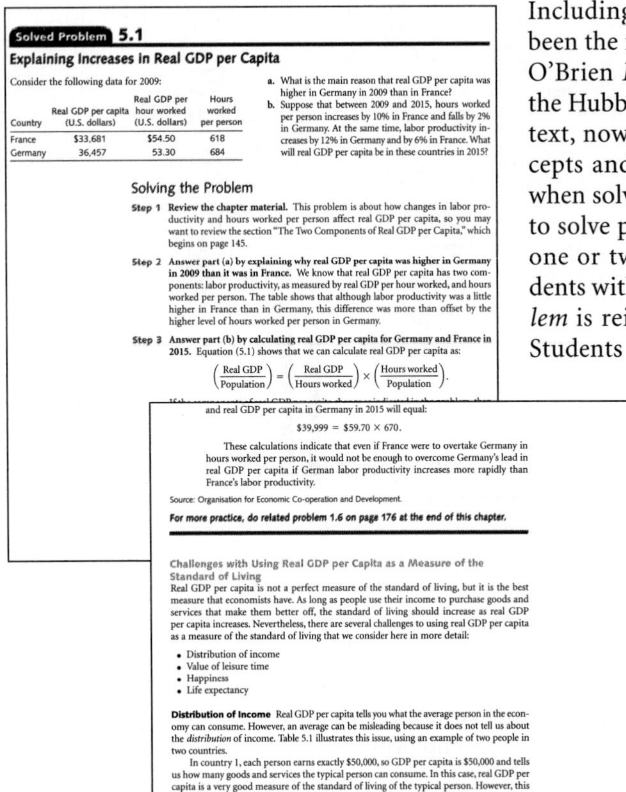

Solved Problem 5.1

Explaining Increases in Real GDP per Capita

Consider the following data for 2009:

Country	Real GDP per capita (U.S. dollars)	Real GDP per hour worked (U.S. dollars)	Hours worked per person
France	$33,681	$54.50	618
Germany	36,457	53.30	684

a. What is the main reason that real GDP per capita was higher in Germany in 2009 than in France?
b. Suppose that between 2009 and 2015, hours worked per person increases by 10% in France and falls by 2% in Germany. At the same time, labor productivity increases by 12% in Germany and by 6% in France. What will real GDP per capita be in these countries in 2015?

Solving the Problem

Step 1 **Review the chapter material.** This problem is about how changes in labor productivity and hours worked per person affect real GDP per capita, so you may want to review the section "The Two Components of Real GDP per Capita," which begins on page 145.

Step 2 **Answer part (a) by explaining why real GDP per capita was higher in Germany in 2009 than it was in France.** We know that real GDP per capita has two components: labor productivity, as measured by real GDP per hour worked, and hours worked per person. The table shows that although labor productivity was a little higher in France than in Germany, this difference was more than offset by the higher level of hours worked per person in Germany.

Step 3 **Answer part (b) by calculating real GDP per capita for Germany and France in 2015.** Equation (5.1) shows that we can calculate real GDP per capita as:

$$\left(\frac{\text{Real GDP}}{\text{Population}}\right) = \left(\frac{\text{Real GDP}}{\text{Hours worked}}\right) \times \left(\frac{\text{Hours worked}}{\text{Population}}\right).$$

and real GDP per capita in Germany in 2015 will equal:

$$\$39{,}999 = \$59.70 \times 670.$$

These calculations indicate that even if France were to overtake Germany in hours worked per person, it would not be enough to overcome Germany's lead in real GDP per capita if German labor productivity increases more rapidly than France's labor productivity.

Source: Organisation for Economic Co-operation and Development.

For more practice, do related problem 1.6 on page 176 at the end of this chapter.

Challenges with Using Real GDP per Capita as a Measure of the Standard of Living

Real GDP per capita is not a perfect measure of the standard of living, but it is the best measure that economists have. As long as people use their income to purchase goods and services that make them better off, the standard of living should increase as real GDP per capita increases. Nevertheless, there are several challenges to using real GDP per capita as a measure of the standard of living that we consider here in more detail:

- Distribution of income
- Value of leisure time
- Happiness
- Life expectancy

Distribution of Income Real GDP per capita tells you what the average person in the economy can consume. However, an average can be misleading because it does not tell us about the *distribution* of income. Table 5.1 illustrates this issue, using an example of two people in two countries.

In country 1, each person earns exactly $50,000, so GDP per capita is $50,000 and tells us how many goods and services the typical person can consume. In this case, real GDP per capita is a very good measure of the standard of living of the typical person. However, this

Including solved problems in the text of each chapter may have been the most popular pedagogical innovation in the Hubbard and O'Brien *Principles of Economics* text, now in its third edition, and the Hubbard and O'Brien *Money, Banking, and the Financial System* text, now in its first edition. Students have fully learned the concepts and theories only when they are capable of applying them when solving problems. Certainly, most instructors expect students to solve problems on examinations. Our *Solved Problems* highlight one or two important concepts in each chapter and provide students with step-by-step guidance in solving them. Each *Solved Problem* is reinforced by a related problem at the end of the chapter. Students can complete related *Solved Problems* on MyEconLab and receive tutorial help. Here are examples of the *Solved Problems* in the book:

- Solved Problem 1.2: Do Rising Imports Lead to a Permanent Reduction in U.S. Employment? (Chapter 1, "The Long and Short of Macroeconomics")
- Solved Problem 3.3: Using the Loanable Funds Model to Analyze the U.S. Economy in 2010 (Chapter 3, "The Financial System")
- Solved Problem 10.4: Did the Federal Reserve Make the Great Depression Worse? (Chapter 10, "Monetary Policy in the Short Run")

Making the Connection Feature

Each chapter includes two to four *Making the Connection* features that present real-world reinforcement of key concepts and help students learn how to interpret what they read on the Web and in newspapers. Most *Making the Connection* features use relevant, stimulating, and provocative news stories, many focused on pressing policy issues. Here are some examples:

- Will China's Standard of Living Ever Exceed That of the United States? (Chapter 5, "Long-Run Economic Growth")
- Job Security and Job Hiring at France Télécom SA (Chapter 7, "The Labor Market")
- The Bankruptcy of Lehman Brothers, the Financial Crisis, and the Financing of Investment (Chapter 9, "*IS–MP*: A Short-Run Macroeconomic Model")
- "Too Big to Fail"—The Legacy of Continental Illinois (Chapter 10, "Monetary Policy in the Short Run")
- State and Local Government Spending During the 2007–2009 Recession (Chapter 11, "Fiscal Policy in the Short Run")

Macro Data Feature

Most chapters include a *Macro Data* feature that explains the sources of macroeconomic data and often cites recent studies using data. This feature helps students apply data to a recent event. An exercise related to each feature appears at the end of the chapter so instructors can test students' understanding.

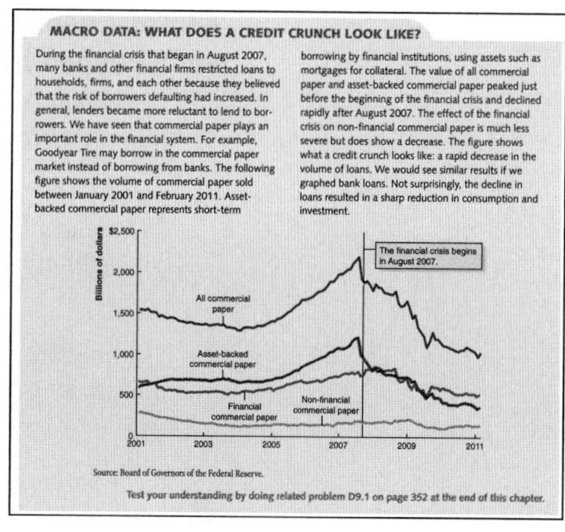

MACRO DATA: WHAT DOES A CREDIT CRUNCH LOOK LIKE?

During the financial crisis that began in August 2007, many banks and other financial firms restricted loans to households, firms, and each other because they believed that the risk of borrowers defaulting had increased. In general, lenders became more reluctant to lend to borrowers. We have seen that commercial paper plays an important role in the financial system. For example, Goodyear Tire may borrow in the commercial paper market instead of borrowing from banks. The following figure shows the volume of commercial paper sold between January 2001 and February 2011. Asset-backed commercial paper represents short-term borrowing by financial institutions, using assets such as mortgages for collateral. The value of all commercial paper and asset-backed commercial paper peaked just before the beginning of the financial crisis and declined rapidly after August 2007. The effect of the financial crisis on non-financial commercial paper is much less severe but does show a decrease. The figure shows what a credit crunch looks like: a rapid decrease in the volume of loans. We would see similar results if we graphed bank loans. Not surprisingly, the decline in loans resulted in a sharp reduction in consumption and investment.

Source: Board of Governors of the Federal Reserve.

Test your understanding by doing related problem D9.1 on page 352 at the end of this chapter.

Graphs and Summary Tables

We use four devices to help students read and interpret graphs:

1. Detailed captions
2. Boxed notes
3. Color-coded curves
4. Summary tables with graphs

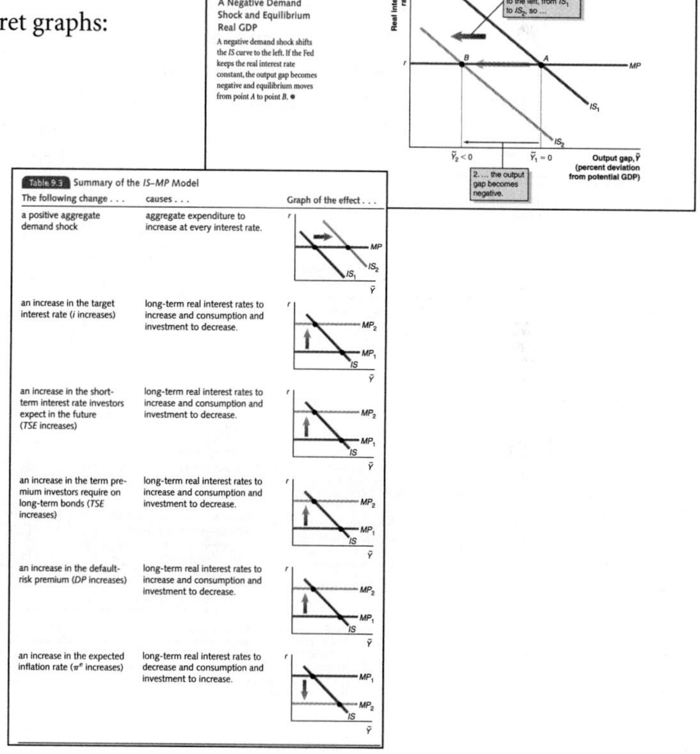

Figure 9.12
A Negative Demand Shock and Equilibrium Real GDP

A negative demand shock shifts the *IS* curve to the left. If the Fed keeps the real interest rate constant, the output gap becomes negative and equilibrium moves from point *A* to point *B*.

Table 9.3 Summary of the *IS–MP* Model

The following change . . .	causes . . .	Graph of the effect . . .
a positive aggregate demand shock	aggregate expenditure to increase at every interest rate.	
an increase in the target interest rate (*i* increases)	long-term real interest rates to increase and consumption and investment to decrease.	
an increase in the short-term interest rate investors expect in the future (*TSE* increases)	long-term real interest rates to increase and consumption and investment to decrease.	
an increase in the term premium investors require on long-term bonds (*TSE* increases)	long-term real interest rates to increase and consumption and investment to decrease.	
an increase in the default-risk premium (*DP* increases)	long-term real interest rates to increase and consumption and investment to decrease.	
an increase in the expected inflation rate (π^e increases)	long-term real interest rates to decrease and consumption and investment to increase.	

End-of-Chapter Problems Written Around the Award-Winning MyEconLab and Grouped by Learning Objective

"I like that this book asks students to interpret quotes from policymakers, speeches and from newspaper articles."

George Hall, Brandeis University

"There are lots of questions and problems for each section and some good data problems also."

Soma Ghosh, Albright College

"Organizing the problems by topic is a wonderful idea that will help both instructors and students."

Kevin Sylwester, Southern Illinois University

"The summary-exercise-summary-exercise breakdown is stellar. This makes it so much easier for students to follow the material and know where to look in the chapter if necessary for additional reinforcement of key ideas."

Francis Mummery, California State University, Fullerton

Each chapter ends with a *Summary, Review Questions, Problems and Applications,* and *Data Exercises.* The problems are written to be fully compatible with MyEconLab, an online course management, testing, and tutorial resource. Using MyEconLab, students can complete select end-of-chapter problems online, get tutorial help, and receive instant feedback and assistance on those exercises they answer incorrectly. Instructors can access sample tests, study plan exercises, tutorial resources, and an online Gradebook to keep track of student performance and time spent on the exercises. MyEconLab has been a successful component of the Hubbard and O'Brien *Principles of Economics* and *Money, Banking, and the Financial System* texts because it helps students improve their grades and helps instructors manage class time.

The *Summary, Review Questions,* and *Problems and Applications* are grouped under learning objectives. The goals of this organization are to make it easier for instructors to assign problems based on learning objectives, both in the book and in MyEconLab, and to help students efficiently review material that they find difficult. If students have difficulty with a particular learning objective, an instructor can easily identify which end-of-chapter questions and problems support that objective and assign them as homework or discuss them in class.

We include one or more end-of-chapter problems that test students' understanding of the content presented in each *Solved Problem, Making the Connection, Macro Data,* and chapter opener. Instructors can cover a feature in class and assign the corresponding problem for homework. The Test Item File also includes test questions that pertain to these special features.

9.1 The *IS* Curve: The Relationship Between Real Interest Rates and Aggregate Expenditure

Explain how the *IS* curve represents the relationship between the real interest rate and aggregate expenditure.

SUMMARY

The ***IS–MP* model** consists of an *IS* curve, an *MP* curve, and a Phillips curve. The ***IS* curve** shows the relationship between the real interest rate and output. The ***MP* curve** shows the relationship between the real interest rate that the central bank targets and the output gap. As the real interest rate increases, consumption and investment expenditures decrease, so real GDP also decreases. As the real interest rate decreases, consumption and investment expenditures increase, so real GDP also increases. Changes in the real interest rate cause movements along an existing *IS* curve. Changes in other de-

1.6 Explain how the *IS* curve represents equilibrium in the goods market.

1.7 Why is the *IS* curve downward sloping?

1.8 Why does investment increase when real interest rates are lower?

1.9 Give an example of a shock that could shift the *IS* curve to the left.

1.10 Give an example of a shock that could shift the *IS* curve to the right.

GDP also decreases. As the real interest rate decreases, consumption and investment expenditures increase, so real GDP also increases. Changes in the real interest rate cause movements along an existing *IS* curve. Changes in other de-terminants of aggregate expenditure—such as wealth and expectations about future income—cause the *IS* curve to shift. The **multiplier effect** explains why changes in autonomous expenditure cause larger changes in real GDP.

Review Questions

1.1 What is the definition of aggregate expenditure?

1.2 How might actual investment spending be different from planned investment spending?

1.3 Explain how equilibrium output is determined in the goods market.

1.4 Why does a change in autonomous expenditure lead to a larger change in real GDP?

1.5 What is the formula for the m… do different values of the marg…

…of a shock that could shift the *IS* curve to the left.

1.10 Give an example of a shock that could shift the *IS* curve to the right.

Problems and Applications

1.11 Draw a graph of the goods market and identify the equilibrium level of GDP. Then use your graph to show the effect of each of the following changes:

a. Households become more pessimistic and decide to buy fewer new homes.

b. The government increases transfer payments without changing taxes.

c. Consumers feel wealthier and want to spend more.

d. Prices rise in the rest of the world, making U.S.

3.3 **[Related to *Solved Problem 9.3* on page 325]** In the early 1990s, Japan's economy experienced a number of shocks due to the bursting of bubbles in real estate and the stock market.

a. Use the *IS–MP* model to show the economy's equilibrium prior to the shocks.

b. Now show how the shocks affected the economy. What happened to the real interest rate, real GDP, and the output gap?

c. The Bank of Japan responded to the shocks by reducing its target interest rate. How would this action affect real GDP and the output gap?

3.4 **[Related to the *Making the Connection* on page 322]** In the early 1990s, Finland experienced a severe recession in which real GDP decreased by 14% and the unemployment rate increased from 3% to nearly 20%. The causes of the depression were in some ways similar to the causes of the 2007–2009 recession in the United States: Earlier financial deregulation led to a boom, in this case largely financed by foreign borrowing. An asset boom caused the prices of most assets, including real estate and stock, to increase rapidly. In addition, the Soviet Union collapsed in 1991, Finland lost its largest trading partner, and at the same time, bank regulations changed, tightening credit standards.

the money supply.

a. What does this increase in the money supply imply about the target federal funds rate?

b. Show the effect in the *IS–MP* model and demonstrate the effect on the output gap.

c. If this increase in the growth rate of the money supply is expected to be permanent, is it likely that the expected inflation rate will remain constant? Briefly explain.

3.7 The effectiveness of monetary policy in changing output depends on the slope of the *IS* curve, which in turn depends on the responsiveness of investment and consumption to the real interest rate. The graph below shows two *IS* curves. IS_1 shows the case where households and firms do not increase consumption and investment much in response to lower interest rates; for IS_2, households and firms are more responsive.

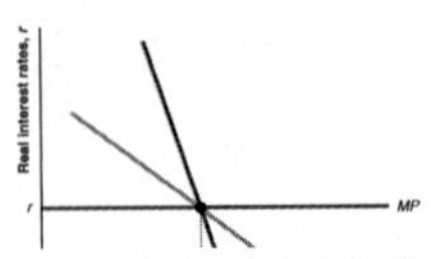

Supplements

The authors and Pearson Education/Prentice Hall have worked together to integrate the text, print, and media resources to make teaching and learning easier.

MyEconLab is a powerful assessment and tutorial system that works hand-in-hand with *Macroeconomics.* MyEconLab includes comprehensive homework, quiz, test, and tutorial options, allowing instructors to manage all assessment needs in one program. Here are the key features of MyEconLab:

- Select end-of-chapter Questions and Problems, including algorithmic, graphing, and numerical questions and problems, are available for student practice or instructor assignment.
- Test Item File multiple-choice questions are available for assignment as homework.
- The Custom Exercise Builder allows instructors the flexibility of creating their own problems or modifying existing problems for assignment.
- The powerful Gradebook records each student's performance and time spent on the Tests and Study Plan and generates reports by student or chapter.

A more detailed walk-through of the student benefits and features of MyEconLab can be found at the beginning of this book. Visit **www.myeconlab.com** for more information on and an online demonstration of instructor and student features.

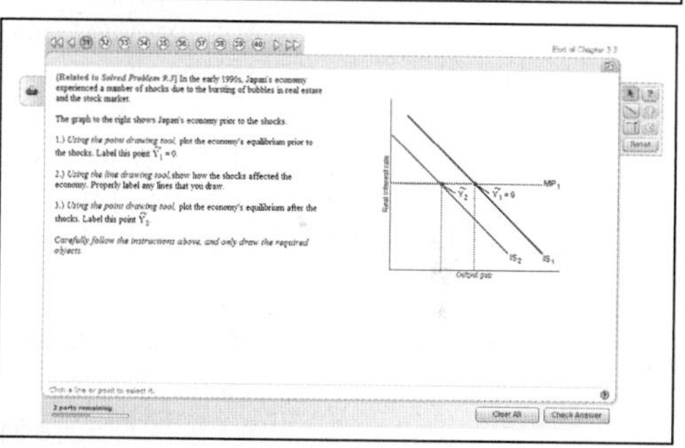

MyEconLab content has been created through the efforts of Melissa Honig, executive media producer; and Noel Lotz and Courtney Kamauf, content leads.

Instructor's Manual

Edward Scahill of the University of Scranton prepared the *Instructor's Manual,* which includes chapter-by-chapter summaries, key term definitions, teaching outlines with teaching tips, and solutions to all review questions and problems in the book. The solutions were prepared by Leonie Stone of State University of New York at Geneseo. The *Instructor's Manual* is available for download from the Instructor's Resource Center (**www.pearsonhighered.com/hubbard**).

Test Item File

Randy Methenitis of Richland College prepared the Test Item File, which includes more than 1,500 multiple-choice, short-answer, and essay questions. Test questions are annotated with the following information:

- **Difficulty:** 1 for straight recall, 2 for some analysis, 3 for complex analysis
- **Type:** Multiple-choice, short-answer, essay
- **Topic:** The term or concept the question supports
- **Learning objective:** The major sections of the main text and its end-of-chapter questions and problems are organized by learning objective. The test item file questions

continue with this organization to make it easy for instructors to assign questions based on the objective they wish to emphasize.

- **Advanced Collegiate Schools of Business (AACSB) Assurance of Learning Standards:** Communication; Ethical Reasoning; Analytic Skills; Use of Information Technology; Multicultural and Diversity; and Reflective Thinking
- **Page number:** The page in the main text where the answer appears allows instructors to direct students to where supporting content appears.
- **Special feature in the main book:** Chapter-opening story, the *Key Issue and Question*, *Solved Problem*, *Making the Connection*, *Macro Data*, and *An Inside Look*.

The Test Item File is available for download from the Instructor's Resource Center (**www.pearsonhighered.com/hubbard**).

The multiple-choice questions in the Test Item File are also available in TestGen software for both Windows and Mac computers, and questions can be assigned via MyEconLab. The computerized TestGen package allows instructors to customize, save, and generate classroom tests. The TestGen program permits instructors to edit, add, or delete questions from the Test Item Files; analyze test results; and organize a database of tests and student results. This software allows for extensive flexibility and ease of use. It provides many options for organizing and displaying tests, along with search and sort features. The software and the Test Item Files can be downloaded from the Instructor's Resource Center (**www.pearsonhighered.com/hubbard**).

PowerPoint Lecture Presentation

The PowerPoint slides were prepared by Andre Neveu of James Madison University. Instructors can use the slides for class presentations, and students can use them for lecture preview or review. These slides include all the graphs, tables, and equations in the textbook.

Student versions of the PowerPoint slides are available as PDF files. These files allow students to print the slides and bring them to class for note taking. Instructors can download these PowerPoint presentations from the Instructor's Resource Center (**www.pearsonhighered.com/hubbard**).

Blackboard and WebCT Course Content

Pearson Education offers fully customizable course content for the Blackboard and WebCT Course Management Systems.

Instructors CourseSmart goes beyond traditional expectations, providing instant online access to the textbooks and course materials you need at a lower cost to students. And, even as students save money, you can save time and hassle with a digital textbook that allows you to search the most relevant content at the very moment you need it. Whether it's evaluating textbooks or creating lecture notes to help students with difficult concepts, CourseSmart can make life a little easier. See how when you visit **www.coursesmart.com/instructors.**

Students CourseSmart goes beyond traditional expectations, providing instant, online access to the textbooks and course materials students need at lower cost. They can also search, highlight, and take notes anywhere, at any time. See all the benefits to students at **www.coursesmart.com/students.**

Class Testers, Reviewers, and Other Contributors

The guidance and recommendations of the following instructors helped us to craft the content, organization, and features of this text. While we could not incorporate every suggestion from every reviewer, we carefully considered each piece of advice we received. We are grateful for the hard work that went into their reviews and truly believe that their feedback was indispensable in developing this text. We appreciate their assistance in making this the best text it could be; they have helped teach a new generation of students about the exciting world of macroeconomics.

Special thanks to Edward Scahill of the University of Scranton for preparing many of the *Making the Connection* features, Randy Methenitis for preparing the *An Inside Look* news feature that ends each chapter, and Leonie Stone of State University of New York at Geneseo for preparing many of the end-of-chapter questions and problems.

Class Testers

We extend special thanks to both the instructors who class tested manuscript chapters and their nearly 200 students for providing recommendations on how to make the chapters engaging and relevant.

Gilad Aharonovitz, Washington State University
Don Coes, University of New Mexico
Kelfala Kallon, University of Northern Colorado
Jeffrey Miller, University of Delaware
Andre Neveu, James Madison University
Walter Park, American University

Reviewers and Focus Group Participants

We also appreciate the thoughtful comments of our reviewers and focus group participants. They brought home to us once again that there are many ways to teach a macroeconomics class. We hope that we have written a text with sufficient flexibility to meet the needs of most instructors. We carefully read and considered every comment and suggestion we received and incorporated many of them into the text. We believe that our text has been greatly improved as a result of the review process.

Gilad Aharonovitz, Washington State University
Francis Ahking, University of Connecticut–Storrs
Nazneen Ahmad, Weber State University
Mohammed Akacem, Metropolitan State College of Denver
Serife Nuray Akin, University of Miami
Laurence Ales, Carnegie Mellon University
David Altig, University of Chicago
J. J. Arias, Georgia College and State University
Mina Baliamoune, University of North Florida
Erol Balkan, Hamilton College
King Banaian, St. Cloud State University
Cynthia Bansak, St. Lawrence University
Eugene Bempong Nyantakyi, West Virginia University
Doris Bennett, Jacksonville State University
Randall Bennett, Gonzaga University
Charles Scott Benson Jr., Idaho State University
Paul Blackely, Le Moyne College
Luisa Blanco, Pepperdine University
Joanne M. Blankenship, State Fair Community College
Emma Bojinova, Canisius College
Inoussa Boubacar, University of Wisconsin–Stout
Mark Brady, San Jose State University
David Brasfield, Murray State University
John Brock, University of Colorado, Colorado Springs
Christopher Burkart, University of West Florida
James Butkiewicz, University of Delaware
Colleen Callahan, American University
Douglas Campbell, University of Memphis
Bolong Cao, Ohio University
Matthew Chambers, Towson University

Marcelle Chauvet, University of California–Riverside
Darian Chin, California State University, Los Angeles
Susanne Chuku, Westfield State University
Donald Coes, University of New Mexico
Olivier Coibion, College of William and Mary
Mark Cullivan, University of San Diego
John T. Dalton, Wake Forest University
H. Evren Damar, State University of New York-Brockport
Stephen Davis, Southwest Minnesota State University
Dennis Debrecht, Carroll University
Greg Delemeester, Marietta College
James Devine, Loyola Marymount University
Dennis Edwards, Coastal Carolina University
Ryan Edwards, Queens College, City University of New York
Wayne Edwards, University of Alaska–Anchorage
Christine Farrell, University of the Ozarks
John Flanders, Central Methodist University
Timothy Ford, California State University–Sacramento
Johanna Francis, Fordham University
Joseph Friedman, Temple University
Timothy Fuerst, Bowling Green State University
William T. Ganley, Buffalo State College
Phillip Garner, Brigham Young University
Doris Geide-Stevenson, Weber State University
Sarah Ghosh, University of Scranton
Satyajit Ghosh, University of Scranton
Soma Ghosh, Albright College
Robert Gillette, University of Kentucky
Tuncer Gocmen, Shepherd University
Robert Godby, University of Wyoming
William Goffe, State University of New York–Oswego
David Gulley, Bentley College
William Hart, Miami University
James Hartley, Mount Holyoke College
Scott Hegerty, Canisius College
Kasthuri Henry, North Park University
Yu Hsing, Southeastern Louisiana University
Kyle Hurst, University of Colorado, Denver
Miren Ivankovic, Anderson University
Aaron Jackson, Bentley University
Louis Johnston, College of Saint Benedict and Saint John's University
Yong-Gook Jung, Wayne State University
Kelfala Kallon, University of Northern Colorado
Lillian Kamal, University of Hartford
Arthur E. Kartman, San Diego State University
John Keating, University of Kansas
Randall Kesselring, Arkansas State University
Yoonbai Kim, University of Kentucky
Sharmila King, University of the Pacific
Janet Koscianski, Shippensburg University
Mikhail Kouliavtsev, Stephen F. Austin State University
Gregory Krohn, Bucknell University
Felix Kwan, Maryville University
Elroy M. Leach, Chicago State University
Jim Leady, University of Notre Dame
Eva Leeds, Moravian College
Liaoliao Li, Kutztown University
Carlos Liard-Muriente, Central Connecticut State University
Chris Lundblad, University of North Carolina
Guangyi Ma, Texas A&M University
Gabriel Martinez, Ave Maria University
Kenneth McCormick, University of Northern Iowa
Fabio Mendez, University of Arkansas University
Diego Mendez-Carbajo, Illinois Wesleyan
Peter Mikek, Wabash College
Fabio Milani, University of California–Irvine
Jeffrey Miller, University of Delaware
Bruce Mizrach, Rutgers University
Francis Mummery, California State University–Fullerton
Andre R. Neveu, James Madison University
Farrokh Nourzad, Marquette University
Eugene Bempong Nyantakyi, West Virginia University
Ronald Olive, University of Massachusetts–Lowell
Esen Onur, California State University–Sacramento
Walter G. Park, American University
Claudiney Pereira, Tulane University
Nathan Perry, Mesa State College

Stephen Pollard, California State University, Los Angeles
Abe Qastin, Lakeland College
Masha Rahnama, Texas Tech University
Rati Ram, Illinois State University
Reza Ramazani, Saint Michael's College
Malcolm Robinson, Thomas More College
Brian Rosario, California State University–Sacramento
Farhad Saboori, Albright College
Nicole Cornell Sadowski, York College of Pennsylvania
Joseph T. Salerno, Pace University
Subarna Samanta, The College of New Jersey
Shane Sanders, Nicholls State University
Mark Scanlan, Stephen F. Austin State University
Buffie Schmidt, Augusta State University
Gary Shelley, East Tennessee State University
Olga Shurchkov, Wellesley College
Tara Sinclair, George Washington University
Fahlino F. Sjuib, Framingham State College
Julie Smith, Lafayette College
Arun Srinivasan, Indiana University Southeast
Kellin Stanfield, DePauw University
Herman Stekler, George Washington University
Paul Stock, University of Mary Hardin–Baylor
Leonie Stone, State University of New York–Geneseo
Georg Strasser, Boston College
Gordon Stringer, University of Colorado, Colorado Springs
Peter Summer, Texas Tech University
Kevin Sylwester, Southern Illinois University
Wendine Thompson, Monmouth College
Kwok Ping Tsang, Virginia Tech
Kristin A. Van Gaasbeck, California State University, Sacramento
John Van Huyck, Texas A&M University
David Vera, California State University, Fresno
Rahul Verma, University of Houston, Downtown
Bhavneet Walia, Nicholls State University
Yaqin Wang, Youngstown State University
Robert Whaples, Wake Forest University
Jeffrey Woods, University of Indianapolis
Guy Yamashiro, California State University, Long Beach
Sheng-Ping Yang, Gustavus Adolphus College
Janice Yee, Worcester State University
Wei-Choun Yu, Winona State University
Erik Zemljic, Kent State University
Christian Zimmermann, University of Connecticut

Accuracy Checkers

In a long and relatively complicated manuscript, accuracy checking is of critical importance. Our thanks go to a dedicated group who provided thorough accuracy checking of both the manuscript and page proof chapters:

Cynthia Bansak, St. Lawrence University
Doris Bennett, Jacksonville State University
Douglas Campbell, University of Memphis
Satyajit Ghosh, University of Scranton
Robert Gillette, University of Kentucky
Robert Godby, University of Wyoming
Anthony Gyapong, Pennsylvania State University
James Moreno, Blinn College
Ronald Olive, University of Massachusetts-Lowell
Nicole L. Cornell Sadowski, York College of Pennsylvania
Robert Whaples, Wake Forest University

Special thanks to Rob Godby of the University of Wyoming and Cynthia Bansak of St. Lawrence University for both commenting on and checking the accuracy of all 15 chapters of the manuscript.

We are grateful to Fernando Quijano of Dickinson State University and Shelly Tefft for their careful accuracy check of the art program in three stages of development. They helped ensure that the graphs are clear, consistent, and accurate.

A Word of Thanks

We benefited greatly from the dedication and professionalism of the Pearson Economics team. Executive Editor David Alexander's energy and support were indispensable. David shares our view that the time has come for a new approach to the macroeconomics textbook. Just as importantly, he provided words of encouragement whenever our energy flagged. Executive Development Editor Lena Buonanno worked tirelessly to ensure that this text was as good as it could be and to coordinate the many moving parts involved in a project of this complexity. We remain astonished at the amount of time, energy, and unfailing good humor she brought to this project. Without Lena, this book would not have been possible. Director of Key Markets David Theisen provided valuable insight into the changing needs of macroeconomics instructors. We have worked with Executive Marketing Manager Lori DeShazo on all three of our books, and we continue to be amazed at her energy and creativity in promoting the field of economics. Market Development Manager Kathleen McLellan developed an innovative marketing plan that promoted our book to instructors. We also appreciate the input of Steve Deitmer, Director of Development. Alison Eusden managed the supplement package that accompanies the book. Lindsey Sloan assisted with the review and marketing programs. Carla Thompson, Kristin Ruscetta, and Jonathan Boylan turned our manuscript pages into a beautiful published book. Fernando Quijano of Dickinson State University and Shelly Tefft diligently accuracy checked the art program in both manuscript and page proof stage. We thank Pam Smith, Elena Zeller, and Jennifer Brailsford for their careful proofreading of two rounds of page proofs.

We extend our special thanks to Wilhelmina Sanford of Columbia Business School, whose speedy and accurate typing of multiple drafts is much appreciated.

A good part of the burden of a project of this magnitude is borne by our families, and we appreciate their patience, support, and encouragement.

CHAPTER 1

The Long and Short of Macroeconomics

LEARNING OBJECTIVES

After studying this chapter, you should be able to:

1.1 Become familiar with the focus of macroeconomics (pages 2–11)

1.2 Explain how economists approach macroeconomic questions (pages 11–16)

1.3 Become familiar with key macroeconomic issues and questions (pages 16–17)

WHEN YOU ENTER THE JOB MARKET CAN MATTER A LOT

If you could choose a year to be born, 1983 or 1984 would have been pretty good choices. If you had been born in those years, you might have graduated college and entered the job market in 2005, which was a great year to begin job hunting. You would be entering the labor force at a time when the economy was expanding: Sales of houses and cars were strong, Wall Street was booming, and unemployment was low and declining. As stock prices and home prices both soared, many people felt wealthier than they had ever been. Born in 1986 or 1987? Well, 2008 was *not* a good year to be graduating and entering the job market. Nor were 2009 and 2010. By 2009, the unemployment rate was higher than it had been in 25 years. By 2010, more people had been out of work for longer than a year than at any time since the Great Depression of the 1930s. From 2008 to 2010, nearly 300,000 more firms closed than opened. Sales of houses and cars were at depressed levels. The prices of homes and shares of stock were well below their levels of a few years earlier, which meant that trillions of dollars of wealth had been wiped out. Many older workers who had expected to retire soon had to rethink their plans. Clearly, this was not the best of times to be entering the labor force.

The U.S. economy has its ups and downs, and the consequences of the ups and downs can significantly affect people's lives. For instance, a recent study found that college students who graduate during an economic recession have to search longer to find a job and end up accepting jobs that, on average, pay 9% less than the jobs accepted by students who graduate during economic expansions. What's more, students who graduate during recessions will continue to earn less for 8 to 10 years after they graduate. But just as recessions can be painful, expansions result in rising income, profits, and employment. Searching for a job or starting a new business is a lot easier during an expansion than during a recession. Clearly, understanding why the economy experiences periods of recession and expansion is important.

Each chapter in this book ends with a feature that we call *An Inside Look*. This feature analyzes a newspaper article on an important macroeconomic issue, typically often a policy issue. Read **AN INSIDE LOOK** on page 18 for a discussion of whether an increase in consumer spending at the end of 2010 was a sign of an expansion of the U.S. economy.

Sources: Philip Oreopoulos, Till von Wachter, and Andrew Heisz, "The Short- and Long-Term Career Effects of Graduating in a Recession: Hysteresis and Heterogeneity in the Market for College Graduates," IZA Discussion Paper No. 3578, June 2008; and Lisa Kahn, "The Long-Term Labor Market Consequences of Graduating from College in a Bad Economy," *Labour Economics*, Vol. 17, No. 2, April 2010, pp. 303–316.

Microeconomics The study of how households and firms make choices, how they interact in markets, and how the government attempts to influence their choices.

Macroeconomics The study of the economy as a whole, including topics such as inflation, unemployment, and economic growth.

How can we understand these fluctuations in the economy? By learning *macroeconomics.* Economics is traditionally divided into the study of **microeconomics**, which is the study of how households and firms make choices, how they interact in markets, and how the government attempts to influence their choices, and **macroeconomics**, which is the study of the economy as a whole, including topics such as inflation, unemployment, and economic growth. Both microeconomics and macroeconomics study important issues, but the very severe recession of 2007–2009 made macroeconomic issues seemed particularly pressing. Although economic theory has the reputation for being dull, there was nothing dull about the events of 2007–2009, which had a major impact on thousands of firms and millions of families.

Many students open an economics textbook and think, "Do I have to memorize all these graphs and equations? How am I going to use this stuff?" Once the final exam is over (at last!) everything learned is quickly forgotten. And it should be forgotten, because economics as an undigested lump of graphs and equations has no value. Graphs and equations are tools; if they are not used for their intended purpose, then they have no more value than a blunt pair of scissors forgotten in the back of a drawer. We have to admit that this textbook has its share of graphs you should know and equations you should memorize. But no more than are necessary. When we present you with a tool, we use it, and we show you how to use it. Our intention is for you to remember these tools long after the final exam, even if this is the last economics course you ever take. With these tools you can make sense of things that will have a huge impact on your life. Studying macroeconomics will be less of a chore if you keep this in mind: By learning this material you will come to understand how and why economic events affect you, your family, and the well-being of people around the world.

We begin the study of macroeconomics in the next section by previewing some of the most important ideas we will discuss in this text.

1.1

Learning Objective

Become familiar with the focus of macroeconomics.

What Macroeconomics Is About

In this text, we will analyze the macroeconomics of the U.S. and world economies. This section provides an overview of some of the important ideas about macroeconomics. We hope it provides you with an overview of what macroeconomics is about. We will discuss these ideas in more detail in the following chapters.

Macroeconomics in the Short Run and in the Long Run

Business cycle Alternating periods of economic expansion and economic recession.

The key macroeconomic issue of the short run—a period of a few years—is different from the key macroeconomic issue of the long run—a period of decades or more. In the short run, macroeconomic analysis focuses on the **business cycle**, which refers to alternating periods of *economic expansion* and *economic recession* experienced by the U.S. and other economies. The U.S. economy has experienced periods of expanding production and employment followed by periods of recession during which production and employment decline dating back to at least the early nineteenth century. The business cycle is not uniform: Each period of expansion is not the same length, nor is each period of recession, but every period of expansion in U.S. history has been followed by a period of recession, and every period of recession has been followed by a period of expansion.

Long-run economic growth The process by which increasing productivity raises the average standard of living.

Labor productivity The quantity of goods and services that can be produced by one worker or by one hour of work.

For the long run, the focus of macroeconomics switches from the business cycle to **long-run economic growth**, which is the process by which increasing productivity raises the average standard of living. A successful economy is capable of increasing production of goods and services faster than the growth in population. Increasing production faster than population growth is the only lasting way that the standard of living of the average person in a country can increase. Achieving this outcome is possible only through increases in *labor productivity.* **Labor productivity** is the quantity of goods and services that can be produced by one worker or by one hour of work. In analyzing long-run growth, economists usually measure labor productivity as output per hour of work to avoid the effects of fluctuations over time in the length of the workday and in the fraction of the population employed. If the quantity of goods and services consumed by the average person is to increase, the quantity of goods and services produced per hour of work must also increase.

Unfortunately, many economies around the world are not growing at all or are growing very slowly. In some countries in sub-Saharan Africa, living standards are barely higher, or are even lower, than they were 50 years ago. Many people in these countries live in the same grinding poverty as their ancestors did. In the United States and other developed countries, however, living standards are much higher than they were 50 years ago. An important macroeconomic topic is why some countries grow much faster than others.

As we will see, one determinant of economic growth is the ability of firms to expand their operations, buy additional equipment, train workers, and adopt new technologies. To carry out these activities, firms must acquire funds from households, either directly through financial markets—such as the stock and bond markets—or indirectly through financial intermediaries—such as banks. Financial markets and financial intermediaries together comprise the *financial system*. As later chapters will show, the financial system has become an increasingly important part of the study of macroeconomics.

The focus of this book will be the exploration of these two key aspects of macroeconomics—the long-run growth that has steadily raised living standards in the United States and some other countries, and the short-run fluctuations of the business cycle. In the following sections, we expand briefly on these two aspects of macroeconomics by looking at some of the topics we will cover in the text.

Long-Run Growth in the United States

By current standards, nearly everyone in the world was poor not very long ago. For instance, in 1900, although the United States was already enjoying the highest standard of living in the world, the typical American was quite poor by today's standards. In 1900, only 3% of U.S. homes had electricity, only 15% had indoor flush toilets, and only 25% had running water. The lack of running water meant that before people could cook or bathe, they had to pump water from wells and haul it to their homes in buckets—on average about 10,000 gallons per year. Not surprisingly, water consumption averaged only about 5 gallons per person per day, compared with about 150 gallons today. The result was that people washed themselves and their clothing only infrequently. A majority of families living in cities had to make use of outdoor toilets, which they shared with other families. Few families had electric lights, relying instead on the limited illumination obtained from candles or from burning kerosene or coal oil in lamps.

Most homes were heated in the winter by burning coal, which was also used as fuel in stoves. In the northern United States, many families saved on fuel costs by heating only the kitchen, abandoning their living rooms and relying on clothing and blankets for warmth in their bedrooms. The typical family used more than seven tons of coal per year just for cooking. Burning so much coal contributed to the severe pollution that fouled the air of most large cities. Poor sanitation and high levels of pollution, along with ineffective medical care, resulted in high rates of illness and premature death. Many Americans became ill or died from diseases such as smallpox, typhus, dysentery, poliomyelitis, measles, and cholera that are now uncommon in developed nations. Life expectancy was about 47 years, compared with 78 years in 2011. In 1900, 5,000 of the 45,000 children born in Chicago died before their first birthday. In 1900, there were, of course, no televisions, radios, computers, air conditioners, washing machines, dishwashers, or refrigerators. Without modern appliances, most women worked inside the home at least 80 hours per week. The typical American homemaker in 1900 baked a half-ton of bread per year.[1]

---

[1]Most of the data on economic conditions in the United States in 1900 come from Stanley Lebergott, *Pursuing Happiness: American Consumers in the Twentieth Century*, Princeton, NJ: Princeton University Press, 1993. Data on economic conditions in 2010 come from the U.S. Census Bureau, *The 2010 Statistical Abstract*, www.census.gov/compendia/statab/; United Nations Development Programme, *Human Development Report, 2010*, New York: Palgrave Macmillan, 2010; and other sources.

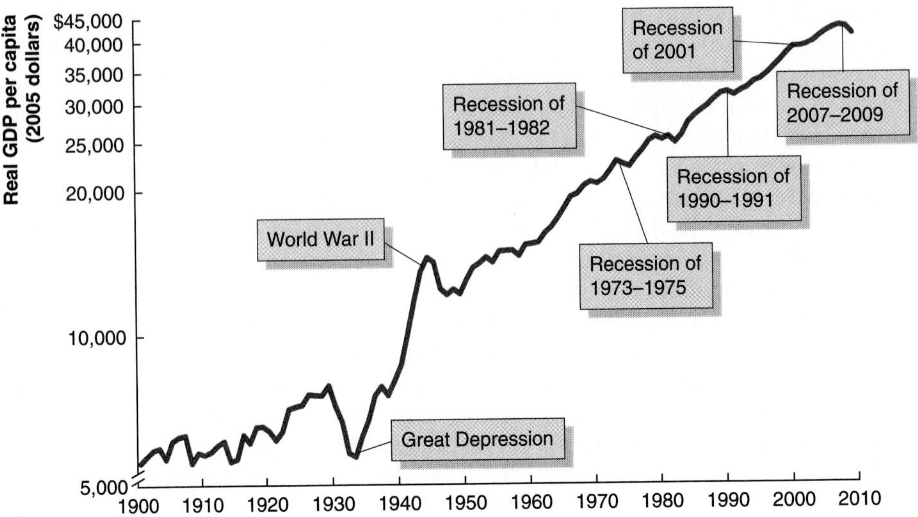

Figure 1.1

The Growth in U.S. Real GDP per Capita, 1900–2010

Measured in 2005 dollars, real GDP per capita in the United States grew from about $5,500 in 1900 to about $42,500 in 2010. The average American in the year 2010 could buy nearly eight times as many goods and services as the average American in the year 1900.

Note: The values in this graph are plotted on a logarithmic scale so that equal distances represent equal percentage increases. For example, the 100% increase from $5,000 to $10,000 is the same distance as the 100% increase from $10,000 to $20,000.

Sources: Louis Johnston and Samuel H. Williamson, "What Was the U.S. GDP Then?" *MeasuringWorth*, 2010, www.measuringworth.org/usgdp/; U.S. Bureau of Economic Analysis; and U.S. Census Bureau. ●

How did the United States get from the relative poverty of 1900 to the relative affluence of today? Will these increases in living standards continue? Will people living in the United States in 2100 look back on the people of 2011 as having lived in relative poverty? The answer to these questions is that changes in living standards depend on the rate of long-run economic growth. Most people in the United States, Western Europe, Japan, and other developed countries expect that over time, their standard of living will improve. They expect that year after year, firms will introduce new and improved products, new prescription drugs and better surgical techniques will overcome more diseases, and their ability to afford these goods and services will increase. For most people, these are reasonable expectations.

The process of long-run economic growth brought the typical American from the standard of living of 1900 to the standard of living of today and has the potential to bring the typical American of 100 years from now to a standard of living that people today can only imagine. **Real gross domestic product (GDP)**, which is the value of final goods and services, adjusted for changes in the price level, provides a measure of the total level of income in the economy. Accordingly, the best measure of the standard of living is real GDP per person, which is usually referred to as *real GDP per capita*. We typically measure long-run economic growth by increases in real GDP per capita over long periods of time, generally decades or more. Figure 1.1 shows real GDP per capita in the United States from 1900 to 2010. The figure shows that the long-run trend in real GDP per capita is strongly upward. The figure also shows that real GDP per capita fluctuates in the short run. For instance, real GDP per capita declined significantly during the Great Depression of the 1930s and by smaller amounts during later recessions, including the recession of 2007–2009. But it is the upward trend in real GDP per capita that we focus on when discussing long-run economic growth.

Real gross domestic product (GDP) The value of final goods and services, adjusted for changes in the price level.

In Chapters 4 and 5 , we will explore in detail *why* the U.S. economy has experienced strong growth over the long run, including the role played by the financial system in facilitating this growth.

Some Countries Have Not Experienced Significant Long-Run Growth

One of the key macroeconomic puzzles that we will examine is why rates of economic growth have varied so widely across countries. Because countries have experienced such different rates of economic growth, their current levels of GDP per capita are also very different, as Figure 1.2 shows. GDP per capita is higher in the United States than in most other countries because the United States has experienced higher rates of economic growth than have most other countries. Figure 1.2 shows that the gap between U.S. GDP per capita and GDP per capita in other high-income countries, such as the United Kingdom and Japan, is relatively small, but the gap between the high-income countries and the low-income countries is quite large. Although China has recently been experiencing rapid economic growth, this rapid

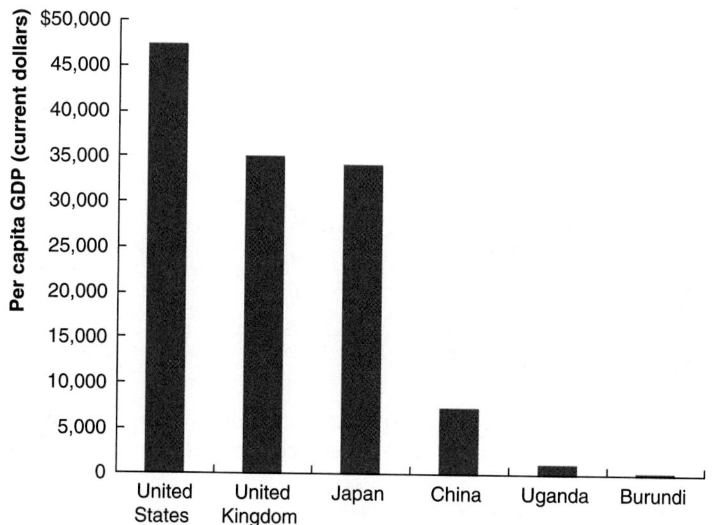

Figure 1.2

Differing Levels of GDP per capita, 2010

Differing levels of long-run economic growth have resulted in countries today having very different levels of GDP per capita.

Note: Values are GDP per capita, measured in dollars corrected for purchasing power parity, where the values have been converted into U.S. dollars using exchange rates and then the values have been corrected for differences in price levels across countries.

Source: U.S. Central Intelligence Agency, *The World Factbook 2011*, Washington, DC: Central Intelligence Agency, 2011. ●

growth began only in the late 1970s, when the Chinese government introduced economic reforms. As a result, GDP per capita in the United States is nearly seven times greater than GDP per capita in China, which is not much smaller than the gap between real GDP per capita in the United States today and real GDP per capita in the United States in 1900. The gap between the United States and the poorest countries is even greater still: U.S. GDP per capita is almost 40 times greater than GDP per capita in the African country of Uganda and a staggering 150 times greater than GDP per capita in the African country of Burundi.

Why is average income in the United States so much higher than that in Uganda and China? Why is China closing the gap with the United States, while Uganda falls further behind? What explains the stark differences in income levels across countries? Why has it been so difficult to raise the incomes of the very poorest countries? In Chapter 5, we will address these important questions about why living standards continue to rise in some countries while other countries appear to be stuck in poverty.

Aging Populations Pose a Challenge to Governments Around the World

The populations of the United States, Japan, and most European countries are aging as birthrates decline and the average person lives longer. Some economists and policymakers fear that aging populations may pose a threat to long-run economic growth. A key part of the problem is that the governments of these countries have programs to make payments to retired workers and to cover some or all of their healthcare cost. For instance, the United States has three programs that fill these roles: *Social Security*, established in 1935 to provide payments to retired workers and the disabled; *Medicare*, established in 1965 to provide health care coverage to people age 65 and older; and *Medicaid*, established in 1965 to provide health care coverage to the poor, including elderly poor in nursing homes and other facilities. Figure 1.3 gives a projection of spending on these three programs as a percentage of GDP.

The figure shows that spending on Social Security, Medicare, and Medicaid was about 3% of GDP in 1962 but is projected to grow to nearly 20% of GDP by 2050. In other words, by 2050, the federal government will be spending, as a fraction of GDP, nearly as much on these three programs as it currently does on all programs. Most of the money for Social Security, Medicare, and Medicaid comes from taxes paid by people currently working. As the population ages, there are fewer workers paying taxes relative to the number of retired people receiving government payments. The result is a funding crisis that countries can solve only by either reducing government payments to retired workers, reducing expenditure on all other programs, or by raising the taxes paid by current workers.

In some European countries and Japan, birthrates have fallen so low that the total population has already begun to decline, which will make the funding crisis for government

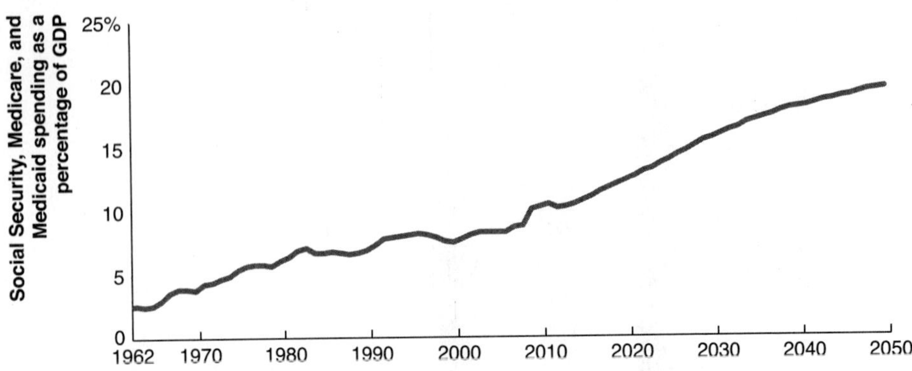

Figure 1.3

Projections of Future Spending on Social Security, Medicare, and Medicaid

Spending on Social Security, Medicare, and Medicaid, which was about 3% of GDP in 1962, is projected to grow to nearly 20% of GDP by 2050.

Source: Congressional Budget Office, *The Long-Term Budget Outlook*, June 2010. ●

retirement programs even worse. How countries deal with the consequences of aging populations will be one of the most important macroeconomic issues of the coming decades.

Unemployment in the United States

The three topics we have just discussed concern the macroeconomic long run. As we already noted, the key macroeconomic issue of the short run is the business cycle. Figure 1.1 on page 4 shows the tremendous increase during the past century in the standard of living of the average American. But close inspection of the figure reveals that real GDP per capita did not increase every year during that century. For example, during the first half of the 1930s, real GDP per capita fell for several years in a row as the United States experienced a severe economic downturn called the Great Depression. The fluctuations in real GDP per capita shown in Figure 1.1 reflect the underlying fluctuations in real GDP caused by the business cycle. Because real GDP is our best measure of economic activity, the business cycle is usually illustrated using movements in real GDP.

Labor force The sum of employed and unemployed workers in the economy.

Unemployment rate The percentage of the labor force that is unemployed.

Most people experience the business cycle in the job market. The **labor force** is the sum of employed and unemployed workers in the economy, and the **unemployment rate** is the percentage of the labor force that is unemployed. As Figure 1.4 shows, the unemployment rate in the United States has risen and fallen with the business cycle. The figure shows that prior to the

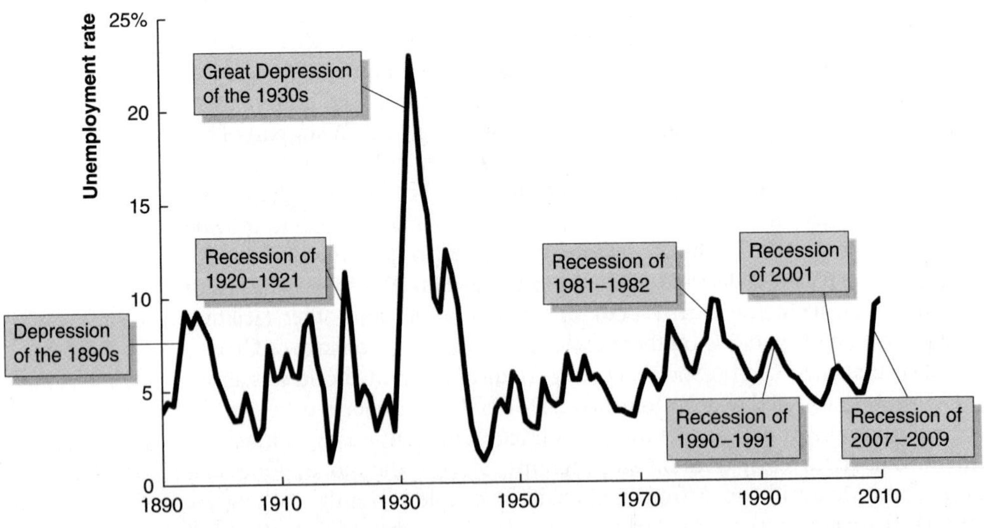

Figure 1.4 Unemployment Rate in the United States, 1890–2010

Unemployment rises and falls with the business cycle.

Sources: Data for 1890–1947 from *Historical Statistics of the United States Millennial Edition Online*, Series Ba475; data for 1948–2010 from the Bureau of Labor Statistics. ●

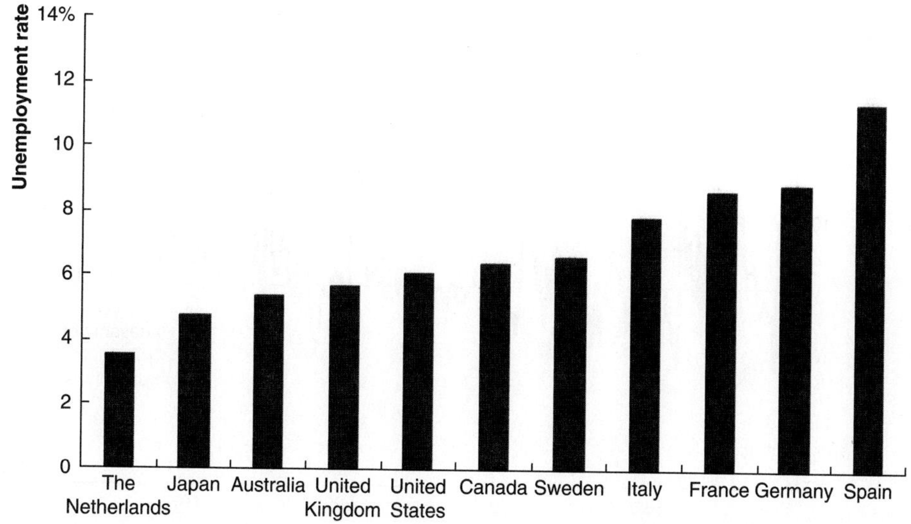

Figure 1.5

Average Unemployment Rates in the United States and Other High-Income Countries, 2001–2010

The average unemployment rate varies significantly across high-income countries. It has been relatively low in the Netherlands, Japan, Australia, the United Kingdom, and the United States, and relatively high in Italy, France, Germany, and Spain. Differences in labor-market policies are the most likely explanation for these differences in unemployment rates.

Sources: U.S. Bureau of Labor Statistics; and International Monetary Fund. ●

1940s, unemployment rates were typically higher during recessions than they have been in the years since. In particular, following the end of the severe 1981–1982 recession, the United States entered into a period of mild business cycles, with relatively low peak unemployment rates. Some economists called this period "the Great Moderation." This period ended in December 2007, with the start of the 2007–2009 recession. During that recession, the unemployment rate soared from less than 5% to more than 10%— more than 8.5 million workers lost their jobs.

In later chapters, we will explore why unemployment has been so much higher in some periods than in others. In particular, we will look at why the unemployment rate in the United States was so low during the Great Moderation and so high during the 2007–2009 recession and its aftermath.

How Unemployment Rates Differ Across Developed Countries

Figure 1.5 shows the average unemployment over the 10-year period from 2001 to 2010 for the United States and several other high-income countries. The average unemployment rates range from a low of 3.5% in the Netherlands to a high of 11.4% in Spain. These differences indicate that although some swings in unemployment are caused by the business cycle, unemployment has been persistently higher in some countries than in others for reasons not connected to the business cycle. What explains these differences? Differences in the labor-market policies governments have pursued seem to be the key to explaining these differences in unemployment rates. As we will see, economists have not yet reached a consensus, though, on which policy differences are most important.

Inflation Rates Fluctuate Over Time and Across Countries

Just as the unemployment rate varies over time in the United States and differs between the United States and other countries, so does the *inflation rate.* Figure 1.6 shows the **inflation rate** in the United States as measured by the percentage change in the average level of prices (here measured by the consumer price index) from one year to the next. The data in this figure stretch all the way back to 1775 to provide a very long-run view of how the inflation rate in the United States has varied over time. There are several points to notice about this figure:

Inflation rate The percentage increase in the price level from one year to the next.

1. Most of the periods of very high inflation have occurred during times of war.
2. An important exception to point 1 is the high levels of inflation in the late 1970s and early 1980s.
3. Periods of falling prices, or **deflation**, were relatively common during most of the country's history, but the United States experienced deflation in 2009 for the first time in more than 50 years.
4. The inflation rate during the past 25 years has generally been below 5%.

Deflation A sustained decrease in the price level.

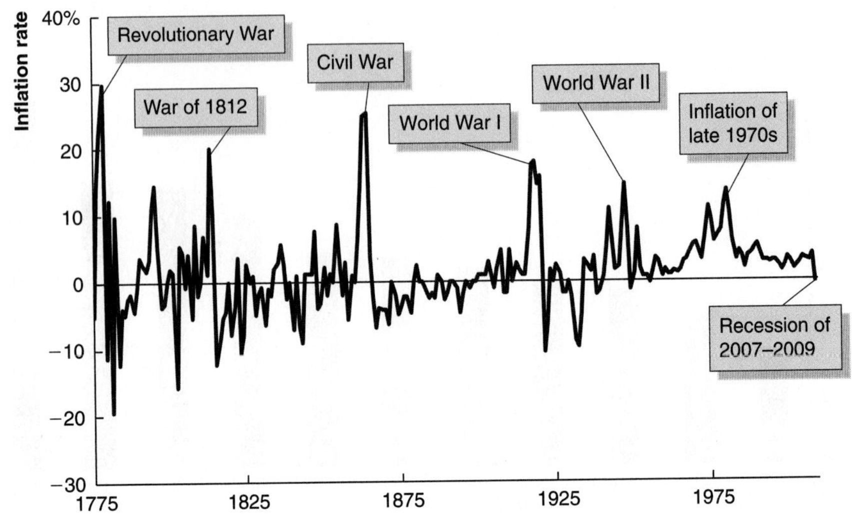

Figure 1.6

Inflation in the United States, 1775–2010

With the exception of the late 1970s and early 1980s, inflation in the United States has generally been high only during wars. Since the 1930s, periods of falling prices, or deflation, have been rare. The inflation rate during the past 25 years has generally been below 5%.

Source: Data for 1775–2003 from *Historical Statistics of the United States Millennial Edition Online*, Series Cc1; data for 2004–2010 from the Bureau of Labor Statistics. ●

In later chapters, we will discuss what determines the inflation rate, why the United States has rarely experienced deflation during the past 50 years, and why inflation has been relatively low during recent years.

While the inflation rate in the United States has generally been below 5% during the past 25 years, the experience in many other countries has been quite different. Figure 1.7 shows inflation during 2010 for several countries around the world. Some countries, including Ireland, Japan, Germany, and the United States experienced either mild deflation, with the price level declining slightly, or mild inflation. Many other countries, though, experienced significantly higher inflation rates, as shown by the values in the figure for India, Nigeria, and Venezuela. In fact, the figure understates how much inflation rates can differ across countries. For instance, the inflation rate in Zimbabwe, not shown in the figure, was an extraordinary 26,470% in 2007! By exploring the reasons for the differences in inflation rates across countries, we will gain better insight into what makes prices increase.

Economic Policy Can Help Stabilize the Economy

A basic measure of economic stability is how much real GDP fluctuates from one year to the next. The more GDP fluctuates, the more erratic firms' sales are and the more likely workers are to experience bouts of unemployment. Figure 1.8 shows year-to-year changes in real GDP in the United States since 1900. Notice that before 1950, real GDP went through much greater

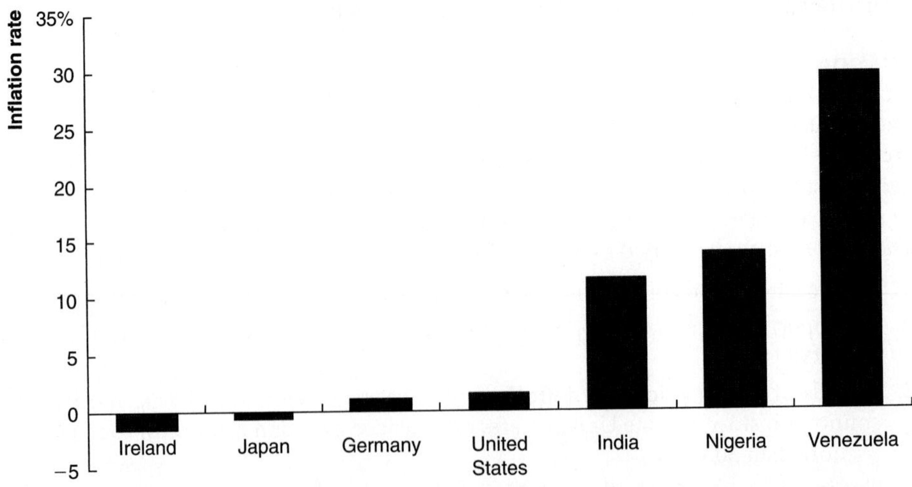

Figure 1.7

Inflation Rates Around the World, 2010

Countries can experience very different inflation rates.

Source: International Monetary Fund. ●

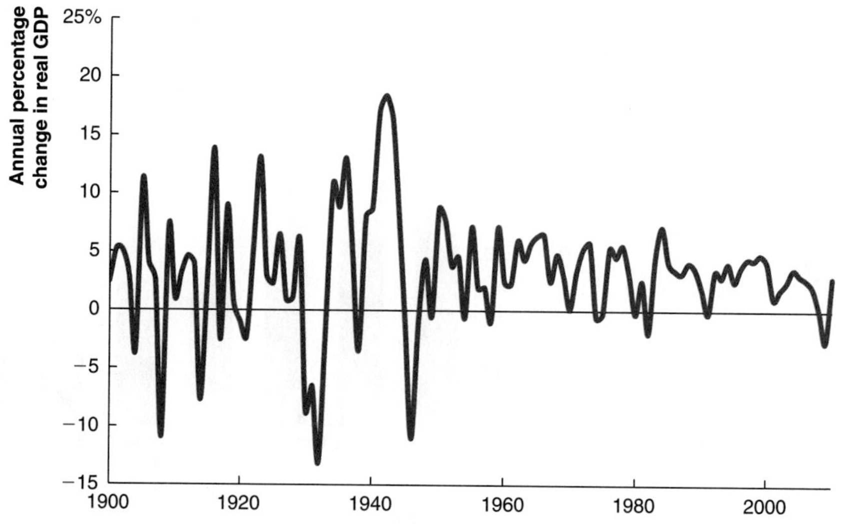

Figure 1.8

Fluctuations in U.S. Real GDP, 1900–2010

Real GDP had much more severe swings in the first half of the twentieth century than in the second half. The severe recession of 2007–2009 interrupted a long period of relative economic stability.

Sources: Louis D. Johnston and Samuel H. Williamson, "What Was the U.S. GDP Then?" *MeasuringWorth*, 2011. www.measuringworth.org/usgdp/; and U.S. Bureau of Economic Analysis. ●

year-to-year fluctuations than it has since that time. In particular, during the past 50 years, the U.S. economy has not experienced anything similar to the sharp fluctuations in real GDP that occurred during the 1930s. The increased stability of the economy since 1950 is also indicated by the increased length of business cycle expansions and decreased length of recessions during these years. From 1950 to 2007, the U.S. economy experienced long business cycle expansions, occasionally interrupted by brief recessions. Most other industrial economies have experienced similar increases in economic stability since 1950. (The period 1984–2007 was particularly stable and is known as the Great Moderation.) This long period of increased stability came to an end with the beginning of the severe 2007–2009 recession. How do we explain the increased stability of the post-1950 period and the severity of the recession of 2007–2009?

Although there are a number of reasons most high-income economies became more stable after 1950, many economists believe that the *monetary policies* and *fiscal policies* governments have pursued played an important role. **Monetary policy** refers to the actions of the central bank to manage the money supply and interest rates to pursue macroeconomic policy objectives. **Fiscal policy** refers to changes in government taxes and purchases that are intended to achieve macroeconomic policy objectives. A major focus of this book will be exploring how macroeconomic policy can be used to stabilize the economy. The severity of the 2007–2009 recession was due to the severity of the accompanying financial crisis. As we will discuss in later chapters, recessions accompanied by financial crises are particularly deep and prolonged and provide challenges to government policymakers.

Monetary policy The actions that central banks take to manage the money supply and interest rates to pursue macroeconomic policy objectives.

Fiscal policy Changes in government taxes and purchases that are intended to achieve macroeconomic policy objectives.

International Factors Have Become Increasingly Important in Explaining Macroeconomic Events

About a year before the financial crisis of 2007–2009, many economists observed that interest rates on mortgage loans in the United States were affected as much by policy actions in China's capital of Beijing as by policy actions in Washington, DC. Federal Reserve Chairman Ben Bernanke spoke of a "global savings glut" that had driven down interest rates in the United States. Thirty years ago, the U.S. economy had been much more insulated from developments abroad.

Economists measure the "openness" of an economy in terms of how much it trades with other economies. Panel (a) of Figure 1.9 shows that for the United States, both imports and exports have been growing as a percentage of GDP. Panel (b) shows that even though the openness of the U.S. economy has increased over time, a number of other developed countries are significantly more open than the United States. Some small countries, such as Belgium, export and import more than 60% of GDP because many firms based in

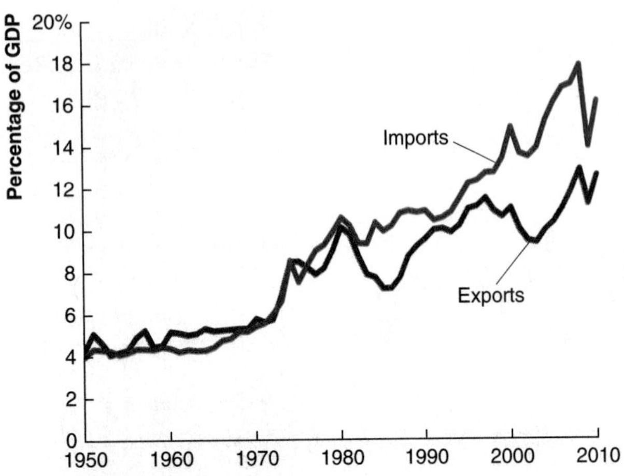

(a) International trade is of increasing importance to the United States

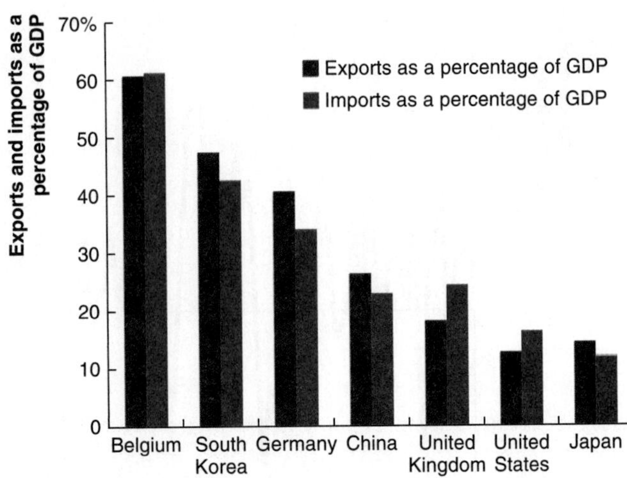

(b) International trade as a percentage of GDP for several countries

Figure 1.9 The Importance of International Trade

Panel (a) shows that since 1950, both imports and exports have been steadily rising as a fraction of U.S. GDP. Panel (b) shows that international trade is still less important to the United States than to many other countries, with the exception of Japan.

Sources: U.S. Department of Commerce; U.S. Bureau of Economic Analysis; and International Monetary Fund. ●

those countries concentrate on exporting rather than on producing for the domestic market. Countries such as South Korea and Germany are heavily dependent on international trade, with exports and imports making up about 40% of GDP. Although China has greatly increased its exports over the past 20 years, in 2010, exports made up about 26% of China's GDP, well below the percentages for Belgium, South Korea, Germany, and a number of other countries not shown in the figure.

As markets in goods and services have become more open to international trade, so have the financial markets that help match savers and investors around the world. Over the past 20 years, there has been an explosion in the buying and selling of financial assets, such as stocks and bonds, as well as in the making of loans across national borders. A *stock* is a financial security that represents part ownership in a firm, while a *bond* is a financial security that represents a promise to repay a fixed amount of funds. Figure 1.10 shows the

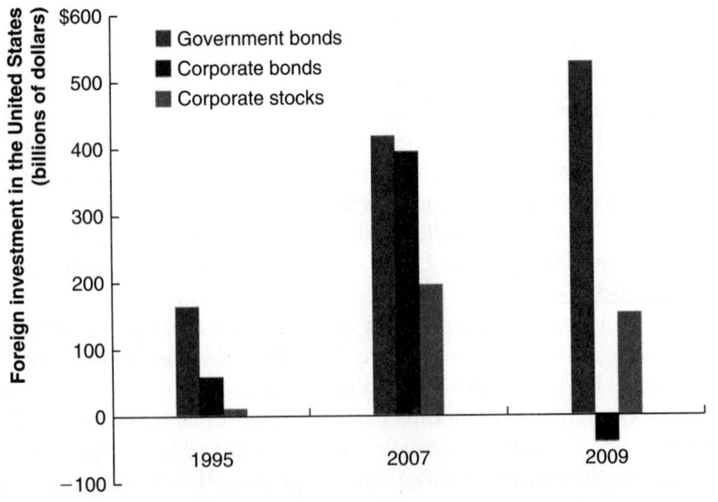

Figure 1.10

Growth of Foreign Financial Investment in the United States

Between 1995 and 2007, a large rise occurred in foreign purchases of stocks and bonds issued by U.S. corporations and bonds issued by the federal government. The financial crisis of 2007–2009 resulted in a sharp decline in foreign purchases of corporate bonds, a small decline in foreign purchases of stock, but an increase in foreign purchases of bonds issued by the federal government.

Sources: International Monetary Fund, *International Capital Markets*, August 2001; and U.S. Department of the Treasury, *Treasury Bulletin*, December 2010. ●

growth of foreign financial investments in the United States. Between 1995 and 2007, a large rise occurred in foreign purchases of stocks and bonds issued by U.S. corporations and bonds issued by the federal government. The financial crisis of 2007–2009 resulted in a sharp decline in foreign purchases of corporate bonds, a small decline in foreign purchases of stock, but an increase in foreign purchases of bonds issued by the federal government.

There has been a similar growth in purchases of foreign financial assets by U.S. investors. The increased openness of the U.S. and other economies has raised incomes and improved economic efficiency around the world. But increased openness also means that macroeconomic problems in one economy can have consequences for other economies. For example, the recession of 2007–2009 reduced the demand for China's exports, and the Greek debt crisis of 2010 caused stock prices to decline around the world. Openness can also complicate the attempts of policymakers to stabilize the economy. In this book, we will explore the macroeconomic implications of increasing trade and investment among countries, as well as the role of the international financial system.

How Economists Think About Macroeconomics

1.2

Learning Objective
Explain how economists approach macroeconomic questions.

Macroeconomics happens to us all: Over the course of your life, you may be laid off from your job during a recession or you will have friends or relatives who are. You are likely to see a stock market investment soar or collapse, find getting a loan to buy a house or car to be easy or difficult, and experience periods when prices of goods and services rise rapidly or slowly. We all have opinions about why these things happen, whether or not we are economists or whether or not we have taken even a single course in economics. What causes inflation? The number one response in a poll of the general public was "corporate greed." When asked what the effect of an increase in inflation would be on wages and salaries, the most popular response was that the main effect of inflation is to increase profits, leaving wages and salaries unchanged. Many people believe that recessions happen only because of mistakes made by Congress and the president and will end only if they implement the correct policies. Many people also tell pollsters that they believe that allowing foreign imports into the country permanently increases the unemployment rate in the United States.

In this section, we explore how macroeconomists analyze macroeconomic issues.

What Is the Best Way to Analyze Macroeconomic Issues?

Because you have already taken a course in principles of economics, you are probably skeptical of the accuracy of the opinions mentioned in the previous paragraph. What accounts for the differences that exist between the opinions of economists and non-economists? Are economists smarter than most people? Actually, the key difference between economists and non-economists is that economists study economic problems systematically by gathering data relevant to the problem and then building a *model* capable of analyzing the data. For instance, suppose we want to look systematically at the claim that inflation is caused by corporate greed. A first step is to look at the data on inflation. Figure 1.6 on page 8 shows the inflation rate for each year dating back to 1775. It is evident from the figure that the inflation rate has varied a lot over this long period. For instance, in the most recent 50 years, inflation varied from below 3% in the 1950s and 1960s to well above 10% in the late 1970s and early 1980s and then returned to relatively low rates below 4% for most of the years after the early 1980s.

By themselves, these data make the corporate greed explanation of inflation unlikely. If corporate greed were the cause of inflation, then greed would have to be fluctuating over time, with corporate managers having been comparatively less greedy in the 1950s and 1960s, more greedy in the late 1970s and 1980s, and then less greedy again beginning in the early 1980s. While a simple examination of the data can often help us to roughly gauge how likely an explanation is, this type of analysis is not completely satisfying for two reasons: First, in many cases just inspecting the data can give misleading results. Second, rather than just rejecting an explanation, it is more useful to provide an alternative explanation. That is, we need to build a *macroeconomic model* that will allow us to explain inflation.

Macroeconomic Models

Economists rely on economic theories, or models, to analyze real-world issues, such as the causes of inflation. (We use the words *theory* and *model* interchangeably.) Economic models are simplified versions of reality. By simplifying, it's possible to move beyond the overwhelming complexity of everyday life to focus on the underlying causes of the issue being studied. For instance, rather than using a model, we could analyze inflation by looking at the details of how every firm in the country decides what price to charge. The problem with that approach is that even if we had the time and money to carry it out, we would end up with a huge amount of detailed information that would be impossible to interpret. And we would end up no closer to understanding why inflation has fluctuated over the years. In contrast, by building an economic model of inflation that simplifies reality by focusing on a few key variables, we would be more likely to increase our understanding of inflation. In particular, we would be better able to predict which factors are likely to make inflation higher or lower in the future. (Remember from your principles of economics class that an *economic variable* is something measurable that can have different values, such as the rate of inflation in a particular year.)

Sometimes economists use an existing model to analyze an issue, but in other cases, they need to develop a new model. To develop a model, economists generally follow these steps:

1. Decide on the assumptions to be used in developing the model and decide which *endogenous variables* will be explained by the model and which *exogenous variables* will be taken as given.
2. Formulate a testable hypothesis.
3. Use economic data to test the hypothesis.
4. Revise the model if it fails to explain the economic data well.
5. Retain the revised model to help answer similar economic questions in the future.

We further explore the basics of economic model building in the next two sections.

In each chapter of this book, you will see the special feature *Solved Problem.* This feature will increase your understanding of the material by leading you through the steps of solving an applied macroeconomic problem. After reading the problem, you can test your understanding by working the related problem that appears at the end of the chapter. You can also complete related Solved Problems on **www.myeconlab.com**, which also allows you to access tutorial help.

Solved Problem 1.2

Do Rising Imports Lead to a Permanent Reduction in U.S. Employment?

Opinion polls show that many people believe that imports of foreign goods lead to a reduction in employment in the United States. On the surface, this claim may seem plausible: If U.S. automobile firms use more imported steel, production at U.S. steel firms declines, and U.S. steel firms will lay off workers. Briefly describe how you might evaluate the claim that employment in the United States has been reduced as a result of imports.

Solving the Problem

Step 1 **Review the chapter material.** This problem is about how economists evaluate explanations of macroeconomic events, so you may want to review the section "What Is the Best Way to Analyze Macroeconomic Issues?" which begins on page 11.

Step 2 **Discuss what data you might use in evaluating this claim.** As a first pass at evaluating this claim, you can look at data showing levels of imports and employment over the years. The U.S. Bureau of Economic Analysis (www.bea.gov) is a good source of data on GDP, including imports, and the U.S. Bureau of Labor Statistics (www.bls.gov) is a good source of data on employment. One way of inspecting whether the data support the claim is to plot the data on a graph. Your graph should look like the one below, which shows for the years 1970 to 2010 imports as a percentage of GDP measured on the left vertical axis and a measure of total employment on the right vertical axis.

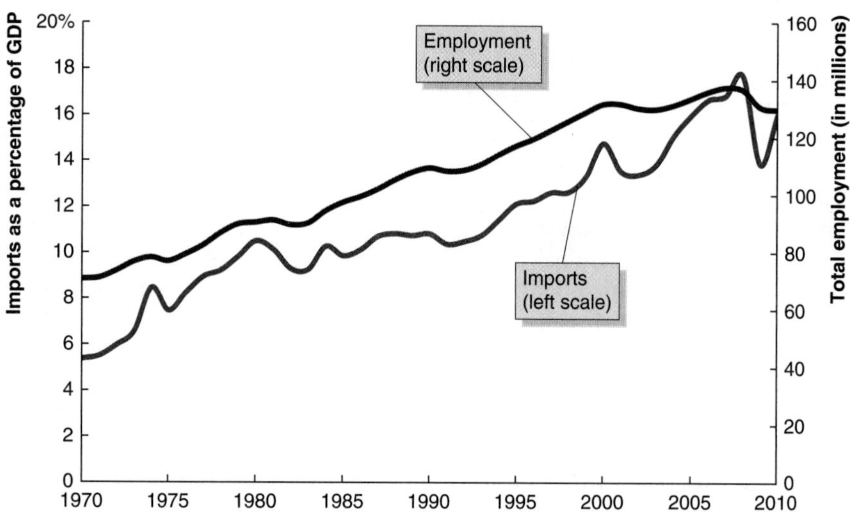

The graph shows that imports and employment have both increased over time, which makes it unlikely that imports have permanently reduced employment.

Step 3 **Discuss what else you might do to evaluate this claim.** Most economists see inspecting the data as only the first step in evaluating a claim about a macroeconomic event. Economists use models to provide systematic explanations. In this case, although the fact that imports and employment have both risen over the past 40 years makes it seem unlikely that rising imports have reduced employment, we can't be entirely sure. It is possible that employment would have risen even more than it did if imports had increased less. In Chapter 7, we will study a model of the labor market to better understand what determines the level of employment in the long run. At that point, it will become more clear that the level of a country's imports has no effect on its level of employment in the long run.

For more practice, do related problem 2.6 on page 22 at the end of this chapter.

Assumptions, Endogenous Variables, and Exogenous Variables in Economic Models

Any model is based on making assumptions because models have to be simplified in order to be useful. We cannot analyze an economic issue unless we reduce its complexity. For example, economic models make behavioral assumptions about the motives of consumers and firms. Economists assume that consumers will buy the goods and services that will maximize their well-being or satisfaction, or *utility*. Similarly, economists assume that firms act to maximize their profits. These assumptions are simplifications because they do not describe the motives of every consumer and every firm. How can we know if the assumptions in a model are too simplified or too limiting? We discover this when we form hypotheses based on these assumptions and test these hypotheses using real-world data.

Exogenous variable A variable that is taken as given and is not explained by an economic model.

Endogenous variable A variable that is explained by an economic model.

In building a model, we must also decide which variables we will attempt to explain with the model and which variables we will take as given. Economists refer to variables that are taken as given as **exogenous variables** and variables that will be explained by the model as **endogenous variables**. For example, suppose we build a macroeconomic model that explores the effect of changes in the money supply on the inflation rate. If we assume that the Federal Reserve determines changes in the money supply, then the money supply is an exogenous variable because we are not using the model to try to explain it. The inflation rate, though, would be an endogenous variable because we are attempting to explain it using the model.

Forming and Testing Hypotheses in Economic Models

A *hypothesis* in an economic model is a statement that may be either correct or incorrect about an economic variable. An example is the statement that the higher the marginal tax rate on income in a country, the higher the country's unemployment rate will be. An economic hypothesis is usually about a *causal relationship.* In this case, the hypothesis states that increases in the marginal tax rate *cause*, or lead to, higher rates of unemployment. A higher marginal tax rate might cause a higher rate of unemployment because the higher the tax rate, the smaller the after-tax wage a person earns from working and the smaller the incentive people have to accept jobs. To evaluate a hypothesis, we need to test it. To test a hypothesis, we need to analyze statistics on the relevant economic variables. In our example, we might gather statistics on tax rates and unemployment rates for different countries. Testing a hypothesis can be tricky. For example, showing that countries with higher tax rates have higher unemployment rates would not be enough to demonstrate that the higher tax rates *caused* the higher unemployment rates. Just because two things are *correlated*—that is, they happen at the same time—does not mean that one caused the other. For example, suppose that many of the countries with high tax rates also have laws that make it difficult for firms to fire workers. In that case, firms in those countries may be reluctant to hire workers because they would have difficulty firing them if they turned out not to be productive. It might be true then that the restrictive laws, rather than the high tax rates, were the cause of the high unemployment rates. Over a period of time, many economic variables change, which complicates testing hypotheses even further. In fact, when economists disagree about a hypothesis, such as the effect of higher tax rates on unemployment rates, it is often because of disagreements over interpreting the statistical analysis used to test the hypothesis.

Note that hypotheses must be statements that could, in principle, turn out to be incorrect. Statements such as "High taxes are good" or "High taxes are bad" are value judgments rather than hypotheses because it is not possible to disprove them. Economists accept and use an economic model if it leads to hypotheses that are confirmed by statistical analysis. In many cases, the acceptance is tentative, however, pending the gathering of new data or further statistical analysis. In fact, economists often refer to a hypothesis having been "not rejected" rather than having been "accepted" by statistical analysis. But what if statistical analysis clearly rejects a hypothesis? For example, perhaps the model used to determine the effect of taxes on unemployment assumed that governments in all countries are equally effective in collecting taxes. If some countries with high tax rates do not enforce their tax laws, few individuals and firms end up paying the high tax rates. This fact may explain why our hypothesis was rejected by the data.

Positive analysis Analysis concerned with what is.

Normative analysis Analysis concerned with what ought to be.

Throughout this book, as we build economic models and use them to answer questions, we need to bear in mind the distinction between *positive analysis* and *normative analysis.* **Positive analysis** is concerned with *what is*, and **normative analysis** is concerned with *what ought to be.* Economics is concerned primarily with positive analysis, which measures the costs and benefits of different courses of action.

In each chapter, the *Making the Connection* feature discusses a news story or another application related to the chapter material. The following *Making the Connection* discusses how well people understand macroeconomic issues.

Making the Connection

What Do People Know About Macroeconomics and How Do They Know It?

Some non-economists seem to know a lot of basic facts about the economy and are familiar with at least some basic macroeconomic ideas. Others, though, seem less well-informed. For example, public opinion polls indicate that in every recession, there are some people who believe that the U.S. economy has gone into permanent decline, apparently not realizing that economic recessions are always followed by economic expansions. Surveys of non-economists also show that they are much less likely to accept propositions accepted by most economists, such as the propositions that international trade increases the average income received by people in a country and that over time the living standard of the typical person in high-income countries increases.

What determines how much people know about macroeconomics? Bryan Caplan of George Mason University and Stephen Miller of Western Carolina University have used data from the General Social Survey (GSS) to explore this question. The GSS is a poll conducted every two years by the National Opinion Research Center (NORC) at the University of Chicago. Previous academic research had indicated that education was the most important factor in explaining who is more likely to understand macroeconomic concepts. Of course, people with more education are more likely to have taken a course in economics. But they are also likely to have developed critical thinking skills that make understanding economic ideas easier, even in the absence of having taken courses in economics. Identifying the gains to education in terms of economic understanding or, more generally, in terms of the higher incomes earned after graduation can be difficult. Do people earn more—or better understand economics—because they have attended college? Or are people with personal characteristics that lead to both success in life and the ability to understand economics—such as a willingness to work hard, having more intellectual curiosity, and having greater intelligence—more likely to attend college? If the second explanation is correct, then a person's characteristics—rather than college attendance—may explain his or her higher earnings and greater understanding of economics.

Caplan and Miller attempt to distinguish the effects of education on economic understanding from the effects of intellectual ability. In addition to asking a large number of questions about economic issues, the GSS contains a question that asks respondents to define 10 words. There is some evidence that the ability to score well on a vocabulary test is related to general intellectual ability, or "intelligence." In statistically analyzing the results of the GSS polls, Caplan and Miller find that when the scores on the vocabulary test are omitted, education is the most important factor explaining understanding of basic economic issues. When including the scores on the vocabulary test in their analysis, Caplan and Miller find that this measure of intelligence becomes more important than education in accounting for economic understanding. So, education, while important, may be less important than previously thought in explaining whether a person understands basic economic analysis.

Caplan and Miller's results are interesting in another respect as well. Economists, naturally, believe that economic analysis is the best way of understanding economic issues. So, when non-economists disagree with economists, economists tend to believe that the views of non-economists are wrong. The economists believe that non-economists would change their views if only they knew more economics. Alternatively, perhaps the views of non-economists are correct, and there are better ways than economic theory for understanding economic issues. Caplan and Miller conclude that:

> The fact that the beliefs of economists and intelligent non-economists dovetail is another reason to accept the "economists are right, the public is wrong" interpretation of [disagreements between economists and non-economists].

Caplan and Miller's conclusion is pleasing to economists, although it may be less so to non-economists!

Sources: Lymari Morales, "Americans More Pessimistic About Emerging from Recession," Gallup.com, September 15, 2010; Bryan Caplan, "Systematically Biased Beliefs About Economics," *Economic Journal*, Vol. 112, No. 479, April 2002, pp. 433–458; and Bryan Caplan and Stephen C. Miller, "Intelligence Makes People Think Like Economists," *Intelligence*, Vol. 38, No. 6, November–December 2010, pp. 636–647.

Test your understanding by doing related problem 2.10 on page 22 at the end of this chapter.

1.3

Learning Objective

Become familiar with key macroeconomic issues and questions.

Key Issues and Questions of Macroeconomics

There are a number of important macroeconomic issues and questions that we will discuss in this text. Beginning with Chapter 2, we will highlight one key issue and related question at the start of each chapter, and end each chapter by using the concepts introduced in the chapter to answer the question. This issue–question framework provides you with a roadmap for the rest of the book and shows why learning macroeconomics gives you the tools to analyze intelligently some of the most important issues of our times. Below is a list of the issues and questions we will discuss:

Chapter 2: Measuring the Macroeconomy

Issue: The unemployment rate can rise even though a recession has ended.
Question: How accurately does the government measure the unemployment rate?

Chapter 3: The Financial System

Issue: The financial system moves funds from savers to borrowers, which promotes investment and the accumulation of capital goods.
Question: Why did the bursting of the housing bubble beginning in 2006 cause the financial system to falter?

Chapter 4: Determining Aggregate Production

Issue: Real GDP has increased substantially over time in the United States and other developed countries.
Question: What are the main factors that determine the growth rate of real GDP?

Chapter 5: Long-Run Economic Growth

Issue: Some countries have experienced rapid rates of long-run economic growth, while other countries have grown slowly, if at all.
Question: Why isn't the whole world rich?

Chapter 6: Money and Inflation

Issue: The Federal Reserve's actions during the financial crisis of 2007–2009 led some economists and policymakers to worry that the inflation rate in the United States would be increasing.
Question: What is the connection between changes in the money supply and the inflation rate?

Chapter 7: The Labor Market

Issue: The unemployment rate in the United States remained about 9% more than 20 months after the end of the 2007–2009 recession.
Question: Should policymakers strive for an unemployment rate of zero?

Chapter 8: Business Cycles

Issue: Economies around the world experience a business cycle.
Question: Why does the business cycle occur?

Chapter 9: *IS-MP*: A Short-Run Macroeconomic Model

Issue: The recession of 2007–2009 was the worst since the Great Depression of the 1930s.
Question: What explains the severity of the 2007–2009 recession?

Chapter 10: Monetary Policy in the Short Run

Issue: The Federal Reserve undertook unprecedented policy actions in response to the recession of 2007–2009.
Question: Why were traditional Federal Reserve policies ineffective during the 2007–2009 recession?

Chapter 11: Fiscal Policy in the Short Run

Issue: During the 2007–2009 recession, Congress and the president undertook unprecedented fiscal policy actions.
Question: Was the American Recovery and Reinvestment Act of 2009 successful in increasing real GDP and employment?

Chapter 12: Aggregate Demand, Aggregate Supply, and Monetary Policy

Issue: Between the early 1980s and 2007, the U.S. economy experienced a period of macroeconomic stability known as the Great Moderation.
Question: Did discretionary monetary policy kill the Great Moderation?

Chapter 13: Fiscal Policy and the Government Budget in the Long Run

Issue: In 2011, the federal government's budget deficit and the national debt were on course to rise to unsustainable levels.
Question: How should the United States solve its long-run fiscal problem?

Chapter 14: Consumption and Investment

Issue: Households and firms make decisions about how much to consume and invest based on expectations about the future.
Question: How does government tax policy affect the decisions of households and firms?

Chapter 15: The Balance of Payments, Exchange Rates, and Macroeconomic Policy

Issue: Some governments allow the value of their currency to fluctuate in foreign-exchange markets, while other governments fix the value of their currency.
Question: How does the choice of exchange-rate system affect monetary policy and fiscal policy?

Before moving on to the next chapter, read *An Inside Look* on the next page for an economic analysis of the state of consumer spending in late 2010.

AN INSIDE LOOK

Will Consumer Spending Nudge Employers to Hire?

THE CHRISTIAN SCIENCE MONITOR

Consumer Spending Hits Four-Year High Thanks to Holiday Splurge

A holiday-season rush pushed consumer US spending to its strongest quarterly gain in more than four years—a display of confidence that adds to other recent signs that an economic recovery is gathering strength.

a Spending grew at an annualized pace of 4.4 percent for the final three months of last year, the best showing since the first quarter of 2006, the Commerce Department reported Monday. . . .

[I]n general, both consumer incomes and spending are on an upward path, and the income gains have increasingly been coming from private-sector wages rather than government-supported programs.

"The growth here was supported by broad-based gains in wages and salaries," said economists Mark Vitner and Tim Quinlan of Wells Fargo Securities. . . . By contrast, "at the outset of this recovery, much of the income growth was concentrated in transfer payments, which includes categories such as social-security payments and unemployment benefits."

That bodes well for the notion . . . that the economy is on track for modest self-sustaining growth—with rising consumer demand nudging businesses toward new hiring, which in turn adds new income for consumers to spend.

b But most economists don't predict a continuation of annualized spending growth of 4.4 percent.

That's the case even though American incomes are poised to get another form of government "stimulus" in 2011: a cut in payroll taxes that was passed by Congress along with extensions of Bush tax cuts. The problem is that many consumers are still weighed down by high levels of debt or the risk of foreclosure, and the unemployment rate is still high. . . .

In general, forecasters envision only a slow recovery for the job market. Consumer incomes simply aren't growing all that fast, adjusted for inflation. Real per capita incomes have grown just 1.5 percent over the past four quarters.

And some big post-recession challenges remain: A high rate of home foreclosures, the risk that Europe's economy could falter amid a debt crisis, and now the spread of unrest—fueled partly by pocketbook anxieties—in the Middle East.

c Still, the recent consumer news is a reminder that US households have been making considerable progress since the recession. The savings rate (the share of disposable income that's not spent) has been hovering in the range of 5 to 6 percent, well above its pre-recession level. That's a sign that families are working to rebuild everything from emergency funds to retirement accounts.

And record debt-to-income ratios, reached before the recession, have declined.

Consider one prominent measure of the household debt burden called the "financial obligations ratio," which looks at key household payments such as mortgages, rent, home insurance, property taxes, and auto loans. Those obligations peaked at 18.9 percent of disposable income in the third quarter of 2007, and now stand at 16.8 percent of income, according to the Federal Reserve. For comparison, this ratio was 16.0 percent of income in the first quarter of 1980.

Source: By Mark Trumbull. Reprinted with permission from the January 31, 2011 issue of *The Christian Science Monitor*.

Key Points in the Article

This article discusses the increase in consumer spending in the last three months of 2010. The increase was just one sign of a growing economic recovery from the recession of 2007–2009. In addition to the rise in spending, consumer income also grew and the personal saving rate remained relatively stable, while debt-to-income ratios declined. Despite these positive signs, some economic challenges remain. Many economists expect growth levels to fall below those of the last part of 2010, high levels of unemployment to persist as job creation remains slow, and home foreclosure rates to remain high.

Analyzing the News

a The recession of 2007–2009 had a profound impact on spending behavior of American consumers. Figure 1 shows the percentage changes in real consumer spending from 2007 to 2010. During most of 2008 and 2009, consumer spending declined, with positive monthly changes returning on a consistent basis only in 2010. The last three months of 2010 saw spending grow at an annualized rate of 4.4%, its best showing in more than four years. The spending increase was accompanied by income growth resulting from an increase in wages and salaries. This growth was a positive economic sign compared to the growth in income at the start of the recovery in June 2009, which was primarily the result of government programs such as Social Security payments and unemployment benefits.

b Although higher spending and income are encouraging signs for the recovery, many economists expect the spending growth at the end of 2010 will not be maintained. Despite the payroll tax reduction and the extension of tax cuts for 2011, many consumers are still saddled with high debt levels and still face the risk of home foreclosure. And the unemployment rate continues to remain high. Although consumer income has been increasing, the level of increase has been modest. Real per capita income grew by only 1.5% in 2010.

c During the recession of 2007–2009, credit markets tightened and Americans changed their spending habits, devoting more of their income to saving. Figure 2 shows a dramatic increase in the personal saving rate in the United States beginning in 2008. The increase in saving continued during the economic recovery in 2010, with the personal saving rate remaining above 5%, well above the pre-recession levels of 2004–2007. The relatively high saving rate during the recovery is an indication that consumers are actively working to restore emergency and retirement funds, many of which became depleted during the recession.

THINKING CRITICALLY

1. During the recession of 2007–2009, consumer spending in the United States declined while the personal saving rate of Americans increased. Suppose a student in your class makes the following statement: "Based on the data for the recession of 2007–2009 presented in Figures 1 and 2, I propose the economic hypothesis that although a decrease in consumer spending is bad for the U.S. economy, the increase in personal saving benefits the economy." Evaluate this statement as an economic hypothesis.
2. Many economists believe that tightening credit markets that occurred during the 2007–2009 recession have played a part in the increase in the personal saving rate. If you wanted to build an economic model based on this hypothesis, explain which variable or variables in the hypothesis would be considered exogenous and which would be considered endogenous.

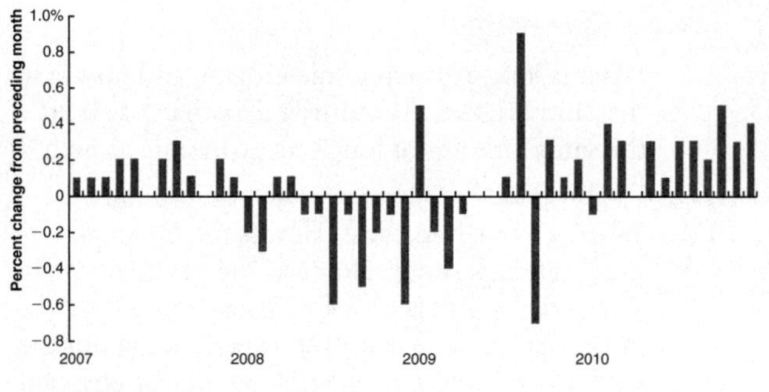

Figure 1

Percent Change in Real Personal Consumption Expenditure for the United States, 2007–2010

Source: U.S. Bureau of Economic Analysis.

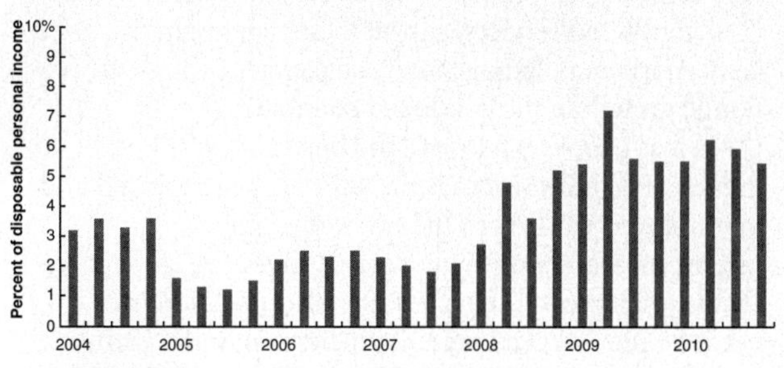

Figure 2

Personal Saving Rate in the United States, 2004–2010

Source: U.S. Bureau of Economic Analysis.

CHAPTER SUMMARY AND PROBLEMS

KEY TERMS

Business cycle, p. 2
Deflation, p. 7
Endogenous variable, p. 14
Exogenous variable, p. 14
Fiscal policy, p. 9
Inflation rate, p. 7
Labor force, p. 6
Labor productivity, p. 2
Long-run economic growth, p. 2
Macroeconomics, p. 2
Microeconomics, p. 2
Monetary policy, p. 9
Normative analysis, p. 14
Positive analysis, p. 14
Real gross domestic product (GDP), p. 4
Unemployment rate, p. 6

1.1 What Macroeconomics Is About

Become familiar with the focus of macroeconomics.

SUMMARY

Economics is traditionally divided into the study of **microeconomics**, which is the study of how households and firms make choices, and **macroeconomics**, which is the study of the economy as a whole, including topics such as inflation, unemployment, and economic growth. The key macroeconomic issue of the short run is the **business cycle**, which refers to alternating periods of economic expansion and economic recession. The key economic issue of the long run is **long-run economic growth**, which is the process by which rising productivity raises the average standard of living. **Labor productivity** is the quantity of goods and services that can be produced by one worker or by one hour of work. Economic growth has greatly improved the standard of living of most people in the United States and other developed countries, but many economies around the world are not growing or are growing only very slowly. Long-run economic growth is usually measured by increase in real gross domestic product per capita. **Real gross domestic product (GDP)** is the value of final goods and services, adjusted for changes in the price level. Aging populations pose a challenge to long-run economic growth in the developed countries.

Most people experience the business cycle in the job market. The **labor force** is the sum of the employed and unemployed workers in the economy. The **unemployment rate** is the percentage of the labor force that is unemployed. There are significant differences between the average unemployment rate in the United States and the average unemployment rate in other countries. The **inflation rate** is the percentage change in the average level of prices from one year to the next. Apart from the late 1970s and early 1980s, most periods of inflation in the United States have happened during times of war. **Deflation**, or a sustained decrease in the price level, was once relatively common in the United States, but it occurred in 2009 for the first time in more than 50 years. Inflation rates vary considerably across countries. The U.S. economy has been more stable since 1950 than before 1950. The period 1984–2007 was particularly stable and has been labeled the Great Moderation. The period of increased stability ended with the severe recession of 2007–2009. **Monetary policy**, which refers to the actions that central banks take to manage the money supply and interest rates to pursue macroeconomic policy objectives, and **fiscal policy**, which refers to changes in government taxes and purchases that are intended to achieve macroeconomic policy objectives, may have contributed to the Great Moderation.

The importance of international trade has increased in recent decades, although international trade remains less important to the U.S. economy than to the economies of many other countries. Foreign financial investments in the United States have significantly increased over the past 20 years.

Review Questions

1.1 What is long-run economic growth, and how is it measured? Have all countries experienced about the same amount of long-run economic growth? Briefly explain.

1.2 What is a business cycle? How is the unemployment rate measured? How has the unemployment rate varied over time in the United States? Do most high-income countries experience about the same average level of unemployment? Briefly explain.

1.3 Describe the average inflation rate in the United States over the past 40 years. When has there been high inflation? When has there been deflation? Are inflation rates roughly the same in countries around the world? Briefly explain.

1.4 Why is spending on programs similar to the Social Security and Medicare programs in the United States increasing in other high-income countries? What problems might this increased spending pose?

1.5 How has the severity of the business cycle varied over time in the United States? What is the Great Moderation?

1.6 What is monetary policy? What is fiscal policy? How are they different?

1.7 How might you identify how "open" an economy is? Is international trade more or less important to the United States than to many other countries?

Problems and Applications

1.8 The average rate of growth of U.S. real GDP is approximately 3%, as measured over long periods of time. China has been averaging growth rates that are considerably higher than this for much of the past two decades, while some sub-Saharan African countries have experienced growth rates that are considerably lower than 3% or even negative.

a. What is happening to the difference in the level of income between the United States and China?

b. What is happening to the difference in the level of income between the United States and these African countries?

c. In general, for countries to "catch up" to higher-income countries, what must happen in terms of growth rates?

1.9 Consider the following statement: "A country like the United States is more open than a country like Belgium because it is larger and has a higher total value of imports and exports." Do you agree with this statement? Explain.

1.10 In an article in the *Economist* magazine, a survey on expectations about standards of living yielded the following conclusion: "Half thought the next generation would have a lower standard of living, double the share that thought living standards would rise." What does this imply about expectations about real GDP growth rates in coming years?

Source: "Upper Bound," *Economist*, April 15, 2010.

1.11 During the 2007–2009 crisis, each of the programs listed below was implemented. Identify whether each of these programs represents monetary policy or fiscal policy.

a. The Federal Reserve decreased interest rates.

b. Congress provided funding for extended payments to unemployed workers.

c. Congress authorized new spending on infrastructure, such as high-speed railway lines.

d. The Federal Reserve took actions that greatly increased the money supply.

1.12 **[Related to the *Chapter Opener* on page 1]** According to the study cited in the chapter opener, "Increasing evidence suggests that even short [recessions] can have substantial . . . effects on workers' careers." Why might graduating into a weak labor market have a substantial affect on a college graduate's career even after the economy has recovered and the job market has improved?

Source: Philip Oreopoulos, Till von Wachter, and Andrew Heisz, "The Short- and Long-Term Career Effects of Graduating in a Recession: Hysteresis and Heterogeneity in the Market for College Graduates," IZA Discussion Paper No. 3578, June 2008.

1.2 How Economists Think About Macroeconomics

Explain how economists approach macroeconomic questions.

SUMMARY

In considering a macroeconomic problem, economists gather data, build a model for analyzing the data, use the model to formulate a testable hypothesis, and then use data to test the hypothesis. Economic models are simplified versions of reality that make it possible to move beyond the details of everyday life to try to find the underlying causes of the issue being studied. Economic models make behavioral assumptions about the motives of consumers and firms. Models also must distinguish between **exogenous variables**, which are taken as given and are not explained by the model, and **endogenous variables**, which are explained by the model. Economic hypotheses are statements that could, in principle, turn out to be incorrect rather than value judgments. **Positive analysis** is concerned with *what is*, and **normative analysis** is concerned with *what ought to be*. Economics is primarily about positive analysis, which measures the costs and benefits of different courses of action.

Review Questions

2.1 Why do economists build models?

2.2 Explain the steps generally used in building an economic model.

2.3 What is the difference between an endogenous variable and an exogenous variable?

2.4 Why is it customary to say that a hypothesis has "not been rejected" rather than "accepted"?

2.5 What is the difference between normative analysis and positive analysis? Is economics concerned primarily with normative analysis or with positive analysis?

Problems and Applications

2.6 **[Related to *Solved Problem 1.2* on page 12]** Many people believe that significant numbers of U.S. jobs have been "outsourced"; that is, firms have relocated operations to countries in which labor is cheaper, so the jobs have moved overseas. While there is no question that there has been some outsourcing, has it been significant relative to the size of the U.S. labor market?

Briefly describe how you would analyze this question. What problems might you expect to encounter in carrying out your analysis?

2.7 Explain which of the following statements would make a reasonable hypothesis to test. Use the concepts of normative and positive statements in your answers.

a. Increases in the duration of unemployment benefits lead to higher rates of unemployment.

b. Immigration is bad for society.

c. Increases in the labor force cause output to rise.

d. Welfare programs make workers lazy.

e. Higher rates of taxation increase work effort.

2.8 If you were studying the following relationships, which variable would be exogenous and which would be endogenous?

a. The effect of investment growth on the growth rate of GDP.

b. The relationship between the amount of sunshine and plant growth.

c. The relationship between hours of studying and GPA.

2.9 Consider the following statement:

"Economic models use many simplifying assumptions. Thus they do not apply to the more complex events in the real world."

Do you agree or disagree with this statement? Explain your answer.

2.10 **[Related to the *Making the Connection* on page 15]** Bryan Caplan of George Mason University and Stephen Miller of Western Carolina University argue that there is substantial evidence that: "Economists and the general public have systematically different beliefs about how the economy works." Briefly discuss why these differences may exist.

Source: Bryan Caplan and Stephen C. Miller, "Intelligence Makes People Think Like Economists," *Intelligence*, Vol. 38, No. 6, November–December 2010, pp. 636–647.

DATA EXERCISES

D1.1: The real GDP data in the chapter come from *MeasuringWorth* (www.measuringworth.org). Go to this Web site and find real GDP from 1900 to the most recent year available.

a. Are there years in which real GDP decreased? With what events are these years associated?

b. Use the calculator feature on the Web site to find the average rate of real GDP growth for the period from 1900 to the most recent year available.

D1.2: *MeasuringWorth* also has data for Japan. Chart the data for real GDP, inflation, and changes in wages for the same period as the U.S. charts shown in Figures 1.1, 1.4, and 1.6.

a. How do these charts compare to the U.S. charts for the same period?

b. What is the average rate of wage change in Japan?

c. What is the average rate of inflation in Japan?

D1.3: **[Excel question]** Use the *MeasuringWorth* data to practice the following Excel skills, which you will need to use in later chapters:

a. Import the data on inflation and wage change from 1990 to 2010 into Excel.

b. Chart the two series on the same graph. How do they compare with each other?

c. Find average wage change and average inflation for the current year. What is the standard deviation of each series?

d. What is the correlation between the two series? What does it mean?

CHAPTER 2

Measuring the Macroeconomy

LEARNING OBJECTIVES

After studying this chapter, you should be able to:

2.1 Explain how economists use gross domestic product (GDP) to measure total production and total income (pages 25–33)

2.2 Discuss the difference between real GDP and nominal GDP (pages 33–41)

2.3 Explain how the inflation rate is measured and distinguish between real and nominal interest rates (pages 41–47)

2.4 Understand how to calculate the unemployment rate (pages 47–49)

HOW DO WE KNOW WHEN WE ARE IN A RECESSION?

President Harry Truman famously remarked: "A recession is when your neighbor loses his job; a depression is when you lose yours." In fact, governments typically do not formally announce when the economy is in recession. Instead, they leave the dating of recessions to economists. In the United States, most economists—inside and outside the government—accept the dates for business cycle recessions and expansions determined by the Business Cycle Dating Committee of the National Bureau of Economic Research (NBER). For example, the committee determined that the business cycle expansion that began in November 2001 ended in December 2007, and it determined that the following recession ended in June 2009, when the next expansion began.

How does the NBER's Business Cycle Dating Committee determine when a recession begins and ends? The committee defines a recession as "a significant decline in economic activity [that] spreads across the economy and can last from a few months to more than a year." Deciding whether a particular economic episode

Continued on next page

Key Issue and Question

At the end of Chapter 1, we noted key issues and questions that serve as a framework for the book. Here are the key issue and question for this chapter:

Issue: The unemployment rate can rise even though a recession has ended.

Question: How accurately does the government measure the unemployment rate?

Answered on page 49

fits this definition requires the committee to examine a broad range of data:

> The Committee does not have a fixed definition of economic activity. It examines and compares the behavior of various measures of broad activity: real GDP measured on the product and income sides, economy-wide employment, and real income. The Committee also may consider indicators that do not cover the entire economy, such as real sales and the Federal Reserve's index of industrial production (IP).

The committee does not focus on any one industry. For example, residential construction fell by 3% during 2010 even though it was a year of economic expansion according to the NBER. The economy was expanding, but it was a difficult recovery for homebuilders. The committee also does not rely entirely on the strength of the labor market. The 2007–2009 recession ended in June 2009 when the unemployment rate was 9.5%. Despite the recession's having ended, the unemployment rate kept increasing during the beginning of the following expansion, peaking at 10.1% in October 2009. By March 2011 the unemployment rate was still 8.8%, much higher than the 4.7% unemployment rate just before the beginning of the recession. Although the economy was in an expansion, the expansion was initially not strong enough to rapidly bring down the unemployment rate.

The economic data the committee relies on are collected primarily by government agencies. Two problems arise in using and interpreting the data: First, there is a lag before the first estimates of production, employment, and other data are released. That is, the data measure economic activity during a period that has already passed. Second, the first estimates by government agencies are based on incomplete data. As the agencies continue to collect additional data and refine their estimates, they issue revised data on production and employment. Revised data continue to be issued over a period of years, with the final estimates often differing substantially from the first estimates. As a result, the NBER committee takes time to consider the revised estimates carefully before announcing that a recession has begun or ended. For example, the committee waited one year—until December 2008—to announce that a recession had begun in December 2007. The committee waited even longer—15 months—to announce that the recession had ended in June 2009.

The Federal Reserve, Congress, and the president of the United States, though, are typically unwilling to wait a year or more to take action when they believe a recession may have begun. Newly issued macroeconomic data—whatever their flaws—end up guiding the actions of these policymakers. Businesses, investors, and households are in a similar position. Businesses often have to make decisions—such as whether to open up new stores or factories or introduce new products—that will turn out to be good ideas if the economy is in an expansion and poor ideas if the economy heads into a recession. For example, at the height of the housing boom in 2004, KB Home and Toll Brothers purchased hundreds of acres of land outside of Las Vegas. The builders planned to construct 14,500 homes. Then the housing bubble burst and the economy entered a severe recession in 2007. Only 635 homes were constructed and the builders suffered heavy losses on the development.

Households are in a similar situation. When they buy houses, cars, or furniture, they may regret the decision if the economy unexpectedly falls into a recession and businesses start laying off workers.

We can conclude that knowledge of key macroeconomic data, including how they are constructed and their possible shortcomings, is important to the study of macroeconomics.

AN INSIDE LOOK on page 50 looks at how the recession of 2007–2009 affected the construction industry for homes and commercial properties.

Sources: National Bureau of Economic Research, "Statement of the NBER Business Cycle Dating Committee on the Determination of the Dates of Turning Points in the U.S. Economy," www.nber.org; and Robbie Whelan, "Builders Face a Desert Reckoning," *Wall Street Journal*, January 5, 2011.

Economists believe that the 2007–2009 recession was one of the worst since the Great Depression of the 1930s, but how do they know that? How do they know how many people lost their jobs during the recession or what happened to the inflation rate? The answer is that economists, consumers, firms, and policymakers all rely on economic data gathered by agencies of the federal government. These data allow us to measure key aspects of the economy, including total production, total employment, and the price level. Economists rely on these data not just to measure the economy but also to test hypotheses derived from macroeconomic models of the economy. As we saw in Chapter 1, macroeconomics is about much more than just describing what has happened. Macroeconomics is also about building models than can help us to understand *why* recessions, periods of high inflation, and other macroeconomic events have happened.

In this chapter, we will focus on the data used in calculating three important measures of the macroeconomic performance of the economy:

1. Gross domestic product (GDP)
2. The unemployment rate
3. The inflation rate

GDP: Measuring Total Production and Total Income

2.1

Learning Objective

Explain how economists use gross domestic product (GDP) to measure total production and total income.

In macroeconomics, we study the economy as a whole, so we need a measure of total production. Economists measure total production by **gross domestic product (GDP)**. GDP is the market value of all final goods and services produced in a country during a period of time. The Bureau of Economic Analysis (BEA) compiles the data needed to calculate GDP and issues reports on GDP and related statistics every three months. Because these reports provide important information on the state of the economy, economists, business managers, policymakers, and investors on Wall Street watch them closely.

How the Government Calculates GDP

Gross domestic product (GDP) The market value of all final goods and services produced in a country during a period of time.

We can note some important facts with respect to the definition of GDP and how the BEA calculates it:

- *GDP is measured using market values, not quantities.* When looking at individual firms or industries, we typically measure output in terms of quantities, such as the number of copies of Windows produced by Microsoft, the number of automobiles produced by Ford, or the number of Big Macs sold by McDonald's. But in measuring total production, we can't just add the quantity of software to the quantity of automobiles to the quantity of hamburgers, and so on because the result would be a meaningless number. Instead, we use market prices and take the *value* in dollar terms of all the goods and services produced. In addition to being convenient, market prices also tell us how much consumers value a particular good or service. If pears sell for $0.50 each and plums sell for $1.00 each, then the market prices tell us that consumers value a plum twice as much as a pear.
- *GDP includes only the market value of final goods.* In measuring GDP, we include only the value of *final goods and services*. A **final good or service** is one that is purchased by its final user and is not included in the production of any other good or service. Examples of final goods are a hamburger purchased by a consumer and a machine tool purchased by Ford. Some goods and services, though, become part of other goods and services; they are **intermediate goods or services**. For example, McDonald's does not produce the buns it uses in making Big Macs. McDonald's purchases the buns from suppliers, so the buns are an intermediate good. In calculating GDP, the BEA includes the value of the Big Mac but not the value of the bun. If we included the bun, we would be *double counting*: The value of the bun would be counted once when McDonald's buys it and again when McDonald's sells the Big Mac to a consumer.
- *GDP measures production within a country.* GDP measures production within a country regardless of who does the production. For example, Toyota is a Japanese automobile company, but it has assembly plants in Indiana, Kentucky, Texas and Mississippi. The automobiles produced at these plants count as part of U.S. GDP because they were produced within the borders of the United States even though Toyota is a Japanese company.[1]

Final good or service A good or service purchased by a final user.

Intermediate good or service A good or service that is an input into another good or service, such as a tire on a truck.

[1]As we note later, the value of imported goods is subtracted from GDP. So, the parts in U.S.-assembled Toyotas that are imported from Japan would be subtracted from GDP.

- *GDP includes some imputed values.* The BEA uses market values for goods and services in computing GDP, but in some cases where there is no market for a good or service, the value has to be *imputed*, or estimated. For example, the rent paid for an apartment or a house is the value of housing services the apartment or house provides. But many people own their own homes, so there is no rent that can be used to value the housing services they receive. The BEA has to impute a value for the rental services generated by owner-occupied housing. Similarly, many government services, such as police and fire services, do not have a market price. The BEA imputes the value of these services as being equal to the cost of providing them.
- *The BEA does not count some types of production.* The BEA does not attempt to impute values for some goods or services that are produced outside the market, such as the services a homemaker provides to the homemaker's family. The BEA also does not impute a value for goods and services produced in the *underground economy*, which refers to buying and selling that is not recorded either to avoid tax payments or because the goods and services—for example, cocaine or heroin—are illegal. Clearly these market transactions are part of the economy, but information on the underground economy is so imperfect that the BEA does not include estimates of it in the official GDP data. Economists Friedrich Schneider of Johannes Kepler University and Dominik Enste of the University of Cologne have surveyed studies estimating the size of the underground economy in countries around the world.[2] They find that estimates for the size of the underground economy in the United States vary widely, but it is probably less than 10% of GDP, or $1.4 trillion. In contrast, the underground economy may be 76% of GDP in Nigeria, 40% in Russia, and 20% in Greece and Italy. Most economists believe that the BEA's decision not to impute values for some goods and services does not present a problem in using GDP data. Typically, we are most interested in using GDP to measure changes in total production over a relatively brief period of time—say, several years. It is unlikely that the total value of goods and services—such as the services of homemakers or goods and services sold in the underground economy— that are not counted by the BEA changes much over a short period. So, our measures of the *changes* in total production would not be much different, even if the BEA were able to impute values for every good and service.
- *GDP includes only current production.* GDP includes only production that takes place during the indicated time period. For example, the sale of a used car would not be included because the production of the car would have already been counted in an earlier period, when the car was first sold. If we counted the sale of a used car, that would be double counting the car: first when it was initially produced and again when it was resold.

Production and Income

National income accounting The rules used in calculating GDP and related measures of total production and total income.

The rules used in calculating GDP are called **national income accounting**. The word *income* in this term indicates that by calculating GDP, the BEA is measuring both total production and total income. Note that nearly all countries around the world use similar rules to produce their *national income accounts*, which is the name given to GDP and other related measures of total production and total income. The BEA refers to the U.S. accounts as the U.S. National Income and Product Accounts (NIPA).

A key fact revealed by national income accounting is that *the value of total production in an economy is equal to the value of total income.* To see why, think about what happens to the money you spend on a single product. For example, if you purchase a Vizio

[2]Friedrich Schneider and Dominik H. Enste, "Shadow Economies: Size, Causes, and Consequences," *Journal of Economic Literature*, Vol. 38, No. 1, March 2000, pp. 73–114.

high-definition television from Best Buy for $1,000, all of the $1,000 must end up as someone's income. Vizio and Best Buy will receive some of the $1,000 as profits, workers at Vizio will receive some as wages, the salesperson who sold you the television will receive some as salary, the firms that sell parts to Vizio will receive some as profits, and the workers at those firms will receive some as wages. Every penny must end up as someone's income.[3] So, we can conclude that the revenues firms receive from selling goods and services are completely distributed to the owners of the inputs that are used to make those goods and services. Therefore, if we add up the total value of every good and service sold in the economy, we must get a total that is exactly equal to the value of all the income in the economy.

The Circular Flow of Income

Figure 2.1 is called a circular-flow diagram, and it uses the flow of spending and money in the economy to illustrate how the total value of spending on goods and services—*total expenditures*—equals the total value of income. Firms sell goods and services to three groups: domestic households and firms, foreign households and firms, and the government. Expenditures by foreign households and firms (shown as the "Rest of the World" in the diagram) on domestically produced goods and services are called *exports*. As we note at the bottom of Figure 2.1, we can measure GDP by adding up the total expenditures of these three groups on goods and services produced in the United States.

Firms use *factors of production* to produce goods and services. A **factor of production** is any input used to produce goods and services. Factors of production are usually divided into three categories: labor, capital, and natural resources. **Capital** refers to physical capital goods, such as machine tools, computers, factories, and office buildings, that are used to produce other goods and services. *Natural resources* refer to land and raw materials, such as coal or iron ore, that are used to produce goods and services. All factors of production are owned by households. It seems natural to say that households own their labor, but we generally think of the capital and natural resources as being owned by firms. Ultimately, though, every firm is owned by households. Even a very large corporation, such as Microsoft, is owned by its shareholders—the people who have bought stock issued by Microsoft. So, in this sense, we can say that households supply all of the factors of production to firms in exchange for income.

Factor of production Any input used to produce goods and services.

Capital Goods, such as machine tools, computers, factories, and office buildings, that are used to produce other goods and services.

We divide income into four categories: wages, interest, rent, and profit. Firms pay wages to households in exchange for labor services, interest for the use of capital, and rent for the use of natural resources. Profit is the income that remains after a firm has paid wages, interest, and rent. Profit is the return to entrepreneurs for organizing the factors of production and for bearing the risk of producing and selling goods and services. As Figure 2.1 shows, federal, state, and local governments make payments of wages and interest to households in exchange for hiring workers and other factors of production. The sum of wages, interest, rent, and profit is the total income received by households.

The circular-flow diagram also allows us to trace the ways that households use their income. Households spend some of their income on goods and services. Some of this spending is on domestically produced goods and services, and some is on foreign-produced goods and services, or *imports*. Households also use some of their income to pay taxes to the government. Some of the income households earn is not spent on goods and services or paid in taxes but is deposited in checking or savings accounts in banks, or other *financial intermediaries*, or used to buy financial assets, such as stocks or bonds, in *financial markets*. Financial intermediaries and financial markets together make up the **financial system**. The flow of funds from households into the financial system makes it

Financial system The financial intermediaries and financial markets that together facilitate the flow of funds from lenders to borrowers.

[3]Note, though, that any sales tax that Best Buy collects on the television will be sent by the store directly to the government, without ending up as anyone's income.

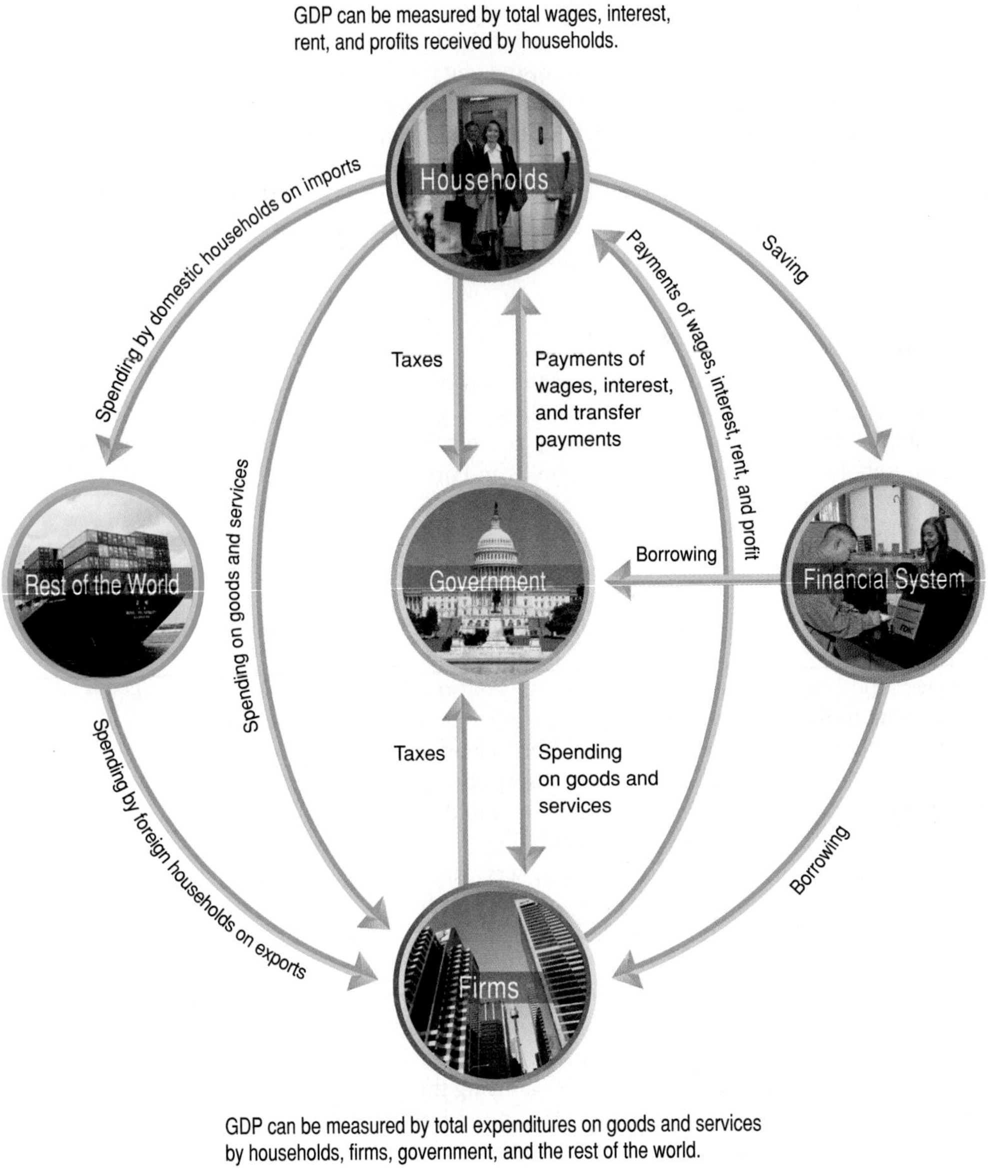

GDP can be measured by total wages, interest, rent, and profits received by households.

Households

Spending by domestic households on imports

Saving

Taxes

Payments of wages, interest, and transfer payments

Payments of wages, interest, rent, and profit

Spending on goods and services

Rest of the World

Government

Borrowing

Financial System

Taxes

Spending on goods and services

Spending by foreign households on exports

Borrowing

Firms

GDP can be measured by total expenditures on goods and services by households, firms, government, and the rest of the world.

Figure 2.1 The Circular Flow of Income and the Measurement of GDP

The circular-flow diagram illustrates the flow of spending and money in the economy. Firms sell goods and services to three groups: domestic households, foreign firms and households, and the government. To produce goods and services, firms use factors of production: labor, capital, natural resources, and entrepreneurship. Households supply the factors of production to firms in exchange for income in the form of wages, interest, profit, and rent. Firms make payments of wages and interest to households in exchange for hiring workers and other factors of production. The sum of wages, interest, rent, and profit is total income in the economy. The diagram also shows that households use their income to purchase goods and services, pay taxes, and save. Firms and the government borrow the funds that flow from households into the financial system. We can measure GDP either by calculating the total value of expenditures on final goods and services or by calculating the value of total income. ●

possible for the government and firms to borrow. As became clear during the 2007–2009 financial crisis, the health of a financial system is of vital importance to an economy. Without the ability to borrow funds through the financial system, firms will have difficulty carrying on their day-to-day operations, much less expanding and adopting new technologies.

An Example of Measuring GDP

As mentioned earlier in this chapter, the BEA gathers data on quantities and prices of final goods and services, multiplies the quantity of each good or service by its price, and adds up the totals to determine the value of GDP. For example, consider a very simple economy in which only two goods are produced: copies of Windows 7 and McDonald's Big Mac hamburgers. The value of GDP could then be calculated as:

$$\text{GDP} = (\text{Quantity of Windows 7} \times \text{Price of Windows 7}) + (\text{Quantity of Big Macs} \times \text{Price of Big Macs})$$

If 1,000 copies of Windows 7 are sold at a price of $100 per copy, and 10,000 Big Macs are sold at a price of $3 per Big Mac, then the value of GDP is:

$$(1{,}000 \times \$100) + (10{,}000 \times \$3) = \$130{,}000$$

By using this method for all final goods and services, the BEA can calculate GDP.

National Income Identities and the Components of GDP

The BEA divides its statistics on GDP into four major categories of expenditures:

1. Personal consumption expenditures, or "Consumption" (C)
2. Gross private domestic investment, or "Investment" (I)
3. Government consumption and gross investment, or "Government purchases" (G)
4. Net exports of goods and services, or "Net exports" (NX)

If we let Y represent GDP, then we have the following *national income identity*:

$$Y = C + I + G + NX.$$

This expression is an identity because the BEA assigns all expenditures on final goods and services into one of the four categories. Table 2.1 shows the values for 2010 of each of the major categories of expenditures, as well as their important subcategories.

We next briefly review some important points about the four categories of expenditures:

Consumption is the purchase of new goods and services by households. Consumption includes the purchase of all new goods and services by household regardless of which country the goods or services were originally produced in.[4] The BEA tracks three categories of consumption: Durable goods are tangible goods with an average life of three years or more, such as cars, toys, and televisions. Nondurable goods are shorter-lived goods, such as food and clothing. Services are consumed at the time and place of purchase, such as haircuts, healthcare, and education. In the United States, as in most other high-income countries, the fraction of services in consumption has risen relative to goods. As people's incomes rise, they tend to buy relatively less food, clothing, and other goods and relatively more healthcare and other services.

Consumption The purchase of new goods and services by households.

Investment is divided into three categories. *Fixed investment* is spending by firms on new factories, office buildings, and machinery used to produce other goods. *Residential investment* is spending by households or firms on new single-family and multi-family homes. Changes in business inventories are also included in investment. *Inventories* are goods that have been produced but not yet sold. For example, if Ford produces 365,000 Mustangs in the United States during 2012 but sells only 350,000, then the BEA counts the 15,000

Investment Spending by firms on new factories, office buildings, machinery, and additions to inventories, plus spending by households and firms on new houses.

[4]Later, we will see that because imports are subtracted out (or netted out), GDP will only reflect the consumption of domestic products.

Table 2.1 GDP in 2010

	Billions of dollars		Percentage of GDP	
Consumption	**$10,349.1**		**70.6%**	
Durable goods	1,089.4		7.4	
Nondurable goods	2,336.3		15.9	
Services	6,923.4		47.2	
Investment	**1,827.5**		**12.5**	
Business fixed investment	1,415.3		9.7	
Structures		383.5		2.6
Equipment and software		1,031.8		7.0
Residential investment	340.5		2.3	
Changes in business inventories	71.7		0.5	
Government purchases	**3,000.2**		**20.5**	
Federal	1,214.3		8.3	
National defense		817.7		5.6
Nondefense		396.6		2.7
State and local	1,786.0		12.2	
Net exports	**–516.4**		**–3.5**	
Exports	1,837.5		12.5	
Imports	2,353.9		16.1	
Gross domestic product	**$14,660.4**		**100.0%**	

Source: U.S. Bureau of Economic Analysis.

unsold Mustangs as investment spending by Ford in the "changes in business inventories" category. In effect, the BEA assumes that Ford "purchased" the Mustangs from itself.

Recall that the BEA wants GDP to measure production during a specific time period. Therefore, the BEA includes inventories as a form of investment. To see why, suppose that a Ford Mustang rolls off the assembly line on December 30, 2011. This is finished production that occurs during 2011, so the BEA counts the Mustang as part of 2011 GDP. However, it takes time for Ford to ship the Mustang to a dealer and for the dealer to sell it. As a result, the Mustang may not sell until June 2012, so the BEA records consumption expenditures as having increased in that month by value of the Mustang, while inventories are recorded as falling by the same amount.

How does the BEA ensure that the Mustang counts as part of 2011 GDP and not 2012 GDP? The BEA assumes that Ford "purchases" the Mustang from itself to hold as inventory on December 31, 2011. Therefore, the "sale" of the Mustang to Ford occurs in 2011, so the Mustang is counted as part of 2011 GDP. When the dealer sells the Mustang in June 2012, the dealer is not selling a new automobile since Ford previously "purchased" the Mustang at the end of 2011. Therefore, the sale of the Mustang by the dealer is the sale of a used good and so does not count as part of GDP in 2012.

The key characteristic of investment goods is that they add to the total amount, or *stock*, of capital goods that provide a flow of services into the future. For example, new capital goods include tools and machines that firms will use to produce goods and services into the future. Similarly, residential *housing* provides housing services for many years, so the production of new residential housing is counted as investment. The BEA classifies inventories as investment because firms plan to sell the inventories in the future.

Government purchases Spending by federal, state, and local governments on newly produced goods and services.

Government purchases are spending by federal, state, and local governments on newly produced goods and services. Some government purchases represent consumption spending,

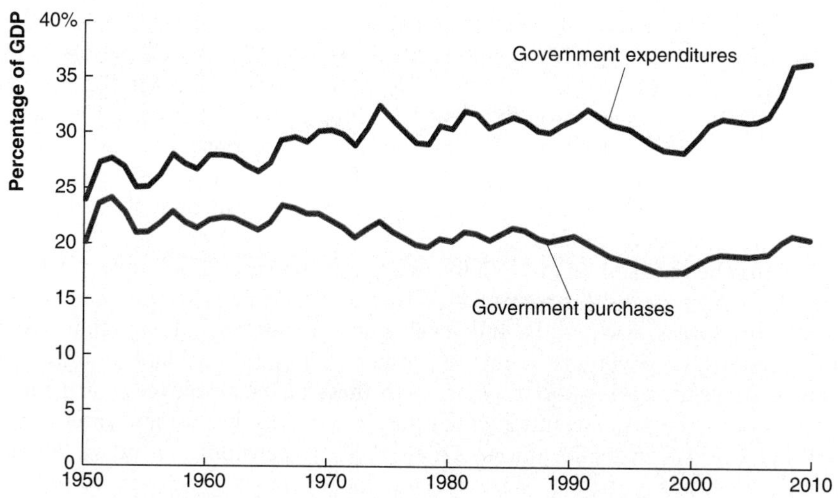

Figure 2.2

Government Purchases and Government Expenditures, 1950–2010

Since 1950, transfer payments have become an increasing fraction of government expenditures, as federal spending on Social Security and Medicare and state and local spending on public employee pensions has increased.

Source: U.S. Bureau of Economic Analysis. ●

as when the government pays the salaries of teachers or FBI agents. Other government purchases represent investment spending, as when the government buys new structures, such as bridges and school buildings, or equipment, such as aircraft carriers. Purchases of this type allow the government to provide services—such as education or national defense—in the future.

It is important to note that *government purchases do not include transfer payments,* which are one of the largest components of the government's budget. **Transfer payments** are payments by the government to individuals for which the government does not receive a new good or service in return. Examples of transfer payments include Social Security payments to retired and disabled people, Medicare payments to provide healthcare services for people 65 years and older, unemployment insurance payments to unemployed workers, and pension payments to retired government workers. Economists often distinguish between government purchases and *government expenditures,* which include government purchases, government transfer payments, and government interest payments on bonds. As Figure 2.2 shows, since 1950, government expenditures have been growing relative to government purchases, as transfer payments have been increasing relative to government purchases of goods and services. In fact, as a percentage of GDP, government purchases in 2010 were the same percentage of GDP that they were in 1950, while government expenditures were 75% greater in 2010 than they were in 1950.

Transfer payments Payments by the government to individuals for which the government does not receive a good or service in return.

Making the Connection

Will Public Employee Pensions Wreck State and Local Government Budgets?

Figure 2.2 shows the substantial growth in government expenditures as a percentage of GDP. Most of this growth resulted from increases in government transfer payments.[5] Increasing transfer payments put a strain on government budgets. As transfer payments increase, governments have to either cut back on purchases of goods and services or raise

[5]Interest payments on government bonds also contributed to a small extent to this growth. Government interest payments rose from 1.4% of GDP in 1951 to 2.6% in 2010.

taxes. Prior to the recession of 2007–2009, most economists focused on the budgetary problems facing the federal government as the aging of the U.S. population results in higher spending on Social Security and Medicare. Clearly there was cause for concern, as the Congressional Budget Office projected that spending on Social Security, Medicare, and Medicaid, which provides healthcare for people with low incomes, would rise to nearly 20% of GDP by 2050. In other words, by 2050, the federal government will be spending as a fraction of GDP nearly as much on these programs as government at all levels currently spends on all purchases of goods and services.

Following the recession of 2007–2009, many economists and policymakers began to focus on the budgetary effects of another type of government transfer payment: pensions for public employees. Most state and local governments, including school districts, provide pensions, or payments to retired workers. The pension plans at most private companies are *defined contribution plans.* With these plans, employees and firms contribute money into a pension fund, which purchase stocks, bonds, and other financial assets. When workers retire, the amounts they receive as pensions depend on the returns on the pension funds' portfolio. Most state and local pension plans—called *public pension plans*—are *defined benefit plans.* With these plans, employees and governments contribute to a pension fund, but workers are guaranteed a certain dollar amount as a pension. If the returns from the pension fund are not sufficient to pay the guaranteed pensions, the plan is said to be *underfunded*, but the government is still legally required to pay the pensions.

The severity of the 2007–2009 recession resulted in falling incomes and falling tax receipts. Personal income tax revenue collected by state and local government dropped by more than 20%. As state and local governments scrambled to meet legal requirements that their budgets be balanced, they faced not only falling revenues but large and increasing pension payments to retired public employees. Many state and local governments were forced to cut their purchases of goods and services and to raise taxes. Looking to the future, many economists and policymakers are worried that state and local governments will have difficulty making their promised pension payments. Many public pension plans are severely underfunded, meaning that state and local governments will need to significantly raise taxes, cut other spending, or raise retirement ages to meet their pension obligations. Robert Novy-Marx of the University of Rochester and Joshua Rauh of Northwestern University have estimated that the value of unfunded public pension obligations amounts to about $4.4 trillion, or about $39,000 per household in the United States.

In 2011, some cities that believed they would be unable to fund their promised pension payments were considering declaring bankruptcy, while others were reducing the value of the pensions that would be earned by newly hired workers or—in some cases—by already retired workers. Some economists and policymakers were urging that public pension plans convert from defined benefit plans to defined contribution plans. In Wisconsin, a major political battle over this issue broke out as Governor Scott Walker proposed reducing benefits to state public employees, as well reducing the ability of their union to collectively bargain with the state government. However the debate is resolved, it has become clear that public pension payments are a pressing issue for nearly all state and local governments.

Sources: Robert Novy-Marx and Joshua Rauh, "Public Pension Promises: How Big Are They and What Are They Worth?" *Journal of Finance*, forthcoming; Steven Malanga, "The 'Build America' Debt Bomb," *Wall Street Journal*, November 22, 2010; and Michael Cooper and Mary Williams Walsh, "Mounting Debts by States Stoke Fears of Crisis," *New York Times*, December 4, 2010.

Test your understanding by doing related problem 1.11 on page 53 at the end of this chapter.

Net exports is the value of all exports of goods and services minus the value of all imports of goods and services. When exports are greater than imports, net exports are positive, and the country runs a trade surplus. When exports are less than imports, net exports are negative, and the country runs a trade deficit. When exports equal imports, net exports are zero, and the trade deficit is zero.

Net exports The value of all exports minus the value of all imports.

If you purchase a Nintendo Wii for $300 at Best Buy, then U.S. consumption increases by $300. Does this lead to higher U.S. GDP? No. The Nintendo Wii is imported from Japan, so imports increase by $300, causing net exports to decrease by $300.[6] Because consumption increases by $300 and net exports decrease by $300, the change in expenditure is zero and GDP does not change.

The Relationship Between GDP and GNP

Prior to 1991, the BEA's main measure of total production was gross *national* product rather than gross *domestic* product. Writers, particularly non-economists, will still sometimes slip and refer to GNP when they should be referring to GDP. **Gross national product (GNP)** is the value of final goods and services produced by residents of a country, even if the production takes place outside that country. GDP measures the production of goods and services within the borders of a country, and GNP measures the production of goods and services by factors of production owned by a country's citizens. For example, the Japanese firm Toyota owns factories in the United States, so the value of the cars produced in those factories is included in U.S. GDP. The profits received by the Japanese owners of Toyota in exchange for the factors of production they supply, however, have to be subtracted from U.S. GNP and added to Japanese GNP. The BEA defines *net factor payments* as being equal to the difference between factor payments from other countries and factor payments to other countries.

Gross national product (GNP) The value of final goods and services produced by residents of a country, even if the production takes place outside that country.

So, GDP and GNP are related by the following identity:

$$\text{GDP} = \text{GNP} + \text{Net factor payments}.$$

In practice, for the United States, net factor payments are small, so the value of GDP is typically within about 1% of the value of GNP. The difference can be quite large for some smaller countries, such as the Netherlands and Ireland, where citizens of other countries own a substantial number of the factories and stores that produce domestic goods and services. For those countries, GDP is a much more accurate measure of the value of total production than is GNP.

Real GDP, Nominal GDP, and the GDP Deflator

2.2

Learning Objective

Discuss the difference between real GDP and nominal GDP.

The *value* of total production as measured by GDP can increase either because the quantity of goods and services increases or because the prices used to value the quantities rise (or because some of both happen). For instance, if the quantities of every good and service remain the same, but all prices double, then the value of GDP will double. Because we are primarily interested in GDP as a measure of production, the BEA separates price changes from quantity changes by calculating a measure of production called *real GDP*. **Nominal GDP** is calculated by summing the current values of final goods and services. **Real GDP** is calculated by designating a particular year as the *base year* and then using

Nominal GDP The value of final goods and services calculated using current-year prices.

Real GDP The value of final goods and services calculated using base-year prices.

[6]Technically, GDP would rise by an amount equal to the difference between what Best Buy pays Nintendo for the Wii and the price you paid for it. This difference represents the value of the service Best Buy has performed by importing the Wii from Japan and making it available for you to buy. We ignore this complication here.

Figure 2.3

Nominal GDP and Real GDP, 1990–2010

Real GDP is calculated using prices from the base year. For years before the base year, real GDP is greater than nominal GDP. For years after the base year, nominal GDP is greater than real GDP.

Source: U.S. Bureau of Economic Analysis. ●

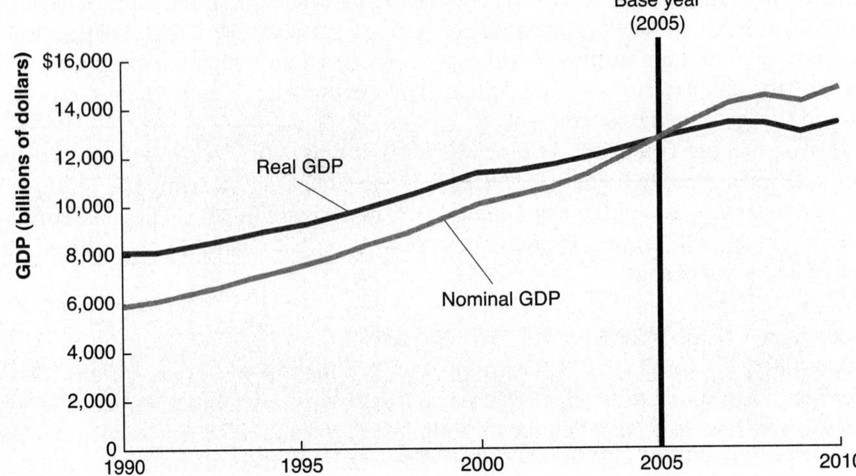

prices in the base year to calculate the value of goods and services in all other years. For instance, currently the BEA has designated 2005 as the base year. So, real GDP for 2012 is calculated by using prices of goods and services from 2005. By keeping prices constant, we know that changes in real GDP represent changes in the quantity of goods and services produced in the economy.

Figure 2.3 shows nominal GDP and real GDP for the years 1990–2010. Note that for years before the base year of 2005, real GDP is greater than nominal GDP; for years after 2005, nominal GDP is greater than real GDP. The lines for real GDP and nominal GDP cross in the base year.

Solved Problem 2.2a

Calculating Real GDP

Consider a very simple economy that produces only four final goods and services: apples, plums, teeth whitening, and hamburgers. Assume that the base year is 2005. Use the information in the following table to calculate nominal and real GDP for 2005 and 2012.

	2005		2012	
Product	**Quantity**	**Price**	**Quantity**	**Price**
Apples	200	$ 0.50	220	$ 0.60
Plums	90	0.40	85	0.35
Hamburgers	60	3.00	70	3.25
Teeth whitening	5	50.00	7	52.00

Solving the Problem

Step 1 **Review the chapter material.** This problem asks you to calculate real GDP, so you may want to review the section "Real GDP, Nominal GDP, and the GDP Deflator," which begins on page 33.

Step 2 **Calculate nominal GDP for the two years.** To calculate nominal GDP, we multiply the quantities produced during a year by the prices for that year to obtain the value of production for each good or service. Then we need to add up the values.

For 2005:

Product	Quantity	Price	Value
Apples	200	$ 0.50	$ 100.00
Plums	90	0.40	36.00
Hamburgers	60	3.00	180.00
Teeth whitening	5	50.00	250.00
Nominal GDP			$ 566.00

For 2012:

Product	Quantity	Price	Value
Apples	220	$ 0.60	$ 132.00
Plums	85	0.35	29.75
Hamburgers	70	3.25	227.50
Teeth whitening	7	52.00	364.00
Nominal GDP			$ 753.25

Step 3 Calculate real GDP for 2012 using the prices for 2005. To calculate real GDP for 2012, we need to multiply the quantities produced in 2012 by the prices for those goods and services in the base year 2005:

Product	Quantity (2012)	Price (2005)	Value
Apples	220	$ 0.50	$110.00
Plums	85	0.40	34.00
Hamburgers	70	3.00	210.00
Teeth whitening	7	50.00	350.00
Real GDP			$704.00

Notice that because the prices of three of the four products increased between 2005 and 2012, for 2012 the value of real GDP is significantly less than the value of nominal GDP.

Step 4 Determine real GDP for 2005. To calculate real GDP, we multiply current year quantities by base year prices. Because 2005 is the base year, our calculation of real GDP would be the same as our calculation of nominal GDP. In fact, nominal GDP will always equal real GDP in the base year.

For more practice, do related problems 2.7, 2.8, and 2.9 on pages 54–55 at the end of this chapter.

Price Indexes and the GDP Deflator

From year to year, the prices of some goods and services rise, while the prices of other goods and services fall. To gauge what is happening to prices in the economy as a whole, economists need a measure of the *price level*, which is an average of the prices of goods and services in the economy. One of the goals of macroeconomic policy is price stability. Economists measure the price level with a *price index*, which is a measure of the average of the prices of goods and services in one year relative to a base year. We can use values for nominal GDP and real GDP to calculate a price index called the *GDP deflator*, which is also called the *GDP implicit price deflator*. We can calculate the **GDP deflator** by using the following formula:

GDP deflator A measure of the price level, calculated by dividing nominal GDP by real GDP and multiplying by 100; also called the GDP implicit price deflator.

$$\text{GDP deflator} = \frac{\text{Nominal GDP}}{\text{Real GDP}} \times 100.$$

Because nominal GDP equals real GDP in the base year, the GDP deflator equals 100 in the base year.

To see why the GDP deflator is a measure of the price level, think about what would happen if prices of goods and services rose while production remained the same. In that case, nominal GDP would increase, but real GDP would remain constant, so the GDP deflator would increase. In fact, in most years, both prices and production increase, but the more prices increase relative to increases in production, the more nominal GDP increases relative to real GDP, and the greater the value for the GDP deflator. Economists measure the inflation rate as the percentage increase in the price level from one year to the next. By calculating the GDP deflator for two consecutive years, we get a measure of the inflation rate in the second year. In symbols, if P_t is the price level in the first year, P_{t+1} is the price level in the second year, and π_{t+1} is the inflation rate during the second year, then:

$$\text{Inflation rate} = \pi_{t+1} = \frac{P_{t+1} - P_t}{P_t} \times 100.$$

Solved Problem 2.2b

Calculating the Inflation Rate

Use the values for nominal GDP and real GDP given in the following table to calculate the inflation rate during 2010.

	2009	2010
Nominal GDP	$14,119.0 billion	$14,660.4 billion
Real GDP	$12,880.6 billion	$13,248.2 billion

Solving the Problem

Step 1 **Review the chapter material.** This problem asks you to calculate the inflation rate using values for the GDP deflator, so you may want to review the section "Price Indexes and the GDP Deflator," which begins on page 35.

Step 2 **Calculate the GDP deflator for each year.** To calculate the GDP deflator, we divide nominal GDP by real GDP and multiply by 100:

$$\text{GDP deflator for 2009} = \frac{\$14{,}119.0 \text{ billion}}{\$12{,}880.6 \text{ billion}} \times 100 = 109.6$$

$$\text{GDP deflator for 2010} = \frac{\$14{,}660.4 \text{ billion}}{\$13{,}248.2 \text{ billion}} \times 100 = 110.7$$

Step 3 **Calculate the inflation rate for 2010 and provide an interpretation of it.** We can calculate the inflation rate for 2010 as the percentage change in the GDP deflator between 2009 and 2010:

$$\left(\frac{110.7 - 109.6}{109.6}\right) \times 100 = 1.0\%.$$

This calculation tells us that an average of the prices of all final goods and services produced in the United States rose 1% between 2009 and 2010.

For more practice, do related problems 2.10 and 2.11 on page 55 at the end of this chapter.

The Chain-Weighted Measure of Real GDP

One drawback to calculating real GDP using base year prices is that over time, prices may change relative to each other. For example, the price of cell phones may fall relative to the price of milk. Because this change in relative prices is not reflected in the fixed prices from the base year, the estimate of real GDP is somewhat distorted. In effect, changes in relative prices reflect changes in consumers' relative valuation of goods and services, and we would like our measure of real GDP to include these changes. An additional difficulty arises because the goods and services that an economy produces change over time, so using prices from 2005 to value output in 2012 is difficult. For example, what was the value of an Apple iPad 2 in 2005? The iPad 2 did not exist in 2005, so we do not have a direct measure of its price in that year.

To address these problems, in 1996, the BEA switched to using *chain-weighted prices*, and it now publishes statistics on real GDP in "chained (2005) dollars." We do not need to go into the details of calculating real GDP using the chain-weighted price index, but the basic idea is straightforward. Starting with the base year, the BEA takes an average of prices in that year and prices in the following year. It then uses this average to calculate real GDP in the year following the base year. For the next year—in other words, the year that is two years after the base year—the BEA calculates real GDP by taking an average of prices in that year and the previous year. In this way, prices in each year are "chained" to prices from the previous year, and the distortion from changes in relative prices is minimized. The key point to remember is that chain-weighting effectively updates the prices for the base year each year and reduces the errors from changes in relative prices and the introduction of new goods and services.[7]

Making the Connection

Trying to Hit a Moving Target: Forecasting with "Real-Time Data"

We saw at the beginning of the chapter that the Federal Reserve, Congress, and the president rely on GDP data in policymaking. Unfortunately for these policymakers, the GDP data provided by the BEA are frequently revised, and the revisions can be large enough that the actual state of the economy can be different from what it at first appeared to be.

The BEA's *advance estimate* of a quarter's GDP is not released until about a month after the quarter has ended. This delay can be a problem for policymakers because it means that, for instance, they will not receive an estimate of GDP for the period from January through March until the end of April. Presenting even more difficulty is the fact that the advance estimate will be subject to a number of revisions. The *second estimate* of a quarter's GDP is released about two months after the end of the quarter. The *third estimate* is released about three months after the end of the quarter. Although the BEA used to refer to the third estimate as the "final estimate," in fact, it continues to revise its estimates through the years. For instance, the BEA releases first annual, second annual, and third annual estimates one, two, and three years after the third estimate. Nor is that the end because *benchmark revisions* of the estimates will occur in later years.

Why so many estimates? Because GDP is such a comprehensive measure of output in the economy, it is very time-consuming to collect the necessary data. To provide the

[7]For more detail on chain-type price indexes and other issues relating to the National Income and Product Account, see the Bureau of Economic Analysis, "Concepts and Methods of the U.S. National Income and Product Accounts," October 2009. Available at: http://www.bea.gov/national/pdf/NIPAhandbookch1-4.pdf.

advance estimate, the BEA relies on surveys carried out by the Commerce Department of retail sales and manufacturing shipments, as well as data from trade organizations, estimates of government spending, and so on. As time passes, these organizations gather additional data, and the BEA is able to refine its estimates.

Do these revisions to the GDP estimates matter? Sometimes they do, as the following example indicates. At the beginning of 2001, there were some indications that the U.S. economy might be headed for recession. The dot-com stock market bubble had burst the previous spring, wiping out trillions of dollars in stockholder wealth. Overbuilding of information technology also weighed on the economy. The advance estimate of the first quarter's GDP, though, showed a reasonably healthy increase in real GDP of 2.0% at an annual rate. It seemed as if there was nothing for government policymakers to be worried about. But, as the graph below shows, that estimate of 2.0% was revised a number of times over the years, mostly downward. Currently, BEA data indicate that real GDP actually *declined* by 1.3% at an annual rate during the first quarter of 2001. This swing of more than 3 percentage points is a large difference—a difference that changes the picture of what happened during the first quarter of 2001 from one of an economy experiencing moderate growth to one of an economy suffering a significant decline. The National Bureau of Economic Research dates the recession of 2001 as having begun in March, but some economists believe it actually began at the end of 2000. The current BEA estimates of GDP provide some support for this view.

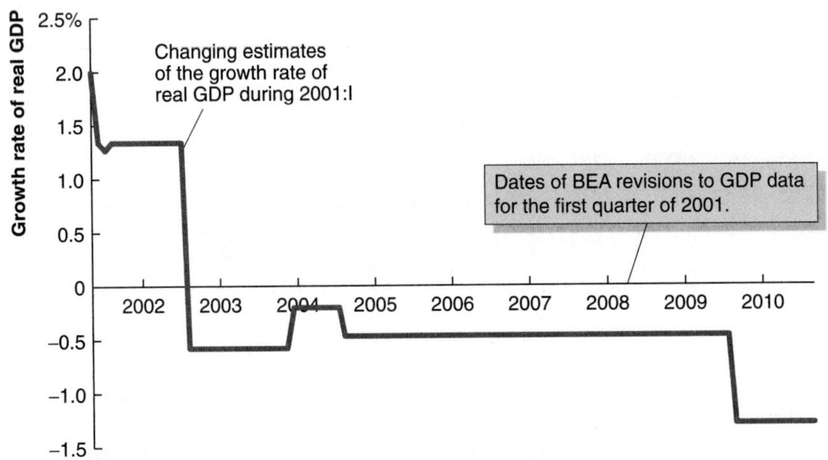

This example shows that in addition to the other problems that the Federal Reserve, Congress, and the president face in successfully conducting macroeconomic policy, they must make decisions using data that may be subject to substantial revisions.

Sources: Federal Reserve Bank of Philadelphia, "Historical Data Files for the Real-Time Data Set," August 24, 2010; and Bruce T. Grimm and Teresa Weadock, "Gross Domestic Product: Revisions and Source Data," *Survey of Current Business*, Vol. 86, No. 2, February 2006, pp. 11–15.

Test your understanding by doing related problem 2.12 on page 55 at the end of this chapter.

Comparing GDP Across Countries

One way of comparing economic activity across countries is by comparing levels of GDP. These comparisons are complicated because countries calculate GDP in terms of their own currencies. For example, for 2010, Chinese GDP was 39,978.3 billion yuan, Indian GDP was 78,799.5 billion rupees, and U.S. GDP was 14,660.4 billion dollars. Which economy was the largest?

We could translate these values into a single currency—say, U.S. dollars—by using exchange rates. For example, if Japanese GDP is ¥200 trillion and the exchange rate between the yen and the dollar is ¥100 = $1, then Japanese GDP in dollar terms equals ¥200 trillion/(¥100/$) = $2 trillion. One problem with this approach is that exchange rates tend to fluctuate widely, so our value for Japanese GDP would depend on which day's exchange rate we used. To get around this problem, rather than use the actual exchange rate, economists use the *purchasing power parity (PPP) exchange rate*, which is the number of units of a country's currency that is required to buy the same amount of goods and services in the country as one U.S. dollar would buy in the United States. Because the purchasing power of a country's currency tends not to change substantially over short periods of time, PPP exchange rates are more stable than actual exchange rates.

The World Bank, an international economic organization, coordinates the International Comparison Program (ICP), which collects data on more than 1,000 goods and services in 146 countries. Based on these surveys, the ICP constructs price levels for each country over time, and economists can use these price levels to calculate GDP for different countries in a common currency.

Making the Connection

The Incredible Shrinking Chinese Economy

Before 2007, China did not participate in the surveys that the ICP uses to construct PPP exchange rates, so the ICP did not have detailed price data on individual goods and services in China. The ICP had to estimate the PPP exchange rate using data provided by the Chinese government on broad categories of goods and services. These data had been first collected by two Chinese economists in 1986 and were not systematically updated. In 2007, the ICP announced the first PPP exchange rate based on detailed surveys of prices and discovered that prices in China were much higher than had been previously estimated. As a result, the previous PPP exchange rates were much too low for China, and the previous estimates for the dollar value of Chinese GDP were much too high.

By how much did the original estimates miss the mark? A lot. Based on the initial data, the ICP estimated that Chinese GDP was $8.8 trillion in 2005, but based on the more detailed data, the ICP estimated that Chinese GDP was actually only $5.3 trillion, or about 40% less. The original estimate indicated that the Chinese economy was 71% as large as the U.S. economy, but the new estimate indicated that the Chinese economy was only 43% as large as the U.S. economy. The adjustment reduced China's share of world GDP from 14% to 10%.

The ICP believes that the new estimates are more accurate, and Eswar Prasad, an economist at Cornell University, has referred to the work involved in gathering them as a "heroic effort." Still, the new price surveys are based on only 11 cities and the surrounding rural areas, so the data may not accurately represent prices in distant rural areas, where a large fraction of the Chinese population lives. As with all macroeconomic data, as time passes, economists refine and improve their estimates. Undoubtedly, future estimates of PPP exchange rates for China will become more accurate. It is unlikely, however, that future changes will have nearly the impact of the one described here.

Sources: World Bank, *International Comparison Program, Preliminary Results*, Washington, DC: World Bank, December 17, 2007; Keith Bradsher, "A Revisionist Tale: Why a Poor China Seems Richer," *New York Times*, December 21, 2007; and "Clipping the Dragon's Wings," *Economist*, December 19, 2007.

Test your understanding by doing related problem 2.13 on page 55 at the end of this chapter.

Figure 2.4

Shares of Global GDP, 1820–2008

As Western Europe and the United States industrialized, these regions increased their shares of world GDP. Industrialization eventually spread to Japan in the late 1800s, China in the late 1970s, and India in the 1990s. As a result, the shares of world GDP produced in Western Europe and the United States have decreased while the share produced in Asia has increased.

Source: Angus Maddison, "Statistics on World Population, GDP, and Per-Capita GDP, 1–2008 A.D.," February 2010, www.ggdc.net/maddison/Historical_Statistics/horizontal-file_02-2010.xls. ●

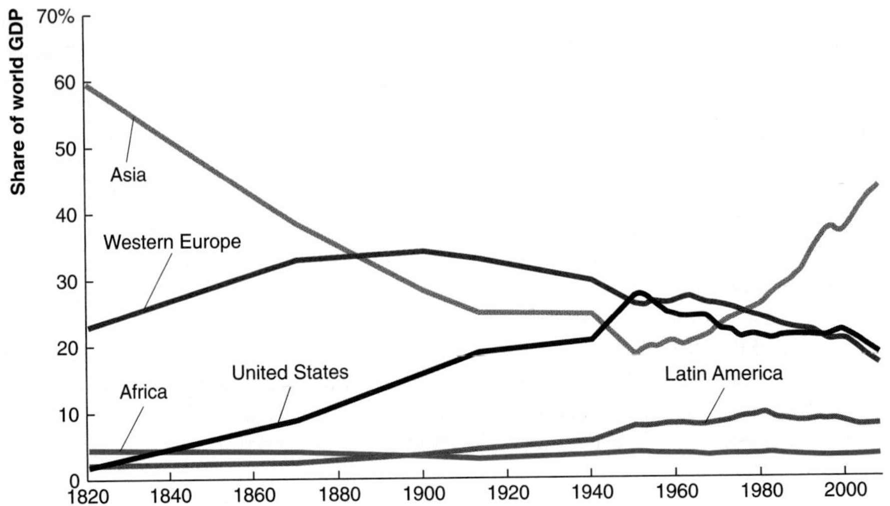

Despite the difficulties in computing PPP measures of GDP, these measures allow economists to compare economic performance across countries and over time. Before his death in 2010, Angus Maddison, an economist at the University of Groningen in the Netherlands, spent decades compiling consistent GDP data on a PPP basis for dozens of countries all the way back to 1820. As Figure 2.4 shows, Maddison's data can be used to track the relative economic performance of different regions of the world. The figure shows the shares of total world GDP for each of four broad regions and for the United States through 2008, the last year for which data are available. Several interesting patterns emerge:

1. Following the Industrial Revolution of the late 1700s, Western Europe's share of world GDP rose until it reached 34% in 1900. Western Europe's share of GDP then declined to 17% in 2008 as other regions started to industrialize.
2. The U.S. share of world GDP grew sharply during the 1800s as the United States industrialized. The U.S. share of world GDP peaked at 27% in 1951, when the economies of Western Europe were still recovering from World War II. Since 1951, the U.S. share of the world economy has declined to about 20%, as the economies of other countries have grown faster than the U.S. economy.
3. Asia's share of GDP declined from nearly 60% in 1820 to less than 20% in 1951 because the United States and Western Europe industrialized before most of Asia. The rapid industrialization of Japan, China, India, and several other Asian countries caused Asia's share to rise to about 44% in 2008.
4. The relatively weak performance of several large Latin American economies caused that region's share of world GDP to decline between 1980 and 2008.
5. The relatively poor economic performance of many African countries has kept that region's share of world GDP below 5% over this period of nearly 200 years.

We will analyze the reasons different countries have experienced different growth rates in Chapters 4 and 5. It's important to note here, though, that studies of economic growth, like studies of other macroeconomic topics, are dependent on the often-difficult job of compiling the necessary statistics.

GDP and National Income

We have seen that GDP is a measure of both the value of total production and the value of total income. GNP is also a measure of total production and total income. In addition

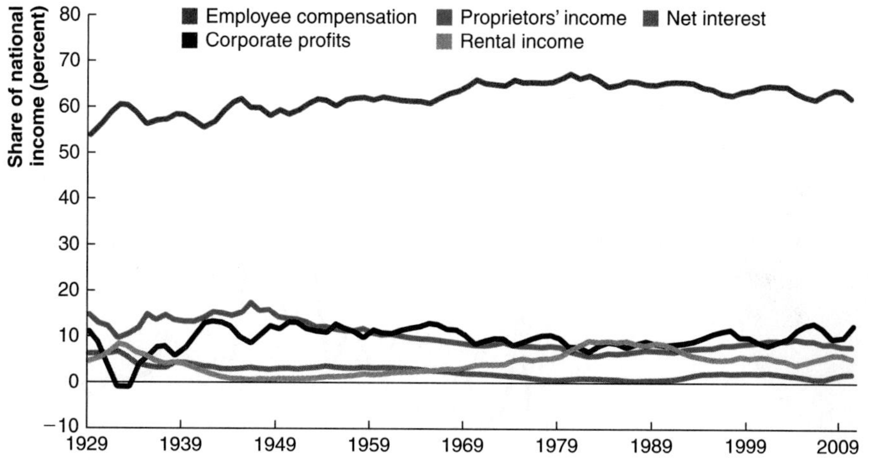

Figure 2.5

Categories of National Income in the United States, 1929–2010

Employee compensation is by far the largest component of national income, averaging 65% since 1969. In contrast, corporate profits averaged just 10%. The compensation of sole proprietors, net interest, and rental income all averaged less than 10% of national income.

Source: U.S. Bureau of Economic Analysis. ●

to GDP and GNP, the BEA publishes data on several additional measures of total income. In producing goods and services, some capital—such as machinery, equipment, and buildings—wears out and has to be replaced. *Depreciation* represents the value of worn-out or obsolete capital. In the data published by the BEA, depreciation is referred to as *consumption of fixed capital.* If we subtract this value from GDP, we are left with *national income.* The BEA publishes data on five categories of income: employee compensation, proprietors' income (which is the income earned by businesses that are not corporations), rental income, corporate profits, and net interest payments.

Figure 2.5 shows the five categories of income as percentages of national income. Employee compensation—mainly wages, salaries, and fringe benefits, such as employer-provided medical insurance and pension contributions—is by far the largest part of national income. Public opinion polls show that many people believe that corporate profits make up 40% or more of national income. In fact, though, over the past 80 years, while employee compensation has made up about 65% of national income, corporate profits have made up slightly less than 10%. The figure shows that, over time, the shares of the different categories of income have remained fairly stable.

The BEA also publishes data on *personal income,* which is income received by households. To calculate personal income, the BEA subtracts from national income the earnings that corporations retain rather than pay to shareholders in the form of dividends. The BEA also adds in household receipts of transfer payments and interest on government bonds. The BEA publishes data on *disposable personal income,* which is equal to personal income minus personal tax payments, such as the federal personal income tax. Disposable personal income is the best measure of the income households have available to spend.

Inflation Rates and Interest Rates

2.3

Learning Objective

Explain how the inflation rate is measured and distinguish between real and nominal interest rates.

We have seen that inflation is measured by the percentage change in the price level from one year to the next. The GDP deflator provides a measure of the price level that allows us to calculate the inflation rate. But for some purposes, the GDP deflator is too broad a measure because it includes the prices of every good and service included in GDP. Economists and policymakers are usually interested in inflation as it affects the prices paid by the typical household. The typical household does not buy large electric generators or 40-story office buildings, among other goods whose prices are included in the GDP deflator. So, economists and policymakers often rely on the *consumer price index,* which includes only good and services consumed by the typical household. The consumer price index does a better job than the GDP deflator at measuring changes in the *cost of living* as experienced by the typical household.

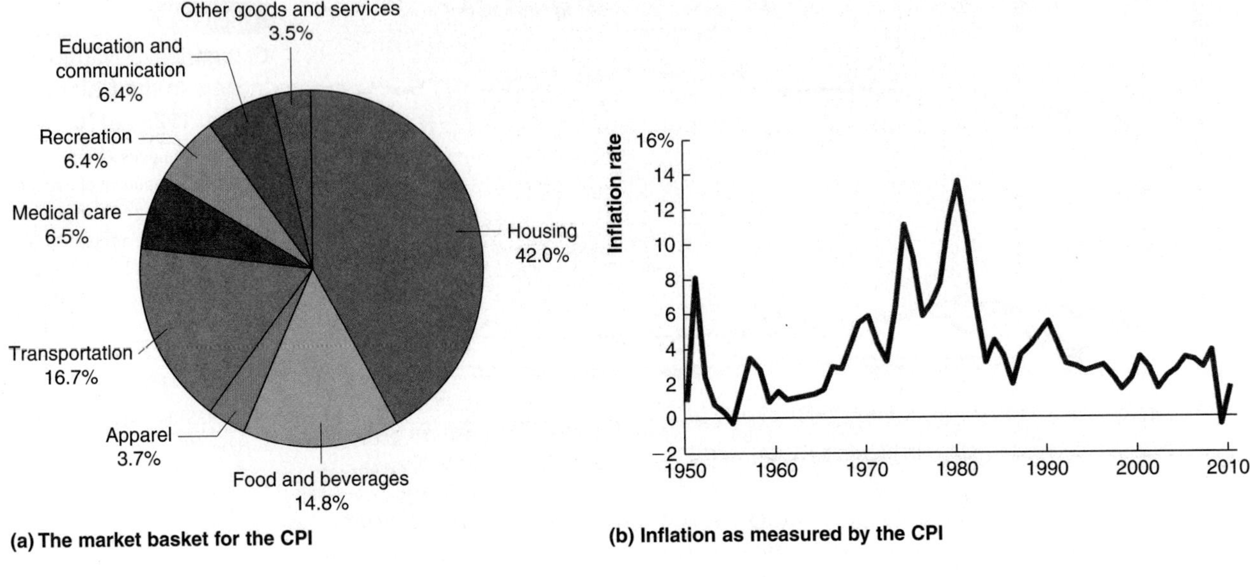

Figure 2.6 The Consumer Price Index

Panel (a) shows the market basket the BLS uses to weight the prices included in the CPI. Panel (b) shows the inflation rate as measured by the annual percentage change in the CPI.

Source: U.S. Bureau of Labor Statistics. ●

Consumer price index (CPI) An average of the prices of the goods and services purchased by the typical urban family of four.

The Consumer Price Index

The **consumer price index (CPI)** is an average of the prices of the goods and services purchased by the typical urban family of four. To obtain information on the goods and services purchased by this typical family, the U.S. Bureau of Labor Statistics (BLS) surveys 30,000 households nationwide on their spending habits.[8] The BLS uses the results of this survey to construct a market basket of 211 types of goods and services purchased by the typical urban family of four. Panel (a) of Figure 2.6 shows the goods and services in the market basket, grouped into eight broad categories. Almost three-quarters of the market basket falls into the categories of housing, transportation, and food. Each month, hundreds of BLS employees visit 23,000 stores in 87 cities and record prices of the goods and services in the market basket. Each price in the CPI is given a weight equal to the fraction of the typical family's budget spent on that good or service. One year is chosen as the base year, and the value of the CPI is set equal to 100 for that year. In any year other than the base year, the CPI is equal to the ratio of the dollar amount necessary to buy the market basket of goods in that year divided by the dollar amount necessary to buy the market basket of goods in the base year, multiplied by 100.

Panel (b) of Figure 2.6 shows the annual inflation rate from 1950 to 2010, as measured by the CPI. The figure shows that inflation rates were high during the late 1970s and early 1980s—reaching above 10%—and typically below 5% since the early 1980s. The severity of the 2007–2009 recession caused the price level to fall—that is, the economy experienced *deflation* according to the CPI—during 2009.

The CPI is widely used in *indexing*, which involves increasing a dollar value to protect against inflation. For example, each year, the federal government increases the Social

[8]Details of how the Bureau of Labor Statistics constructs the CPI can be found at: http://www.bls.gov/cex/.

Security payments it sends to retired workers by the percentage increase in the CPI during the previous year. If the CPI increases by 3%, then increasing Social Security payments by 3% should keep the purchasing power of the payments from declining. The federal government does not reduce Social Security payments when—as in 2009—the CPI declines during a year. The federal government also indexes the dollar thresholds that determine the federal tax rates individuals pay. Some union wage contracts are also indexed.

Making the Connection

Does Indexing Preserve the Purchasing Power of Social Security Payments?

If your salary increases at the same rate as the CPI, then the purchasing power of your salary should be unchanged. In 1975, Congress decided to index Social Security payments to keep the purchasing power of the payments constant. Has this cost-of-living adjustment (COLA) succeeded in protecting retired workers from the effects of inflation? The CPI is a good measure of changes in the cost of living for people who come close to consuming the same market basket of goods and services as the typical consumer. The CPI is not as good a measure for people whose purchases do not match those of the typical consumer. For example, as a college student, the mix of goods and services you buy may not match the CPI market basket shown in panel (a) of Figure 2.6. The percentage of your budget that you spend on housing and medical care may be lower, and the percentage you spend on food and beverages and apparel may be higher.

We might suspect that just as the budget of the average college student may not match the CPI market basket, the same may be true of retirees. (Although the most familiar version of the CPI is based on a market basket consumed by "all urban consumers," CPI-U, Congress chose to index Social Security to a slightly different version of the CPI that is based on a market basket consumed by "urban wage earners and clerical workers," CPI-W.) Economists Gopi Goda and John Shoven of Stanford University and Sita Slavov of Occidental College argue that indexing Social Security payments to the CPI does not fully protect retirees against inflation because retirees spend a much larger fraction of their budgets on medical services than does the average consumer, and the prices of medical services have tended to rise faster than other prices. The longer a person has been receiving Social Security payments, the greater the erosion in purchasing power. Goda, Shoven, and Slavov estimate that in 2007, the average 89-year old man would have needed a Social Security payment 20% higher than actually received in order to have kept pace with inflation. For a woman of the same age, the payment would have needed to be 27% higher. The BLS gathers information on a price index, CPI-E, that tracks a market basket of goods that better reflects the goods and services purchased by the elderly. If Congress changed the law to have Social Security payments indexed to CPI-E, Social Security payments would still not be completely protected against inflation, but the shortfall would be cut about in half.

If the calculations of Goda, Shoven, and Slavov are correct, then Congress has not managed to fully protect Social Security payments against the effects of inflation by indexing the payments to the CPI.

Sources: U.S. Social Security Administration, "Cost-of-Living Adjustment (COLA)," www.ssa.gov/oact/COLA/colasummary.html; and Gopi Shah Goda, John B. Shoven, and Sita Nataraj Slavov, "How Well Are Social Security Recipients Protected from Inflation?" *National Tax Journal*, Vol. 64, No. 2, June 2011, pp. 429–450.

Test your understanding by doing related problem 3.7 on page 56 at the end of this chapter.

How Accurate Is the CPI?

Because the CPI is the most widely used measure of the inflation rate, it is important that it be accurate. Most economists believe, however, that there are four reasons the CPI *overstates* the true inflation rate. First, the CPI suffers from *substitution bias.* In constructing the CPI, the BLS assumes that each month, consumers purchase the same quantity of each product in the market basket. In fact, though, consumers are likely to buy less of the products whose prices increase the most and more of the products whose prices increase the least. For example, if the price of pears increases much more than the price of plums, consumers are likely to buy more plums and fewer pears. Because the BLS assumes that consumers buy fixed quantities of pears and plums, the CPI will overstate the price increase in the market basket that consumers actually buy.

Second, the CPI suffers from a bias due to the *introduction of new goods* because the market basket is updated only every two years. The prices of many new goods, such as smart phones, Blu-ray players, and high-definition televisions decrease significantly in the months after being introduced, but these price decreases will not be reflected in the CPI if the goods are not included in the market basket.

Third, the *quality of goods and services* changes over time, and these changes are not completely reflected in the CPI. For example, if you spend $2,000 on a high-definition television in 2012, you will get a much better television than if you had spent $2,000 on a high-definition television in 2006, which means that, in effect, the price of a television of constant quality has decreased. The BLS attempts to make adjustments for changes in the quality of products, but doing so is difficult. The failure to fully adjust prices for changes in the quality of products results in a upward bias in the CPI.

Fourth, there is an *outlet bias* in the CPI data. That is, the BLS collects price data primarily from traditional retail outlets such as supermarkets and department stores. However, many households shop at large discount stores such as Costco or BJ's or on the Internet, and these sources are underrepresented in the sample of prices the BLS gathers.

The BLS is working continually to improve the accuracy of the CPI, but many economists still believe that CPI inflation overstates the true inflation rate by 0.5 percentage point to 1 percentage point. That is, when the BLS reports an inflation rate of 2%, the actual inflation rate is probably 1% to 1.5%. Do such small differences matter? They can when compounded over long periods of time. For example, suppose that a Social Security payment starts out at $1,000 in 2012. If over the following 20 years, the CPI indicates that inflation has been 2%, the federal government will have increased the payment to $1,486. If the inflation rate is actually only 1%, then the payment should have grown to $1,220, or about 18% less. Multiplied by millions of Social Security recipients, the effect on the federal government's budget could be substantial.

The Way the Federal Reserve Measures Inflation

Federal Reserve The central bank of the United States; usually referred to as "the Fed."

Personal consumption expenditures (PCE) price index A price index similar to the GDP deflator, except that it includes only the prices of goods from the consumption category of GDP.

The **Federal Reserve** (the Fed) is the central bank of the United States. One of the Fed's main policy goals is price stability. To meet this goal, the Fed has an informal target for the inflation rate of about 2%. So, the Fed has to consider carefully the best way to measure the inflation rate. Because the CPI suffers from biases that cause it to overstate the true underlying rate of inflation, the Fed announced in 2000 that it would rely more on the **personal consumption expenditures (PCE) price index** than on the CPI in tracking inflation. The PCE is a measure of the price level that is similar to the GDP deflator, except that it includes only the prices of goods from the consumption category of GDP.

The Fed believes that there are three advantages to using the PCE:

1. The PCE is a chain-type price index, as opposed to the market-basket approach used in constructing the CPI. Because consumers shift the mix of products they buy each year, the market-basket approach causes the CPI to overstate actual inflation. A chain-type price index allows the mix of products to change each year.

2. The PCE includes the prices of more goods and services than the CPI, so it is a broader measure of inflation.
3. Past values of the PCE can be recalculated as better ways of computing price indexes are developed and as new data become available. Much of the survey information that the BEA uses to construct GDP or the PCE Index comes from firms. The sample of firms that the BEA uses does not include some new firms. Over time, however, the BEA revises its estimates as data from these new firms becomes available. The BLS is unable to make similar adjustments to the CPI. Therefore, the PCE index allows the Fed to better track historical trends in inflation.

Since 2004, the Fed has focused on a subcategory of the PCE: the so-called *core PCE*, which excludes food and energy prices. Prices of food and energy tend to fluctuate up and down for reasons that may not be related to the causes of general inflation and that cannot easily be controlled by the Fed's actions. These events include severe weather, such as droughts in farm areas or hurricanes along the Gulf Coast, or political events, such as unrest in oil-producing countries, which temporarily disrupts oil production. Figure 2.7 shows the inflation rate as measured by the CPI, the PCE, and the core PCE. Although the three measures of inflation move roughly together, the core PCE has been more stable than the other indexes. Note in particular that during most of 2009, when the CPI and the PCE were indicating that the economy was experiencing deflation, the core PCE was still showing moderate inflation of greater than 1.5%. If you want to know what the Fed thinks the current inflation rate is, the best idea is to look at data on the core PCE. The BEA publishes these data monthly.

Interest Rates

The financial crisis and severe recession of 2007–2009 showed that what happens in the financial system can be of crucial importance for the rest of the economy. A key economic variable in understanding the financial system is the interest rate. The **interest rate** is the cost of borrowing funds, usually expressed as a percentage of the amount borrowed. For example, if you borrow \$100 and have to pay back \$105 in one year, then you have paid \$5 in interest, and the interest rate on the loan is 5%: (\$5 / \$100) × 100 = 5%. Similarly, if you deposit money in a savings account or a certificate of deposit in a bank, the interest rate you earn is the return to your savings.

Interest rate The cost of borrowing funds, usually expressed as a percentage of the amount borrowed.

The **nominal interest rate** is the stated interest rate you pay on a loan or receive on your savings. Inflation reduces the purchasing power of interest payments. For example, suppose that you buy a \$1,000 certificate of deposit bond that pays you \$50 in interest

Nominal interest rate The stated interest rate on a loan.

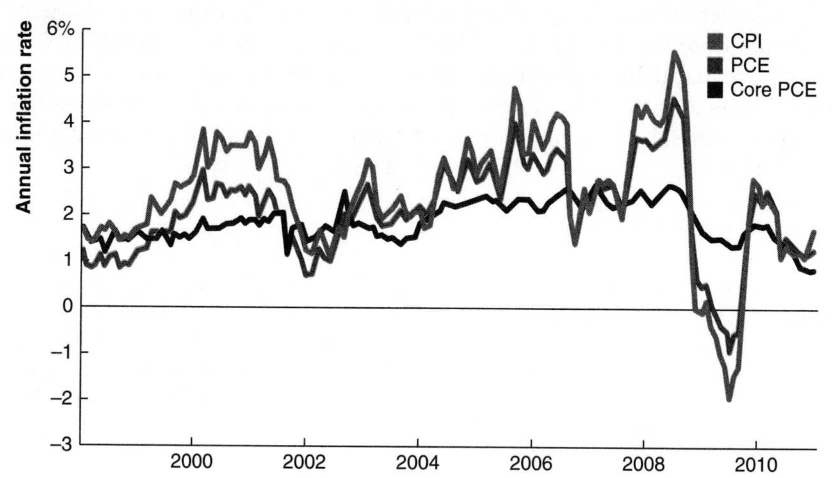

Figure 2.7

The Measures of the Inflation Rate, 1998–2011

The Federal Reserve measures inflation using the core personal consumption expenditures (PCE) price index, which is more stable than the CPI or the personal consumption expenditures (PCE) price index.

Source: Federal Reserve Bank of St. Louis.

each year for five years. If the purchasing power of the dollars that you receive declines over time, you are, in effect, losing part of your interest income to inflation. In addition, inflation causes the purchasing power of the $1,000—the *principal*—to decline as well. For example, if inflation is 3% per year, the purchasing power of your $1,000 principal falls by $30 each year. Lenders and borrowers know that inflation reduces the purchasing power of interest income, so they base their decisions not on the nominal interest, but on the **real interest rate**, which is the nominal interest rate adjusted for the effects of inflation.

Real interest rate The nominal interest rate adjusted for the effects of inflation.

Because borrowers and lenders don't know with certainty what the inflation rate will be during the period of a loan, they don't know what the *actual* real interest rate will be. So, they must make borrowing or investing decisions on the basis of what they *expect* the real interest rate to be. To estimate the expected real interest rate, savers and borrowers must decide what they expect the inflation rate to be. Therefore, we can say that the expected real interest rate, r, equals the nominal interest rate, i, minus the expected rate of inflation, π^e, or[9]:

$$r = i - \pi^e.$$

Note that this equation also means that the nominal interest rate equals the real interest rate plus the expected inflation rate:

$$i = r + \pi^e.$$

For example, suppose you take out a car loan from your local bank. You are willing to pay, and the bank is willing to accept, a real interest rate of 3%. Both you and the bank expect that the inflation rate will be 2%. Therefore, you and the bank agree on a nominal interest rate of 5% on the loan. What happens if the actual inflation rate turns out to be 4%, which is higher than you and the bank had expected? In that case, the actual real interest rate that you end up paying (and the bank ends up receiving) equals 5% − 4% = 1%, which is less than the expected real interest rate of 3%. Because the inflation rate turns out to be higher than you and the bank expected, you gain by paying a lower real interest rate, and the bank loses by receiving a lower real interest rate.

We can generalize by noting that the actual real interest rate equals the nominal interest rate minus the actual inflation rate. If the actual inflation rate is greater than the expected inflation rate, the actual real interest rate will be less than the expected real interest rate; in this case, borrowers will gain and lenders will lose. If the actual inflation rate is less than the expected inflation rate, the actual real interest rate will be greater than the expected real interest rate; in this case, borrowers will lose, and lenders will gain.

For the economy as a whole, economists often measure the nominal interest rate as the interest rate on U.S. Treasury bills that mature in three months. In Figure 2.8, we show the nominal interest rate, the actual real interest rate, and the expected real interest rate for the period from the first quarter of 1982 through the fourth quarter of 2010. To calculate the actual real interest rate, we used the actual inflation rate as measured by percentage changes in the CPI. To calculate the expected real interest rate, we used the expected percentage change in the CPI, as reported in a survey of professional forecasters conducted by the Federal Reserve Bank of Philadelphia.

---

[9]To fully account for the effect of changes in purchasing power on the nominal interest rate, we should use the equation. $\frac{1+i}{1+\pi^e} = 1 + r$. Rearranging terms gives us $1 + i = 1 + r + \pi^e + r\pi^e$, or $r = i - \pi^e - r\pi^e$. This equation is the same as the one in the text except for the term $r\pi^e$. The value of this term is usually quite small. For example, if the real interest rate is 2% and the expected inflation rate is 3%, then $r\pi^e = 0.02 \times 0.03 = 0.0006$. So, as long as the inflation rate and the real interest rate are relatively low, the equation for the real interest rate given in the text is a close approximation.

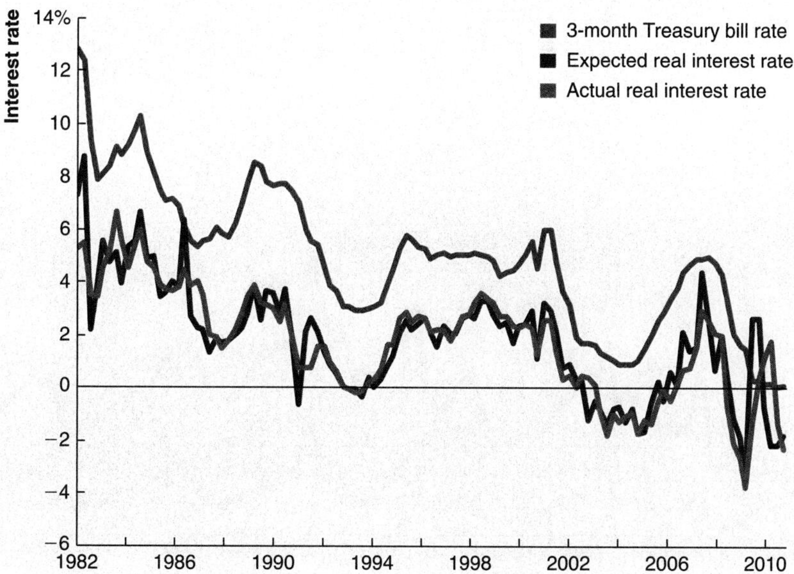

Figure 2.8

Nominal and Real Interest Rates, 1982–2010

In this figure, the nominal interest rate is the interest rate on 3-month U.S. Treasury bills. The actual real interest rate is the nominal interest minus the actual inflation rate, as measured by changes in the consumer price index. The expected real interest rate is the nominal interest rate minus the expected rate of inflation as measured by a survey of professional forecasters. When the U.S. economy experienced deflation during 2009, the real interest rate was greater than the nominal interest rate.

Sources: Federal Reserve Bank of St. Louis; and Federal Reserve Bank of Philadelphia. ●

Figure 2.8 shows that the nominal and real interest rates tend to rise and fall together. The figure also shows that the actual and expected real interest rates follow each other closely, which is an indication that during most of this period, expectations of the inflation rate were fairly accurate. Note that in some periods, particularly after the beginning of the recession in late in 2007, the real interest rate was negative. Finally, note that it is possible for the nominal interest rate to be lower than the real interest rate. For this outcome to occur, the nominal interest rate has to be less than the inflation rate.

Measuring Employment and Unemployment

2.4

Learning Objective

Understand how to calculate the unemployment rate.

When most people think about an economic recession, they don't think about declines in GDP as much as they think about problems with finding and keeping a job. In fact, the unemployment rate can have important political implications. In most presidential elections, the incumbent president is reelected if unemployment is falling early in the election year but is defeated if unemployment is rising. Investors also closely monitor the reports the U.S. Department of Labor issues each month on changes in employment and unemployment as the investors try to gauge the health of the economy. The levels of employment and unemployment are key macroeconomic variables, so it is important to have some familiarity with how the federal government measures them.

Each month, the U.S. Bureau of the Census conducts the *Current Population Survey* (often referred to as the *household survey*) to collect data needed to compute the unemployment rate. The BLS uses these data to calculate the monthly unemployment rate. People are considered *employed* if they worked during the week before the survey or if they were temporarily away from their jobs because they were ill, on vacation, on strike, or for other reasons. People are considered *unemployed* if they did not work in the previous week but were available for work and had actively looked for work at some time during the previous four weeks. The **labor force** is the sum of employed and unemployed workers. The **unemployment rate** is the percentage of the labor force that is unemployed, or:

Labor force The sum of employed and unemployed workers in the economy.

Unemployment rate The percentage of the labor force that is unemployed.

$$\text{Unemployment rate} = \left(\frac{\text{Number of unemployed}}{\text{Labor force}}\right) \times 100.$$

For example, in March 2011, there were 13,542,000 unemployed workers in a labor force of 153,406,000, so the unemployment rate was $(13{,}542{,}000/153{,}406{,}000) \times 100 = 8.8\%$.

Figure 2.9

Alternative Measures of the Unemployment Rate, 1948–2011

Because of the uncertainty about the best way to measure the unemployment rate, the BLS publishes data on alternative measures.

Source: U.S. Bureau of Labor Statistics. ●

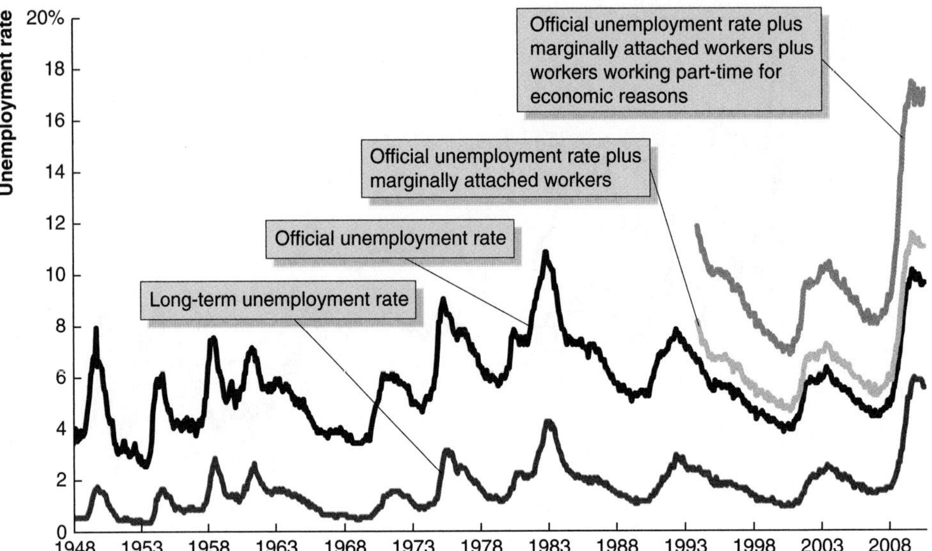

One problem the BLS has in measuring the unemployment rate is distinguishing between unemployed workers and people who are not in the labor force. The official unemployment rate includes just those workers who have looked for work in the past four weeks. But some *discouraged workers* might prefer to have a job but have given up looking because they believe finding a job is too difficult. Because these workers are not actively looking for a job, they are not considered to be in the labor force and so aren't counted as unemployed. Therefore, the unemployment rate as measured by the BLS may understate the true degree of joblessness in the economy. A second problem arises because the BLS also counts people with part-time jobs as being employed, even if they would prefer to hold full-time jobs. Counting as employed a part-time worker who wants to work full time tends to understate the degree of joblessness in the economy and make the employment situation appear better than it is. For example, the official unemployment rate for March 2011 was 8.8%. However, the unemployment rate when including discouraged workers was 9.4%. The unemployment rate when taking into account both discouraged workers and part-time workers who would have preferred to work full time was 15.7%.[10]

As a result of problems with the official unemployment rate measure, the BLS publishes data on several different measures of the unemployment rate. Figure 2.9 shows several of these alternative measures of the unemployment rate. The long-term unemployment rate in the figure shows the percentage of the labor force that has been unemployed for 15 weeks or more. The alternative series are higher than the official unemployment rate—and sometimes substantially higher. These alternative measures of unemployment have been available only since 1994, but the data show that the alternative measures tend to rise

[10]The BLS refers to the official unemployment rate as the U-3 measure of unemployment. The broader unemployment rate given in this paragraph is called the U-6 measure and includes *marginally attached workers* and part-time workers who would prefer to work full time. This is BLS's definition of marginally attached workers: "Persons marginally attached to the labor force are those who currently are neither working nor looking for work but indicate that they want and are available for a job and have looked for work sometime in the past 12 months. Discouraged workers, a subset of the marginally attached, have given a job-market related reason for not currently looking for work."

and fall with the official unemployment rate. This means changes in the official unemployment rate accurately reflect changes in the difficulty of finding a job. Most economists believe that the official unemployment rate is a useful, although not perfect, measure of conditions in the labor market.

In addition to the household survey, the BLS uses the *establishment survey*, sometimes called the *payroll survey*, to measure total employment in the economy. This monthly survey samples about 300,000 business establishments. The establishment survey provides information on the total number of persons who are employed and on a company payroll. The establishment survey has three drawbacks. First, the survey does not provide information on the number of self-employed persons because they are not on a company payroll. Second, the survey may fail to count some persons as employed at newly opened firms that are not included in the survey. Third, the survey provides no information on unemployment. Despite these drawbacks, the establishment survey has the advantage of being determined by actual payrolls rather than by unverified answers to survey questions, as is the case with the household survey. In recent years, some economists have come to rely more on establishment survey data than on household survey data in analyzing current labor market conditions. Some financial analysts who forecast the future state of the economy to help forecast stock prices have also begun to rely more on establishment survey data than on household survey data.

Answering the Key Question

Continued from page 23

At the beginning of this chapter, we asked the question:

"How accurately does the government measure the unemployment rate?"

We have just seen that in measuring the unemployment rate, the BLS has not been given an easy task. Clearly, not everyone without a job should be counted as unemployed. Some people are full-time homemakers, others suffer from chronic illnesses that leave them unable to work, and some are retired. People in these groups are voluntarily without jobs and so should not be counted as in the labor force or as unemployed. The gray areas involve people who respond to the household survey that they want a job and are available to take one, but who have not actively searched for a job during the previous four weeks, and part-time workers who can't find a full-time job. Whether and how to count these people in the unemployment statistics remains open to debate.

In addition, the household survey does not verify the responses of people included in the survey. Some people who claim to be unemployed and actively looking for work may not be actively looking. A person might claim to be actively looking for a job to remain eligible for government payments to the unemployed. In this case, a person who is actually not in the labor force is counted as unemployed. Other people might be employed but engaged in illegal activity—such as drug dealing—or might want to conceal a legitimate job to avoid paying taxes. In these cases, individuals who are actually employed are counted as unemployed.

We can conclude that, although the unemployment rate provides some useful information about the employment situation in the country, it is far from an exact measure of joblessness in the economy.

Before moving on to the next chapter, read *An Inside Look* on the next page for a discussion of how the recession of 2007–2009 affected the construction industry.

Weak Construction Market Persists

ASSOCIATED PRESS

Builders Began Work on Fewer Projects in 2010

Builders began work on fewer homes, shopping centers and other projects in 2010, pushing total building activity down to the lowest point in a decade.

a Construction spending dropped 10.3 percent last year, marking the fourth annual decline, the Commerce Department said Tuesday. It fell to $814.18 billion in 2010, the lowest level since 2000.

And the year ended on a weak note. Builders started fewer homes and other projects in December, pushing activity down 2.5 percent for the month.

Builders have struggled with falling demand since the housing bubble burst, triggering a deep recession. The downturn sharply lowered overall economic activity and that cut into demand for office buildings, hotels and shopping centers.

Analysts said harsh winter weather had some impact on the weak December numbers. But other factors are likely to keep the industry from seeing significant gains in the early months of this year.

b Homebuilders are having a hard time competing with the record number of foreclosures and declining home prices. The budget crises at the state and local level, along with fading federal stimulus money, have governments pulling back on projects. Rising vacancy rates and declining rents are dragging on commercial real estate construction.

David Wyss, an economist for Standard & Poor's in New York, said a healthy level for the construction industry would have spending around $1.5 trillion annually—almost double the level in 2010. He said it will probably take until the middle of this decade to reach that point.

"We still have a big overhang of unsold homes out there," Wyss said. "And on the nonresidential side, the question is jobs. You don't need to build another office building until you get the jobs back."

c For 2010, home construction fell 1.7 percent and nonresidential projects plunged 23.3 percent. Spending for the category that includes shopping centers dropped 26 percent.

Government projects slid 2.7 percent.

The December drop in construction left spending at a seasonally adjusted annual rate of $787.9 billion, the lowest monthly level since July 2000. That surpassed the previous low hit in August and underscored that conditions in the building industry remain extremely weak.

For the month, builders spent 4.1 percent less for residential projects. Work on nonresidential projects dropped 0.5 percent, with work on hotels and shopping centers both declining.

Builders have had trouble obtaining financing for projects since the recession began. Banks have tightened lending standards in response to higher default rates.

Spending on government projects fell in December 2.8 percent. State and local spending dropped 1.8 percent and spending by the federal government plunged 11.6 percent to the lowest level since October 2004.

Source: Martin Krutsinger, "Builders began work on fewer projects in 2010," *Associated Press*, February 1, 2011. Used with permission of The Associated Press.

Key Points in the Article

This article discusses the continued weakness in the construction and real-estate markets during 2010, as spending on the construction of residential housing and commercial buildings reached their lowest levels since 2000. The year 2010 marked the fourth straight year of decline for new construction, with residential, nonresidential, and government projects all falling below their 2009 levels. Existing inventories of residential and commercial properties, foreclosures, decreased demand, and tightening credit markets have all contributed to the slowdown in new construction.

Analyzing the News

a According to the Commerce Department, spending on construction projects fell to \$814.18 billion in 2010, down 10.3% from the previous year, its lowest level in the past ten years. Demand for new construction has fallen since the beginning of the recession of 2007–2009, following the burst in the housing market bubble. According to the Federal Reserve Bank of St. Louis, the number of building permits issued monthly for new home construction between 2007 and 2010 declined over 60% from more than 1,600,000 in January 2007 to just over 600,000 in December 2010.

b The large inventory of unsold homes in 2010 put a damper on new construction. Builders of new homes found it difficult to compete against the number of existing homes for sale, including an increasing number of foreclosures and their respective falling prices. The figure below shows the existing inventory of unsold homes from 2002 through 2010. After reaching its lowest point in almost three years in December 2009, the existing housing inventory, measured in months of supply, jumped significantly during the first half of 2010, peaking at a supply of more than 12 months before dropping in the last half of 2010 to a supply of 9.4 months.

c Compared to figures for 2009, new home construction fell 1.7% in 2010, and budget deficits were partly responsible for the 2.7% decline in the construction of government projects, but these paled in comparison to the drop in nonresidential construction. In 2010, nonresidential construction projects fell by more than 23%, and spending on these projects dropped by 26%. Since 2009 was also considered a weak year for new construction, the figures for 2010 are further indication of the continuation of an anemic construction market.

THINKING CRITICALLY

1. The value of new construction is included in the various components of gross domestic product (GDP). Explain where the following types of new construction are included in GDP calculations:
   a. A single-family home
   b. A commercial office building
   c. A public school
   d. An interstate highway
   e. A private hospital
   f. An apartment building
   g. A manufacturing factory with warehouse space
2. The decline in new construction has been accompanied by a decline in sales of new homes. According to the U.S. Census Bureau, an estimated 191,000 new homes were for sale at the end of December 2010. Based on the sales rate at the time, this represented a 9.4 month supply of new residential construction. Assume that all of these new homes were built in 2010 and that 90% of these homes were sold in 2011, with the remaining 10% sold in 2012. Explain when the value of these new homes would be included in GDP.

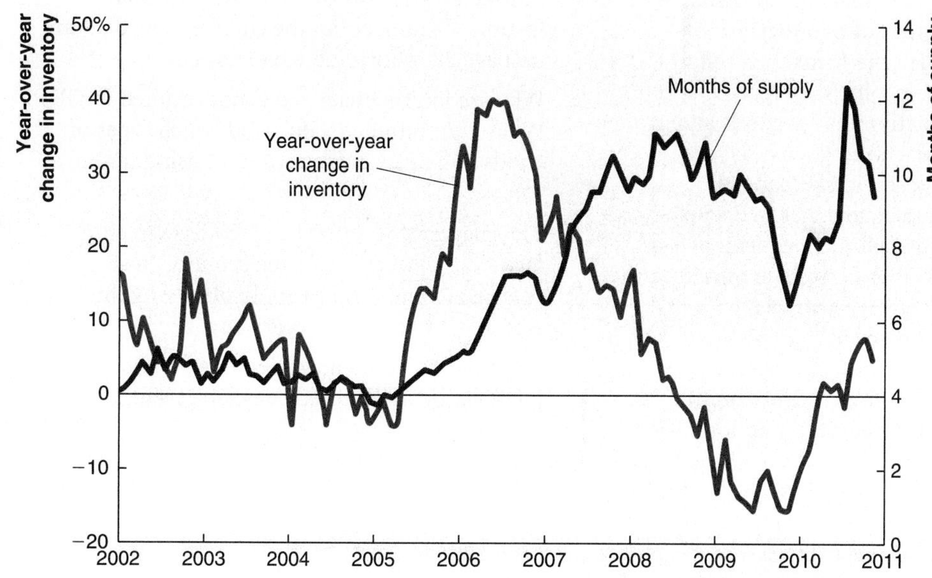

Existing Home Inventory, 2002–2011

Source: calculatedriskblog.com using data from the National Association of Realtors. ●

CHAPTER SUMMARY AND PROBLEMS

KEY TERMS

Capital, p. 27
Consumer price index (CPI), p. 42
Consumption, p. 29
Factor of production, p. 27
Federal Reserve, p. 44
Final good or service, p. 25
Financial system, p. 27
GDP deflator, p. 35
Government purchases, p. 30
Gross domestic product (GDP), p. 25
Gross national product (GNP), p. 33
Interest rate, p. 45
Intermediate good or service, p. 25
Investment, p. 29
Labor force, p. 47
National incomc accounting, p. 26
Net exports, p. 33
Nominal GDP, p. 33
Nominal interest rate, p. 45
Personal consumption expenditures (PCE) price index, p. 44
Real GDP, p. 33
Real interest rate, p. 46
Transfer payments, p. 31
Unemployment rate, p. 47

2.1 GDP: Measuring Total Production and Income

Explain how economists use gross domestic product (GDP) to measure total production and total income.

SUMMARY

Economists at the U.S. Bureau of Economic Analysis (BEA) measure total production based on **gross domestic product (GDP)**, which is the market value of all final goods and services produced in a country during a period of time. A **final good or service** is one that is purchased by its final user and is not included in the production of any other good or service. An **intermediate good** is a good or service that is an input into another good or service. The rules used in calculating GDP are called **national income accounting**. A key fact revealed by national income accounting is that the value of total production in an economy is equal to the value of total income. The circular-flow diagram illustrates how firms use the **factors of production** to produce goods and services, which the firms then sell to households. Households use the income they receive from selling the factors of production to buy goods and services. **Capital** refers to manufactured goods that are used to produce other goods and services. Financial intermediaries and financial markets together make up the **financial system**. GDP contains four categories of expenditures: **Consumption** *(C)* is the purchase of new goods and services by households. **Investment** *(I)* is spending by firms on new factories, office buildings, machinery, and additions to inventories, plus spending by households and firms on new houses. **Government purchases** *(G)* are spending by federal, state, and local governments on goods and services. Government purchases do not include **transfer payments**, which are payments by the government to individuals for which the government does not receive a good or service in return. **Net exports** *(NX)* is the value of all exports of goods and services minus the value of all imports of goods and services. **Gross national product (GNP)** is the value of final goods and services produced by residents of a country, even if the production takes place outside the country.

Review Questions

1.1 What is GDP? In what ways is it both a measure of total production and a measure of total income? (Think about the circular-flow diagram on page 28 in forming your answer.)

1.2 Why are intermediate goods not counted in GDP? What is an imputed value, and which types of goods and services are measured using imputed values?

1.3 The chapter states that households own all the factors of production in the economy and receive income from them. Explain why this is true.

1.4 What are the four categories of expenditures included in GDP? Briefly describe each.

Visit www.myeconlab.com to complete these exercises online and get instant feedback.

1.5 What is the difference between GDP and GNP? Briefly explain whether the difference is important for the United States.

Problems and Applications

1.6 How would each of the following events change measured GDP?

a. There is an increase in illegal drug sales.

b. More women stop being full-time homemakers and enter the labor force.

c. An oil spill causes pollution on beaches in California.

d. More families prepare meals at home instead of eating out.

1.7 By the 1960s, a larger percentage of women were entering the labor force. Because more women were working, their production of services within the home, such as cooking and cleaning, may have fallen. In addition, they may have employed others to do some tasks that they had previously done themselves, including caring for their children.

a. How did these changes affect GDP as measured by the BEA?

b. If we define "actual GDP" as GDP measured with the inclusion of such things as household production, illegal goods and services, and other typically excluded variables, how would actual GDP have changed?

1.8 Which of the following goods and services are included in GDP? If a good or service is not included, state why.

a. Cynthia buys some house paint.

b. Cynthia uses the paint that she purchased to paint her own house.

c. Bruce hires a painter to paint his house.

d. Randy sells the house that he bought 10 years ago.

e. Don buys a new Toyota Prius.

f. Don buys a 2005 Dodge truck to drive on the weekends.

1.9 Suppose that a simple economy produces pizza, video games, and candy. The following table gives quantities and prices for each good in three successive years:

	2010		2011		2012	
	Quantity	Price	Quantity	Price	Quantity	Price
Pizza	100	$0.50	125	$0.50	125	$0.60
Video games	75	1.00	85	1.00	85	1.25
Candy	20	5.00	30	5.00	30	6.00

a. Calculate GDP in 2010, 2011, and 2012.

b. What is the growth rate of GDP between 2010 and 2011?

c. What is the growth rate of GDP between 2011 and 2012?

d. Does GDP, measured in this way, show the change in quantity of goods produced from 2010 to 2011? From 2011 to 2012? Briefly explain.

1.10 Consider the following statement: "The BEA revises GDP data several times. Since preliminary estimates of GDP are likely to be incorrect, they should not be used for policymaking." Explain whether the statement is true, false, or uncertain.

1.11 **[Related to the *Making the Connection* on page 31]** According to financial journalist Roger Lowenstein writing in the *New York Times*,

> "The budgetary math is irrefutable: generous [public employee] pensions end up draining money from schools, social services and other programs."

a. Is spending by state and local governments on public employee pensions counted in GDP? Briefly explain.

b. How do generous public employee pensions end up draining money from other programs?

c. Does the federal government face the same problem? Why or why not?

Source: Roger Lowenstein, "The Next Crisis: Public Pension Fund," *New York Times*, June 25, 2010.

Real GDP, Nominal GDP, and the GDP Deflator

Discuss the difference between real GDP and nominal GDP.

SUMMARY

Nominal GDP measures the market value of final goods and services produced within a country, using prices from the current year. **Real GDP** measures the market value of final goods and services produced within a country, using prices from a base year. Real GDP is a measure of the total amount of goods and services produced. Real GDP allows us to compare total production in an economy over time. To compare the size of economies across countries, economists measure the size of the economy at purchasing power parity. Economists measure the price level with a *price index*. We can use the values for nominal GDP and real GDP to calculate a price index called the **GDP deflator**. To compare GDP across countries, economists use the purchasing power parity (PPP) exchange rate. In addition to publishing data on GDP and GNP, the BEA also publishes data on other measures of total income, including national income, personal income, and personal disposable income. Employee compensation is the largest category of national income. The shares of the different categories of income have remained fairly stable over the past 40 years.

Review Questions

2.1 What is the difference between nominal GDP and real GDP? Why do changes in nominal GDP usually overstate changes in total production in the economy?

2.2 What is a price index? How can values for nominal GDP and real GDP be used to calculate a price index?

2.3 What is a purchasing power parity exchange rate? How can it be used to compare GDP across countries?

2.4 What is the difference between GDP and national income? What is the difference between national income and personal income?

2.5 What are the five main categories of national income? Which category is the largest? Has any of the categories significantly increased or decreased its share over the past 40 years?

Problem and Applications

2.6 In January 2010, the approximate value of U.S. oil imports was $26.5 billion. In January 2011, the approximate value of U.S. oil imports was $35.2 billion.

a. Given the information above, can you conclude that there has been a significant increase in the number of barrels of oil that the United States is importing? Briefly explain.

b. The average price per barrel of crude oil in January 2010 was $75. By January 2011, the price had risen to approximately $91 per barrel. By what percentage had the *quantity* of oil imported changed?

Source: U.S. Department of Energy.

2.7 **[Related to *Solved Problem 2.2a* on page 34]** Use the information in the table to answer the following questions. Assume that 2010 is the base year.

	2010		2011		2012	
	Quantity	Price	Quantity	Price	Quantity	Price
Grapes	100	$0.50	125	$0.50	125	$0.60
Raisins	75	1.00	85	$1.00	85	1.25
Oranges	20	5.00	30	$5.00	30	6.00

a. Calculate real GDP in 2010, 2011, and 2012.

b. Did output in the economy grow by more in percentage terms between 2010 and 2011 or between 2011 and 2012? Briefly explain.

2.8 **[Related to *Solved Problem 2.2a* on page 34]** Use the information in the following table to calculate nominal and real GDP for 2005 and 2012. Assume that 2005 is the base year.

	2005		2012	
Product	Quantity	Price	Quantity	Price
Oranges	400	$ 0.50	440	$ 0.75
Plums	90	0.50	85	0.60
Haircuts	7	30.00	10	32.00
Pizza	60	8.00	70	8.25

2.9 **[Related to *Solved Problem 2.2a* on page 34]** The answer to Solved Problem 2.2a includes the following statement: "Notice that because the prices of three of the four products increased between 2005 and 2012, for 2012 the value of real GDP is significantly less than the value of nominal GDP."

Construct an example similar to the one in the problem for an economy with only four products. Show that it is possible to choose prices in 2012 so that although only one price increases, nominal GDP in 2012 is still greater than real GDP.

2.10 **[Related to *Solved Problem 2.2b* on page 36]** In the fourth quarter of 2009, U.S. GDP was $14,453.8 billion. Real GDP for the same quarter was $13,149.5 billion. Based on this information, what was the GDP deflator for the fourth quarter of 2009?

2.11 **[Related to *Solved Problem 2.2b* on page 36]** Use the values for nominal GDP and real GDP given in the following table to calculate the inflation rate during 1930:

	1929	1930
Nominal GDP	$103.6 billion	$91.2 billion
Real GDP	$977.0 billion	$892.8 billion

2.12 **[Related to the *Making the Connection* on page 37 and the *Chapter Opener* on page 23]** If policymakers are aware that GDP data is sometimes subject to large revisions, how might it affect their views about how best to conduct policy?

2.13 **[Related to the *Making the Connection* on page 39]** Suppose that the current exchange rate between the Chinese yuan and the U.S. dollar is 10 yuan = $1. Suppose that you can buy more goods and services in China with 1,000 yuan than you can in the United States with $100. Will China's GDP in dollars be greater if the current exchange rate is used to convert yuan to dollars or if the PPP exchange rate it used? Briefly explain.

2.14 In 2008, the World Bank estimated that, at current exchange rates, Kenya's GDP per capita (in U.S. dollars) was $730. For the same year, U.S. GDP per capita was $47,580.

a. The World Bank uses the Atlas method to convert data into U.S. dollars at current exchange rates. The Atlas method uses an average of three years of exchange rates plus adjustments for inflation and other factors. Why would it be desirable to use a method like this?

b. What problems do you see in comparing GDP per capita in the United States to GDP per capita in Kenya using these data?

c. Adjusting for purchasing power parity, the World Bank calculates Kenya's GDP per capita to be $1,580. Why is this number so different from the original figure? Explain.

d. How many times larger is GDP per capita in the United States than GDP per capita in Kenya before the purchasing power adjustment? After the adjustment?

Source: The World Bank.

2.15 The text states that: "For years before the base year, real GDP is greater than nominal GDP; for years after the base year, nominal GDP is greater than real GDP." Suppose that the economy experiences *deflation*, with the price level falling. In this case, will the relationship between real GDP and nominal GDP for years before and after the base year still hold? Briefly explain.

2.3 Inflation Rates and Interest Rates

Explain how the inflation rate is measured and distinguish between real and nominal interest rates.

SUMMARY

The **consumer price index (CPI)** is an average of the prices of the goods and services purchased by the typical urban family of four. The percentage increase in the CPI from one year to the next is the most common measure of the inflation rate. Biases in the way the CPI is measured may cause it to overstate the actual inflation rate by between one-half and one percentage point. The Federal Reserve prefers to measure the inflation rate by using the **personal consumption expenditure (PCE) price index**. The **interest rate** is the cost of borrowing funds, usually expressed as a percentage of the amount borrowed. The **nominal interest rate** is

myeconlab Visit www.myeconlab.com to complete these exercises online and get instant feedback.

the stated interest rate on a loan. The **real interest rate** is the nominal interest rate adjusted for the effects of inflation. Because borrowers and lenders don't know with certainty what the inflation rate will be during the period of a loan, they must make borrowing or lending decisions on the basis of what they expect the real interest rate to be.

Review Questions

3.1 What is the difference between the price level and the rate of inflation?

3.2 How is the CPI calculated? What biases in the way the CPI is calculated may cause it to overstate the actual inflation rate?

3.3 How is the PCE calculated? What is the difference between the PCE and the GDP deflator? What is the difference between the PCE and the core PCE?

3.4 What is the difference between real and nominal interest rates? If the actual inflation rate is greater than the expected inflation rate, do borrowers gain or lose? Briefly explain.

Problems and Applications

3.5 Explain the major difference between the CPI and the PCE deflator. Why does the Federal Reserve prefer to use the core PCE to measure the inflation rate?

3.6 Suppose that a virus wipes out half the apple crop, causing the quantity produced to go down and the price to increase. Other fruits can be substituted for apples in many cases, so some consumers will switch to other items. What would be the effect of this on the CPI? On the PCE deflator? [Hint: in each case, consider how the quantity of apples measured by the price index does or does not change.]

3.7 **[Related to the *Making the Connection* on page 43]** This *Making the Connection* indicates that indexing Social Security payments to the CPI has resulted in a reduction in the standard of living for retirees, because their benefits have not kept up with the rising cost of medical care.

a. Do you think that this situation will improve or worsen in coming years? Briefly explain.

b. Can you think of other groups for whom changes in the CPI are a poor measure of changes in the cost of living? Briefly explain.

3.8 During the 2007–2009 crisis, nominal interest rates fell to nearly 0%, while the rate of inflation remained positive.

a. What happened to the real interest rate?

b. How would this affect savers and borrowers?

c. If *nominal* interest rates were negative, what would happen if you put money in a savings account in the bank?

2.4 Measuring Employment and Unemployment

Understand how to calculate the unemployment rate.

SUMMARY

Each month, the U.S. Bureau of the Census conducts the Current Population Survey (also called the household survey) to collect the data needed to compute the unemployment rate. The **unemployment rate** measures the percentage of the labor force that is unemployed. The **labor force** is the sum of employed and unemployed workers. The official unemployment rate is not a perfect measure of the true unemployment rate because it ignores discouraged workers and counts a part-time worker as fully employed even if the worker would prefer a full-time job. The BLS does provide alternative measures of the unemployment rate that include discouraged and part-time workers. These unemployment rates are higher than the official measure, but changes in the official measure closely track changes in the alternative measures. So, the official unemployment rate is useful but not perfect. In addition to the household survey, the BLS uses the establishment survey, sometimes called the payroll survey, to measure total employment in the economy.

Review Questions

4.1 How is the unemployment rate calculated?

4.2 What is meant by discouraged workers?

4.3 Why might the unemployment rate understate the extent of unemployment?

4.4 What is the difference between the household survey and the establishment survey? Why do some economists prefer to use the employment data from the establishment survey?

Problems and Applications

4.5 For each of the following, state whether the individual is included or not included in the labor force and, if included, whether that person is counted as employed or unemployed.

a. Soma is employed as a chef at a restaurant in Maine.

b. Randy is working part time but is looking for a full-time job.

c. Bruce would like a job but has stopped looking.

d. Jessie won the lottery and quit her job. She is not seeking a new job.

e. Jose is in college.

f. Christina just graduated from college and is applying for jobs.

4.6 During recessions, industries such as construction often cut back on employees. The newly unemployed workers may seek jobs for a while and then become discouraged if they do not find new jobs.

a. If workers are seeking jobs, how does the BLS count those workers?

b. If workers have stopped seeking jobs, how does the BLS count those workers?

c. Use this information to explain why, when the economy begins to recover from a recession, the unemployment rate may initially worsen.

4.7 Suppose that all workers in the economy are currently working 40 hours a week.

a. If all employers cut worker hours so that each employee is working 20 hours a week, what would happen to the unemployment rate?

b. What would happen to real GDP?

c. The unemployment rate is sometimes used as a measure of the slack in the economy or how far the economy is below potential GDP. How do parts a. and b. of this question suggest that this might be misleading?

DATA EXERCISES

D2.1: Go to the Bureau of Economic Analysis Web site (www.bea.gov) and find the most recent GDP figures.

a. Do the figures for the most recent quarter available represent an advance estimate, a third estimate, or something in between? Would it be reasonable to base economic policy on these figures? Explain. (You can find current data in the most recent press release.)

b. How has real GDP changed over the past year? (You can find data for more than one quarter in the GDP and the National Income and Product Accounts [NIPA] Historical Tables.)

c. Is the economy in a recession or a recovery? (Hint: see the nber.org for official definitions of business cycle turning points.) Based on the GDP deflator, what is the inflation rate?

D2.2: Go to the Web site of the *Economist* (www.economist.com) and find the most recent Big Mac index.

a. Which country's currency is the most overvalued? Which is the least?

b. What factors do you think cause countries to have particular relative positions on the list? Do certain types of countries (for example, larger countries, poorer countries) have currencies that are typically overvalued or undervalued?

c. If you were to live in your favorite country on the list, what would the cost be, relative to what it costs you to live in the United States? What factors about that specific country do you think cause this?

D2.3: Go to the Statistics Canada Web site of the Canadian government (www.statcan.gc.ca).

a. Search for Income and Expenditure Accounts. What percentage of GDP is accounted for by each of the major GDP subcategories in Canada, and how do those those percentages compare to the United States?

b. What do you think are the reasons for the differences between the figures for Canada and the United States?

c. Because Canada is closely tied to the United States in terms of trade and proximity, business cycles in Canada are often very similar to those in the United States. How does the trend in Canada's GDP compare with that in the United States?

CHAPTER 3

The Financial System

LEARNING OBJECTIVES

After studying this chapter, you should be able to:

- **3.1** Describe the financial system and explain the role it plays in the economy (pages 60–69)
- **3.2** Understand the role of the central bank in stabilizing the financial system (pages 69–75)
- **3.3** Explain how nominal and real interest rates are determined in financial markets (pages 76–85)
- **3.4** Understand how to calculate interest rates (pages 85–93)
- **3A** Understand the term structure of interest rates (pages 103–104)

THE WONDERFUL WORLD OF CREDIT

In late 2010, a curious thing happened: Consumers substantially increased their purchases of cars. Normally, car sales rise rapidly when employment and income are increasing. In late 2010, with the unemployment rate still well above 9%, and household income growing only slowly, many people were surprised to see car sales soar. The reason that car sales rose was not primarily because households saw their incomes rise and their employment prospects improve, but because they had an easier time obtaining credit. Most people have to borrow money to buy a car, and during the financial crisis that accompanied the recession of 2007–2009, most banks had tightened their requirements for obtaining loans. People who could have borrowed money to purchase a car in 2007 could not do so in 2009. As a result, car sales had plummeted.

Car buyers aren't the only ones dependent on bank loans. Most small businesses have to finance their

Continued on next page

Key Issue and Question

At the end of Chapter 1, we noted key issues and questions that serve as a framework for the book. Here are the key issue and question for this chapter:

Issue: The financial system moves funds from savers to borrowers, which promotes investment and the accumulation of capital goods.

Question: Why did the bursting of the housing bubble beginning in 2006 cause the financial system to falter?

Answered on page 93

operations either through the profits they earn or by borrowing from banks. As banks tightened their lending requirements, many small businesses found themselves strapped for the funds needed to meet their payrolls, pay their suppliers, and cover their other expenses. Not surprisingly, these small businesses had to cut back their purchases from suppliers and lay off workers to avoid bankruptcy. During the worst period of the financial crisis—from the last quarter of 2008 through the last quarter of 2009—businesses employing fewer than 50 workers laid off a staggering 17 *million* workers. This was 70% more than the number laid off by firms that employ more than 250 workers, even though these larger firms employed twice as many workers.[1]

The difficulty car buyers and small businesses had in securing loans is an indication of why the recession of 2007–2009 was so severe: It was accompanied by the worst financial crisis since the Great Depression of the 1930s. No modern economy can prosper without a well-functioning financial system. The financial system provides the means by which funds can flow from savers to borrowers. A significant disruption in that flow invites economic disaster, as the world learned again during the financial crisis.

AN INSIDE LOOK on page 94 explores the improving credit market for small businesses after the financial crisis ended and the effect that this has had on investment expenditure.

Sources: Bill Vlasic and Nick Bunkley, "Detroit Carmakers Post Sales Gains as Toyota Lags," *New York Times*, January 4, 2011; Lawrence Ulrich, "Clouds Parted to a Forecast of Sunnier Days," *New York Times*, December 31, 2010; and Sharon Terlep, "GM Again Sees Need for GMAC," *Wall Street Journal*, January 11, 2011. Data on employment by firm size are from U.S. Bureau of the Census, *2007 Economic Census*; data on employment losses by firm size are from U.S. Bureau of Labor Statistics, "Business Employment Dynamics."

The financial system channels funds from those who want to save to those who want to borrow. Households borrow to purchase new cars and houses, among other durable goods. Firms such as Ford Motor Company use the financial system to obtain funds to expand and modernize factories and meet payrolls, among other purposes. Most governments, including the state, local, and federal governments in the United States, use the financial system to obtain funds to build new roads, bridges, and schools; to purchase goods and services; and to make payments to the elderly and the poor. When the financial system operates well, funds move smoothly from savers to borrowers, which enhances economic activity. When the financial system does not work well, the economy can experience a recession. In extreme cases, the recession can be severe as with the Great Depression of the 1930s and the 2007–2009 recession. In this chapter, we describe how the financial system works and explore some of the problems that can occur if the flow of funds through the system is disrupted. Understanding how the financial system works will be important for understanding the material in later chapters on long-run economic growth, the business cycle, and fiscal and monetary policy.

3.1 Overview of the Financial System

Learning Objective
Describe the financial system and explain the role it plays in the economy.

Financial system The financial intermediaries and financial markets that together facilitate the flow of funds from lenders to borrowers.

The **financial system** is the network of banks, stock and bond markets, and other financial markets and institutions that make it possible for money to flow from lenders to borrowers. Households and firms depend heavily on the financial system to attain their goals. For instance, consider how the financial system works for you. When you begin your career, you will probably want to save some of your income to buy a car or a house. Through the financial system, you can save in many ways, including by putting money in a savings account in a bank or by buying stocks or bonds. At certain points in your life, you are also likely to be a borrower. You may need to buy a car without saving enough to pay for it completely, so you borrow the money from a bank. If you start a business, it is unlikely that you will be able to finance the startup costs for the business out of your savings, so once again, you are likely to borrow money from a bank. Large businesses are often in a similar situation. To find the money they need to expand and grow, businesses tap the savings of households.

[1]These numbers are *gross* layoffs, which means they do not take into account any hiring of workers that these firms may have done during this period.

Large businesses sometimes acquire funds by borrowing from banks, while at other times they sell stocks and bonds directly to savers. In fact, without a well-functioning financial system, economic growth is difficult because firms will be unable to expand and adopt new technologies. History shows that only countries with well-developed financial systems have been able to sustain high levels of economic growth.

Financial Markets and Financial Intermediaries

The financial system consists of *financial markets* and *financial intermediaries.* An **asset** is anything of value owned by a person or a firm. A **financial asset** is a financial claim, which means that if you have a financial asset, you have a claim on someone else to pay you money. For instance, a bank checking account is a financial asset because it represents a claim you have against the bank to pay you an amount of money equal to the dollar value of your account. *Financial securities* are *tradable* financial assets, which means they can be bought and sold. Stocks, bonds, and other financial securities are bought and sold in **financial markets**, such as the New York Stock Exchange. **Stocks** are financial securities that represent partial ownership of a firm. If you buy one share of stock in General Electric (GE), you become one of millions of owners of that firm, and you have a legal claim to your portion of anything GE owns and to its profits. **Bonds** are financial securities that represent promises to repay a fixed amount of funds. When GE sells a bond, the firm promises to pay the purchaser of the bond an interest payment each year for the term of the bond, as well as a final payment equal to the face value of the bond. In a financial market, borrowers can obtain money directly from lenders. This happens, for example, when GE sells a bond to someone who wants to invest by purchasing the bond.[2]

Asset Anything of value owned by a person or a firm.

Financial asset A financial claim.

Financial market A place or channel for buying or selling stocks, bonds, or other financial securities.

Stock A financial security that represents a legal claim on a share in the profits and assets of a firm.

Bond A financial security issued by a corporation or government that represents a promise to repay a fixed amount of funds.

Some financial assets—such as a checking account or a saving account in a bank—are not financial securities because they cannot be resold in a financial market. When a financial asset is first sold, the sale takes place in the *primary market.* Subsequent sales take place in the *secondary market.* Financial securities can be resold in the secondary market. Primary markets and secondary markets can exist in the same physical place. For instance, if IBM issues new stock on the New York Stock Exchange, the sale is in the primary market. When investors resell those shares of stock on the New York Stock Exchange, the sales are in the secondary market.

A **financial intermediary** is an institution that borrows funds from savers and lends them to borrowers. The most important financial intermediaries are commercial banks. Other financial intermediaries include mutual funds, hedge funds, pension funds, investment banks, and insurance companies. See Table 3.1 for brief descriptions of several important financial intermediaries. Financial intermediaries act as go-betweens for borrowers and lenders. In effect, financial intermediaries borrow funds from savers and lend them to borrowers. For example, suppose Cindy wants to open a café. Although you may be reluctant to lend money directly to Cindy, you may end up doing so indirectly: You deposit money in a bank, which then combines your deposit with money from other depositors to make a loan to Cindy. In general, intermediaries pool the funds of many small savers and lend the funds to many individual borrowers. The intermediaries earn a profit by paying savers less for the use of their funds than the intermediaries receive from borrowers. For example, a bank might pay you as a depositor a 3% interest rate, while it lends money to Cindy's Café at a 6% interest rate.

Financial intermediary An institution, such as a commercial bank, that borrows funds from savers to lend to borrowers.

Some financial intermediaries, such as mutual funds, hedge funds, pension funds, and insurance companies, make investments in stocks and bonds on behalf of savers. For example,

[2]A brief note on terminology: In this chapter when we refer to "investors" we mean households and financial firms who buy stocks, bonds, and other securities as financial investments. It is important not to confuse financial investment with the macroeconomic term "investment," which, as we saw in Chapter 2, refers to spending by households and firms on *investment goods*, such as houses, factories, machinery, and equipment.

Table 3.1 Important Financial Intermediaries

Type of financial intermediary	Description	Examples
Commercial bank	A company that takes in deposits and makes loans to households and firms.	Bank of America, Wells Fargo
Mutual fund	A company that sells shares to investors and uses the funds to buy stocks, bonds, or other financial securities.	Vanguard, T. Rowe Price
Hedge fund	A company that is similar to a mutual fund but that obtains funds primarily from wealthy investors and uses the funds to make complicated—and often risky—investments.	Soros Fund Management, Paulson & Co.
Pension fund	An institution that receives contributions from workers and uses the funds received to invest in financial securities to fund retirement benefits.	California Public Employees' Retirement System, Federal Retirement Thrift
Insurance company	A company that sells insurance policies to households and firms and uses the funds received to invest in financial securities.	Travelers, The Hartford, Aetna
Investment bank	A company that provides advice to firms issuing new securities, underwrites the issuing of securities, and develops new securities.	Goldman Sachs, Morgan Stanley

mutual funds sell shares to savers and then use the funds to buy a *portfolio* of stocks, bonds, mortgage loans, and other financial securities. Most mutual funds issue shares that the funds will buy back—or *redeem*—at a price that represents the underlying value of the financial securities owned by the fund. Large mutual fund companies, such as Fidelity, Vanguard, and T. Rowe Price, offer many alternative stock and bond funds. Over the past 30 years, the role of mutual funds in the financial system has increased dramatically. By 2011, competition among hundreds of mutual fund firms gave investors thousands of funds from which to choose.

Financial intermediaries play a key role in the economy because they are the main source of loans to households and small businesses. Because they usually cannot borrow money directly from savers, households and small firms have to do so indirectly by getting loans from banks. Therefore, when banks decide to tighten their requirements for loans, many consumers are unable to obtain the credit they need to buy cars and houses, and small businesses have trouble financing their operations.

Making the Connection

Is General Motors Making Cars or Making Loans?

Alfred Sloan, the legendary CEO of General Motors (GM) from the 1920s to the 1950s, was once quoted as saying, "General Motors is not in the business of making cars, it is in the business of making money." His point was that manufacturing cars was not enough; the cars had to be sold to customers at a profit. Selling cars at a profit was difficult for GM and other automobiles companies during the 2007–2009 recession. In fact, GM went through bankruptcy and was saved from being liquidated only after the federal government agreed to bail out the company by investing $50 billion in it.

As a result of the financial crisis that accompanied the recession, banks tightened their requirements for loans. This hurt automobile companies in two ways. First, automobile companies don't sell cars directly to customers. Instead, they rely on franchised dealers, who are independent businesspeople who buy cars from the manufacturers and then resell them to consumers. Car dealers need access to credit to bridge the time between when they buy cars from manufacturers and when they finally sell them to customers weeks or even months later. Second, many consumers rely on loans to finance 80% or more of the price of a new car. When banks tightened their requirements for obtaining loans, consumers had trouble buying cars from dealers, and dealers had trouble financing their purchases of cars from manufacturers.

Early in the history of the industry, automobile manufacturers realized that forcing their dealers and customers to rely on banks for credit was not likely to be successful. As the volume of production increased, dealers often could not obtain large enough loans to finance their purchases from manufacturers. Similarly, only car buyers with high incomes and perfect credit histories were able to obtain car loans from banks. Automobile manufacturers responded to these problems by setting up subsidiaries that would directly make loans to both dealers and car buyers. In 1919, GM established the General Motors Acceptance Corporation (GMAC) to make loans to dealers and buyers. As the decades passed and it became easier for dealers and car buyers to obtain loans from banks, some automobile executives questioned whether it was necessary for their firms to continue to operate finance companies. Some finance companies began making loans outside of the automobile business, including residential mortgage loans to homebuyers. During the housing boom of the mid-2000s, GMAC began making residential mortgage loans to "subprime" homebuyers. Subprime borrowers have flawed credit histories, perhaps because they have a history of failing to pay their bills on time. During the recession that began in 2007, many of these subprime borrowers defaulted on their loans, causing GMAC to suffer heavy losses. GM sold most of its ownership in GMAC, which was renamed Ally Financial and survived only after the federal government agreed to invest in it.

By early 2011, though, GM was considering buying back part of Ally Financial. As we saw in the chapter opener, car sales had begun to revive in late 2010, as banks became more willing to make loans to car buyers. GM believed, though, that to meet its sales goals, it might have to provide more credit directly to its customers. As the automobile companies had found out the hard way during the 2007–2009 recession, a disruption in the flow of funds from savers to borrowers can have severe consequences for the economy.

Sources: Sharon Terlep, "GM Again Sees Need for GMAC," *Wall Street Journal*, January 11, 2011; Daniel Indiviglio, "In Defense of Subprime Auto Lending, but Not of GM," www.theatlantic.com, July 22, 2010; Eric Dash, "U.S. Unveils Plan to Sell Stake in Ally, Once GMAC," *New York Times*, December 30, 2010; and Steven M. Davidoff, "Valuing Ally Financial," *New York Times*, January 3, 2011; Sloan quote from Jonathan Rowe, "Why the Engineers Left the Shop Floor," *Washington Monthly*, June 1984, pp. 12–21.

Test your understanding by doing related problem 1.17 on page 97 at the end of this chapter.

Stocks, Bonds, and Stock Market Indexes A financial security can be thought of as a document, which may be in electronic form, that states the terms under which funds pass from the buyer of the security—who is supplying the funds—to the seller—who is demanding the funds. Buying stock gives you the opportunity to be a part owner of a firm. Granted, if you are buying a few shares of stock in Apple, you own only a very small piece of the firm. But that ownership allows you to participate in the growth and increased profits the firm may experience. For reasons we will discuss later in this chapter, only a relatively small number of U.S. firms—about 5,100 out of the millions of firms in the United States—are *publicly traded companies* that sell stock on one of the U.S. stock markets. When

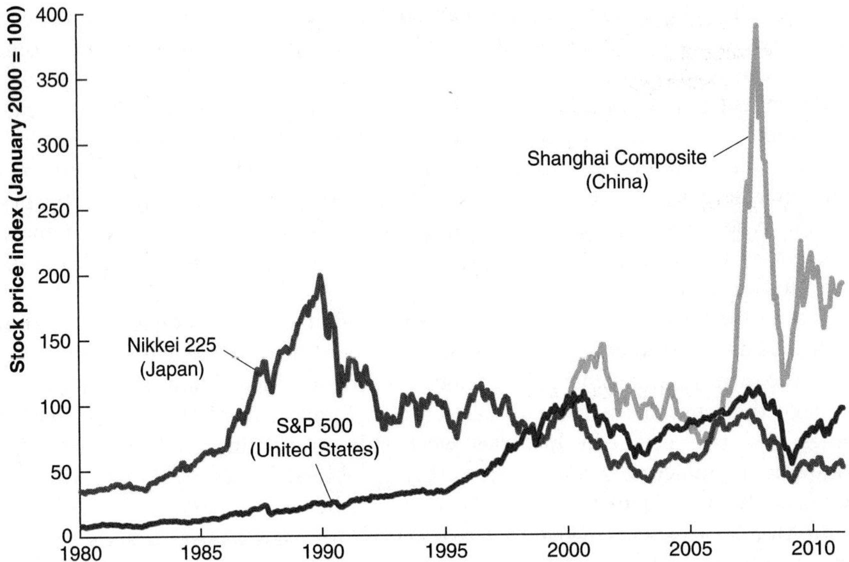

Figure 3.1

Stock Prices in the United States, Japan, and China, 1980–2011

Stock prices tend to rise and fall with the general economy. The Japanese stock market rose to high levels in the 1980s, during a period of rapidly rising real estate values. The Chinese stock market boomed during 2006 and 2007, before declining sharply during the financial crisis of 2007–2009.

Source: finance.yahoo.com. ●

many people think of the "stock market," they think of the New York Stock Exchange (NYSE) building located on Wall Street in New York City. Many of the largest and oldest U.S. corporations, such as General Electric, IBM, and ExxonMobil, are listed on the NYSE's Big Board. Although in recent years trading at the NYSE has become increasingly electronic, some buying and selling still takes place on the floor of the exchange. By contrast, the NASDAQ stock market, which is named for the National Association of Securities Dealers, is entirely electronic. As an "over-the-counter" market, buying and selling on NASDAQ is carried out between dealers who are linked together by computer. High-tech firms such as Apple, Microsoft, and Google dominate the listings on NASDAQ.

The performance of the U.S. stock market is often measured using stock market indexes. Like other indexes, stock market indexes are weighted averages of stock prices, with the index set equal to 100 for the base year. Figure 3.1 shows movements from 1980 to 2011 in the three stock indexes: the U.S. Standard & Poor's (S&P) 500, the Japanese Nikkei 225, and (beginning in 2000) the Chinese Shanghai Composite.

Stock prices tend to mirror what is happening in the economy. When an economy is expanding, profits and expected future profits rise, causing stock prices to increase. During an economic recession, the opposite occurs. Notice in Figure 3.1 that all three stock market indexes peaked at about the same time in 2000 and then again in 2007. These common movements in stock prices suggest that the forces affecting the business cycle and financial markets can be global in nature. In addition, factors specific to each economy can cause movements in stock prices. For example, during the 1980s, Japan experienced a surge in the value of real estate and stocks before both markets crashed. The increase in stock prices in China during 2006 and 2007 was particularly large, reflecting the optimism many investors had about the future growth of the Chinese economy.

Making the Connection

Investing in the Worldwide Stock Market

Suppose you decide to invest in stocks. How would you go about it? Traditionally, an investor would establish an account with a stock broker, such as Merrill Lynch, who would purchase the stock for the investor in exchange for a payment or commission. Today, many investors who want to buy the stocks of individual companies use online brokerage firms, such as E*Trade or TD Ameritrade, which typically charge much lower commissions than traditional brokerage firms but also do not offer personal investment advice and other services offered by traditional brokers. Investors can also purchase shares in mutual funds, which invest in a portfolio of stocks. For instance, the Vanguard mutual fund company offers the Index 500 fund, which buys shares in the 500 firms represented in the S&P 500. Buying mutual funds allows savers with small amounts of money to reduce their risk by spreading their savings across the stocks of the many firms included in the fund. So-called no-load mutual funds also allow investors to avoid the commissions they would have to pay to buy individual stocks using brokers.

What about investing in firms headquartered outside the United States? The 5,100 publicly traded U.S. firms represent only about 10% of all the firms listed on stock exchanges worldwide. The following table lists world stock markets, by total value of the shares of the listed firms at the end of 2010. Although the New York Stock Exchange still remains the world's largest stock market, foreign stock markets have been rapidly increasing in size. The shares of the largest foreign firms, such as Sony, Toyota, and Nokia, do trade indirectly on the New York Stock Exchange in the form of American Depository Receipts, which are receipts for shares of stock held in a foreign country. Some mutual funds also invest in the stock of foreign firms. It is possible to buy individual stocks listed on foreign stock exchanges by setting up an account with a local brokerage firm in the foreign country. Although at one time only the wealthy invested directly in foreign stock markets, the rise in popularity of the Internet has made it much easier for people of more moderate income to establish foreign brokerage accounts and to research foreign companies.

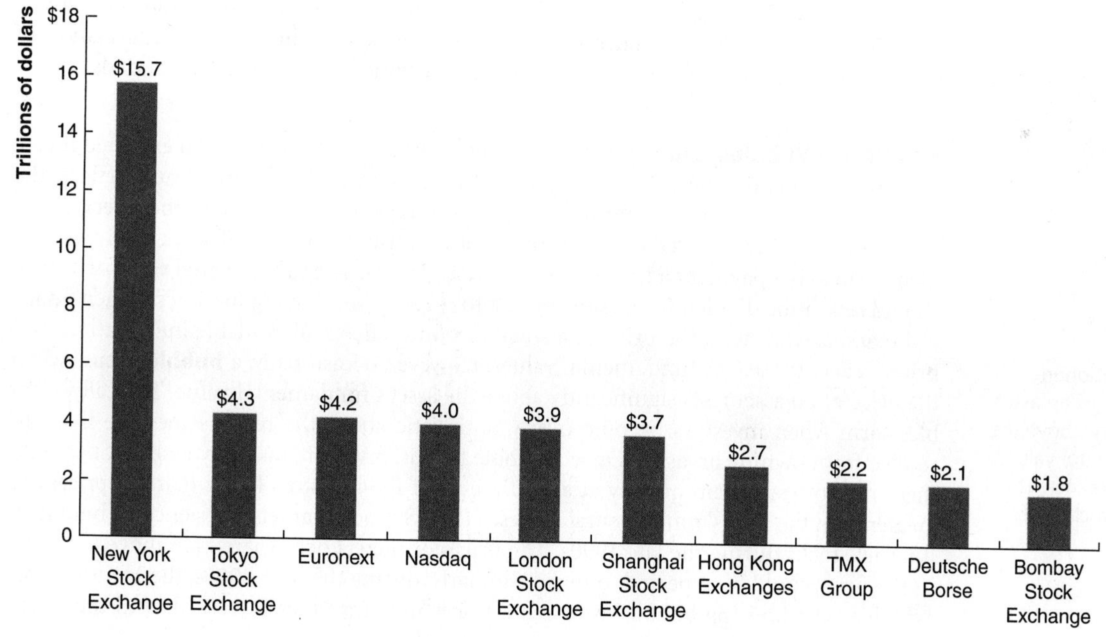

Source: www.world-exchanges.org

Test your understanding by doing related problem 1.18 on page 97 at the end of this chapter.

Services Provided by the Financial System In addition to matching households that have funds to lend with households and firms that want to borrow funds, the financial system provides three key services to savers and borrowers: *risk sharing*, *liquidity*, and *information*. In financial markets, **risk** is the chance that the value of a financial security will change relative to what you expect. For example, you may buy a share of stock in Google at a price of $450, only to have the price fall to $100. Most individual savers prefer to avoid risk and seek a steady return on their savings rather than experience erratic swings between high and low earnings. The financial system provides *risk sharing* by allowing savers to spread their money among many financial investments. For example, you can divide your money among a bank savings account, individual bonds, and a mutual fund to reduce the risk you face. Dividing your investment funds among different assets is called *diversification*, or, as the old saying has it, "Don't put all of your eggs in one basket."

Risk The degree of uncertainty in the return on an asset.

Liquidity The ease with which an asset can be exchanged for cash.

Liquidity is the ease with which an asset can be exchanged for cash. The financial system provides the service of liquidity through markets in which savers can sell their holdings of financial securities. For example, savers can easily sell their holdings of the stocks and bonds issued by large corporations on the major stock and bond markets. Savers value liquidity because they want the reassurance that if they need money to buy goods and services, they can easily convert their assets into cash. For instance, Barnes & Noble's retail stores and inventories of books are not very liquid because they cannot be easily converted into cash. The financial system, however, allows you to buy and sell the stock and bonds of Barnes & Noble, thereby making your savings much more liquid than if you directly owned stores and books.

The financial system also provides savers with a third service by collecting and communicating *information*, or facts about borrowers and expectations about returns on financial securities. If you read a newspaper headline announcing that an automobile firm has invented a car with an engine that runs on water, how would you determine the effect of this discovery on the firm's profits? Financial markets do that job for you by incorporating information into the prices of stocks, bonds, and other financial securities. In this example, expectation of higher future profits would boost the prices of the automobile firm's stock and bonds.

Asset Price Bubbles The fundamental value of an asset reflects the total expected future returns from owning the asset. For example, the fundamental value of a house reflects the housing services the homeowner receives. We could measure the value of these services by looking at the price required to rent a comparable house. The owner of stock receives a dividend, which is a payment a firm makes out of its profits. The fundamental value of a stock should reflect the dividends investors expect to receive from buying the stock. When financial markets work well, the price of a stock or bond reflects all available information, and prices reflect the asset's fundamental values. However, occasionally, a **bubble** occurs when the price of an asset rises significantly above the asset's fundamental value. Typically, bubbles form when investors become overly optimistic about the returns they are likely to receive from owning an asset. Once a bubble begins, investors may buy assets not to hold them but to resell them quickly at a profit, even if the investors know that the prices are greater than the assets' fundamental values. The U.S. stock market experienced a bubble in Internet stocks during the late 1990s. The prices of these stocks soared far above the profits the firms could be expected to make. Similarly, during the mid-2000s, the United States experienced a housing bubble, as housing prices in many cities increased until they were far above the levels implied by rents on comparable houses.

Bubble A situation in which the price of an asset rises significantly above the asset's fundamental value; an unsustainable increase in the price of a class of assets.

Bubbles can be bad for two reasons. First, a bubble will eventually collapse as some investors begin to doubt that the prices of the assets will continue to rise. As investors begin to sell the assets, their prices start to fall. Falling prices can lead to panic selling, which eventually drives prices back to fundamental values. If investors become as overly pessimistic as they once were overly optimistic, prices may even fall below their fundamental values. By 2011, housing prices in some markets in the United States appeared to be below their fundamental values. The collapse of the bubble can wipe out the wealth of investors who own the assets and can harm banks and other financial institutions that may have made loans to finance purchases of the assets. As we will discuss later, the collapse of the housing bubble in the United States caused significant harm to the financial system. Second, bubbles lead to a misallocation of resources. For example, during the late 1990s, a bubble in the price of stock for Internet companies caused a significant amount of funds to flow to Internet companies that eventually failed. Investors could have better used those funds for either consumption or investment in other firms.

Banking and Securitization

Typically, when we refer to "banks," we are thinking of *commercial banks*, which are financial firms that take in deposits and make loans to households and firms. Today, many financial institutions engage not just in commercial banking but also in *investment banking*. Investment banking typically involves several functions. One is to provide advice to firms issuing stocks and bonds or considering mergers with other firms. Investment banks also *underwrite* new issues of stock and bonds. In underwriting, banks charge firms a fee to guarantee a certain price for the stocks and bonds the firms issue.

In recent years, investment banks became heavily involved in *securitization*. **Securitization** involves creating secondary markets for financial assets that previously could not be bought and sold and so were not considered financial securities. Until about 1970, most loans made by banks were financial assets to the banks, but they were not securities because they could not be sold in a market. For instance, when a bank granted a car loan, it would keep the loan and collect the payments until the loan *matured* when the borrower made the last payment. Today, many bank loans are bundled together into securities that are resold to investors. When this happens, the banks that make the loans collect the payments from borrowers and send those payments to the investors who have bought the securities based on the loans. This change in financial structure means that there is a good chance that when you take out a car loan at a local bank, you will write a check to the bank each month as payment on your loan, but someone else who bought a security backed by your loan will ultimately receive your payment. Securitization has been particularly important in the market for mortgage loans taken out by households to buy new and existing homes. Securitization allows banks to make more loans. When a bank sells a mortgage, the bank receives funds that allow it to make additional loans. So, securitization made it easier for banks to expand the number of loans they make and to earn larger profits.

Securitization The process of converting loans and other financial assets that are not tradable into securities.

The Mortgage Market and the Subprime Lending Disaster

The process of securitizing mortgages began when Congress created two institutions that would stand between the investor and the bank granting the mortgage. These institutions are the Federal National Mortgage Association (nicknamed "Fannie Mae") and the Federal Home Loan Mortgage Corporation (nicknamed "Freddie Mac") The goal of Congress in creating Fannie Mae and Freddie Mac was to increase homeownership in the United States by reducing the risks to financial institutions of issuing mortgages and by increasing the funds available to be lent as mortgages. Fannie Mae and Freddie Mac sell bonds to investors and use the funds to purchase mortgages from banks and savings and loans. From a modest start in 1970, by the 1990s, a large secondary market existed in mortgages, with funds flowing from investors through Fannie Mae and Freddie Mac to banks and savings and loans and, ultimately, to individuals and families borrowing money to buy houses.

By the 2000s, investment banks began buying mortgages, bundling large numbers of them together as bonds known as *mortgage-backed securities*, and reselling them to investors. Mortgage-backed securities became very popular with investors because they often paid higher interest rates than other securities that appeared to have comparable risk that the seller of the security would default, or stop making the promised payments. In the mid-2000s, the U.S. economy underwent a housing bubble during which the number of new homes constructed and the prices of homes increased sharply in most parts of the country. At the height of the housing bubble in 2005 and early 2006, banks and other lenders had greatly loosened the standards for obtaining a mortgage loan. By 2006, more than 40% of mortgages were being issued to subprime borrowers with flawed credit histories or to borrowers who did not document their incomes with copies of pay stubs and tax returns (who are known as Alt-A borrowers). In addition, lenders created new types of mortgages that, rather than charging a fixed interest rate for the life of the loan, allowed borrowers to pay a very low interest rate for the first few years of the mortgage before paying a higher rate in later years. Many borrowers expected that housing prices would rise, and they would be able to take out a new loan—or "refinance" their existing loan at a lower interest rate—before the time came to pay the higher interest rates.

But rather than continuing to increase, housing prices fell. The housing bubble began to burst in 2006, leading to a decline in housing prices and to rising default rates among subprime and Alt-A borrowers. The default rates made investors less likely to purchase mortgage-backed securities, so the prices of the securities decreased. Because many commercial and investment banks owned these mortgage-backed securities, the decline in their value caused the banks to suffer losses, amounting to billions of dollars for the largest banks. The decline in the value of mortgage-backed securities and the large losses suffered by commercial and investment banks caused turmoil in the financial system.

Asymmetric Information and Principal–Agent Problems in Financial Markets

Securitization was at the heart of the financial crisis of 2007–2009. In this section, we describe key difficulties that investors encounter in financial markets and how those difficulties led to the financial crisis.

Asymmetric Information *Asymmetric information* is a problem in many financial transactions. **Asymmetric information** refers to a situation in which one party to an economic transaction has better information than does the other party. For example, households and firms that want to borrow money know more about their true financial condition than do lenders. A firm wanting to borrow money to avoid bankruptcy has a strong incentive to conceal its shaky financial state from potential lenders. Similarly, an investment bank that wants to sell a security has an incentive to make the security appear less risky than it is. Economists refer to this situation where one party to a transaction takes advantage of knowing more than the other party as **adverse selection**. For example, adverse selection results in the people who most want to borrow money often being the people lenders would least want to loan money to if they had full information on the borrowers' true financial condition. Asymmetric information can also lead to problems of **moral hazard**, which refers to actions people take after they have entered into a transaction that make the other party to the transaction worse off. For instance, once a firm or household has borrowed money, what will it do with the funds? The owner of a small firm may have told the bank that she would use a loan to expand her business, but it is possible that, in fact, she intends to visit Las Vegas and gamble with the money.

Asymmetric information A situation in which one party to an economic transaction has better information than does the other party.

Adverse selection The situation where one party to a transaction takes advantage of knowing more than the other party.

Moral hazard Actions people take after they have entered into a transaction that make the other party to the transaction worse off.

Principal–Agent Problems In many large corporations, asymmetric information leads to a *principal–agent problem.* Although the shareholders actually own a large corporation, top managers control the day-to-day operations of the firm. Because top managers do not own the firm, they may be more interested in increasing their own pay than in maximizing the profits of the firm. This separation of ownership of the firm from control of the firm can lead to a principal–agent problem because the agents—the firm's top management—pursue their own interests rather than the interests of the principals who hired them—the shareholders of the corporation. Some economists believe that principal–agent problems were at the heart of the financial meltdown of 2007–2009. Top managers of many financial firms, particularly investment banks, received large salaries and bonuses from creating, buying, and selling securities. Because these managers did not own the firms, they were less concerned with the degree of risk involved with securities backed by subprime mortgages.

In fact, when the value of these securities declined, the shareholders of many banks and other financial institutions who had invested in the securities suffered large losses.

By 2008, increased awareness of principal–agent problems led many investors to realize that many securities were riskier than they had previously believed. As investors became more reluctant to invest in any but the safest securities, many financial firms found it difficult to raise the funds necessary for them to carry out their role of financial intermediation.

As problems in the financial system increased during 2007–2009, the attempts of the Federal Reserve—the central bank of the United States—to increase financial stability became the focus of economists and policymakers. In the next section, we briefly explore the role of a central bank as a lender of last resort in a financial system.

The Role of the Central Bank in the Financial System

3.2

Learning Objective

Understand the role of the central bank in stabilizing the financial system.

A central bank is an institution established by the government to operate as a 'banker's bank' rather than as a bank to households and firms. Central banks, such as the Federal Reserve in the United States, the Bank of Japan in Japan, or the European Central Bank in Europe, perform the following functions:

- Regulating the money supply
- Acting as a lender of last resort to the banking system
- Acting as the government's bank by playing a role in the collection and disbursement of government funds
- Facilitating the payment system by providing banks with check-clearing and other services

Central Banks as Lenders of Last Resort

At this point, we are most concerned with how the central bank can help stabilize a financial system, so we focus on the central bank's role as a *lender of last resort.* In this role, a central bank can stabilize the financial system by making loans to financial institutions—particularly commercial banks—that are having temporary problems. To understand the role of a lender of last resort, consider the situation of commercial banks. The United States, like nearly all other countries, has a fractional reserve banking system where banks keep less than 100% of deposits as *reserves,* which are funds physically present in the bank or on deposit with the central bank. When people deposit money in a bank, the bank loans out most of the money. While the deposits may be withdrawn at any time, the loans are typically long term, with the bank having to wait months or years before being fully paid back. What happens if depositors want their money back? This possibility would seem to be a problem because banks have loaned out most of the money and can't easily get it back.

In practice, withdrawals are usually not a problem for banks because on a typical day, about as much money is deposited as is withdrawn. Sometimes, though, depositors lose confidence in a bank if the bank's assets—such as loans and securities—lose value. When many depositors simultaneously decide to withdraw their money from a bank, there is a **bank run.** If many banks experience runs at the same time, the result is a **bank panic.** It is possible for one bank to handle a run by borrowing from other banks, but if many banks simultaneously experience runs, the banking system may be in trouble. When banks experience a run, they are said to be experiencing *liquidity problems* because their loans cannot be easily sold to provide funds to pay off depositors. In other words, the banks do not have enough liquid assets to pay off all the depositors who want their deposits back.

Bank run The process by which depositors who have lost confidence in a bank simultaneously withdraw their funds.

Bank panic A situation in which many banks simultaneously experience runs.

A central bank, such as the Federal Reserve in the United States, can help stop a bank panic by acting as a lender of last resort in making loans to banks that cannot borrow funds elsewhere. The bank can use these loans to pay off depositors. When the panic ends and the depositors put their money back in their accounts, the bank can repay the loan to the central bank. In fact, a series of bank panics in the late nineteenth century and early twentieth century led Congress to establish the Federal Reserve in 1913 and grant it the authority to make *discount loans* to banks experiencing liquidity problems.

Bank Runs, Contagion, and Asset Deflation

An economy requires a stable banking system to operate efficiently, but why should the Federal Reserve be concerned when only one bank or a few banks experience problems? One key reason that Congress established the Fed to act as a lender of last resort was to prevent *contagion*, the process by which a run on one bank spreads to other banks, resulting in a bank panic. When one or a few banks suffer a run, depositors may interpret the run as indication of a general problem with the banking system. Because of asymmetric information, banks always know more about their true financial situation than do depositors. Therefore, depositors have difficulty separating "good banks" from "bad banks" and may decide that the best policy is to withdraw their deposits from all banks.

Once a bank panic begins, some banks will be forced to permanently close, which can lead to a process called *asset deflation*. When a bank closes, its assets are sold to raise the funds necessary to pay off its depositors. If a large number of banks close, then many similar assets, such as loans and bonds, will be sold at the same time. These sales may cause the price of these assets to fall (or deflate), which in turn causes difficulties for other banks. Ultimately, a bank's assets provide the means for the bank to pay off depositors in the event of withdrawals. If the value of the bank's assets declines, depositors will become more concerned about the ability of the bank to have funds on hand to cover deposit withdrawals, which will make depositors more likely to withdraw funds, which can lead to more bank runs, more assets being sold, and so on, in a vicious cycle.

It became clear during the 2007–2009 crisis that other financial institutions besides commercial banks could also be vulnerable to runs. In fact, any financial institution that borrows money short-term and lends it long-term is vulnerable to a run. For instance, many investment banks and hedge funds borrow short-term from banks and other financial firms and use the funds to make long-term investments. Some of the long-term investments made by investment banks and hedge funds are in securities that are difficult to sell quickly, except at sharply discounted prices. Deposits in commercial banks are insured by the Federal Deposit Insurance Corporation (FDIC) up to $250,000 per depositor. This federal deposit insurance provides some reassurance to depositors that they do not need to pull their funds out of a commercial bank even if they suspect that it may soon fail. Investment banks, hedge funds, and other nonbank financial institutions are more vulnerable to runs because there is no government insurance on the loans made to investment banks. As a result, if lenders begin to doubt the ability of an investment bank or hedge fund to repay its loans, a run may take place.

Government "Bailouts" and Moral Hazard Should government policymakers worry about the failure of a large financial institution? In a market system, we do not ordinarily expect the government to intervene to save a failing business. If you open a car dealership, restaurant, or hardware store, you take on the risk of losing your investment if the business fails, just as you will gain the profits if the business succeeds. In the United States, many businesses fail—and many new businesses are started—every day. But at least since the founding of the Federal Reserve in 1913, the government has decided that allowing commercial banks to fail may sometimes cause wider problems in the economy and that intervening to save a bank that would otherwise fail may be justified.

When Congress established the FDIC in 1934, it reduced the likelihood that deposit withdrawals would set off a series of commercial bank runs and lead to asset deflation and bank failures. Congress did not extend government insurance, like that offered by the FDIC, to other financial institutions. As a result, financial firms, such as the investment banks Bear Stearns and Lehman Brothers, remained vulnerable to the equivalent of a bank run if investors decided not to renew their short-term loans to these firms. Declines during 2008 in the prices of securities backed by subprime mortgages resulted in many financial firms having difficulties. The federal government was left with the policy dilemma of either helping these firms, thereby limiting the cycle of asset deflation and averting a financial crisis, or allowing them to fail, with the owners and investors in these firms bearing the full consequences of the decisions made by the firms' managers. Moral hazard was an important consideration in the government's deliberations because aiding troubled financial firms might make their managers more likely to undertake risky investments in the future, in the expectation that should the investments result in losses, the government would bail out the firms.

During 2008, then President George W. Bush, a majority of Congress, the Federal Reserve, the Treasury Department, and the FDIC became convinced that the risk from the increased moral hazard that might result from aiding financial firms was outweighed by the risk of a severe disruption of the U.S. financial system of a kind that had not been seen since the Great Depression of the 1930s. Although the details of federal aid to troubled financial firms are too complex to go into here, several key steps included:

- In March 2008, the Fed extended its role as a lender of last resort to investment banks by allowing them to receive discount loans, which had been previously available only to commercial banks.
- In September 2008, the Fed began lending to non-financial corporations—such as General Electric and IBM—for the first time since the Great Depression by buying commercial paper issued by those firms. Commercial paper is a security that is the corporate equivalent of a U.S. Treasury bill.
- The Treasury and Fed took steps to help a number of financial firms—including Bear Stearns in March 2008 and AIG, the country's largest insurance company, in September 2008—by providing them loans or arranging for them to be merged with other firms.
- Congress passed the Troubled Asset Relief Program (TARP) in October 2008, under which the U.S. Treasury purchased stock in a large number of banks with the intention of increasing their stability and making them more likely to make loans to households and firms.

Although most of these steps were temporary policies in response to the financial crisis, critics argued that the federal government was insuring financial firms against failure, which would increase the level of moral hazard in the financial system. Moral hazard is a common problem with insurance because once people are insured, they often change their behavior in a way that makes the insured event more likely to occur. For example, a business that has a fire insurance policy may decide not to install an expensive fire sprinkler system in its warehouse. But not having a sprinkler system increases the chances of a disastrous fire. Similarly, if the result of bad investment decisions is bankruptcy, managers of financial firms may be more cautious than if they believe the Fed and the Treasury have effectively insured them against bankruptcy. If the federal government's policies increase moral hazard and artificially increases risk taking, the financial system may become less stable.

Federal policymakers continue to weigh the tradeoffs involved in attempting to avoid the repercussions from large financial firms failing, while also avoiding unduly increasing moral hazard in the financial system. The evolution of the financial system and its increasing complexity ensure that policymakers will be grappling with these issues for the foreseeable future.

Making the Connection

Panics Then and Now: The Collapse of the Bank of United States in 1930 and the Collapse of Lehman Brothers in 2008

Although the Federal Reserve was established in 1913 to stop bank panics, in fact, the worst bank panic in U.S. history occurred during the early 1930s, and the Fed did little to stop it. The panic was the result of the Great Depression, which began in August 1929. By the fall of 1930, many commercial banks found that their assets had declined significantly in value, as both households and firms had difficulty repaying loans. In October 1930, the Bank of United States, a private commercial bank in New York City, experienced a bank run. It appealed to the Fed for loans that would allow it to survive the liquidity crisis caused by deposit withdrawals. The term *moral hazard* had not yet been coined, but Fed officials were clearly familiar with the concept because they declined to save the Bank of United States on the grounds that the bank's managers had made risky mortgage loans to borrowers investing in apartment houses and other commercial property in New York City. The Fed believed that saving the Bank of United States would reward the poor business decisions of the bank's managers. The Fed also doubted that if the bank's assets were sold, the amount raised would be sufficient to pay off depositors.

Although the Fed's reasons for failing to save the Bank of United States were legitimate, there were adverse financial consequences for the entire economy. When the bank failed, the faith of depositors in the commercial banking system was shaken. Because deposit insurance did not yet exist, depositors were afraid that if they delayed in withdrawing their money and their bank failed, they would receive only part of their money back—and only after a delay. In fact, depositors at the Bank of United States received back only about 75 cents per dollar of deposits, and final payments to depositors were made 14 years after the bank failed. Further waves of bank failures took place over the next few years, culminating in the "bank holiday" of 1933, when President Franklin Roosevelt ordered every bank in the country shut down for a week so that emergency measures could be taken to restore the banking system. Although the Fed's actions during the bank panic had avoided the moral hazard problem, they resulted in a catastrophic meltdown of the U.S. financial system, which most economists believe significantly worsened and lengthened the Great Depression.

The figure below shows for each year from 1920 through 1939 the number of banks that were forced to temporarily or permanently suspend allowing depositors to withdraw funds.

The figure reveals that bank runs in the United States went from being fairly common in the 1920s, to reaching very high levels in the early 1930s, to practically disappearing after the FDIC was established in 1934. In fact, the Fed's role as a lender of last resort was used infrequently over the next 75 years.

In 2008, the Fed was once again confronted with the dilemma of how to deal with financial firms whose failures might be a significant blow to the financial system. In the spring, Bear Stearns, a large investment bank, ran into difficulty as the declining prices for many of the mortgage-backed securities it held made other financial firms reluctant to lend it money. The Fed and the U.S. Treasury responded by arranging for Bear Stearns to be purchased by JPMorgan Chase, a commercial bank, for the low price of $2 per share of stock. That fall, though, fear of increasing moral hazard led the Fed and the Treasury to allow Lehman Brothers, also a large investment bank, to declare bankruptcy.

The Lehman Brothers bankruptcy had an immediate negative effect on financial markets. The two graphs below indicate the impact. Panel (a) shows the difference between the three-month London Interbank Offered Rate (LIBOR), which is the interest rate at which banks can borrow from each other, and the interest rate on three-month T-bills. The difference in these two interest rates is called the TED spread and provides a measure of how risky banks consider loans to each other compared with loans to the U.S. government. After fluctuating in a narrow range around 0.5 percentage point during 2005, 2006, and the first half of 2007, the TED spread rose as problems in financial markets began in the second half of 2007, and then it soared to record levels immediately following the failure of Lehman Brothers. These problems spread to nearly all financial markets. Panel (b) shows the decline in issuing of securities backed by credit card debt. The increase in perceived risk following the failure of Lehman Brothers meant that issuance of these securities plummeted to zero in the last quarter of 2008. Since banks could not sell new credit card loans, banks became reluctant to issue new credit cards or increase credit limits on existing accounts. This restricted the access of households to financial markets. Many on Wall Street saw the bankruptcy of Lehman Brothers as such a watershed in the financial crisis that they began to refer to events as having happened either "before Lehman" (declared bankruptcy) or "after Lehman."

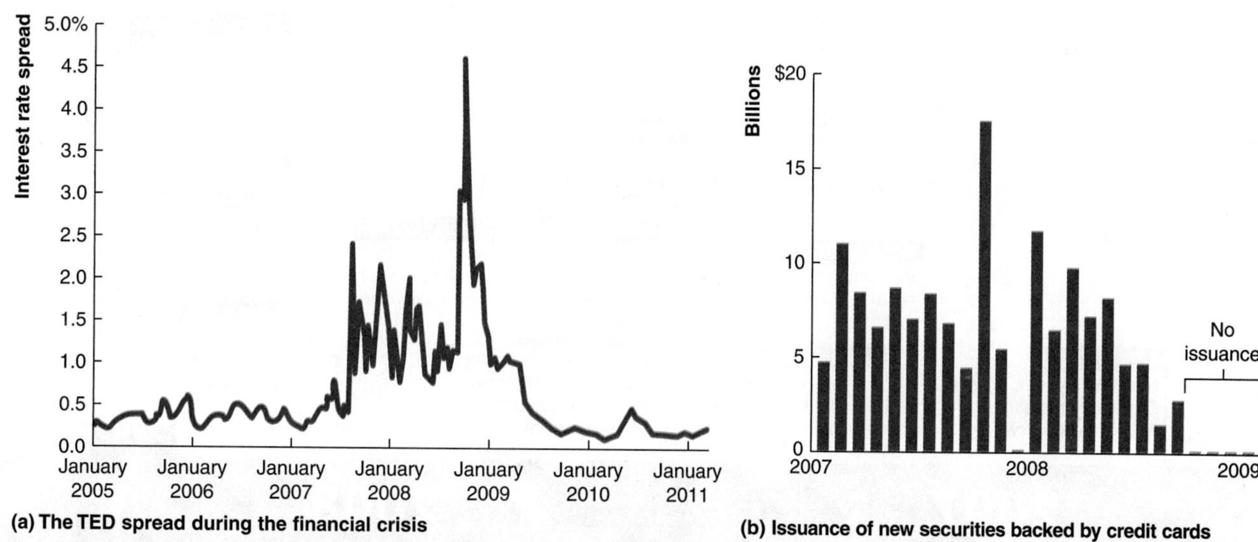

(a) The TED spread during the financial crisis

(b) Issuance of new securities backed by credit cards

Having failed to intervene to save Lehman Brothers from bankruptcy, the Treasury and the Fed reversed course later that same week to provide aid to AIG—the largest U.S. insurance company—that saved the firm from bankruptcy. For the remainder of 2008 and into 2009, the Treasury and the Fed appeared to have set aside concerns about moral hazard as they gave no indication that they would allow another large financial firm to fail. It remains to be seen whether the failure of Lehman Brothers will be viewed as being as significant an event in the 2008–2009 financial crisis as the failure of the Bank of United States was in the 1929–1933 crisis.

Sources: TED spread: Authors' calculations from British Bankers' Association data and Federal Reserve data; Credit card securitization: Peter Eavis, "The Fed Goes for Brokerage," *Wall Street Journal*, March 4, 2009. U.S. Federal Reserve System, Board of Governors, "Bank Suspensions, 1921–1936," *Federal Reserve Bulletin*, Vol. 23, September 1937, p. 907.

Test your understanding by doing related problem 2.7 on page 98 at the end of this chapter.

Figure 3.2 provides a timeline of the financial crisis of 2007–2009.

Figure 3.2 A Timeline of the Financial Crisis of 2007–2009 and Surrounding Events

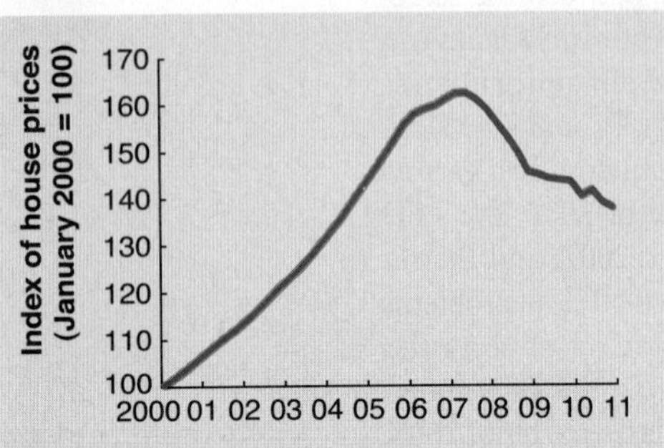

▲ Housing prices, as measured by the Federal Housing Finance Agency index, begin to fall as early as August 2006, signaling the end of the boom in the housing market.

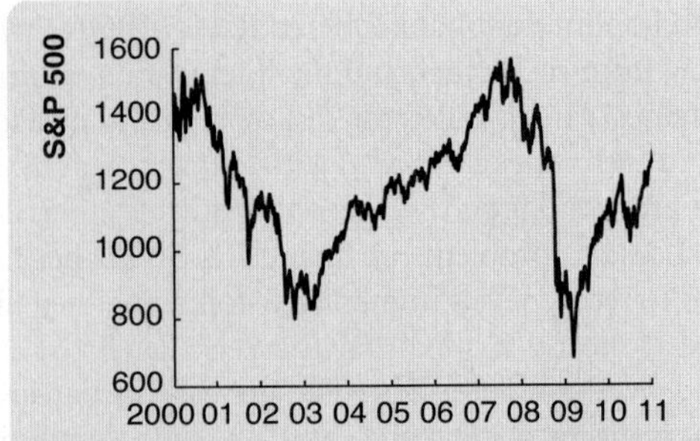

▲ Stock market prices reflect the unfolding crisis and enter a free fall in September and October 2008.

2007

April 2, 2007 New Century Financial Corporation files for bankruptcy

August 6, 2007 American Home Mortgage Investment Corporation files for bankruptcy

August 9, 2007 BNP Paribas closed two of its investment funds

September 14, 2007 Bank of England provides liquidity for Northern Rock

September 18, 2007 Fed reduces federal funds rate to 4.75%

December 12, 2007 Fed creates Term Auction Facility

2008

February 13, 2008 President Bush signs Economic Stimulus Act of 2008

March 16, 2008 Fed creates Primary Dealer Credit Facility

March 24, 2008 Fed provides financing to facilitate JPMorgan Chase's acquisition of Bear Stearns

July 11, 2008 Indy Mac is closed by the Office of Thrift Supervision

September 7, 2008 Fannie Mae and Freddie Mac placed in government conservatorship

September 15, 2008 Lehman Brothers files for bankruptcy

September 16, 2008 Fed authorizes lending to AIG

September 16, 2008 Investors in Reserve Primary Money Fund suffer losses

September 19, 2008 Fed creates the Asset-Backed Commercial Paper Money Market Mutual Fund Liquidity Facility

September 29, 2008 Treasury creates the Temporary Guarantee Program for Money Market Funds

October 3, 2008 President Bush signs Emergency Economic Stabilization Act of 2008

October 7, 2008 Fed creates Commercial Paper Funding Facility

October 14, 2008 Treasury launches Troubled Asset Relief Program and makes $250 billion available for purchasing stock of U.S. financial institutions

October 21, 2008 Fed creates Money Market Investor Funding Facility

November 25, 2008 Fed creates Term Asset-Backed Securities Lending Facility

December 16, 2008 FOMC reduces federal funds rate to between 0 and 0.25%

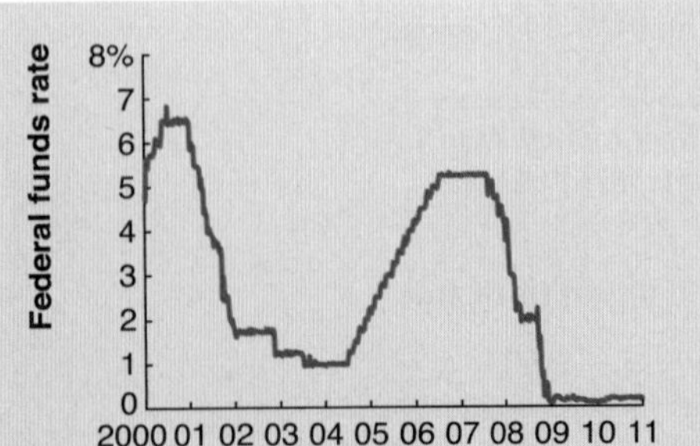

▲ Between September 2007 and December 2008, the Fed decreased the target for the federal funds rate in a series of steps from 5.25% to 0–0.25%.

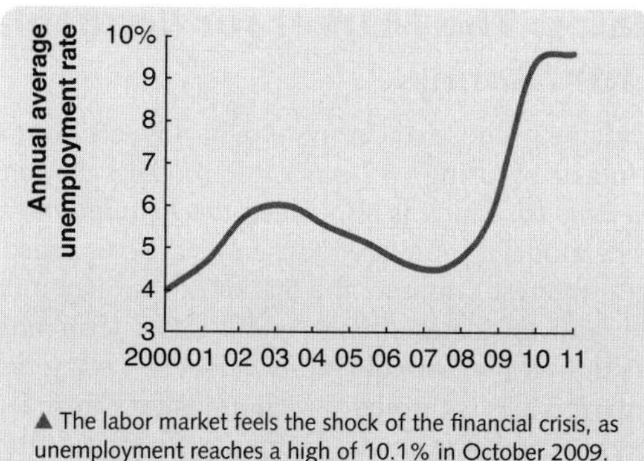

▲ The labor market feels the shock of the financial crisis, as unemployment reaches a high of 10.1% in October 2009.

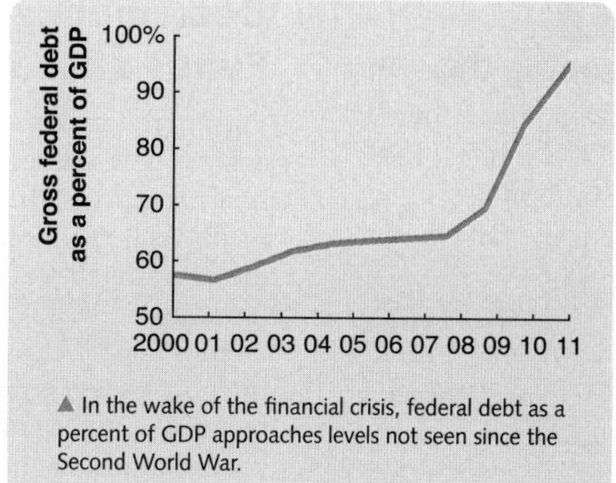

▲ In the wake of the financial crisis, federal debt as a percent of GDP approaches levels not seen since the Second World War.

2009

February 17, 2009
President Obama signs American Recovery and Reinvestment Act of 2009

March 3, 2009
Treasury and Fed create Term Asset-Backed Securities Loan Facility

May 20, 2009
President Obama signs Helping Families Save Their Homes Act of 2009

June 1, 2009
General Motors files for bankruptcy

September 18, 2009
Temporary Guarantee Program for Money Market Funds expires

2010

January 13, 2010
Financial Crisis Inquiry Commission holds its first hearing

February 1, 2010
Many programs created during the financial crisis expire, including the Commercial Paper Funding Facility, Asset-Backed Commercial Paper Money Market Mutual Fund Liquidity Facility, Primary Dealer Credit Facility, and Term Securities Lending Facility

May 9, 2010
EU and IMF provide loan assistance to Greece in an effort to stabilize the Euro countries

July 21, 2010
President Obama signs Dodd-Frank Wall Street Reform and Consumer Protection Act

November 3, 2010
Fed announces "QE2"

November 22, 2010
EU and IMF provide loan assistance to Ireland

December 17, 2010
President Obama signs 2010 tax bill that extends tax cuts and unemployment benefits

2011

January 27, 2011
Financial Crisis Inquiry Commission releases final report on the financial crisis

3.3

Learning Objective

Explain how nominal and real interest rates are determined in financial markets.

Determining Interest Rates: The Market for Loanable Funds and the Market for Money

The interest rate is a key economic variable in the financial system. In this section, we will analyze how interest rates are determined by using two economic models: the *loanable funds model* and the *market for money model*, which is also called the *liquidity preference model*. As we will see, the loanable funds model is more useful when we are concerned with the determinants of the long-term real interest rate, and the market for money model is more useful when we are concerned with the determinants of the short-term nominal interest rate.[3] We can begin our discussion of the loanable funds model by noting that the financial system is composed of the many markets through which funds flow from lenders to borrowers: the market for certificates of deposit at banks, the market for stocks, the market for bonds, the market for mutual fund shares, and so on. For simplicity, we can combine these markets into a single market for loanable funds. In the model of the market for loanable funds, the interaction of borrowers and lenders determines the market real interest rate and the quantity of loanable funds exchanged, as illustrated in Figure 3.3.

Saving and Supply in the Loanable Funds Market

The supply of loanable funds is equal to the supply of saving in the economy. The supply of saving represents the total flow of funds into financial markets from all sources. It's useful to divide total saving into three sources:

1. *Saving from households* ($S_{\text{Households}}$), which equals the funds households have left from their incomes (including transfer payments received from the government) after buying goods and services and paying taxes to the government.
2. *Saving from the government* ($S_{\text{Government}}$), which equals the difference between the government's tax receipts and its spending on goods and services and on transfer payments to households. Typically, the government spends more than it receives in taxes, so government saving is often negative.
3. *Saving from the foreign sector* (S_{Foreign}), which equals net exports, or the difference between exports and imports, but with opposite sign. (Or, saving from the foreign sector $= -1 \times$ net exports.) To see why foreign saving equals the negative of net exports, consider that if the United States imports more than it exports, more dollars flow out of the country to purchase imports than flow back in as foreign firms and foreign households buy U.S. exports. These extra dollars held by people outside the United States are available to be reinvested back into U.S. financial markets. So, for instance, in 2010, U.S. net exports equaled −$516 billion. As a consequence, in 2010, people outside the United States had an additional $516 billion available to invest in U.S. financial markets. Saving from the foreign sector is referred to as a net *capital inflow*.

   Using symbols for these sources of saving, we have:

$$S = S_{\text{Households}} + S_{\text{Government}} + S_{\text{Foreign}}.$$

For the United States in 2010, the total saving available for investment from these three sources was $2,669 billion. We can look more closely at the components of saving. Recall from Chapter 2 the basic national income identity:

$$Y = C + I + G + NX,$$

[3] Recall from Chapter 2 that the nominal interest rate is the stated interest rate on a loan, while the real interest rate is the nominal interest rate adjusted for the effects of inflation.

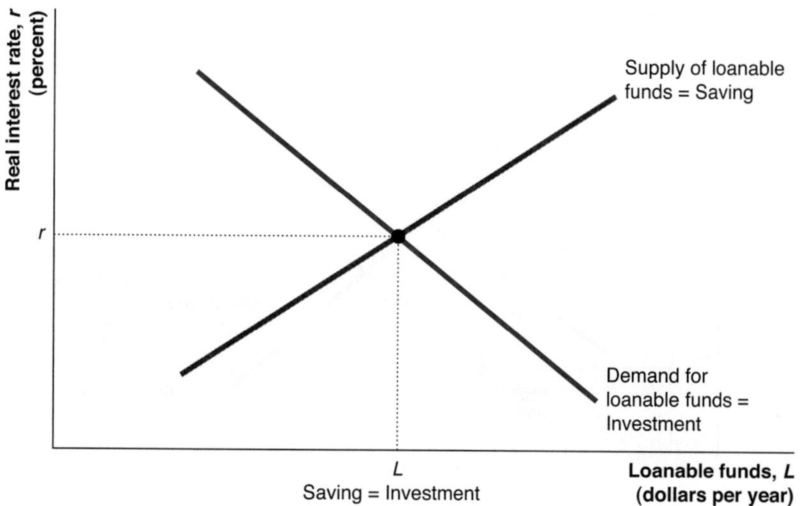

Figure 3.3

The Market for Loanable Funds

The supply of loanable funds is determined by the willingness of households to save, by the extent of government saving, and by the extent of foreign saving that is invested in U.S. financial markets. The demand for loanable funds is determined by the willingness of firms to borrow money to engage in new investment projects. Equilibrium in the market for loanable funds determines the real interest rate and the quantity of loanable funds exchanged. At equilibrium in the loanable funds market, the total quantity of saving must equal the total quantity of investment. ●

which states that GDP, or national income (Y), equals the sum of consumption expenditures (C); investment expenditures (I) on capital goods, such as factories, houses, and machinery, and changes in business inventories; government purchases of goods and services (G); and net exports (NX).

Household income equals the amount of funds received by households from the sale of goods and services (Y), plus what is received from the government as transfer payments (TR) such as Social Security payments or unemployment insurance payments. Using these definitions and letting T stand for households' tax payments to government, we can make more precise our definitions of the three sources of saving:

$$S_{\text{Households}} = (Y + TR) - (C + T)$$
$$S_{\text{Government}} = T - (G + TR)$$
$$S_{\text{Foreign}} = -NX$$

In Figure 3.3, we showed the supply of loanable funds, or saving, as an upward-sloping line. The quantity of saving supplied increases as the interest rate increases for two reasons:

1. When households save, they reduce the amount of goods and services they can consume and enjoy today. The willingness of households to save rather than consume their incomes today will be determined in part by the interest rate they receive when they lend their savings. The higher the interest rate, the greater the reward to saving and the larger the quantity of funds households will save.
2. Foreign saving depends on the size of net exports. When the U.S. interest rate rises, foreign investors increase their demand for dollars in order to buy U.S. financial assets, such as Treasury bills. An increased demand for dollars increases the foreign exchange value of the dollar, reducing U.S. exports and increasing U.S. imports. A fall in exports and a rise in imports makes net exports a larger negative number, which increases the dollars available for people outside the United States to invest in U.S. financial markets. So, the higher the interest rate, the greater the quantity of foreign saving.

Investment and the Demand for Loanable Funds

The demand for loanable funds is determined by the willingness of firms to borrow money to engage in new investment projects, such as building new factories or carrying out

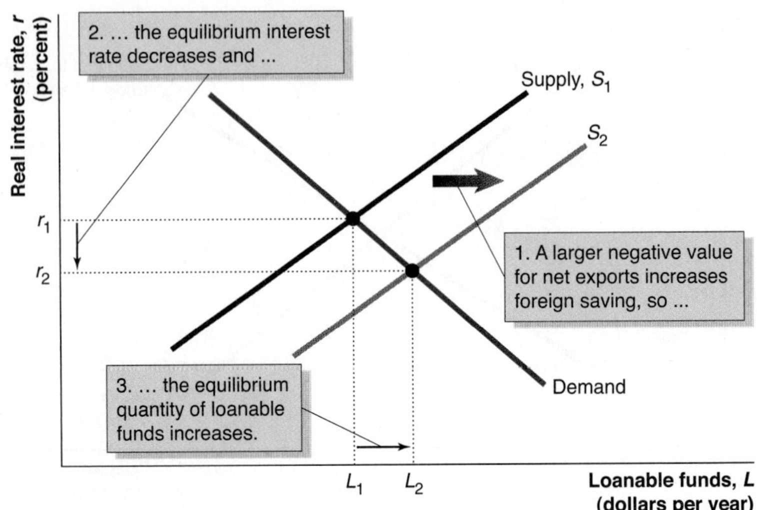

Figure 3.4

An Increase in the Supply of Loanable Funds

An increase in the supply of loanable funds decreases the equilibrium real interest rate from r_1 to r_2 and increases the equilibrium quantity of loanable funds from L_1 to L_2. As a result, saving and investment expenditures both increase. ●

research and development of new products, and by the demand by households for new houses.[4] In determining whether to borrow funds, firms compare the real return (or return accounting for inflation) they expect to make on an investment with the real interest rate they must pay to borrow the necessary funds. For example, suppose that Home Depot is considering opening several new stores and expects to earn a real return of 8% on its investment. That investment will be profitable if Home Depot can borrow the funds at a real interest rate of 6% but will not be profitable if the real interest rate is 10%. In Figure 3.3, the demand for loanable funds is downward sloping because the lower the real interest rate, the more investment projects firms can profitably undertake, and the greater the quantity of loanable funds they will demand.

Explaining Movements in Saving, Investment, and the Real Interest Rate

Equilibrium in the market for loanable funds determines the quantity of loanable funds that will flow from lenders to borrowers each period. It also determines the real interest rate that lenders will receive and that borrowers must pay. Also notice that because the supply of loanable funds represents saving, and the demand for loanable funds represents investment, in equilibrium, the value of saving equals the value of investment.

We draw the demand curve for loanable funds by holding constant all factors, other than the interest rate, that affect the willingness of borrowers to demand funds. For example, we have assumed that risk, taxes on businesses, and expectations about the profitability of investment projects are constant. We draw the supply curve by holding constant all factors, other than the real interest rate, that affect the willingness of lenders to supply funds. For example, we have assumed that taxes on households, government expenditure, and the desire for households to consume today relative to consuming in the future are constant. We have also assumed the level of national income or GDP remains constant. A shift in either the demand curve or the supply curve will change the equilibrium interest rate and the equilibrium quantity of loanable funds.

For example, during the mid-2000s, the negative value of net exports in the United States surged to record levels, peaking at −$769 billion in 2006. The resulting capital inflows shifted the supply of loanable funds to the right. Figure 3.4 shows that the impact of this increase in supply was to reduce the equilibrium real interest rate from r_1 to r_2 and to increase the equilibrium quantity of loanable funds from L_1 to L_2. Notice that an increase in the quantity

[4]Once again, be alert to the important difference between *financial investment* in stock, bonds, and other securities and *investment expenditures* on houses, factories, machinery, equipment, and inventories.

of loanable funds means that both the quantity of saving and the quantity of investment expenditures by firms have increased. In fact, investment spending in the United States rose during this period, particularly spending on residential construction. There was also an increased capital inflow, representing saving from the foreign sector, as a result of the large negative value for net exports. Some economists have argued that the ready availability of funds from foreign savers was a key reason why interest rates in the United States were low during the early to mid-2000s. And low interest rates on mortgage loans may have contributed to the housing bubble.

We can also use the market for loanable funds to examine the impact of a government budget surplus or deficit. When the government's tax receipts exceed its spending, the government's budget is in *surplus*, and the total amount of saving in the economy is increased. In the more common situation where the government's spending exceeds its tax receipts, the budget is in *deficit*, and the total amount of saving in the economy is reduced. In 2010, the federal government's budget deficit was $1.5 trillion. Holding constant other factors that affect the demand and supply of loanable funds, Figure 3.5 shows the effects of a budget deficit as a shift to the left in the supply of loanable funds, from S_1 to S_2. In the new equilibrium, the real interest rate is higher, and the equilibrium quantity of loanable funds is lower. Running a deficit has reduced the level of total saving in the economy and, by increasing the interest rate, it has also reduced the level of investment expenditures by firms. By borrowing to finance its budget deficit, the government will have *crowded out* some firms that would otherwise have been able to borrow to finance investment. **Crowding out** refers to the reduction in private investment spending that results from an increase in government purchases. Figure 3.5 shows the decline in investment spending due to crowding out by the movement from L_1 to L_2 on the demand for loanable funds curve.

Crowding out The reduction in private investment that results from an increase in government purchases.

Figure 3.5 shows that an increase in the budget deficit will reduce national savings, leading to higher real interest rates and lower investment expenditures. However, beyond budget deficits, government policy can have more subtle effects on national savings. For example, the government gives special tax incentives for savings, such as 401(k) retirement accounts. These accounts allow individuals to delay paying taxes on income put into retirement accounts until they actually retire. The delay in paying taxes increases the after-tax return to savings, so the policy encourages individuals to save. We discuss these policies in more detail in Chapter 14.

Table 3.2 summarizes the key factors that cause shifts in the demand and supply of loanable funds.

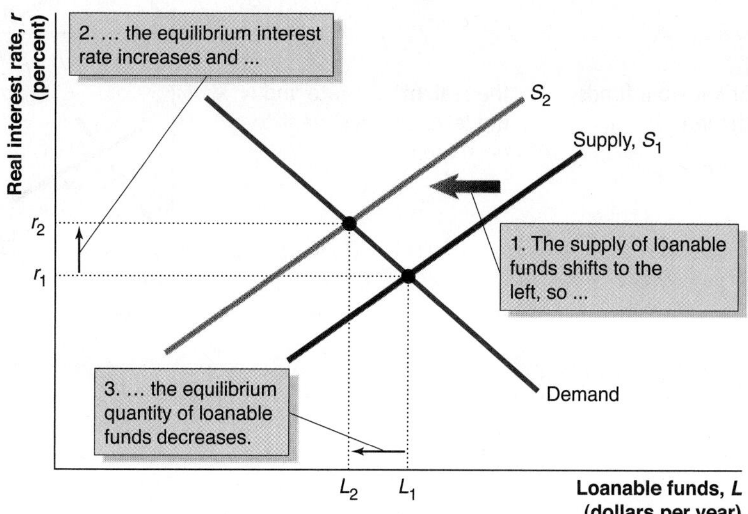

Figure 3.5

The Effect of a Budget Deficit on the Market for Loanable Funds

When the government runs a budget deficit, the supply of loanable funds shifts to the left. The equilibrium real interest rate increases from r_1 to r_2, and the equilibrium quantity of loanable funds falls from L_1 to L_2. As a result, saving and investment both decline. ●

Table 3.2 Summary of the Loanable Funds Model

An increase in . . .	will shift the . . .	causing . . .	Graph of the effect on equilibrium in the loanable funds market
the government's budget deficit	supply of loanable funds curve to the left	the real interest rate to increase and investment to decrease.	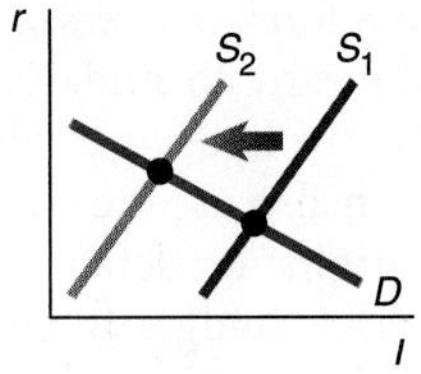 r, S_2, S_1, D, I
net exports	supply of loanable funds curve to the left	the real interest rate to increase and investment to decrease.	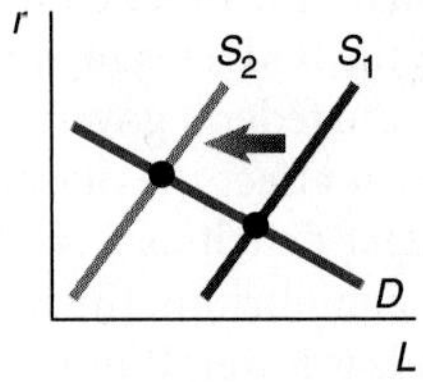 r, S_2, S_1, D, L
the desire of households to consume today	supply of loanable funds curve to the left	the real interest rate to increase and investment to decrease.	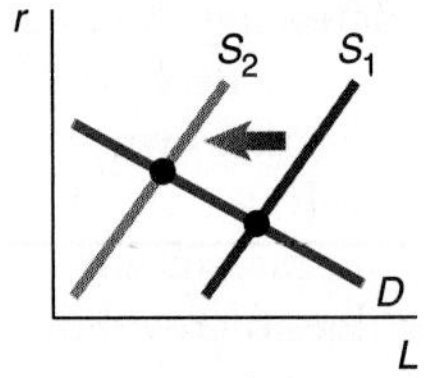 r, S_2, S_1, D, L
tax credits for savings, such as 401(k) retirement accounts, which increases the incentive to save	supply of loanable funds curve to the right	the real interest rate to decrease and investment to increase.	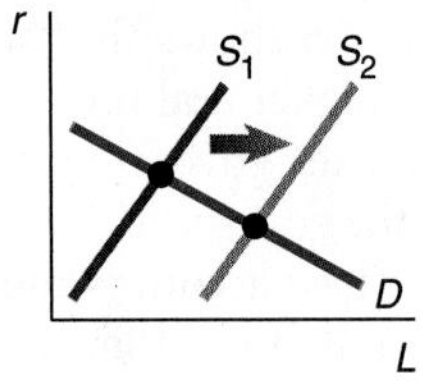 r, S_1, S_2, D, L
expected future profits	demand of loanable funds curve to the right	the real interest rate and the level of investment to increase.	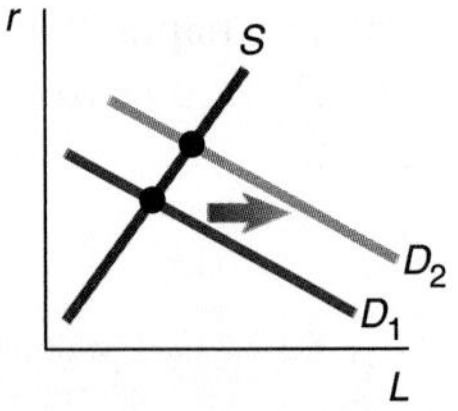 r, S, D_2, D_1, L
corporate taxes	demand of loanable funds curve to the left	the real interest rate and the level of investment to decrease.	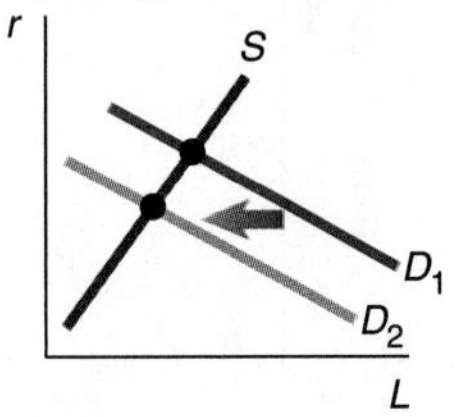 r, S, D_1, D_2, L

Solved Problem 3.3

Using the Loanable Funds Model to Analyze the U.S. Economy in 2010

During 2010, the U.S. economy experienced all of the following: a large federal budget deficit, a large negative value for U.S. net exports, and a falling demand for housing. Use the loanable funds model to explain how each of these events affected the demand and supply of loanable funds. Use a graph to illustrate your answer. Be sure to state the predictions of the model with respect to changes in the equilibrium interest rate and the equilibrium levels of saving and investment.

Solving the Problem

Step 1 **Review the chapter material.** This problem is about applying the market for loanable funds model, so you may want to review the section "Explaining Movements in Saving, Investment, and the Real Interest Rate," which begins on page 78.

Step 2 **Explain the effects on demand and supply of loanable funds of each of the events listed in the problem.** Two of the events—the large federal budget deficit and the negative value for net exports—affect the supply of loanable funds—and the other event—the falling demand for housing—affects the demand. The decline in demand for housing will shift the demand for loanable funds to the left, as households demand fewer mortgage loans. The two events affecting the supply of loanable funds pull in opposite directions: The budget deficit will cause the supply of loanable funds to shift to the left, while the inflow of capital resulting from net exports being negative will cause the supply curve to shift to the right. In 2010, the budget deficit was greater than net exports. Therefore, the net effect of these two factors was a shift in the supply of loanable funds to the left.

Step 3 **Draw a graph of the loanable funds market to illustrate your answer.** The graph shows our assumption that the net impact of the federal budget deficit and the

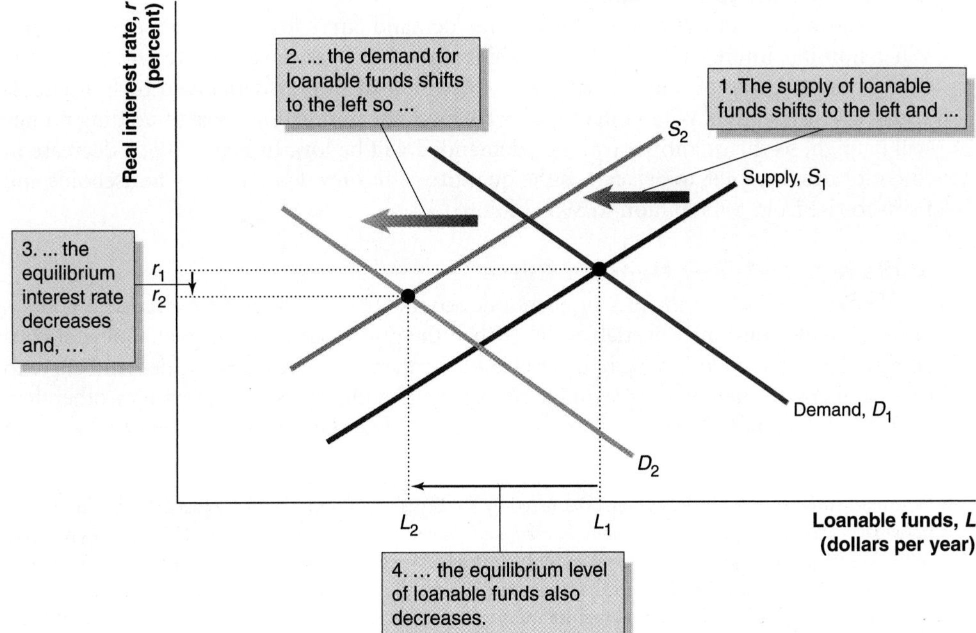

capital inflow from negative net exports is to shift the supply curve to the left. As households reduce their demand for loanable funds, the levels of saving and investment expenditure will decrease. Whether the equilibrium interest rate will decrease depends on whether the shift in the demand for loanable funds is less than or greater than the shift in supply. We have drawn the graph with the shift in demand being greater than the shift in supply, so the real interest rate falls from r_1 to r_2. For additional practice, draw the case where the shift in supply is greater than the shift in demand, causing the equilibrium real interest rate to rise.

For more practice, do related problem 3.7 on page 99 at the end of this chapter.

The Market for Money Model

The market for money model focuses on how the interaction of the demand and supply for money determines the short-term nominal interest rate.[5] Figure 3.6 shows the demand curve for money. The nominal interest rate is on the vertical axis, and the quantity of money is on the horizontal axis. Here we are using the M1 definition of money, which equals currency in circulation plus checking account deposits. To understand why the demand curve for money is downward sloping, consider that households and firms have a choice between holding money and holding other financial assets, such as U.S. Treasury bills. Money has one particularly desirable characteristic: It is perfectly liquid, so you can use it to buy goods, services, or financial assets. Money also has one undesirable characteristic: It earns either no interest or a very low rate of interest. The currency in your wallet earns no interest, and the money in your checking account earns either no interest or very little interest. Alternatives to money, such as U.S. Treasury bills, pay interest, but you have to sell them if you want to use the funds to buy goods or services. When nominal interest rates rise on financial assets such as U.S. Treasury bills, the amount of interest that households and firms lose by holding money increases. When nominal interest rates fall, the amount of interest households and firms lose by holding money decreases. Remember that *opportunity cost* is what you have to forgo to engage in an activity. The nominal interest rate is the opportunity cost of holding money.

We now have an explanation for why the demand curve for money slopes downward: When nominal interest rates on Treasury bills and other financial assets are low, the opportunity cost of holding money is low, so the quantity of money demanded by households and firms will be high. When interest rates are high, the opportunity cost of holding money will be high, so the quantity of money demanded will be low. In Figure 3.6, a decrease in interest rates from 4% to 3% causes the quantity of money demanded by households and firms to rise from $900 billion to $950 billion.

Shifts in the Money Demand Curve

You know from your principles of economics course that the demand curve for a good is drawn holding constant all variables, other than the price, that affect the willingness of consumers to buy the good. Changes in variables other than the price cause the demand curve to shift. Similarly, the demand curve for money is drawn holding constant all variables, other than the interest rate, that affect the willingness of households and firms to hold money. Changes in

[5]The market for money model was first discussed by the British economist John Maynard Keynes in his book *The General Theory of Employment, Interest, and Money*, which was published in 1936. Keynes referred to the model as the "liquidity preference model," a term still used by some economists. You should note one possible source of confusion: Economists sometimes use the phrase "money market" to refer to the market for bonds, such as Treasury bills, that mature in one year or less. The market for money in the sense of the demand and supply for money is sometimes also—confusingly!—referred to as the money market.

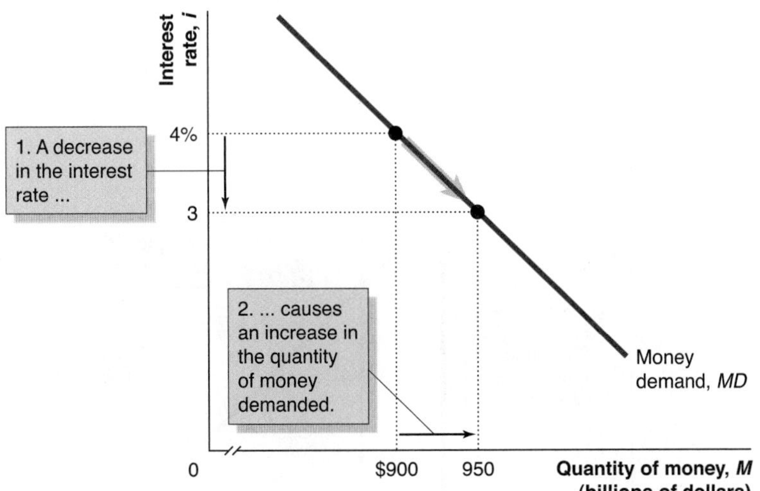

Figure 3.6

The Demand for Money

The money demand curve slopes downward because lower nominal interest rates cause households and firms to switch from financial assets such as U.S. Treasury bills to money. All other things being equal, a fall in the interest rate from 4% to 3% will increase the quantity of money demanded from $900 billion to $950 billion. An increase in the interest rate will decrease the quantity of money demanded. ●

variables other than the interest rate cause the demand curve to shift. The two most important variables that cause the money demand curve to shift are real GDP and the price level.

An increase in real GDP means that the amount of buying and selling of goods and services will increase. Households and firms need more money to conduct these transactions, so the quantity of money households and firms want to hold increases at each interest rate, shifting the money demand curve to the right. A decrease in real GDP decreases the quantity of money demanded at each interest rate, shifting the money demand curve to the left. A higher price level increases the quantity of money required for a given amount of buying and selling. Eighty years ago, for example, when the price level was much lower, a salary of $30 per week put you in the middle class, and you could purchase a new car for $500. As a result, the quantity of money demanded by households and firms was much lower than it is today, even adjusting for the effect of the lower real GDP and the smaller population of those years. An increase in the price level increases the quantity of money demanded at each interest rate, shifting the money demand curve to the right. A decrease in the price level decreases the quantity of money demanded at each interest rate, shifting the money demand curve to the left. Figure 3.7 illustrates shifts in the money demand curve. An increase in real GDP or an increase in

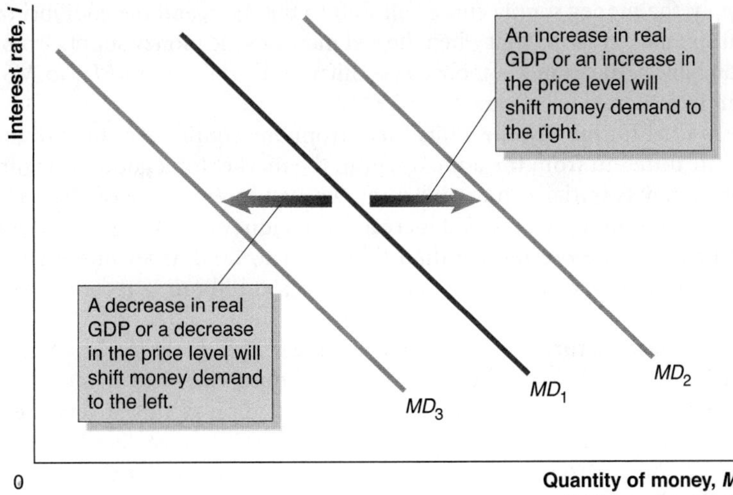

Figure 3.7

Shifts in the Money Demand Curve

Changes in real GDP or the price level cause the money demand curve to shift. An increase in real GDP or an increase in the price level will cause the money demand curve to shift to the right, from MD_1 to MD_2. A decrease in real GDP or a decrease in the price level will cause the money demand curve to shift to the left, from MD_1 to MD_3. ●

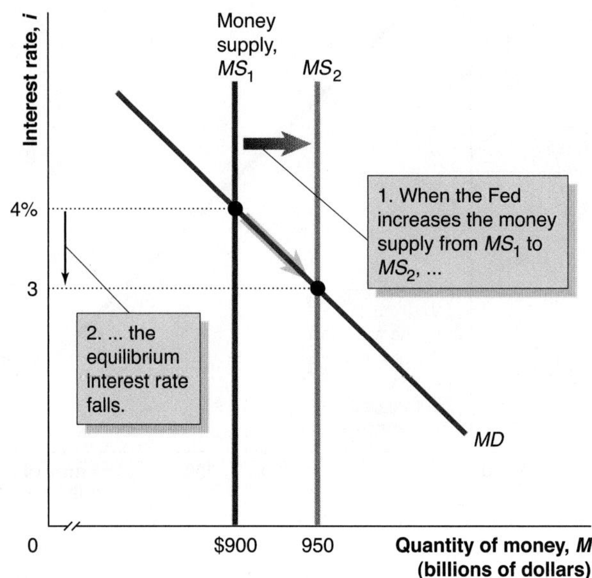

Figure 3.8

The Effect on the Interest Rate When the Fed Increases the Money Supply

When the Fed increases the money supply from \$900 billion to \$950 billion, the money supply curve shifts to the right from MS_1 to MS_2, and the equilibrium nominal interest rate falls from 4% to 3%. ●

the price level will cause the money demand curve to shift to the right, from MD_1 to MD_2. A decrease in real GDP or a decrease in the price level will cause the money demand curve to shift to the left, from MD_1 to MD_3.

Equilibrium in the Market for Money

In Chapter 10, we will discuss in more detail how central banks, including the U.S. Federal Reserve, are able to control the supply of money. At this point, we assume that the Federal Reserve is able to set the supply of money at whatever level it chooses. Therefore, the money supply curve is a vertical line, and changes in the nominal interest rate have no effect on the quantity of money supplied. Figure 3.8 includes both the money demand and money supply curves to show how the equilibrium nominal interest rate is determined in the market for money model. Just as in other markets, equilibrium in the market for money occurs where the money demand curve crosses the money supply curve. If the Fed increases the money supply, the money supply curve will shift to the right, and the equilibrium interest rate will fall. Figure 3.8 shows that when the Fed increases the money supply from \$900 billion to \$950 billion, the money supply curve shifts to the right, from MS_1 to MS_2, and the equilibrium interest rate falls from 4% to 3%.

In the market for money, the adjustment from one equilibrium to another equilibrium is a little different from the adjustment in the market for a good. In Figure 3.8, the market for money is initially in equilibrium, with an interest rate of 4% and a money supply of \$900 billion. When the Fed increases the money supply by \$50 billion, households and firms have more money than they want to hold at an interest rate of 4%. What do households and firms do with the extra \$50 billion? They are most likely to use the money to buy short-term financial assets, such as Treasury bills. Short-term financial assets have maturities—the date when the last payment by the seller is made—of one year or less. By buying short-term assets, households and firms drive up their prices and drive down their interest rates. We will discuss this inverse relationship between the prices of financial assets and interest rates in more detail in the next section. Table 3.3 summarizes the key factors that cause shifts in the demand and supply of loanable funds.

Table 3.3 **Summary of the Market for Money Model**

An increase in . . .	will shift the . . .	causing . . .	Graph of the effect on equilibrium in the money market
real GDP	money demand curve to the right	the nominal interest rate to increase.	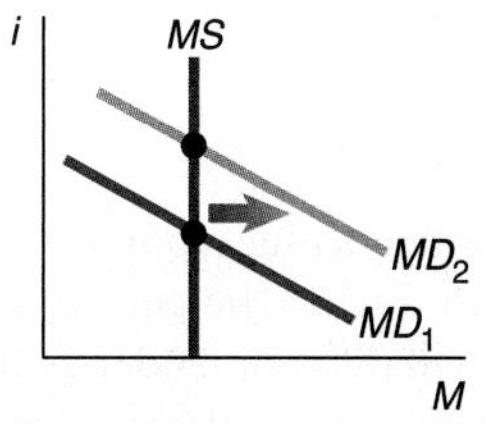 i, MS, MD_2, MD_1, M
the price level	money demand curve to the right	the nominal interest rate to increase.	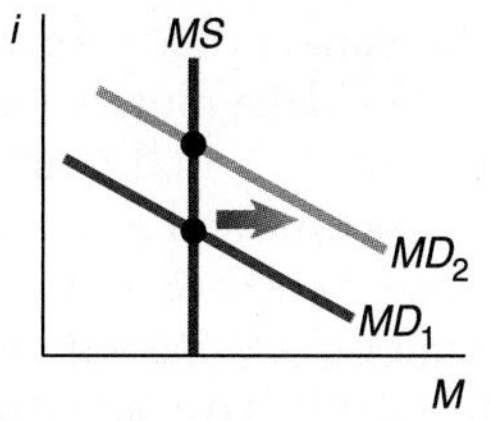 i, MS, MD_2, MD_1, M
money supply	money supply curve to the right	the nominal interest rate to decrease and the quantity of money to increase.	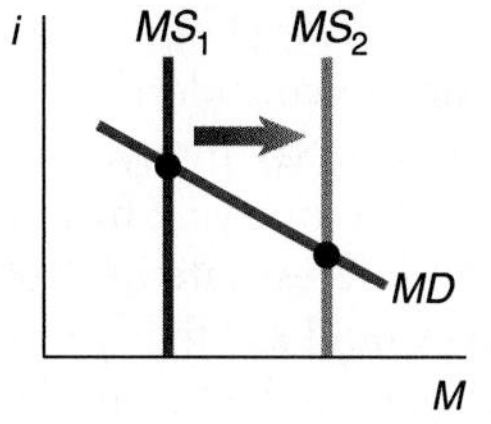 i, MS_1, MS_2, MD, M

Calculating Interest Rates

3.4

Learning Objective
Understand how to calculate interest rates.

To better understand interest rates, we need to look more closely at how to calculate one key set of interest rates: the interest rates on bonds. Corporations and governments sell bonds to raise funds. Investors who buy bonds when they are first issued often later resell them to other investors, who in turn may also resell them. An individual bond may be resold many times. This buying and selling will cause the interest rate on the bond to change. To understand this process, we need to look more closely at the relationship between bond prices and interest rates.

The Concept of Present Value

Present value The value today of funds that will be received in the future.

The relationship between bond prices and interest rates depends on an important concept called **present value**, which is the value today of funds that will be received in the future. Most people value funds they already have more highly than funds they will not receive until sometime in the future. Consider the following situation: You make a $1,000 loan to a friend who promises to pay back the money in one year. There are three key facts you need to take into account when deciding how much interest to charge him: (1) By the time your friend pays you back, prices are likely to have risen, so you will be able to buy fewer goods and services than you could have if you had spent the money rather than lending it; (2) your friend might not pay you back; in other words, he might default on the loan; and (3) during the period of the loan, your friend has use of your money, and you don't. If he uses the money to buy a computer, he gets the use of the computer for a year, while you wait for him to pay you back. In other words, lending your money involves the opportunity cost of not being able to spend it on goods and services today.

So, we can think of the interest you charge on the loan as being the result of:

1. Compensation for inflation
2. Compensation for default risk—the chance that the borrower will not pay back the loan
3. Compensation for the opportunity cost of waiting to spend your money

Notice two things about this list. First, even if lenders are convinced that there will be no inflation during the period of the loan and even if they believe there is no chance the borrower will default, lenders will still charge interest to compensate them for waiting for their money to be paid back. Second, these three factors vary from person to person and from loan to loan. For instance, during periods when lenders believe that inflation will be high, they will charge more interest. Lenders will also charge more interest to borrowers who seem more likely to default. The reward lenders require for waiting to be repaid can also vary across time and across lenders.

The longer you have to wait to receive a payment, the less value it will have for you. One thousand dollars you will receive in one year is worth less to you than one thousand dollars you already have, and one thousand dollars you will not receive for two years is worth less to you than one thousand dollars you will receive in one year.

When you buy a bond, you are lending money to the company or government selling the bond. Before considering bonds, though, let's consider the more straightforward case of a simple loan. Say that you decide that you are willing to lend $1,000 today if you are paid back $1,100 one year from now. In this case, you are receiving an interest payment of $100 and an interest rate of $100/$1,000 = 0.10, or 10%, on the $1,000 you have loaned. Economists would say that you value $1,000 today as equivalent to the $1,100 you would receive one year in the future.

Notice that $1,100 can be written as $1,000 (1 + 0.10). That is, the value of money received in the future is equal to the value of money in the present multiplied by 1 plus the interest rate, with the interest rate expressed as a decimal, or:

$$\$1{,}100 = 1{,}000\,(1 + 0.10).$$

Notice also that if we divide both sides by (1 + 0.10), we can rewrite this formula as:

$$\$1{,}000 = \frac{\$1{,}100}{(1 + 0.10)}.$$

The rewritten formula states that the present value is equal to the future value to be received in one year divided by one plus the interest rate. This formula is important because you can use it to convert any amount to be received in one year into its present value. Writing the formula generally, we have:

$$\text{Present value} = \frac{\text{Future value}_1}{(1 + i)}.$$

The present value of funds to be received in one year—Future value$_1$—can be calculated by dividing the amount of those funds to be received by 1 plus the interest rate. With an interest rate of 10%, the present value of $1,000,000 to be received one year from now is:

$$\frac{\$1{,}000{,}000}{(1 + 0.10)} = \$909{,}090.91.$$

This method is a very useful way of calculating the value today of funds that will be received in one year. But bonds often involve promises to pay funds over many years.

Present Value and the Prices of Stocks and Bonds

It is easy to expand the present value formula to cover multiple years. Suppose, for example, that you are willing to loan money for two years if you receive 10% interest in each of the two years. That is, you are lending $1,000, which at 10% interest will grow to $1,100 after one year, and you are agreeing to loan that $1,100 out for a second year at 10% interest. So, after two years, you will be paid back $1,100 (1 + 0.10), or $1,210. Or:

$$\$1{,}210 = \$1{,}000(1 + 0.10)(1 + 0.10),$$

or:

$$\$1{,}210 = \$1{,}000(1 + 0.10)^2.$$

This formula can be rewritten as:

$$\$1{,}000 = \frac{\$1{,}210}{(1 + 0.10)^2}.$$

To put this formula in words, the $1,210 you receive two years from now has a present value equal to $1,210 divided by the quantity 1 plus the interest rate squared. We can generalize the concept to say that the present value of funds to be received n years in the future—whether n is 1, 20, or 85 does not matter—equals the amount of the funds to be received divided by the quantity 1 plus the interest rate raised to the nth power. For instance, with an interest rate of 10%, the present value of $1,000,000 to be received 25 years in the future is:

$$\text{Present value} = \frac{\$1{,}000{,}000}{(1 + 0.10)^{25}} = \$92{,}296.$$

Or, more generally:

$$\text{Present value} = \frac{\text{Future value}_n}{(1 + i)^n},$$

where Future value$_n$ represents funds that will be received in n years. Notice that present value depends on the interest rate used. For example, if we change the interest rate used in the example from 10% to 5%, the present value of $1,000,000 to be received 25 years in the future changes to:

$$\text{Present value} = \frac{\$1{,}000{,}000}{(1 + 0.05)^{25}} = \$295{,}303.$$

This example illustrates an important fact: *The higher the interest rate, the lower the present value of a future payment, and the lower the interest rate, the higher the present value of a future payment.*

Anyone who buys a financial asset, such as a share of stock or a bond, is really buying a promise to receive certain payments in the future. Investors receive the interest on a bond in the form of a *coupon,* which is a flat dollar amount that is paid each year and that does not change during the life of the bond. Similarly, investors receive a *dividend* payment from a firm when they buy a firm's stock. The price investors are willing to pay for a bond or a stock (or other financial asset) should be equal to the value of the payments they will receive as a result of owning the bond or stock. Because most of the coupon payments on a bond or dividend payments on a stock will be received in the future, it is the present value of the payments that matters. In other words: *The price of a financial asset should equal the present value of the payments to be received from owning that asset.*

Take the case of a five-year coupon bond that pays an annual coupon of $60 and has a face value of $1,000, which the owner of the bond will receive when the bond matures in five years. The expression for the price, P, of the bond is the sum of the present values of the six payments the investor will receive:

$$P = \frac{\$60}{(1+i)} + \frac{\$60}{(1+i)^2} + \frac{\$60}{(1+i)^3} + \frac{\$60}{(1+i)^4} + \frac{\$60}{(1+i)^5} + \frac{\$1{,}000}{(1+i)^5}.$$

We can use this reasoning to arrive at a general expression for the price of a bond that makes coupon payments, C, has a face value, FV, and matures in n years:

$$P = \frac{C}{(1+i)} + \frac{C}{(1+i)^2} + \frac{C}{(1+i)^3} + \cdots + \frac{C}{(1+i)^n} + \frac{FV}{(1+i)^n}.$$

The dots (ellipsis) indicate that we have omitted the terms representing the years between the third year and the nth year—which could be the tenth, twentieth, thirtieth, or other, year.

The fact that present value depends on the interest rate used to calculate it leads to another important fact: *An increase in interest rates reduces the prices of existing financial assets, and a decrease in interest rates increases the prices of existing financial assets.* Consider a simple example: U.S. Treasury bills are *discount bonds*, which means they do not pay a coupon but are sold at a discount to their face value. Suppose, for instance, that you pay a price of \$961.54 for a \$1,000 face value one-year Treasury bill. So, in exchange for your investment of \$961.54, you will receive \$1,000 from the U.S. Treasury in one year. The interest rate, i, on the Treasury bill is equal to the \$38.46 in interest you will receive divided by the price you paid (multiplied by 100):

$$i = \left(\frac{\$38.46}{\$961.54}\right) \times 100 = 4\%.$$

Suppose that the day after you purchase your Treasury bill, investors decide they will only buy one-year Treasury bills if they receive an interest rate of 5% on their investment. Why might investors increase the interest rate they require on Treasury bills? Possibly, new information might convince investors that inflation will be higher during the year than they had previously expected. With a higher inflation rate, the nominal interest rate must rise to keep the real interest rate unchanged. If the interest rate rises to 5%, what will be the effect on the price at which you could sell your Treasury bill to another investor? The answer is that the price will have to fall enough so that another investor would receive an interest rate of 5% from buying your bond. We can calculate that price by noting that the new price will be the present value of \$1,000 to be received in one year with an interest rate of 5%:[6]

$$\text{Price} = \frac{\$1{,}000}{(1 + 0.05)} = \$952.38.$$

So, as a result of the market interest rate for Treasury bills having risen from 4% to 5%, the price of your Treasury bill—should you decide to sell it—has fallen from \$961.54 to \$952.38. You have suffered a *capital loss* of \$9.16. If the market interest rate for Treasury bills had fallen, say, to 3%, then the price of your Treasury bill would have risen, and you would have received a *capital gain*.

[6]Technically, we should take into account that one day has passed since you bought your Treasury bill, which means that anyone buying your Treasury bill will have to wait only 364 days to receive the \$1,000 payment from the Treasury. Because making this adjustment would have only a tiny affect on the result, we ignore it in the calculation.

Solved Problem 3.4

Interest Rates and Treasury Bond Prices

The U.S. Treasury issues a variety of securities, including Treasury notes, which have maturities from 2 years to 10 years, and Treasury bonds, which have maturities of 30 years. Suppose that a Treasury bond was issued 28 years ago, so it will mature in 2 years. If the bond pays a coupon of $45 per year and will make a final par value, or face value, payment of $1,000 at maturity, what is its price if the relevant market interest rate is 5%? What is its price if the relevant market interest rate is 10%?

Solving the Problem

Step 1 **Review the chapter material.** This problem is about the relationship between interest rates and bond prices, so you may want to review the section "Present Value and the Prices of Stocks and Bonds," which begins on page 87.

Step 2 **Explain what determines the price of a Treasury bond.** The price of a financial asset should equal the present value of the payments to be received from owning that asset. So, the price of the Treasury bond being considered here should be equal to the present value of the two coupon payments and the face value payment that the owner of the bond would receive.

Step 3 **Determine the price of the Treasury bond if the interest rate is 5%.** To determine the price of the bond, calculate the sum of the present values of the three payments an owner of the bond would receive:

$$\text{Bond price} = \frac{\$45}{(1 + 0.05)} + \frac{\$45}{(1 + 0.05)^2} + \frac{\$1{,}000}{(1 + 0.05)^2}$$
$$= \$990.70$$

Step 4 **Determine the price of the Treasury bond if the interest rate is 10%.** Substituting 10% for 5% in the expression in step 3, we have:

$$\text{Bond price} = \frac{\$45}{(1 + 0.10)} + \frac{\$45}{(1 + 0.10)^2} + \frac{\$1{,}000}{(1 + 0.10)^2}$$
$$= \$904.55$$

Notice that increasing the interest rate reduces the price of the bond. This confirms the general point that an increase in interest rates reduces the prices of existing financial assets.

For more practice, do related problem 4.7 on page 101 at the end of this chapter.

The Economy's Many Interest Rates

For simplicity, economists refer to "the" interest rate in the economy, as if there were only one interest rate. In fact, of course, there are many interest rates. In the lobby of your local bank, you will probably find one poster showing the interest rate you will receive if you put money in a certificate of deposit and another poster showing the (higher) interest rate you will pay if you take out a car loan. We have already noted that in macroeconomics, the interest rates paid on bonds are of particular importance. The interest rates investors receive can vary substantially. Panel (a) of Figure 3.9 shows the interest rates that prevailed on April 15, 2011, for four bonds that all mature in 2016. Economists refer to the relationship among

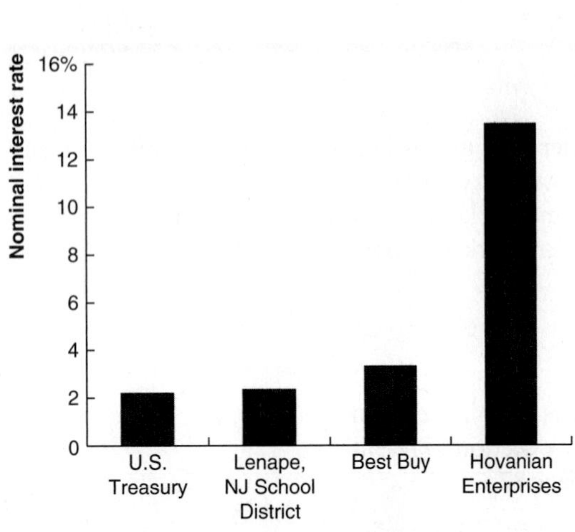

(a) The risk structure of interest rates

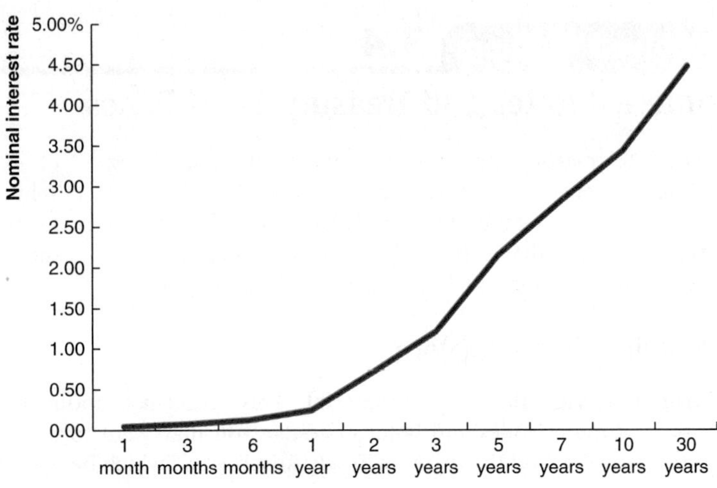

(b) The term structure of interest rates

Figure 3.9 The Term Structure and the Risk Structure of Interest Rates

Panel (a) shows an example of the risk structure of interest rates, which is the relationship among interest rates on bonds that all mature at the same time. Panel (b) shows an example of the term structure of interest rates, which is the relationship among interest rates on bonds that have the same characteristics except for having different maturities.

Sources: Panel (a): Yahoo.com, bond screener; panel (b): U.S. Department of the Treasury, "Daily Treasury Yield Curve Rates." ●

interest rates on bonds that all mature at the same time, such as those shown in panel (a), as the **risk structure of interest rates**. The relationship among interest rates on bonds that have the same characteristics except for having different maturities is called the **term structure of interest rates**. A common way to analyze the term structure is by looking at the *Treasury yield curve*, which is the relationship on a particular day among the interest rates on U.S. Treasury bonds with different maturities. Panel (b) of Figure 3.9 shows the interest rates on April 15, 2011, for Treasury bonds of different maturities.[7] Panel (b) shows the typical relationship, with the shorter-maturity bonds having lower interest rates than the longer maturity bonds.

Risk structure of interest rates The relationship among interest rates on bonds that have different characteristics but the same maturity.

Term structure of interest rates The relationship among the interest rates on bonds that are otherwise similar but that have different maturities.

In the next sections, we look more closely at the risk structure and the term structure of interest rates.

The Risk Structure of Interest Rates Investors naturally prefer a higher rate of return on their investments to a lower rate of return. So, everything else being equal, when considering bonds with the same maturity, they will prefer bonds with higher interest rates to bonds with lower interest rates. But everything else is usually not equal, because bonds differ in important characteristics. In particular, investors are interested in the following characteristics of bonds:

- *Default risk.* Default risk refers to the chance that the firm issuing the bond will declare bankruptcy and stop paying interest on the bond at some time before it matures.

[7]Treasury bonds with a maturity of 1 year or less are *bills*, those with a maturity of 2 years to 10 years are *notes*, and those with a maturity of more than 10 years are *bonds*. For simplicity, economists often refer to all these securities as *bonds*.

Because the bond issued by home builder Hanovian Enterprises shown in panel (a) of Figure 3.9 has a relatively high default risk, it also has a high interest rate.

- *Liquidity.* As we have seen, bonds can be bought and sold in secondary markets. The more buyers and sellers there are in a market for a bond, the easier it is for an investor to sell the bond and the more liquid the bond is. One reason Treasury bonds, such as the one shown in panel (a) of Figure 3.9, have low interest rates is that they are very liquid.
- *Tax treatment of interest.* The interest you earn from owning a bond is usually counted as part of your taxable income. But the government does not treat all interest the same. For example, the interest on bonds issued by state and local governments, called *municipal bonds,* is usually not taxed. Because the interest on the bond issued by the Lenape Regional High School District in New Jersey shown in panel (a) of Figure 3.9 is not subject to tax, the interest rate on the bond is low.

Investors prefer to receive a high interest rate on a bond, but they also prefer the bond to have low default risk, high liquidity, and favorable tax treatment. In general, bonds with unfavorable characteristics—for example, higher default risk—have higher interest rates to compensate investors for these unfavorable characteristics. Bonds with favorable characteristics have lower interest rates.

The Term Structure of Interest Rates Panel (b) of Figure 3.9 illustrates the term structure of interest rates by showing the interest rates on bonds issued by the Treasury. One mystery of the term structure is why an investor would be willing to buy a one-month Treasury bill with an interest rate of only 0.04% when the investor could have purchased a 30-year Treasury bond with an interest rate of 4.47%. To understand why an investor might be perfectly rational in making this decision, consider the following simple example. Suppose you intend to invest $1,000 for two years. You are weighing two options:

Option 1. Buying a bond that matures in two years—a two-year bond
Option 2. Buying a one-year bond, and when it matures in one year, investing your money in another one-year bond

The *expectations hypothesis* of the term structure of interest rates asserts that the relationship between the interest rate on the one-year bond and the interest rate on the two-year bond should be such that the *average* of the interest rate on the current one-year bond and the interest *expected* on a one-year bond one year from now should equal the interest rate on the two-year bond. For example, the following information would be consistent with the expectations theory:

1. Interest rate on the one-year bond today: 4%
2. Interest rate investors expect on the one-year bond one year from now: 6%
3. Interest rate (per year) on the two-year bond today:

$$5\% = \left(\frac{4\% + 6\%}{2}\right)$$

The logic of the expectations theory is straightforward: If an investor intends to invest over a period of years, the investor has the choice of buying one bond with a maturity equal to the desired period of investment or a sequence of shorter-term bonds. The expectations hypothesis holds that because investors have no reason to prefer buying a long-term bond to buying a series of short-term bonds, competition among investors will ensure that they receive the same interest rate either way they invest. To see why the expected returns must be equal, consider what would happen if, for example, investors expected to receive a higher return from Option 2 (buying two one-year bonds). In that case, investors would increase their demand for one-year bonds. This increased demand would drive up the price of one-year bonds, and—because bond prices and interest rates move in opposite directions—drive down their interest rate. Eventually, the interest rate on the one-year bond would fall to the point where investors would expect to receive the same return from pursuing either strategy.

We now have an explanation for why investors would buy a one-month Treasury bill with an interest rate of 0.04% when they could buy a 30-year Treasury bond with an interest rate of 4.47%: When interest rates on long-term bonds are higher than interest rates on short-term bonds, investors must be expecting that interest rates on short-term bonds will be higher in the future. In other words, an *upward-sloping yield curve*, such as the one shown in panel (b) of Figure 3.9, reflects the expectations of investors that short-term interest rates will be higher in the future. Similarly, if the yield curve was downward-sloping—with interest rates on short-term bonds being *higher* than interest rates on long-term bonds—investors must be expecting short-term interest rates will be lower in the future.

The expectations hypothesis does not completely explain the term structure of interest rates because it fails to take into account the important fact that long-term bonds are riskier than short-term bonds. The risk involved here is not default risk but *interest-rate risk*. **Interest-rate risk** refers to the risk that the price of a financial asset will fluctuate in response to changes in interest rates. For instance, if you own a Treasury bond with an interest rate of 4% and new Treasury bonds are issued with the same maturity but with an interest rate of 6%, the price at which you could sell your bond to other investors will fall. This fall in price would be necessary to compensate investors for buying a bond with a lower interest rate than newly issued bonds.

Interest-rate risk The risk that the price of a financial asset will fluctuate in response to changes in market interest rates.

Although all bonds are subject to interest-rate risk, the longer the term of the bond, the greater the risk. We explain more completely why the extent of interest-rate risk varies with the maturity of a bond in the appendix to this chapter, but we can offer a basic explanation here: If you own a 30-year bond with an interest rate of 4%, and newly issued 30-year bonds have interest rates of 6%, then any investor you sold your bond to would be receiving a lower-than-market interest rate for 30 years. An investor would be willing to do this only if you offered to sell the bond at a significantly lower price. But if you sold a one-year bond, the buyer would be receiving a lower-than-market interest rate for only one year and would be willing to buy the bond with a proportionally smaller price cut. We can conclude that investors are exposed to greater interest-rate risk when they buy long-term bonds than when they buy short-term bonds. So, we expect that investors will be willing to buy long-term bonds issued by the Treasury—or anyone else—only if the interest rate is higher than on a short-term bond. The **term premium** is the additional interest investors require in order to be willing to buy a long-term bond rather than a comparable sequence of short-term bonds.

Term premium The additional interest investors require in order to be willing to buy a long-term bond rather than a comparable sequence of short-term bonds.

We now have a more complete explanation for the term structure of interest rates. (This more complete explanation is often referred to as the *liquidity premium theory*.) Long-term interest rates are the average of expected short-term interest rates *plus* a term premium. For example, assume that the term premium for a two-year bond is 0.25%. If the interest rate on the current one-year bond is 4%, and the expected interest rate on the one-year bond next year is 6%, then the interest rate on the two-year bond will be 5.25%. Or:

$$\text{Interest rate on two-year bond} = \left(\frac{\text{Interest rate on one-year bond today} + \text{Interest rate expected on one-year bond next year}}{2}\right) + \text{Term premium}$$

Or:

$$5.25\% = \left(\frac{4\% + 6\%}{2}\right) + 0.25\%.$$

The term premium explains why the yield curve is typically upward sloping, like the one in panel (b) of Figure 3.9: Because investors require a term premium to buy long-term bonds, the interest rates on long-term bonds will be above the interest rates on short-term bonds not only when investors expect future short-term rates to be higher, but also when investors expect future short-term rates to be constant or even when they expect them to be somewhat lower than current short-term rates. The yield curve will be downward sloping only when investors expect future short-term rates to be significantly lower than current short-term rates.

As we will see in Chapter 9, both the term-structure and the risk-structure of interest rates play important roles in the Federal Reserve's attempts to use monetary policy to affect the levels of real GDP, employment, and prices.

Answering the Key Question

Continued from page 59

At the beginning of the chapter, we asked the question:

"Why did the bursting of the housing bubble beginning in 2006 cause the financial system to falter?"

When housing prices began to fall in 2006, home buyers, particularly subprime borrowers, who had bought when prices were near their peak, began to default on their mortgage loans. At first, many economists and policymakers did not think that the defaults would have an effect outside of the housing market. However, it soon became clear that many financial firms had significant investments in mortgage-backed securities that contained subprime mortgages.

As the prices of mortgage-backed securities declined rapidly, many financial firms suffered heavy losses and some were forced into bankruptcy. The problems at these financial firms led to a decline in the flow of funds through the financial system. The Federal Reserve took steps to contain these problems, but it was more than a year before the financial crisis was ended. The effects of the financial crisis on the economy continued to be felt for several more years.

Before moving on to the next chapter, read *An Inside Look* on the next page for a discussion about the improving credit market for small businesses.

Credit Market Easing for Small Businesses

USA TODAY

As Small Businesses Get Loans, Job Outlook Shows Promise

Some small businesses say they're finding it easier to get loans, a development that could help jump-start a tepid recovery and sluggish job market.

a Small firms with fewer than 100 workers employ half the labor force and typically account for two-thirds of jobs created in a recovery. So far, though, they've benefited far less from the upswing that began in mid-2009 than larger firms. That's because they generally haven't taken part in the export surge, and they rely on banks rather than corporate bond markets to borrow money.

Many small businesses still complain credit is tight. But in a survey released this month by the National Federation of Independent Business (NFIB), the portion saying loans were harder to get than three months earlier was the lowest since September 2008. And senior loan officers surveyed by the Federal Reserve said their standards for small-business loans eased for the second-straight quarter in the three months ending Sept. 30.

"This looks to us like the start of a serious improvement," says Chief Economist Ian Shepherdson of High Frequency Economics. . . .

b Financial institutions are on stronger financial footing, with more capital and fewer bad loans. The amount of loans that banks charged off in the third quarter fell vs. a year ago for the second-straight quarter after rising steadily since late 2006, the Federal Deposit Insurance Corp. said this week.

"Banks have worked through a lot of their problems," says Paul Merski, chief economist of the Independent Community Bankers of America (ICBA). "The industry is in a better position to increase lending."

Furthermore, interest rates are so low that banks can scarcely make a profit by investing depositors' money in Treasury bonds. "Eventually, for banks to become profitable, you have to start taking on some risk," Merski says.

Commercial and industrial loans by small banks, which largely serve small firms, grew at a 4.1% annual rate in October, the most since 2008, according to a UBS analysis of Fed data. . . .

Even so, most lenders are still tight-fisted. Credit conditions aren't nearly as favorable as they were before the 2008 financial crisis. . . .

c Meanwhile, most small businesses aren't trying to borrow, as they have yet to see a robust pickup in sales, says NFIB Chief Economist William Dunkelberg.

"Demand is a bigger issue than borrowing," says Roger Harris, president of Padgett Business Services, a small-business consultant.

Still, even a gradual improvement in banks' willingness to lend could fuel small-business expansions as demand grows. When the economy is shaky, lenders may require a borrower to put up more collateral or boast a higher credit score.

Rockland Trust in Massachusetts is lending more to home builders this year and is even funding speculative construction. "We have more confidence," says Executive Vice President Gerard Nadeau. Home "prices aren't collapsing. . . ."

Source: Paul Davidson, "As small businesses get loans, job outlook shows promise," *USA Today*. November 26, 2010. Reprinted with Permission.

Key Points in the Article

This article discusses the improving credit market for small businesses. Financial institutions are becoming stronger, with fewer bad loans on their books and more capital to lend, and they have been easing their standards for making small business loans. Although credit conditions are still not as favorable as they were prior to the financial crisis and demand for loans is still sluggish, the increase in the availability of loans for small businesses is seen as a positive sign for the job market and the economic recovery from the recession of 2007–2009.

Analyzing the News

a During the financial crisis that began in 2007, commercial and industrial bank loans decreased dramatically and small businesses did not see much improvement in the availability of bank loans until 2010. Although credit remained tight in 2010, banking standards for small business loans began to ease in the second and third quarters, making it easier for small businesses to obtain bank loans. Small businesses with fewer than 100 employees not only account for over half of the U.S. labor force, but also two-thirds of jobs created in a typical recovery. It is therefore important for the economic recovery that small businesses have access to credit.

b Banks began to increase their business lending in 2010 following almost two years of decline. The figure on the right shows that since 2005, commercial and industrial loans peaked in October 2008, plummeted for the duration of the recession, and continued to fall until October 2010. In 2010, lending began to slowly recover. Banks found themselves carrying fewer bad loans and more funds to distribute. With the financial situation in the country becoming more stable, banks were more willing to increase lending, taking on more risk in an effort to increase profits.

c Although lending to small businesses did increase in late 2010 as credit markets became less restrictive, many small businesses were not in the market for loans. Until sales significantly increase, many of these businesses are reluctant to borrow money, concerned that the return they expect to make on their investments may not be enough to justify the rate of interest they have to pay on the loans. Banks becoming more willing to lend to businesses is a positive sign for the economic recovery, but businesses will also have to become more willing to borrow to have a significant impact on the economy.

THINKING CRITICALLY

1. During 2010, the supply of loanable funds expanded as credit markets became less restrictive. Go to the website of the Bureau of Economic Analysis at http://www.bea.gov/ and research the changes in the federal deficit, net exports, and personal saving in the United States at the beginning and end of 2010 and explain the impact that each of these changes would have on the supply of loanable funds, the real interest rate, and investment.
2. As credit markets became less restrictive in late 2010, banks were more willing to make small business loans. Holding other factors that affect the demand and supply of loanable funds constant, explain what effect this should have on the equilibrium interest rate and the equilibrium quantity of loanable funds. Draw a graph that shows the effect on the market for loanable funds of the increased willingness of banks to lend and the increased willingness of businesses to borrow, with the interest rate remaining unchanged.

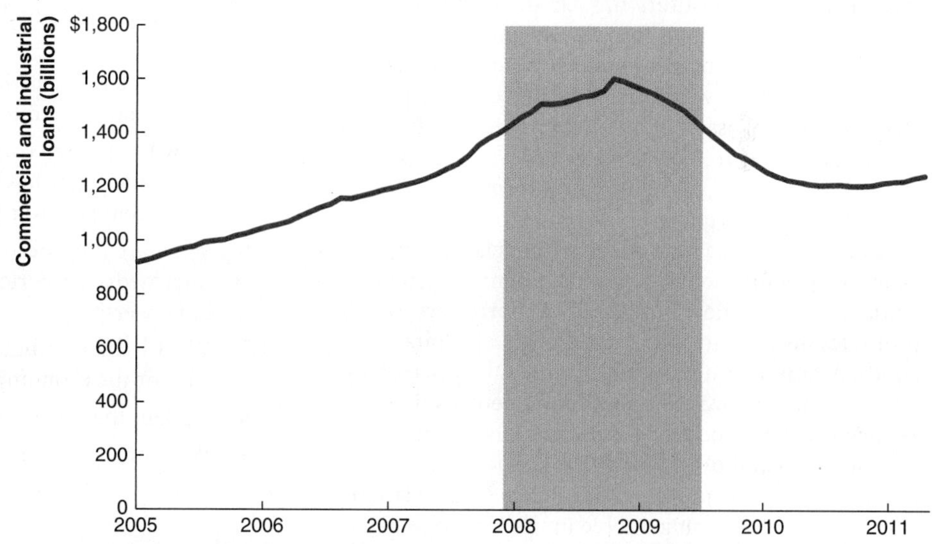

Commercial and Industrial Loans, 2005–2011

Source: Board of Governors of the Federal Reserve System (research.stlouisfed.org)

CHAPTER SUMMARY AND PROBLEMS

KEY TERMS

Adverse selection, p. 68
Asset, p. 61
Asymmetric information, p. 68
Bank panic, p. 69
Bank run, p. 69
Bond, p. 61
Bubble, p. 66
Crowding out, p. 79
Financial asset, p. 61
Financial intermediary, p. 61
Financial market, p. 61
Financial system, p. 60
Interest-rate risk, p. 92
Liquidity, p. 66
Moral hazard, p. 68
Present value, p. 85
Risk, p. 66
Risk structure of interest rates, p. 90
Securitization, p. 67
Stock, p. 61
Term premium, p. 92
Term structure of interest rates, p. 90

3.1 Overview of the Financial System

Describe the financial system and explain the role it plays in the economy.

SUMMARY

An **asset** is anything of value owned by a household or firm. The **financial system** consists of **financial markets** and **financial intermediaries. Financial assets,** such as **stocks** and **bonds**, are traded in financial markets, such as the New York Stock Exchange. A financial intermediary is an institution, such as a commercial bank, that borrows funds from savers and lends them to borrowers. The financial system has become increasingly international, with citizens of one country purchasing financial assets in other countries. The financial system provides three key services to savers and borrowers: risk sharing, liquidity, and information. **Risk** is the degree of uncertainty in the return on an asset. **Liquidity** is the ease with which a financial security can be exchanged for money. When the financial system works well, funds flow from savers to borrowers, which promotes investment and accumulation of capital goods. A **bubble** is a situation in which the price of an asset rises well above the asset's fundamental value. **Securitization** is the process of converting loans, such as mortgages, and other assets that are not tradeable into securities. The process of mortgage securitization contributed to a housing bubble in the United States during the early 2000s. **Asymmetric information** refers to the situation where one party to an economic transaction has better information than does the other party. Many economists believe that asymmetric information problems contributed to the financial crisis of 2007–2009.

Review Questions

1.1 What purpose does the financial system serve in the economy?

1.2 Is there a difference between financial assets and other types of assets?

1.3 Explain the roles of primary and secondary markets in the purchase and sale of financial assets.

1.4 What is a financial intermediary, and what are some examples of financial intermediaries?

1.5 How has foreign ownership of U.S. assets changed over time? How has U.S. ownership of foreign assets changed over time?

1.6 What are the three key services that financial intermediaries perform for savers and borrowers?

1.7 What is an asset bubble, and why are asset bubbles bad for the economy?

1.8 Explain the process of securitization.

1.9 What are adverse selection and moral hazard? What causes them?

Problems and Applications

1.10 Could an economy function without a financial system? Briefly explain.

1.11 For each of the following transactions, identify whether a financial intermediary is

myeconlab Visit www.myeconlab.com to complete these exercises online and get instant feedback.

involved and, if it is a market transaction, state whether it occurs in a primary or secondary market:

a. A bank makes a mortgage loan to a home buyer.
b. The bank sells the mortgage loan to Fannie Mae.
c. A startup company obtains financing by selling shares of stock to private investors.
d. One of the investors of a startup company resells the stock to someone else.
e. The federal government sells Treasury bills at a weekly auction, where they are purchased by a pension fund.
f. The pension fund resells the Treasury bills to a bank.
g. A saver purchases 1,000 shares of Microsoft stock on the NASDAQ stock exchange.
h. Microsoft issues new stock, which it sells on the NASDAQ.

1.12 For each of the following cases, explain what service the financial intermediary is providing to savers or borrowers: risk sharing, liquidity, or information

a. A mutual fund allows savers to purchase shares in a large basket of stocks.
b. A bank takes in small deposits and makes large mortgage loans.
c. A life insurance company offers consumers life insurance, auto insurance, and fire insurance.
d. Workers have part of their paychecks deducted and placed into pension funds.
e. Banks provide depositors with research about investment opportunities.
f. An investment bank underwrites a new issue of stock.

1.13 Many banks sell most of the mortgage loans that they originate within a few years. Assuming that a bank is not worried about default risk, why would it want to sell the mortgage loans it makes rather than hold them in its portfolio?

1.14 Are high interest rates good for banks? Explain your answer.

1.15 In testimony to Congress on the failure of Lehman Brothers, former CEO Richard Fuld stated:

> As C.E.O., I ran more of a "what do I really need to be focused on" mentality. . . . I was focused on less-liquid assets—commercial real estate, residential mortgages, leveraged loans. I was not focused on the most highly liquid securities. I was not focused on government securities that could vary between $50 billion and $100 billion a day.

How does this testimony illustrate a principal–agent problem?

Source: "Lehman Examiner: Fuld Probably Knew of Repo 105," April 20, 2010, http://dealbook.blogs.nytimes.com/2010/04/20/lehman-examiner-fuld-probably-knew-of-repo-105.

1.16 Checking accounts and savings accounts at banks are insured by the FDIC, up to at least $250,000. How might the knowledge that deposits are insured create a moral hazard problem?

1.17 **[Related to the *Making the Connection* on page 62]** For years, General Motors was willing to make car loans through its GMAC subsidiary to car buyers who could not borrow money from a bank. If a bank fails to make a loan to someone who wants to borrow money to buy a car, the bank is giving up the profit it could earn by making the loan. If the bank finds the loan to be too risky, why would GMAC be willing to make it?

1.18 **[Related to the *Making the Connection* on page 64]** How does the globalization of financial markets improve the ability of intermediaries to provide risk-sharing, information, and liquidity?

3.2 The Role of the Central Bank in the Financial System

Understand the role of the central bank in stabilizing the financial system.

SUMMARY

When people deposit money in a bank, the bank loans out most of the money. While the deposits may be withdrawn at any time, the loans are typically long term with the bank having to wait months or years before being fully paid back. When many depositors simultaneously decide to withdraw their money from a bank, there is a **bank run**. If many banks experience runs at the same time, the result is a **bank panic**. Once a bank panic begins, some banks will be forced to close permanently, which leads to another difficulty known as *asset deflation.* When a bank closes, its assets are sold to raise the funds necessary to pay off its depositors. These sales may cause the price of these assets to fall (or deflate), which in turn causes difficulties for other banks. A central bank, such as the Federal Reserve in the United States, can help stop a bank panic by acting as a lender of last resort in making loans to banks that cannot borrow funds elsewhere. Economists worry that aiding troubled financial firms may increase *moral hazard* in the financial system because the managers of financial firms may be more likely to undertake risky investments if they expect the government to bail them out if the investments result in losses.

Review Questions

2.1 How are the functions of a central bank different from those of a conventional bank?

2.2 Why is it desirable to have a lender of last resort in a financial system?

2.3 How does a bank run cause a bank to fail?

2.4 What is the difference between a bank run and a bank panic? How might a bank run lead to a bank panic?

2.5 Why do the government bailouts during the 2007–2009 financial crisis create worries about moral hazard?

Problems and Applications

2.6 The Fed used broad powers to act as a lender of last resort during the 2007–2009 financial crisis. If there had not been a lender of last resort, what would the effect have been on banks and other financial firms? What would the effect have been on the U.S. economy?

2.7 **[Related to the *Making the Connection* on page 71]** During the Great Depression of the 1930s, prices of many assets, including stocks, bonds, real estate, and farm land, fell rapidly.

a. What problems did banks encounter during the Great Depression?

b. How did these problems contribute to asset price deflation?

c. Compare the effects of the problems with commercial banks during the Great Depression with the effects of the bankruptcy of Lehman Brothers.

2.8 An article in the *New York Times* states:

> In the last year and a half, the largest financial institutions have only grown bigger, mainly as a result of government-brokered mergers. They now enjoy borrowing at significantly lower rates than their smaller competitors, a result of the bond markets' implicit assumption that the giant banks are "too big to fail."

a. Why are large banks able to borrow at lower rates than smaller banks?

b. Why does the bond market assume that these banks are too big to fail?

c. What are some of the possible consequences for the banking industry if the too-big-to-fail policy continues?

Source: David M. Herszenhorn and Sewell Chan, "Financial Debate Renews Scrutiny on Banks' Size," *New York Times*, April 21, 2010.

2.9 **[Related to the *Chapter Opener* on page 59]** Bank failures are caused by banks having insufficient funds to cover withdrawals of deposits.

a. Should Congress require banks to hold 100% of deposits as reserves instead of the 10% now required?

b. What would happen to the availability of credit if banks held 100% reserves?

3.3 Determining Interest Rates: The Market for Loanable Funds and the Market for Money

Explain how nominal and real interest rates are determined in financial markets.

SUMMARY

The long-term real interest rate is determined in the loanable funds market. The short-term nominal interest rate is determined in the market for money. The supply of loanable funds comes from domestic households, the government, and the foreign sector, while the demand for loanable funds comes from the willingness of firms and households to borrow to finance investment expenditures. When the government increases its spending, holding everything else constant, the supply of loanable funds available to the private sector decreases. As a result, the real interest rate increases, so investment spending decreases. This phenomenon is called **crowding out** because increases in government spending reduce private investment expenditures. The Federal Reserve determines the supply of money. The nominal interest rate is the opportunity cost of holding money because by holding money you give up the interest you could have earned on another financial asset, such as a Treasury bill. Individuals and groups hold money to conduct market transactions, so the price level and real GDP determine the demand for money. The Federal Reserve determines the supply of money. The intersection of the demand for money and the supply of money determines the short-term nominal interest rate.

Review Questions

3.1 What determines the demand for loanable funds?

3.2 What determines the supply of loanable funds?

3.3 How is the market for money model different from the loanable funds model?

3.4 Why is the demand for money downward sloping?

3.5 How is the equilibrium real interest rate determined? How is the equilibrium nominal interest rate determined?

Problems and Applications

3.6 Draw a graph of the market for loanable funds. Show the effect on the equilibrium real interest rate and quantity of funds loaned and borrowed of each of the following events:

a. Consumers decide to spend less.

b. The government decreases its spending.

c. Businesses become pessimistic about future profitability.

d. Imports increase.

e. The government's budget deficit increases, and at the same time, investment in new capital goods becomes more profitable.

3.7 **[Related to *Solved Problem 3.3* on page 81]** During the late 1990s, U.S. asset markets were growing rapidly, making the United States attractive to foreign savers. At the same time, strong economic growth made firms optimistic about the future, and the government was reducing the size of its budget deficit.

a. Use the loanable funds model to show the probable effect of these events on interest rates and the quantity of loanable funds.

b. Use your results from part a. to explain why the U.S. trade deficit grew rapidly during this period.

3.8 Suppose that the domestic quantity of loanable funds supplied equals the domestic quantity of loanable funds demanded. In other words, there is no foreign lending or borrowing. If the government budget deficit increases, what will happen in the market for loanable funds? Will the country lend or borrow internationally? Briefly explain.

3.9 Assume that initially the government has a balanced budget. However, to finance infrastructure investment, the government decides to increase spending. Show the effect on the loanable funds market in each of the following cases:

a. The government raises taxes on consumers.

b. The government raises taxes on businesses.

c. The government borrows, leaving taxes unchanged.

3.10 The price of a bond is inversely related to its return, or interest rate. Using the market for money model, explain why, all other things held constant, an increase in real GDP causes a fall in bond prices.

3.11 Draw a graph of the market for money. Show the effect on the money demand curve, the money supply curve, and the equilibrium nominal interest rate of each of the following:

a. The Fed decreases the money supply.

b. A recession causes real GDP to fall.

c. The price level increases.

d. The Fed increases the money supply at the same time that the price level falls.

3.12 During the 2007–2009 financial crisis, the Fed increased the money supply. In the same period, real GDP declined.

a. Assuming the price level remained constant, use a graph of the market for money to analyze the effect of these events on the equilibrium nominal interest rate.

b. During the financial crisis of 2007–2009, the Fed stated that it was concerned about the possibility of deflation. How would a falling price level change your answer to part a?

3.13 Suppose that the loanable fund market is in equilibrium at real interest rate r_1. The government then decides to spend more, increasing the budget deficit. The new supply curve (S_2) is shown in the graph below:

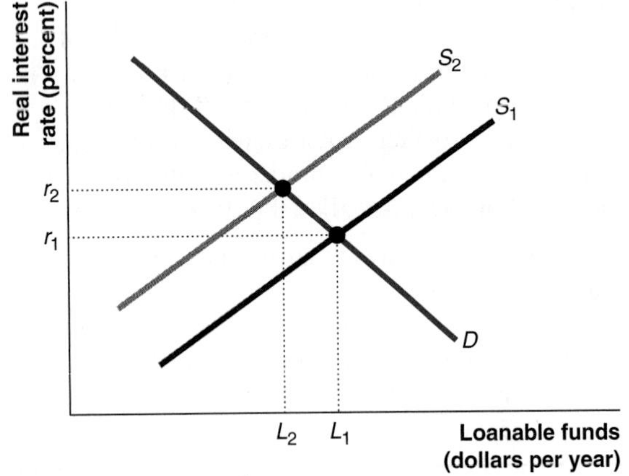

a. Identify the new equilibrium real interest rate and quantity of loanable funds.

b. How would your answer change if the increase in the budget deficit was accompanied by a significant increase in imports to the United States?

c. During the early 1980s, large government budget deficits were accompanied by large trade deficits. Use your analysis in parts a. and b. to explain why real interest rates did not rise significantly even with a major increase in government borrowing.

3.4 Calculating Interest Rates

Understand how to calculate interest rates.

SUMMARY

Financial instruments such as bonds make payments to the owners in the present and in the future. The price of a bond and the interest rate on the bond are related through the concept of **present value**. The price of a bond equals the present value of all future payments to the owner of the bond. The **term structure of interest rates** shows the relationship among bonds that have the same characteristics except for having different maturities. The interest rate on a long-term bond is equal to the average of the short-term interest rates over the duration of the long-term bond plus a premium to compensate for **interest-rate risk**, which is the risk that the price of a financial asset will fluctuate in response to changes in interest rates. The **risk structure of interest rates** is the relationship among the interest rates on bonds of different default risks. The **term premium** is the additional interest investors require in order to be willing to buy a long-term bond rather than a comparable sequence of short-term bonds.

Review Questions

4.1 Why are there many different interest rates in the economy?

4.2 How do interest rates change with the riskiness of lending?

4.3 How does the maturity of a bond affect its interest rate?

4.4 What is the Treasury yield curve?

Problems and Applications

4.5 During the 2007–2009 crisis, the interest rates on short-term U.S. Treasury bills fell to near zero. What does this tell us about the riskiness of U.S. government debt?

4.6 Imagine that you have won the lottery. You get to choose between a prize of $100,000 today or a total of $200,000 paid in 10 annual payments of $20,000 (paid at the end of each year). Which

prize would you choose if the interest rate is 5%? Would your answer change if the interest rate is 20%?

4.7 **[Related to *Solved Problem 3.4* on page 89]** Suppose that a Treasury bond was issued 27 years ago, so it will mature in three years. If the bond pays a coupon of $50 per year and will make a final face value payment of $1,000 at maturity, what is its price if the relevant market interest rate is 5%? What is its price if the relevant market interest rate is 10%?

4.8 Bonds and loans have interest rates that vary according to how many years until they mature, their risk, and their liquidity. For each of the following pairs of loans and bonds, explain which would be likely to have the higher interest rate.

a. A credit card and an auto loan

b. A 10-year Treasury bond and a 10-year Chrysler bond

c. A 1-year U.S. Treasury bill and a 10-year U.S. Treasury note

d. A 1-year personal loan to a friend and a 1-year corporate bond

4.9 Credit cards are often issued with an initial interest rate but include the provision that the interest rate will rise if the borrower makes a certain number of late payments. Why do credit card companies increase interest rates for borrowers who miss payments?

4.10 Yield curves generally slope upward. A downward-sloping, or "inverted," yield curve is often thought to signal a future recession. Why might this be true?

4.11 With a zero-coupon bond, the buyer receives only the face value of the bond at maturity—the bond pays no coupons. Suppose that for a price of $675, you buy a 10-year, zero-coupon with a $1,000 face value.

a. What interest rate will you receive over the life of the bond if you hold the bond to maturity?

b. Now suppose that interest rates on equivalent bonds have risen to 10% after one year. If you decide to sell the bond, what price can you sell it for?

DATA EXERCISES

D3.1: The federal government's deficits must be financed by the sale of Treasury bills and bonds. Go to the U.S. Treasury Web site (www.treasurydirect.gov) and search for the *Monthly Statement of the Public Debt.*

a. How large is the U.S. debt? How large is the U.S. debt relative to U.S. GDP?

b. What percentage of the debt is financed by short-term instruments (Treasury bills)?

c. What percentage of the debt is financed by medium-term instruments (Treasury notes)?

d. What percentage of the debt is financed by long-term instruments (Treasury bonds)?

D3.2: At the Treasury Web site (www.treasury.gov), go to the Resources tab, and find Data and Charts Center. Then locate the Daily Treasury Yield Curve Rates.

a. For the most recent date, graph the yield curve. Then explain how yield changes with the maturity of the Treasury security.

b. This site gives about two weeks of data. Is the yield curve changing? How? Can you infer anything about the current state of the economy?

D3.3: The U.S. Treasury also provides data on the external holdings of U.S. debt. You can find this data usually through the following link: www.treas.gov/tic/mfh.txt.

a. What countries are the top five holders of U.S. debt?

b. Using the loanable funds model, explain how U.S. government debt relates to the loanable funds market. What effect does this have on funds available for domestic businesses to borrow?

c. What percentage of the U.S. government debt is held outside the United States? Of this amount, what percentage is held by foreign governments?

D3.4: Go to www.bloomberg.com. In the Rates & Bonds menu at the bottom of the page, find Government Bonds. This section gives yields and the yield

myeconlab Visit **www.myeconlab.com** to complete these exercises online and get instant feedback.

curves for the United States, Australia, Brazil, Germany, Hong Kong, Japan, and the United Kingdom. How do the yield curves of the different countries vary?

D3.5: Go to http://www.treasury.gov/initiatives/financial-stability/about/Pages/default.aspx to find information about the Emergency Economic Stabilization Act of 2008 (EESA). The Troubled Asset Relief Program (TARP) is the best-known so-called government bailout program.

a. How did TARP work?

b. Original estimates of the cost of TARP have fallen as financial institutions have repaid funds. Can you find current figures on the cost of TARP?

c. Do you think that TARP created moral hazard problems for the future?

D3.6: **[Excel exercise]** The Federal Reserve Bank of St. Louis offers a wide range of economic data at its Web site called FRED (http://research.stlouisfed.org/fred2/). Find the data for U.S. three-month and one-year Treasury bill rates from 1990 to the most recent date available and download these data into an Excel file.

a. What is the average interest rate on each type of Treasury bill over this period?

b. What is the standard deviation? Which series is more volatile?

c. Graph the data. Do the rates move together?

d. Calculate the mean and standard deviation again, but end the series at 2006 rather than the current date. How does this change the mean and standard deviation? Briefly explain.

APPENDIX

More on the Term Structure of Interest Rates

3A **Understand the term structure of interest rates.**

As we saw in the chapter, the term structure of interest rates is the relationship among interest rates on bonds of different maturities. Because the term structure of interest rates plays an important role in monetary policy, it is useful to look at it more closely. First, consider again the situation you face if you want to invest funds over a two-year period and you are considering whether to pursue a strategy of buying a two-year bond or a strategy of buying a one-year bond today and another one-year bond one year from now. To work out the arithmetic, let's use the following notation, where time t is the present and time $t+1$ is one year from now:

$$i_{1t} = \text{interest rate on a one-year bond at time } t$$
$$i_{2t} = \text{interest rate (per year) on a two-year bond at time } t$$
$$i^e_{1t+1} = \text{interest rate that investors expect on a one-year bond at time } t+1$$

To keep things simple, let's assume that you are investing \$1.What are the expected returns on a \$1 investment after two years for each strategy? If you buy a two-year bond, your \$1 is worth $\$1(1 + i_{2t})$ after the first year and $\$1(1 + i_{2t})(1 + i_{2t})$ after two years. If you buy two one-year bonds, your \$1 is worth $\$1(1 + i_{1t})$ after the first year, and you expect it will be worth $\$1(1 + i_{1t})(1 + i^e_{1t+1})$ after two years. According to the expectations theory, investors in the bond market expect the return from the two strategies to be the same. Therefore, we can equate the two returns:

$$\$1(1 + i_{2t})(1 + i_{2t}) = \$1(1 + i_{1t})(1 + i^e_{1t+1}).$$

Simplifying the expression, we get:

$$2i_{2t} + i^2_{2t} = i_{1t} + i^e_{1t+1} + i_{1t}(i^e_{1t+1}).$$

Because the product of two interest rates is very small—for instance, $0.02 \times 0.04 = 0.0008$—we can ignore the products on each side of the equation without significantly affecting the result. We are then left with:

$$i_{2t} = \frac{i_{1t} + i^e_{1t+1}}{2}.$$

We again see the result of the expectations hypothesis: The interest rate on a two-year bond should equal the average of the interest rate on a one-year bond that can be purchased today and the expected interest rate on a one-year bond that can be purchased one year from now. We could easily extend this reasoning to demonstrate that the interest rate on a bond that matures after n years—an n-year bond—is the average of the expected one-year interest rates over the life of the bond. So, for instance, the interest rate on a 10-year bond should equal the average of the interest rate on the one-year bond today and the expected interest rates on the other nine one-year bonds during this 10-year period.

We saw in the chapter, though, that the liquidity premium theory argues that because investors are subject to greater interest-rate risk on a long-term bond than on a short-term bond, they require a risk premium to buy the long-term bond. We can look more closely at why investors require a risk premium. Consider the following example: Suppose you purchased a one-year bond for \$1,000 that has a \$100 coupon and a principal, or face value, of \$1,000. The interest rate on this bond, then, will be \$100/\$1,000 = 0.10, or 10%. Now suppose that immediately after you purchase this bond, new bonds are issued that are otherwise identical, except they have coupons of \$150, so buyers of these bonds will receive an interest rate of \$150/\$1,000 = 0.15, or 15%. What will happen to the price of your bond? If you sell your bond, buyers will only pay a price that will give them a 15% interest rate because that is the interest rate they could receive if they were to buy a newly issued bond rather than your bond. Therefore, the price of your bond will fall to:

$$\text{Price} = \frac{\$100}{(1 + 0.15)} + \frac{\$1{,}000}{(1 + 0.15)} = \$956.52.$$

So, you will have suffered a loss of \$1,000 − \$956.52 = \$43.48 on your investment. As a percentage of your investment, your loss equals −\$43.48/\$1,000 = −0.043, or −4.3%.

Now, suppose that instead of buying a one-year bond with a 10% interest rate, you buy a two-year bond with a 10% interest rate, and, once again, immediately after you buy your bond, new bonds are issued with 15% interest rates. In this case, what will happen to the price of your bond? Once again, we can calculate that the price must be such that potential buyers would receive a 15% interest rate from buying your bond:

$$\text{Price} = \frac{\$100}{(1 + 0.15)} + \frac{\$100}{(1 + 0.15)^2} + \frac{\$1{,}000}{(1 + 0.15)^2} = \$918.71.$$

So, now you have suffered a loss of \$1,000 − \$918.71 = \$81.29 on your investment. In percentage terms, your loss equals −\$81.29/\$1,000 = −0.081, or −8.1%. Your loss from an increase in interest rates is significantly greater if you hold a two-year bond than if you hold a one-year bond. Because investors know this fact, they will buy a two-year bond only if they receive a higher interest rate—the term premium—than they would receive on a one-year bond.

If we denote the term premium on a two-year bond at time t as i^{TP}_{2t}, then we have the following expression for the yield on a two-year bond:

$$i_{2t} = \frac{i_{1t} + i^{e}_{1t+1}}{2} + i^{TP}_{2t}.$$

Once again, we could extend this analysis to show that according to the liquidity premium theory, the interest rate on an n-year bond is the average of the expected short-term interest rates over the life of the bond plus the risk premium for an n-year bond at time t.

CHAPTER 4

Determining Aggregate Production

LEARNING OBJECTIVES

After studying this chapter, you should be able to:

4.1 Describe the aggregate production function (pages 106–116)

4.2 Explain how real GDP is determined in the long run (pages 116–120)

4.3 Discuss the contributions of capital, labor, and efficiency to the growth rate of real GDP (pages 120–126)

4.4 Understand that differences in efficiency explain differences in labor productivity across countries (pages 127–131)

4A Derive important properties of the Cobb–Douglas production function (pages 140–142)

THE SURPRISING ECONOMIC RISE OF INDIA

When you have a computer problem and need technical support, the person who takes your call may well be in India. This is one indication of how Indian information technology firms have been expanding relative to U.S.-based firms. The largest steel company in the world, Arcelor Mittal, although now headquartered in Luxembourg, was founded in India by the Mittal family. In 2011, *Forbes* magazine listed Lakshmi Mittal, Arcelor Mittal's chairman and CEO, as the sixth richest person in the world. The ninth richest person in the world is Mukesh Ambani, the CEO of Reliance Industries, an oil firm, based in Mumbai, India, which is the country's largest private firm. Tata Motors, India's largest automobile company, made headlines in 2009, when it introduced the Nano car, which it sold in India at the very low price of $2,200. Tata also owns Jaguar and Land Rover. Increasingly, U.S. consumers find themselves buying Indian goods and services, and U.S. firms find themselves competing against Indian firms.

To many people in the United States, the rapid economic rise of India was unexpected. In 1950, India was

Continued on next page

Key Issue and Question

At the end of Chapter 1, we noted key issues and questions that serve as a framework for the book. Here are the key issue and question for this chapter:

Issue: Real GDP has increased substantially over time in the United States and other developed countries.

Question: What are the main factors that determine the growth rate of real GDP?

Answered on page 131

desperately poor. India's real GDP per capita in 1950 was less than $1,000 measured in 2010 dollars, or less than 7% of 1950 U.S. real GDP per capita. Twenty-five years later, India had fallen even further behind the United States, with GDP per capita only 5.5% of U.S. GDP per capita. Recent years tell a much different story. Between 1990 and 2010, real GDP per capita in India grew at an average annual rate of 4.7%, well above the average growth rate of 1.4% experienced by the United States. In early 2011, PwC, a consulting firm, projected that between 2010 and 2050, the Indian economy would grow three times as fast as the U.S. economy. After centuries of extreme poverty, India has finally begun to close the gap between its standard of living and the standard of living in high-income countries such as the United States and the countries of Western Europe.

India remains a very poor country, however. It has a population of 1.2 billion, more than half of whom are employed in agriculture and, in many cases, produce barely enough to feed themselves. Infant mortality remains high, and as many as half of all adult women and one-quarter of adult men are unable to read and write. Still, the rapid economic growth that began in the early 1990s provides hope for a better life for India's population. What explains the higher growth rates in India during the past 20 years? Clearly, an increase in growth was not inevitable. Prior to 1947, India was part of the colony of British India, which also included the modern countries of Pakistan and Bangladesh. In 1950, real GDP per capita was about the same in all three countries. By 2010, however, as India experienced much faster economic growth, real GDP per capita in Pakistan was 30% lower than in India, and real GDP per capita in Bangladesh was 50% lower.

So, countries very close geographically and sharing the same colonial history can have very different experiences with economic growth. Explaining economic growth can be complex. In this chapter, we begin the process of explaining economic growth by focusing on a few key ideas that explain what determines the level of real GDP in the long run.

AN INSIDE LOOK on page 132 explores why General Motors is expanding production in India.

Sources: "Business in India," *Economist*, September 30, 2010; Angus Maddison, *Contours of the World Economy*, New York: Oxford University Press, 2007; "The World's Billionaires," forbes.com, March 10, 2010; "GDP per Person Forecasts," *Economist*, January 13, 2011; and www.cia.gov/library/publications/the-world-factbook/index.html.

Economic growth is a key macroeconomic issue because it determines the standard of living of the average person in a country. Although the United States, Japan, Western Europe, and certain other countries have attained high standards of living, billions of people remain stuck in grinding poverty. In fact, the standard of living in some countries in Asia, Africa, and Latin America has increased relatively little in hundreds of years. Why are some countries rich and others poor? In this chapter, we begin building a model that can help answer that question.

The Aggregate Production Function

4.1

Learning Objective
Describe the aggregate production function.

In looking at economic growth, we are most interested in long-run increases in real GDP *per capita* because that is the best measure of the quantity of goods and services available per person. We begin, though, by developing a model to explain real GDP and then adjust the model to explain real GDP per capita.

Figure 4.1 shows how real GDP increased in the United States from 1949 to 2010. The figure shows that because of the business cycle, real GDP has decreased in some years, but overall, the trend has been strongly upward. Measured in 2005 dollars, real GDP was just $1.8 trillion at the beginning of 1949, but it had increased to $13.4 trillion by the beginning of 2011. This increase represents an average annual growth rate of 3.3%. Before we can explain why real GDP grows over time, though, we first have to explain how real GDP is determined at any point in time.

First, think about how an individual firm combines land, labor, natural resources, and capital—such as machinery, equipment, factories, and office buildings—to produce goods and services. The relationship between the inputs employed by a firm and the maximum output it can produce with those inputs is called the firm's *production function*. A firm's *technology* is the processes it uses to turn inputs into outputs of goods and services. Notice that this economic definition of technology is broader than the everyday definition. When we use the word *technology* in everyday language, we usually refer only to the development

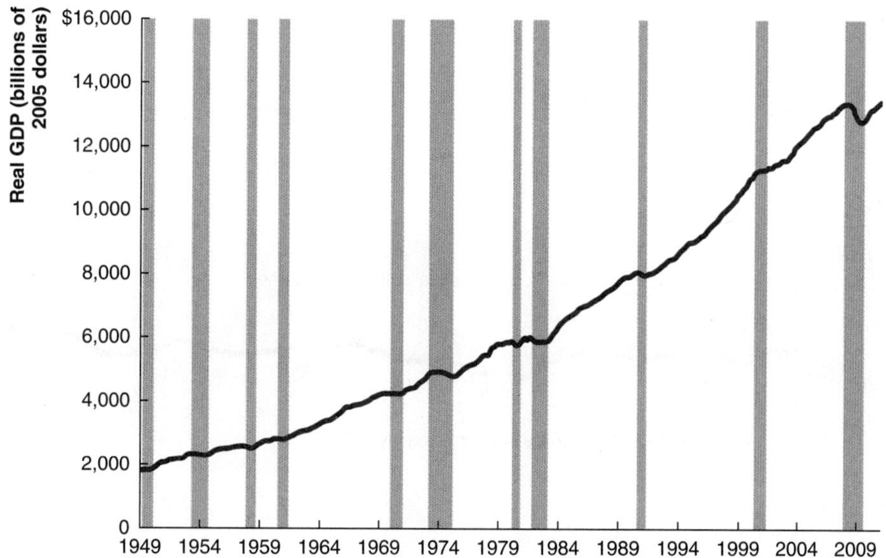

Figure 4.1

Real GDP for the United States, 1949–2010

The dominant feature of this graph is the increase in real GDP over time. Real GDP was just \$1.8 trillion at the beginning of 1949 and increased to \$13.4 trillion by the beginning of 2011. Real GDP increases during some years and decreases during other years, but the average annual growth rate of real GDP was 3.3% during the 1949–2010 period. The shaded areas show periods of recession.

Source: U.S. Bureau of Economic Analysis. ●

of new products. In the economic sense, a firm's technology depends on many factors, such as the skills of its managers, the training of its workers, and the speed and efficiency of its machinery and equipment. The technology of pizza production, for example, includes not only the capacity of the restaurant's pizza ovens and how quickly they bake the pizza but also how quickly the cooks can prepare the pizza for baking, how well the manager motivates the workers, and how well the manager has arranged the facilities to allow the cooks to quickly prepare the pizzas and get them in the ovens. Because a firm's technology is the processes it uses to turn inputs into output, the production function represents the firm's technology.

The production function is a microeconomic concept when we apply it to an individual firm, but on a macroeconomic level, we can think about how an economy turns the total available inputs into goods and services. So, we can say that the **aggregate production function** is an equation that shows the relationship between the inputs employed by firms and the maximum output firms can produce with those inputs. At the macroeconomic level, we measure output as real GDP, and we include only labor and capital as inputs because land and natural resources are relatively minor components of production in advanced economies such as the United States, Japan, and Germany.

Aggregate production function An equation that shows the relationship between the inputs employed by firms and the maximum output firms can produce with those inputs.

We can write a general version of the aggregate production function as:

$$Y = A \times F(K, L), \text{ or } Y = AF(K, L),$$

where:

Y = real GDP

K = quantity of capital goods available to firms, or the *capital stock*

L = quantity of labor

A = index of how efficiently the economy transforms capital and labor into real GDP

The higher the level of the index, A, the more efficient is the economy and the higher is real GDP. Technology, government regulations and institutions, the quality of the labor force, and the effect of a nation's geography are some of the factors that can affect the value of A. In fact, A measures the influence of any factor that determines real GDP other than the quantities of capital and labor. For the sake of simplicity, for the rest of this book, we will refer to the aggregate production function simply as the *production function*.

Constant returns to scale A property of a production function such that if all inputs increase by the same percentage, real GDP increases by the same percentage.

The Cobb–Douglas Production Function

The model of economic growth that we will build in this chapter assumes that the production function has **constant returns to scale**, which means that if all inputs increase by the

Figure 4.2

Capital's and Labor's Shares of Income in the United States, 1949–2010

Capital's and labor's shares of income in the United States vary from year to year, but they have been relatively stable since 1949. Capital has received about a one-third share of income, and labor has received about a two-thirds share.

Source: U.S. Bureau of Economic Analysis. ●

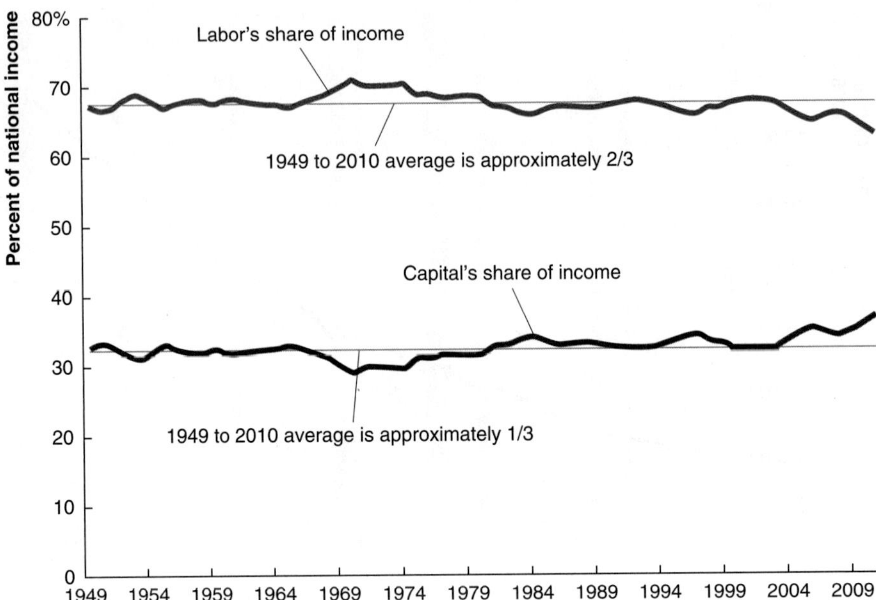

same percentage, real GDP increases by that percentage. For example, under constant returns to scale, if the quantity of capital and the quantity of labor both double, then real GDP will also double. Or:

$$2Y = AF(2K, 2L).$$

Macroeconomists often work with a particular production function called the *Cobb–Douglas production function*, which has constant returns to scale and does a good job of accounting for U.S. data on the growth of real GDP. The **Cobb–Douglas production function** takes the general form:

Cobb–Douglas production function A production function that takes the form $Y = AK^{\alpha}L^{1-\alpha}$.

$$Y = AK^{\alpha}L^{1-\alpha},$$

where:

α = capital's share in national income

$1 - \alpha$ = labor's share in national income

Notice that $\alpha + (1 - \alpha) = 1$. For a Cobb–Douglas production function with constant returns to scale, the exponents on the labor and capital variables sum to one.

Equation (4.1) is the Cobb–Douglas production function with α having a value of one-third:

$$Y = AK^{\frac{1}{3}}L^{\frac{2}{3}}, \tag{4.1}$$

where 1/3 is the share of national income going to the owners of capital goods, and 2/3 is the share of national income going to labor. In this form of the Cobb–Douglas production function, *A* is called **total factor productivity (*TFP*)**, which is an index of the overall level of efficiency of transforming capital and labor into real GDP.

Total factor productivity (*TFP*) An index of the overall level of efficiency of transforming capital and labor into real GDP.

Figure 4.2 shows why in Equation (4.1) we chose one-third as capital's share of income and two-thirds as labor's share of income. The shares of income going to the owners of capital and to labor vary from year to year, but they have been relatively stable since 1949. The average share of income has been about one-third (or 33%) for capital and about

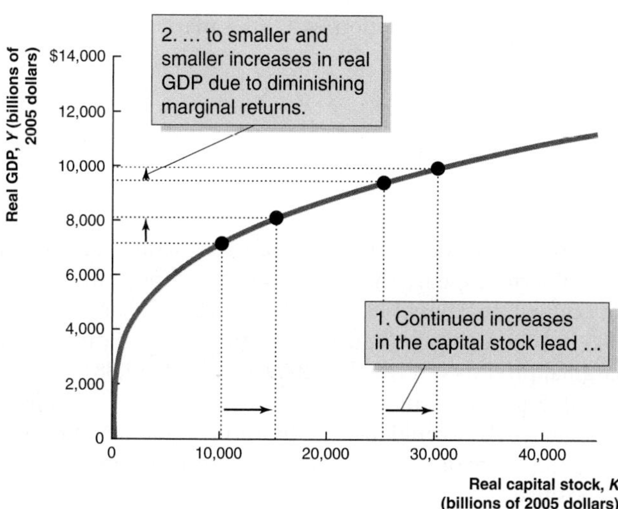

(a) Aggregate production function, holding labor and total factor productivity constant

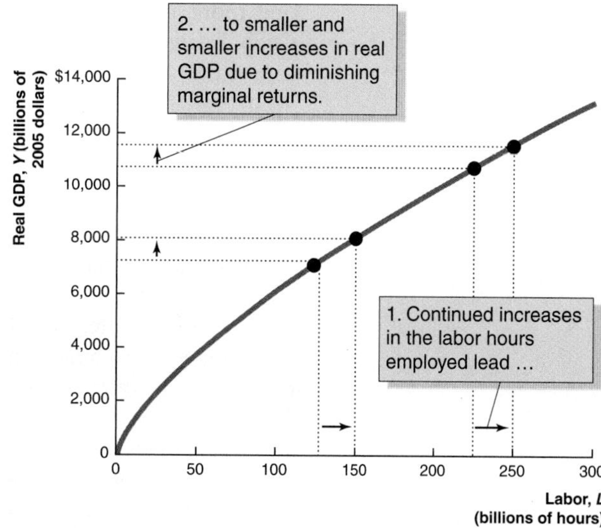

(b) Aggregate production function, holding capital and total factor productivity constant

Figure 4.3 Aggregate Production Functions for the United States During 2009

Panel (a) shows the aggregate production function for the United States, with total factor productivity and labor constant at their 2009 values but allowing the capital stock to vary. Panel (b) shows the aggregate production function for the United States, holding total factor productivity and the capital stock constant at their 2009 values but allowing labor to vary. The production functions in Panels (a) and (b) are two different ways of showing the same relationship. Notice that the production function becomes flatter as firms accumulate more capital and hire more labor.

Sources: U.S. Bureau of Economic Analysis; and Congressional Budget Office. ●

two-thirds (or 67%) for labor. These values are similar in many other developed countries, so we use them throughout this chapter and the next.

Notice that if capital, labor, or total factor productivity increase, real GDP also increases. Therefore, the Cobb–Douglas production function in Equation (4.1) is just another way of saying that when firms use more inputs or become more efficient, real GDP increases.

Panel (a) in Figure 4.3 shows a graph of the aggregate production function for the United States, with the level of real GDP (Y) on the vertical axis and the value of the capital stock (K) on the horizontal axis. This is the estimated production function for the United States based on actual data.

By showing the production function this way, we are holding total factor productivity (A) and labor (L) constant. As the level of the capital stock increases, real GDP increases. Panel (b) of Figure 4.3 is an alternative way of showing the production function. In this case, we show the value for labor on the horizontal axis while holding total factor productivity and the capital stock constant. As the quantity of labor increases, real GDP increases. The production functions in panels (a) and (b) are two different ways of showing the same relationship.

The Marginal Products of Capital and Labor

There are three important features of the production function in panel (a) of Figure 4.3. First, the production function slopes upward, indicating that, all else being equal, real GDP increases as the economy accumulates more capital goods. We can understand better why the production functions slopes upward by considering the marginal product of capital. The **marginal product of capital (*MPK*)** is the extra output a firm receives from adding

Marginal product of capital (*MPK*) The extra output a firm receives from adding one more unit of capital, holding all other inputs and efficiency constant.

one more unit of capital, holding all other inputs and efficiency constant. For the Cobb–Douglas production function shown in Equation (4.1), the marginal product of capital is[1]:

$$MPK = \left(\frac{1}{3}\right)\left(\frac{Y}{K}\right). \tag{4.2}$$

(In general, the marginal product of capital for a Cobb–Douglas production function is equal to the exponent on the capital term, capital's share of income, multiplied by (Y/K).) For the United States in 2009, the capital stock was \$40,084 billion in 2005 dollars, and real GDP was \$12,881 billion in 2005 dollars. Using the equation for the marginal product of capital, we can calculate the marginal product of capital in 2009 as 1/3 × (\$12,881 billion/ \$40,084 billion) = \$0.107 of real GDP per dollar of the capital stock. That is, if the capital stock were to increase by \$1 billion, real GDP would increase by \$0.107 billion. Notice that real GDP, the capital stock, and capital's share of income are always positive, so the marginal product of capital is also always positive.

The second important feature of the aggregate production function is that the production function as shown in panel (a) of Figure 4.3 flattens out as the capital stock increases. In other words, the slope of the production function decreases as the capital stock increases. This flattening occurs because capital goods experience diminishing marginal returns, which means that, holding labor and efficiency constant, the marginal product of capital decreases as the capital stock increases. Capital experiences diminishing marginal returns because labor and total factor productivity are fixed, so as the economy adds more capital goods, there are fewer workers per machine. With fewer workers per machine, the machines are not used as efficiently, so the marginal product of capital decreases.

To illustrate this point, consider a simple example of two administrative assistants named Cynthia and Dan who have to put together an accounting report for their boss. If Cynthia and Dan do not initially have a computer, then they will have to write the report on typewriters and do not have access to spreadsheets to do the accounting. As a result, it will take Cynthia and Dan a long time to write a report. However, if Cynthia and Dan had one computer then Cynthia could use a spreadsheet to do the accounting and when she took breaks, Dan could use the computer to write the report. Now, the computer is in constant use, and the marginal product of capital for the computer is high. Consider what happens when we add a second computer. Now Dan can do the writing while Cynthia does the accounting, so the marginal product of capital for the second computer is positive. However, now when Cynthia or Dan takes a break, his or her computer is also "resting" and not adding to the goal of writing the accounting report because there is no worker available to use the computer during the break. As a result, the marginal product of capital for a second computer remains positive but is less than the marginal product of capital for the first computer. Adding a third computer helps them even less because neither of them is available to use the new computer. In effect, the third computer is always "resting." The marginal product of capital decreases as we add more computers, holding constant the number of workers and total factor productivity. Economists call this phenomenon *diminishing marginal returns.*

What happens to the marginal product of capital if we keep total factor productivity and labor at their 2009 values but allow the capital stock to increase to \$42,000 billion and then to \$45,000 billion? Using Equation (4.1) for the aggregate production function and Equation (4.2) for the marginal product of capital, we can show that the marginal product

[1]We can demonstrate this result mathematically: The marginal product of capital is the rate at which output is changing as capital is changing, or $MPK = \frac{\partial F(K,L)}{\partial K}$. For the production function in Equation (4.1), we have $MPK = 1/3AK^{-2/3}L^{2/3}$. Substituting in $Y = AK^{1/3}L^{2/3}$, we get Equation (4.2). We can generalize that for a Cobb–Douglas production function, $MPK = \alpha\left(\frac{Y}{K}\right)$.

of capital would have been \$0.103 of GDP per dollar of capital in the first instance, at \$42,000 billion, and \$0.099 of real GDP per dollar of capital in the second instance, at \$45,000 billion. This pattern illustrates diminishing marginal returns for capital: Holding labor and total factor productivity constant, the marginal product of capital decreases as the economy accumulates more capital.

The third feature of the production function in panel (a) of Figure 4.3 is the relationship between the marginal product of capital and the slope of the production function. Because we have real GDP, Y, on the vertical axis, and the capital stock is on the horizontal axis, the slope of the production function is:

$$\frac{\text{Change in real GDP}}{\text{Change in capital stock}}.$$

This expression is another way of representing the extra output the firm gets from adding capital, so it is also an expression for the marginal product of capital. Due to diminishing marginal returns, the marginal product of capital decreases as the economy accumulates more capital goods, so the slope of the production function also decreases as the economy accumulates more capital goods. The result is that the production function flattens as the capital stock increases.

Everything we just discussed about capital also applies to labor. The **marginal product of labor (*MPL*)** is the extra output a firm receives from adding one more unit of labor, holding all other inputs and efficiency constant. For the Cobb–Douglas production function shown in Equation (4.1), the marginal product of labor is:

Marginal product of labor (*MPL*) The extra output a firm receives from adding one more unit of labor, holding all other inputs and efficiency constant.

$$MPL = \left(\frac{2}{3}\right)\left(\frac{Y}{L}\right). \tag{4.3}$$

(In general, the marginal product of labor for a Cobb–Douglas production function is equal to the exponent on the labor term, or labor's share of income, multiplied by (Y/L).) For the United States in 2009, total labor input, L, was 244 billion hours. So, with real GDP of \$12,881 billion, the marginal product of labor was 2/3 × (\$12,881 billion/244 billion hours) = \$35.19 per hour of labor. As a consequence, if the economy employed one more hour of labor, real GDP would increase by \$35.19. Notice that real GDP, labor hours, and labor's share of income are always positive, so the marginal product of capital is also always positive.

Solved Problem 4.1

Calculating the Marginal Product of Labor and the Marginal Product of Capital

Suppose that the production function for the economy is:

$$Y = AK^{1/2}L^{1/2}.$$

Assume that real GDP is \$12,000 billion, the capital stock is \$40,000 billion, and the labor supply is 200 billion hours.

a. Calculate the value of the marginal product of capital. Given this value, if the capital stock increases by \$1 billion, by how much will real GDP increase?

b. Calculate the value for the marginal product of labor. Given this value, if the labor supply increases by one hour, by how much will real GDP increase?

Solving the Problem

Step 1 **Review the chapter material.** This problem is about calculating values for the marginal products of capital and labor, so you may want to review the section "The Marginal Products of Capital and Labor," which begins on page 109.

Step 2 **Answer part (a) by calculating the value of the marginal product of capital and use the value to determine how much real GDP will increase if the capital stock increases by $1 billion.** We know that the marginal product of capital for a Cobb–Douglas production function is equal to the exponent on the capital term multiplied by (Y/K). Or, in this case:

$$MPK = 1/2\,(Y/K).$$

Substituting the given values, we have:

$$\begin{aligned} MPK &= 1/2\,(\$12{,}000 \text{ billion}/\$40{,}000 \text{ billion}) \\ &= \$0.15 \text{ per dollar of capital} \end{aligned}$$

So, in this case, an increase of $1 billion in the capital stock would increase real GDP by $0.15 billion.

Step 3 **Answer part (b) by calculating the value of the marginal product of labor and use the value to determine how much real GDP will increase if the labor supply increases by one hour.** We know that the marginal product of labor for a Cobb–Douglas production function is equal to the exponent on the labor term multiplied by (Y/L). Or, in this case:

$$MPL = 1/2\,(Y/L).$$

Substituting the given values, we have:

$$\begin{aligned} MPL &= 1/2\,(\$12{,}000 \text{ billion}/200 \text{ billion}) \\ &= \$30 \text{ per hour of labor} \end{aligned}$$

So, in this case, an increase of one hour of labor would increase real GDP by $30.

For more practice, do related problems 1.7 and 1.8 on page 134 at the end of this chapter.

Panel (b) of Figure 4.3 shows that the shape of the aggregate production function flattens out as the quantity of labor increases. In other words, the slope of the aggregate production function decreases as the quantity of labor increases. Therefore, the marginal product of labor decreases as more labor is added, so labor experiences diminishing marginal returns similar to those experienced by capital. What would have happened to the marginal product of labor if capital and total factor productivity remained at their 2009 values but the amount of labor employed increased from 244 billion hours to 250 billion hours? Using Equation (4.1) for the aggregate production function and Equation (4.3) for the marginal product of labor, we find out that with a labor supply of 250 billion hours the marginal product of labor would have been $34.77 per hour. If the quantity of labor employed increased to 260 billion hours, the marginal product of labor would drop to $34.32 per hour. So, there are diminishing marginal returns: Holding capital and total factor productivity constant, the marginal product of labor decreases as labor hours increase.

Panels (a) and (b) of Figure 4.4 show the marginal product of capital and marginal product of labor curves for the United States in 2009. The marginal product of capital is always positive, but it decreases as the capital stock increases. Similarly, the marginal product of labor is always positive, but it decreases as the labor stock increases. All countries have downward-sloping marginal product of capital and marginal product of labor curves because diminishing returns apply to all types of capital and labor. Notice that these curves slope downward very much like demand curves do. In fact, the marginal product of capital *is* the demand curve for capital, and the marginal product of labor *is* the demand curve for labor. We explain why the marginal product curves are also demand curves in the next section.

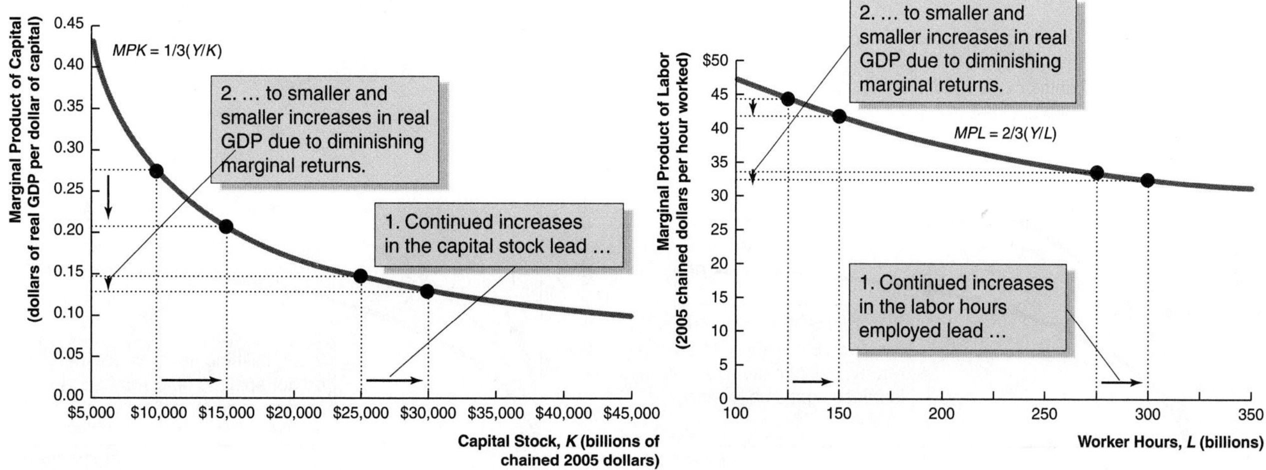

Figure 4.4 The Marginal Product of Capital and Marginal Product of Labor Curves for the United States in 2009

In panel (a), the marginal product of capital is always positive, but it decreases as the capital stock increases. Similarly, in panel (b), the marginal product of labor decreases as the quantity of labor increases. The downward slope for the marginal product of capital and marginal product of labor curves is the result of diminishing marginal returns. All countries have similarly shaped marginal product of capital and marginal product of labor curves.

Sources: U.S. Bureau of Economic Analysis; and Congressional Budget Office. ●

Calculating Total Factor Productivity

The Cobb–Douglas production function in Equation (4.1) shows real GDP as a function of the three variables: total factor productivity, capital, and labor. Unlike capital, labor, and real GDP, it is not possible to observe the "overall level of efficiency" to calculate total factor productivity directly. However, because we observe real GDP, capital, labor, labor's share of income, and capital's share of income, we can use Equation (4.1) for the aggregate production function to calculate A as:

$$A = \frac{Y}{K^{\frac{1}{3}}L^{\frac{2}{3}}}. \tag{4.4}$$

To find total factor productivity for the year 2009, we can plug the values of real GDP, capital, and labor for the year 2009 into Equation (4.4) to find:

$$A_{2009} = \frac{Y_{2009}}{K_{2009}^{\frac{1}{3}} L_{2009}^{\frac{2}{3}}} = \frac{\$12{,}881 \text{ billion}}{\left(\$40{,}084 \text{ billion}^{\frac{1}{3}}\right)\left(244.0 \text{ billions of hours}^{\frac{2}{3}}\right)} = 9.6.^{[2]}$$

In 1949, real GDP was $1,845 billion, the capital stock was $5,417 billion and labor hours were 127 billion. Therefore, total factor productivity for 1949 was 4.2. Total factor productivity has grown by 1.4% per year on average, and the U.S. economy has become 2.3 times as efficient as it was in 1949.

[2]In what units is total factor productivity measured? Some arithmetic shows us that the unit of measurement for total factor productivity is $\left(\frac{\$}{hours}\right)^{\frac{2}{3}}$. But this expression is awkward to use, so we will ignore it for convenience.

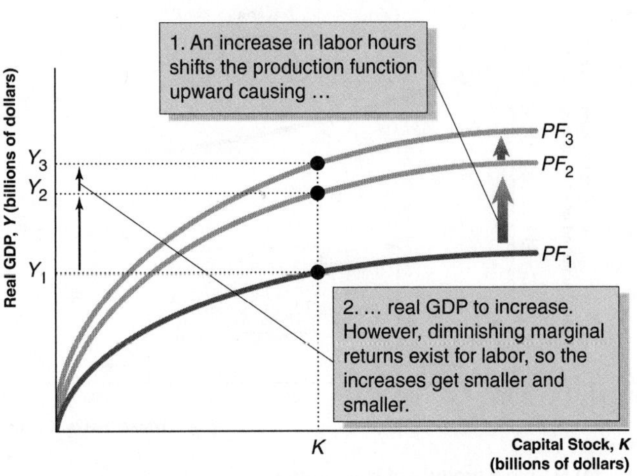

(a) Increases in labor, holding capital and total factor productivity constant

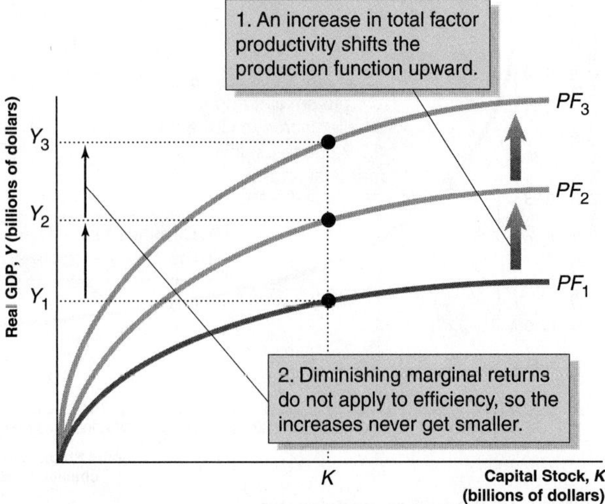

(b) Increases in total factor productivity, holding capital and labor constant

Figure 4.5 The Effect of an Increase in Labor and Total Factor Productivity in the Aggregate Production Function

In panel (a), an increase in labor hours will shift the production function up and increase real GDP, but labor experiences diminishing marginal returns. As a result, increases in labor hours will lead to smaller and smaller increases in real GDP. In panel (b), an increase in total factor productivity will shift the production function up and increase real GDP. In contrast to labor, total factor productivity does not experience diminishing marginal returns, so the increases in real GDP do not get smaller. ●

Changes in Capital, Labor, and Total Factor Productivity

The production function in panel (a) of Figure 4.3 on page 109 shows that an increase in the capital stock will increase real GDP, holding labor and total factor productivity constant. But what happens if either labor or total factor productivity increases? We drew the production function in Figure 4.3, holding labor and total factor productivity constant so that if either of them increases, the production function shifts upward, and real GDP increases. Figure 4.5 shows how an upward-shifting aggregate production function increases real GDP.

Panel (a) shows that if labor hours increased from, say, 150 billion hours to 200 billion hours, real GDP would increase from Y_1 to Y_2. If labor hours increased from 200 billion hours to 250 billion hours, real GDP would increase again from Y_2 to Y_3, but by a smaller amount due to diminishing marginal returns. Panel (b) shows that if total factor productivity increased from, say, 9.6 to 10.6, real GDP would increase from Y_1 to Y_2. If total factor productivity increased from 10.6 to 11.6, real GDP would increase again from Y_2 to Y_3. The increases would be the same size because diminishing marginal returns do not exist for total factor productivity.

Making the Connection

Foreign Direct Investment Increases Real GDP Growth in China

Prior to Chinese President Hu Jintao's visit to the United States in January 2011, China's Commerce Ministry announced that *foreign direct investment*, which is the purchase or building of capital goods by a foreign firm, in China had reached \$100 billion for the first time in 2010. This amount represented an increase of over 17% from 2009. This was good news for China because investment in manufacturing plants by foreign firms such as PepsiCo Inc. and AU Optronics Corp. increases China's stock of capital goods. The increase in the Chinese capital stock causes a movement along an existing production function. Because new capital goods are subject to diminishing marginal returns, however, we know that the rapid growth the Chinese economy has experienced in recent years must be due to more than the accumulation of capital goods. As panel (b) of Figure 4.5 shows, increases in total factor productivity are not subject to diminishing marginal returns. When foreign firms build new factories in China, those factories typically embody new technology. Technology is an important component of total factor productivity, so the transfer of technology from other countries to China is an important means of increasing total factor productivity. To encourage foreign firms to make additional investments, China has pledged to protect the intellectual property rights of foreign companies. In 2009, China announced that patent applications rose by 41%, to 580,000, and many of the patent applications came from foreign firms doing business or research in China. Drug giant Pfizer and software giant Microsoft are two of the firms conducting research and applying for patents in China. Increases in total factor productivity have played a large part in the increase in China's real GDP.

Sources: Loretta Chao, "China Issued a Record Number of Patents in 2009," *Wall Street Journal*, February 4, 2010; Owen Fletcher, "Foreign Direct Investment in China Rises 17%," *Wall Street Journal*, January 19, 2011; Chinmei Sung, Zheng Lifei, and Li Yanping, "Foreign Direct Investment in China in 2010 Rises to Record $105.7 Billion," *Bloomberg News*, January 17, 2011; and "India, China Top Global Labour Production," *The Economic Times*, January 19, 2011.

Test your understanding by doing related problem 1.11 on page 135 at the end of this chapter.

Table 4.1 summarizes the changes to an aggregate production function graph drawn with capital on the horizontal axis.

Table 4.1 Summary of Changes to an Aggregate Production Function Graph with Capital on the Horizontal Axis

Increases in . . .	will . . .	and lead to an increase in real GDP by . . .	Graph of effect on an aggregate production function
the capital stock	cause a movement along the production function	smaller and smaller amounts due to diminishing marginal returns.	Y, PF, K
labor hours employed	shift the aggregate production function up	smaller and smaller amounts due to diminishing marginal returns.	Y, PF_2, PF_1, K
total factor productivity	shift the aggregate production function up	the same amount because increases in total factor productivity are not subject to diminishing marginal returns.	Y, PF_2, PF_1, K

In Figure 4.5, we used a production function drawn with capital on the horizontal axis because that is the production function we will use the most in this chapter. If we had put labor on the horizontal axis, the results would have been very similar. In that case, increases in the capital stock would shift the production function upward and increase real GDP. Because of diminishing marginal returns, the increases in real GDP would get smaller and smaller. Increases in total factor productivity would still shift the production function upward and would still not experience diminishing marginal returns.

4.2

Learning Objective

Explain how real GDP is determined in the long run.

Profit Total revenue minus total cost.

A Model of Real GDP in the Long Run

The aggregate production function in Equation (4.1) on page 108 shows how real GDP is determined by the quantities of capital and labor, as well as the level of total factor productivity. To fully explain how real GDP is determined, we need to explain how firms choose the quantities of capital goods to purchase and labor to hire. We adopt the usual economic assumption that firms are motivated by the desire to maximize **profit**, which is the total revenue received by a firm minus the total cost a firm pays to produce output. We can think of the level of real GDP as resulting from the profit-maximizing decisions by individual firms. Economists assume that (1) firms purchase capital and hire labor only if doing so maximizes profits, (2) firms operate in *perfectly competitive markets*, so each firm is a *price taker*, that is, small relative to the market, and takes the market price of the goods and services it sells as given, or fixed, (3) firms take the prices of capital goods and labor, as given, and (4) firms decide how much capital and labor to hire and how much output to produce using the available technology based on the prices of output and inputs.

A model that describes the behavior of every single firm in the economy would be too complex to work with, so instead we use a simplified model. We consider the behavior of a single representative firm and assume that all firms behave the same as that firm. The firm produces output, Y, and sells it at the perfectly competitive nominal price, P. In addition, the firm takes the *nominal wage rate*, W, and the *nominal rental cost of capital*, R, as given. We measure the cost of capital using the rental cost, rather than the purchase price because the rental cost represents the use of capital services for a given period just as the wage represents the cost of labor services. If firms do not own capital, they can rent capital and *pay* the rental cost. If they currently own capital, they could have chosen to rent out their capital and *receive* the rental cost. So the rental cost is the opportunity cost to the firm of using its own capital.

The firm receives revenue by selling output, so total revenue is PY. The firm has to hire labor and capital to produce output, so total cost is $WL + RK$. Profits are therefore:

$$\text{Profit} = \text{Revenue} - \text{Cost}$$

$$\text{Profit} = PY - (WL + RK)$$

$$\text{Profit} = PY - WL - RK.$$

The Markets for Capital and Labor

Firms hire capital and labor in markets, so we can use the model of demand and supply to explain the quantities of capital and labor firms hire. At any given time, there are given amounts of capital goods and workers available, so we treat the supply of capital and labor as fixed and unresponsive to market prices. Therefore, the "supply side" of these markets is simple, but the "demand side" is more interesting.

To understand the demand for capital and labor, we need to think of the markets for capital and labor from the point of view of the firm doing the hiring. We are assuming that the firm is small relative to the market, so it cannot influence the price of output, the wage, or the rental cost of capital. If the firm hires one more worker, it can produce more output, so the revenue from hiring one more worker equals the price of output multiplied by the extra output from hiring the worker. To hire that worker, the firm must pay the nominal wage of W. Therefore, the change in profit from hiring one more worker is the difference between the additional revenue earned and the additional cost paid:

$$\Delta\text{Profit} = P \times MPL - W.$$

The firm maximizes profit, so it will hire labor whenever the change in profit is greater than zero. In other words, the firm will hire additional workers as long as $P \times MPL > W$.

The *real wage, w,* is the nominal wage divided by the price of output. So, we can say that the firm will hire additional workers as long as the marginal product of labor is greater than the real wage:

$$MPL > \frac{W}{P}.$$

Stated another way, the firm will hire workers as long as the additional output produced by another worker is greater than the cost of hiring the worker. The firm cannot affect the real wage because it is perfectly competitive, so the real wage is constant. However, the marginal product of labor is not constant because it will decrease as the firm hires more workers—due to diminishing marginal returns. The firm will continue to hire more labor until:

$$MPL = \frac{W}{P}.$$

If the real wage decreases, the firm will hire additional workers until the marginal product of labor falls enough to restore the above equality. If the real wage increases, the firm will lay off workers until the marginal product of labor rises enough to restore the equality. *Therefore, the marginal product of labor curve is the demand curve for labor.* We have already calculated that the marginal product of labor in the United States is $35.19 per hour worked, so we can say that the real wage is also $35.19 per hour. We can make a similar argument about a firm hiring capital. The change in profit from purchasing one more unit of capital, holding the quantity of labor constant, is:

$$\Delta\text{Profit} = P \times MPK - R.$$

The firm maximizes profit, so it will purchase capital goods whenever the change in profit is greater than zero. In other words, the firm will purchase capital goods whenever $P \times MPK > R$.

The *real rental price of capital, r,* is the nominal rental price divided by the price of output. The firm maximizes profit, so the firm will purchase capital goods whenever

$$MPK > \frac{R}{P}.$$

This equation means that the firm will continue purchasing units of capital as long as the additional output produced by another unit of capital is greater than the real rental price of capital. The firm cannot affect the real rental cost because it is perfectly competitive. However, the marginal product of capital will decrease as the firm purchases more units of capital due to diminishing marginal returns. If the marginal product of capital is greater than the real rental cost of capital, the firm will purchase more units of capital, and the marginal product of capital will decrease. The firm will continue to purchase capital until:

$$MPK = \frac{R}{P}.$$

If the real rental cost of capital decreases, the firm will purchase more units of capital until the marginal product of capital falls enough to again equal the real rental cost, and if the real

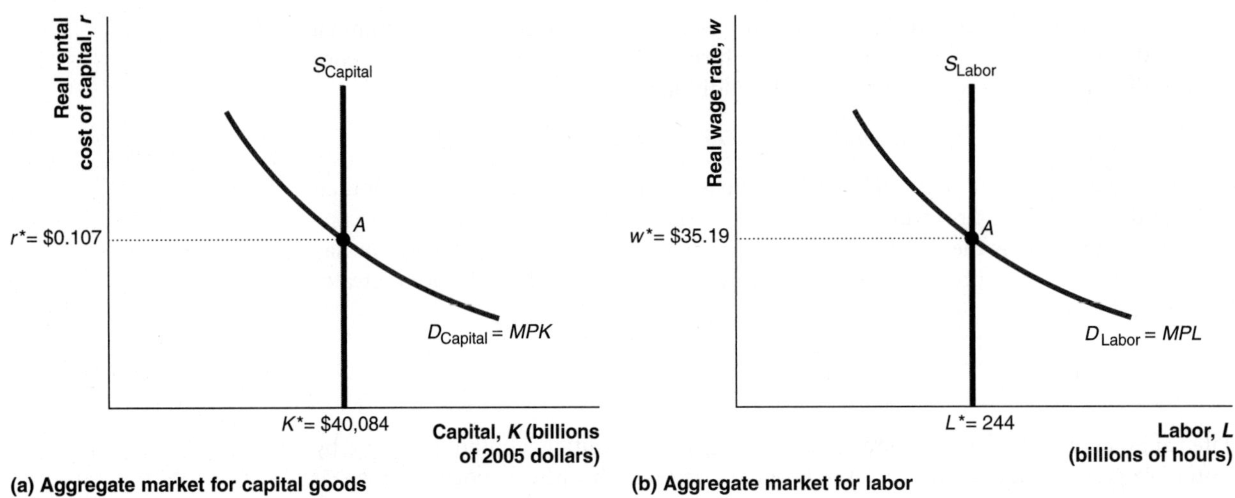

Figure 4.6 Aggregate Capital and Labor Markets for the United States, 2009

Panel (a) shows the aggregate market for capital goods, and panel (b) shows the aggregate market for labor in the United States in 2009. The demand curves slope downward, reflecting diminishing marginal returns to capital and labor. The supply curves for capital and labor are vertical lines, reflecting the assumption that the quantity supplied does not respond to changes in prices. The intersection of the demand and supply curves determine the equilibrium quantities of capital and labor.

Sources: U.S. Bureau of Economic Analysis; and Congressional Budget Office. ●

rental cost rises, the firm will let its capital stock wear out, or depreciate, until the marginal product of capital rises enough to again equal the real rental cost. *Therefore, the marginal product of capital curve is the demand curve for capital goods.* We have already calculated that the marginal product of capital in the United States is $0.107 of real GDP per dollar of the capital stock, so the real rental cost of capital is also $0.107 per dollar of capital.

Everything we have discussed so far about a single firm is also true, by assumption, for every firm in the economy. Therefore, economists often talk about the *aggregate labor market* and the *aggregate capital market.* Figure 4.6 shows these two markets for the United States in 2009. The real rental cost of capital is *r*, and the real wage rate is *w*. We have already calculated that the real wage was $35.19 per hour and the real rental cost of capital was $0.107 of real GDP per dollar of capital. The values of the capital stock and labor supply in the figure are also equal to their 2009 values. The demand curves slope downward, reflecting diminishing marginal returns to capital and labor. The supply curves for capital and labor are vertical lines, reflecting our assumption that the quantity supplied does not respond to changes in price. The intersections of the demand and supply curves determine the equilibrium quantities of capital and labor. In the next section, we substitute those quantities into the aggregate production function in Equation (4.1) to determine real GDP.

Combining the Factor Markets with the Aggregate Production Function

Factor markets determine the equilibrium prices and quantities of capital and labor. We can combine the equilibrium quantities of capital and labor with the aggregate production function to determine the long-run equilibrium level of real GDP. Figure 4.7 panel (a) shows how real GDP is determined when we measure the capital stock on the horizontal axis. In this case, the quantity of labor is assumed to be fixed at L^*, while the equilibrium quantity and rental cost of capital are determined in the aggregate capital market. Once the equilibrium quantity of capital is determined, we can use that quantity to determine real GDP. Panel (b) shows how real GDP is determined when we measure the quantity of labor on the horizontal axis. In this case, we assume the capital stock is fixed at K^*, while the equilibrium quantity and real wage are determined in the aggregate labor market. Once the equilibrium quantity of labor is determined, we can use that quantity to determine real GDP.

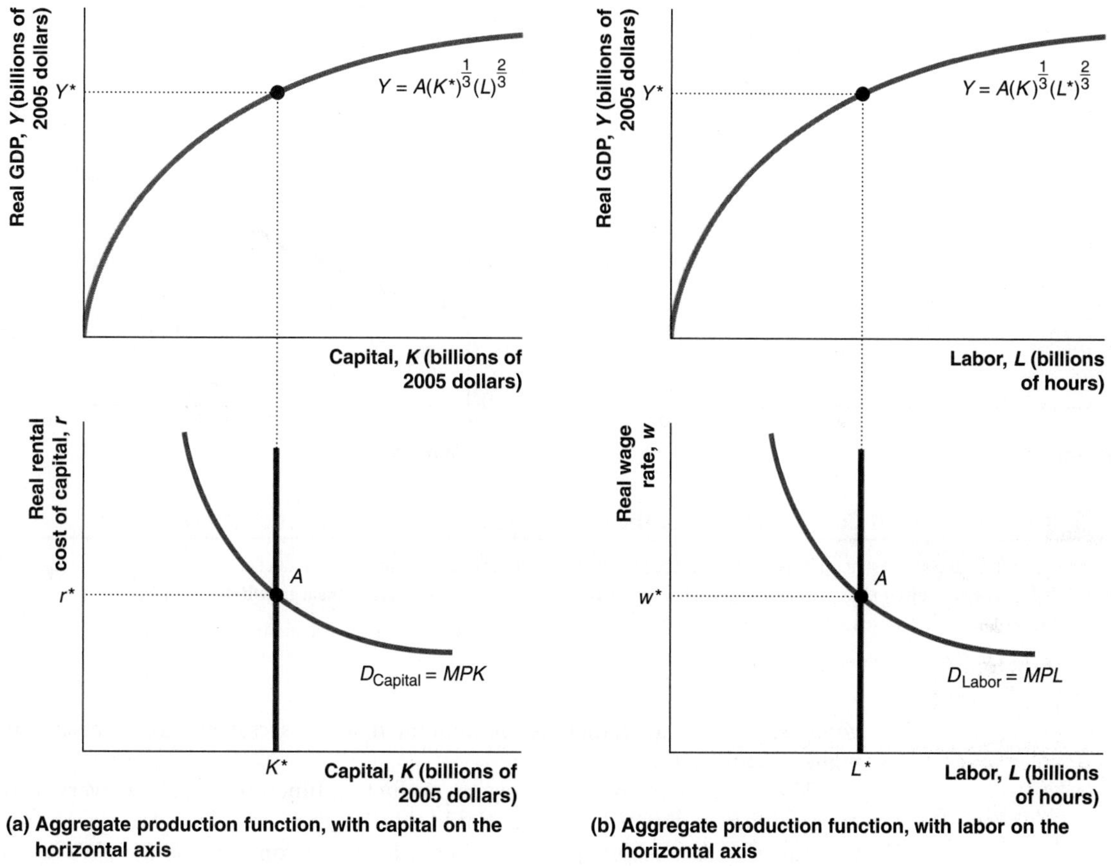

Figure 4.7 Determination of Long-Run Real GDP

Panel (a) shows how potential real GDP is determined when we measure the capital stock on the horizontal axis. Panel (b) shows how potential real GDP is determined when we measure the quantity of labor on the horizontal axis. ●

What Has Happened to the Real Wage and the Real Rental Cost of Capital Over Time?

In competitive markets, we know that the marginal product of capital equals the real rental cost of capital, and the marginal product of labor equals the real wage. Figure 4.8 shows both the real rental cost of capital and the real wage from 1949 to 2009. Panel (a) shows that the real rental cost of capital, calculated as the marginal product of capital, has averaged $0.116 of real GDP per dollar of capital since 1949 and has never been far from this average. However, panel (b) shows that the real wage, calculated as the marginal product of labor, has increased dramatically since 1949. The real wage was $9.69 per hour in 1949, and it rose to $35.19 per hour in 2009, for an average annual growth rate of 2.2%.

Aggregation

The notion of an aggregate labor market or aggregate capital market is a simplification. In reality, it is sometimes inaccurate to assume an aggregate labor or capital market because workers and firms are typically not interchangeable. For example, many financial firms, such as Citigroup and Bank of America, laid off workers during 2007–2009 due to the financial crisis and the falling demand for financial services. These workers have a specific set of skills related to the financial sector that do not readily transfer to other sectors, such as construction, so it is unlikely that former investment bankers will seek jobs building highways or bridges. Therefore, a change in the demand for workers who build highways will have little effect on the employment of former investment bankers. Similarly, capital

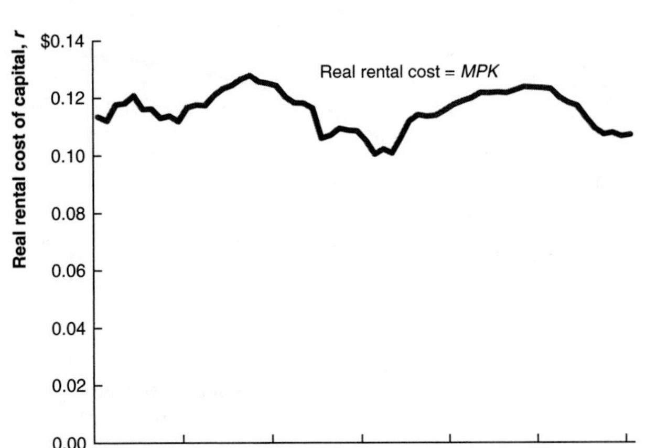

(a) Real rental cost of capital

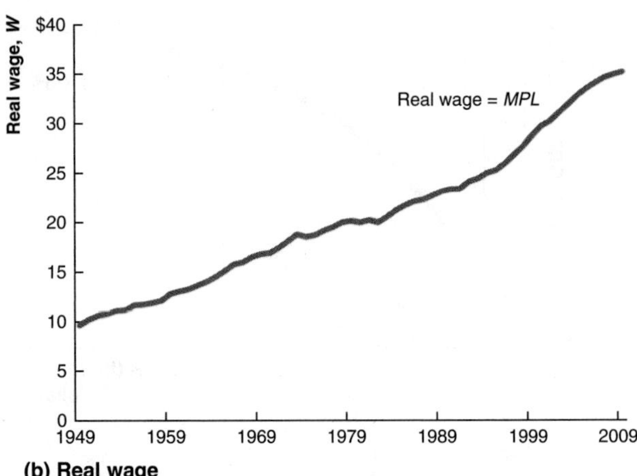

(b) Real wage

Figure 4.8 The Real Rental Cost of Capital and the Real Wage in the United States, 1949–2009

Panel (a) shows that the real rental cost of capital, calculated as the marginal product of capital, has been relatively constant, averaging $0.116 of real GDP per dollar of capital since 1949. However, panel (b) shows that the real wage, calculated as the marginal product of labor, has increased steadily since 1949, with an average annual growth rate of 2.2%.

Sources: U.S. Bureau of Economic Analysis. ●

goods, such as software, that are useful in the financial sector, are not necessarily useful in highway construction.

The same is true for the aggregate production function. In reality, every firm has its own production function. So, we should think of the Cobb–Douglas aggregate production function as a useful approximation of how the economy operates. We have already encountered one important piece of evidence that suggests that an aggregate Cobb–Douglas production function is a close approximation of how real GDP is determined. The Cobb–Douglas production function predicts that the shares of income going to capital and labor should be constant. Figure 4.2 on page 108 supports this prediction, so there is reason to think that an aggregate Cobb–Douglas production function is a reasonable approximation for the U.S. economy. Studies have shown that the Cobb-Douglas production function is also a reasonable approximation for other developed economies.

4.3

Learning Objective

Discuss the contributions of capital, labor, and efficiency to the growth rate of real GDP.

Accounting for Growth in Real GDP

Figure 4.9 shows that for the United States, labor hours, the capital stock, and total factor productivity as calculated by Equation (4.4) have all increased since 1949. The capital stock was 7.4 times larger in 2009 than it was in 1949, while labor and total factor productivity were both about twice as large in 2009 as in 1949. Therefore, all three inputs into the aggregate production function have contributed to the growth of real GDP. Nobel Laureate Robert Solow of MIT developed a procedure known as *growth accounting* that allows us to determine how much of the growth rate in real GDP is due to each of these three causes.[3] In this section, we use growth accounting to show that total factor productivity has been the most important determinant of economic growth.

[3]Robert Solow, "Technical Change and the Aggregate Production Function," *Review of Economics and Statistics*, Vol. 39, No. 3, August 1957, pp. 312–320.

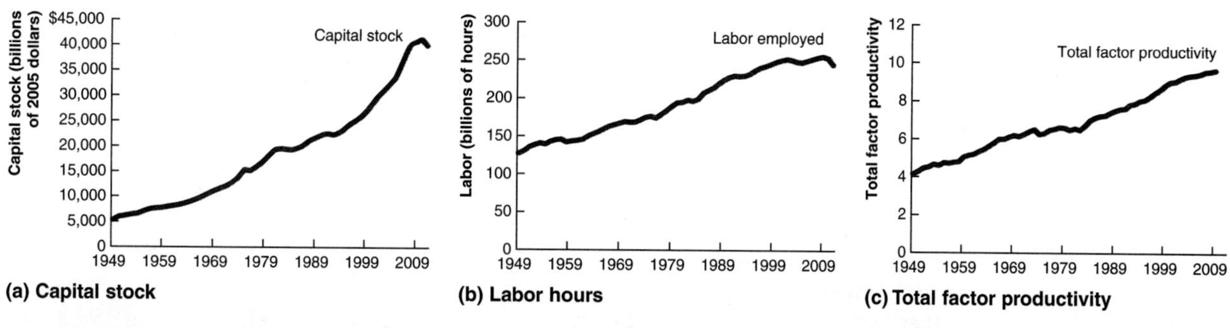

Figure 4.9 Capital Stock, Labor Hours, and Total Factor Productivity for the United States, 1949–2009

Capital stock, labor supply, and total factor productivity have all increased significantly since 1949. All three inputs have contributed to the growth of real GDP.

Sources: U.S. Bureau of Economic Analysis; and Congressional Budget Office. ●

Accounting for Real GDP Growth

We will use the following symbols in this section:

g_Y = growth rate of real GDP
g_K = growth rate of the capital stock
g_L = growth rate of labor hours
g_A = growth rate of total factor productivity

To determine the contribution of capital, labor, and total factor productivity to the growth rate of U.S. real GDP, we need to know the above four growth rates. For the 1949–2009 period these growth rates were:

$g_Y = 3.29\%$
$g_K = 3.39\%$
$g_L = 1.09\%$
$g_A = 1.41\%$

Now we need a method to determine how much of the 3.29% average annual growth rate of real GDP is due to each of these factors.

The production function in Equation (4.1) shows how capital, labor, and total factor productivity determine the *level* of real GDP. In this section, we switch our focus from the level of real GDP to the *growth rate* of real GDP by using an equation that is similar to Equation (4.1):[4]

$$g_Y = g_A + \left(\frac{1}{3}\right)g_K + \left(\frac{2}{3}\right)g_L \qquad (4.5)$$

This equation is the *basic growth accounting equation.* It allows us to determine the contribution of each component of the production function to the growth of real GDP. Using the above growth rates and Equation (4.5), we can calculate that:

Contribution of total factor productivity: $g_A = 1.41\%$,

Contribution of capital: $\left(\frac{1}{3}\right)g_K = \left(\frac{1}{3}\right)(3.39) = 1.13\%$, and

Contribution of labor: $\left(\frac{2}{3}\right)g_L = \left(\frac{2}{3}\right)(1.09) = 0.73\%$.

[4]Further discussion of the relationship between Equation (4.1) and Equation (4.5) appears in the appendix to this chapter, which begins on page 140.

Table 4.2 **Contributions to the Growth Rate of Real GDP in the United States, 1949–2009**

	Capital Stock (*K*)	Labor Hours (*L*)	Total Factor Productivity (*A*)	Total
Absolute (percent)	1.13%	0.73%	1.41%	3.27%
Relative share of real GDP growth (percent)	34.3%	22.1%	42.9%	99.3%

Note: The percentages do not add to 100 due to rounding.

In other words, of the 3.29% average annual growth rate of real GDP, 1.41% was due to the growth in total factor productivity, 1.13% was due to the growth in the capital stock, and 0.73% was due to the growth in hours worked.

The relative share to the growth rate of real GDP equals that component's contribution divided by the growth rate of real GDP. To find the relative share of capital, labor, and total factor productivity, we can divide Equation (4.5) by g_Y to obtain:

$$1 = \left(\frac{g_A}{g_Y}\right) + \left(\frac{1}{3}\right)\left(\frac{g_K}{g_Y}\right) + \left(\frac{2}{3}\right)\left(\frac{g_L}{g_Y}\right). \tag{4.6}$$

Substituting the values from Table 4.2 into Equation (4.6), the relative share of total factor productivity growth is:

$$\left(\frac{g_A}{g_Y}\right) = \left(\frac{1.41}{3.29}\right) = 0.429, \text{ or } 42.9\%.$$

The relative share of capital growth is:

$$\left(\frac{1}{3}\right)\left(\frac{g_K}{g_Y}\right) = \left(\frac{1}{3}\right)\left(\frac{3.39}{3.29}\right) = 0.343, \text{ or } 34.3\%.$$

The relative share of labor growth is:

$$\left(\frac{2}{3}\right)\left(\frac{g_L}{g_Y}\right) = \left(\frac{2}{3}\right)\left(\frac{1.09}{3.29}\right) = 0.221, \text{ or } 22.1\%.$$

Table 4.2 shows the contributions of capital, labor, and total productivity to the growth of real GDP over the 1949–2009 period. The message from Table 4.2 is clear: *The two most important determinants of the growth rate of real GDP are the growth rate of the capital stock and the growth rate of total factor productivity.* Together they account for over 75% of the growth in real GDP. Total factor productivity growth alone accounts for nearly 43% of the growth in U.S. real GDP. That means that the most important determinants of economic growth have been those things, such as changes in technology, increases in the skill level of the labor force, and improvements in managerial techniques, that have contributed to increases in total factor productivity.

Accounting for Labor Productivity Growth

So far we have found that total factor productivity and the capital stock are the two most important determinants of the growth rate of real GDP. We now turn to discussing real GDP per hour worked, a measure of labor productivity, because it will be critical to our discussion of long-run growth in Chapter 5 and to explaining why the standard of living varies across countries. To explain the growth of labor productivity, we work with a slightly modified version of the Cobb–Douglas production function. Because the Cobb–Douglas production function has constant returns to scale, we know that if we multiply both K and L by $(1/L)$, the value of Y will change to Y/L:

$$\frac{Y}{L} = AF\left(\frac{K}{L}, \frac{L}{L}\right) = AF\left(\frac{K}{L}, 1\right).$$

We can define output per hour worked—which is also labor productivity—as:

$$y = \frac{Y}{L}.$$

We can define capital per hour worked, or the **capital–labor ratio**, as:

Capital–labor ratio The dollar value of capital goods per unit of labor; measured as either the dollar value of capital divided by the total number of hours worked, or as the dollar value of capital divided by the total number of workers.

$$k = \frac{K}{L}.$$

We can safely ignore the 1 because it is a constant, which leaves us with:

$$y = Af(k).$$

Given that the share of capital in income is one-third, we have:

$$y = Ak^{\frac{1}{3}}. \tag{4.7}$$

Equation (4.7) tells us that labor productivity depends on total factor productivity and the capital–labor ratio.

In the appendix to this chapter, which begins on page 140, we show that the equations for the absolute and relative contributions to the growth rate of real GDP per hour worked are:

$$g_y = g_A + \left(\frac{1}{3}\right)g_k \tag{4.8}$$

and:

$$1 = \left(\frac{g_A}{g_y}\right) + \left(\frac{1}{3}\right)\left(\frac{g_k}{g_y}\right). \tag{4.9}$$

Labor productivity plays a key role in determining the standard of living, so Equations (4.8) and (4.9) allow us to analyze the factors that are important for increasing the standard of living. We leave this analysis to you in the following Solved Problem.

Solved Problem 4.3

Accounting for Labor Productivity Growth

Real GDP per hour worked in the United States grew by 2.17% per year from 1949 to 2009, and capital per hour worked grew at the rate of 2.27% per year during the same years. As we saw earlier, total factor productivity grew at a rate of 1.41% per year. We also saw that total factor productivity growth was the most important determinant of real GDP growth. Is total factor productivity growth also the most important determinant of real GDP per hour worked?

Solving the Problem

Step 1 **Review the chapter material.** This problem asks you to determine the absolute and relative contributions to the growth rate of real GDP per worker, so you may want to review the sections "Accounting for Real GDP Growth," which begins on page 121, and "Accounting for Labor Productivity Growth," which begins on page 122.

Step 2 **Determine the contributions to growth in real GDP per hour worked of the capital–labor ratio and total factor productivity.** Equation (4.8) shows us that the contribution of the capital–labor ratio to the growth rate of real GDP per hour worked is:

$$g_k = \left(\frac{1}{3}\right)(2.27) = 0.76\%,$$

The contribution of total factor productivity is:

$$g_A = 1.41\%.$$

The contribution of total factor productivity is larger than the contribution of capital per hour worked.

Step 3 **Determine the relative shares of total factor productivity and capital per hour worked in explaining growth in real GDP per hour worked.** Equation (4.9) shows us that the relative share of the capital–labor ratio in explaining the growth rate of real GDP per hour worked is:

$$\left(\frac{1}{3}\right)\left(\frac{g_k}{g_y}\right) = \left(\frac{1}{3}\right)\left(\frac{2.27}{2.17}\right) = 0.349, \text{ or } 34.9\%,$$

The relative share of total factor productivity is:

$$\left(\frac{g_A}{g_y}\right) = \left(\frac{1.41}{2.17}\right) = 0.650, \text{ or } 65.0\%.$$

The relative share of total factor productivity is larger than the relative share of the capital per hour worked.

Both capital per hour worked and total factor productivity help determine real GDP per hour worked. However, the calculations in steps 2 and 3 indicate that total factor productivity is the most important determinant.

For more practice, do related problem 3.5 on page 137 at the end of this chapter.

Making the Connection

What Explains Recent Economic Growth in India?

Economists Barry Bosworth of the Brookings Institution and Susan Collins of the University of Michigan used a growth accounting procedure similar to the one described here to explain recent economic growth in India. They showed that the growth rate of labor productivity increased from 2.4% per year between 1978 and 1993 to 4.6% per year between 1993 and 2004. What accounts for this 2.2% increase in the growth rate of labor productivity?

Bosworth and Collins report that total factor productivity growth increased from 1.4% per year before 1993 to 2.7% per year after 1993. That means that 1.3% of the increase in labor productivity (over half the increase) was due to faster total factor productivity growth. The rest came from an increase in the growth rate of the capital stock. Since 2004, total factor productivity growth has slowed. A report by The Conference Board, a business research firm, found that from 2005 to 2010, "India's transition to a higher growth path had been . . . resource-consuming and . . . constrained by a continuing need for reforms."

Although Bosworth and Collins believe that the future prospects for India's economy are good, they point out that the country has devoted much of its high level of private saving to finance a large public-sector debt. Bosworth and Collins also note that without an expansion of India's production of goods—rather than services—the country will have difficulty absorbing a large number of underemployed and undereducated workers.

Nicholas Eberstadt, of the American Enterprise Institute, has pointed to another area of concern regarding India's economy. Although population growth is projected to be positive and will result in a relatively large working-age population, population growth rates are very different in the northern and southern parts of the country. In the northern part of India fertility rates are relatively high, while population growth is slower in the south. However, much of the future prospects for economic growth are in the south and in the large urban areas in the north. About one-third of the working-age population has no education at all. Policymakers in India must meet these demographic and educational challenges for the country to continue its strong rates of growth in labor productivity and real GDP per hour worked.

Sources: Barry Bosworth and Susan Collins, "Accounting for Growth: Comparing China and India," *Journal of Economic Perspectives*, Vol. 22, No. 1, Winter 2008, pp. 45–66; Sudeshna Sen, "India, China, Top Global Labor Productivity," *The Economic Times of India*, January 19, 2011; and Nicholas Eberstadt, "The Demographic Future," *Foreign Affairs*, Vol. 89, No. 6, November/December 2010, pp. 54–64.

Test your understanding by doing related problem 3.6 on page 137 at the end of this chapter.

Total Factor Productivity as the Ultimate Source of Growth

Is it possible for a government to cause rapid economic growth by encouraging the accumulation of capital goods such as factories and machines? Yes, but only for a period of time. Capital accumulation is subject to diminishing marginal returns, so growth driven by the accumulation of more factories and machines eventually diminishes to zero. Not surprisingly, our growth accounting exercises for the United States show that capital accumulation is not as important as total factor productivity in explaining growth. In fact, for economic growth to be sustainable, it must be driven by increases in total factor productivity. We can illustrate this point with an important historical example: the Soviet Union.

Table 4.3 uses data from Nicholas Crafts of the University of Warwick to show what growth accounting can tell us about one of the most striking events of the twentieth century: the economic collapse of the Soviet Union.[5] The data on the contributions of capital growth and total factor productivity growth are derived using an equation very similar to Equation (4.8) on page 123.

The Soviet Union was formed from the old Russian Empire following the Communist revolution of 1917. Under Communism, the Soviet Union was a centrally planned economy where the government owned nearly every business and made all production and pricing decisions. In 1960, Nikita Khrushchev, the leader of the Soviet Union, addressed the United Nations in New York City. He declared to the United States and the other democracies, "We will bury you. Your grandchildren will live under Communism."

Many people at the time took Khrushchev's boast seriously. After all, labor productivity growth in the Soviet Union was extremely rapid following World War II. Labor productivity growth averaged 4.0% per year during the 1950–1970 period when Khrushchev made his boast. This growth rate far exceeded that of the United States and many other Western

[5]Nicholas Crafts, "Solow and Growth Accounting: A Perspective from Quantitative Economic History," *History of Political Economy*, Vol. 41, Supplement 1, 2009, pp. 200–220.

Table 4.3 **Accounting for Labor Productivity Growth in the Soviet Union, 1920–1985**

	Labor Productivity Growth	Contribution from Capital	Contribution from Total Factor Productivity
1928–1940	2.5%	2.0%	0.5%
1940–1950	1.5	−0.1	1.6
1950–1970	4.0	2.6	1.4
1970–1985	1.6	2.0	−0.4

Source: Nicholas Crafts, "Solow and Growth Accounting: A Perspective from Quantitative Economic History," *History of Political Economy*, Vol. 41, Supplement 1, 2009, pp. 200–220.

countries and caused some economists in the Union States to predict incorrectly that the Soviet economy would someday surpass the U.S. economy. But if you look closely at the data in Table 4.3, you can see that Soviet labor productivity growth was driven primarily by capital accumulation. The Soviet economic system was quite good at accumulating more and more capital goods, such as factories. Unfortunately for them, though, diminishing returns to capital meant that the additional factories the Soviet Union was building resulted in smaller and smaller increases in real GDP per hour worked. To keep labor productivity growth high, the Soviet Union had to devote more and more resources to accumulating capital goods, which meant diverting resources away from private consumption.

The Soviet Union did experience increases in total factor productivity, but for a fifteen-year period leading up to its collapse, total factor productivity *decreased* by 0.4% per year. Why did the Soviet Union fail the crucial requirement for growth: developing new ways to make the economy efficient? The key reason is that in a centrally planned economy, the persons in charge of running most businesses are government employees and not entrepreneurs or independent businesspeople, as is the case in market economies. Soviet managers had little incentive to adopt new ways of doing things. Their pay depended on producing the quantity of output specified in the government's economic plan, not on discovering new, better, and lower-cost ways to produce goods. In addition, these managers did not have to worry about competition from either domestic or foreign firms.

Entrepreneurs and managers of firms in the United States, by contrast, are under intense competitive pressure from other firms. They must constantly search for better ways of producing the goods and services they sell. Developing and using new technologies is an important way to gain a competitive edge and higher profits. The drive for profit provides an incentive for technological change that centrally planned economies are unable to duplicate. In market economies, decisions about which investments to make and which technologies to adopt are made by entrepreneurs and managers who have their own money on the line. In the Soviet system, these decisions were usually made by salaried bureaucrats trying to fulfill a plan formulated in Moscow. Nothing concentrates the mind like having your own funds at risk.

In hindsight, it is clear that a centrally planned economy, such as the Soviet Union's, could not, over the long run, grow faster than a market economy. The Soviet Union collapsed in 1991, and contemporary Russia now has a more market-oriented system, although the government continues to play a much larger role in the economy than does the government in the United States.

The example of the Soviet Union helps explain why capital accumulation alone cannot explain labor productivity *growth*. Next we use the aggregate production function to explain why total factor productivity is also the most important determinant of the *level* of labor productivity.

GDP per Hour Worked Among Countries

4.4

Learning Objective
Understand that differences in efficiency explain differences in labor productivity across countries.

In the previous section, we saw that real GDP per hour worked is determined by total factor productivity and capital per hour worked. We also saw that total factor productivity growth is the most important determinant of the growth rate of real GDP per hour worked in the United States. In this section, we explain why differences in total factor productivity help explain the differences in GDP per hour worked across countries. As we will see in Chapter 5, differences in labor productivity are crucial for understanding why some countries are rich and other countries are poor.

Differences in capital per hour worked do not explain differences in real GDP per hour worked among countries. To see why, consider an example with just two countries: the United States and Mexico. To focus on the role of capital per hour worked, we assume that the United States and Mexico have the same level of total factor productivity and that capital's share of income is the same in both countries. Given these two assumptions, the only way that real GDP per hour worked can differ is if capital per hour worked is different in the two countries. One of the important determinants of total factor productivity is the level of knowledge, which flows freely across borders. For example, the fact that someone in the United States knows calculus does not prevent someone in Mexico from learning calculus from a textbook or on the Internet. In fact, the person from Mexico could go to a U.S. university and learn calculus. So, all countries have access to a similar stock of knowledge.

Figure 4.10 shows what would happen if $k_{US} > k_{Mexico}$. Mexico and the United States have the same level of total factor productivity and capital's share of income. Initially, Mexico is at point *B*, and the United States is at point *A*. Mexico has a higher rate of return than the United States. Why? We know that the rate of return to capital, *r*, equals the marginal product of capital. We also know that the marginal product of capital equals the slope of the production function: A steep production function indicates a high rate of return, and a flat production function indicates a low rate of return. The production function is steeper at point *B* than at point *A*, so $MPK_{Mexico} > MPK_{US}$. Because the rate of return to

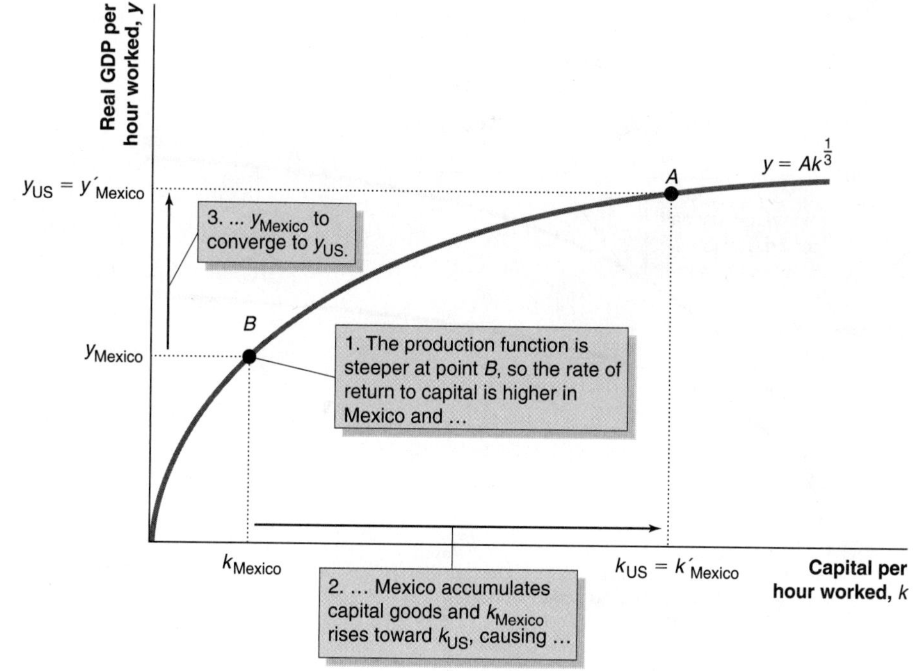

Real GDP per hour worked, y
$y = Ak^{\frac{1}{3}}$
A
$y_{US} = y'_{Mexico}$
3. ... y_{Mexico} to converge to y_{US}.
B
y_{Mexico}
1. The production function is steeper at point B, so the rate of return to capital is higher in Mexico and ...
k_{Mexico}
2. ... Mexico accumulates capital goods and k_{Mexico} rises toward k_{US}, causing ...
$k_{US} = k'_{Mexico}$
Capital per hour worked, k

Figure 4.10

Mexico and the United States, Assuming the Same Level of Total Factor Productivity

Mexico and the United States have the same level of total factor productivity and capital's share of income. Initially, Mexico is at point *B*, and the United States is at point *A*, so the slope of the production function is steeper for Mexico than for the United States. The rate of return to capital is the slope of the production function, so $r_{Mexico} > r_{US}$. Therefore, capital would flow to Mexico, so GDP per hour worked in Mexico and the United States would converge to the same level. ●

capital is the marginal product of capital, $r_{\text{Mexico}} > r_{\text{US}}$. So, we would expect new capital to flow to Mexico and for k_{Mexico} to increase toward k_{US}. Capital per hour worked is a determinant of real GDP per hour worked, so as capital per hour worked increases in Mexico, y_{Mexico} converges to y_{US}. However, y_{Mexico} will not rise above y_{US} because diminishing marginal returns exist for capital. As Mexico accumulates more capital goods, r_{Mexico} decreases, and this adjustment would continue until $r_{\text{Mexico}} = r_{\text{US}}$, which occurs when $k'_{\text{Mexico}} = k_{\text{US}}$. Both countries are at point A, so $y'_{\text{Mexico}} = y_{\text{US}}$. When total factor productivity is the same in both countries, differences in k do not persist because capital flows to the country with the low k and high r. This means that if there are persistent differences in output per worker across countries, the difference must be due to differences in total factor productivity. This point is important, and we will return to it in Chapter 5 when we explain why total factor productivity differs across countries.

This example about the United States and Mexico shows that differences in capital per hour worked alone cannot explain differences in real GDP per hour worked. The only two possible explanations are therefore differences in total factor productivity and in capital's share of income. In practice, differences in capital's share of income are not large enough to be important, so we focus on differences in total factor productivity and continue to assume that capital's share of income is the same in both countries. Figure 4.11 shows how differences in total factor productivity can explain differences in real GDP per worker. In this example, $A_{\text{US}} > A_{\text{Mexico}}$, so the production function for the United States lies above the production function for Mexico. Capital still flows to Mexico until $r_{\text{Mexico}} = r_{\text{US}}$, causing capital per hour worked in Mexico to rise to k'_{Mexico}. However, now the rates of return are equal when $k_{\text{US}} > k'_{\text{Mexico}}$. Why is this answer different from our previous answer? The higher level of total factor productivity in the United States increases y and the marginal product of capital for any given k in the United States. If $k_{\text{US}} = k'_{\text{Mexico}}$, the marginal product of capital would be higher in the United States due to the higher level of total factor productivity. Therefore, the rates of return to capital are equalized when $k_{\text{US}} > k'_{\text{Mexico}}$. So, real GDP per hour worked stops rising in Mexico when $y_{\text{US}} > y'_{\text{Mexico}}$.

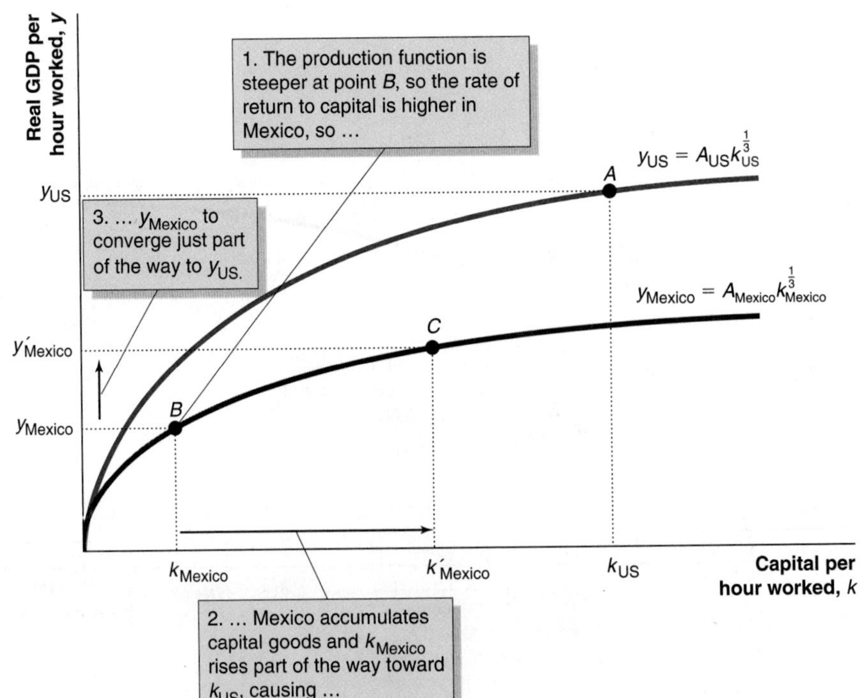
Real GDP per hour worked, y
1. The production function is steeper at point B, so the rate of return to capital is higher in Mexico, so ...
$y_{US} = A_{US}k_{US}^{\frac{1}{3}}$
A
y_{US}
3. ... y_{Mexico} to converge just part of the way to y_{US}.
$y_{Mexico} = A_{Mexico}k_{Mexico}^{\frac{1}{3}}$
C
y'_{Mexico}
B
y_{Mexico}
k_{Mexico}
k'_{Mexico}
k_{US}
Capital per hour worked, k
2. ... Mexico accumulates capital goods and k_{Mexico} rises part of the way toward k_{US}, causing ...

Figure 4.11

Mexico and the United States, Assuming Different Levels of Total Factor Productivity

The United States has a higher level of total factor productivity than Mexico. Initially, Mexico is at point B, and the United States is at point A, so the slope of the production function is steeper for Mexico than for the United States. Because the rate of return to capital is the slope of the production function, $r_{\text{Mexico}} > r_{\text{US}}$. Therefore, capital would flow to Mexico, so GDP per hour worked in Mexico would rise toward the level of GDP per hour worked in the United States. However, because total factor productivity is higher in the United States, Mexico stops accumulating more capital when Mexico reaches point C, and the rates of return on capital and the slopes of the production function are equal in the two countries. ●

Why would Mexico and the United States have different levels of total factor productivity? Total factor productivity includes all factors that determine real GDP per worker, other than capital per worker and capital's share of income. Therefore, total factor productivity includes the effect not only of knowledge but also of government institutions—including the level of corruption among government officials—macroeconomic policies, geography, and the quality of the labor force. The United States and Mexico may have access to the same stock of knowledge, but these other differences may persist for years and explain why GDP per hour worked varies between the countries. We explore these differences among countries in greater detail in Chapter 5.

Making the Connection

Will Indian Workers Become More Productive Than U.S. Workers?

According to the Conference Board, labor productivity growth in India averaged 5.8% annually between 2005 and 2010. Can the country sustain this rapid growth in productivity, and can Indian workers eventually become as productive as, or more productive than, U.S. workers? There are reasons to support both negative and positive responses to this question. Those who see continued growth in the productivity of the Indian labor force point to favorable demographic factors. Unlike in China, the working age population in India is destined to grow over the next several decades. In addition to adding to the labor force, this should lead to greater saving and investment as workers' per capita incomes rise. Much of India's labor force is still employed in agriculture, where productivity is relatively low. If these workers can shift into more productive jobs in manufacturing and services—which is by no means a certainty—this shift will further add to overall productivity growth. However, India faces obstacles that the country must overcome if growth is to continue. The *Economist* magazine noted that one of these obstacles is India's infrastructure: "its lousy roads, ports and power. India spends 4% of its GDP on infrastructure investment, compared with China's 9%. In absolute dollars terms, China spends seven times as much on its infrastructure."

Another problem facing India is its strict labor laws. Firms that employ more than 100 people are not allowed to fire anyone without the permission of the central government. This and other restrictions discourage private businesses from investing and expanding. Reform of labor laws will be difficult to achieve as long as the central government seeks the favor of the country's politically powerful Communist Party. India also suffers from the poor quality of its public services. Of particular concern are the ability of the government to provide clean water—a problem that may become worse as population grows—and education. Although India can boast of having trained millions of scientists, engineers, and researchers, these people represent a small fraction of the labor force. About one-third of the working-age population has had no formal education.

Despite the challenges India faces, the prospects for continued robust increases in economic growth and worker productivity are good. Goldman Sachs recently forecast that India could sustain 8% real GDP growth until 2020, provided that the government continues with labor market and education reforms and continues reducing restrictions on private business.

Sources: "Total Economy Database and 2011 Productivity Brief," *The Conference Board*, January 2011; Nicholas Eberstadt, "The Demographic Future," *Foreign Affairs*, Vol. 89, No. 6, November/December 2010, pp. 54–64; and "India on Fire," *Economist*, February 1, 2007.

Test your understanding by doing related problem 4.7 on page 138 at the end of this chapter.

Table 4.4 **Total Factor Productivity, GDP per Worker, and Capital per Worker for the United States and Mexico**

Country	Real GDP per worker (thousands of dollars)	Capital per worker (thousands of dollars)	TFP
United States	$57.3	$125.6	11.4
Mexico	21.4	44.2	6.1

Note: The total factor productivity for the United States differs from the value in panel (c) of Figure 4.9 on page 121 because Caselli and Feyrer use real GDP per worker and capital per worker rather than real GDP per hour worked and capital per hour worked. For simplicity, we assume that capital's share of income is one third for both countries.

Sources: Francesco Caselli and James Feyrer, "The Marginal Product of Capital," *Quarterly Journal of Economics*, Vol. 122, No. 2, May 2007, pp. 535–568; and authors' calculations.

A Numerical Example

Francesco Caselli of the London School of Economics and James Feyrer of Dartmouth College provide data that illustrate the example of the United States and Mexico. Table 4.4 shows their data for real GDP per worker and capital per worker for the United States and Mexico.[6] In Figure 4.10, total factor productivity and capital's share of income are the same for both countries. However, Mexico has a lower level of capital per worker. Using the data from Table 4.4, the rates of return for capital for the two countries are:

$$r_{\text{Mexico}} = \left(\frac{1}{3}\right)\left[\frac{A(k_{\text{Mexico}})^{\frac{1}{3}}}{k_{\text{Mexico}}}\right] = \left(\frac{1}{3}\right)\left[\frac{11.4(44.2)^{\frac{1}{3}}}{44.2}\right] = 0.304$$

$$r_{\text{US}} = \left(\frac{1}{3}\right)\left[\frac{A(k_{\text{US}})^{\frac{1}{3}}}{k_{\text{US}}}\right] = \left(\frac{1}{3}\right)\left[\frac{11.4(125.6)^{\frac{1}{3}}}{125.6}\right] = 0.152.$$

In this situation, investors have an incentive to shift capital to Mexico, so capital per worker increases in Mexico and, due to diminishing marginal returns, r_{Mexico} decreases toward r_{US}. Capital keeps flowing to Mexico until $r_{\text{Mexico}} = r_{\text{US}}$. Because total factor productivity and capital's share of income are the same in the two countries, this equality must occur when $k_{\text{Mexico}} = k_{\text{US}}$. So, capital flows to Mexico until $y_{\text{Mexico}} = y_{\text{US}}$.

If the levels of total factor productivity are not the same, Mexico's GDP per hour worked will not converge to the same level of GDP per hour worked as in the United States. The level of total factor productivity in the United States is 11.4, so the rate of return to capital in the United States remains 0.152. However, total factor productivity in Mexico is just 6.1, so the initial rate of return on capital in Mexico is:

$$r_{\text{Mexico}} = \left(\frac{1}{3}\right)\left[\frac{A(k_{\text{Mexico}})^{\frac{1}{3}}}{k_{\text{Mexico}}}\right] = \left(\frac{1}{3}\right)\left[\frac{6.4(44.2)^{\frac{1}{3}}}{44.2}\right] = 0.171.$$

This value is still higher than r_{US}, so capital will still flow to Mexico, but not to the same extent. As a result, k_{Mexico} never rises to the level of k_{US}, and y_{Mexico} never converges to y_{US}. In fact, k_{Mexico} rises to only $52.6 per worker, and y_{Mexico} rises to $24.0 per worker, both of

[6]Caselli and Feyrer did not have data on number of hours worked, so the discussion in this section is in terms of real GDP per worker and capital per worker. The figures for total factor productivity in Table 4.4 are based on the assumption that capital's share of income is one-third for both Mexico and the United States. Neither of these differences from the original paper is critical here.

which are far below the U.S. levels shown in Table 4.4. Therefore, when total factor productivity varies across countries, rates of return to capital do converge to the same values, but levels of GDP per worker do not converge.

MACRO DATA: HOW WELL DO INTERNATIONAL CAPITAL MARKETS ALLOCATE CAPITAL?

The example in Figure 4.10 shows that capital flows to low-income countries can increase real GDP per hour worked in those countries. If there are no barriers to capital mobility and capital markets are functioning well, capital should move to the countries with the highest rates of return until the rates of return on capital are equal in all countries. When rates of return to capital are not equal, world real GDP will increase if capital moves from countries with low rates of return to countries with high rates of return. When differences in rates of return to capital are large enough, the flow of capital from high-income to low-income countries has the potential to substantially increase world real GDP.

In fact, though, Francesco Caselli and James Feyrer found that the rate of return to capital is essentially the same in all countries. So, reallocating capital from low- to high-rate-of-return countries would increase real GDP per worker in the world by just 0.1%. Therefore, international capital markets appear to do a good job of allocating capital across countries.

This finding by Caselli and Feyrer is important because it tells us something about why some countries have persistently low levels of real GDP per worker. Poor countries with profitable investment opportunities are generally able to attract the funds to pursue those opportunities. However, there tend to be relatively few good investment opportunities in poor countries because total factor productivity is lower than in rich countries. The following figure illustrates this point by showing that high-income countries also have marginal products of capital.

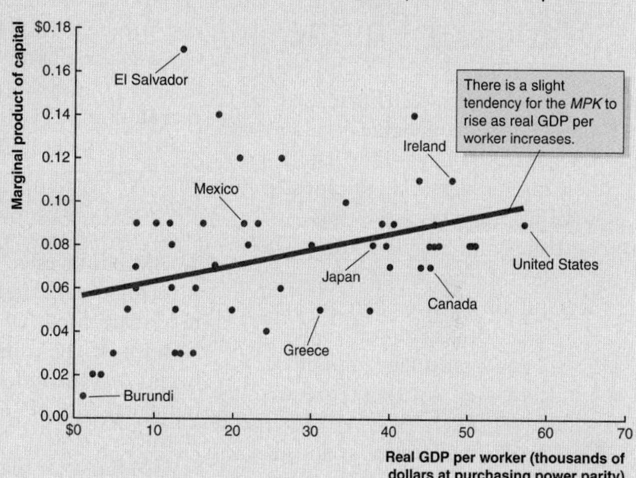

To understand why some countries have persistently lower levels of real GDP per worker, we need to understand why total factor productivity is lower in those countries. We address this issue in the next chapter.

Source: Francesco Caselli and James Feyrer, "The Marginal Product of Capital," *Quarterly Journal of Economics*, Vol. 122, No. 2, May 2007, pp. 535–568.

Test your understanding by doing related problem 4.6 on page 138 at the end of this chapter.

Answering the Key Question

Continued from page 105

At the beginning of this chapter, we asked:

"What are the main factors that determine the growth rate of real GDP?"

In this chapter, we saw that a model based on the aggregate production function for the economy allowed us to analyze the determinants of growth in real GDP. The three determinants of growth in real GDP are growth in the capital stock, growth in the number of hours worked, and growth in total factor productivity. We saw that for the United States during the period from 1949 to 2009, growth in total factor productivity was the most important determinant of the growth rate of real GDP.

Before moving on to the next chapter, read *An Inside Look* on the next page for a discussion of why General Motors has car manufacturing facilities in India.

GM Expanding Production in India

WALL STREET JOURNAL

General Motors Unveils India-Made Car Engine

General Motors Co. Thursday unveiled the first engine developed by its Indian unit, as the Detroit auto maker takes a significant step to expand its presence in this emerging automobile market.

The 1.2-liter gasoline engine will initially be offered in the Chevrolet Beat small car from Feb. 1 and later extended to other models as well, company executives said.

a Introducing locally developed engines will help GM utilize the lower-cost and skilled manpower in the south Asian country to produce new cars that are priced competitively to take on rivals such as Suzuki Motor Corp., Hyundai Motor Co. and Ford Motor Co.

"India is a key market for General Motors," said Tim Lee, GM's president for international operations.

"We are focusing on leveraging our unmatched global resources, as well as our growing local capabilities to develop vehicles and powertrains in India, for India," Mr. Lee said.

The new so-called Smartech gasoline engine will be produced at GM's engine plant at Talegaon, in the western state of Maharashtra. The auto maker also has a technical center and a design studio in India's technology hub of Bangalore, where it has 2,000 employees.

b GM has invested more than $230 million on the new factory in Maharashtra that opened last November. The company previously said that the unit will have an initial capacity of 160,000 engines a year.

GM has a car manufacturing plant at Halol in the western state of Gujarat and another at Talegaon.

General Motors India Pvt. Ltd. makes and sells eight car models locally under its Chevrolet brand, namely the Spark, Beat and Aveo U-VA hatchbacks, the Optra, Cruze and Aveo sedans, the Captiva sport-utility vehicle and multi-purpose vehicle Tavera.

"India and the rest of emerging markets, are very important to us. The business model after the IPO [initial public offering] is to focus on and leverage on these growth markets," Mr. Lee said.

c Separately, Karl Slym, president and managing director of GM India, said the company will introduce six new vehicles in the next two years. Four of the new models will be passenger vehicles and the other two will be commercial vehicles.

Also, Mr. Slym said GM plans to start selling its first light truck with partner SAIC Motor Corp. by the end of December. . . .

"We have a portfolio planned for the next 5 years which focuses on the growth market of India," he said, adding that the auto maker aims to sell 300,000 vehicles in India in 2013.

Sales of GM cars in the country rose to 110,804 vehicles in 2010 from 69,579 in 2009. The 2010 sales figure is the highest since the company began operations in 1996.

Source: Nikhil Gulati and Santanu Choudhury, "General Motors Unveils India-Made Car Engine," *Wall Street Journal*, January 27, 2011. *The Wall Street Journal* by Dow Jones & Co.

Key Points in the Article

This article discusses General Motors' (GM) continued expansion in India. In 2011, GM introduced its 1.2 liter Smartech gasoline engine, which is being produced in its new engine plant in Talegaon, India. The engine factory is the latest addition to GM's growing presence in India, which also includes car manufacturing facilities in Talegaon and Halol, and a technical center and design studio in Bangalore. Presently, GM produces 8 models for the local Indian market, with plans to introduce another 6 new Indian-built vehicles by 2013. GM's car sales in India rose by over 50% from 2009 to 2010, and the company has set a sales target of nearly triple its 2010 figure by 2013.

Analyzing the News

a India has one of the world's fastest growing economies, and is a key to expansion for many of the world's major companies. Expanding operations in India allows GM to take advantage of the country's lower-cost, skilled labor and be more competitive in the sale of automobiles in the Indian market. Developing and producing vehicles in India for the Indian market will provide benefits for GM as well as increasing India's capital stock and access to technology.

b GM's president for international operations emphasized the importance of expanding in India and other emerging markets, and this is evident with the company's investment of over $230 million in its new engine factory in Talegaon. GM's increased investment brings new capital goods and technology to India. Figure 1 shows this increase in capital. Holding labor and technology constant, the increase in capital is shown in Figure 1 by a movement along the per-worker production function from point *A* to point *B*. As capital per worker increases from k_1 to k_2, real GDP per worker increases from y_1 to y_2. Holding labor and capital constant, the increase in technology is shown in Figure 2 as an upward shift of the per-worker production function, with a movement from point *A* to point *C*, and an increase in real GDP per worker from y_1 to y_3. As the figures show, both the increase in capital and the increase in technology result in an increase in real GDP per worker.

c GM has developed a five-year plan for its growing Indian market, and intends to continue its investment in India with the introduction of six new vehicles by 2013, at which time it hopes to reach an annual sales rate of 300,000 new vehicles. The continued investment will further expand capital and technology in this rapidly growing economy.

THINKING CRITICALLY

1. The figures below represent the per-worker production function in India when either technology or capital is held constant along with labor. General Motors' increased investment will bring new capital goods *and* technology to India. Explain how the increases in both capital goods and technology will affect real GDP per worker in India, and use a graph to illustrate your explanation.
2. General Motors is just one of many companies investing in India. As more companies invest, India receives additional capital goods and new technology. Explain how these increases in capital goods and new technology will affect the aggregate production function in India, and holding other factors constant, describe how each of these changes will affect real GDP.

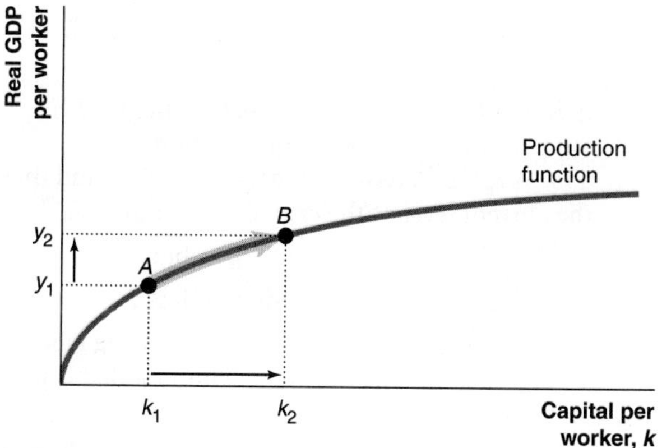

Figure 1 An increase in capital, holding labor and technology constant

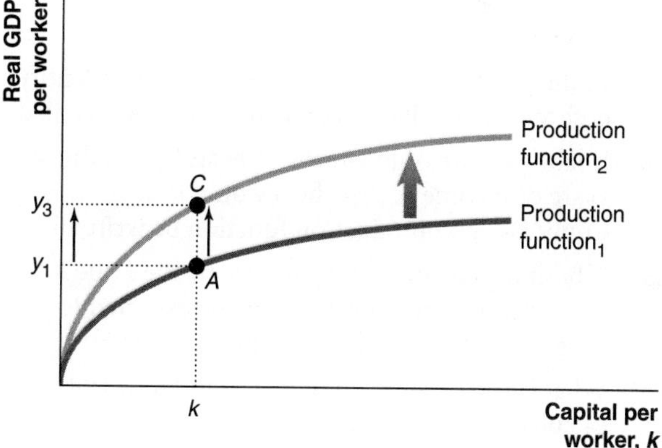

Figure 2 An increase in technology, holding labor and capital constant

CHAPTER SUMMARY AND PROBLEMS

KEY TERMS

Aggregate production function, p. 107
Capital-labor ratio, p. 123
Cobb–Douglas production function, p. 108
Constant returns to scale, p. 107
Marginal product of capital (*MPK*), p. 109
Marginal product of labor (*MPL*), p. 111
Profit, p. 116
Total factor productivity (*TFP*), p. 108

4.1 The Aggregate Production Function

Describe the aggregate production function.

SUMMARY

The **aggregate production** function shows the relationship between the inputs of capital and labor and the output of real GDP. The **Cobb–Douglas production function** is a production function commonly used in economics. This production function has **constant returns to scale.** For example, if both capital and labor inputs are doubled, then real GDP also doubles. **Total factor productivity (*TFP*)** is an index of the overall level of efficiency of transforming capital and labor into real GDP. The **Marginal product of capital (*MPK*)** is the extra output a firm receives from adding one more unit of capital, holding all other inputs and efficiency constant. The **marginal product of labor (*MPL*)** is the extra output a firm receives from adding one more unit of labor, holding all other inputs and efficiency constant.

Review Questions

1.1 In the production function, $Y = A\ F(K, L)$, identify each variable. What does an increase in *A* mean?

1.2 If labor's share of income is 80% and capital's share of income is 20%, how would the Cobb–Douglas production function be written?

1.3 If both capital and labor increase by the same proportion, would the economy be expected to experience diminishing marginal returns?

1.4 What is total factor productivity, and how is it calculated?

1.5 Suppose that it is known that labor receives 25% of national income. With a Cobb-Douglas production function and an initial level of real GDP of $10,000, what happens to real GDP if both capital and labor double?

Problems and Applications

1.6 Draw a graph of the aggregate production function with capital, *K*, on the horizontal axis.

a. Why does it have the shape that you have drawn?

b. How would the graph change if there is an improvement in technology?

c. How would the graph change if there is an increase in the productivity of labor?

1.7 **[Related to *Solved Problem 4.1* on page 111]** Suppose that the production function is $Y = A\ K^{1/4}L^{3/4}$.

a. What is the marginal product of labor (*MPL*)?

b. What is the marginal product of capital (*MPK*)?

c. Graph the approximate shapes of the *MPL* and *MPK* curves.

1.8 **[Related to *Solved Problem 4.1* on page 111]** Suppose that the production function were $Y = A\ K^{1/4}L^{3/4}$. Assume that $A = 100{,}000$, and that the current level of the capital stock is 10,000.

a. Find the marginal product of labor.

b. Graph the marginal product of labor.

c. Graph the production function, putting labor on the horizontal axis and assuming that capital is constant.

d. What would happen to the marginal product of labor and the production function if the capital stock increased to 20,000?

1.9 Current labor hours worked are 50,000 per year. The capital stock is $100,000. Real GDP is $1,000,000.

a. If the production function is $Y = A K^{1/2}L^{1/2}$, what is total factor productivity?

b. If the production function is $Y = A K^{1/4}L^{3/4}$, what is total factor productivity?

1.10 Current labor hours worked are 50,000 per year. The capital stock is $100,000. Total factor productivity is 2.

a. If the production function is $Y = A K^{1/3}L^{2/3}$, what is real GDP?

b. If the labor force increases to 100,000, what will happen to real GDP?

c. If total factor productivity doubles, what will happen to real GDP?

d. Graph the production function, with capital on the horizontal axis, and use your graph to explain the difference between a doubling of the labor force and a doubling of total factor productivity.

1.11 **[Related to the *Making the Connection* on page 114]** In the 1950s, China had a very rapid population growth rate, which it was able to reduce dramatically over the next half century. Over the past two decades, China has experienced rapid growth in both technology and the capital stock.

a. Draw a graph of China's aggregate production function. Put labor on the horizontal axis. Show why a rapid increase in population did not result in a rapid increase in real GDP.

b. Show how moderate population growth combined with increases in technology and the capital stock would result in much faster real GDP growth. Explain why your results are different than in your answer to part a.

1.12 The Organisation for Economic Co-operation and Development (OECD) measures the productivity of its member countries as GDP per hour worked. The highest productivities reported in 2007 were in Luxemburg and Norway, and the lowest were in Poland and Mexico. Measured in U.S. dollars, the highest productivities were nearly four times the lowest productivities. What factors might account for these productivity differences?

A Model of Real GDP in the Long Run
Explain how real GDP is determined in the long run.

SUMMARY

Economists assume that firms maximize **profit**, which is total revenue minus total cost. When the marginal product of labor is greater than the real wage, firms hire more workers, and when the marginal product of labor is less than the real wage, firms lay off workers. When the marginal product of capital is greater than the real rental cost of capital, firms purchase more capital goods, and when the marginal product of capital is less than the real rental cost of capital, firms let the capital stock depreciate. The marginal product of capital curve is the demand curve for capital goods, and the marginal product of labor curve is the demand curve for labor. The supply of capital and labor are fixed at the current values at any given point in time. The real rental cost of capital and the real wage are determined in the markets for capital and labor.

Review Questions

2.1 Write the equation for a firm's profit in terms of input costs.

2.2 Explain how firms choose the amount of capital and labor to use.

2.3 How do individual markets for capital and labor relate to aggregate capital and labor markets?

2.4 Why is the aggregate supply curve of labor vertical?

2.5 Show how the markets for labor and capital are related to the aggregate production function and real GDP.

Problems and Applications

2.6 The graph below shows the production function and the labor market. The labor market is currently in equilibrium at point A.

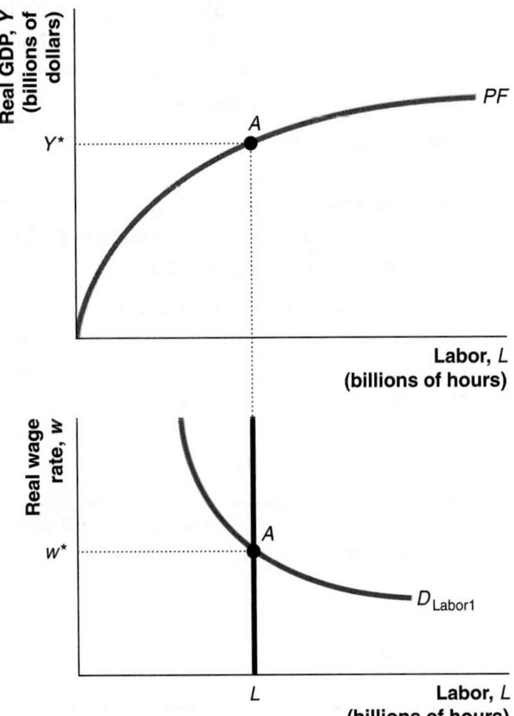

Suppose that total factor productivity decreases.

a. Show the effect on the real wage rate and on real GDP.

b. Now suppose that, at the same time, there is an increase in the labor force. Show the effect on the graphs, and explain your results.

c. Why is the effect on output different in these two cases?

2.7 Suppose that the production function is given by $Y = A\,K^{1/5}L^{4/5}$.

a. If $A = 1$, $K = 10{,}000$, and $L = 10{,}000$, what is real GDP?

b. The demand for labor in this economy is given by $MPL = \frac{(4/5)AK^{1/5}}{L^{1/5}}$. Find the real wage.

c. The demand for capital in this economy is given by $MPK = \frac{(1/5)AL^{4/5}}{K^{4/5}}$. Find the real rental cost of capital.

d. Graph the relationship between the production function and the labor and capital markets.

2.8 Consider the economy described in problem 2.7. Graph and explain the likely changes in output, the real wage, and the real rental cost of capital under each of the following scenarios:

a. There are breakthroughs in technology that improve the productivity of all factors of production. Technological breakthroughs cause A to increase to 2.

b. A devastating earthquake causes the capital stock to decrease to 5,000.

c. A wave of immigration causes the labor force to increase to 15,000.

2.9 The productivity of labor is usually a function of at least three factors: available technology, the amount of capital available to use, and the human capital (skills) of the workforce. Compare the likely real wages in the following pairs of countries, assuming that all other things are identical, and draw a graph to support your answer.

a. Country A is more technologically advanced than Country B.

b. Country C has a larger labor force than Country D.

c. Country E has more skilled workers than Country F.

2.10 Some firms produce in both China and the United States. Suppose that the marginal product of capital in the United States is 100 units of output per hour, and the real rental cost of capital is \$50. Assume further that the marginal product of capital in China is 20, and the real rental rate on capital is \$5.

a. All other things being equal and assuming that labor cannot be moved from one country to another, should firms move production from the United States to China or vice versa? Explain your answer in terms of profit-maximizing employment decisions for firms.

b. What would happen to the marginal product of capital in each country if this reallocation occurred? What would happen to real wages?

2.11 International data on labor's share of total national income shows variation between countries and over time. In Europe, for example, in 2006, labor's share was between 60% and 70% for most countries. While labor's share is similar today, its share varied widely in these countries some years ago. In Greece in the early 1970s, labor's share was less than 50%, while in France in the 1980s, labor's share was close to 80%. Using the model developed in this chapter, how can you best explain these changes over time?

Source: Organisation for Economic Co-operation and Development.

4.3 Accounting for Growth in Real GDP

Discuss the contributions of capital, labor, and efficiency to the growth rate of real GDP.

SUMMARY

Capital, labor, and total factor productivity all contribute to the growth rate of real GDP. The **capital–labor ratio** is the dollar value of capital goods per unit of labor and is measured as either the dollar value of capital divided by the total number of hours worked, or as the dollar value of capital divided by the total number of workers. We can use growth accounting to determine the size of the contribution of each one. Growth accounting shows that capital stock growth and total factor productivity growth are the two most important determinants of the growth rate of real GDP. Growth accounting shows that total factor productivity is the most important determinant of real GDP per hour worked.

Review Questions

3.1 What is growth accounting?

3.2 How have U.S. capital, labor, and total factor productivity changed over time?

3.3 How have capital, labor, and total factor productivity contributed to U.S. real GDP growth?

Problems and Applications

3.4 From 1990 to 2004, labor's share of income averaged 60% in Ireland, while real GDP grew at an average annual rate of 6.7%.

a. Write an equation similar to Equation (4.5) on page 121 to show growth accounting for this economy.

b. The average annual growth of the capital stock over this period was 4.8%, and the average annual growth rate of hours worked was 2.0%. What was the contribution of technological growth?

c. Find the relative share of real GDP growth accounted for by the three determinants of real GDP.

3.5 **[Related to *Solved Problem 4.3* on page 123]** Calculate the following growth rates for Ireland.

a. Based on problem 3.4, write Ireland's growth accounting equation for labor productivity growth.

b. Find the relative contribution of growth in the capital–labor ratio to the growth rate of real GDP per hour worked.

c. Find the relative contribution of growth in total productivity to the growth rate of real GDP per hour worked.

d. Compare the two rates in parts b. and c.

3.6 **[Related to the *Making the Connection* on page 124]** In the study discussed on page 124, the authors found a real GDP growth rate of 9.3% for China from 1978 to 2004. In terms of the simple growth equation discussed, 2 percentage points of the growth was due to adding workers, 3.2 percentage points was due to capital accumulation, and 3.9 percentage points was due to increases in total factor productivity. A more complex version of the authors' results shows that 1.2 percentage points of total factor productivity growth's contribution resulted from the movement of workers from agricultural to industrial sectors.

a. Why would reallocating workers between sectors in the economy increase economic growth?

b. All other things being equal, if moving workers from agriculture to industry increases output, what does this imply about the marginal productivity of labor in agriculture prior to the move?

Source: Barry Bosworth and Susan M. Collins, "Accounting for Growth: Comparing China and India," *Journal of Economic Perspectives*, Vol. 22, No. 1, Winter 2008, pp. 45–66.

3.7 Ray J. Barrell, Catherine Guillemineau, and Dawn Holland Barrell, economists at the National Institute of Social and Economic Research in the United Kingdom, studied the growth rates of Germany and the United Kingdom from 1993 to 2005. Prior to 1993, both countries grew at about the same rate. After 1993, the United Kingdom grew at an average annual rate of about 3%, while Germany's growth rate fell to an average rate of 1.5%. The following table gives a summary of their results:

	Germany	United Kingdom
Total GDP growth	1.5%	3%
Labor growth	–0.8	0.8
Capital growth	1.2	0.4
Total factor productivity growth	1.1	1.9

Based on the table, discuss why the German economy grew more slowly after 1993 than did the British economy.

Source: Ray J. Barrell, Catherine Guillemineau, and Dawn Holland Barrell, "Decomposing Growth in France, Germany and the United Kingdom Using Growth Accounting and Production Function Approaches," *National Institute Economic Review*, Vol. 199, No. 1, January 2007, pp. 99–113.

3.8 Section 4.3 of this chapter showed that real wages have risen over time, while the real rental cost of capital has remained roughly constant. Can you explain this through the relative growth of the capital stock and the labor force? What role does technology play in explaining the relative growth of real wages and returns to capital?

4.4 GDP per Hour Worked Among Countries

Understand that differences in efficiency explain differences in labor productivity across countries.

SUMMARY

Differences in real GDP per hour worked are due to either differences in capital per hour worked, total factor productivity, or capital's share of income. It is not possible for differences in capital per hour worked by themselves to explain most of the differences in real GDP per hour worked across countries. Differences in capital's share of income tend to be relatively unimportant, so differences in total factor productivity are the primary cause of differences in real GDP per hour worked across countries.

Review Questions

4.1 What are the three sources of differences in real GDP per worker?

4.2 Why would increases in hours worked tend to increase GDP but not GDP per worker?

4.3 If countries have different rates of return on capital, what will happen to the allocation of capital between countries over time?

Problems and Applications

4.4 Graphically show the following:

a. Why countries with higher capital-labor ratios will have higher levels of real GDP per worker.

b. How differences in technology can cause countries with identical capital-labor ratios to have different levels of real GDP per worker.

4.5 The share of income going to physical capital in both Colombia and Costa Rica is about 10%, so we can represent the production function for real GDP per worker as $y = Ak^{1/10}$. The capital–labor ratio is \$15.25 for Colombia, and it is \$23.12 for Costa Rica. Real GDP per worker is \$12.18 in Colombia and \$13.31 in Costa Rica.

a. Calculate total factor productivity for each country.

b. Calculate the return on capital in each country.

4.6 **[Related to the *Macro Data* feature on page 131]** If the rates of return on capital in Colombia and Costa Rica are what you found in problem 4.5b, what will happen to the capital stocks of the two countries over time? How is this likely to change output per worker in each country?

4.7 **[Related to the *Making the Connection* on page 129]** Briefly explain whether you agree with the following statement: "Because capital will move to the location in which it receives the highest return, over time, per capita incomes of all countries should become the same."

4.8 **[Related to the *Chapter Opener* on page 105]** Between 1990 and 2010, real GDP per capita grew much more rapidly in India than in the United States. Based on the discussion in this chapter, do you think that India's growth rate will be permanently higher than the U.S. growth rate? Briefly explain.

DATA EXERCISES

D4.1: Go to the Bureau of Labor Statistics Web site (www.bls.gov) and examine the graphical representation of changes in overall productivity and manufacturing productivity. (www.bls.gov/lpc/prodybar.htm).

a. How has overall productivity changed in the United States from 1947 to the present?

b. Why do you think that overall productivity is so different from manufacturing productivity?

c. How can you account for the drop in manufacturing productivity in the 2007–2009 period? Why didn't overall productivity show the same drop?

D4.2: The World Bank collects data on per capita output (see http://data.worldbank.org/data-catalog). Instead of GDP per capita, the World Bank uses gross domestic income (GDI) adjusted for purchasing power and other factors.

a. Using this method, what countries have the highest per capita incomes? The lowest?

b. Can you explain these differences based on labor, capital, and total factor productivity?

D4.3: The Bureau of Labor Statistics publishes data on compensation and productivity for a variety of countries. Go to the international section (International Labor Comparisons, www.bls.gov/fls/home.htm) and find data on hourly compensation and productivity for other countries. In order to compare countries, it is necessary to use a common currency, such as dollars. What is the relationship between productivity and wages around the world?

D4.4: **[Excel question]** Go to the Bureau of Labor Statistics Web site (www.bls.gov). Find data for real wages (earnings in constant dollars) and productivity for 2002–2009. Then use these data to find the growth rates of real wages and productivity.

a. Graph your results.

b. What is the correlation between productivity growth and real wage growth over this period?

APPENDIX

The Cobb–Douglas Production Function and Constant Returns to Scale

4A **Derive important properties of the Cobb–Douglas production function.**

Constant returns to scale exist if all inputs change by the same percentage and real GDP changes by the same percentage. For example, if we were to double both capital and labor inputs, then according to the Cobb–Douglas aggregate production function in Equation (4.1), output would equal:

$$= A(2K)^{\frac{1}{3}}(2L)^{\frac{2}{3}}.$$

We can factor out the 2 to obtain:

$$A2^{\frac{1}{3}}K^{\frac{1}{3}}2^{\frac{2}{3}}L^{\frac{2}{3}} = AK^{\frac{1}{3}}L^{\frac{2}{3}}2^{\frac{1}{3}+\frac{2}{3}} = 2AK^{\frac{1}{3}}L^{\frac{2}{3}}$$
$$= 2Y.$$

Therefore, doubling both capital and labor doubles output, so constant returns to scale exist.

Deriving the Marginal Product of Capital

To find the marginal product of capital, we make use of partial derivatives from calculus:

$$MPK = \frac{\partial Y}{\partial K} = \frac{\partial AK^{\frac{1}{3}}L^{\frac{2}{3}}}{\partial K} = \left(\frac{1}{3}\right)AK^{-\frac{2}{3}}L^{\frac{2}{3}}.$$

Now, we multiply this expression by K/K to get:

$$MPK = \left(\frac{(\frac{1}{3})AK^{-\frac{2}{3}}L^{\frac{2}{3}}}{1}\right)\left(\frac{K}{K}\right) = \frac{(\frac{1}{3})AK^{\frac{1}{3}}L^{\frac{2}{3}}}{K}.$$

Using the Cobb–Douglas production function, the numerator simplifies to Y so:

$$MPK = \left(\frac{1}{3}\right)\frac{Y}{K}.$$

Deriving the Marginal Product of Labor

We can use the same method to find the marginal product of labor:

$$MPL = \frac{\partial Y}{\partial L} = \frac{\partial AK^{\frac{1}{3}}L^{\frac{2}{3}}}{\partial L} = \left(\frac{2}{3}\right)AK^{\frac{1}{3}}L^{-\frac{1}{3}}.$$

Now, we multiply this expression by L/L to get:

$$MPL = \left(\frac{(\frac{2}{3})AK^{\frac{1}{3}}L^{-\frac{1}{3}}}{1}\right)\left(\frac{L}{L}\right) = \frac{(\frac{2}{3})AK^{\frac{1}{3}}L^{-\frac{2}{3}}}{L}.$$

Using the Cobb–Douglas production function, the numerator simplifies to Y so:

$$MPL = \left(\frac{2}{3}\right)\frac{Y}{L}.$$

Deriving the Growth Accounting Equation for the Aggregate Production Function

The first step in deriving the growth accounting equation is to recognize that all inputs grow over time, so we can think of them as being functions of time:

$$Y_t = A_t K_t^{\frac{1}{3}} L_t^{\frac{2}{3}},$$

where the t subscript indicates that the variable is a function of time. Next, take the natural logarithm of the aggregate production function to get:

$$\ln Y_t = \ln A_t + \left(\frac{1}{3}\right)\ln K_t + \left(\frac{2}{3}\right)\ln L_t.$$

The derivative of the natural logarithm of the variable X_t with respect to time is:

$$\frac{d\ln X_t}{dt} = \frac{1}{X_t}\frac{dX_t}{dt} = \frac{dX_t/dt}{X_t} = g_X.$$

Taking the derivative with respect to time and applying the above rule to the production function in natural logarithms produces:

$$g_Y = g_A + \left(\frac{1}{3}\right)g_K + \left(\frac{2}{3}\right)g_L.$$

Deriving the Real GDP per Hour Worked Form of the Production Function

To find the form of the production function with real GDP per hour worked, we divide Equation (4.1) by the quantity of labor to find:

$$\frac{Y}{L} = \frac{AK^{\frac{1}{3}}L^{\frac{2}{3}}}{L}.$$

Labor appears in both the numerator and the denominator. Using our rules for exponents, this equation becomes:

$$\frac{Y}{L} = \frac{AK^{\frac{1}{3}}L^{\frac{2}{3}}}{L} = AK^{\frac{1}{3}}L^{\frac{2}{3}}L^{-1} = AK^{\frac{1}{3}}L^{\frac{2}{3}-1} = AK^{\frac{1}{3}}L^{-\frac{1}{3}} = A\left(\frac{K}{L}\right)^{\frac{1}{3}}.$$

Given the definitions of output per hour worked and the capital–labor ratio, we see that:

$$y = Ak^{\frac{1}{3}}.$$

Deriving the Growth Accounting Equation for the Real GDP per Hour Worked Form of the Production Function

The first step is to recognize that all inputs grow over time, so we can think of them as a function of time:

$$y_t = A_t k_t^{\frac{1}{3}},$$

Next, we take the natural logarithm of the aggregate production function to get:

$$\ln y_t = \ln A_t + \left(\frac{1}{3}\right)\ln k_t.$$

Taking the derivative with respect to time, we see that:

$$g_y = g_A + \left(\frac{1}{3}\right)g_k.$$

Showing That the Rate of Return to Capital Is Equal to the Marginal Product of the Capital–Labor Ratio

To see that the rate of return to capital is equal to the marginal product of the capital–labor ratio, we take the derivative of real GDP per hour worked form of the production function with respect to capital per worker, k, to get:

$$\frac{\partial y}{\partial k} = \left(\frac{1}{3}\right)Ak^{-\frac{2}{3}}.$$

Next, we multiply and divide by the capital–labor ratio to get:

$$= \left(\frac{1}{3}\right)\left(\frac{Ak^{-\frac{2}{3}}}{1}\right)\left(\frac{k}{k}\right).$$

Then, we multiply through the parentheses:

$$= \left(\frac{1}{3}\right)\left(\frac{Ak^{\frac{1}{3}}}{k}\right).$$

Next, we use the fact that $y = Ak^{\frac{1}{3}}$:

$$= \left(\frac{1}{3}\right)\left(\frac{y}{k}\right).$$

Then, we use the definitions of output per hour worked and the capital–labor ratio:

$$= \left(\frac{1}{3}\right)\left(\frac{Y/L}{K/L}\right).$$

Now cancel the terms for labor hours:

$$\frac{\partial y}{\partial k} = \left(\frac{1}{3}\right)\left(\frac{Y}{K}\right).$$

Therefore, the marginal product of capital is exactly equal to the marginal product of capital per hour worked.

CHAPTER 5

Long-Run Economic Growth

LEARNING OBJECTIVES

After studying this chapter, you should be able to:

- **5.1** Discuss the connection between labor productivity and the standard of living (pages 144–151)
- **5.2** Use the Solow growth model to explain the effect of capital accumulation on labor productivity (pages 151–161)
- **5.3** Explain how total factor productivity affects labor productivity (pages 162–168)
- **5.4** Explain the balanced growth path, convergence, and long-run equilibrium (pages 168–173)
- **5A** Describe how capital accumulation causes endogenous growth (pages 182–184)
- **5B** Solve for the steady-state capital–labor ratio and real GDP per hour worked (pages 185–187)

WHO IS NUMBER ONE?

What is the leading economy in the world today? In ranking the economic performance of countries, economists generally use two related measures: GDP and GDP per capita. (Recall from Chapter 1 that GDP per capita is GDP divided by population.) The following table shows the top 10 economies in 2010, based on these two measures (for GDP per capita, only countries having a population of at least 1 million are included):

Rank	GDP	GDP per Capita
1	United States	Norway
2	China	Singapore
3	Japan	Kuwait
4	India	United States
5	Germany	Switzerland
6	Russia	Australia
7	Brazil	Netherlands
8	United Kingdom	Austria
9	France	Canada
10	Italy	Sweden

Continued on next page

Key Issue and Question

At the end of Chapter 1, we noted key issues and questions that serve as a framework for the book. Here are the key issue and question for this chapter:

Issue: Some countries have experienced rapid rates of long-run economic growth, while other countries have grown slowly, if at all.

Question: Why isn't the whole world rich?

Answered on page 173

Both of these measures have some value. The sheer size of an economy, as measured by GDP, can help a country's firms achieve economies of scale, and a large economy may be better able to support a large military, thereby increasing the country's political influence in the world. From the point of view of the average person living in a country, however, GDP per capita is the most important measure. GDP per capita measures the quantity of goods and services available to the average person in the country and, therefore, is a good measure of the standard of living of the typical person. A country can have a large economy, as measured by GDP, but a low standard of living, as measured by GDP per capita (or per person). Notice, for instance, that China has the second-largest economy and India has the fourth-largest economy, as measured by GDP, but as the following table shows, in 2010, both countries lagged far behind the United States in GDP per capita:

Country	GDP	GDP per capita
United States	$14.7 trillion	$47,400
China	9.9 trillion	7,400
India	4.0 trillion	3,400

The table shows that while in 2010, GDP in the United States was only about 50% higher than in China, the standard of living of the typical person in the United States was more than six times higher than the standard of living of the typical person in China. The difference in GDP per capita actually understates the true difference in living standards between the two countries. For example, the average person in the United States lives longer, has more years of education, is much less likely to die in infancy or during childbirth, and is much less likely to suffer serious medical problems because of pollution than is the average person in China.

Is the United States likely to maintain its current economic lead over China? Since the Chinese government first introduced market-oriented reforms in 1978, the Chinese economy has grown more rapidly than the U.S. economy. So, part of the gap between the two economies has already closed. The projected growth rate of real GDP in China is nearly three times greater than the growth rate of real GDP in the United States. If those projections are accurate, Chinese real GDP should be larger than U.S. real GDP by 2018. Closing the gap in real GDP per capita will be much more difficult for China. Long-range growth forecasts can be inaccurate because the factors that determine economic growth can change in ways that are difficult to predict. But a recent forecast by the consulting firm PwC indicated that by 2050, Chinese real GDP per capita will still be only about 50% of U.S. real GDP per capita.

As we will discuss in this chapter, even relatively small growth rates, when compounded over many years, can result in tremendous increases in living standards. The more than 200 years of growth experienced by the United States have resulted in a living standard that the more rapid growth experienced by China during the past 30 years has not been able to match.

AN INSIDE LOOK on page 174 compares the economic growth of China and India.

Sources: U.S. Central Intelligence Agency, *World Factbook*, 2010; United Nations Development Program, *Human Development Report, 2010*, New York: Palgrave Macmillan, November 2010; "GDP per Person, Forecasts," *Economist*, January 13, 2011; and authors' calculations.

In Chapter 4, we saw that capital per hour worked and total factor productivity (TFP) are the key determinants of labor productivity. In this chapter, we explain why capital per hour worked and total factor productivity vary across countries. By doing so, we can explain why some countries are rich and other countries are poor.

5.1

Learning Objective

Discuss the connection between labor productivity and the standard of living.

Labor Productivity and the Standard of Living

In Chapter 2, we saw that real GDP equals the income generated in an economy. So, real GDP per capita is a measure of both the income available to the average person in the country and of how many goods and services the average person can purchase. Clearly, real GDP per capita is not a perfect measure of the standard of living, much less the average level of well-being. As we will discuss later, the measurement of GDP neglects the value of leisure and is not adjusted for pollution or other negative effects of production, or for changes in crime or other social problems. Although far from perfect, real GDP per capita remains the most widely available measure of the standard of living.

Figure 5.1 provides some long-run perspective on economic growth by showing real GDP per capita from 1820 to 2008 for several countries and regions around the world. Even

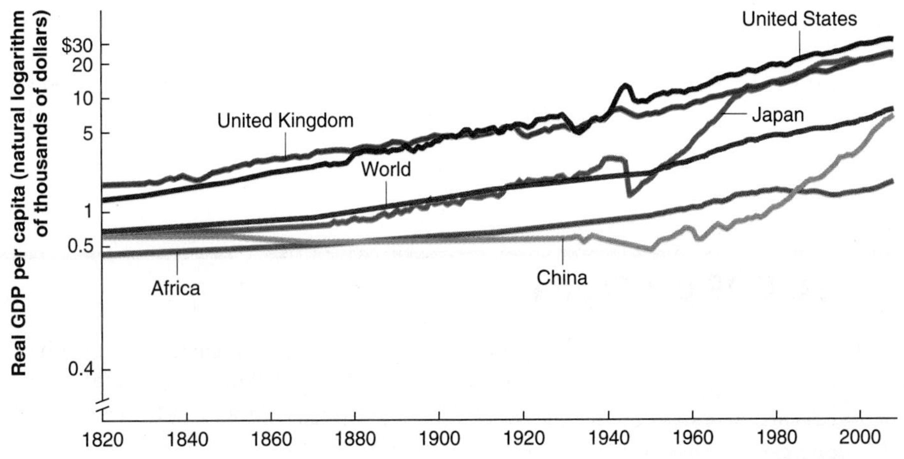

Figure 5.1

Real GDP per Capita, 1820–2008

Real GDP per capita varied significantly in 1820 but has increased for most regions of the world since 1820. However, the growth has not been evenly distributed or constant over time. For example, although the average annual growth rate of real GDP per capita for the world during these years was 1.3%, it was just 0.8% for Africa. Real GDP data in this figure are purchasing power parity values using 1990 prices.

Source: Angus Maddison, www.ggdc.net/maddison/. ●

as far back as 1820, levels of real GDP per capita varied significantly. For instance, measured in 1990 dollars, in 1820, real GDP per capita in the United Kingdom was about $1,700. While this is low by modern standards—real GDP in the United Kingdom is about 14 times greater today—it was more than 4 times the level in Africa. Over time, the rankings of countries and regions by real GDP per capita have changed because the growth rates of real GDP per capita have varied. For example, over this nearly 200-year period, the growth rate of real GDP per capita has averaged just 0.8% per year in Africa. In 2010, some African countries, such as Zimbabwe, Niger, and Somalia, still have levels of GDP per capita of *less than* $900. In contrast, Japan's growth rate averaged 1.9% per year, so real GDP per capita in Japan rose from $669 in 1820 to $22,816 in 2008. Real GDP per capita in China was stagnant until the 1970s but has been growing at a rate of over 8% per year since then. As we saw in the chapter opener, these rapid rates of growth have allowed China to close some of the gap between its living standards and those of high-income countries.

The Two Components of Real GDP per Capita

Labor productivity measures how much output, or real GDP, the economy can produce per hour of work:

$$\frac{\text{Real GDP}}{\text{Hours worked}}.$$

Because the standard of living in an economy can be measured as real GDP per capita, we can relate the standard of living to labor productivity as follows:

Real GDP per capita = Labor productivity × Hours worked per person, or

$$\left(\frac{\text{Real GDP}}{\text{Population}}\right) = \left(\frac{\text{Real GDP}}{\text{Hours worked}}\right) \times \left(\frac{\text{Hours worked}}{\text{Population}}\right). \tag{5.1}$$

Both labor productivity and the number of hours worked per person affect real GDP per capita, but labor productivity has the larger effect. This conclusion is true because while there is a limit to how many hours people can work, there is no limit to how much labor productivity can increase. As long as labor productivity increases, real GDP per capita will also increase, and the standard of living will rise. So, once we have explained what determines labor productivity, we have explained most of what determines real GDP per capita and the standard of living.

Consider the case of the United States: Labor productivity rose (in 2005 dollars) from $15 per hour worked in 1949 to $53 per hour worked in 2009, but hours worked per person actually fell from 852 hours in 1949 to 795 hours in 2009. (We will discuss the reasons for this decline in Chapter 7.) Holding labor productivity constant, the decrease in hours worked would have reduced the real GDP per capita. So, the entire increase in real GDP per capita from $12,365 in 1949 to $41,947 in 2009 was due to increased labor productivity.

Solved Problem 5.1

Explaining Increases in Real GDP per Capita

Consider the following data for 2009:

Country	Real GDP per capita (U.S. dollars)	Real GDP per hour worked (U.S. dollars)	Hours worked per person
France	$33,681	$54.50	618
Germany	36,457	53.30	684

a. What is the main reason that real GDP per capita was higher in Germany in 2009 than in France?

b. Suppose that between 2009 and 2015, hours worked per person increases by 10% in France and falls by 2% in Germany. At the same time, labor productivity increases by 12% in Germany and by 6% in France. What will real GDP per capita be in these countries in 2015?

Solving the Problem

Step 1 **Review the chapter material.** This problem is about how changes in labor productivity and hours worked per person affect real GDP per capita, so you may want to review the section "The Two Components of Real GDP per Capita," which begins on page 145.

Step 2 **Answer part (a) by explaining why real GDP per capita was higher in Germany in 2009 than it was in France.** We know that real GDP per capita has two components: labor productivity, as measured by real GDP per hour worked, and hours worked per person. The table shows that although labor productivity was a little higher in France than in Germany, this difference was more than offset by the higher level of hours worked per person in Germany.

Step 3 **Answer part (b) by calculating real GDP per capita for Germany and France in 2015.** Equation (5.1) shows that we can calculate real GDP per capita as:

$$\left(\frac{\text{Real GDP}}{\text{Population}}\right) = \left(\frac{\text{Real GDP}}{\text{Hours worked}}\right) \times \left(\frac{\text{Hours worked}}{\text{Population}}\right).$$

If the components of real GDP per capita change as indicated in the problem, then because Labor productivity = (real GDP/Hours worked), in 2015 we will have:

$$\text{France: } \frac{\text{Hours worked}}{\text{Population}} = 618 \times 1.10 = 680$$

$$\text{France: } \frac{\text{Real GDP}}{\text{Hours worked}} = \$54.50 \times 1.06 = \$57.77$$

$$\text{Germany: } \frac{\text{Hours worked}}{\text{Population}} = 684 \times 0.98 = 670$$

$$\text{Germany: } \frac{\text{Real GDP}}{\text{Hours worked}} = \$53.30 \times 1.12 = \$59.70$$

Therefore, real GDP per capita in France in 2015 will equal:

$$\$39{,}284 = \$57.77 \times 680,$$

and real GDP per capita in Germany in 2015 will equal:

$$\$39{,}999 = \$59.70 \times 670.$$

These calculations indicate that even if France were to overtake Germany in hours worked per person, it would not be enough to overcome Germany's lead in real GDP per capita if German labor productivity increases more rapidly than France's labor productivity.

Source: Organisation for Economic Co-operation and Development.

For more practice, do related problem 1.6 on page 176 at the end of this chapter.

Challenges with Using Real GDP per Capita as a Measure of the Standard of Living

Real GDP per capita is not a perfect measure of the standard of living, but it is the best measure that economists have. As long as people use their income to purchase goods and services that make them better off, the standard of living should increase as real GDP per capita increases. Nevertheless, there are several challenges to using real GDP per capita as a measure of the standard of living that we consider here in more detail:

- Distribution of income
- Value of leisure time
- Happiness
- Life expectancy

Distribution of Income Real GDP per capita tells you what the average person in the economy can consume. However, an average can be misleading because it does not tell us about the *distribution* of income. Table 5.1 illustrates this issue, using an example of two people in two countries.

In country 1, each person earns exactly $50,000, so GDP per capita is $50,000 and tells us how many goods and services the typical person can consume. In this case, real GDP per capita is a very good measure of the standard of living of the typical person. However, this approximation is not very good for country 2. In country 2, person 1 has an income of $99,000, and person 2 has an income of just $1,000. GDP per capita is still $50,000, but person 1 can consume much more than that amount, and person 2 can consume much less. Person 1 has a higher standard of living, and person 2 has a lower standard of living than GDP per capita indicates. The possibility that the distribution of income may be unequal is important to keep in mind when using GDP per capita as a measure of the standard of living of the typical person.

How much do concerns about the distribution of income affect conclusions about the benefits of economic growth? Certainly, if all the gains from economic growth went only to those individuals at the top of the income distribution, then increases in real GDP per capita would have little benefit for those at the bottom of the income distribution. Do people with lower incomes actually benefit from increases in real GDP per capita? There is considerable evidence that lower-income individuals do, in fact, benefit from economic growth. For

Table 5.1 Income Distribution and Real GDP per Capita

	Country 1	Country 2
Person 1	$50,000	$99,000
Person 2	50,000	1,000
GDP per capita	50,000	50,000

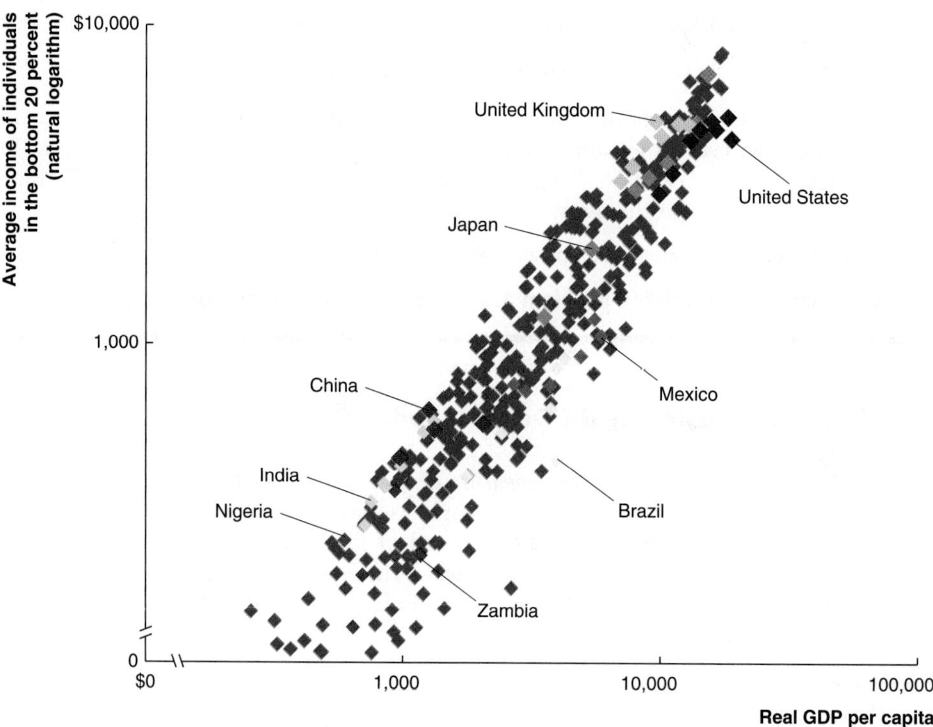

Figure 5.2

Relationship Between Real GDP per Capita and Average Income of Individuals in the Lowest 20% of the Income Distribution

The countries with the highest levels of real GDP per capita are also the countries in which the incomes of individuals in the bottom 20% of the income distribution are highest. The figure includes data for 137 countries during the 1956 to 1999 time period. Some countries, such as the United States, are represented by up to eight observations, while other countries have just one observation. Most observations appear in blue, but we put the observations for nine countries in a different color to show the relationship within these countries over time.

Source: David Dollar and Aart Kraay, "Growth Is Good for the Poor," *Journal of Economic Growth*, Vol. 7, No. 3, September 2002, pp. 195–225. ●

example, data collected by the World Bank show that as real GDP per capita for the world grew at an average annual rate of 1.8% between 1981 and 2005, the number of people living on less than $1.25 per day fell from 1.9 billion in 1981 to 1.4 billion in 2005.[1] That represents a 26% decrease in the number of very low-income individuals in just 24 years. In addition, David Dollar and Aart Kraay, economists with the World Bank, found that as real GDP per capita in a country increases by 1%, the income of the individuals in the bottom 20% of the income distribution in the country also increases by 1%.[2] Figure 5.2 shows the relationship Dollar and Kraay determined between real GDP per capita and average income for the bottom 20% of the income distribution. The figure shows that the countries with the highest levels of real GDP per capita are also the countries in which the incomes of individuals in the bottom 20% of the income distribution are highest. Therefore, the evidence indicates that economic growth raises the incomes of the poor as well as the rich.

Value of Leisure Time Because real GDP per capita measures the income of the average person in a country, it tells us how many goods and services the average person can consume. But people care about more than the goods and services they can purchase. For one thing, people value having leisure time to spend with their friends and family. As we saw earlier, all of the increase in real GDP per capita in the United States since 1949 has come from increased productivity, with the annual average hours worked per capita having declined by about 7%. So, the average person in the United States can purchase many more goods and services than in 1949, while having more leisure time. Figure 5.3 shows long-run trends in average annual hours worked per worker for several high-income countries: France, Germany, Italy, the United Kingdom, and the United States. Hours per year for the average worker in the United States decreased from 3,096 hours in 1870 to 1,878 hours in 2000. This nearly 40% decrease in the amount of time working represents a

[1]Data are from the World Bank's PovcalNet, available at http://web.worldbank.org.

[2]David Dollar and Aart Kraay, "Growth Is Good for the Poor," *Journal of Economic Growth*, Vol. 7, No. 3, September 2002, pp. 195–225.

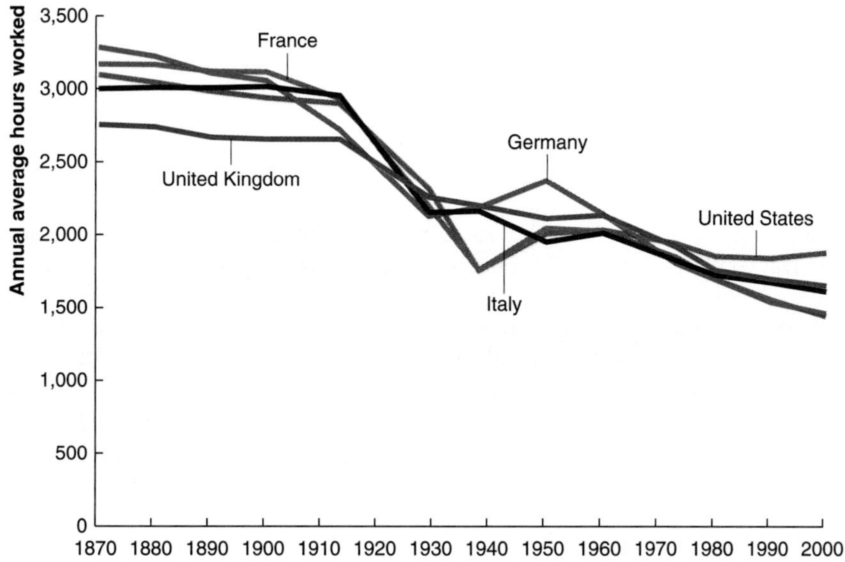

Figure 5.3

Annual Average Hours Worked per Worker in High-Income Countries, 1870–2000

As real GDP per capita has increased, annual average hours worked per worker has tended to decrease, increasing leisure time. Hours worked per year for the average worker in the United States decreased from 3,096 hours in 1870 to 1,878 hours in 2000.

Source: Michael Huberman and Chris Minns, "The Times They Are Not Changin': Days and Hours of Work in Old and New Worlds, 1870–2000," *Explorations in Economic History*, Vol. 44, No. 4, October 2007, pp. 538–567. ●

significant amount of time available for leisure activities and, correspondingly, a significant increase in the standard of living of the average person. Other high-income countries experienced similar decreases in average hours worked per worker. For example, hours per year for the average worker in France decreased from 3,168 in 1870 to 1,443 in 2000. We will analyze the reasons for this long-run decrease in the hours worked per worker in Chapter 7.

We can conclude that because leisure time has increased substantially in the United States and other developed countries, increases in real GDP per capita understate the true increases in well-being due to economic growth.

Happiness Does economic growth increase happiness? About 30 years ago, Richard Easterlin of the University of Pennsylvania found that, surprisingly, there appears to be little relationship across countries between how happy people say they are when surveyed and the level of real GDP per capita. The average person in a rich country was apparently no happier than the average person in a poor country.[3] The lack of correlation between income and happiness across countries is called the *Easterlin paradox* because it seems the opposite of what most people would expect. What explains the paradox? Easterlin argues that individuals judge themselves relative to their peer groups. Therefore, if your income increases by 10%, but the income of all your peers also increases by 10%, you will not report yourself as being any happier because you have not improved relative to your peers. However, if your income increases by 10% while everyone else's income remains constant, you have improved relative to your peers, so you will report yourself as happier.[4] Because increased real GDP per capita does not lead to increased happiness, Easterlin argues that economists and policymakers place too much emphasis on economic growth. Richard Layard of the London School of Economics has found that the Easterlin paradox does not hold at low levels of real GDP per capita. At these low levels, an increase in income does

[3]Richard Easterlin, "Does Economic Growth Improve the Human Lot? Some Empirical Evidence," in Paul David and Melvin Reder (eds.), *Nations and Households in Economic Growth: Essays in Honor of Moses Abramowitz*, New York: Academic Press, 1974.

[4]Richard Easterlin, "Will Raising the Incomes of All Increase the Happiness of All?" *Journal of Economic Behavior and Organization*, Vol. 27, No. 1, June 1995, pp. 35–47.

lead to increased happiness.[5] However, he also finds that there is little relationship between average income and happiness once real GDP per capita exceeds $15,000 per year. At low levels of income, economic growth improves the ability of people to purchase essential goods and services such as food, shelter, and clothing. But once these basic necessities are met, economic growth tends to produce luxuries that may not necessarily make individuals happier.

Recently, Betsey Stevenson and Justin Wolfers of the Wharton School at the University of Pennsylvania have called into question whether the Easterlin paradox holds, even for higher levels of real GDP per capita. Stevenson and Wolfers reexamined the relationship between real GDP per capita and happiness using a wider range of countries.[6] They found a positive relationship between how happy people reported themselves to be and GDP per capita across 131 countries. In addition, Stevenson and Wolfers also found a positive relationship between economic growth and happiness within a country. Because Stevenson and Wolfers improved on Easterlin's research by using complete surveys of people's attitudes and a larger sample of countries, their results are more likely to accurately represent the relationship between the level of income and happiness. If Stevenson and Wolfers are correct, the higher levels of income that result from economic growth do make people happier.

Life Expectancy Some people have argued that economic growth reduces the quality of life by generating pollution and increasing the stress workers feel. Consumers create air pollution by burning gasoline to power their cars and natural gas to heat their homes. Firms create air pollution when they produce electricity, pesticides, and plastics. This pollution affects the air we breathe, the water we drink, and the food we eat. Sometimes pollution is a minor irritant that spoils scenic views, but pollution can also contribute to dangerous diseases such as cancer. In addition, compared with earlier times, some people argue that jobs today create more stress, which may have negative health consequences that could potentially shorten life spans. Therefore, the costs to higher real GDP per capita might offset the benefits of the increase in the amount of goods and services that people can purchase.

Many economists are skeptical of these criticisms of economic growth. Most types of pollution have actually declined in the United States and other developed countries over the past few decades. The higher levels of income that result from economic growth have made it easier for the governments of these countries to devote additional resources to fighting pollution. Although some types of pollution, including those that contribute to global warming, remain a serious problem in developed countries, the negative health effects of pollution appear to be declining. Many types of pollution are actually more severe in lower-income, developing countries than in developed countries, because lower-income countries have fewer resources to devote to reducing pollution. In other words, a clean environment is a *normal good*, which is a good for which the demand increases as income rises. The idea that a clean environment is a normal good lies behind the *environmental Kuznets curve.* The relationship depicted by the curve states that as an economy grows, pollution initially increases as countries industrialize and air and water pollution increase, but then begins to decline as individuals choose to spend more of their income on a cleaner environment. If developing countries are able to experience economic growth, they may well follow the path of the currently developed countries and see their levels of pollution fall as their incomes rise.

In addition, although the jobs of many workers in high-income countries can be stressful, jobs in early times could also be stressful. For instance, economic growth has resulted in a sharp decline in the number of jobs in the developed countries that require long hours of hard physical labor. In the nineteenth century, the majority of Americans

[5]Richard Layard, "Happiness: Has Social Science a Clue?" Lionel Robbins Memorial Lecture, 2002/2003, http://cep.lse.ac.uk/events/lectures/layard/RL030303.pdf.

[6]Betsey Stevenson and Justin Wolfers, "Economic Growth and Subjective Well-Being: Reassessing the Easterlin Paradox," *Brookings Paper on Economic Activity*, Spring 2008, pp. 1–87.

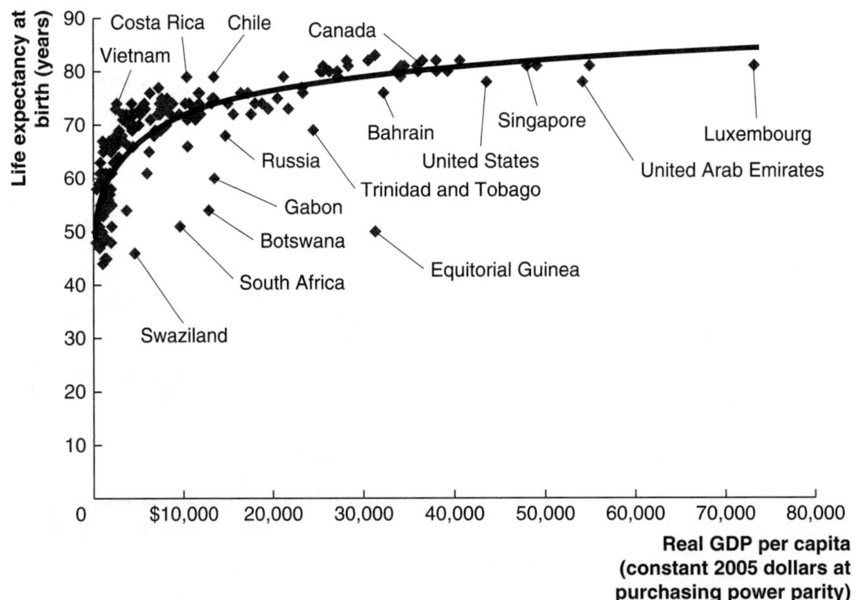

Figure 5.4

Relationship Between Real GDP per Capita and Life Expectancy at Birth, 2009

There is a clear tendency for life expectancy to increase as GDP per capita increases, but at a decreasing rate.

Source: The World Bank, *World Development Indicators.* ●

worked on farms where the hours were long and the work strenuous. As recently as the 1920s, steelworkers typically worked 12-hour days, six days per week.

One possible measure of the effects of economic growth on health is life expectancy. As real GDP per capita increases, life expectancy at birth increases, suggesting that health actually improves as real GDP per capita increases. Figure 5.4 shows the relationship between life expectancy at birth and GDP per capita for 185 countries in 2009. There is a clear tendency for life expectancy to increase as GDP per capita increases. For instance, for countries with real GDP per capita of about $5,000, life expectancy is 67 years, but it rises to 74 years as real GDP per capita increases to $15,000. As real GDP per capita increases by another $10,000, to $25,000, life expectancy increases only to 77. So, life expectancy increases at a decreasing rate with real GDP per capita. The higher real GDP per capita, the longer the average person can expect to live.

One reason that life expectancy increases as per capita real GDP increases is people with higher incomes have more money to spend on health care and on more nutritious food. In addition, they have more leisure time to devote to exercising.

As real GDP per capita increases, all of the following typically happen: Leisure time increases, people report that they are happier, life expectancy increases, and the income for the lowest-income members of society increases. While real GDP per capita may not be a perfect measure of the standard of living, it is a useful measure. There is good reason to believe that increases in real GDP per capita increase not just the goods and services that the typical person can purchase, but also increase the typical person's overall level of well-being.

Our next task is to develop a model to explain differences in real GDP per capita across time and across countries.

The Solow Growth Model

5.2 Learning Objective

Use the Solow growth model to explain the effect of capital accumulation on labor productivity.

Labor productivity is the key determinant of real GDP per capita and, therefore, of the standard of living in a country. In Chapter 4, we saw that capital accumulation and changes in total factor productivity (TFP) are the primary determinants of changes in labor productivity. So, if we want to understand why the standard of living increases over time, we need to understand capital accumulation and the determinants of total factor productivity. In this section, we use the *Solow growth model* to explain how capital accumulation

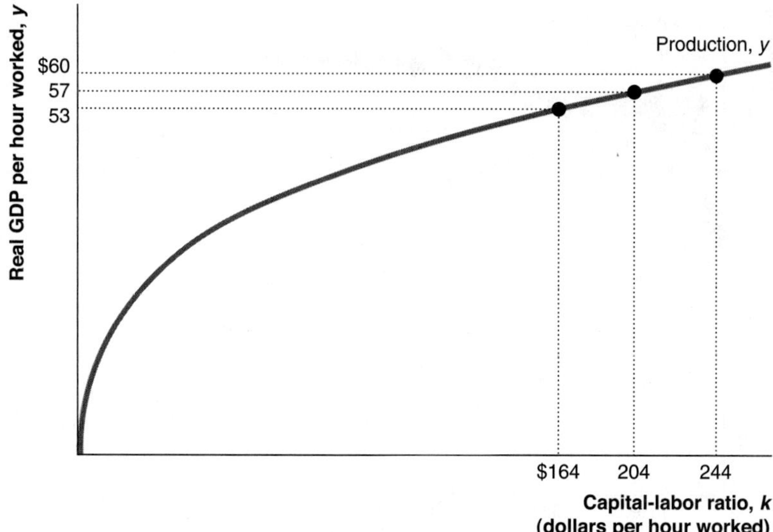

Figure 5.5

The Aggregate Production Function for the United States, 2009

The capital–labor ratio for the United States was $164 per hour in 2009, and real GDP per hour worked was $53. If the capital–labor ratio increases to $204 per hour, labor productivity increases to $57, so $40 per hour more of capital per hour worked increases output by $4 per hour. If the capital–labor ratio increases again by $40, to $244 per hour, labor productivity increases by only $3 per hour to $60 per hour. The extra real GDP from an additional $40 of capital per hour worked decreases due to diminishing marginal returns. ●

affects labor productivity when total factor productivity is constant. Developed by Nobel Laureate Robert Solow of the Massachusetts Institute of Technology during the 1950s, this model has become the foundation for how economists think about economic growth.[7]

The model begins with the aggregate production function for real GDP per hour worked that we introduced on page 123 of Chapter 4, where y is real GDP per hour worked and k is capital per hour worked, or the capital–labor ratio:

$$y = Ak^{\frac{1}{3}}, \tag{5.2}$$

where A is total factor productivity and capital's share of income is one-third. Figure 5.5 shows the aggregate production function for the United States in 2009. Measured in 2005 dollars, the capital–labor ratio for the United States was $164 per hour worked in 2009, total factor productivity was 9.6, and real GDP per hour worked was $53. The production function shows what happens to labor productivity as the capital–labor ratio increases while keeping total factor productivity constant. If the capital–labor ratio increases to $204 per hour, labor productivity increases to $57, so $40 per hour more of capital per hour worked increases output by $4 per hour. If the capital–labor ratio increases again by $40, to $244 per hour, labor productivity increases by only $3 per hour to $60 per hour. Real GDP per hour increases at a decreasing rate as the capital–labor ratio increases, which indicates that the marginal product of capital is decreasing. The marginal product of capital decreases when total factor productivity is constant—that is, when moving along a given production function, as in Figure 5.5—due to diminishing marginal returns. Eventually, the contribution of capital accumulation to labor productivity growth becomes zero, which means that adding more machines, computers, and factories will not produce any additional increases in real GDP per hour worked. Because capital experiences diminishing marginal returns, the sustained increases in labor productivity and the standard of living that the United States and other countries have experienced must be due more to increases in total factor productivity than to capital accumulation. We will return to this issue in Section 5.3.

[7]Robert Solow, "A Contribution to the Theory of Economic Growth," *Quarterly Journal of Economics*, Vol. 70, No. 1, February 1956, pp. 65–94.

Capital Accumulation

Labor productivity is the critical determinant of the standard of living, and we saw in Chapter 4 that capital accumulation is one determinant of labor productivity. So, our next step in building the Solow growth model is to explain capital accumulation.

Investment An economy accumulates capital when it increases the stock of machines, computers, buildings and other investment goods faster than it increases the number of hours worked. In other words, an economy accumulates capital when its capital–labor ratio increases. The loanable funds model from Chapter 3 told us that financial markets operate to ensure that saving equals investment. For simplicity, we assume that the economy saves a constant fraction, s, of real GDP per hour worked, y, where the value of s is between zero and one. So, if the saving rate is 10%, then s equals 0.10; if the saving rate is 20%, then s equals 0.20; and so on. (We will use "output" and "real GDP" interchangeably; note also that real GDP, output and income are all equal.) Because saving and investment are equal, investment per hour worked, i, equals:

$$i = sy. \tag{5.3}$$

Investment in the United States averages about 20% real GDP, so:

$$i = 0.20y.$$

Remember that we are assuming the Cobb-Douglas production function:

$$y = Ak^{\frac{1}{3}},$$

so, substituting, the *investment function* is:

$$i = s\left(Ak^{\frac{1}{3}}\right),$$

which for the United States is:

$$i = (0.20)\left(9.6k^{\frac{1}{3}}\right) = 1.9k^{\frac{1}{3}}.$$

Figure 5.6 plots the values for the Cobb–Douglas production function and the investment function given above. The figure shows how investment per hour worked increases as the capital–labor ratio increases. Notice that the investment function has the same general shape as the production function. This similarity occurs because we have assumed a constant saving rate for the economy. As the capital–labor ratio increases, real GDP per hour worked also increases, which causes investment per hour worked to increase. Because of

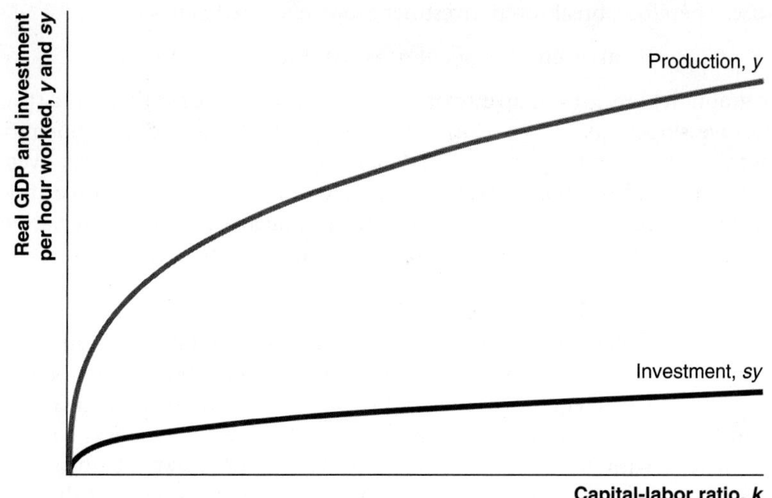

Figure 5.6

Investment per Hour Worked, Real GDP per Hour Worked, and the Capital–Labor Ratio

The production function shows that as the capital–labor ratio increases, real GDP per hour worked also increases and that causes investment per hour worked to increase. Because of diminishing marginal returns, the increase in investment per hour worked gets smaller and smaller as the capital–labor ratio increases. ●

diminishing marginal returns, increasing the capital–labor ratio causes smaller and smaller increases in real GDP per hour worked. Because investment per hour worked equals the saving rate multiplied by real GDP per hour worked, the increase in investment per hour worked also gets smaller and smaller as the capital–labor ratio increases.

Break-Even Investment *Break-even investment* is the level of investment necessary to keep the capital–labor ratio constant. When investment is greater than the break-even level, the capital–labor ratio increases; when investment is less than the break-even level, the capital–labor ratio decreases. Two factors determine the break-even level of investment. First, the capital stock *depreciates* over time. **Depreciation** refers to the reduction in the capital stock that occurs either because machinery, equipment, and other capital goods become worn out by use or because they become obsolete. For instance, a business may find its computers are obsolete if they are too slow or have too little memory to be used with new software programs. We assume that the depreciation rate, d, is a constant fraction of the capital–labor ratio and that the depreciation rate, expressed as a decimal, is between zero and one, so:

Depreciation The reduction in the capital stock that occurs either because capital goods become worn out by use or because they become obsolete.

$$\text{Depreciation} = dk.$$

Second, the capital–labor ratio can decrease when the capital stock is constant and the amount of labor increases. In this case, the capital–labor ratio decreases because the existing capital stock is spread across more labor. You can think of this as the *dilution* of the existing capital stock. We use n to represent the growth rate of the labor force. We measure n as a decimal, so its values are between zero and one. We can define dilution as:

$$\text{Dilution} = nk.$$

Therefore, we can think of break-even investment as:

$$\begin{aligned}\text{Break-even investment} &= \text{Depreciation} + \text{Dilution} \\ &= dk + nk = (d + n)k.\end{aligned} \tag{5.4}$$

Notice that break-even investment is a constant fraction of the capital–labor ratio, so at higher levels of the capital–labor ratio, the break-even investment is higher. For the United States, the growth rate of labor hours averaged 1.0%, or 0.01, per year from 1949 to 2009. The depreciation rate depends on the type of capital good. For example, while buildings can last decades, computers may be useful for only a few years, so computers depreciate much more quickly than buildings. A depreciation rate of 10%, or 0.10, is a common value to use. Therefore, break-even investment for the United States is:

$$\text{Break-even investment} = (0.10 + 0.01)k = 0.11k.$$

When we graph the break-even investment line in Figure 5.7, we see that it is a straight line with a positive slope equal to $(d + n)$. At higher levels of the capital–labor ratio, more investment is required to keep the capital–labor ratio constant, so the break-even level of investment is also higher. An increase in either the depreciation or labor force growth rates leads to a steeper break-even investment line, while a decrease in the depreciation rate or labor force growth rate leads to a flatter break-even investment line.

Equilibrium and the Steady State

Equilibrium in the Solow growth model occurs when the capital–labor ratio is constant. Economists call this equilibrium a *steady state*. In a **steady state** in the Solow growth model, the economy is in equilibrium with the capital–labor ratio and real GDP per hour worked constant but with capital, labor, and real GDP growing. One way to think about this steady state is with an analogy to a bathtub. Figure 5.8 shows a bathtub with water flowing into the tub through the faucet, and water flowing out through the drain. The level of water is a stock variable because we measure it *at a point* in time, while the water flowing

Steady state An equilibrium in the Solow growth model in which the capital–labor ratio and real GDP per hour worked are constant but capital, labor, and output are growing.

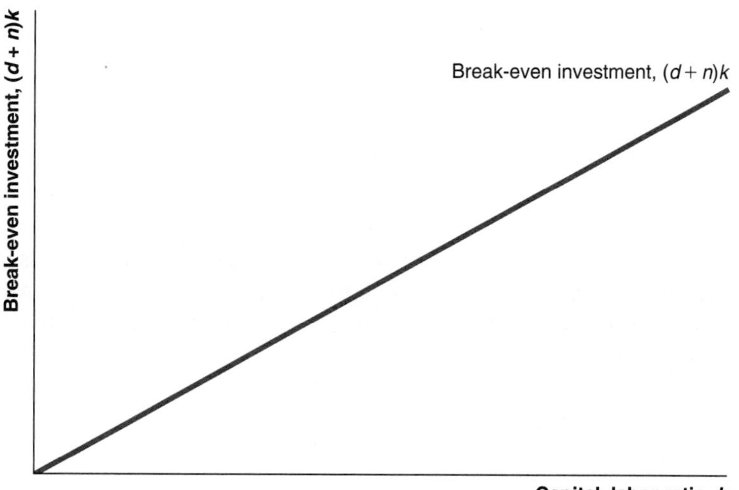

Figure 5.7

Break-Even Investment and the Capital–Labor Ratio

The break-even investment line has a slope equal to the sum of the depreciation rate and the labor force growth rate. At higher levels of the capital–labor ratio, more investment is required to keep the capital–labor ratio constant, so the break-even level of investment is also higher. An increase in the depreciation or labor force growth rates leads to a steeper break-even investment line, while a decrease in the depreciation or labor force growth rates leads to a flatter break-even investment line. ●

into and out of the tub are flow variables that are measured *per time period*. The level of the water in the tub is constant when the water flowing into the tub is exactly equal to the water flowing out of the tub. The level of water in the tub increases when the water flowing into the tub is greater than the water flowing out of the tub and decreases when the water flowing out of the tub is greater than the water flowing into the tub.

For the level of water in the tub to remain constant, the water flowing into the tub must equal the water flowing out of the tub. Think of this as the equilibrium for the bathtub. In terms of the Solow growth model, the level of water is the capital–labor ratio, so equilibrium occurs when the capital–labor ratio is constant. Investment is water flowing into the tub, and the sum of depreciation plus dilution is the water flowing out of the tub. The steady state is the long-run equilibrium, so an economy not at the steady state will gradually move toward it, as we explain later. To find the steady state capital–labor ratio, we first need to find an equation for the change in the capital–labor ratio. The change in the capital–labor ratio equals investment minus the sum of depreciation plus dilution, or break-even investment:

$$\text{Change in level of water} = \text{Water flowing in} - \text{Water flowing out}$$

$$\text{Change in capital–labor ratio} = \text{Investment} - \text{Depreciation plus dilution (or, break-even investment)}$$

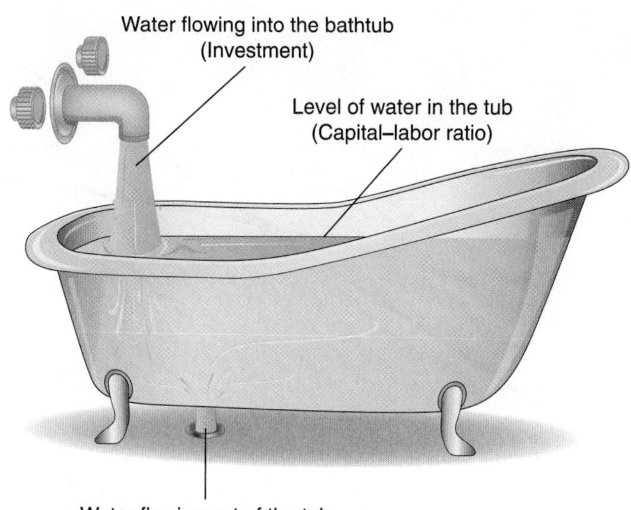

Figure 5.8

Steady State and the Bathtub Analogy

Investment per hour worked is like the water flowing into a bathtub, and depreciation plus dilution (break-even investment) is like the water flowing out of the tub. The level of water in the tub is the capital–labor ratio. When the level of water is constant, the tub is in a steady state. ●

We can express the relationship for a change in the capital-labor ratio as:

$$\Delta k = i - (d + n)k.$$

If we substitute the expressions for investment per hour worked and the production function into the equation above, we get:

$$\Delta k = sy - (d + n)k = s\left(Ak^{\frac{1}{3}}\right) - (d + n)k. \tag{5.5}$$

Equation (5.5) is the key equation for the Solow growth model because it tells us how the capital–labor ratio changes over time and allows us to determine equilibrium. We know that in the steady state, $\Delta k = 0$. Substituting into Equation (5.5), we can solve for the steady-state capital–labor ratio k^* as:

$$k^* = \left[\frac{sA}{d + n}\right]^{\frac{3}{2}}. \tag{5.6}$$

Using the aggregate production function, the steady-state real GDP per hour worked is:

$$y^* = A^{\frac{3}{2}}\left[\frac{s}{d + n}\right]^{\frac{1}{2}}. \tag{5.7}$$

For the United States, the formula for the steady-state values is:

$$k^* = \left[\frac{0.20A}{0.11}\right]^{\frac{3}{2}} = 2.5A^{\frac{3}{2}},$$

and:

$$y^* = 1.3A^{\frac{3}{2}}.$$

Figure 5.9 shows both the investment and break-even investment lines. In the steady state, the capital–labor ratio is constant, so the change in the capital–labor ratio is zero. The steady state occurs where the investment line intersects the break-even investment line, because at this point, investment equals the sum of depreciation plus dilution. If the

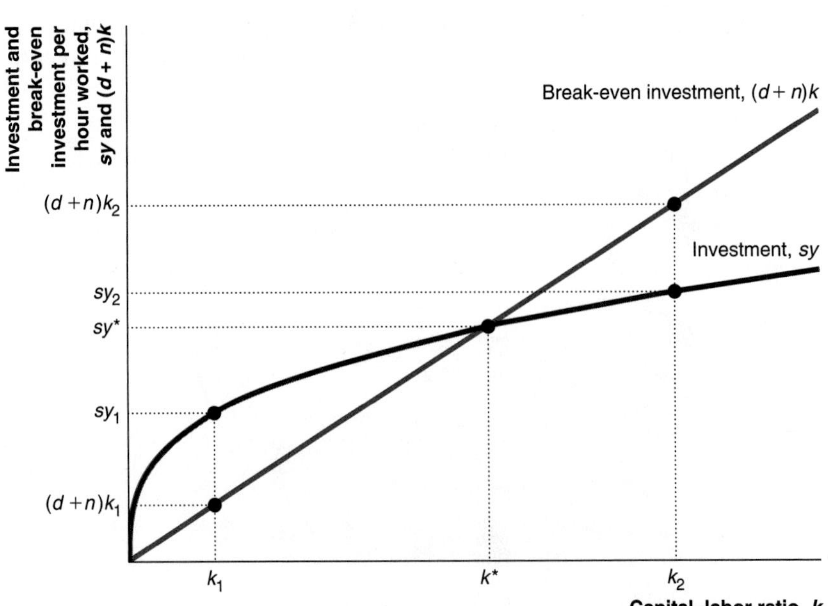

Figure 5.9

Equilibrium in the Solow Growth Model

In the steady state, the capital–labor ratio is constant, so the change in the capital–labor ratio is zero. The steady state occurs where the investment line intersects the break-even investment line. If the capital–labor ratio is below the steady-state value, investment per hour worked, sy_1, is greater than break-even investment, so the capital–labor ratio increases toward the steady-state capital–labor ratio, k^*. If the capital–labor ratio is above the steady-state value, investment per hour worked, sy_2, is less than break-even investment, so the capital–labor ratio decreases toward the steady-state capital–labor ratio, k^*. ●

capital–labor ratio is below the steady-state value, investment per hour worked, sy_1, is greater than break-even investment, $(d + n)k_1$, so $\Delta k > 0$, and the capital–labor ratio increases toward the steady-state capital–labor ratio, k^*. If the capital–labor ratio is above the steady-state value, investment per hour worked, sy_2, is less than break-even investment, $(d + n)k_2$, so $\Delta k < 0$, and the capital–labor ratio decreases toward the steady-state capital–labor ratio, k^*.

The steady state is stable because there is an automatic tendency for the economy to move toward the equilibrium. For example, suppose that the initial capital–labor ratio is k_1 in Figure 5.9. At that ratio, the level of investment, sy_1, is greater than the break-even level of investment, $(d + n)k_1$. According to Equation (5.5), $\Delta k > 0$, and the capital–labor ratio increases toward the steady-state capital–labor ratio, k^*. The increase in the capital–labor ratio is the vertical distance between the investment and break-even investment lines. Notice that this vertical distance decreases as the capital–labor ratio increases. Why does this happen? As the economy accumulates more capital goods per hour worked, capital goods become less productive because of diminishing marginal returns. As a result, the extra output and investment that the economy receives from additional capital decreases as the economy accumulates more capital. The increase in the capital–labor ratio continues until $\Delta k = 0$, which occurs when the capital–labor ratio equals k^*.

Now suppose that the initial capital–labor ratio is k_2 in Figure 5.9. At that capital–labor ratio, the level of investment, sy_2, is less than the break-even level of investment, $(d + n)k_2$. According to Equation (5.5), $\Delta k < 0$, and the capital–labor ratio decreases toward the steady-state capital–labor ratio, k^*. The decrease in the capital–labor ratio is the vertical distance between the investment and break-even investment lines. The decrease in the capital–labor ratio continues until $\Delta k = 0$, and that occurs when the capital–labor ratio equals k^*. So, the steady state is the equilibrium for the economy. We will come back to this point in Section 5.3.

The Saving Rate and Real GDP per Hour Worked

Now that we have an equilibrium model for the capital–labor ratio and real GDP per hour worked, we can ask what causes the equilibrium to change. Figure 5.10 shows what happens when the saving rate increases from s_1 to s_2, thereby increasing investment.

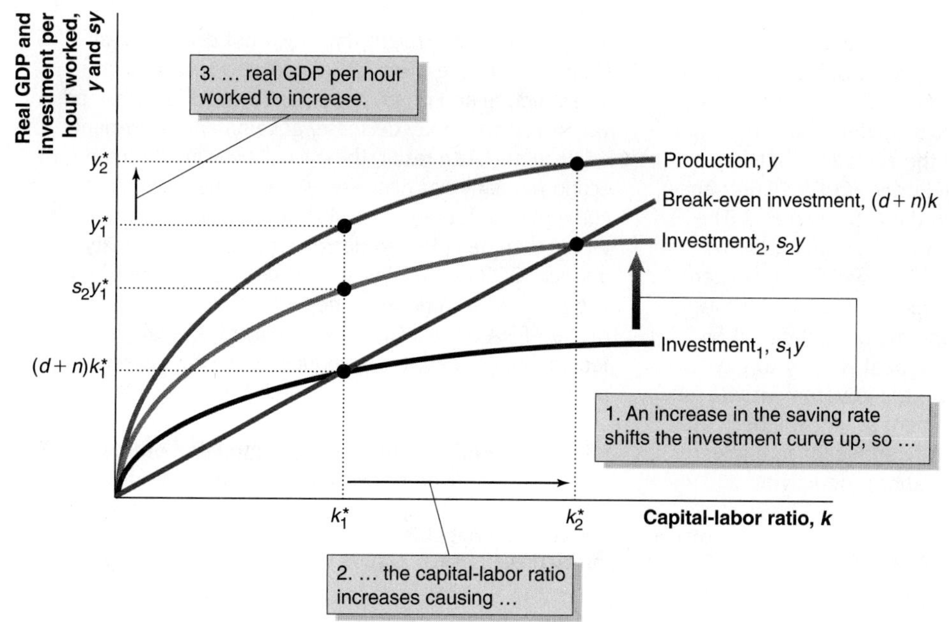

Figure 5.10

An Increase in the Saving Rate

An increase in the saving rate from s_1 to s_2 shifts the investment curve up, from Investment$_1$ to Investment$_2$, so the level of investment is now greater than the break-even level of investment. As a result, the capital–labor ratio increases from the original steady-state value, k_1^*, to the new steady-state value, k_2^*, and real GDP per hour worked increases from y_1^*, to y_2^*. ●

MACRO DATA: WHAT ARE THE LONG-RUN EFFECTS OF GOVERNMENT BUDGET DEFIICTS?

We saw in Chapter 3 that the supply of loanable funds to the domestic economy is the sum of private, government, and foreign saving. When the government runs a budget deficit, government saving decreases so national saving decreases as well. In the Solow growth model, we would represent this change as a decrease in the saving rate:

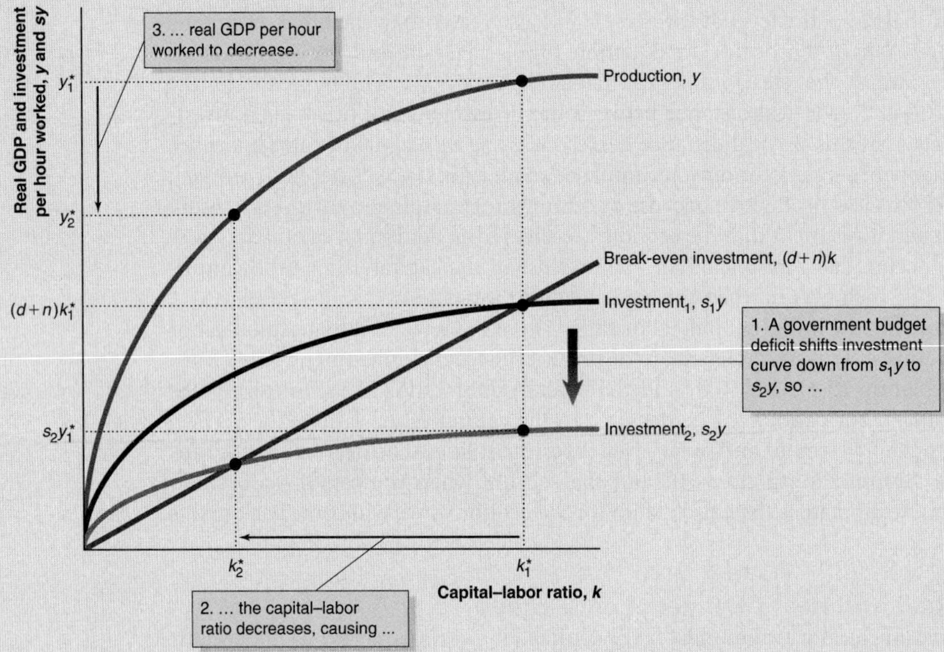

The above graph shows the long-run cost of government budget deficits: a lower capital-labor ratio, which leads to lower labor productivity and a lower standard of living. However, budget deficits do have short-run benefits, which we discuss in Chapters 9 and 11.

What does our analysis imply about the American Recovery and Reinvestment Act (ARRA) that Congress passed and President Obama signed into law in February 2009? At the time the act was debated in Congress, the Congressional Budget Office (CBO) analyzed the effect of the act on the U.S. economy. The CBO estimated that the act will *reduce* real GDP by between 0.0% and 0.2% in 2019, which is consistent with the above graph.[8] Why did the CBO reach this estimate? The act will increase the budget deficit by $814 billion, which the government is likely to pay for by borrowing. In other words, the government will run a budget deficit, and government saving will decrease, which decreases the saving rate and leads to a lower capital-labor ratio and lower labor productivity.

While the findings of the CBO are consistent with the above graph, it is important to note that the CBO estimates only a small decrease in real GDP. In fact, the CBO believes the ARRA may not decrease real GDP at all in the future. Why might the ARRA not decrease real GDP in the future? The ARRA increased spending on infrastructure and other investment projects, so while private investment may decrease, government investment will increase. As a result, the overall investment rate in the economy many not decrease much, so the investment curve may shift down only slightly, if at all. The end result would then be either no decrease in labor productivity and real GDP or a relatively small decrease. There is not yet a consensus among economists about the net effect of the ARRA on real GDP. The key point, though, is that a federal budget deficit may reduce real GDP, depending on how the federal government spends the funds it borrows.

Test your understanding by doing related problem 2.9 on page 178 at the end of this chapter.

[8]"Estimated Macroeconomic Impacts of the American Recovery and Reinvestment Act of 2009." Letter from Douglas Elmendorf, Director of the Congressional Budget Office, to Senator Charles E. Grassley (Iowa), March 2, 2009 www.cbo.gov/ftpdocs/100xx/doc10008/03-02-Macro_Effects_of_ARRA.pdf.

First, the investment curve shifts upward, from s_1y to s_2y, so the economy is now producing more investment goods for any given level of the capital–labor ratio. The level of investment is now greater than the break-even level of investment. As a result, the capital–labor ratio begins to rise from the original steady-state value of k_1^* to the new steady-state value of k_2^*, and real GDP per hour worked increases from y_1^* to y_2^*. An increase in the saving rate increases the steady-state level of real GDP per hour worked but does not affect the steady-state growth rate. Therefore, policies that change the saving rate have a *level effect.* Policies that change the steady-state growth rate of real GDP per hour worked have a *growth effect.* We discuss policies that are intended to increase economic growth in Section 5.3.

Depreciation, the Labor Force Growth Rate, and Real GDP per Hour Worked

Figure 5.11 shows what happens when the depreciation rate decreases. The break-even investment line flattens, and the capital–labor ratio increases. The level of investment is now greater than the break-even level of investment. As a result, the capital–labor ratio begins to rise from the original steady-state value of k_1^* to the new steady-state value of k_2^*. Because the capital–labor ratio is one of the inputs of the production function, the higher capital–labor ratio increases real GDP per hour worked. Therefore, the Solow growth model predicts that a lower depreciation rate will lead to higher productivity and a higher standard of living.

Notice that the growth rate of the labor force and the depreciation rate both affect the slope of the break-even investment line in the same way: A decrease in the labor force growth rate will have exactly the same effect on the standard of living as a decrease in the depreciation rate. Therefore, the Solow growth model predicts that a lower labor force growth rate will lead to higher productivity and a higher standard of living.

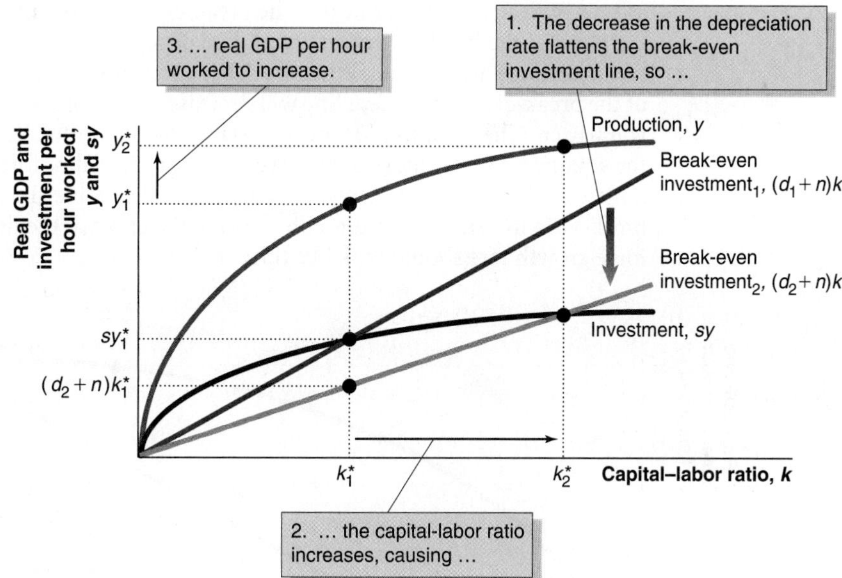

Figure 5.11 A Decrease in the Depreciation Rate

A decrease in the depreciation rate flattens the break-even investment line and the capital–labor ratio increases because the level of investment is now greater than the break-even level of investment. As a result, the capital–labor ratio begins to rise from the original steady-state value of k_1^* to the new steady-state value of k_2^*. Because the capital–labor ratio is one of the inputs of the production function, the higher capital–labor ratio increases real GDP per hour worked. ●

Solved Problem 5.2

A Decrease in the Labor Force Growth Rate and Real GDP per Hour Worked

According to the United Nations' Population Division, the world's population growth rate averaged 1.7% per year between 1950 and 2005. The following table shows the Population Division's forecasts for the population growth rates for different regions in the world:

In every region, the forecast is for slower population growth. The slower population growth should reduce the growth rate of the labor force. What effect will this reduction have on labor productivity and the standard of living in the world?

Period	Africa	Asia	Europe	North America	South America	World
1950–2005	2.6	1.9	0.5	2.2	1.2	1.7
2005–2050	1.7	0.6	−0.1	0.6	0.6	0.8
Change in the population growth rate	−0.9%	−1.3%	−0.6%	−1.6%	−0.6%	−0.9%

Sources: United Nations, Population Division; and calculations based on the median variant forecast.

Solving the Problem

Step 1 **Review the chapter material.** The problem asks you to determine the effect of a decrease in the labor force growth rate on labor productivity and the standard of living, so you may want to review the section "Depreciation, Labor Force Growth Rate, and Real GDP per Hour Worked," which begins on page 159.

Step 2 **Use a graph to determine the effects of a decrease in the labor force growth rate in the Solow model.** The Solow growth model consists of three curves: (1) the aggregate production function, (2) the investment curve, and (3) the break-even investment line. To determine the effect of a decrease in the labor force growth rate, we must determine which, if any, of these curves the labor force growth rate affects. In Section 5.2, we saw that the break-even investment line is $(n + d)k$, so the slope of the break-even investment line depends on the depreciation rate and the labor force growth rate. When the labor force growth rate decreases, the slope of the break-even investment line will decreases so the break-even investment line will flatten. The equation for the aggregate production function is $y = Ak^{\frac{1}{3}}$, and the equation for the investment curve is $i = sy$. The labor force growth rate does not affect either of these curves. Therefore, the labor force growth rate affects only break-even investment. Your graph showing the effect of the decrease in the labor force growth rate should look like this:

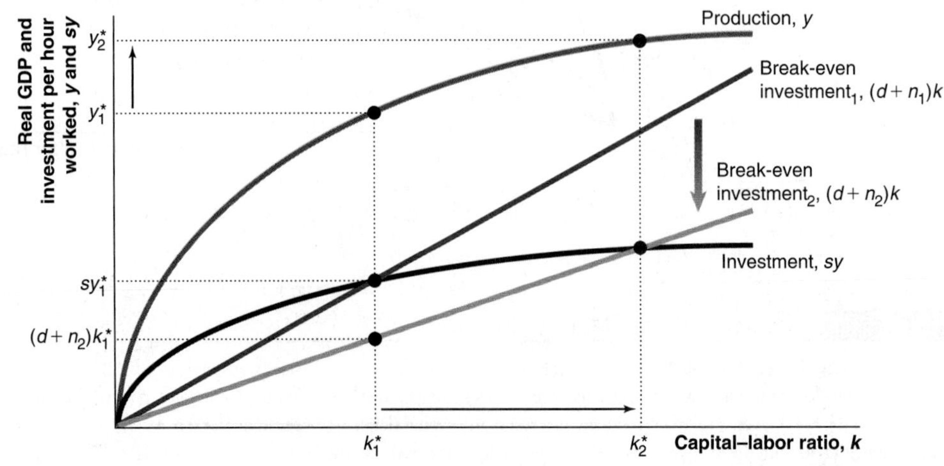

Step 3 Determine the effect on the capital–labor ratio. The break-even investment line flattens, so at the initial capital–labor ratio, k_1^*, the level of investment, sy_1^* is now greater than the new level of break-even investment, $(d + n_2)k_1^*$. Equation (5.5) tells us how the capital–labor ratio changes over time. Using that equation and what we know about the initial levels of investment and break-even investment:

$$\Delta k = sy_1^* - (d + n_2)k_1^* > 0.$$

As a result, the capital–labor ratio begins to increase toward the new steady-state capital–labor ratio, k_2^*. The change in the capital–labor ratio is the vertical distance between the investment curve and the break-even investment line. The vertical distance gets smaller as the capital–labor ratio increases due to diminishing marginal returns, so the increase in the capital–labor ratio gets smaller and smaller as the economy approaches the new steady state. Growth stops when the economy reaches the new steady state where the new capital-labor ratio is k_2^*. The steady-state level of labor productivity has increased from y_1^* to y_2^*.

Step 4 Determine the effect of the capital–labor ratio on the standard of living. Economists use real GDP per capita to measure the standard of living, and Equation (5.1) tells us that real GDP per capita equals labor productivity multiplied by annual hours worked per person. If hours worked per person remains constant, the increase in labor productivity from y_1^* to y_2^* will increase the standard of living. The ultimate effect of the decrease in the population growth rate is to increase the standard of living for the average person.

The United Nations predicts that the population growth rate will decrease during the 2005–2050 period for all regions of the world. However, the table at the beginning of this Solved Problem shows that the decrease in the population growth rate will vary across regions of the world. The largest decrease in the population growth rate is expected to occur in North America, so, all else being equal, you should expect that the increases in labor productivity and in the standard of living that result from slower labor force growth rates will be highest in North America.

For more practice, do related problem 2.8 on page 178 at the end of this chapter.

Table 5.2 summarizes how changes in the Solow growth model change the steady-state real GDP per hour worked. Increases in the investment rate and total factor productivity lead to higher real GDP per hour worked in the steady state, while increases in the depreciation rate and the growth rate of the labor force lead to lower real GDP per hour worked in the steady state.

Table 5.2 Summary of Changes in the Steady State

An increase in ...	will ...	causing the capital–labor ratio to ...	and the real GDP per hour worked to ...
the investment rate	shift up the investment curve	increase	increase.
the level of total factor productivity	shift up the investment curve	increase	increase.
the depreciation rate	make the break-even investment line steeper	decrease	decrease.
the labor force growth rate	make the break-even investment line steeper	decrease	decrease.

5.3

Learning Objective

Explain how total factor productivity affects labor productivity.

Total Factor Productivity and Labor Productivity

Total factor productivity growth and capital accumulation are the two sources of increases in labor productivity. We have seen that increases in labor productivity from capital accumulation eventually decrease to zero due to diminishing marginal returns. As a consequence, increases in total factor productivity are the ultimate source of sustained increases in labor productivity growth and, therefore, of increases in the standard of living.

Total Factor Productivity and Real GDP per Hour Worked

Figure 5.12 shows the effect of an increase in total factor productivity for the United States in 2009, assuming that the capital–labor ratio equals \$164 per hour. Total factor productivity is initially 9.6, so real GDP per hour worked is \$53, and the economy is at point *A* in Figure 5.12. If the capital–labor ratio remains constant and total factor productivity increases by 1 point, to 10.6, the production function shifts up, with the economy now at point *B* and real GDP per hour worked at \$58. In this example, an increase in total factor productivity has a similar effect to an increase in the investment rate. But there is an important difference: The marginal product of capital decreases as the economy accumulates more capital, holding all else constant, but the extra output from increasing total factor productivity does not. If total factor productivity increases by another point, to 11.6, the economy moves to point *C*, and real GDP per hour worked increases to \$63. Therefore, each time total factor productivity increases by 1 point, real GDP per hour worked increases by about \$5. Unlike with capital goods, there are no diminishing marginal returns to total factor productivity. Therefore, there is no limit to growth from increases in total factor productivity, and total factor productivity growth must be the explanation for increases in labor productivity and the standard of living.

New technology is one source of higher total factor productivity. Suppose that a new technology is discovered that increases the processing power of computers, and total factor productivity increases from 9.6 to 10.6. The production function will shift upward, and real GDP per hour worked will increase. Similarly, suppose that if a second technology is discovered that reduces congestion on the Internet, the productivity of all existing computers will increase, so total factor productivity will increase from 10.6 to 11.6. The production function shifts upward again, and real GDP per hour worked increases again.

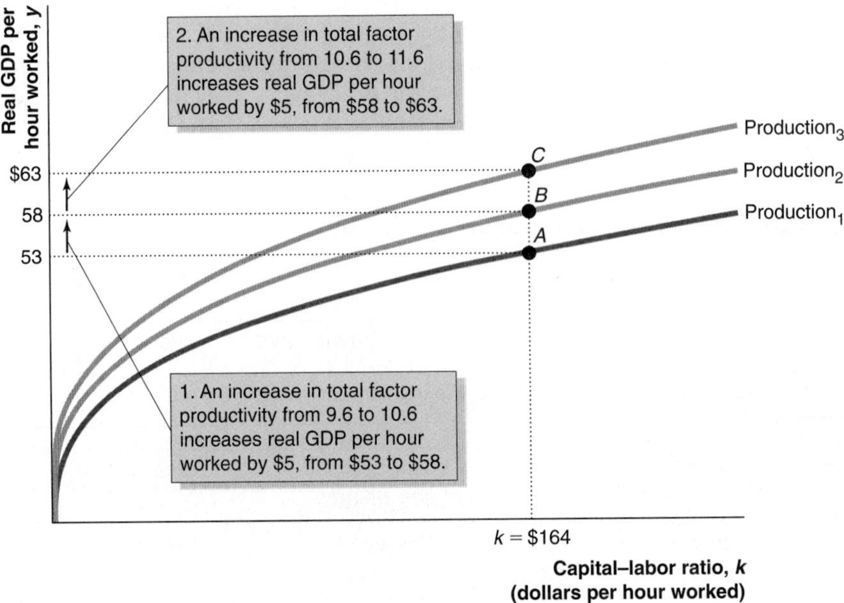

Figure 5.12

An Increase in Total Factor Productivity for the United States, 2009

For the United States in 2009, total factor productivity is initially 9.6, and the capital–labor ratio is \$164 per hour, so real GDP per hour worked is \$53, and the economy is at point *A*. If total factor productivity increases by 1 point, to 10.6, the production function shifts up, and the economy is now at point *B*. If total factor productivity increases by another point, to 11.6, the economy moves to point *C*. Every time total factor productivity increases by 1, real GDP per hour worked increases by about \$5. ●

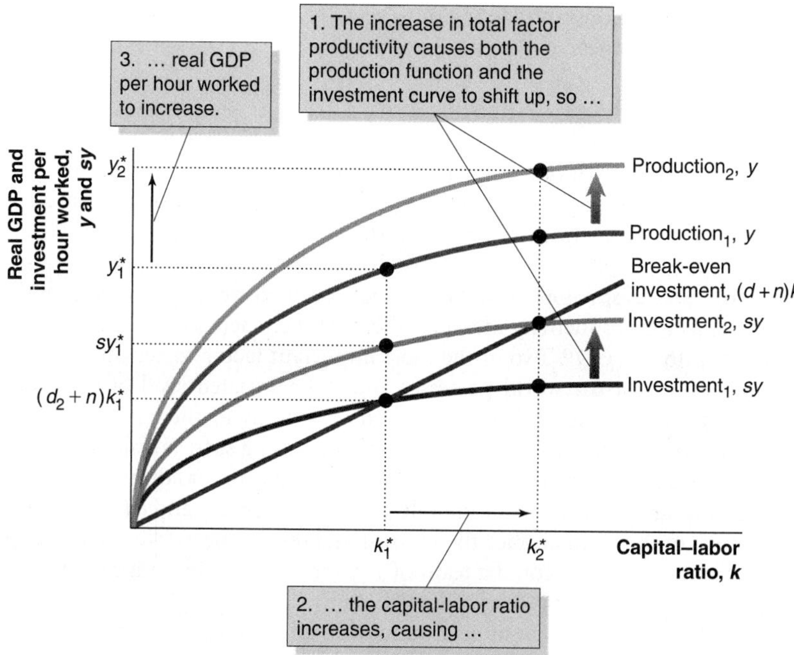
1. The increase in total factor productivity causes both the production function and the investment curve to shift up, so ...
3. ... real GDP per hour worked to increase.
2. ... the capital-labor ratio increases, causing ...
Real GDP and investment per hour worked, y and sy
y_2^*
y_1^*
sy_1^*
$(d_2 + n)k_1^*$
Production$_2$, y
Production$_1$, y
Break-even investment, $(d + n)k$
Investment$_2$, sy
Investment$_1$, sy
k_1^*
k_2^*
Capital–labor ratio, k

Figure 5.13

A One-Time Increase in Total Factor Productivity

The one-time increase in total factor productivity shifts the production function from Production$_1$ to Production$_2$. At the initial capital–labor ratio, investment is now greater than break-even investment, so the capital–labor ratio increases, causing real GDP per hour worked to increase. ●

Figure 5.13 shows that a one-time increase in total factor productivity shifts the production function from Production$_1$ to Production$_2$. At the initial capital–labor ratio, investment is now greater than the break-even level of investment, so the capital–labor ratio increases, causing real GDP per hour worked to increase.

In fact, the growth rate of total factor productivity, g_A, is the key determinant for labor productivity growth and the growth rate of the standard of living, assuming that hours worked per person are constant.

Table 5.3 shows the steady-state growth rates for the capital–labor ratio and real GDP per hour worked. (Appendix B at the end of the chapter shows how to derive the steady-state growth rates.) For the United States, capital's share of income is one-third, total factor productivity growth has averaged 0.014, or 1.4%, per year, and the growth rate of labor hours, n, averaged 0.011, or 1.1%, per year. So, for the United States:

$$g_k = g_y = 1.5(1.4) = 2.1\% \text{ per year},$$

and:

$$g_K = g_Y = 1.5(1.4) + 1.1 = 3.2\%, \text{ per year}.$$

Labor productivity increases by about 2.1% per year, and if hours worked per capita are constant, real GDP per capita also grows at about 2.1% per year. Similarly, when hours

Table 5.3 Steady-State Growth Rates

Variable	Symbol	Steady-State Growth Rate
Capital–labor ratio	$k = \frac{K}{L}$	$1.5g_A$
Real GDP per hour worked	$y = \frac{Y}{L}$	$1.5g_A$
Capital stock	$K = k \times L$	$1.5g_A + n$
Real GDP	$Y = y \times L$	$1.5g_A + n$

worked per person are constant, labor hours grow at about 1.1% per year, so real GDP grows at about 3.2% per year.

What Explains Total Factor Productivity?

Now that we know that total factor productivity growth is the key factor in labor productivity growth and the growth rate of the standard of living, we need to determine why TFP increases over time. Although no single theory has emerged, economists have identified several important factors, which we discuss next.

Research and Development and the Level of Technology As we mentioned in Chapter 4, total factor productivity measures the overall efficiency of the economy in transforming inputs into real GDP. Two of the most important factors determining TFP are the stock of knowledge that the world possesses and the associated level of technology. The invention of computers made workers more productive by giving them new and better types of capital goods to work with. For example, word processing software allows one administrative assistant today to do work that would have taken a team of administrative assistants in 1949. Assembly-line workers in automobile plants now operate and oversee robots rather than doing much of the manual labor themselves. As a result, one worker today can produce many more automobiles than could a team of workers in 1949. In both examples, the new capital goods have made labor more productive.

New capital goods do not just appear out of thin air. Private firms and the government devote a significant amount of resources to research and development (R&D) activities to come up with ideas for new capital goods or new consumption goods. The United States spent about $405 billion on R&D in 2011, with the private sector responsible for about 72% and the government responsible for about 28%.[9]

Making the Connection

Research and Development Expenditures and Labor Productivity Differences Between China and the United States

China's population and its labor force are much larger than the U.S. population and labor force. However, U.S. real GDP per capita is larger than China's. Because of its higher labor productivity, the United States is able to maintain a higher standard of living than China. A key reason labor productivity is higher in the United States is because it devotes more resources than does China to developing new technology and accumulating human capital. For example, in 2011, the United States devoted 2.7% of GDP to research and development, while China devoted just 1.4%. And, as recently as 1996, China devoted just 0.6% of GDP to research and development. The higher level of investment in new technology in the United States helps increase knowledge and total factor productivity, so U.S. workers are more productive. Why doesn't the Chinese government do more to encourage private businesses to devote more resources to spending on research and development? Despite the strides China has made toward liberalizing its economy since the 1970s, the Heritage Foundation's *2011 Index of Economic Freedom* ranked China only 135th out of 179 countries in economic freedom. This index is used to evaluate countries on the basis of 10 criteria, including property rights, business and investment freedom, and freedom from corruption. China scores low because the Chinese Communist Party maintains tight controls on political expression and economic decision-making. The government decides

[9]Battelle, *2011 Global R&D Funding Forecast*, December 2010.

which businesses receive access to loans based on political, as well as economic, criteria, and efforts to enact economic reforms have stalled in recent years.

Although a number of foreign companies, such as BP, Exxon, General Motors, and Alcoa, have invested heavily in China, the Chinese government has not allowed the companies to exercise full control of their operations, despite the capital, technology, and management skills the companies bring with them.

China has been successful in weaning manufacturing industries away from government control. Private firms produce about two-thirds of the country's manufacturing output. But state-owned enterprises still control much of the banking, telecommunications, and energy industries. Even in the agricultural sector, where China has been given credit for dismantling communes and allowing farmers to raise grain prices, land remains collectively owned and leased to individual households.

China has made remarkable progress since the 1970s in moving toward greater economic liberalization, but the extent to which the government still exercises control over the economy has hindered investment in research and development. The result is that labor productivity in China remains relatively low.

Sources: The World Bank, *World Development Indicators*; Heritage Foundation, *2011 Index of Economic Freedom*, www.heritage.org/index/; "The Second Long March," *Economist*, December 11, 2008; and "Even Harder Than It Looks," *Economist*, September 16, 2010.

Test your understanding by doing related problem 3.9 on page 179 at the end of this chapter.

Quality of Labor The quality of labor, like the quality of capital goods, can change over time. Workers become more productive as they acquire *human capital.* **Human capital** is the accumulated knowledge and skills that workers acquire from education and training or from life experiences. There are two basic ways for workers to acquire human capital.

Human capital The accumulated knowledge and skills that workers acquire from education and training or from life experiences.

First, a worker can go to college for formal training to gain skills that are useful in the workplace. Students go to college to learn science, math, and other subjects that make them better workers. As students acquire new skills, their human capital increases, and they become more productive workers. Through this learning, education transforms low-skilled high school graduates into high-skilled engineers, scientists, and teachers.

Second, as Nobel Laureate Kenneth Arrow of Stanford University has argued, workers can accumulate skills through *learning by doing.*[10] Arrow noted that the more often workers perform a task, the more they learn to do the task quickly—thereby improving their productivity. Arrow cited evidence from engineering studies showing that the amount of time it takes to build an airplane decreases as workers build more airplanes. This relationship emerges because the workers have acquired knowledge and skills through building the previous airplanes, making them more productive.

Government and Social Institutions Nobel Laureate Douglass North of the Hoover Institution and Robert Paul Thomas of the University of Washington have emphasized the importance of government and social institutions in explaining differences in labor productivity and the standard of living across countries.[11] North and Thomas, along with many other economists, believe that markets and property rights are important institutions that lead to economic growth. Individuals and firms are unlikely to risk their own funds,

[10]Kenneth J. Arrow, "Economic Implications of Learning by Doing," *Review of Economic Studies*, Vol. 29, No. 3, June 1962, pp. 155–173.

[11]Douglass North and Robert Paul Thomas, *The Rise of the Western World: A New Economic History*, New York: Cambridge University Press, 1973.

and investors are unlikely to lend them funds, unless the profits from risky investment projects are safe from being seized by the government or by criminals. In other words, property rights must be secure to encourage investment and capital accumulation. In some countries, property rights are not secure, so individuals are reluctant to devote the resources required to develop new goods and services or expand existing businesses.

The case of North and South Korea provides a good example of the importance of government institutions. Japan had occupied the Korean peninsula since 1905. After Japan's surrender to the Allies at the end of World War II in 1945, Soviet troops occupied what would become North Korea, while U.S. troops occupied what would become South Korea. North Korea was a communist dictatorship without strong markets or secure property rights, while South Korea had strong markets and secure property rights. Although economic data for North Korea are unreliable because its government does not make official data available, in 2010, real GDP per capita for South Korea is estimated to have been 15 times the level in North Korea.

Economists Daron Acemoglu and Simon Johnson of Massachusetts Institute of Technology and James Robinson of the University of California at Berkeley have analyzed the effects of government and social institutions on real GDP per capita.[12] European countries colonized large regions of the world between the 1600s and the 1800s. In countries such as the United States, Australia, and New Zealand, Europeans came as settlers and established institutions that enforced the rule of law. These favorable institutions encouraged investment, which led to faster economic growth and higher real GDP per capita. In Africa and other areas, Europeans came only to extract natural resources and so did not establish government institutions that favored investment. Acemoglu, Johnson and Robinson find that the areas of the world in which the Europeans established strong property rights are generally rich today, while the regions in which Europeans did not establish strong property rights are generally poor.

The experiences of the Germany, Korea, and the former European colonies have reinforced the view of many economists that government institutions play a critical role in encouraging economic growth.

Geography Some economists argue that geography plays an important role in explaining the standard of living. In fact, as long ago as Adam Smith's 1776 book *An Inquiry into the Nature and Causes of the Wealth of Nations*, economists have pointed out that geography affects a country's potential for growth. For example, access to navigable rivers and having a coastline makes trade easier and should increase labor productivity and the standard of living. The United States has a long coastline and extensive navigable rivers, while countries such as Bolivia and Niger are landlocked and mountainous, so transportation is difficult. Jeffrey Sachs of Columbia University argues that geography plays an important role in economic growth for another reason. Sachs, along with economists Andrew Mellinger of Harvard and John Gallup of Portland State University, argues that tropical climates experience higher rates of infectious disease such as malaria.[13] Many countries that are poor today have had high rates of infectious disease, such as malaria, in the past. Infectious disease affects health especially for infants and young children, and these health problems can affect labor productivity later in life. For example, children with serious illnesses often

---

[12]Daron Acemoglu, Simon Johnson, and James Robinson, "The Colonial Origins of Comparative Development: An Empirical Investigation," *American Economic Review*, Vol. 91, No. 5, December 2001, pp. 1369–1401.

[13]Jeffrey Sachs, Andrew Mellinger, and John Gallup, "Climate, Coastal Proximity, and Development," in *Oxford Handbook of Economic Geography*. New York: Oxford University Press, 2000.

grow up to be shorter than healthy children. If someone is short due to extensive childhood illness or nutritional deficiency as a child, that person is often not as physically strong as he or she otherwise would have been. Workers who are shorter due to physical illness are often less productive in agricultural or manufacturing jobs that require strength. This adverse link may explain why agricultural productivity is lower in tropical areas, such as Burundi, Malawi, Uganda, and Zambia. Low agricultural productivity increases the likelihood of famines and has a further negative effect on health, labor productivity, and the standard of living.

Making the Connection

How Important Were the Chinese Economic Reforms of 1978?

For much of its history, China was ruled by hereditary dynasties. The last of these, the Qing Dynasty, ended in 1911, at which time the Republic of China was established. The Republic of China had difficulty extending its authority over the whole of the country. By the 1930s, the government had become involved in a civil war with the Communist Party led by Mao Zedong. The Communists eventually won the civil war and established the People's Republic of China in 1949. The government under Mao created a socialist economy based on state ownership of major industries. Without a system of secure property rights, markets in China were relatively limited and unimportant. For example, agricultural workers had to turn over their crops to the Chinese government, which then distributed the food to its citizens. The Chinese government allowed few foreign firms or individuals to purchase financial or physical assets in the country. The Chinese government launched what it called the Great Leap Forward in 1958, which forced Chinese peasants to move from their farms into cities to build roads and other infrastructure projects. This resulted in a decline in agricultural output and widespread famine. Mao Zedong started another movement, the Cultural Revolution, in 1966 to further advance socialism and rid China, often by violent means, of those who were suspected of advocating free market capitalism. After Mao's death in 1976, a power struggle resulted in Deng Xiaoping becoming the leader of the Communist Party in 1978. Under Deng's leadership, China instituted many economic reforms, including allowing private ownership of farms and businesses and the establishment of special economic zones that foreign investors could use to establish joint venture enterprises with Chinese firms. Economic research tells us that government institutions are important determinants of economic growth and the standard of living.

Figure 5.1 on page 145 shows that economic growth accelerated in China about the time the country began instituting major economic reforms. The economic reforms opened China to international trade and investment, which allowed foreign technology to flow into the country more easily and also allowed agricultural workers to sell some of their crops at markets and keep the proceeds from the sales. This reform provided agricultural workers with a financial incentive to work harder. The reforms accelerated in the 1980s and 1990s to allow a greater role for the market. The reforms that began in the 1970s allowed total factor productivity and real GDP per capita to increase rapidly in China.

Sources: Mark Williams, "Foreign Investment in China: Will the Anti-Monopoly Law Be a Barrier or a Facilitator?" *Texas International Law Journal,* Vol. 45, No. 1, Fall 2009, pp. 127–155; and "The Second Long March," *Economist*, December 11, 2008.

Test your understanding by doing related problem 3.11 on page 179 at the end of this chapter.

The Financial System The role of the financial system is to help the economy allocate resources by matching borrowers with lenders. When the financial system works well, individuals who want to borrow to finance the accumulation of physical or human capital can find lenders. To the extent that firms and the government pay for R&D with funds obtained through the financial system, a well-functioning financial system can also lead to more investment in R&D. The financial system can also affect total factor productivity by improving the efficiency of the economy. The financial system allocates funds to the individuals and firms who are willing to pay the most to obtain the funds. These individuals and firms are also those whose investment projects have the best likelihood of success. Therefore, a good financial system ensures that resources flow to their most productive uses, and total factor productivity for the economy increases. As a consequence, labor productivity and the standard of living are higher.

Research by Thorsten Beck of the World Bank, Ross Levine of the University of Minnesota, and Norman Loayza of the Central Bank of Chile has shown that the financial system has a significant effect on total factor productivity growth.[14] Interestingly, it is not just banks that matter for economic growth. Ross Levine and Sara Zervos of the World Bank have found that stock market liquidity also affects productivity and capital accumulation.[15] The more liquid a stock market, the easier it is for investors to sell stocks. Investors are more likely to purchase stocks that they know are easy to sell. As a consequence, stock prices are higher, and it is less costly for firms to issue new stock to pay for investment projects. This research tells us that the development of financial markets plays an important role in sustaining economic growth in both developed and developing economies.

5.4

Learning Objective

Explain the balanced growth path, convergence, and long-run equilibrium.

The Balanced Growth Path, Convergence, and Long-Run Equilibrium

Balanced growth A situation in which the capital–labor ratio and real GDP per hour worked grow at the same rate.

The steady state is the equilibrium for the economy; however, it is an equilibrium in which the key economic quantities such as the capital–labor ratio and real GDP per hour worked are growing. **Balanced growth** occurs when the capital–labor ratio and real GDP per hour worked grow at the same rate. The *balanced growth path* shows how real GDP per hour worked grows over time when the economy is in the steady state and experiencing balanced growth. We can think of the balanced growth path as the equilibrium time path for real GDP per hour worked. We can also think of each steady state as having its own unique balanced growth path. Understanding the equilibrium time path is critical for understanding the long-run behavior of real GDP per hour worked and real GDP.

Convergence to the Balanced Growth Path

Figure 5.1 on page 145 shows that the growth rates for most countries have been roughly constant since 1820, which suggests that most of these countries have typically been on or near their balanced growth paths. Just as the steady state is the equilibrium for the economy at a point in time, the balanced growth path is the equilibrium for the economy over time. However, some countries, such as Japan, appear to have been off their balanced growth paths for extended periods of time.

The experiences of Germany and Japan after World War II provide a good example of how an economy that is off its balanced growth path eventually converges back to that path. By the end of World War II, both Germany and Japan had experienced large decreases in

[14]Thorsten Beck, Ross Levine, and Norman Loayza, "Finance and the Sources of Growth," *Journal of Financial Economics*, Vol. 58, No. 1-2, October–November 2000, pp. 261–300.

[15]Ross Levine and Sara Zervos, "Stock Markets, Banks, and Economic Growth," *American Economic Review*, Vol. 88, No. 3, June 1998, pp. 537–558.

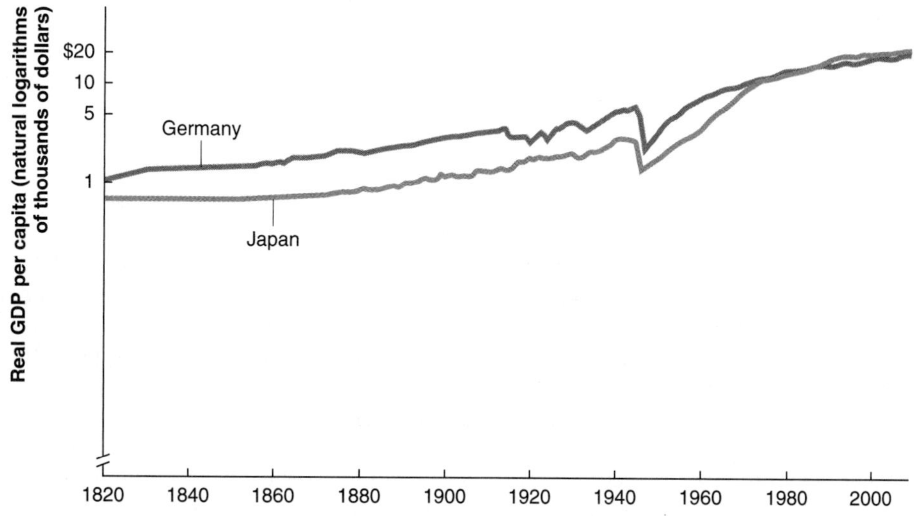

Figure 5.14

Post–World War II Convergence in Germany and Japan

Germany and Japan experienced a large decrease in real GDP per capita at the end of World War II due to destruction of their capital stock. Germany grew rapidly from the end of the war until about 1960. After 1960, Germany appears to have grown at the same rate as it did prior to the war. Japan grew rapidly from the end of the War until the mid-1970s, but it appears to have moved to a higher balanced growth path compared to the one it was on before the war.

Source: Total Economy Database, The Conference Board: http://www.conference-board.org/data/economydatabase/.

their capital–labor ratios as the United States and its allies bombed the factories, bridges, and transportation networks in both countries. Figure 5.14 shows real GDP per capita over time for both Germany and Japan. Both countries experienced a large decrease in real GDP per capita at the end of World War II, due to the destruction of their capital stock. However, after the war, both countries grew much more rapidly than they did before the war. Germany grew rapidly from the end of the war until about 1960. After 1960, Germany appears to have grown at the same rate as it did prior to the war. In fact, Germany appears to have been on the same growth path since 1960 that it was on before World War II. Japan had a similar experience. The country grew rapidly from the end of the war until the mid-1970s when it appears to have moved to a higher balanced growth path compared to the one it was on before the war. Therefore, the country's steady-state capital–labor ratio and real GDP per hour worked must have increased.

Why do countries return to the balanced growth path? We can use the Solow growth model and the experiences of Germany and Japan to explain why. Figure 5.15 shows for

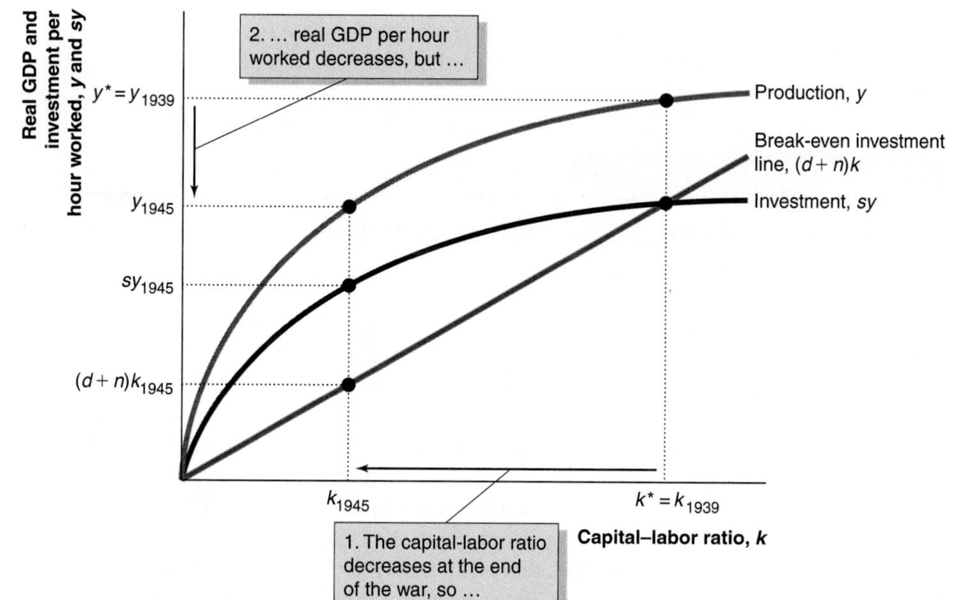

Figure 5.15

The Solow Growth Model and Post-World War II Convergence in Germany

The destruction of Germany's capital stock at the end of World War II caused the capital–labor ratio to decrease from k^* to k_{1945}, and real GDP per hour worked to decrease from y^* to y_{1945}. At that point, Germany was below its balanced growth path. Postwar Germany experienced very fast growth rates of real GDP as the country rapidly accumulated capital goods while approaching its balanced growth path.

Germany the effect of the destruction of the capital on real GDP per hour worked. Germany started off in the steady state prior to World War II, with a capital labor ratio, $k^* = k_{1939}$, and real GDP per hour worked, $y^* = y_{1939}$. Because the country was in the steady state, it was also on the balanced growth path, so according to Table 5.3 on page 163, the capital–labor ratio and real GDP per hour worked both grew at a rate of $1.5g_A$. By the end of the war, large portions of Germany's capital stock had been destoyed. As a result, the capital–labor ratio decreased from k^* to k_{1945}, and real GDP per hour worked decreased from y^* to y_{1945}. The decrease in labor productivity caused the decrease in real GDP per capita at the end of World War II that we see in Figure 5.14. After the war had ended, total factor productivity continued to grow, which caused real GDP per hour worked and real GDP per capita to grow. However, because the capital–labor ratio had fallen to k_{1945}, the German economy grew for an additional reason: It accumulated capital more quickly than it had along the balanced growth path.

At k_{1945}, the level of investment, sy_{1945}, was greater than the break-even level of investment, $(d + n)k_{1945}$, so the capital–labor ratio increased toward the steady-state value of k^*. From 1945 to 1960, the capital–labor ratio in Germany increased for two reasons. First, total factor productivity growth was positive, so the growth rate of the capital–labor ratio along the balanced growth path was positive. Second, Germany was converging from the capital–labor ratio of k_{1945} toward the steady-state capital–labor ratio of k^*. Because the growth rate of the capital–labor ratio determines the growth rate of real GDP per hour worked, the growth rate of real GDP per hour worked was also the result of balanced growth due to total factor productivity growth and growth due to the convergence of y_{1945} to y^*. In general, we can think of the growth rate of real GDP per hour worked as:

$$g_y = (\text{Balanced growth rate}) + (\text{Growth from convergence}).$$

As long as the capital–labor ratio is less than k^*, growth from convergence is positive, so the German economy was growing more rapidly than it did along the balanced growth path. Therefore, real GDP per hour worked converged toward y^*, so real GDP per capita converged toward the balanced growth path. In the very different situation where an economy starts off with a capital–labor ratio that is greater than k^*, the capital–labor ratio will decrease over time, so growth from convergence will be negative. As a result, the economy will grow more slowly than along the balanced growth path, so real GDP per worker will converge to the balanced growth path.

Figure 5.14 shows that Japan experienced a similar decrease in real GDP per capita at the end of the War and then rapid growth after the War.

Making the Connection

Will China's Standard of Living Ever Exceed that of the United States?

In 2010, GDP per capita in the United States was more than six times higher than GDP per capita in China. However, the growth rate of real GDP per capita in the United States has averaged only 1.9% per year since 1980 compared to China's average rate of 8.9% per year over the same time period. Because China's standard of living is growing more rapidly than in the United States, we could predict that China's standard of living will exceed the U.S. standard of living in the year 2038. However, for China to maintain its high rates of growth in real GDP per capita, it would have to maintain high rates of growth for total factor productivity, which is unlikely for several reasons. First, the United States invests more in activities, such as research and development, that result in new technologies and increases in total factor productivity. Second, much of China's growth is likely due to the transition from a centrally planned economy to a market economy, so China's growth rate is likely to decrease as the transition is completed. It is probably best to think of the transition to a market economy as moving China's balanced growth path higher. The high rates of growth in real GDP per capita are due to convergence to the higher growth path. As China approaches the new higher balanced growth path, we would expect China's growth rate to decrease to a more sustainable rate.

Another looming problem is demographic. Because of China's low birthrate, it will soon experience a decline in its labor force. Over the next two decades, the population of men and women between 15 and 29 years will fall by about 100 million, or about 30%. China will also experience a large increase in older workers, a group that will likely be less educated and less healthy than younger workers. Given current trends, the U.S. Census Bureau projects fewer people under age 50 in China in 2030 than today, with fewer in their 20s and early 30s and many more in their 60s and older. More ominous is that China has no national public pension system. China still has potential sources for enhancing productivity, including the migration of rural workers to more productive urban jobs and wider application of technical know-how. These factors can fuel future growth, but at some point, China's demographic problems could slow growth.

The experience of Japan in the last two decades offers a sobering lesson: Throughout the 1970s, Japan grew faster than the United States, and there was much discussion about when Japan would surpass the United States in real GDP per capita. But in the 1990s, Japan's average annual growth rate of per capita GDP was only 0.5%, well below the rate of growth of the United States, and Japan experienced a decrease in the rate of growth of total factor productivity. Although growth in Japan increased during the early 2000s, the country has never approached the growth rates of the years before 1990. Whether China will also suffer a rapid decline in growth rates remains to be seen.

Sources: Nicholas Eberstadt, "The Demographic Future," *Foreign Affairs*, Vol. 89, No. 6, November/December 2010, pp. 54–64; and Fumio Hayashi and Edward C. Prescott, "The 1990s in Japan: A Lost Decade;" www.minneapolisfed.org/research/wp/wp607.pdf.

Test your understanding by doing related problem 4.9 on page 180 at the end of this chapter.

Figure 5.16 shows what the time paths of real GDP per capita would look like for an economy initially on the balanced growth path, an economy initially below the balanced growth path, and an economy initially above the balanced growth path. If an economy is on the balanced growth path, it remains on the path until an event moves the economy off the path. When the economy is on the balanced growth path, the growth rate of real GDP

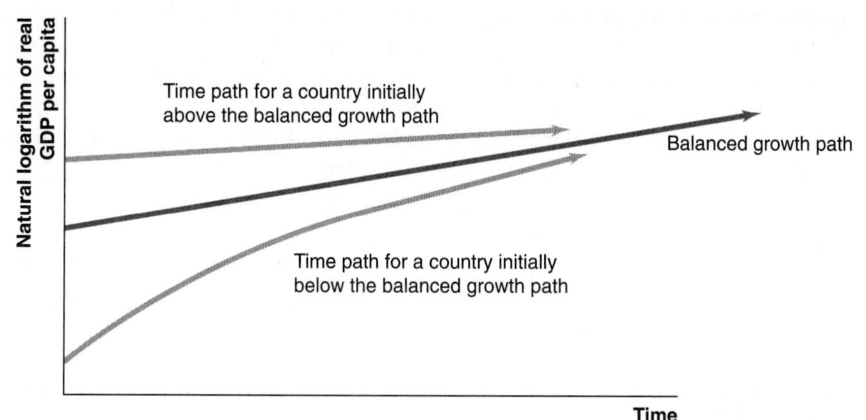

Figure 5.16

Potential Time Paths for Real GDP per Capita

If an economy is on the balanced growth path, it remains on the path until an event moves the economy off the path. If an economy starts off below the balanced growth path, the economy grows faster than it would along the balanced growth path. If an economy starts off above the balanced growth path, the economy grows more slowly than it would along the balanced growth path. ●

Table 5.4 Summary of Adjustments to the Steady State

If ...	the capital labor ratio ...	so growth from convergence is ...	and the growth rate of the economy ...
$k = k^*$	equals the steady-state value	zero	equals the balanced growth rate, and the economy remains on the balanced growth path.
$k > k^*$	is greater than the steady-state value	negative	is less than the balanced growth rate, so the economy converges to the balanced growth path.
$k < k^*$	is less than the steady-state value	positive	is greater than the balanced growth rate, so the economy converges to the balanced growth path.

per capita is determined by the growth rate of total factor productivity. If an economy starts off below the balanced growth path, growth from convergence is positive, so the economy grows faster than it would along the balanced growth path, and it eventually converges to the balanced growth path. If an economy starts off above the balanced growth path, growth from convergence is negative, so the economy grows more slowly than it would along the balanced growth path, and it eventually converges to the balanced growth path. Table 5.4 provides a summary of adjustments to the steady state.

Do All Countries Converge to the Same Balanced Growth Path?

Our discussion so far suggests that countries eventually converge to their balanced growth paths. But does this mean that all countries converge to the *same* balanced growth path and the same level of real GDP per capita'? That seems unlikely because real GDP per capita varies dramatically among countries. In 2010, real GDP per capita for the average country in the world was \$9,400. Real GDP per capita in the United States was \$47,400. The country with the lowest real GDP per capita was the Democratic Republic of the Congo, at \$300, so the average person in the United States had an income 158 times that of the average person in the Congo. Economists have spent a great deal of time and effort studying whether poor countries such as the Congo eventually converge to the same real GDP per capita as countries that are already rich such as the United States. Economists use the term *convergence* to describe the process of poor countries catching up to the real GDP per capita of rich countries.

Figure 5.1 on page 145 makes it clear that convergence does not seem to be occurring. Japan caught up to the rich Western countries during the twentieth century, and there are signs that China is catching up to rich countries now. However, many countries in sub-Saharan Africa such as the Democratic Republic of the Congo seem to have persistently low real GDP per capita over long periods of time. These regions and countries are not converging to the rich nations. Why?

The prediction of convergence comes from the Solow growth model, when all countries have the same balanced growth path. However, if the balanced growth path differs among countries due to different saving rates, labor force growth rates, or growth rates of total factor productivity, countries will not have the same balanced growth path. Instead of convergence, countries exhibit *conditional convergence*, where each country converges to its own balanced growth path. Research by N. Gregory Mankiw of Harvard University, David Romer of the University of California at Berkeley, and David Weil of Brown University shows that once you account for differences in the balanced growth path due to differences in saving rates, human capital, social institutions, and so on, countries converge at a rate of about 2% per year.[16] This rate of convergence is so slow that it will take about 35 years for a poor country to close half the gap between its current real GDP per capita and the real GDP per capita on the balanced growth path. Moreover, if low-income countries do not

[16]N. Gregory Mankiw, David Romer, and David Weil, "A Contribution to the Empirics of Economic Growth," *Quarterly Journal of Economics*, Vol. 107, No. 2, May 1992, pp. 407–437.

increase their saving rates, increase human capital, or take other measures to increase total factor productivity, the gap in real GDP per capita between high-income and low-income countries will never disappear.

Answering the Key Question

Continued from page 143

At the beginning of this chapter, we asked the question:

"Why isn't the whole world rich?"

Our discussion has shown that the growth rate of labor productivity is the key determinant of the growth rate of the standard of living. But what determines the growth rate of labor productivity? According to the Solow growth model, the growth rate of total factor productivity is *the* determinant of the growth rate of labor productivity. As a result, total factor productivity growth causes improvements in the standard of living and economic growth over the long run. We also saw that there is no single factor that causes total factor productivity to grow. The level of technology, the quality of the labor force, the quality of government and social institutions, geography, and the quality of financial institutions all play an important role in explaining differences in total factor productivity across countries. If a country fails to achieve sustained economic growth then, it is due to its failure in one or more of these areas. Therefore, while some countries are simply unlucky because of their geography, other countries are poor because of institutions that their governments are unable, or unwilling to reform.

Before moving on to Chapter 6, read *An Inside Look* on the next page for a comparison of projected economic growth rates in India and China.

Will India Catch Up With China?

THE ECONOMIST

The Fastest Lap: India's Economy Is Racing with China's

No other pair of countries invites such frequent comparison yet share so little in common. China is bigger, stronger, richer and better organised than India, the only other country with over a billion people. And yet Indians, it is fair to say, enjoy the comparisons with their northern neighbour more than the Chinese do. It was an Indian who coined the word Chindia. India relishes being in the same league as China, even if it loses most of the games.

In 2011, however, India may win a round. According to some projections, its economy may grow as fast as China's. It may even grow a little faster.

a By the conventions of Indian national accounting, next year begins on April 1st and ends on March 31st 2012. Over that period, the World Bank expects India's economy to grow by 8.7%, slightly faster than the 8.5% growth it has forecast for China over the calendar year. That is hardly the consensus view. But it is not an isolated one either. . . .

Although only a handful of economists think India's growth will outpace China's next year, a larger number believe it will do so this decade. The reasons are largely demographic. China's economy cannot go on rapidly expanding once its labour force starts shrinking. Thanks to its one-child policy, introduced in 1978, the number of young Chinese (15-29-year-olds) will fall quite sharply after 2011, depriving the country's factories of nomadic, nimble-fingered workers. Within a couple of years, Chinese youngsters will be outnumbered by their Indian peers, even though India's population will not match China's until about 2025.

b India may also outpace China this decade for the simple reason that it is poorer, giving it more scope to catch up. India's income per head would have to grow at 8% a year for 17 years to match the level China enjoys today. One year of faster growth does not, then, mean that India is somehow overtaking China. Rather, it is like a 5,000-metre runner doing a faster lap than the frontrunner, who is five laps ahead.

c It would, nonetheless, be a rare achievement. India has not grown faster than China since 1990. . . . If India is to pip China again in 2011, several stars will also have to fall into alignment. . . .

India's economy must maintain its momentum, despite its central bank's campaign against stubbornly high inflation. And China's must slow appreciably. CLSA forecasts that the Chinese economy will grow by 8% in 2011, down from 10% in 2010.

Such a (relatively) low expectation for growth reflects a high opinion of China's leaders. That sounds paradoxical—surely slower growth is a sign of policy failure, not success? But China's leaders no longer seek growth at any cost. If they believe what they say, they would welcome a less breakneck pace of economic expansion. . . .

India still has massive catching up to do in infrastructure. It is not yet clear, with due respect to Indian nationalists, whether India will become the world's fastest-growing big economy in 2011. . . .

Source: "The fastest lap: India's economy is racing with China's," *The Economist*, November 22, 2010.

Key Points in the Article

This article discusses projected economic growth in India and China. After more than 20 years of trailing China in annual growth, some economic projections show India's growth rate may actually equal or surpass that of China during this decade. Several factors have led economists to this conclusion, including (1) the growing size of India's labor force and (2) the fact that per capita income is less in India than in China, leading to a more rapid rate of convergence between the two nations.

Analyzing the News

a Although China's overall population is expected to outnumber India's for the next 15 years, the size of the Chinese labor force will soon decline due to the country's one-child policy, a population-control measure instituted in 1978 that limits most Chinese families to only one child per household. Within the next few years, India's population of 15-to-29-year-olds is projected to surpass that of China, giving India a younger, larger, healthier, and possibly more educated workforce. These demographic changes will give India a better opportunity to experience faster economic growth in the coming decades.

b According to the CIA's *World Factbook*, India's real GDP per capita was $3,400 in 2010, less than one-half of China's $7,400 real GDP per capita. With significantly lower per capita income, less total economic growth is needed in India than in China for the annual percentage increases in growth in these two nations to converge. Even if India does surpass China in annual economic growth, India has a long way to go to overtake China in per capita income. At an annual growth rate of 8%, India would still need just over 10 years to equal the per capita income in China in 2010.

c Even with a considerably lower per capita income, surpassing China's annual growth rate would be a significant economic milestone for India, as this feat has not been achieved in more than 20 years. The figure shows actual and projected growth in GDP for India and China from 2006 through 2016. The actual figures through 2009 show a consistently higher GDP growth rate in China than in India—with projections that the gap will narrow considerably in 2011; the gap will disappear in 2015; and India will overtake China in 2016. A few economists predict that this gap will close even faster, perhaps as soon as 2011, but for this outcome to occur India must maintain its growth momentum while growth in China will need to substantially subside.

THINKING CRITICALLY

1. Labor productivity in emerging nations such as India and China has grown significantly in recent years. The growth rate of total factor productivity is the key determinant for labor productivity growth and the growth rate of the standard of living when labor inputs per person are constant. Using the formulas for steady-state growth rates and the data in the table for 2008, calculate the annual increases in labor productivity and real GDP for both India and China. Based on your answers, explain which of these countries has a higher rate of growth in its standard of living.

	India	China
Capital's share of income	0.37	0.58
Total factor productivity growth rate	0.010	0.013
Potential labor hours growth rate	0.058	0.065

2. Total factor productivity in emerging economies like those of India and China is growing significantly, leading to increased efficiency for both workers and firms. What effect does an increase in total factor productivity have on the steady-state values of the capital–labor ratio and real GDP per hour worked? Why? Use a graph showing a one-time increase in total factor productivity to illustrate your answer.

Actual and projected growth in GDP, 2006–2016

Source: © The Economist Newspaper Limited, London (November 22, 2010). ●

CHAPTER SUMMARY AND PROBLEMS

KEY TERMS

Balanced growth, p. 168
Depreciation, p. 154
Human capital, p. 165
Steady state, p. 154

5.1 Labor Productivity and the Standard of Living

Discuss the connection between labor productivity and the standard of living.

SUMMARY

Real GDP per capita refers to the quantity of goods and services that the average person in an economy can consume. So, real GDP per capita is a useful measure of the standard of living. Real GDP per capita equals labor productivity multiplied by average hours worked per capita. The population is finite, and there are just 24 hours in a day, so there is a limit to how much increasing labor inputs can increase the standard of living. However, labor productivity can increase indefinitely, and as long as labor productivity increases, the standard of living can increase. Real GDP per capita is not a perfect measure of the standard of living because it ignores the distribution of income, the value of leisure time, whether people are happy, and life expectancy. Nevertheless, the incomes of the poor, leisure time, self-reported happiness, and life expectancy all tend to increase as real GDP per capita increases. Although imperfect, real GDP per capita remains a very good measure of the standard of living.

Review Questions

1.1 In what sense is real GDP per capita a measure of the standard of living?

1.2 Describe how real GDP per capita has changed throughout the world from 1820 to the present.

1.3 How is labor productivity related to the standard of living?

1.4 In what ways is real GDP per capita a poor measure of the standard of living?

Problems and Applications

1.5 Use the equation that relates the standard of living to labor productivity to describe the probable effect on the standard of living of each of the following:

a. There is a baby boom, causing the population to increase.

b. The length of the average workweek decreases.

c. The capital stock rises.

1.6 **[Related to *Solved Problem* 5.1 on page 146]** In 2000, France shortened the legal workweek to 35 hours (from the previous workweek of 39 hours). Hours worked in excess of 35 would require payment of overtime.

a. All other things being equal, how would you expect this measure to change the standard of living?

b. One reason for this change in work hours was to attempt to reduce the problem of relatively high unemployment occurring at the same time as some workers were working long hours. If this measure simply redistributed hours of work among workers, would it change the average standard of living?

c. Are there any other reasons to think that a shorter workweek might benefit the population of France?

1.7 Consider the following statement: "Leisure time is not counted in real GDP because it is not a productive activity. So, it should not be part of the measurement of the standard of living, either." Do you agree with this statement? Briefly explain.

1.8 Measures of income distribution from the CIA *World Factbook* show that the most unequal income distribution in the world in 2009 was in Namibia. Namibia is also a relatively poor country, with per capita GDP of $6,900 in 2010. Brazil is considered to be one of the fastest growing of the newly industrializing countries, with a per capita GDP of $10,900. But Brazil also has the 10th most unequal income distribution in the world. Are the poorest people in Brazil likely to be better or worse off than the poorest people in Namibia? Briefly explain.

Source: U.S. Central Intelligence Agency, *World Factbook.*

1.9 Economist Robert Frank and others suggest that some goods are "positional." In other words, their value comes largely from their relative desirability, such as the best house in the neighborhood, the newest car, the largest yacht. Frank contends that such goods result in a wasteful "arms race" of spending and that taxation of these goods would reduce the inefficiencies of the market and reduce income inequality.

a. If happiness derives from position rather than absolute quantity of income, how would a tax that makes income more equal be likely to affect happiness?

b. If Frank's claims are correct, how would a tax on positional goods change the standard of living?

Source: Robert H. Frank, *Falling Behind: How Rising Inequality Harms the Middle Class*, Berkeley, CA: University of California Press, 2007.

1.10 According to the CIA *World Factbook*, Kuwait has the 8th highest per capita GDP in the world. However, life expectancy in Kuwait is only 66th in the world. Briefly discuss whether per capita real GDP or life expectancy is likely to be a better measure of the standard of living in Kuwait.

Source: U.S. Central Intelligence Agency, *World Factbook.*

1.11 In the spring of 2010, a large oil spill threatened the coasts of Louisiana and surrounding areas. The oil company in charge, BP, and various environmental agencies spent millions of dollars on the cleanup.

a. What happened to the usual measure of real GDP per capita in the area for this period?

b. What does this episode suggest about relying on real GDP per capita as a measure of the standard of living?

5.2 The Solow Growth Model

Use the Solow growth model to explain the effect of capital accumulation on labor productivity.

SUMMARY

Labor productivity depends on the capital–labor ratio and the level of total factor productivity. The break-even level of investment is the level of investment necessary to keep the capital–labor ratio constant. Break-even investment is equal to depreciation plus dilution. **Depreciation** is the reduction in the capital stock that occurs either because capital goods become worn out or because they become obsolete. The **steady state** occurs when investment equals break-even investment and the capital–labor ratio is constant. An increase in the investment rate leads to a higher capital–labor ratio and a higher level of labor productivity. Because financial markets work to ensure that savings flow into investment, anything that increases the saving rate will lead to a higher investment rate, a higher capital–labor ratio, and a higher level of labor productivity. Anything that decreases the saving rate, such as a government budget deficit, will cause the reverse to happen. The break-even level of investment is determined by the growth rate of the labor force and the depreciation rate. A decrease in either the depreciation rate or the labor force growth rate decreases the break-even level of investment. As a consequence, the capital–labor ratio and level of labor productivity are higher. Increases in the depreciation rate or labor force growth rate cause the reverse to happen.

Review Questions

2.1 Why does the marginal product of capital decrease as more capital is added?

2.2 What is the difference between a stock variable and a flow variable?

2.3 Describe the relationship between the investment function and the production function.

2.4 How do government budget deficits affect capital accumulation?

2.5 Explain the concepts of depreciation and dilution.

2.6 How is the steady state defined in the Solow growth model?

2.7 Use the bathtub analogy to explain the steady-state capital-labor ratio.

Problems and Applications

2.8 **[Related to *Solved Problem 5.2* on page 160]** Following World War II, many countries, including the United States, experienced a baby boom—an increase in the growth rate of the population.

a. Use the Solow model to demonstrate the effect of a baby boom on the steady-state capital–labor ratio.

b. Explain the effect of the baby boom on real GDP and on the standard of living.

c. The U.S. economy experienced strong growth in real GDP per capita during the years of the baby boom. Reconcile this fact with your answer to part b.

2.9 **[Related to *the Macro Data feature* on page 158]** Following the 2007–2009 financial crisis, interest rates on many investments declined to historically low levels.

a. Assume that savers respond to low interest rates by reducing their saving rate. Use the Solow model to demonstrate the effect of a reduction in the saving rate on the steady-state capital–labor ratio.

b. Explain the effect of a reduction in the saving rate on real GDP and on the standard of living.

2.10 Some countries experiencing low birthrates are offering women incentives to have children, such as income subsidies and other benefits. Does the analysis in this section suggest that a decline in the birthrate is bad for the standard of living? Why do governments worry about population declines?

2.11 Suppose that the per hour worked form of the production function for an economy is given by $y = 10k^{1/4}$. The depreciation rate is 10%, the investment rate is 20%, and the growth rate of labor hours is 2%.

a. Find the steady-state capital-labor ratio for this economy.

b. Find the steady-state real GDP per hour worked for this economy.

2.12 Suppose that the economy described in problem 2.11 is at the steady-state capital-labor ratio. A change in preferences causes the investment rate to rise to 25%.

a. Describe the forces that will move the economy to the new steady state.

b. Find the new steady-state capital–labor ratio and level of real GDP per hour worked.

2.13 It is often said that economies with larger investment rates will grow both faster and for a longer time. Imagine two economies both of which have a capital–labor ratio that is less than the steady-state ratio. Assume that these economies have identical production functions, rates of growth of labor hours, and depreciation rates. Use the Solow model to demonstrate that if country 1 has a greater investment rate than country 2, country 1 will both have a higher rate of growth in the next period and will grow to a higher level of real GDP per hour worked.

2.14 The former Soviet Union, a planned economy, was able to maintain consistently high rates of investment for decades. Use the Solow growth model to explain the limitations of growth through an expansion of the capital stock.

5.3 Total Factor Productivity and Labor Productivity

Explain how total factor productivity affects labor productivity.

SUMMARY

Total factor productivity measures the overall efficiency of the economy in transforming inputs into goods and services. Total factor productivity (*TFP*) is not subject to diminishing marginal returns, so increases in total factor productivity can explain sustained increases in labor productivity. Because labor productivity is the key determinant of the standard of living, total factor productivity growth also explains sustained increases in the standard of living. TFP also explains the large differences in labor productivity and the standard of living across countries. To understand labor productivity and the standard of living fully, we must understand why total factor productivity changes over time and why it is higher in some countries than in others. Although economists do not have a complete explanation for why total factor productivity differs over time and across countries, they have identified five important factors: (1) Investment in R&D leads to new ideas and new products that make workers more productive. (2) Education and learning by doing increase the skill level of the labor force. (3) Good government and social institutions channel resources toward wealth-creating activities. (4) Geography and climate determine a nation's natural resources and the rate of infectious disease among the population. (5) A well-functioning financial system ensures that savings flow to the individuals with the most productive investment projects and may lead to higher levels of physical and **human capital**.

Review Questions

3.1 How do increases in total factor productivity increase the standard of living?

3.2 What factors cause total factor productivity to change?

3.3 What is human capital, and how is it accumulated?

3.4 How can government institutions promote economic growth?

3.5 What role does geography play in economic growth?

3.6 How do financial institutions promote economic growth?

Problems and Applications

3.7 Consider the economy described in Problem 2.11. Suppose that total factor productivity increases to 15.

a. Find the new levels of the steady-state capital–labor ratios and real GDP per hour worked.

b. Would a similar increase in the growth rate of labor hours have the same effect? Explain.

3.8 One comprehensive study of contributions to growth in recent years found that the majority of growth in China over the 2005–2007 period was due to increases in the capital stock, although there was also a significant amount of growth due to increases in total factor productivity. In contrast, during these years Russia's capital stock actually declined, and Russia's growth was solely attributable to increases in total factor productivity.

a. Use the Solow growth model to depict graphically what happened in China.

b. Use the Solow growth model to depict graphically what happened in Russia.

c. China and Russia have very different levels of real GDP per hour worked, as well as many other differences, and China's growth rate was considerably higher than that of Russia over this period. It also could be argued that Russia is closer to its steady-state capital stock than is China. Use a graph to illustrate and explain these differences between Russia and China.

Source: Vivian Chen, Abhay Gupta, Andre Therrien, Gad Levanon, and Bart van Ark, "Recent Productivity Developments in the World Economy: An Overview from The Conference Board Total Economy Database," *International Productivity Monitor*, Spring 2010.

3.9 **[Related to the *Making the Connection* on page 164]** Investment in research and development is strongly linked to growth in total factor productivity. Governments usually support research and development activities because firms will tend to underinvest in such projects. Why would firms tend to underinvest, and why is it beneficial for government funds to be directed to what are often private projects?

3.10 Consider the following statement: "Without a well-functioning financial system, it is not possible for an economy to reach its full potential for economic growth."

a. Briefly explain whether you agree with this statement.

b. How does a well-functioning financial system help to explain why so many governments devoted resources to financial market stabilization during the 2007–2009 crisis?

3.11 **[Related to the *Making the Connection* on page 167]** Most countries that have experienced high rates of economic growth have economies that can roughly be characterized as free market. China's economy is one of the most rapidly growing in the world, yet parts of that economy are state controlled.

a. How did the 1978 economic reforms change the structure of the Chinese economy?

b. What advantages might state control of some parts of the economy have in increasing economic growth? Are these advantages likely to persist in the long run?

5.4 The Balanced Growth Path, Convergence, and Long-Run Equilibrium

Explain the balanced growth path, convergence, and long-run equilibrium.

SUMMARY

Real GDP and real GDP per hour worked both grow when the economy is in equilibrium; when they grow at the same rate, the economy experiences **balanced growth**. The equilibrium growth rate is determined by the growth rate of total factor productivity. When an economy initially has a capital–labor ratio that is below the steady-state value, the capital–labor ratio grows quickly, so real GDP per hour worked converges to the balanced growth path. When an economy initially has a capital–labor ratio that is above the steady-state value, the capital–labor ratio grows slowly or falls, so real GDP per hour worked converges to the balanced growth path.

Review Questions

4.1 What is a balanced growth path?

4.2 Is the world on a balanced growth path? What evidence do we have?

4.3 Are all countries on a balanced growth path? What evidence do we have?

4.4 What determines the growth rate of an economy when it is on the balanced growth path?

4.5 How did Germany diverge from a balanced growth path? How did it return?

4.6 Japan diverged from a balanced growth path and apparently returned to a higher growth path. What changed?

Problems and Applications

4.7 Consider the following statement: "If the economy is at the steady state, it must not be growing." Is this statement true, false, or uncertain? Explain.

4.8 Consider the economy described in problems 2.11. Suppose that annual growth in total factor productivity is 2%.

a. What is the steady-state growth rate of real GDP?

b. What is the steady-state growth rate of the capital–labor ratio?

4.9 **[Related to *The Making the Connection* on page 170]** Suppose that all economies have the following production function: $Y = K^{1/2}L^{1/2}$. A developed country has a saving rate of 28% and a population growth rate of 1% per year. A less-developed country has a saving rate of 10% and a population growth rate of 4% per year. In both countries, total factor productivity grows at 2% per year, and capital depreciates at 4% per year. Use the information in the question and the Solow model to explain whether it is likely that per capita GDP in these two countries will converge.

4.10 Suppose that an economy is growing at its steady-state rate of 4% per year when a natural disaster destroys one-quarter of its capital stock, leaving all other factors of production unchanged.

a. What will be the immediate effect on the capital–labor ratio and real GDP per hour worked?

b. After the disaster, will the economy grow at the same 4% rate in the short run? Explain.

c. What will be the long-run growth rate of the economy?

4.11 How would your answer to problem 4.10 change if, in addition to the loss of capital stock, the natural disaster also caused a permanent reduction in the growth rate of total factor productivity?

4.12 Prior to 2009, Zimbabwe experienced a decade of negative economic growth. Although there were many causes of these problems, two prominent causes were misguided land reforms that removed considerable agricultural land from production and hyperinflation that destroyed the financial system.

a. Use Table 5.3 on page 163 to explain how a negative growth rate of real GDP per capita can occur.

b. The coalition government that was formed in Zimbabwe in 2009 is apparently making some progress in restoring economic institutions and controlling inflation. If this government's actions are successful, what would you expect to happen to Zimbabwe's growth rate?

c. Is Zimbabwe's situation best described as a case of an economy that has temporarily diverged from its balanced growth path or a permanent change in the growth path?

4.13 On average, growth rates for high-income economies are much lower than growth rates for low-income economies. How does the Solow model explain this?

4.14 [Related to the *Chapter Opener* on page 143] The average growth rate in the United States is about 2.9%, and real GDP per capita is about $47,400. The average growth rate in China is 8.5%, and real GDP per capita is about $7,400. The average growth rate in Kenya is less than 2%, and real GDP per capita is about $1,600. Is it possible that the per capita real GDPs of these countries will converge, given enough time? Briefly explain.

Source: U.S. Central Intelligence Agency, *World Factbook.*

4.15 The following graph shows an economy that is at the steady-state capital–labor ratio. Suppose that an increase in the rate at which capital depreciates causes the break-even investment line to become steeper, as shown.

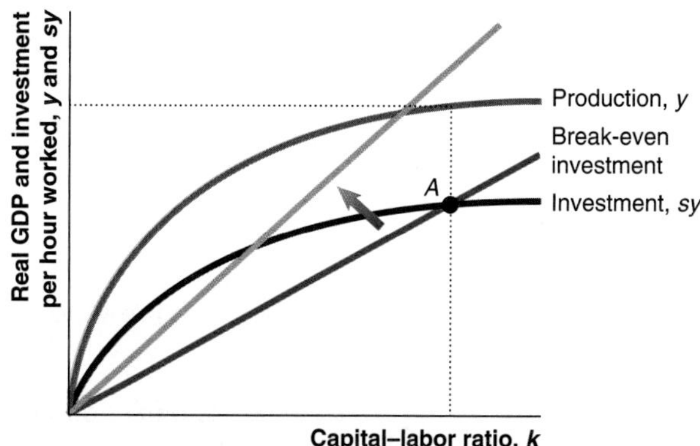

a. How will the steady-state capital–labor ratio and real GDP per hour worked change?

b. Carefully describe the path that the economy will take to reach the new steady state.

DATA EXERCISES

D5.1: The U.S. Central Intelligence Agency's *World Factbook* (https://www.cia.gov/library/publications/the-world-factbook//) offers many comparative tables of world data. Go to this site and find the following:

a. The countries with the highest and lowest real GDPs

b. The countries with the highest and lowest per capita real GDPs, adjusted for purchasing power

c. The countries with the most equal and least equal income distributions

d. The countries with the highest and lowest real GDP growth rates

e. Where does the United States rank in these categories?

D5.2: One determinant of the productivity of labor is the human capital, or the skills and education of the labor force. Return to the CIA *World Factbook* Web site and look up education expenditures as a percentage of GDP. Which countries spend the most on education? The least? Are there any general relationships between the level of development and the amount spent on education?

D5.3: A 2007 World Bank development report titled "Development and the Next Generation" suggests that countries with rapidly growing populations could achieve more rapid economic growth by investing in education and health care for their 15- to 24-year-old populations.

a. Find the press release related to this report on the World Bank's Web site (www.worldbank.org).

b. What does the report mean when it calls these young populations a "development dividend"? Is it also possible that these populations could be a drag on economic growth?

D5.4: Go to the World Bank's Web site and look up the most recent *World Development Report.* What are the current challenges for global growth? At what rate is the world expected to grow, and how are growth rates different in different regions?

D5.5: **[Excel question]** The Federal Reserve Bank of St. Louis offers data on U.S. real GDP at its Web site (http://research.stlouisfed.org/fred2/). Look at the data from 1950 to the present.

a. Use the data to calculate the growth rate of real GDP. Graph your results. Calculate the long-run growth trend by calculating the average growth rate over this time period.

b. What is the standard deviation of real GDP growth?

c. What happened to the economy in 2001? Did the economy return to its long-run growth trend after this period?

d. Has the economy returned to its long run growth path since the 2007–2009 financial crisis?

APPENDIX A

Capital Accumulation and Endogenous Growth

5A Describe how capital accumulation causes endogenous growth.

Capital accumulation and total factor productivity growth are the two determinants of labor productivity and the standard of living. Due to diminishing marginal returns, growth from capital accumulation eventually dies out, so total factor productivity growth is the ultimate determinant of sustained increases in labor productivity and the standard of living. According to the Solow growth model, a low growth rate of total factor productivity causes a low growth rate of the standard of living. The answer is very clear and precise, but where does total factor productivity growth come from? The Solow model does not explain why growth rates in total factor productivity differ over time and across countries. In other words, the Solow model does not fully explain why some countries are rich and others are poor.

Endogenous growth theory A theory of economic growth that tries to explain the growth rate of total factor productivity.

Endogenous growth theory tries to improve on this shortcoming of the Solow growth model by explaining the growth rate of total factor productivity. There are many different endogenous growth models, and we do not have space to explain them all. Instead, we concentrate on a relatively simple theory that focuses on the importance of capital accumulation. To highlight how capital accumulation can lead to productivity growth, we assume that the quantity of labor is fixed at a value of 1 and that total factor productivity is also fixed. Given these two assumptions, the only way that labor productivity and the standard of living can increase is if the capital stock increases. A common aggregate production function in endogenous growth models is:

$$Y = AK. \tag{5A.1}$$

Notice that there are no diminishing marginal returns to capital in this aggregate production function. In fact, the marginal product of capital always equals A, so the marginal product of capital is constant. Because the marginal product of capital is constant, unlike in the basic Solow model, capital accumulation can drive sustained productivity growth.

Assuming a constant marginal product of capital makes sense if we use a broader interpretation of the K term in the aggregate production function.[17] For example, K may include not just physical capital but also human capital, which may not be subject to diminishing marginal returns. Recall that human capital is the knowledge and skills that the workers in the economy possess. If an economy accumulates physical and human capital at the same rate, the ratio of physical to human capital remains constant, and the marginal product of capital may not decline. Why would human capital increase with physical capital? As physical capital increases, a country becomes richer, and the country may invest more in education and devote more resources to on-the-job training. Increased education and on-the-job training should both lead to more human capital. In addition, as an

[17] Paul Romer, "Crazy Explanations for the Productivity Slowdown," in Stanley Fischer (ed.), *NBER Macroeconomics Annual 1987*, Vol. 2, Cambridge, MA: MIT Press, 1987; and Sergio Rebelo, "Long-Run Policy Analysis and Long-Run Growth," *Journal of Political Economy*, June 1991, pp. 500–521.

economy accumulates more capital goods of a given type, learning by doing occurs, so the existing workers become more proficient at using the capital goods. The more highly skilled workers can keep the marginal product of capital from declining. Finally, we may consider the stock of knowledge as one type of capital good. As the stock of knowledge increases, the economy can produce new and better types of capital goods and, as a consequence, the marginal product of capital will not decline.

The aggregate production function with a broader definition of capital has important consequences for our theory of economic growth. To see these consequences, think in terms of the bathtub analogy that we introduced on pages 154–155. The investment rate, s, is still a constant fraction of output. Given our aggregate production function, water flowing into the bathtub is now:

$$\text{Water flowing in} = sY = sAK.$$

We have assumed a constant labor force, so the growth rate of the labor force, n, equals zero, and water flowing out of the bathtub is now:

$$\text{Water flowing out} = dK.$$

So, the change in the level of water in the bathtub, ΔK, equals:

$$\Delta K = sAK - dK.$$

We can divide each side of the equation by the capital stock to find an expression for the growth rate of the capital stock:

$$\frac{\Delta K}{K} = sA - d.$$

Given the new production function in Equation (5A.1), the growth rate of real GDP is:

$$\frac{\Delta Y}{Y} = sA - d. \tag{5A.2}$$

Because we have assumed a constant labor force, Equation (5A.2) also tells us the long-run growth rate of labor productivity. In the Solow growth model, the growth rate of labor productivity depends on an assumed rate of TFP growth. However, Equation (5A.2) tells us that the growth rate of productivity depends on the investment rate, so the investment rate emerges as an important determinant of the growth rate of labor productivity and the standard of living. In addition, government policies that either increase or decrease the investment rate become important determinants of the standard of living. For example, some governments have special tax credits designed to promote investment in capital goods and research and development. This endogenous growth model provides an answer to why countries experience high or low growth rates of the standard of living: Countries with high investment rates experience high growth rates, and countries with low investment rates experience low growth rates.

The Evidence on Endogenous Growth Theory

The endogenous growth model we just described predicts that as the investment rate increases, the growth rate of labor productivity also increases. All else being equal, the higher investment rate should lead to a higher growth rate of real GDP per capita. Charles Jones of Stanford University examined this prediction using data from advanced economies. He found that growth rates of real GDP per capita are roughly constant over long periods of time but that the investment rates increased significantly during the post-World War II era.[18] If the endogenous growth model is correct, then Jones should have found that the increases in the investment rates were associated with higher growth rates of real GDP per capita. Instead, he found that growth rates of real GDP per capita have been constant over time. He interprets this finding as evidence against the simple endogenous growth model that we have discussed here. The evidence that Jones presents suggests that the simple model of endogenous growth does not explain the long-run performance of advanced economies. The model does capture one of the basic insights of the endogenous growth literature: If diminishing marginal returns do not apply to capital, then capital accumulation and government policies that affect capital accumulation can permanently affect the growth rate of real GDP and not just the level of real GDP. Research on endogenous growth has moved beyond the simple model described here to more advanced models that fit the data better.

KEY TERM

Endogenous growth theory, p. 182

[18]Charles Jones, "Time Series Tests of Endogenous Growth Models," *Quarterly Journal of Economics*, Vol. 110, No. 2, May 1995, pp. 495–525.

APPENDIX B

Steady-State Capital–Labor Ratio and Real GDP per Hour Worked

5B Solve for the steady-state capital–labor ratio and real GDP per hour worked.

Equation (5.5) describes how the capital–labor ratio changes over time:

$$\Delta k = s\left(Ak^{\frac{1}{3}}\right) - (d + n)k.$$

In the steady state, the capital–labor ratio is constant. Therefore, to find the steady-state capital–labor ratio, we first set $\Delta k = 0$, so:

$$0 = s\left(Ak^{\frac{1}{3}}\right) - (d + n)k.$$

Next, we divide by k on each side of the equation:

$$0 = s\left(Ak^{-\frac{2}{3}}\right) - (d + n).$$

Isolating the capital–labor on the right-hand side, we have:

$$\frac{d + n}{sA} = k^{-\frac{2}{3}}.$$

Raising each side of the equation to the $\frac{-3}{2}$ power yields:

$$k^* = \left[\frac{d + n}{sA}\right]^{-\frac{3}{2}}.$$

We can transform this into:

$$k^* = \left[\frac{sA}{d + n}\right]^{\frac{3}{2}}.$$

To find the steady-state real GDP per hour worked, we plug this expression into the production function $y = Ak^{\frac{1}{3}}$ to get:

$$y^* = A\left\{\left[\frac{sA}{d + n}\right]^{\frac{3}{2}}\right\}^{\frac{1}{3}} = A\left[\frac{sA}{d + n}\right]^{\frac{1}{2}}.$$

Now we just rearrange terms so that there is just one term representing A, total factor productivity:

$$y^* = A^{\frac{3}{2}}\left[\frac{s}{d + n}\right]^{\frac{1}{2}}.$$

Calculating the Steady-State Growth Rates

Capital–Labor Ratio

The steady-state capital–labor ratio is:

$$k^* = \left[\frac{sA}{d + n}\right]^{\frac{3}{2}}.$$

In the steady state, capital's share of income, the investment rate, the depreciation rate, and the growth rate of the labor force are all constant. However, total factor productivity may increase. Therefore, it will be helpful to rewrite the equation for the steady-state capital–labor ratio as:

$$k_t^* = A_t^{\frac{3}{2}}\left[\frac{s}{d+n}\right]^{\frac{3}{2}},$$

where we include the t subscript to emphasize that the capital–labor ratio and total factor productivity change over time. We can take the natural logarithm of each side of the above equation to get:

$$\ln k_t^* = (1.5)\ln A_t + (1.5)\ln\left[\frac{s}{d+n}\right].$$

The derivative of the natural logarithm of the variable X_t with respect to time is:

$$\frac{d\ln X_t}{dt} = \frac{1}{X_t}\frac{dX_t}{dt} = \frac{dX_t/dt}{X_t} = g_X.$$

Applying this rule, we get:

$$g_k^* = 1.5g_A.$$

Real GDP per Hour worked

The steady-state real GDP per hour worked is:

$$y^* = A^{\frac{3}{2}}\left[\frac{s}{n+d}\right]^{\frac{1}{2}}.$$

Just as it was helpful to use time subscripts for the expression for the steady-state capital–labor ratio, it is also helpful here to emphasize that real GDP per hour worked and total factor productivity may change over time:

$$y_t^* = A_t^{\frac{3}{2}}\left[\frac{s}{d+n}\right]^{\frac{1}{2}}.$$

Following what we saw in the Chapter 4 appendix, we can take the natural logarithm of each side of the above equation to get:

$$\ln y_t^* = (1.5)\ln A_t + (0.5)\ln\left[\frac{s}{d+n}\right].$$

Applying the rule for taking the derivative of a variable with respect to time, we find that the growth rate for the steady-state real GDP per hour worked is:

$$g_y^* = (1.5)g_A.$$

Real GDP

Real GDP per hour worked is defined as $y = \frac{Y}{L}$. We can rewrite this definition by multiplying by labor on each side of the equation to obtain:

$$Y = yL.$$

The labor force and real GDP per hour worked grow over time, so we write the above equation as:

$$Y_t = y_t L_t.$$

Applying the rule for taking the derivative of a variable with respect to time, we find that the growth rate for the steady-state real GDP is:

$$g_Y = g_y + g_L.$$

The labor force grows at a constant rate of n, so the above equation becomes:

$$g_Y = g_y + n.$$

When the economy is in the steady state, the growth rate of real GDP per hour worked is $g_y{}^*$, so the growth rate for real GDP in the steady state is:

$$g_Y^* = g_y^* + n.$$

Now we can substitute the expression for the steady-state growth rate of real GDP per hour worked to obtain:

$$g_Y^* = 1.5g_A + n.$$

CHAPTER 6

Money and Inflation

LEARNING OBJECTIVES

After studying this chapter, you should be able to:

6.1 Define money and explain its functions (pages 189–194)

6.2 Explain how the Federal Reserve changes the money supply (pages 194–197)

6.3 Describe the quantity theory of money and use it to explain the connection between changes in the money supply and the inflation rate (pages 197–201)

6.4 Discuss the relationships among the growth rate of money, inflation, and nominal interest rates (pages 202–205)

6.5 Explain the costs of a monetary policy that allows inflation to be greater than zero (pages 206–212)

6.6 Explain the causes of hyperinflation (pages 212–214)

6A Explain how the formula for the money multiplier is derived (pages 226–229)

6B Derive the percentage change version of the quantity equation (page 230)

USING MONEY AS TOILET PAPER?

In Germany in 1923, people burned paper currency, rather than wood or coal, in their stoves. In Zimbabwe in 2009, people used currency for toilet paper. There was no shortage of wood or coal in Germany during the 1920s, and there was no shortage of toilet paper in Zimbabwe in more recent years. In both cases, the purchasing power of paper currency had fallen so low that the currency was worth more as paper than as money.

People in most countries are used to some inflation. Even a moderate inflation rate will gradually reduce the purchasing power of money. For example, if the United States experiences an inflation rate that averages only

Continued on next page

Key Issue and Question

At the end of Chapter 1, we noted key issues and questions that serve as a framework for the book. Here are the key issue and question for this chapter:

Issue: The Federal Reserve's actions during the financial crisis of 2007–2009 led some economists and policymakers to worry that the inflation rate in the United States would be increasing.

Question: What is the connection between changes in the money supply and the inflation rate?

Answered on page 215

3% per year over the next 30 years, it will take $2.43 to buy the same amount of goods and services 30 years from now that $1.00 can buy today. Germany and Zimbabwe experienced the much higher inflation rates known as *hyperinflation*, which is defined as very high rates of inflation reaching 50% or more per month. The inflation rates suffered by these two countries were extreme even by the standards of hyperinflations: The consumer price index in Germany, which had been 100 in 1914, had risen to 1,440 in January 1922, and then to 126,160,000,000,000 by December 1923. The German mark had become nearly worthless. In Zimbabwe, the inflation rate had reached 15 billion percent by 2008. A U.S. tourist visiting the Victoria Falls Hotel in Zimbabwe during the summer of 2008 ordered dinner, two beers, and a mineral water. He received a bill for $1,243,255,000.00 in Zimbabwean dollars.

Countries suffer from hyperinflations when their governments allow the money supply to grow too rapidly. Between 1999 and 2008, the Reserve Bank of Zimbabwe (RBZ), the central bank for Zimbabwe, increased the money supply by more than 7,500% per year. In Germany, the money supply rose from 115 million marks in January 1922 to 1.3 billion in January 1923 and to 497 billion billion—or 497,000,000,000,000,000,000—in December 1923. Why would a government create so much money when it knows that doing so will destroy the money's purchasing power? In this chapter, we will explore this and other issues involving the relationship between money and prices.

AN INSIDE LOOK AT POLICY on page 216 explores why rapid lending and increases in the growth rate of the money supply in China have raised fears of inflation.

Sources: Steven D. Levitt and Stephen J. Dubner, "Freak Shots: $1 Billion Dollars and Other African Pricing Problems," *New York Times*, June 2, 2008; Thomas Sargent, "The Ends of Four Big Hyperinflations," in Robert E. Hall, ed., *Inflation: Causes and Effects*, Chicago: University of Chicago Press, 1982; and "What Can You Do with a Zimbabwean Dollar?" *Economist*, July 26, 2010.

In the previous chapters, we focused on real GDP and real GDP per hour worked. These are real variables because they represent quantities. In this chapter, we focus on the behavior of nominal variables such as the price level, the inflation rate, and the nominal interest rate. In the long run, changes in nominal variables are caused by changes in the *money supply*. We begin with a discussion of the basic role that money plays in the economy and with a review of how the Federal Reserve measures the money supply.

What Is Money, and Why Do We Need It?

6.1
Learning Objective
Define money and explain its functions.

A major objective of central banks, such as the Federal Reserve in the United States, is to control the inflation rate. As we will see, in the long run, the inflation rate is determined by the growth rate of the money supply. To understand why we need money, we need to understand the functions of money.

The Functions of Money

Economies can function without money. In the early stages of an economy's development, individuals often exchange goods and services by trading output directly with each other. This type of exchange is called *barter*. For example, on the frontier in colonial America, a farmer whose cow died might trade several pigs to a neighboring farmer in exchange for one of the neighbor's cows. In principle, people in a barter economy could satisfy all their needs by trading for goods and services, in which case they would not need money. In practice, though, barter economies are inefficient because each party must want what the other party has available to trade. That is, there must be a *double coincidence of wants*. Because of the time and effort spent searching for trading partners in a barter economy, the *transactions costs*—or the costs in time or other resources of making a trade or exchange—will be high.

To improve on barter, people had an incentive to identify a specific product that most people would accept in an exchange. In other words, they had a strong incentive to invent money. For example, in colonial times, animal skins were very useful in making clothing, so many people were willing to accept them in exchange for goods and services. A good, such as animal skins, that is used as money while also having value independent of its use

Commodity money A good used as money that has value independent of its use as money.

as money is called a **commodity money**. Historically, once a good became widely accepted as money, people who did not have an immediate use for it were still willing to accept it. A colonial farmer might not want a deerskin for his own use, but as long as he knew he could use it to buy other goods and services, he would be willing to accept it in exchange for what he had to sell.

Once money is invented—as it has been many times and in many places around the world—transactions costs are greatly reduced, as are the other inefficiencies of barter. People can take advantage of *specialization*, producing the good or service for which they have relatively the best ability. The high income levels in modern economies are based on the specialization that money makes possible. So, the answer to the question "Do we need money?" is "Yes, because money allows for specialization, higher productivity, and higher incomes."

Economists think of money as serving four functions in the economy:

1. It acts as a medium of exchange.
2. It is a unit of account.
3. It is a store of value.
4. It offers a standard of deferred payment.

Medium of exchange Something that is generally accepted as payment for goods and services; a function of money.

Medium of Exchange If you are a teacher or an accountant, you are paid money for your services. You then use that money to buy goods and services. You essentially exchange your teaching or accounting services for food, clothing, rent, and other goods and services. But unlike with barter, where goods and services are exchanged directly for other goods and services, the exchanges you participate in involve money. Money acts as a **medium of exchange**. That is, money is the medium through which exchange takes place. Because, by definition, money is generally accepted as payment for goods and services or as payment for debts, you know that the money your employer pays you will be accepted at the stores where you purchase food, clothing, and other goods and services. In other words, you can specialize in producing teaching or accounting services without having to worry about directly producing the other goods and services you require to meet your needs, as you would in a barter economy.

Unit of account A way of measuring value in an economy in terms of money; a function of money.

Unit of Account Money serves as a **unit of account**, which means it is a way of measuring value in an economy. For example, when you purchase an iPad, the Apple store posts a price in terms of dollars rather than shares of Apple stock or ounces of gold. Having an agreed-upon unit of account makes an economy more efficient because goods and services have a single price rather than many prices.

Store of value The accumulation of wealth by holding dollars or other assets that can be used to buy goods and services in the future; a function of money.

Store of Value Money provides a **store of value** by allowing for the accumulation of wealth that can be used to buy goods and services in the future. For example, suppose you want to purchase an iPad next year that has a price of $500. If you have $500 in currency, you can put it aside and purchase the iPad in one year. Note, though, that if prices in an economy rise rapidly over time, as happened recently in Zimbabwe, the quantity of goods and services a given amount of money can purchase declines, and money's usefulness as a store of value is reduced. In that case, you would need more than $500 to purchase the iPad. Of course, money is only one of many assets that can be used to store value. In fact, any asset—shares of Apple stock, Treasury bonds, real estate, or Renoir paintings, for example—represents a store of value. Money, though, has the advantage of being perfectly liquid. When you exchange other assets for money, you incur transactions costs. For example, when you sell bonds or shares of stock to buy a car, you pay a fee, or commission, online or to your broker. To avoid such transactions costs, people are willing to hold some money, even though other assets offer a greater return as a store of value.

Standard of Deferred Payment Money acts as a medium of exchange to facilitate exchange at a point in time but also as a **standard of deferred payment** to facilitate exchange over time. For example, if you purchase an iPad for $500 today, the store may allow you several months to pay that amount. For an asset, such as money, to fulfill this function, the value of the asset must be stable over time—or changes in its value must be predictable.

Standard of deferred payment An asset that facilitates transactions over time; a function of money.

Commodity Money Versus Fiat Money

To be considered money, an asset must fulfill the four functions that we described in the previous sections. Because the function of a medium of exchange is so important, we will examine that further. An asset can be used as a medium of exchange if it is:

- *Acceptable* to most people.
- *Standardized in terms of quality*, so that any two units are identical.
- *Durable*, so its value is not quickly lost due to wear and tear.
- *Valuable* relative to its weight, so that amounts large enough to be useful in trade can be easily transported.
- *Divisible*, because prices of goods and services vary.

There are two types of assets with these five characteristics: commodity money and fiat money. Throughout history, gold has been a common form of commodity money. However, the value of gold depends on its purity. If you mixed gold with a metal of lesser value, then you could make a profit by deceiving others into accepting impure gold as payment for goods and services. Therefore, anyone accepting gold would need to verify its purity. In addition, the supply of gold fluctuates with unpredictable discoveries of gold and changes in the technology for extracting gold from existing mines. Gold also has the disadvantage that large quantities can be heavy and, therefore, difficult to transport.

Because of its convenience and because it meets all five characteristics of money listed above, paper currency has been widely used as money during the past 200 years. **Fiat money** is money, such as paper currency, that has no value apart from its use as money. In most countries, including the United States, during the late nineteenth and early twentieth centuries, paper currency could be redeemed for gold or silver. Today, however, paper currency is not backed by gold, silver, or anything else of value. In the modern economy, people are generally willing to accept paper currency for two reasons. First, fiat currency is *legal tender*. If you look at a U.S. dollar, you will see the words "This note is legal tender for all debts, public and private." This expression means that the federal government requires that cash or checks denominated in dollars be used in payment of taxes and that dollars must be accepted in private payments of debt. Private businesses, though, are not legally obliged to accept dollars in exchange for goods and services, although most businesses do so most of the time. Second, households and firms have confidence that if they accept paper dollars in exchange for goods and services, then the dollars will not lose much value during the time they hold them. Without this confidence, dollar bills would not serve as a medium of exchange or fulfill the other functions of money. As we saw at the beginning of the chapter, in Germany and Zimbabwe, paper currency lost its value so quickly during periods of **hyperinflation** that it ceased to function as money. Hyperinflation occurs when the inflation rate becomes extremely high, exceeding 50% or more per month.

Fiat money Money, such as paper currency, that has no value apart from its use as money.

Hyperinflation Extremely high rates of inflation, exceeding 50% or more per month.

Making the Connection

When Money Is No Longer Money: Hyperinflation in Zimbabwe

At the time of its independence from Great Britain in 1980, Zimbabwe was poor by the standards of the high-income countries, but it was relatively well off by the standards of sub-Saharan Africa. Its GDP per capita was 35% higher than that of Kenya and 20% higher than that of Nigeria. The following three decades were not good ones for Zimbabwe, however, as its real GDP per capita declined by 45%. By 2010, real GDP per capita was only about $400, one of the lowest in the world. In that year, the level of real GDP per capita was five times higher in Nigeria than in Zimbabwe and it was four times higher in Kenya. What happened to Zimbabwe's economy?

Zimbabwe has suffered from a long period of economic mismanagement and, in recent years, political strife as long-time president Robert Mugabe has attempted to maintain power in the face of widespread opposition. Since 2004, the country's problems have been made much more acute by hyperinflation. As noted in the chapter opener, the Zimbabwean central bank, the Reserve Bank of Zimbabwe (RBZ), caused the money supply to increase at an annual rate of 7,500%. The result was an increase in the inflation rate from an already high 130% to more than 15 billion percent in 2008. The exchange rate between the Zimbabwean dollar and the U.S. dollar changed from about 1,000 Zimbabwean dollars per U.S. dollar at the beginning of 2004 to 10,000,000,000,000,000 Zimbabwean dollars by the end of 2009. As the Zimbabwean dollar lost nearly all of its value, the economy reverted to barter or used as money the limited amounts of foreign currency that were available. Because exchanging Zimbabwean dollars for foreign currency was so difficult, imports plunged, and shortages of food and other basic goods became widespread. Reliable statistics on Zimbabwe's economy are difficult to find, but in 2008, one journalist described a situation bordering on economic collapse: "Zimbabwe is in the midst of a dire economic crisis with unemployment at almost 80%, most manufacturing at a halt and basic foods in short supply." Some estimates put the unemployment rate as high as 95%. Nearly the entire labor force had to scratch out a subsistence living as best they could. Many unemployed Zimbabweans were reported as surviving only by growing vegetables in vacant lots or along roads.

Why would the RBZ allow such high rates of growth in the money supply if the result was a ruinous hyperinflation? The answer is that the RBZ was not independent of the rest of the Zimbabwean government. When the Zimbabwean government decided in the mid-2000s to greatly increase its spending, primarily to support the efforts of Robert Mugabe to retain power, it did so not by raising taxes or borrowing by selling government bonds to investors, but by having the RBZ increase the money supply.

In early 2009, a new government in Zimbabwe took the drastic step of abandoning its own currency and making the U.S. dollar the country's official currency. By 2011, the economy was showing signs of recovery as the inflation rate declined to about 5% and real GDP per capita was projected to rise by 13% from the very low levels of 2008. Still, the political situation remained uncertain, and many Zimbabweans did not trust the government to control the money supply responsibly.

Sources: "Zimbabwe's Independence: Thirty Years On," *Economist*, April 20, 2010; Angus Maddison, *Contours of the World Economy*, New York: Oxford University Press, 2007; "Zimbabwe Inflation Rockets Higher," news.bbc.co.uk, August 19, 2008; "What a Full-Fledged Economic Collapse Looks Like," *Economist*, May 6, 2009; Michael Hartnack, "Zimbabwe Inflation Tops 1,000 Percent," Associated Press, May 13, 2006; and International Monetary Fund, "Statement of the IMF's Mission to Zimbabwe," Press Release No. 10/420, November 8, 2010.

Test your understanding by doing related problem 1.10 on page 219 at the end of this chapter.

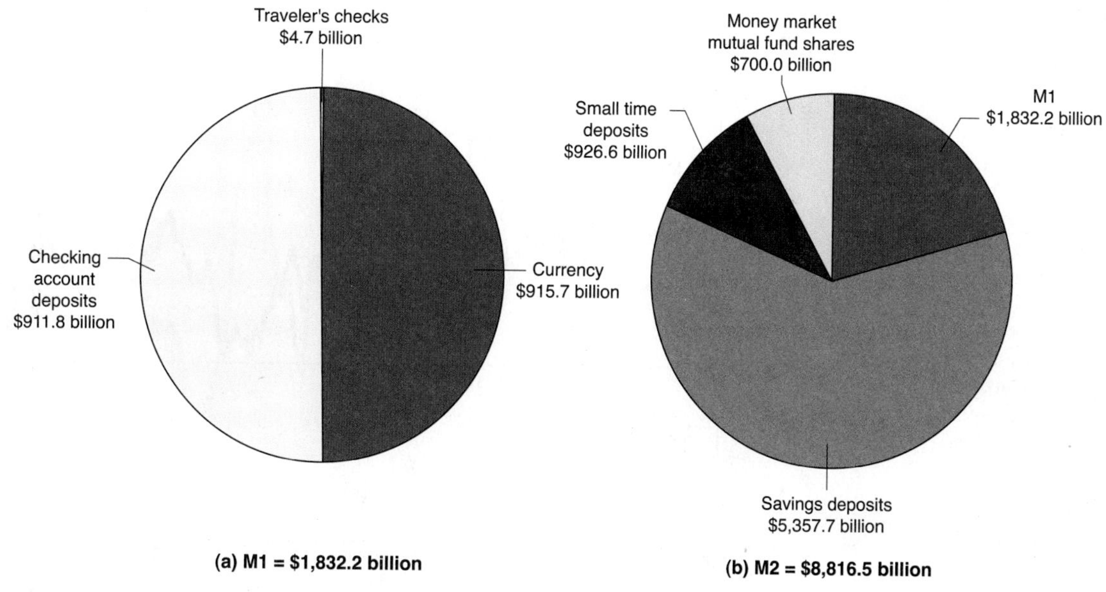

Figure 6.1 M1 and M2 in the United States, December 2010

The Federal Reserve uses two different measures of the money supply: M1 and M2. M1 includes currency, checking account deposits, and traveler's checks. M2 includes all the assets in M1, as well as the additional assets shown in panel (b). Savings deposits include money market deposit accounts.

Source: Board of Governors of the Federal Reserve System, *Federal Reserve Statistical Release, H6*, January 20, 2011. ●

How Is Money Measured?

Households, firms, and policymakers are all interested in measuring money because, as we will see, changes in the quantity of money are associated with changes in nominal interest rates and prices. If the only function of money were to serve as a medium of exchange, then money should include only currency, checking account deposits, and traveler's checks because households and firms can easily use these assets to buy goods and services. But many other assets can be used as a medium of exchange, even though they are not as liquid as cash or checking account deposits. For example, you can easily convert your savings account at a bank into cash. Likewise, if you own shares in a *money market mutual fund*—which is a mutual fund that invests exclusively in short-term bonds, such as Treasury bills—you can write checks against the value of your shares. So, assets such as savings accounts and money market mutual fund shares can plausibly be considered part of the medium of exchange.

As part of its responsibility to regulate the quantity of money in the United States, the Federal Reserve publishes data on two different measures of the money supply: *M1* and *M2*. These definitions are referred to as *monetary aggregates*. Figure 6.1 shows both these measures graphically. **M1** is a narrower measure of the money supply: It is the sum of currency in circulation, checking account deposits, and holdings of traveler's checks. M1 comes closest to the role of money as a medium of exchange. **M2** is a broader measure of the money supply than M1 and includes accounts that many households treat as short-term investments. Households can easily convert these accounts into currency, although not as easily as the components of M1. As shown in panel (b) of Figure 6.1, in addition to the assets included in M1, M2 includes:

- Time deposits with a value of less than $100,000, primarily certificates of deposits in banks.
- Savings accounts and money market deposit accounts at banks.
- Noninstitutional money market mutual fund shares. *Noninstitutional* means that the money market fund shares are owned by individual investors rather than by institutional investors, such as pension funds. Noninstitutional is also sometimes referred to as *retail*.

M1 A narrower measure of the money supply: The sum of currency in circulation, checking account deposits, and holdings of traveler's checks.

M2 A broader measure of the money supply: All the assets that are included in M1, as well as time deposits with a value of less than $100,000, savings accounts, money market deposit accounts at banks, and noninstitutional money market mutual fund shares.

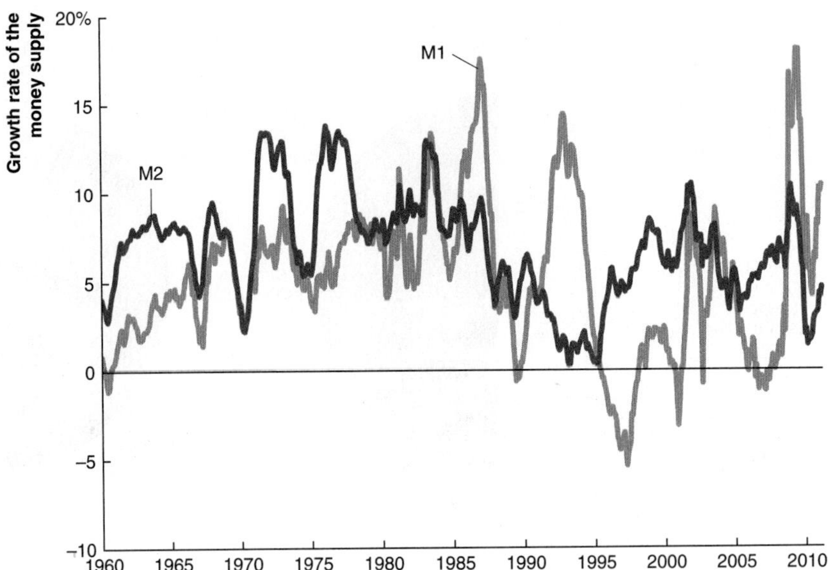

Figure 6.2

Growth Rates of M1 and M2 in the United States, 1960–2011

M1 and M2 have similar growth rates much of the time, but significant differences can emerge over short periods of time. For example, the growth rate of M1 fell from nearly 14.4% in November 1992 to negative growth rates in June 1995, reaching a low of −5.4% in April 1997. In contrast, the growth rate of M2 rose from 1.8% to 4.6% during the same period.

Source: Board of Governors of the Federal Reserve System. ●

Which Measure of the Money Supply Should We Use?

Which measure of the money supply is most useful is still an open question among economists. Figure 6.2 shows that M1 and M2 have similar growth rates most of the time, although significant differences in their growth rates occur during certain periods. For example, M2 grew much more rapidly than M1 for much of the 1970s, and during the 1990s, the growth rate of M1 fell, while the growth rate of M2 increased.

At one time, fluctuations in the money supply were a major source of discussion among macroeconomists, investment analysts, and policymakers. This interest arose from the fact that for most of the post-World War II period, there had been a stable short-run relationship between M1 and M2 and economic variables such as inflation, interest rates, and real GDP. Whether this relationship was stronger for M1 or for M2 was the subject of considerable debate. However, beginning in 1980, the emergence of new financial assets, such as checking accounts that pay interest and money market deposit accounts, provided alternatives to traditional checking accounts. As a result, the relationship between M1 and M2 and many economic variables became unreliable. More importantly, the experience of the 1980s suggests that as banks and other financial firms respond to the demands of households and firms by developing new assets, the relationship between whatever we define as *money* and economic variables may break down. Changes in the money supply, however defined, are no longer as closely connected to other economic variables. Since the early 1990s, the Fed has therefore de-emphasized the roles of M1 and M2 in monetary policymaking.

6.2

Learning Objective

Explain how the Federal Reserve changes the money supply

The Federal Reserve and the Money Supply

To understand how the Federal Reserve controls the money supply, we need to describe the *monetary base* and then investigate how it is linked to the money supply. We present a simple model of how the money supply is determined that includes the behavior of three actors:

1. The Federal Reserve, which is responsible for controlling the money supply and regulating the banking system.
2. The banking system, which creates the checking accounts that are the most important component of the M1 measure of the money supply.

3. The nonbank public, which refers to all households and firms. The nonbank public decides the form in which they wish to hold money (for instance, as currency or as checking accounts).

The process of determining the money supply begins with the **monetary base** (also called **high-powered money**), which is equal to the amount of currency in circulation plus the reserves of the banking system:

Monetary base (or high-powered money) The sum of currency in circulation and bank reserves.

$$\text{Monetary base} = \text{Currency in circulation} + \text{Reserves}.$$

Reserves are a bank asset consisting of vault cash plus bank deposits with the Federal Reserve. The Fed requires banks to hold reserves against checking account deposits. The link between the monetary base and money supply is called the **money multiplier**, which tells us how much the money supply increases when the monetary base increases by $1:

Reserves A bank asset consisting of vault cash plus bank deposits with the Federal Reserve.

$$\text{Money supply} = \text{Money multiplier} \times \text{Monetary base}. \quad (6.1)$$

Money multiplier The number indicating how much the money supply increases when the monetary base increases by $1.

How the Fed Changes the Monetary Base

By controlling the reserves in the banking system, the Fed is able to control the monetary base and, therefore, the money supply. The Federal Open Market Committee (FOMC) is the decision-making body inside the Fed for monetary policy. The FOMC consists of the seven members of the Board of Governors (who are chosen by the president of the United States and confirmed by the U.S. Senate to 14-year terms), the president of the Federal Reserve Bank of New York, and presidents from 4 of the other 11 regional Federal Reserve Banks. The FOMC meets eight times per year and makes decisions that affect the money supply.

The FOMC controls the monetary base through **open market operations**, which are the Fed's purchases and sales of securities, usually U.S. Treasury securities, in financial markets. When the Fed buys Treasury securities, it pays for them by increasing banks' reserves. When the banks' reserves increase, they usually increase the loans they make, which in turn increases the money supply. For example, if the Fed purchases $1 million worth of Treasury securities from JP Morgan, the bank's reserves increase by $1 million. JP Morgan may then, if it chooses, increase the loans it makes to households and firms. If JP Morgan makes new loans, the funds it lends out end up either as currency or as deposits in checking accounts. In either case, a component of the money supply increases. If the Fed sells $1 million of Treasury securities to JP Morgan, the bank pays for the securities by decreasing its reserves and reducing its loans to households and firms. As a result, either the amount of currency in circulation or deposits in checking accounts decrease—so the money supply decreases.

Open market operations The Federal Reserve's purchases and sales of securities, usually U.S. Treasury securities, in financial markets.

The Process of Money Creation

Because an open market purchase increases either currency or bank reserves by the amount of the purchase, the Fed controls the monetary base. As we indicated above, an increase in the monetary base usually results in an increase in the money supply, and a decrease in the monetary base usually results in a decrease in the money supply. For example, if the Fed decides to increase the monetary base by $1 million, it can achieve its objective by carrying out a $1 million open market purchase. As Equation (6.1) shows, however, to know the effect of the open market purchase on the money supply, the Fed needs to know the value of the money multiplier. What follows is a brief description of how banks and the nonbank public also affect the money supply through the money multiplier. We provide a more detailed explanation of the money multiplier in Appendix A to this chapter.

If we let M stand for the money supply, MB stand for the monetary base, and m stand for the money multiplier, we can rewrite Equation (6.1) as:

$$M = m \times MB,$$

and, rearranging this expression, we can see that the money multiplier is the ratio of the money supply to the monetary base:

$$m = \frac{M}{MB}.$$

If we use the M1 definition of the money supply, then M is the sum of currency in circulation, C, and checking account deposits, D, (for simplicity, we are ignoring traveler's checks) while the monetary base is the sum of currency in circulation and bank reserves, R. Reserves consist of required reserves, RR, that the Fed requires banks to hold, and excess reserves, ER, that banks hold above the required amount. So, we can expand the expression for the money multiplier to:

$$m = \frac{C + D}{C + RR + ER}.$$

The nonbank public—that is, households and firms—determines how much currency they wish to hold relative to checking account deposits. We can take into account both the nonbank public's desire to hold currency relative to checking account deposits and banks' desire to hold excess reserves relative to checking account deposits in the expression for the money multiplier. To do so, we want to include the currency-to-deposit ratio (C/D), which measures the nonbank public's holdings of currency relative to its holdings of checking account deposits, and the excess reserves-to-deposit ratio (ER/D), which measures banks' holdings of excess reserves relative to their checking account deposits. To include these ratios in the expression for the money multiplier, we can rely on the basic rule of arithmetic that multiplying the numerator and denominator of a fraction by the same variable preserves the value of the fraction. So, we can introduce the deposit ratios into our expression for the money multiplier this way:

$$m = \left(\frac{C + D}{C + RR + ER}\right) \times \frac{(1/D)}{(1/D)} = \frac{(C/D) + 1}{(C/D) + (RR/D) + (ER/D)}.$$

The Fed calls the ratio of required reserves to checking account deposits the *required reserve ratio*, rr_D. We can use this fact to arrive at our final expression for the money multiplier:

$$m = \frac{(C/D) + 1}{(C/D) + rr_D + (ER/D)}. \tag{6.2}$$

So, we can say that because:

$$\text{Money supply} = \text{Money multiplier} \times \text{Monetary base},$$

then:

$$M = \left(\frac{(C/D) + 1}{(C/D) + rr_D + (ER/D)}\right) \times MB. \tag{6.3}$$

For example, if the value of the monetary base is $1 trillion and the money multiplier is 2, the value of the money supply will be $2 trillion.

There are several points to note about our expression linking the money supply to the monetary base:

1. The money supply will increase if either the monetary base or the money multiplier increases in value, and it will decrease if either the monetary base or the money multiplier decreases in value.
2. An increase in the currency-to-deposit ratio (C/D) causes the value of the money multiplier to decline and, if the monetary base is unchanged, it also causes the value of the money supply to decline. This result makes economic sense: If households and firms increase their holdings of currency relative to their holdings of checking account deposits, banks will have a relatively smaller amount of funds they can lend out, which reduces the money multiplier.

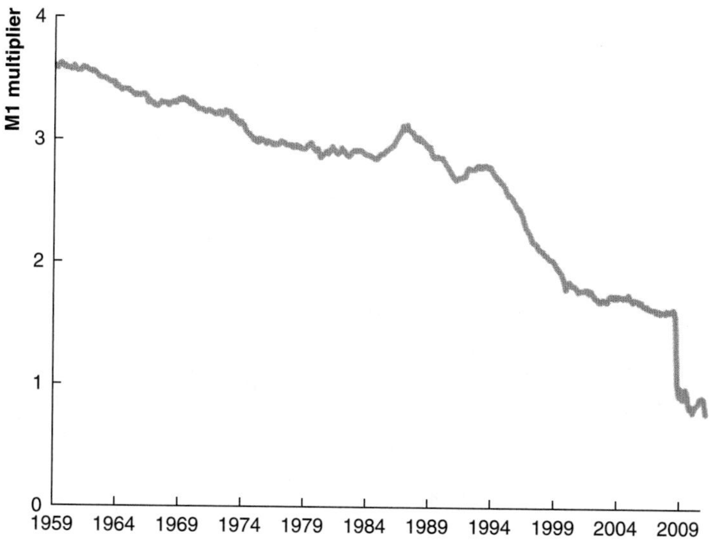

Figure 6.3

The M1 Multiplier for the United States, 1959–2011

There has been a long-term downward trend in the M1 multiplier, as households and firms have begun to rely on financial assets other than cash and checking accounts to conduct market transactions. However, there was a very steep drop in the value of the multiplier during 2008, when the financial crisis caused banks to become reluctant to lend to households and firms.

Source: Board of Governors of the Federal Reserve System. ●

3. An increase in the required reserve ratio, rr_D, causes the value of the money multiplier to decline and, if the monetary base is unchanged, it also causes the value of the money supply to decline. An increase in rr_D means that for any increase in reserves banks receive, a larger fraction must be held as required reserves and these funds, therefore, are not available to be loaned, which reduces the multiplier.
4. An increase in the excess reserves-to-deposit ratio (*ER/D*) causes the value of the money multiplier to decline and, if the monetary base is unchanged, it also causes the value of the money supply to decline. An increase in *ER/D* means that banks are holding relatively more excess reserves, so they are not using these funds to make loans, which reduces the multiplier.

Figure 6.3 shows values of the money multiplier for M1 since the late 1950s. There has been a long-term downward trend in the M1 multiplier, as households and firms have begun to rely on financial assets other than currency and checking accounts in buying and selling. During the financial crisis of 2007–2009, banks tightened the guidelines for households and firms to qualify for loans to avoid having customers default on them. Banks had become concerned about the quality of the loans they had made in the mid-2000s, and they wanted to keep extra reserves to help protect themselves in case households and firms did not repay their current loans. As a result, *ER/D* soared and the money multiplier decreased dramatically.

The Quantity Theory of Money and Inflation

6.3 Learning Objective
Describe the quantity theory of money and use it to explain the connection between changes in the money supply and the inflation rate.

The connection between increases in the money supply and increases in the price level have been discussed by writers dating back at least as far as the Greek philosopher Aristotle in the fourth century B.C. During the sixteenth century, the Spanish conquest of Mexico and Peru resulted in huge quantities of gold and silver being exported to Europe, where they were minted into coins. Many writers noted that this sharp increase in the money supply had resulted in an increase in inflation. Early in the twentieth century, Yale economist Irving Fisher formalized the relationship between money and prices by using the *quantity equation*. The **quantity equation** (also called the **equation of exchange**) is an identity that states that the money supply, *M*, multiplied by the *velocity of money*, *V*, equals the price level, *P*, multiplied by real GDP, *Y*:

Quantity equation (or equation of exchange) An identity that states that the money supply multiplied by the velocity of money equals the price level multiplied by real GDP.

$$M \times V = P \times Y. \tag{6.4}$$

Velocity of money The average number of times each dollar in the money supply is used to purchase goods and services included in GDP.

Fisher defined the **velocity of money**—or, simply, *velocity*—as the average number of times each dollar in the money supply is used to purchase a good or service that is included in GDP. Rewriting Equation (6.4) by dividing each side by the money supply, we have an equation for velocity:

$$V = \frac{P \times Y}{M}.$$

Recall that the price level multiplied by real GDP equals nominal GDP. So, we can think of velocity as being equal to nominal GDP divided by the money supply. If we use M1 as our measure of the money supply, the value of velocity in 2010 was:

$$V = \frac{\text{Nominal GDP}}{\text{M1}} = \frac{\$14{,}660.4 \text{ billion}}{\$1{,}832.2 \text{ billion}} = 8.0.$$

This result tells us that, on average during 2010, each dollar of M1 was spent about eight times on goods and services included in GDP.

The Quantity Theory of Money

Quantity theory of money A theory about the connection between money and prices that assumes that the velocity of money is constant.

Because Fisher defined velocity to be equal to PY/M, Equation (6.4) is an identity that must always be true: The left side of the equation must always be equal to the right side. A theory is a statement about the world that could be either true or false. The quantity *equation* is always true, so it does not qualify as a theory. Irving Fisher turned the quantity equation into the **quantity theory of money** by assuming that velocity is constant. Fisher argued that the average number of times a dollar is spent depends on factors that do not change very often, such as how often people get paid, how often they go grocery shopping, and how often businesses mail bills. Because this assertion that velocity is constant may be either true or false, the quantity theory of money is a theory. As we will see, even if velocity is not constant, the quantity theory may still prove to be useful in predicting future inflation rates.

The Quantity Theory Explanation of Inflation

The quantity equation gives us a way of showing the relationship between changes in the money supply and the inflation rate. To see this relationship more clearly, we can use a mathematical rule that states that an equation where variables are multiplied together is approximately equal to an equation where the *growth rates* of variables are *added* together.[1] Using this rule, and recalling that the growth rate of a variable is the same as the percentage change in a variable, we can rewrite Equation (6.4) as:

$$\%\text{ Change in } M + \%\text{ Change in } V = \%\text{ Change in } P + \%\text{ Change in } Y. \quad (6.5)$$

The quantity theory assumes that velocity is constant, so the % Change in $V = 0$. The percentage change in the price level is the inflation rate, which we represent by π. Therefore, we can rewrite Equation (6.5) as:

$$\%\text{ Change in } M = \pi + \%\text{ Change in } Y.$$

This equation tells us that the growth rate of the money supply equals the inflation rate plus the growth rate of real GDP. Rewriting it, we have:

$$\pi = \%\text{ Change in } M - \%\text{ Change in } Y.$$

This equation tells us that inflation results from the money supply growing faster than real GDP. For example, if the money supply grows by 5%, while real GDP grows by 3%, the inflation rate will be 2%. If the Fed were to double the growth rate of the money supply from

[1]See Appendix B to this chapter for the derivation.

5% to 10%, the quantity theory predicts that the inflation rate would increase from 2% to 7%. In other words, the quantity theory predicts that a one-percentage-point increase in the growth rate of the money supply will cause a one-percentage-point increase in the inflation rate.

Making the Connection

Is the Inflation Rate Around the World Going to Increase in the Near Future?

Through 2010, central banks increased bank reserves to help their economies recover from the financial crisis. In addition, the European Central Bank (ECB) bought bonds in 2010 to support financial markets after investors sold the bonds of some weaker European economies. The resulting increase in bank reserves *necessarily* increased the monetary base, which *can* lead to an increase in the money supply and higher prices, but not necessarily. The ECB's actions surprised some observers who had become accustomed to the central bank's anti-inflation stance. "The sovereign crisis has pushed the ECB into flooding the system with even more liquidity," Morgan Stanley economist Joachim Fels wrote. "Global excess liquidity should grow by even more, lifting the prices of commodities and other risky assets and adding to global inflation pressures." By the end of 2010, the euro-zone inflation rate rose to 2.2%, the highest reading in two years.

There was less evidence of higher inflation in the United States. During 2008, the Fed reduced the short-term nominal interest rate to near 0% and started a new policy of purchasing long-term bonds, a process known as *quantitative easing*, in an attempt to improve the performance of the economy. Quantitative easing resulted in a large increase in the monetary base and could have been inflationary. Although officials at the Federal Reserve noted that commodity prices had risen in 2010, the underlying rate of inflation—excluding volatile food and energy prices—had been trending downward. Because the U.S. economy was slow to recover from the 2007–2009 recession, the Fed embarked on a new round of bond buying in late 2010 and the first half of 2011, known as *quantitative easing II*, as the inflation rate stayed below 2%.

The increase in the monetary base did not lead to large increases in the money supply in either the United States or Europe because most banks held on to their new reserves. Therefore, the money multiplier decreased, while the monetary base increased. When the economies of the United States and Europe begin to recover, however, banks will be more willing to loan out their new reserves, which will increase the possibility of a sudden rapid rise in the money supply. Vincent Reinhart, a former chief economist for the Federal Reserve's Federal Open Market Committee, said "What you worry about is we have a lot of reserves in the banking system. Ultimately they'll get used and create a multiplier expansion of the money supply." Equation (6.5) on page 198 tells us that in the long run a sudden increase in the money supply will cause an increase in the inflation rate. Although inflation was still relatively low in 2011, there were fears that it would increase as the economies of the world were recovering and banks were becoming more willing to lend.

Sources: Kevin Hall, "Bernanke Unveils Plan to Unwind Fed's Massive Asset Purchases," *McClatchy—Tribune Business News*, February 10, 2010; Heil Shah and Katie Martin, "Europe's Newest Risk: Inflation," *Wall Street Journal*, May 14, 2010; and Dave Kansas, "Whiffs of Inflation from Europe," *Wall Street Journal*, January 4, 2011.

Test your understanding by doing related problem 3.9 on page 221 at the end of this chapter.

Solved Problem 6.3

The Effect of a Decrease in the Growth Rate of the Money Supply

The average annual growth rate of real GDP for the United States since World War II has been 3%. Suppose that the growth rate of velocity is 0%. What happens to the inflation rate if the money supply growth rate decreases from 5% to 2%? Assume that the growth rate of velocity remains 0% and that changes in the growth rate of the money supply do not affect the growth rate of real GDP.

Solving the Problem

Step 1 **Review the chapter material.** The problem asks you to determine the effect of a decrease in the growth rate of the money supply on the inflation rate, so you may want to review the section "The Quantity Theory Explanation of Inflation," which begins on page 198.

Step 2 **Calculate the initial inflation rate.** Equation (6.5) tells us that:

$$\%\text{ Change in } M + \%\text{ Change in } V = \%\text{ Change in } P + \%\text{ Change in } Y,$$

so if the growth rate of velocity is 0%, we have:

$$\%\text{ Change in } M = \pi_1 + \%\text{ Change in } Y,$$

where π_1 = the initial inflation rate. We already know that the growth rate of real GDP is 3%, so the % Change in $Y = 3\%$.

We also know that the growth rate of the money supply is initially 5%, so the % Change in $M = 5\%$. We can plug these two values into the above equation to get:

$$5\% = \pi_1 + 3\%, \text{ or}$$

$$\pi_1 = 5\% - 3\% = 2\%.$$

Step 3 **Calculate the new inflation rate.** If the growth rate of the money supply decreases from 5% to 2%, then, given that velocity is unchanged, the inflation rate will also decrease. We assume that changing the growth rate of the money supply does not change the growth rate of real GDP, which, therefore, remains 3%. Equation (6.5) tells us:

$$\%\text{ Change in } M = \pi_2 + \%\text{ Change in } Y,$$

where the % Change in M is now 2%, and π_2 is the new inflation rate.

We can solve for the new inflation rate:

$$2\% = \pi_2 + 3\%$$

$$\pi_2 = 2\% - 3\% = -1\%.$$

The 3-percentage-point decrease in the growth rate of the money supply led to a 3-percentage-point decrease in the inflation rate. In this case, the inflation rate is negative, so the price level is decreasing. In other words, deflation occurs.

For more practice, do related problem 3.5 on page 220 at the end of this chapter.

Can the Quantity Theory Accurately Predict the Inflation Rate?

Velocity does not have to be constant in order for an increase in the growth rate of the money supply to cause an increase in the inflation rate. As long as velocity grows at a constant rate, there will be a close relationship between increases in the money supply and increases in the inflation rate. However, when the growth rate of velocity changes, it is difficult for the central bank to predict how changes in the growth rate of the money supply will affect the inflation rate. For instance, an increase in the growth rate of the money supply might be offset by a decline in velocity, leaving the inflation rate unaffected.

What can we conclude, then, about the link between the growth rate of the money supply and the inflation rate? Because velocity sometimes moves erratically over short periods, we would not expect the quantity equation to provide good forecasts of inflation in the short run. Over the long run and across countries, there is evidence of a strong link between the growth rate of the money supply and the inflation rate. Panel (a) of Figure 6.4 shows the relationship between the growth rate of the M2 measure of the money supply and the inflation rate by decade in the United States. (We use M2 here because data on M2 are available for a longer period of time than for M1.) Because of variations in the rate of growth of real GDP and in velocity, there is not an exact relationship between the growth rate of M2 and the inflation rate. But there is a clear pattern that decades with higher growth rates in the money supply were also decades with higher inflation rates. In other words, most of the variation in inflation rates across decades can be explained by variation in the rates of growth of the money supply.

Panel (b) provides further evidence consistent with the quantity theory by looking at rates of growth of the money supply and rates of inflation for 40 countries between 1995 and 2009. Although there is not an exact relationship between rates of growth of the money supply and rates of inflation across countries, panel (b) shows that countries where the money supply grew rapidly tended to have high inflation rates, while countries where the money supply grew more slowly tended to have much lower inflation rates. We can conclude that the basic prediction of the quantity theory is one of the most reliable relationships in macroeconomics: If the central bank increases the growth rate of the money supply, then in the long run, this increase will lead to a higher inflation rate.

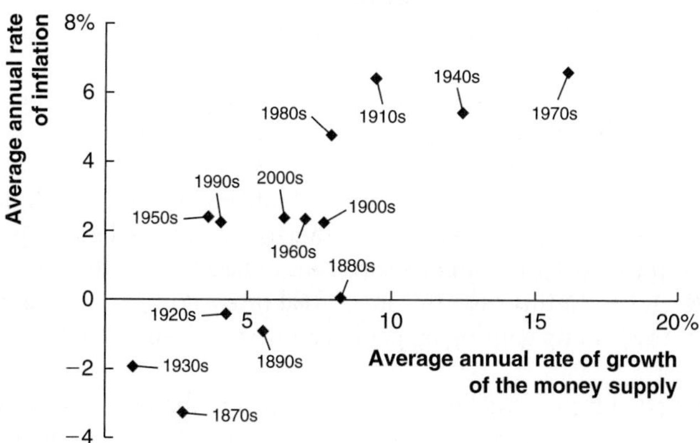

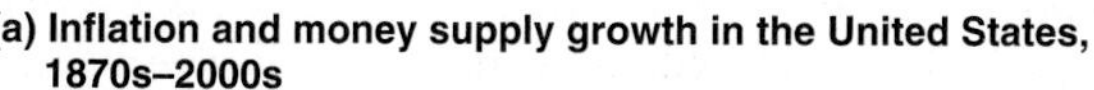
(a) Inflation and money supply growth in the United States, 1870s–2000s

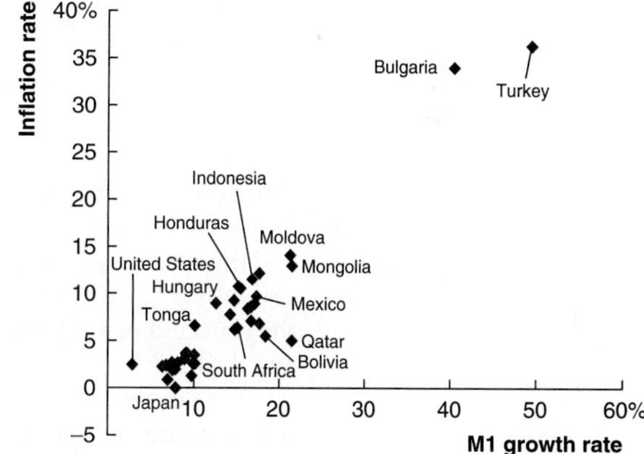

(b) Inflation and money supply growth in 40 countries, 1995–2009

Figure 6.4 The Relationship Between Money Growth and Inflation Over Time and Around the World

Panel (a) shows the relationship between the growth rate of M2 and the inflation rate for the United States from the 1870s to the 2000s. Panel (b) shows the relationship between the growth rate of M1 and inflation for 40 countries during the 1995-2009 period. In both panels, high money growth rates are associated with higher inflation rates.

Source: Panel (a): for 1870s to 1960s, Milton Friedman and Anna J. Schwartz, *Monetary Trends in the United States and United Kingdom: Their Relation to Income, Prices, and Interest Rates, 1867–1975*, Chicago: University of Chicago Press, 1982, Table 4.8; for the 1970s to 2000s: Federal Reserve Board of Governors and U.S. Bureau of Economic Analysis; Panel (b): International Monetary Fund, *International Financial Statistics*. ●

6.4

Learning Objective

Discuss the relationships among the growth rate of money, inflation, and nominal interest rates.

The Relationships Among the Growth Rate of Money, Inflation, and Nominal Interest Rates

We saw in Chapter 3 that interest rates are critical for allocating resources in the economy. In this section, we discuss how the central bank by changing the money supply can affect the inflation rate and interest rates.

Actual and Expected Real Interest Rates

Recall from Chapter 2 that the real interest rate is the nominal interest rate minus the inflation rate:

$$r = i - \pi.$$

Expected real interest rate The nominal interest rate minus the expected inflation rate.

Also recall that the **expected real interest rate** is the real interest rate borrowers and lenders expect at the time that a loan is made. The expected real interest rate on a loan equals the nominal interest rate minus the *expected* inflation rate, π^e:

$$\text{Expected } r = i - \pi^e. \tag{6.6}$$

Actual real interest rate The nominal interest rate minus the actual inflation rate.

The **actual real interest rate** on a loan equals the nominal interest rate minus the actual inflation rate:

$$\text{Actual } r = i - \pi. \tag{6.7}$$

If the actual inflation rate and the expected inflation rate are equal, the expected and actual real interest rates are also equal. But if, as is frequently the case, the actual inflation rate does not equal the expected inflation rate, then the actual real interest rate will be higher or lower than the expected real interest rate. The real interest rate is the cost of borrowing. When the actual real interest rate is less than the expected real interest rate, borrowers benefit because the loan is cheaper than they originally expected. By the same token, lenders lose because when the loan is cheaper for the borrower, it is also less profitable for the lender.

For example, if you take out a mortgage loan with a nominal interest rate of 6% when you and the bank making the loan expect the inflation rate to be 2%, then you expect to pay (and the bank expects to receive) a real interest rate of: 6% − 2% = 4%. If the actual inflation rate turns out to be 0%, then the actual real interest rate equals 6%, which is higher than you expected. You end up losing by paying a higher-than-expected real rate, and the bank gains. However, if the actual inflation rate turns out to be 5%, then the actual real interest rate is: 6% − 5% = 1%. In this case, the actual real interest rate is less than the expected real interest rate. You end up gaining by paying a lower-than-expected rate, and the bank loses.

We can generalize by noting that if the actual inflation rate is greater than the expected inflation rate, the actual real interest rate will be less than the expected real interest rate; in this case, borrowers will gain, and lenders will lose. If the actual inflation rate is less than the expected inflation rate, the actual real interest rate will be greater than the expected real interest rate; in this case, borrowers will lose, and lenders will gain. Table 6.1 summarizes the important relationships among nominal interest rates, expected real interest rates, and actual real interest rates.

The Fisher Effect

In the mortgage interest rate example, the nominal mortgage interest rate was fixed, so we could see what happens to the real interest rate when the actual inflation rate rises above or falls below the expected inflation rate. However, the mortgage interest rate, as with other

Table 6.1 The Relationships Among the Nominal Interest Rate and the Expected and Actual Real Interest Rates

If . . .	then . . .	so, . . .
the actual inflation rate is greater than the expected inflation rate	the actual real interest rate will be less than the expected real interest rate	borrowers will gain and lenders will lose.
the actual inflation rate is less than the expected inflation rate	the actual real interest rate will be greater than the expected real interest rate	borrowers will lose and lenders will gain.

interest rates, is fixed only when the borrower signs a mortgage contract. Before the borrower and lender agree on an interest rate, they are free to negotiate an interest rate based on their assessments of market conditions, including the expected inflation rate over the duration of the loan. To determine what nominal interest rate will be acceptable to borrowers and lenders, we can rearrange Equation (6.6) as follows:

$$i = \text{Expected } r + \pi^e. \tag{6.8}$$

Equation (6.8) states that the nominal interest rate is the sum of the expected real interest rate and the expected inflation rate. This equation is called the *Fisher equation*, after the same Irving Fisher associated with the quantity theory of money. The **Fisher equation** states that the nominal interest rate is the sum of the expected real interest rate and the expected inflation rate. Therefore, the nominal interest rate changes when the expected real interest rate changes or when the expected inflation rate changes.

Fisher equation The equation stating that the nominal interest rate is the sum of the expected real interest rate and the expected inflation rate.

As we saw in Chapter 3, there are many different real interest rates in the economy. If we think of the market for Treasury securities, then r is the real interest rate that the Treasury must pay to borrow funds. This real interest rate is determined in the market for loanable funds. That is, factors such as the willingness of households to save and the government's spending and taxing decisions affect the real interest rate. For example, if a budget deficit results from the federal government raising expenditures or cutting taxes, it finances this deficit by borrowing. So, the supply of loanable funds will decrease, causing the real interest rate to increase. According to the Fisher equation, the nominal interest rate will also rise, as long as the expected inflation rate doesn't change.

With the expected real interest rate determined in the market for loanable funds, the Fisher equation tells us that the nominal interest rate changes when the expected inflation rate changes. For example, assume the real interest rate in the market for loanable funds is 4%, and the expected inflation rate is 2%. In that case, the nominal interest rate on a loan is: $4\% + 2\% = 6\%$. If the expected inflation rate rises from 2% to 3%, the nominal interest rate will also rise by 1%, to 7%. This adjustment of the nominal interest rate to changes in the expected inflation rate is called the *Fisher effect*. The **Fisher effect** holds that the nominal interest rate rises or falls point-for-point with changes in the expected inflation rate.

Fisher effect The assertion by Irving Fisher that the nominal interest rate rises or falls point-for-point with changes in the expected inflation rate.

Do the data support the Fisher effect? Figure 6.5 shows the relationship between the inflation rate and the nominal interest rate for 89 countries over the period 1995–2009. There is a clear positive relationship between inflation and the nominal interest rate, with nominal interest rates increasing by about 1 percentage point for each 1-percentage-point increase in the inflation rate. Therefore, the Fisher effect and Equation (6.8) provide a good approximation of how inflation rates affect nominal interest rates around the world.

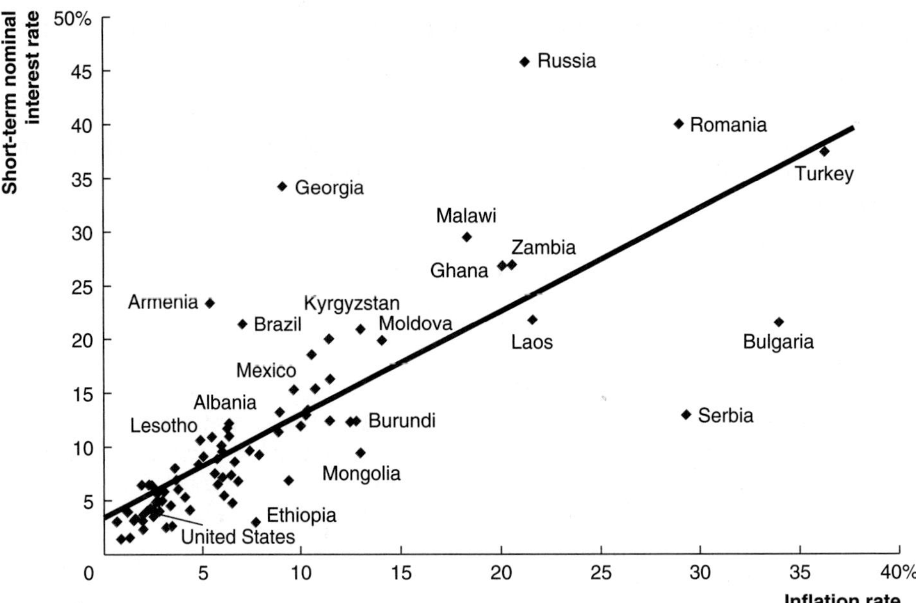

Figure 6.5

The Relationship Between the Inflation Rate and the Nominal Interest Rate, 1995–2009

The figure shows a positive relationship between the inflation rate and the nominal interest rate for 89 countries. This relationship is consistent with the Fisher effect.

Source: International Monetary Fund, *International Financial Statistics*. ●

Money Growth and the Nominal Interest Rate

If we combine the quantity theory of money with the Fisher effect, we learn an important relationship: In the long run, an increase in the growth rate of the money supply causes the inflation rate to increase, which then causes the nominal interest rate to increase. We can conclude that because the inflation rate varies across time and countries as a result of changes in the growth rate of the money supply, nominal interest rates will also vary across time and countries.

Consider the United States. From 1919 to 2011, the growth rate of M2 velocity was approximately 0%, the growth rate of real GDP was 3%, and the expected real interest rate on Aaa corporate bonds averaged 2.8%.[2] Suppose that the Fed sets the growth rate of the money supply at 5%. According to the Fisher equation, what should be the nominal interest rate on a Aaa corporate bond? To answer this question, we must first calculate the expected inflation rate. For simplicity, we will assume that the actual and expected inflation rates are the same. So, we can use Equation (6.5), which is the quantity equation in growth rates, to find the inflation rate. The quantity equation in growth rates is:

$$\%\text{ Change in } M + \%\text{ Change in } V = \%\text{ Change in } P + \%\text{ Change in } Y.$$

The growth rate of the price level is the inflation rate, and we are assuming that the growth rate of velocity is zero, so:

$$\%\text{ Change in } M = \pi + \%\text{ Change in } Y\text{, or}$$
$$5\% = \pi + 3\%\text{, so that}$$
$$\pi = 5\% - 3\% = 2\%.$$

[2]We measure the expected real interest rate as the nominal interest rate minus the inflation rate during the previous year. The inflation rate is calculated as the growth rate of the consumer price index.

If we are willing to assume that this is also the expected inflation rate, we can use the Fisher equation in Equation (6.8) to calculate the nominal interest rate on a corporate Aaa bond as:

$$i = r + \pi^e, \text{ or}$$
$$i = 2.8 + 2 = 4.8\%.$$

Note that the relationship between the rate of growth of the money supply and the inflation rate described by the quantity equation is best thought of as a long-run relationship. Therefore, we would not expect that an increase in the rate of growth of the money supply would necessarily result in an immediate increase in nominal interest rates.

Solved Problem 6.4

The Effect of an Increase in the Growth Rate of the Money Supply on the Interest Rate

As we have seen, in the long run, the average annual growth rate of real GDP for the United States has been about 3%, and the expected real interest rate on corporate bonds with Aaa ratings has averaged 2.8%. Suppose that the growth rate of velocity is 0%, and the growth rate of real GDP remains unchanged.

a. Use the Fisher equation to determine the value of the nominal interest rate on Aaa bonds if the money supply grows at an annual rate of 6%.

b. What will happen to the nominal interest rate in the long run if the growth rate of the money supply increases to 10%?

Solving the Problem

Step 1 **Review the chapter material.** This problem asks you to determine the effect of an increase in the growth rate of the money supply on the interest rate, so you may want to review the section "Money Growth and the Nominal Interest Rate," which begins on page 204.

Step 2 **Use the quantity equation to determine the inflation rate.** The quantity equation tells us that with constant velocity, real GDP growing at a rate of 3%, and the money supply growing at a rate of 6%, the initial inflation rate, π_1, will equal $6\% - 3\% = 3\%$.

Step 3 **Use the result from step 2 and the Fisher equation to answer part (a) by calculating the initial nominal interest rate.** The Fisher equation tells us that the nominal interest rate should equal the expected real interest rate plus the expected inflation rate:

$$i = \text{Expected } r + \pi^e.$$

The expected real interest rate is given as 2.8%, and in step 2 we calculated the inflation rate as 3%. Therefore, the nominal interest rate should equal 2.8% + 3% = 5.8%.

Step 4 **Answer part (b) by calculating the effect of the increase in the growth rate of the money supply on the nominal interest rate.** We know from the quantity equation that, with velocity constant, an increase in the rate of growth of the money supply from 6% to 10% will increase the inflation rate from 3% to 7%. The Fisher equation tells us that an increase of 4 percentage points in the inflation rate should result in an increase of 4 percentage points in the nominal interest rate. Therefore, in the long run, the nominal interest rate should rise from 5.8% to 9.8%.

For more practice, do related problem 4.7 on page 221 at the end of this chapter.

6.5

Learning Objective

Explain the costs of a monetary policy that allows inflation to be greater than zero.

The Costs of Inflation

In the previous sections, we discussed the quantity theory of money, the inflation rate, and nominal interest rates. We also saw how to use equations to predict the long run rate of inflation. We now explain the costs of inflation and the benefits of reducing inflation. As it turns out, the costs of inflation depend on whether the inflation is expected or unexpected. The costs arise partly because inflation interferes with the ability of money to serve its four functions that we discussed on page 190.

Figure 6.6 shows the inflation rates for Japan, Mexico, and the United States from 1961 to 2010. For most nations, the inflation rate rose from the late 1960s to the early 1980s as central banks allowed the growth rate of the money supply to increase, before decreasing to much lower levels in the 1990s and 2000s. In fact, Japan experienced deflation during part of the 1990s and 2000s. In contrast, some countries, such as Mexico, experienced very high rates of inflation. The United States experienced an increase in the inflation rate during the 1970s and then a decrease during the 1980s and 1990s. However, the changes in the U.S. inflation rate were small relative to countries such as Mexico.

Costs of Expected Inflation

Seigniorage The government's profit from issuing fiat money; also called inflation tax.

There are four costs of expected inflation: seigniorage, shoe-leather costs, tax distortions, and menu costs. **Seigniorage** refers to the government's profit from issuing fiat money. Seigniorage is also known as the *inflation tax.* When the government increases the money supply, it gets to use the extra money to purchase goods and services or pay for transfer programs such as Social Security and unemployment insurance. However, we have also seen that an increase in the money supply causes inflation. Inflation causes the purchasing power of money to decrease. Suppose you want to purchase an iPad next year. The current price of the iPad is $500, and you decide to keep $500 in your checking account for one year and then purchase the device. If the government finances its expenditures by increasing the money supply to the extent that the inflation rate is 10% for the year, then the price of the iPad will rise to $550. Your $500 can no longer purchase the iPad, so the purchasing

Figure 6.6

Inflation Rates in Japan, Mexico, and the United States, 1961–2010

Inflation rates around the world increased during the 1970s, but the inflation rate increased much more in countries such as Mexico than in higher-income economies. Many low-income countries experienced periods of very high inflation rates and even hyperinflation before making the transition to lower inflation rates. Inflation rates are measured as the annual growth rates of the consumer price index.

Source: International Monetary Fund, *International Financial Statistics.* ●

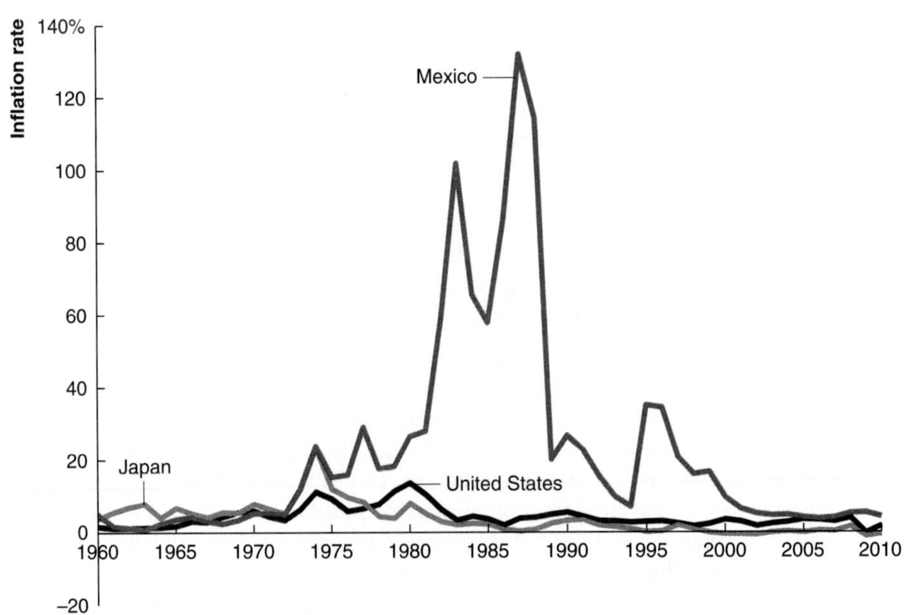

power of your money has decreased. The government's actions caused the decrease in the purchasing power of your $500, so the increase in inflation is essentially a tax. Therefore, inflation acts like a transfer of wealth from the holders of money to the government. What the government gains in revenues, the holders of money lose so seigniorage does not directly decrease aggregate well-being.

Households and firms change their behavior to avoid the inflation tax by choosing to hold less of their wealth as money. The nominal interest rate on money is 0%, so if the expected inflation rate is 3%, the expected real interest rate for money is 0% minus 3%, or −3%. Other assets, such as savings accounts, certificates of deposits, and bonds, have a nominal interest rate greater than zero. To protect themselves from seigniorage, households and firms transfer their wealth from money to interest-bearing assets. Unfortunately, these other assets are less liquid than money. When people want to use their wealth to purchase goods and services, they must first transfer their wealth from the less liquid interest-bearing assets into money. This transfer takes time and effort, so it is costly. Economists use the term **shoe-leather costs** to refer to the costs of inflation to households and firms from holding less money and making more frequent trips to the bank.

Shoe-leather costs The costs of inflation to households and firms from holding less money and making more frequent trips to the bank; costs related to expected inflation.

Expected inflation also creates inefficiencies in the tax system by distorting individual behavior. The first distortion involves the tax system. In addition to taxing income, the federal government also taxes *capital gains.* A capital gain is the increase in the price of an asset. If you buy a share of Apple stock for $100 and sell it 10 years later for $300, you are taxed on the whole $200 gain, even though part of the price increase may be due to inflation. The failure to adjust the value of capital gains for inflation increases the tax burden on investors and may reduce the level of saving in the economy. In addition, the tax code fails to adjust the values of inventories and the value of depreciation allowances for inflation, which also makes the economy less efficient by raising the corporate tax burden when prices rise and depressing business investment during periods of high inflation.

Expected inflation also can distort financial decisions because lenders pay taxes on nominal rather than real returns. Suppose that expected inflation is 4% and that an individual faces a tax rate of 30%. On an investment with a nominal interest rate of 8%, the individual realizes a real after-tax return of $(1 - 0.30)(8\%) - 4\% = 1.6\%$. Suppose that the expected inflation rate rises to 8% and that the nominal interest rate rises by the same amount, to 12%. The investor's real after-tax return falls to $(1 - 0.30)(12\%) - 8\% = 0.4\%$. Therefore, nominal interest rates would have to increase by more than the change in inflation $(8\% - 4\%)$ to maintain the real return of 1.6%. But there are winners as well as losers during a period of high inflation. Borrowers such as corporations and individual home buyers benefit from expected inflation because borrowers deduct nominal interest payments (*not* real interest payments) in calculating their income tax liabilities. Changes in expected inflation can change the real after-tax cost of borrowing. For example, with high expected inflation, corporations find selling bonds or taking out loans more attractive because nominal interest payments are deductible. Households find housing investment more attractive relative to investing in stocks because home mortgage interest is tax deductible.

Menu costs are the costs to firms of changing prices due to reprinting price lists, informing customers, and angering customers by frequent price changes. The higher the inflation rate, the more frequently firms change prices, so the greater the menu costs. In addition, not all firms have the same menu costs, so when expected inflation occurs, some firms will change prices and others will not. For example, restaurants often have to pay to have new menus printed up, so the menu costs for restaurants are high, and restaurants therefore do not change prices frequently. However, the price of a gallon of gas can change every day because it is relatively cheap and easy for gasoline stations to change posted

Menu costs The costs to firms of changing prices due to reprinting price lists, informing customers, and angering customers; costs related to expected inflation.

prices. Therefore, gasoline prices often respond quickly to inflation, while prices at restaurants do not respond quickly. This distortion causes relative prices in the economy to change, and the economy's allocation of resources to become less efficient. The phenomenon is very similar to what happens with real interest rates. In this case, firms set nominal prices partly based on what they think the inflation rate will be. If inflation is higher or lower than expected, the real price of a firm's product is also higher or lower than expected. Firms with low menu costs are likely to adjust their prices to the desired level quickly, but firms with high menu costs will not. As a result, the relative price of goods and services can change and make markets less efficient.

How Large Are the Costs of Expected Inflation?

Inflation has averaged around 2% in the United States for the past 20 years. That inflation rate is low, but the rate is still positive, so the average price of goods and services rises over time. Martin Feldstein of Harvard University has argued that there would be substantial benefit to the economy of going from 2% to 0% inflation.[3] Feldstein believes that even at a 2% inflation rate, the welfare costs from inflation range from 0.63% to 1.01% of GDP. Given the size of U.S. economic activity in 2010, the welfare costs of 2% inflation range from \$92 billion to \$148 billion per year.[4] And these costs are paid every year, which makes the present value of the welfare gain of going from 2% to 0% inflation 35% of GDP, or more than \$5.1 trillion.

The welfare costs are large because the distortions caused by inflation persist into the future. When inflation combines with the tax code to reduce the incentive for firms to invest, the capital stock falls over time. In addition, if individuals save less because inflation lowers returns to saving, the supply of loanable funds falls. This decline will raise real interest rates and reduce investment expenditures. The reduction in the capital stock depresses economic activity today and into the future. Because real GDP grows over time, even a 1% welfare loss is very large in an economy the size of the U.S. economy.

Costs of Unexpected Inflation

When the inflation rate turns out to be higher or lower than expected, wealth is redistributed. For example, suppose you borrowed \$500 to purchase an iPad instead of paying cash for it. The bank charges you a nominal interest rate of 10%, and you repay the loan after one year. That is, you pay the bank \$550 at the end of the year in exchange for the bank giving you \$500 at the beginning of the year to purchase the iPad. If the expected inflation rate for the year is 4%, then the expected real interest rate is: $10\% - 4\% = 6\%$. That means you expect to pay—and the bank expects to receive—a 6% real interest rate. The nominal compensation to the bank for the loan is \$50, but the real compensation is \$30. What happens if the inflation rate turns out to be 8%? In that case, the actual real interest rate is: $10\% - 8\% = 2\%$. While the nominal compensation to the bank remains \$50, the real compensation is just \$10. You gain, and the bank loses. As we saw in Table 6.1 on page 203, when inflation is higher than expected, borrowers gain, and creditors lose.

---

[3]Martin Feldstein, "The Costs and Benefits of Going from Low Inflation to Price Stability," in Christina Romer and David Romer (eds.), *Reducing Inflation: Motivation and Strategy*, Chicago: University of Chicago Press, 1997. See also Darrell Cohen, Kevin Hassett, and R. Glenn Hubbard, "Inflation and the User Cost of Capital: Does Inflation Still Matter?" in Martin Feldstein (ed.), *The Costs and Benefits of Price Stability*, Chicago: University of Chicago Press, 1999.

[4]Data are in chained 2005 dollars.

MACRO DATA: WHAT IS THE EXPECTED INFLATION RATE?

The expected inflation rate is clearly important. Although we cannot directly observe a person's expectations, we can infer the inflation rate that the market as a whole expects. In 1997, the U.S. government started issuing Treasury Inflation Protected Securities (TIPS). Most Treasury securities have a fixed nominal face value, so when the Treasury sells these securities in auctions, we learn the nominal interest rate. In contrast, TIPS have a fixed real face value that increases with the inflation rate, so when they are sold, we learn the expected real interest rate. The Fisher equation states:

$$i = \text{Expected}\, r + \pi^e.$$

We can use this relationship to determine the expected inflation rate. When the Treasury auctions standard securities, i is set in the market; when the Treasury auctions TIPS, expected r is set in the market. The difference between these two market interest rates is an estimate of the expected inflation rate in the bond market. For example, on January 18, 2011, the nominal interest rate on a standard 10-year Treasury bond was 3.4%, and the expected real interest rate on a 10-year TIPS Treasury bond was 1.0%. As a result, the average annual expected inflation rate for the next 10 years in the market was: 3.4% − 1.0% = 2.4%.

The following figure shows the expected inflation rate over the following 5 years and 10 years, calculated using the interest rates on standard 5-year and 10 -year Treasury notes and TIPS with the same maturities. Inflationary expectations were stable from 2003 through the fall of 2008, then as a result of the worsening of the financial crisis, expected inflation plummeted and actually became negative before rebounding to previous levels. In Chapter 9, we discuss why economic downturns can decrease expected inflation.

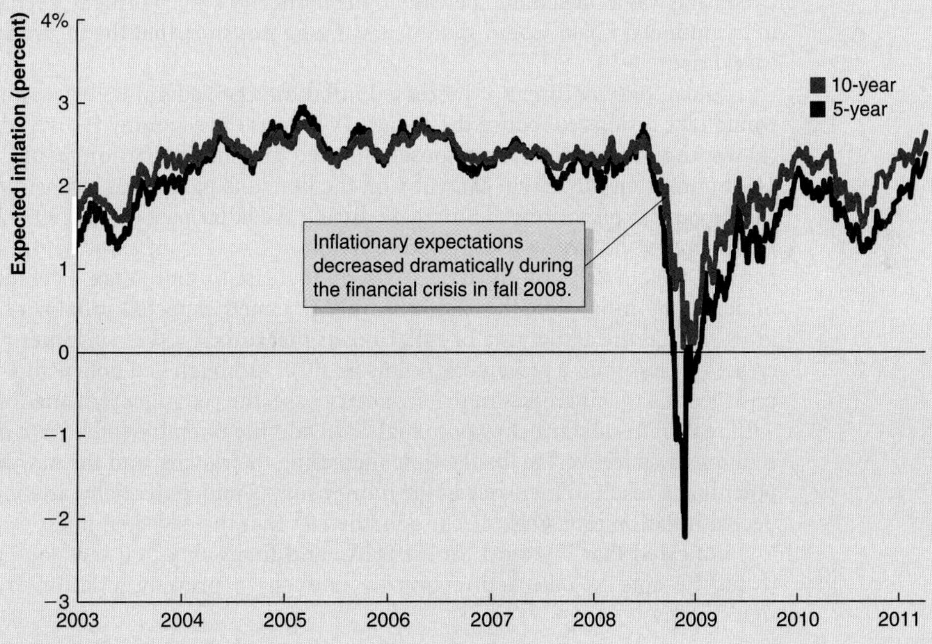

Source: Federal Reserve Bank of Saint Louis FRED database.

Test your understanding by doing related problem D6.4 on page 225 at the end of this chapter.

So, if inflation is higher than expected, there is a redistribution of wealth from lenders to borrowers. As with seigniorage, the total wealth in the economy does not change. Nevertheless, unexpected inflation can generate true costs for the economy. First, both lenders and borrowers devote resources to forecasting inflation and avoiding the costs of unexpectedly high or low inflation. These resources could be used elsewhere to produce goods and services. Second, one way in which lenders and borrowers can avoid the costs associated with unexpected inflation is not to borrow or lend. Unexpected inflation can therefore reduce economic activity—investment activity in particular.

Making the Connection

Did the Fed's Actions During the Financial Crisis of 2007–2009 Increase the Expected Inflation Rate?

In 2008, the U.S. economy was in a financial crisis and the worst recession since the 1930s. Federal Reserve officials believed they should take bold action by undertaking a program known as *quantitative easing*. Under this program, the Federal Reserve began to purchase more than $1 trillion of U.S. Treasury bonds and mortgaged-backed securities in order to reduce long-term interest rates and increase the growth of output. The result of quantitative easing was a substantial increase in the monetary base. Normally, such a large increase in the monetary base would spark fears among investors that the future rate of inflation would rise.

To combat the threat of increased inflation, the Federal Reserve announced that it would take actions to reduce the monetary base as the economy recovered. How successful was the Fed in convincing households and firms that inflation would not accelerate? The figure from the *Macro Data* box on the previous page helps us answer this question. Inflationary expectations did increase during the latter part of the 2007–2009 recession. For example, the five-year expected inflation rate rose from a low of −2.2% on November 28, 2008, to 2.0% on April 6, 2010—an increase of more than 4 percentage points in under 18 months—but this increase only returned expected inflation to its pre-crisis level. In fact, the actual rate of inflation, as measured by the consumer price index, increased by less than 2 percentage points in 2010. Although Fed policy during the financial crisis led to large increases in the monetary base, the economy remained weak into 2011, with real GDP still far below potential GDP and the unemployment rate near 9%. As the economy was recovering, banks were increasing their loans, and the new lending had the potential to result in increases in the money supply and, potentially, an increase in the expected inflation rate. Overall, though, the fact that the expected inflation rate remained low indicated that investors, households, and firms expected that the Federal Reserve would be able to take action quickly enough to prevent inflation from increasing significantly.

Sources: Board of Governors of the Federal Reserve System; Ben S. Bernanke, "Aiding the Economy: What the Fed Did and Why," *Washington Post*, November 4, 2010; and Sudeep Reddy, "Unanimous Fed Keeps Buying Bonds," *Wall Street Journal*, January 27, 2011.

Test your understanding by doing related problem 5.8 on page 222 at the end of this chapter.

Inflation Uncertainty

Relative prices play an important role in allocating resources. For example, suppose that the price of a new residential house is $300,000, and the price of a new retail store is also $300,000. This means the relative price of residential housing is one retail store. If the population increases because many young families move into an area, then the price of residential housing is likely to rise relative to the price of retail stores. Suppose the price of residential housing doubles to $600,000, while the price of a retail store remains $300,000. As a result, the relative price of residential housing is now two. Building residential housing is now more profitable relative to building retail stores, so resources will flow into the construction of residential housing to satisfy the demand for housing by the young families. The relative price of residential housing plays a critical role in allocating resources to the construction of residential housing to satisfy the increased demand. In a market economy, relative prices help guide resources to those activities in which the resources improve welfare the most.

When the inflation rate fluctuates significantly from year to year, relative prices become distorted and can send misleading signals to households and firms. As we discussed earlier, when inflation occurs, not all prices rise by the same amount, so relative prices can change, and markets may misallocate resources. Consider the previous example of residential housing and retail stores. Suppose there is no increase in the number of young families in the area, but inflation occurs. We traditionally think of menu costs as the dollar cost of changing prices, but the term is actually much broader than that. When a firm increases prices, it runs the risk of losing customers to its competitors. This is also a cost of increasing prices, so it is a menu cost. When builders increase prices, they also run the risk of losing customers to their competitors. If the menu costs are higher for retail stores than for residential housing because firms are not tied to one locality while households often choose to locate near their place of business, the builders of retail stores will increase prices more slowly than will the builders of residential housing. As a result, the price of residential housing may rise to $600,000 while the price of retail stores remains at $300,000. The relative price of residential housing has again risen to two, so resources will flow into the construction of residential housing. However, relative prices have not changed as a result of changes in the number of young families, so the new residential housing does not satisfy increased demand from consumers. In this situation, the economy's resources can be misallocated.

The more the inflation rate changes from year to year, the more likely it is to distort relative prices. We can measure the volatility of inflation using the statistical measure, standard deviation. Figure 6.7 shows the relationship between the average inflation rate and the volatility of the inflation rate for countries around the world. There is a clear tendency for the volatility of inflation to increase as the average annual inflation rate increases. Therefore, as the inflation rate increases, it becomes less predictable. In this situation, the ability of market prices to help households and firms allocate resources is reduced, as with the previous example about the rise in residential housing prices.

Benefits of Inflation

So far, we have emphasized the costs of inflation. However, some economists believe that there are benefits to low inflation because it can allow for adjustments in relative prices in situations where nominal prices are sticky. For example, it is the real wage—the nominal wage divided by the price level—that determines how many workers a firm will hire. In a situation where the real wage needs to decrease to restore equilibrium in a labor market, this can happen either by cutting the nominal wage or by keeping the nominal wage constant while inflation causes the real wage to decline. Workers are often more reluctant to see their nominal wages cut than they are to see their real wages fall as a result

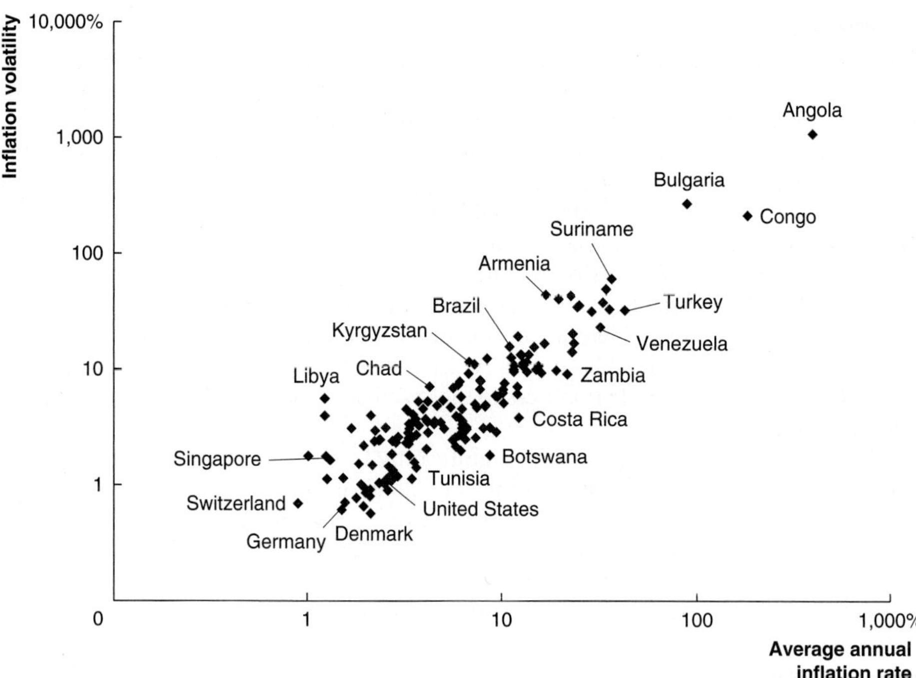

Figure 6.7

Inflation and Inflation Volatility Around the World, 1996–2009

The volatility of inflation tends to increase as the average annual inflation rate increases. As the inflation rate increases, it becomes less predictable. The figure measures the volatility of inflation as the standard deviation of annual inflation rates. Note that the axes are in log base 10 scale.

Sources: International Monetary Fund, *International Financial Statistics*. ●

of inflation, even though in the end the result can be equivalent. For example, in 2010, Dr Pepper Snapple Group tried to cut the nominal wages of its workers by $1.50 per hour, or about $3,000 per year for the typical worker at a plant producing Mott's apple juice near Rochester, New York. The company argued that workers at the plant were overpaid compared to similar workers in the Rochester area. The workers went on strike to resist the nominal wage cuts. In September 2010, the company and the union agreed not to cut nominal wages but did agree to freeze nominal wages for three years. During the three years that the nominal wages are frozen, inflation will reduce the real wages of the workers and bring them closer to those of similar workers in the Rochester area. As the real wage falls at the Mott's plant, the Dr Pepper Snapple Group should become more willing to hire additional workers and make the labor market in the Rochester area operate more efficiently.[5]

6.6

Learning Objective

Explain the causes of hyperinflation.

Hyperinflation and Its Causes

Hyperinflation occurs when the inflation rate is extremely high. At such high rates of inflation, the volatility of inflation is also typically high, so there is a great deal of misallocation of resources in the economy because households and firms have difficulty determining relative prices of goods and services. Firms, for example, may be led by rising prices to think that the demand for their product has increased, when, in fact, the demand for their product is unchanged and the rising price level is solely due to inflation. When a country experiences hyperinflation, its currency will eventually cease to function as money, which is what happened in Germany in 1923 and more recently in Zimbabwe.

[5]Debra Groom, "Mott's Strike Ends in Williamson as Union Approves Contract," *The (Syracuse) Post-Standard*, September 13, 2010; and Steven Greenhouse, "In Mott's Strike, More Than Pay at Stake," *New York Times*, August 18, 2010.

Prices rise rapidly during a hyperinflation, so households and firms try to minimize how much currency they hold, and firms must pay employees frequently. Employees must spend money quickly or convert it to more stable foreign currencies before prices increase further. Merchants raise prices as quickly as possible. The government's tax-collecting ability diminishes significantly during a hyperinflation. Because tax bills typically are fixed in nominal terms, households and firms have an incentive to delay their payments to reduce their real tax burden.

Causes of Hyperinflation

Hyperinflations begin when governments rapidly increase the growth rate of the money supply, and hyperinflations end when governments reverse course and reduce the growth rate of the money supply. While hyperinflations are caused by rapid increases in the money supply, ultimately, hyperinflations are typically due to persistently large budget deficits. To understand why large budget deficits cause hyperinflations, first look at the government's budget constraint. Governments purchase goods and services, G, and make transfer payments, TR. A government must raise the funds for these expenditures by collecting taxes, T; issuing more bonds; or printing money, M. So, in any given year:

$$G + TR = T + \text{Change in } B + \text{Change in } M.$$

The government's budget deficit is the difference between its expenditures, $G + TR$, and its tax revenues, T. We can therefore rewrite the above equation with the government's budget deficit on the left side as:

$$G + TR - T = \text{Change in } B + \text{Change in } M. \quad (6.9)$$

A government with a large budget deficit can finance it either by issuing bonds or by printing money. Some governments, however, may have trouble selling bonds because investors believe that the government may not pay them back. If investors won't buy the government's bonds and the government is unable or unwilling to raise taxes or cut expenditures, the government can finance the budget deficit only by printing money. In this case, to finance a large budget deficit the growth rate of the money supply will have to increase dramatically, leading to higher inflation.

German Hyperinflation After World War I

At the end of World War I, the German government was unable to balance its budget by raising taxes or cutting expenditures. Once inflation began to accelerate, the government's budget deficit was made worse by the structure of the tax system. Taxes were levied in nominal terms, and there were lags between when the government levied the tax and when the government collected the tax revenue. In addition, the German government consistently underestimated the inflation rate, and individuals had a strong incentive to delay paying taxes, so real tax revenues lagged behind real government expenditures. As a result, the German government was forced to print money to finance the budget deficit, until eventually it was financing nearly 100% of its expenditures by printing money.

By the time the hyperinflation ended in Germany, the price level was *50 billion times higher* than before the hyperinflation. The inflation rate reached 41% *per day* during October 1923, so prices doubled every two days. A similar hyperinflation today in the United States would cause a pack of gum to go from a price of $1.50 to over $75 billion in just 15 months! Such rapid increases in the price level make currency almost worthless.

The hyperinflation ended in November 1923, after the German government made the following policy changes:

- Established a new central bank called the Rentenbank to control a new currency, the Rentenmark, which was worth 1 trillion of the old German marks (October 15, 1923). In just a few months after the establishment of the Rentenbank, the German government stopped borrowing from the central bank, the government balanced its budget, and the hyperinflation ended.
- Limited the ability of the Rentenbank to issue new currency to just 3.2 billion Rentenmarks.
- Limited the ability of the Rentenbank to extend loans to the German government to only 1.2 billion Rentenmarks.
- Cut the number of its employees by 25% in October 1923 and by another 10% in January 1924.
- Negotiated relief from the reparation payments it was making to France and the United Kingdom as part of the treaty to end World War I.

These steps were enough to bring the hyperinflation to an end—but not before the savings of anyone holding the old German currency had been wiped out. Most middle-income Germans were extremely resentful of this outcome. Many historians believe that the hyperinflation greatly reduced the allegiance of many Germans to the Weimar Republic, the government at that time, and may have helped pave the way for Adolph Hitler and the Nazis to seize power 10 years later.

Answering the Key Question

Continued from page 188

At the beginning of the chapter, we asked the question:

"What is the connection between changes in the money supply and the inflation rate?"

In this chapter, we saw how the growth rate of the money supply determines the inflation rate in the long run. Central banks control bank reserves with open market operations. An open market purchase of government securities increases bank reserves, and, as banks use the reserves to make loans, the increase in reserves usually results in an increase in the money supply. The quantity theory tells us that this increase in the money supply will then increase the price level. Therefore, if the central bank allows the money supply to grow, the price level will grow, and the economy experiences inflation. Hyperinflation occurs when the government is forced to finance budget deficits through the printing of money. During a hyperinflation, currency ceases to function as a useful medium of exchange or store of value.

In Chapter 7, we cover labor markets and explain how government policy affects wages and employment. Before moving to that chapter, read *An Inside Look at Policy* on the next page to learn about China's monetary policy to deal with a growing rate of inflation without impeding growth.

Growing Economy Fuels Inflation Concerns in China

NEW YORK TIMES

China's Economy Grew 10.3 Percent in 2010

China's economy continued to accelerate in the fourth quarter, as inflation is easing only slightly, showing that a series of cooling measures by Beijing over the last year have had only a limited effect.

Data released by the National Bureau of Statistics on Thursday put the pace of growth at 10.3 percent for the full year, up from 9.2 percent in 2009. . . .

Taken together, the data and a number of other statistics in recent days supported the view of many economists who believe that the government will have to further tighten monetary policy. . . .

a Inflation, which has become a major concern for the authorities in recent months, came in at 3.3 percent for the full year, above the official target of 3 percent, while the data for December showed consumer prices were up 4.8 percent from a year earlier.

This was lower than the 5.1 percent inflation seen in November, but still a worrying one in the eyes of ordinary Chinese, who have been complaining of rising food prices, with some staples increasing 25 percent in the last few months.

Moreover, many economists expect the pace of inflation to pick up again in coming months because of adverse weather conditions and other seasonal factors. . . . Rising wages also have fanned inflation pressures in recent months.

"It's clear that the government policy stance has shifted" from worrying about growth to controlling inflation, said Arthur Kroeber, head of the economics research company Dragonomics, based in Beijing.

b Over the last year, the government has taken a series of incremental steps to tighten growth and curb inflation. The so-called reserve requirement ratio for state-controlled banks—which effectively dictates the amount that lenders have to set aside against loans, limiting how much they can lend—has been raised seven times since early 2010. . . .

However, these steps have had only a moderate effect on the pace of growth. Bank lending continues to surge. . . .

c "In sum, growth has not been significantly impacted by tightening measures. Instead, it continues to fuel inflation by boosting demand for both producer and consumer goods and services," Ken Peng, an economist at Citigroup, commented in a note on Thursday. "This should give the green light for authorities to continue to tighten policy to contain inflation expectations."

Many analysts believe that another rate increase, a higher reserve ratio for banks and other measures aimed more specifically at sectors like housing could come within weeks. . . .

Some analysts also say that one way to combat inflation would be to allow the Chinese currency to strengthen. A stronger renminbi would make it cheaper for Chinese companies to import raw materials and goods from abroad, helping keep down the price inflation of finished goods at home. . . .

Source: Ian Johnson and Bettina Wassener, "China's Economy Grew 10.3 % in 2010," From *The New York Times*, January 21, 2011.

Key Points in the Article

This article discusses why the continued rapid lending and increases in the growth rate of the money supply in China have raised fears of inflation and the expectations that the Chinese government will need to further tighten its monetary policy. The Chinese economy grew by more than 10% in 2010 and experienced an annual inflation rate of 3.3%. The inflation rate grew to over 5% in November, and many analysts expect this rate to continue to increase. China enacted measures in 2010 to curb inflation, but the high rates of inflation indicate that additional money tightening policies may need to be implemented.

Analyzing the News

a The 3.3% annual inflation rate in 2010 exceeded the government's official target rate of 3%. While the annual rate was only slightly higher than the target, the inflation rate continued to increase throughout the year, as shown in Figure 1, rising to 5.1% in November, its highest level in over two years. With predictions of further increases continuing into 2011, the Chinese government has expressed concerns about the price level increases and has taken measures to attempt to bring the inflation rate down to its official target.

b The global financial crisis of 2008–2009 prompted the Chinese government to take significant measures to stimulate its economy, measures which helped China continue its rapid economic growth during these years. Through generous lending by state banks, the money supply grew rapidly in 2009, as is shown in Figure 2, increasing by over 30% by the end of the year. Concerned that this increase in the money supply would generate too much inflation, the government took steps to tighten monetary policy, including increasing the reserve ratio seven times in 2010 as well as raising interest rates. Despite these steps, bank lending continued to increase throughout the year.

c With inflation on the rise, the government is contemplating further money tightening measures, including additional increases in the bank reserve ratio. The continued growth in the money supply has caused significant increases in consumer prices since mid-2009. As Figure 1 shows, consumer price inflation has jumped from being negative in 2009 to nearly 5% and on the rise by the end of 2010.

THINKING CRITICALLY *ABOUT POLICY*

1. If the Chinese government continues to tighten its monetary policy by increasing the reserve requirement ratio for state-controlled banks, what will be the likely effect on the ability of these banks to make loans and the money supply? What effect will this have on inflation?
2. During 2010, real GDP increased by 10.3% from 2009, M2 increased by 19%, and the inflation rate was 3.3%. Using these figures, calculate the growth rate of velocity during 2010. Suppose that velocity had been constant during 2010 and that real GDP growth remained 10.3% and the growth rate of the money supply remained 19%. What would the inflation rate have been? Use the quantity equation to derive your answer.

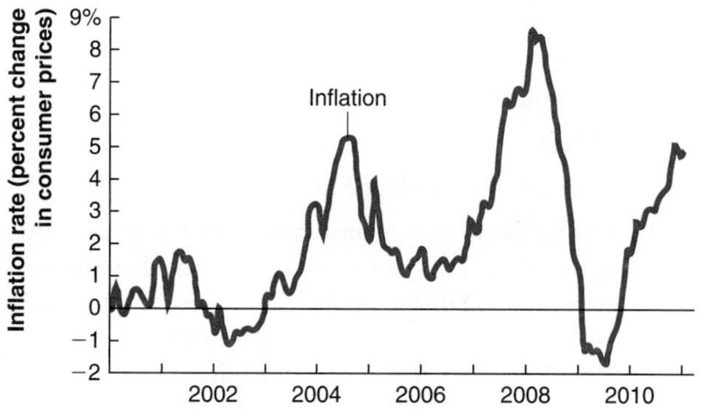

Figure 1 Consumer price inflation in China

Source: Reuters

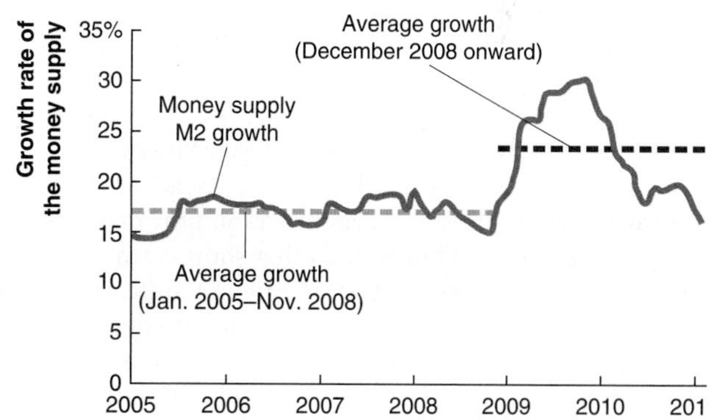

Figure 2 M2 year-over-year growth

Source: Also Sprach Analyst http://www.alsosprachanalyst.com

CHAPTER SUMMARY AND PROBLEMS

KEY TERMS

Actual real interest rate, p. 202
Commodity money, p. 190
Expected real interest rate, p. 202
Fiat money, p. 191
Fisher effect, p. 203
Fisher equation, p. 203
Hyperinflation, p. 191
Medium of exchange, p. 190
Menu costs, p. 207
M1, p. 193
M2, p. 193
Monetary base (or high-powered money), p. 195
Money multiplier, p. 195
Open market operations, p. 195
Quantity equation (or equation of exchange), p. 197
Quantity theory of money, p. 198
Reserves, p. 195
Seigniorage, p. 206
Shoe-leather costs, p. 207
Standard of deferred payment, p. 191
Store of value, p. 190
Unit of account, p. 190
Velocity of money, p. 198

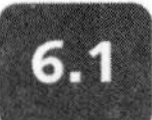

6.1 What Is Money, and Why Do We Need It?

Define money and explain its functions.

SUMMARY

Money is the most liquid of all assets. Money acts as a **store of value**, **unit of account**, **medium of exchange**, and **standard of deferred payment**. **Commodity money** is an asset used as money that also has value independent of its use as money. Gold is the most common form of commodity money. **Fiat money** has no value apart from its use as money. Fiat money is valuable because the government makes it legal tender, and individuals have confidence that the currency will maintain its value. Very high rates of inflation are called **hyperinflation**, and when hyperinflation occurs, fiat money no longer functions as an effective medium of exchange. The **M1** measure of the money supply consists of currency plus checking accounts and traveler's checks. These are the most liquid assets because they are widely accepted as payment for goods and services. **M2** consists of all the assets in M1 plus savings accounts, small-denomination time deposits, money market mutual funds, and other short-term deposits. The additional assets in M2 are not quite as liquid as the assets in M1. However, today's automated teller machines and online banking make it easy for households and firms to convert the additional assets in M2 into currency and checking accounts.

Review Questions

1.1 What is a store of value? What types of assets act as a store of value?

1.2 What is a medium of exchange? Why must money act as a medium of exchange?

1.3 What is a standard of deferred payment, and why is it important?

1.4 What is a unit of account, and why is it important?

1.5 What is the difference between commodity money and fiat money?

1.6 List the components of M1 and M2.

Problems and Applications

1.7 Each of the following has been used as money at some time in the past. Comment on how well each fulfills the four functions of money and why it might be used as money.

a. Gold or silver

b. Cigarettes

c. Salt

d. Native American beads

1.8 People living in Yap, an island group in the Pacific, at one time used as money large stone disks known as Rai. These disks can be up to 12 feet in diameter and were made of a stone that is not native to the islands, so they had to be transported by canoe with great difficulty and risk. The stones were valued both due to their scarcity and because of the history of their acquisition.

a. How well do large stones fulfill the functions of money?

b. In 1874, a Western immigrant to the islands used ships to transport more stones to Yap.

While these stones were larger, they did not have the history of risk and hardship associated with them.

i. What happened to Yap's money supply and to the overall value of stones?

ii. How does what happened to Yap's money illustrate a central problem of commodity monies?

iii. How would you expect old stones to be valued relative to new stones? Briefly explain.

1.9 A *New York Times* column in the fall of 2009 reported that the value of the dollar was falling, in part, because "investors who had sought shelter in the American currency's perceived stability were beginning to funnel their money into hard assets like gold." What does the article mean by "hard assets"? Why is the dollar not a hard asset?

Source: "Times Topics: Dollar," *New York Times*, October 12, 2009.

1.10 **[Related to the *Making the Connection* on page 192]** After the French Revolution in 1789, France experienced a hyperinflation similar to Zimbabwe's (although much smaller in magnitude). At one point, the French currency was worth so little that people used it for fuel rather than spending it.

a. What function(s) of money did the French currency fail to fulfill during the hyperinflation?

b. Eventually, France issued a new currency, backed by gold. Why did the new currency need to be backed by gold?

6.2 The Federal Reserve and the Money Supply

Explain how the Federal Reserve changes the money supply.

SUMMARY

The **monetary base** is the sum of currency in circulation and bank **reserves**. The central bank determines the monetary base through **open market operations**. The money supply equals the monetary base times the **money multiplier**. The central bank, the nonbank public, and private banks together determine the value of the money multiplier. Therefore, the central bank does not have complete control over the money supply. For example, the Fed increased the monetary base dramatically during the 2007–2009 recession. However, the money supply increased by much less because the money multiplier fell as banks decided to increase their excess reserves.

Review Questions

2.1 What is the monetary base?

2.2 What is the formula for the money multiplier?

2.3 How does the Fed control the monetary base?

2.4 How does the money multiplier change when banks decide to hold more excess reserves relative to deposits?

2.5 How does the money multiplier change when the nonbank public decides to hold more currency relative to deposits?

2.6 Why does the Fed have greater control over the monetary base than over the money supply?

Problems and Applications

2.7 In April 2011, the money supply, as measured by M1, was approximately $1,917 billion. The monetary base was approximately $2,494 billion.

a. What was the value of the money multiplier?

b. Why is the value of the money multiplier typically greater than 1? What is the key reason that it was less than 1 in 2011?

Source: Federal Reserve Bank of St. Louis.

2.8 As of early 2011, banks continued to hold large amounts of excess reserves, leading to concern that potential increases in lending activity could increase the money supply and the inflation rate.

a. Use the money multiplier to explain how a reduction in excess reserves could lead to an increase in the money supply.

b. What tools does the Fed have to change the money supply?

c. How might the Fed use these tools to offset the effects of a surge in bank lending?

2.9 Consider the following statement: "The central bank is the only entity that can print money. Therefore, the central bank has complete control over the money supply."

Do you agree with this statement? Explain.

2.10 Briefly explain why the monetary base is often called "high-powered money."

2.11 Suppose that the required reserve ratio is 8%, banks hold 5% of deposits as excess reserves, and the currency-to-deposit ratio is 2.

a. What is the value of the money multiplier?

b. If the Fed conducts open market operations and buys bonds from banks, what will happen to the money supply?

c. How would your answer to part b. change if banks become concerned about making loans and now choose to hold 20% of deposits as excess reserves?

6.3 The Quantity Theory of Money and Inflation

Describe the quantity theory of money and use it to explain the connection between changes in the money supply and the inflation rate.

SUMMARY

The **quantity equation** states that the money supply multiplied by the velocity of money equals nominal GDP. The **velocity of money** is the average number of times each dollar in the money supply is used to purchase goods and services included in GDP. The **quantity theory of money** assumes a constant or predictable velocity of money. If velocity is constant, there is a close relationship between the rate of growth of the money supply and inflation. If velocity is constant and the growth rate of real GDP is not affected by the rate of growth of money supply, then a 1-percentage-point increase in the growth rate of the money supply causes the inflation rate to increase by 1 percentage point.

Review Questions

3.1 State the quantity equation.

3.2 What is the velocity of money?

3.3 What is the difference between the quantity equation and the quantity theory of money?

3.4 According to the quantity theory, what is the relationship between the rate of growth of the money supply and inflation?

Problems and Applications

3.5 **[Related to *Solved Problem 6.3* on page 200]** The average annual growth rate of real GDP for the United States is about 3%. Assume that the growth rate of velocity is 0%, and the rate of growth of the money supply is 4%.

a. What is the current rate of inflation?

b. What will happen to the inflation rate if the rate of growth of the money supply increases to 7%?

c. What will happen to the inflation rate if the rate of growth of the money supply increases to 7%, and, at the same time, the growth rate of velocity increases to 2%?

3.6 In 2010, the money supply, M1, was $1,832 billion. Nominal GDP was $14,660 billion.

a. What was the velocity of money measured using M1?

b. In 2010, M2 was $8,816 billion. What was the velocity of money measured using M2?

c. Why are these measures of velocity different?

Source: Federal Reserve Bank of St. Louis.

3.7 A *Wall Street Journal* article on the Fed's options for reducing inflationary pressure stated: "In the old days, when the Fed wanted to tighten . . . the task was easy. It pulled a few billion dollars out of short-term lending markets by selling Treasury bonds." Why does the Fed's selling Treasury bonds "pull" money out of the system?

Source: Jon Hilsenrath, "As the Fed Uses Fewer Tools, Exit Plan Emerges," *Wall Street Journal*, December 15, 2009.

3.8 During the late nineteenth century, the United States experienced a period of sustained *deflation*, or a falling price level. Explain using the quantity theory of money how deflation is possible. Is it necessary for the quantity of money to decline for deflation to occur?

3.9 **[Related to the *Making the Connection* on page 199]** The quantity theory of money states that changes in the money supply have predictable effects on the price level, or, in other words, that money growth determines inflation in the long run. Under what circumstances might this theory be incorrect? Briefly explain.

6.4 The Relationships Among the Growth Rate of Money, Inflation, and Nominal Interest Rates

Discuss the relationships among the growth rate of money, inflation, and nominal interest rates.

SUMMARY

The **expected real interest rate** equals the nominal interest rate minus the expected inflation rate, and the **actual real interest rate** equals the nominal interest rate minus the actual inflation rate. The expected and actual real interest rates are the same if the inflation rate equals the expected inflation rate. The **Fisher equation** states that the nominal interest rate is the sum of the expected real interest rate and the expected inflation rate. The **Fisher effect** states that if the expected inflation rate increases by 1 percentage point, the nominal interest rate also increases by 1 percentage point. The quantity theory of money and the Fisher effect together predict that in the long run a 1-percentage-point increase in the growth rate of the money supply causes a 1-percentage-point increase in the expected inflation rate and the nominal interest rate.

Review Questions

4.1 Explain the difference between the expected real interest rate and the actual real interest rate.

4.2 If the actual inflation rate turns out to be greater than the expected inflation rate, will the expected real interest rate be higher or lower than the actual real interest rate?

4.3 What is the Fisher equation?

4.4 What is the Fisher effect?

4.5 Do the data in Figure 6.5 on page 204 support the Fisher effect?

4.6 How does an increase in the rate of growth of the money supply affect the nominal interest rate?

Problems and Applications

4.7 **[Related to *Solved Problem 6.4* on page 205]** The long run growth rate of real GDP for the United States is about 3%, and the expected real interest rate on corporate Aaa bonds has averaged 2.8%.

a. If the growth rate of velocity is 0% and the rate of growth of the money supply is 6%, in the long run what is the nominal interest rate?

b. What will happen to the nominal interest rate in the long run if the rate of growth of the money supply falls to 3%?

c. What will happen to the nominal interest rate in the long run if the rate of growth of the money supply falls to 3% and the growth rate of real GDP falls to 2.5%?

4.8 Suppose that inflation has been equal to 3% per year for several years and that the real interest rate that banks require on typical mortgage loans is 2%.

a. What nominal interest rate would banks currently be charging on typical mortgages?

b. The Federal Reserve unexpectedly increases the rate of growth of the money supply by 1%, and this change is expected to be permanent. What nominal interest rate will banks charge on new mortgages?

c. What is the actual real return on mortgages made prior to the increase in the growth rate of the money supply?

4.9 In the spring of 2011, as worries about the possibility of the Greek government defaulting on its sovereign debt rose, the nominal interest rate on Greek bonds increased sharply.

a. Why did the nominal interest rate increase?

b. Would you expect there to be a difference between actual and expected real interest rates in this situation?

4.10 During the Great Depression, the price level fell during some years.

a. With a falling price level, what happens to the actual real interest rate? Does your answer depend on what happens to the nominal interest rate? Briefly explain.

b. In contrast, during the 2007–2009 financial crisis, nominal interest rates on Treasury bills were close to zero, and inflation remained positive. What was the actual real interest rate on Treasury bills during this period?

c. Why would savers be willing to hold Treasury bills with a negative real interest rate?

6.5 The Costs of Inflation

Explain the costs of a monetary policy that allows inflation to be greater than zero.

SUMMARY

When inflation occurs, money becomes less valuable, so individuals choose to hold less of their wealth in the form of money. **Seigniorage** is the government's profit from issuing fiat money. Households and firms incur the costs of holding less money and making more frequent trips to the bank. These costs are called **shoe-leather costs**. Expected inflation also interacts with the tax system to increase the tax on capital income. There are also costs to firms from changing prices due to reprinting price lists, informing customers, and angering customers. Economists call these costs **menu costs**. The existence of menu costs means that not all prices rise at the same rate because not all firms face identical menu costs, so inflation causes relative prices to change, and this makes the economy less efficient. When inflation is greater than or less than expected, there is a transfer of wealth among borrowers and lenders. As a result, both borrowers and lenders devote resources to predicting inflation that could be used to produce goods and services. In some cases, unexpected inflation can lead to reduced borrowing and lending and reduced investment activity. When inflation fluctuates significantly from year to year, it is difficult to predict, so large changes in relative prices may occur. Large fluctuations in relative prices mean the economy does not allocate resources efficiently.

Review Questions

5.1 What is seigniorage? In what sense is it an inflation tax?

5.2 What are shoe-leather costs?

5.3 What are menu costs?

5.4 What are the costs of unexpected inflation?

5.5 How can the expected inflation rate be determined?

5.6 How does inflation uncertainty affect the allocation of resources?

5.7 Are there any benefits to inflation?

Problems and Applications

5.8 **[Related to the *Making the Connection* on page 210]** Some central banks set an explicit inflation target, essentially committing themselves to attempting to keep inflation within a certain range. How might an explicit inflation target affect inflationary expectations?

5.9 Forty years ago, it was typical for grocery stores to post prices by labeling each individual can or box. When prices changed, an employee would have to relabel every item in the store so that the cashier could ring them up correctly. Today, most prices are posted on shelf labels and scanned into cash registers using bar codes.

a. How has this change to pricing items in stores affected menu costs?

b. Are menu costs the same for all grocery store items? Briefly explain.

5.10 Suppose that consumer preferences are changing, so that more consumers want to buy chicken and fish and fewer want to buy beef and pork.

a. If inflation is low and fully anticipated, how would you expect the relative price of these goods to change, and how would that affect production of these goods?

b. Suppose now that inflation is volatile, so that it is difficult to tell the difference between an increase in the price of an individual good and an increase in the overall price level. How might volatile inflation lead to a misallocation of resources?

5.11 It is often said that inflation "greases the wheels of the labor market." Explain what this statement means.

5.12 Suppose that the inflation rate in an economy has been 4% for several years. The central bank unexpectedly increases the rate of growth of the money supply by 2%. Describe the effect on each of the following.

a. The inflation rate

b. Lenders

c. Borrowers

d. People with fixed incomes

5.13 The idea of shoe-leather costs is that people wear out their shoes going back and forth to the bank. While this is unlikely in reality, what are some examples of actual costs that you might incur by trying to reduce the costs to you of inflation?

Hyperinflation and Its Causes
Explain the causes of hyperinflation.

SUMMARY

With hyperinflation, the rate of inflation is so high that money loses nearly all of its value. Hyperinflation almost always has a fiscal cause. If the central government runs large persistent budget deficits that it is unable or unwilling to eliminate, then it must rely on the central bank to finance the budget deficits by increasing the money supply. Hyperinflation occurs when the central bank allows the rate of growth of the money supply to rise to very high rates to finance these budget deficits. The experience of Germany after World War I shows that once the budget deficits end and the central bank commits to moderate rates of money growth, the hyperinflation ends very quickly.

Review Questions

6.1 What is hyperinflation?

6.2 How does hyperinflation occur?

6.3 How can hyperinflation be stopped?

Problems and Applications

6.4 While hyperinflations are always caused by rapid growth in the money supply, they can be intensified by the actions of households and firms trying to protect themselves from inflation by spending money as soon as they receive it.

a. What is likely to happen to the velocity of money during a hyperinflation?

b. Use the quantity equation to show how the change in velocity affects the inflation rate.

6.5 If hyperinflations are caused by governments printing money, why don't the governments of these countries simply choose to reduce the rate of the growth of the money supply? Carefully explain the consequences of such actions.

6.6 One problem with hyperinflation is that it reduces economic growth, both through resource misallocation and by reducing saving and investment.

a. Why does hyperinflation cause misallocation of resources?

b. Why does hyperinflation reduce saving and investment?

c. What effects do the misallocation of resources and reduced saving and investment have on economic growth?

6.7 Hyperinflation occurred in the South during the U.S. Civil War (1861–1865). Unable to tax effectively in a largely agricultural economy, the Confederate government was forced to print money, eventually creating a money supply of approximately $1.5 billion Confederate dollars.

a. Explain how the rapid increase in the money supply combined with wartime scarcity of goods would cause prices to escalate.

b. In 1864, the Confederate government attempted to reduce inflation by reducing the money

supply by approximately one-third. The Confederacy forced paper currency to be converted into bonds by a specific date (or converted at a penalty after that date). What do you expect that the immediate effect of this policy would be?

6.8 **[Related to the *Chapter Opener* on page 188]** The following table shows the approximate *daily* rates of inflation from some of the worst hyperinflation episodes in history:

Country	Month with highest inflation rate	Daily inflation rate
Hungary	July 1946	195%
Zimbabwe	November 2008	98
Yugoslavia	January 1994	64.6
Germany	October 1923	20.9
Greece	October 1944	17.1
Taiwan (Republic of China)	May 1949	13.4

A simple way of calculating the approximate amount of time it will take prices to double is to divide 70 by the growth rate; this is called the Rule of 70. For each of the hyperinflations shown in the table, calculate the amount of time it would take prices to double. (Hint: Because these are daily rates, in some cases, prices will double in a matter of hours.)

Source: Steve H. Hanke and Alex K. F. Kwok, "On the Measurement of Zimbabwe's Hyperinflation," *Cato Journal*, Vol. 29, No. 2, Spring/Summer 2009.

6.9 **[Related to the *Chapter Opener* on page 188]** By early 2009, Zimbabwe was experiencing inflation that was estimated to be 231 million percent per year. Because of the rapidly falling value of paper money, the government was forced to issue currency in larger and larger denominations, including a $50 billion note. At the time, a $50 billion note would purchase about two loaves of bread. An economist in Zimbabwe was quoted as saying, "It is a waste of resources to print Zimbabwe dollar notes now. Who accepts a currency that loses value by almost 100 percent daily?"

a. Why would printing notes be a waste of resources?

b. The government of Zimbabwe authorized many stores to make transactions in foreign currencies. What difficulties would this cause stores and consumers?

Source: "Zimbabwe Introduces $50 Billion Note,"CNN.com, January 10, 2009.

DATA EXERCISES

D6.1: The Federal Reserve Bank of St. Louis offers data on monetary aggregates at its Web site (research.stlouisfed.org/fred2/). Look at the data from 1995 to the present.

a. What is the relationship between M1 and M2? Which is more volatile?

b. The monetary base is called M0. Look at the data for M0 and compare these data with the M1 and M2 measures you found in part a.

i. In general, what happens to M1 and M2 as the monetary base increases?

ii. Is the relationship that you found in part i. different during the 2007–2009 period?

D6.2: Steve Hanke at the Cato Institute (www.cato.org/zimbabwe) has calculated a hyperinflation index for Zimbabwe and other countries suffering from hyperinflations.

a. Where does Zimbabwe rank in Hanke's index? How long did it take for prices to double at the peak of the hyperinflation?

b. Search media sources to find out what the current state of Zimbabwe's economy is. How did the government get to this point?

D6.3: The World Bank (www.worldbank.org) has data on money growth rates for different countries. These data are listed under "Money and Quasi-Money" growth, which is roughly the same as M2 in the United States.

a. Which countries have the most rapid rates of money growth? The slowest?

b. Is there a relationship between the growth rate of the money supply and level of development?

c. Compare these data with the growth rate of consumer prices. Does this comparison seem to be consistent or inconsistent with the quantity theory?

D6.4: **[Related to the *Macro Data* box on page 209]** As discussed in the chapter, one way of measuring expectations of inflation is by looking at the difference between the interest rate on a Treasury bond and on a TIPS Treasury bond of the same maturity. Return to the St. Louis Fed site and find the current rate of expected inflation for 10-year bonds. What is the real interest rate?

D6.5: **[Excel question]** Use the World Bank data you found in Data Exercise D6.3.

a. Find the correlation coefficient for M2 growth and consumer price growth for each country in the group of 10 high-income countries.

b. Find the correlation coefficient for each country in the group of 10 low-income countries.

c. Now find the correlation coefficient for the entire group of 20 countries.

d. If you have had a statistics class covering regression analysis, run a regression using money growth as the independent variable and the average price growth as the dependent variable. Explain your results.

APPENDIX A

The Money Multiplier

6A Explain how the formula for the money multiplier is derived.

There is a close connection between the monetary base and the Fed's balance sheet, which lists the Fed's assets and liabilities. In Table 6A.1, we show a simplified version of the Fed's balance sheet that includes only the four entries that are most relevant to the Fed's actions in increasing and decreasing the monetary base. In most years, the Fed's most important assets are its holdings of U.S. Treasury securities—Treasury bills, notes, and bonds—and the discount loans it has made to banks. Recall from Chapter 3 that discount loans are loans that the Fed makes to troubled financial institutions such as commercial banks. The Fed's two most important liabilities are currency in circulation and bank reserves.

Table 6A.1 A Simplified Federal Reserve Balance Sheet

Assets	Liabilities
U.S. Treasury securities	Currency in circulation
Discount loans to banks	Reserves

Notice that the sum of currency in circulation and bank reserves, the Fed's two liabilities shown in Table 6A.1, equals the monetary base.

Open Market Operations

The Fed can increase the money supply using open market operations, which involve buying and selling Treasury securities. Suppose that the Fed buys $1 million worth of Treasury securities from Bank of America. We can illustrate the effect of the Fed's open market purchase by using a *T-account,* which is a stripped down version of a balance sheet. We will use T-accounts to show only how a transaction *changes* a balance sheet. Although in our example, the Fed purchased securities from only one bank, in practice, the Fed typically buys securities from multiple banks at the same time. So, we use a T-account for the whole banking system to show the results of the Fed's open market purchase: The banking system's balance sheet shows a decrease in security holdings of $1 million and an increase in reserves of the same amount (note that the banking system's balance sheet simply adds together the assets and liabilities of all of the commercial banks in the United States):

Banking System

Assets	Liabilities
Securities − $1 million	
Reserves + $1 million	

We can use another T-account to show the changes in the Fed's balance sheet. The Fed's holdings of securities (an asset) increase by $1 million, and bank reserve deposits (a liability) also increase by $1 million:

Federal Reserve

Assets	Liabilities
Securities + $1 million	Reserves + $1 million

The Fed's open market purchase from Bank of America increases reserves by $1 million and, therefore, the monetary base increases by $1 million. A key point is that *the monetary base increases by the dollar amount of an open market purchase.* The whole process also works in reverse, so if the Fed sells $1 million of securities in an open market sale, the monetary base will decrease by $1 million.

The Simple Deposit Multiplier

In this section, we describe how the money supply can be increased or decreased through a process of *multiple deposit expansion.* What happens to the money supply when the Fed increases bank reserves through an open market purchase? To answer this question, we first analyze the changes that occur at a single bank and then look at changes for the whole banking system.

How a Single Bank Responds to an Increase in Reserves Suppose that the Fed purchases $100,000 in Treasury bills (or T-bills) from Bank of America, increasing the bank's reserves by $100,000. We can use a T-account to show how Bank of America's balance sheet changes to reflect these transactions:

Bank of America

Assets	Liabilities
Securities − $100,000	
Reserves + $100,000	

The Fed's purchase of T-bills from Bank of America increases the bank's excess reserves but not its required reserves. The reason is that required reserves are determined as a percentage of the bank's checking accounts. Because this transaction has no effect on Bank of America's checking accounts, it doesn't change the amount of reserves that the bank is required to hold. Bank of America earns only a low interest rate from the Fed on the additional reserves obtained from the T-bill sale and therefore has an incentive to loan out or invest these funds.

Suppose that Bank of America loans $100,000 to Rosie's Bakery to enable it to install two new ovens. We will assume that Bank of America extends the loan by creating a checking account for Rosie's and depositing the $100,000 principal of the loan in it. Both the asset and liability sides of Bank of America's balance sheet increase by $100,000:

Bank of America

Assets	Liabilities
Securities − $100,000	Checking accounts + $100,000
Reserves + $100,000	
Loans + $100,000	

Recall that the money supply—using the M1 definition—equals currency in circulation plus checking accounts. By lending money to Rosie's, Bank of America creates checking accounts and, therefore, increases the money supply. Suppose that Rosie's then spends the loan proceeds by writing a check for $100,000 to buy the ovens from Bob's Bakery Equipment. Bob's deposits the check in its account with PNC Bank. Once the check has cleared and PNC Bank has collected the funds from Bank of America, Bank of America will have lost $100,000 of reserves and checking account deposits:

Bank of America

Assets	Liabilities
Securities − $100,000	Checking accounts $0
Loans + $100,000	
Reserves $0	

Bank of America is now satisfied because it has exchanged some of its low-interest Treasury bill holdings for a higher-interest loan. But the impact of the open market purchase on the banking system is not finished.

How the Banking System Responds to the Increase in Reserves We can trace the further impact of the open market operation by considering the situation of PNC Bank after it has received the check for $100,000 from Bob's Bakery Equipment. After PNC has cleared the check and collected the funds from Bank of America, PNC's balance sheet changes as follows:

PNC Bank

Assets	Liabilities
Reserves + $100,000	Checking accounts + $100,000

PNC's deposits and reserves have both increased by $100,000. For simplicity, let's assume that when it received Bob's deposit, PNC had no excess reserves. If the required reserve ratio is 10%, PNC must hold $10,000 (= 0.10 × $100,000) against its increase of $100,000 in checking account deposits. The other $90,000 of the reserves PNC has gained are excess reserves. PNC knows that it will lose reserves equal to the amount of any loan it grants because the amount of the loan will be spent and the funds will be deposited in another bank. So, *PNC can only safely lend out an amount equal to its excess reserves.* Suppose that PNC makes a $90,000 loan to Jerome's Printing to purchase new office equipment. Initially, PNC's assets (loans) and liabilities (checking account deposits) rise by $90,000. But this is temporary because Jerome's will spend the loan proceeds by writing a $90,000 check for equipment from Computer Universe, which has an account at SunTrust Bank. When SunTrust clears the $90,000 check against PNC, PNC's balance sheet changes as follows:

PNC Bank

Assets	Liabilities
Reserves + $10,000	Checking accounts + $100,000
Loans + $90,000	

These are the changes in SunTrust's balance sheet:

SunTrust Bank

Assets	Liabilities
Reserves + $90,000	Checking accounts + $90,000

To this point, checking account deposits in the banking system have risen by $190,000 as a result of the Fed's $100,000 open market purchase. SunTrust faces the same decisions that confronted Bank of America and PNC. SunTrust wants to use the increase in reserves to expand its loans, but it can safely lend only the increase in excess reserves. With a required reserve ratio of 10%, SunTrust must add ($90,000 × 0.10) = $9,000 to its required reserves and can lend only $81,000. Suppose that SunTrust lends the $81,000 to Howard's Barber Shop to use for remodeling. Initially, SunTrust's assets (loans) and liabilities (checking account deposits) rise by $81,000. But when Howard's spends the loan proceeds and a check for $81,000 clears against it, the changes in SunTrust's balance sheet will be as follows:

SunTrust Bank

Assets	Liabilities
Reserves + $9,000	Checking accounts + $90,000
Loans + $81,000	

Table 6A.2 Multiple Deposit Creation, Assuming a Fed Open Market Purchase of $100,000 and a Required Reserve Ratio of 10%

Bank	Increase in deposits	Increase in loans	Increase in reserves
PNC Bank	$100,000	$90,000	$10,000
SunTrust Bank	90,000	81,000	9,000
Third Bank	81,000	72,900	8,100
Fourth Bank	72,900	65,610	7,290
Fifth Bank	65,610	59,049	6,561
.	.	.	.
.	.	.	.
.	.	.	.
Total Increase	$1,000,000	$900,000	$100,000

If the proceeds of the loan to Howard's Barber Shop are deposited in another bank, checking account deposits in the banking system will rise by another $81,000. To this point, the $100,000 increase in reserves supplied by the Fed has increased the level of checking account deposits by $100,000 + $90,000 + $81,000 = $271,000. This process is called *multiple deposit creation*. The money supply is growing with each loan. The initial increase in bank reserves and in the monetary base is resulting in a multiple change in the money supply.

The process still isn't complete. The recipient of the $81,000 check from Howard's Barber Shop will deposit it, and checking account deposits at some other bank will expand. The process continues to ripple through the banking system and the economy. We illustrate the results in Table 6A.2. Note from the table that new checking account deposits continue to be created each time checks are deposited and banks make new loans, but the size of the increase gets smaller each time because banks must hold part of the money at each step as required reserves.

Notice that the initial increase in reserves was $100,000, so the monetary base increased by $100,000, but the ultimate increase in checking account deposits was $1,000,000, so the money supply increased by $1,000,000. Therefore, the *simple deposit multiplier*, the ratio of the amount of deposits created by banks to the amount of new reserves, is ($1,000,000/$100,000) = 10.

A More Realistic Money Multiplier

The simple deposit multiplier assumed that banks hold no excess reserves and that the nonbank public chooses to keep its holdings of currency constant. Equation 6.2 on page 196 shows how we can derive a more realistic money multiplier by relaxing these assumptions.

APPENDIX B

The Growth Rate Version of the Quantity Equation

6B Derive the percentage change version of the quantity equation.

The first step to deriving the percentage change version of the quantity equation is to recognize that money, velocity, the price level, and real GDP all change over time, so we can think of them as a function of time:

$$M_tV_t = P_tY_t,$$

where the *t* subscript indicates that the variable is a function of time. Next, we can take the natural logarithm of each side of the above equation to get:

$$\ln M_t + \ln V_t = \ln P_t + \ln Y_t.$$

The derivative of the natural logarithm of the variable X_t with respect to time is:

$$\frac{d\ln X_t}{dt} = \frac{1}{X_t}\frac{dX_t}{dt} = \frac{dX_t/dt}{X_t} = \frac{\text{Change in } X_t}{X_t} = \%\text{ Change in } X_t.$$

Applying this rule to the previous equation we get:

$$\%\text{ Change in } M_t + \%\text{ Change in } V_t = \%\text{ Change in } P_t + \%\text{ Change in } Y_t,$$

which is equation (6.5) on page 198.

CHAPTER 7

The Labor Market

LEARNING OBJECTIVES

After studying this chapter, you should be able to:

- **7.1** Use the model of demand and supply to explain how wages and employment are determined (pages 232–239)
- **7.2** Define unemployment and explain the three categories of unemployment (pages 239–246)
- **7.3** Explain the natural rate of unemployment (pages 246–253)
- **7.4** Explain how government policies affect the unemployment rate (pages 253–257)
- **7.5** Describe how economic policy explains differences in unemployment rates between Europe and the United States (pages 257–260)

ERNST & YOUNG AND PHARMACEUTICAL FIRMS ARE HIRING, SO WHAT'S THE PROBLEM?

The economic recession of 2007–2009 was the most severe the United States had experienced since the Great Depression of the 1930s. Real GDP declined by 4.1% during the recession and the unemployment rate rose to over 10%. According to the National Bureau of Economic Research (NBER), the recession had ended in June 2009, but the unemployment rate remained at 9% as late as April 2011. A broader measure of the unemployment rate counts as unemployed some people who have become discouraged and stopped looking for work and people who are working part time because they can't find full-time jobs. This measure of the unemployment rate stood at 15.9% in April 2011, not far below the rate of 16.6% in June 2009. And the unemployed were staying unemployed for longer periods as well. In April 2011, 43% of the unemployed had been out of work for at least six months, compared with

Continued on next page

Key Issue and Question

At the end of Chapter 1, we noted key issues and questions that serve as a framework for the book. Here are the key issue and question for this chapter:

Issue: The unemployment rate in the United States remained about 9% more than 20 months after the end of the 2007–2009 recession.

Question: Should policymakers strive for an unemployment rate of zero?

Answered on page 261

33% in June 2009 and only 17.5% in April 2007. Unemployment had been so high for so long that some economists had begun speaking of the "new normal," in which unemployment rates might be stuck at higher levels for many years.

But despite the severity of the recession, some firms continued to hire workers. For instance, Ernst & Young, the accounting and consulting firm, continued to hire thousands of new graduates each year. Many firms even reported shortages of skilled workers, while millions remained unemployed. Astro Manufacturing & Design had trouble finding workers qualified to operate its computer numerical control machines to make medical and aerospace parts. Similarly, Ben Venue Laboratories, a pharmaceutical firm, had difficulty finding qualified workers from the thousands of job applications it received.

The experiences of these firms reflected two aspects of the U.S. labor market. First, economists agree that during recessions and expansions alike, the U.S. labor market creates and destroys millions of jobs every month. For example, during the worst part of the recession, from the fourth quarter of 2008 through the third quarter of 2009, more than 32 million workers lost their jobs. During the same period, though, more than 25 million workers found jobs. Net employment declined by 7 million, but even these very high job losses took place in the context of millions of workers finding jobs.

The second aspect of the labor market involves structural unemployment, which arises from a persistent mismatch between the skills of workers and the requirements of jobs. No one doubted that part of the high unemployment rates during and after the recession represented *cyclical unemployment*, or unemployment due to the severity of the recession. But was the level of structural unemployment unusually high? Economists and policymakers debated this question in 2011.

Narayana Kocherlakota, president of the Federal Reserve Bank of Minneapolis, argued that the U.S. labor market was in the unusual situation of suffering from high rates of unemployment in some industries while at the same time having large numbers of job openings in other industries, particularly in manufacturing, oil exploration, and other industries that required more skilled workers than were available. In other words, Kocherlakota argued that there was an unusually large mismatch between workers' skills and the available jobs. If Kocherlakota was correct, the process of adjusting to structural changes in the economy would likely take considerable time, leaving the unemployment rate stuck at high levels. Other economists were skeptical, however, that structural unemployment could account for more than a small percentage of the overall increase in unemployment.

This disagreement was not just a debate over how best to categorize the unemployed. The types of economic policies Congress, the president, and the Federal Reserve might use depended at least in part on what was causing the high rates of unemployment. Clearly, understanding the causes of unemployment remains an important part of macroeconomics.

AN INSIDE LOOK on page 262 discusses the U.S. jobless rate in December 2010 and the challenges facing the long-term unemployed.

Sources: U.S. Bureau of Labor Statistics, "Business Employment Dynamics—Second Quarter 2010," February 1, 2011; David Leonhardt, "Debating the Causes of Joblessness," *New York Times*, January 21, 2011; Motoko Rich, "Factory Jobs Return, but Employers Find Skills Shortage," *New York Times*, July 1, 2010; Neal Conan, "Job Pool for 2010 Grads Crowded with 2009 Grads," www.npr.org, May 24, 2010; and Narayana Kocherlakota, "Back Inside the FOMC," speech delivered in Missoula, Montana, September 8, 2010.

When we discussed economic growth in Chapters 4 and 5, we assumed that all resources are fully employed. In this chapter, we discuss what economists mean by the phrase *full employment*. As it turns out, full employment does not mean that every worker who wants a job has a job. The U.S. labor market is dynamic, with millions of workers entering and leaving employment every year. Economists use a definition of full employment that reflects the fact that workers are constantly entering and leaving employment.

7.1

Learning Objective

Use the model of demand and supply to explain how wages and employment are determined.

The Labor Market

Economists rely on the basic model of demand and supply to analyze markets. We can use basic demand and supply analysis to analyze the market for labor, although this market differs from the markets for final goods and services. The most obvious difference is that in the market for labor, firms are demanders, and households are suppliers. The demand for labor and other factors of production is a *derived demand*, in that it depends on the

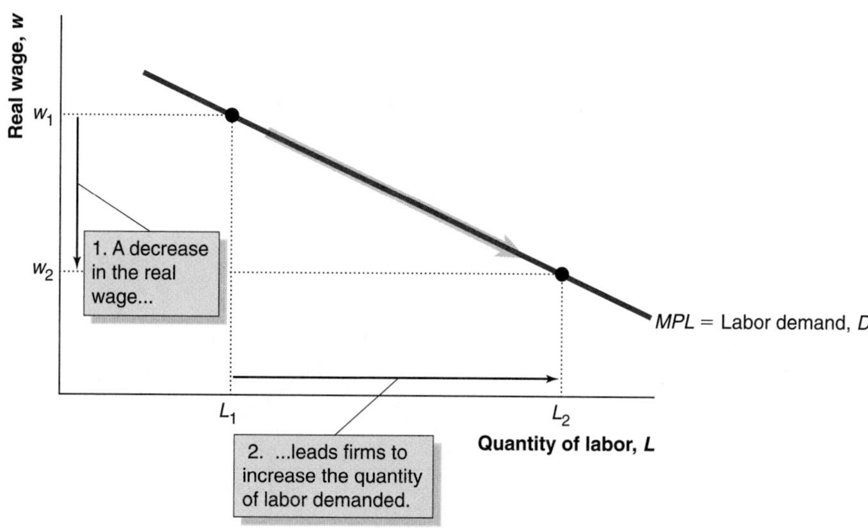

Figure 7.1

The Labor Demand Curve

The demand curve for labor is the marginal product of labor curve. The demand curve slopes downward due to diminishing marginal returns. As the real wage decreases from w_1 to w_2, firms increase the quantity of labor demanded from L_1 to L_2. As firms hire more workers, the marginal product of labor decreases. ●

demand for the goods that labor produces. We briefly discuss the demand for labor, which is discussed in greater detail in chapter 4, before discussing the supply of labor.

Nominal and Real Wages

In our analysis, the price of labor is the wage, which includes "fringe benefits," such as medical insurance, retirement benefits, and bonuses. The nominal wage (W) is how much workers are paid in dollars. The real wage, w, represents the purchasing power of the nominal wage. As Equation (7.1) shows, the real wage is the nominal wage divided by the price level, P:

$$\text{Real wage} = w = \frac{W}{P}. \tag{7.1}$$

For example, if the nominal wage in 2012 is \$40 per hour and the price level is 1, then the real wage is also \$40.[1] If the economy experiences an inflation rate of 3% while the nominal wage remains unchanged, then the real wage will fall:

$$\frac{\$40}{1.03} = \$38.83.$$

The Demand for Labor Services

The labor demand curve is the same as the **marginal product of labor (*MPL*)** curve where the marginal product of labor is the extra output a firm receives from adding one more unit of labor, holding all other inputs and efficiency constant. Therefore, due to diminishing marginal returns, the marginal product of labor will decrease as firms hire more workers. Figure 7.1 shows that diminishing marginal returns cause the demand curve for labor to slope downward.

Marginal product of labor (*MPL*) The extra output a firm receives from adding one more unit of labor, holding all other inputs and efficiency constant.

Shifting the Demand Curve

The demand curve for labor shows the relationship between the real wage rate and the quantity of labor demanded, holding everything else constant. For labor demand, "everything else" is any variable that affects the willingness of firms to hire workers other than

[1]Note that we often express the price level in the base year as 100, rather than 1. In that case, we can think of the real wage as being calculated as $(W/P) \times 100$.

Figure 7.2

Shifting the Labor Demand Curve

If technology improves, the marginal product of labor increases, which shifts the labor demand curve to the right, from D_1 to D_2. Similar reasoning shows that an increase in the capital stock or an improvement in efficiency also shifts the labor demand curve to the right. ●

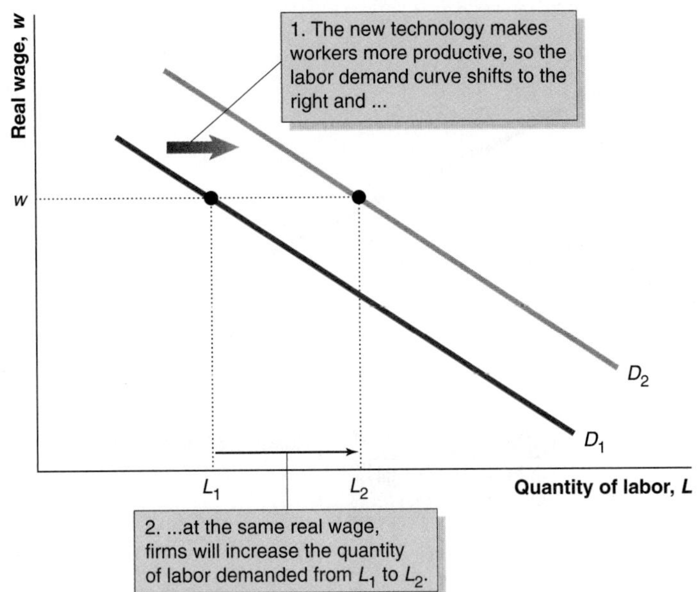

Real wage, w
1. The new technology makes workers more productive, so the labor demand curve shifts to the right and ...
w
D_2
D_1
L_1
L_2
Quantity of labor, L
2. ...at the same real wage, firms will increase the quantity of labor demanded from L_1 to L_2.

the real wage. These variables include the quantity of capital and the overall level of efficiency with which workers transform inputs into finished goods and services. In particular, the technology of production and the skill level of the workers determine their efficiency. We hold these variables constant when we draw the demand curve. Changes in these variables cause the demand curve to shift.

For example, suppose that the accounting firm Ernst & Young purchases new computer software that allows its workers to audit financial statements more quickly, thereby increasing the marginal product of labor. What happens to the demand curve for labor? Remember that the marginal product of labor curve is the labor demand curve. Anything that increases the marginal product of labor will shift the labor demand curve to the right. Figure 7.2 shows the shift of the labor demand curve to the right, from D_1 to D_2. If the real wage remains fixed at w, the quantity of labor demanded will increase from L_1 to L_2. By similar reasoning, an increase in the capital stock would also increase the quantity of labor demanded. If Ernst & Young gave its workers more computers to work with, each worker could carry out more audits, so the marginal product of labor would increase. The labor demand curve would shift to the right, from D_1 to D_2, and the quantity of labor demanded would increase from L_1 to L_2.

Efficiency can also decrease in some circumstances and make workers less productive. For example, suppose the government passes new regulations that force Ernst & Young and other accounting firms to ensure that they follow federal guidelines for audits. This change would require Ernst & Young to divert workers from doing audits to complying with government regulations. The workers dealing with government regulation are not producing measurable output, so the marginal product of labor will decrease. In general, if efficiency decreases or the capital stock decreases—perhaps because of a natural disaster such as a major earthquake or flood—the marginal product of labor would decrease, and the labor demand curve would shift to the left.

To understand why the demand curve for labor shifts, think from the firm's point of view. Firms hire workers to produce goods and services. Anything that makes workers more productive will make the workers more valuable to the firm. The more productive workers become, the more workers the firm is willing to hire at the current real wage, so the labor demand curve shifts to the right. Similarly, anything that makes workers less productive also makes them less valuable to the firm, so the labor demand curve shifts to the left.

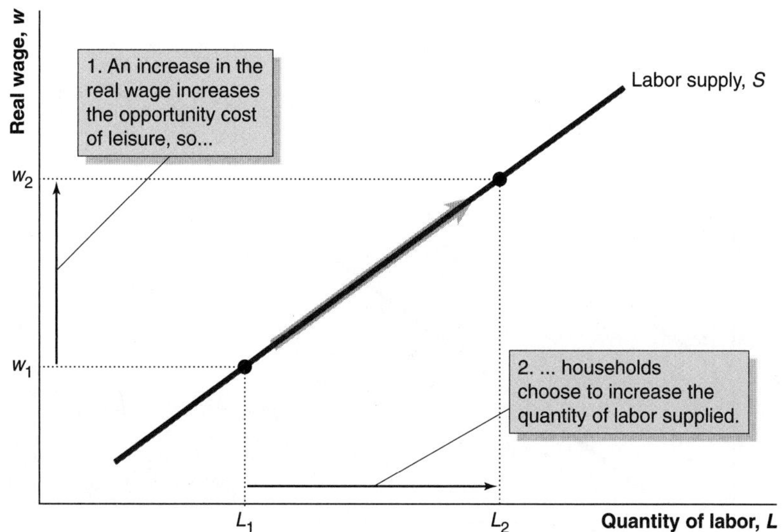
Real wage, w
1. An increase in the real wage increases the opportunity cost of leisure, so...
Labor supply, S
w_2
w_1
2. ... households choose to increase the quantity of labor supplied.
L_1
L_2
Quantity of labor, L

Figure 7.3

The Labor Supply Curve

Assuming the substitution effect is stronger than the income effect, an increase in the real wage from w_1 to w_2, causes the quantity of labor supplied to increase from L_1 to L_2 and the labor supply curve to slope upward. ●

The Supply of Labor Services

We turn now to considering how households decide the quantity of labor to supply. Of the many trade-offs each of us faces in life, one of the most important is how to divide up the 24 hours in a day between labor and leisure. Every hour spent sleeping, reading, watching television, playing sports, or in other forms of leisure is an hour less spent working. Because in devoting an hour to leisure we give up an hour's earnings from working, *the wage is the opportunity cost of leisure.* In that sense, we can consider the wage to be the price of leisure.

To understand the effect of an increase in the real wage on the quantity of labor supplied, imagine that you work for Ernst & Young and that you just received a pay increase of 10%. Would you be willing to work more hours or fewer hours? Microeconomics tells us that we consume less of a good when its price increases. Because the price of leisure increases as the wage rate increases, the wage increase should lead us to devote less time to leisure and more time to work. This response to a wage increase is called the *substitution effect* because we substitute work for leisure. However, the substitution effect is not the entire story. Microeconomics also tells us that we consume more of normal goods when our income rises. The higher wage rate increases your income, so you should consume more leisure. More time spent at leisure means less time spent working. This response to a wage increase is called the *income effect* because you are using your higher income to purchase more leisure.

The substitution effect and the income effect are pushing the quantity of hours you supply in opposite directions: Following an increase in your real wage, the substitution effect leads you to supply more hours of labor, while the income effect leads you to supply fewer hours of labor. As a worker at Ernst & Young, whether you would increase or decrease the quantity of hours you supply in response to a 10% increase in your real wage depends on which of these tendencies is strongest *for you.*[2] If you prefer more time with your family, you may decrease the quantity of labor supplied, but if you want to purchase a new car or save more to send your children to college, you may increase the quantity of labor supplied. For the aggregate labor market, which includes all the workers in the country, evidence suggests that in the short run, the substitution effect is stronger than the income effect, so an increase in the real wage leads to an increase in the quantity of labor supplied. In other words, the labor supply curve slopes upward, as shown in Figure 7.3. As the real wage increases from w_1 to w_2, the quantity of labor supplied increases from L_1 to L_2.

[2]It also depends on whether Ernst & Young allows you the flexibility to adjust the number of hours that you work.

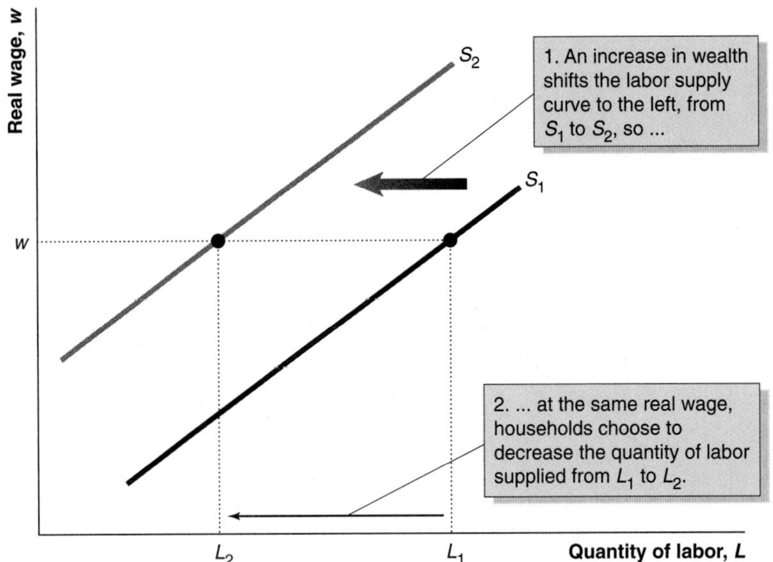
Real wage, w
w
S2
S1
1. An increase in wealth shifts the labor supply curve to the left, from S1 to S2, so ...
2. ... at the same real wage, households choose to decrease the quantity of labor supplied from L1 to L2.
L2
L1
Quantity of labor, L

Figure 7.4

Shifting the Labor Supply Curve

The labor supply curve shifts to the left, from S_1 to S_2, if wealth increases, income taxes increase, or there is a shift in preference toward leisure. As a result, the quantity of labor that households supply decreases from L_1 to L_2 at the fixed real wage, w. ●

Factors That Shift the Labor Supply Curve

The supply curve shows the relationship between the real wage and the quantity of labor supplied, holding constant other factors that might affect the willingness of households to supply labor, such as households' wealth, preferences for leisure over labor, and income taxes. When these other factors change, the supply curve shifts. For instance, an increase in wealth makes it easier to buy homes, cars, or vacations at any given wage rate. Households typically respond to an increase in wealth by "purchasing" more leisure time and supplying fewer hours of labor. The result is that when household wealth increases, the labor supply curve shifts to the left, as shown in Figure 7.4.

An increase in income taxes will also shift the labor supply curve to the left. An increase in income tax rates will reduce after-tax income so the opportunity cost of leisure decreases. As a result, households will purchase more leisure and decrease the quantity of labor supplied, so the labor supply curve will shift to the left. This explanation assumes, once again, that the substitution effect is larger than the income effect. Similarly, an increased preference for leisure will shift the labor supply curve to the left. In Figure 7.4, the labor supply curve shifts to the left, from S_1 to S_2, and the quantity of labor that households supply decreases from L_1 to L_2.

Equilibrium in the Labor Market

Figure 7.5 shows equilibrium in the labor market. The intersection of the demand and supply curves, point A, represents an equilibrium wage rate, w^*, and an equilibrium quantity of labor, L^*. At a real wage, such as w_1, that is less than the equilibrium real wage, the quantity of labor demanded, L_2, would exceed the quantity of labor supplied, L_1. At w_1, firms cannot hire all the labor they want, so competition among firms will drive up the real wage. As the wage rises, the quantity of labor demanded will decline as some firms decide that it is no longer profitable to hire workers at the higher wage. In addition, the quantity of labor supplied will increase because the higher real wage leads some individuals to substitute work for leisure. Firms keep bidding up the real wage as long as it is below equilibrium. When the real wage is bid up to w^*, the quantity of labor demanded equals the quantity of labor supplied, eliminating the upward pressure on wages.

If the real wage started above the equilibrium real wage, the quantity of labor supplied would exceed the quantity of labor demanded. Not all workers who want jobs would be able to find them. Some workers would offer to work for a lower real wage, which would bid down the real wage, decreasing the quantity of labor supplied, and increasing the quantity

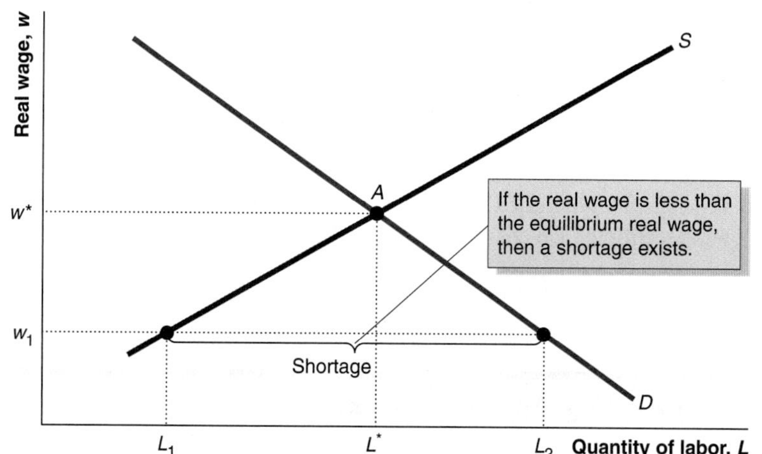

Figure 7.5

Equilibrium in the Labor Market

If the real wage equals w^*, the labor market is in equilibrium. At the real wage, w_1, the quantity of labor demanded, L_2, would exceed the quantity of labor supplied, L_1, resulting in a shortage of labor. ●

of labor demanded. When the real wage is bid down to w^*, the quantity of labor demanded equals the quantity of labor supplied, eliminating the downward pressure on real wages.

A change in a variable, apart from the real wage, will cause the demand curve for labor or the supply curve for labor to shift. Consider the situation we discussed earlier, where Ernst & Young buys software that makes its workers more efficient at conducting audits. We have already seen that the result is a shift to the right of the labor demand curve. In Figure 7.6, the equilibrium real wage and the equilibrium quantity of hours worked are both higher in the new equilibrium at point *B*. Not only is more labor hired, but workers receive higher real wages after the introduction of the improved software. This effect

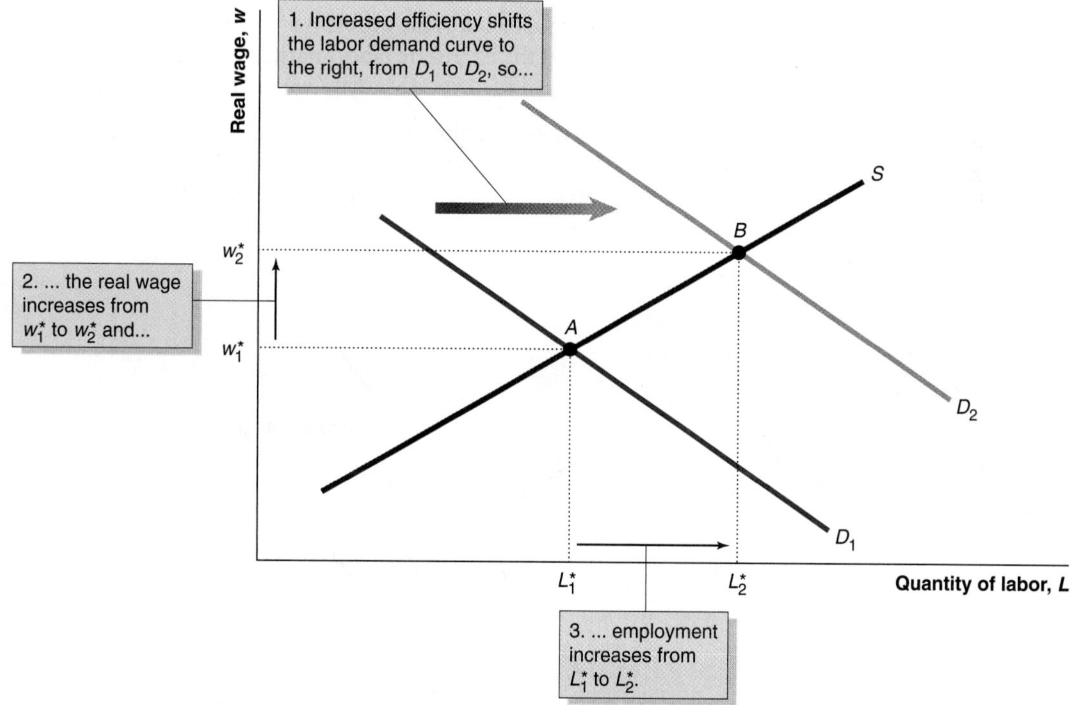

Figure 7.6 The Effect of Technology on Labor Market Equilibrium

New software enables employees of Ernst & Young to conduct audits more quickly. The marginal product of labor increases, so the labor demand curve shifts to the right, from D_1 to D_2. As a result, the real wage increases to w_2^*, and the quantity of labor increases to L_2^*. ●

suggests that all workers gain from the new software. However, when we look at individual labor markets as opposed to the labor market as a whole, we can see that technological change may hurt some workers. For example, the development of the automobile led to unemployment among workers employed assembling carriages and wagons pulled by horses. Similarly, most workers employed assembling and repairing typewriters eventually lost their jobs following the introduction of personal computers. So, while the analysis in Figure 7.6 allows us to conclude that the real wage in the aggregate labor market will increase following technological change, in the markets for some jobs, the real wage may fall.

Solved Problem 7.1

The Effect of Increased Wealth on the Aggregate Labor Market

Douglas Holtz-Eakin of the American Action Forum, David Joulfaian of the U.S. Treasury Department, and Harvey Rosen of Princeton University examined the effect of inheritances on labor supply decisions in the United States. They found that the larger the inheritance, the more likely the recipient was to reduce his or her labor supply. The likely explanation is that individuals who receive large inheritances can use those funds to purchase goods and services, thereby reducing the need to work as many hours. This result applies to individuals, but also raises the issue of what will happen in the aggregate labor market as a country becomes wealthier. From 1950 to 2008, total wealth in the United States increased from $1,046 billion to $51,309 billion, in 2005 dollars. Predict the effect this increase in wealth had on the equilibrium real wage and the level of employment. Use a graph to support your answer.

Solving the Problem

Step 1 **Review the chapter material.** This problem is about determining the effect of an increase in wealth on the aggregate labor market, so you may want to review the section "Equilibrium in the Labor Market," which begins on page 236.

Step 2 **Draw a graph that shows the effect of the increase in wealth on the labor demand and labor supply curves.** The labor demand curve shows the relationship between the real wage and the quantity of labor that firms want to hire, holding capital, technology, and the level of efficiency constant. The increase in wealth

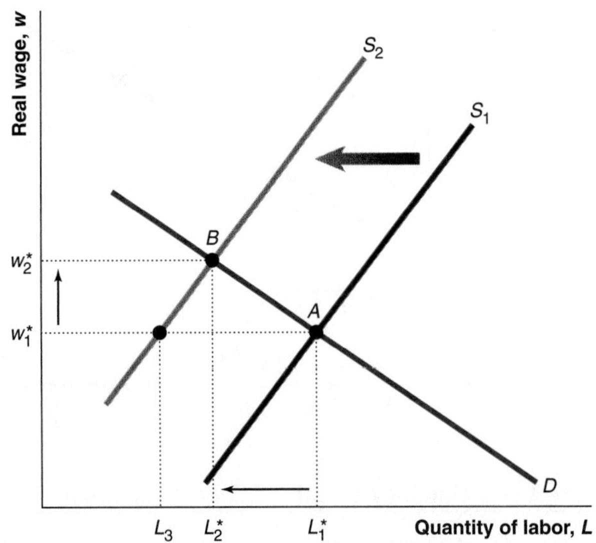

should not affect the marginal product of labor, so the labor demand curve should not shift. The labor supply curve will shift, however. The labor supply curve shows the relationship between the real wage and the quantity of labor supplied, holding constant other factors such as the willingness of individuals to work. When wealth increases, individuals can purchase the same quantity of goods and services that they currently buy while working fewer hours. So, we would expect individuals to reduce the quantity of labor supplied at each real wage, which you should show on your graph as the labor supply curve shifting to the left from S_1 to S_2.

Step 3 Use your graph to explain the effect on the real wage and quantity of labor. The graph shows that at the original real wage of w_1^*, a shortage of labor would exist. At the original equilibrium real wage of w_1^*, the quantity of labor supplied is L_3, and the quantity of labor demanded is L_1^*. Because firms cannot hire all the labor they want at the original equilibrium real wage, firms have an incentive to bid up the real wage as they try to attract workers from other firms or lure individuals away from leisure and into labor. As a result, the equilibrium real wage will rise, while the equilibrium quantity of labor will decrease from to L_1^* to L_2^*.

The amount of leisure time has increased in high-income countries such as France, Germany, and the United States. This Solved Problem helps explain why: As wealth has increased, individuals have used the increase in wealth to "purchase" more leisure time, thereby decreasing the number of hours spent working.

Source: Holtz-Eakin, Douglas; Joulfaian, David; and Rosen, Harvey. "The Carnegie Conjecture: Some Empirical Evidence," *Quarterly Journal of Economics*, Vol. 108, No. 2, May 1993, pp. 413–35

For more practice, do related problem 1.5 on page 264 at the end of this chapter.

Categories of Unemployment

7.2

Learning Objective

Define unemployment and explain the three categories of unemployment.

The demand and supply model suggests that when the labor market is in equilibrium, every worker who wants a job can find one. This observation means that any worker who does not have a job must prefer leisure to working at the prevailing real wage. If this analysis is true, then the unemployment we observe must be voluntary. There are good reasons, though, to be skeptical that all unemployment is voluntary. For instance, it seems implausible that when the unemployment rate in the United States increased from 4.6% during June 2007 to 10.1% in October 2009, it was due to a sudden increase in people's preference for leisure over work. It is difficult to believe that millions of workers suddenly decided to engage in leisure, especially when the loss of a job can lead to bankruptcy, the loss of a home, or other severe consequences. Some of the increase in the unemployment rate was almost certainly involuntary, which means that workers who wanted jobs at the current wage could not find them. In this section, we discuss three categories of unemployment that economists have found useful in analyzing the labor market. We continue the discussion in Section 7.3 by looking at explanations of involuntary unemployment. First, though, we look at how unemployment rates vary across countries.

Unemployment Around the World

Figure 7.7 shows monthly unemployment rates for the United States, the United Kingdom, Japan, Canada, and the 17 countries that use the euro for their currency. In all countries, the unemployment rate has fluctuated over time. For example, the unemployment rate for the United Kingdom varied from a low of about 2% in the mid-1970s to nearly 12% in the

Figure 7.7

Monthly Unemployment Rates Around the World, 1955–2011

The unemployment rate fluctuates over time for all countries, rising during recessions and falling during expansions.

Source: Organisation for Economic Co-operation and Development.

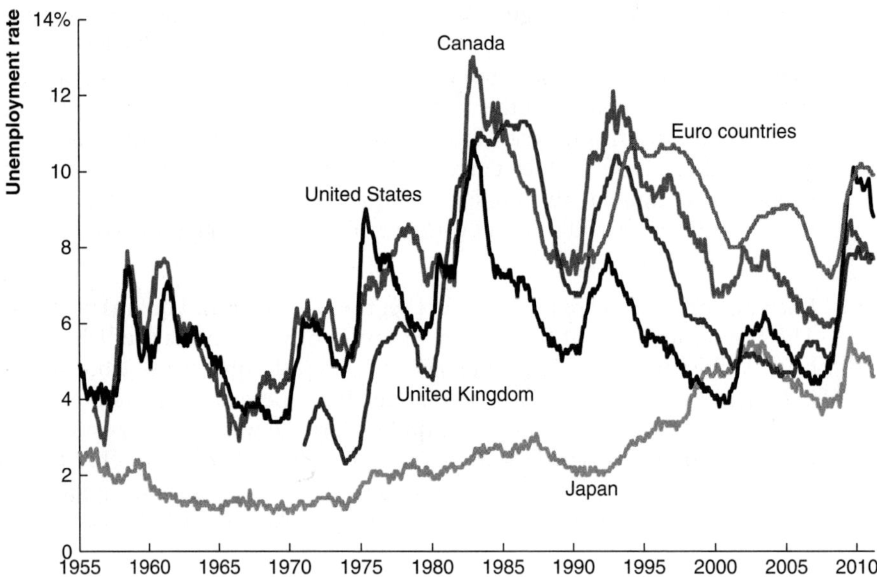

mid-1980s. The figure also shows that the average unemployment rate has varied substantially across countries. For example, since January 1978, the unemployment rate has averaged 8.6% in Canada, 3.4% in Japan, 6.3% in the United States, 7.5% in the United Kingdom, and 9.1% for countries using the euro. The differences in average unemployment rates can change. The United Kingdom and France had lower unemployment rates than the United States before the early 1980s but have had higher unemployment rates since that time. In Section 7.5, we explain why the unemployment rates in the United Kingdom, France, and some other European countries rose above the unemployment rate in the United States.

Figure 7.7 illustrates that the unemployment rate rises and falls over time, but it never falls to zero. To understand why this is true, we need to discuss the three categories of unemployment:

1. Frictional unemployment
2. Structural unemployment
3. Cyclical unemployment

Frictional Unemployment and Job Search

Workers have different skills, interests, and abilities, and jobs have different skill requirements, working conditions, and wages. As a result, most workers spend at least some time engaging in *job search*, just as most firms spend time searching for new persons to fill job openings. **Frictional unemployment** is short-term unemployment that arises from the process of matching the job skills of workers to the requirements of jobs. It takes time for workers to search for a job and for firms to search for a new employees, so there will always be some workers who are frictionally unemployed because they are between jobs and in the process of searching for new ones.

Frictional unemployment Short-term unemployment that arises from the process of matching the job skills of workers to the requirements of jobs.

Some unemployment is due to seasonal factors, such as weather or fluctuations in demand for certain goods or services during different times of the year. For example, stores located in beach resort areas reduce their hiring during the winter, and ski resorts reduce their hiring during the summer. Department stores increase their hiring in

November and December and reduce their hiring after New Year's Day. In agricultural areas, employment increases during harvest season and declines thereafter. Construction workers experience greater unemployment during the winter than during the summer. *Seasonal unemployment* refers to unemployment due to factors such as weather, variations in tourism, and other calendar-related events. Because seasonal unemployment can make the unemployment rate seem artificially high during some months and artificially low during other months, the Bureau of Labor Statistics reports two unemployment rates each month—one that is *seasonally adjusted* and one that is not seasonally adjusted. The seasonally adjusted data eliminate the effects of seasonal unemployment. Economists and policymakers rely on the seasonally adjusted data as a more accurate measure of the current state of the labor market.

Would eliminating all frictional unemployment be good for the economy? No, because some frictional unemployment actually increases economic efficiency. Frictional unemployment occurs because workers and firms take the time necessary to ensure a good match between the skills of workers and the requirements of jobs. By devoting time to job search, workers end up with jobs they find satisfying and in which they can be productive. Of course, having more productive and more satisfied workers is also in the best interest of firms.

As we saw in Section 7.1, when workers are more productive, they have a higher marginal product of labor, so the demand curve shifts to the right. This shift should lead to higher real wages and more employment. Therefore, **unemployment insurance**, a government program that allows workers to receive benefits for a period of time after losing their jobs, can increase the efficiency of labor markets and the economy. Without unemployment insurance, an unemployed worker would be under severe financial pressure to accept the first job offer he or she received, regardless of whether the job suited the worker's skills and paid the most. Unemployment insurance reduces this financial pressure by providing workers with some income during the job search. As a result, workers can afford to search for jobs that suit their skills. It is possible, though, that providing unemployment insurance for too long a period may lead unemployed workers to take too much time searching for a new job, which would reduce economic efficiency. During the aftermath of the 2007–2009 recession, the federal government extended the normal period for receiving unemployment insurance benefits on three separate occasions. Economists debated the merits of these extensions. In addition to their effects on economic efficiency, unemployment insurance payments may increase the level of consumption spending by unemployed workers, thereby speeding economic recovery. We will return to this point in Chapter 11.

Unemployment insurance A government program that allows workers to receive benefits for a period of time after losing their jobs.

Structural Unemployment

Structural unemployment arises from a persistent mismatch between the job skills or attributes of workers and the requirements of jobs. Although frictional unemployment is short term, structural unemployment can last for longer periods because workers need time to learn new skills. According to the Bureau of Economic Analysis, employment in the motor vehicle industry, which includes the major automobile producers and their suppliers, fell from 1.32 million in 1977 to 0.99 million in 2007—a nearly 25% decrease in employment. In addition, during this period, automobile production in the United States began to shift from domestic automobile firms, such as General Motors, located near Detroit and elsewhere in the Midwest to non-U.S. firms, such as Toyota, operating factories that are concentrated in the South. The automobile workers near Detroit either had to move to the South or seek employment in new industries near where they lived. In either case, the workers were likely to be unemployed for a period. For example, it might take months for a General Motors worker who installed car doors to learn the skills needed to obtain a new job in a different sector, such as health care.

Structural unemployment Unemployment that arises from a persistent mismatch between the job skills or attributes of workers and the requirements of jobs.

MACRO DATA: IS THE DECLINE OF GOODS-PRODUCING INDUSTRIES A RECENT PHENOMENON?

Industries that produce goods, such as cars, computers, and appliances, have become less important over time as a share of both GDP and total employment in the United States as well as other high-income countries. Correspondingly, the share of services, such as haircuts or investment advice, has grown. The figure shows that in the United States, the percentage of workers in goods-producing industries decreased from 37.1% of total employment in January 1939 to 13.7% in April 2011. Goods-producing industries have been in relative decline since the end of World War II in 1945, a trend that seems unlikely to be reversed. Although the *relative share* of employment in goods-producing industries has declined, the *absolute number* of workers employed in these industries has increased. Employment in goods-producing industries increased from 11.1 million workers in January 1939 to 18.0 million workers in April 2011. This increase, though, is swamped by the increase in employment in services-producing industries from 18.8 million workers in January 1939 to 113.0 million workers in April 2011.

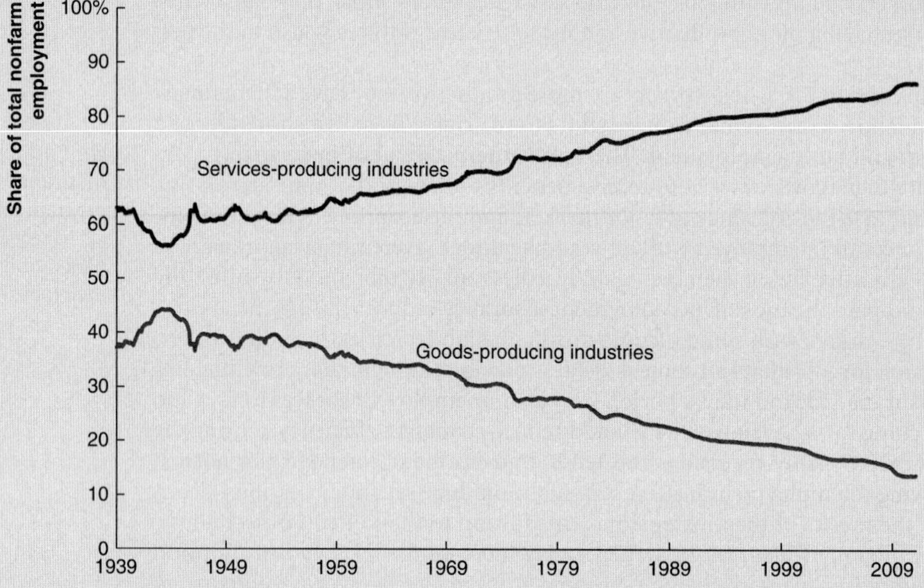

Source: U.S. Bureau of Labor Statistics.

What explains the decline in the share of employment in goods-producing industries in the United States? Given that the decline dates back at least as far as the 1940s, recent developments, such as competition from China or other effects of globalization, cannot be the cause. Instead, many economists believe that the decreasing importance of the goods-producing sector is likely due to differences in productivity growth between the goods-producing and service-producing sectors. Productivity growth has been much faster in goods-producing industries than in service-producing industries. For example, it still takes just as many members of an orchestra to play Beethoven's Ninth Symphony in 2011 as it did in 1939. However, each manufacturing worker is much more productive today than in 1939. As a result, the need for manufacturing workers has not grown as rapidly as the need for service workers.

The figure makes another important point. Using employment as the measure, the United States has been a service economy for a long time. In fact, services employment in 1939 was actually greater than goods employment in 2011, despite the growth in the economy and the population over the intervening 72 years.

Test your understanding by doing related problem D7.1 on page 270 at the end of this chapter.

Technological change is another possible cause of structural unemployment. Technological change in the United States has tended to eliminate unskilled jobs, while increasing the demand for skilled jobs. For example, computers and information technology have eliminated many unskilled jobs, such as typists, and reduced the demand for clerical staff. At the same time, these innovations have increased the demand for workers who produce computers, computer software, and other related products. These latter jobs often require more skills than the jobs computers and information technology have eliminated. Low-skilled workers who are unable to acquire the skills necessary to find employment are structurally unemployed.

Some workers lack even basic skills, such as literacy, or have addictions to drugs or alcohol that make it difficult for them to perform adequately the duties of almost any job. These workers may remain structurally unemployed for years.

Cyclical Unemployment

When the economy moves into recession, many firms find their sales falling and cut back on production. As production falls, firms lay off workers. Workers who lose their jobs because of a recession experience *cyclical unemployment.* Economists define **cyclical unemployment** as the difference between the actual level of unemployment and the level of unemployment when the unemployment rate equals the natural rate of unemployment. The **natural rate of unemployment** is the normal rate of unemployment, consisting of frictional unemployment plus structural unemployment. It is the long-run equilibrium unemployment rate. So, when the unemployment rate equals the natural rate, cyclical unemployment is zero. Most economists believe that the natural rate of unemployment is equal to a measured unemployment rate of 5% to 6%.

Cyclical unemployment Unemployment caused by a recession; measured as the difference between the actual level of unemployment and the level of unemployment when the unemployment rate equals the natural rate of unemployment.

Natural rate of unemployment The normal rate of unemployment, consisting of frictional unemployment plus structural unemployment.

Although cyclical unemployment is caused by a recession, it doesn't end when the recession ends. For example, Figure 7.8 shows that the unemployment rate in the United States continued to be well above the natural rate for many months after the recession of 2007–2009 had ended in June 2009. In 2011, the Federal Reserve was forecasting that the unemployment rate might not return to the full employment rate until 2013 or later. The forecasts of White House economists were even more pessimistic, with the unemployment rate projected to be at 6.8% at the end of 2013—four and a half years after the recession ended. Some economists believed that even these gloomy forecasts might be optimistic. These economists had begun speaking of the "new normal," in which unemployment rates might be stuck at higher levels for many years.

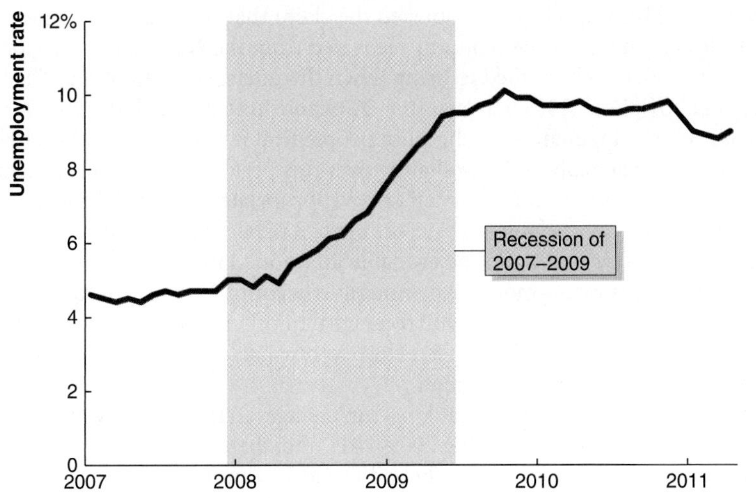

Figure 7.8

High Unemployment Rates After the End of the 2007–2009 Recession

Although the recession ended in June 2009, the unemployment rate remained quite high for many months thereafter.

Source: U.S. Bureau of Labor Statistics.

Making the Connection

Did the Structural Unemployment Rate Rise During the Recession of 2007–2009?

We saw in the chapter opener that as the unemployment rate remained high long after the end of the 2007–2009 recession, some economists argued that the level of structural unemployment might have increased. Cyclical unemployment rises and falls with the business cycle. It typically takes several years following the end of a recession before unemployment returns to the normal level represented by the natural rate. But the decline in unemployment following the end of the recession in June 2009 seemed particularly slow. For example, during the severe recession of 1981–1982, the unemployment rate peaked at 10.8% in November 1982. Twenty-two months later, in September 1984, the unemployment rate had declined by 3.5 percentage points, to 7.3%. After the 2007–2009 recession, the unemployment rate continued to rise and peaked at 10.1% in October 2009. Twenty-two months after the end of the recession, in April 2011, the unemployment rate had declined by only 1.1 percentage points, to 9.0%. Why did the unemployment rate fall so slowly during the recovery from the 2007–2009 recession?

Some economists and policymakers believed that the unemployment rate remained at high levels because the extent of structural unemployment in the economy had increased. Economists taking this position tended to stress one of two points. Some economists argued that certain industries had been severely affected by the recession and that the recovery of jobs and employment in these industries would be very slow. These industries might even permanently contract in size. Most notably, the residential construction industry was devastated by the recession as the housing bubble burst. From a peak in the spring of 2006, the number of jobs in residential construction declined by an extraordinary 44%. Residential and commercial construction typically decline during recessions as incomes and profits fall and families become more cautious about investing in new homes and firms reduce spending on factories and office buildings. But some economists believed that in this case, it would take years for spending on residential construction to again reach its 2005 level. As a result, many people who had worked in this sector would need to find jobs elsewhere. Doing so might require workers to learn new skills or to move to other parts of the country. The situation was similar for people who worked in industries that depend on construction, such as mortgage lending, real estate appraisals, and manufacturing of furniture, appliances, and construction equipment.

As we noted in the chapter opener, Narayana Kocherlakota, president of the Federal Reserve Bank of Minneapolis, has supported the claim that the rise in unemployment was structural. He argued that as the economy recovered from the 2007–2009 recession, new job openings appeared, but they failed to bring down the unemployment rate: "The job openings rate [rose] by about 20% between July 2009 and June 2010. Under this scenario, we would expect unemployment to fall because people find it easier to get jobs. However, the unemployment rate actually went up slightly over this period." The problem, Kocherlakota argued, was that "firms have jobs, but can't find appropriate workers. The workers want to work, but can't find appropriate jobs." According to Kocherlakota, the unusually large mismatch between workers' skills and the available jobs added more than 3 percentage points to the unemployment rate—more than enough to account for the difference between the 2007–2009 recession and the 1981–1982 recession. In other words, during 2010 and 2011, the unemployment rate would have been close to normal, at approximately 6%, if not for the increase in structural unemployment.

Other economists have argued that long-run changes in the economy might account for the slow growth of employment during 2009–2011 and, therefore, the slow decline in unemployment. For example, Daron Acemoglu and David H. Autor of MIT have argued that the long-run decline in jobs in manufacturing and related industries reduced earnings of workers, particularly males, who lack education beyond high school. These lower earnings resulted in more workers from these groups dropping out of the labor force. This trend, which dates back to the 1970s, was accelerated by the recession of 2007–2009, during which predominantly male jobs in manufacturing and construction were particularly hard hit. Erica Groshen and Simon Potter of the Federal Reserve Bank of New York have argued that over time, many firms moved away from using a system of temporary layoffs to deal with a decline in demand. When firms use temporary layoffs, workers are likely to be rehired quickly once demand increases during an economic expansion. If firms use permanent layoffs following declines in demand, an "unusually high share of unemployed workers must now find new positions in different firms or industries," according to Groshen and Potter. If these arguments are correct, then the U.S. economy may face a future of "jobless recoveries" as increases in employment lag behind increases in GDP and high rates of unemployment persist for years.

Some economists, though, have been skeptical of these explanations. These economists argue that the severity of the 2007–2009 recession was caused by a particularly large decline in total spending, or *aggregate demand*. Because aggregate demand increased only slowly following the recession, GDP also grew slowly, hindering the growth in employment and keeping the unemployment rate high. In other words, the unemployment was cyclical rather than structural. For example, Christina Romer, former chair of the Council of Economic Advisers, argued that "the rise in long-term unemployment is the almost-inevitable consequence of the severe recession. We do not need to appeal to any underlying structural changes to understand it, and there is every reason to expect that long-term unemployment will come back down when aggregate demand recovers."

Economists Mary Daly, Bart Hobijn, and Rob Valletta of the Federal Reserve Bank of San Francisco have argued that the level of structural unemployment increased because of the 2007–2009 recession, but only by about 1.25 percentage points. They estimated that the natural rate of unemployment increased from 5% to 6.25% as a result, although they forecast that this increase would be reversed within five years.

As we will see when we discuss short-run monetary and fiscal policies in Chapters 10 and 11, understanding the reasons for changes in the unemployment rate is of crucial importance to policymakers.

Sources: Narayana Kocherlakota, "Back Inside the FOMC," speech delivered in Missoula, Montana, September 8, 2010; Daron Acemoglu and David H. Autor, "Skills, Tasks and Technologies: Implications for Employment and Earnings," in Orley Ashenfelter and David Cards (eds.). *Handbook of Labor Economics*, Vol. 4, Amsterdam: Elsevier–North Holland; Erica L. Groshen and Simon Potter, "Has Structural Change Contributed to a Jobless Recovery?" Federal Reserve Bank of New York, *Current Issues in Economics and Finance*, Vol. 9, No. 8, August 2003, pp. 1–7; Mary Daly, Bart Hobijn, and Rob Valletta, "The Recent Evolution of the Natural Rate of Unemployment," Federal Reserve Bank of San Francisco, Working Paper 2011-05, January 2011; and Christina D. Romer, "Back to a Better Normal: Unemployment and Growth in the Wake of the Great Recession," speech delivered at the Woodrow Wilson School of Public and International Affairs, April 17, 2010.

Test your understanding by doing related problem 2.6 on page 265 at the end of this chapter.

Full Employment

The frequently used term *full employment* does not mean that every worker has a job. Instead, the economy is at *full employment* when the cyclical unemployment rate is zero, or, in other words, when the unemployment rate is equal to the natural rate of unemployment. Economists sometimes call the natural rate of unemployment the *full-employment rate of unemployment*. The fluctuations in the unemployment rate that we see in Figure 7.7 on page 240 are mainly due to the changes in the level of cyclical unemployment. We discuss what determines the natural rate of unemployment further in Section 7.3.

Figure 7.9

Unemployment Duration Around the World, 1968–2009

The average duration of unemployment is higher in Europe than in the United States. The difference has decreased over time but remains large. The average duration of unemployment during these years was 11.9 months in Europe, but just 5.6 months in the United States.

Source: Organisation for Economic Co-operation and Development. ●

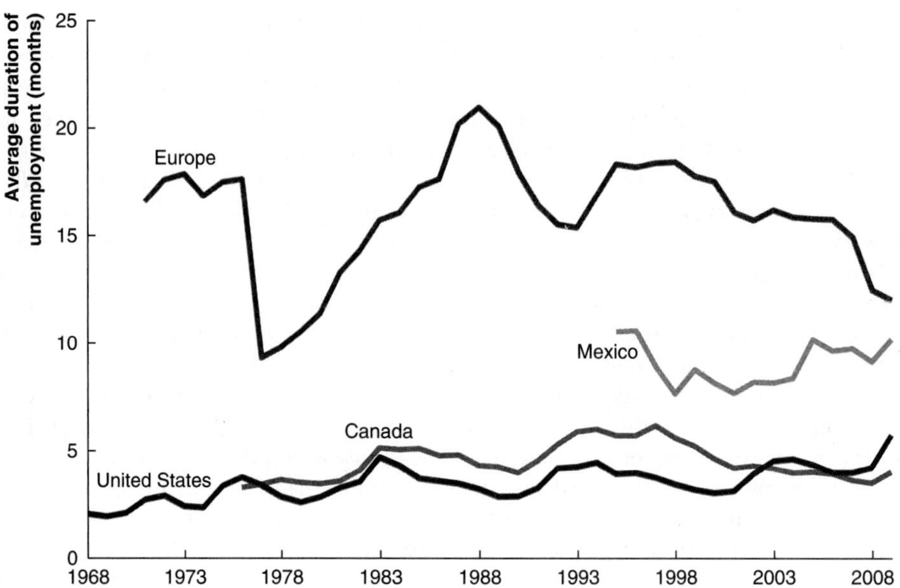

Duration of Unemployment Around the World

In addition to the variation in the average unemployment rates across countries, there is also variation in the average amount of time a worker is unemployed, or the *duration* of unemployment. Figure 7.9 shows the average duration of unemployment, measured in months, for a number of countries for the years from 1968 to 2009. Although unemployment rates in Europe were as low as or lower than those in the United States during the 1960s and early 1970s, before becoming higher in recent years, the average duration of unemployment was higher in Europe even in the early 1970s. For example, in 1971, the average duration of unemployment in Europe was 16.5 months, but it was just 2.6 months in the United States. This large difference in the average duration of unemployment has decreased but was still large in 2009. The average duration of unemployment in Europe was 11.9 months in 2009 but just 5.6 months in the United States. In addition, long periods of unemployment have been more common in Europe than in the United States. In 2009, 28.1% of unemployed workers were unemployed three months or less in Europe, and 30.9% were unemployed for more than one year. By contrast, in the same year, 48.3% of unemployed workers in the United States were unemployed for three months or less, and just 16.4% of unemployed workers were unemployed for more than one year.

Differences in the average duration of unemployment have important policy implications. Workers who are unemployed for long periods of time are more likely to be unemployed for structural reasons than for frictional or cyclical reasons. So, policies designed to help the long-term unemployed are more likely to be effective if they involve retraining programs or other programs that help workers move from declining industries into expanding ones.

7.3

Learning Objective

Explain the natural rate of unemployment.

The Natural Rate of Unemployment

As we discussed in Section 7.2, there are three categories of unemployment: cyclical, frictional, and structural. Economists call the long-run equilibrium unemployment rate the natural rate of unemployment, and measure it as the sum of structural and frictional unemployment. Figure 7.7 on page 240 shows that the average unemployment rate varies across countries, with European countries generally having higher average unemployment rates, and the United States and Japan generally having a lower unemployment rate. One explanation for the differences in average unemployment rates is that the natural rate of unemployment also varies across countries. In this section, we explain what determines the natural rate of unemployment.

A Model of the Natural Rate of Unemployment

Each month, the Bureau of Labor Statistics collects employment data from about 140,000 businesses and government agencies for the *Current Employment Statistics* survey, also known as the *establishment survey.* The survey sample covers approximately one-third of all nonfarm payroll workers. According to this survey, total nonfarm employment increased by 221,000 employees during March 2011. It is important to interpret this number correctly in order to understand the labor market. The number does not mean that no workers lost their jobs or that only 221,000 workers found new ones. Rather, this number represents a *net change.* Each month, some people find jobs and so move from being unemployed to being employed, while some workers quit or are fired and so move from being employed to being unemployed. The establishment survey measures the net change in employment and not these total flows of workers into and out of employment.

Even in the best economic times, some workers leave one job for another or stop working to return to school or pursue other activities, while other workers lose jobs as their firms close or productivity improvements make their jobs unnecessary. As a result, there is a constant flow of workers from employment to unemployment and from unemployment to employment, even when cyclical unemployment is zero.

The Bureau of Labor Statistics uses the *Job Openings and Labor Turnover Survey* (*JOLTS*) to measure job flows. The JOLTS survey consists of a sample of 16,000 business establishments made up of private businesses and government offices. According to JOLTS, during March 2011, 4.043 million workers found jobs, and 3.836 million workers left their jobs or were fired. This difference indicates that total employment increased by 207,000 during that month.[3]

Solved Problem 7.3

How Many Jobs Does the U.S. Economy Create Every Month?

The following data on total private-sector employment are from the establishment survey, as given in a BLS Employment Situation report:

Total private-sector employment (in thousands)

April	May	June
107,584	107,617	107,700

A newspaper article on the report commented, "The 83,000 private sector jobs created in June more than doubled the count in May." Is the reporter accurately interpreting the data? Did the private sector create 83,000 jobs during June of that year?

[3]Note that the employment increase for March 2011 from the establishment survey was 221,000, while the increase from the JOLTS survey was 207,000. Because the JOLTS survey covers many fewer firms, it is less likely to give accurate estimates of month-to-month changes in employment than is the establishment survey. For more information, see John Wolford, Mary Phillips, Richard Clayton, and George Werking, "Reconciling Labor Turnover and Employment Statistics," *Proceedings of the Section on Government Statistics*, 2003. This article is available at www.bls.gov/osmr/pdf/st030080.pdf.

Solving the Problem

Step 1 **Review the chapter material.** This problem is about understanding employment flows in the U.S. labor market, so you may want to review the section "A Model of the Natural Rate of Unemployment," which begins on page 247.

Step 2 **Answer the problem by explaining how to interpret the data in the BLS Employment Situation report.** The BLS Employment Situation report provides data on total employment each month, as determined by the establishment survey. The change in total employment from one month to the next tells us the *net* change in employment. The change does *not* tell us the *total* number of jobs created during a given month. So, while the reporter is correct that the change in private-sector employment during June was 83,000 (= 107,700,000 − 107,617,000), he is incorrect in saying that 83,000 private-sector jobs were created in June. As our discussion of the JOLTS data indicates, in a typical month, millions of jobs are created (and millions of jobs are lost). This reporter is making a common mistake of confusing the net change in employment with the total amount of job creation.

Sources: Bureau of Labor Statistics, "Employment Situation—June 2010," July 2, 2010; and Michael Powell, "Recovery Slows with Weak Job Creation in June," *New York Times*, July 2, 2010.

For more practice, do related problem 3.13 on page 267 at the end of this chapter.

One way to think of the natural rate of unemployment is as the rate of unemployment that exists in the long run when the economy is in a steady state and the flow of workers into employment equals the flow of workers into unemployment. Let's explore this point further. First, assume for simplicity that the labor force is constant, so that there are no new entrants into the labor force each month and that no one leaves the labor force. Because the labor force is the sum of unemployed and employed workers, we know that:

$$\text{Labor force} = \text{Employed} + \text{Unemployed}.$$

Every month, some of the unemployed workers find jobs. We call the percentage of unemployed individuals who find jobs the *rate of job finding*, or f. Every month, some employed workers leave, or separate from, their jobs either voluntarily or involuntarily. We call the percentage of employed workers who separate from jobs the *rate of job separation*, or s.

The total number of workers moving from unemployed to employed status is:

$$f \times \text{Unemployed},$$

while the total number of workers moving from employed to unemployed status is:

$$s \times \text{Employed}.$$

When the labor market is in equilibrium and unemployment is at the natural rate, the number of workers finding jobs equals the number of workers separating from jobs, so:

$$f \times \text{Unemployed} = s \times \text{Employed}. \tag{7.2}$$

We can again use the bathtub analogy from Chapter 5 to understand what determines the number of unemployed workers: The stock variable (the level of water in the bathtub) is the number of unemployed workers. The number of workers separating from their jobs (the water flowing into the bathtub) is the flow of workers into the stock of unemployed workers. The number of workers finding jobs (the water flowing out of the bathtub) is the flow of workers out of the stock of unemployed. When these two flows are equal, the number of unemployed workers is constant, the labor market is in equilibrium, and unemployment is at the natural rate.

In Section 7.2, we saw that the unemployment rate equals the number of unemployed workers divided by the labor force. Using this definition and Equation (7.2), we can derive an expression of the natural rate of unemployment, U:[4]

$$U = \frac{s}{s+f} = \frac{1}{1+(f/s)}. \tag{7.3}$$

This equation tells us that the natural rate of unemployment depends on the rate at which workers find jobs and the rate at which workers separate from jobs. As the rate of workers finding jobs increases, the unemployment rate decreases. As the rate of workers separating from jobs increases, the unemployment rate increases.

The job-finding and separation rates fluctuate with economic conditions. When these rates are constant and the flows into and out of employment are equal, the unemployment rate equals the natural rate of unemployment. So, Equation (7.3) represents a model for the natural rate of unemployment. The model tells us that if policymakers are going to lower the natural rate, they must find ways either to reduce the rate of job separation or increase the rate of job finding.

The Natural Rate of Unemployment in the United States

Figure 7.10 plots estimates for the natural rate of unemployment by the Congressional Budget Office (CBO) against the actual rate of unemployment. The CBO is a nonpartisan agency of Congress that, among other things, gathers data to help the federal government carry out economic policy. Figure 7.10 shows that while the natural rate of unemployment is not constant, it fluctuates much less than does the actual unemployment rate. The structural unemployment rate is one of the key determinants of the natural rate of unemployment. The factors that determine the structural unemployment rate change more slowly than the factors that determine cyclical unemployment.

The natural rate of unemployment changes when either structural or frictional unemployment changes. Structural and frictional unemployment vary based on:

1. *Demographics*, including changes in the age, gender, and race of the population
2. *Public policy*, including changes in unemployment insurance and laws governing the labor market
3. *Technological change*, including the introduction of new products that displace old products and increases in labor productivity
4. *Sectoral shifts*, including growth and decline in different industries and changes in where industries locate

---

[4]This is how we arrived at Equation (7.2): We know that Employed = Labor force − Unemployed, so

$$f(\text{Unemployed}) = s(\text{Labor force} - \text{Unemployed}).$$

Next, we can divide each side of the above equation by the labor force to obtain:

$$f\left(\frac{\text{Unemployed}}{\text{Labor force}}\right) = s\left(1 - \frac{\text{Unemployed}}{\text{Labor force}}\right).$$

Because the unemployment rate equals

$$\frac{\text{Unemployed}}{\text{Labor force}},$$

we can write this as:

$$f(U) = s(1 - U).$$

If we solve for the natural rate of unemployment, U, we get Equation (7.2).

Figure 7.10

The Actual and Natural Rates of Unemployment for the United States

The natural rate of unemployment is not constant, but it fluctuates much less than the actual unemployment rate. The Congressional Budget Office estimates that the natural rate of unemployment is currently 5% for the United States.

Sources: U.S. Bureau of Labor Statistics; and U.S. Congressional Budget Office. ●

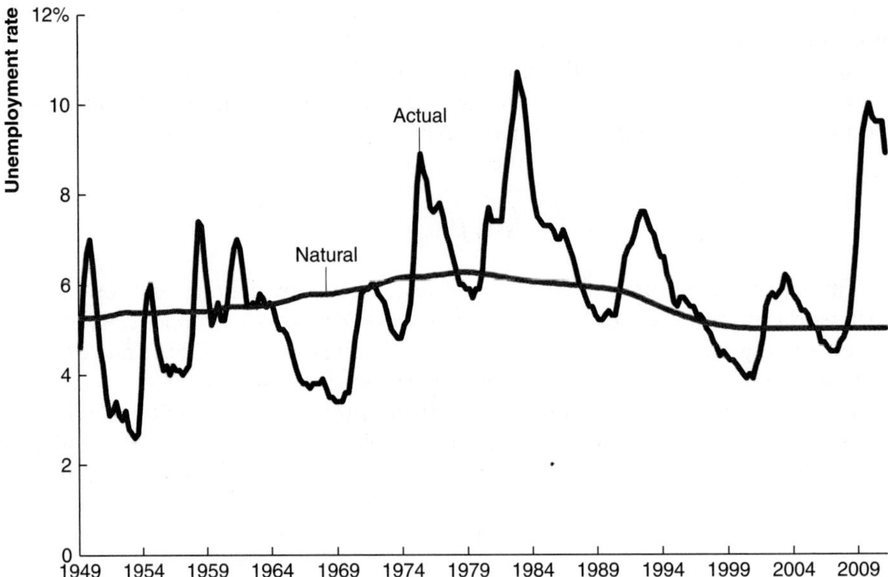

Demographics Younger workers have lower skills and change jobs more frequently than do older workers. In addition, it often takes younger workers longer to obtain an initial job when entering the labor force. As the workforce ages, the average worker finds a job more easily, so frictional and structural unemployment decline. As a result of these factors, the unemployment rate for people aged 16 to 24 averaged 11.7% from January 1948 to April 2011. During the same time period, the unemployment rate for people aged 25 and older averaged just 4.4%. The birthrate in the United States declined during the 1960s; as a result, the average age of the U.S. labor force has been rising since the 1970s. This aging has reduced the natural rate of unemployment by about 0.4%.[5]

The unemployment rate also varies by gender, so the percentage of men and women in the labor force also affects the natural rate of unemployment. The percentage of the labor force made up of women increased from 33.0% in 1959 to 46.7% in 2010. Since 2000, women have typically had lower unemployment rates than men. For example, in April 2011, the unemployment rate for men was 9.4%, while the unemployment rate for women was 8.4%. So, as women have become a larger share of the labor force, the natural rate of unemployment has decreased. In 2011, many state and local governments were significantly reducing their labor forces. Because state and local government employees are disproportionally women, if this trend continues, the gap between the unemployment rate for men and the unemployment rate for women may narrow.

Race and ethnicity also may affect the natural rate of unemployment. African Americans and Hispanics have grown as a percentage of the labor force and have higher unemployment rates than do Asian Americans and Whites. For example, from March 1973 to April 2011, the unemployment rate for Whites has averaged 5.6%, the unemployment rate for African Americans has averaged 12.3%, and the unemployment rate for Hispanics and Latinos has averaged 9.1%. So, holding other factors constant, the increase in African Americans and Hispanics in the labor force has increased the natural rate of unemployment.

[5]Lawrence Katz and Alan Krueger, "The High-Pressure Labor Market of the 1990s," *Brookings Papers on Economic Activity*, Vol. 1, 1999, pp. 1–65; and Robert Shimer, "Why Is the U.S. Unemployment Rate So Much Lower?" in Ben Bernanke and Julio Rotemberg (eds.), *NBER Macroeconomics Annual*, Vol. 13, Cambridge, MA: MIT Press, 1998, pp. 11–61.

Finally, the prison population increased from about 0.5 million in 1980 to 2.3 million in 2009. Most of this increase came from young males with low skills. If these inmates had been in the labor force rather than in prison, many would have been unemployed. Therefore, the increase in the size of the prison population has likely reduced the natural rate of unemployment by 0.1 to 0.2 percentage points.[6]

Public Policy Public policies, such as unemployment insurance and disability benefits, affect the natural rate of unemployment. Unemployment insurance is a government program that allows unemployed workers to receive benefits for a period of time after losing their jobs. In the United States, unemployment insurance is a joint federal and state program, so benefits vary by state, although workers are usually eligible to receive a portion of their previous salary for up to 26 weeks. During economic downturns, the federal government often extends the duration of unemployment insurance. During the economic downturn of 2007 to 2009, some workers have been eligible for up to 99 weeks of insurance. Unemployment insurance makes it easier for workers to remain unemployed, and so it reduces the probability that a worker will accept any given job offer. Holding other factors constant, this insurance therefore reduces the rate of job finding and increases the natural rate of unemployment.[7] For example, if you lose your job as an accountant at Ernst & Young and are receiving unemployment insurance, you are less likely to accept a job working at Wal-Mart. However, if you do not have unemployment insurance, then you may accept a job at Wal-Mart because otherwise you may lack the income to pay for food and rent. If you have unemployment insurance and do not take a job at Wal-Mart, the unemployment rate will be higher than if you did take the job, so unemployment insurance has led to a higher unemployment rate.

Economists have long known that unemployment insurance may decrease the incentive to find a job and so may increase the unemployment rate. However, there is no consensus on how large this effect is. Raj Chetty of Harvard University has found that a 10% increase in the value of unemployment benefits increases the duration of unemployment by 4% to 8%.[8] Rob Valletta and Katherine Kuang of the Federal Reserve Bank of San Francisco estimate that the extension of unemployment insurance from the standard 26 weeks to 99 weeks during the 2007–2009 economic downturn may have increased the unemployment rate by as much as 0.4% by the end of 2009.[9] This increase means the unemployment rate would have been about 9.5% without the extension of unemployment benefits rather than 9.9% by the end of 2009. Because the unemployment rate increased from 5.0% to 9.9% from the beginning of the downturn in December 2007 to December 2009, the extension of unemployment benefits made only a minor contribution to the overall increase in the unemployment rate; most of the rise in the unemployment rate was caused by the large decline in GDP during the recession.

In 1984, the federal government passed the Social Security Disability Reform Act, which made it easier for workers to receive a portion of their wages when physically or psychologically unable to work. The act caused the number of workers on disability to increase by 60% from 1984 to 2001. People on disability are not in the labor force, so they do not count as unemployed. Low-skilled workers are more likely to perform physically

[6]Lawrence Katz and Alan Krueger, "The High-Pressure Labor Market of the 1990s," *Brookings Papers on Economic Activity*, Vol. 1, 1999, pp. 1–65.

[7]Stephen Woodbury and Robert Spiegelman, "Bonuses to Workers and Employers to Reduce Unemployment: Randomized Trials in Illinois," *American Economic Review*, Vol. 77, No. 4, September 1987, pp. 513–530.

[8]Raj Chetty, "Moral Hazard Versus Liquidity and Optimal Unemployment Insurance," *Journal of Political Economy*, Vol. 116, No. 2, April 2008, pp. 173–234.

[9]Rob Valletta and Katherine Kuang, "Extended Unemployment and UI Benefits," *Federal Reserve Bank of San Francisco Economic Letter*, April 19, 2010.

demanding jobs, such as construction and manufacturing work, so they account for most of the increase in those receiving disability benefits. When disabled low-skilled workers left the labor force, the natural rate of unemployment fell by about 0.5%.[10]

The growing importance of temporary employment agencies has also affected the natural rate of unemployment. Temporary workers allow firms to increase output without committing to hiring workers who receive full benefits such as health insurance or pension contributions. Temporary employment provides a means for workers who cannot find full-time jobs to still find some employment. In addition, temporary jobs can enable young workers to make the transition to full-time employment. As a result, as temporary employment has become more common since the 1980s, the job-finding rate has increased, and the natural rate of unemployment has decreased by 0.2–0.4 percentage points.[11]

Technological Change Research by Jordi Gali of Pompeu Fabra University has found that increases in productivity reduce employment in the short run because new technology and other sources of improved productivity make some jobs obsolete.[12] However, new technology also creates the demand for new products. For example, employment in the newspaper business has declined over the past two decades, as many people get their news online or from cable television channels. But the growth of online news and cable television has created new jobs. The workers who lost their jobs running the newspaper printing presses are not necessarily the same ones who will write the software for the new Web sites or help produce cable news. Workers who lose their jobs producing newspapers and who cannot make the transition to the new jobs online or on cable may become structurally unemployed, which would cause the natural rate of unemployment to increase. However, as labor and resources flow from the old to the new industries, the new technology actually leads to *higher* overall employment in the following way: In the long run, technological change and increased labor productivity lead to higher real wages. Higher real wages increase the quantity of labor that workers are willing to supply. We can conclude that *technological change and increases in labor productivity ultimately make workers as a group better off*, even though some individual workers may be made worse off. The loss of jobs by workers at newspapers and the increase in jobs for workers in online and cable news is an example of what economists call *creative destruction*, a phrase first used by the Austrian economist Joseph Schumpeter, who taught for many years at Harvard. New technology destroys existing jobs but simultaneously creates jobs making new and better products elsewhere in the economy. Overall, technological change has a large effect on the mix of employment across industries, but it probably has at most a small effect on the natural rate of unemployment.

Sectoral Shifts Changes in the prices of key raw materials, such as oil, can also cause employment to shift across sectors and increase structural unemployment. The price of a barrel of oil rose from $2.00 in December 1973 to $32.63 in July 1980. U.S. households responded to the large price increase by conserving energy, by, for example, switching from large automobiles with low gas mileage to smaller automobiles—often imported from Japan—with high gas mileage. As a result, the demand for autoworkers in the United States

---

[10]David Autor and Mark Duggan, "The Rise in the Disability Roles and the Decline in Unemployment," *Quarterly Journal of Economics*, Vol. 118, No. 1, February 2003, pp. 157–205.

[11]Lawrence Katz and Alan Krueger, "The High-Pressure Labor Market of the 1990s," *Brookings Papers on Economic Activity*, Vol. 1, 1999, pp. 1–65; and Maria Otoo, "Temporary Employment and the Natural Rate of Unemployment," *Finance and Economics Discussion Series*, Paper No. 1999-66, Washington, DC: Board of Governors of the Federal Reserve System, December 1999.

[12]Jordi Gali, "Technology, Employment, and the Business Cycle: Do Technology Shocks Explain Aggregate Fluctuations?" *American Economic Review*, Vol. 89, No. 1, March 1999, pp. 249–271.

decreased dramatically. Autoworkers who could not develop the new skills needed for another career became structurally unemployed.

Economists refer to the process of output and employment increasing in some industries while declining in other industries as *sectoral shifts*. As sectoral shifts occur, markets work to move labor from one industry to another. During the transition, some workers will have difficulty finding new jobs and may become structurally unemployed. The figure in the Macro Data box on page 242 showed a long-term movement of labor from the goods-producing sector to the service-producing sector in the United States. This trend is not unique to the United States. We see a similar decline in the importance of goods production for almost all countries. For example, the World Bank estimates that output in the manufacturing sector decreased from 20% of world GDP in 1998 to 17% in 2008. The decrease in the relative importance of the manufacturing sectors is particularly evident in high-income countries. For countries in the Organisation of Economic Co-operation and Development (OECD) such as France, Germany, and the United States, manufacturing as a percentage of GDP decreased from 20% in 1998 to 16% in 2008. This decline does not mean that the absolute level of manufacturing production is shrinking in high-income countries. During this same time period, manufacturing output in OECD countries increased from $4.1 trillion to $5.3 trillion when measured in 2000 U.S. dollars. Because nonmanufacturing output—in particular, services such as accounting, business consulting, and health care—increased even faster, the relative importance of manufacturing declined. In contrast, the manufacturing sector has been relatively constant in countries such as China and India. The Chinese manufacturing sector was 32% of GDP in 1998 and 33% of GDP in 2008, while the Indian manufacturing sector was 16% of GDP in both 1998 and 2008. In high-income countries, labor has been flowing from the manufacturing sector to the service sector, while in many low-income countries, labor has been flowing from the agricultural sector to the manufacturing sector. As these reallocations take place, the natural rate of unemployment may temporarily increase.

Why Does Unemployment Exist?

7.4

Learning Objective

Explain how government policies affect the unemployment rate.

Our labor market model suggests that at equilibrium, all workers who want jobs can find them. If our model is correct, why do the three categories of unemployment described in Section 7.2 exist? A model is a simplified version of reality. In reality, there are many types of *frictions* that prevent the real wage from adjusting to maintain the labor market continually at equilibrium. As a result, unemployment can exist.

Equilibrium Real Wages and Unemployment

Figure 7.11 shows a labor market with unemployment. At point *A*, the labor market is in equilibrium because the quantity of labor demanded and the quantity of labor supplied both equal L^*. All the workers who want jobs can find them, so there is no unemployment. However, if the real wage, $\overline{w}$, is above the equilibrium real wage, w^*, the quantity of labor supplied by households, L_2, is greater than the quantity of labor demanded by firms, L_1. Because the quantity of labor employed cannot be greater than the quantity of labor demanded, L_1 also represents employment in the economy. As a result, some workers would like to have a job at the prevailing wage, $\overline{w}$, but cannot find one. In other words, some workers are unemployed. Why doesn't the real wage quickly decline to restore equilibrium in the labor market and eliminate unemployment? In the next section, we explain why the real wage may remain above the equilibrium real wage for a period of time.

Efficiency Wages

Some firms can ensure that workers work hard by supervising them. For example, a telemarketing firm can monitor workers electronically to ensure that they make the required number of phone calls per hour. Most firms, however, must rely on workers being motivated to

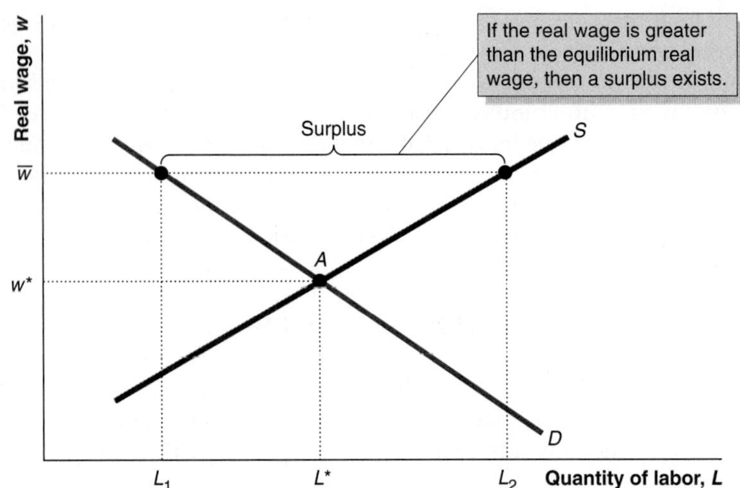

Figure 7.11

A Labor Market with Unemployment

If the real wage, $\overline{w}$, is at a level above the equilibrium real wage, w^*, then the quantity of labor supplied is greater than the quantity of labor demanded. This surplus means that some workers who would prefer to have a job at a real wage of $\overline{w}$ cannot find one. ●

Efficiency wage A higher-than-market wage that a firm pays to motivate workers to be more productive.

work hard. Therefore, some firms voluntarily pay an **efficiency wage**, which is a higher-than-market wage that a firm pays to motivate workers to be more productive. Efficiency wages can arise for four reasons. First, an efficiency wage can motivate workers to work harder: If you receive an efficiency wage that is more than you would earn at your next best alternative job, you are less likely to take actions that will get you fired. For example, you are more likely to show up on time, take only necessary sick days, and work harder when you are at the job.

Second, an efficiency wage makes workers less likely to switch jobs because most alternative jobs will pay only the market wage. When a worker quits a job, the firm incurs the cost of finding and training a new worker. If the costs of finding and training new workers are high enough, the efficiency wage may actually increase profits. In that case, the firm will voluntarily pay a higher-than-equilibrium real wage.

Third, firms may also pay efficiency wages to improve the quality of their workers. If wages are currently above the equilibrium real wage and a firm *reduces* its wage, some of the best workers are likely to quit and work for competitors that are paying higher wages.

The fourth explanation for efficiency wages applies mostly to low-income nations. In this explanation, higher real wages mean that workers can afford to purchase more food and more nutritious food so that they are healthier and more productive. Therefore, a firm may choose to pay an efficiency wage to improve the health of its workers.

Firms hope that the increase in productivity that results from paying the high wage can more than offset the extra cost of the wage, thereby lowering the firm's production cost. Because the efficiency wage is above the market wage, it results in the quantity of labor supplied being greater than the quantity of labor demanded. Efficiency wages, therefore, provide one explanation of why an economy can experience unemployment even when cyclical unemployment is zero.

Labor Unions Around the World

Labor unions are organizations of workers that bargain with employers over wages and working conditions for their members. In the United States, the National Labor Relations Act requires firms to allow unions to organize and requires firms to negotiate with unions. Therefore, unions can typically bargain for a wage that is above the market level. The higher wages result in firms in unionized industries hiring fewer workers. But do unions increase the overall unemployment rate in the economy? In the United States, fewer than 7% of workers in the private sector belong to a union. So, it seems likely that workers who cannot find jobs in unionized industries, such as the airlines and telecommunications industries, can find jobs in other industries.

In the United States, unionization rates are much higher in the public sector, where more than 36% of workers are members of unions. In 2011, as state and local governments attempted to deal with budget deficits, some economists and policymakers argued that public-sector unions had succeeded in bargaining for wages and benefits—particularly pension benefits—that were far above those being paid by private firms. There remained some disagreements about the extent to which this observation was correct because some government jobs do not have direct counterparts at private firms. In any event, after many years of steady increases, employment by state and local governments declined about 500,000 between the summer of 2008 and early 2011. These job losses contributed to the high levels of unemployment during this period.

Unionization rates vary across counties. In Canada and the United Kingdom, 27% of workers are unionized, 19% of workers are unionized in Germany, and 18% of workers are unionized in Japan. In contrast, just 12% of workers (in the public and private sectors combined) are unionized in the United States, and 10% of workers are unionized in South Korea. The relative strength of unions has declined dramatically in recent years for most countries due to globalization and the slow growth in the demand for labor in goods-producing industries. These factors have reduced the effect of union bargaining power on national unemployment rates.

Minimum Wage Laws

A *minimum wage* is a legal minimum hourly wage rate that employers are required to pay employees. The federal government has had a national minimum wage law since 1938. In 2011, the federal minimum wage was $7.25 per hour. Some state and local governments also impose minimum wages. For example, in 2011, the minimum wage in California was $8.00 per hour and the minimum wage in San Francisco was $9.92.

If the minimum wage is set above the market wage determined by the demand and supply of labor, the quantity of labor supplied will be greater than the quantity of labor demanded. As a result, some workers will be unemployed who would have been employed if there had been no minimum wage. Figure 7.12 shows the nominal minimum wage as set by the federal government and the real value of the minimum wage in 2010 dollars. The nominal national minimum wage increased from $0.25 per hour in 1938 to $7.25 per hour in 2010. In contrast, the real minimum wage increased in value from 1938 to 1968,

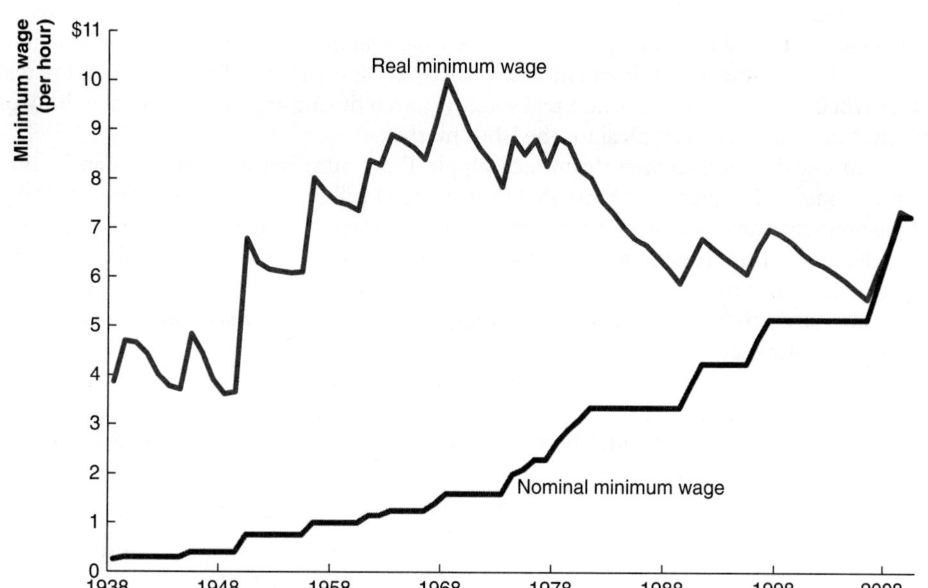

Figure 7.12

The Federal Minimum Wage, 1938–2010

The nominal minimum wage has increased significantly since 1938. However, the real minimum wage measured in 2010 dollars is lower than it was in 1968 because the nominal minimum wage has increased more slowly than the price level.

Source: U.S. Bureau of Labor Statistics.

but it has been declining on average since then. Initially, the real minimum wage was $3.87 per hour in 2010 dollars. It rose to $10.02 per hour in 1968, before declining to $7.25 per hour in 2010, as the average price level rose more than did the nominal minimum wage.

How much does the federal minimum wage increase unemployment? Relatively few workers earn the federal minimum wage. In 2009, fewer than 5% of workers received the federal minimum wage. By itself, this low fraction suggests that the federal minimum wage may not have an important effect on the overall unemployment rate. However, the minimum wage may significantly increase the unemployment rate for certain groups of low-skilled workers. For example, education level is an important determinant of whether a worker earns the minimum wage. During 2009, 10.2% of workers without a high school degree earned the minimum wage, while just 2.5% of workers with a bachelor's degree or higher earned the minimum wage. Minimum wage workers are also primarily young workers. For workers under age 25, 12.1% earned the minimum wage, but just 3.2% of workers age 25 and older earned the minimum wage. So, the minimum wage law may have important effects on young, less educated workers. But because teenagers and other workers receiving the minimum wage are a relatively small part of the labor force, most economists believe that, at its present level, the effect of the minimum wage on the unemployment rate in the United States is fairly small.

Monetary Policy, Unemployment, and the Classical Dichotomy

In the long run, the inflation rate is determined by the growth rate of the money supply. Therefore, in the long run, the Federal Reserve can use monetary policy to control the inflation rate. Can the Federal Reserve also use monetary policy to affect the unemployment rate in the long run? The **classical dichotomy** is the assertion that in the long run, nominal variables, such as the money supply or the price level, do not affect real variables, such as the levels of employment or real GDP. If the classical dichotomy is correct, then monetary policy will not affect the unemployment rate in the long run.[13] We can use our labor market model to understand when the classical dichotomy should apply.

Classical dichotomy The assertion that in the long run, nominal variables, such as the money supply or the price level, do not affect real variables, such as the levels of employment or real GDP.

Figure 7.11 on page 254 shows that there is typically unemployment in labor markets for a variety of reasons, including the existence of efficiency wages and labor unions. Although it is the real wage that determines employment in the labor market, workers and firms typically negotiate over the nominal wage. Because monetary policy can affect the price level, in the short run it can also affect the real wage and the level of employment.

Figure 7.13 is similar to Figure 7.11 in showing a labor market with unemployment. If there is always some unemployment due to frictional and structural reasons, then the real wage will be above the equilibrium real wage, w^*, even during expansions. We can think of point A in Figure 7.13 as typical for the labor market.

Suppose the Fed increases the money supply. From our discussion of the quantity theory of money in Chapter 6, we know that the price level will eventually increase from P_1 to P_2. If the nominal wage remained at its initial level of W_1, then the real wage will decrease to w_2. The decrease in the real wage will lead firms to hire more workers, so employment increases. The labor market is at point B. The key point is that if the nominal wage is fixed at its initial level, then an increase in the money supply can decrease the real wage and increase employment.

However, the real wage does not stay at w_2 forever. For example, firms that were paying efficiency wages will find that the real wage of w_2 is not high enough to achieve the efficiency gains that they want. These firms will increase the nominal wage to W_2, which

[13]In macroeconomics, "classical" is generally used to apply to theories that were first widely discussed before the 1930s. Economists first discussed the classical dichotomy during that period.

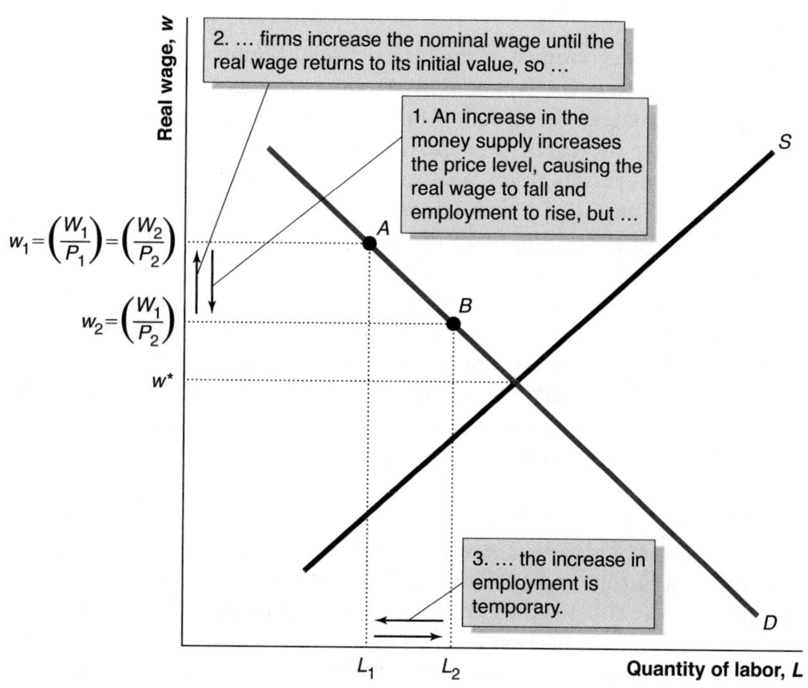
Real wage, w
2. ... firms increase the nominal wage until the real wage returns to its initial value, so ...
1. An increase in the money supply increases the price level, causing the real wage to fall and employment to rise, but ...
$w_1 = \left(\frac{W_1}{P_1}\right) = \left(\frac{W_2}{P_2}\right)$
$w_2 = \left(\frac{W_1}{P_2}\right)$
w^*
A
B
S
D
3. ... the increase in employment is temporary.
L_1
L_2
Quantity of labor, L

Figure 7.13

Labor Markets and Monetary Policy

An increase in the money supply temporarily reduces the real wage and increases employment. However, in the long run the nominal wage increases so the real wage and employment return to their initial levels. ●

will cause the real wage to increase back towards its initial value. The labor market is back at the original point *A*. Therefore, after nominal wages adjust to the higher price level, the increase in the money supply does not affect the real wage and employment.

An increase in the money supply increases *nominal* variables. But in the long run, the price level and the nominal wage both increase so as to leave the real wage unchanged. Because the real wage does not change, the level of employment remains unchanged. With employment constant, holding other factors constant, the level of real GDP will not change. The real wage, employment, and real GDP are all real variables because they represent quantities. Therefore, we can conclude that an increase in the money supply does not increase *real* variables.

Our labor market model shows that the classical dichotomy applies in the long run when prices have sufficient time to adjust to the increase in the money supply, but that the dichotomy does not apply in the short run when prices do not have enough time to fully adjust to the increase in the money supply. We discuss the flexibility of nominal wages and prices in greater detail in Chapter 8.

Comparisons of Unemployment Rates in Western Europe and the United States

7.5

Learning Objective

Describe how economic policy explains differences in unemployment rates between Europe and the United States.

In this chapter, we have developed models of the labor market and of the determinants of the natural rate of unemployment. We have also seen that average unemployment rates and the average duration of unemployment are higher in Western Europe than in the United States. Households in Western Europe consume more leisure than do households in the United States, but this development is relatively recent. There appear to be significant differences between the Western European and U.S. labor markets. Economists have examined three potential explanations for the differences:

1. Preferences of workers
2. Income tax rates
3. Strength of labor unions

Preferences of Workers

Olivier Blanchard, chief economist at the International Monetary Fund, argues that differences in cultural preferences explain why Western Europeans work less than do individuals in the United States.[14] In both the United States and Europe, real GDP per person and the real wage have increased over the decades due to the accumulation of capital goods and increases in productivity. As a result, incomes and wealth are higher today than they were in the past. In Section 7.1, we saw that an increase in the real wage has both a substitution effect, leading to an increase in the quantity of labor supplied, and an income effect, leading to a decrease in the quantity of labor supplied. How strong each of these effects is depends on the preferences of workers in a country. Blanchard argues that as real GDP per person has increased, Western Europeans have simply used the increase in income to "purchase" more leisure than have Americans. However, for Blanchard's explanation to be correct, the difference in preferences must be a recent development, because as recently as the 1960s, Western Europeans worked as many hours as, or even more hours than, Americans.

Income Tax Rates

Nobel Laureate Edward Prescott of Arizona State University believes that higher income tax rates in Western Europe can explain why Western Europeans work fewer hours than do Americans.[15] If the substitution effect is stronger than the income effect, then our model of the labor market in Section 7.1 indicates that an increase in income tax rates will reduce the incentive to work and lead to a reduction in the amount of labor supplied. Prescott points out that the differences in income tax rates between Western Europe and the United States were smaller in the 1960s and early 1970s, when the amount of leisure time was similar in both areas. During the 1970s, income tax rates rose much more rapidly in Western Europe at the same time as the amount of leisure in Europe was increasing. This finding supports Prescott's emphasis on income tax rates. However, for Prescott's explanation to be correct, declines in the after-tax wage resulting from tax increases should have resulted in the quantity of labor supplied declining significantly. In other words, the *elasticity* of labor supply with respect to the after-tax wage would have to be large. Many estimates of the elasticity of labor supply with respect to the after-tax wage indicate that it is very low. As a result, the observed increases in income tax rates in Western Europe do not appear to be large enough by themselves to explain the large increases in leisure taken by workers in those countries.

Strength of Labor Unions

Figure 7.14 shows that the extent of unionization is greater in the United Kingdom, Germany, Canada, and Japan than in the United States and South Korea. Economists Alberto Alesina and Edward Glaeser of Harvard University and Bruce Sacerdote of Dartmouth College argue that this difference in unionization rates can explain much of the difference between U.S. and European labor markets.[16] Strong labor unions in Europe negotiate for a large number of mandatory holidays, long vacations, and short workweeks. Strong labor unions may push the wage above the equilibrium real wage and cause unemployment. Unions are also politically powerful and can use that influence to pressure

---

[14]Olivier Blanchard, "The Economic Future of Europe," *Journal of Economic Perspectives*, Vol. 18, No. 4, Fall 2004, pp. 3–26.

[15]Edward Prescott, "Why Do Americans Work So Much More Than Europeans?" *Federal Reserve Bank of Minneapolis Quarterly Review*, Vol. 28, No. 1, July 2004, pp. 2–13.

[16]Alberto Alesina, Edward Glaeser, and Bruce Sacerdote, "Work and Leisure in the U.S. and Europe: Why So Different?" *NBER Macroeconomic Annual 2005*, Vol. 20, 2006, pp. 1–64.

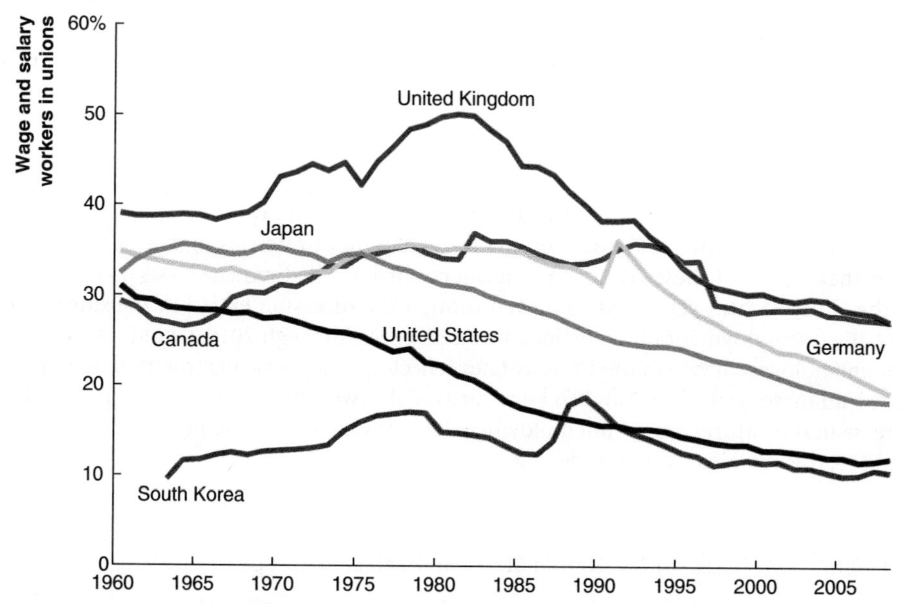

Figure 7.14

Unionization Rates Around the World, 1960–2008

A larger percentage of the workforce in Europe belongs to unions than in the United States, although the relative strength of unions has declined dramatically in recent years for most countries.

Source: Organization for Economic Co-operation and Development.

politicians for regulations that make it difficult for firms to fire workers. Equation (7.2) from page 248 tells us that

$$U = \frac{1}{1 + (f/s)}.$$

You might think that a decrease in the separation rate, s, would reduce the natural rate of unemployment, U. However, this is not necessarily the case because firms will respond to the regulation in ways that reduce the rate of job finding, f. Firms may adopt more capital-intensive technology that reduces the need to hire workers, or they may be reluctant to expand operations. Both of these actions may decrease the rate of job finding and therefore increase the natural rate of unemployment. In addition, labor unions have pushed for generous unemployment insurance, which reduces the incentive for workers to accept job offers, further reducing the job finding rate.

Making the Connection

Job Security and Job Hiring at France Télécom SA

In 2006, France Télécom SA was the world's fifth-largest telecommunications company. Because it was a formerly state-owned company, two-thirds of its employees were covered by civil service contracts, which meant the workers were guaranteed jobs for life. Not surprisingly, France Télécom found it very difficult to adapt to changes in the telecommunications industry. To encourage workers to quit, the company provided employees with funds to start up their own businesses and provided help writing business plans and obtaining loans. If these new businesses did not work out within the first three years, the employees could return to work for French Télécom.

The French government also makes it difficult to fire workers even if they do not have civil service contracts. Unless employees steal or are extremely negligent, it is difficult for any firm in France to fire workers. While an extreme case, the experience of France Télécom demonstrates how difficult it can be for European firms to fire workers. Economist Elie Cohen, a former board member of France Télécom said, "In France, you can't fire people just because your industry or technology is changing." Not surprisingly, many firms are reluctant to hire in the first place. This can reduce the rate of job finding and increase the natural rate of unemployment. This chapter examines some of the reasons economists have offered for the differences between unemployment rates in Western Europe and the United States, including different preferences among workers, differences in tax rates, and the influences of labor unions. The table below confirms that the unemployment rate in the United States was lower than the unemployment rate in France, Germany, and Italy from 2005 to 2008. In 2009, however, the unemployment rate was higher in the United States than in any of these Western European countries. The financial crisis of 2007–2009 hit the United States very hard, and even though the recession ended in the summer of 2009, the unemployment rate remained in excess of 9% through 2010. Could it be that the high unemployment rate in the United States reflected an increase in structural unemployment—an increase in the mismatch between available workers and job openings—and an increase in the natural rate of unemployment? As we saw in the *Making the Connection* on page 244, this remains a point of debate among economists.

Unemployment Rates for the United States and Selected European Countries

Year	United States	France	Germany	Italy
2005	5.1%	9.0%	11.2%	7.8%
2006	4.6	8.9	10.3	6.9
2007	4.6	8.1	8.7	6.2
2008	5.8	7.5	7.6	6.8
2009	9.3	9.2	7.8	7.9
2010	9.6	9.4	7.2	8.6

Sources: Lelia Abboud "At France Télécom, Battle to Cut Jobs Breeds Odd Tactics," *Wall Street Journal*, August 14, 2006; U.S. Bureau of Labor Statistics, *International Comparisons of Annual Labor Force Statistics, Adjusted to U.S. Concepts, 10 Countries, 1970–2010*, www.bls.gov/fls/flscomparelf/unemployment.htm; and Rob Valletta and Katherine Kuang, "Is Structural Unemployment on the Rise?" *Economic Letter*, Federal Reserve Bank of San Francisco, November 8, 2010.

Test your understanding by doing related problem 5.4 on page 269 at the end of this chapter.

Answering the Key Question

Continued from page 231

At the beginning of the chapter, we asked the question:

"Should policymakers aim for an unemployment rate of zero?"

There are three categories of unemployment: cyclical, frictional, and structural. Cyclical unemployment occurs when workers lose their jobs due to a recession, and structural unemployment occurs when workers lack the skills necessary to find new jobs. Reducing these categories of unemployment will increase the level of well-being in the economy. Frictional unemployment occurs as workers and firms look for better job matches. Eliminating all frictional unemployment would clearly reduce the efficiency of the economy. Better job matches make workers more productive and increase the efficiency of the economy. Therefore, policymakers should *not* aim for an unemployment rate of zero.

Before moving on to Chapter 8, read *An Inside Look* on the next page for a discussion of the U.S. jobless rate in December 2010 and the challenges facing the long-term unemployed.

Unemployment Rate Falls, yet Remains Significantly Lower than Underemployment Rate

WALL STREET JOURNAL

Why Did the Unemployment Rate Drop?

The U.S. jobless rate dropped substantially to 9.4% in December, but the government's broader measure of unemployment dropped at a more modest pace to 16.7%, highlighting the problem of the long-term unemployed.

The comprehensive gauge of labor underutilization, known as the "U-6" for its data classification by the Labor Department, accounts for people who have stopped looking for work or who can't find full-time jobs.

a The key to the discrepancy between the two numbers was an increase in the number of workers considered marginally attached to the labor force. The figure increased in December. The number of workers part-time for economic reasons fell slightly.

The increase in the number of discouraged workers highlights the problem of the long-term unemployed. Some four million people have been without a job for 52 weeks or longer in December, according to the Labor Department. That's a decline from November, but there are indications that those people are dropping out of the labor force.

b The big drop in the overall unemployment rate and the U-6 measure was primarily due to a decline in the number of unemployed, which fell by 556,000 in December. That's good news since the number of people who are employed increased by nearly 300,000. But that still leaves over 250,000 workers leaving the labor force altogether. That likely means a substantial part of the drop was due to workers giving up. Anyone unemployed over 99 weeks has no access to unemployment benefits and many lose access even earlier. Once those benefits expire, the unemployed may stop considering themselves part of the labor force.

To be sure, declines in the labor force also come from workers who decide to go back to school, go on disability, leave to raise children or retire.

The overall unemployment rate is calculated based on people who are without jobs, who are available to work and who have actively sought work in the prior four weeks. The "actively looking for work" definition is fairly broad, including people who contacted an employer, employment agency, job center or friends; sent out resumes or filled out applications; or answered or placed ads, among other things. The rate is calculated by dividing that number by the total number of people in the labor force.

c The U-6 figure includes everyone in the official rate plus "marginally attached workers"—those who are neither working nor looking for work, but say they want a job and have looked for work recently; and people who are employed part-time for economic reasons, meaning they want full-time work but took a part-time schedule instead because that's all they could find. People who drop out of the labor force completely aren't included in this tally.

Source: Phil Izzo, "Why Did the Unemployment Rate Drop?," *Wall Street Journal*, January 7, 2011.

Key Points in the Article

This article discusses unemployment and underemployment in the United States in December, 2010. The U.S. Department of Labor reported that the U.S. jobless rate dropped to 9.4% in December, but the broader measure of unemployment, a comprehensive gauge of underemployment known as the U-6, only declined to 16.7%. The decreases in these two figures can be explained by an increase in available jobs and a decrease in the size of the labor force.

Analyzing the News

a Although the jobless rate declined to 9.4% in December 2010, a wide gap remained between this figure and the Labor Department's broader measure of unemployment, known as the U-6. The U-6 measurement includes not only those workers who are unemployed, but also those who are working part time because they cannot find full-time employment and those who are considered marginally attached workers. The graph shows both measurements of unemployment from 2006 through 2010. Throughout 2006 and 2007, the gap remained relatively constant at approximately 4%, but since the recession began in December 2007, the gap between these two figures has grown significantly, widening to more than 7% by the end of 2010. One reason for this growing disparity is the extended length of time many workers have gone without employment. As of December 2010, approximately 4 million people had been without work for a year or longer, and this seems to have resulted in an increase in the total number of discouraged workers who had dropped out of the labor force.

b The number of unemployed workers fell by 556,000 in December 2010, but of this total, only 300,000 found employment. The remaining 256,000 workers dropped out of the labor force. The lingering effects of the recession, including long-term unemployment, are likely responsible for a large portion of this exodus from the labor force. After 99 weeks of unemployment, workers are no longer eligible for unemployment benefits, and many of these workers drop out of the labor force. As a result, the unemployment rate falls even though the number of employed workers does not increase.

c Discouraged workers who have been out of the labor force for more than one year are not included in the labor force and are therefore not included in either the jobless rate or the U-6 measure of unemployment. An alternative unemployment measurement, called the SGS Alternate, includes these long-term discouraged workers. In December 2010, this measure of the unemployment rate was greater than 22%, further highlighting the economic challenges of the long-term unemployed.

THINKING CRITICALLY

1. According to the article, the number of people employed increased by nearly 300,000 and over 250,000 left the labor force in December 2010. Using a labor market graph, illustrate these changes and explain how these changes will affect the real wage and the quantity of labor.
2. According to the figure showing the unemployment rate below and the article, the unemployment rate increased from approximately 5% at the beginning of 2008 to 9.4% in December 2010. Was the increase in the unemployment rate due to frictional, structural, or cyclical reasons? Did the natural rate of unemployment increase?

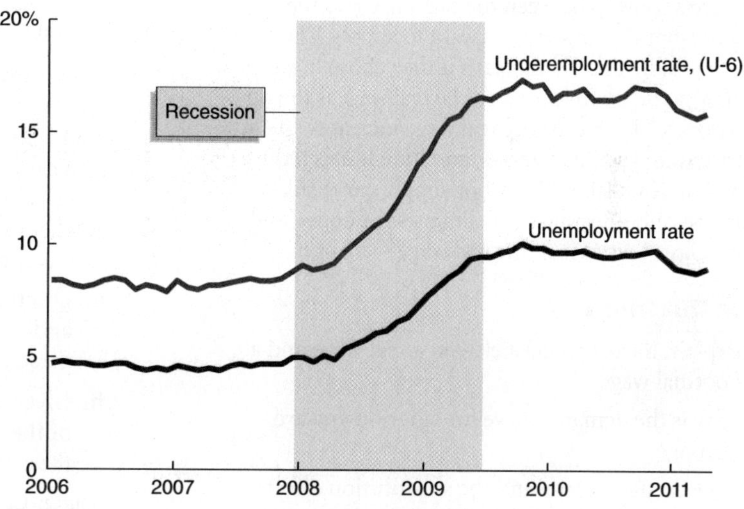

Unemployment Rate and Underemployed (U-6) Rate, 2006–2010.

Source: Reprinted with permission of *The Wall Street Journal*, Copyright © 2011 Dow Jones & Company, Inc. All Rights Reserved Worldwide.

CHAPTER SUMMARY AND PROBLEMS

KEY TERMS

Classical dichotomy, p. 256
Cyclical unemployment, p. 243
Efficiency wage, p. 254
Frictional unemployment, p. 240
Marginal product of labor (*MPL*), p. 233
Natural rate of unemployment, p. 243
Structural unemployment, p. 241
Unemployment insurance, p. 241

7.1 The Labor Market

Use the model of demand and supply to explain how wages and employment are determined.

SUMMARY

We can use the model of demand and supply to explain the real wage and the quantity of labor. The labor demand curve shows the relationship between the real wage and the quantity of labor that firms want to hire. The labor demand curve is the **marginal product of labor** curve and is downward sloping because of diminishing marginal returns. The labor demand curve shifts when any variable affecting the willingness of firms to hire workers—other than the real wage—changes. The labor supply curve shows the relationship between the real wage and the quantity of labor that individuals want to supply. The real wage is what individuals could earn if they chose to work rather than to engage in leisure, so the real wage is the opportunity cost of leisure. As the real wage increases, the opportunity cost of leisure increases, and individuals reduce leisure and increase labor. The labor supply curve shifts when any variable affecting the willingness of households to supply labor—other than the real wage—changes.

Review Questions

1.1 Explain the difference between a real wage and a nominal wage.

1.2 Why is the demand curve for labor downward sloping?

1.3 How do the income and the substitution effects determine the slope of the labor supply curve?

1.4 When the labor market is in equilibrium, are all workers employed?

Problems and Applications

1.5 **[Related to *Solved Problem 7.1* on page 238]** Draw a graph of the aggregate labor market in equilibrium. Then consider each of the following scenarios. In each case, show the effect on the market and explain what will happen to the real wage and the equilibrium quantity of labor.

a. A technological change occurs that increases the productivity of all workers.
b. The government increases income tax rates.
c. Worker preferences change so that they prefer consumption of market goods to consumption of leisure.
d. The government reduces payroll taxes firms pay when they hire workers.

1.6 According to Claudia Goldin of Harvard University, in the United States prior to 1940, most married women who worked had limited education and came from lower-income families. She argues that: "Their decisions were made as secondary workers and their market work evaporated when family incomes rose sufficiently."

a. Discuss the likely relative sizes of the income and substitution effects for women during these years.
b. Given your answer to part a., discuss the shape of the labor supply curve for women during these years.

Source: Claudia Goldin, "The Quiet Revolution That Transformed Women's Employment, Education, and Family," *American Economic Review, Papers and Proceedings*, Vol. 96, No. 2, May 2006, pp. 1–21.

1.7 Suppose that workers become concerned about the future and therefore wish to increase their hours of work relative to leisure. At the same time, there is an increase in the capital stock, making workers more productive.

a. Draw a graph of the labor market, showing the effect of these changes.

b. Can you predict the effect on equilibrium employment? On the real wage?

1.8 In countries with declining populations, governments have begun to offer income subsidies for families with children. What impact is this subsidy likely to have on the labor market, all other things being equal? Support your answer with a graph.

1.9 Discussing job openings during the recession, Cheryl Peterson, a director of the American Nurses Association, was quoted as saying: "Until the downturn, it was easy for [nurses] to find employment. . . . Now it is a little more difficult because the number of job openings has fallen and we have more retired nurses . . . coming back."

a. Why might retired nurses reenter the job market during a recession?

b. Use a graph to explain what is happening in the labor market.

Source: Louis Uchitelle, "Despite Recession, High Demand for Skilled Labor," *New York Times*, June 23, 2009.

1.10 Consider the following statement: "Increases in the capital stock are harmful to workers because they allow firms to substitute capital for labor, thus reducing overall employment." Do you agree with this statement? Briefly explain.

1.11 The graph below shows the labor market. The initial equilibrium is at point *A*. The new equilibrium is at point *B*.

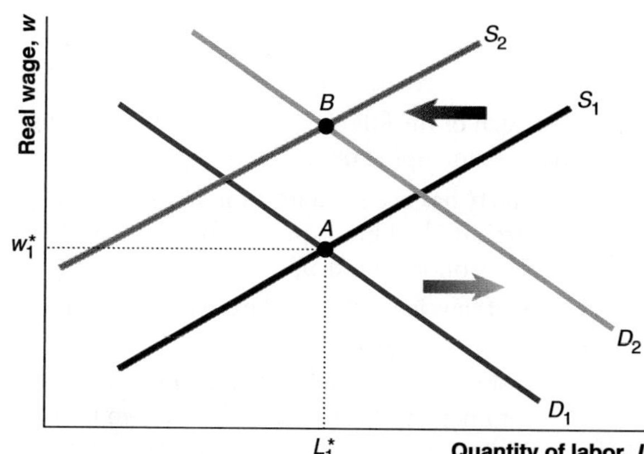

a. What factors could have caused the shifts shown on the graph?

b. Show the new equilibrium real wage and quantity of labor on the graph. Have wages and employment increased or decreased?

c. How would your answer to part b. change if the size of the labor demand shift had been greater than the size of the labor supply shift?

7.2 Categories of Unemployment

Define unemployment and explain the three categories of unemployment.

SUMMARY

There are three categories of unemployment: cyclical, frictional, and structural. You are **cyclically unemployed** if you are unemployed due to current economic conditions, such as a recession. You are **frictionally unemployed** if you are unemployed for a short period of time while looking for a better job match. You are **structurally unemployed** if you lack the skills necessary to find a job. Full employment occurs when cyclical unemployment is zero. The **natural rate of unemployment** is the normal rate of unemployment that exists when cyclical unemployment is zero. **Unemployment insurance**, a government program that allows workers to receive benefits for a period of time after losing their jobs, can increase the efficiency of labor markets and the economy.

Review Questions

2.1 What is frictional unemployment?

2.2 What is structural unemployment?

2.3 What is cyclical unemployment?

2.4 When the economy is at full employment, are all workers employed? Briefly explain.

2.5 Compare the average duration of unemployment in the United States and Europe.

Problems and Applications

2.6 **[Related to the *Making the Connection* on page 244]** Increases in structural unemployment can result from a recession but are more commonly associated with other changes, such as the development of new products that replace old products. A classic example of this is typewriters and computers.

a. How might technological change cause structural unemployment?

b. Would you expect a similar effect on unemployment when new types of cereal or styles of clothing are developed?

2.7 For each of the following examples, identify the type of unemployment.

a. Marty has been laid off from her job at an aircraft plant but expects to be recalled when the economy picks up.

b. Scott has just graduated from college and hasn't found a job yet.

c. Kishore works as a lobsterman in Maine in the summer, but the industry shuts down in the winter.

d. Doug worked in an automobile plant in Michigan, but the plant was shut down permanently.

2.8 Suppose that the government wished to reduce the rate of frictional unemployment.

a. What types of measures might target frictional unemployment?

b. There is some evidence that frictional unemployment has decreased over the past two decades. What would explain that?

2.9 Suppose that the government wants to reduce the rate of structural unemployment.

a. What types of measures might target structural unemployment?

b. Do measures such as the extension of unemployment insurance in industries affected by technological change tend to increase or decrease structural unemployment?

2.10 Consider the following statement: "Because there will always be frictional and structural unemployment, there is no reason for government policymakers to be concerned about them. They should target cyclical unemployment instead." Do you agree with this statement? Briefly explain.

2.11 **[Related to the *Chapter Opener* on page 231]** In February 2010, the average duration of unemployment increased to 30.5 weeks, a record high. According to *CNN Money*, "It's no wonder unemployed workers are getting discouraged: It's never taken longer to find a new job."

a. What type of unemployment is the quote referring to?

b. What may happen if workers become discouraged?

Source: Jessica Dickler, "Countdown to a New Job . . . . . . 211 Days," *CNN Money*, money.cnn.com/2010/02/05/news/economy/unemployment_duration/index.htm.

7.3 The Natural Rate of Unemployment

Explain the natural rate of unemployment.

SUMMARY

There is a significant amount of job turnover every quarter in the economy, with millions of workers finding employment and millions of workers leaving employment. When the rate of job finding increases, the natural rate of unemployment decreases, and when the rate of job separation increases, the natural rate of unemployment increases. Demographic, institutional, and economic factors cause the natural rate of unemployment to rise and fall. Technological change can increase unemployment in the short run as new technology eliminates the demand for some products and the workers who make those products. However, technological change also creates the demand for new products. In the long run, by increasing the real wage, technological change ultimately increases employment.

Review Questions

3.1 Define the natural rate of unemployment in terms of flows into and out of the labor market.

3.2 What are the key factors that determine the structural and frictional unemployment rates?

3.3 How does the natural rate of unemployment change as the demographic composition of the population changes?

3.4 What is the effect of unemployment insurance on the natural rate of unemployment?

3.5 Explain the ways in which technological change might alter the natural rate of unemployment.

Problems and Applications

3.6 Suppose that the rate of job separation is 2% and the job-finding rate is 18%.

a. What is the natural rate of unemployment?

b. If the job-finding rate doubles, what is the new natural rate of unemployment?

c. Return to the original scenario. If the rate of job separation is cut in half, what is the new natural rate of unemployment?

d. Which has more impact: a doubling of the job-finding rate or a halving of the job-separation rate? Does your result have any implications for government policy?

3.7 How would you expect each of the following factors to affect the natural rate of unemployment?

a. There is an increase in the rate of technological change.

b. The minimum wage falls.

c. Unemployment benefits (that is, the percentage of wages replaced by unemployment) are increased.

d. Improvements in information technology speed the matching of jobs and workers.

e. There is a recession.

3.8 The CBO estimated that the natural rate of unemployment was 6.8% in 1979 and 5.0% in 2001. If you examine Figure 7.10 on page 250 carefully, you can see that the natural rate remained relatively constant during the 1980s and then fell more rapidly during the 1990s.

a. Considering only the frictional component of the natural rate of unemployment, what might explain this change?

b. Productivity growth was slow during the 1980s. One theory about this slow growth was that innovations in computer technology were not increasing productivity in ways that were directly measurable. Productivity growth increased in the 1990s, and at the same time, the natural rate fell. Does this fact suggest anything about structural unemployment in the 1980s and 1990s?

3.9 Increases in the generosity (percentage of wages replaced) and duration of unemployment benefits are associated with increases in the natural rate of unemployment.

a. Why do governments provide unemployment benefits if they may increase unemployment rates?

b. Among the measures passed by the U.S. government during the 2007–2009 recession were temporary increases in the duration of unemployment benefits. Would you expect these measures to increase the natural rate?

3.10 In countries with high birthrates, such as many of the Central and South American nations, unemployment rates are typically far higher than in countries with lower birthrates. Explain why.

3.11 Demographic studies show that the Hispanic population of the United States is increasing. Traditionally, Hispanics have had higher-than-average rates of unemployment. However, it is also true that Hispanic women tend to have lower labor force participation rates (in other words, are less likely to enter the labor force) than women of other ethnic groups. How would these demographic trends be likely to affect the natural rate of unemployment?

3.12 In an article about the impact of the 2007–2009 recession on the labor market, Bloomberg quotes Lawrence Mishel, president of the Economic Policy Institute in Washington, as saying: "People tend to think that when you come out of a recession you get the labor market you had when you entered it. This time you may get something quite different." Why might a prolonged recession cause changes in the natural rate of unemployment?

Source: Matthew Benjamin and Rich Miller, "'Great' Recession Will Redefine Unemployment as Jobs Vanish," Bloomberg.com, May 3, 2009.

3.13 **[Related to *Solved Problem 7.3* on page 247]** The following table, based on data from the Bureau of Labor Statistics, gives total nonfarm employment in October, November, and December 2010:

Total nonfarm employment (in thousands)

October	November	December
130,538	130,609	130,712

Source: Bureau of Labor Statistics.

a. Calculate the change in nonfarm employment between October and November and between November and December.

b. Because new workers constantly enter the labor market, the economy must create approximately 150,000 jobs each month to keep unemployment constant, all other things being equal. What would you expect to have happened to the unemployment rate during November and December?

7.4 Why Does Unemployment Exist?

Explain how government policies affect the unemployment rate.

SUMMARY

Unemployment exists when the real wage is above the equilibrium real wage. When this occurs, a surplus of workers exists, and the surplus is equivalent to the unemployed in the household survey by the Bureau of Labor Statistics. An **efficiency wage** is a higher-than-equilibrium real wage that firms voluntarily pay. This wage may reduce quit rates, increase worker productivity, and improve the average quality of the workforce, which can increase firms' profits. Labor unions can have market power and drive the real wage above the equilibrium real wage. Minimum wage laws force some firms to pay a wage higher than the equilibrium real wage. The **classical dichotomy** asserts that in the long run, nominal variables, such as the money supply or the price level, do not affect real variables, such as the levels of employment or real GDP.

Review Questions

4.1 How does a real wage above equilibrium cause unemployment?

4.2 What is an efficiency wage, and how do efficiency wages affect the labor market?

4.3 How might labor unions contribute to unemployment?

Problems and Applications

4.4 Suppose the equations for the demand and supply of labor are given by:

$$L_D = 100 - 2w$$
$$L_S = 10 + 3w$$

where w is the real wage and L_D and L_S are the quantity of labor demanded and supplied, respectively.

a. Solve for the equilibrium wage and the quantity of employment and graph your results.

b. Assume that the government imposes a \$20 minimum wage. Find the new quantity of labor demanded and supplied.

c. How many people lose their jobs because of the minimum wage? How many workers are now unemployed?

4.5 In 1914, Ford Motor Company doubled its wage to \$5 per day, a rate that was considerably above the average wage at that time.

a. In terms of efficiency wages, explain why Ford would have had an incentive to do this.

b. What data would you look for to determine whether Ford's wage increase was successful in achieving its goals?

4.6 Minimum wage laws are controversial for many reasons. One is that they may not be beneficial to the workers that they are most intended to help.

a. What type of workers are most likely to be paid the minimum wage?

b. What happens to employment of these workers when a minimum wage is enacted (or increased)?

c. Overall, who gains and who loses from a minimum wage law?

4.7 Some economists studying the effects of the minimum wage law have found that it tends to reduce the employment of black teenagers relative to white teenagers. Briefly explain the economics behind this finding.

4.8 Some craft unions, such as electricians, restrict the number of workers who can join the union and then negotiate with employers to hire only union workers. Use a demand and supply graph to illustrate the effect of a craft union on emoloyment and wages in an industry.

4.9 Traditionally, unions have been strongest in manufacturing industries. In the United States, unionism reached its peak in 1945, and it has been falling since then.

a. How does the changing sectoral composition of the U.S. economy help to explain this trend?

b. Two industries in which, traditionally, unions have been very strong are automobile manufacturing and airlines. Why has union power weakened in these industries?

4.10 Unemployment in the labor market is increased by forces that keep wages from falling to the equilibrium level. Other than efficiency wages, unionism, and minimum wages, what other factors might cause this wage stickiness?

7.5 Comparisons of Unemployment Rates in Western Europe and the United States

Describe how economic policy explains differences in unemployment rates between Europe and the United States.

SUMMARY

Western European countries have higher average unemployment rates than does the United States, and workers in Western Europe work fewer hours. There are three broad explanations for why this is the case. First, workers in Western Europe may simply choose to work fewer hours than workers in the United States. However, the differences in unemployment rates and leisure time are recent developments, so the differences in preferences must have been a recent development. Second, income tax rates are higher in Western Europe, which reduces the opportunity cost of leisure. The tax rates in Western Europe rose relative to the rates in the United States in the 1970s and 1980s as the differences in unemployment rates and leisure started to develop. However, given what economists know about how much leisure responds to tax rates, the increase in Western European tax rates may not be large enough by itself to explain the differences in leisure and unemployment that we observe. Finally, labor unions are stronger in Western Europe and may negotiate higher-than-equilibrium real wages, long vacations, more holidays, and shorter workweeks. In addition, strong unions may pressure politicians into passing regulations that make it difficult to fire workers. Firms may respond by being reluctant to hire workers in the first place. This reluctance would reduce the rate of job finding and increase the natural rate of unemployment.

Review Questions

5.1 How might differences in preferences explain the difference between European and U.S. unemployment rates?

5.2 Why would tax rates have an impact on unemployment rates?

5.3 Does the extent of labor unionism explain the difference between European and U.S. unemployment rates?

Problems and Applications

5.4 **[Related to the *Making the Connection* on page 259]** Some European companies have U.S. subsidiaries, and the labor practices they employ in the U.S. may be very different from those they employ in Europe. *Bloomberg Businessweek* reports: "With more than 5 million Americans now employed by foreign-owned companies, U.S. labor unions are starting to export their grievances." If U.S. unions are successful in getting these companies to follow European practices, what would you expect to see happen to the natural rate of employment in the United States?

Source: Carol Matlack, "U.S. Labor Takes Its Case to European Bosses," *Bloomberg Businessweek*, January 22, 2010.

5.5 Discussing the recovery of the labor market in Europe, the European Central Bank (ECB) noted: "Hourly wages adjusted earlier and more sharply in the United States than in the euro area. . . . Different labor market policies and a greater degree of wage flexibility . . . played a role." What did the ECB mean by "different labor market policies?"

Source: European Central Bank, *Monthly Bulletin*, May 13, 2010.

5.6 In Japan, relationships between labor unions and management tend to be less adversarial and more cooperative than those in the United States and Europe. What are the implications of this observation for the size of Japan's natural rate of unemployment, relative to the natural rates of unemployment in the United States and Europe?

5.7 The number of U.S. autoworkers has decreased considerably, in part due to the decline of the auto industry but also due to changes in the way that automobiles are manufactured. In light of the information presented in this chapter on European unionism, how might the strength of U.S. autoworkers' unions actually have caused some of the long-run trends in employment in that industry?

DATA EXERCISES

D7.1: **[Related to *Macro Data* on page 242]** The CIA *World Factbook* (https://www.cia.gov/library/publications/the-world-factbook/) gives the sectoral composition of GDP for most countries.

a. Examine the sectoral compositions for high-income countries. Are they similar to or different from those of the United States?

b. Examine the sectoral compositions for low-income countries. How are these distributions different?

c. What implications might the different sectoral distributions have for natural rates of unemployment?

D7.2: Under the World Bank's Labor and Social Protection data (see http://data.worldbank.org/topic/labor-and-social-protection), there is information on long-term unemployment by country.

a. In what countries is the percentage of long-term unemployed individuals (as a percentage of total unemployed individuals) the highest? The lowest?

b. Can you relate the differences in the duration of unemployment to differences in labor markets in these countries?

D7.3: How has the 2007–2009 recession affected U.S. unemployment? Go to the Bureau of Labor Statistics Web site (www.bls.gov) and find monthly unemployment rates for the past decade.

a. What was the average rate of unemployment for the 2002–2006 period?

b. What has been the average rate of unemployment from 2007 to the present?

c. At this time, does it appear that the labor market has recovered from the 2007–2009 recession?

d. Search the Web to find the most recent government projections for unemployment in the coming years.

D7.4: Return to the Bureau of Labor Statistics Web site and look for data on the duration of unemployment.

a. What percentage of unemployment is accounted for by spells lasting less than five weeks.

b. What percentage of unemployment is accounted for by spells lasting over 26 weeks?

c. If you chart unemployment spells, you observe that, during normal periods, many workers become unemployed and reemployed relatively quickly. Others do not find jobs until just before or after the 26-week mark. What does this suggest about the relationship between unemployment benefits and longer spells of unemployment?

D7.5: **[Excel question]** The standard measure of unemployment is called the U-3 rate in data from the Bureau of Labor Statistics. There is a broader measure, U-6, which includes those measured as unemployed under the U-3 rate plus workers who are underemployed and marginally attached to the labor force.

a. Go to the Web site for the Bureau of Labor Statistics and find the definition of the U-6 rate.

b. Use Excel to chart the U-3 and U-6 data for the past ten years.

c. How do the U-3 and U-6 measures move during the business cycle?

d. What is the average level of unemployment, as based on each rate? Is one more volatile than the other?

e. To what extent are the U-3 and U-6 rates correlated?

myeconlab Visit **www.myeconlab.com** to complete these exercises online and get instant feedback.

CHAPTER 8

Business Cycles

LEARNING OBJECTIVES

After studying this chapter, you should be able to:

8.1 Explain the difference between the short run and the long run in macroeconomics (pages 272–277)

8.2 Understand what happens during a business cycle (pages 278–289)

8.3 Explain how economists think about business cycles (pages 290–293)

8A Derive the formula for the expenditure multiplier (page 301)

FORD RIDES THE BUSINESS CYCLE ROLLERCOASTER

The graph on the next page shows sales of Ford cars and trucks in the United States from the early 1960s through 2010.

A firm's sales can be affected by many factors, such as the prices it charges relative to its competitors, how innovative its products seem to consumers, and the effectiveness of its advertising campaigns. But for firms like Ford that sell consumer durables that buyers may have to borrow money to purchase, sales are heavily affected by the business cycle. The ups and downs in Ford's sales shown in the graph mirror the business cycle. For instance, the two most severe business cycle recessions since World War II occurred during 1981–1982 and 2007–2009. During each period, Ford's sales declined by more than 40%. Although rising gasoline prices also hurt Ford's sales during these periods, the largest effect was from the business cycle.

The causes and consequences of the business cycle were not always a significant part of the study of economics. Modern macroeconomics began during the 1930s, as economists and policymakers struggled to understand why the Great Depression was so severe. During just the first two years of the Great Depression, from 1929 to 1931,

Continued on next page

Key Issue and Question

At the end of Chapter 1, we noted key issues and questions that serve as a framework for the book. Here are the key issue and question for this chapter:

Issue: Economies around the world experience a business cycle.

Question: Why does the business cycle occur?

Answered on page 293

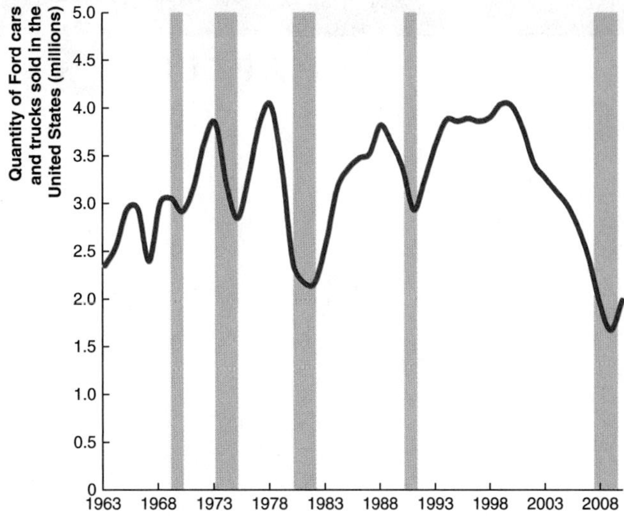

Note: Shaded areas represent recessions.

Ford's sales declined by almost two-thirds. Ford was hardly alone. During the same two years, General Motors' sales fell by nearly one-half, and U.S. Steel's sales declined by nearly three-quarters. From the business cycle peak in 1929 to the business cycle trough in 1933, real GDP declined by 27%, real investment spending declined by an astonishing 81%, and the S&P 500 stock price index declined by 85%—the largest decline in U.S. history. Unemployment soared from less than 3% in 1929 to more than 20% in 1933, and it remained above 11% as late as 1939.

As economists studied the events of the Great Depression, they came to understand more clearly that although in the long run real GDP experiences an upward trend, in the short run real GDP fluctuates around this trend. These short-run fluctuations in real GDP consisting of alternating periods of expansion and recession are what economists mean by the *business cycle*. Research has shown that the U.S. economy has experienced business cycles dating back to at least the early nineteenth century. The business cycle is not uniform: Periods of expansion are not all the same length, nor are periods of recession, but every period of expansion in U.S. history has been followed by a period of recession, and every period of recession has been followed by a period of expansion.

Economists have developed short-run macroeconomic models to analyze the business cycle. British economist John Maynard Keynes developed a particularly influential model in 1936 in direct response to the Great Depression. In this chapter, we begin our discussion of the macroeconomic short run.

AN INSIDE LOOK on page 294 analyzes why auto sales rose in the United States in 2010 for the first time since the recession that began in 2007.

Sources: Ford Motor Company, *Annual Report*, various years; U.S. Bureau of Economic Analysis; David R. Weir, "A Century of U.S. Unemployment, 1890–1990," in Roger L. Ransom, Richard Sutch, and Susan B. Carter (eds.), *Research in Economic History*, Vol. 14, Westport, CT: JAI Press, 1992, Table D3, pp. 341–343; and Robert J. Shiller, *Irrational Exuberance*, Princeton, NJ: Princeton University Press, 2005, as updated at www.econ.yale.edu/~shiller/data.htm.

In Chapters 4 and 5, we developed a model of long-run economic growth. As we have seen, the analysis of long-run economic growth is a key part of modern macroeconomics. In this chapter and the four that follow, we shift our focus from the long run to the short run. We begin our analysis in this chapter by identifying the ways in which the short run differs from the long run in macroeconomics.

The Short Run and the Long Run in Macroeconomics

8.1

Learning Objective

Explain the difference between the short run and the long run in macroeconomics.

In microeconomic analysis, economists rely heavily on the model of demand and supply. Economists usually assume that the markets they are analyzing are in equilibrium: For example, they assume that the quantity of apples demanded equals the quantity of apples supplied. Put another way, economists typically assume that markets *clear* because prices rise to eliminate shortages and fall to eliminate surpluses. We know that it is not literally true that all markets for goods are in equilibrium all the time. If you can't find a popular toy during the holidays or can't get a reservation at a favorite restaurant on a Saturday night or are waiting in line to buy Apple's latest electronic gadget, you know that prices do *not* adjust continually to keep all markets cleared all the time. Still, these examples of *nonmarket clearing*, or *disequilibrium*, are exceptions to typical market behavior, and assuming that markets are in equilibrium does not distort in any significant way our usual microeconomic analysis.

We made the same assumption of market clearing in analyzing long-run economic growth in Chapters 4 and 5, when we ignored the fact that unemployment sometimes exists in labor markets and that the level of real GDP does not always equal *potential GDP*. Recall that **potential GDP** is the level of real GDP attained when firms are producing at capacity and labor is fully employed. We could safely ignore unemployment and the possibility that firms may produce below capacity because these are not factors that affect the long-run growth rate of an economy. In this chapter, though, we are shifting our focus to the short run. In particular, we want to begin the process of explaining the **business cycle**, or the alternating periods of **expansion** and **recession** that the U.S. economy has experienced for more than 200 years. Two key facts about the business cycle are:

Potential GDP The level of real GDP attained when firms are producing at capacity and labor is fully employed.

Business cycle Alternating periods of expansion and recession.

Expansion The period of a business cycle during which real GDP and employment are increasing.

Recession The period of a business cycle during which real GDP and employment are decreasing.

1. Unemployment rises—and employment falls—during a recession, and unemployment falls—and employment rises—during an expansion.
2. Real GDP declines during a recession, and real GDP increases during an expansion.

The Keynesian and Classical Approaches

Do the movements in employment and output during the business cycle represent equilibrium, market-clearing, behavior? Or do these movements represent disequilibrium, nonmarket-clearing, behavior? Economists have debated these questions for many years. Modern macroeconomics began in 1936, when the British economist John Maynard Keynes published *The General Theory of Employment, Interest, and Money*. In that book, Keynes argued that the high levels of unemployment and low levels of output that the world economy was experiencing during the Great Depression represented disequilibrium. He labeled the perspective that the economy was always in equilibrium as *classical economics*. These labels have stuck, and down to the present **Keynesian economics** stands for the perspective that business cycles represent disequilibrium or nonmarket-clearing behavior, and **classical economics** represents the perspective that business cycles can be explained using equilibrium analysis.

Keynesian economics The perspective that business cycles represent disequilibrium or nonmarket-clearing behavior.

Classical economics The perspective that business cycles can be explained using equilibrium analysis.

If the Keynesian view is correct, then the increase in cyclical unemployment during a recession primarily represents *involuntary unemployment*, or workers who would like to find jobs at the current wage rate but who are unable to. So, the quantity of labor supplied is greater than the quantity of labor demanded. Similarly, the decline in real GDP occurs primarily because some firms would like to sell more goods or services at prevailing prices but are unable to do so. So, in the markets for some goods and services, the quantity supplied is greater than the quantity demanded. If the classical view is correct, the labor market and the markets for goods and services remain in equilibrium during the business cycle. Although employment and output decline during a recession, they do so because of the voluntary decisions of households to supply less labor and firms to supply fewer goods and services.

The majority of economists believe that the basic Keynesian view of the business cycle is correct, although the details of their explanations of the business cycle are significantly different from those that Keynes offered in 1936. A significant minority of economists, however, believes that the classical view is correct. The views of these economists are sometimes called the *new classical macroeconomics*, where the word *new* is used to distinguish their views from the views of economists writing before 1936. In this and the following chapters, we will focus on the Keynesian view. In later chapters, we will discuss the classical view further.

Macroeconomic Shocks and Price Flexibility

The word *cycle* in the phrase *business cycle* can be misleading if it suggests that the economy follows a regular pattern of recessions and expansions of the same length and intensity in a self-perpetuating cycle. Although decades ago some economists thought of business cycles in more or less this way, today most do not. Instead, most economists—of both the Keynesian and classical schools—see the business cycle as resulting from the response of households

Macroeconomic shock
An unexpected exogenous event that has a significant effect on an important sector of the economy or on the economy as a whole.

and firms to *macroeconomic shocks*. A **macroeconomic shock** is an unexpected exogenous event that has a significant effect on an important sector of the economy or on the economy as a whole.[1] Examples of macroeconomic shocks are a financial crisis, the collapse of a housing bubble, a significant innovation in information technology, a significant unexpected increase in oil prices, or an unexpected change in monetary or fiscal policy.

Macroeconomic shocks require many households and firms to change their behavior. For example, the collapse of the housing bubble in the United States during 2006 reduced the demand for housing. Firms engaged in residential construction and workers employed by those firms had to adjust to the decline in demand. Similarly, as use of personal computers spread during the 1980s, firms making large mainframe computers, typewriters, and other office equipment had to adjust to a decline in demand. One of the benefits of the market system is its flexibility. Every month in the United States, new firms open and existing firms expand their operations, creating millions of jobs, while at the same time other firms close or contract their operations, destroying millions of jobs. Generally, a market system handles well the flow of resources—labor, capital, and raw materials—from declining industries to expanding industries.

A macroeconomic shock, however, requires an economy to make these adjustments quickly, so the results can be disruptive. For example, at the height of the housing bubble in the United States from 2004 to 2006, residential construction averaged more than 6% of GDP. By the first half of 2011, with the housing bubble having burst, residential construction was only about 2.2% of GDP. That decline may sound small, but it amounted to reduced spending on new houses of over $480 *billion.* If total output and total employment in the U.S. economy were not to decline, then substantial resources, including more than 2 million workers, would have to leave the construction industry and find employment elsewhere—a difficult task to accomplish in a short period of time. In fact, the economy did not adjust smoothly to the collapse of the housing bubble. As a result, employment and output in the U.S. economy declined substantially.

We know from microeconomic analysis that markets adjust to changes in demand and supply through changes in prices. One reason an economy may have difficulty smoothly adjusting to a macroeconomic shock is that prices and wages may not fully adjust to the effects of the shock in the short run. In fact, many economists believe that a key difference between the macroeconomic short run and the macroeconomic long run is that *in the short run prices and wages are "sticky," while in the long run prices and wages are flexible.* By "sticky," economists mean that prices and wages do not fully adjust in the short run to changes in demand or supply, while in the long run they do fully adjust.

Recall the important distinction between nominal and real variables. A nominal price is the stated price of a product, not corrected for changes in the price level, while a real price is corrected for changes in the price level. Similarly, a nominal wage is not corrected for changes in the price level, while a real wage is corrected. When we refer to price and wage stickiness, we are referring to nominal prices and wages, not real prices and wages. Economists call the slow adjustment of nominal prices and wages to shocks *nominal price and wage rigidity* or *nominal price and wage stickiness.*

Why Are Prices Sticky in the Short Run?

The fact that prices are often sticky in the short run is a key reason macroeconomic shocks can result in fluctuations in total employment and total output. So, understanding why prices can be sticky is an important macroeconomic issue. Two key factors cause price stickiness. First, we need to note that in reality most firms are in *imperfectly competitive* markets. Recall from your principles of economics course that a firm is in a *perfectly competitive* market if the market has many buyers and sellers and the firm is competing with other firms

[1]Recall from Chapter 1 that economists refer to something that is taken as given as *exogenous*, and something that will be explained by the model as *endogenous*.

selling identical products. In a perfectly competitive market, a firm cannot affect the price of its product. In an imperfectly competitive market, however, a firm has some control over price. Second, there are often costs to firms from changing prices. If changing prices is costly, firms face a trade-off when demand or supply curves shift. For example, when the demand curve for a firm's product shifts to the left, a firm will benefit from cutting prices because quantity demanded does not fall by as much as it would if the firm held price constant. So, a firm will hold price constant only if it incurs a cost to changing the price. We would expect that a firm will lower its price following a decline in demand if the benefit to doing so would be greater than the cost. The firm will not lower its prices if the benefit would be less than the cost. The same is true following an increase in demand: If the benefit from raising the price does not exceed the cost, the firm will hold its price constant.

Why is it costly for firms to change prices? Firms such as JCPenney and IKEA print catalogs and create Web sites that list the prices of their products. If prices change, these firms must take the time and incur the cost to reprint their catalogs, update their Web sites, and change the prices marked on their store merchandise. Customers may also be angered if a firm raises prices, as might happen, for instance, if a hardware store raised the price of snow shovels after a winter storm. Customers and firms may also agree to long-term contracts. For instance, customers of some fuel oil companies have signed contracts to buy home heating oil at a fixed price during the coming year. In addition, before firms adjust their prices, they must figure out how much demand and supply have shifted in their individual markets and how long-lived these shifts might be. For example, the manager of a hotel may realize that the economy has moved into a recession and may expect that demand for rooms in the hotel has declined. But rather than lower prices right away—and run the risk of annoying customers by quickly raising them again—the manager may want to see how much the recession affects tourism and business travel in that city. In this case, we can think of the cost of changing prices as the cost of determining how the firm should respond to a macroeconomic shock. These various costs to firms of changing prices are called *menu costs*. Economists call these costs **menu costs** because one example of menu costs is the cost of printing up new restaurant menus.

Menu costs The costs to firms of changing prices.

How Long Are Prices Sticky? Economic research has shown that most firms in Western Europe and the United States change prices just once or twice a year, with firms in the service sector typically changing prices less frequently than manufacturing firms.[2] Economists have also found that firms are more likely to change prices as a result of shocks to the firm's sector than to shocks to the aggregate economy.[3]

Making the Connection

The Curious Case of the 5-Cent Coke

There is price stickiness and then there is the case of the price of a bottle of Coke. As we have seen, there are reasons firms may not fully adjust the prices of their products to changes in demand and supply in the short run. The period involved, though, is usually a year or two. After that amount of time has passed, firms will typically have fully adjusted their prices. Over a period of decades, most firms experience many shifts in demand and

[2]Alan Blinder, "On Sticky Prices: Academic Theories Meet the Real World," in N. Gregory Mankiw (ed.), *Monetary Policy*, Chicago: University of Chicago Press, 1994; and Campbell Leith and Jim Malley, "A Sectoral Analysis of Price-Setting Behavior in U.S. Manufacturing Industries," *Review of Economics and Statistics*, Vol. 89, No. 2 March 2007, pp. 335–342.

[3]Jean Boivin, Marc Giannoni, and Ilian Mihov, "Sticky Prices and Monetary Policy: Evidence from Disaggregated U.S. Data," *American Economic Review*, Vol. 99, No. 1, March 2009, pp. 350–384.

supply. Despite short-run price stickiness, these shifts ought to result in the prices of the firm's products changing many times. Not so with a bottle of Coca-Cola, however. Between 1886 and 1955, the price of a standard, 6.5-ounce glass bottle of Coke remained unchanged, at 5 cents.

During this long period, World War I and World War II occurred, as did the Great Depression of the 1930s, other severe recessions, Prohibition—which lasted from 1919 to 1933 and during which sales of alcoholic beverages were illegal in the United States—a tripling of the price of sugar, and tremendous changes in the structure of the soft drink industry as well as in the technology of producing soft drinks. In other words, the demand for Coke and the cost of producing it went through many changes during this 70-year period, but Coca-Cola held the price of its most important product constant.

Coca-Cola was introduced in 1886 by an Atlanta, Georgia, druggist named John Stith Pemberton. At first he sold it as a "patent medicine." Patent medicines were bottled liquids that their sellers claimed would cure a variety of physical ailments. Pemberton claimed that Coca-Cola acted as a nerve tonic and stimulant and could cure headaches. Although patent medicines were typically sold in large bottles for a price of $0.75 to $1.00, Pemberton hit on the idea of selling Coca-Cola in single servings for a nickel, thereby expanding the number of consumers who could afford to buy it. At first, most Coke was sold by the glass at soda fountains, drug stores, and restaurants. Following the introduction of the distinctive 6.5-ounce "hobble skirt" bottle in 1916, bottle sales, particularly through vending machines, became increasingly important.

Daniel Levy and Andrew T. Young of Emory University have provided the most careful account of why Coca-Cola kept the price of its most important product fixed for decades. Levy and Young argue that three main factors account for this extraordinary episode of price rigidity: First, from 1899 to 1921, the firm was obligated by long-term contracts to provide its bottlers with the syrup that Coca-Cola is made from at a fixed price of $0.92 per gallon. Although Coca-Cola manufactured the syrup, the bottlers that actually produced the soft drink and distributed it for sale were independent businesses. After 1921, the price Coca-Cola charged its bottlers for syrup varied, and this no longer became an important reason for inflexibility in the retail price. Second, the technology of vending machines was such that for years they could accept only a single coin and could not make change. Coca-Cola, therefore, could not adjust the price of a bottle in penny increments. Third, Coca-Cola believed that it was important that consumers be able to buy the signature 6.5-ounce Coke bottle using a single coin. This meant that to raise the price from a nickel, the firm would have to start charging a dime, which would be a 100% increase in price. During the 1950s, Robert Woodruff, who was then president of Coca-Cola, tried to get around this problem by urging newly elected President Eisenhower, who happened to be Woodruff's friend and hunting companion, to have the U.S. Treasury begin issuing a 7.5-cent coin. Eisenhower forwarded the proposal to the Department of the Treasury, but the Treasury did not pursue the idea further.

Ultimately, rising costs and advances in vending machine technology led Coca-Cola to abandon its fixed-price strategy. By 1955, Coke was selling for 5, 6, 7, or even 10 cents in different parts of the country. In 1959, 6.5-ounce bottles of Coke were no longer selling for 5 cents anywhere in the United States.

The saga of the nickel Coke provides an extreme example of why a firm may consider it profitable to hold the price of a product constant, despite large swings in demand and costs.

Sources: Daniel Levy and Andrew T. Young, "'The Real Thing': Nominal Price Rigidity of the Nickel Coke, 1886–1959," *Journal of Money, Credit, and Banking*, Vol. 36, No. 4, August 2004, pp. 765–799; Richard S. Tedlow, *New and Improved: The Story of Mass Marketing in America*, New York: Basic Books, 1990; and E. J. Kahn, Jr., *The Big Drink: The Story of Coca-Cola*, New York: Random House, 1960.

Test your understanding by doing related problem 1.6 on page 296 at the end of this chapter.

Long-term labor contracts help explain why nominal wages can be sticky. For example, when a firm negotiates a long-term labor contract with a labor union, the contract fixes the nominal wage for the duration of the contract, which is typically several years. Even if economic conditions change, it is often difficult and costly to renegotiate long-term contracts. In addition to formal contracts, firms often arrive at *implicit contracts* with workers. An implicit contract is not a written, legally binding agreement. Instead, it is an informal arrangement a firm enters into with workers in which the firm refrains from making wage cuts during recessions in return for workers being willing to accept smaller wage increases during expansions. Firms may also refrain from cutting wages during recessions for fear that their best workers will quit to find jobs at other firms once an economic expansion improves conditions in the labor market. As we saw in Chapter 7, firms sometimes pay higher than equilibrium real wages known as *efficiency wages* to motivate workers to be more productive. Efficiency wage considerations can also lead firms to maintain wages during a recession. All these reasons help to explain why nominal wages are typically sticky in the short run.

Making the Connection

Union Contracts and the U.S. Automobile Industry

U.S. automobile companies have been losing market share to foreign competition since the 1970s. Along with the decline in market share has come a decrease in employment. At General Motors (GM) alone, employment went from 618,000 workers 30 years ago to fewer than 100,000 in 2009. The failure of U.S. automobile companies to bring their costs under control is part of the reason for these declines. In particular, Chrysler, Ford, and GM signed labor contracts with the United Automobile Workers union (UAW) that provided generous healthcare and retirement benefits. These contracts made it difficult for the companies either to reduce wages and benefits or to shed unnecessary workers. When the companies did lay off workers, the union contracts ensured that the workers received up to 95% of their pay. Therefore, the U.S. automobile companies found it very difficult to reduce labor costs when the demand for automobiles changed.

Not surprisingly, the rigid cost structure hindered the ability of U.S. firms to adjust to changes in the automobile market. The recession of 2007–2009 was so severe that Chrysler and GM declared bankruptcy and were saved from shutting down only when the federal government agreed in 2009 to invest in the firms. As part of the agreement that brought the firms out of bankruptcy, the UAW agreed to changes in labor contracts that reduced the healthcare benefits for existing retirees and made it easier to lay off workers. The changes to retiree benefits reduced GM's costs by nearly $3 billion per year, and it expects to reduce its U.S. workforce by more than half of its 2009 level, to 40,000 workers. While GM had been losing money when U.S. auto sales were 15 million vehicles per year, the company now believes that with the changes in labor contracts it can turn a profit if U.S. auto sales exceed 10.5 million vehicles per year. The rigid cost structures at Chrysler and GM prevented those companies from responding quickly to the 2007–2009 recession. However, once the companies faced bankruptcy and liquidation, they were able to alter their cost structures by negotiating with the UAW to achieve lower labor costs.

Sources: David Robinson, "Bankruptcy Puts GM at Rock Bottom," *McClatchy—Tribune Business News*, May 31, 2009; and Sharon Terlep and Mike Ramsey, "Auto Makers Reverse Skid," *Wall Street Journal*, May 10, 2010.

Test your understanding by doing related problem 1.7 on page 296 at the end of this chapter.

What Happens During a Business Cycle?

8.2
Learning Objective
Understand what happens during a business cycle.

Economists think of the business cycle as resulting from macroeconomic shocks that push real GDP away from potential GDP. For example, the United States experienced three large shocks during 2007–2009: the collapse of the housing bubble, a financial crisis that increased the cost of obtaining loans, and a large increase in the price of imported oil. As a result of these shocks, the growth rate of real GDP decreased from 2.9% during the fourth quarter of 2007 to −6.8% during the fourth quarter of 2008. The financial crisis and the increase in oil prices were global shocks that affected most countries. For instance, among countries using the euro for their currency, the growth rate of real GDP decreased from 1.7% during the fourth quarter of 2007 to −7.1% during the fourth quarter of 2008.

Figure 8.1 illustrates the phases of the business cycle. Panel (a) shows an idealized business cycle, with real GDP increasing smoothly in an expansion to a business cycle peak and then decreasing smoothly in a recession to a business cycle trough, followed by another expansion. Panel (b) shows the period before and during the recession of 2007–2009. The figure shows that a business cycle peak was reached in December 2007. The following recession was the most severe since the Great Depression of the 1930s. Panel (b) also shows the growth of potential GDP during this period. Recall that potential GDP is the level of real GDP when all resources are fully employed. Notice that even when the economy was in a business cycle expansion after the second quarter of 2009, real GDP remained well below potential GDP.

Why do we care about the business cycle? Declining real GDP is always accompanied by declining employment. As people lose jobs, their incomes and standard of living decline. In severe recessions, the long-term unemployed can encounter severe financial hardship, even destitution. Declining GDP also increases business bankruptcies, with some entrepreneurs having a lifetime's investment in a business wiped out in a year or two. The failure of a large firm can bring economic decline to a whole geographical area. Expanding

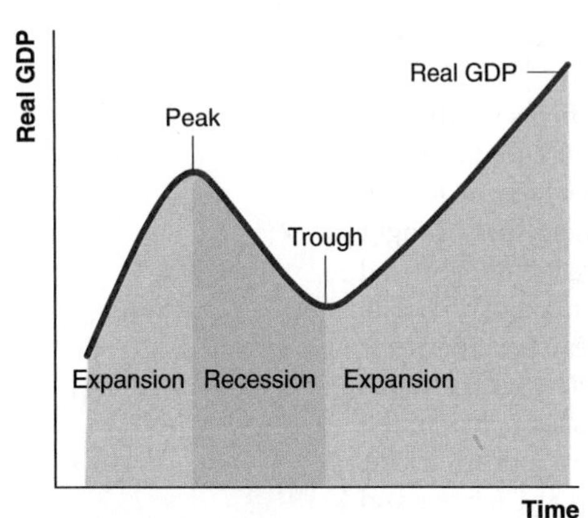

(a) An idealized business cycle

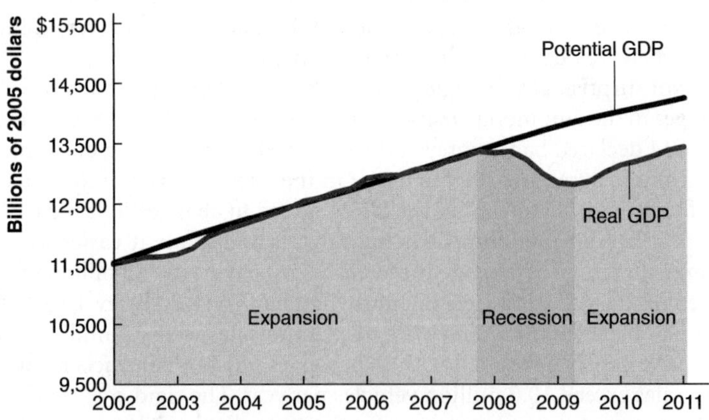

(b) Actual movements of real GDP and of potential GDP for 2002–2011

Figure 8.1 The Business Cycle

Panel (a) shows an idealized business cycle, with real GDP increasing smoothly in an expansion to a business cycle peak and then decreasing smoothly in a recession to a business cycle trough, followed by another expansion. The periods of expansion are shown in green, and the period of recession is shown in red.

Panel (b) shows the severe recession of 2007–2009, with real GDP remaining below potential GDP well into the expansion.

Sources: U.S. Bureau of Economic Analysis; Congressional Budget Office; and National Bureau of Economic Research. ●

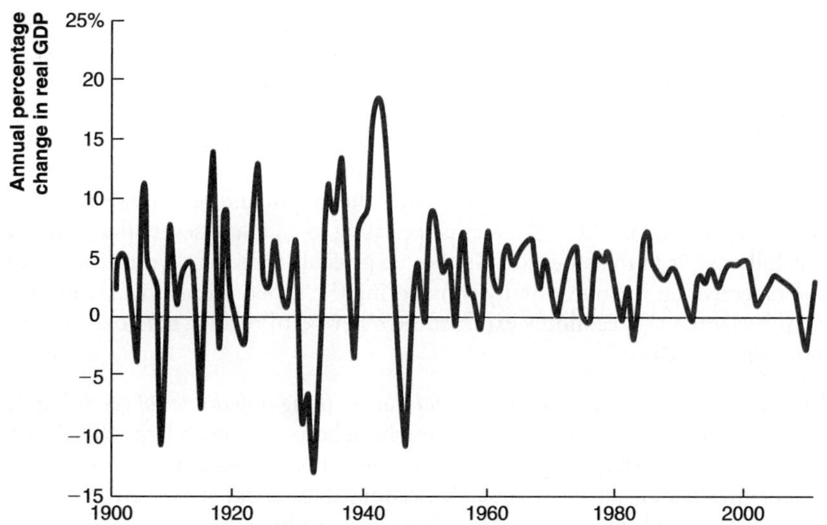

Figure 8.2

Fluctuations in Real GDP, 1900–2010

The annual growth rate of real GDP fluctuated more before 1950 than it has since 1950.

Sources: For 1900–1928: Louis D. Johnston and Samuel H. Williamson, "What Was the U.S. GDP Then?" www.measuringworth.org/usgdp, 2010; and for 1929–2010: U.S. Bureau of Economic Analysis. ●

GDP, on the other hand, opens up employment opportunities to millions of additional workers and makes it possible for more entrepreneurs to realize the dream of opening a business.

The Changing Severity of the U.S. Business Cycle

One way to gauge the severity of the economic fluctuations caused by a business cycle is to look at annual percentage changes, or growth rates, in real GDP. Figure 8.2 shows the annual growth rates for real GDP between 1900 and 2010. The fluctuations in real GDP were clearly more severe before 1950 than after 1950. In particular, there were eight years before 1950 during which real GDP declined by 3% or more, but there were no years with such declines after 1950. The increased stability of real GDP after the early 1980s, as well as the mildness of the recessions of 1991–1992 and 2001, led some economists to describe the period as the "Great Moderation." The recession that began in December 2007, though, was the most severe since the Great Depression of the 1930s, suggesting that the Great Moderation was over.

The unusual severity of the 2007–2009 recession can also be seen by comparing its length to the lengths of other recent recessions. Table 8.1 shows that in the late nineteenth century, the average length of recessions was the same as the average length of expansions. During the first half of the twentieth century, the average length of expansions decreased slightly, and the average length of recessions decreased significantly. As a result, expansions were about six months longer than recessions during those years. The most striking change came after 1950, when the length of expansions greatly increased and the length

Table 8.1 Until 2007, the Business Cycle Had Become Milder

Period	Average length of expansions	Average length of recessions
1870–1900	26 months	26 months
1900–1950	25 months	19 months
1950–2010	62 months	11 months

Note: The World War I and World War II periods have been omitted from the computations in the table.

Source: National Bureau of Economic Research.

of recessions decreased. In the second half of the twentieth century, expansions were more than six times as long as recessions. In other words, in the late nineteenth century, the U.S. economy spent as much time in recession as it did in expansion, but after 1950, the U.S. economy experienced long expansions interrupted by relatively short recessions.

The recession of 2007–2009 is an exception to this experience of relatively short, mild recessions. This recession lasted 18 months, making it the longest since the 43-month recession that began the Great Depression. Does the length and severity of the 2007–2009 recession indicate that the United States is returning to an era of severe fluctuations in real GDP? A full answer to this question will not be possible for several years. But we can gain some perspective on the question by considering the explanations that economists have offered for why the U.S. economy experienced a period of relative macroeconomic stability from 1950 to 2007:

- *The increasing importance of services and the declining importance of goods.* As services, such as medical care or investment advice, have become a much larger fraction of GDP, there has been a corresponding relative decline in the production of goods. For example, at one time, manufacturing production accounted for about 40% of GDP, whereas today it accounts for only about 12%. Manufacturing production, particularly production of durable goods such as automobiles, fluctuates more than does the production of services.
- *The establishment of unemployment insurance and other government transfer programs that provide funds to the unemployed.* Before the 1930s, programs such as unemployment insurance, which provides government payments to workers who lose their jobs, and Social Security, which provides government payments to retired and disabled workers, did not exist. These and other government programs make it possible for workers who lose their jobs during recessions to have higher incomes and, therefore, to spend more than they would otherwise spend. This additional spending may have helped to shorten recessions.
- *Active federal government policies to stabilize the economy.* Before the Great Depression of the 1930s, the federal government did not attempt to end recessions or prolong expansions. Because the Great Depression was so severe, with the unemployment rate rising to more than 20% of the labor force and real GDP declining by almost 30%, public opinion began favoring government attempts to stabilize the economy. In the years since World War II, the federal government has actively tried to use policy measures to end recessions and prolong expansions. Many economists believe that these government policies have played a key role in stabilizing the economy. Some economists note that during the period of the Great Moderation, both the average inflation rate and the volatility of the inflation rate decreased, suggesting that monetary policy had become more effective. Other economists, however, argue that active policy has had little effect. This macroeconomic debate is an important one, and we will consider it further in Chapters 10 to 12 when we discuss the federal government's monetary and fiscal policies.
- *The increased stability of the financial system.* The severity of the Great Depression of the 1930s was caused in part by instability in the financial system. More than 5,000 banks failed between 1929 and 1933, reducing the savings of many households and making it difficult for households and firms to obtain the credit needed to maintain their spending. In addition, a decline of more than 80% in stock prices greatly reduced the wealth of many households and made it difficult for firms to raise funds by selling stock. In Chapter 10, we will discuss some of the institutional changes that resulted in increased stability in the financial system during the years after the Great Depression. Most economists believe that the return of financial instability during the 2007–2009 recession is a key reason the recession was so severe. If the United States is to return to macroeconomic stability, stability will first have to return to the financial system.

How Do We Know the Economy Is in an Expansion or a Recession?

The federal government produces many statistics that make it possible to monitor the economy. But the federal government does not officially decide when a recession begins or when it ends. Instead, most economists accept the decisions of the Business Cycle Dating Committee of the National Bureau of Economic Research (NBER), a private research group located in Cambridge, Massachusetts. Nine economists on the NBER's Business Cycle Dating Committee determine the beginning and ending of recessions. Although newspaper reporters often define a recession as two consecutive quarters of declining real GDP, the NBER has a broader definition:

> A recession is a significant decline in economic activity spread across the economy, lasting more than a few months, normally visible in production, employment, real income, and other indicators. A recession begins when the economy reaches a peak of activity and ends when the economy reaches its trough. Between trough and peak, the economy is in an expansion.[4]

The Business Cycle Dating Committee declares a recession when its members conclude that there is enough evidence that a recession has started, which is typically months after the recession has begun. For example, in December 2008, the committee announced that a recession had begun in December 2007—a year earlier. Although the committee regards gross domestic product (GDP) and gross domestic income (GDI) as the "two most reliable comprehensive estimates of aggregate domestic production," it does not use these two data series exclusively when dating the beginning and ending of recessions. The official GDP and GDI data are available only quarterly, and the committee dates the beginning and ending of recessions to a specific month. Therefore, the committee looks at monthly data on payroll employment, industrial production, real personal income, real manufacturing production, and wholesale and retail sales. The committee also considers monthly estimates of real GDP constructed by Macroeconomic Advisers, a private, nonpartisan economic research group and a second monthly real GDP series constructed by James Stock and Mark Watson, two economists on the committee.

Measuring Business Cycles

Looking at panel (b) of Figure 8.1 on page 278, you can think of actual real GDP as being composed of two parts, both of which change over time. The first part is potential GDP, and the second part is the deviation of actual real GDP from potential GDP. Economists typically use the deviation of real GDP from potential GDP as the best measure of the size of the economic fluctuations associated with a business cycle. For a particular calendar quarter, t, we can write:

$$\text{Real GDP}_t = \text{Potential GDP}_t + \text{Deviation from potential GDP}_t$$

or:

$$Y_t = Y_t^P + (Y_t - Y_t^P),$$

where Y_t is real GDP, Y_t^P is potential GDP, and $(Y_t - Y_t^P)$ is the deviation of real GDP from its potential level.

[4]Business Cycle Dating Committee, National Bureau of Economic Research, September 20, 2010. www.nber.org/cycles/sept2010.html.

Solved Problem 8.2

Dating U.S. Recessions

You may have heard a recession defined as two consecutive quarters of negative real GDP growth. In fact, though, the NBER does not use this rule of thumb in dating recessions. According to the NBER, the U.S. economy was in a recession from March 2001 to November 2001. The following table shows the growth rate of real GDP for the United States around the time of the recession. Use the rule of thumb to date the beginning and end of the 2001 recession. Based on the rule of thumb, did the United States experience a recession in 2001? Why is there a difference between the dates using the rule of thumb and the dates from the NBER?

Quarter	Growth Rate of Real GDP	Quarter	Growth Rate of Real GDP	Quarter	Growth Rate of Real GDP
2000 Q1	1.0%	2001 Q1	−1.3%	2002 Q1	3.5%
2000 Q2	8.0	2001 Q2	2.6	2002 Q2	2.1
2000 Q3	0.3	2001 Q3	−1.1	2002 Q3	2.0
2000 Q4	2.4	2001 Q4	1.4	2002 Q4	0.1

Solving the Problem

Step 1 **Review the chapter material.** The problem asks you to think about dating business cycles, so you may want to review the section "How Do We Know the Economy is in an Expansion or a Recession?" which begins on page 281.

Step 2 **Use the rule of thumb to determine if a recession occurred.** The rule of thumb states that a recession begins with two consecutive negative quarters of real GDP growth. Although economic growth slowed dramatically in 2000 from the late 1990s, the first quarter of negative real GDP growth occurs during the first quarter of 2001. However, economic growth was positive during the second quarter before becoming negative again during the third quarter. Therefore, according to the rule of thumb, there was no recession during 2001.

Step 3 **Explain why there is a difference between the rule of thumb and the NBER dates.** As noted in the text, the NBER defines a recession as "a significant decline in economic activity . . . lasting more than a few months . . . ." In determining whether a recession has occurred, the NBER looks at many data series, not just real GDP. So, it is possible, as happened during 2001, for the NBER to decide a recession has occurred even during a period when real GDP did not decline for two consecutive quarters.

For more practice, do related problem 2.9 on page 297 and problem D8.1 on page 299 at the end of this chapter.

Output gap The percentage deviation of actual real GDP from potential GDP.

Because potential GDP grows over time, economists measure economic fluctuations as the percentage deviation of actual real GDP from potential GDP, rather than the absolute dollar difference. This percentage deviation of real GDP from potential GDP is called the **output gap**. To obtain this measure, we divide $(Y_t - Y_t^P)$ by potential output:

$$\text{Output gap} = \frac{Y_t - Y_t^P}{Y_t^P}. \tag{8.1}$$

The output gap measures how fully the economy is employing its resources, such as labor, natural resources, and physical and human capital. For example, in the first quarter of 2011, actual real GDP was $13,439 billion and potential GDP was $14,256 billion. Therefore, the deviation from potential was $13,439 billion − $14,256 billion = −$817 billion, so the output gap was:

$$-\$817 \text{ billion}/\$14{,}256 \text{ billion} = -0.057 \text{ or } -5.7\%.$$

When the output gap equals zero, the economy is producing at its long-run capacity, and so is producing the maximum sustainable level of goods and services. If the output gap is greater than zero, the economy is operating at a level that is greater than it can sustain in the long run. If the output gap is less than zero, the economy is operating below its capacity.

Figure 8.3 shows the output gap for the United States from the first quarter of 1949 to the first quarter of 2011. The shaded areas represent recessions. During a recession, real GDP declines below potential GDP, and the output gap becomes negative. Even after an expansion begins and real GDP begins to increase, it typically remains below potential GDP for a considerable time, so the output gap remains negative. Eventually, as the expansion continues, real GDP will rise above potential GDP, and the output gap will become positive.

Costs of the Business Cycle

Should we care about the fluctuations in real GDP that occur during the business cycle? We saw in Chapter 1 that real GDP per capita grows over time. These increases are large enough that, over time, the effects of economic growth should overwhelm the effects of the business cycle on the average person's well-being. Moreover, the business cycle results in real GDP sometimes being below potential GDP, but it also results in periods during which real GDP is above potential GDP. It might seem as if the costs of economic fluctuations will average out across the business cycle. Actually, though, economic research and simple observations of the effects of recessions on workers and firms indicate that economic fluctuations have costs—and the costs can be large. Furthermore, recent research suggests that the business cycle may affect the level of potential GDP. We discuss the costs of the business cycle in the sections that follow.

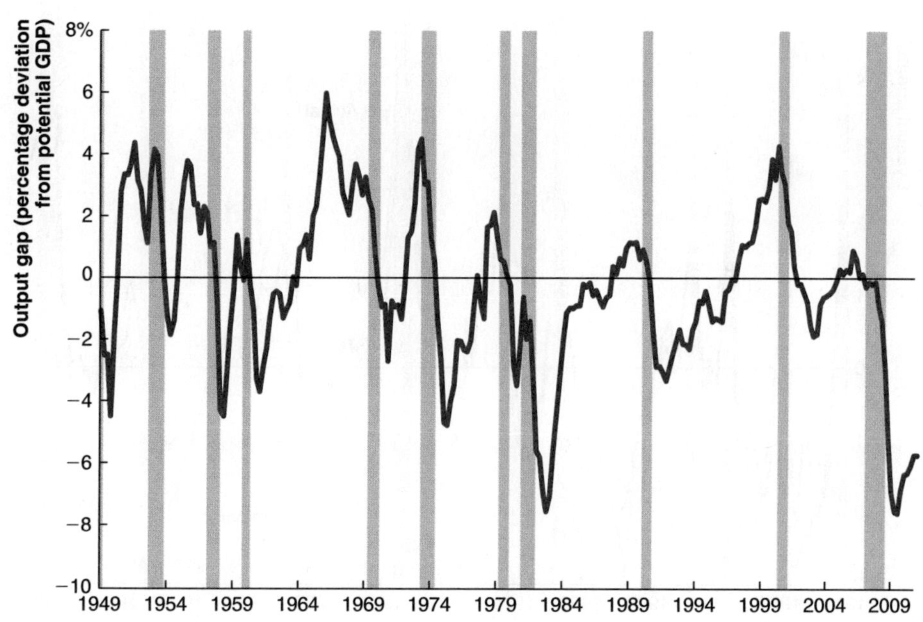

Figure 8.3

The Output Gap for the United States, 1949–2011

During a recession, real GDP declines below potential GDP, and the output gap becomes negative. Even after an expansion begins and real GDP begins to increase, real GDP typically remains below potential GDP for a considerable time, so the output gap remains negative. Eventually, as the expansion continues, real GDP will rise above potential GDP, and the output gap will become positive. The potential GDP data are estimates from the Congressional Budget Office.

Sources: U.S. Bureau of Economic Analysis; Congressional Budget Office; and National Bureau of Economic Research. ●

Okun's Law and Unemployment Economists and policymakers focus on two key costs of the business cycle: the lost income that occurs when real GDP is below potential GDP and the inflation that often develops when the economy is operating above potential GDP. To explain the costs of operating below potential GDP, we focus on labor markets.

Cyclical unemployment rate The difference between the actual unemployment rate and the natural unemployment rate.

When real GDP falls below potential GDP during a recession, firms lay off workers, so the unemployment rate rises, and households earn less income. The **cyclical unemployment rate** is the difference between the actual unemployment rate and the natural unemployment rate. (We discussed the natural unemployment rate in Chapter 7.) The cyclical unemployment rate increases during recessions. As the economy enters an expansion, cyclical unemployment may continue to rise for a period, before falling later in the expansion.

Okun's law A statistical relationship discovered by Arthur Okun between the cyclical unemployment rate and the output gap.

Arthur Okun, who served as chairman of the President's Council of Economic Advisers in the 1960s, carefully studied the relationship between real GDP and unemployment. He discovered that over the course of the business cycle, the relationship between the output gap and cyclical unemployment remained fairly close. This relationship, which Okun first wrote about in 1962, has remained reasonably stable to the present. **Okun's law**, as it is now known, conveniently summarizes the relationship between cyclical unemployment and the output gap. According to Okun's Law, as real GDP increases by 1 percentage point relative to potential GDP, cyclical unemployment decreases by 0.5 percentage point:

$$\text{Cyclical unemployment rate} = -0.5 \times \text{Output gap.} \quad (8.2)$$

Figure 8.4 shows the actual cyclical unemployment rate and the rate calculated using Okun's law for the period from the first quarter of 1949 to the first quarter of 2011. The figure shows that Okun's law provides a reasonable approximation of the behavior of unemployment during the business cycle.

Figure 8.4

Actual and Predicted Cyclical Unemployment Rates Based on Okun's Law

The simple relationship in Equation (8.2) does a good job expressing how the output gap and cyclical unemployment are related: As real GDP increases by 1 percentage point relative to potential GDP, cyclical unemployment decreases by 0.5 percentage point. Shaded areas represent recessions.

Sources: U.S. Bureau of Economic Analysis; and Congressional Budget Office. ●

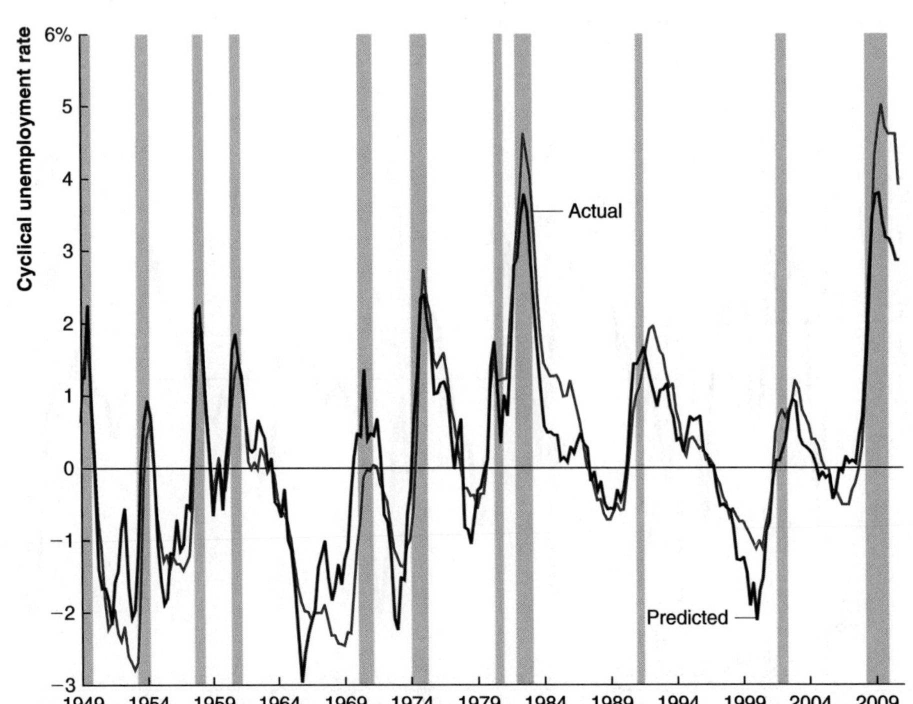

Making the Connection

Did the 2007–2009 Recession Break Okun's Law?

During 2009 and 2010, White House economists were criticized for their inaccurate predictions of the unemployment rate. In early 2009, Christina Romer, who was then chair of the President's Council of Economic Advisers, and Jared Bernstein, economic adviser to Vice President Joe Biden, predicted that if Congress passed President Barack Obama's stimulus program of higher federal government spending and tax cuts, unemployment would peak at about 8% in the third quarter of 2009 and then decline in the following quarters. Although Congress passed the stimulus program, the unemployment rate was 9.7% in the third quarter of 2009. It rose to 10.0% in the fourth quarter of 2009 and was still at 9.6% in the fourth quarter of 2010.

Romer and Bernstein were hardly alone in failing to forecast the severity of unemployment during 2009 and 2010. One reason for the faulty forecasts was that the unemployment rate was significantly higher than would have been expected from the size of the output gap, given Okun's law. Figure 8.4 shows that for the whole period since 1949, Okun's law does a good job of accounting for movements in the unemployment rate. The graph below, which covers just the period from the first quarter of 2007 through the first quarter of 2011, shows that Okun's law does not do as well in accounting for movements in the unemployment rate during the recession of 2007–2009 and its immediate aftermath.

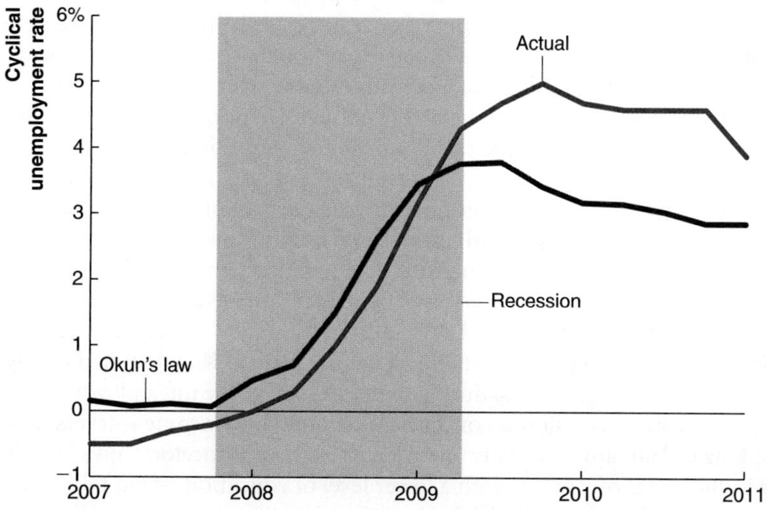

The graph shows that beginning in mid 2009, Okun's law indicates that cyclical unemployment should have been about 1% lower than it actually was. In late 2009 and 2010, the gap between actual cyclical unemployment and the level indicated by Okun's law widened to about 1.5%. What explains the relatively poor performance of Okun's law during this period? Economists were still debating this point during 2011, but some saw rising labor productivity during 2009 and early 2010 as the main explanation. When labor productivity—or the amount of output produced per worker—increases, firms can produce either more output with a given number of workers or the same amount of output with fewer workers. During 2009 and 2010, many firms appear to have taken the second option—maintaining their production levels with fewer workers—thereby leading to a larger increase in unemployment than many economists had forecast.

Economists have mixed opinions about whether the surge in productivity during 2009–2010 was temporary and whether Okun's law would return to reliably accounting for movements in the unemployment rate. Economist Robert J. Gordon of Northwestern University argues that a decline in unionization and other developments have increased the willingness of firms to lay off workers in recessions, thereby making it likely that Okun's law will continue to have difficulty accounting for unemployment increases during recessions.

Other economists argue that the unusual severity of the recession may account for the inaccuracy of Okun's law during 2009–2010. Okun's law had similar difficulty in accounting for the unemployment rate following the severe recession of 1981–1982.

Sources: Christina Romer and Jared Bernstein, "The Job Impact of the American Recovery and Reinvestment Plan," January 10, 2009, Available at: http://otrans.3cdn.net/45593e8ecbd339d074_l3m6bt1te.pdf.; Mary Daly and Bart Hobjin, "Okun's Law and the Unemployment Surprise of 2009," *Federal Reserve Bank of San Francisco Economic Letter*, March 8, 2009; and Robert J. Gordon, "The Demise of Okun's Law and of Procyclical Fluctuations in Conventional and Unconventional Measures of Productivity," paper presented at the NBER Summer Institute, July 21, 2010.

Test your understanding by doing related problem 2.15 on page 298 at the end of this chapter.

Okun's law illustrates the ebb and flow of cyclical unemployment across the business cycle. The lost income suffered by unemployed workers is one of the most important costs of the business cycle. Although cyclical unemployment falls and household incomes rise during expansions, the costs of the business cycle do not necessarily average out across the cycle for four reasons: First, a business cycle consists of an expansion and a recession, but recessions do not necessarily have the same magnitude as expansions. As a result, real GDP may be below potential GDP more than half the time. For example, real GDP rose above potential GDP only briefly and by a small amount during the expansion that began in November 2001. Second, if workers are unemployed for long periods of time, their skills may deteriorate. In the extreme case, this deterioration can be severe enough to make some workers structurally unemployed and increase the natural rate of unemployment. Some economists believe that a prolonged period of unemployment can result in *hysteresis*, in which the natural rate of unemployment may increase for a number of years. Hysteresis may have occurred in the United States during the 1930s and in some Western European countries during the 1980s. In the case of Western Europe, an increase in unemployment initially due to recessions brought on by sharp increases in oil prices persisted for years. For example, while the unemployment rate in France had averaged 3.8% during the 1970s, it averaged 9.0% during the 1990s. Similarly, while the unemployment rate in the United Kingdom had averaged 4.4% during the 1970s, it averaged 10.1% during the 1980s. Third, the unemployment and lost income resulting from a recession is concentrated among low-income workers. Research by Lawrence Katz of Harvard University and Alan Krueger of Princeton University shows that increases in the wages of workers with a lower level of education—who typically also have low incomes—are affected more by high unemployment than are increases in wages of workers with a higher level of education. Katz and Krueger also show that low-income workers and workers who lack skills do particularly well during periods of low unemployment, such as the late 1990s, but much more poorly during periods of high unemployment.[5] Fourth, the negative effects of recessions on workers can last many years. Economist Lisa Kahn of Yale University recently studied the effects on workers of graduating from college during a recession. Not surprisingly, Kahn found that graduating during a recession reduced a worker's wage and job prospects. However, what is surprising is that these effects lasted for up to 15 years.[6] Therefore, recessions can have very long-lasting effects on particular groups of workers.

[5]Lawrence P. Katz and Alan B. Krueger, "The High-Pressure Labor Market of the 1990s," *Brookings Papers on Economic Activity*, Vol. 1999, No. 1, 1999, pp. 1–87.

[6]Lisa Kahn, "The Long-Term Labor Market Consequences of Graduating from College in a Bad Economy," *Labour Economics*, Vol. 17, No. 2, April 2010, pp. 303–316.

Inflation Business cycles typically affect the inflation rate. As actual GDP increases relative to potential GDP, resources become fully employed, so it becomes difficult for firms to find idle labor, capital, and natural resources to produce goods and services. As a result, the prices of these inputs begin to rise, and firms try to pass along the cost increases to consumers in the form of higher prices, thereby increasing inflation. We discussed the costs of inflation in Chapter 6, and we will more fully examine the link between business cycles and inflation in Chapter 9.

Links Between Business Cycles and Growth It is possible that business cycles affect the balanced growth path of real GDP that we described in Chapter 5. A reduction in the balanced growth path would be another cost of economic fluctuations that would not average out over the business cycle. The Solow growth model from Chapter 5 shows that if the investment rate changes, the level of real GDP along the balanced growth path also changes. The uncertainty associated with business cycles can affect firms' investment expenditures, providing one possible link between business cycles and long-run economic growth. Ben Bernanke, the current Chairman of the Federal Reserve, while an economics professor at Princeton University, argued that the greater the uncertainty about the future demand for a firm's product, the more difficult it is for the firm to determine whether investment in machinery or a new factory will be profitable.[7] This uncertainty also makes it difficult for the firm to determine the size of the factory to build and the most appropriate technology to use in the factory. Because of uncertainty, the firm may choose not to pursue the investment at all. Business cycles, particularly when they are severe, can cause uncertainty about future demand. An economy with more severe business cycles experiences greater uncertainty about future demand, so it may invest less than an economy with milder business cycles. For example, Heartland Precision Fasteners, Inc., a Kansas-based distributor of fasteners used by airlines, was planning a $1.5 million expansion of its factory, but the financial market shock of 2008 led the company to delay its plans. David Rose, the company's president, was quoted as saying that the financial market crisis and the economic downturn "is making us think twice; this is a big investment for us."[8] In Chapter 5, we showed that a decline in the investment rate will reduce the level of GDP along the balanced growth path. So, an economy with severe business cycles may have a permanently lower level of potential GDP. As a consequence, average income for households in that economy will be permanently lower, reducing the average standard of living.

Garey Ramey and Valerie Ramey of the University of California, San Diego have found that average growth rates of real GDP are lower for countries with more severe business cycles, such as the Democratic Republic of the Congo, Guyana, and Zambia.[9] Gadi Barlevy of the Federal Reserve Bank of Chicago shows that eliminating business cycles would raise the growth rate of per capita consumption by 0.35% per year.[10] While this percentage may seem small, small changes in growth rates become large differences in the standard of living over time due to the power of compounding. So, an increase in the growth rate of this magnitude would have a very large effect on households' well-being in the long run.

---

[7]Ben Bernanke, "Irreversibility, Uncertainty, and Cyclical Investment," *Quarterly Journal of Economics*, Vol. 98, No. 1, February 1983, pp. 85–106.

[8]Justin Lahart, Timothy Aeppel, and Conor Dougherty, "The Financial Crisis: U.S. Economy's Prospects Worsen," *Wall Street Journal*, September 19, 2008.

[9]Garey Ramey and Valerie Ramey, "Cross-Country Evidence on the Link Between Volatility and Growth," *American Economic Review*, Vol. 85, No. 5, December 1995, pp. 1138–1151.

[10]Gadi Barlevy, "The Cost of Business Cycles Under Endogenous Growth," *American Economic Review*, Vol. 94, No. 4, September 1994, pp. 964–990.

Movements of Economic Variables During the Business Cycle

Procyclical variable An economic variable that moves in the same direction as real GDP—increasing during expansions and decreasing during recessions.

Countercyclical variable An economic variable that moves in the opposite direction as real GDP—decreasing during expansions and increasing during recessions.

Leading indicators Economic variables that tend to rise and fall in advance of real GDP.

Coincident indicators Economic variables that tend to rise and fall at the same time as real GDP.

In studying business cycles, economists are interested in movements of economic variables relative to the cycle. An economic variable is a **procyclical variable** if it moves in the same direction as real GDP and other measures of aggregate economic activity: increasing during business cycle expansions and decreasing during recessions. For example, employment, investment expenditures, and expenditures on durable goods tend to increase during expansions and decrease during recessions, so these variables are procyclical. A variable is a **countercyclical variable** if it moves in the opposite direction from real GDP and other measures of aggregate economic activity: decreasing during expansions and increasing during recessions. For example, the unemployment rate tends to decrease during expansions and increase during recessions, so the unemployment rate is countercyclical.

Economists also study the timing of fluctuations in economic variables relative to the timing of fluctuations in real GDP. The Conference Board, a private nonprofit economic research firm, classifies economic variables by whether the fluctuations in the variables lead, lag, or occur at the same time as fluctuations in real GDP. Table 8.2 shows the Conference Board's classification of economic variables. **Leading indicators** are economic variables that tend to rise and fall in advance of real GDP and other measures of aggregate economic activity. For example, stock prices, such as the S&P 500, tend to peak and then decrease prior to the start of a recession. The S&P 500 peaked at a value of 1,527.46 on March 24, 2000, a full year before the 2001 recession began, and it bottomed at 965.80 on September 21, 2001, two months before the recession ended. **Coincident indicators** are economic variables that tend to rise and fall at the same time as real GDP and other measures of aggregate economic

Table 8.2 Movements of Economic Variables Relative to Real GDP

Leading economic indicators

1. Average weekly hours in the manufacturing sector
2. Average weekly initial claims for unemployment insurance
3. Building permits for new private housing units
4. Interest rate spread, which is the interest rate on 10-year Treasury bonds minus the federal funds rate
5. Index of consumer expectations
6. Index of supplier deliveries
7. Manufacturers' new orders received for consumer goods and materials
8. Manufacturers' new orders received for nondefense capital goods
9. Money supply, M2
10. Stock prices of 500 common stocks

Coincident economic indicators

1. Employees on nonagricultural payrolls
2. Industrial production
3. Manufacturing and trade sales
4. Personal income minus transfer payments

Lagging economic indicators

1. Average duration of unemployment
2. Average prime interest rate charged by banks
3. Commercial and industrial loans
4. Consumer price index for services
5. Inventories-to-sales ratio in manufacturing and trade
6. Labor cost per unit of output in the manufacturing sector
7. Ratio of consumer installment credit—such as credit card balances—to personal income

Source: The Conference Board; http://www.conference-board.org/data/bci/index.cfm?id=2160.

activity. The coincident indicators that the Conference Board follows are virtually identical to the four data series that the Business Cycle Dating Committee of the NBER relies on most heavily when determining the official beginning and ending dates of recessions. **Lagging indicators** are economic variables that tend to rise and fall after real GDP and other measures of aggregate economic activity have already risen or fallen. For example, the median duration of unemployment was 6.6 weeks at the beginning of the 2001 recession in March 2001, but it fell to 6.0 weeks in June 2001, during the middle of the recession. Therefore, unemployment duration was falling during the first months of the 2001 recession. By the end of the recession, in November 2001, the median duration of unemployment was 7.7 weeks. The duration of unemployment kept rising after the expansion began, and it peaked at 11.5 weeks in June 2003—a full 19 months after the end of the recession.

Lagging indicators
Economic variables that tend to rise and fall after real GDP.

The Global Business Cycle

The U.S. economy is not alone in experiencing business cycles. Figure 8.5 shows the deviation of real GDP from potential GDP from 1965 to 2010 for the United States, Japan, and the European countries using the euro.

Business cycles across countries are related but not perfectly synchronized. For example, business cycles in Japan and the United States seem to have been synchronized from the 1970s to the mid-1980s, but during the 1990s the relationship was not as strong. Business cycles in the countries using the euro and the United States appear to have been synchronized between 1991 and 2002, but the relationship was weaker between 2002 and 2008. From 2008 to 2010 all three areas experienced a large decrease in real GDP relative to potential GDP due to the financial crisis.

Several factors explain why business cycles are related across countries. First, countries trade with one another. If the United States enters a recession, then U.S. imports from Canada, Japan, and European countries decline. For example, the decrease in the demand for automobiles in the United States during the 2007–2009 recession reduced imports into the United States from Japanese automobile companies, such as Toyota and Honda, and European automobile companies, such as BMW and Mercedes. As a result, real GDP in those countries decreased as well. Second, shocks, such as the oil price shocks of 1973 and 1990 and the financial market shock of 2007–2009, are often global in nature. In such cases, all countries experience a similar shock at the same time, so it is not surprising that business cycles appear to be synchronized across countries.

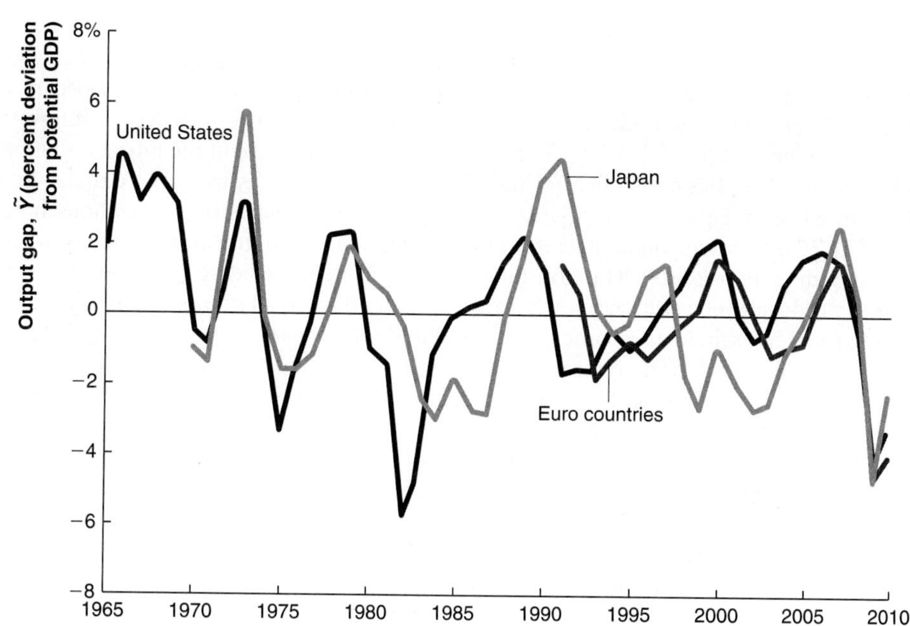

Figure 8.5

The International Business Cycle, 1965–2010

Business cycles in Japan and the United States seem to have been synchronized from the 1970s to the mid-1980s, but during the 1990s, the relationship was not as strong. Business cycles in the euro countries and the United States appear to have been synchronized between 1991 and 2002, but the relationship was weaker between 2002 and 2008.

Source: Organisation for Economic Co-operation and Development.

8.3

Learning Objective

Explain how economists think about business cycles.

How Economists Think About Business Cycles

The many markets that make up the national and global economy are constantly buffeted by shocks that affect the consumption and investment decisions of firms and households. Some shocks affect many markets in the economy at once. For example, the Organization of Petroleum Exporting Countries (OPEC) instituted an oil embargo of several countries, including the United States, in 1973, which caused oil prices to spike. Households faced higher gasoline prices, and firms faced higher fuel costs and higher costs for goods, such as plastics, that are made from oil. Households responded to this shock by reducing consumption spending on products other than gasoline, and firms reduced production as their costs rose. These reductions in spending contributed to the 1973–1975 recession. Iraq's invasion of Kuwait in August 1990 caused a spike in oil prices and a drop in consumer confidence that some economists believe contributed to the 1990–1991 recession. The terrorist attacks of September 11, 2001, in the United States led to a dramatic decline in consumption for that month, which worsened the 2001 recession. Some shocks arise in financial markets. The collapse of stock prices that began in March 2000 following the end of the "dotcom bubble" likely contributed to the 2001 recession in the United States. Natural disasters can also act as shocks. When Hurricane Katrina hit the Gulf Coast region in 2005, it reduced consumer confidence and disrupted the availability of refined oil products in the United States, although this shock was not large enough to cause a recession.

Shocks also have ripple effects in the economy. Although the collapse in stock market prices starting in March 2000 was a financial market event, stocks are a component of household wealth, so when stock prices decline, household wealth also declines. When their wealth declines, households have fewer resources to finance consumption either today or in the future. As a result, households cut back on consumption.

When nominal wages and prices are flexible, markets absorb shocks, so the shocks do not have a large effect on real GDP. However, when nominal wages and prices are sticky, quantities in individual markets respond to these shocks. Changes in quantities reverberate through the economy because, as output changes, so does income. Changes in income can lead to changes in spending and further changes in output and employment.

Multiplier Effects

Multiplier effect A series of induced increases (or decreases) in consumption spending that results from an initial increase (or decrease) in autonomous expenditure; this effect amplifies the effect of economic shocks on real GDP.

The effects of shocks are amplified through **multiplier effects**, which refers to a series of induced increases (or decreases) in consumption spending that results from an initial increase (or decrease) in spending. Multiplier effects occur when there is a change in *autonomous expenditure*, which refers to spending that does not depend on income. Examples of changes in autonomous expenditure include a change in government purchases or taxes, a decline in consumer spending as a result of a decline in consumer confidence, or a decline in investment spending resulting from firms becoming more pessimistic about the future profitability of capital. The basic idea behind the multiplier effect comes from the circular-flow diagram shown in Figure 2.1 on page 28. That diagram shows that every \$1 that households spend on consumption goods generates \$1 of revenues for some firm (for simplicity, we ignore spending on imports). The firm then uses that \$1 to hire labor, capital, and other inputs to produce goods and services. Because households own all inputs, the \$1 ultimately goes to some household as income. That household spends part of the increase in income, while using the rest of the increase to pay taxes or to save. This extra spending initiates a second round of expenditure and income changes in the circular flow, and so on.

Consider an example of the multiplier effect. To keep the example simple, we will assume that when households receive an increase in income, they spend part of it on domestically produced goods and services and save the rest—so we will ignore taxes and spending on imports. We will assume that households spend \$0.90 of each additional dollar of income and save the remaining \$0.10.

Suppose a shock, such as an increase in consumer confidence, causes households to increase spending on goods and services by \$1 billion. The circular-flow diagram shows that this extra $1 billion in spending generates $1 billion in revenues for firms. Firms hire labor, capital, and natural resources to produce goods and services, so the $1 billion in revenues generates $1 billion in income for households, who are the owners of labor, capital, and natural resources. Households use this increase in income to purchase additional goods and services, such as appliances, furniture, and vacations, so the initial increase in expenditures generates a second round of spending. The new spending during the second round is $1 billion × 0.90 = $900 million, which, in turn, provides $900 million in additional revenues to firms and $900 million in additional income for households. These households spend 90% of this extra $900 million in income on goods and services. Therefore, there is a third round through the circular flow in which spending increases by $900 million × 0.90 = $810 million. Each time through the circular flow, the increase in income and spending gets smaller because households spend only 90% of an increase in income, saving the other 10%. So, the new income generated eventually becomes zero as the number of rounds increases. The total change in income is large, however, because additional income is generated during each round through the circular flow:

$$\begin{aligned}\text{Total income generated} &= \$1\text{ billion} + \$900\text{ million} + \$810\text{ million}\\ &\quad + \$729\text{ million} + \$656\text{ million} + \ldots = \$10\text{ billion.}\end{aligned}$$

Because the change in total income equals the change in GDP, in this example, a $1 billion increase in consumption spending results in a $10 billion increase in GDP. In the appendix to this chapter, we demonstrate why the total increase in GDP in this example is $10 billion. The fact that the total income generated is greater than the initial change in household spending is the result of the multiplier effect.

Any shock that initially increases spending by $1 billion would have a similar multiplier effect: The multiplier effect is the same whether government purchases increase by $1 billion, the government cuts taxes so investment or consumption increase by $1 billion, or consumers become optimistic about the future and decide to increase spending by $1 billion.

Our example shows a multiplier of 10. In practice, however, expenditure multipliers are much smaller, partly because of the effects of taxes and expenditures on imports. Because economists measure the magnitude of the business cycle relative to potential GDP, they often measure the multiplier effect relative to potential GDP as well. In that case, we would have:

$$\left(\frac{\text{Change in autonomous expenditure}}{\text{Potential GDP}}\right) \times \text{Multiplier effect} = \left(\frac{\text{Change in real GDP}}{\text{Potential GDP}}\right).$$

Table 8.3 shows for the United States estimates of the multiplier measured in this way, based on an economic model that the Organisation for Economic Co-operation and Development (OECD) uses. The estimates allow for the possibility of income taxes and household purchases of imported goods, as well as other factors that can reduce the size of the multiplier effect.

Table 8.3 Expenditure Multiplier Estimates for the United States (percentage point of real GDP)

	Years after the shock				
	1	2	3	4	5
Increase in expenditure by 1 percentage point of potential real GDP	1.1	1.0	0.5	0.2	0.1

Source: Thomas Dalsgaard, Christophe Andre, and Peter Richardson, "Standard Shocks in the OECD Interlink Model," Organisation for Economic Co-operation and Development Working Paper 306, September 6, 2001.

The estimate for the expenditure multiplier in the first year is 1.1, which means a 1-percentage-point increase in expenditure as a percentage of real GDP increases real GDP by 1.1 percentage points. Notice that the effect gets smaller over time because nominal wages and prices adjust to the shock as the economy moves from the short run to the long run. The estimates in the table show the multiplier effect resulting from an increase in government purchases, but these estimates would also apply to changes in consumption, investment, and net exports.

The values for the multiplier in Table 8.3 are estimates based on historical data. The actual value of the multiplier may be larger or smaller, depending on the circumstances. For the multiplier effect to operate, there must be some idle resources so that firms can hire more labor, capital, and other inputs when demand increases. The further real GDP is below potential GDP, the greater the amount of idle resources and the larger the multiplier effect may be. Put another way, the worse the economy is performing, the larger the multiplier effect may be.

We can summarize our account of economic fluctuations during a business cycle with the following simple schematic:

Shock → Spending response by households and firms → Multiplier effect → Change in real GDP.

An Example of a Shock with Multiplier Effects

In this section, we continue our discussion of the multiplier effect using an example of a recent shock to the U.S. economy. The Federal Reserve Board estimates that measured in 2005 dollars, the value of real estate owned by households declined by $2,330 billion from the first quarter of 2007 to the first quarter of 2008.[11] According to the Congressional Budget Office, for every $1 change in real estate wealth, consumption changes by $0.07.[12] So, the change in total consumption is $-\$2{,}330$ billion $\times$ 0.07 = $-\$163.1$ billion. This amount represents an initial reduction in expenditure in the circular flow, which then had multiplier effects. Potential GDP was $13,590 billion in 2008 (measured in 2005 dollars), so the initial change in consumption represents $-\$163.1$ billion/$13,590 billion = -1.2% of potential GDP. The estimate of the multiplier for the first year after an expenditure shock in Table 8.3 is 1.1, so a 1-percentage-point change in expenditure causes a 1.1-percentage-point change in real GDP. Using this value for the multiplier, we have:

Total change in real GDP relative to potential GDP

$$= \text{Initial change in expenditure relative to potential GDP} \times \text{Multiplier}$$
$$= (-1.2\%) \times 1.1.$$
$$= -1.3\%.$$

Output was -0.1% below its potential level at the end of 2007, so holding everything else constant, we would have expected the output to fall further below potential in 2008. The multipliers in Table 8.3 decrease as we move from year 1 to year 5, so the effect of the decrease in housing prices on output becomes smaller over time. This effect occurs because nominal wages and prices adjust to the shock and help move real GDP back to

[11]Calculated using the Flow of Funds Account from June 5, 2008. The data for the value of real estate owned by households come from Table B.100, line 4. Nominal values were converted to real values using the chain-type price index for real GDP.

[12]Congressional Budget Office, "Housing Wealth and Consumer Spending," January 2001. The CBO considers two estimates: a high estimate of 0.07, which we use here, and a low estimate of 0.03. Table 1 of the report discusses recent estimates for the multiplier effect that range from a low of 0.017 to a high of 0.21.

potential GDP. Our estimates of the multiplier effect suggest that the collapse in housing prices would reduce real GDP relative to its potential level by the following:

$$(-1.2) \times 1.0 = -1.2\% \text{ in } 2009$$
$$(-1.2) \times 0.5 = -0.6\% \text{ in } 2010$$
$$(-1.2) \times 0.2 = -0.2\% \text{ in } 2011$$
$$(-1.2) \times 0.1 = -0.1\% \text{ in } 2012$$

Because of the multiplier effect, a reduction in construction activity may reduce real GDP for years into the future.

Answering the Key Question

Continued from page 271

At the beginning of this chapter, we asked the question:

"Why does the business cycle occur?"

The business cycle occurs due to the combined effects of shocks and nominal price and wage stickiness. Shocks alter the decisions of households and firms about how much to consume and invest given current nominal prices and wages. When nominal prices and wages are sticky, shocks cause output to fluctuate. Therefore, a shock that, for instance, reduces the willingness of households to spend or firms to invest will cause real GDP to decrease. This initial decrease in real GDP will be amplified by the multiplier.

Before moving to the next chapter, read *An Inside Look* on the next page for a discussion of why automobile sales rose in the United States in 2010 for the first time since the recession that began in 2007.

AN INSIDE LOOK

New Vehicle Sales Increase by 11 Percent in 2010

ASSOCIATED PRESS

Auto Sales Up for First Time Since the Recession

Auto sales rose in the United States last year for the first time since the recession. They're still far from what they were just a few years ago — but that's just fine with the downsized auto industry, which can post profits even if it sells millions fewer cars and trucks.

a For the year, new car and truck sales came in at 11.6 million, up 11 percent from last year. . . . For December alone, sales were 1.14 million, also up 11 percent from a year earlier.

While the figures have some in the industry talking about a return to the glory days, it's a fragile idea. Rising gas prices or more economic trouble could still shake the confidence of American car buyers.

But for now, executives are optimistic about this year. General Motors, Ford and Toyota all predict sales will come in at 12.5 million to 13 million for 2011. It will take years, analysts expect, to get back to the peak sales of 17 million reached in the middle of the decade.

"The economic downturn has lasted quite a while," says Jessica Caldwell, director of pricing and analysis for consumer website Edmunds.com. "It's going to be slow and gradual rather than a fast bounceback. . . ."

b U.S. automakers are relieved to have the past two years behind them. When the financial crisis hit in the fall of 2008, car sales plummeted. GM and Chrysler were on the brink of death, saved by a $60 billion government bailout and speedy bankruptcies that helped both companies close plants and eliminate debt. Ford didn't declare bankruptcy or take a bailout, but it closed plants, laid off employees, and worked to lower its overall cost structure.

As a result, those companies can now make money even if sales hover below pre-recession levels.

c Over the past two years, many Americans, even those who had enough money to buy a car during the recession, had been wary to commit to monthly car payments, so they put off making such a large purchase. Many opted to repair or make do with what they had.

Those buyers are easing back into the market, replacing aging vehicles. The average vehicle on U.S. roads is now 10.2 years old — the oldest since 1997 and a full year older than in 2007, before the recession, according to the National Automobile Dealers Association.

"With 240 million vehicles out there on the road, a lot of them are going to be ripe for replacement," says Ellen Hughes-Cromwick, Ford's chief economist.

Auto sales peaked in 2005 at 17.4 million and bottomed out at 10.6 million in 2009. The peak was fueled, in part, by big incentives — like the employee-discounts-for-everyone schemes that were popular in the summer of 2005. But those deals may be a thing of the past. . . .

The figures include only sales made in the United States. . . . Globally, auto sales should hit around 65 million this year.

The U.S. car market is considered the most profitable market in the world, because buyers tend to pay higher prices for vehicles and opt for add-ins that bring up the cost.

Source: Sharon Silke Carty, "Auto sales up for first time since the recession," *Associated Press*, January 4, 2011. Used with permission of The Associated Press.

Key Points in the Article

This article discusses vehicle sales in 2010. Sales were up for the first time since the recession, with new car and truck sales reaching 11.6 million, an increase of 11% from 2009. Auto sales in the United States peaked at 17.4 million in 2005 and experienced a rapid decline during the recession, with sales bottoming out at 10.6 million in 2009. Auto executives were optimistic that the rise in sales will continue for 2011, predicting that sales for the year will increase to as many as 13 million new vehicles.

Analyzing the News

a The rise in sales of new vehicles in 2010 boded well for the economic recovery, and some industry executives expected this sales trend to continue into 2011. With sales up 11% from the previous year, some in the industry spoke of a return to the peak sales days of the mid-2000s, yet analysts believe that could take years to happen. And while the economy did improve in 2010, rising gas prices in early 2011 had the potential to slow down or even stall the recovery. Figure 1 shows that the average price of gasoline rose to more than $4.00 per gallon in July 2008, and then dropped significantly, playing a role in the rebound in new car sales. In 2011, gas prices were again on the rise, topping the $3.00 per gallon mark in January and rising to over $3.50 per gallon by March.

b The financial crisis and recession severely damaged the automobile industry. New vehicle sales in the United States fell dramatically, as shown in Figure 2. GM and Chrysler were only able to survive with the help of a $60 billion bailout and major restructuring via bankruptcy. Ford was able to avoid the bailout and bankruptcy route, but did lower costs with plant closings and layoffs. The restructuring in the industry has allowed companies to profit with lower sales figures. As the chapter states on page 277, GM believes it can now earn a profit if sales exceed 10.5 million cars, a much lower figure than before the recession.

c During the recession, orders for durable goods in the United States declined by more than 35%, with automobile orders falling by an even greater amount. Feeling the effects of the recession, many consumers chose to avoid being saddled with new car payments, opting instead to keep and maintain their existing vehicles. By 2010, the average age of vehicles on U.S. roads was 10.2 years, the oldest average in 13 years. A combination of easing credit markets, lower gas prices, and an improving economy saw consumers beginning to replace their aging vehicles, increasing new car production and sales during 2010.

THINKING CRITICALLY

1. From December 2007 to July 2008, the average price of gasoline rose by more than $1.00 per gallon to over $4.00 per gallon, and new automobile sales fell dramatically. In December 2010, the average price of gasoline was again below $3.00 per gallon, and automobile sales were rising. What might this information indicate about real GDP and the output gap from July 2008 through December 2010? How might the rapid increase in gasoline prices in the first three months of 2011 affect automobile sales, real GDP, and the output gap?
2. The changes in the price of gasoline and in the production and sales of new automobiles from July 2008 to December 2010 appear to have had a positive effect on the economy. Explain how these changes can affect the economy, and how the multiplier effect would be involved.

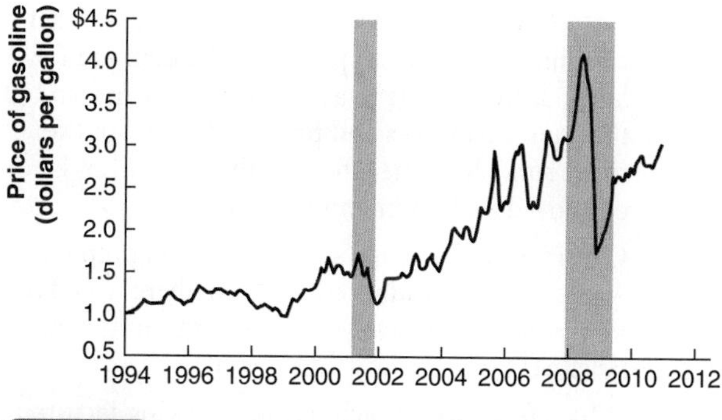

Figure 1 U.S. Gasoline Prices, January 1994–January 2011

Source: United States Department of Energy

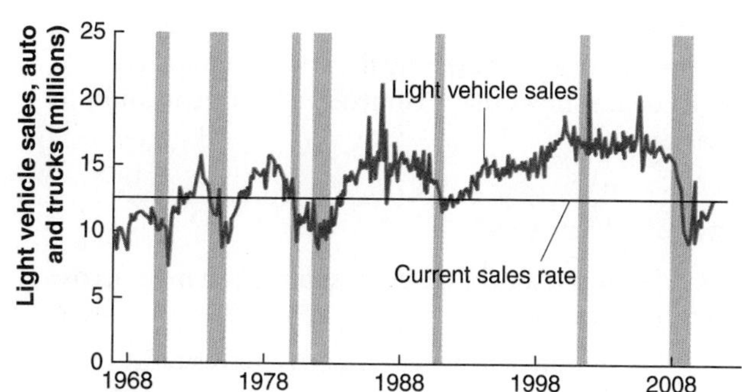

Figure 2 U.S. Light Vehicle Sales, January 1967–January 2011

Source: www.calculatedriskblog.com

CHAPTER SUMMARY AND PROBLEMS

KEY TERMS

Business cycle, p. 273
Classical economics, p. 273
Coincident indicators, p. 288
Countercyclical variable, p. 288
Cyclical unemployment rate, p. 284
Expansion, p. 273
Keynesian economics, p. 273
Lagging indicators, p. 289
Leading indicators, p. 288
Macroeconomic shock, p. 274
Menu costs, p. 275
Multiplier effect, p. 290
Okun's law, p. 284
Output gap, p. 282
Potential GDP, p. 273
Procyclical variable, p. 288
Recession, p. 273

8.1 The Short Run and the Long Run in Macroeconomics

Explain the difference between the short run and the long run in macroeconomics.

SUMMARY

The **business cycle** refers to alternating periods of economic **expansion** and economic **recession**. According to **Keynesian economics**, business cycles represent disequilibrium or nonmarket-clearing behavior. According to **classical economics**, business cycles can be explained using equilibrium analysis. Nominal wages and prices are flexible in the long run but sticky in the short run due to menu costs and long-term contracts. **Menu costs** represent all the costs firms incur to change prices, including printing new catalogs and changing the prices in stores, costs due to angering customers with price increases, and the difficulty of changing long-term contracts. Because nominal wage and price stickiness exist, **macroeconomic shocks** can cause business cycles. However, nominal wages and prices are not permanently fixed, and they do respond to shocks over time. Economists dispute how long the adjustment takes, but evidence shows that a complete adjustment could take years.

Review Questions

1.1 What is a shock? Give an example of a macroeconomic shock.

1.2 What is an expansion? What is a recession?

1.3 Why are nominal prices and wages sticky in the short run?

1.4 Why is it costly for firms to change prices?

1.5 What is the main difference between the Keynesian and the classical views of the business cycle?

Problems and Applications

1.6 **[Related to the *Making the Connection* on page 275]** The price of a bottle of Coke remained constant for nearly 70 years, but the prices of other types of goods can also be very sticky. Identify at least two products that have prices that change infrequently, and explain why the companies that produce those products might choose price stickiness as a strategy.

1.7 **[Related to the *Making the Connection* on page 277]** In Chapter 7, we saw that one possible explanation for higher natural rates of unemployment in Western Europe than the United States was stronger unions. Strong unions may also increase the severity of a business cycles by increasing wage stickiness.

Draw a graph of the aggregate labor market in equilibrium. Then suppose that the demand for labor decreases due to an economic downturn but that nominal wages and prices are sticky in the short run. Show the effect on the amount of labor employed and on unemployment.

1.8 Consider the following statement: "If all nominal wages and prices adjusted instantly, there would be no business cycle." Do you agree with this statement? Briefly explain.

1.9 What effect would each of the following factors have on the stickiness of nominal wages and prices? Would these factors increase or decrease the severity of the business cycle?

a. Grocery stores change from stamping individual prices on products to using bar codes to scan prices into a computer.

b. The size of the unionized manufacturing sector increases relative to the size of the nonunionized service sector.

c. More firms move to selling via the Internet rather than using printed catalogs.

1.10 An Associated Press article about sticky prices states: "That's what analysts call it when companies slap higher prices on products and keep them there even though the rationale for the price hikes . . . is gone."

a. Prices for goods such as cereal and toothpaste did not fall during the 2007–2009 recession. Why might these prices be sticky?

b. Prices for goods such as oil and wheat did fall during the 2007–2009 recession. Why are these prices different from the prices for goods such as cereal and toothpaste?

Source: Christopher Leonard, "Despite Threat of Recession, 'Sticky Prices' Keep Bills High," *Associated Press*, October 19, 2008.

8.2 What Happens During a Business Cycle?
Understand what happens during a business cycle.

SUMMARY

The National Bureau of Economic Research (NBER) defines a **recession** as a "period of falling economic activity spread across the economy, lasting more than a few months," and defines an **expansion** as the period between two recessions. A recession combined with the subsequent expansion make up one business cycle. The **output gap** allows us to measure the magnitude of an economic fluctuation. The costs of business cycles include lost income, the increased unemployment during recessions described by **Okun's law,** and the increase in inflation during expansions. The increased unemployment during recessions is concentrated among low-income households. If the period of unemployment persists long enough, the skills of the workers may deteriorate, and the natural rate of unemployment may rise. Severe business cycles can reduce the investment rate and, therefore, reduce potential GDP. A **procyclical variable** moves in the same direction as real GDP, and a **countercyclical variable** moves in the opposite direction as real GDP. Economists classify some economic variables as **leading indicators**, **coincident indicators**, and **lagging indicators** depending on how they fluctuate relative to the business cycle. Business cycles appear to be somewhat, but not completely, synchronized across countries.

Review Questions

2.1 How does the National Bureau of Economic Research (NBER) define a recession? What data do the NBER consider when determining whether the economy is in a recession?

2.2 How is the output gap measured?

2.3 What is cyclical unemployment?

2.4 What is Okun's law?

2.5 How might economic uncertainty resulting from business cycles affect long-term economic growth?

2.6 What has been the average duration of U.S. recessions since World War II? What has been the average duration of U.S. expansions since World War II? What factors have contributed to the moderating of recessions?

2.7 Give examples of a procyclical and a countercyclical variable. Give examples of a leading, a lagging, and a coincident indicator.

2.8 What is the relationship between business cycles in different countries?

Problems and Applications

2.9 **[Related to *Solved Problem 8.2* on page 282]** The following table shows data on the quarterly growth rate of real GDP for the U.S. economy:

Year	Quarter	Growth rate (percentage)
1973	1	10.6%
1973	2	4.7
1973	3	−2.1
1973	4	3.9
1974	1	−3.5
1974	2	1.0
1974	3	−3.9
1974	4	−1.6
1975	1	−4.8
1975	2	3.1
1975	3	6.9
1975	4	5.3

a. Using the rule-of-thumb definition of a recession, did this economy experience any recessions during this period? Briefly explain.

b. The NBER says that a recession began during the fourth quarter of 1973 and ended during the first quarter of 1975. How does your answer in part a. compare to the official NBER dates.

2.10 Suppose that potential GDP in a small country is \$10,000 in year 1 and real GDP is also \$10,000. Potential GDP grows at a rate of 3% per year.

a. Calculate potential GDP for the next six years.

b. If real GDP in year 4 is \$10,500, what is the output gap?

c. If real GDP in year 6 is \$11,700, what is the output gap?

2.11 Refer to problem 2.10. Using Okun's law, determine the cyclical unemployment rate in the small country.

a. What is the cyclical rate of unemployment in year 1?

b. What is the cyclical rate of unemployment in year 4?

c. What is the cyclical rate of unemployment in year 6?

2.12 Consider the following statement: "In a business cycle, recessions are followed by expansions. Therefore, it is not necessary to be concerned about the costs of business cycles, because they will average out." Do you agree with this statement? Briefly explain.

2.13 Explain how each of the following workers may be permanently affected by the situation described.

a. Satyajit loses his job during a recession and remains unemployed for a long period of time.

b. Lena graduates from college during a recession.

2.14 In problem 2.13, explain whether Satyajit's and Lena's situations are an issue for the economy as a whole.

2.15 **[Related to the *Making the Connection* on page 285]** Some economists believe that the severity of the 2007–2009 recession may have permanently changed Okun's Law. Okun's law states that as real GDP increases by 1 percentage point relative to potential GDP, cyclical unemployment decreases by 0.5 percentage point. How might the recession have changed this relationship? Briefly explain.

2.16 For each of the following, define the variable and state why it is a leading, lagging, or coincident indicator.

a. Average duration of unemployment

b. Stock prices

c. Personal income minus transfer payments

d. Index of consumer expectations

e. Ratio of consumer installment credit to personal income

2.17 What would each of the following tend to indicate about the state of the economy? That is, in each of these situations, is the economy likely to be headed for a recession, in a recession, headed for an expansion, or in an expansion?

a. A sharp decline in real GDP

b. A rise in the inflation rate

c. A decrease in international trade

d. A decrease in the unemployment rate below the natural rate

2.18 Consider the following statement: "Large countries such as the United States, in which a relatively small portion of GDP comes from international trade, are not likely to be affected by business cycles in other countries." Briefly explain whether you agree with this statement.

2.19 In the spring of 2011, the U.S. unemployment rate was around 9%. If the natural rate of unemployment is assumed to be 5.5%, what is the output gap?

2.20 Discussing business cycles, an article from the Federal Reserve Bank of Dallas stated: "Volatility can also spill over into real and financial asset markets, where severe price movements can produce seemingly arbitrary redistributions of wealth."

a. What does the article mean when it says that price movements can produce arbitrary wealth redistributions?

b. This article was written before the 2007–2009 recession. Do you think that this recession caused arbitrary redistributions of wealth? What evidence would support your answer?

Source: Evan Koenig and Nicole Ball, "The 'Great Moderation' in Output and Unemployment Volatility: An Update," *Economic Letter*, Vol. 2, No. 9, September 2007.

8.3 How Economists Think About Business Cycles

Explain how economists think about business cycles.

SUMMARY

Markets are interconnected, so shocks in one market can affect other markets and reverberate throughout the economy. The **multiplier effect** represents one way that shocks in one market affect other markets. For example, the decline in housing prices during 2006–2009 reduced household wealth, which reduced the income for other households, which then reduced their consumption spending, and so on. In this way, the effect of shocks can spill over from one market to the rest of the economy. As nominal wages and prices in markets adjust to the shock, real GDP moves back toward potential GDP. As a result, the multiplier effect declines over time and is zero in the long run.

Review Questions

3.1 What is a multiplier effect? Give an example.

3.2 What factors affect the size of the multiplier?

3.3 Why are the full effects of a shock on real GDP not felt immediately?

Problems and Applications

3.4 One factor in the 2007–2009 recession was the decline in housing prices due to the bursting of the housing bubble. The housing industry is closely linked to many other markets and to the spending and saving decisions of households. Carefully explain some of the ways in which a decline in housing prices may affect the rest of the economy.

3.5 Suppose that the federal government decides to increase purchases by $10 billion. Briefly explain why this increase in purchases is likely to have a multiplier effect. If the tax rate on personal income is relatively low, will the size of the multiplier effect be larger or smaller than if the tax rate is relatively high? Briefly explain.

3.6 A decline in stock prices reduces household wealth and consumption spending. Estimates of U.S. stock market losses in 2008 are around $7,000 billion.

a. It is estimated that the propensity to spend out of stock market wealth is relatively small. Assume that consumers spent $0.03 out of every additional $1 of stock market wealth. Estimate the GDP loss due to the fall in the stock market during 2008.

b. Assuming that potential GDP was $13,610 billion in 2008, what effect did the loss of wealth from the stock market have on the output gap?

3.7 The costs of the Japanese earthquake and tsunami of March 2011 include the direct cost of cleanup and additional costs, such as the loss of revenues from seafood harvests, tourism, and related industries. Using the concept of multipliers, explain how this disaster may affect the Japanese economy as a whole.

3.8 **[Related to the *Chapter Opener* on page 271]** In 2011, the U.S. automobile industry appeared to be recovering as the overall economy improved. Suppose, though, that the following unlikely event had occurred: Because of the severity of the 2007–2009 recession, all U.S.-based automobile firms had closed.

a. What would be the direct impact of the failure of the automobile industry?

b. What other industries are closely connected to the automobile industry? How would these industries have been affected by the failure of the U.S. automobile firms?

c. Would there have been other multiplier effects? If so, briefly describe what they would have been.

DATA EXERCISES

D8.1: **[Related to *Solved Problem 8.2* on page 282]** The National Bureau of Economic Research's (NBER's) Web site is located at www.nber.org.

a. Find the NBER listing of all business cycle peaks and troughs since 1854. Do these data support the claim that the length of recessions has moderated? Do expansions last as long as contractions, on average?

b. What is the most recent NBER announcement on the business cycle?

D8.2: The index of Leading Economic Indicators (LEI) is published by the Conference Board (www.conference-board.org).

a. Go to the Conference Board's Web site and find the 10 components of the LEI. Why is each component important?

b. What does the most recent value for the index indicate about the state of the economy? Are all components of the index moving in the same direction?

D8.3: The Conference Board also publishes indices of indicators for other countries. Consider the LEI for the euro zone.

a. How is this index calculated compared to the LEI for the United States?

b. What does the most recent value indicate? What impact is this value likely to have on the United States?

D8.4: The Federal Reserve Bank of St. Louis offers data on both real GDP and potential GDP at its Web site (research.stlouisfed.org/fred2/). Look at the data for 2007 to the present.

a. Use the data to calculate the output gap.

b. Assume that the natural rate of unemployment for the United States is 5.5%. Based on the GDP gap that you found in (a), what does Okun's law predict about cyclical unemployment?

c. What was the actual unemployment rate during this period?

D8.5: **[Excel question]** While it is preferable to use quarterly data to follow business cycles, it is often difficult to find consistent data for a broad range of countries. The World Bank (www.worldbank.org) has annual real GDP data for most countries.

a. Choose two countries that you think have interrelated economies (for example, the United States and Canada) and download real GDP data from 1972 to the present.

1. Calculate annual real GDP growth rates for each country.
2. Graph the data and calculate the correlation coefficient. How closely correlated are growth rates for these countries? Do their growth rates move together? Do business cycles appear to be related in the two countries?

b. Repeat the steps above for two countries that you think are less likely to be closely related, such as the United States and Chile. Briefly explain how your answers here are different from your answers in part (a).

APPENDIX

The Formula for the Expenditure Multiplier

8A Derive the formula for the expenditure multiplier.

The total increase in real GDP resulting from an increase in autonomous expenditure is found using the formula for an infinite series. Suppose that there is an initial increase of \$1,000 in government purchases and that households spend \$0.90 of each additional dollar of income. In each subsequent round through the circular flow, new spending is 90% of the spending from the previous round. Therefore:

$$\begin{aligned}\text{Total increase in spending} &= \$1{,}000 + 0.9 \times \$1{,}000 + 0.9 \times (0.9 \times \$1{,}000) + \ldots \\ &= \$1{,}000 + 0.9 \times \$1{,}000 + 0.9^2 \times \$1{,}000 \\ &\quad + 0.9^3 \times \$1{,}000 + \ldots \\ &= (1 + 0.9 + 0.9^2 + 0.9^3 + \ldots) \times \$1{,}000.\end{aligned}$$

The expression in parentheses is an infinite series, and it equals:

$$(1 + 0.9 + 0.9^2 + 0.9^3 + \ldots) = 1/(1 - 0.9) = 10.$$

Therefore, the total change in real GDP is:

$$\text{Total increase in spending} = \text{Total increase in real GDP} = 10 \times \$1{,}000 = \$10{,}000,$$

where 10 is the value of the multiplier.

To derive a general formula for the multiplier, let b represent the fraction of income spent during each round through the circular flow (0.9 in the above example). The infinite sum m in parentheses represents the multiplier:

$$m = (1 + b + b^2 + b^3 + \ldots).$$

To solve for the value of the multiplier, multiply both sides of the equation by b to get:

$$bm = (b + b^2 + b^3 + b^4 + \ldots).$$

Now, subtract bm from m to get:

$$m - bm = (1 + b + b^2 + b^3 + \ldots) - (b + b^2 + b^3 + b^4 + \ldots) = 1.$$

Now, solve for m to get:

$$m = 1/(1 - b).$$

So, if $b = 0.9$, then $m = 10$. We could introduce the effects of income taxes and spending on imports into the b term, but the procedure for arriving at a value for the multiplier would not change.

CHAPTER 9

IS–MP: A Short-Run Macroeconomic Model

LEARNING OBJECTIVES

After studying this chapter, you should be able to:

9.1 Explain how the *IS* curve represents the relationship between the real interest rate and aggregate expenditure (pages 304–312)

9.2 Use the monetary policy, *MP*, curve to show how the interest rate set by the central bank helps to determine the output gap (pages 312–319)

9.3 Use the *IS–MP* model to understand why real GDP fluctuates (pages 319–327)

9.4 Understand the role of the Phillips curve in the *IS–MP* model (pages 327–338)

9.5 Use the *IS–MP* model to understand the performance of the U.S. economy during the recession of 2007–2009 (pages 339–342)

9A Use the *IS–LM* model to illustrate macroeconomic equilibrium (pages 353–362)

THE LEHMAN BROTHERS BANKRUPTCY AND THE GREAT RECESSION OF 2007–2009

In December 1930, the Bank of United States, a large private bank located in New York City, collapsed. The bank ran into trouble in part because an unusually high percentage of its loans were in real estate. By the fall of 1930, the prices of houses, as well as office buildings and other commercial real estate, were falling, and borrowers were defaulting on mortgages. The failure of the Bank of United States triggered a wave of banking failures that helped turn a severe recession into the Great Depression. Nearly 78 years later, the bankruptcy of Wall Street investment bank Lehman Brothers on Monday, September 15, 2008, helped turn a serious financial situation into a financial crisis that severely worsened the recession that had begun in December 2007. At the time, Lehman Brothers was the fourth-largest U.S. investment bank. The bankruptcy of Lehman Brothers was linked in part to its role in the market for mortgage-backed securities. Lehman Brothers had purchased mortgages, bundled

Continued on next page

Key Issue and Question

At the end of Chapter 1, we noted key issues and questions that serve as a framework for the book. Here are the key issue and key question for this chapter:

Issue: The recession of 2007–2009 was the worst since the Great Depression of the 1930s.

Question: What explains the severity of the 2007–2009 recession?

Answered on page 343

large numbers of them together as mortgage-backed securities, and resold them to investors. When housing prices fell, beginning in 2006, homeowners began defaulting on mortgage payments, and the prices of mortgage-backed securities declined sharply, reducing the value of Lehman Brothers' holdings of these securities. Lehman Brothers' investments were financed, in part, by short-term borrowing from other financial firms. When these financial firms began to doubt the ability of Lehman Brothers to pay back loans, the firms refused to extend Lehman Brothers any additional credit. Without access to credit, Lehman Brothers was forced to declare bankruptcy, causing most of the firm's 26,000 workers around the world to immediately lose their jobs.

Many economists believe that the failure of Lehman Brothers helped lead to a crisis of confidence in the financial system, with financial firms becoming very reluctant to lend to each other. The result was a wave of bankruptcies or near bankruptcies involving commercial banks, investment banks, and other financial firms. In the days after Lehman's bankruptcy, prices on world stock markets declined by almost $2.85 trillion, which represented about 6% of the value of these markets. The flow of funds through the financial system was disrupted, causing real GDP and employment in the United States to decline sharply. Some economists believe that the failure of Lehman Brothers was a symptom of the underlying problems in the financial system. These economists argue that even if Lehman Brothers had avoided bankruptcy, the results for the financial system and the economy would have been much the same. In any event, it is clear that the financial crisis and the economic recession became much more severe beginning about the time that Lehman Brothers failed.

U.S. real GDP had fallen by less than 0.1% between the beginning of the recession in the fourth quarter of 2007 and the end of the second quarter of 2008, just before Lehman's bankruptcy. Following the bankruptcy, however, real GDP declined at an annual rate of 6.8% during the fourth quarter of 2008 and 4.9% during the first quarter of 2009. This was the largest decline in real GDP over such a short period since the Great Depression. The damage from the financial crisis spread from the United States to the global economy. In August 2008, the International Monetary Fund (IMF) forecast global GDP growth of 3.9% for 2009, but, in fact, global GDP actually fell by 2% during that year.

Is it possible that the collapse of one financial firm could lead to a crisis of confidence so severe that it dramatically worsened a global recession? The financial system plays an important role in the transfer of funds from savers to borrowers, who use the funds to buy consumption and investment goods. More important than its direct effects, the Lehman Brothers bankruptcy generated doubt about the ability of other investment banks, as well as many commercial banks and other financial institutions to survive. As a result, it became very difficult for many financial institutions to borrow from each other or from investors, as lenders feared that borrowers would not pay them back. When financial institutions have difficulty borrowing, they reduce lending to households and firms, so consumption and investment expenditures decrease. The reduction in these expenditures deepened the global recession.

AN INSIDE LOOK AT POLICY on page 344 discusses the financial reform bill signed into law by President Obama in July 2010.

Sources: Bob Ivry, Christine Harper, and Mark Pittman, "Missing Lehman Lesson of Shakeout Means Too Big Banks May Fail," *Bloomberg.com*, September 7, 2009; "What If?" *Economist*, September 12, 2009; Chris Giles, "Bank Failure That Triggered the Panic," *Financial Times*, September 14, 2009; Gary Duncan, "Lehman Brothers Collapse Sends Shockwaves Round World," *Times Online*, September 16, 2008; and U.S. Bureau of Economic Analysis.

In Chapter 8, we looked at the basic facts of the business cycle. We saw that the unemployment rate and the inflation rate rise and fall during recessions and expansions. During the Great Depression of the 1930s, the most severe economic downturn in U.S. history, the unemployment rate rose above 20%. While the unemployment rate in the United States has never again been as high as 20%, the unemployment rate did rise to 10.8% during the 1981–1982 recession and to 10.1% during the recession of 2007–2009. Although the unemployment rate during the 2007–2009 recession was not as high as during the 1981–1982 recession, the decline in real GDP was larger. In fact, by most measures, the recession of 2007–2009 was the worst since the Great Depression. High rates of unemployment and large declines in output can result in severe hardships for many households and can drive firms into bankruptcy. In this chapter, we develop the *IS–MP* model to explain changes in real GDP, the inflation rate, and interest rates. This model will help us to understand why economic fluctuations occur and how policymakers use monetary policy and fiscal policy to help reduce the severity of recessions.

9.1

Learning Objective

Explain how the *IS* curve represents the relationship between the real interest rate and aggregate expenditure.

IS–MP model A macroeconomic model consisting of an *IS* curve, which represents equilibrium in the goods market; an *MP* curve, which represents monetary policy; and a Phillips curve, which represents the short-run relationship between the output gap (which is the percentage difference between actual and potential real GDP) and the inflation rate.

***IS* curve** A curve in the *IS–MP* model that shows the combination of the real interest rate and aggregate output that represents equilibrium in the market for goods and services.

***MP* curve** A curve in the *IS–MP* model that represents Federal Reserve monetary policy.

Phillips curve A curve that represents the short-run relationship between the output gap (or the unemployment rate) and the inflation rate.

The *IS* Curve: The Relationship Between Real Interest Rates and Aggregate Expenditure

The ***IS–MP* model** is a macroeconomic model that analyzes the determinants of real GDP, the inflation rate, and the real interest rate in the short run.[1] We will use the *IS–MP* model to show why real GDP fluctuates in the short run and to analyze the effects of *monetary policy* and *fiscal policy*. To be useful, every model must simplify reality. The *IS–MP* model is less complete than some other macroeconomic models, including some that the Fed uses to prepare its forecasts. Whether a model is too simplified—or not simplified enough—depends on the context in which the model is being used. For our purposes, the *IS–MP* model is sufficiently complete to explain the main reasons real GDP fluctuates and to allow us to understand the key aspects of monetary policy and fiscal policy. Modern central banks, such as the Federal Reserve, set interest rates to achieve macroeconomic objectives such as price stability and high employment. Using the *IS–MP* model is an effective way of showing how central banks attempt to affect the economy. The *IS* curve also allows us to understand how governments can use their ability to tax and spend to achieve macroeconomic objectives.

The *IS–MP* model consists of three parts:

1. The ***IS* curve**, which represents equilibrium in the market for goods and services
2. The ***MP* curve**, which represents Federal Reserve monetary policy
3. The **Phillips curve**, which represents the short-run relationship between the output gap (which is the percentage difference between real GDP and potential GDP) and the inflation rate

We begin by analyzing the *IS* curve.

Equilibrium in the Goods Market

Economists define *aggregate expenditure* on real GDP as the sum of consumption demand, C; demand for investment in business plant and equipment, inventories, and housing, I; government purchases of goods and services, G; and net exports (or exports of goods and services minus imports of goods and services), NX. So, we can write that aggregate expenditure, AE, is:

$$AE = C + I + G + NX.$$

Recall that gross domestic product (GDP) is the market value of all final goods and services produced in a country during a period of time. Nominal GDP is calculated using the current year's prices, while real GDP is calculated using the prices in a base year. Because real GDP gives a good measure of a country's output, corrected for changes in the price level, it is the measure of aggregate output that we will use initially. The *goods market* includes trade in all final goods and services that the economy produces during a particular period of time—in other words, all goods that are included in real GDP. Equilibrium occurs in the goods market when the value of goods and services demanded—aggregate expenditure, AE—equals the value of goods and services produced—real GDP, Y. So, at equilibrium:

$$AE = Y.$$

What if aggregate expenditure is less than real GDP? In that case, some goods that were produced are not sold, and inventories of unsold goods will increase. For example, if General Motors (GM) produces and ships to dealers 250,000 cars in a particular month but sells only 225,000, inventories of cars on the lots of GM's dealers will rise by 25,000 cars. (Notice that because inventories are counted as part of investment, in this situation, *actual investment spending* will be greater than *planned investment spending*.) If the decline in demand is affecting not just automobiles but other goods and services as well, firms are

[1]Economists love acronyms, even if they can sometimes be mysterious. In this case, *IS* stands for *investment and saving*, and *MP* stands for *monetary policy*.

Table 9.1 The Relationship Between Aggregate Expenditure and GDP

If aggregate expenditure is . . .	then . . .	and . . .
equal to GDP	there are no unexpected changes in inventories	the goods market is in equilibrium.
less than GDP	inventories rise	GDP and employment decrease.
greater than GDP	inventories fall	GDP and employment increase.

likely to reduce production and lay off workers: Real GDP and employment will decline, and the economy will be in a recession.

If aggregate expenditure is greater than GDP, however, spending will be greater than production, and firms will sell more goods and services than they had expected to sell. If GM produces 250,000 cars but sells 300,000, then inventories of cars on dealers' lots will decline by 50,000 cars. (In this case, because dealers are unexpectedly drawing down inventories, actual investment spending will be less than planned investment spending.) The dealers will be likely to increase their orders from GM's factories. If sales exceed production not just for automobiles but for other goods and services as well, firms will increase production and hire more workers: Real GDP and employment will increase, and the economy will be in an expansion.

Only when aggregate expenditure equals GDP will firms sell what they expected to sell. In that case, firms will experience no unexpected changes in their inventories, and they will not have an incentive to increase or decrease production. The goods market will be in equilibrium. Table 9.1 summarizes the relationship between aggregate expenditure and GDP.

We can use a simple *45°-line diagram* to illustrate equilibrium in the goods market. The 45°-line diagram analysis is based on the simplifying assumption that of the four components of aggregate expenditure—*C*, *I*, *G*, and *NX*—changes in real GDP affect only *C*, consumption spending. To see why consumption depends on GDP, remember that when we measure the value of total production, we are at the same time measuring the value of total income. This is true because, for example, when you buy a DVD at Best Buy for $10, the entire $10 becomes someone's income. Some of the $10 becomes wages for the person working the cash register, some becomes profit for Best Buy, some becomes wages for the workers who produced the DVD, and so on. If we add up the value of all the goods and services purchased, we have also added up all the current income produced during that period in the economy. (Sales taxes and some other relatively minor items cause a difference between the value for GDP and the value for *national income*, as shown in the federal government's statistics. But this difference is not important for our analysis.)

Studies have shown that households spend more when their current disposable income, Y^D, increases, and spend less when their current disposable income decreases.[2] Recall that disposable income equals total income (Y) plus transfer payments (TR) minus taxes (T), or:

$$Y^D = Y + TR - T.$$[3]

The relationship between current consumption spending and current income, or GDP, is called the *consumption function*. Algebraically, we can write:

$$C = \overline{C} + MPC \times Y^D,$$

[2]Many economists believe that consumption is better explained by a household's *permanent income* than by its current income. A household's permanent income is the level of income that it expects to receive over time. A household's current income might differ from its permanent income due to a temporary job loss, an illness, winning a lottery, having a year of particularly high or low investment income, and so forth. For our analysis, we ignore this complication here. We provide a more detailed discussion of the determinants of consumption in Chapter 14.

[3]Keep in mind that we are using Y to stand for *both* real GDP and total income. At this point, it may be helpful to review the discussion in Chapter 2, pages 33–41, of the relationship among GDP and the different measures of income.

where $\overline{C}$ represents consumption expenditures that are independent of the level of income. (We use the "bar" designation over the C to indicate that these expenditures are *autonomous*, or independent of changes in income.) The **marginal propensity to consume (*MPC*)** equals

Marginal propensity to consume (*MPC*) The slope of the consumption function: The amount by which consumption spending changes when disposable income changes.

$$\frac{\Delta C}{\Delta Y^D},$$

so it is the slope of the consumption function and shows the change in consumption when disposable income changes. The *MPC* will have a value between 0 and 1. For instance, if the *MPC* is equal to 0.90, then households are spending \$0.90 of every additional dollar they earn. If taxes and transfer payments are constant, then a change in disposable income is the same as a change in total income, so the consumption function shows the relationship between consumption and total income, holding taxes and transfer payments constant. Therefore, we can also write that

$$MPC = \frac{\Delta C}{\Delta Y}.$$

Because we are focusing on the effect of changes in GDP on aggregate expenditure, assuming that *I*, *G*, and *NX* don't depend on GDP is the same as assuming that their values are fixed. Just as we do with consumption, we can designate a variable whose value is autonomous—or, in this case, fixed with respect to GDP—by placing a bar over it. So, we have the following expression for aggregate expenditure, substituting in the expression above for *C*:

$$AE = \overline{C} + (MPC \times Y^D) + \overline{I} + \overline{G} + \overline{NX},$$

where $\overline{I}$ represents investment expenditures that are independent of GDP, $\overline{G}$ represents government expenditures that are independent of GDP, and $\overline{NX}$ represents net exports that are independent of GDP.

Panel (a) of Figure 9.1 graphically shows equilibrium in the goods market using the 45°-line diagram. On the vertical axis, we measure aggregate expenditure. On the horizontal

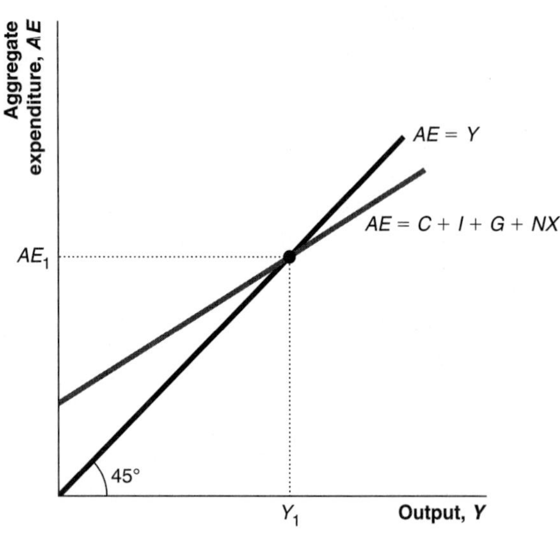

(a) Equilibrium in the goods market

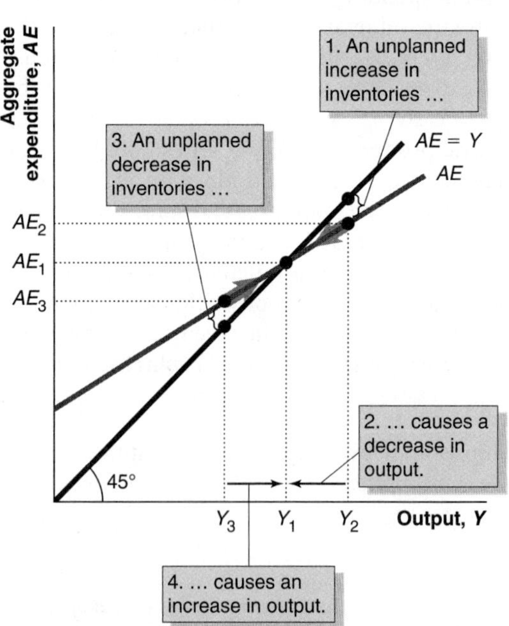

(b) Adjustment to equilibrium in the goods market

Figure 9.1 Illustrating Equilibrium in the Goods Market

Panel (a) shows that equilibrium in the goods market occurs at Y_1, where the *AE* line crosses the 45° line. In panel (b), if the level of real GDP is initially Y_2, aggregate expenditure is AE_2. Rising inventories cause firms to cut production, and the economy will move down the *AE* line until it reaches equilibrium at Y_1. If real GDP is initially Y_3, aggregate expenditure is AE_3. Falling inventories cause firms to increase production, and the economy will move up the *AE* line until it reaches equilibrium at Y_1. ●

axis, we measure real GDP, or real total income, Y. The 45° line represents all points that are equal distances from the two axes, or in this case, all the points where $AE = Y$. Therefore, any point along the 45° line is potentially a point of equilibrium in the goods market. At any given time, though, equilibrium is the point where the aggregate expenditure line crosses the 45° line. We draw the aggregate expenditure line as upward sloping because as GDP increases, consumption spending increases, while the other components of aggregate expenditure remain constant.

Panel (a) of Figure 9.1 shows that equilibrium in the goods market occurs at Y_1, where the AE line crosses the 45° line. Panel (b) shows why the goods market is not in equilibrium at other levels of real GDP. For example, if real GDP is initially Y_2, aggregate expenditure is only AE_2. With spending less than production, there is an unexpected increase in inventories. Rising inventories cause firms to cut production, and the economy will move down the AE line until it reaches equilibrium at Y_1. If real GDP is initially Y_3, aggregate expenditure is AE_3. With spending greater than production, there is an unexpected decrease in inventories. Falling inventories cause firms to increase production, and the economy will move up the AE line until it reaches equilibrium at Y_1.

The Multiplier Effect

In Figure 9.1, Y_1 is the equilibrium level of GDP, but it is not necessarily the level policymakers want to achieve. The Fed's goal is to have equilibrium GDP close to potential GDP, which is the level of real GDP attained when all firms are producing at capacity. The capacity of a firm is *not* the maximum output the firm is capable of producing. Rather, it is the firm's production when operating at normal hours, using a workforce of normal size. At potential GDP, the economy achieves full employment, and cyclical unemployment is reduced to zero. So, potential GDP is sometimes called *full-employment GDP*. The level of potential GDP increases over time as the labor force grows, new factories and office buildings are built, new machinery and equipment is installed, and technological change takes place.

In Figure 9.2, we see what happens if the economy is initially in equilibrium at point A, with real GDP, Y_1, equal to potential GDP, Y^P, and then aggregate expenditure falls. Assume that spending on residential construction declines, so the investment component, I, of aggregate expenditure falls. As a result, the aggregate expenditure line shifts from AE_1 to AE_2, and equilibrium is now at point B. With spending below production, there is an unintended increase in inventories. Firms respond to the inventory buildup by cutting production, and

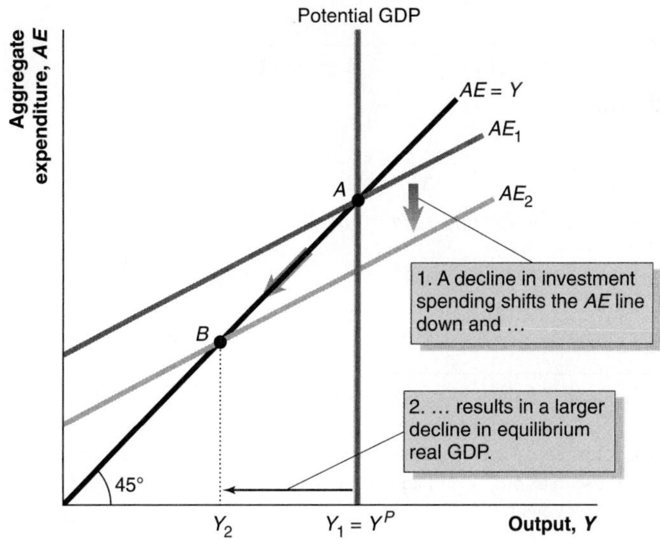

Figure 9.2

The Multiplier Effect

Point A shows the economy initially at equilibrium with real GDP, Y_1, equal to potential GDP, Y^P. Then investment, I, declines. As a result, the aggregate expenditure line shifts from AE_1 to AE_2. Short-run equilibrium is now at point B, with a new level of real GDP, Y_2. The decline in GDP is greater than the initial decline in investment spending that caused it. ●

the economy's new short-run equilibrium is at point *B*, with real GDP equal to, Y_2. Note that the decline in GDP is greater than the decline in investment spending that caused it.

Remember that we are assuming that investment spending, government purchases, and net exports are all autonomous, while consumption spending consists of an autonomous component, $\overline{C}$, and a component that depends on—or is *induced* by—total income, $(MPC \times Y)$. A decline in autonomous expenditure results in an equivalent decline in income, which leads to an *induced* decline in consumption. For example, as spending on residential construction declines, homebuilders cut production, lay off workers, and cut their demand for construction materials. Falling incomes in the construction industry lead households to reduce their spending on cars, furniture, appliances, and other goods and services. As production declines in those industries, so does income, leading to further declines in consumption, and so on.

Multiplier The change in equilibrium GDP divided by the change in autonomous expenditure.

Multiplier effect The process by which an initial change in autonomous expenditure leads to a larger change in equilibrium GDP.

The **multiplier** is the change in equilibrium GDP divided by the initial change in autonomous expenditure. The series of induced changes in consumption spending that result from an initial change in autonomous expenditure is called the **multiplier effect**. In symbols, the multiplier for a change in investment spending is:

$$\text{Multiplier} = \frac{\Delta Y}{\Delta \overline{I}}.$$

How large is the multiplier? It is quite large in our simple model. To see this, recall that our expression for aggregate expenditure is:

$$AE = \overline{C} + MPC \times Y^D + \overline{I} + \overline{G} + \overline{NX},$$

and that at equilibrium:

$$AE = Y.$$

So, substituting, we have:

$$Y = \overline{C} + MPC \times Y^D + \overline{I} + \overline{G} + \overline{NX},$$

and using the definition for disposable income, we get:

$$Y = \overline{C} + MPC \times (Y + \overline{TR} - \overline{T}) + \overline{I} + \overline{G} + \overline{NX},$$

where we put bars above taxes and transfers to indicate that we are assuming that they too are autonomous and independent of the current level of income. Rearranging terms, we get:

$$Y = \frac{\overline{C} + \overline{I} + \overline{G} + \overline{NX} + (MPC \times \overline{TR}) - (MPC \times \overline{T})}{(1 - MPC)}. \quad (9.1)$$

If investment changes, while everything else remains constant, then we have:

$$\Delta Y = \frac{\Delta \overline{I}}{(1 - MPC)},$$

or, rearranging terms:

$$\frac{\Delta Y}{\Delta \overline{I}} = \frac{1}{(1 - MPC)}.$$

In general, we can write the expenditure multiplier as:[4]

$$\frac{\Delta Y}{\Delta \text{ Autonomous expenditure}} = \frac{1}{(1 - MPC)}. \quad (9.2)$$

[4]There is also a multiplier for changes in autonomous taxes: $\frac{\Delta Y}{\Delta \overline{T}} = \frac{-MPC}{(1 - MPC)}$, and a multiplier for transfer payments: $\frac{\Delta Y}{\Delta \overline{TR}} = \frac{MPC}{(1 - MPC)}$. Each of these multipliers is smaller than the autonomous expenditure multiplier because when households receive a tax cut or an increase in transfer payments, they save part of the dollar amount. Therefore, households only spend an amount equal to the *MPC* multiplied by the dollar amount of the tax cut or transfer payment.

If, as we assumed earlier, the *MPC* is equal to 0.90, then the value of the multiplier for investment expenditure equals:

$$\frac{\Delta Y}{\Delta \bar{I}} = \frac{1}{(1 - 0.90)} = \frac{1}{0.10} = 10.$$

So, a decline in investment spending of $1 billion would lead to a decline in equilibrium real GDP of $10 billion. When multiplier analysis was first developed in the 1930s by the British economist John Maynard Keynes and his colleagues, they believed that a large multiplier effect helped to explain the severity of the Great Depression: With a large multiplier, a relatively small decline in investment spending could have led to the large declines in GDP experienced in the United States and Europe.

Constructing the *IS* Curve

To understand how monetary policy and financial markets affect output, we need to explore the effect of interest rates on spending. Changes in the real interest rate affect three of the components of aggregate expenditure: consumption, *C*; investment, *I*; and net exports, *NX*. We focus on the effect of changes in the real interest rate because it is the interest rate most relevant to the spending decisions of households and firms. Recall that the real interest rate equals the nominal interest rate minus the expected inflation rate. A decrease in the real interest rate makes firms more willing to invest in plant and equipment and makes households more likely to purchase new houses, so *I* increases. Similarly, a decrease in the real interest rate gives consumers an incentive to spend rather than save and reduces their cost of borrowing, so *C* increases. And a lower domestic real interest rate makes returns on domestic financial assets less attractive relative to those on foreign assets, decreasing the exchange rate. The decrease in the exchange rate decreases imports and increases exports, thereby increasing *NX*. An increase in the real interest rate will have the opposite effect—decreasing *I*, *C*, and *NX*.

Panel (a) of Figure 9.3 uses the 45°-line diagram to show the effect of changes in the real interest rate on equilibrium in the goods market. With the real interest rate initially

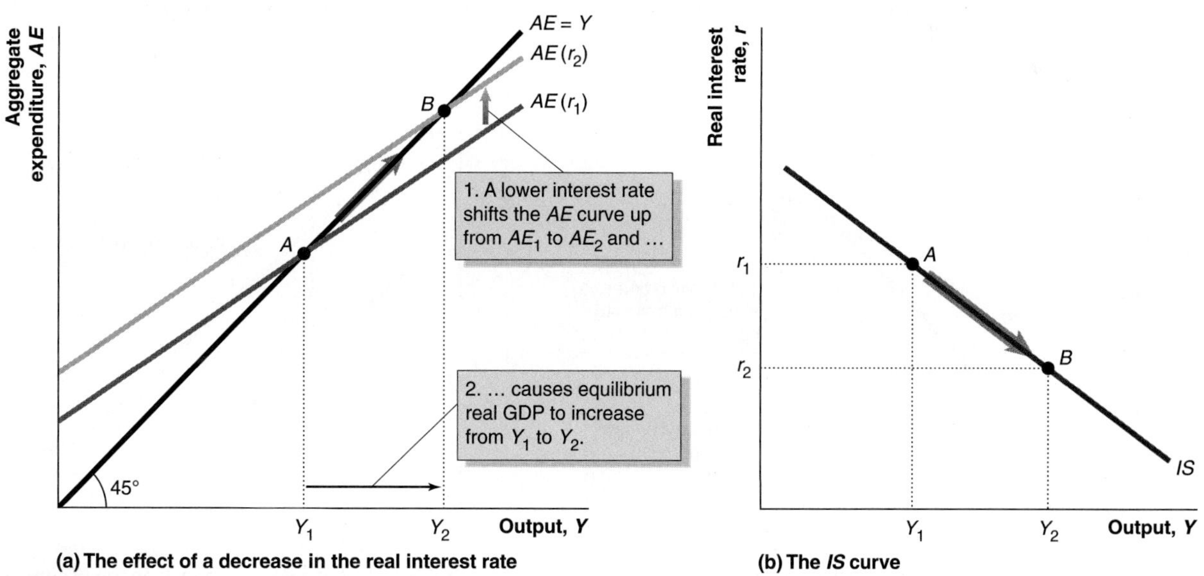

Figure 9.3 Deriving the *IS* Curve

Panel (a) uses the 45°-line diagram to show the effect of changes in the real interest rate on equilibrium in the goods market. With the real interest rate initially at r_1, the aggregate expenditure line is $AE(r_1)$, and the equilibrium level of real GDP is Y_1 (point *A*). If the interest rate falls from r_1 to r_2, the aggregate expenditure line shifts upward from $AE(r_1)$ to $AE(r_2)$, and the equilibrium level of real GDP increases from Y_1 to Y_2 (point *B*). In panel (b), we plot the points from panel (a) to form the *IS* curve. The points *A* and *B* in panel (b) correspond to the points *A* and *B* in panel (a). ●

at r_1, the aggregate expenditure line is $AE(r_1)$, and the equilibrium level of real GDP is Y_1 (point *A*). If the interest falls from r_1 to r_2, the aggregate expenditure line shifts upward from $AE(r_1)$ to $AE(r_2)$, and the equilibrium level of real GDP increases from Y_1 to Y_2 (point *B*).

In panel (b), we use the results from panel (a) to construct the *IS* curve, which shows the combinations of the real interest rate and real GDP where the goods market is in equilibrium. We know that at every equilibrium point in the 45°-line diagram in panel (a), aggregate expenditure equals real GDP. In panel (b), we plot these points on a graph with the real interest rate on the vertical axis and the level of real GDP on the horizontal axis. The points *A* and *B* in panel (b) correspond to the points *A* and *B* in panel (a). The *IS* curve is downward sloping because a lower interest rate causes an increase in aggregate expenditure and a higher equilibrium level of real GDP.

Shifts of the *IS* Curve

The *IS* curve summarizes the goods market by showing the effect of changes in the real interest rate on aggregate expenditure, holding constant all other factors that might affect the willingness of households, firms, and governments to spend. Therefore, an increase or a decrease in the real interest rate results in *a movement along the IS curve.* Changing other factors that affect aggregate expenditure will cause a *shift of the IS curve.* These other factors—other than a change in the real interest rate—that lead to changes in aggregate expenditure are called *demand shocks.* For example, spending on new residential construction in the United States declined by 7% in 2006, 19% in 2007, 24% in 2008, and 23% in 2009. This decline in a component of *I* was a *negative demand shock* that, holding all other factors constant, shifted the *IS* curve to the left. During late 2009 and the first half of 2010, more rapid economic recoveries in China and Europe than in the United States resulted in U.S. exports increasing at an annual rate of 24% during the fourth quarter of 2009 and 11% during the first quarter of 2010. This increase in *NX* was a *positive demand shock* that, holding all other factors constant, shifted the *IS* curve to the right.

Figure 9.4 shows that for any given level of the real interest rate, a positive demand shock shifts the *IS* curve to the right. To see the effect of the shock on output, assume that

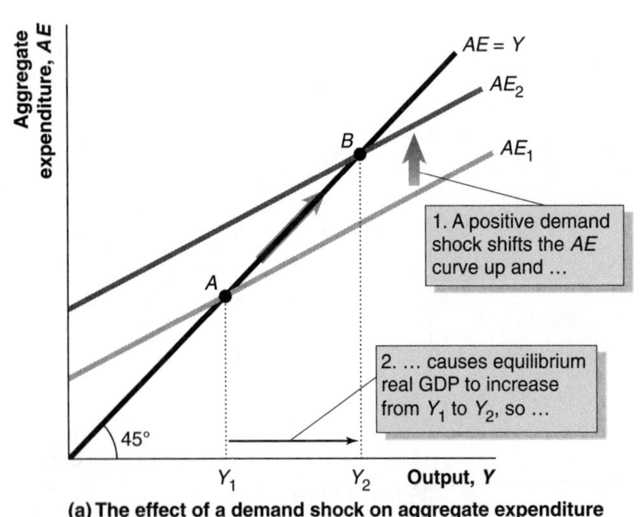

(a) The effect of a demand shock on aggregate expenditure

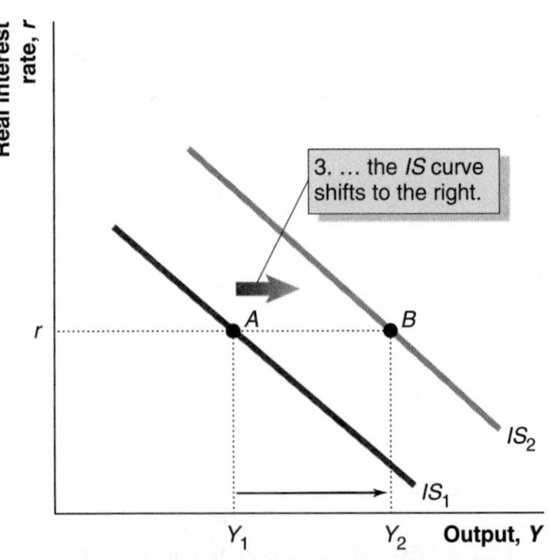

(b) The effect of a demand shock on the *IS* curve

Figure 9.4 A Positive Demand Shock and the *IS* Curve

In panel (a), the positive demand shock shifts up the *AE* curve, and equilibrium moves from point *A* to point *B*. In panel (b), the *IS* curve shifts from IS_1 to IS_2. Points *A* and *B* represent the same combination of the real interest rate and level of real GDP in both panels. ●

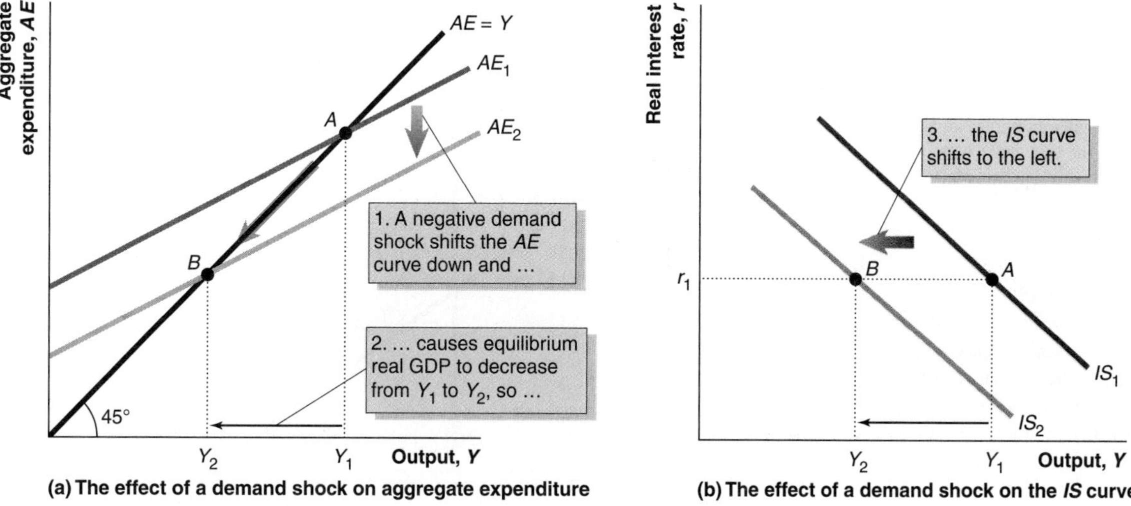

Figure 9.5 A Negative Demand Shock and the *IS* Curve

In panel (a), the negative demand shock shifts down the *AE* curve, and equilibrium moves from point *A* to point *B*. In panel (b), the *IS* curve shifts from IS_1 to IS_2. Points *A* and *B* represent the same combination of the real interest rate and level of real GDP in both panels. ●

the real interest rate is unchanged at r_1. In panel (a), the initial aggregate expenditure curve is AE_1, so the economy is at point *A* and real GDP is Y_1. A positive demand shock, such as an increase in net exports or an increase in government purchases, will cause the aggregate expenditure curve to shift up from AE_1 to AE_2, so equilibrium in the goods market now occurs at point *B*, with a higher level of real GDP, Y_2. In panel (b), the economy begins at the combination of r_1 and Y_1. Given the assumption of a constant real interest rate, the positive demand shock moves equilibrium to point *B*, where real GDP has increased from Y_1 to Y_2, so the *IS* curve has shifted to the right, from IS_1 to IS_2.

Figure 9.5 shows the effect of a negative demand shock on the *IS* curve. In panel (a), a negative demand shock, such as a decrease in spending on residential housing or an increase in taxes, will cause the aggregate expenditure curve to shift down from AE_1 to AE_2, so equilibrium in the goods market now occurs at point *B*, with a lower level of real GDP, Y_2. In panel (b), equilibrium has moved from point *A* to point *B*, and real GDP has fallen from Y_1 to Y_2. So, the *IS* curve has shifted to the left, from IS_1 to IS_2.

When working with the *IS* curve, you should remember this simple rule: If a demand shock increases aggregate expenditure, the *IS* curve will shift to the right, and if a demand shock decreases aggregate expenditure, the *IS* curve will shift to the left.

The *IS* Curve and the Output Gap

In Chapter 8, we explained that economists measure the economic fluctuations that occur during a business cycle using the output gap, which is the percentage difference between real GDP and potential GDP. When output decreases during a recession, the output gap becomes negative when real GDP is below potential GDP. When output increases during an expansion, the output gap eventually becomes positive as real GDP rises above potential GDP. Because economists measure economic fluctuations using the output gap and because the Federal Reserve focuses on the output gap rather than on the level of real GDP when conducting monetary policy, it would be useful to incorporate the output gap into our macroeconomic model. The graph of the *IS* curve shown in the previous figures has the level of real GDP, rather than the output gap, on the horizontal axis. Can we replace the level of real GDP with the output gap in the *IS* curve graph? Yes, we can, with the

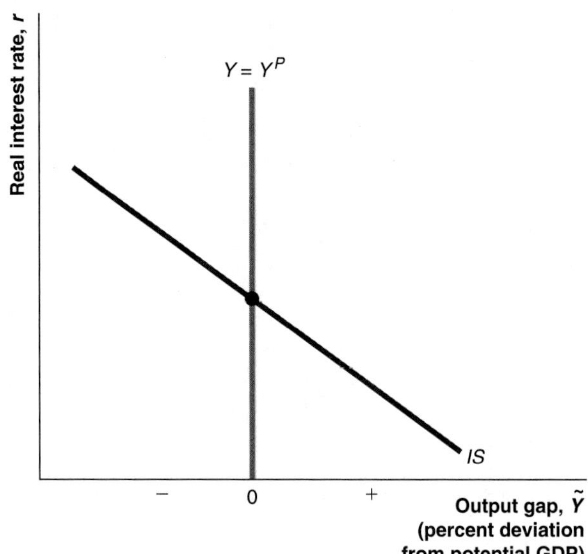

Figure 9.6

The *IS* Curve Using the Output Gap

The graph shows the output gap, rather than the level of real GDP, on the horizontal axis. Values to the left of zero on the horizontal axis represent negative values for the output gap—periods during which real GDP is below potential GDP—and values to the right of zero on the horizontal axis represent positive values for the output gap—periods during which real GDP is above potential GDP. The vertical line, $Y = Y^P$, is also the point where the output gap is zero. ●

following qualification: We should think of changes in the real interest rate as affecting the level of investment spending, consumption spending, and net exports *relative to potential GDP*. For instance, when the real interest rate falls and *C*, *I*, and *NX* increase, the increase in aggregate expenditure will cause real GDP, *Y*, to increase relative to potential GDP, Y^P. In that case, when we graph the *IS* curve with the real interest rate on the vertical axis and the output gap on the horizontal axis, the *IS* curve is still downward sloping.

Figure 9.6 shows the *IS* curve graph with the output gap on the horizontal axis. We use the symbol $\tilde{Y}$ to distinguish the output gap from real GDP, *Y*. As a reference, we have included a vertical line where $Y = Y^P$, which is also the point where the output gap is zero. Normally, we draw graphs with the vertical axis beginning at a value of zero on the horizontal axis. In this case, though, our graphs are easier to understand if we move the vertical axis to the left, leaving zero in the middle of the horizontal axis. It's important to note that values to the left of zero on the horizontal axis represent negative values for the output gap, and values to the right of zero on the horizontal axis represent positive values for the output gap.

9.2

Learning Objective

Use the monetary policy, *MP*, curve to show how the interest rate set by the central bank helps to determine the output gap.

The Monetary Policy Curve: The Relationship Between the Central Bank's Target Interest Rate and Output

The second part of the *IS–MP* model is the monetary policy, or *MP*, curve. The Fed conducts monetary policy by managing the money supply and interest rates to pursue macroeconomic policy objectives such as price stability, high employment, and high rates of growth. During the past several decades, the Fed, like most other central banks, has focused its monetary policy actions on interest rates. Therefore, we call the curve showing the effect of the real interest rate on the output gap the monetary policy, or *MP*, curve. One problem the Fed faces in carrying out monetary policy is that it controls a key short-term nominal interest rate, the *federal funds rate*, but not long-term real interest rates. It is the long-term real interest rate on mortgage loans or on corporate bonds that is relevant to households when they make decisions about buying houses and to firms when they make decisions about investing in new factories, equipment, and office buildings. As we will discuss in more detail in the next chapter, the federal funds rate is the interest rate that banks charge each other on short-term loans. To explain the link between the federal funds rate that the Fed controls and long-term real interest rates that affect aggregate expenditures, we need to review the Fisher effect from Chapter 6 and the link between short-term and long-term interest rates, known as the *term structure of interest rates*, from Chapter 3. After this discussion, it should be clear that the Fed *influences* long-term real interest rates, but the Fed does not have complete *control* over these interest rates.

The Link Between the Short-Term Nominal Interest Rate and Long-Term Real Interest Rate

In Chapter 3, we discussed the **term structure of interest rates**, which is the relationship among the interest rates on bonds that are otherwise similar but that have different maturities. As we saw, the interest rate on a long-term bond equals the average of the expected interest rates on short-term bonds plus a *term premium* to compensate lenders for the possibility that interest rates will change while they own the long-term bond. Recall that when interest rates fluctuate, so do the prices of bonds, thereby potentially causing losses to investors in bonds. The **term premium** is the additional interest that investors require in order to be willing to buy a long-term bond rather than a comparable sequence of short-term bonds. Therefore, if there is a difference between the short-term nominal interest rate—say, the interest rate on a three-month Treasury bill—and the long-term nominal interest rate—say, the interest rate on a 10-year Treasury note—the difference is due to two factors:

Term structure of interest rates The relationship among the interest rates on bonds that are otherwise similar but that have different maturities.

Term premium The additional interest that investors require in order to be willing to buy a long-term bond rather than a comparable sequence of short-term bonds.

1. Investors' expectations of future short-term interest rates, as given by the term structures
2. The term premium

We can combine these two factors into what we will call the *term structure effect*, or *TSE*. So, we can say that the difference between the short-term nominal interest rate, i, and the long-term nominal interest rate, i_{LT}, is:

$$i_{LT} = i + TSE.^5$$

This equation shows that if the Fed increases the short-term nominal interest rate today and the term structure effect stays constant, the long-term nominal interest rate will also increase. The equation also shows that lower expected short-term interest rates in the *future* will reduce long-term interest rates *today* because the term structure effect will become smaller. That is, expectations about the future can have an important effect on interest rates today and, therefore, on current spending. (If you are having trouble understanding how expectations of future short-term rates affect long-term rates today, you may want to review the discussion of the term structure in Chapter 3 on pages 90–92.) Similarly, if the term premium that investors require to invest in long-term bonds increases, then *TSE* will increase, which increases the long-term nominal interest rate, i_{LT}.

Chapter 3 also explained the **risk structure of interest rates**, which shows the relationship among interest rates on bonds that have different characteristics but the same maturity. As we saw, a key way in which bonds differ is with respect to **default risk**, which is the risk that a borrower will fail to make payments of interest or principal. The bonds of private corporations have higher interest rates than do comparable bonds issued by the

Risk structure of interest rates The relationship among interest rates on bonds that have different characteristics but the same maturity.

Default risk The risk that a borrower will fail to make payments of interest or principal.

[5]This equation is a useful simplification that highlights the relationship between short-term and long-term nominal interest rates. There is one technical detail that we should mention. In the simplest case, where the long-term bond is a two-year bond, the equation for the *TSE* is: $TSE = \frac{i^e_{t+1}}{2} - \frac{i_t}{2} + i^{TP}$, where i_t is the interest rate on the one-year bond today, i^e_{t+1} is the interest rate expected on the one-year bond one year from now, and i^{TP} is the term premium on the two-year bond. The equation shows that an increase in the short-term nominal interest rate reduces the *TSE* term. However, a 1-percentage-point increase in the short-term nominal interest rate will decrease the *TSE* term by just 0.5 percent point. So, an increase in the short-term nominal interest rate will still increase the long-term nominal interest rate, and the basic message of the equation in the text is correct: Increases in the short-term nominal interest rate will increase the long-term nominal interest rate.

U.S. Treasury, to compensate investors for the possibility that the corporations might default on the bonds. This higher interest rate is called a *default-risk premium.* Households must also pay a default-risk premium when they borrow money because they may not be able to make all the interest and principal payments on loans that they receive. If we let *DP* stand for the default-risk premium, then we have the following relationship between the long-term nominal interest rates and the short-term nominal interest rates:

$$i_{LT} = i + TSE + DP. \tag{9.3}$$

Finally, we need to consider the link between the long-term *nominal* interest rate and the long-term *real* interest rate. As we saw in Chapter 2, to calculate the expected real interest rate we subtract the expected inflation rate from the nominal interest rate:

$$r = i - \pi^e.$$

This relationship holds for both short-term and long-term interest rates. So, we can say that the long-term real interest rate equals the long-term nominal interest rate minus the expected inflation rate, or:

$$r_{LT} = i_{LT} - \pi^e.$$

Combining this equation and Equation (9.3), we can come up with our final equation for the real interest rate:

$$r_{LT} = i + TSE + DP - \pi^e. \tag{9.4}$$

Because the Fed has good control over the short-term nominal interest rate, it controls the long-term real interest rate as well, *provided that term structure effects, the default-risk premium, and the expected inflation rate all remain unchanged.* In practice, the Fed's job is complicated by the fact that these other three factors may move in ways that offset the Fed's policy action. For example, the Fed might want to stimulate the economy by lowering the real interest rate so that households and firms increase their spending on houses, factories, office buildings, and other investment goods. To bring about this outcome, the Fed lowers the short-term nominal interest rate. However, the long-term real interest rate may not decline if one of these three events occurs: (1) lenders, including investors in the bond market, believe that future short-term nominal rates will be higher; or (2) lenders require a higher default-risk premium; or (3) lenders lower their expectations of the future inflation rate. If one of these three events occurs, the Fed's attempts to stimulate the economy may be ineffective.

These other three factors are not entirely independent of Fed actions. For instance, if the Fed is able to convince lenders that it will keep short-term nominal rates low for an extended period of time, then the term structure effect will likely be unchanged. The Fed may actually bring about a reduction in the default-risk premium if lenders believe that the Fed's expansionary policy will bring the economy out of a recession, thereby reducing the probability that borrowers will default on loans. Still, events beyond the control of the Fed can drive the default-risk premium.

The effect of Fed actions on the expected inflation rate can be complex. If the Fed lowers the short-term nominal interest rate to stimulate the economy, lenders, households, and firms may believe that increased economic activity will lead to a higher inflation rate. Equation (9.4) shows that an increase in the expected inflation rate would reinforce the Fed's action by further decreasing the real interest rate. Similarly, if the Fed increases the short-term nominal interest rate to slow down the economy, the expected inflation rate may fall. A decrease in the expected inflation rate would reinforce the Fed's action by further increasing the real interest rate. As we saw in Chapter 6, however, the *Fisher effect* indicates that increases in expected inflation typically result in increases in long-term nominal interest rates. In the long run, the Fisher effect works exactly, so a 1-percentage-point increase in the expected inflation rate will result in a 1-percentage-point increase in the long-term nominal interest rate, leaving the real interest rate unchanged. In this case, the effect of Fed policy on the expected inflation rate would not affect the real interest rate because there would be offsetting movements in the long-term nominal interest rate. For example, assume that the long-term nominal interest rate is 5% and the expected inflation rate is 2%, so the long-term real interest rate is 3%. If as a result of Fed policy, the expected inflation rate increases from 2% to 4%, the long-term nominal interest rate will increase from 5% to 7%, leaving the long-term real interest rate unchanged, at 3%. However, in the short-run, the Fisher effect does not typically work exactly because the long-term nominal interest rate usually does not rise and fall percentage point-for-percentage point with the expected inflation rate. Therefore, an increase in the expected inflation rate may result in a decrease in the real interest rate, and a decrease in the expected inflation rate may result in an increase in the real interest rate.

Interest Rate Movements During the 2007–2009 Recession

The behavior of interest rates during the 2007–2009 financial crisis and recession can illustrate the point that the Fed can influence long-term interest rates but does not have complete control of those interest rates. During the financial crisis, the Fed reduced the federal funds rate to nearly zero and indicated that this interest rate would remain near zero for a long time. However, the interest rates that households and firms paid did not fall to zero because they had to pay a term premium on long-term loans and a default-risk premium to compensate for the possibility that they would be unable to repay the loans. For example, the default-risk premium as measured by the spread between the interest rate on an Aaa corporate bond, the lowest default-risk corporate bond, and a 10-year Treasury note rose from 0.9% on August 1, 2007, before the beginning of the financial crisis, to 3.0% on March 18, 2009. (Recall that Aaa is the highest rating that a credit rating agency—such as Moody's—gives a bond.) This increase in the default-risk premium offset some of the efforts of the Fed to keep interest rates low.

The default-risk premium did not increase steadily through the entire financial crisis. Instead, there were episodes of sudden large increases in the default-risk premium, such as the one that occurred following the bankruptcy of Lehman Brothers in September 2008, when that investment bank defaulted on its bonds, loans, and other debts. The interest rate on Aaa-rated corporate bonds increased by nearly 1 percentage point from 5.5% on September 2 to 6.6% on October 17, even as the Fed was taking actions to reduce short-term interest rates. Most of this increase was due to an increase in the default-risk premium from 1.8% on September 2, 2008, to 2.6% on October 17, 2008. The default-risk premium increased to compensate investors for what they saw as the increased likelihood that borrowers might default.

Deriving the *MP* Curve Using the Money Market Model

The Fed and other central banks have explicit interest rate targets and adjust the money supply to keep interest rates at those targets. We discuss interest rate targets in Chapter 10. For now, we assume that the Fed has determined a target interest rate and adjusts the money supply to hit that target rate. In practice, the Fed targets the federal funds rate, while movements in the money supply have a greater effect on other short-term nominal interest rates, such as the interest rate on three-month Treasury bills. Figure 9.7 shows three short-term nominal interest rates: the federal funds rate, the three-month Treasury bill rate, and the three-month commercial paper rate. (Corporations use *commercial paper* to borrow funds for a short period, generally three months or less.) The figure shows that the three rates moved very closely together between 1997 and 2011. Therefore, the Fed can be confident that when it takes actions to increase or decrease one short-term rate, other short-term rates will move in the same direction, and which short-term nominal interest rate we focus on is not particularly important.

Figure 9.7

Short-Term Nominal Interest Rates Typically Move Together

The federal funds rate, the three-month Treasury bill rate, and the three-month commercial paper rate all move closely together. The Fed can therefore be confident that when it takes actions to increase or decrease one short-term rate, other short-term rates will move in the same direction.

Source: Federal Reserve Bank of St. Louis. ●

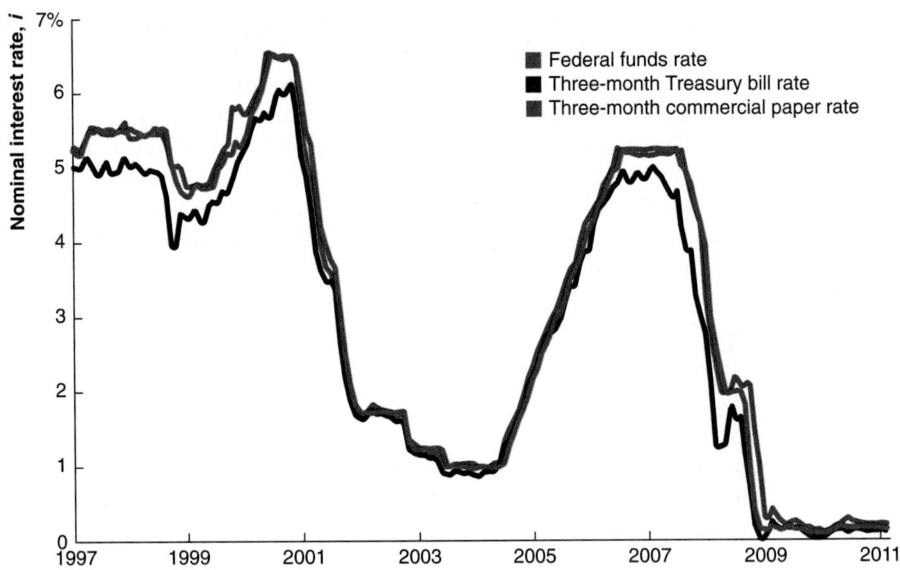

When we derive the *MP* curve, we make the following assumptions:

1. The *TSE* and *DP* terms in Equation (9.4) on page 314 are constant.
2. The expected inflation rate, π^e, is constant.

Given these assumptions, by changing the short-term nominal interest rate, the Fed can change the long-term real interest rate that is relevant for consumption and investment expenditures.

Figure 9.8 shows how we can derive the *MP* curve by using our model for the money market from Chapter 3. Remember that if the expected inflation rate, the term structure

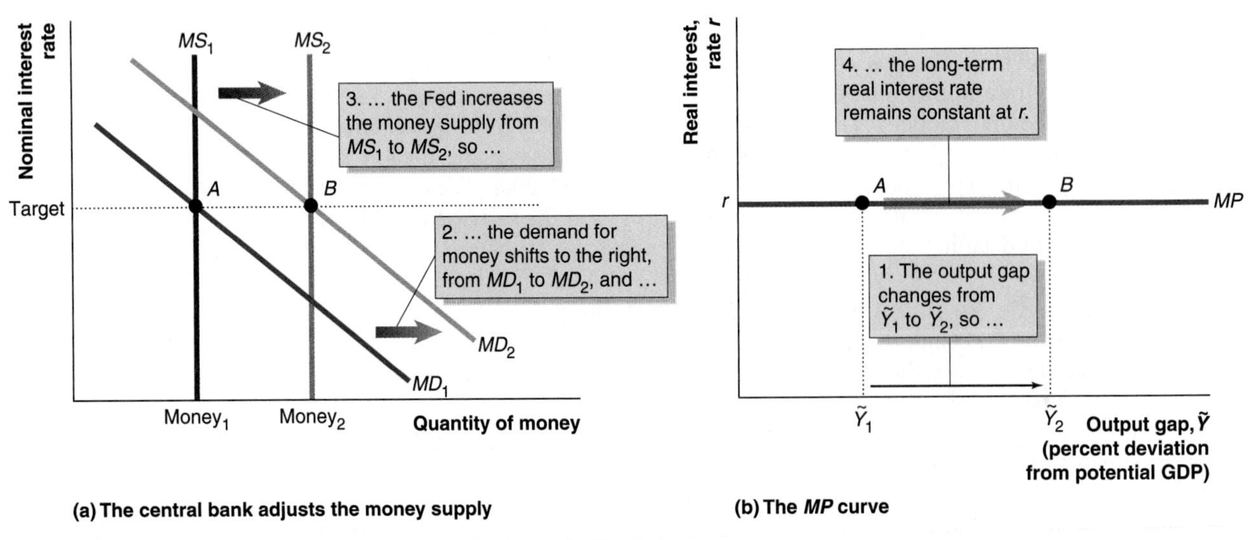

Figure 9.8 Deriving the *MP* Curve

As the output gap changes from $\tilde{Y}_1$ to $\tilde{Y}_2$ in panel (b), the money demand curve shifts to the right in panel (a). The central bank increases the money supply in panel (a) to keep the short-term nominal interest rate at the target interest rate. If the short-term nominal interest rate is constant, then so is the long-term nominal interest rate. If expected inflation is also constant, then the long-term real interest rate also remains constant, and equilibrium moves from point *A* to point *B* in both panels. ●

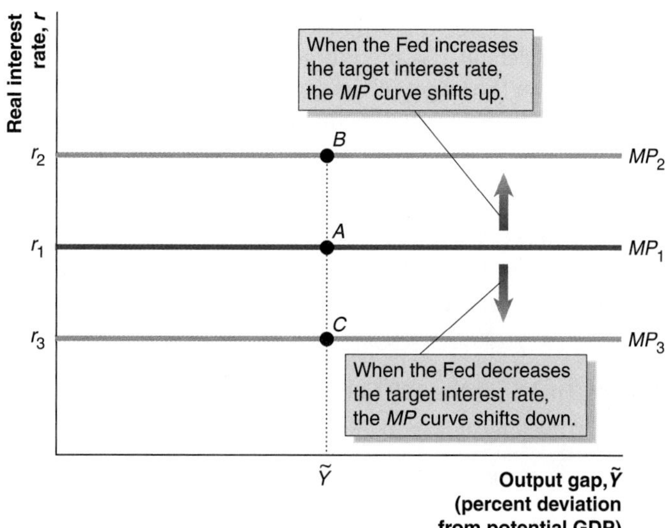

Figure 9.9

Changes in the Interest Rate Target and the *MP* Curve

When the Fed increases its target for the short-term nominal interest rate, the long-term nominal interest rate increases. Assuming that expected inflation, the term structure effect, and the default-risk premium are constant, the long-term real interest rate increases, so the *MP* curve shifts up, from MP_1 to MP_2. When the Fed decreases its target for the short-term nominal interest rate, the long-term nominal interest rate decreases, and the *MP* curve shifts down, from MP_1 to MP_3. ●

effect, and the default-risk premium are all constant, then the short-term nominal interest rate determines the long-term real interest rate. The economy's equilibrium starts off at point *A* in panel (b), where the output gap equals $\tilde{Y}_1$. Suppose that real GDP increases so that the output gap changes from $\tilde{Y}_1$ to $\tilde{Y}_2$. The increase in real GDP leads households and firms to purchase more goods and services, so the demand for money in panel (a) shifts to the right, from MD_1 to MD_2. If the Fed kept the money supply constant, then the increase in the demand for money would cause nominal interest rates to increase. However, the Fed has a target nominal interest rate, so it increases the money supply to keep the interest rate at the target. As a result, the short-term nominal interest rate remains constant, and with the term structure effect and the default-risk premium remaining constant, the long-term nominal interest rate will also remain constant. We have assumed that the expected inflation rate is constant, so the long-term real interest rate is also constant. With the real interest rate constant and the output gap at $\tilde{Y}_2$, the economy is now at point *B* in panel (b), given the assumption that the *MP* curve is horizontal at *r*.

Shifts of the *MP* Curve

The *MP* curve is determined by the Fed's target short-term nominal interest rate along with the term structure effect, *TSE*, the default-risk premium, *DP*, and the expected inflation rate, π^e. If any of these four variables change, the *MP* curve will shift. For example, in Figure 9.9, we begin at point *A* because the Fed has an initial interest rate target consistent with a real interest rate of r_1, so the *MP* curve is MP_1.[6]

Suppose that the Fed then decides to increase its interest rate target. If expected inflation, the term structure effect, and the default-risk premium are constant, then the increase in the target for the short-term nominal interest rate will increase the long-term real interest rate from r_1 to r_2. As a result, we will be at point *B* because the *MP* curve will shift up from MP_1 to MP_2. Similarly, if the Fed decides to decrease its target for the short-term nominal interest rate, the long-term real interest rate will decrease from r_1 to r_3. As a result, the *MP* curve will shift down, from MP_1 to MP_3, and we will be at point *C*.

[6]For simplicity, we are dropping the *LT* subscript from *r*. For the remainder of this chapter and in the following chapters, *r* will be the long-term real interest rate.

Of course, Fed policy is not the only factor that affects the real interest rate. For instance, increases in the default-risk premium increase the real interest rate in much the same way as an increase in the target interest rate. As we have seen, the default-risk premium increased after the bankruptcy of Lehman Brothers in September 2008, so real interest rates in financial markets increased, shifting up the *MP* curve. Table 9.2 summarizes the factors that cause the *MP* curve to shift. (Note that the table shows the shift in the *MP* curve that results from an *increase* in each of the factors. A *decrease* in these factors would cause the *MP* curve to shift in the opposite direction.)

Central banks adjust the target short-term nominal interest rate as economic conditions change, usually increasing it during expansions and decreasing it during recessions.

Table 9.2 Factors That Shift the *MP* Curve

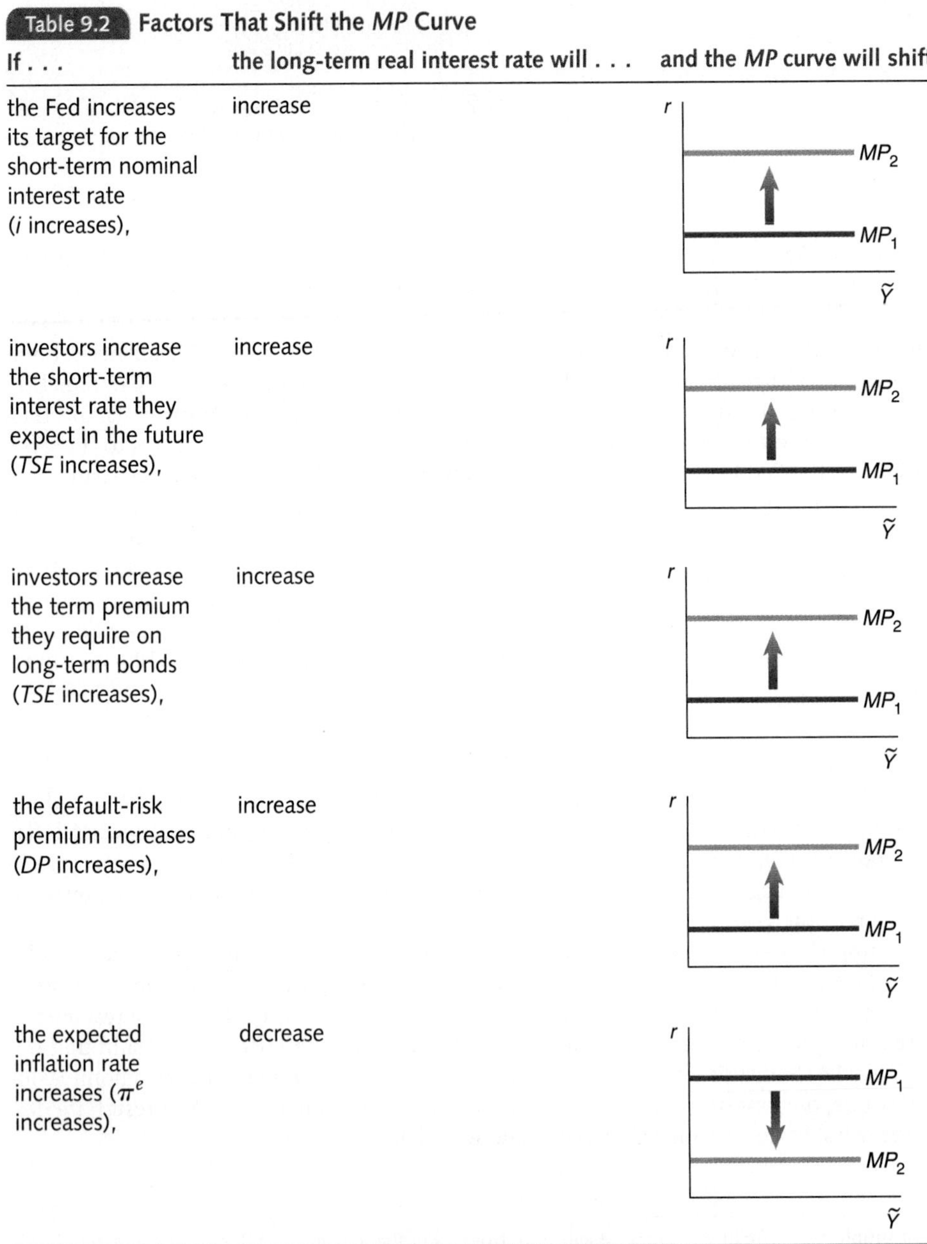

If . . .	the long-term real interest rate will . . .	and the *MP* curve will shift
the Fed increases its target for the short-term nominal interest rate (i increases),	increase	up, from MP_1 to MP_2 (graph: r vs. $\tilde{Y}$)
investors increase the short-term interest rate they expect in the future (TSE increases),	increase	up, from MP_1 to MP_2 (graph: r vs. $\tilde{Y}$)
investors increase the term premium they require on long-term bonds (TSE increases),	increase	up, from MP_1 to MP_2 (graph: r vs. $\tilde{Y}$)
the default-risk premium increases (DP increases),	increase	up, from MP_1 to MP_2 (graph: r vs. $\tilde{Y}$)
the expected inflation rate increases (π^e increases),	decrease	down, from MP_1 to MP_2 (graph: r vs. $\tilde{Y}$)

For example, in a series of interest rate hikes, the Federal Reserve increased its target interest rate from 1.0% in June 2004 to 5.25% on June 29, 2006 during the economic expansion. The target rate was still 5.25% at the beginning of the financial crisis, but the Fed reduced it in a series of steps until, by December 2008, it had been lowered to between 0% and 0.25%. The target interest rate for the Bank of Japan followed a similar pattern. The Bank of Japan increased its target interest rate from essentially 0% at the end of 2001 to about 0.5% at the beginning of the financial crisis in 2007. Then the Bank of Japan reversed course and started decreasing the target interest rate to about 0.1% on December 19, 2008. In Chapter 10, we discuss in more detail how central banks adjust their target interest rates.

Monetary Policy and the *MP* Curve

The *MP* curve shows the long-term real interest rate. Monetary policy is one of the factors that affects the real interest rate, which is why we call this curve the *MP* curve. Although in deriving the *MP* curve in Figure 9.8, we assumed that the interest rate that the Fed sets does not respond to the level of real GDP, strictly speaking, this is not true. As we will see in Chapters 10 and 12, monetary policy responds to the level of real GDP, inflation, financial market instability, and many other factors. However, the *MP* curve as we have drawn it is still useful for discussing policy for two reasons. First, it is the simplest way to start thinking about monetary policy. Second, we have not specified how the central bank changes interest rates in response to the economy, so our approach is flexible. For example, if the central bank focuses just on inflation, then if inflation increases, we can just show the central bank responding with an upward shift in the *MP* curve. However, if the central bank has chosen to place more emphasis on movements in real GDP than on inflation, then our approach is flexible enough to account for that as well. In short, our approach allows us to analyze the typical situation where the central bank has the *discretion* to focus on different policy goals if it chooses to.

Equilibrium in the *IS–MP* Model

9.3

Learning Objective

Use the *IS–MP* model to understand why real GDP fluctuates.

In Chapter 8, we defined *macroeconomic shocks* as exogenous events that cause economic fluctuations. Examples of shocks are a collapse in housing prices that reduces wealth, an increase in net exports due to higher incomes abroad, and an increase in government purchases due to a war. In this section, we combine the *IS* and *MP* curves in order to understand how these shocks can affect the output gap and how government policy can respond to the effects of shocks. We start by explaining equilibrium in the *IS–MP* model.

Figure 9.10 shows equilibrium in the *IS–MP* model. If the Fed sets the real interest rate at r_1, then real GDP equals potential GDP, and we have the desirable outcome that the output gap equals zero. For a given *IS* curve, the Fed's choice of the real interest rate determines the equilibrium output gap.

In the *IS–MP* model, financial markets set the long-term real interest rate, which then determines the level of aggregate expenditures and real GDP. By its control of the short-term interest rate, the Fed has an important effect on the long-term real interest rate, but as we have seen, the Fed's policy is not the only factor that affects the long-term real interest rate. As these other factors change, the *MP* curve will shift, which will cause the level of real GDP and the output gap to change. Similarly, demand shocks will shift the *IS* curve and cause fluctuations in real GDP. We begin our discussion of fluctuations in real GDP and the output gap by discussing the effects of monetary policy.

Monetary Policy and Fluctuations in Real GDP

One of the Fed's monetary policy goals is to stabilize the price level by keeping the inflation rate low. Accordingly, the Fed adjusts its target for the short-term nominal interest rate

Figure 9.10

Equilibrium in the *IS–MP* Model

The economy is in equilibrium where *MP* and *IS* curves intersect at point *A*, with real GDP equal to potential GDP, so the output gap equals 0. ●

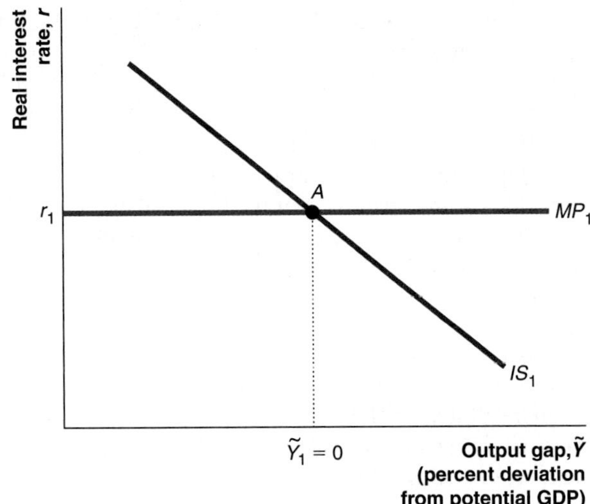

in response to changes in the inflation rate. When the inflation rate is high, the Fed typically increases its target interest rate. In this section, we consider the effect on the equilibrium output gap of a change in the target interest rate. In Chapter 10, we discuss why and how the Fed adjusts the target interest rate.

Figure 9.11 shows the effect of an increase in the Fed's target interest rate on the equilibrium output gap. The economy is initially at equilibrium at point *A*, where real GDP equals potential GDP, so $\tilde{Y}_1 = 0$. Assuming that the expected inflation rate, the term structure effect, and the default-risk premium are constant, an increase in the Fed's target short-term nominal interest rate increases the long-term real interest rate from r_1 to r_2. The *MP* curve shifts up from MP_1 to MP_2, and short-run equilibrium is now at point *B*, where real GDP is less than potential GDP so the output gap, $\tilde{Y}_2$, is less

Figure 9.11

The Fed Increases the Target Short-Term Nominal Interest Rate

An increase in the target short-term nominal interest rate causes the long-term real interest rate to increase from r_1 to r_2. As a result, aggregate expenditure falls, causing real GDP to drop below potential GDP, so the output gap becomes negative and equilibrium moves from point *A* to point *B*. ●

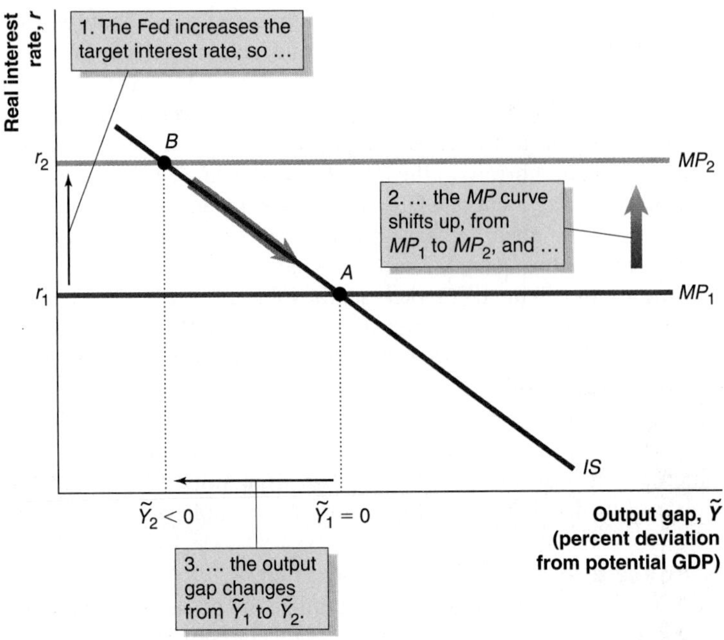

than zero. Why has real GDP decreased below its potential level? The higher long-term real interest rate has reduced consumption, investment, and net exports. A lower level of aggregate expenditure leads to a reduction in real GDP, causing it to fall below potential GDP.

Figure 9.11 suggests that the Fed can cause recessions by increasing the target short-term nominal interest rate, which will cause real GDP to decrease. As we will see in Section 9.4, the Fed may cause a recession to reduce the inflation rate. Although the Fed did not have an explicit nominal interest rate target during the 1981–1982 recession, it allowed short-term nominal interest rates to increase to over 21%! As a result, consumption and investment expenditures decreased dramatically, real GDP fell to 7.5% below potential GDP, and the unemployment rate peaked at 10.8%.

If the Fed decreases the target short-term nominal interest rate, the opposite will happen. Assuming that the expected inflation rate, the term structure effect, and the default-risk premium are constant, a decrease in the Fed's target short-term nominal interest rate decreases the long-term real interest rate. As a result, the *MP* curve shifts down. The lower real interest rate increases aggregate expenditure. When aggregate expenditure increases, firms expand production, so real GDP increases relative to potential GDP.

The Fed can help offset the effects on real GDP of a recession by reducing its target for the short-term nominal interest rate. In practice, this is what the Fed does. The Fed's target for the federal funds rate was 6.5% just before the 2001 recession. To stimulate the economy, the Fed reduced this target interest rate to 2.0% by the end of the recession in November 2001, and it further reduced the target rate to 1.0% by June 2003 to help speed the following economic expansion. As we will see in Section 9.4, the downside of reducing interest rates is that low interest rates can cause the inflation rate to increase. Other central banks, such as the Bank of Japan, also use reductions in short-term nominal interest rates to fight recessions. During the early 1990s, Japan experienced the collapse of both real estate and stock prices, so the Japanese economy grew very slowly during the 1990s. In an attempt to increase the growth rate of the economy, the Bank of Japan lowered its target short-term nominal interest rate in a series of steps to essentially 0% by 1999. Unfortunately, there are many complications to effectively implementing monetary policy, which we will discuss in Chapter 10. In this case, the Japanese economy did not fully recover and has been experiencing a nearly 20-year period of extremely sluggish economic growth.

Demand Shocks and Fluctuations in Output

In Section 9.1, we saw how demand shocks affect the *IS* curve. We now explain how these shocks will cause real GDP to fluctuate if the Fed keeps the real interest rate constant. For example, suppose that a collapse in consumer confidence leads households to reduce consumption expenditures. Many economists believe that a drop in consumer confidence contributed to the 1990–1991 recession. Iraq invaded Kuwait on August 1990. Fears that the invasion would lead to sharply higher gasoline prices helped push the University of Michigan's Index of Consumer Sentiment down from 88.2 during July 1990 to 63.9 during October 1990. The decrease in consumer sentiment contributed to the 3.1% decrease in consumption expenditures during the fourth quarter of 1990, which helped cause the recession.

Figure 9.12 shows the effect of the decrease in consumer optimism using the *IS–MP* model. The economy's equilibrium starts at point *A*, with real GDP equal to potential GDP, so $\tilde{Y}_1 = 0$. Concern about rising gasoline prices causes households to reduce consumption spending, so the *IS* curve shifts to the left, from IS_1 to IS_2. Assuming that the Fed does not adjust its target short-term nominal interest rate, the economy is now at point *B*. The decrease in consumption spending leads firms to reduce output, so real GDP falls below potential GDP, making $\tilde{Y}_2 < 0$. A reduction in consumer confidence is just one example of a

Figure 9.12

A Negative Demand Shock and Equilibrium Real GDP

A negative demand shock shifts the *IS* curve to the left. If the Fed keeps the real interest rate constant, the output gap becomes negative and equilibrium moves from point *A* to point *B*. ●

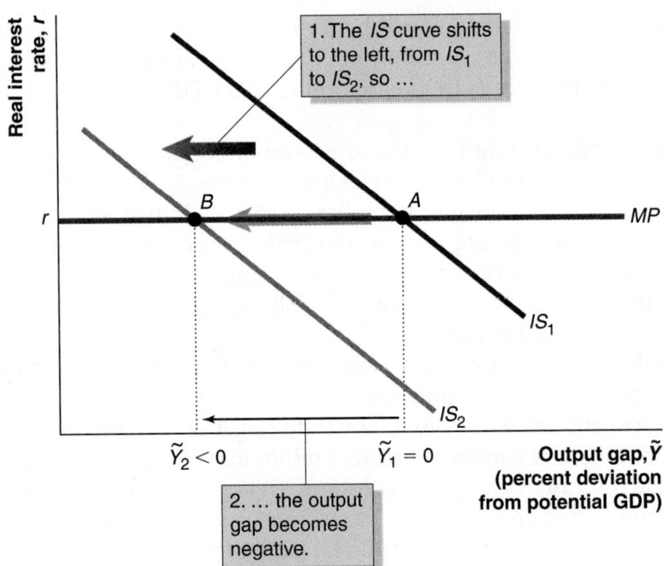

negative demand shock that shifts the *IS* curve to the left. Any negative demand shock would have a similar effect. Similarly, any positive demand shock, such as a surge in investment spending by firms, would increase aggregate expenditure and shift the *IS* curve to the right.

Making the Connection

The Bankruptcy of Lehman Brothers, the Financial Crisis, and the Financing of Investment

We discussed in the chapter opener that the failure of the Lehman Brothers investment bank in September 2008 was a severe blow to the financial system. Money market mutual funds were particularly hard hit by the financial panic following Lehman's bankruptcy. Mutual funds allow savers to purchase shares in a portfolio of assets, such as stocks, bonds, and mortgage-backed securities. Money market mutual funds invest exclusively in high-quality, short-term assets, such as Treasury bills, negotiable certificates of deposit, and commercial paper. These funds provide higher returns to savers than do commercial banks and provide risk-sharing benefits by offering a diversified portfolio of assets and liquidity benefits because savers can easily sell the shares. Companies that manage mutual funds for investors include Fidelity Investments, Putnam Investments, and Vanguard.

Many companies, such as Goodyear Tire and Rubber Company, deposit their spare cash in money market mutual funds. The money market mutual funds take the deposits of Goodyear, along with those of other companies and individuals, and purchase Treasury bills and other short-term financial assets, particularly commercial paper issued by both financial and non-financial firms. The funds earn profits by paying Goodyear and other investors a lower interest rate than the funds receive from their investments. Unfortunately for Goodyear and other investors, many money market mutual funds held securities issued by Lehman Brothers. For example, the Reserve Primary Fund had purchased about $786 million of Lehman Brothers commercial paper. When Lehman Brothers went bankrupt on September 15, 2008, because it could not pay its creditors, the Reserve Primary Fund could not reimburse Goodyear, which had invested $360 million in that fund, or other companies and individuals who had invested in it. In November 2009, a federal judge ruled that all of the investors in the Reserve Primary Fund would share equally in its losses, and the fund has since been liquidated.

The fact that investors in a well-known fund had suffered losses and had been unable to redeem their shares caused large withdrawals from other money market funds. These panicked withdrawals from money market funds led the U.S. Treasury to announce that it would guarantee the holdings of money market funds against losses, thereby insuring that investors in other funds would not suffer a loss of principal. Although the Treasury's guarantee slowed withdrawals from money market mutual funds, the funds cut back significantly on their purchases of commercial paper. Because the funds made up such a large fraction of the market for commercial paper and because many firms had become heavily dependent on sales of commercial paper to finance their operations, the adverse consequences for the financial system were severe. In October 2008, the Federal Reserve stepped in to stabilize the market by directly purchasing commercial paper for the first time since the Great Depression of the 1930s. The Fed's actions helped restore the flow of funds to firms that were dependent on commercial paper.

Although through these and other actions, the Fed and the U.S. Treasury lessened the most severe consequences of the financial crisis, the collapse of a number of financial institutions and a crisis of confidence among lenders led to a significant reduction in the flow of funds from savers to borrowers. Households and firms that were unable to borrow funds cut back on their investment. Non-inventory investment in the United States decreased at an annual rate of 25% during the fourth quarter of 2008, 35% during the first quarter of 2009, and 10% during the second quarter of 2009. By the third quarter of 2009, U.S. real GDP was 7.6% below potential GDP, and the United States was experiencing its worst recession since the Great Depression.

Sources: U.S. Bureau of Economic Analysis; Bob Ivry, Christine Harper, and Mark Pittman, "Missing Lehman Lesson of Shakeout Means Too Big Banks May Fail," *Bloomberg.com*, September 7, 2009; Dale Kasler, "One Year After Lehman Brothers' Fall, a Citrus Heights Merchant Struggles to Survive," *McClatchy—Tribune Business News*, September 15, 2009; and Pallavi Gogoi, "A Year After Lehman's Fall," *USA Today*, September 14, 2009.

Test your understanding by doing related problem 3.4 on page 349 at the end of this chapter.

Table 9.3 summarizes the effects of different shocks and changes in policy on real GDP and the real interest rate in the *IS–MP* model. Keep Equation 9.4 from page 314 in mind as you read the table.

The *IS-MP* model that we have developed explains fluctuations in real GDP as being the result of macroeconomic shocks combined with nominal price and wage stickiness. Based on our discussion in Chapter 8, that puts our model in the *Keynesian* tradition because it regards the business cycle as a departure from long-run equilibrium. More specifically, the *IS-MP* model is a *new Keynesian* model because, unlike the original Keynesian models developed in the 1930s and 1940s, the *IS-MP* model is based on the assumption that individual households maximize utility and firms maximize profits. We discuss these *microfoundations* of the model in more detail in Chapter 14.

We also mentioned the *classical* tradition in Chapter 8, which emphasizes the importance of nominal price and wage flexibility in maintaining equilibrium. There are several different types of classical models of the business cycle, but the most influential emphasizes the importance of productivity shocks. (This and related models are sometimes referred to as *new classical models* to distinguish them from the classical models of the 1930s and earlier.) In this view, recessions occur when economies experience negative productivity shocks that lead households to choose to work less and firms to choose to produce less output. Because, in this view, productivity shocks drive the business cycle and productivity is a key determinant of potential GDP, the business cycle consists of short-run fluctuations

Table 9.3 Summary of the *IS–MP* Model

The following change . . .	causes . . .	Graph of the effect . . .
a positive aggregate demand shock	aggregate expenditure to increase at every interest rate.	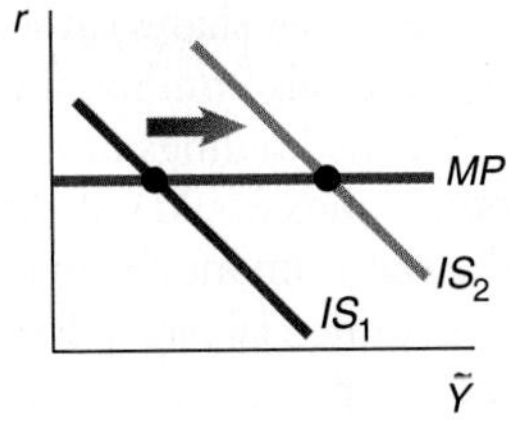
an increase in the target interest rate (*i* increases)	long-term real interest rates to increase and consumption and investment to decrease.	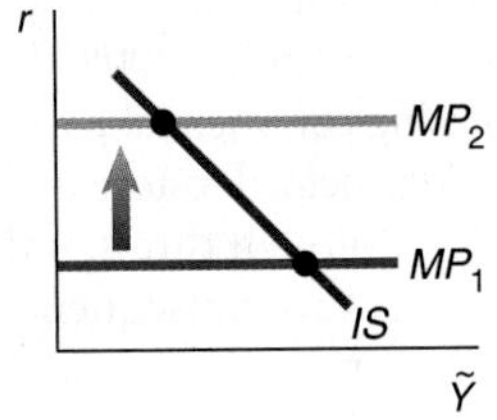
an increase in the short-term interest rate investors expect in the future (*TSE* increases)	long-term real interest rates to increase and consumption and investment to decrease.	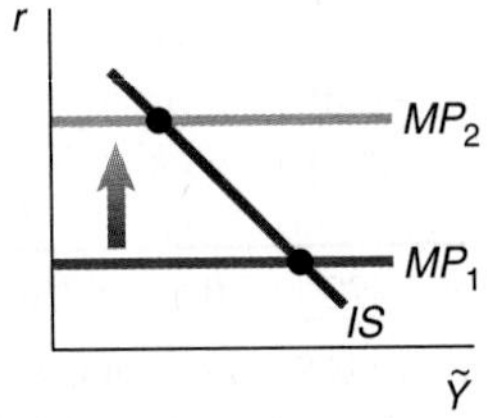
an increase in the term premium investors require on long-term bonds (*TSE* increases)	long-term real interest rates to increase and consumption and investment to decrease.	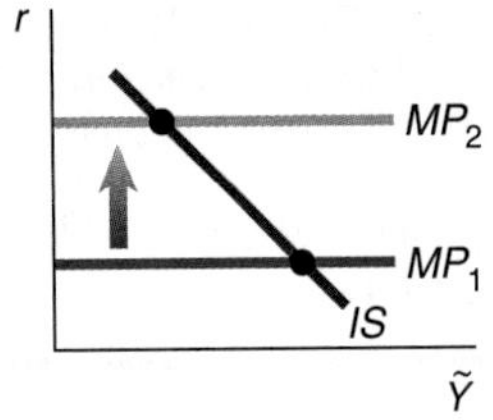
an increase in the default-risk premium (*DP* increases)	long-term real interest rates to increase and consumption and investment to decrease.	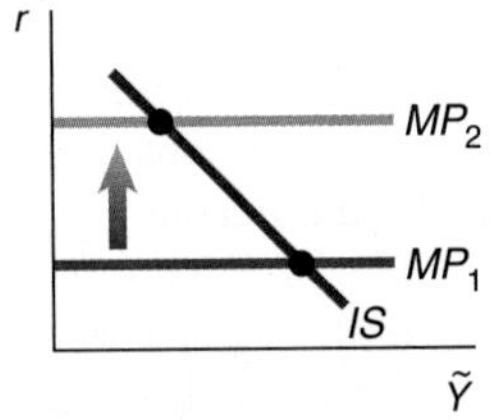
an increase in the expected inflation rate (π^e increases)	long-term real interest rates to decrease and consumption and investment to increase.	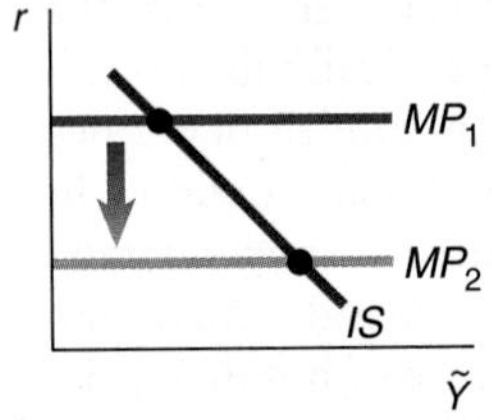

in potential GDP. In effect, the output gap is always zero because wage and price flexibility is assumed to always keep real GDP equal to potential GDP. Proponents of the new classical model have developed many of the most important tools of modern macroeconomics, but only a minority of economists accept the view that the business cycle consists of fluctuations in potential GDP. We will discuss the new classical model again in Chapter 12, where we complete our discussion of the business cycle.

MACRO DATA: WHAT DOES A CREDIT CRUNCH LOOK LIKE?

During the financial crisis that began in August 2007, many banks and other financial firms restricted loans to households, firms, and each other because they believed that the risk of borrowers defaulting had increased. In general, lenders became more reluctant to lend to borrowers. We have seen that commercial paper plays an important role in the financial system. For example, Goodyear Tire may borrow in the commercial paper market instead of borrowing from banks. The following figure shows the volume of commercial paper sold between January 2001 and February 2011. Asset-backed commercial paper represents short-term borrowing by financial institutions, using assets such as mortgages for collateral. The value of all commercial paper and asset-backed commercial paper peaked just before the beginning of the financial crisis and declined rapidly after August 2007. The effect of the financial crisis on non-financial commercial paper is much less severe but does show a decrease. The figure shows what a credit crunch looks like: a rapid decrease in the volume of loans. We would see similar results if we graphed bank loans. Not surprisingly, the decline in loans resulted in a sharp reduction in consumption and investment.

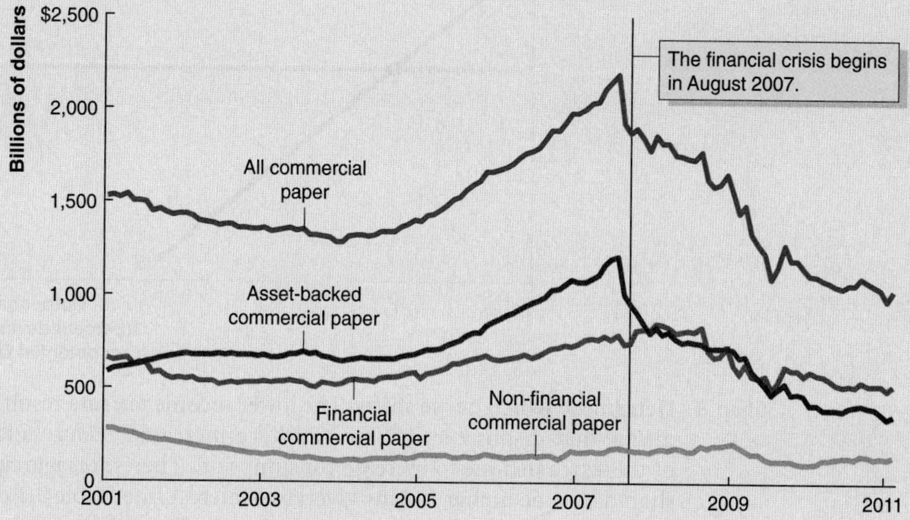

Source: Board of Governors of the Federal Reserve.

Test your understanding by doing related problem D9.1 on page 352 at the end of this chapter.

Solved Problem 9.3

Using the *IS–MP* Model to Analyze the 2001 Tax Cut

The National Bureau of Economic Research dates the 2001 recession as starting in March 2001 and ending in November 2001. The output gap became negative during the recession and remained negative until 2005. On June 7, 2001, Congress passed and President George W. Bush signed into law the Economic Growth and Tax Relief Reconciliation Act. The act reduced the income tax rates that households pay. For example, the top income tax rate, which at that time was levied on income above $288,350, was reduced from 39.6% to 35%, and the lowest income tax rate, levied on income below $26,250, was reduced from 15% to 10%. As a result, U.S. households experienced an increase in disposable income, which led them to increase their expenditures on cars, clothes, household appliances, and other consumption goods and services. Use the *IS-MP* model to analyze the effect of the tax on real GDP and the output gap. Be sure to show any shifts in the *IS* curve and the *MP* curve, as well as the old and new equilibrium values of the output gap. Also state any assumptions that you are making about monetary policy.

Solving the Problem

Step 1 Review the chapter material. This problem is about using the *IS* and *MP* curves to determine the effect of a tax cut on real GDP and the output gap, so you may want to review the section "Demand Shocks and Fluctuations in Output," which begins on page 321.

Step 2 Draw a graph that shows the initial equilibrium. The problem states that the economy was in a recession at the time that the act was passed. As a result, we can assume that real GDP was less than potential GDP, so the output gap was negative. Therefore, your initial graph should look like this:

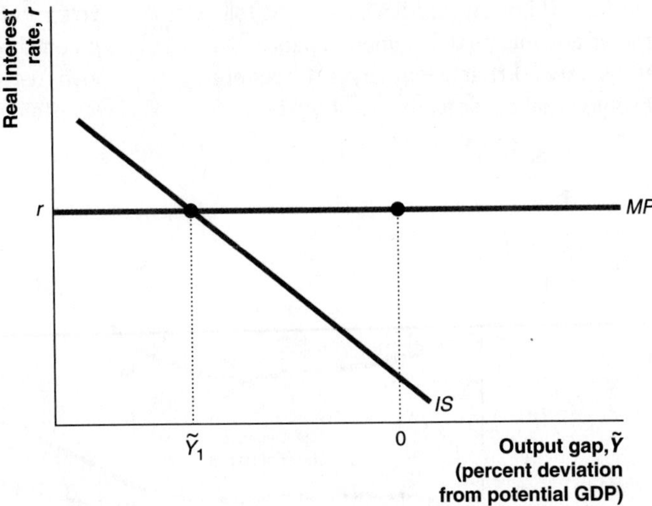

Step 3 Determine which curve shifts. The lower income tax rate resulting from the act means that disposable income will have increased. Households will use part of this extra income to increase consumption. Therefore, aggregate expenditure should now be higher for any given real interest rate. Table 9.3 on page 324 tells us that a shock that increases aggregate expenditure will shift the *IS* curve to the right, from IS_1 to IS_2.

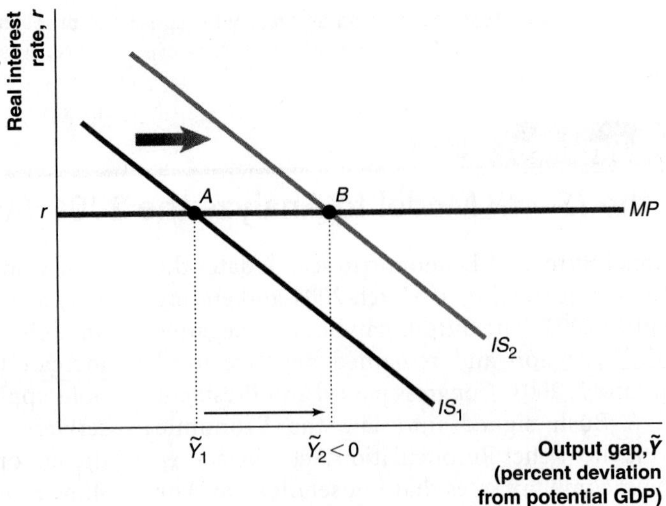

Step 4 State your assumption about monetary policy and explain the effect of the act on real GDP and on the output gap. The simplest assumption is that the Fed keeps the real interest rate constant. In that case, if the *IS* curve shifts to the right, short-run equilibrium will move from point *A* to point *B* in the graph in step 3. The higher level of consumption causes real GDP to increase relative to potential GDP, so the equilibrium output gap changes from $\tilde{Y}_1$ to $\tilde{Y}_2 < 0$. The problem states that the output gap in the United States remained negative until 2005, so your graph in Step 3 should show that the output gap is still negative after the effect of the tax cut.

This analysis indicates that the 2001 tax cut increased consumption and real GDP. As a result, the tax cut made the 2001 recession less severe.

EXTRA CREDIT: Although the 2001 tax cuts served in the short run to increase disposable income and aggregate expenditure, they had another purpose—increasing economic growth. As we will discuss in Chapter 13, some macroeconomic policies have effects in the long run. In this case, President Bush and the members of Congress who voted for the act hoped that cutting tax rates would increase the incentive to work, save, and invest, which would in the long run increase potential GDP.

For more practice, do related problem 3.3 on page 349 at the end of this chapter.

The *IS–MP* Model and the Phillips Curve

9.4

Learning Objective
Understand the role of the Phillips curve in the *IS–MP* model.

An important observation about the economy is that when output and employment are increasing, the inflation rate tends to increase, and when output and employment are decreasing, the inflation rate tends to decrease. The first economist to systematically analyze this relationship was the New Zealand economist A.W.H. Phillips in 1958.[7] Phillips plotted data on the growth rate of nominal wages and the unemployment rate in the United Kingdom and drew a curve showing their average relationship. Firms generally pass increases in costs, such as higher nominal wages, along to consumers in the form of higher prices. As a result, most economists interpreted Phillips's results as showing a tendency for the inflation rate to increase as the unemployment rate decreases. Since that time, a graph showing the short-run relationship between the unemployment rate and the inflation rate has been called a *Phillips curve.* Figure 9.13 is similar to the graph that Phillips prepared. Each point on the Phillips curve represents a combination of the inflation rate and the unemployment rate that might be observed in a particular year. For example, point *A* represents the combination of a 3% unemployment rate and a 5% inflation rate in one year, and point *B* represents the combination of a 6% unemployment rate and a 2% inflation rate in another year.

Economists and policymakers initially viewed the Phillips curve as a *structural relationship* in the economy. A structural relationship depends on the basic behavior of households and firms and remains unchanged over long periods. If the Phillips curve is a structural relationship, policymakers face a stable trade-off between inflation and unemployment. The Fed could *permanently* reduce the unemployment rate if it were willing to accept a higher inflation rate, and it could *permanently* reduce the inflation rate if it were willing to accept a higher unemployment rate. Two events changed the view that the

[7]A.W.H. Phillips, "The Relationship Between Unemployment and the Rate of Change of Money Wages in the United Kingdom 1861–1957," *Economica*, Vol. 25, No. 100, November 1958, pp. 283–299.

Figure 9.13

The Traditional Phillips Curve

The traditional Phillips curve shows an inverse relationship in the short run between the inflation rate and the unemployment rate. ●

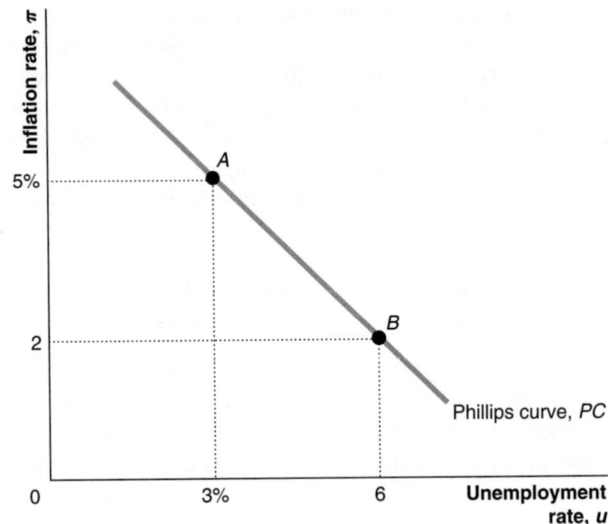

Phillips curve represented a stable trade-off for policymakers. First, in 1968, Nobel Laureates Milton Friedman and Edmund Phelps argued that, while in constructing the Phillips curve economists assumed that expected inflation was constant, it was more likely that expected inflation adjusts if current inflation rates are different from past inflation rates.[8] In other words, Friedman and Phelps believed that if inflation is higher in 2012 than it has been in the past, households and firms will expect the higher inflation to persist in 2013. Because expected inflation should affect the prices that firms charge and the wages that workers seek, higher expected inflation in 2013 may also increase the actual inflation rate in 2013. Friedman and Phelps believed that as the inflation rate in the United States increased during the 1960s, it was only a matter of time before the stable inverse relationship between unemployment and inflation embodied in the Phillips curve broke down.

The second event that undermined the view that the Phillips curve represented a stable trade-off between inflation and unemployment was the increase in *both* the inflation rate and the unemployment rate during the 1970s. The annual inflation rate as measured by changes in the consumer price index (CPI) was just 1.9% during January 1966, but eventually rose to 12.2% during November 1974 and then to 14.6% during April 1980. Instead of decreasing, the unemployment rate actually rose. The unemployment rate was 4.0% in January 1966, rose to 6.6% in November 1974, and 6.9% in April 1980. Over this entire period, the unemployment rate rose by 2.9 percentage points, and in contrast to the prediction of a stable Phillips curve, the inflation rate actually rose by 12.7 percentage points! It seemed impossible to reconcile actual macroeconomic data with a stable Phillips curve.

Friedman's and Phelps's criticism of the theory behind the Phillips curve and the actual experience of the U.S. economy during the 1970s convinced economists that the Phillips curve did not represent a stable relationship. Economists who have studied the Phillips curve have concluded that the position of the Phillips curve can shift over time in response to *supply shocks*, such as an increase in the price of oil, and changes in the expected inflation rate. Once we account for these two factors, the Phillips curve remains a useful tool for explaining the *short-run* tradeoff between the unemployment rate and the inflation rate.

[8] Milton Friedman, "The Role of Monetary Policy," *American Economic Review*, Vol. 58, No. 1, March 1968, pp.1–17; and Edmund Phelps, "Money–Wage Dynamics and Labor Market Equilibrium," *Journal of Political Economy*, Vol. 76, No. 4, Part 2, July/August 1968, pp. 678–711.

Changes in households' and firms' expectations about the inflation rate will shift the position of the Phillips curve. For example, if workers and firms expect that the inflation rate will be 2% per year, but they experience an extended period of 4% inflation, they are likely to adjust their expectations of future inflation from 2% to 4%. Expectations of inflation can become embedded in the economy. So, if workers believe that the future inflation rate will be 4%, rather than 2%, they know that unless their nominal wage increases by at least 4%, their real wage—their nominal wage divided by the price level—will decline. Similarly, we saw in Chapter 6 that the Fisher effect indicates that an increase in the expected inflation rate will cause an increase in nominal interest rates. As workers, firms, and investors adjust from expecting an inflation rate of 2% to expecting an inflation rate of 4%, at any given unemployment rate, the inflation rate will be 2% higher. In other words, the Phillips curve will have shifted up by 2%.

Most economists believe that the best way to capture the effect of changes in the unemployment rate on the inflation rate is by looking at the gap between the current unemployment rate and the unemployment rate when the economy is at full employment, which is called the *natural rate of unemployment.* The gap between the current rate of unemployment and the natural rate represents *cyclical unemployment* because it is unemployment caused by a business cycle recession raising the unemployment rate above its full employment level. When the current unemployment rate equals the natural rate, the inflation rate typically does not change, holding constant expectations of inflation and the effects of supply shocks. When the current unemployment rate is greater than the natural rate, some workers have trouble finding jobs, so wage increases will be limited, as will increases in firms' costs of production. As a result, the inflation rate will decrease. When the current unemployment rate is less than the natural rate of unemployment, labor market conditions will be tight, and wages are likely to increase, which pushes up firms' costs of production. So, the inflation rate will increase.

Taking all these factors into account gives us the following equation for the Phillips curve:

$$\pi_t = \pi_t^e - a(U_t - U^N) - s_t,$$

where:

$\pi_t =$ current inflation rate
$\pi_t^e =$ expected inflation rate
$U_t =$ current unemployment rate
$U^N =$ natural rate of unemployment
$s_t =$ variable representing the effects of a supply shock (s will have a negative value for a negative supply shock and a positive value for a positive supply shock.)
$a =$ constant that represents how much the gap between the current rate of unemployment and the natural rate affects the inflation rate

The equation tells us that an increase in expected inflation or a negative supply shock such as an increase in oil prices will shift the Phillips curve up, while a decrease in expected inflation or a positive supply shock such as an increase in the growth rate of productivity will shift the Phillips curve down.

What might cause the expected rate of inflation to change? Many economists believe that the main reason households and firms adjust their expectations of inflation is that they experience persistent rates of actual inflation that are above the rates they had expected. The experience of the U.S. economy during the 1960s and 1970s provides an example of this point. Inflation during the 1960s averaged about 2% per year but accelerated to 5% per year from 1970 to 1973 and to 8.5% per year from 1974 to 1979. These persistently high rates of inflation led households and firms to revise upward their expectations of inflation, and the Phillips curve shifted up. Notice that once the Phillips curve has shifted up, the economy is worse off. That is, every unemployment rate becomes associated with a higher inflation rate. The decline in the inflation rate during the 1980s provides an example of how a decrease in expected inflation can lead to lower inflation. Paul Volcker became Federal Reserve chairman in August 1979, with a mandate from President Jimmy Carter to bring down the inflation rate. When the economy experienced the severe recession of 1981–1982, the inflation rate declined sharply as the unemployment rate soared and firms experienced excess capacity. From 1983 to 1986, the inflation rate averaged 3.3% per year. Accordingly, households and firms lowered their expectations of future inflation, and the Phillips curve shifted down.

Figure 9.14 shows the shifts of the Phillips curve associated with supply shocks and changes in expected inflation. An increase in the expected inflation rate such as the one that occurred during the 1960s and 1970s will shift the Phillips curve up, from PC_1 to PC_2. A decrease in the expected inflation rate such as the one that occurred after the 1981–1982 recession will shift the Phillips curve down, from PC_1 to PC_3.

Okun's Law and an Output Gap Phillips Curve

The Phillips curve shows the short-run relationship between the inflation rate and the unemployment rate. We saw in Figure 9.10 how we can use the *IS* curve and the *MP* curve to explain equilibrium real GDP and the real interest rate. If we could show the relationship between the output gap and the inflation rate, we could integrate the Phillips curve into our *IS–MP* model. That would allow us to illustrate the effects of changes in the inflation rate on Fed policy and the effects of changes in Fed policy on the inflation rate. Fortunately, there is a straightforward way of modifying the Phillips curve to change it from a relationship between the inflation rate and the unemployment rate to a relationship between the inflation rate and the output gap. This approach relies on Okun's law, which we discussed in Chapter 8.

Okun's law conveniently summarizes the relationship between the output gap, $\tilde{Y}_t$, and the gap between the current and natural rates of unemployment, or cyclical unemployment:

$$(U_t - U^N) = -0.5\tilde{Y}_t,$$

which we can rewrite as:

$$\tilde{Y}_t = -2(U_t - U^N).$$

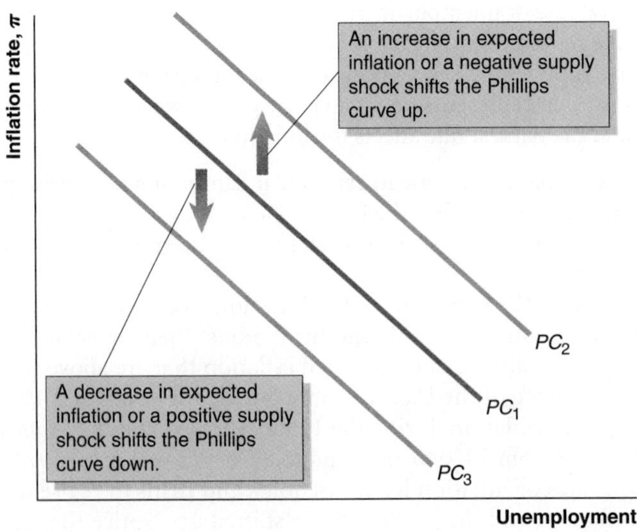

Figure 9.14

Shifts of the Phillips Curve

An increase in expected inflation or a negative supply shock will shift the Phillips curve up, so the inflation rate is now higher for any given unemployment rate. A decrease in expected inflation or a positive supply shock will shift the Phillips curve down, so the inflation rate is now lower for any given unemployment rate. ●

We can substitute the Okun's law relationship into the equation for the Phillips curve using unemployment to obtain:

$$\pi_t = \pi_t^e + b\widetilde{Y}_t - s_t. \quad (9.5)$$

Equation (9.5) is a Phillips curve incorporating the output gap. The coefficient b in the equation represents the effect of changes in the output gap on the inflation rate. The term $b\widetilde{Y}_t$ represents the effect of demand shocks on inflation, and the term s_t represents the effects on inflation of supply shocks that increase firms' costs of production. As before, the term π^e shows the effect of expected inflation on the current inflation rate.

The Effects of Demand Shocks on Inflation Inflation often increases during expansions. For example, real GDP was about equal to potential GDP during the fourth quarter of 1963, but by the first quarter of 1966, real GDP was 5.9% above potential GDP. The inflation rate as measured by changes in the CPI increased from 1.7% at the end of 1963 to 3.8% by October 1966. Inflation often decreases during recessions, as happened during the 1981–1982 recession. Real GDP was 0.6% below potential GDP during the first quarter of 1981, but 7.5% below potential GDP by the end of the recession in the fourth quarter of 1982. As a result, the inflation rate fell from 11.8% during January 1981 to 3.8% during December 1982. These two experiences illustrate that when real GDP increases relative to potential GDP during economic expansions, the inflation rate typically increases as well. And when real GDP falls relative to potential GDP during recessions, the inflation rate typically decreases.

The Effect of Supply Shocks on Inflation Inflation does not always decrease during recessions, however. Inflation actually increased during the 1973–1975, 1980, and 1990–1991 recessions. Not coincidentally, each of these recessions was accompanied by a supply shock. Supply shocks raise firms' costs of production, which the firms typically pass along as increases in the prices of the goods they sell. For example, as oil prices increase, firms will try to pass along their higher costs to consumers in the form of higher prices for goods and services. Through this mechanism, a supply shock can increase the inflation rate.

Increases in productivity represent positive supply shocks that can reduce firms' costs and decrease the inflation rate. Productivity growth reduces costs per unit of output, so firms can produce more goods and services with the same number of workers. For example, improvements in information technology help firms produce more goods and services without incurring higher costs. Competition among firms ensures that these cost reductions are passed along to consumers in the form of lower prices.

Two examples illustrate the effects of supply shocks. First, as oil prices rose from \$3.56 per barrel to \$11.16 per barrel during the 1973–1975 recession, the inflation rate increased from 8.3% at the beginning of the recession in November 1973 to 10.5% at the end of the recession in March 1975. The U.S. economy was described as experiencing **stagflation**, which is a combination of inflation and recession, usually resulting from a supply shock such as an increase in oil prices. The tripling of the price of oil during the 1973–1975 recession significantly increased the costs of production and caused the inflation rate to increase, even though real GDP fell relative to potential GDP.

Stagflation A combination of inflation and recession, usually resulting from a supply shock.

The United States experienced an increase in the growth rate of labor productivity beginning in the late 1990s. From 1973 to 1995, labor productivity growth averaged just 1.4% per year. But from 1996 to 2010 the growth rate of labor productivity increased, averaging 2.7% per year. Many economists believe that labor productivity growth increased during the 1990s because of the spread of information technology. The increase in Internet use during the 1990s brought changes to the ways firms sell to consumers and to each other.

Cell phones, laptop computers, and wireless Internet access allow people to work away from the office, both at home and while traveling. These developments significantly increased labor productivity.

The nearly doubling of the growth rate of labor productivity has helped keep the growth rate of costs per unit of output low. From 1973 to 1995, when labor productivity growth was low, costs per unit of output grew at a rate of 4.7% per year, but costs per unit of output grew at a rate of just 1.3% per year from 1996 to 2009, when labor productivity growth was high. The rapid productivity growth since 1996 represents a positive supply shock that helped keep the inflation rate low.

Expectations of Inflation Unlike prices and quantities of goods in individual markets, we cannot observe the expected inflation rate directly. However, two surveys provide us with some data. The Federal Reserve Bank of Philadelphia conducts a survey called the *Survey of Professional Forecasters.* This survey provides a consensus estimate of professional economic forecasters of the expected inflation rate over the next year. In addition, the University of Michigan conducts a monthly survey of households that includes a question about their expectations of the inflation rate for the upcoming year. Figure 9.15 shows the actual inflation rate and the expected inflation rate as measured by these two surveys. (The University of Michigan survey data only began in 1978.) The figure shows that the two measures of the expected inflation rate track the actual inflation rate fairly closely.

The expected inflation rate rose rapidly during the late 1960s and early 1970s, but then fell dramatically during the early 1980s, and has been low and fairly stable since 1990. The decrease in the expected inflation rate was part of the Great Moderation that we discussed in Chapter 8 and is attributable to a combination of improved monetary policy performance; good luck in the form of milder shocks; improved business management techniques, such as just-in-time inventory methods; and the movement of the economy from producing goods to producing services.

Adaptive expectations The assumption that people make forecasts of future values of a variable using only past values of the variable.

Adaptive Expectations We have seen that changes in the expected inflation rate can have an important effect on the actual inflation rate. How do households and firms form their expectations of future inflation rates? Some economists believe that households and firms have **adaptive expectations**, which is the assumption that people make forecasts of future values of a variable using only past values of the variable. The simplest form of adaptive expectations is that people expect that the value of a variable, such as the inflation rate, from last year should occur again this year. For example, using the GDP chain-type price index,

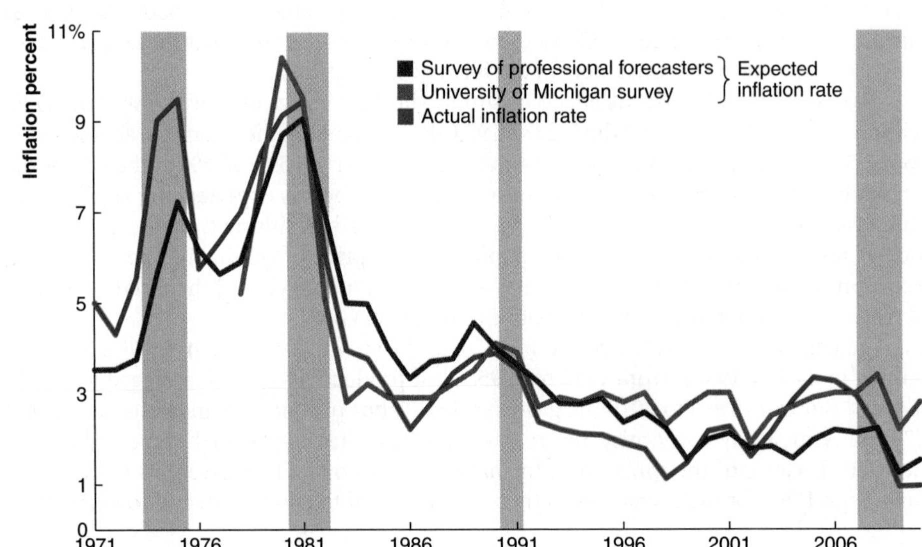

Figure 9.15

Measures of Expected Inflation for the United States, 1971–2010

Two measures of the expected inflation rate—one from the University of Michigan survey and one from a survey of professional forecasters—track the actual inflation rate fairly closely. Shaded areas represent recessions, as determined by the National Bureau of Economic Research.

Sources: U.S. Bureau of Labor Statistics; Federal Reserve Bank of Philadelphia; and University of Michigan.

the inflation rate for 2010 was 1.0%. With adaptive expectations, individuals would expect an inflation rate of 1.0% for 2011. We can express adaptive expectations as:

$$\pi_t^e = \pi_{t-1}.$$

When inflation rose during the late 1960s and 1970s, the rise in the actual inflation rate increased the expected inflation rate, which drove the actual inflation rate even higher. The inflation rate was 0.9% during the third quarter of 1963, but eventually rose to 11.1% during the third quarter of 1980. During the late 1960s and 1970s both demand shocks and supply shocks led to higher inflation. When expectations adjusted to these higher inflation rates, the inflation rate rose even more.

Assuming adaptive expectations, we can rewrite the Phillips curve in Equation (9.5) as:

$$\pi_t = \pi_{t-1} + b\widetilde{Y}_t - s_t. \tag{9.6}$$

Movement Along an Existing Phillips Curve

Figure 9.16 shows the Phillips curve in Equation (9.6). For simplicity, we assume that there are no supply shocks, so $s_t = 0$. At point *A*, real GDP equals potential GDP, so $\widetilde{Y}_1 = 0$, and the inflation rate during the current year equals the inflation rate from the previous year, so $\pi_1 = \pi_0$. Because the inflation rate is unchanged, there are no supply shocks, and the output gap equals 0, the expected inflation rate equals the actual inflation rate, $\pi_1 = \pi^e$. Therefore, point *A* represents equilibrium. Suppose a positive demand shock, such as a surge in household wealth, causes real GDP to increase above potential GDP, and the output gap to change from $\widetilde{Y}_1$ to $\widetilde{Y}_2$. As firms produce beyond their normal capacity, input prices rise, which firms pass on to consumers by increasing the prices of goods and services. In Equation (9.6), $b\widetilde{Y}_t$ is greater than zero, so the inflation rate rises from π_1 to π_2, and the economy moves along an existing Phillips curve from point *A* to point *B*.

The experience of the United States during the 1960s illustrates a movement along an existing Phillips curve. During the third quarter of 1963, real GDP equaled potential GDP, so the economy was at point *A*, with an inflation rate of 0.9%. However, as the expansion continued, real GDP rose relative to potential GDP, and by the first quarter of 1969, real

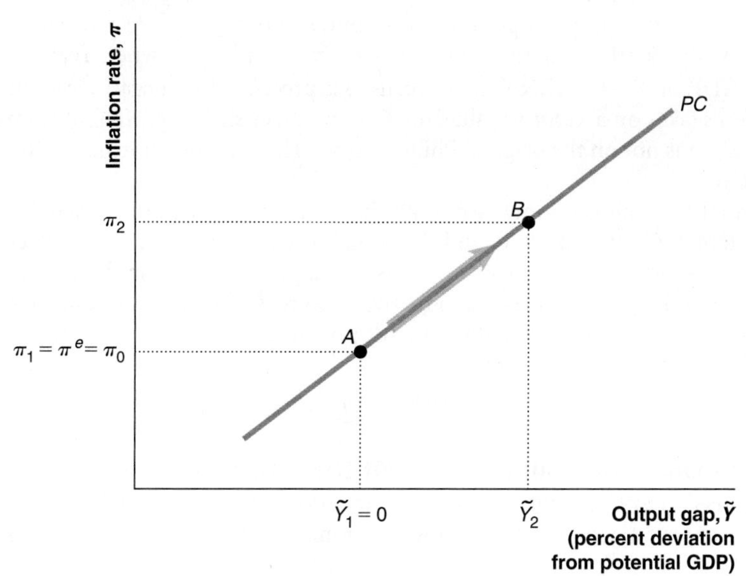

Figure 9.16

An Increase in the Output Gap Increases the Inflation Rate

The economy's equilibrium moves along an existing Phillips curve from point *A* to point *B*. ●

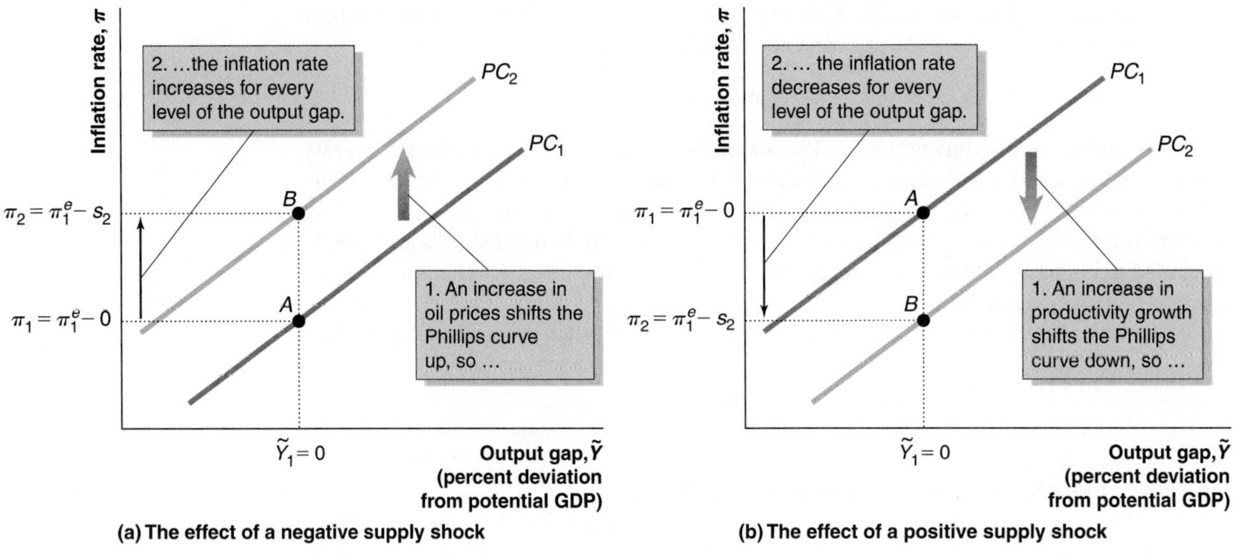

Figure 9.17 Shifts of the Phillips Curve

In panel (a), a negative supply shock, such as an increase in oil prices, shifts the Phillips curve up. In panel (b), a positive supply shock, such as an increase in labor productivity, shifts the Phillips curve down. ●

GDP was 3.2% above potential GDP, and the inflation rate had increased to 4.6%. The economy was now at point *B*.

Shifts of the Phillips Curve

Changes in the expected inflation rate and supply shocks cause the Phillips curve to shift. The United States experienced supply shocks when oil prices increased in 1973–1975 and again in 1980. Figure 9.17 illustrates how such a supply shock affects the Phillips curve.

In panel (a), the economy is initially in equilibrium at point *A*, where real GDP equals potential GDP, so $\tilde{Y}_1 = 0$, and the actual inflation rate equals the expected inflation rate, $\pi_1 = \pi_1^e$. Initially the economy is not experiencing a supply shock, so $s_1 = 0$. An increase in oil prices increases the cost per unit of output, so now $s_2 < 0$. As a result of the negative supply shock, the inflation rate rises to $\pi_2 = \pi_1^e - s_2$, when real GDP equals potential GDP, or $\tilde{Y}_1 = 0$. (Recall that because *s* is preceded by a negative sign in Equation (9.6), when *s* takes on a *negative* value, the Phillips curve shifts up.) Equilibrium is now at point *B*, which is not on the original Phillips curve. The Phillips curve has shifted up, from PC_1 to PC_2.

In panel (b), the economy is initially in equilibrium at point *A*, where real GDP equals potential GDP, so $\tilde{Y}_1 = 0$, and the actual inflation rate equals the expected inflation rate, $\pi_1 = \pi_1^e$. Initially the economy is not experiencing a supply shock, so $s_1 = 0$. An increase in the growth rate of productivity decreases the cost per unit of output, so now $s_2 > 0$. As a result of the positive supply shock, the inflation rate decreases to $\pi_2 = \pi_1^e - s_2$. Equilibrium is now at point *B*, which is not on the original Phillips curve, so the Phillips curve has shifted down, from PC_1 to PC_2.

How Well Does the Phillips Curve Fit the Inflation Data?

One of the Fed's responsibilities is to keep the inflation rate low and stable, so it is important for the Fed to have a good model for how inflation is determined. Chairman Ben Bernanke

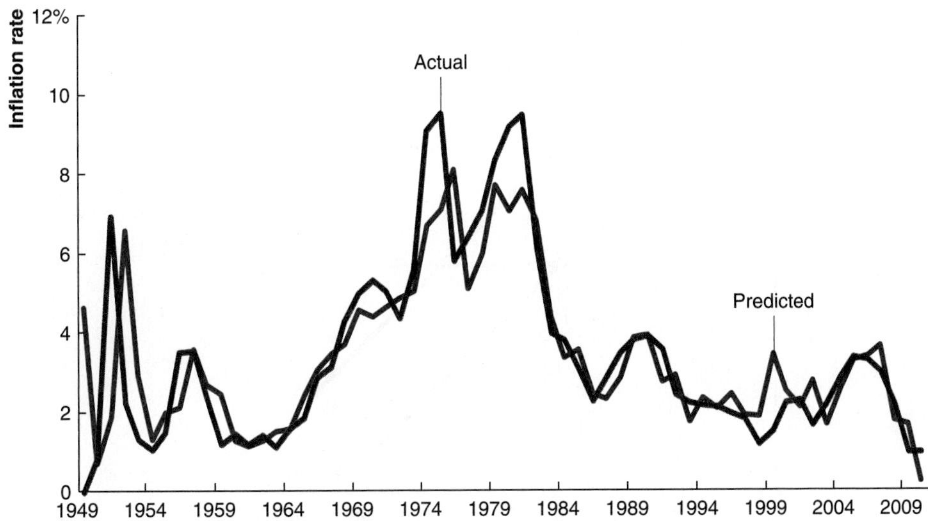

Figure 9.18

Actual and Predicted Inflation, Using the Phillips Curve with Adaptive Expectations for the United States, 1949–2010

A Phillips curve with simple adaptive expectations and using the growth rate of nominal oil prices to measure supply shocks can explain most of the variation in the inflation rate measured by the growth rate of the chain-type GDP price index.

Sources: U.S. Bureau of Economic Analysis; U.S. Bureau of Labor Statistics; Congressional Budget Office; and Federal Reserve Bank of Saint Louis. ●

and other members of the Fed use a version of the Phillips curve when conducting monetary policy. Therefore, it is useful to know how well the Phillips curve explains the inflation rate.

To see whether the predictions of the Phillips curve are accurate, we will use the following procedure:

1. Plug U.S. data from the 1949–2010 time period into Equation (9.6).
2. Measure the cost shock, s_t, using data on the growth rate of nominal oil prices.
3. Assume that households and firms have adaptive expectations where the expected inflation rate equals the actual inflation rate from the previous year.

Figure 9.18 shows the actual inflation rate and the inflation rate that the Phillips curve predicts. Notice that the predicted inflation rate closely tracks the actual inflation rate. Therefore, the Phillips curve in Equation (9.6) provides reasonable, though not perfect, predictions for the inflation rate.

Using Monetary Policy to Fight a Recession

In this section, we combine the *IS* and *MP* curves and the Phillips curve to explain how monetary policy responds to demand shocks. Figure 9.19 shows how the Fed can try to use monetary policy to move the economy back to potential GDP following a negative demand shock.

Suppose that the economy begins in equilibrium at point *A* in panel (a) of Figure 9.19. The economy then experiences a negative demand shock, such as the one that occurred in 2007, when spending on residential construction declined following the bursting of the housing bubble. Panel (a) shows that the demand shock causes the *IS* curve to shift to the left, from IS_1 to IS_2. Real GDP falls below potential GDP, so the economy enters a recession at point *B*. Panel (b) shows the decrease in real GDP as a movement down the Phillips curve from point *A* to point *B*, lowering the inflation rate from π_1 to π_2. The Fed typically fights recessions by lowering its target for the federal funds rate. As we have seen, this action lowers the real interest rate, shifting the monetary policy curve down from MP_1 to MP_2. A lower real interest rate leads to increases in consumption spending, investment spending, and net exports, causing a movement down the *IS* curve from point *B* to point *C* in panel (a). Real GDP returns to its potential level, so the output gap again equals 0. In panel (b), the inflation rate rises from π_2 back to π_1, causing a movement back up the Phillips curve from point *B* to point *C*.

Figure 9.19

Monetary Policy Responds to a Negative Demand Shock

A negative demand shock leads to lower real GDP and inflation. The Fed responds by decreasing real interest rates, so real GDP and inflation both rise back to their original levels. ●

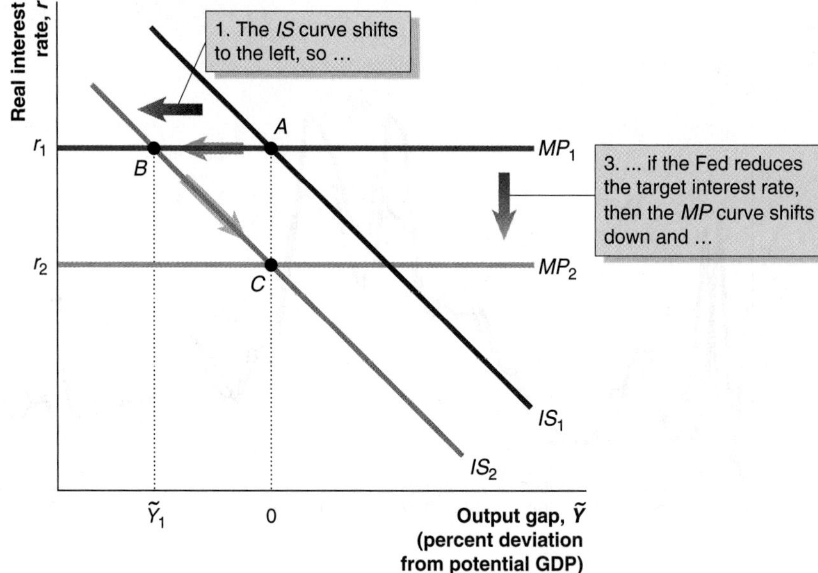
Real interest rate, r
1. The IS curve shifts to the left, so ...
A
r_1
B
MP_1
3. ... if the Fed reduces the target interest rate, then the MP curve shifts down and ...
r_2
C
MP_2
IS_1
IS_2
$\tilde{Y}_1$
0
Output gap, $\tilde{Y}$ (percent deviation from potential GDP)

(a) The Fed offsets a shift in the *IS* curve

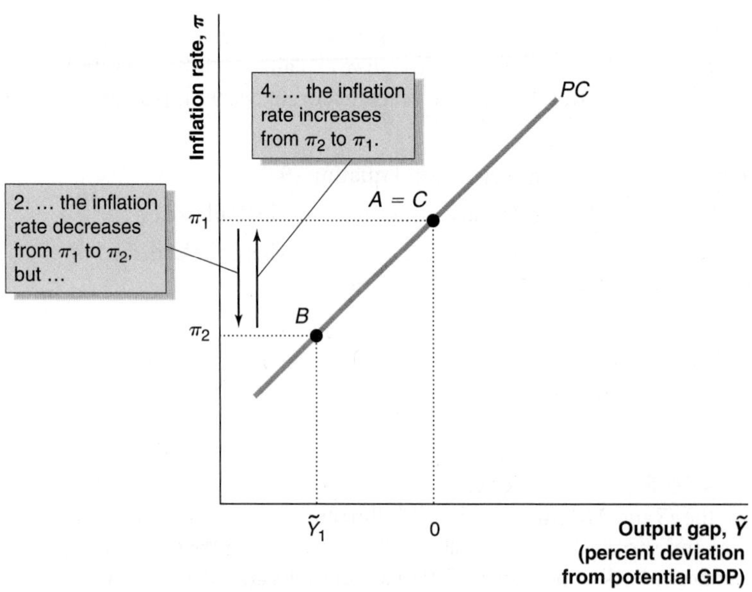
Inflation rate, π
4. ... the inflation rate increases from π_2 to π_1.
PC
2. ... the inflation rate decreases from π_1 to π_2, but ...
A = C
π_1
B
π_2
$\tilde{Y}_1$
0
Output gap, $\tilde{Y}$ (percent deviation from potential GDP)

(b) Inflation first falls and then rises

Solved Problem 9.4

Fed Policy to Keep Inflation from Increasing

During the expansion of the 1990s, the stock market boomed, increasing household wealth and the willingness of households to spend. As a result, the inflation rate accelerated from 1.0% during the fourth quarter of 1998 to 2.4% during the fourth quarter of 2000. What policy could the Fed have pursued to keep the inflation rate from rising? Use the *IS-MP* model to answer this question. Be sure to show any shifts in or movements along the *IS* curve, the *MP* curve, and the Phillips curve.

Solving the Problem

Step 1 **Review the chapter material.** This problem is about using the *IS-MP* model to analyze how the Fed can keep inflation from rising, so you may want to review the section "Using Monetary Policy to Fight a Recession," which begins on page 335.

Step 2 **Draw a graph that shows the initial equilibrium and the effect of the increase in household wealth.** Before the stock market boom, output equals potential output, and the inflation rate is 1%. An increase in consumption expenditures is a positive demand shock, so the *IS* curve should shift to the right, and the inflation rate should increase to 2.4%, as shown by the Phillips curve graph. Therefore, your initial graphs should look like this:

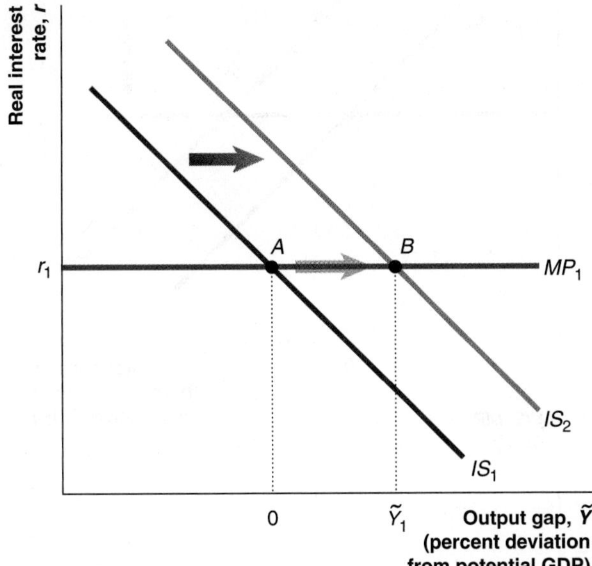

(a) *IS–MP*

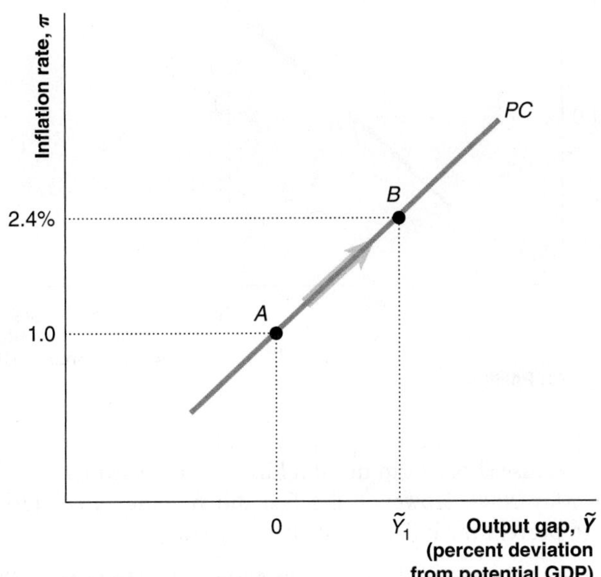

(b) Phillips curve

Step 3 Determine the Fed's response. What would the Fed have to do to keep the inflation rate from increasing? The Phillips curve shows that the output gap would have to remain equal to 0 to keep the inflation rate at 1.0%. The Fed affects the output gap by changing the real interest rate and the position of the *MP* curve. To keep the output gap at 0, the real interest rate would have to increase, so the *MP* curve must shift upward. Your graphs should now look like this:

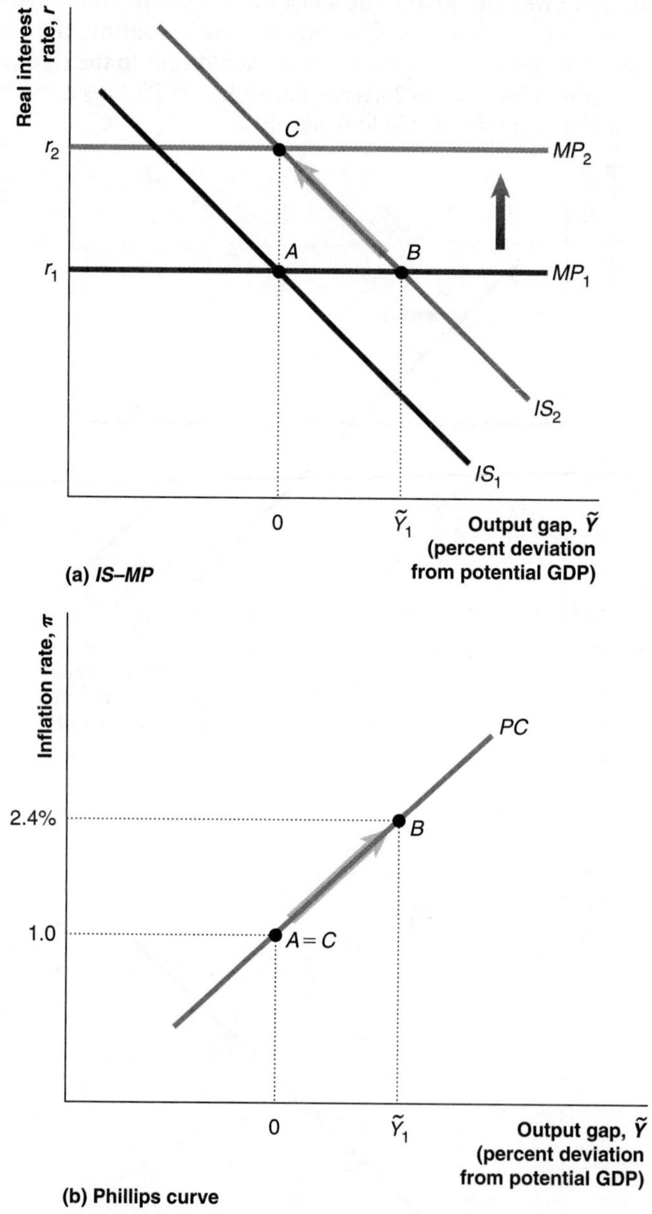

In principle, the Fed could have prevented the increase in the inflation rate. The Fed did increase short-term nominal interest rates from 4.75% in June 1999 to 6.5% in May 2000. However, the Fed did not increase interest rates quickly enough to prevent the inflation rate from increasing.

For more practice, do related problem 4.13 on page 351 at the end of this chapter.

The Performance of the U.S. Economy During 2007–2009

9.5

Learning Objective

Use the *IS–MP* model to understand the performance of the U.S. economy during the recession of 2007–2009.

The U.S. economy experienced three shocks during the 2007–2009 period:

- A financial crisis, which increased the risk premium investors required before making loans
- A decrease in real estate values, which affected the *IS* curve
- A surge in oil prices, which affected the Phillips curve

As a result of these shocks, real GDP fell from 0.2% below potential GDP during the second quarter of 2007 to 7.6% below potential GDP during the third quarter of 2009. The inflation rate rose from 1.8% during the fourth quarter of 2006 to 4.4% during the third quarter of 2008, before decreasing to 0.3% during the second quarter of 2009. In this section, we use the *IS–MP* model to explain both the decrease in real GDP and the temporary increase in the inflation rate caused by the three shocks.

The *IS–MP* Model and the Financial and Real Estate Shocks

The risk premium is measured as the difference between the interest rate on Aaa corporate bonds and the interest rate for a 10-year Treasury note. On June 7, 2007, the risk premium was 0.65%, which was just below the average level over the 1953–2008 period of 0.77%. On August 21, the risk premium rose to 1.25% as investors became increasingly concerned that conditions in the real estate market would spill over into the financial market. The risk premium continued to rise until it peaked at 2.13% on March 17, 2008 the day on which JPMorgan Chase offered to purchase the investment bank Bear Stearns for $2 per share, thereby saving Bear Stearns from bankruptcy. Because investors had become very concerned that firms might default on their bonds, they were unwilling to purchase corporate bonds except at higher interest rates. So, the risk premium rose, and many firms were unable to obtain financing for investment projects. Problems in financial markets also affected households as banks began to demand more collateral for loans and to increase interest rates. These changes restricted the ability of households to borrow and caused consumption expenditures and housing sales to decline. So, the financial market shock reduced both consumption and investment. If financial market turbulence had lasted a brief period, it would probably not have significantly affected investment expenditures—because it can take months or longer for firms to plan investment projects or for individuals to purchase a home. However, the risk premium continued to rise to 2.73% on November 26, 2008, and it remained elevated at 1.56% as late as May 13, 2010.

Housing prices began to decline in 2006, as the housing bubble burst. The value of a home is a major component of a household's wealth, and when wealth decreases, so does household consumption. In addition, as sales of new homes decreased, builders cut back on construction of new housing. The growth rate of residential construction went from 6.2% during 2006 to −22.9% during 2008, and it was still −3.0% in 2010. The rapid decrease in housing prices reduced both consumption and investment.

Figure 9.20 uses the *IS–MP* model to show the effects of the housing and financial shocks. Panel (a) shows the effect of these shocks on the *IS* curve. The economy starts off in equilibrium at point *A*, where real GDP equals potential GDP, so $\tilde{Y}_1 = 0$. The financial market shock increases the default-risk premium, so the *MP* curve shifts up, from MP_1 to MP_2. The real estate shock reduces wealth and residential construction, causing the *IS* curve to shift to the left, from IS_1 to IS_2. The economy's equilibrium is now at point *B*, where real GDP has fallen below potential GDP and the output gap has changed from $\tilde{Y}_1$ to $\tilde{Y}_2$. Panel (b) uses the Phillips curve to show the effect of the change in the output gap on the inflation rate. The economy's equilibrium moves down the Phillips curve from point *A* to point *B*, so the inflation rate falls from π_1 to π_2. The *IS–MP* model predicts

Figure 9.20

The Financial and Real Estate Market Shocks and the U.S. Economy, 2007–2009

The financial crisis shifts the *MP* curve upward, and the collapse in housing prices shifts the *IS* curve to the left in panel (a). As a result, the real interest rate increases and the output gap becomes negative in panel (a), and the inflation rate decreases in panel (b). ●

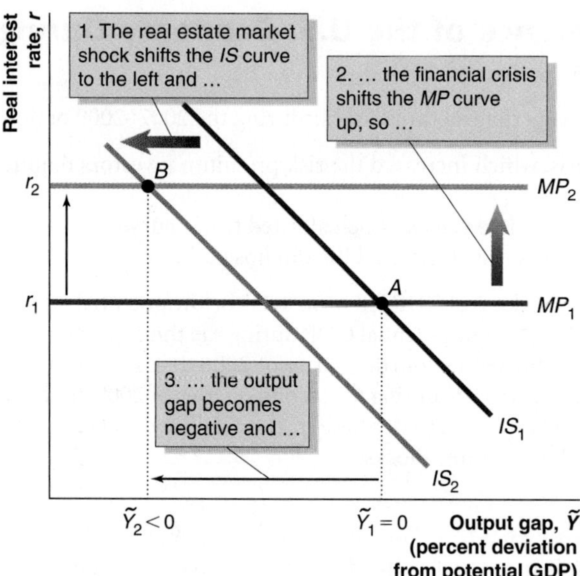

(a) *IS–MP*

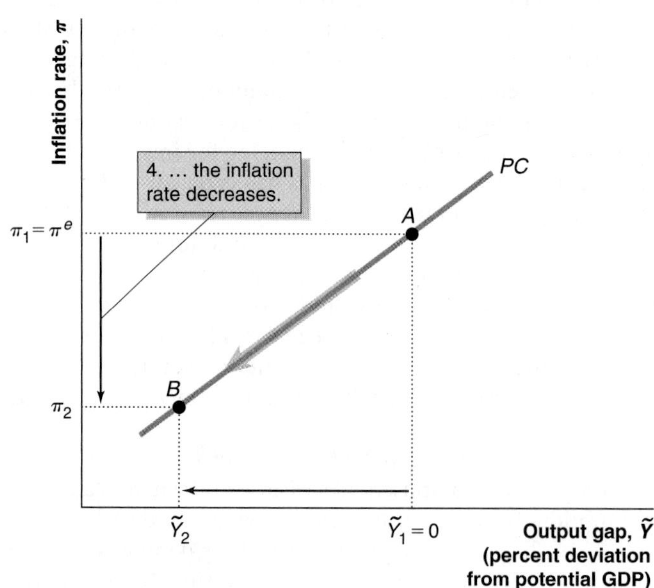

(b) Phillips curve

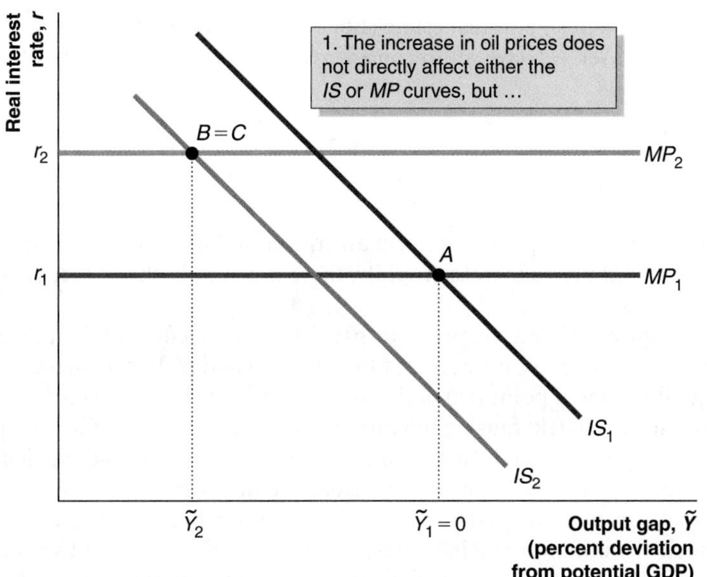

(a) *IS–MP*

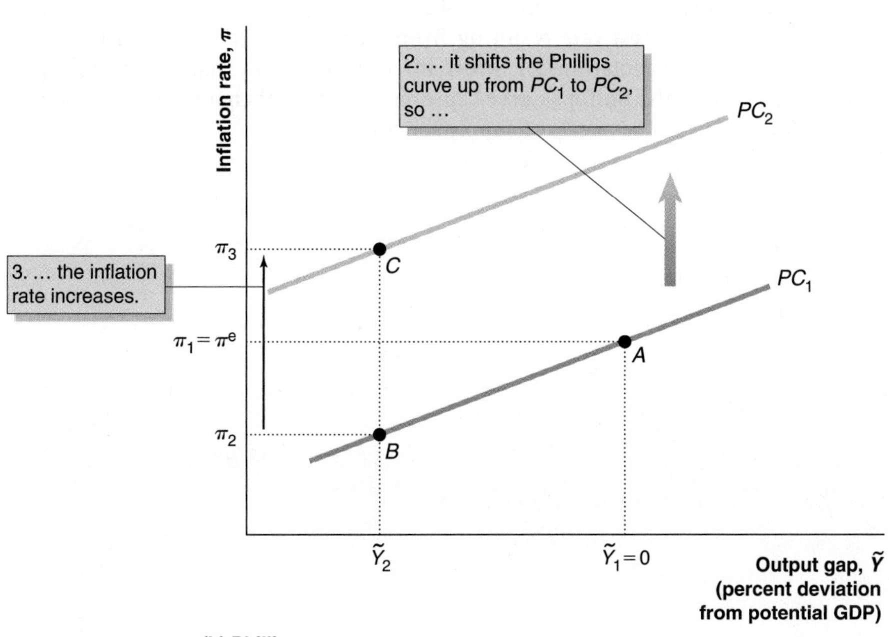

(b) Phillips curve

Figure 9.21

The Oil Price Shock and the U.S. Economy, 2007–2009

The increase in the price of oil does not shift the curves in panel (a). However, the increase shifts the Phillips curve up in panel (b), which puts upward pressure on inflation. ●

that the financial and real estate shocks should have reduced real GDP *and* the inflation rate. However, we have yet to consider the effect on the economy of the surge in oil prices during 2008.

The *IS–MP* Model and the Oil Shock of 2007–2008

The price of oil rose from $56.60 a barrel on March 19, 2007 to a high of $145.66 on July 11, 2008 before decreasing to $30.81 on December 22, 2008. The more than doubling of oil prices had important effects on inflation. Oil is an important cost of production, so when oil prices increase rapidly, there is a supply shock that causes the inflation rate to increase.

Figure 9.21 (on the previous page) shows the effect of the oil price shock, using the *IS–MP* model. After the effects of the financial and real estate market shocks, the short-run equilibrium is at point *B* in both panel (a) and panel (b). The increase in oil prices is a negative supply shock, causing inflation to increase. As a result, the Phillips curve will shift up from PC_1 to PC_2, so the inflation rate increases to π_3, output remains at $\tilde{Y}_2$, and short-run equilibrium is now at point *C*. Because the increase in inflation does not cause an additional decline in real GDP, point *C* is also point *B* in panel (a). As a result of the supply shock, the inflation rate increases, and our model is consistent with the experience of the economy from 2007 to mid 2008. After mid-2008, oil prices fell, as did the inflation rate.

The *IS-MP* model is a useful tool for analyzing short-run fluctuations in the output gap and in the inflation rate. The *IS* curve captures the effect of demand shocks that can temporarily push short-run macroeconomic equilibrium away from a zero output gap. The *MP* curve captures the effects not only of monetary policy, but also the effects of fluctuations in the real interest rate resulting from changes in the default-risk premium, changes in investors' expectations of future interest rates, and changes in the expected inflation rate. Finally, the Phillips curve captures the effect of changes in the output gap on the inflation rate and the effects of supply shocks.

Answering the Key Question

Continued from page 302

At the beginning of this chapter, we asked the question:

"What explains the severity of the 2007–2009 recession?"

Most economists were surprised by the severity of the 2007–2009 recession. During the previous 25 years of the Great Moderation, the U.S. economy had experienced only the mild recessions of 1990–1991 and 2001. It appeared that the Fed had learned to tame the business cycle. Even in early 2007, after it had become clear that significant problems had developed in the subprime mortgage market, many economists and policymakers, including Fed Chairman Ben Bernanke, were uncertain that a recession would occur at all, much less a recession more severe than any since the Great Depression of the 1930s. As we have seen in this chapter, the key reason the recession was so severe is that it was accompanied by a financial crisis. It is not a coincidence that the Great Depression and the recession of 2007–2009 were both accompanied by financial crises.

This chapter has discussed how a financial panic reduces the effectiveness of the Fed's key policy tool: reducing short-term nominal interest rates. Although the Fed reduced short-term rates to historic lows, a sharp increase in the default-risk premium led to increases in the long-term real interest rates that households and firms pay when borrowing. These high real interest rates combined with the reluctance of many banks and other financial firms to make loans at any rate of interest led to sharp declines in consumption and investment spending and a severe recession.

In the next chapter, we will discuss how monetary policy attempts to minimize the effect of shocks on the output gap and on the inflation rate. When evaluating policy, remember that shocks cause economic fluctuations because nominal wages and prices are sticky. This tendency for the economy to only gradually self-correct poses one of the biggest challenges to successful macroeconomic policy.

Read an *Inside Look at Policy* on the next page for a discussion of the financial reform bill that President Obama signed into law in 2010.

Largest Financial Overhaul Package since Great Depression Signed Into Law

CHRISTIAN SCIENCE MONITOR

Financial Reform Law: What's In It and How Does It Work?

The financial reform bill signed into law by President Obama Wednesday constitutes a sweeping attempt to reallocate power from Wall Street to Washington and prevent future financial crises. . . .

What's in the bill? Here are some of its major provisions:

• *New consumer watchdog.* The bill establishes a Consumer Financial Protection Bureau within the Federal Reserve. This agency will enforce existing consumer-oriented regulations that apply to big financial firms, mortgage-related businesses, and payday and student lenders. It will also ensure that the fine print on financial services is clear and accurate, and will maintain a single toll-free hotline for consumers to report possibly deceptive practices.

a • *Financial early warning system.* The law sets up a Financial Services Oversight Council that is intended to work as a sort of bureaucratic early warning radar that scans the horizons looking for trouble in financial markets. Composed largely of existing officials, such as the Secretary of the Treasury, the group could require Federal Reserve oversight for big nonbank financial firms whose failure might destabilize the US economy. The council could also vote to require big, troubled companies to sell off assets–but only as a last resort.

b • *Breakup authority.* Federal regulators will have the power to seize and dismantle troubled financial firms whose collapse might pull other companies down as well. This resolution authority would be overseen by the Federal Deposit Insurance Corporation. Taxpayers would pay for upfront costs but regulators would then be required to recoup the money by levying fees on financial firms with more than $50 billion in assets.

• *Tighter leash for financial firms.* The bill establishes tight restrictions on the ability of banks to trade in financial markets with their own funds. Proprietary trading–when banks place market bets for their own profits, instead of their customers–will be banned. Banks will be able to invest sums equal to only 3 percent of their capital in hedge and private equity investment instruments. In addition, the complex financial risk swaps known as derivatives will face comprehensive regulation for the first time. Most will have to be traded through public clearinghouses or exchanges.

c • *Mortgage reforms.* In the years leading up to the financial meltdown it seemed as if banks and other financial firms would give a mortgage to any person with a pulse. Those loose practices are supposed to end, under the terms of the financial overhaul bill. Banks and other financial companies must review the income and credit histories of mortgage applicants, to ensure they can afford payments. Firms that bundle mortgages into pooled investment instruments must keep at least 5 percent of these instruments on their books. This is intended to serve as an incentive for the firms to make solid loans– not questionable ones that are then dumped entirely on outside investors. . . .

Source: "Financial Reform Law: What's In It and How Does It Work?" By Peter Grier. Reprinted with permission from the July 21, 2010 issue of *The Christian Science Monitor*.

Key Points in the Article

This article discusses new financial regulations included in the financial reform bill that President Obama signed into law on July 21, 2010. The legislation, which is designed to address issues that contributed to the 2008 financial crisis, is the largest overhaul of U.S. financial regulations since the Great Depression. The law attempts to reallocate power from Wall Street to Washington. Among the items addressed in the legislation are increased regulations and oversight of financial firms, additional consumer protection measures, greater supervisory responsibilities for the Fed, and reforms of the mortgage industry.

Analyzing the News

a The financial reform law includes establishing a Financial Services Oversight Council to monitor and assess risks to the nation's financial stability. The council will allow the Fed to impose stricter rules on large financial firms. The legislation also gives the Fed supervisory powers over large financial firms, a move designed to ensure that the government has a better understanding of the risks and complexities of firms that could pose a risk to the economy as a whole.

b One of the major provisions in the financial reform law gives federal regulators the authority to seize and break up large troubled financial institutions in cases where a firm's collapse could destabilize the financial system. Regulators will have the authority to accomplish this without resorting to taxpayer bailouts of these institutions. Following the bankruptcy of Lehman Brothers in September 2008, many large institutions, including Citigroup and Bank of America, received bailout funds from the federal TARP program. The FDIC lists more than 330 banks that have failed from the date of the collapse of Lehman Brothers through the end of February 2011. The figure below shows the number of bank failures in the United States, by year, from 2001 until February 2011, with very few failures recorded from 2001 until the financial crisis began in 2008.

c The legislation also addresses mortgage reforms. Loose lending practices should become less common after this legislation, with banks and other financial institutions being required to ensure that mortgage applicants can afford mortgage payments by reviewing their income and credit histories. Also included in the law is an incentive for financial firms to make safer loans. Those firms that securitize mortgages will be required to hold at least 5% of the risk on their own balance sheets.

THINKING CRITICALLY *ABOUT POLICY*

1. Financial markets play an important role in determining consumption. The legislation establishing new regulations for the financial industry is designed to prevent a repeat of a financial crisis like the one that occurred in 2008. Assume the legislative changes are effective in stabilizing financial markets and lead to an increase in consumption expenditures. Use the *IS-MP* model to explain the efffects on the output gap and the equilibrium real interest rate.
2. The severity of the financial crisis that began in 2008 prompted the passage of the financial reform bill. The financial crisis is, in large part, responsible for the length and severity of the recession of 2007–2009, a time when the Federal Reserve lowered its target for the federal funds rate to 0.00–0.25%, where it remained for all of 2009 and 2010 and into 2011. Assume that the real interest rate also remained constant during this timeframe. Use the *IS-MP* model to demonstrate the effect of the financial shock during 2009.

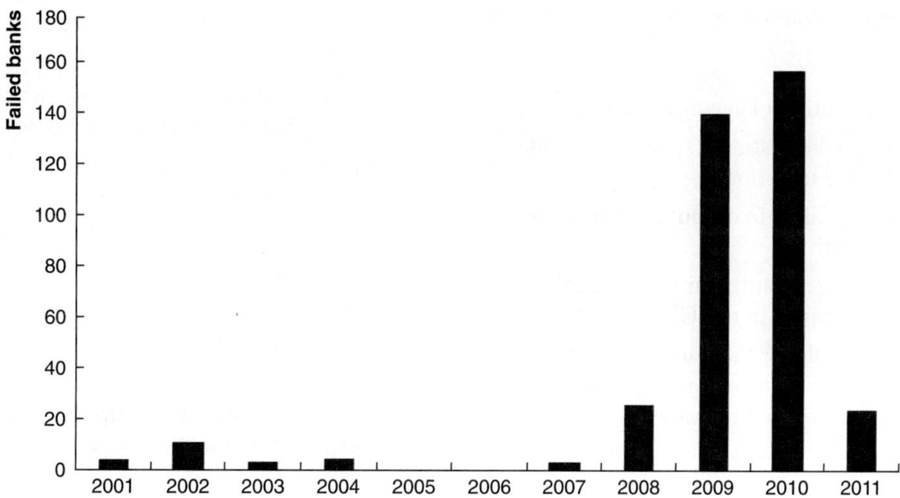

U.S. Bank Failures by year, 2001–February 2011

Source: FDIC Failed Bank List

CHAPTER SUMMARY AND PROBLEMS

KEY TERMS AND CONCEPTS

Adaptive expectations, p. 332
Default risk, p. 313
IS–MP model, p. 304
IS curve, p. 304
Marginal propensity to consume (*MPC*), p. 306
MP curve, p. 304
Multiplier, p. 308
Multiplier effect, p. 308
Phillips curve, p. 304
Risk structure of interest rates, p. 313
Stagflation, p. 331
Term premium, p. 313
Term structure of interest rates, p. 313

9.1 The *IS* Curve: The Relationship Between Real Interest Rates and Aggregate Expenditure

Explain how the *IS* curve represents the relationship between the real interest rate and aggregate expenditure.

SUMMARY

The ***IS–MP*** model consists of an *IS* curve, an *MP* curve, and a Phillips curve. The ***IS* curve** shows the relationship between the real interest rate and output. The ***MP* curve** shows the relationship between the real interest rate that the central bank targets and the output gap. As the real interest rate increases, consumption and investment expenditures decrease, so real GDP also decreases. As the real interest rate decreases, consumption and investment expenditures increase, so real GDP also increases. Changes in the real interest rate cause movements along an existing *IS* curve. Changes in other determinants of aggregate expenditure—such as wealth and expectations about future income—cause the *IS* curve to shift. The **multiplier effect** explains why changes in autonomous expenditure cause larger changes in real GDP.

Review Questions

1.1 What is the definition of aggregate expenditure?

1.2 How might actual investment spending be different from planned investment spending?

1.3 Explain how equilibrium output is determined in the goods market.

1.4 Why does a change in autonomous expenditure lead to a larger change in real GDP?

1.5 What is the formula for the multiplier? What effect do different values of the marginal propensity to consume (*MPC*) have on the value of the multiplier?

1.6 Explain how the *IS* curve represents equilibrium in the goods market.

1.7 Why is the *IS* curve downward sloping?

1.8 Why does investment increase when real interest rates are lower?

1.9 Give an example of a shock that could shift the *IS* curve to the left.

1.10 Give an example of a shock that could shift the *IS* curve to the right.

Problems and Applications

1.11 Draw a graph of the goods market and identify the equilibrium level of GDP. Then use your graph to show the effect of each of the following changes:

a. Households become more pessimistic and decide to buy fewer new homes.

b. The government increases transfer payments without changing taxes.

c. Consumers feel wealthier and want to spend more.

d. Prices rise in the rest of the world, making U.S. exports more desirable.

1.12 The graph on the next page shows the goods market in equilibrium at output Y_1. Then the aggregate expenditure function shifts to AE_2.

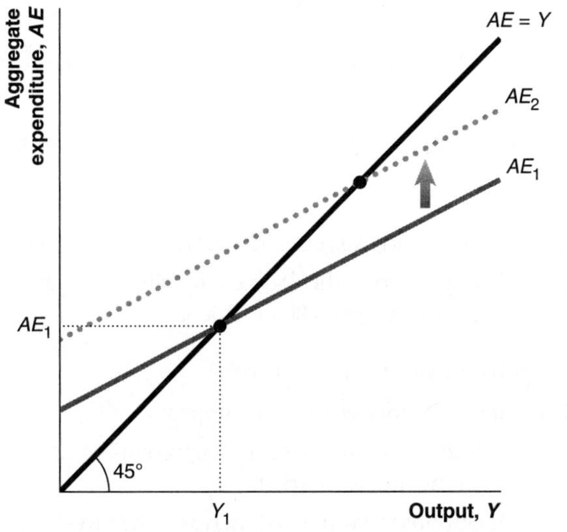

Aggregate expenditure, AE

$AE = Y$

AE_2

AE_1

AE_1

45°

Y_1

Output, Y

a. What could have caused this shift in aggregate expenditures?

b. Carefully explain the process by which the economy will adjust to the new equilibrium.

1.13 For each of the following values of the marginal propensity to consume (*MPC*), find the value of the multiplier. Use the equation from footnote 4 on page 308 to also calculate the value of the tax multiplier for each value of the *MPC*.

a. $MPC = 0.8$

b. $MPC = 0.75$

c. $MPC = 0.6$

1.14 Suppose that the marginal propensity to consume is 0.8.

a. If the government increases spending by \$100 million, what is the change in output?

b. If the government increases taxes by \$100 million, what is the change in output?

c. If the government increases taxes by \$100 million *at the same time* that it increases spending by \$100 million (so the budget deficit does not increase), what is the change in output?

1.15 The *IS* curve shows the equilibrium combinations of the real interest rate and real GDP.

a. Demonstrate using graphs how the *IS* curve represents equilibrium in the goods market.

b. Now suppose that firms become more optimistic about future profits. Show the effect on the goods market and derive the new *IS* curve.

1.16 For each of the following changes, identify (1) whether there is a shift in the *IS* curve or a movement along the curve, and (2) if the curve shifts, state the direction in which it shifts.

a. The real interest rate increases.

b. Firms become more pessimistic about future profitability.

c. Government spending increases.

d. Real GDP falls.

1.17 Consider the following statement: "The *IS* curve slopes downward because a fall in short-term nominal interest rates increases the money supply and decreases investment spending." Do you agree with this statement? Briefly explain.

1.18 The Great Depression began in the summer of 1929, but the stock market crash of October 1929 may have deepened the initial recession. The stock market crash increased the pessimism of both households and firms and decreased household wealth.

a. Which component of real GDP changed as a result of the stock market crash?

b. How did the crash affect the goods market?

c. Did the crash affect the *IS* curve? Briefly explain.

1.19 During the 1960s, a major restructuring of the tax code decreased taxes for most people. Also during these years, the war in Vietnam required increased government purchases.

a. Which components of real GDP were affected by these events?

b. How did these events affect the goods market?

c. Would these events affect the *IS* curve? Briefly explain.

1.20 The name of the *IS* curve derives from the relationship between investment and saving.

a. What is the relationship between investment and saving along the *IS* curve?

b. Why must this relationship hold?

9.2 The Monetary Policy Curve: The Relationship Between the Central Bank's Target Interest Rate and Output

Use the monetary policy, *MP*, curve to show how the interest rate set by the central bank helps to determine the output gap.

SUMMARY

Central banks control only the short-term nominal interest rate. However, when the default risk premium, the term structure effect, and the expected inflation rate are constant, changes in the short-term nominal interest rate cause changes in the long-term real interest rate. If the central bank increases its target interest rate, the *MP* curve shifts up; if the central bank decreases its target interest rate, the *MP* curve shifts down. Similarly, if the default risk premium increases, the *MP* curve will shift up, and if the default risk premium decreases, the *MP* curve will shift down. If the **term premium** or expected future short-term nominal interest rates increase, the *MP* curve will shift up, and if either of them decreases, the *MP* curve will shift down. Finally, if the expected inflation rate decreases, the *MP* curve will shift up, and if the expected inflation rate increases, the *MP* curve will shift down.

Review Questions

2.1 Over which interest rates does the central bank have the most control?

2.2 What are the key differences between the short-term nominal interest rate and the long-term real interest rate?

2.3 What must we assume in order for the *MP* curve to be horizontal?

2.4 What would cause the *MP* curve to shift up? Down?

2.5 Briefly describe the Fed's changes in its target interest rate from 2004 to 2008.

Problems and Applications

2.6 Show the following using graphs:

a. Show how the *MP* curve represents equilibrium in the money market.

b. Suppose that the Fed increases the target for the federal funds rate. Show the effect on the money market and derive the new *MP* curve.

2.7 For each of the following changes, identify (1) whether there is a shift in the *MP* curve or a movement along the curve, and (2) if the curve shifts, state the direction in which it shifts.

a. The Fed decreases the target federal funds rate.

b. Real GDP increases.

c. Government purchases increase.

2.8 Consider the following statement: "Central banks control only short-term interest rates, but long-term interest rates are most important for economic activity. Therefore, monetary policy is not important in determining output." Do you agree with this statement? Briefly explain.

Equilibrium in the *IS–MP* Model

Use the *IS–MP* model to understand why real GDP fluctuates.

SUMMARY

The economy is in long-run equilibrium when real GDP equals potential GDP, or the output gap is zero. If the central bank increases its target interest rate, households and firms find it more costly to borrow. As a result, consumption and investment decrease, so real GDP decreases and the output gap becomes negative. If the central bank decreases its target interest rate, households and firms find it cheaper to borrow. As a result, consumption and investment increase, so real GDP and the output gap increase. A positive demand shock—such as an increase in wealth that increases consumption—shifts the *IS* curve to the right. If the central bank keeps the target interest rate constant, real GDP and the output gap will increase. A negative demand shock—such as a decrease in wealth that decreases consumption—shifts the *IS* curve to the left. If the central bank keeps the target interest rate constant, real GDP and the output gap will decrease.

Visit **www.myeconlab.com** to complete these exercises online and get instant feedback.

Review Questions

3.1 How does a shift to the right of the *IS* curve affect the output gap and the real interest rate?

3.2 How does a shift up of the *MP* curve affect the output gap and the real interest rate?

Problems and Applications

3.3 **[Related to *Solved Problem 9.3* on page 325]** In the early 1990s, Japan's economy experienced a number of shocks due to the bursting of bubbles in real estate and the stock market.

a. Use the *IS–MP* model to show the economy's equilibrium prior to the shocks.

b. Now show how the shocks affected the economy. What happened to the real interest rate, real GDP, and the output gap?

c. The Bank of Japan responded to the shocks by reducing its target interest rate. How would this action affect real GDP and the output gap?

3.4 **[Related to the *Making the Connection* on page 322]** In the early 1990s, Finland experienced a severe recession in which real GDP decreased by 14% and the unemployment rate increased from 3% to nearly 20%. The causes of the depression were in some ways similar to the causes of the 2007–2009 recession in the United States: Earlier financial deregulation led to a boom, in this case largely financed by foreign borrowing. An asset boom caused the prices of most assets, including real estate and stock, to increase rapidly. In addition, the Soviet Union collapsed in 1991, Finland lost its largest trading partner, and at the same time, bank regulations changed, tightening credit standards.

a. Explain the effect of a large decrease in international trade on the economy of Finland.

b. Explain the effect of a tightening of credit standards.

c. Use the *IS–MP* model to show why Finland experienced a depression.

3.5 Consider the following statement: "Expectations about future events, such as the profitability of firms or projected income, are important to economic activity only when the expected events occur, not in the present." Do you agree or disagree with this statement? Explain your answer.

Source: Alan Greenspan, "The Challenge of Central Banking in a Democratic Society," Speech to the American Enterprise Institute, December 5, 1996.

3.6 Suppose that a central bank wants to increase economic activity by increasing the rate of growth of the money supply.

a. What does this increase in the money supply imply about the target federal funds rate?

b. Show the effect in the *IS–MP* model and demonstrate the effect on the output gap.

c. If this increase in the growth rate of the money supply is expected to be permanent, is it likely that the expected inflation rate will remain constant? Briefly explain.

3.7 The effectiveness of monetary policy in changing output depends on the slope of the *IS* curve, which in turn depends on the responsiveness of investment and consumption to the real interest rate. The graph below shows two *IS* curves. IS_1 shows the case where households and firms do not increase consumption and investment much in response to lower interest rates; for IS_2, households and firms are more responsive.

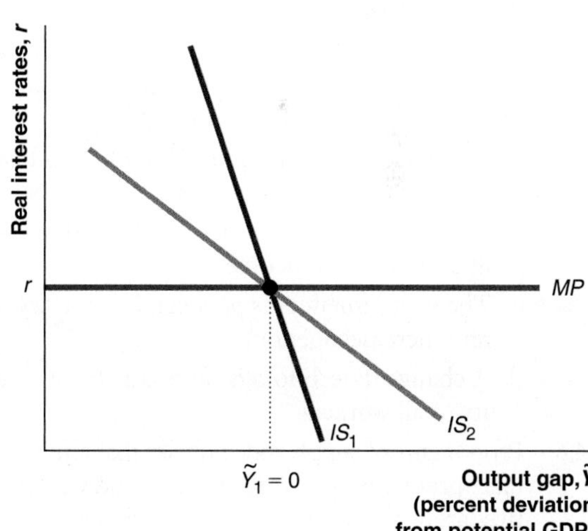

a. Show the effect on the output gap of a decrease in the target federal funds rate, given each of the *IS* curves.

b. How does the slope of the *IS* curve affect the ability of monetary policy to change real GDP?

9.4 The *IS–MP* Model and the Phillips Curve

Understand the role of the Phillips curve in the *IS–MP* model.

SUMMARY

The traditional **Phillips curve** shows the relationship between the unemployment rate and the inflation rate. In this chapter, we use Okun's law to derive a Phillips curve that shows the relationship between the output gap and the inflation rate. This Phillips curve shows that the inflation rate depends on the expected inflation rate, the output gap, and supply shocks. Changes in the output gap cause a movement along an existing Phillips curve, while changes in expected inflation and supply shocks cause the Phillips curve to shift. The simplest way to model inflation is with **adaptive expectations**, which assume that the expected inflation rate this year is the same as last year's inflation rate. A Phillips curve using adaptive expectations provides a good explanation of the inflation rate for the United States.

Review Questions

4.1 What does the Phillips curve represent?

4.2 What is the equation for the Phillips curve?

4.3 How is the expected inflation rate measured?

4.4 What are adaptive expectations?

Problems and Applications

4.5 For each of the following scenarios, state the likely effect on the price level and whether it is cost related or demand related.

a. Unions in the airline and automobile industries successfully strike for higher wages.

b. Consumers decide to spend more and save less at every level of income.

c. The government cuts personal income taxes and increases spending.

d. A change in technology increases the productivity of all workers.

4.6 Proponents of supply-side policies that aim to stimulate productivity through tax cuts and work incentives argue that changes in the individual and corporate tax codes and cuts in capital gains taxes set the stage for productivity gains during the 1990s.

a. What effect would an increase in productivity have on the Phillips curve? Illustrate your answer with a graph.

b. What effect would the productivity increase have on inflation?

4.7 Suppose that the economy is known to be producing at potential output. In other words, the output gap is zero.

a. Graph the economy's initial equilibrium using the *IS–MP* model including the Phillips curve.

b. Now suppose that the government increases spending due to a war. Show the effect on output and inflation, using both of your graphs.

4.8 Consider the following statement: "Because wages and prices are sticky, the Phillips curve relationship between inflation and the output gap is valid only when the output gap is positive." Do you agree with this statement? Briefly explain.

4.9 Recent evidence suggests that the Phillips curve has flattened. An article in the *Economist* states: "A flatter Phillips curve is good news when unemployment is falling. But it also implies bad news if inflation rises significantly."

a. If firms find it difficult to raise prices, why might the result be a flatter Phillips curve?

b. How would the effect of a demand shock be different if the Phillips curve is relatively flat than if its relatively steep?

c. Why does the article argue that a flatter Phillips curve may be bad news if there is high inflation?

Source: "Curve Ball," *Economist*, September 28, 2006.

4.10 In a speech at the Monetary Economics Workshop of the National Bureau of Economic Research, Fed Chairman Ben Bernanke said: "With inflation expectations well anchored, a one-time increase in energy prices should not lead to a permanent increase in inflation but only to a change in relative prices." What does it mean to say that inflation expectations are *well anchored*?

Source: Ben S. Bernanke, "Inflations Expectation and Inflation Forecasting," Monetary Economics Workshop of the National Bureau of Economic Research Summer Institute, Cambridge, MA, July 10, 2007.

4.11 Problem 4.10 discussed the language that the Fed uses to describe stable inflationary expectations: the idea that expectations are "well anchored." If

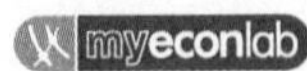

Visit www.myeconlab.com to complete these exercises online and get instant feedback.

expectations are adaptive, are they likely to be well anchored? Briefly explain.

4.12 **[Related to the *Chapter Opener* on page 302]** The Lehman Brothers bankruptcy helped set off a wave of demand shocks around the world.

a. Use the *IS-MP* model to show the effects of these shocks.

b. Why was the Fed worried about deflation in the wake of the Lehman Brothers bankruptcy?

4.13 **[Related to *Solved Problem 9.4* on page 336]** In the aftermath of the 2007–2009 financial crisis, the Fed became concerned about deflation.

a. Use the *IS–MP* model including the Phillips curve to show how a decrease in aggregate expenditure could cause deflation.

b. What policies should the Fed pursue to attempt to prevent deflation? Use the *IS-MP* model including the Phillips curve in your answer.

9.5 The Performance of the U.S. Economy During 2007–2009

Use the *IS–MP* model to understand the performance of the U.S. economy during the recession of 2007–2009.

SUMMARY

The financial crisis and the bursting of the real estate bubble led to a fall in consumption and investment that shifted the *IS* curve to the left, reducing real GDP, and making the output gap negative. The change in the output gap put downward pressure on inflation. The rapid increase in oil prices during the first part of 2008 acted as a supply shock that increased the inflation rate and offset the downward pressure on inflation caused by the real estate market and financial market shocks.

Review Questions

5.1 What were the three shocks that the U.S. economy experienced during the 2007–2009 period?

5.2 Why did the default-risk premium increase during 2007–2009. How did that increase affect interest rates?

5.3 How did the collapse in housing prices after 2006 alter the composition of GDP?

5.4 What was the effect of the increase in oil prices during 2008 on the Phillips curve?

Problems and Applications

5.5 China experienced many negative effects of the U.S. recession of 2007–2009. Like the United States, China was faced with higher oil prices. Unlike the U.S. case, housing prices in China did not fall. However, China's exports fell sharply as the recession lowered incomes in the United States and other trading partners. Assume that China was producing at potential GDP prior to the recession. Use the *IS–MP* model including the Phillips curve to show the effects of the recession in China.

5.6 Prior to the 2007–2009 recession, China's inflation rate appeared to be increasing.

a. What would a high and increasing rate of inflation imply about China's output gap?

b. What would you expect to happen to China's inflation rate as a result of the U.S. recession?

5.7 Some economists were concerned that the financial crisis of 2007–2009 would lead to problems with deflation. The Federal Reserve Bank of San Francisco's *Economic Letter* stated: "A popular version of the well-known Phillips curve model of inflation predicts that we are on the cusp of a deflationary spiral in which prices will fall at ever-increasing rates over the next several years."

a. How might a deflationary spiral occur in the Phillips curve model?

b. Why do you think that a deflationary spiral did not happen?

Source: "The Risk of Deflation," *FRBSF Economic Letter*, March 27, 2009.

5.8 **[Related to the *Chapter Opener* on page 302]** Consider the following statement: "The event that caused the recession of 2007–2009 was the failure of Lehman Brothers. If Lehman Brothers had not been allowed to fail, there would have been no effect on the risk premium and thus no demand shock." Do you agree with this statement? Briefly explain.

DATA EXERCISES

D9.1: [Related to the *Macro Data* feature on page 325] One measure of the tightness of credit is called the TED spread, which refers to the difference between the interbank loan rate and the short-term government debt rate. The TED spread is usually measured as the difference between the London Interbank Offered Rate (LIBOR) and the three-month Treasury bill rate. This spread measures the size of the gap between a rate that reflects some credit risk (the LIBOR) and a riskless rate (the Treasury bill rate).

A current chart of the TED spread can be found at Bloomberg.com (www.bloomberg.com/apps/cbuilder?ticker1=.TEDSP%3AIND). Reset the chart to show the spread over the past five years.

a. What happened to the TED spread during 2007–2008?

b. What is the value of the TED spread now?

D9.2: In problem 4.6, you drew graphs to show the effects of the positive technology shock in the 1990s. Look up inflation rate data for 1980–2000. What happened to inflation over this time period? Can you relate it to the productivity shock? (Hint: Inflation data can be found at the Bureau of Labor Statistics Web site, at www.bls.gov.)

D9.3: During the 2007-2009 period, the United Kingdom had been affected by shocks in ways that were fairly similar to those in the United States. As in the United States, oil prices were high, and housing prices had sharply escalated after 2000.The financial crisis in the United States also affected investment in the United Kingdom, both by limiting credit and increasing risk premiums.

U.K. data can be found at the Web site of the U.K. National Statistics, at www.statistics.gov.uk. What has happened to real GDP growth in the United Kingdom from 2007 to the present? To the inflation rate and the unemployment rate? How does this macroeconomic performance compare with that of the United States?

D9.4: [Excel exercise] Another way of viewing the Phillips curve relationship is to relate the inflation rate to the unemployment rate. (Hint: Inflation and unemployment data can be found at the Bureau of Labor Statistics Web site, at www.bls.gov.)

a. Find annual inflation and unemployment rate data for the United States from 1960 to the present. Chart the relationship, putting the inflation rate on the vertical axis and the unemployment rate on the horizontal axis.

b. For what periods does there appear to be a clear inverse relationship between the inflation rate and the unemployment rate?

c. How closely correlated are the inflation and unemployment rates over the entire period? What about over the periods for which you can identify a distinct inverse relationship?

APPENDIX

IS–LM: An Alternative Short-Run Macroeconomic Model

9A Use the *IS–LM* model to illustrate macroeconomic equilibrium.

The *IS–MP* model that we developed in this chapter assumes that the Fed adjusts the money supply in order to hit its target for the short-term nominal interest rate. We presented the *IS–MP* model in the chapter because many central banks today do target short-term nominal interest rates. However, central banks may target economic variables other than the short-term nominal interest rate. For example, the Federal Reserve did not have an official short-term nominal interest rate target until 1990. In this appendix, we examine the ***IS–LM* model**, which assumes that the central bank targets the money supply.[9] Whether the Fed targets interest rates or the money supply, it affects the economy by first intervening in the market for money. Therefore, the *IS–MP* model and *IS–LM* model are similar. In fact, we can derive the *MP* curve by using the *IS–LM* model. As a result, *you should think of the models as being complementary models, rather than competing models.*

***IS–LM* model** A macroeconomic model that assumes that the central bank targets the money supply.

As the names suggest, both the *IS–MP* model and *IS–LM* model use the *IS* curve to show the negative relationship between the real interest rate and aggregate expenditure: Households and firms purchase fewer goods and services when interest rates are high, and they purchase more goods and services when interest rates are low. The two models differ in the ways they include financial markets. While the *IS–MP* model analyzes the market for money using the *MP* curve, which assumes that the Fed has a short-term nominal interest rate target, the *IS–LM* model analyzes the market for money by using the *LM* curve, which assumes that the Fed has a target level of the money stock. The ***LM* curve** shows the combinations of the interest rate and output that result in equilibrium in the market for money. We start the discussion by deriving the *LM* curve.

***LM* curve** A curve that shows the combinations of the real interest rate and output that result in equilibrium in the market for money.

Asset Market Equilibrium

Savers have a variety of ways to allocate their wealth. We can think of savers as choosing between two broad categories of assets: money assets, such as checking accounts and cash, and non-money assets, such as stocks and bonds. Each household and firm decides how to allocate its wealth. The markets for money and non-money assets are in equilibrium when the total quantities demanded equal the total quantities supplied. Therefore, for the economy as a whole, the total demand for money balances, M_d, and non-money assets, N_d, equals total wealth, W, or:

$$M_d + N_d = W.$$

On the supply side, total wealth, W, equals the sum of the total quantity of money supplied, M_s, and the total quantity of non-money assets supplied, N_s, or:

$$M_s + N_s = W.$$

[9] *LM* refers to liquidity and money.

In equilibrium, the quantity of an asset demanded equals the quantity of the asset supplied. Combining the equations for the demand and supply for assets, we get:

$$M_d + N_d = M_s + N_s.$$

We can combine terms to show the *excess demand* for each type of asset:

$$(M_d - M_s) + (N_d - N_s) = 0,$$

so the excess demand for the different types of assets must sum to zero. Alternatively, we can write this equation as:

$$M_d - M_s = N_s - N_d. \tag{9A.1}$$

So, an excess demand for money is an excess supply of non-money assets, and an excess supply for money is an excess demand for non-money assets.

When the total quantity of money demanded exceeds the quantity supplied, or $M_d > M_s$, the expression on the left side of Equation (9A.1) is positive, representing an excess demand for money. When the total quantity of non-money assets supplied exceeds the quantity demanded, or $N_s > N_d$, there is an excess supply of non-money assets. Therefore, Equation (9A.1) states that the *excess demand* for one of the two assets (money or non-money) equals the *excess supply* of the other. In equilibrium, asset prices adjust so that there is no excess demand or supply in either market. In other words, the left side of Equation (9A.1) and the right side of Equation (9A.1) must both equal zero. So, the market for money is in equilibrium only if the market for non-money assets is in equilibrium. Knowing that the equilibrium in one of the two asset markets is related to the equilibrium in the other, we can make an important simplification: Any combination of real GDP and the real interest rate that results in an equilibrium in the market for money also results in an equilibrium in the market for non-money assets. We use this simplification to focus on the variables that determine equilibrium in the market for money.

Deriving the *LM* Curve

To derive the *LM* curve, we use a modified version of our market for money model from Chapter 3. In that chapter, we used a nominal money demand curve and a nominal money supply curve to determine the short-term nominal interest rate. Because equilibrium in the goods market, as shown by the *IS* curve, depends on the real interest rate, we will make the simplifying assumption that the expected inflation rate is constant, so that a change in the nominal interest rate is equivalent to a change in the real interest rate. In addition, we will assume that a change in short-term nominal interest rates results in a change in long-term nominal interest rates in the same direction. If these two conditions hold, the equilibrium real interest rate is determined in the market for money.

We will use the real money supply curve and the real money demand curve to determine the short-term real interest rate. The real money supply is the nominal money supply divided by the aggregate price level, and real money demand is nominal money demand divided by the aggregate price level. The nominal money demand curve depends on the nominal interest rate and the level of nominal income, but the real money demand curve depends on the real interest rate and the level of real income, or real GDP. If we assume that the price level is initially constant, there is little difference between the real money supply and the nominal money supply and, similarly, for money demand. In constructing the *LM* curve, we assume that the central bank keeps the nominal money supply constant. In both panel (a) and panel (b) of Figure 9A.1, the economy begins in equilibrium at point *A*. If real GDP increases relative to potential GDP,

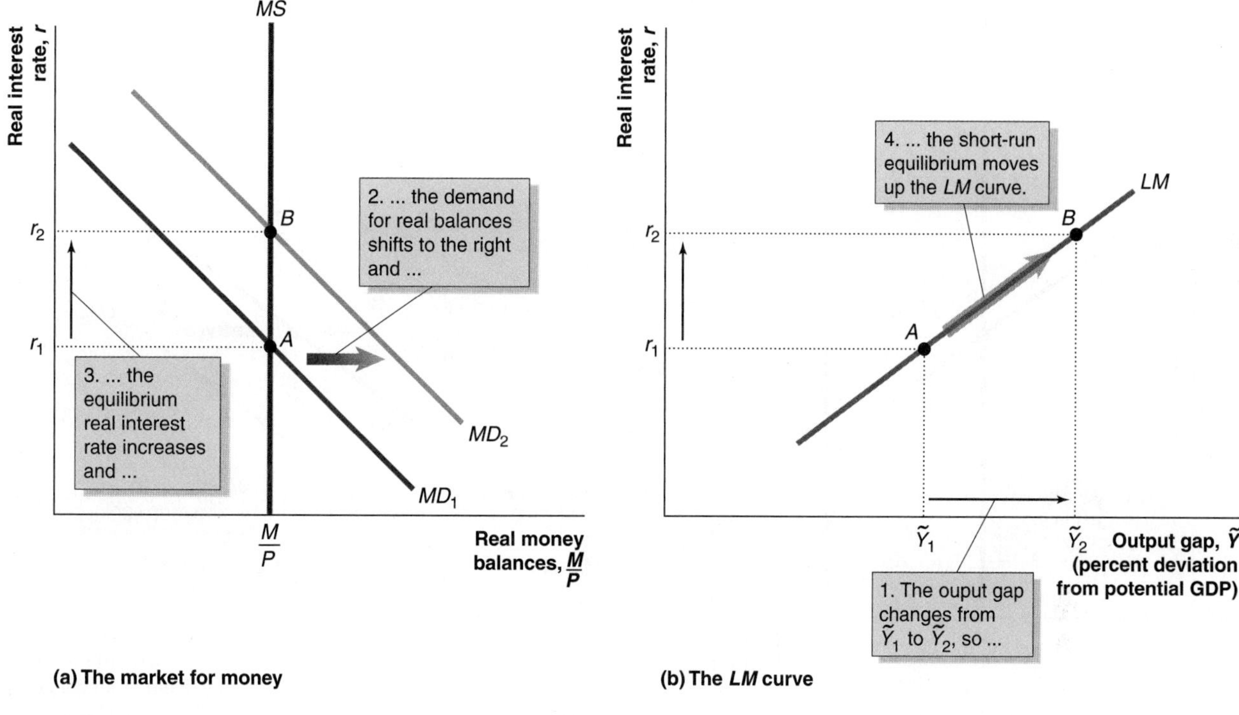

Figure 9A.1 Deriving the *LM* Curve

As real GDP increases relative to potential GDP, the output gap changes from $\widetilde{Y}_1$ to $\widetilde{Y}_2$ in panel (b), and households purchase more goods and services, so the real money demand curve shifts to the right and the equilibrium real interest rate increases in panel (a). As a result, the real interest rate also increases in panel (b) and the *LM* curve shows a positive relationship between the equilibrium combinations of the output gap and the real interest rate. ●

the output gap changes from $\widetilde{Y}_1$ to $\widetilde{Y}_2$, and households and firms make more purchases. The demand for money in panel (a) shifts from MD_1 to MD_2 as these purchases occur. The Fed keeps the real money supply constant, so the equilibrium real interest rate increases from r_1 to r_2. The economy's equilibrium is now at point *B* in both panel (a) and panel (b). Therefore, as real GDP increases, the interest rate necessary to keep the market for money in equilibrium also increases.

Shifting the *LM* Curve

The *LM* curve shows the combinations of the output gap and the real interest rate that result in equilibrium in the market for money. If factors that affect the market for money (other than the output gap) change, the *LM* curve will shift. For example, Figure 9A.2 shows the effect of an increase in the money supply on the *LM* curve. The economy begins in equilibrium at point *A*, with the output gap equal to $\widetilde{Y}_1$ and the real interest rate equal to r_1. In panel (a), suppose that the Fed decides to increase the nominal money supply. If the price level remains constant, the real money supply increases, so the money supply curve shifts to the right, from MS_1 to MS_2. The equilibrium real interest rate decreases from r_1 to r_2, and equilibrium in the market for money is at point *B*. The increase in the real money supply reduces the equilibrium real interest rate from r_1 to r_2. In panel (b), if output remains at $\widetilde{Y}_1$ and the equilibrium real interest rate is now r_2, the economy's equilibrium is at point *B*. Point *B* is not on the original *LM* curve, so the *LM* curve shifts

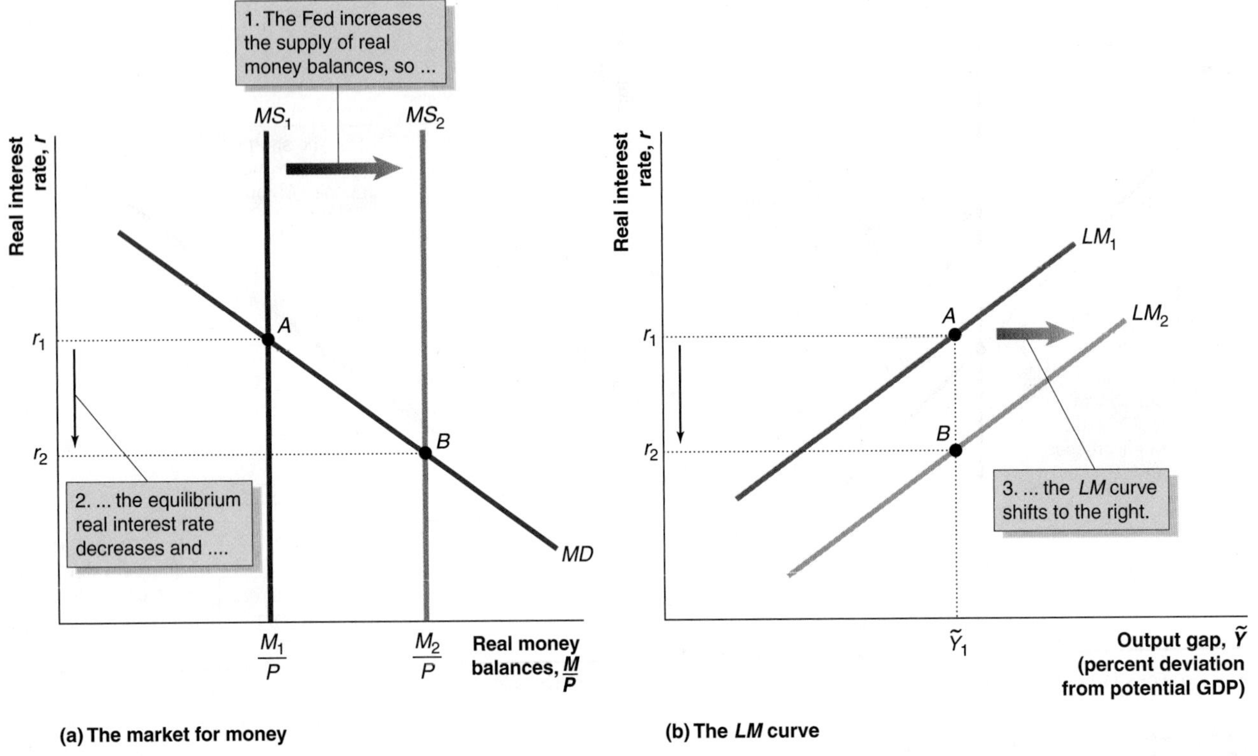

Figure 9A.2 An Increase in the Money Supply and the *LM* Curve

In panel (a), the price level is constant. An increase in the nominal money supply shifts the real money supply curve to the right, from MS_1 to MS_2, and lowers the real interest rate. The real interest rate is now lower for any given level of the output gap, so the *LM* curve shifts to the right in panel (b). ●

to the right, from LM_1 to LM_2. Table 9A.1 summarizes the factors that shift the *LM* curve.

Equilibrium in the *IS–LM* Model

In the *IS–LM* model, the *IS* curve shows the relationship between changes in the real interest rate and the output gap, and the *LM* curve shows the effect of changes in the output gap on the real interest rate. The market for goods and services and the market for money are both in equilibrium at the point where the *IS* curve intersects the *LM* curve in Figure 9A.3 (on the bottom of the next page). At point *A*, the real interest rate equals the equilibrium real interest rate r_1, and real GDP equals potential GDP, so $\tilde{Y} = 0$.

Using Monetary Policy to Increase Output We derived the *LM* curve by assuming that the Fed kept the nominal money supply constant. Of course, the Fed can always change the nominal money supply, and we have already seen that when the nominal money supply increases, the *LM* curve shifts to the right. Figure 9A.4 on page 358 shows the effect of an increase in the nominal money supply on the equilibrium output gap and the real interest rate. The economy is initially in short-run macroeconomic equilibrium at point *A*. The Fed increases the nominal money supply, so the *LM* curve shifts to the right, from LM_1 to LM_2. At the initial equilibrium real interest rate, there is now an excess supply of money, so the real interest rate falls. The lower real interest rate leads to higher consumption and investment, so real GDP increases relative to potential GDP,

Table 9A.1 Summary of the *IS-LM* Model

All else being equal, an increase in . . .	causes . . .	and the *LM* curve shifts . . .
the nominal money supply (*M* increases)	the real interest rate to decrease at every level of the output gap	r, LM_1, LM_2, $\tilde{Y}$
the price level (*P* increases)	the real interest rate to increase at every level of the output gap	r, LM_2, LM_1, $\tilde{Y}$
the expected inflation rate (π^e increases)	the real interest rate to decrease at every level of the output gap	r, LM_1, LM_2, $\tilde{Y}$
the nominal interest rate on money (*i* increases)	the real interest rate to increase at every level of the output gap	r, LM_2, LM_1, $\tilde{Y}$

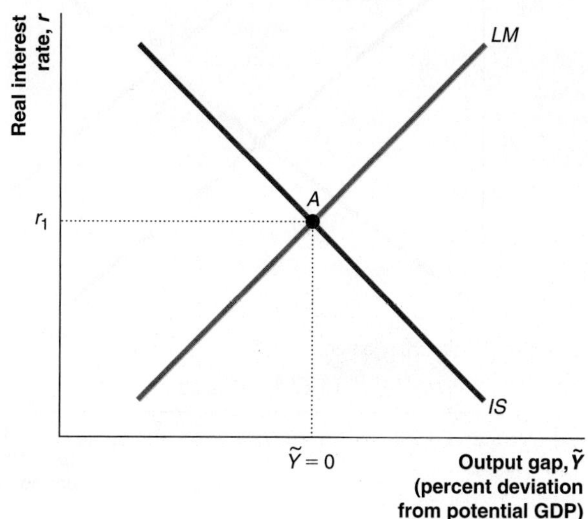

Figure 9A.3

Equilibrium in the *IS–LM* Model

Equilibrium occurs at point *A*, the *IS* and *LM* curves intersect, and both the goods market and the market for money are in equilibrium. ●

Figure 9A.4

An Increase in the Nominal Money Stock and Equilibrium

Holding everything else constant, if the Fed increases the nominal money supply, the *LM* curve will shift to the right. As a result, the equilibrium real interest rate will decrease, and the output gap changes from $\tilde{Y}_1$ to $\tilde{Y}_2$. ●

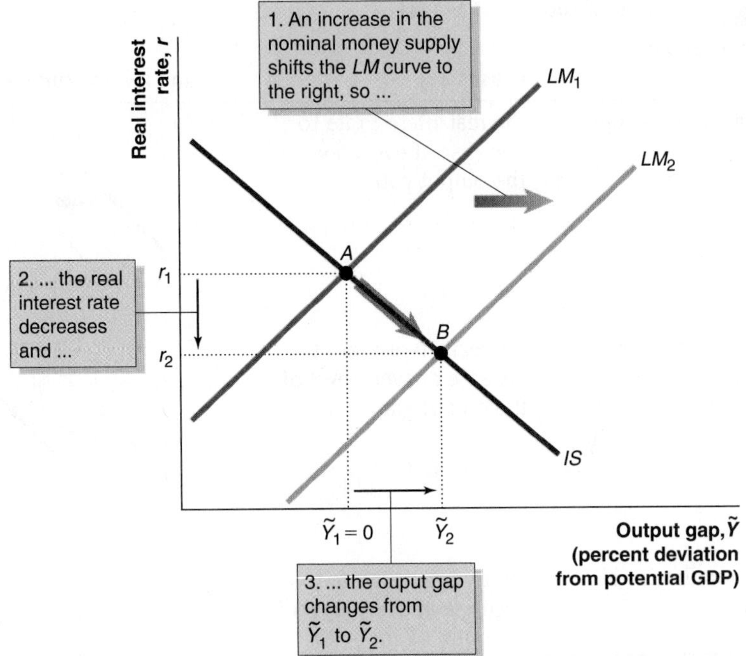

and the output gap changes from $\tilde{Y}_1$ to $\tilde{Y}_2$. The new short-run macroeconomic equilibrium is at point *B*.

A Positive Demand Shock Suppose that the economy experiences a positive demand shock due to a stock market boom and increased optimism of households and firms. Figure 9A.5 shows the economy initially in short-run macroeconomic equilibrium at point *A*. A positive demand shock leads to higher consumption and investment, so the

Figure 9A.5

The Effect of a Positive Demand Shock on Equilibrium

Holding everything else constant, a positive demand shock will shift the *IS* curve to the right, so the equilibrium real interest rate will increase from r_1 to r_2 and the equilibrium output gap changes from $\tilde{Y}_1$ to $\tilde{Y}_2$. ●

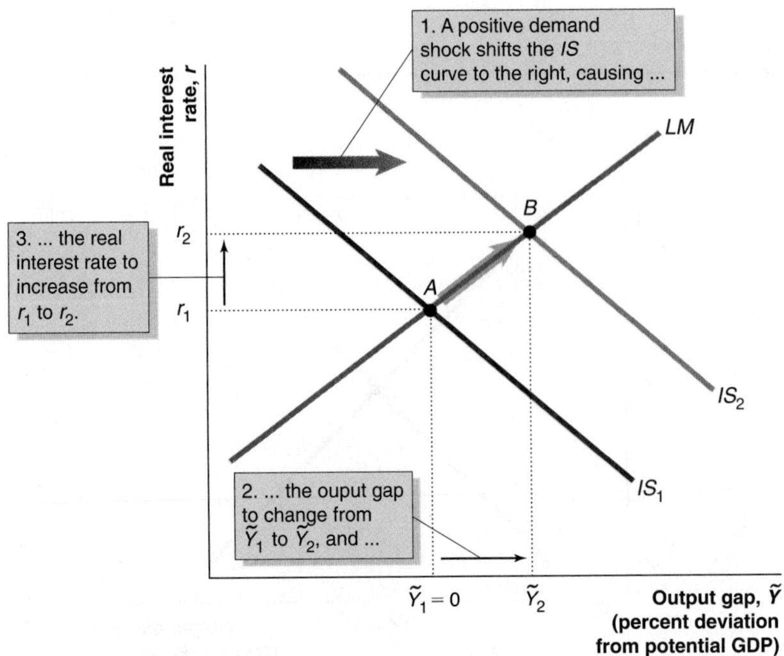

IS curve shifts to the right, from IS_1 to IS_2. As a result, real GDP increases relative to potential GDP and the real interest rate also increases. The new short-run macroeconomic equilibrium is at point *B*.

Solved Problem 9A.1

Monetary Policy During the Great Depression

Nobel Laureate Milton Friedman criticized the Federal Reserve for allowing the money supply to decrease during the Great Depression. The nominal money supply decreased from $26.2 billion during the third quarter of 1929 to $18.9 billion during the first quarter of 1933—a 27% decrease in just four years. Real interest rates on corporate bonds rose from 6% to about 17%, and real GDP fell by more than 25%. Real GDP equaled potential GDP at the beginning of the Great Depression, but real GDP may have been as much as 35% below potential GDP during the first quarter of 1933! In Friedman's view, the decrease in the money supply played an important role in the decrease in real GDP during the Great Depression. Is Friedman's view consistent with the *IS–LM* model?

Solving the Problem

Step 1 **Review the chapter material.** This problem is about applying the *IS-LM* model, so you may want to review the section "Equilibrium in the *IS–LM* Model," which begins on page 356.

Step 2 **Draw a graph that shows the initial equilibrium in 1929.** Draw the initial equilibrium with the *IS–LM* graph for the year 1929. Because real GDP was equal to potential GDP at the beginning of the Great Depression, make the initial equilibrium occur where the output gap equals zero. The real interest rate was about 6% in 1929, so make the initial equilibrium occur where the real interest rate is 6%. Your graph should look like this:

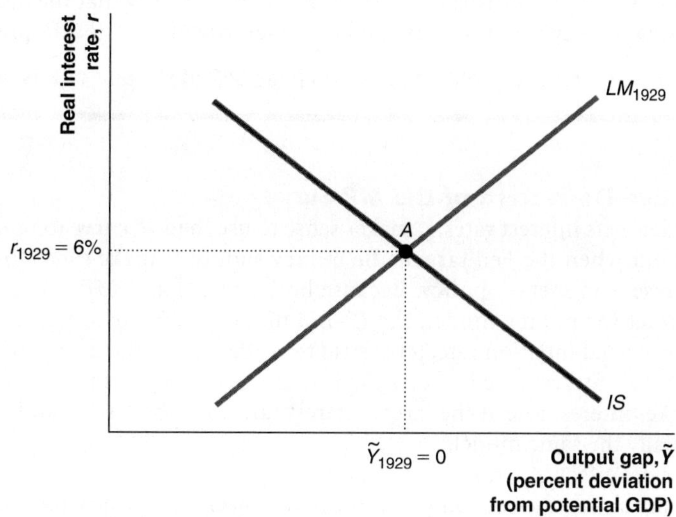

Step 3 **Determine the effect of the decrease in the nominal money supply.** The nominal money supply decreased by about 27% between 1929 and 1933. The nominal money supply is one of the factors that we hold constant when we draw the *LM*

curve. Therefore, you should show the effect of the decrease in the money supply by shifting the *LM* curve to the left, from LM_{1929} to LM_{1933}. Label the new equilibrium interest rate r_{1933} and the new equilibrium output gap, $\tilde{Y}_{1933}$. Your graph should look like this:

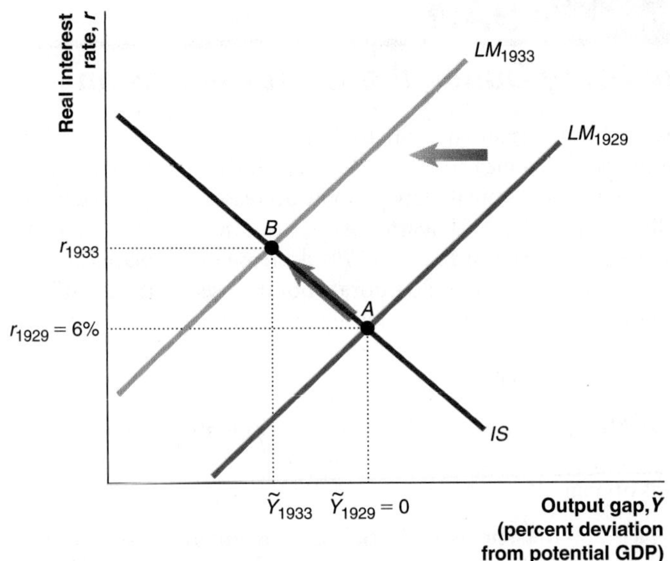

Step 4 **Compare your graph to the actual experience.** Your graph should show that a decrease in the nominal money supply will lead to higher real interest rates and lower real GDP. This is in fact what happened. The real interest rate rose from 6% to about 17%, while the output gap fell from 0% to about −35%. Therefore, the *IS–LM* model is consistent with Milton Friedman's view that the decrease in the nominal money supply contributed to the severity of the Great Depression.

For more practice, do related problem 9A.10 on page 362 at the end of this appendix.

An Alternative Derivation of the *MP* Curve

When the Fed targets interest rates, it makes sense to use the *MP* curve to represent monetary policy, but when the Fed targets the money supply, it make sense to use the *LM* curve to represent monetary policy. Because both the *LM* and *MP* curves are derived from the market for money model, the *IS–LM* model is similar to the *IS–MP* model. Holding the expected inflation rate, term structure effects, and the default-risk premium constant, the real interest rate is set by the Fed. If the Fed adjusts the money supply to keep the market interest rate at the target interest rate, then the *IS–LM* and *IS–MP* models are essentially the same model.

Consider the effect of a positive demand shock as shown in Figure 9A.6. Before the positive demand shock, the economy is in short-run macroeconomic equilibrium at point *A*, where the real interest rate equals the Fed's target real interest rate, r^{target}, and real GDP equals potential GDP. If the Fed keeps the money supply constant, then the positive demand shock will cause the real interest rate to rise to r_2, which is above the target real interest rate, and the economy will be in short-run macroeconomic equilibrium at point *B*. If, on the other hand, the Fed targets the real interest rate, the money supply and the *LM*

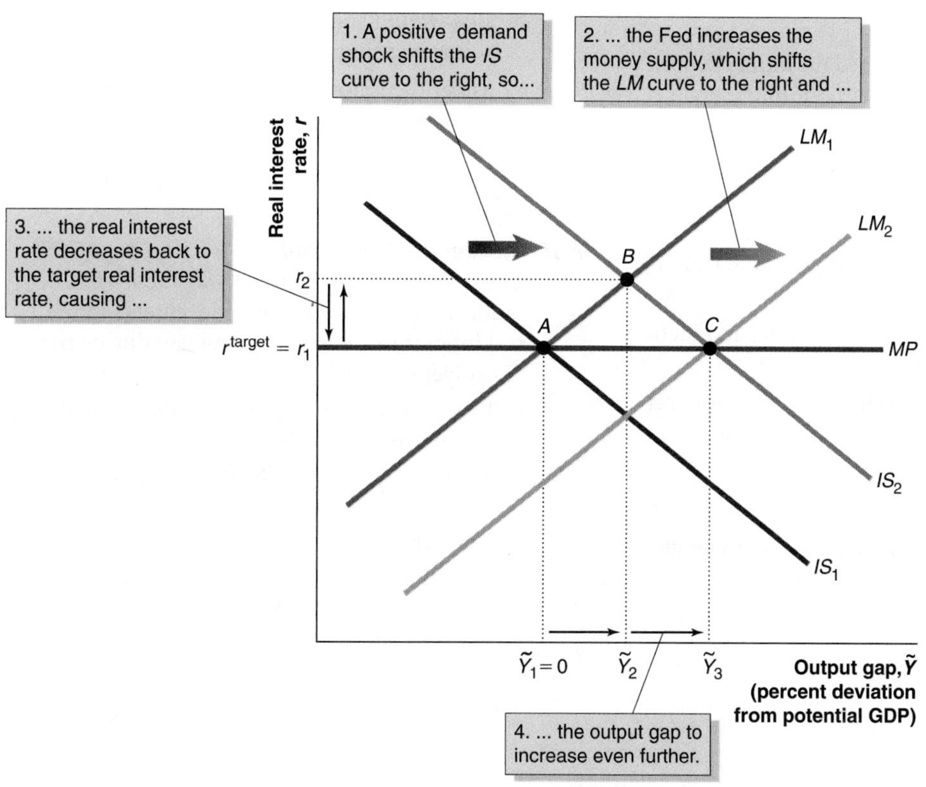

1. A positive demand shock shifts the IS curve to the right, so...
2. ... the Fed increases the money supply, which shifts the LM curve to the right and ...
3. ... the real interest rate decreases back to the target real interest rate, causing ...
4. ... the output gap to increase even further.
Real interest rate, r
r2
rtarget = r1
LM1
LM2
MP
IS2
IS1
A
B
C
Ỹ1 = 0
Ỹ2
Ỹ3
Output gap, Ỹ (percent deviation from potential GDP)

Figure 9A.6

An Alternative Derivation of the *MP* Curve

If the Fed targets the real interest rate, the money supply and the *LM* curve must adjust to keep the real interest rate equal to the target real interest rate. Therefore, in response to a positive demand shock, the Fed must increase the money supply, which shifts the *LM* curve to the right and reduces the real interest rate back to the target real interest rate. ●

curve must adjust to keep the real interest rate at r^{target}. To maintain the target real interest rate, the Fed must increase the money supply, shifting the *LM* curve to the right, from LM_1 to LM_2. This shift causes the real interest rate to decrease from r_2 to r^{target}. If the Fed acts quickly enough, the real interest rate never increases at all, and the economy moves directly from point *A* to point *C*. If we connect those two points, we have a horizontal line at the target real interest rate, which we have previously called the *MP* curve.

We can see that the *LM* and *MP* curves are really not very different. Using the *LM* curve is a convenient way to represent monetary policy when the Fed targets the money supply. Using the *MP* curve is a convenient way to represent monetary policy when the Fed targets the interest rate.

KEY TERMS

IS–LM model, p. 353

LM curve, p. 353

Review Questions

9A.1 What is the difference between how the *IS–LM* and the *IS–MP* models analyze the market for money?

9A.2 How is equilibrium in the market for money related to equilibrium in the market for non-money assets?

9A.3 Explain how the *LM* curve represents equilibrium in the market for money.

9A.4 What factors shift the *LM* curve?

9A.5 Explain how an increase in the money supply affects the *LM* curve and equilibrium in the *IS–LM* model.

9A.6 How can the *MP* curve be derived from the *IS–LM* model?

Problems and Applications

9A.7 In earlier periods, the Fed targeted the money supply. More recently, the Fed has targeted the interest rate.

a. Which model best represents the United States today? Which model would you use in explaining earlier periods?

b. Use the *IS–LM* model to explain why the Fed cannot target the money supply and the real interest rate at the same time.

9A.8 Draw a graph showing the *IS–LM* model and identify the initial equilibrium.

a. For each of the following changes, show the effect on the output gap and the real interest rate.

i. The government increases taxes.

ii. The Fed decreases the money supply.

iii. Consumers experience an increase in wealth due to increases in stock prices.

b. How would your answers above be different if you were using the *IS–MP* model?

9A.9 Consider the following statement: "Because interest rates in the real world change, it is more appropriate to use the *IS–LM* model than the *IS–MP* model." Do you agree with this statement? Briefly explain.

9A.10 **[Related to *Solved Problem 9A.1* on page 359]** This appendix demonstrates why the *IS–LM* model accurately represents movements in the real interest rate and the output gap during the Great Depression.

a. Use the *IS–LM* model to show the approximate movements of real interest rates and the output gap during the 2007–2009 financial crisis.

b. Design a change in monetary policy that would have prevented the change in the output gap.

CHAPTER 10

Monetary Policy in the Short Run

LEARNING OBJECTIVES

After studying this chapter, you should be able to:

10.1 Understand the structure of the Federal Reserve (pages 365–367)

10.2 Describe the goals of monetary policy (pages 367–370)

10.3 Explain the Fed's monetary policy tools (pages 370–376)

10.4 Use the *IS–MP* model to understand how monetary policy affects the economy in the short run (pages 376–386)

10.5 Explain the challenges to using monetary policy effectively (pages 386–394)

10.6 Evaluate the arguments for and against central bank independence (pages 394–397)

WHAT DID THE GREAT DEPRESSION TEACH BEN BERNANKE?

In the early 1960s, Milton Friedman of the University of Chicago and Anna Schwartz of the National Bureau of Economic Research published an influential discussion of the importance of bank panics in their book, *A Monetary History of the United States, 1867–1960.* Friedman and Schwartz focused on the period before the federal government began insuring deposits in banks in 1934. During that period, if depositors lost confidence in banks and began withdrawing their deposits, the result would be a bank panic, which would lead to many, perhaps all, banks in the system closing. In *A Monetary History* and later writings, Friedman and Schwartz singled out the failure in December 1930 of the Bank of United States, a large private bank located in New York City, as being particularly important:

> [The bank's] failure on Dec. 11, 1930, marked a basic change in character of the contraction that had started in August 1929, from a severe recession, with no sign of any financial crisis, to a catastrophe that reached its climax in the banking holiday of March 1933, when all banks were closed for a week. . . .

Continued on next page

Key Issue and Question

At the end of Chapter 1, we noted key issues and questions that serve as a framework for the book. Here are the key issue and question for this chapter:

Issue: The Federal Reserve undertook unprecedented policy actions in response to the recession of 2007–2009.

Question: Why were traditional Federal Reserve policies ineffective during the 2007–2009 recession?

Answered on page 397

For Friedman and Schwartz, the failure of the Federal Reserve to stop the bank panics of the early 1930s was the key reason the Great Depression was so severe.

In 2002, when Ben Bernanke was a member of the Fed's Board of Governors, but not yet the chairman, he told Friedman, "Regarding the Great Depression, you're right, we did it. We're very sorry. But thanks to you, we won't do it again." When the financial crisis started in August 2007, Bernanke's words were put to the test. At that point, Bernanke faced a dilemma similar to the one Fed officials faced in the 1930s: If the Fed moved to save failing financial firms, it could reduce the severity of the financial crisis, but it might also increase the extent of *moral hazard* in the financial system. As we saw in Chapter 3, in this context, moral hazard refers to the possibility that by intervening to save failing firms, the Fed would change the behavior of the firms' managers. Moral hazard was an important consideration in the Fed's deliberations because aiding troubled financial firms might make their managers more likely to undertake risky investments in the future in the expectation that, should the investments result in losses, the Fed would bail out the firms.

The Fed's handling of the investment banks Bear Stearns and Lehman Brothers when these firms ran into problems during the crisis demonstrates the Fed's need to balance the needs of the financial system with the problems that arise due to moral hazard. In March 2008, lenders became concerned that Bear's investments in mortgage-backed securities had declined in value to the extent that the investment bank was insolvent. Rather than see the financial system disrupted by Bear's failure, the Fed saved Bear from bankruptcy by helping to arrange for its purchase by the bank JPMorgan Chase at a price of $10 per share (raised from an initial offer of $2 per share); one year earlier, Bear's shares had sold for $170. By August 2008, the financial crisis was deepening, as nearly 25% of subprime mortgages were at least 30 days past due. When Lehman Brothers appeared likely to fail, the Fed and the U.S. Treasury decided that to avoid moral hazard problems they would take the opposite position to the one they had taken with respect to Bear Stearns and decline to commit the funds necessary to entice a private buyer to purchase the firm. As we saw in Chapter 9, the failure of Lehman Brothers on September 15, 2008, marked a turning point in the crisis. Many parts of the financial system became frozen, and large firms as well as small ones had difficulty arranging for even short-term loans.

Under Bernanke's leadership, the Fed then decided to put aside concerns about moral hazard and act aggressively to stabilize the financial system. Among other actions, the Fed began making loans to financial institutions beyond just commercial banks, saved the insurance giant American International Group (AIG) by lending it $85 billion in exchange for the federal government's receiving ownership of 80% of the firm, and provided short-term financing for corporations by buying the firms' commercial paper.

Although the Fed eventually took aggressive policy actions during the financial crisis, it was initially slow to recognize the threat the crisis posed to the U.S. financial system. For example, just days before the start of the crisis, the Fed indicated that it was more concerned about inflation than about a potential recession. In May 2007, Ben Bernanke gave a speech indicating that the housing market problems developing at that time would have little effect on financial markets and the broader economy. Bernanke was wrong, as were many other economists. The collapse in housing prices in 2006 and 2007 helped trigger a massive financial crisis. Some economists and policymakers criticized the Fed for being slow to recognize the problems in financial markets and for having potentially increased the extent of moral hazard in the financial system by "bailing out Wall Street" in saving Bear Stearns and AIG. As a result of the financial crisis and the criticisms of the Fed's actions during the crisis, Bernanke's confirmation by Congress to a second term as Fed chairman in early 2010 was contentious, with strong opposition from some Democrats and Republicans. Senator Richard Shelby of Alabama accused Bernanke of sitting idly by while financial problems developed that "greatly exacerbated the crisis." In some ways, these criticisms were like those made by Friedman and Schwartz of Fed policy during the Great Depression. Ultimately, 70 senators voted to confirm Bernanke, but the 30 votes against his confirmation represented the most "no" votes that any nominee for Fed chair had ever received.

As we will see in this chapter, the monetary policy actions the Fed took during the financial crisis remain controversial.

AN INSIDE LOOK AT POLICY on page 398 discusses the Fed's view of the economy in the spring of 2011 and assesses whether the Fed should begin reversing its $600 billion bond purchase program.

Sources: Milton Friedman and Anna Schwartz, *A Monetary History of the United States, 1867–1960*, Princeton, NJ: Princeton University Press, 1963, pp. 308–313; Friedman quote from Milton Friedman, "Anti-Semitism and the Great Depression," *Newsweek*, Vol. 84, November 16, 1974; "The Very Model of a Modern Central Banker," *The Economist*, August 29, 2009; Tom Braithwaite and James Politi, "Bernanke Wins New Term as Fed Chief," *Financial Times*, January 29, 2010; David Wessel, "Financial Crisis: Inside Dr. Bernanke's E.R.," *The Wall Street Journal*, July 18, 2009; and Ben Bernanke, "The Subprime Mortgage Market," speech at the Federal Reserve Bank of Chicago's 43rd Annual Conference on Bank Structure and Competition, Chicago, May 17, 2007.

In Chapter 9, we introduced the *IS–MP* model to explain the causes of economic fluctuations. In this chapter, we use this model to explain how the Fed can use monetary policy to help stabilize the economy and the financial system and reduce the severity of economic fluctuations. **Monetary policy** refers to the actions the Federal Reserve takes to manage interest rates and the money supply to pursue macroeconomic goals. We will also discuss how in practice it can be difficult for the Fed and other central banks to implement effective policies.

Monetary policy The actions the Federal Reserve takes to manage interest rates and the money supply to pursue macroeconomic goals.

The Federal Reserve System

10.1
Learning Objective
Understand the structure of the Federal Reserve.

The organization of the Federal Reserve plays a significant role in how monetary policy is conducted. To understand why the Fed is organized as it is, we need to look briefly at earlier attempts to create a central bank in the United States.

Creation of the Federal Reserve System

Not long after the United States won its independence, Treasury Secretary Alexander Hamilton organized the Bank of the United States, which was meant to perform functions similar to those of a modern central bank.[1] The Bank of the United States was not entirely a government agency in that it had both government and private shareholders. The Bank attempted to stabilize the financial system by taking steps to ensure that local banks did not extend excessive amounts of loans. Congress granted the Bank a 20-year charter in 1791, making it the only federally chartered bank. Local banks resented the Bank's supervision of their operations. Many advocates of a limited federal government distrusted the Bank's power, and important figures such as Thomas Jefferson believed that the Bank of the United States was unconstitutional. Farmers and owners of small businesses, particularly in the West and South, resented the Bank's interfering with their ability to obtain loans from their local banks. There was not enough congressional support to renew the charter, so the Bank ceased operations in 1811.

Partly because of the federal government's problems in financing the War of 1812, political opinion in Congress shifted back toward the need for a central bank. In 1816, Congress established the Second Bank of the United States, also under a 20-year charter. The Second Bank of the United States encountered many of the same controversies as the First Bank of the United States. Although Congress passed a bill to recharter the Bank, President Andrew Jackson vetoed the bill, and the Bank's charter expired in 1836.

The disappearance of the Second Bank of the United States left the nation without a central bank and, therefore, without an official lender of last resort to make loans to banks during **bank runs**, when large numbers of depositors would lose confidence in banks leading the depositors to withdraw their funds. Without a lender of last resort, banks suffering temporary problems with deposit withdrawals could be forced to close. Private institutions, such as the New York Clearing House, attempted to fill the void by lending to troubled banks, but severe nationwide financial panics in 1873, 1884, 1893, and 1907—and accompanying economic downturns—raised fears in Congress that the U.S. financial system was unstable. The severity of the panic of 1907 convinced many that the United States needed a central bank to make loans to banks experiencing runs. In 1913, President Woodrow Wilson signed the Federal Reserve Act into law. The act established the **Federal Reserve System** (the Fed) as the central bank of the United States.

Bank run The process by which depositors who have lost confidence in a bank simultaneously withdraw enough funds to force the bank to close.

Federal Reserve System The central bank of the United States; commonly referred to as "the Fed."

[1]Note that this bank is unrelated to the bank with similar name that failed during the 1930s, as mentioned in the chapter opener.

The Structure of the Federal Reserve System

Many in Congress believed that a unified central bank based in Washington, DC would concentrate too much economic power in the hands of the officials running the bank. Congress also wanted to avoid having a single central bank with branches, which had been the structure of the First and Second Banks of the United States. So, the Federal Reserve Act divided the United States into 12 Federal Reserve districts, each of which has a *Federal Reserve Bank* in one city. Among other responsibilities, the Federal Reserve Bank in each district makes short-term loans called *discount loans* to banks within the district. These loans were intended to help provide liquidity to banks, thereby fulfilling, in a decentralized way, the system's role as lender of last resort and making bank panics less likely. Figure 10.1 shows the Federal Reserve districts and the locations of the Federal Reserve Banks. Although the federal government created these banks, technically Federal Reserve Banks have a certain degree of independence from the government. Federal Reserve Banks are owned by commercial banks within their districts. In addition, each Federal Reserve Bank selects its own president to oversee operations and take part in monetary policy decisions. We discuss central bank independence in more detail in section 10.6.

Board of Governors The governing board of the Federal Reserve System, consisting of seven members appointed by the president of the United States.

In addition to the 12 regional Federal Reserve Banks, the Fed has the **Board of Governors** headquartered in Washington, DC. Its seven members are appointed by the president of the United States and confirmed by the U.S. Senate. Governors serve nonrenewable terms of 14 years that are staggered so that one term expires every other

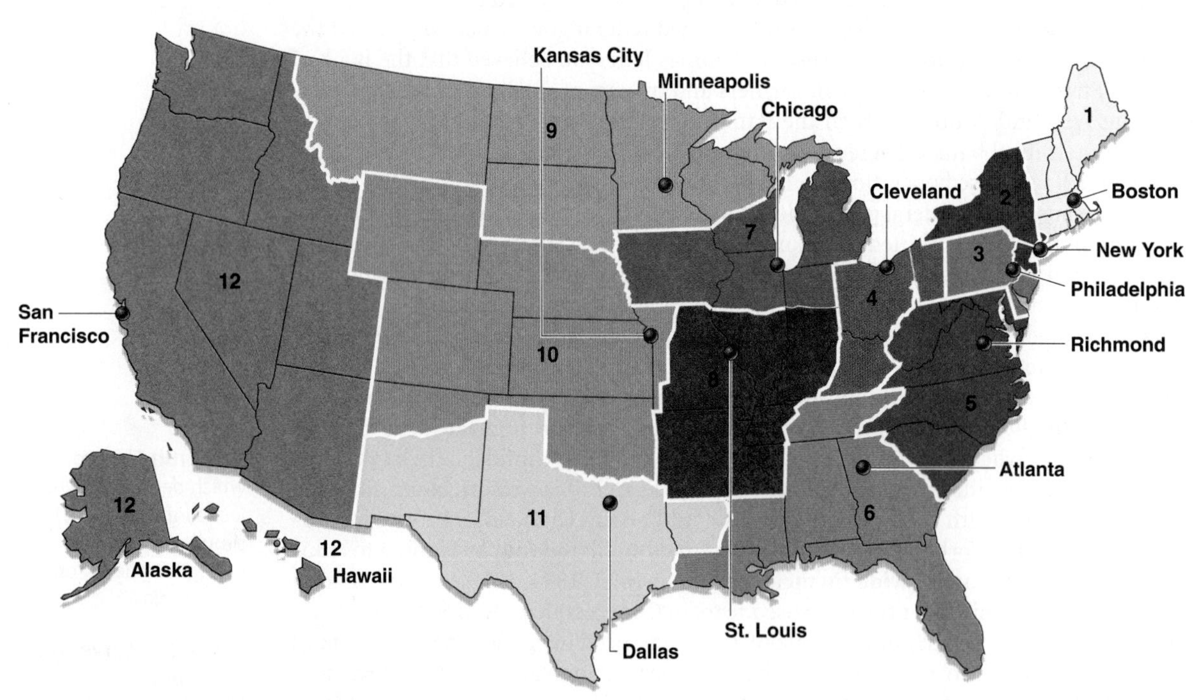

Figure 10.1 Federal Reserve Districts and Banks

The Federal Reserve System is divided into 12 districts, each of which has a district bank identified by a purple dot in the figure. The federal government created the Federal Reserve System, but each regional Federal Reserve Bank is owned by the commercial banks within its district. Note that Hawaii and Alaska are included in the Twelfth Federal Reserve District. ●

January.[2] The result is that one U.S. president typically does not appoint a full Board of Governors. In an unusual occurrence in 2010, President Barack Obama had an opportunity to appoint three members. The president appoints one member of the Board to serve as the chairman for a renewable four-year term. For instance, Ben Bernanke was appointed chair in January 2006 by President George W. Bush and reappointed in January 2010 by President Barack Obama. The chairman acts as the public face of the Federal Reserve and often testifies before Congress on monetary policy and the state of the U.S. economy.

The Board of Governors oversees the entire Federal Reserve System. In recent decades, however, the 12-member **Federal Open Market Committee (FOMC)** has been at the center of Fed policymaking. The FOMC conducts **open market operations**, the buying and selling of U.S. Treasury securities, which we first discussed in Chapter 6. Members of the FOMC are the chair of the Board of Governors, the other 6 Fed governors, the president of the Federal Reserve Bank of New York, and the presidents of 4 of the other 11 Federal Reserve Banks (who serve on a rotating basis). Only 5 Federal Reserve Bank presidents are voting members of the FOMC, but all 12 attend meetings and participate in discussions. The committee is scheduled to meet eight times a year, but it may meet more frequently as economic conditions warrant.

Federal Open Market Committee (FOMC) The 12-member Federal Reserve committee that directs open market operations.

Open market operations The Federal Reserve's purchases and sales of securities, usually U.S. Treasury securities, in financial markets.

Until the financial crisis of 2007–2009, the Fed's most important policy tool was setting the target for the **federal funds rate**, which is the interest rate that banks charge each other on short-term loans. During the financial crisis, Fed Chairman Ben Bernanke needed to make decisions rapidly and to use new policy tools. As a result, the focus of monetary policy moved away from the federal funds rate. As more normal conditions returned to the economy and financial system, the federal funds rate began to resume its previous importance.

Federal funds rate The interest rate that banks charge each other on short-term loans.

The Goals of Monetary Policy

10.2
Learning Objective
Describe the goals of monetary policy.

Most economists and policymakers agree that the overall aim of monetary policy is to advance the economic well-being of the population. Although there are many ways to assess economic well-being, it is typically determined by the quantity and quality of goods and services that individuals can enjoy. Economic well-being arises from the efficient employment of labor and capital and the steady growth in output. In addition, stable economic conditions—minimal fluctuations in production and employment, steady interest rates, and smoothly functioning financial markets—are qualities that enhance economic well-being. The Federal Reserve has several goals intended to promote a well-functioning economy: (1) price stability, (2) high employment, (3) economic growth, (4) financial market stability, (5) interest rate stability, and (6) foreign-exchange market stability.

Price Stability

Inflation, or persistently rising prices, erodes the value of money. Especially since inflation rose dramatically and unexpectedly during the 1970s, policymakers in most industrial economies have set price stability as a policy goal. In a market economy, in which prices communicate information about costs and about demand for goods and services to households and firms, inflation makes prices less useful as signals for resource allocation.

[2]Technically, a governor could resign before the term expired and then be reappointed, thereby lengthening the term. Since 1970, this practice has been rare. If a governor resigns during his or her term, a new governor can be appointed to complete the term. The new governor is then entitled to his or her own fourteen-year term. In this way, Alan Greenspan was able to serve as chairman of the Board of Governors from 1987 to 2006.

When the overall price level changes, families have trouble deciding how much to save for their children's education or for retirement, and firms facing uncertain future prices hesitate to enter into long-term contracts with suppliers or customers. Fluctuations in inflation can also arbitrarily redistribute income, as when lenders suffer losses when inflation is higher than expected.

In practice, the Fed's goal of price stability means that it attempts to achieve low and stable inflation rather than zero inflation. With low and stable inflation, market prices efficiently allocate resources in the economy, so the economy is more productive and living standards are higher in the long run. Although the Fed has never formally announced a target for the inflation rate, many economists believe that the Fed considers an inflation rate of roughly 2% to be consistent with price stability. Since the early 1980s, the Fed has by and large been successful in meeting its goal of price stability. Between 1984 and 2010, the inflation rate in the United States averaged 2.2% per year.

High Employment

The second goal of the Federal Reserve is high employment, or a low rate of unemployment. Unemployed workers and underused factories and machines lower output. Unemployment causes financial distress and decreases the self-esteem of workers who lack jobs. Congress and the president share responsibility with the Fed for the goal of high employment. Congress enacted the Employment Act of 1946 and the Full Employment and Balanced Growth Act of 1978 (the Humphrey–Hawkins Act) to promote high employment and price stability.

If the Fed were completely successful in maintaining high employment, then cyclical unemployment would equal zero, and real GDP would always equal potential GDP. Because we know that the U.S. economy has experienced recessions, it's clear that the Fed has not always been able to keep the cyclical unemployment rate at zero. Nevertheless, until the recession of 2007–2009, the Fed seemed increasingly successful at meeting this goal. In the severe recession of 1981–1982, the cyclical unemployment rate peaked at about 4.6%. The following two recessions were much milder, however, with the cyclical unemployment rate peaking at about 2.0% in the 1990–1991 recession and at about 1.2% in the 2001 recession. This downward trend in cyclical unemployment during recessions was part of the period that economists call the *Great Moderation* due to the reduction in the severity of business cycles. Unfortunately, however, the recession of 2007–2009 reversed this trend, with the cyclical unemployment rate peaking at about 5.1% in late 2009.

The Fed does not aim for zero unemployment. Indeed, if the unemployment rate were zero, then cyclical unemployment would be negative, and real GDP would be far above potential GDP. The Phillips curve analysis from Chapter 9 tells us that the result would be an increase in the inflation rate. So, zero unemployment is not compatible with the Fed's goal of price stability. Instead, the Fed attempts to keep the cyclical unemployment as close to zero as possible, or, looked at another way, the Fed attempts to keep the actual unemployment rate equal to the natural rate of unemployment. Currently, most economists estimate that the natural rate of unemployment is between 5% and 6%. For example, in 2011, the Congressional Budget Office used 5.0% as its estimate of the natural rate of unemployment.

Economic Growth

Policymakers seek steady *economic growth.* As we discussed in Chapter 5, economic growth provides the only source of sustained real increases in household incomes. High employment facilitates economic growth. With high employment, businesses are likely to be more confident that demand for their products will remain strong, and so will be willing to engage in the long-term investment necessary for growth. With high unemployment, businesses have unused productive capacity and are much less likely to engage in long-term investment. Policymakers attempt to encourage *stable* economic growth because a stable business environment allows firms and households to plan accurately and encourages the long-term investment that is needed to sustain growth.

Financial Market Stability

When financial markets and institutions are not efficient in matching savers and borrowers, the economy loses resources. Firms with the potential to produce high-quality products and services cannot obtain the financing they need to design, develop, and market these products and services. Savers waste resources looking for satisfactory investments. The stability of financial markets and institutions makes possible the efficient matching of savers and borrowers.

Congress and the president created the Federal Reserve in response to the financial market turmoil of 1907, so it is not surprising that financial market stability is a goal of monetary policy. As we discussed in Chapter 3, banks and financial institutions are prone to *liquidity problems* because they borrow short-term—sometimes overnight—and use the funds to make long-term investments. Therefore, if a large number of depositors want to withdraw funds, the bank may have trouble providing the funds because they have been invested in long-term loans and securities. In a system without deposit insurance, depositors may worry that unless they are among the first to withdraw their money, they may not be able to retrieve all of it. If many depositors try to withdraw their funds at the same time, the result is a bank run that may cause the bank to fail. The failure of one bank may lead depositors at other banks to withdraw their money in a process called *contagion.* Many banks may be forced to close in a *bank panic.* A central bank can aim to head off such a panic by acting as a *lender of last resort* to help troubled banks get through temporary liquidity problems. As the 2007–2009 financial crisis showed, any financial firm that borrows short term and uses the funds to lend long term can be subject to a run.

Although the Fed responded vigorously to the financial crisis that began in 2007, it initially underestimated the severity of the crisis and was unable to head off the deep recession of 2007–2009. The financial crisis led to renewed debate over whether the Fed should take action to forestall asset price bubbles such as those associated with the dot-com boom on the U.S. stock market in the late 1990s and the U.S. housing market in the 2000s. Fed policymakers and many economists have generally argued that asset bubbles are difficult to identify ahead of time and that actions to deflate them may be counterproductive. But the severity of the 2007–2009 recession led some economists and policymakers to reassess this position. Financial stability has clearly become a more important Fed policy goal.

Interest Rate Stability

Like fluctuations in price levels, fluctuations in interest rates make planning difficult for households and firms. Increases and decreases in interest rates make it hard for firms to plan investments in plant and equipment and make households more hesitant about long-term investments in houses. Because people often blame the Fed for increases in interest rates, the Fed's goal of interest rate stability is motivated by political pressure as well as by a desire for a stable saving and investment environment. In addition, sharp interest rate fluctuations cause problems for banks and other financial firms that borrow in short-term markets and lend in long-term markets. So, stabilizing interest rates can help to stabilize the financial system.

Foreign-Exchange Market Stability

In the global economy, foreign-exchange market stability, or limited fluctuations in the foreign-exchange value of the dollar, is an important monetary policy goal of the Fed. A stable dollar simplifies planning for commercial and financial transactions. In addition, fluctuations in the dollar's value change the international competitiveness of U.S. industry: A rising dollar makes U.S. goods more expensive abroad, reducing exports, and a falling dollar makes foreign goods more expensive in the United States. In practice, the U.S. Treasury often originates changes in foreign-exchange policy, although the Fed implements these policy changes.

10.3
Learning Objective
Explain the Fed's monetary policy tools.

Monetary Policy Tools

To achieve its six goals, the Fed has a variety of policy tools. The three traditional monetary policy tools are (1) open market operations, (2) discount loans, and (3) reserve requirements. Of the three traditional monetary policy tools, open market operations, which we first discussed in Chapter 6, are by far the most important. In this section, we discuss the Fed's three traditional policy tools and two new policy tools that the Fed introduced starting in the fall of 2008.

Open Market Operations

The FOMC conducts open market operations—the purchase and sale of government securities in financial markets—with the goal of affecting the federal funds rate. The FOMC sets a target for the federal funds rate, but the actual rate is determined by the interaction between the demand and supply for bank reserves in the *federal funds market.* Banks demand reserves both to meet their legal obligation to hold required reserves and because they might want to hold excess reserves to meet their short-term liquidity needs. When interest rates are very low, as they were during and after the financial panic of 2007–2009, banks may also decide to hold onto reserves if they cannot find sufficiently profitable lending opportunities. If a bank finds that it has insufficient reserves, it can borrow reserves from other banks. Similarly, if a bank has more reserves than it needs, it can loan reserves to other banks. In the United States, the funds banks borrow and lend to each other are called *federal funds,* and the market in which they are traded is called the federal funds market. The Fed supplies bank reserves through open market operations. So, although the Fed controls the supply of reserves, banks control the demand for reserves. The result is that the Fed can usually come close to hitting its target for the federal funds rate, but is not always able to hit the target exactly.

The Fed can decrease the federal funds rate by increasing the supply of bank reserves, and it can increase the federal funds rate by decreasing the supply of bank reserves. To decrease bank reserves, the Fed engages in an *open market sale.* To increase bank reserves, the Fed engages in an *open market purchase.* For example, suppose the Fed wants to buy $1 billion of Treasury bills from Citigroup. Citigroup has an account with the Fed, so the easiest way for the Fed to pay for the securities is to increase Citigroup's account by $1 billion. Doing so increases reserves in the banking system by $1 billion. This increase in the supply of reserves reduces the federal funds rate. If the Fed wanted to increase the federal funds rate, it could sell $1 billion in Treasury bills to Citigroup or another bank. In paying for the Treasury bills, Citigroup will reduce its reserves by $1 billion. The decrease in the supply of reserves increases the federal funds rate.

At the end of each of its meetings, the FOMC issues a statement that includes its target for the federal funds rate and its assessment of the economy, particularly with respect to its policy goals of price stability and economic growth. In addition, the FOMC issues a *policy directive* to the Federal Reserve System's account manager, who is a vice president of the Federal Reserve Bank of New York and who is responsible for implementing open market operations and hitting the FOMC's target for the federal funds rate. The Open Market Trading Desk at the New York Federal Reserve Bank carries out open market operations. The trading desk is linked electronically through a system called the Trading Room Automated Processing System (TRAPS) to about 20 primary dealers, who are private securities firms that the Fed has selected to participate in open market operations. Each morning, the trading desk notifies the primary dealers of the size of the open

MACRO DATA: DOES THE FEDERAL RESERVE HIT ITS FEDERAL FUNDS RATE TARGET?

The FOMC conducts monetary policy by setting a target for the federal funds rate. The Open Market Trading Desk at the New York Federal Reserve Bank then conducts open market operations each morning to keep the federal funds rate close to the target rate. Although the Federal Reserve controls the supply of bank reserves, the federal funds rate is a market interest rate that is determined by both demand and supply. Fluctuations in the demand for bank reserves may cause the federal funds rate in the market to deviate from the target federal funds rate. The following figure shows the relationship between the target federal funds rate set by the Federal Reserve and the federal funds rate in the market using daily data from 1986 to 2011. The Federal Reserve has been generally successful at keeping the market rate close to the target rate by using daily open market operations. The Fed can offset changes in the demand for reserves with changes in the supply of reserves. Beginning in September 2008, however, the federal funds rate persistently fell below the target rate as the Federal Reserve injected reserves into the banking system. For example, the target federal funds rate was 2.0% on October 2, but the effective federal funds rate in the market was just 0.7%. In December 2008, the Fed temporarily abandoned having a single target for the federal funds rate in favor of a target *range* between 0.00% and 0.25%. The actual federal funds rate has remained in the target range every week through May 2011.

Test your understanding by doing related problem D10.1 on page 406 at the end of this chapter

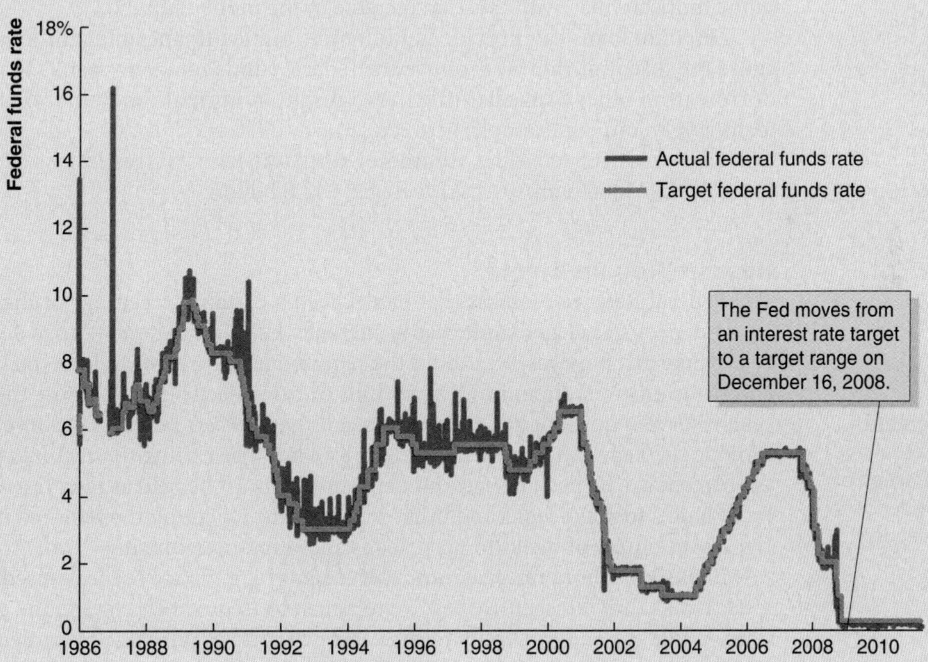

Source: Board of Governors of the Federal Reserve System.

market purchase or sale being conducted and asks them to submit offers to buy or sell Treasury securities. The dealers have just a few minutes to respond. Once the dealers' offers have been received, the Fed's account manager goes over the list, accepts the best offers, and has the trading desk buy or sell the securities until the volume of reserves reaches the Fed's desired goal.

How does the account manager know what to do? The manager interprets the FOMC's most recent policy directive, holds daily conferences with two members of the FOMC, and personally analyzes financial market conditions. Then the manager compares the level of reserves in the banking system with the level the trading desk staff estimates will be necessary to hit (or maintain) the target federal funds rate. If the level of reserves needs to be increased over the current level, the account manager orders the trading desk to purchase securities. If the level of reserves needs to be decreased, the account manager orders the trading desk to sell securities.

Discount Loans and the Lender of Last Resort

The Federal Reserve was founded to act as a *lender of last resort* for commercial banks. Banks can borrow from the *discount window* at their regional Federal Reserve Bank. The loans the Fed makes to banks are discount loans, and they are typically for very short periods, usually overnight, although they can be as long as 90 days. The interest rate the Fed charges on discount loans is called the **discount rate**. Because the Federal Reserve provides discount loans to banks in the form of increases in the banks' reserves, an increase in the quantity of discount loans from the Fed to banks will increase the monetary base, unless the Fed offsets the effect through another policy action.[3] All else held constant, an increase in the monetary base will cause an increase in the money supply.

Discount rate The interest rate that the Federal Reserve charges on discount loans.

Discount loans can provide liquidity to troubled financial institutions. However, because the discount rate is set above the federal funds rate, only banks that are unable to borrow from other banks use them. As a result, in normal times, the volume of discount loans is very low. For example, between January 2000 and July 2007—the month before the financial crisis started—the volume of discount loans averaged just $219 million per month, while total bank reserves averaged $42.8 billion.

Reserve Requirements

The Federal Reserve requires that banks hold a certain percentage of their checking account deposits as either vault cash—currency held in the bank—or as deposits with the Fed. Banks that have reserves above the required levels are free to loan them to households and firms or invest them in Treasury bills or other securities.[4] Because these reserves exceed reserve requirements, economists call them *excess reserves.* **Reserve requirements** provide the Fed with a monetary policy tool because raising the *required reserve ratio*, or the percentage of checking account deposits that must be held as reserves, reduces the ability of banks to make loans and other investments. Lowering the required reserve ratio increases the ability of banks to make loans and other investments.

Reserve requirements Regulations that require banks to hold a fraction of checking account deposits as vault cash or deposits with the Fed.

Banks must hold reserves, but reserve requirements are the least-used policy tool because banks find it disruptive to have to adjust to frequent changes in the required reserve ratio. While the Fed can easily reverse an open market purchase by carrying out an open market sale, quickly reversing an increase or a decrease in the required reserve ratio would cause significant problems for banks. As a result, the Fed has not changed the required reserve ratio since 1992.

---

[3]Recall from Chapter 6 that the monetary base is equal to currency in circulation plus bank reserves.

[4]U.S. law does not allow commercial banks to own the stock of non-financial firms.

New Monetary Policy Tools in Response to the 2007–2009 Financial Crisis

The traditional monetary policy tools allow the Fed to respond to most economic problems. However, the financial market crisis that started in August 2007 forced the Fed to develop new policy tools to achieve its goals. The Fed used some of the policy tools for just a short period of time, but it is still using two new tools that involve paying interest to banks:

1. Interest on bank reserves
2. Interest on funds deposited at the Fed for more than one day

Interest on Bank Reserves Banks had long complained that the Fed's failure to pay interest on the banks' reserve deposits amounted to a tax. To respond to banks' complaints and to give the Fed greater control over movements in bank reserves, Congress, in 2006, authorized the Fed to begin paying interest on bank reserve deposits beginning in October 2011. In response to the financial market crisis, Congress moved this date forward to October 2008, and the Fed immediately began to pay interest on reserves. Paying interest on reserve balances gives the Fed another monetary policy tool. By increasing the interest rate, the Fed can increase the level of reserves banks are willing to hold, thereby restraining bank lending and the increases in the money supply that would result. Lowering the interest rate would have the opposite effect.[5]

Interest on Funds Deposited at the Fed for More than One Day To provide greater control over bank reserve accounts, the Fed created a second policy tool, the Term Deposit Facility (TDF). Term deposits are similar to the certificates of deposit that banks offer to households and firms. The Fed offers term deposits to banks in periodic auctions. The interest rates are determined by the auctions and have been slightly above the interest rate the Fed offers on reserve balances. For example, in March 2011, the interest rate on the Fed's auction of $5 billion in 28-day term deposits was 0.26%, which was higher than the interest rate of 0.25% the Fed was paying on reserve deposits. The TDF gives the Fed another tool in managing bank reserve holdings because the funds that banks place in term deposits are removed from their reserve accounts. So, the more funds banks place in term deposits, the less they will have available to expand loans and the money supply.

Other Nontraditional Policy Actions From its founding in 1913 until 1980, with a few brief exceptions, the Fed made loans only to members of the Federal Reserve System. In 1980, Congress authorized the Fed to make loans to all depository institutions. By the beginning of the financial crisis in 2007, however, a *shadow banking system* of investment banks, money market mutual funds, hedge funds, and other nonbank financial firms had grown to be as large as the commercial banking system. The initial stages of the financial crisis involved these shadow banks rather than commercial banks. When the crisis began, the Fed was handicapped in its role as a lender of last resort because it had no recent tradition of lending to anyone but banks.

The Fed did, however, have the authority to lend more broadly. Section 13(3) of the Federal Reserve Act authorizes the Fed in "unusual and exigent circumstances" to lend to any "individual, partnership, or corporation" that could provide acceptable collateral and

[5]Technically, the Fed can set separate interest rates on required reserve balances and on excess reserve balances. As of June 2011, the interest rate on both types of balances has been the same: 0.25%.

could demonstrate an inability to borrow from commercial banks. The Fed used this authority to set up several temporary lending facilities:

- *Primary Dealer Credit Facility*. Under this facility, primary dealers—those securities firms that trade directly with the Fed in the conduct of open market operations—could borrow overnight using mortgage-backed securities as collateral. This facility was intended to allow the investment banks and large securities firms that are primary dealers to obtain emergency loans. The facility was established in March 2008 and closed in February 2010.
- *Term Securities Lending Facility*. Under this facility, the Fed would loan up to $200 billion of Treasury securities in exchange for mortgage-backed securities. By early 2008, selling mortgage-backed securities had become difficult. This facility was intended to allow financial firms to borrow against those illiquid assets. It was established in March 2008 and closed in February 2010.
- *Commercial Paper Funding Facility*. Under this facility, the Fed purchased three-month commercial paper issued by nonfinancial corporations. As we discussed in Chapter 9, when Lehman Brothers defaulted on its commercial paper in September 2008, many money market mutual funds suffered significant losses. As investors began redeeming their shares in these funds, the funds stopped buying commercial paper. Many corporations had come to rely on selling commercial paper to meet their short-term financing needs, including funding their inventories and their payrolls. By buying commercial paper directly from these corporations, the Fed allowed these firms to continue normal operations. This facility was established in October 2008 and closed in February 2010.
- *Term Asset-Backed Securities Loan Facility (TALF)*. Under this facility, the Federal Reserve Bank of New York extended three-year or five-year loans to help investors fund the purchase of asset-backed securities. Asset-backed securities are securitized consumer and business loans, apart from mortgages. For instance, some asset-backed securities consist of consumer automobile loans that have been bundled together as a security to be resold to investors. Following the financial crisis, the market for asset-backed securities largely dried up. This facility was announced in November 2008, and the last loans were made in June 2010.

In addition to these new lending facilities, the Fed set up a new way for banks to receive discount loans under the *Term Auction Facility*. In this facility, the Fed for the first time began auctioning discount loans at an interest rate determined by banks' demand for the funds. All banks eligible to borrow under the regular discount loan program could participate in the auctions. Depository institutions could pledge mortgage-backed securities, including those that were not otherwise marketable, as collateral for the loans. The length of the loans was 28 days or 84 days. Typically, the interest rate from these auctions was below the official discount rate. The length of the loans, the low interest rate, and the broader acceptability of collateral made these loans attractive to many banks during the crisis. The facility was established in December 2007 and closed in March 2010.

The Fed ended these innovative discount programs in 2010, with the financial system having recovered from the worst of the crisis.

Figure 10.2 shows that there was an explosion in all types of lending by the Fed during the financial crisis. Borrowing from the Fed amounted to just $2.2 billion as late as December 5, 2007. However, as the financial crisis worsened during the first months of 2008, financial institutions borrowed more and more from the Fed. Just after the collapse of Bear Stearns on March 19, 2008, total borrowing from the Fed had increased to $108.9 billion. On September 17, 2008, just days after Lehman Brothers filed for bankruptcy, total borrowing had reached $271.3 billion, skyrocketing from there to $993.5 billion on December 10, 2008 during the worst part of the financial crisis. Since that time, borrowing from the Fed has decreased steadily; it had fallen to $15.3 billion on May 11, 2011. However, even this low level is nearly 65 times larger than pre-crisis levels.

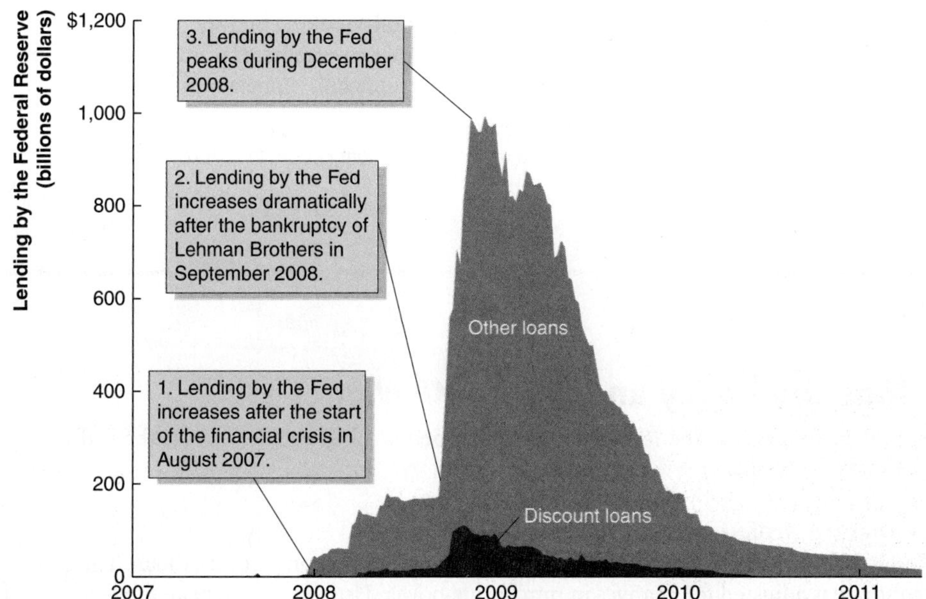
Lending by the Federal Reserve (billions of dollars)
$1,200
1,000
800
600
400
200
0
2007
2008
2009
2010
2011
3. Lending by the Fed peaks during December 2008.
2. Lending by the Fed increases dramatically after the bankruptcy of Lehman Brothers in September 2008.
1. Lending by the Fed increases after the start of the financial crisis in August 2007.
Other loans
Discount loans

Figure 10.2

Lending by the Fed During the Financial Market Shock

During the financial crisis, lending by the Federal Reserve increased from just a few hundred million dollars to $993.5 billion during December 2008. Since that time, lending by the Fed has steadily decreased.

Source: Board of Governors of the Federal Reserve System. ●

Making the Connection

On the Board of Governors, Four Can Be a Crowd

Because the Fed's most important monetary policy tool is setting the target for the federal funds rate, by the 1980s, the key monetary policy debates within the Fed took place during meetings of the FOMC. Economists and Wall Street analysts closely watched the outcome of each meeting for clues about the direction of Fed policy. During the financial crisis of 2007–2009, however, it became clear that the Fed could not confine its actions to changes in the target for the federal funds rate. As in other recessions, the FOMC moved quickly to cut the target beginning in September 2007. But by December 2008, the target had effectively been cut to zero, yet the economy continued to contract, and the financial system was in crisis.

As discussed earlier, during the financial crisis, Fed Chairman Ben Bernanke instituted a series of policy actions, some of which were unprecedented. Because events were moving swiftly, waiting for the next FOMC meeting to discuss potential policy moves was not feasible. In addition, because the FOMC consists of all the members of the Board of Governors and five of the 12 district bank presidents, its size was a barrier to quick decision making. The alternative of relying on the Board of Governors was also problematic. In 1976, Congress passed the Government in the Sunshine Act, which requires most federal government agencies to give public notice before a meeting. If four or more members of the Board of Governors meet to consider a policy action, it is considered an official meeting under the act and cannot be held without prior public notice. Given that Bernanke needed to make decisions rapidly as events unfolded hour by hour, the requirement of prior public notice made it infeasible for him to meet with more than two other members of the Board of Governors.

As a result, Bernanke relied on an informal group of advisers consisting of Board of Governors members Donald Kohn and Kevin Warsh and Federal Reserve Bank of New York president Timothy Geithner. Geithner was a member of the FOMC but not of the Board of Governors, so his presence at meetings did not trigger the Sunshine Act requirement. The "four musketeers," as they came to be called, were the key policymaking body at the Fed during the crisis. The unintended consequence of the Sunshine Act requirements was to drastically limit the input of the other members of the Board of Governors into monetary policymaking.

Source: David Wessel, *In Fed We Trust: Ben Bernanke's War on the Great Panic*, New York: Three Rivers Press, an imprint of Crown Publishing Group, a division of Random House, Inc., 2009, 2010.

Test your understanding by doing related problem 3.9 on page 402 at the end of this chapter.

10.4

Learning Objective

Use the *IS–MP* model to understand how monetary policy affects the economy in the short run.

Monetary Policy and the *IS–MP* Model

In this section, we use the *IS–MP* model developed in Chapter 9 to analyze the Fed's monetary policy actions.

Monetary Policy and Aggregate Expenditure

Recall that the nominal interest rate is the stated interest rate on a bond or loan. The real interest rate is adjusted for changes in purchasing power. Usually, we calculate the real interest rate by subtracting the expected inflation rate from the nominal interest rate. As we have seen, the Fed is able to keep the nominal federal funds rate close to its target. But, long-term real interest rates, such as those a homebuyer would pay on a 30-year mortgage or a firm would pay on a 30-year bond, are more relevant in determining consumption and investment. Long-term nominal interest rates are linked to short-term nominal interest rates through the *term structure of interest rates*, which we first introduced in Chapter 3 and discussed further in Chapter 9, and the default risk premium. As we saw in Chapter 9, the long-term nominal interest rate, i_{LT}, equals the short-term nominal interest rate, i, plus the term structure effect, TSE, and the default-risk premium, DP:

$$i_{LT} = i + TSE + DP. \tag{10.1}$$

We will typically assume that if the Fed increases its target for the short-term nominal interest rate, the term structure effect and the default-risk premium will remain unchanged. Therefore, an increase or decrease in the Fed's target for the federal funds rate will result in an increase or decrease in the long-term nominal interest rate.

The long-term real interest rate is important in determining consumption and investment expenditures. As we saw in Chapter 9, the long-term real interest rate, r, equals the long-term nominal interest rate minus the expected inflation rate, π^e:

$$r = i_{LT} - \pi^e.$$

For simplicity, we will assume that households and firms expect the inflation rate next year to be the same as the inflation rate this year. In other words, we will assume that households and firms have *adaptive expectations*. Adaptive expectations imply that, because the expected inflation rate is constant, any increase in nominal interest rates will also increase real interest rates. If at the beginning of 2012, a bank is offering car loans with a nominal interest rate of 5% when the expected inflation rate is 2%, then the real interest rate is $5\% - 2\% = 3\%$. If at the beginning of 2013, the bank increases the nominal interest rate to 6%, then, because the expected inflation rate is unchanged, the real interest rate increases to $6\% - 2\% = 4\%$. Therefore, if the nominal interest rate increases by a given number of percentage points, the real interest rate will increase by that same number of percentage points. Similarly, any decrease in the nominal interest rate will result in a decrease in the real interest rate.

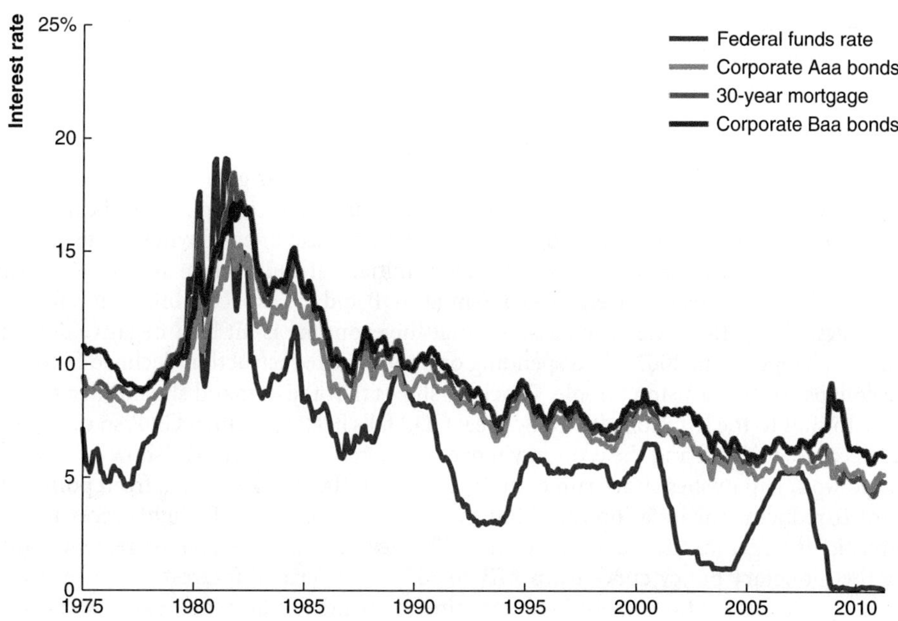

Figure 10.3

The Federal Funds Rate and the Interest Rates on Corporate Bonds and Mortgages

The Fed controls the federal funds rate. The long-term interest rates that households pay to purchase a house or that corporations pay to finance investment generally rise and fall with the federal funds rate.

Source: Board of Governors of the Federal Reserve System. ●

The Fed conducts monetary policy in large part by setting a target federal funds rate. Although households and firms cannot borrow or lend at the federal funds rate, as Figure 10.3 shows, it is closely linked to long-term interest rates. The figure shows that the federal funds rate, the mortgage interest rate, and the interest rates on corporate bonds generally move together. Note, though, that the federal funds rate often increases and decreases more than these long-term rates. For example, for several years after 2000, all interest rates fell, but the interest rates on mortgages and corporate bonds did not fall by as much or as rapidly as the federal funds rate. In this case, investors did not believe that these low short-term rates would persist for very long. In other words, investors expected that future short-term rates would increase, increasing the *TSE* term in Equation (10.1) on the previous page. Generally, though, if the Fed increases or decreases its target for the federal funds rate, long-term nominal interest rates—for example, the interest rate on a 30-year mortgage—will also increase or decrease. If the expected inflation rate is constant, then the long-term real interest rate will also increase or decrease.

If the Fed increases its target for the federal funds rate, it will become more expensive for households and firms to borrow, so consumption and investment expenditures decrease, which will decrease aggregate expenditure. As we saw in Chapter 9, a decrease in aggregate expenditure will cause real GDP to also decrease. When the Fed lowers its target for the federal funds rate in an attempt to increase real GDP and employment, it is conducting an *expansionary monetary policy*. When the Fed raises its target for the federal funds rate—typically in response to a rising inflation rate—in an attempt to decrease real GDP and employment, it is conducting a *contractionary monetary policy*. Table 10.1 summarizes

Table 10.1 **Open Market Operations and Real GDP**

When the Fed . . .	banking reserves and the money supply . . .	causing the federal funds rate and long-term real interest rates to . . .	and causing consumption and investment to . . .	so, real GDP . . .
Sells government bonds	decrease	increase	decrease	decreases.
Buys government bonds	increase	decrease	increase	increases.

how the Fed conducts monetary policy by using open market operations, its main policy tool, to affect real GDP.

Using Monetary Policy to Fight a Recession

One of the Fed's goals is high employment and to achieve this goal, the Fed attempts to keep the cyclical unemployment rate close to zero. During a recession, the Fed carries out an expansionary monetary policy to try to reduce the cyclical unemployment rate.

In Figure 10.4, suppose that the economy is initially at equilibrium at point *A* in panels (a) and (b), with real GDP equal to potential GDP and the expected inflation rate equal to the actual inflation rate. Then assume that the economy is hit by a negative demand shock, as happened in 2007 when spending on residential construction declined following the collapse of the housing bubble. Panel (a) shows that the demand shock causes the *IS* curve to shift to the left, from IS_1 to IS_2. Real GDP falls below potential GDP, so the output gap becomes negative and the economy moves into a recession. Panel (b) shows that a negative output gap pushes short-run equilibrium down the Phillips curve, from point *A* to point *B*, reducing the inflation rate from π_1 to π_2. The Fed typically fights recessions by lowering its target for the federal funds rate. This action lowers the real interest rate, shifting the monetary policy curve from MP_1 to MP_2. A lower real interest rate leads to increases in consumption spending, investment spending, and net exports, moving short-run equilibrium from point *B* to point *C* on the *IS* curve. Real GDP returns to its potential level, so the output gap is again zero. In panel (b), the inflation rate rises from π_2 back to π_1.

Using Monetary Policy to Fight Inflation

During the economic expansion of the 1990s, real GDP in the United States increased from 1.1% above potential GDP in 1998 to 4.2% above potential GDP during the second quarter of 2000. During the same period, the inflation rate as measured using the CPI rose from 1.6% to 3.8%. Figure 10.5 on page 380 shows how the Fed can use monetary policy to reduce the inflation rate and achieve its goal of price stability.

Suppose a positive demand shock has pushed real GDP above potential GDP, so that short-run equilibrium is at point *A* in panels (a) and (b). At point *A*, the output gap is positive and the inflation rate is greater than expected, $\pi_1 > \pi^e$. To reduce the inflation rate, the Fed increases the interest rate from r_1 to r_2, causing the *MP* curve to shift up from MP_1 to MP_2. Short-run equilibrium is now at point *B*, and real GDP equals potential GDP, so $\tilde{Y}_2 = 0$. Along the Phillips curve, the output gap changes from $\tilde{Y}_1$ to $\tilde{Y}_2$, so the inflation rate decreases to π_2. At point *B* in panels (a) and (b), both the inflation rate and the output gap have been reduced.

Using Monetary Policy to Deal with a Supply Shock

In the two previous examples, the Fed used changes in its target interest rate to offset the effects on the economy of demand shocks. In theory, when changes in aggregate expenditure cause the output gap and the inflation rate to fluctuate, the policy for the Fed to use to achieve its goals is clear. But what should the Fed do when dealing with a supply shock, such as a significant increase in oil prices? The correct policy for the Fed to pursue following an supply shock is less clear.

The U.S. economy suffered from large supply shocks in the 1970s when the price of a barrel of oil nearly tripled from $3.56 per barrel in July 1973 to $11.16 per barrel in October 1974. This increase in oil prices significantly raised the costs of production for many firms. As firms raised prices in response to these higher costs, the inflation rate rose. Figure 10.6 on page 381 illustrates the effects of a supply shock. The short-run equilibrium before the supply shock is shown by point *A* in both panels. As panel (b) shows, the supply shock causes the Phillips curve to shift up, from PC_1 to PC_2, as the inflation rate increases for every value of the output gap.

Panel (b) of Figure 10.6 on page 381 illustrates the dilemma that supply shocks pose for the Fed. If the Fed keeps the real interest rate unchanged, then the inflation rate will rise, undermining the Fed's goal of price stability. The Fed could attempt to maintain the inflation rate at its initial level by raising the real interest rate from r_1 to r_2. But, as shown

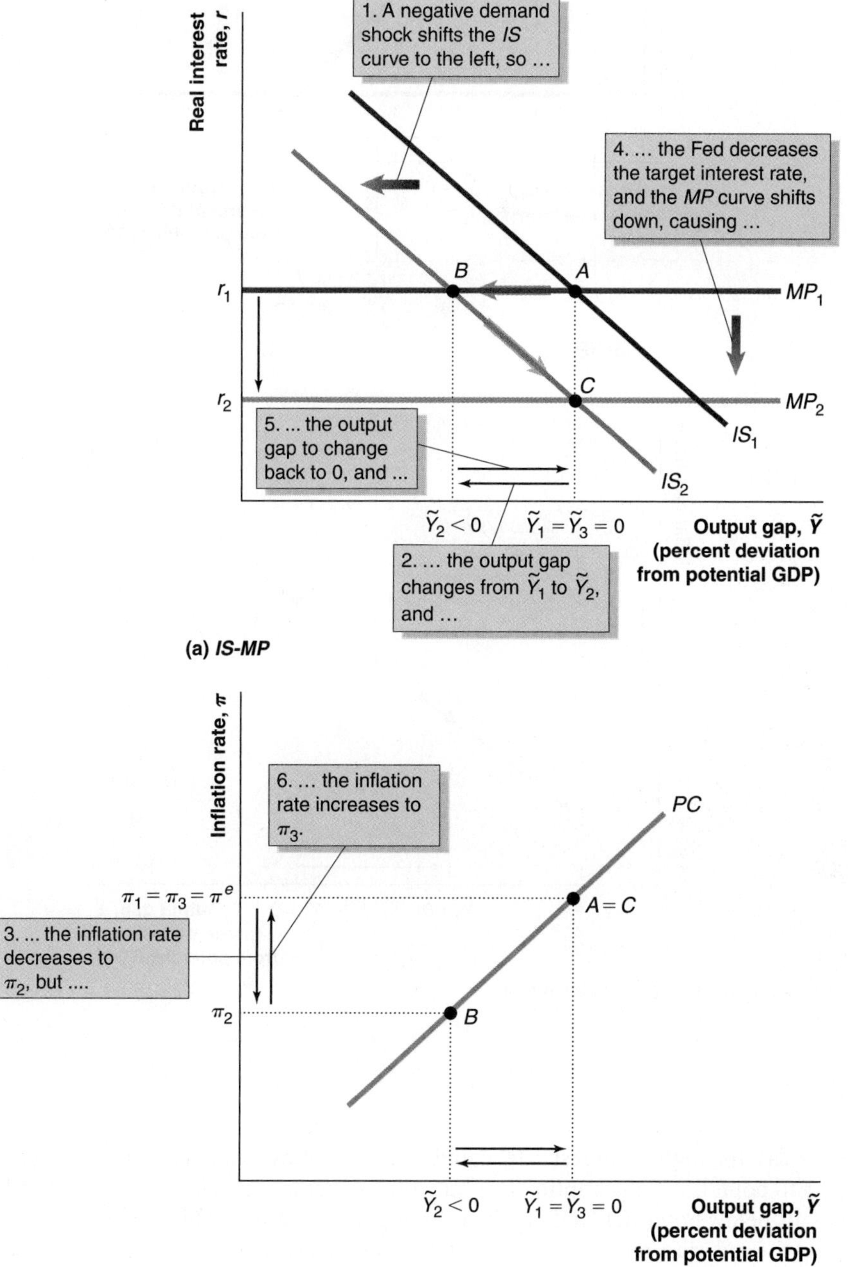

Figure 10.4

Expansionary Monetary Policy

In panel (a), a demand shock causes the *IS* curve to shift to the left, from IS_1 to IS_2. Real GDP falls below potential GDP, so the economy has a negative output gap at $\tilde{Y}_2$ and moves into a recession. Panel (b) shows that a negative output gap results in a movement down the Phillips curve, lowering the inflation rate from π_1 to π_2. The Fed lowers the real interest rate, shifting the monetary policy curve down from MP_1 to MP_2, causing a movement down the *IS* curve. Real GDP returns to its potential level, so the output gap is again zero. In panel (b), the inflation rate rises from π_2 back to π_1. ●

Figure 10.5

Contractionary Monetary Policy

After a positive demand shock, the economy is at point *A* in panels (a) and (b), where the output gap is positive and inflation is greater than expected. To reduce inflation, the Fed increases the real interest rate, which shifts up the *MP* curve in panel (a). As a result, the output gap changes from $\tilde{Y}_1$ to $\tilde{Y}_2$. The Phillips curve in panel (b) shows us that the inflation rate will also decrease. ●

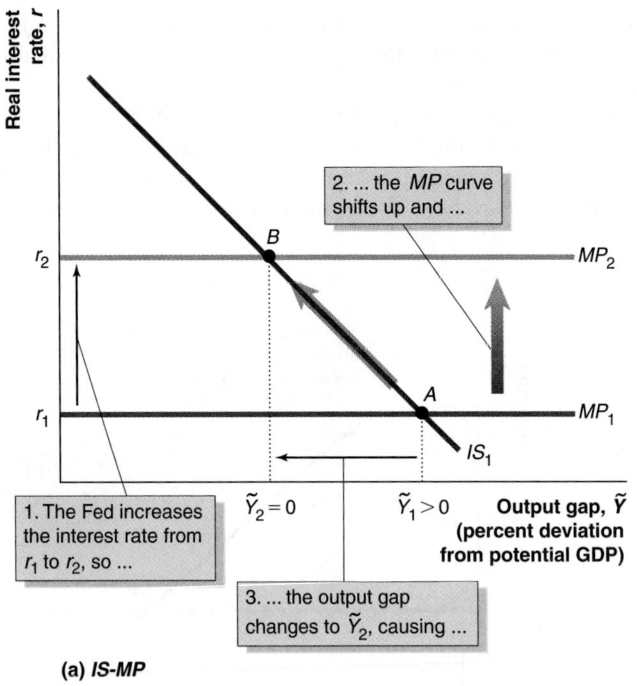

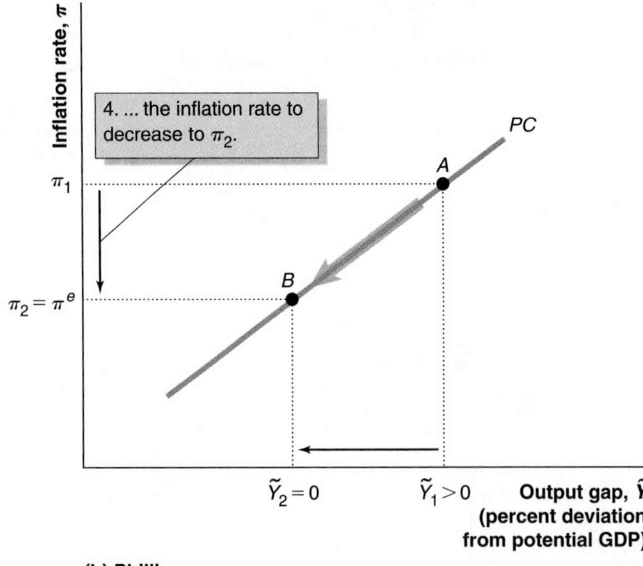

in panel (a), the higher interest rate would result in a movement along the *IS* curve from point *A* to point *C* as consumption, investment, and net exports all decline. At point *C*, real GDP falls below potential GDP, so the output gap is negative. The Fed has succeeded in keeping the inflation rate constant at point *C* in panel (b), but only by failing to meet its goal of high employment. Unfortunately for the Fed, supply shocks require it to choose between its goals of price stability and high employment.

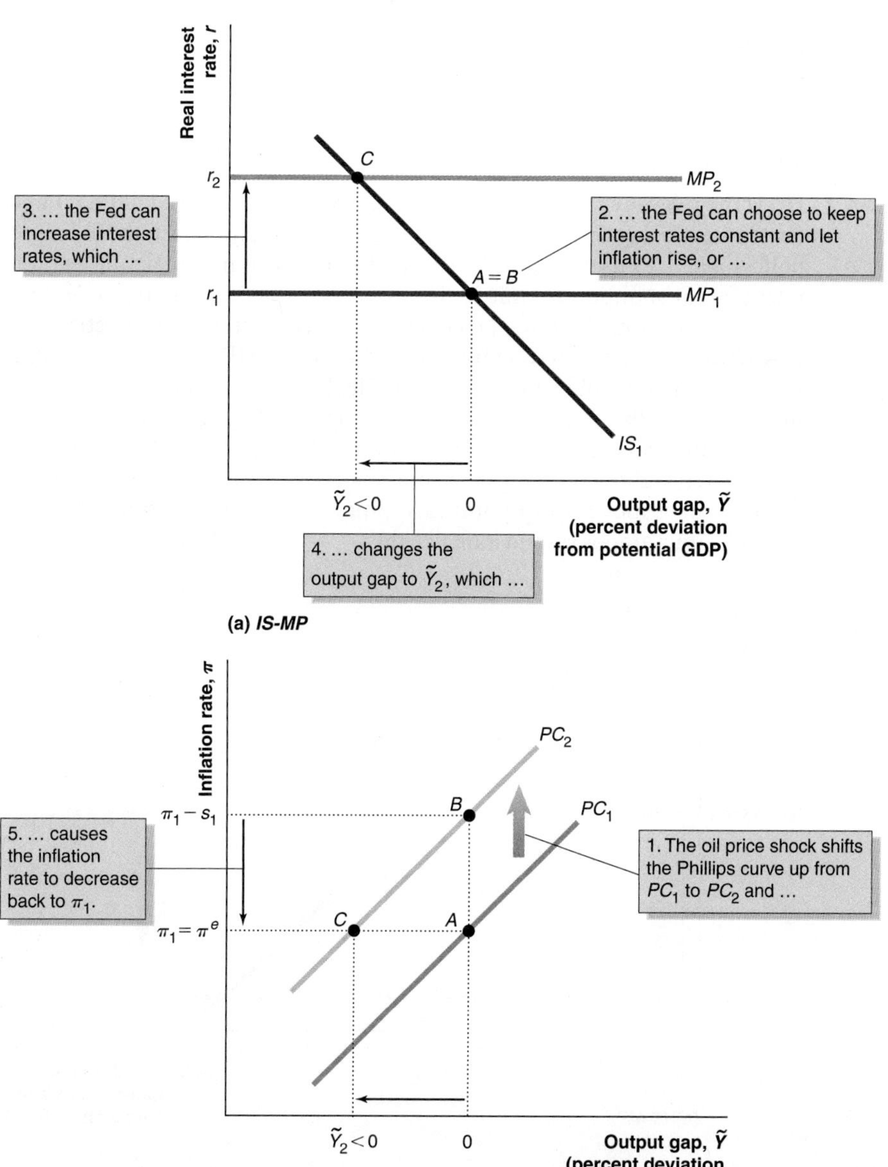

Real interest rate, r
r2
r1
C
MP2
MP1
A = B
IS1
3. … the Fed can increase interest rates, which …
2. … the Fed can choose to keep interest rates constant and let inflation rise, or …
Ỹ2 < 0
0
Output gap, Ỹ (percent deviation from potential GDP)
4. … changes the output gap to Ỹ2, which …
(a) IS-MP
Inflation rate, π
π1 − s1
π1 = πe
5. … causes the inflation rate to decrease back to π1.
PC2
PC1
B
C
A
1. The oil price shock shifts the Phillips curve up from PC1 to PC2 and …
Ỹ2 < 0
0
Output gap, Ỹ (percent deviation from potential GDP)
(b) Phillips curve

Figure 10.6

Monetary Policy and an Increase in Oil Prices

After an increase in oil prices, the economy's equilibrium is at point *B* in panels (a) and (b), where the actual inflation rate is greater than the expected inflation rate. In this situation, the Fed faces a choice. The Fed can increase the real interest rate to decrease the inflation rate, which would move short-run equilibrium to point *C* in panels (a) and (b), but this measure comes at the cost of lower real GDP. Alternatively, the Fed can keep interest rates constant, so the economy remains at point *B* in panels (a) and (b), but this action leaves the economy with a higher inflation rate. ●

Solved Problem 10.4

Did the Federal Reserve Make the Great Depression Worse?

The Great Depression was the most severe economic contraction that the United States has ever experienced. During the first years of the Great Depression in the early 1930s, the Fed thought that its monetary policy was expansionary because interest rates were low and stable. For example, the *nominal* interest rate on the safest corporate bonds varied from 4.4% to 5.4%. The Fed thought that these low interest rates represented an expansionary policy, so that there was no need to change policy. Because the United States experienced deflation during these years, however, the *real* interest rate on the safest corporate bonds increased from 4.8% in October 1929 when the stock market crashed to 15.8% in May 1932! Use the *IS–MP* model to show the effect of a monetary policy that allowed the real interest rate to increase from 4.8% to 15.8%.

Solving the Problem

Step 1 **Review the chapter material.** The problem asks you to explain the effect of the Fed's allowing real interest rates to increase, so you may want to review the section "Monetary Policy and Aggregate Expenditure," which begins on page 376.

Step 2 **Draw the relevant *IS–MP* and Phillips curve graphs.** The Fed did not target interest rates during the Great Depression as it does today. In fact, the failure of Fed policymakers to understand the distinction between nominal and real interest rates played an important role in the monetary policy failures that worsened the Great Depression. To show the effect of the Fed's action—or inaction!—draw *IS–MP* and Phillips curve graphs with the initial *MP* curve, MP_{1929}, at 4.8%. Label the initial equilibrium as point *A*. The Fed allowed the real interest rate to increase to 15.8%, so draw a second *MP* curve, MP_{1932}, at a real interest rate of 15.8%. Short-run equilibrium is now at point *B*. As real GDP falls relative to potential GDP and the output gap becomes negative, short-run equilibrium on the Phillips curve moves from point *A* to point *B*, and the inflation rate becomes negative. Your graphs should look like this:

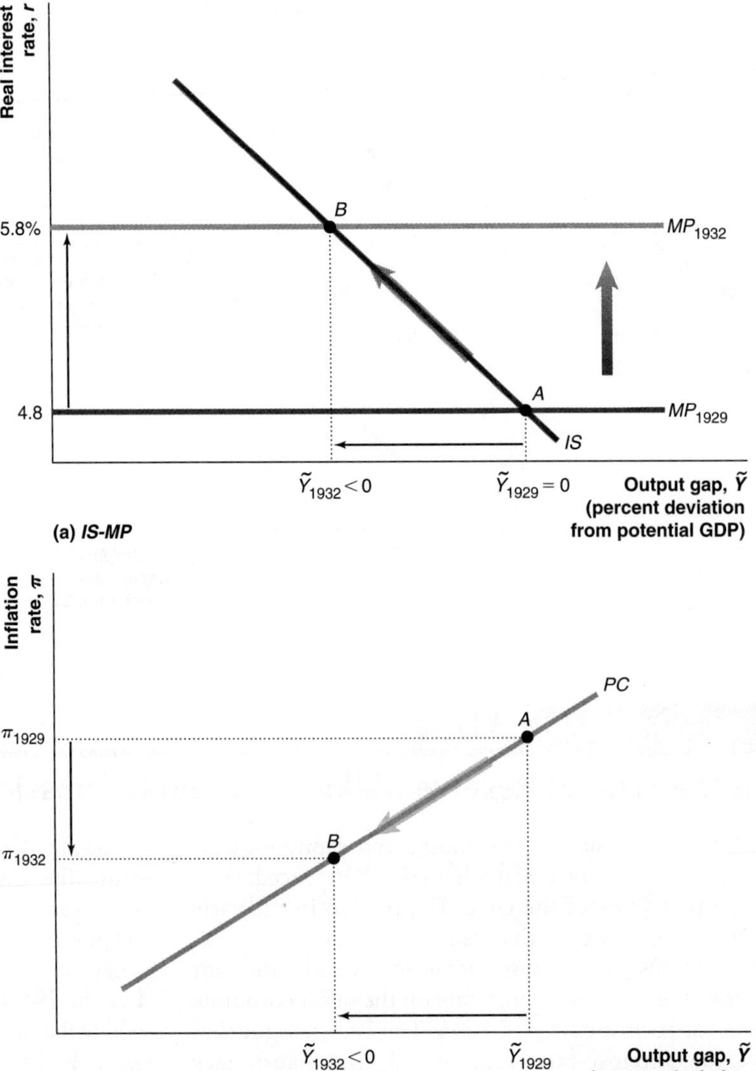

Step 3 **Discuss the effects of a rising real interest rate on the economy.** If the Fed's policy made the Great Depression worse, then the increase in the real interest rate should have led to lower real GDP. In fact, real GDP did fall. The increase in the real interest rate made it more expensive for households and firms to borrow to finance consumption and investment expenditures, so aggregate expenditure decreased and real GDP fell between 1929 and 1932. The Phillips curve in panel (b) shows that as real GDP declined far below potential GDP, the economy experienced deflation, or a falling price level.

As Milton Friedman argued, the Fed's policies were at least partly responsible for the severity of the Great Depression. Friedman emphasized the Fed's failure to stop the bank panics and the decline in the money supply, but the Fed's failure to distinguish real interest rates from nominal interest rates was also an important policy mistake. The Fed did learn from the experience of the Great Depression, which is why Ben Bernanke is quoted as saying at the start of the chapter, "we won't do it again."

For more practice, do related problems 4.7 and 4.8 on page 403 at the end of this chapter.

Alternative Channels of Monetary Policy

Economists refer to the ways in which monetary policy can affect output and prices as the *channels of monetary policy.* In the *IS–MP* model, monetary policy works as follows: Using open market operations, the Fed changes the target for the federal funds rate, which causes a change in the long-term real interest rate. A change in the long-term real interest rate affects the components of aggregate expenditure, thereby changing the output gap and the inflation rate. We call this channel the *interest rate channel.* If the Fed wants to increase output, it reduces the short-term nominal interest rate. Through the term structure of interest rates, the decrease in short-term nominal interest will decrease long-term nominal interest rates. If the default-risk premium and the expected inflation rate remain constant, then the long-term real interest rate also decreases. A lower real interest rate leads to increases in consumption and investment spending and net exports, which leads firms to increase output.

Nominal interest rates almost never fall below zero. A negative federal funds interest rate, for example, implies that one bank is willing to *pay* another bank for lending the other bank reserves. That effect would be similar to the unlikely event of a bank paying a household to take out a car loan or a student loan. As a consequence, when short-term nominal interest rates are already at 0%, the Fed cannot decrease them further. The inability of the Fed to lower interest rates to negative values is referred to as the *zero bound constraint.* At the zero bound constraint, the Fed cannot decrease real interest rates by decreasing nominal interest rates. Does this inability mean that monetary policy cannot increase aggregate expenditure and real GDP when the short-term nominal interest rate equals 0%?

Not necessarily. With standard open market operations, the central bank buys and sells government securities to change the quantity of bank reserves to keep the short-term nominal interest rate at the target rate. The effect of open market operations on interest rates is important, but the fact that open market operations also change the level of bank reserves provides two additional channels through which monetary policy can affect real GDP and the inflation rate:

1. The bank lending channel
2. Quantitative easing

The Bank Lending Channel The *bank lending channel* of monetary policy emphasizes the behavior of borrowers who depend on bank loans. This channel exists due to *asymmetric information* in the financial system. **Asymmetric information** occurs when one party in an economic transaction has better information than the other

Asymmetric information The situation in which one party to a transaction has better information than the other party.

party. Firms have much better information about their true financial condition than do potential investors who might be willing to buy their stocks or bonds. Some firms such as Starbucks or Google are so large and well known that most of the information investors need is publicly available, and the firms can borrow directly from financial markets by selling corporate bonds. However, some firms are not well-known, and investors are not willing to buy their bonds. These firms are forced to rely on banks and other financial intermediaries for loans. Banks develop specialized knowledge about firms. For example, a local bank may have made loans to a neighborhood bakery or beauty salon over a period of years, so the bank knows the owner's history of repaying loans and the owner's general creditworthiness. Many households also use the bank lending channel to finance consumption and investment, by borrowing money to buy cars and homes.

Now consider how the open market purchase of government securities affects the bank lending channel. The Fed purchases government securities, so bank reserves increase. Banks can use the increased reserves to make new loans. Borrowing from banks increases, so consumption and investment increase. The increase in expenditure leads firms to increase output. An open market sale of government securities would have the opposite effect: The sale of government securities to banks reduces reserves and leads banks to decrease lending. As a result, some households and firms will not be able to obtain loans, so consumption and investment will decrease. The decrease in expenditure leads firms to decrease output. The bank lending channel provides one explanation for why monetary policy may still be effective even when short-term nominal interest rates equal 0%. Notice, though, that the bank lending channel operates even when the short-term nominal interest rate is greater than 0%.

Quantitative Easing If the short-term nominal interest rate is already zero, then the central bank can still add reserves to the banking system through open market purchases of long-term securities. By December 2008, the Fed had driven the target for the federal funds rate nearly to zero, while the financial crisis and the economic recession had deepened. These continuing problems led the Fed to take the unusual step of buying more than $1.7 trillion in mortgage-backed securities and longer-term Treasury securities during 2009 and early 2010. This policy of a central bank attempting to stimulate the economy by buying long-term securities is called **quantitative easing**. The Fed's objective was to reduce the interest rates on mortgages and on 10-year Treasury notes. Lower interest rates on mortgages could help to spur new home sales. And lower interest rates on 10-year Treasury notes could help to lower interest rates on corporate bonds, thereby increasing investment spending on physical capital. In November 2010, the Fed announced a second round of quantitative easing (dubbed QE2). With QE2, the Fed would buy an additional $600 billion in long-term Treasury securities through June 2011. QE2 was the Fed's response to the economy's slow recovery from the recession.

Quantitative easing
A central bank policy that attempts to stimulate the economy by buying long-term securities.

We can use our discussion of the *MP* curve in Chapter 9 to analyze the effects of quantitative easing. Recall that the expression for the long-run real interest rate, r, is:

$$r = i + TSE + DP - \pi^e. \qquad (10.2)$$

With conventional monetary policy, the Fed reduces r by lowering its target for the federal funds rate, i, thereby shifting down the *MP* curve. This strategy will be successful if the expected inflation rate, the term structure effect, and the default risk premium, remain unchanged. During the 2007–2009 financial crisis and its aftermath, however, the Fed had already pushed the federal funds rate as low as it could. Therefore, to increase real GDP and employment, the Fed needed another means of shifting down the *MP* curve. Quantitative easing gave the Fed the means to do so. By purchasing long-term securities such as 10-year U.S. Treasury notes, the Fed would increase demand for them, which would increase their price. Recall from Chapter 3 that the price and the interest rate on a financial asset, such as a bond, move in opposite directions: When the price of a Treasury note increases, its interest rate decreases. The interest rate on the 10-year Treasury note plays a particularly important role in the financial system because it is a benchmark default-free interest rate. The interest rate on the 10-year Treasury note is considered free of default risk because investors do not believe that the federal government will default on its debts. A falling interest rate on a long-term bond such as a U.S. Treasury note can reduce the real interest rate, causing the *MP* curve to shift down. In practice, the market for U.S. Treasury securities is very large, so the Fed's purchases had only limited effectiveness in driving down the interest rate on 10-year Treasury notes. Therefore, quantitative easing did not necessarily have a large effect on the economy.

The Bank of Japan tried using quantitative easing in an attempt to revive the Japanese economy from a decade of extremely slow economic growth throughout the 1990s. During 2001–2006, the Bank of Japan set targets for the volume of bank reserves and purchased long-term government securities until reserves hit the target level. At one point, the Bank of Japan set a target of 30–35 trillion yen for bank reserves when the required level of bank reserves was just 6 trillion yen. The target created a huge supply of excess reserves that Japanese banks could lend to households and firms if they so chose. During this experiment with quantitative easing, the Bank of Japan purchased not only government securities but also equities and commercial paper. Economists still debate whether the Bank of Japan's quantitative easing helped the economy, but the Japanese economy has yet to return to the growth rates it experienced prior to the 1990s.

Figure 10.7 shows the effects of the Fed's policies during the financial crisis of 2007–2009 and the immediately following period on the value of assets on the *Fed's balance sheet.* The turmoil following the collapse of Lehman Brothers on September 15, 2008 led to a dramatic change in Fed policy. The Fed's assets exploded from $959 billion before

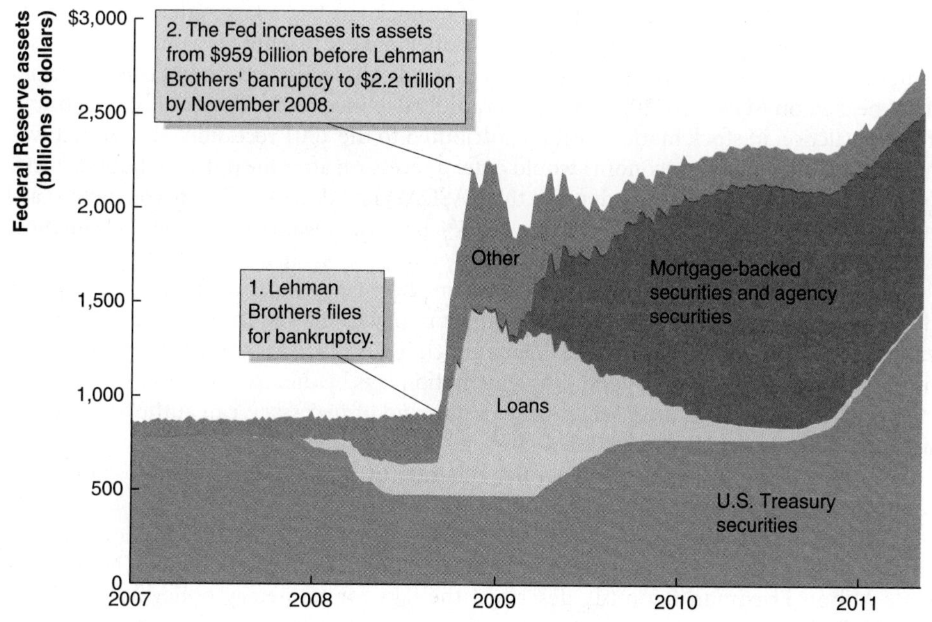

Figure 10.7

Federal Reserve Assets, 2007–2011

After the collapse of Lehman Brothers, the Fed dramatically increased the assets it owned from $959 billion to $2.2 trillion. Some of the increase came from loans to financial institutions and the rest came from purchases of assets such as commercial paper and mortgage-backed securities.

Source: Board of Governors of the Federal Reserve System. ●

the Lehman Brothers bankruptcy to $2.2 trillion on November 12, 2008. The increase came primarily from new loans to financial institutions and attempts to increase the liquidity of key markets such as commercial paper. Access to the commercial paper market is critical to the day-to-day operations of many large firms.

10.5

Learning Objective

Explain the challenges to using monetary policy effectively.

The Limitations of Monetary Policy

Our discussion thus far may make it seem easy for central banks to eliminate economic fluctuations and achieve price stability, high employment, and stable interest rates following a demand shock. In fact, though, central banks face several important challenges to implementing policy successfully.

The Fed's ability to recognize quickly the need for a change in monetary policy is a key to its success. If the Fed is late in recognizing that a recession has begun or that the inflation rate is increasing, it may not be able to implement a new policy soon enough to avoid a significant recession or a significant increase in inflation. In fact, particularly when dealing with small demand shocks, if the Fed implements a policy too late, it may actually destabilize the economy.

Policy Lags

In practice, the Fed is not instantly aware that a demand shock or supply shock has occurred that is large enough to cause a recession or to cause inflation to accelerate. Even after the Fed becomes aware that a demand shock or supply shock has occurred, it takes time to decide on an appropriate change in policy. Then, it takes time for the new policy to actually affect real GDP, employment, and inflation. Due to *lags* between the time a shock occurs and the effects of the policy change, monetary policy cannot immediately offset the effects of demand and supply shocks. In this section, we discuss policy lags further.

Recognition lag The period of time between when a shock occurs and when policymakers recognize that the shock has occurred.

Recognition lags are the period of time between when a shock occurs and when policymakers recognize that the shock has occurred. Recall from Chapter 2 that economic data become available to policymakers with a delay of up to several months. In addition, there is a great deal of uncertainty about initial estimates of economic variables, such as employment and real GDP, so it is difficult to know if a shock has had a large effect on the economy. This uncertainty makes it difficult for policymakers to know if a shock requires a policy response. For example, NASDAQ (a stock index based largely on high-tech companies) peaked on March 10, 2000, and then rapidly declined as the dot-com bubble burst. The destruction in stock market wealth contributed to the 2001 recession. However, it was not initially clear that the economy would enter a recession after the dot-com bubble burst. In fact, on May 16, 2001, at which point the NASDAQ had decreased by 26.4%, the Fed actually increased interest rates from 6.0% to 6.5% because it was still worried that inflation was accelerating.

Implementation lag The period of time between when policymakers recognize that a shock has occurred and when they adjust policy to the shock.

Implementation lags are the period of time between when policymakers recognize that a shock has occurred and when they adjust policy to the shock. Implementation lags exist because once the Fed recognizes that a shock has occurred it still takes time to determine whether and how to respond. Implementation lags by themselves are short for monetary policy. The FOMC meets eight times a year and, if necessary, can authorize changes in policy between regularly scheduled meetings. For example, in response to the financial crisis, the FOMC cut the target federal funds rate by 0.50% on October 8, 2008, even though the FOMC was not scheduled to meet until October 28, 2008.

Impact lag The period of time between a policy change and the effect of that policy change.

Impact lags are the period of time between a policy change and the effect of that policy change on real GDP, employment, inflation, and other economic variables. Nobel Laureate Milton Friedman famously described the lags for monetary policy as "long and variable," which means that it can take months or years for changes in monetary policy to affect real GDP and inflation and that the lags vary based on historical circumstances. Figure 10.3 on page 377 illustrates part of the reason these lags exist. Once the Fed reduces the target federal funds rate, it takes time for the interest rates that affect corporate and household behavior to also decline. Then, it takes time for corporations to identify newly profitable investment projects, obtain loans from banks or arrange to sell corporate bonds, and start spending the borrowed funds. Similarly, it takes time for families to respond to lower mortgage interest rates by buying houses. As a result, the full effect of a change in monetary policy is typically spread out over several years.

Economic Forecasts

It can take a long time for the effect of a change in monetary policy to affect real GDP. Therefore, central banks do not respond to the current state of the economy. Instead, they respond to the state of the economy they think will exist in the future when the policy actually affects the economy. For example, the Fed cut its federal funds rate target by 0.5% on October 8, 2008. Given the impact lags associated with monetary policy, the full effect of that rate cut on real GDP was likely to be spread out over some period of time. In making that cut, the Fed was thinking about the economy's future performance.

For a central bank to succeed in reducing the severity of business cycles, it must often act *before* the severity of a shock is apparent in the economic data. So, good policy requires good economic forecasts based on models that describe accurately how the economy functions. Unfortunately, economic forecasts and models can be unreliable because the factors determining economic growth can change quickly. Shocks by their nature are unpredictable. For example, the forecasts of most economists at the end of 2006 and the beginning of 2007 did not anticipate the severity of the economic slowdown that began in December 2007. Only after financial market conditions began to deteriorate rapidly after August 2007, did economists significantly reduce their forecasts of GDP growth in 2008 and 2009.

Table 10.2 shows the Fed's estimates for the growth rate of real GDP for 2007 and 2008 in its *Monetary Policy Report to Congress.* The actual growth rate for real GDP was 1.9% during 2007 and 0.0% during 2008. To avert the economic slowdown in 2007, the Fed would have had to change policy before 2007. However, in February 2006, the Fed expected the economy to grow by 3% to 4% in 2007, so it had little reason to change policy. Similarly, the Fed could have changed policy in an attempt to keep the economy growing in 2008, but it would have had to change policy before 2008, and as late as July 2007, the Fed still expected the economy to grow by 2.5% to 3.0% in 2008. In principle, the Fed could have taken actions to avert or at least greatly reduce the severity of the 2007–2009 recession. In practice, the Fed could not prevent the recession because it did not see the recession coming.

Table 10.2 **Federal Reserve Forecasts for Real GDP Growth During 2007 and 2008**

	Forecasted growth rate	
Forecast date	**2007**	**2008**
February 2006	3% to 4%	—
July 2006	2.5% to 3.25%	—
February 2007	2.25% to 3.25%	2.5% to 3.25%
July 2007	2% to 2.75%	2.5% to 3.0%
February 2008	—	1.0% to 2.2%
July 2008	—	1.0% to 1.6%

Source: Board of Governors of the Federal Reserve System, *Monetary Report to the Congress,* various dates.

Model Uncertainty

An issue related to poor economic forecasts is model uncertainty. Even if the Fed is convinced that the economy will enter a recession or that inflation will accelerate next year, it still faces problems in implementing monetary policy. Why? Economic models are just approximations of how the world works. As a result, economists do not know precisely how any given event will change real GDP and inflation; how any change in the target short-term nominal interest rate will change the long-term real interest rate; how much consumption and investment will respond to changes in the long-term real interest rate; or how much inflation will respond to changes in real GDP.

Economic models are not sophisticated enough to tell us precisely how much an event will change aggregate expenditure. For example, we know that consumption responds to changes in wealth, so a reduction in real estate values should reduce consumption expenditures. The key question for central bankers is, By how much? According to the Congressional Budget Office, recent estimates of the responsiveness of consumption to a $100 increase in real estate wealth range from $1.70 to $21. The high estimate is more than 10 times larger than the low estimate, so it is difficult for the Fed to know exactly how much a change in housing wealth will affect consumption, real GDP, and inflation. In addition, there is only a *tendency* for long-term interest rates to decrease as the Fed reduces its target short-term nominal interest rate. Figure 10.3 on page 377 shows that the interest rates are related but that the relationship is not perfect. As a result, the Fed does not know for certain how much it must reduce its target short-term nominal interest rate to get the long-term real interest rate to be at the desired level. Economic models have not advanced to the point where economists know exactly how responsive consumption and investment are to interest rates, so the Fed does not know exactly how much to reduce interest rates to prevent a recession. Finally, economic models also cannot tell us exactly how much inflation will respond to changes in real GDP.

Consequences of Policy Limitations

Policy lags and the inherent uncertainty of economic forecasts mean that policymakers may make mistakes. Figure 10.8 provides an example of a poorly timed monetary policy. Suppose that stock market wealth falls by 10% on a single day. Based on its models and economic forecasts, suppose the Fed believes the result will be reduced consumption spending leading to a recession. Therefore, the Fed believes that short-run equilibrium will occur at point *A* in panels (a) and (b).

At point *A*, real GDP is below potential GDP, so $\tilde{Y}_1 < 0$, and cyclical unemployment is positive. In response, the Fed decreases the target interest rate to increase consumption, investment, and net exports—and move the economy's short-run equilibrium to point *B*. If the *IS* curve remains at IS_1, then when the Fed reduces interest rates, real GDP increases relative to potential GDP and the output gap moves to $\tilde{Y}_2$. Therefore, the inflation rate increases to π_2. Short-run equilibrium is now at point *B*, and the recession has ended. The lags for monetary policy are long and variable, so it takes time for the change in monetary policy to increase output. If the stock market recovers or other events increase aggregate expenditure during that time, short-run equilibrium will be at point *C* when real GDP responds to policy. The recession will be over *before* the change in policy affects real GDP. Therefore, the change in policy will move the short-run equilibrium to point *D* in panel (a), where $\tilde{Y}_4 > 0$. When the change in policy finally increases real GDP, the output gap has changed to $\tilde{Y}_4$. The inflation rate increases to π_4. Short-run equilibrium is now at point *D* in panel (b). In this case, monetary policy has pushed the economy beyond potential GDP, which causes the inflation rate to increase.

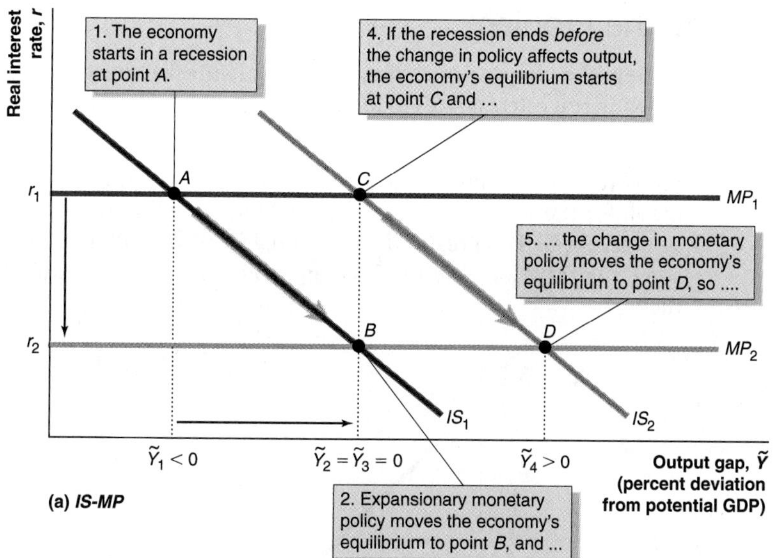

Real interest rate, r
1. The economy starts in a recession at point A.
4. If the recession ends *before* the change in policy affects output, the economy's equilibrium starts at point C and ...
A
C
r_1
MP_1
5. ... the change in monetary policy moves the economy's equilibrium to point D, so ....
B
D
r_2
MP_2
IS_1
IS_2
$\tilde{Y}_1 < 0$
$\tilde{Y}_2 = \tilde{Y}_3 = 0$
$\tilde{Y}_4 > 0$
Output gap, $\tilde{Y}$ (percent deviation from potential GDP)
(a) *IS-MP*
2. Expansionary monetary policy moves the economy's equilibrium to point B, and ...

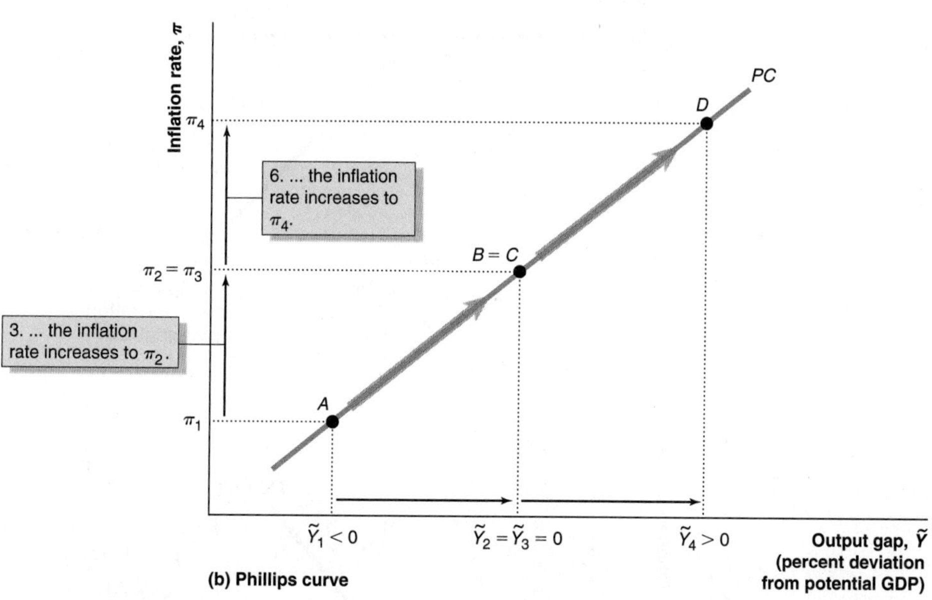

Inflation rate, π
PC
D
π_4
6. ... the inflation rate increases to π_4.
$B = C$
$\pi_2 = \pi_3$
3. ... the inflation rate increases to π_2.
A
π_1
$\tilde{Y}_1 < 0$
$\tilde{Y}_2 = \tilde{Y}_3 = 0$
$\tilde{Y}_4 > 0$
Output gap, $\tilde{Y}$ (percent deviation from potential GDP)
(b) Phillips curve

Figure 10.8

Monetary Policy That Is Poorly Timed

Expansionary monetary policy results in short-equilibrium moving from point *A* to point *B* in panels (a) and (b) and end a recession. If a recession ends before the change in monetary policy affects the economy, the policy change will move the short-run equilibrium from point *C* to point *D* in panels (a) and (b). As a result of poor timing, the policy will increase the inflation rate after the recession has already ended. ●

Solved Problem 10.5

Did the Fed Help Cause the 2001 Recession?

Real GDP was essentially equal to potential GDP during the first quarter of 1999, but rose to 4.2% above potential GDP by the second quarter of 2000. With real GDP above potential GDP, the inflation rate began to increase. The inflation rate as measured by the CPI increased from 1.7% during January 1999 to 3.7% during June 2000. The Fed responded by increasing the target federal funds rate from 4.75% in January 1999 to 6.5% in May 2000. The last increase in the target came after the dot-com bubble burst and all major stock indexes started to decline. By March 2001, the U.S. economy had entered a recession that worsened after the terrorist attacks on September 11, 2001, led households and firms to reduce consumption and investment. The recession was short, ending in November 2001, but the economy recovered slowly, and real GDP was 1.9% below potential GDP as late as the first quarter of 2003. Did the Fed's decision to increase the federal funds rate contribute to the recession and the slow recovery? Use the *IS–MP* model to show the effect of the Fed's policy.

Solving the Problem

Step 1 **Review the chapter material.** The problem asks you to explain the effect of allowing real interest rates to increase, so you may want to review the section "The Limitations of Monetary Policy," which begins on page 386.

Step 2 **Draw the initial equilibrium using an *IS-MP* graph.** Draw an initial *IS–MP* graph for the second quarter of 2000. Make sure that you draw the equilibrium so that real GDP is greater than potential GDP. Your Phillips curve graph should show the inflation rate for 2000 as being 3.7%. Your graphs should look like these:

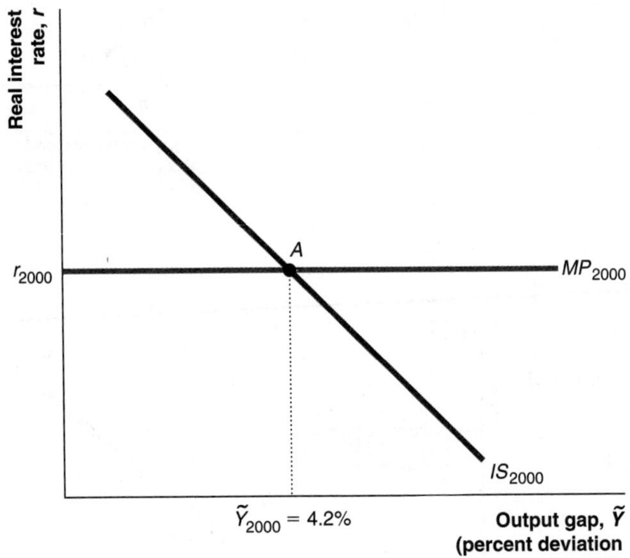

(a) *IS-MP*

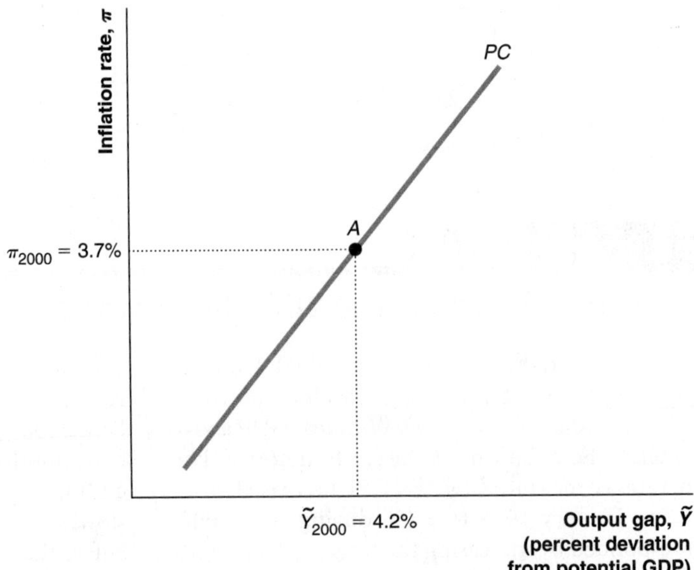

(b) Phillips curve

Step 3 **Show the effect of the increase in interest rates.** The Fed increased the federal funds rate, which should increase long-term real interest rates. Assume that the Fed knows exactly how much to increase interest rates to move real GDP to potential GDP. Therefore, you should shift the *MP* curve up on the *IS-MP* graph and you should show the short-run equilibrium moving down the Phillips curve. Your graphs should now look like these:

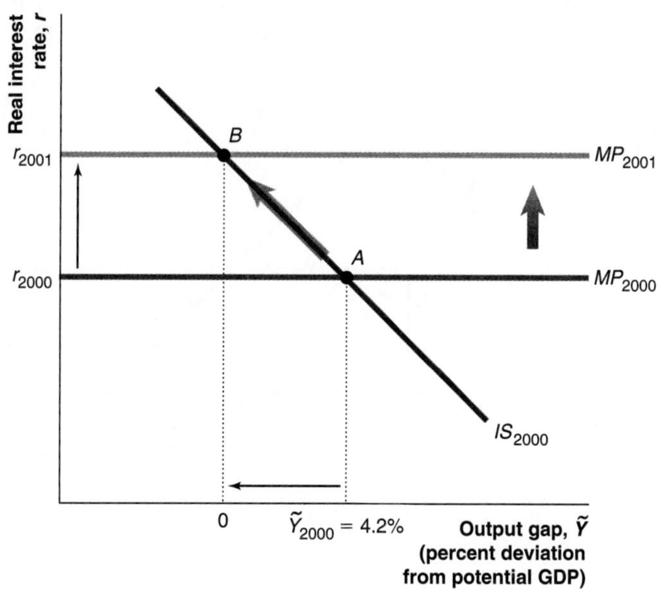

(a) *IS-MP*

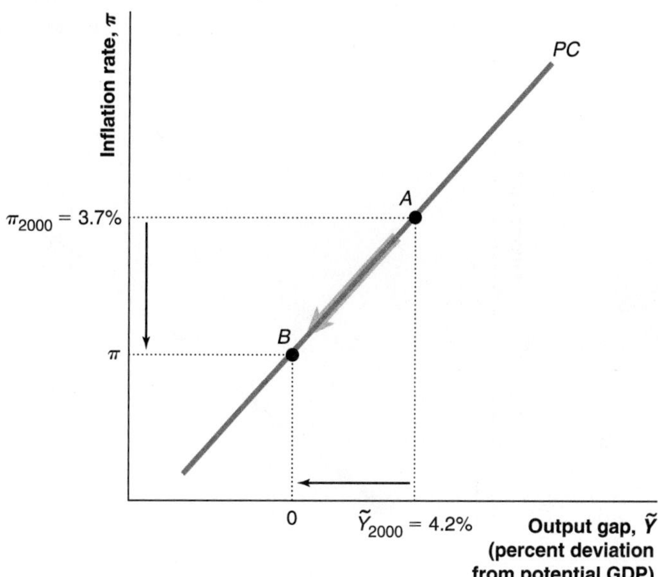

(b) Phillips curve

Step 4 **Show the effect of the collapse in stock prices and the terrorist attacks.** A stock market collapse such as the one that occurred in 2000 reduces household wealth, which reduces consumption. The stock market collapse also increases uncertainty about the future, leading firms to reduce investment spending and leading households to further reduce consumption. The terrorist attacks also increased uncertainty, leading firms and households to reduce expenditures on goods and services. Show the effect of the decrease in aggregate expenditure by shifting the *IS* curve to the left in the *IS-MP* graph and by moving the short-run equilibrium further down the Phillips curve. Your graphs should look like these:

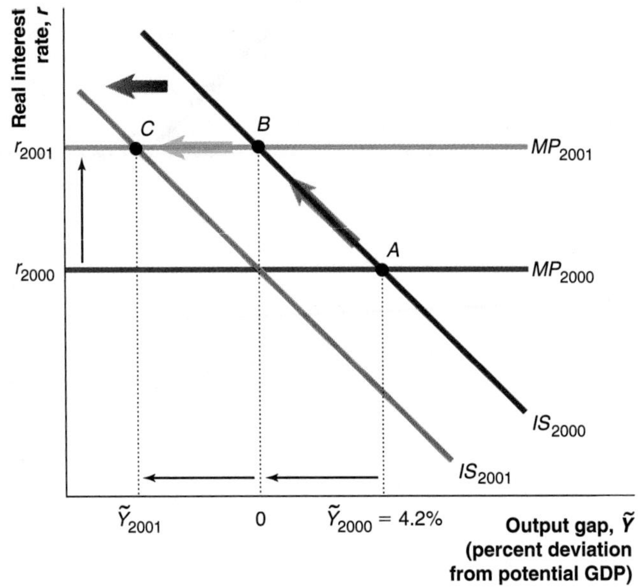

(a) *IS-MP*

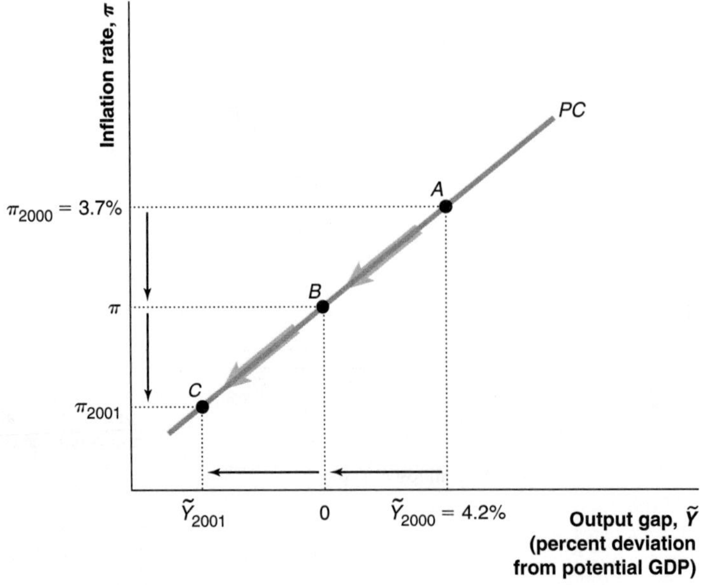

(b) Phillips curve

The Fed could not be certain where the *IS* curve would be for the year 2001. Therefore, it based its policy decisions in 2000 on where it *thought* the *IS* curve would be. The Fed may have underestimated the effect of the stock market collapse on consumption and investment, but could not have anticipated the terrorist attacks or their effect on the U.S. economy. The Fed may have anticipated that the *IS* curve would remain at IS_{2000}, but the actual *IS* curve was IS_{2001}. As a result, the Fed's decision to increase the federal funds rate during 2000 may have contributed to the 2001 recession and to the slow recovery.

For more practice, do related problem 5.8 on page 405 at the end of this chapter.

Moral Hazard

Investments in financial markets are inherently risky, and it is possible for financial institutions to earn huge profits. It is often the case, however, that the larger the potential profits, the larger the risk of losses. When financial institutions earn profits *and* suffer losses because of their decisions, they have a strong financial incentive to carefully balance potential reward against risk. Sometimes, however, a financial institution becomes so large that its failure would damage the financial system and, potentially, the broader economy. If the federal government adopts a **too-big-to-fail policy**, it does not allow large financial firms to fail for fear of damaging the financial system. A goal of monetary policy is financial market stability, so the Fed and central banks in other countries often make loans to troubled financial institutions during a crisis. By saving troubled financial institutions, central banks may achieve financial stability in the short run, but their actions may encourage even riskier behavior on the part of financial institutions in the future. This risk is known as **moral hazard**.

Too-big-to-fail policy A policy in which the federal government does not allow large financial firms to fail for fear of damaging the financial system.

Moral hazard The risk that people will take actions after they have entered into a transaction that will make the other party worse off.

Making the Connection

"Too Big to Fail"—The Legacy of Continental Illinois

The Federal Reserve responded to the 2007–2009 financial crisis very aggressively in 2008, providing loans not only to commercial banks but also to investment banks and private companies. While many analysts credit the Fed's actions with preventing the crisis from worsening, these actions also reinforced the belief that there were institutions that were "too big to fail." Therefore, it came as a great shock in the fall of 2008, when the Fed allowed the investment bank Lehman Brothers to declare bankruptcy.

According to Neil McLeish, an analyst at Morgan Stanley, "Prior to Lehman, there was an almost unshakable faith that the senior creditors and counterparties of large, systemically important financial institutions would not face the risk of outright default." This "almost unshakable faith" was partly the result of the failure of another financial institution. Continental Illinois Bank, one of the largest banks in the United States, had suffered large losses on its loans, and many of its customers withdrew their deposits in 1984 after the bank's weakened financial condition became known. Many other smaller banks held deposits in Continental Illinois, and there was concern among regulators that these banks might go down with Continental Illinois if it failed. To avoid these losses to the banking system and the economy, the Federal Deposit Insurance Corporation (FDIC) seized the assets of Continental Illinois. The FDIC is an agency Congress created to insure deposits at commercial banks. When a bank fails, the FDIC pays back depositors and helps to settle the bank's other debts. The creditors of the bank are typically paid less than the face value of the obligations. The possibility of such losses discourages creditors from buying the bonds of or making loans to institutions that are poorly managed. But in the case of Continental Illinois, bondholders were fully paid out. In effect, the bank's creditors did not pay a penalty for the failure of Continental Illinois.

Although neither the federal government nor the Federal Reserve had an official too-big-to-fail policy, the government's response to Continental Illinois encouraged executives at other large financial firms and their creditors to assume that policymakers would rescue them in the event of another crisis. This approach, which some refer to as "constructive ambiguity," proved to be unworkable in 2008. The Federal Reserve and other banking regulators were challenged to find alternatives to constructive ambiguity. There remain many institutions that are "too big to fail." Some analysts have suggested that these institutions be reduced in size in order to improve the credibility of a government pledge to allow them to fail. Another suggestion is to more heavily regulate institutions to reduce the risk of failure.

Sources: Gerald P. Dwyer, "Too Big to Fail," *Notes from the Vault*, Federal Reserve Bank of Atlanta, February 2010; and "The Hazard in Moral Hazard," *Economist*, October 13, 2008.

Test your understanding by doing related problem 5.10 on page 405 at the end of this chapter.

In pursuing the goals of monetary policy, central banks may inadvertently create moral hazard and make the financial system and the economy less stable. In July 2010, Congress passed the Wall Street Reform and Consumer Protection Act, often referred to as the Dodd–Frank Act. The act contained provisions intended to eliminate the too big-to-fail policy. Some economists were skeptical, though, that when faced with the failure of a large financial firm the federal government would not still feel obliged to take action to rescue it.

10.6

Learning Objective

Evaluate the arguments for and against central bank independence.

Central Bank Independence

Central banks are created by governments and the heads of central banks are appointed by the government. This process does not necessarily mean, however, that governments control the decisions of central bankers. The Federal Reserve System of the United States provides a good example of how a central bank that is created by the government can nevertheless maintain substantial independence in how it conducts monetary policy.

The Independence of the U.S. Federal Reserve

Congress created the Federal Reserve System in 1913, and mandated that the Fed seek price stability, high employment, and financial market stability. The president nominates and the Senate confirms members of the Federal Reserve's Board of Governors. The chairman of the Federal Reserve is required to testify before Congress twice each year to explain monetary policy decisions. So, the Federal Reserve acts within boundaries established by Congress and the president. The Fed, though, has a great deal of flexibility in meeting the goals of monetary policy. The Federal Open Market Committee decides the target federal funds rate without direct input from either the president or Congress. During the financial crisis of 2007–2009, the Fed developed a number of new policy tools without direct approval from either the president or Congress. Chairman Ben Bernanke did have to explain the Fed's actions to Congress, but the Fed was able to pursue major new policies without approval from the government.

Congress intended that the structure of the Fed would insulate it from political pressure. The members of the Federal Reserve Board are appointed to 14-year nonrenewable terms, so once confirmed, they are relatively free of political pressure. The Fed is not dependent on the federal government for funding. The Fed owns a large amount of U.S. Treasury securities and pays for its operations with the interest income from these securities. Unlike federal agencies such as the Department of Defense or the Department of the Treasury, the Fed does not have to go to Congress each year to request funding. In fact, the Fed typically spends less than it earns. The Fed returns these profits to the Treasury. Because the Fed greatly increased its holdings of securities during the financial crisis, it was able to return $47 billion to the U.S. Treasury in 2009, and $78 billion in 2010.

If Congress and the president become dissatisfied with the Fed's performance, they are free to change how the Fed operates by amending the Federal Reserve Act. As we saw in the chapter opener, the reappointment of Ben Bernanke in 2010 was politically contentious. During the debate over the Dodd–Frank Act in 2010, there were several proposals to substantially reduce the Fed's independence, although none of the proposals was included in the final bill. The debate over the Fed's independence is likely to continue. In the next two sections, we briefly review some arguments for and against Fed independence.

The Case for Fed Independence The main argument for Fed independence is that monetary policy—which affects inflation, interest rates, exchange rates, and economic growth—is too important and technical to be determined by politicians. Because of the frequency of elections, politicians may be concerned with short-term benefits without regard for potential long-term costs. The short-term desire of politicians to be reelected may clash with the country's long-term interest in low inflation. Therefore, the Fed cannot assume that the objectives of politicians are consistent with the nation's long-term interests. The public may well prefer that the experts at the Fed, rather than politicians, make monetary policy decisions.

Another argument for Fed independence is that complete control of the Fed by elected officials increases the likelihood of fluctuations in the money supply caused by political pressure. For example, particularly just before an election, those officials might pressure the Fed to assist the Treasury's borrowing efforts by buying government bonds, which would increase the money supply and temporarily increase real GDP and employment, but at the risk of increasing inflation in the long run.

The Case Against Fed Independence The importance of monetary policy for the economy is also the main argument against central bank independence. Supporters claim that in a democracy, elected officials should make public policy. Because the public holds elected officials responsible for perceived monetary policy problems, some analysts advocate giving those officials more control over monetary policy. While some economists argue that monetary policy is too technical for elected officials, other economists argue that elected officials have experience dealing with equally complex tasks, such as fiscal policy, national security, and foreign policy. In addition, critics of central bank independence argue that placing the central bank under the control of elected officials could confer benefits by coordinating and integrating monetary policy with government taxing and spending policies.

Those who argue for greater government control make the case that the Fed has not always used its independence well. For example, some critics note that the Fed's concern about inflation prevented it from assisting the banking system during the Great Depression. Another example that many economists cite is that Fed policies were too inflationary in the 1960s and 1970s. Some analysts believe that the Fed acted too slowly in addressing credit problems during the recession of the early 1990s. Finally, some analysts believe that the Fed kept interest rates too low for too long after the 2001 recession, which helped fuel the housing market bubble.

These examples illustrate that central bank independence is by no means a guarantee of sound monetary policy. However, research on central bank independence indicates that

Figure 10.9

Central Bank Independence and the Average Inflation Rate

For 16 high-income countries, the greater the degree of central bank independence from the rest of the government, the lower the inflation rate.

Source: "Central Bank Independence and Macroeconomic Performance: Some Comparative Evidence" by Alberto Alesina and Lawrence Summers. *Journal of Money, Credit, and Banking*, May 1993, pp. 151–162. Copyright © 1993. Reproduced with permission of Blackwell Publishing Ltd. ●

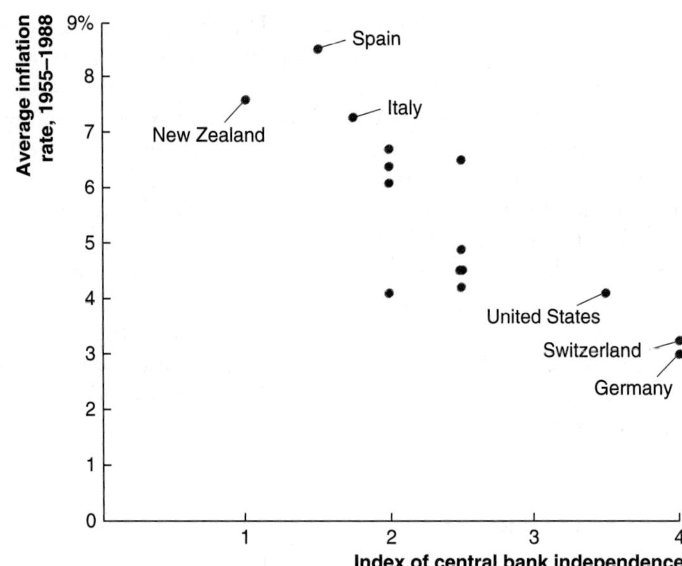

the more independent the central bank, the better the economy's performance. Alberto Alesina and Lawrence Summers, economists at Harvard University, examined the relationship between central bank independence and macroeconomic performance for 16 high-income countries from 1955 to 1988. Figure 10.9 shows their findings on the relationship between central bank independence and average inflation rates. Alesina and Summers measured central bank independence using an index ranging from 1 (minimum independence) to 4 (maximum independence). Their results show that the more independent the central bank, the lower the average inflation rate. During the time period 1955–1988, New Zealand's central bank had the lowest independence, 1, and the inflation rate averaged 7.6%. In contrast, the central banks for Germany and Switzerland had the most independence, 4, and average inflation rates of about 3%. This result is consistent with the view that independent central banks resist political pressure to stimulate the economy in the short run at the cost of higher inflation in the long run. Alesina and Summers also found that central bank independence reduces the volatility of both the inflation rate and the real interest rate. More stable prices and real interest rates makes it easier for households and firms to make long-term plans such as saving for retirement or deciding to build a new factory. Therefore, central bank independence improves the performance of the economy. However, the benefits of improved economic performance must be weighed against the cost of having an undemocratic central bank conduct monetary policy.

Answering the Key Question

Continued from page 363

At the beginning of this chapter, we asked the question:

"Why were traditional Federal Reserve policies ineffective during the 2007–2009 recession?"

The traditional Fed policy response to a recession is to reduce the short-term nominal interest rate. Normally, this policy will decrease the long-term real interest rate, provided that term structure effects, the default-risk premium, and the expected inflation rate remain constant. This traditional interest rate channel could not operate through much of the 2007–2009 recession because by December 2008, the Fed had pushed its target for the federal funds rate nearly to zero. As a result, the Fed was forced to turn to new policies to attempt to increase real GDP and employment.

Before moving to the next chapter, read *An Inside Look at Policy* for a discussion of the Fed's evaluation of the economy in early 2011 and plans for the future.

Will the Fed Reverse Its Current Monetary Policy?

BLOOMBERG

Fed Signals More Stimulus Unlikely as Recovery Picks Up Steam in U.S.

a Federal Reserve officials signaled they're unlikely to expand a $600-billion bond purchase plan as the recovery picks up steam and the threat that inflation will fall too low begins to wane.

The economy is on a "firmer footing, and overall conditions in the labor market appear to be improving gradually," the Federal Open Market Committee said in a statement yesterday after a one-day meeting in Washington. While commodity prices have "risen significantly," inflation expectations have "remained stable. . . ."

Their statement reveals confidence that the plan to buy Treasury securities through June will be enough to achieve the self-sustaining expansion that they say is vital before reversing record stimulus, said analysts including Josh Feinman, global chief economist for DB Advisors, a unit of Deutsche Bank AG. . . .

b Too Slow

Chairman Ben S. Bernanke and his Fed colleagues removed language from their January statement which said that the recovery is "disappointingly slow" and that "tight credit" is holding back consumer spending. They also dropped references to "modest income growth" and "lower housing wealth."

"Certainly, this is the most optimistic Fed officials have sounded since asset purchases began in November and, at a minimum, that's consistent with the expectation there will be no third round of purchases," said Jim O'Sullivan, chief economist at MF Global Inc. in New York.

Even so, the statement echoed caution from the January release, saying that "the unemployment rate remains elevated, and measures of underlying inflation continue to be somewhat low, relative to levels that the Committee judges to be consistent, over the longer run, with its dual mandate" for stable prices and maximum employment. Policy makers also said they'll "pay close attention" to inflation trends.

c 'Easy Policy'

"Inflation is rising and they are running an easy policy," said Julia Coronado, North America chief economist at BNP Paribas in New York. "They are betting their credibility that inflation expectations won't become unhinged. They had to balance that against global developments taking the wind out of sails."

The Fed left its benchmark interest rate in a range of zero to 0.25 percent, where it's been since December 2008, and retained a pledge in place since March 2009 to keep it "exceptionally low" for an "extended period. . . ."

Unanimous Decision

The FOMC decision was unanimous for a second consecutive meeting. That means Dallas Fed President Richard Fisher and Philadelphia Fed President Charles Plosser, both skeptics of the second round of so-called quantitative easing who voted for the statement today, don't disagree strongly enough with the path of policy to dissent. . . .

The central bank, through the New York Fed's traders, has enlarged its balance sheet by $304 billion through its Treasury purchases since Nov. 12. Including securities bought by reinvesting proceeds of maturing mortgage debt the Fed has purchased $426 billion of Treasuries. . . .

Source: Joshua Zumbrun, "Fed Signals More Stimulus Unlikely as Recovery Picks Up Steam in U.S.," *Bloomberg*, March 15, 2011. Reprinted from the March 15, 2011 issue of *Bloomberg Businessweek* by special permission,

Key Points in the Article

This article discusses the unanimous opinion of the Federal Open Market Committee in early 2011 that the economy had sufficiently recovered that they would not need to extend the most recent stimulus package, a $600 billion bond-purchase program, beyond its scheduled expiration date of June 2011. The FOMC implemented stimulus programs in an attempt to aid recovery from the recession and financial crisis, and believes that achieving a self-sustaining expansion is vital to the health of the economy.

Analyzing the News

a The Fed's $600 billion bond-purchase plan was the most recent action taken to stimulate the economy. The chapter mentions that the Fed can attempt to stimulate the economy by increasing bank reserves, and one way to accomplish this goal is by purchasing assets. As Figure 1 below shows, since the start of the financial crisis in 2008, the Fed dramatically increased its purchases of assets. Prior to the beginning of the crisis, the Fed's balance sheet remained consistently below $1 trillion. In the last four months of 2008, Fed asset purchases more than doubled, and the balance sheet topped $2 trillion. Following a slight dip in early 2009, the balance sheet again moved beyond $2 trillion, growing to over $2.6 trillion by March 2011. The balance sheet was expected to exceed $2.7 trillion by June 2011.

b The Fed's statement in March was more optimistic than its statement two months earlier and led to the expectation that a third round of purchases would not occur. Despite this more optimistic tone, the Fed remained cautious in its evaluation of the economy, pointing out that the unemployment rate has continued to remain high and inflation continued to remain low. The Fed indicated that it will closely monitor inflation trends and employment.

c Through its bond purchases and by keeping the federal funds rate between zero and 0.25%, the Fed has been undertaking an expansionary monetary policy. Some FOMC members were critical of the Fed's most recent asset purchases and expressed concerns about the size of the Fed's balance sheet, suggesting that the time had arrived to begin tightening monetary policy. Maintaining a large balance sheet and a low target for the federal funds rate has some analysts concerned about the potential for inflation to eventually rise to an unacceptable level.

THINKING CRITICALLY *ABOUT POLICY*

1. The Fed has held its target for the federal funds rate at 0% to 0.25% since December 2008 and during this time has raised the discount rate once, from 0.50% to 0.75% in February 2010. Some analysts have called on the Fed to raise interest rates and begin tightening monetary policy. All else being equal, what impact would an increase in interest rates have on an economy that is currently experiencing cyclical unemployment and producing below potential GDP? Use the *IS-MP* model including the Phillips curve to explain your answer.
2. Since the Fed began engaging in quantitative easing in late 2008, it has purchased over $1.5 trillion in long-term securities. How does the Fed's purchases of these assets affect economic activity?

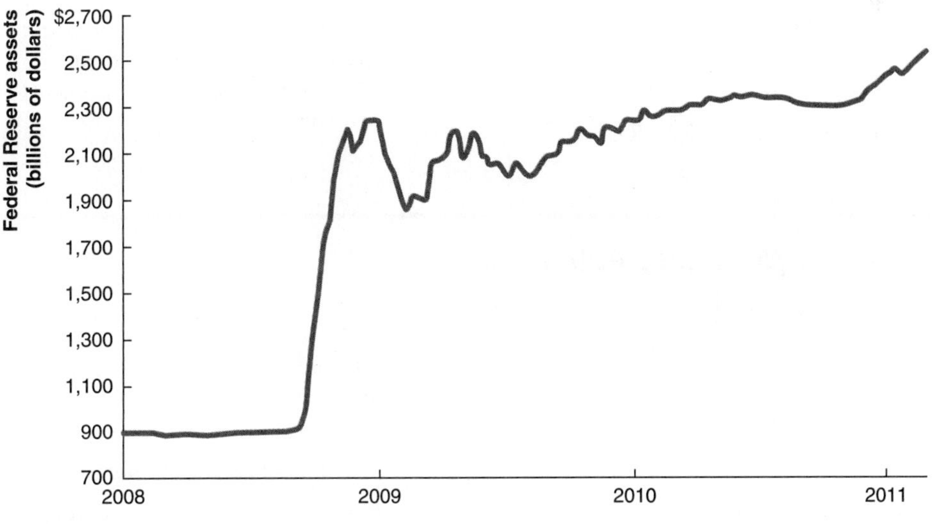

Figure 1 Federal Reserve Balance Sheet, January 2008 to March 2011

Source: Reprinted with permission from NumberNomics.

CHAPTER SUMMARY AND PROBLEMS

KEY TERMS

Asymmetric information p.383
Bank run, p. 365
Board of Governors, p. 366
Discount rate, p. 372
Federal funds rate, p. 367
Federal Open Market Committee (FOMC), p. 367
Federal Reserve System, p. 365
Impact lag, p. 386
Implementation lag, p. 386
Monetary policy, p. 365
Moral hazard, p. 393
Open market operations, p. 367
Quantitative easing, p. 384
Recognition lag, p. 386
Reserve requirements, p. 372
Too-big-to-fail policy, p. 393

10.1 The Federal Reserve System
Understand the structure of the Federal Reserve.

SUMMARY

The **Federal Reserve System** is the central bank of the United States. The system consists of 12 district Federal Reserve Banks, a **Board of Governors** located in Washington, DC, and member banks. **Monetary policy** refers to the actions the Federal Reserve takes to manage the money supply and interest rates to pursue macroeconomic goals. A key part of the Fed is the **Federal Open Market Committee (FOMC)**, which conducts **open market operations**, the buying and selling of U.S. Treasury securities. The FOMC consists of the 7 members of the Board of Governors, the president of the New York Federal Reserve Bank, and the presidents of 4 of the other 11 Federal Reserve Banks, who serve on a rotating basis.

Review Questions

1.1 Why did Congress create the Federal Reserve System?

1.2 What is a discount loan?

1.3 Explain the structure of the Federal Reserve.

1.4 What are open market operations?

1.5 What is the Federal Open Market Committee (FOMC), and why is it important?

Problems and Applications

1.6 Why are the terms of members of the Board of Governors both very long and staggered?

1.7 In 1913, Congress created 12 Federal Reserve districts spread over the country.

a. Why did Congress divide the country into districts?

b. Some argue that Fed districts should change. Why might this change make sense?

1.8 Consider the following statement: "Because the Chairman of the Fed is appointed by the president of the United States and serves a four-year term, the president controls the Fed." Do you agree with this statement? Briefly explain.

10.2 The Goals of Monetary Policy
Describe the goals of monetary policy.

SUMMARY

The goals of monetary policy are:

1. *Price stability.* To keep the inflation rate low and stable.
2. *High employment.* To keep the cyclical unemployment rate close to zero.
3. *Economic growth*: To increase the economy's output of goods and services over time.
4. *Financial market stability.* To ensure the efficient matching of savers and borrowers.
5. *Interest rate stability.* To aid the spending and investing decisions of households and firms.

 Visit www.myeconlab.com to complete these exercises online and get instant feedback.

6. *Foreign-exchange market stability.* To help simplify planning for commercial and financial transactions.

Because inflation increases when the output gap increases and the cyclical unemployment rate decreases, there is a short-run trade-off between the goals of price stability and high employment.

Review Questions

2.1 What are the primary goals of the Fed?

2.2 What does the Fed consider to be "price stability"?

2.3 Would the Fed consider zero unemployment to be a desirable goal? Explain.

2.4 How are the goals of high employment and economic growth related?

2.5 In general, how does a central bank help to ensure the stability of a financial system?

2.6 What problems can interest rate fluctuations cause?

Problems and Applications

2.7 The Fed views price stability as keeping inflation in the range of 1% to 3%. Why doesn't the Fed target a 0% rate of inflation?

2.8 Consider the following statement: "On average, rates of unemployment in Europe are higher than rates of unemployment in the United States. Thus, the Fed must be doing a good job of maintaining high employment." Do you agree or disagree with this statement? Explain your answer.

2.9 During the Great Depression, banks were subject to runs.

a. Explain how a bank run can occur.

b. How does the term structure of a bank's assets and liabilities create the possibility of liquidity problems?

c. How can a lender of last resort (usually a central bank that can lend when no other credit sources are available) solve bank runs and liquidity problems?

2.10 The Congressional Budget Office uses 5% as its estimate of the natural rate of unemployment. Most economists estimate that the natural rate is between 5% and 6%. However, some evidence suggests that the natural rate of unemployment may have increased after the recession of 2007–2009. If the Fed believed that the natural rate of unemployment was lower than the true rate and tried to maintain that rate, what would be the consequences for the economy?

2.11 When financial markets do not function well, savers and investors waste resources, and the economy is less efficient.

a. How might problems in financial markets affect employment and economic growth?

b. Some argue that the Fed should not interfere in financial markets. Why is maintaining the stability of financial markets important to the Fed's other goals?

10.3 Monetary Policy Tools
Explain the Fed's monetary policy tools.

SUMMARY

Monetary policy has three traditional tools:

1. *Open market operations.* This is the most important tool of monetary policy. Central banks use open market operations to keep the short-term nominal interest rate close to the target rate.
2. *Discount loans.* Banks can borrow directly from the Fed and pay the **discount rate**.
3. *Reserve requirements.* This tool is the one least used.

The financial market crisis of 2007–2009 led the Fed to develop new monetary policies, most of which have expired. The Fed now pays interest on reserves that financial institutions deposit with the Fed, and it purchases securities backed by assets such as home mortgages. This last tool allows the Fed to keep an important financial market liquid and encourages banks to issue new mortgages.

Monetary policy affects the economy by causing changes in interest rates. When the central bank changes short-term nominal interest rates, it also changes long-term real interest rates assuming the term structure effect, the default-risk premium, and expected inflation are constant. Therefore, there is a tendency for an increase in short-term nominal interest rates to increase long-term real interest rates and for a decrease in short-term

nominal interest rates to decrease long-term real interest rates. An increase in long-term real interest rates decreases consumption and investment, all else being equal. A decrease in long-term real interest rates increases consumption and investment, all else being equal.

Review Questions

3.1 Explain how the Fed uses open market operations to target the federal funds rate. Why does the value of the federal funds rate matter?

3.2 What is the discount rate? How is it different from the federal funds rate?

3.3 Why is it important to have a central bank to act as a lender of last resort?

3.4 What is the direct effect of changes in reserve requirements?

3.5 What are the new tools of monetary policy? How do these new tools differ from the conventional tools?

Problems and Applications

3.6 Suppose that the Fed wants to reduce the federal funds rate.

a. Explain how the Fed would achieve this reduction.

b. If the Fed successfully lowers the federal funds rate, how would this be expected to affect banks?

c. Briefly explain why the Fed might perform the same actions you described in (a), even if the federal funds rate were already zero?

3.7 Explain how each of the following tools allows the Fed to fine-tune its control of bank reserves:

a. The ability to pay interest on reserves

b. The Term Deposit Facility (TDF)

3.8 The goal of the Term Asset-Backed Securities Loan Facility (TALF) was to allow financial institutions to borrow against a variety of illiquid assets.

a. Why were these assets illiquid?

b. How does the ability to borrow against these assets improve financial market stability?

3.9 **[Related to the *Making the Connection* on page 375]** The FOMC currently releases a statement after each meeting, releases a summary of the meeting three weeks later, and releases a full transcript five years later.

a. Some economists have argued in favor of a more rapid release of the full minutes of the meetings. Why might the Fed oppose this rapid release?

b. FOMC meetings were considerably more secretive in the past than they are today, before the Fed implemented policies that increased openness ("transparency"). Why might increased transparency make monetary policy actions more effective?

10.4 Monetary Policy and the *IS–MP* Model

Use the *IS–MP* model to understand how monetary policy affects the economy in the short run.

SUMMARY

Central banks usually decrease interest rates during a recession. Lower interest rates lead to increased consumption and investment, which increases real GDP and so helps to end the recession. When inflation is high, the central bank increases interest rates. Higher interest rates lead to decreased consumption and investment, which decreases real GDP and so helps to reduce inflation. When a supply shock, such as an increase in oil prices, increases the inflation rate, the Fed has a choice. It can do nothing and allow the inflation rate to increase. Alternatively, the Fed could increase real interest rates to decrease the inflation rate, but this comes at the cost of lower real GDP and lower employment.

Central banks tend to decrease interest rates during recessions—when real GDP is below potential GDP—in order to increase expenditures. Central banks also increase interest rates when real GDP is above its potential GDP and inflation is high. The response to an aggregate supply shock is less clear, and the central bank must choose between pursuing the goal of price stability and pursuing the goal of high employment.

Review Questions

4.1 What interest rate does monetary policy most directly affect? How does a change in that interest rate affect other interest rates?

4.2 Monetary policy targets the federal funds rate, a rate that only banks pay. Why does the federal funds rate have an impact on household spending?

4.3 How is the federal funds rate related to other important interest rates?

4.4 What is the usual monetary policy response to a recession? What is the usual monetary policy response to inflation?

4.5 What challenge does a negative supply shock create for monetary policy?

4.6 What is the bank lending channel of monetary policy? What is quantitative easing?

Problems and Applications

4.7 **[Related to *Solved Problem 10.4* on page 381]** In 1999 and early 2000, the Fed increased the target federal funds rate repeatedly, in part because it believed that the economy was overheating and that inflation would rise. The graph below shows the position of the economy prior to the Fed's actions.

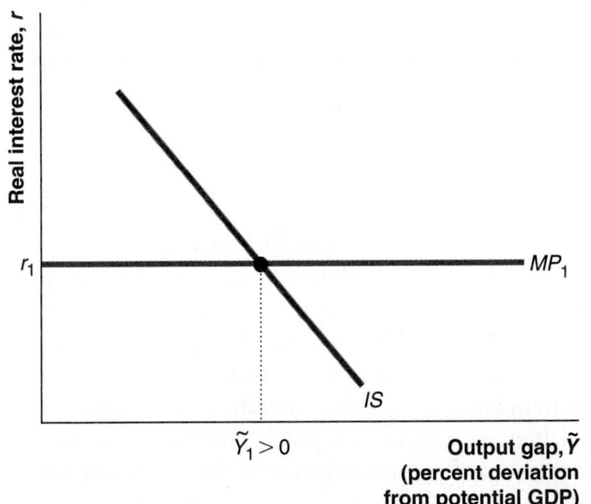

a. Explain how the Fed's actions would be expected to affect the economy, being careful to explain all the steps.

b. Show the effect of the Fed's actions on the *IS–MP* graph and then relate your answer to the Phillips curve.

4.8 **[Related to *Solved Problem 10.4* on page 381]** Economic activity in the United States peaked in March 2001 and then began to decline with the NASDAQ crash resulting from the collapse of the dot-com bubble. The terrorist attacks on the United States on September 11, 2001 worsened the recession.

a. Use the *IS–MP* model to show the position of the economy in late 2001.

b. What actions would you expect the Fed to have taken in this situation?

c. Use your *IS–MP* graph from part a, to show the effect of the Fed's actions.

4.9 Not all changes in production costs are bad for the economy. During the 1990s, changes in technology lowered costs. Use the *IS–MP* model including the Phillips curve to analyze the situations described below.

a. Suppose the Fed does not change the real interest rate. What will happen to the inflation rate?

b. Suppose that the Fed does not want the inflation rate to change. What should it do to the real interest rate?

4.10 Suppose that expectations are not adaptive and that increases in the money supply cause the expected inflation rate to increase.

a. In this case, when the Fed increases the money supply, what happens to long-term real interest rates?

b. How does the link between money supply increases and expected inflation change the Fed's ability to affect the economy through the interest rate channel?

4.11 During the 2007–2009 financial crisis, banks faced liquidity problems, in part due to the illiquidity of some of their assets. This in turn made some banks reluctant to lend, causing problems for households and firms that needed to borrow funds, which in turn caused economic activity to decline.

a. Explain how the Fed can use the bank lending channel to solve this problem.

b. Even with increased liquidity due to the Fed's actions, it appeared that banks became so risk averse that they were reluctant to lend. Evaluate the effectiveness of the bank lending channel in stimulating economic activity during this period.

4.12 Consider the following statement: "If the short-term nominal interest rate is zero, monetary policy can have no further expansionary effect on the economy." Do you agree with this statement? Briefly explain.

4.13 In early 2011, unrest in the Middle East caused a sharp increase in the price of oil. Suppose that the economy was below potential GDP at $\tilde{Y}_1$ prior to the oil shock, as shown at point *A* on the following Phillips curve graph:

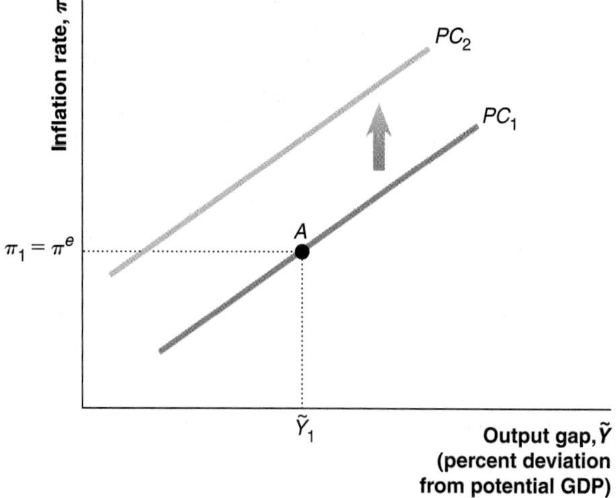

a. If the Fed keeps the real interest rate constant, show on the graph a possible short-run equilibrium inflation rate and output gap.

b. If the Fed acts to keep the inflation rate constant, show the new short-run equilibrium.

10.5 The Limitations of Monetary Policy

Explain the challenges to using monetary policy effectively.

SUMMARY

In principle, it may seem easy for the central bank to achieve its policy goals. However, the practice of monetary policy is much more complicated because of lags in the policy process. Because of the **recognition lag**, it takes time for the central bank to know that a problem has developed. An **implementation lag** is the period of time it takes for the central bank to change policy once it knows a problem has developed. An **impact lag** is the period of time it takes for a change in policy to affect real GDP and the inflation rate. Because of these lags, the central bank must adjust policy not to the current state of the economy but to the state of the economy it thinks will exist in the future. Therefore, monetary policy requires good economic forecasts based on models that accurately describe the way the economy works. Unfortunately, economic models are not sophisticated enough to allow the central bank to conduct monetary policy with certainty. As a result, a change in monetary policy designed to end a recession may actually cause inflation to accelerate.

The central bank's pursuit of financial market stability can lead the central bank to save large financial institutions from bankruptcy when problems develop. Essentially, this is a **too-big-to-fail policy**. This policy may have encouraged financial institutions to pursue risky investment strategies, such as investing in mortgage-backed securities. As a result, this policy may have increased **moral hazard** and contributed to the financial market crisis of 2007–2009.

Review Questions

5.1 What is a recognition lag, and why is it a challenge for monetary policy?

5.2 What is an implementation lag, and why is it a challenge for monetary policy?

5.3 What is an impact lag, and why is it a challenge for monetary policy?

5.4 Why are economic forecasts often inaccurate? Why is this a challenge to monetary policy?

5.5 What is moral hazard? How does a too-big-to fail policy contribute to moral hazard?

Problems and Applications

5.6 For each of the following cases, identify the type of lag involved.

a. Although changes in policy have taken place, it takes time for businesses and consumers to react to these changes.

b. Data on GDP growth during a quarter is published months after the quarter has ended and is repeatedly revised.

c. In order to change monetary policy, a meeting of the FOMC must usually take place.

5.7 Economist Milton Friedman was credited with the "fool in the shower" analogy, which compares policymakers to a fool in the shower, who, thinking that the water is too cold, might turn up the hot water very fast, thus scalding himself. What was Friedman trying to suggest about economic policymaking?

5.8 **[Related to *Solved Problem* 10.5 on page 389]** The rise in housing prices in 2001–2006 was a key factor in setting the stage for the financial crisis of 2007–2009. Low interest rates is one possible cause for the rise in housing prices. Because most housing is financed with long-term mortgages, small increases in mortgage rates lead to large increases in the cost of purchasing a house.

a. Why might the Fed have kept interest rates too low for too long? Frame your answer in terms of policy lags and the uncertainty of modeling.

b. Illustrate your answer with the *IS–MP* model.

5.9 Consider the following statement. "Because economic models cannot precisely predict the effect of policy changes, policymakers should not use them to make predictions about the economy." Do you agree with this statement? Explain why or why not.

5.10 **[Related to the *Making the Connection* on page 393]** Discussing the bailouts of insurance giant AIG and the auto companies, a *New York Times* article stated: "Policymakers fear companies like these are so enormous and so intertwined in the fabric of the economy that their collapse would be catastrophic." How do companies that are "too big to fail" create a moral hazard problem?

Source: Eric Dash, "If It's Too Big to Fail, Is It Too Big to Exist?" *New York Times*, June 10, 2009.

5.11 **[Related to the *Chapter Opener* on page 363]** The chapter opener says that Senator Richard Shelby of Alabama accused Chairman Bernanke of sitting idly by while financial problems developed, which "greatly exacerbated the crisis." In the early 1960s, Milton Friedman made the same criticism of the Fed's monetary policy during the Great Depression. In light of the problems of lags, forecasting, and economic uncertainty presented in Section 10.5, to what extent do you think it is reasonable to hold the Fed accountable for the policy failures that led to the financial crisis of 2007–2009 and the Great Depression?

10.6 Central Bank Independence

Evaluate the arguments for and against central bank independence.

SUMMARY

Governments create central banks, but governments usually do not directly control monetary policy. Central bank independence helps reduce the inflation rate and makes the inflation rate and real interest rates less volatile. But central bank independence comes at the cost of removing a major component of economic policy from democratic control. The empirical evidence suggests that countries with independent central banks have lower and less volatile inflation rates and less volatile real interest rates. This makes long-term planning, such as retirement planning by households and the building of new factories by firms, easier and contributes to a well-functioning economy.

Review Questions

6.1 What does it mean to say that a central bank is independent?

6.2 In what ways is the Fed independent from the rest of the federal government?

Visit www.myeconlab.com to complete these exercises online and get instant feedback.

6.3 In what ways is the Fed accountable to the rest of the federal government?

6.4 Why is it desirable for a country to have an independent central bank?

Problems and Applications

6.5 In 2010, the European Central Bank (ECB) purchased bonds issued by Greece and other euro zone economies with excessive government debt. This bailout raised a number of concerns, as discussed in the *Economist.* "Even as the bank's dealers were pushing cash into the bond markets of selected euro-zone countries, its president . . . was trying to reassure Germans that the ECB had not lost . . . its independence."

a. What risks would be created by a loss of ECB independence?

b. Does it matter what people think of ECB independence?

Source: "After the Fall," *Economist,* May 10, 2010.

6.6 It is frequently said that people "vote with their pocketbooks."

a. What monetary policies would a president who was solely interested in reelection wish to pursue?

b. What risks for the economy would such monetary policies present?

DATA EXERCISES

D10.1: **[Related to the *Macro Data* box on page 371]** The *Macro Data* box shows the relationship between the actual federal funds rate and the target rate. Data for the target rate and the actual federal funds rate can be found at the Board of Governors Web site (www.federalreserve.gov). Find the daily rate data from the beginning of 2010 to the present. How close has the actual rate come to the target range for this period?

D10.2: Go to the Web site of the Bank of England, www.bankofengland.co.uk. Search for charts of the Bank of England's balance sheet. Plot the Bank of England's assets over time. What happened to the bank's balance sheet after 2007? How does this compare to the changes in the Fed's balance sheet?

D10.3: **[Excel question]** The text discussion of discount loans states that average monthly borrowing of banks from the Fed from 2000 to 2007 was $219 million.

a. Data on discount window borrowing can be found at the St. Louis Fed Web site (research.stlouisfed.org). Collect monthly data from 2000 to the present.

b. What was the average monthly level of discount loans for 2007–2009, based on these data? What was the standard deviation?

c. Graph your data. What happened to average monthly borrowings between 2007 and the present?

CHAPTER 11

Fiscal Policy in the Short Run

LEARNING OBJECTIVES

After studying this chapter, you should be able to:

11.1 Explain the goals and tools of fiscal policy (pages 408–413)

11.2 Distinguish between automatic stabilizers and discretionary fiscal policy and understand how the budget deficit is measured (pages 414–420)

11.3 Use the *IS–MP* model to understand how fiscal policy affects the economy in the short run (pages 421–432)

11.4 Use the *IS–MP* model to explain the challenges to using fiscal policy effectively (pages 432–438)

DID THE AMERICAN RECOVERY AND REINVESTMENT ACT ACHIEVE ITS GOALS?

The global financial crisis that began in August 2007 ended nearly 25 years of economic stability in the United States and other developed countries. The crisis led to a severe recession that many economists refer to as the "Great Recession." The Great Recession was worldwide, affecting Asian countries, including Japan, Singapore, and Hong Kong; European countries, including Germany, Ireland, Greece, and the United Kingdom; and countries in the Americas, including Canada, Mexico, and the United States. In the United States, real GDP decreased by 4.1%—the largest decline since the Great Depression of the 1930s. The unemployment rate rose from 4.4% in May 2007 to a peak of 10.1% in October 2009—the highest unemployment rate since the severe recession of 1981–1982. Although the unemployment rate was even higher—10.8%—in December 1982, the decline in the unemployment rate was much more rapid following the end of the 1981–1982 recession than following the end of the Great Recession. By June 1984, 19 months after the end of the recession, the unemployment rate had dropped by 3.6 percentage points, to 7.2%. By contrast, in

Continued on next page

Key Issue and Question

At the end of Chapter 1, we noted key issues and questions that serve as a framework for the book. Here are the key issue and key question for this chapter:

Issue: During the 2007–2009 recession, Congress and the president undertook unprecedented fiscal policy actions.

Question: Was the American Recovery and Reinvestment Act of 2009 successful at increasing real GDP and employment?

Answered on page 439

January 2011, 19 months after the end of the Great Recession, the unemployment rate was 9.0%, just 1.1 percentage points below its peak. The persistence of high unemployment meant that during the Great Recession, the unemployed were out of work for an average of 25.5 weeks—nearly half a year—compared with only 12.3 weeks during the 1981–1982 recession.

As we have seen in Chapters 9 and 10, the federal government uses macroeconomic policies to attempt to shorten the length and lessen the severity of recessions. In Chapter 10, we considered the *monetary policy* actions the Federal Reserve used during the Great Recession. In addition, Congress and Presidents George W. Bush and Barack Obama also implemented *fiscal policy* actions. In 2008, during the early stages of the recession, Congress and President Bush enacted tax cuts in an attempt to increase aggregate expenditure. By the time President Obama took office in January 2009, it had become apparent that the recession was going to be very severe. So, President Obama proposed, and Congress passed, the American Recovery and Reinvestment Act (often referred to as "the stimulus package") in February 2009. This act involved increases in government spending and tax cuts that totaled $814 billion. The goal was to increase aggregate expenditure enough to end the Great Recession. In January 2009, President Obama's economic team forecast that passage of the act would keep the unemployment rate from rising above 8%. Despite passage of the act, however, the unemployment rate rose to more than 10%, and was still 9.0% in April 2011.

Did the Obama administration's stimulus package fail? Clearly, the unemployment rate increased more than the administration had forecast, but Obama administration economists were hardly alone in failing to anticipate the severity of the recession. Many other economists, policymakers, and business leaders also failed to anticipate the recession's severity. So, although the stimulus package did not keep the unemployment rate from rising above 10%, Christina Romer, who served as chair of President Obama's Council of Economic Advisers, argued that the bill had succeeded in keeping the economy from plunging into a second Great Depression. Shortly before leaving office in September 2010, Romer argued that the stimulus package would ultimately increase real GDP by 3.5% and employment by 3.5 million jobs. Other economists, however, were skeptical of Romer's estimates and argued that the stimulus bill had done little to lessen the severity of the recession while significantly increasing the federal government's budget deficit. Economists will undoubtedly continue to debate the impact of the stimulus bill for years to come.

AN INSIDE LOOK AT POLICY on page 440 presents Christina Romer's evaluation of the American Recovery and Reinvestment Act.

Sources: U.S. Bureau of Economic Analysis; U.S. Bureau of Labor Statistics; Christina Romer and Jared Bernstein, "The Job Impact of the American Recovery and Reinvestment Plan," January 9, 2009; Christina D. Romer, "Not My Father's Recession: The Extraordinary Challenges and Policy Responses of the First Twenty Months of the Obama Administration," speech given at the National Press Club, September 1, 2010.

Fiscal policy Changes in federal government taxes, purchases of goods and services, and transfer payments intended to achieve macroeconomic policy objectives.

In Chapter 10, we discussed how the Federal Reserve uses monetary policy to pursue macroeconomic policy goals, including high employment and price stability. We used the *IS–MP* model to explain the effect of monetary policy on the economy in the short run. In this chapter, we use this model to explain how *fiscal policy* affects the economy in the short run. **Fiscal policy** refers to changes the federal government makes in taxes, purchases of goods and services, and transfer payments that are intended to achieve macroeconomic policy objectives. As we will see, fiscal policy encounters many of the same problems in achieving its goals that we saw monetary policy encountering in Chapter 10.

11.1

Learning Objective

Explain the goals and tools of fiscal policy.

The Goals and Tools of Fiscal Policy

Long before the Great Recession of 2007–2009, there was the Great Depression of the 1930s. The Great Depression was the worst economic downturn in U.S. history. Real GDP decreased from $977 billion (measured in 2005 dollars) in 1929 to $716 billion in 1933, a 27% decrease, or about six times the decrease in real GDP that the economy suffered from 2007 to 2009. The unemployment rate, which had been 3% in 1929, soared to over 20% in 1933. And the Great Depression was prolonged, with the unemployment rate not returning to 3% until 1942, after the United States had entered World War II. The dramatic increase in government spending on goods and services to fight World War II caused real GDP to increase by 48.9% from 1941 to 1944, and the unemployment rate fell to about 1%.

Some economists and policymakers were concerned that the end of the war and the demobilization of the military might cause a return to the high unemployment rates of the 1930s. In response to these concerns, Congress and President Harry Truman enacted the Employment Act of 1946. This act stated:

> The Congress hereby declares that it is the continuing policy and responsibility of the Federal Government to use all practicable means . . . to promote maximum employment, production, and purchasing power.

What "all practicable means" might be is unclear, but this act was important because for the first time, the federal government explicitly took responsibility for achieving macroeconomic policy goals. This responsibility continues today. As we saw at the start of the chapter, the U.S. government took several macroeconomic policy actions, including passing the American Recovery and Reinvestment Act, to reduce the severity of the 2007–2009 recession.

Who Conducts Fiscal Policy?

In most countries, the central government conducts fiscal policy. The specific structure and mechanisms through which the central government conducts fiscal policy vary from country to country. In the United States, fiscal policy requires agreement between the Congress and the president. Members of the House of Representatives and the Senate introduce bills to change government spending and taxes, debate their differences over the bills, and revise the bills. For a bill passed by Congress to become law, either the president must sign it, or, if the president vetoes the bill, Congress must override the president's veto with two-thirds majorities in the House and Senate. This process normally takes considerable time and can slow the response of fiscal policy to changes in economic conditions.

In the United States, the federal, state, and local governments all have responsibility for taxing and spending. Economists typically use the term *fiscal policy* to refer only to the actions of the federal government. State and local governments sometimes change their taxing and spending policies to aid their local economies, but these are not fiscal policy actions because they are not intended to affect the national economy. The federal government makes many decisions about taxes and spending, but not all of these decisions are fiscal policy actions because they are not intended to achieve macroeconomic policy goals. For example, a decision to cut the taxes of people who buy hybrid cars is an environmental policy action, not a fiscal policy action. Similarly, the spending increases to fund the wars in Iraq and Afghanistan were part of defense and homeland security policy, not fiscal policy. While changes in tax policy to help the environment and military expenditures on a war may affect the national economy, they are not fiscal policy in the strict sense of the term.

Just as with monetary policy, the goal of fiscal policy is to reduce the severity of economic fluctuations. Typically, though, in the United States and most other countries, fiscal policy focuses on employment and production and leaves price stability to the central bank.

Traditional Tools of Fiscal Policy

Fiscal policy can affect the economy in the short run by causing changes in aggregate expenditure. Recall that the expression for aggregate expenditure is:

$$AE = C + I + G + NX, \tag{11.1}$$

where:
$C =$ consumption
$I =$ investment
$G =$ government purchases
$NX =$ spending on exports minus spending on imports.

In the sections that follow, we discuss three fiscal policy tools that affect real GDP:

1. Government purchases
2. Taxes
3. Transfer payments

Government Purchases The federal government purchases goods, such as computers for government offices and aircraft carriers, and services, such as those provided by soldiers and FBI agents. Holding everything else constant, an increase in government purchases, *G*, will increase aggregate expenditure, *AE*. The increase in aggregate expenditure means that firms sell more goods and services, which leads them to expand production, increasing real GDP. Governments have traditionally used spending on infrastructure projects to try to stimulate the economy during a recession. For example, the Japanese government during the 1990s and the U.S. government during 2007–2009 spent billions of dollars on building and repairing domestic infrastructure, including roads and bridges. While building and repairing infrastructure may be valuable in its own right, the specific reason the Japanese and U.S. governments increased infrastructure spending was to provide a stimulus to the economy in the short run. Holding all else constant, we would expect:

An increase in government purchases → an increase in aggregate expenditure → an increase in real GDP and employment.

Taxes Governments obtain tax revenue from many different sources. The U.S. government levies a *personal income tax*, a *payroll tax*, and a *corporate income tax*. Some governments also tax consumption. For example, most of the states in the United States have a sales tax that applies to most consumer purchases. Most European countries have a *value-added tax* (VAT), which is collected from firms, rather than from consumers, and is paid on the difference between the price consumers pay and the cost firms incur to produce the good or service. The federal government does not have a national sales tax or a VAT, but it does levy excise taxes on specific goods, such as gasoline and alcohol.

Changes in taxes affect the consumption and investment components of aggregate expenditure.

Disposable income
National income plus transfer payments minus personal tax payments.

Consumption Changes in taxes on personal income increase or decrease *disposable income*. As we saw in Chapter 2, to calculate **disposable income**, the U.S. Bureau of Economic Analysis adds transfer payments to national income and subtracts personal tax payments. Households can do one of two things with their disposable income: They can either spend it on goods and services, such as clothes and vacations, or they can save it. When their disposable income increases, households usually spend part and save part. When their disposable income decreases, households usually decrease spending and decrease saving. If income taxes increase, then, holding everything else constant, disposable income decreases so household spending and saving both decrease. As a result, consumption, *C*, and aggregate expenditure, *AE*, decrease, which reduces spending on goods and services, leading firms to decrease production and employment. Similarly, a decrease in taxes will increase disposable income, which will increase consumption and aggregate expenditure, leading firms to increase production and employment. Governments sometimes decrease personal income taxes to fight recessions. For example, the Economic Growth and Tax Relief Reconciliation Act of 2001 reduced tax rates on personal income for all households. (Changing tax rates can also have important effects on the willingness of households to work and invest. We discuss these long-run effects later in this chapter and in Chapter 13.) To summarize, holding all else constant, we would expect:

A decrease in the tax rate on personal income → an increase in disposable income → an increase in consumption → an increase in aggregate expenditure → an increase in real GDP and employment.

Taxes on consumption such as sales taxes or a VAT affect consumption. An increase in these taxes makes goods and services more expensive by raising prices, so households reduce their consumption. As a result, *C* decreases in Equation (11.1) and aggregate expenditure decreases, which leads firms to decrease production and employment. Holding all else constant, we would expect:

> An increase in consumption taxes → an increase in prices of consumption goods → a decrease in consumption → a decrease in aggregate expenditure → a decrease in real GDP and employment.

Investment An increase in corporate income taxes reduces the *after-tax* profitability of investment projects. So, an increase in corporate income tax rates will cause firms to abandon their least profitable investment projects, reducing spending on new plant and equipment. As a result, investment, *I*, and aggregate expenditure decrease. This decrease in aggregate expenditure reduces firms' sales, leading them to reduce production and employment. Holding all else constant, we would expect:

> An increase in corporate income taxes → a decrease in the after-tax profitability of investment projects → a decrease in investment → a decrease in aggregate expenditure → a decrease in real GDP and employment.

Transfer Payments *Transfer payments*, such as unemployment insurance, are payments by the government to individuals for which the individuals do not provide a good or service in return. Transfer payments are an important component of disposable income. For example, unemployment insurance payments keep a worker's disposable income from decreasing to zero when he or she loses a job. An increase in transfer payments will increase disposable income and lead to more spending on goods and services. As a result, consumption and aggregate expenditure increase, leading firms to increase production and employment. During the 2007–2009 recession, both President Bush and President Obama signed laws that extended the duration of unemployment benefits for unemployed workers whose benefits had expired. Holding all else constant, we would expect:

> An increase in transfer payments → an increase in disposable income → an increase in consumption → an increase in aggregate expenditure → an increase in real GDP and employment.

Expansionary Policy and Contractionary Policy Economists distinguish between *expansionary fiscal policy* and *contractionary fiscal policy*. Expansionary fiscal policy is intended to increase real GDP and employment by increasing aggregate expenditure. Expansionary fiscal policy actions include increases in government purchases, reductions in taxes, and increases in transfer payments. Contractionary fiscal policy is intended to reduce increases in aggregate expenditure that seem likely to lead to inflation. Contractionary fiscal policy actions include decreases in government purchases, increases in taxes, and reductions in transfer payments.

TARP: An Unconventional Fiscal Policy During the 2007–2009 Financial Crisis

During the financial crisis, the federal government undertook an unconventional fiscal policy action. Recall from Chapter 3 that the financial crisis began when homeowners started defaulting on their mortgages. Mortgage-backed securities declined in value, adversely affecting financial firms that had invested in them. The investment bank Bear Stearns was saved from bankruptcy when the U.S. Treasury and the Federal Reserve arranged for it to merge with JPMorgan Chase in March 2008. But the financial crisis worsened that fall after the bankruptcy of Lehman Brothers and the government bailouts of AIG, Fannie Mae, and Freddie Mac. Many economists and policymakers began to fear that a wave of failures of financial firms might occur.

In October 2008, to deal with the problems banks were facing, Congress passed the *Troubled Asset Relief Program (TARP)*. TARP provided the Treasury and the Fed with $700 billion in funding to help restore the market for mortgage-backed securities and other "toxic assets" in order to provide relief to financial firms that had trillions of dollars worth of these assets on their balance sheets. Unfortunately, no good way of restoring a market for these assets was developed, so some of the funds were used instead for "capital injections" into banks. Under this program, called the Capital Purchase Program (CPP), the Treasury purchased stock in hundreds of banks, thereby increasing the banks' capital, just as any issuance of new stock would have. Participating banks were obligated to pay the Treasury a yearly dividend equal to 5% of the value of the stock and to issue warrants that would allow the Treasury to purchase additional shares equal to 15% of the value of the Treasury's original investment. Although the Treasury stock purchases amounted to partial government ownership of hundreds of banks, the Treasury did not attempt to become involved in the management decisions of any of the banks. The federal government later used TARP funds to purchase stock in the automobile companies Chrysler and General Motors and the insurance company Hartford Financial Services.

Some economists and policymakers criticized the TARP/CPP program as a "bailout" of banks or a bailout of Wall Street. These economists argued that by providing funds to banks that had made bad loans and invested in risky assets, the Treasury was encouraging bad business decisions, thereby increasing the extent of moral hazard in the financial system. Fears were also raised that the managers of banks that had received Treasury investments might feel pressure to make lending and investment decisions on the basis of political, rather than business, concerns. Treasury and Fed officials feared that a surge in bank failures might plunge the U.S. economy into another Great Depression and argued that the program was justified, given the severity of the financial downturn. Criticism of the program lessened as the economy and banking system began to revive and many banks bought back the Treasury's stock investment. Ultimately, most of the banks that received funds under TARP repaid the funds. In mid-2011, it appeared the Treasury would earn a profit on the program.

Should we classify TARP as fiscal policy? Government purchases of financial mortgage-backed securities and stock in banks are not changes in taxes, T, or transfer payments, TR. Purchases of these assets are not government spending on goods and services, so these purchases are not part of G. Therefore, the government's actions under the Emergency Economic Stabilization Act are not *traditional* fiscal policy. TARP did, however, represent an intervention by the Treasury that involved spending, although in the form of asset purchases, that was intended to stabilize the economy. So, in that sense, most economists consider TARP to be an example of fiscal policy.

Making the Connection

Why Was the Severity of the 2007–2009 Recession So Difficult to Predict?

We saw in the chapter opener that at the time the Obama administration prepared the stimulus bill in early 2009, the administration's economists presented economic forecasts that turned out to be much too optimistic. Other policymakers, economists, and corporate CEOs also were surprised by the severity of the 2007–2009 recession in the United States. A key reason for the surprise was that the United States had not experienced a financial panic since the 1930s.

Business cycles can have a number of causes. The recession of 2001 was caused by a decline in investment spending after many firms had overspent on information technology during the dot-com boom of the late 1990s. Spikes in oil prices have also caused recessions. But recessions in the United States between 1933 and 2007, regardless of their cause, were not accompanied by bank panics. In contrast, the beginning of the Great Depression of the 1930s did see a series of bank panics. The recession of 2007–2009 was also accompanied by a bank panic, although it was primarily in the "shadow banking system" of investment banks, mutual funds, hedge funds, and insurance companies rather than in the commercial banking system. Both the Great Depression and the recession of 2007–2009 were severe. Was their severity the result of the accompanying bank panics? More generally, do recessions accompanied by bank panics tend to be more severe than recessions that do not involve bank panics?

Carmen Reinhart of the University of Maryland and Kenneth Rogoff of Harvard University have gathered data on recessions and bank panics, or bank crises, in a number of countries in an attempt to answer this question. The table below shows the average change in key economic variables during the period following a bank crisis for the United States during the Great Depression and a variety of other countries in the post–World War II era, including Japan, Norway, Korea, and Sweden. The table shows that for these countries, on average, the recessions following bank crises were quite severe. Unemployment rates increased by 7 percentage points—for example, from 5% to 12%—and continued increasing for nearly five years after a crisis had begun. Real GDP per capita also declined sharply, and the average length of a recession following a bank crisis has been nearly two years. Adjusted for inflation, stock prices dropped by more than half, and housing prices dropped by more than one-third. Government debt soared by 86%. The increased public debt was partly the result of increased government spending, including spending to bail out failed financial institutions. But most of the increased debt was the result of government budget deficits resulting from sharp declines in tax revenues as incomes and profits fell as a result of the recession.

Economic variable	Average change	Average duration of change	Number of countries involved
Unemployment rate	+7 percentage points	4.8 years	14
Real GDP per capita	−9.3%	1.9 years	14
Real stock prices	−55.9%	3.4 years	22
Real house prices	−35.5%	6 years	21
Real government debt	+86%	3 years	13

The table above does not include data for the United States during the 2007–2009 recession because that recession was still under way when Reinhart and Rogoff were compiling their data. The table below shows some key indicators for the 2007–2009 U.S. recession compared with other U.S. recessions of the post–World War II period:

	Duration	Decline in real GDP	Peak unemployment rate
Average for postwar U.S. recessions	10.4 months	−1.7%	7.6%
U.S. recession of 2007–2009	18 months	−4.1%	10.1%

Note: In the second table, the duration of recessions is based on National Bureau of Economic Research (NBER) business cycle dates; the decline in real GDP is measured as the simple percentage change from the quarter of the cyclical peak to the quarter of the cyclical trough; and the peak unemployment rate is the highest unemployment rate in any month following the cyclical peak.

Consistent with Reinhart's and Rogoff's findings that recessions that follow bank panics tend to be unusually severe, the 2007–2009 recession was the worst in the United States since the Great Depression of the 1930s. The recession lasted nearly twice as long as the average of earlier postwar recessions, GDP declined by more than twice the average, and the peak unemployment rate was about one-third higher than the average.

A key reason that most people did not anticipate the severity of the 2007–2009 recession is that they failed to see the financial crisis coming.

Sources: The first table is adapted from data in Carmen M. Reinhart and Kenneth S. Rogoff, *This Time Is Different: Eight Centuries of Financial Folly*, Princeton, NJ: Princeton University Press, 2009, Figures 14.1–14.5; the second table uses data from the U.S. Bureau of Economic Analysis and National Bureau of Economic Research.

Test your understanding by doing related problem 1.11 on page 443 at the end of this chapter.

11.2

Learning Objective

Distinguish between automatic stabilizers and discretionary fiscal policy and understand how the budget deficit is measured.

Budget Deficits, Discretionary Fiscal Policy, and Automatic Stabilizers

Some changes in government spending and taxes occur due to the effects of existing law, and some changes occur because the government decides to change current law to achieve its macroeconomic policy objectives, such as reducing the severity of the business cycle. In this section, we distinguish between these two types of fiscal policies.

Discretionary Fiscal Policy and Automatic Stabilizers

Discretionary fiscal policy Government policy that involves deliberate changes in taxes, transfer payments, or government purchases to achieve macroeconomic policy objectives.

Discretionary fiscal policy is the deliberate change in taxes, transfer payments, or government purchases to achieve macroeconomic policy objectives. The American Recovery and Reinvestment Act of 2009 is an example of discretionary fiscal policy that both increased government purchases and decreased taxes in an attempt to increase real GDP and employment. On rare occasions, governments have used fiscal policy to try to contain inflation. For example, in 1968, the federal government levied a temporary 10% surcharge on personal and corporate income in an attempt to reduce aggregate expenditure and prevent inflation from accelerating. For the most part, however, Congress and the president have let the Federal Reserve take the lead in controlling inflation.

Automatic stabilizers Taxes, transfer payments, or government expenditures that automatically increase or decrease along with the business cycle.

Some types of government spending and taxes automatically respond to changes in output. **Automatic stabilizers** refer to taxes, transfer payments, or government expenditure that automatically increases or decreases along with the business cycle. In Chapter 8, we described how unexpected events—"shocks"—along with the multiplier effect cause business cycles. Automatic stabilizers help reduce the severity of the business cycle by reducing the size of the multiplier. Consider the case of unemployment insurance, a government program that replaces a portion of the lost wages of recently unemployed workers. Without this insurance, the disposable income of a worker who loses her job may drop to zero. She would have to pay for food, clothing, and rent by drawing down savings or by borrowing. As a result, she would likely decrease consumption significantly. With unemployment insurance, the unemployed worker's disposable income would decline, but not all the way to zero. Therefore, consumption would not fall by as much as it would without unemployment insurance. So, the size of the multiplier effect is reduced, as is the total effect on real GDP of any initial decrease in aggregate expenditure.

The income tax system in the United States also acts as an automatic stabilizer. During a recession, as unemployment rises, household income falls, but personal income taxes will also automatically fall. The effect is similar to a tax cut, so disposable income and consumption spending will decrease less than they otherwise would have. Similarly, during an economic expansion, as households incomes rise, so will personal income taxes, restraining the growth of disposable income and spending.

The Budget Deficit and the Budget Surplus

Budget deficit The situation in which the government's expenditure is greater than its tax revenue.

Budget surplus The situation in which the government's expenditure is less than its tax revenue.

The federal government's budget shows the relationship between its expenditure—including both federal government purchases of goods and services and transfer payments—and its tax revenue. If the federal government's expenditure is greater than its tax revenue, a **budget deficit** results. If the federal government's expenditure is less than its tax revenue, a **budget surplus** results.

As with other macroeconomic variables, it is useful to consider the size of the surplus or deficit relative to the size of the overall economy. Figure 11.1 shows that, as a percentage of GDP, the largest deficits of the twentieth century came during World Wars I and II. During major wars, higher taxes only partially offset massive increases in government expenditure, leaving large budget deficits. Figure 11.1 also shows large deficits during recessions. During recessions, government spending increases and tax revenues fall, increasing the budget deficit. In 1970, the federal government entered into a long period of continuous budget deficits. From 1970 through 1997, the federal government's budget was in deficit

Figure 11.1

The Federal Budget Surplus and Deficit, 1901–2010

During wars, government spending increases far more than tax revenues, increasing the budget deficit. The budget deficit also increases during recessions, as government spending increases and tax revenues fall.

Sources: *Budget of the United States Government, Fiscal Year 2009, Historical Tables*, Washington, DC: U.S. Government Printing Office, 2008; and U.S. Bureau of Economic Analysis. ●

every year. From 1998 through 2001, there were four years of budget surpluses. The recessions of 2001 and 2007–2009, tax cuts, and increased government spending on the wars in Iraq and Afghanistan helped keep the budget in deficit in the years after 2001. The effects on the federal budget deficit of the Obama administration's American Recovery and Reinvestment Act can also be seen in Figure 11.1. In 2009, the federal budget deficit reached 10% of GDP for the first time since World War II. During 2011, both President Obama and Republican members of Congress put forward plans to reduce the federal budget deficit in the long run. We discuss these plans in Chapter 13.

Making the Connection

How Did the Federal Government Run a Budget Surplus in the Late 1990s and Early 2000s?

When the federal government is running annual budget deficits of over $1 trillion, as it has been doing since 2009, it is difficult to believe that the government had a budget surplus as recently as fiscal year 2001.[1] In fact, as the table below shows, 2001 was the fourth consecutive year of budget surpluses:

Fiscal year	Federal budget surplus
1998	$69.3 billion
1999	125.6 billion
2000	236.2 billion
2001	128.2 billion

Before 1998, the federal government had not had a budget surplus since 1969, so this four-year period was unusual. There are several explanations for the surplus years. The U.S. economy emerged from a brief recession in 1991, when the budget deficit was $269.2 billion.

[1]The federal government's *fiscal year* does not correspond to the calendar year. The federal government's fiscal year begins on October 1 and extends to the following September 30. For example, fiscal 2011 began on October 1, 2010 and ended on September 30, 2011.

The 1990–1991 recession was followed by a ten-year expansion that added 24 million jobs. As a result, federal tax receipts in fiscal year 2001 were $1,991.1 billion, about 89% higher than in 1991. But the increase in revenue was not the only reason for the budget surpluses. In 1990, Congress passed the Budget Enforcement Act (BEA). The law had two significant parts: It placed a limit on annual federal expenditure, and it also required that any revenue or spending legislation that would increase the deficit (or decrease the surplus) be offset by a reduction in expenditures or an increase in revenue elsewhere in the budget. Although the federal government did not always meet the "pay-as-you-go" rules, the rules did check federal spending somewhat, and the presence of large deficits when the act was passed made it politically difficult for legislators to recommend new spending programs. The BEA was extended by Congress several times, but expired in 2002.

Several factors made it easier to control the growth of federal expenditure during the 1990s. The sudden collapse of the Soviet Union in the late 1980s and early 1990s allowed the United States to reduce defense spending. Adjusted for inflation, defense outlays in 1998 were about $100 billion less than they were in 1989. During President Clinton's administration, the federal government's main transfer program to low-income households, Aid to Families with Dependent Children (AFDC), was revised. There were 6.5 million fewer recipients of federal funding under the new program, Temporary Assistance for Needy Families (TANF), in 1996 than there had been under AFDC in 1993. In addition to these developments on the expenditure side of the budget, the federal government increased taxes during the administrations of President George H. W. Bush in 1990 and Bill Clinton in 1993.

Federal budget surpluses came to an end in 2001, in part because the recession that began that year reduced revenue and increased expenditures on transfer programs. Congress also approved income tax reductions and increases in defense and national security spending after the terrorist attacks on September 11, 2001. The recession of 2007–2009 and the expenditure programs enacted to pull the economy out of the recession sent the federal budget deficit to record levels. By early 2011, the U.S. Congressional Budget Office projected that the deficit for the fiscal year would be $1.5 trillion. It may be a long time before we see another federal budget surplus.

Sources: Allen Schick, "A Surplus, if We Can Keep It: How the Federal Budget Surplus Happened," Winter 2000, www.brookings.edu; *Economic Report of the President*, Washington, DC: U.S. Government Printing Office, 2011, Table B-80, p. 285; "The Budget Surplus," *Economist*, February 10, 2000; and Mark Memmott, "Deficit Projections: See Them Grow," *National Public Radio*, January 26, 2011.

Test your understanding by doing related problem 2.10 on page 444 at the end of this chapter.

Looking at the budget deficit in isolation can provide a misleading picture of discretionary fiscal policy because the budget deficit automatically rises and falls with the business cycle. When the economy enters an expansion, output, employment, and income increase. The higher level of income means that the government will receive more tax revenue, and the higher level of employment means that payments for unemployment insurance and other transfer payments, such as Temporary Assistance for Needy Families and Medicaid, decrease. Therefore, an economic expansion automatically reduces a budget deficit (or increases a budget surplus). By the same token, when the economy moves into recession, the budget deficit automatically increases (or the surplus decreases) as tax revenues fall and expenditures on unemployment insurance and other programs rise. Notice that these changes in the budget deficit happen automatically without Congress or the president undertaking discretionary fiscal policy.

The tax systems, the unemployment insurance systems, and programs to provide income to low-income households vary from country to country, and the strength of automatic stabilizers also varies from country to country. In general, policies in Europe provide more of an automatic fiscal stimulus than do those in the United States. As the global economy experienced a recession during 2008 and 2009, the spending increases and tax reductions due to automatic stabilizers increased by 1.6% of potential GDP in the United States and 1.8% in Japan, but they increased by 2.7% in France and Germany and by 2.9% in the United Kingdom.

We can think of the government's actual budget deficit in any particular year as resulting from two factors: discretionary fiscal policy and the response of automatic stabilizers to the state of the economy. To focus on that part of the budget deficit that is due to discretionary fiscal policy, economists often use the **cyclically adjusted budget deficit or surplus**, which measures what the deficit or surplus in the federal government's budget would be if real GDP equaled potential GDP. Economists sometimes call the cyclically adjusted budget deficit the *full-employment budget deficit* because it is the budget deficit that would exist if workers were fully employed. In other words:

Cyclically adjusted budget deficit or surplus The deficit or surplus in the federal government's budget if real GDP equaled potential GDP; also called the full-employment budget deficit or surplus.

$$\text{Budget deficit} = \text{Cyclically adjusted budget deficit} + \text{Effect of automatic stabilizers.} \quad (11.2)$$

Because the cyclically adjusted budget deficit removes the effects of economic fluctuations—and therefore automatic stabilizers—on the budget deficit, the cyclically adjusted budget deficit tells us whether discretionary fiscal policy is expansionary or contractionary. If the government is running a cyclically adjusted budget deficit, discretionary fiscal policy is expansionary because the effect of fiscal policy is to increase aggregate expenditure. If the government is running a cyclically adjusted budget surplus, discretionary fiscal policy is contractionary because the effect of fiscal policy is to decrease aggregate expenditure.

Figure 11.2 shows the cyclically adjusted budget deficits for Japan, the United Kingdom, the United States, and countries using the euro, such as France and Germany, from 1992 to 2010. A positive number indicates a cyclically adjusted budget surplus, so discretionary fiscal policy is contractionary. A negative number indicates a cyclically adjusted budget deficit, so discretionary fiscal policy is expansionary. Each country experienced an increase in its cyclically adjusted budget deficit during the 2007–2009 period, but the size of the deficits differed across countries. From 2007 to 2009, the cyclically adjusted budget deficit increased by 6.4% of potential GDP in the United Kingdom and 6.1% in the United States, but by just 2.8% in Japan and 2.3% for countries using the euro. Figure 11.2 shows that the United Kingdom and the United States had particularly large cyclically adjusted

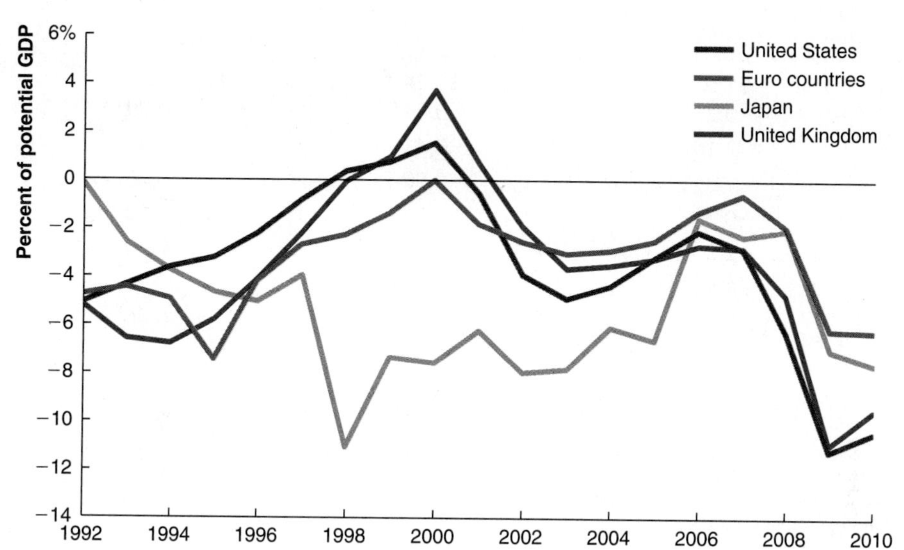

Figure 11.2

Cyclically Adjusted Budget Deficit or Surplus for Euro Countries, Japan, the United Kingdom, and the United States, 1992–2010

The United States and the United Kingdom used discretionary fiscal policy to a greater extent during the 2007–2009 financial crisis than did the other countries shown. As a result, these two countries experienced a much larger increase in the cyclically adjusted budget deficit than did the countries using the euro and Japan.

Source: Organisation for Economic Co-operation and Development. ●

MACRO DATA: DID FISCAL POLICY FAIL DURING THE GREAT DEPRESSION?

Modern macroeconomic analysis began during the 1930s, with the publication of *The General Theory of Employment, Interest, and Money* by John Maynard Keynes. One conclusion that many economists drew from Keynes's book was that an expansionary fiscal policy would be necessary to pull the United States out of the Great Depression. When Franklin D. Roosevelt became president in 1933, federal government expenditure increased as part of his New Deal program. The United States experienced a federal budget deficit each remaining year of the decade, except for 1937. The U.S. economy recovered very slowly, however, and did not reach potential GDP again until the United States entered World War II in 1941.

Some economists and policymakers at the time argued that because the economy recovered slowly, despite increases in government spending, fiscal policy had been ineffective. During the debate over President Obama's 2009 stimulus package, some economists again raised the argument that fiscal policy failed during the Great Depression. Economic historians have argued, however, that despite the increases in government spending, Congress and the president had not, in fact, implemented an expansionary fiscal policy during the 1930s. In separate studies, economists E. Cary Brown of the Massachusetts Institute of Technology and Larry Peppers of Washington and Lee University argued that there was a cyclically adjusted budget deficit during only one year of the 1930s—and that this one deficit was small. The table below provides data supporting their arguments. (Dollar values in the table are presented in nominal rather than real terms.) The second column shows that federal government expenditure increased from 1933 to 1936, fell in 1937, and then increased in 1938 and 1939. The third column shows a similar pattern, with the federal budget being in deficit each year after 1933, except for 1937. The fourth column, however, shows that in each year after 1933, the federal government ran a cyclically adjusted budget *surplus*. Because the level of income was so low and the unemployment rate was so high during these years, tax collections were far below what they would have been if the economy had been at potential GDP. As the fifth column shows, in 1933 and again in the years 1937 to 1939, the cyclically adjusted surpluses were quite large relative to GDP.

Although President Roosevelt proposed many new government spending programs, he had also promised during the 1932 presidential election campaign to balance the federal budget. He achieved a balanced budget only in 1937, but his reluctance to allow the actual budget deficit to grow too large helps explain why the cyclically adjusted budget remained in surplus. Therefore, rather than reduce the severity of the Great Depression, fiscal policy may have helped to slow the recovery.

Year	Federal government expenditure (billions of dollars)	Actual federal government budget deficit or surplus (billions of dollars)	Cyclically adjusted budget deficit of surplus (billions of dollars)	Cyclically adjusted budget deficit or surplus as a percentage of GDP
1929	$2.6	$1.0	$1.24	1.20%
1930	2.7	0.2	0.81	0.89
1931	4.0	−2.1	−0.41	−0.54
1932	3.0	−1.3	0.50	0.85
1933	3.4	−0.9	1.06	1.88
1934	5.5	−2.2	0.09	0.14
1935	5.6	−1.9	0.54	0.74
1936	7.8	−3.2	0.47	0.56
1937	6.4	0.2	2.55	2.77
1938	7.3	−1.3	2.47	2.87
1939	8.4	−2.1	2.00	2.17

Sources: E. Cary Brown, "Fiscal Policy in the 'Thirties: A Reappraisal," *American Economic Review*, Vol. 46, No. 5, December 1956, pp. 857–879; Larry Peppers, "Full Employment Surplus Analysis and Structural Changes," *Explorations in Economic History*, Vol. 10, No, 2, Winter 1973, pp. 197–210; and U.S. Bureau of Economic Analysis.

Test your understanding by doing related problem 2.11 on page 444 at the end of this chapter.

budget deficits during the 2007–2009 recession, which means that they relied much more on fiscal policy than did the other countries. Figure 11.2 also shows that in the United States discretionary fiscal policy may have contributed to the recession of 2001. The cyclically adjusted budget went from a deficit equal to −0.9% of potential GDP in 1997 to a surplus equal to 1.5% of potential GDP in 2000; so discretionary fiscal policy moved from being expansionary to being contractionary just before the start of the 2001 recession.

The Deficit and the Debt

Every time the federal government runs a budget deficit, the U.S. Treasury must borrow funds from investors by selling Treasury securities. For simplicity, we will refer to all Treasury securities as "bonds." When the federal government runs a budget surplus, the Treasury pays off some existing bonds. Figure 11.1 on page 415 shows that there are many more years of federal budget deficits than years of federal budget surpluses. As a result, the total number of Treasury bonds has grown over the years. The total value of U.S. Treasury bonds outstanding is referred to as the *federal government debt* or, sometimes, as the *national debt.* Formally, **gross federal debt held by the public** includes U.S. Treasury bonds and a small amount of securities issued by other federal agencies.[2] Each year the federal budget is in deficit, the federal government debt grows. Each year the federal budget is in surplus, the debt shrinks.

Gross federal debt held by the public Debt that includes the debt securities issued by the U.S. Treasury and a small amount of securities issued by federal agencies not held by the federal government; also called national debt.

Figure 11.3 shows the gross federal debt held by the public as a percentage of GDP since 1790. Over the long run, the federal debt has increased during wars and decreased during peace. The debt increased during the Great Depression of the 1930s, reflecting the large federal budget deficits of those years. After the end of World War II, GDP grew faster than the debt until the early 1970s, which caused the ratio of debt to GDP to fall. The large budget deficits of the 1980s and early 1990s sent the debt-to-GDP ratio climbing. The budget surpluses of 1998 to 2001 caused the debt-to-GDP ratio to fall, but it rose again with the return of deficits beginning in 2002. There were major tax cuts in 2001 and 2003, and further tax cuts in 2008, 2009, and 2011 in response to the recession of 2007–2009 and its aftermath. There were also several major increases in government spending during these years. In 2004, President George W. Bush and Congress enacted a new prescription drug benefit for Medicare patients. Both President Bush and President Obama extended unemployment benefits, and President Obama increased spending on infrastructure projects and other programs during the 2007–2009 recession. Finally, the wars in Afghanistan and Iraq increased defense spending during this period.

The dollar value of federal debt held by the public in 1945 was \$251.7 billion, versus \$7,544.7 billion in 2009. This comparison makes the debt in 2009 look much larger than the debt in 1945. However, a comparison of the dollar value of the debt across time can be misleading. If we look at the debt relative to GDP, we can see that it was 57.0% of GDP in 2009, but 112.7% of GDP in 1945!

Is the Federal Debt a Problem?

Debt can be a problem for a government for the same reasons it can be a problem for a household or a business. If members of a family have difficulty making the monthly mortgage payment, they will have to cut back spending on other things. If they are unable

[2]Some federal government debt is owned by the Federal Reserve System and some is held by the Social Security trust fund (formally called the Old-Age and Survivors Insurance [OASI] Trust Fund) or other federal trust funds. The Federal Reserve has accumulated Treasury bonds in the course of conducting monetary policy, while the Social Security Administration has accumulated bonds in anticipation of the effect on the Social Security system of the retirements of millions of baby boomers. When the baby boomers retire, the trust fund will sell Treasury bonds to make payments to retirees. However, ultimately it is taxpayers in the future who will have to provide the tax revenue to repay the Treasury bonds.

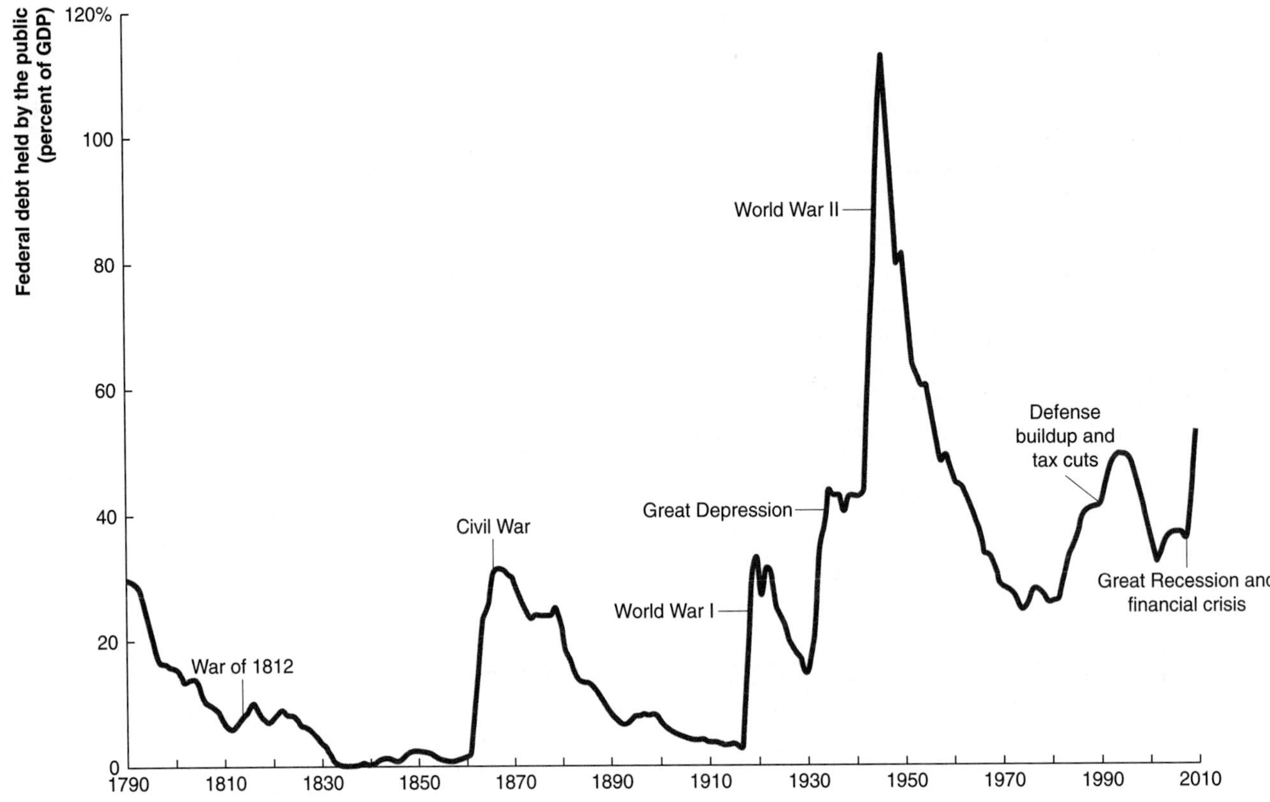

Figure 11.3 Federal Debt Held by the Public as a Percentage of GDP for the United States, 1790–2009

The federal debt increased during the Great Depression and also during the recession of 2007–2009 due to declining tax revenue and increased federal spending. The federal debt also rose in the 1980s due to tax cuts and increased military spending.

Source: Congressional Budget Office. ●

to make the payments, they will have to default on the loan and will probably lose their house. The federal government is in no danger of defaulting on its debt. Ultimately, the government can raise the funds it needs through taxes to make the interest payments on the debt. If the debt becomes very large relative to the economy, however, the government may have to raise taxes to high levels or cut back on other types of spending to make the interest payments on it. Interest payments were about 6% of total federal expenditure in 2011. At this level, large tax increases or significant cutbacks in other types of federal spending are not required.

In the long run, a debt that increases in size relative to GDP can pose a problem. If an increasing debt raises interest rates, it may *crowd out* investment spending. Lower investment spending means a lower capital stock in the long run and a reduced capacity of the economy to produce goods and services. This effect is somewhat offset if some of the government debt is incurred to finance improvements in infrastructure, such as bridges, highways, and ports; to finance education; or to finance research and development. Improvements in infrastructure, a better-educated labor force, and additional research and development can add to the productive capacity of the economy.

We will provide a more complete discussion of the long-run effects of government debt in Chapter 13.

The Short-Run Effects of Fiscal Policy

11.3

Learning Objective

Use the *IS–MP* model to understand how fiscal policy affects the economy in the short run.

We can use the *IS–MP* model introduced in Chapter 9 to show the effect of fiscal policy on real GDP and inflation. Fiscal policy may also have an effect on potential GDP by changing the incentives of households and firms to save and invest. We discuss the effect of fiscal policy on aggregate expenditure, real GDP, and employment in the short run first and then turn to the effects of fiscal policy on potential GDP.

Fiscal Policy and the *IS* Curve

Governments can use fiscal policy to reduce the severity of economic fluctuations. Some governments, including those of many countries in Western Europe, have relied more on automatic stabilizers, while other governments, such as the United States, have relied more on discretionary fiscal policy. Table 11.1 shows the size of fiscal policy actions as measured by changes in the budget deficit for the euro countries, Japan, the United Kingdom, and the United States from 2008 to 2009, as the global economy deteriorated. Table 11.1 shows that the total size of the fiscal policy action was somewhat smaller in the euro countries than in other countries because the euro countries chose to rely much more on automatic stabilizers than did other countries. We turn now to analyzing how both automatic stabilizers and discretionary fiscal policy can be useful in reducing the severity of economic downturns.

Fiscal policy affects aggregate expenditure, which causes the *IS* curve to shift. All else being equal, an increase in government purchases causes aggregate expenditure to increase, and firms respond by increasing output. Graphically, we can show an increase in government purchases as a shift of the *IS* curve to the right. A decrease in taxes or an increase in transfer payments will also shift the *IS* curve to the right. The key point is that fiscal policy affects the *IS* curve by changing aggregate expenditure. Table 11.2 on page 422 summarizes the relationship between fiscal policy and real GDP.

Using Discretionary Fiscal Policy to Fight a Recession

Many governments used discretionary fiscal policy to try to reduce the severity of the 2007–2009 economic downturn. For example, as we mentioned at the start of the chapter, President Obama signed the $814 billion American Recovery and Reinvestment Act into law on February 17, 2009. The act consisted of increases in transfer payments, increases in spending on goods and services, tax cuts to households and firms, and aid to state and local governments. China passed a similar $586 billion stimulus package in 2009. Given the financial commitments of governments to large fiscal stimulus packages, it is important to understand the effect of these policies on the economy. We can use the *IS–MP* model to analyze these effects.

Table 11.1 Fiscal Policy in Advanced Economies, 2008–2009

	Change in the cyclically adjusted budget deficit (as a percentage of potential GDP)	Change in automatic stabilizers (as a percentage of potential GDP)	Change in the budget deficit (as a percentage of potential GDP)
Euro countries	−1.5%	−2.7%	−4.1%
Japan	−2.8	−1.8	−4.6
United Kingdom	−4.5	−2.9	−7.4
United States	−3.1	−1.6	−4.7

Note: Negative numbers indicate that the budget deficit became larger, and so fiscal stimulus increased.

Sources: Organisation for Economic Co-operation and Development; and authors' calculations.

Table 11.2 Fiscal Policy Tools and Real GDP

An increase in . . .	results in . . .	which then causes the *IS* curve to shift to the . . .
personal income taxes or payroll taxes	a decrease in disposable income, so consumption decreases	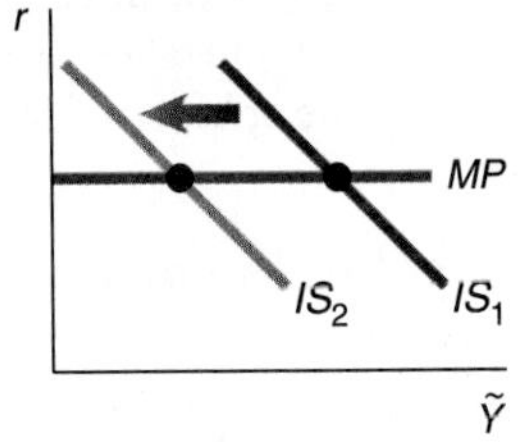
corporate taxes	a decrease in profitability of investment projects, so investment decreases	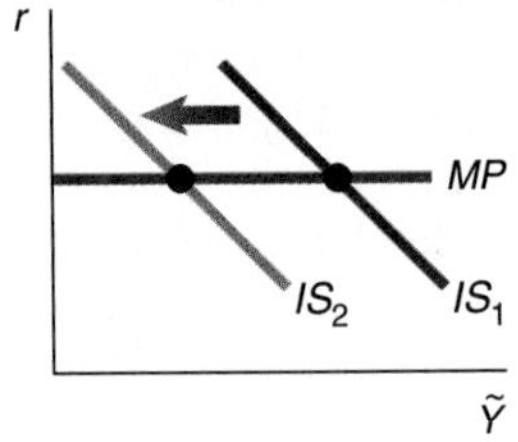
transfer payments	an increase in disposable income, so consumption increases	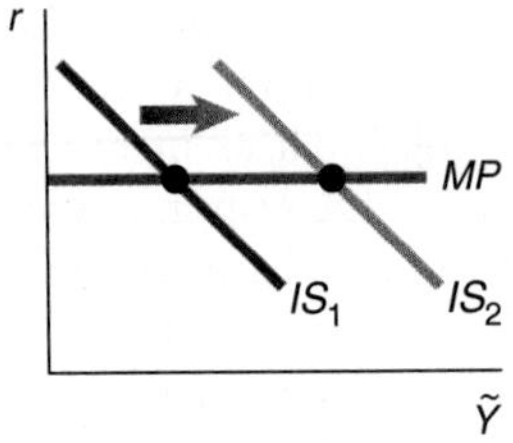
government purchases	an increase in aggregate expenditure	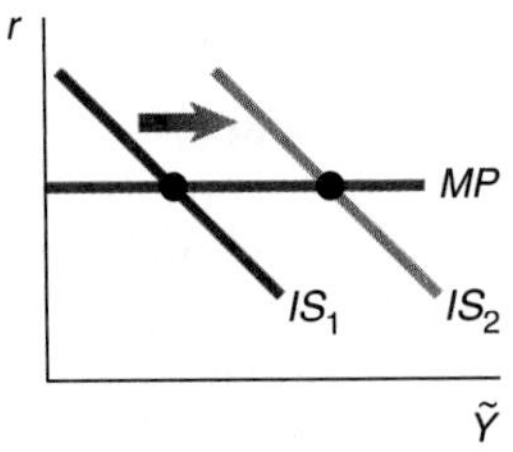

The U.S. and Chinese fiscal stimulus packages increased aggregate expenditure and caused the *IS* curve to shift. Figure 11.4 shows how discretionary fiscal policy can help end a recession. For simplicity, we show the effect of an increase in government purchases, but a decrease in taxes or an increase in transfer payments would have similar effects.

We assume that the economy is already in a recession, so in panel (a) it is initially in short-run equilibrium at point *A*, where $\tilde{Y}_1 < 0$. Real GDP is less than its potential level, so cyclical unemployment is greater than zero. Because the economy is in a recession and real GDP is less than potential GDP, in panel (b) the inflation rate, π_1, is less than it would be at potential GDP. Government purchases increase, so the *IS* curve shifts to the right, from IS_1 to IS_2. Real GDP increases back to potential GDP, so the output gap changes from $\tilde{Y}_1$ to $\tilde{Y}_2$, and in panel (b) the inflation rate increases to π_2. The short-run equilibrium is now at point *B* and the recession has ended. The government has achieved the goal of higher real GDP and employment, with the inflation rate returning to its value before the recession.

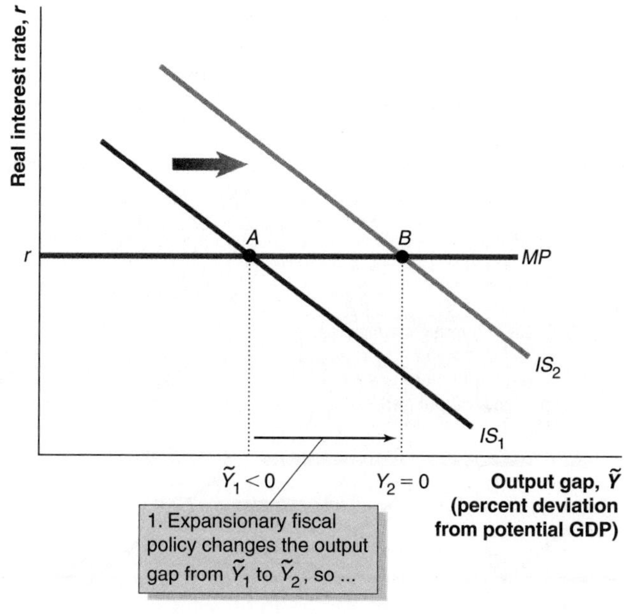

(a) *IS-MP*

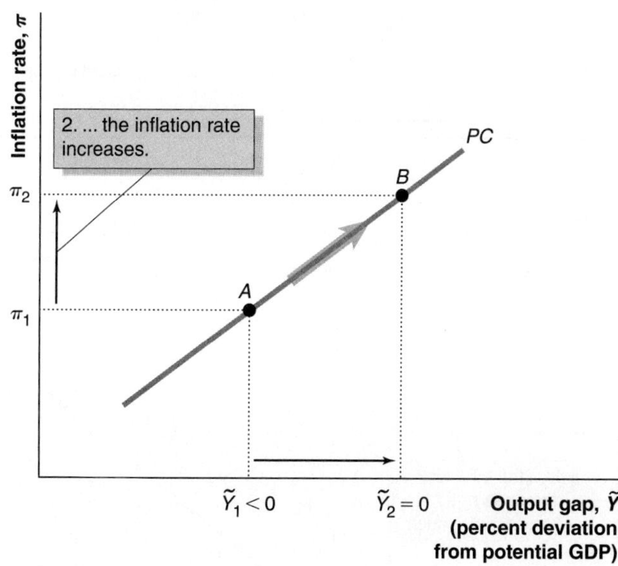

(b) Phillips curve

Figure 11.4

Discretionary Fiscal Policy to End a Recession

Increases in government purchases and transfer payments or decreases in taxes all increase aggregate expenditure and shift the *IS* curve to the right, from IS_1 to IS_2, as shown in panel (a). As a result, real GDP again equals potential GDP, ending the recession and increasing the inflation rate from π_1 to π_2, which was its value before the recession, as shown in panel (b). ●

Automatic Stabilizers

The size of the expansionary impact of automatic stabilizers varies from recession to recession. During the severe recessions of 1973–1975, 1981–1982, and 2007–2009, automatic stabilizers in the United States were 2.1%, 1.6%, and 2.1% of potential GDP, respectively, but during the milder recessions of 1990–1991 and 2001, automatic stabilizers were just 0.8% and 1.1% of potential GDP, respectively. We can also use the *IS–MP* model to analyze the effects of automatic stabilizers on the economy.

Because of automatic stabilizers, there is an immediate fiscal policy response to a decline in aggregate expenditure, even without Congress and the president taking deliberate action. This automatic fiscal response reduces the adverse consequences of the initial shock, so any given decrease in aggregate expenditure has a smaller effect on real GDP and employment. Figure 11.5 shows the automatic stabilizers at work in response to an increase in uncertainty that leads to reduced investment spending.

In panel (a), the economy begins in short-run equilibrium at point *A* with real GDP equal to potential GDP. If uncertainty about the economy increases, investment will decrease. If there are no automatic stabilizers, the *IS* curve shifts to the left, from

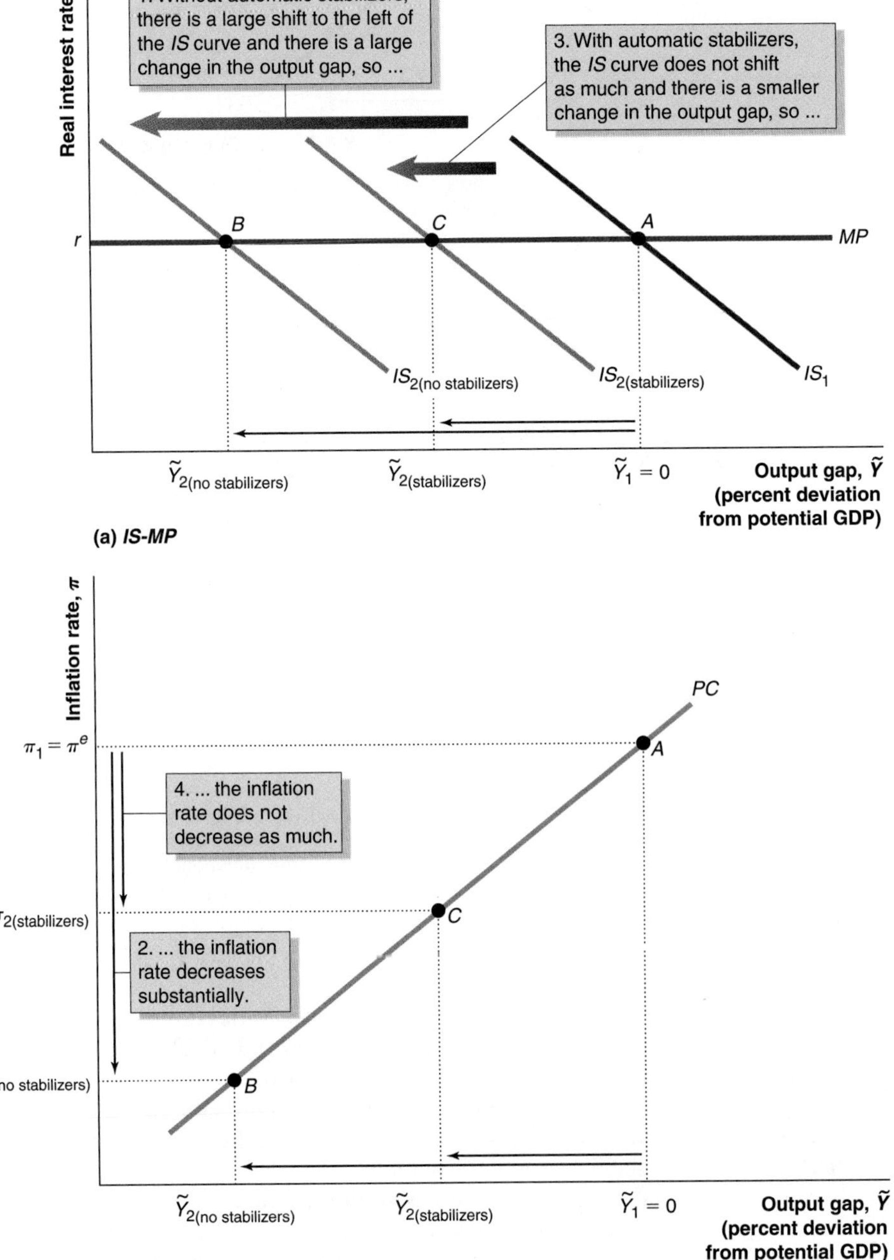

Figure 11.5

Automatic Stabilizers and a Decrease in Aggregate Expenditure

Automatic stabilizers reduce the size of the multiplier. As a result, a shock such as an increase in uncertainty has a smaller effect on real GDP and the output gap. Without automatic stabilizers, the *IS* curve shifts to $IS_{2(\text{no stabilizers})}$ and the output gap moves to $\tilde{Y}_{2(\text{no stabilizers})}$. With automatic stabilizers, though, the *IS* curve shifts only to $IS_{2(\text{stabilizers})}$, so real GDP declines by less and the output gap moves only to $\tilde{Y}_{2(\text{stabilizers})}$ in panel (a) and the inflation rate only decreases to $\pi_{2(\text{stabilizers})}$ in panel (b). ●

IS_1 to $IS_{2(\text{no stabilizers})}$, which equals the decline in investment spending times the multiplier. Real GDP decreases, so the output gap changes to $\tilde{Y}_{2(\text{no stabilizers})}$, cyclical unemployment is greater than zero, and the economy is in a recession. In panel (b), as the output gap changes from $\tilde{Y}_1$ to $\tilde{Y}_{2(\text{no stabilizers})}$, there is a movement down the Phillips curve from point *A* to point *B*, so the inflation rate declines to $\pi_{2(\text{no stabilizers})}$, which is less than the initial inflation rate, π_1. Short-run equilibrium is now at point *B* in both panel (a) and panel (b). If there are automatic stabilizers such as unemployment insurance, then the initial decrease in investment is the same, but the multiplier is smaller, so the effect of the shock on the economy is smaller. To see why, recall the expression for disposable income: $Y^D = Y + TR - T$. Disposable income will not fall as much when automatic stabilizers are triggered because some decreases in income from higher unemployment are offset by higher transfers and lower taxes. So, the automatic stabilizers cause a smaller shift in the *IS* curve, to $IS_{2(\text{stabilizers})}$. Real GDP falls, but not by as much, so the recession is less severe. Automatic stabilizers reduce the magnitude of the multiplier and so reduce the size of the decline in real GDP. In panel (b), the smaller decline in real GDP means that the inflation rate only decreases to $\pi_{2(\text{stabilizers})}$. The economy's short-run equilibrium is now at point *C* in panel (a) and panel (b).

How effective are automatic stabilizers? Economists Darrel Cohen and Glenn Follette of the Federal Reserve Board estimate that automatic stabilizers in the United States reduce the multiplier associated with shocks to aggregate expenditure by 10%, but do not reduce the effect of supply shocks, such as increases in the price of oil.[3] The findings of Cohen and Follette suggest that automatic stabilizers have a modest effect on reducing the severity of business cycles, but that such stabilizers are nonetheless important because they represent an immediate policy response that does not require direct government action. In addition, even if automatic stabilizers such as unemployment insurance and assistance to low-income households do not reduce the severity of business cycles, these policies still help reduce the negative effect of economic fluctuations on lower-income groups and those who lose their jobs. As we saw in Table 11.1 on page 421, automatic stabilizers are stronger in European countries than in the United States and are therefore likely to have more of an effect on European economies.

Solved Problem 11.3A

Should the Government Reduce the Budget Deficit During a Recession?

Due to the effects of the 2007–2009 recession and the American Recovery and Reinvestment Act, the United States ran a $1.4 trillion budget deficit in 2009 and a $1.3 trillion deficit in 2010. As a result, the amount of federal government debt held by the public increased from $6.4 trillion in 2008 to $9.4 trillion in 2010, and the number is expected to reach $14.0 trillion in 2020. The projected increases in the debt are so large that some people believe that the government should immediately reduce the budget deficit to zero. What would be the effect on economic activity and employment if the government eliminated a budget deficit when real GDP was below potential GDP?

Solving the Problem

Step 1 **Review the chapter material.** The problem asks you to determine how eliminating a budget deficit when real GDP is below potential GDP will affect the economy, so you may want to review the section "The Short-Run Effects of Fiscal Policy," which begins on page 421.

---

[3]Darell Cohen and Glenn Follette, "The Automatic Fiscal Stabilizers: Quietly Doing Their Thing," *Economic Policy Review*, Vol. 6, No. 1, April 2000, pp. 35–68.

Step 2 Draw the *IS–MP* model with the economy experiencing a negative output gap. Make sure that you label each curve and indicate that the initial equilibrium occurs where real GDP is less than potential GDP. Your graph should look like this:

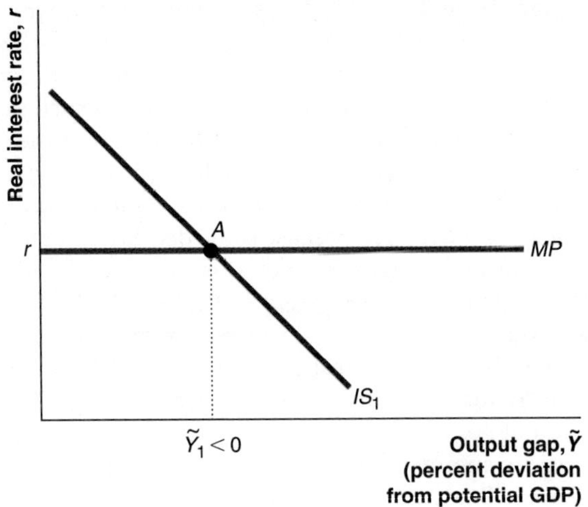

Step 3 Determine the effect on the *IS* curve of eliminating the budget deficit. Begin by recalling that a budget deficit exists when government purchases plus transfer payments exceed tax revenue. Therefore, to eliminate the budget deficit, the government must decrease government purchases, decrease transfer payments, increase taxes, or some combination of the three. Now consider the effect of eliminating the budget deficit on aggregate expenditure. Decreasing government purchases reduces aggregate expenditure, all else being equal. Decreasing transfer payments reduces disposable income, which leads households to consume less, so aggregate expenditure decreases. If the government increases taxes on households, then disposable income also decreases, so consumption and aggregate expenditure will decrease. If the government increases taxes on firms, then investment is less profitable and investment and aggregate expenditure decrease. This reasoning suggests that regardless of how the government decides to eliminate the budget deficit, aggregate expenditure decreases. So, eliminating the budget deficit will cause the *IS* curve to shift to the left.

Step 4 Draw the *IS–MP* graph with the new *IS* curve. The size of the output gap has increased, so real GDP is now further away from potential GDP:

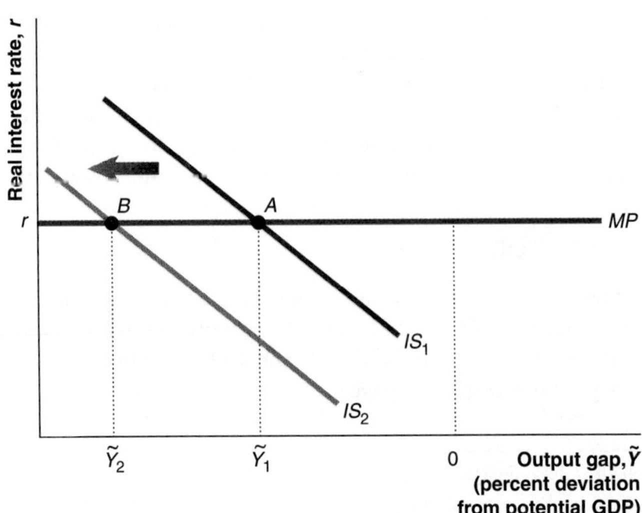

This example shows that eliminating a budget deficit during a recession may actually make the recession worse. Another example occured in 1937, when the federal government raised taxes during the Great Depression. This tax increase contributed to a 3.4% decline in real GDP the following year. Japan had a similar experience in 1997, when the government increased the national sales tax to balance the budget, after which real GDP decreased by 2.0% in 1998 and 0.1% in 1999. Nevertheless, sometimes reducing the budget deficit is necessary during recessions, especially for developing countries such as Mexico, South Korea, and Thailand. These economies do not have a long track record of sound fiscal policies, so they are often unable to borrow in international financial markets during recessions because investors fear that the countries may default on their debts. To maintain access to international financial markets, the governments in these countries may be forced to reduce their budget deficits even during a recession. Even high-income countries such as Germany, Japan, and the United States may in the future face limits on their ability to borrow. The willingness of investors to lend depends on investors' confidence that a country will repay the loan as promised. Once that confidence disappears, it can become very difficult for a country to borrow additional funds, and even developed economies may be forced to reduce deficits.

For more practice, do related problem 3.5 on page 445 at the end of this chapter.

Conceptually, using fiscal policy to reduce the severity of economic fluctuations is straightforward: The government uses fiscal policy to offset the effect of an increase or a decrease in aggregate expenditure by adjusting government purchases of goods and services, transfer payments, and taxes. In practice, implementing a successful fiscal policy may be difficult for many of the same reasons that monetary policy is difficult to implement. We discuss these difficulties in the next section.

Making the Connection

State and Local Government Spending During the 2007–2009 Recession

The recession that began in late 2007 severely reduced the tax revenues of state governments and increased the demand for their public services. The decline in state and local tax receipts was the most severe since World War II. The budget deficit—the difference between tax revenue and expenditure—for all states at the beginning of fiscal 2010 was about $200 billion, or 30% of their total spending. Most state governments in the United States have balanced-budget requirements that prevent planned spending from exceeding expected revenues. The details of the restrictions vary, but they limit the ability of states to run budget deficits during recessions. Recessions reduce state revenues for the same reason that recessions reduce federal revenues: As people lose their jobs and firms' profits decline during recessions, the state government has less income and profits to tax, so tax revenues decrease. Another problem for the states was that at the beginning of the recession, most had only small "rainy day" funds—revenues set aside during times of budget surpluses for use in leaner years.

The budget crisis forced lawmakers to make difficult spending decisions. California was one of many states that instituted involuntary furloughs for state employees. The furloughs forced nearly 200,000 state employees to take Fridays off without pay in 2008. While furloughs help to reduce state expenditure, they also reduce the incomes of state employees. These employees and their families are forced to cut back on expenditures, which hurts local businesses. For example, in California in 2008, business on Fridays in restaurants that state employees frequent was off nearly 65%. Then Governor Arnold Schwarzenegger ended the furlough policy in the summer of 2010 but began a new furlough policy later that year that affected 144,000 workers and was projected to save the state over $135 million per month.

Research by economists Joshua Aizenman of the University of California, Santa Cruz and Gurnain Pasricha of the Bank of Canada shows that the positive effect on real GDP from the increased federal spending and lower taxes from the American Recovery and Reinvestment Act was mostly offset by the negative effects of state and local governments reducing spending and raising taxes. For example, spending on goods and services for all levels of government in the United States was only $47.6 billion higher in 2009 than in 2008. This offset helps to explain why the recovery from the recession was not more robust through 2010.

Sustained improvement in the national economy needed to occur for states to increase their tax receipts and decrease their spending on transfer payments, which was the key to improving their fiscal condition.

Sources: Joshua Aizenman and Gurnain Pasricha, "On the Ease of Overstating the Fiscal Stimulus in the U.S., 2008-9," National Bureau of Economic Research Working Paper 15784; U.S. Bureau of Economic Analysis; Jeremy Gerst and Daniel Wilson, "Fiscal Crises of the States: Causes and Consequences," *Federal Reserve Bank of San Francisco Economic Letter*, June 28, 2010; and Jon Ortiz and Jim Wasserman, "State Furloughs: Unpaid Fridays May Not Be Over," *Sacramento Bee*, June 19, 2010.

Test your understanding by doing related problem 3.6 on page 445 at the end of this chapter.

Personal Income Tax Rates and the Multiplier

A change in personal income tax rates has a more complicated effect on real GDP than does a tax cut of a fixed dollar amount, such as the targeted tax cuts that were part of President Obama's 2009 stimulus plan. The *marginal income tax rate*, which is the fraction of each additional dollar of income that must be paid in taxes, is one of the automatic stabilizers in the economy. Recall that automatic stabilizers, such as the income tax, reduce the size of the expenditure multiplier. Why do taxes have this effect?

To answer this question, we return to our example from Chapter 9, in which a marginal propensity to consume (*MPC*) of 0.9 resulted in an expenditure multiplier of 10. The *MPC* is the amount by which consumption changes when disposable income changes, so an *MPC* of 0.9 means that households spend $0.90 out of each additional dollar of disposable income. In our Chapter 9 discussion of the multiplier, we ignored income taxes so we did not have to distinguish between total income and disposable income. Once we incorporate income taxes, we can show that the expenditure multiplier is smaller.

If the income tax rate is 20%, the government takes 20% of a household's income in taxes. The remaining 80% remains with the household, and the household can decide to either spend it or save it. Therefore, if total income is *Y*, then disposable income is given by:

$$Y^D = (1 - t)Y.$$

where t is the marginal income tax rate and a 20% tax rate means that t equals 0.20. Consumption is based on disposable income rather than total income, so:

$$C = \overline{C} + MPC(Y^D) = \overline{C} + MPC(1 - t)Y.$$

Therefore, aggregate expenditure is given by:

$$AE = \overline{C} + MPC(1 - t)Y + \bar{I} + \overline{G} + \overline{NX}.$$

In equilibrium:

$$Y = AE.$$

So, substituting, we have:

$$Y = \overline{C} + MPC(1 - t)Y + \bar{I} + \overline{G} + \overline{NX},$$

or, rearranging terms:

$$Y = \frac{\overline{C} + \bar{I} + \overline{G} + \overline{NX}}{[1 - (1 - t)MPC]}.$$

If investment changes, while autonomous consumption, government purchases, and net exports remain unchanged, we have:

$$\Delta Y = \frac{\Delta \bar{I}}{[1 - (1 - t)MPC]},$$

or, rearranging terms:

$$\frac{\Delta Y}{\Delta \bar{I}} = \frac{1}{[1 - (1 - t)MPC]}.$$

In Chapter 9, we set the tax rate equal to 0, and the MPC was 0.9, so the multiplier equaled:

$$\frac{\Delta Y}{\Delta \bar{I}} = \frac{1}{[1 - (1 - 0)0.9]} = \frac{1}{[1 - 0.9]} = \frac{1}{0.1} = 10.$$

If the tax rate were to increase from 0 to 0.20, then the multiplier would equal:

$$\frac{\Delta Y}{\Delta \bar{I}} = \frac{1}{[1 - (1 - 0.2)0.9]} = \frac{1}{[1 - (0.8)0.9]} = \frac{1}{[1 - 0.72]} = \frac{1}{0.28} = 3.6.$$

Taking account of the income tax significantly reduces the value of the multiplier. Other automatic stabilizers, such as unemployment insurance, similarly reduce the value of the multiplier. With unemployment insurance, rising real GDP and employment will cause a less than proportional increase in disposable income because rising employment means a lower level of unemployment insurance payments.

Our example was for a change in autonomous investment. However, as we explained in Chapter 9, the formulas are equally valid for autonomous changes in government purchases, consumption, and net exports. Therefore, marginal income tax rates and other automatic stabilizers reduce the ultimate effect of shocks on the economy.

Solved Problem 11.3B

Calculating Equilibrium Real GDP and the Expenditure Multiplier with Income Taxes

Use the following data to calculate the equilibrium level of real GDP and the value of the investment spending multiplier:

$$C = \bar{C} + MPC(1 - t)Y = \$1.0 \text{ trillion} + 0.8(1 - 0.2)Y$$
$$I = \$1.6 \text{ trillion}$$
$$G = \$1.3 \text{ trillion}$$
$$NX = -\$0.4 \text{ trillion}$$

Solving the Problem

Step 1 Review the chapter material. The problem asks you to calculate equilibrium real GDP and the value of the expenditure multiplier, so you may want to review the section "Personal Income Tax Rates and the Multiplier," which begins on page 428.

Step 2 Use the data to calculate equilibrium real GDP. We know that in equilibrium, aggregate expenditure equals real GDP. The expression for aggregate expenditure is:

$$AE = \bar{C} + MPC(1 - t)Y + \bar{I} + \bar{G} + \overline{NX}.$$

So, at equilibrium:

$$Y = AE = \bar{C} + MPC(1 - t)Y + \bar{I} + \bar{G} + \overline{NX}.$$

Substituting the values above gives us:

$$Y = \$1.0 \text{ trillion} + 0.8(1 - 0.2)Y + \$1.6 \text{ trillion} + \$1.3 \text{ trillion} - \$0.4 \text{ trillion}$$

$$Y = 0.64Y + \$3.5 \text{ trillion}$$

$$0.36Y = \$3.5 \text{ trillion}$$

$$Y = \frac{\$3.5 \text{ trillion}}{0.36} = \$9.7 \text{ trillion}.$$

Step 3 Calculate the value of the multiplier from the data given. The expression for the investment spending multiplier is:

$$\frac{\Delta Y}{\Delta I} = \frac{1}{[1 - (1 - t)MPC]}.$$

With $MPC = 0.8$ and $t = 0.2$, the value of the multiplier is:

$$\frac{\Delta Y}{\Delta I} = \frac{1}{[1 - (1 - 0.2)0.8]} = \frac{1}{[1 - (0.8)0.8]} = \frac{1}{[1 - 0.64]} = \frac{1}{0.36} = 2.8.$$

For more practice, do related problem 3.10 on page 446 at the end of this chapter.

The Effects of Changes in Tax Rates on Potential GDP

So far, we have concentrated on the effect of fiscal policy on aggregate expenditure. However, changes in the marginal tax rate may also have important effects on potential GDP. In Chapter 4, we saw that potential GDP is determined by the quantity of labor available, the quantity of capital goods, and the overall level of efficiency in the economy. To the extent that marginal tax rates affect these three factors, changes in marginal tax rates will affect potential GDP.

The difference between the before-tax and after-tax return to an economic activity is known as the **tax wedge**. For example, the U.S. federal income tax has several tax brackets, which are the income ranges within which a tax rate applies. In 2010, for a single taxpayer, the tax rate was 10% on the first $8,350 earned during the year. The tax rate rose for higher income brackets, until it reached 35% on income earned above $373,650. Suppose you are paid a wage of $20 per hour. If your marginal income tax rate is 25%, then for every additional hour you work, your after-tax wage is $15, and the tax wedge is $5. When we discussed labor markets in Chapter 7, we saw that cutting the marginal tax rate on income would result in a larger quantity of labor supplied because the after-tax wage would be higher. Similarly, a reduction in the income tax would increase the after-tax return to saving, causing an increase in the supply of loanable funds, a lower equilibrium interest rate, and an increase in investment spending. In general, economists believe that the smaller the tax wedge for any economic activity—such as working, saving, investing, or starting a business—the more of that economic activity that will occur.

Tax wedge The difference between the before-tax and after-tax return to an economic activity.

We can look briefly at the effects on potential GDP of cutting each of the following taxes:

- *Individual income tax.* As we have seen, reducing the marginal tax rates on individual income will reduce the tax wedge faced by workers, thereby increasing the quantity of labor supplied. The increase in the labor supplied by households will increase potential GDP. Many small businesses are *sole proprietorships*, whose profits are taxed at the individual income tax rates. Therefore, cutting the individual income tax rates also raises the return to entrepreneurship, encouraging the opening of new businesses and increasing employment. Most households are also taxed on their returns from saving at the individual income tax rates. Reducing marginal income tax rates, therefore, also increases the return to saving. If households save more, then the loanable funds model tells us that investment will increase. As the economy accumulates more capital goods, potential GDP will increase.
- *Corporate income tax.* The federal government taxes the profits earned by corporations under the corporate income tax. In 2010, most large corporations faced a marginal corporate tax rate of 35% at the federal level. Cutting this tax rate would encourage investment spending by increasing the return corporations receive from new investments in equipment, factories, and office buildings. Because innovations are often embodied in new investment goods, cutting the corporate income tax rate can potentially increase the pace of technological change. Decreases in the corporate income tax rate can lead to more capital goods and improved technology, so the overall level of efficiency in the economy will increase. In Chapter 4, we saw that both increased capital and increased efficiency will increase potential GDP.
- *Taxes on dividends and capital gains.* Corporations distribute some of their profits to shareholders in the form of payments known as *dividends*. Shareholders also may benefit from higher corporate profits by receiving capital gains. A *capital gain* is the change in the price of an asset, such as a share of stock. Rising profits usually result in rising stock prices and capital gains to shareholders. Individuals pay taxes on both dividends and capital gains (although the tax on capital gains can be postponed if the stock is not sold). As a result, the same earnings are, in effect, taxed twice—once when corporations pay the corporate income tax on their profits and a second time when the profits are received by individual investors in the form of dividends or capital gains. Economists debate the costs and benefits of a separate tax on corporate profits. With the corporate income tax remaining in place, one way to reduce the "double taxation" problem is to reduce the taxes on dividends and capital gains. These taxes were, in fact, reduced in 2003, and currently the marginal tax rates on dividends and capital gains are well below the top marginal tax rate on individual income. Lowering the tax rates on dividends and capital gains increases the supply of loanable funds, increasing saving and investment, and lowering the equilibrium real interest rate. Therefore, all else being equal, decreasing taxes on capital gains and dividends leads to a larger capital stock and increases potential GDP.

The increases in potential GDP due to the increases in capital, labor, and the overall level of efficiency are sometimes referred to as *supply-side effects* of fiscal policy. Most economists would agree that there is a supply-side effect from reducing taxes, but, as with the effect of tax cuts on aggregate expenditure, the magnitude of the effect is the subject of considerable debate. For example, some economists argue that the increase in the quantity of labor supplied following a tax cut will be limited because many people work a number of hours set by their employers and lack the opportunity to work additional hours. Similarly, some economists believe that tax changes have only a small effect on saving and investment and the capital stock. In this view, saving and investment are affected much more by changes in income or changes in expectations of the future profitability of new investment due to technological change or improving macroeconomic conditions than they are by tax changes.

Ultimately, the size of the supply-side effects of tax policy can be resolved only through careful study of the effects of differences in tax rates on labor supply and on saving and investment decisions. Some recent studies have arrived at conflicting conclusions, however. For example, a study by Nobel Laureate Edward Prescott of Arizona State University concludes that the differences between the United States and Europe with respect to the average number of hours worked per week and the average number of weeks worked per year are due to differences in taxes. The lower marginal tax rates in the United States compared with Europe increase the return to working for U.S. workers and result in a larger quantity of labor supplied. But another study by Alberto Alesina and Edward Glaeser of Harvard University and Bruce Sacerdote of Dartmouth College argues that the more restrictive labor market regulations in Europe explain the shorter workweeks and longer vacations of European workers and that differences in tax rates have only a small effect. We will discuss the supply-side effect of tax cuts further in Chapter 13.

11.4

Learning Objective

Use the *IS–MP* model to explain the challenges to using fiscal policy effectively.

The Limitations of Fiscal Policy

Fiscal policy, like monetary policy, faces many challenges in attempting to reduce the severity of business cycles. For a fiscal policy to be implemented successfully, Congress and the president must quickly recognize that a recession has started. If Congress and the president are late to respond, then the policy may not be of much help. In fact, if Congress and the president respond slowly enough, policy may actually destabilize the economy.

Policy Lags

In Chapter 10, we saw with respect to monetary policy that three policy lags make it difficult to reduce the severity of economic fluctuations: recognition, implementation, and impact lags. *Recognition lags* exist because it takes time for an event such as a stock market crash or a housing market crash to show up in the data on consumption, investment, output, and employment. *Implementation lags* exist because it takes time for policymakers to decide how to respond to events such as demand shocks and supply shocks. *Impact lags* exist because it takes time for a change in policy to have an effect on output, employment, and inflation. These three policy lags limit the effectiveness of fiscal policy, just as they limit the effectiveness of monetary policy.

Congress and the president have access to the same information as does Ben Bernanke and the other monetary policymakers at the Fed, so the recognition lag is the same for both monetary and fiscal policy: typically several months.

The response lag is different for automatic stabilizers than for discretionary fiscal policy. As we noted earlier, in the United States, discretionary fiscal policy requires coordination between Congress and the president, so the lag for discretionary fiscal policy can be several months or longer. By contrast, automatic stabilizers respond immediately, without the need for political coordination.

The impact lag for fiscal policy can last up to several months. The government can often immediately adjust taxes and transfer payments, which result in immediate changes in disposable income. However, there is no guarantee that households will immediately use their extra disposable income to consume more goods and services; indeed, households may instead choose to save the extra disposable income. In addition, if the government cuts tax rates on corporate profits, it takes time for firms to evaluate and pursue new investment projects. Therefore, the impact lags for discretionary changes to taxes and transfer programs can be long. The impact lag for government purchases can also be long because even after the federal government authorizes new expenditures on, say, roads and bridges, it takes time to plan the new projects.

The American Recovery and Reinvestment Act of 2009 provides an example of the lags associated with discretionary fiscal policy. The act was intended to stimulate the economy and to help reduce the severity of the 2007–2009 recession. Ideally, the act should have had its greatest effect during 2009, but much of the effect appears to have occurred *after* 2009. Table 11.3 shows that just 20.9% of the spending and 30.9% of the tax cuts authorized by the act occurred in 2009. The act provided tax cuts to households and firms, including incentives for first-time homebuyers to purchase new homes. However, it takes time for households to find a home that they want and can afford, and it takes time for firms to find new investment projects. In addition, the act provided funds for additional spending on infrastructure projects, but the projects needed to be planned and coordinated with state and local governments and appropriate regulatory agencies before they could begin. Much of the debate over the act centered on whether there were enough "shovel-ready projects" in 2009—that is, infrastructure projects that had received all the necessary regulatory approval so they could start at any time but were waiting for government funding—to have a sufficiently large effect on the economy. Not many shovel-ready projects were available in 2009, so most of the spending from the 2009 act occurred in 2010 and 2011, after the recession had ended. In this case, though, the impact lag was not as significant because the recession had been so severe that real GDP was still well below potential GDP in 2010 and 2011.

Economic Forecasts

Because of lags, Congress and the president must make changes to discretionary fiscal policy based on their forecasts of how the economy will be performing several months or years in the future. In this respect, Congress and the president face the same problem the Federal Reserve faces in conducting monetary policy: They must rely on economic forecasts

Table 11.3 Initial Estimates of the Timing of Government Expenditure and Tax Changes from the American Recovery and Reinvestment Act

	Billions of dollars per year			Percentage		
Year	Expenditure	Taxes	Total	Expenditure	Taxes	Total
2009	$120.1	−$64.8	$184.9	20.9%	30.6%	23.5%
2010	219.3	−180.1	399.4	38.1	85.0	50.7
2011	126.2	−8.2	134.4	21.9	3.9	17.1
2012	46.1	10.0	36.1	8.0	−4.7	4.6
2013	30.3	2.7	27.6	5.3	−1.3	3.5
2014	27.9	5.5	22.4	4.8	−2.6	2.8
2015	11.7	7.0	4.7	2.0	−3.3	0.6

Note: The CBO estimated the cost of the ARRA over the 2009 to 2019 period. We show only the cost over the years from 2009 to 2015 so the percentages in the last three columns do not necessarily add to 100. The values in the tax column are positive after 2011 because some of the changes to the tax code resulted in higher taxes in those years.

Source: U.S. Congressional Budget Office.

that are not always accurate. If an economic forecast indicates that a drop in stock prices or a similar event will have only a small effect on real GDP, then Congress and the president are unlikely to undertake a discretionary fiscal policy action. If the effect of the drop in stock prices has a larger effect on GDP than forecast, the result may be that, in the absence of the fiscal policy action, the economy will enter a recession. Similarly, if the drop in stock prices has a smaller effect than forecast, Congress and the president may end up having increased spending or cut taxes more than was required. Therefore, mistakes in economic forecasts may limit the effectiveness of fiscal policy in reducing the severity of economic fluctuations. For example, in November 2008, the professional forecasters surveyed by the Federal Reserve Bank of Philadelphia expected real GDP to decrease by 0.2% in 2009 and the unemployment rate to increase to 7.4%. As it turns out, these forecasts were extremely optimistic. Real GDP actually decreased by 2.6% during 2009, and the unemployment rate rose to 10.1% in October and averaged 9.3% for the entire year. Even after the severe financial distress following the bankruptcy of Lehman Brothers in September 2008, most forecasters failed to predict the severity of the economic downturn.

The Uncertainty of Economic Models

We discussed in Chapter 10 that uncertainty makes monetary policy challenging because the central bank does not know exactly how much a change in household wealth, for example, will affect output or inflation. Fiscal policy faces similar challenges, but recent debates about fiscal policy have centered on the magnitude of the multipliers for changes in government purchases and taxes.

In Chapter 8, we showed estimates of the expenditure multiplier equal to 1.1 during the first year. However, as Table 11.4 shows, estimates of the size of the multiplier vary. It is not even clear whether tax cuts or spending increases have a larger effect on GDP. The uncertainty over the magnitude of the multipliers made it difficult for economists to provide policymakers with clear advice on whether the American Recovery and Reinvestment Act should contain more increases in government spending or more tax cuts. However, as Table 11.3 on page 433 shows, the final act relied more heavily on spending increases than it did on tax cuts.

Crowding Out and Forward-Looking Households

Crowding out A reduction in private investment caused by government budget deficits.

Two phenomena help explain why the multiplier may not be large (and possibly even less than one): crowding out and the forward-looking behavior of households and firms. **Crowding out** is a reduction in private investment caused by government budget deficits. If the government runs a deficit by either cutting taxes or increasing government spending, this affects the ability of households and firms to borrow. For example, suppose the government borrows $100 billion to spend on infrastructure projects. Holding everything else constant, aggregate expenditure will increase by $100 billion. However, in this case, everything else is not constant. In Chapter 3, we saw that a $100 billion increase in government purchases will reduce national saving by $100 billion, and, according to the loanable funds model, this reduction should lead to higher real interest rates. When real interest rates increase, firms find it more expensive to borrow to finance investment, so investment expenditures decrease. As a result of crowding out, aggregate expenditure does not increase by $100 billion. Instead, if the budget deficit crowds out, say, $30 billion of private investment, aggregate expenditure increases by $70 billion (the $100 billion increase in government purchases minus the $30 billion decrease in private investment). Therefore, crowding out may partially offset the expansionary effects of fiscal policy. The exact degree of crowding out depends on how much of the deficit is financed by households, firms, and governments outside the United State; how much real interest rates increase; and the sensitivity of investment to the real interest rate. Higher real interest rates may also encourage households to save rather than consume, so consumption may also decrease.

Table 11.4 Estimates of the Multiplier from Various Academic and Government Sources

Economist or Organization	Type of multiplier studied	Estimated size of multiplier
Christina Romer (prior to serving as chair of the Council of Economic Advisers from 2009–2010) and David Romer, University of California, Berkeley	Tax multiplier	Between 2 and 3
Congressional Budget Office	Government purchases	1.0–2.5
Congressional Budget Office	Tax multiplier	0.6–1.5 (two-year tax cut for lower- and middle-income people) and 0.2–0.6 (one-year tax cut for higher-income people)
Tommaso Monacelli, Roberto Perotti, and Antonella Trigari, Universita Bocconi	Government purchases	1.2 (after one year) and 1.5 (after two years)
Ethan Ilzetzki, London School of Economics, Enrique G. Mendoza and Carlos A. Vegh, University of Maryland	Government purchases	0.8
Valerie Ramey, University of California, San Diego	Military expenditure	Between 0.6 and 1.1
Robert J. Barro, Harvard University, and Charles J. Redlick, Bain Capital, LLC	Military expenditure	0.4–0.5 (after one year) and 0.6–0.7 (after two years)
Robert J. Barro, Harvard University, and Charles J. Redlick, Bain Capital, LLC	Tax multiplier	1.1
John Cogan and John Taylor, Stanford University, and Tobias Cwik and Volker Wieland, Gothe University	A permanent increase in government purchases	0.4
Christina Romer, University of California, Berkeley, and Jared Bernstein, Chief Economist and Economic Policy Adviser to Vice President Joseph Biden	A permanent increase in government purchases	1.6

Sources: Tommaso Monacelli, Roberto Perotti, and Antonella Trigari, "Unemployment Fiscal Multipliers," *Journal of Monetary Economics*, Vol. 57, No. 5, July 2010, pp. 531–553; Ethan Ilzetzki, Enrique G. Mendoza, and Carlos A. Vegh, "How Big (Small?) Are Fiscal Multipliers?" National Bureau of Economic Research, Working Paper No. 16479, December 2001; Robert J. Barro and Charles J. Redlick, "Macroeconomic Effects from Government Purchases and Taxes," National Bureau of Economic Research Working Paper 15369, September 2009; Congressional Budget Office, *Estimated Impact of the American Recovery and Reinvestment Act on Employment and Economic Output from April 2010 Through June 2010*, August 2010; Jared Bernstein and Christina Romer, "The Job Impact of the American Reinvestment and Recovery Plan," January 9, 2009; John Cogan, Tobias Cwik, John Taylor, and Volker Wieland, "New Keynesian Versus Old Keynesian Government Spending Multipliers," *Journal of Economic Dynamics and Control*, Vol. 34, No. 3, March 2010, pp. 281–295; Valerie Ramey, "Identifying Government Spending Shocks: It's All in the Timing," *Quarterly Journal of Economics*, Vol. 126, No. 1, February 2011, pp. 1–50; Christina Romer and David Romer, "The Macroeconomic Effects of Tax Changes: Estimates Based on a New Measure of Fiscal Shocks," *American Economic Review*, Vol. 100, No. 3, June 2010, pp. 763–801; U.S. Congressional Budget Office, "Estimated Impact of the American Recovery and Reinvestment Act on Employment and Economic Output from October 2009 through December 2009," February 2010.

Most economists believe that households and firms are forward-looking in the sense that they care about the future when they make decisions about how much to consume and invest. Households need to save for future spending on things such as cars, homes, college educations, and retirement. That is, households care not only about taxes this year, but also about taxes in the future. Similarly, the profits earned from investing in factories and other capital goods can continue to be earned for many years into the future, so firms care not just about taxes this year, but they also care about taxes in the future. When the government borrows to run a budget deficit, the government must pay back the loans at some point in the future, and this may require higher taxes. As households and firms anticipate paying higher taxes in the future, they may reduce consumption and investment expenditures today. Robert J. Barro of Harvard University calls the idea that households reduce consumption when the government cuts taxes *Ricardian equivalence* because it was first discussed in the early nineteenth century by British economist David Ricardo. In principle, Ricardian equivalence might reduce to zero the multiplier effect of increases in government spending or cuts in taxes. The multiplier would be zero if a decrease in taxes led households and firms to reduce current spending by exactly the amount of the tax cut. Most economists doubt that Ricardian equivalence reduces multipliers to zero, but opinions differ over how important Ricardian equivalence is. We discuss Ricardian equivalence at greater length in Chapter 13.

When Will Fiscal Multipliers Be Large?

Economists have identified two situations under which expenditure and tax multipliers are likely to be large. First, multipliers are likely to be large during severe recessions when there are substantial unemployed resources in the economy. The multiplier story depends on the ability of firms to use additional revenue to hire resources, such as labor, to produce more goods and services. For example, if the government spends an additional $10 billion on building roads, the revenue for the firms that build roads increases by $10 billion. The firms then hire $10 billion of labor, material, and equipment to build roads. Imagine what would happen if all workers were already employed at the time the government increases expenditures by $10 billion. Firms would go to the labor market to hire unemployed workers, but would not find any. Therefore, to produce the $10 billion in goods and services that the government wants, firms would have to hire workers away from other firms that produce goods and services for the private sector. In this case, goods and services for the private sector would decrease as goods and services for the government increased, so real GDP would not increase much, if at all. If the economy is already at full employment, the likely effect of an expansionary fiscal policy would be to increase nominal wages and prices but leave output unchanged. So, the further away from full employment the economy is, the larger the multiplier is likely to be.

Second, if the central bank keeps real interest rates constant, then the multipliers for fiscal policy are more likely to be large. Crowding out occurs when government borrowing increases the real interest rate that firms must pay when borrowing to finance investment. The crowding out of private investment offsets part of the increase in government spending or the cut in taxes, and the multiplier is small. However, if monetary policy keeps real interest rates from rising, the multiplier should be relatively large in the short run.

Fiscal policy may be especially effective when the short-term nominal interest rate that the central bank controls has reached zero and is expected to remain there for an extended time. Under these conditions, an increase in government purchases will increase both real GDP and the inflation rate. With short-term nominal interest rates fixed at 0%, any increase in the inflation rate will reduce the real interest rate and encourage households and firms to increase consumption and investment. Therefore, the multiplier should be larger when short-term nominal interest rates are at or close to 0%.

Moral Hazard

Fiscal policy, like monetary policy, creates moral hazard because it can insulate households and firms from the consequences of poor decisions. If the result of fiscal policy is to reduce the cost of making poor decisions, it makes these decisions more likely. The eventual result of this consequence of fiscal policy could be more severe economic fluctuations.

Recall that the Emergency Economic Stabilization Act of 2008 created the $700 billion Troubled Asset Relief Program (TARP) to help stabilize financial markets. On the theory that some firms are too big to fail because their bankruptcy would cause severe disruption to the financial system or the broader economy, the government used TARP funds to purchase stock in banks such as Citigroup and Bank of America, the insurance company AIG, and the automobile companies Chrysler and General Motors. To the extent that TARP funds prevented those firms from going bankrupt, TARP reduced the severity of the 2007–2009 recession. However, TARP may also have sent a signal from the federal government to U.S. firms that if they are large enough, the federal government will not let them go bankrupt. As a result, large firms have less incentive to avoid risky investments. If their investments work out well, the firms get to keep the profits, but if the investments fail, taxpayers may protect them from bankruptcy.

The federal government has recognized the risks inherent in programs such as TARP, and it has taken steps to reduce moral hazard. First, the government restricted the ability of firms receiving TARP funds to pay dividends to shareholders until the funds were repaid. Not receiving expected dividend payments hurts the shareholders of the firm. Second, the government placed limits on executive compensation for firms that accepted TARP funds. Because executives do not want limits on their compensation, these limits represent a cost to executives of seeking government funds. It is not yet clear how much moral hazard TARP has created or how much limits on dividends and executive compensation reduced moral hazard.

Consequences of Policy Limitations

During 2009, real GDP in the United States was 7.2%, or about $1 trillion, below potential GDP. How much would the U.S. government have had to increase government expenditures to eliminate the gap between actual and potential real GDP? The answer depends on the size of the multiplier associated with government expenditures. Refer again to Table 11.4 on page 435. If the government expenditure multiplier is at the high end of the CBO's estimates, the government would have had to increase spending by $1 trillion divided by 2.5, or $400 billion. In contrast, if the expenditures multiplier is on the low end of the CBO's estimates, the government would have had to increase expenditures by $1 trillion ($1 trillion divided by 1). If the still lower estimates for the multiplier by Valerie Ramey are correct, the government would have had to spend nearly $1 trillion divided by 0.6, or $1.7 trillion, to eliminate the gap, and if the estimates of John Cogan et al. are correct, the government would have had to increase expenditures by $1 trillion divided by 0.4, or $2.5 trillion. Therefore, the estimates of the magnitude of government spending increase necessary to have ended the 2007–2009 recession in the United States range from $400 billion to $2.5 trillion! This simple example tells us that the size of the government spending increase or tax cut required to increase output to potential and end a recession is far from certain. This uncertainty makes it difficult to design a fiscal policy to reduce the severity of economic fluctuations.

The American Recovery and Reinvestment Act: An Early Evaluation

When President Obama first proposed the American Recovery and Reinvestment Act, his economic team forecast that the act would keep the unemployment rate from rising over 8%. Economists, policymakers, and political commentators have advanced two opposed interpretations for why this did not happen:

1. The act did not succeed in increasing real GDP and employment.
2. The act worked exactly as intended, but the recession turned out to be much more severe than policymakers realized at the start of 2009.

It still remains unclear which of these two interpretations is correct.

Appraising exactly the effect of the act is difficult. First, we cannot go back in time and see what would have happened to real GDP and the unemployment rate if there had been no stimulus package. Second, as we saw earlier, estimates of the size of fiscal policy multipliers vary widely.

Studies examining the effect of the act have used different approaches. First, separate studies by the CBO and by Alan Blinder of Princeton University and Mark Zandi of Moody's Analytics have found that the act had a large positive effect on real GDP and employment.[4] The CBO found that during 2010, the act increased real GDP by between

[4]Congressional Budget Office, "Estimated Impact of the American Recovery and Reinvestment Act on Employment and Economic Output from January 2010 Through March 2010," May 2010; and Alan Blinder and Mark Zandi, "How the Great Recession was Brought to an End," Economy.com, July 27, 2010.

1.5% and 4.2%, increased employment by between 1.9 million and 4.8 million workers, and reduced the unemployment rate by between 0.7 percentage points and 1.8 percentage points. Blinder and Zandi found similar results. However, both these studies are based on economic models that assume large multiplier effects. The studies tell us the effect of the act if the multipliers are what they were assumed to be. If the multipliers are smaller than assumed in the studies, the impact of the act will be correspondingly smaller.

A second approach to determining the effect of the act is to compare the historical paths for real GDP and employment with a forecast of GDP and employment, assuming that the act had not been passed. This approach has the advantage that it does not assume that multipliers are large or small. Instead, it calculates the magnitude of the multiplier by looking at the difference between the historical path and the forecast path. President Obama's Council of Economic Advisers used this approach to estimate the effect of the act on GDP and employment.[5] The Council's estimates show that the act increased GDP by 3.2% and employment by 3.6 million by the second quarter of 2010. However, as the Council itself points out, its approach cannot distinguish between the effects of the act and other policy changes, such as changes in monetary policy and other government policies, such as TARP. At best, the Council's report shows that the total effect of all fiscal policy and monetary policy actions to fight the 2007–2009 recession was to increase real GDP and employment significantly.

Moreover, the analysis of Cogan, Taylor, Cwik, and Wieland mentioned in Table 11.4 suggests that the multipliers for the act were as small as 0.4. If this analysis is correct, then the effect of the act is likely to have been even smaller than the lower estimates made by the CBO. The varying estimates of the effect of the act indicate that there is no consensus among economists on the effectiveness of fiscal policy or even which fiscal policy tools are likely to have the largest effect. Economists will likely be analyzing the effect of the American Recovery and Reinvestment Act for many years to come.

---

[5]Council of Economic Advisers, "The Economic Impact of the American Recovery and Reinvestment Act of 2009: Fourth Quarterly Report," July 14, 2010.

Answering the Key Question

Continued from page 407

At the beginning of this chapter, we asked the question:

"Was the American Recovery and Reinvestment Act of 2009 successful at increasing real GDP and employment?"

In the short run, fiscal policy affects aggregate expenditure, which then causes changes in real GDP and employment. An increase in government purchases will increase aggregate expenditure, which will cause an increase in real GDP and employment. A decrease in personal taxes increases disposable income so consumption spending increases, which will increase aggregate expenditure, which will cause an increase in real GDP and employment.

The American Recovery and Reinvestment Act tried to increase real GDP and employment by both increasing government purchases and cutting taxes. As the discussion in the text makes clear, economists have not yet come to a consensus on how effective the Act was. If the expenditure multiplier is as large as the Obama Administration and Congressional Budget Office believe, then the act substantially increased both real GDP and employment. However, if the expenditure multiplier is smaller, as other studies indicate, then the act increased real GDP and employment by a relatively modest amount.

Read *An Inside Look at Policy* on the next page for an evaluation of the 2009 stimulus package by Christina Romer, who was then chair of President Obama's Council of Economic Advisers.

Obama Advisor Claims Stimulus Package Successful Despite Original Unemployment Projections

NEW YORK TIMES

Stimulus Averted Depression, Romer Says

(a) Christina D. Romer, chairwoman of President Obama's Council of Economic Advisers, said in a farewell speech on Wednesday that the administration's stimulus policies averted "a second Great Depression."

But she also gave her most detailed explanation yet for why her original forecast that unemployment would peak at 8 percent "was so far off."

Ms. Romer's last day as one of the four principals on Mr. Obama's economic team is Friday, which means one of her last acts will be to provide the administration's reaction to the latest unemployment report.

For the last year those reports have been a monthly refutation of her early projection. . . .

With Republicans continually reminding voters of the erroneous forecast, it undercut Ms. Romer's effectiveness as a public spokeswoman for administration policies. Within White House economic debates, however, she proved to be more active than most predecessors in past administrations.

(b) The economic projections that were the basis for Mr. Obama's $787 billion stimulus package of spending and tax cuts were based on data from late 2008, before Mr. Obama took office. Ms. Romer, in her speech at the National Press Club, said that she, like most analysts, had underestimated American businesses' reaction to the near collapse of the financial system in 2008 and the global nature of the recession.

"What was not clear at the time was how quickly and strongly the financial crisis would affect the economy," she said. Because such financial shocks are rare, she added, "to this day economists don't fully understand why firms cut production as much as they did, and why they cut labor so much more than they normally would. . . ."

"In any event," she added, "almost all analysts were surprised by the violent reaction."

(c) The analysts, and the new Obama economic team, also were surprised that the reaction turned out to be global, Ms. Romer said. She recalled that until reports in 2009 showed slowdowns in Asian and European countries, she and Mr. Obama's other advisers had anticipated that those trading partners would help bolster the American economy.

Even so, by then the advisers had greatly increased the size of the proposed stimulus package by hundreds of billions of dollars; Congress passed it within a month of Mr. Obama's inauguration.

Against Republicans' continued claims in this campaign season that the stimulus package was a waste—a claim many nonpartisan analyses dispute—Ms. Romer offered an emphatic affirmation.

"I am proud of the recovery actions we have taken," she said. "I believe they have made the difference between a second Great Depression and a slow but genuine recovery. . . ."

Congress is divided over further action. "Concern about the deficit cannot be an excuse for leaving unemployed workers to suffer," Ms. Romer said. "We have tools that would bring unemployment down without worsening our long-run fiscal outlook, if we can only find the will and the wisdom to use them. . . ."

Source: Jackie Calmes, "Stimulus Averted Depression, Romer Says." From *The New York Times*, September 2, 2010.

Key Points in the Article

Christina D. Romer was chair of President Obama's Council of Economic Advisers from 2008–2010. This article presents Romer's view that the American Recovery and Reinvestment Act prevented the recession of 2007–2009 from becoming another Great Depression in the United States. Romer had remained under fire for her original projections of the unemployment rate, which were significantly below what the actual unemployment rate turned out to be beginning in January 2009. Romer stated that the disparity is due to her originally underestimating the severity of the recession.

Analyzing the News

a Despite Romer's initial forecast that unemployment would peak at 8% in the third quarter of 2009, the unemployment rate has remained significantly higher than that. Figure 1 below shows the initial Obama administration estimates of the unemployment rate with and without the recovery plan. Included in Figure 1 is actual unemployment data through December 2010, showing that the actual unemployment rate was not only higher than the estimate with the stimulus package, but also higher than the estimate without the package. The article and figure indicate that the initial administration estimates were clearly too low, yet many analysts believe the projected rate without the stimulus was also too low and the actual unemployment rate remains below what would have occurred without the recovery plan.

b The American Recovery and Reinvestment Act, which President Obama signed into law on February 17, 2009, was composed of increases in spending and tax cuts. Economic projections made at the time were based on data from late 2008, before most analysts understood the severe consequences the financial crisis would have on the economy. Romer implied that the unexpected reaction of businesses to the financial crisis, which involved greater-than-expected cuts in production and employment, explains why the initial projections of unemployment have remained significantly below the actual unemployment rate.

c Another explanation for the unexpected severity of the recession was the global reaction to the financial crisis. Romer stated that prior to the economic slowdown in Europe and Asia, she and other advisors had expected foreign trading partners to help strengthen the U.S. economy through an increase in U.S. exports, thereby boosting domestic GDP.

THINKING CRITICALLY *ABOUT POLICY*

1. The article indicates that the unemployment rate rose above projections because the government underestimated the severity of the recession. All else being equal, show how the American Recovery and Reinvestment Act would affect the economy if the government did underestimate the recession's severity. Use the *IS-MP* model to explain your answer.
2. Suppose that the original projection for the unemployment rate without the stimulus was correct. Is it possible that the American Recovery and Reinvestment Act could have *increased* the unemployment rate from the "Projected unemployment without the stimulus" to the "Actual unemployment with the stimulus"? Hint: Consider what the value of the multiplier would have to be for the unemployment rate to increase.

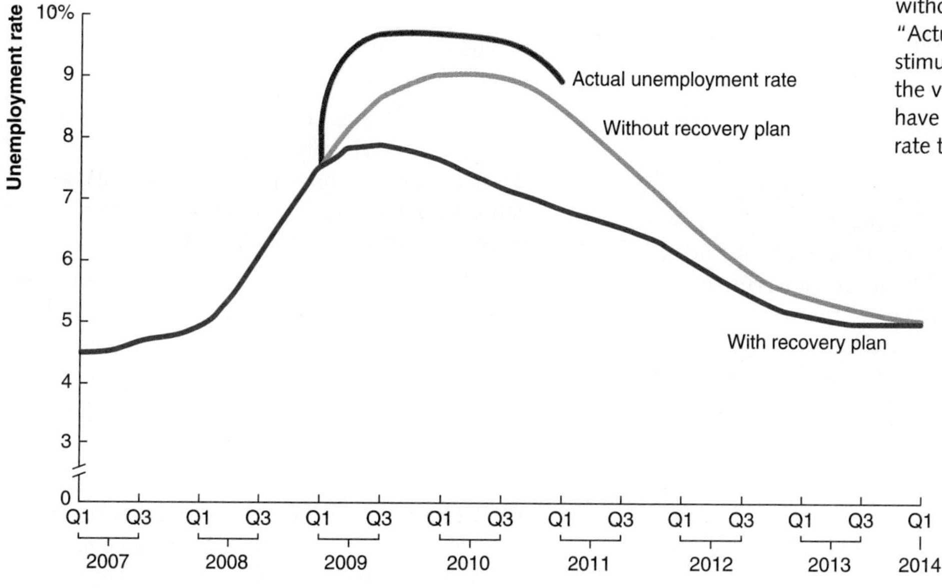

Figure 1 Estimates of the unemployment rate with and without the recovery plan

Sources: Christina Romer and Jared Bernstein, "The Job Impact of the American Recovery and Reinvestment Plan," January 9, 2009; and U.S. Bureau of Labor Statistics. ●

CHAPTER SUMMARY AND PROBLEMS

KEY TERMS

Automatic stabilizers, p. 414
Budget deficit, p. 414
Budget surplus, p. 414
Crowding out, p. 434
Cyclically adjusted budget deficit or surplus, p. 417
Discretionary fiscal policy, p. 414
Disposable income, p. 410
Fiscal policy, p. 408
Gross federal debt held by the public, p. 419
Tax wedge, p. 431

The Goals and Tools of Fiscal Policy

Explain the goals and tools of fiscal policy.

SUMMARY

The government conducts **fiscal policy** to "promote maximum employment, production, and purchasing power." The traditional tools of fiscal policy are government purchases of goods and services, transfer payments to households and firms, and taxes. These tools allow Congress and the president to affect aggregate expenditure. There are four components of aggregate expenditure (*AE*): consumption (*C*), investment (*I*), government purchases (*G*), and net exports (*NX*). Government purchases are a component of aggregate expenditure, so an increase in government purchases increases aggregate expenditure. Increasing transfer payments and decreasing taxes on households increases **disposable income** and consumption, so aggregate expenditure increases. Decreasing taxes on corporate income increases investment and aggregate expenditure. During the 2007–2009 recession, the federal government created the Troubled Asset Relief Program (TARP) to purchase equity in institutions that were deemed too big to fail, such as Citigroup, AIG, and General Motors. TARP is a new fiscal policy tool in that the government purchased financial assets rather than goods or services, such as a new road or bridge. The federal government adopted this too-big-to-fail policy to prevent the recession from worsening. However, the policy protects financial firms from the consequences of their own actions and so may have encouraged moral hazard.

Review Questions

1.1 How severe was the Great Depression? Use output and unemployment data to support your answer.

1.2 What is fiscal policy? Who is responsible for conducting fiscal policy?

1.3 What are the goals of fiscal policy?

1.4 What tools have policymakers traditionally used to try to achieve the goals of fiscal policy?

1.5 What is a consumption tax, and how is it different from an income tax?

1.6 Name and describe a new tool of fiscal policy used during the 2007–2009 recession.

Problems and Applications

1.7 For each of the following situations, choose a fiscal policy and explain how it could be used to correct the economic problem.

a. Real GDP is above potential GDP after a stock market boom.

b. The economy is in a recession due to a decline in investment spending.

1.8 In the United States, consumption taxes (such as sales taxes) are typically state rather than federal taxes. In Europe, consumption taxes are imposed nationally rather than regionally, and they are mostly far higher than U.S. consumption taxes.

a. If the United States were to reduce income taxes and impose a national sales tax, what would be the primary effects on consumption and investment? Briefly explain.

b. Would you expect a consumption tax to have a different effect on consumer savings than an income tax? Briefly explain.

1.9 The United Kingdom faced a fiscal crisis during 2010 and 2011. The government had a large budget deficit, which it believed needed to be reduced. At the time, though, the United Kingdom had only barely recovered from the 2007-2009 recession.

a. What fiscal policies would achieve the U.K. government's budget goal?

b. What effect would these policies have on the British economy?

1.10 Consider the following statement: "Monetary policy and fiscal policy are really the same thing because they both can involve the buying and selling of U.S. Treasury securities." Do you agree or disagree with this statement? Explain your answer.

1.11 **[Related to the *Making the Connection* on page 412]** The chapter suggests that one reason it was difficult to predict the severity of the 2007–2009 recession is that the financial crisis was not anticipated by most economists, and thus the severity of the recession was also not anticipated.

a. What might the failure to anticipate the recession imply about the effectiveness of fiscal policy in preventing or reducing the severity of the recession?

b. What fiscal policies might have been implemented earlier if the recession had been anticipated?

11.2 Budget Deficits, Discretionary Fiscal Policy, and Automatic Stabilizers

Distinguish between automatic stabilizers and discretionary fiscal policy and understand how the budget deficit is measured.

SUMMARY

There are two types of fiscal policy: **Discretionary fiscal policy** is a deliberate change in taxes, transfer payments, and government purchases to reduce the severity of economic fluctuations; **Automatic stabilizers** are the change in taxes, transfer payments, and government expenditures that occur without any direct action by the government. Automatic stabilizers, such as unemployment insurance, reduce the severity of economic fluctuations by reducing the size of the expenditure multiplier. If there is a **budget deficit**, government purchases of goods and services plus transfer payments are greater than tax revenue. If there is a **budget surplus**, tax revenue is greater than the government purchases of goods and services plus transfer payments. Due to automatic stabilizers, the budget automatically responds to the state of the economy. The **cyclically adjusted budget deficit or surplus** is the deficit or surplus that would exist if real GDP equaled potential GDP.

Review Questions

2.1 How is discretionary policy different from an automatic stabilizer?

2.2 How do automatic stabilizers work? Relate your answer to the multiplier.

2.3 What is a cyclically adjusted budget deficit or surplus? How is it used to determine whether fiscal policy is expansionary or contractionary?

2.4 Describe the pattern of cyclically adjusted deficits and surpluses in the United States since 1992.

Problems and Applications

2.5 Briefly explain whether each of the following is (1) a discretionary fiscal policy, (2) an automatic stabilizer, or (3) not a fiscal policy.

a. Government spending on rebuilding highways

b. Sales and purchases of government securities on the open market

c. Unemployment insurance

d. Proportional income taxes

e. Changes in the federal funds rate

f. A 5% increase in all income tax rates.

2.6 According to the chapter, contractionary fiscal policy is rarely used. But during the late 1990s, the U.S. government had a budget surplus. Does this surplus imply that fiscal policy in this period was contractionary?

2.7 As mentioned in the chapter, in 1968, the U.S. government placed a temporary 10% surcharge on personal and corporate income in an attempt to prevent the economy from overheating and causing inflation to accelerate.

a. How would you describe this policy?

b. Economic research has shown that consumers are more likely to make changes in consumption spending when there is a permanent change in their income. Based on this idea, would you expect this surcharge to have the desired result?

c. How would your answer be different if the surcharge were permanent?

2.8 Most of the programs that we think of as automatic stabilizers did not exist in 1929. How might the existence of automatic stabilizers have affected the severity of the Great Depression?

2.9 **[Related to the *Chapter Opener* on page 407]** The George W. Bush administration (2001–2009) passed a variety of tax cuts. For example, the highest marginal tax rate was lowered from 39.6% to 35%. However, these tax cuts were set to expire automatically at the end of 2010. According to the *New York Times*, the fight in Congress over what to do about these cuts has "such substantial economic and political consequences that it could shape the fall elections and fiscal policy for years to come."

a. What do you expect that the effect of the original tax cuts would have been?

b. What would be the effect of allowing the tax cuts to expire?

c. The final agreement in Congress allowed for a two-year extension of the tax cuts. Problem 2.7 discusses the difference between permanent and temporary policy changes. Do you think that this distinction is relevant in the case of the Bush tax cuts? Briefly explain.

Source: David M. Herszenhorn, "Next Big Battle in Washington: Bush's Tax Cuts," *New York Times*, July 24, 2010.

2.10 **[Related to the *Making the Connection* on page 415]** One reason given for the Bush tax cuts in 2001 was to reduce the size of the government budget surplus.

a. Why might the government want to reduce the size of the budget surplus?

b. Shortly after the tax cuts were passed, various changes occurred that policymakers could not have predicted, such as the terrorist attacks on September 11, 2001. What happened to the government's budget surplus?

2.11 **[Related to the *Macro Data* feature on page 418]** Consider the following statement: "The U.S. government is running a large budget deficit, so fiscal policy must be expansionary." Do you agree with this statement? Briefly explain.

11.3 The Short-Run Effects of Fiscal Policy

Use the *IS–MP* model to understand how fiscal policy affects the economy in the short run.

SUMMARY

The tools of fiscal policy affect aggregate expenditure and, therefore, the *IS* curve. To reduce the severity of a recession, discretionary fiscal policy needs to increase aggregate expenditure and shift the *IS* curve to the right, which requires increasing government purchases, increasing transfer payments, decreasing taxes, or some combination of the three. Automatic stabilizers such as unemployment insurance automatically increase or decrease transfer payments and tax payments based on the state of the economy. Research shows that automatic stabilizers have a relatively modest effect on the severity of economic fluctuations. Marginal income tax rates have additional effects on the economy in two ways. First, increasing personal income tax rates reduces the size of the expenditure multiplier. Second, marginal income tax rates can have important supply-side effects. The **tax wedge** is the difference between the before-tax and after-tax return to an economic activity. Increasing tax rates increases the tax wedge. Increases in personal income tax rates reduce the incentive for households to supply labor, which reduces potential GDP. Increases in personal income tax rates also reduce the incentive of households to save, which reduces the supply of loanable funds, the capital stock, and potential GDP. Increases in corporate income taxes reduce the incentive to invest and the rate at which new technologies are adopted, which reduces the capital stock and potential GDP. Increases in taxes on capital gains and dividends reduce the incentive of households to supply loanable funds, reducing the capital stock and reducing potential GDP.

Review Questions

3.1 How is a change in discretionary fiscal policy shown in the *IS–MP* model?

3.2 How do automatic stabilizers affect the *IS–MP* graph? The Phillips curve?

3.3 How does a change in the personal tax rate affect the multiplier? How does a change in the size of the multiplier affect the economy?

3.4 Explain the three ways in which a change in the marginal income tax rate affects the economy. How are these effects different from a change in the multiplier?

Problems and Applications

3.5 **[Related to *Solved Problem 11.3A* on page 425]** As mentioned in the chapter and in problem 2.7, in 1968, the U.S. government placed a temporary 10% surcharge on personal and corporate income in an attempt to prevent the economy from overheating and inflation from accelerating. The graph below shows a possible short-run equilibrium prior to the surcharge. Assume that the economy was already experiencing inflation at this point. Use the graph to illustrate the effect of the surcharge on the economy.

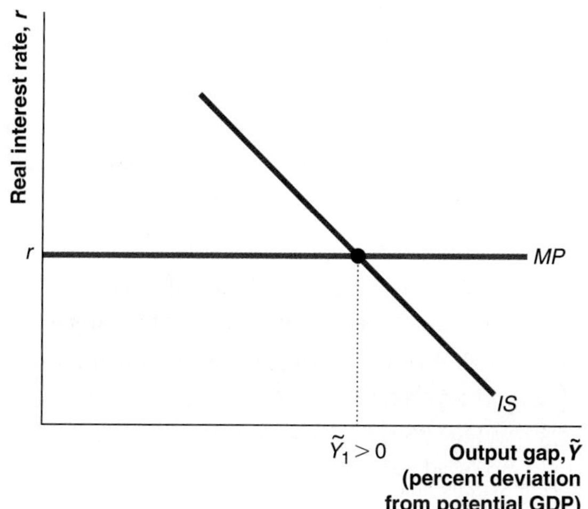

3.6 **[Related to the *Making the Connection* on page 427]** From 1991 to 2000, the Japanese economy grew so slowly that those years have become known as the "Lost Decade." Nevertheless, the Japanese government increased the national sales tax in 1997 because it had become concerned about its budget deficit. As a result, real GDP decreased by 2.0% in 1998 and 0.1% in 1999. The graph below shows short-run equilibrium in the Japanese economy in 1997 prior to the sales tax increase. The graph assumes that growth had been slow but not negative, so the economy was at or near full employment.

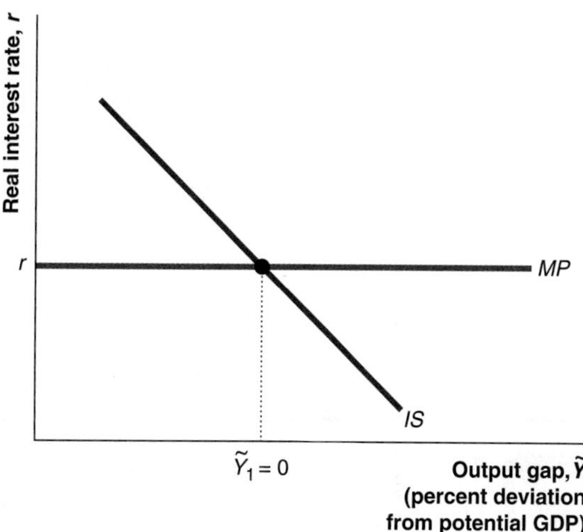

a. Show the effect of the sales tax on an *IS–MP* graph.

b. If the primary goal of the government is full employment, was increasing the national sales tax in 1997 a wise policy? Briefly explain.

3.7 Consider the following statement: "Because automatic stabilizers are built into the economy, there is no need for discretionary fiscal policy." Do you agree with this statement? Briefly explain.

3.8 Section 11.1 describes the use of "new" tools of fiscal policy, as demonstrated by the Troubled Asset Relief Program (TARP). Is it possible to show the effects of TARP by using the *IS–MP* model? Explain.

3.9 Unemployment insurance usually expires at approximately 26 weeks. During the 2007–2009 crisis, unemployment benefits were extended for some workers. The extended benefits expired in June 2010, but Congress passed a new extension in July. Discussing this extension, an article in the *Economist* states, "Congress had never before failed to extend benefits when unemployment remained above 7.2%, and this week's action marked the seventh extension in this recession."

a. Use the *IS–MP* graph to show how an automatic stabilizer such as unemployment benefits works.

b. What would have been the consequences of having let unemployment insurance benefits expire after 26 weeks?

c. Can you think of any reason why extensions of unemployment insurance benefits might be harmful to the economy?

Source: "Read This Shirt," *Economist*, July 22, 2010.

3.10 **[Related to *Solved Problem 11.3B* on page 430]** An economy can be described by the following data:

$$C = \overline{C} + MPC(1 - t)Y$$
$$= \$1.0 \text{ trillion} + 0.758(1 - 0.25)Y$$
$$I = \$2.0 \text{ trillion}$$
$$G = \$3.0 \text{ trillion}$$
$$NX = \$0.5 \text{ trillion}$$

a. Calculate the equilibrium level of real GDP.

b. Suppose that the government increases purchases by $1 trillion. Calculate the change in real GDP.

c. What is the value of the multiplier?

3.11 An economy has a marginal propensity to consume of 0.90. The tax rate is 0.10.

a. What is the value of the multiplier?

b. What would the value of the multiplier be if the tax rate increased to 0.15?

c. Suppose that the government increases purchases by $2 billion in (a) and (b). What is the change in real GDP in each case?

d. How do changes in the tax rate affect the amount by which equilibrium real GDP changes as government purchases change?

11.4 The Limitations of Fiscal Policy

Use the *IS–MP* model to explain the challenges to using fiscal policy effectively.

SUMMARY

The same policy lags that limit the effectiveness of monetary policy also limit the effectiveness of fiscal policy. The *recognition lag* is the time between the occurrence of an economic shock and when the effects of the shock appear in economic data. The *implementation lag* is the time between when a shock appears in data and when policymakers can change policy. The *impact lag* is the time between the change in policy and when the policy has an effect on real GDP and inflation. In the case of government expenditures, an impact lag can be over a year. The advantage of automatic stabilizers is that they respond immediately as output falls and individuals lose their jobs. Recognition lags and implementation lags are extremely short for automatic stabilizers.

Fiscal policymakers are also limited by the quality of economic forecasts and by model uncertainty. For example, there is not currently a consensus among economists about the size of the expenditure and tax multipliers or about which of the two multipliers is larger. As a result of these uncertainties, it is difficult to know how much the government needs to increase spending or cut taxes to end a recession. There are two reasons why the multiplier may be small. First, **crowding out**, which is the reduction in private investment caused by budget deficits, may occur and offset some of the effects of fiscal policy. Second, households and firms are forward-looking, so they may view a deficit today as an indication that taxes will be higher in the future. Households may reduce consumption now to save to pay higher future taxes, and firms may reduce investment in anticipation of lower future profits. Fiscal policy, like monetary policy, can also increase moral hazard. Some economists worried that TARP, which helped save firms that were considered too big to fail, may have significantly increased moral hazard.

Review Questions

4.1 How are lags different for fiscal policy than for monetary policy? How are they the same?

4.2 How does the accuracy of economic forecasts present a problem for fiscal policy?

4.3 What is model uncertainty, and how is it relevant to fiscal policy?

4.4 What is crowding out?

4.5 Why is the extent to which households are forward-looking important for the size of the multiplier?

4.6 Under what circumstances will multipliers be large?

4.7 How do the uncertainties involved in policymaking limit the use of fiscal policy?

Problems and Applications

4.8 During the 2007–2009 financial crisis, among policymakers, the Fed was the first to respond with a reduction in short-term nominal interest rates in September 2007. Fiscal policy actions came later. Comment on the length of fiscal and monetary policy lags and why monetary action occurred first.

4.9 The size of the federal budget deficit increased sharply in 2010 due to (1) the stimulus package of 2009, (2) reduced tax collections, and (3) increased spending due to the sluggish economy.

a. If households are forward-looking, what effect will increased budget deficits have on their spending and saving choices?

b. Comment on how these spending and saving choices might affect the effectiveness of the stimulus package.

4.10 Consider the following statement: "Fiscal policy that involves increases in government purchases always carries a risk of crowding out private investment. Therefore, fiscal policy is not desirable because investment spending is preferable to government spending." Do you agree with this statement? Briefly explain.

4.11 While it is too soon to fully determine the effects of the American Recovery and Reinvestment Act, some argue that the multiplier effects of this stimulus have been limited.

a. Under what circumstances will multiplier effects be relatively large?

b. As of the summer of 2010, were these circumstances in existence?

c. Are there other factors that you think might limit the size of multiplier effects?

4.12 Spending multipliers are larger when the Fed keeps interest rates low. Why might the Fed choose *not* to keep interest rates low? Briefly explain.

DATA EXERCISES

D11.1: The International Monetary Fund publishes the World Economic Outlook. Go to www.imf.org and look at the most recent version available. What does the World Economic Outlook indicate about stimulus spending across countries and the recoveries these countries have made from the 2007–2009 recession? Explain.

D11.2: Go to www.recovery.gov, where you will find information about the American Recovery and Reinvestment Act. According to this site, how were the recovery dollars spent? According to the site, how many jobs has the economy gained or saved?

D11.3: Go to the U.S. Bureau of Economic Analysis Web site (www.bea.gov) and find data on real federal government receipts and expenditure. Answer the follow questions with a graph:

a. How do federal government expenditures vary with the business cycle? How do government receipts change? All other things being equal, does this show some of the effect of automatic stabilizers?

b. Go to the Congressional Budget Office Web site (www.cbo.gov) and search the Publications section for "The Effects of Automatic Stabilizers on the Federal Budget." What does the CBO data in the appendix to this article show?

D11.4: **[Excel question]** The Congressional Budget Office provides data on the actual and cyclically adjusted budget deficit. Find data from 1959 to 2008 by linking to this Excel file: www.cbo.gov/doc.cfm?index=10544&type=2.

a. Graph the budget deficit or surplus and the cyclically adjusted deficit or surplus for this period. (Note that the deficit or surplus is called "Government Saving" in this file.)

b. What was the average surplus or deficit? What was the average cyclically adjusted surplus or deficit? How closely are these figures correlated?

c. Calculate the standard deviation for each series and comment on your results.

Visit **www.myeconlab.com** to complete these exercises online and get instant feedback.

CHAPTER 12

Aggregate Demand, Aggregate Supply, and Monetary Policy

LEARNING OBJECTIVES

After studying this chapter, you should be able to:

- **12.1** Describe monetary policy rules and how they affect aggregate demand (pages 450–456)
- **12.2** Explain the relationship between aggregate supply and the Phillips curve (pages 456–458)
- **12.3** Use the aggregate demand and aggregate supply model to analyze macroeconomic conditions (pages 459–469)
- **12.4** Define rational expectations and explain how it affects policymaking (pages 469–472)
- **12.5** Discuss the pros and cons of the central bank's operating under policy rules rather than using discretionary policy (pages 472–477)

DID THE FED CREATE AND THEN KILL THE GREAT MODERATION?

The key short-run macroeconomic problem is the business cycle. Most economists believe that business cycles make households and firms worse off. So, if macroeconomic policy can reduce those fluctuations, it can improve the economic well-being of households and firms. Macroeconomic policy has often failed to accomplish this result, however. In some periods, monetary and fiscal policy appear to have actually made macroeconomic conditions worse rather than better. For example, the Federal Reserve failed to stop the collapse of the banking system in the early 1930s and raised reserve requirements in 1936, which may have caused the severe recession of 1937–1938. President Herbert Hoover and Congress may have contributed to the severity of the 1929–1933 downturn by sharply raising federal income tax rates in 1932.

Continued on next page

Key Issue and Question

At the end of Chapter 1, we noted key issues and questions that serve as a framework for the book. Here are the key issue and question for this chapter:

Issue: Between the early 1980s and 2007, the U.S. economy experienced a period of macroeconomic stability known as the Great Moderation.

Question: Did discretionary monetary policy kill the Great Moderation?

Answered on page 477

Many economists have also been critical of the macroeconomic policy employed during the 1970s. Until the 1970s, the United States had experienced high inflation rates only during wartime. In 1972, the inflation rate averaged a comparatively low 3.3%, but by 1974, the inflation rate soared to more than 10%. The inflation rate declined during the next few years, only to rise again sharply beginning in 1978. In early 1980, the inflation rate was above 14% for five months. These high inflation rates imposed serious costs on many households and firms. Workers whose nominal wages did not keep pace with these high inflation rates suffered large declines in real wages. Bondholders, people receiving fixed-dollar pensions, and banks and other financial intermediaries that had made fixed-interest-rate loans all suffered losses. Although the Fed faced a policy dilemma because some of the inflation was due to the supply shocks caused by the rapid increase in oil prices during this period, most economists believe that monetary policy could have been used more skillfully to keep inflation from reaching such high levels. To add to the problems of the 1970s and early 1980s, the economy suffered severe recessions in 1973–1975 and 1981–1982. In late 1982, the unemployment rate hit a peak of 10.8%, which remains the highest unemployment rate since the 1930s. This combination of high inflation and high unemployment, dubbed *stagflation*, left much of the general public wondering whether the Federal Reserve was capable of implementing effective macroeconomic policies.

After the early 1980s, however, the performance of the economy improved, and so did the reputation of Fed policymakers. Following the end of the 1981–1982 recession, the United States experienced 92 straight months of economic expansion, ending with the brief and mild recession of 1990–1991. The following expansion was 120 months long—the longest in U.S. history—and was followed by another short and mild recession during 2001. The inflation rate was also well under control, averaging just 2.6% between December 1982 and December 2007. This 25-year run of long expansions, short and mild recessions, and low inflation was arguably the longest period of macroeconomic stability in the history of the United States. The period was a sufficiently sharp break with the past that economists James Stock of Harvard University and Mark Watson of Princeton University named it the "Great Moderation." Having received a good share of the blame for previous periods of macroeconomic instability, should the Fed receive credit for the Great Moderation? Certainly many economists, Wall Street analysts, and members of Congress seemed convinced that Alan Greenspan, who served as Fed chair from 1987 to 2006, had somehow managed to tame the business cycle. As we will see in this chapter, however, some economists were skeptical that better Fed policy was the key to the Great Moderation.

In any event, the Great Moderation ended abruptly in 2007. As we have seen in earlier chapters, the 2007–2009 recession was the worst since the Great Depression of the 1930s. Did Fed policies play a role in ending the Great Moderation? In hindsight, a number of economists and policymakers argued that Fed policies during the early 2000s, although widely seen as successful at the time, actually led to the recession of 2007–2009. To some economists, Alan Greenspan's reputation was turned on its head—from hero to villain—in just a few years.

As we have already seen, explaining business cycles is not an easy task. In this chapter, we will look more closely at monetary policy, with the aim of being better able to evaluate the Fed's role in the Great Moderation and in the severe recession of 2007–2009.

AN INSIDE LOOK AT POLICY on page 478 explores consumers' expectations of inflation for 2011 and the Fed's efforts to increase economic growth.

Sources: U.S. Bureau of Economic Analysis; U.S. Bureau of Labor Statistics; and James Stock and Mark Watson, "Has the Business Cycle Changed and Why?" *NBER Macroeconomics Annual*, 2002, pp. 159–218.

In Chapters 10 and 11, we used the *IS–MP* model to explain how monetary and fiscal policy affect real GDP and the inflation rate. We saw that policymakers rely more on monetary policy than on fiscal policy to reduce the severity of business cycles. In this chapter, we build an *aggregate demand and aggregate supply model*, which explicitly incorporates the Fed's use of a *monetary policy rule*. **Aggregate demand** is the level of planned aggregate expenditure in the economy. **Aggregate supply** is the total quantity of goods and services that firms are willing to supply. The model presented in this chapter completes our discussion of business cycles.

Aggregate demand The level of planned aggregate expenditure in the economy.

Aggregate supply The total quantity of goods and services that firms are willing to supply.

12.1

Learning Objective

Describe monetary policy rules and how they affect aggregate demand.

Monetary Policy Rules and Aggregate Demand

We have seen how the Fed attempts to affect interest rates, which in turn affect the level of real GDP. In this chapter, we explain how central banks can use a monetary policy rule to select an interest rate target.

Monetary Policy Rules

All else being equal, an increase in the short-term nominal interest rate will increase the long-term real interest rate and, therefore, decrease consumption, investment, net exports, and real GDP. Similarly, a decrease in the short-term nominal interest rate decreases the long-term real interest rate and, therefore, increases consumption, investment, net exports, and real GDP.

One of the main goals of central banks is price stability. To achieve this goal, the central bank sets either an implicit or explicit inflation target, π_{Target}. Some central banks, such as the Federal Reserve in the United States, have implicit inflation targets that they do not make public. Most economists believe the Fed's target inflation rate is approximately 2%. Other central banks, such as the Reserve Bank of New Zealand, have an explicit inflation target specified by law. When inflation is greater than the target rate, central banks increase interest rates to reduce aggregate expenditure and real GDP, which in turn will reduce the inflation rate. When inflation is less than the target rate, central banks decrease interest rates to increase aggregate expenditure and real GDP, which in turn will raise the inflation rate.

Monetary policy rule A rule or formula that a central bank uses to set interest rates in response to changing economic conditions.

We can think of the central bank's response to changes in inflation as a **monetary policy rule**, which is a rule or formula that a central bank uses to set interest rates in response to changing economic conditions. The line in Figure 12.1 illustrates the central bank's monetary policy rule. When the real interest rate, r, equals r_1, the level of aggregate expenditure is consistent with the central bank's target inflation rate, π_{Target}. The monetary policy rule slopes upward because the central bank increases the real interest rate as the inflation rate increases and decreases the real interest rate as the inflation rate decreases. There are two key components of the monetary policy rule. First, the target inflation rate is the inflation rate that the central bank wants to achieve in the long run. Second, the slope of the monetary policy rule indicates how much the central bank responds to short-run deviations of the actual inflation rate from the target inflation rate: The steeper the monetary policy rule, the more the central bank increases the interest rate in response to the current inflation rate being above the target inflation rate and the more the central bank decreases the real interest rate in response to the actual inflation rate being below the target inflation rate. The flatter the monetary policy rule, the smaller the changes the central bank makes in the real interest rate in response to deviations of the actual inflation rate

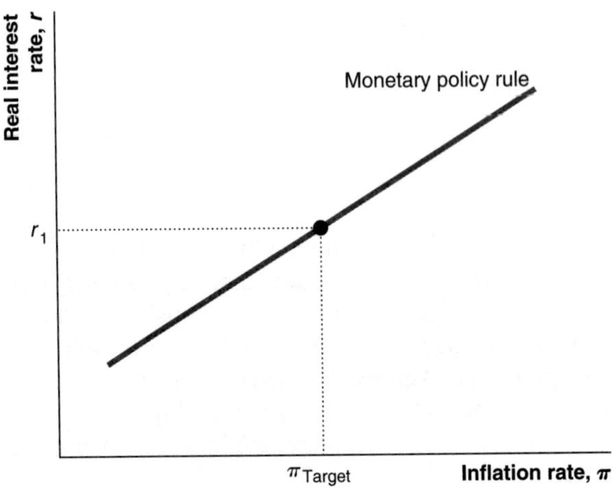

Figure 12.1

The Central Bank's Monetary Policy Rule

The monetary policy rule slopes upward, indicating that the central bank increases the real interest rate as the inflation rate increases and decreases the real interest rate as the inflation rate decreases. ●

from the target inflation rate. In other words, if the monetary policy rule is steep, the central bank responds more aggressively to deviations between the actual inflation rate and the target inflation rate than if the monetary policy rule is flat.

The monetary policy rule in Figure 12.1 somewhat simplifies the actual policy situation that central banks face. For one thing, central banks typically have goals beyond just price stability. The Federal Reserve, for example, is charged by Congress with achieving stable economic growth, high employment, and financial market stability, as well as price stability. So, in some circumstances, a monetary policy rule focusing on just inflation may not be consistent with the Fed's other goals. We consider more complicated policy rules later in this chapter. The monetary policy rule illustrated in Figure 12.1 also assumes that the central bank controls the *long-term real interest rate*, but the Fed, like other central banks, actually controls the *short-term nominal interest rate*. Recall from Chapter 10 that the long-term real interest rate depends on the short-term nominal interest rate, the term structure effect, the default risk premium, and the expected inflation rate. At this point, we are assuming that these factors are unchanged, so a change in the short-term nominal interest rate will change the long-term real interest rate.

The Aggregate Demand Curve

The monetary policy rule shows how the Fed adjusts its target for the real interest rate in response to changes in the inflation rate. The Fed's raising its target for the real interest rate makes it more costly for households and firms to borrow to finance consumption and investment. A higher real interest rate also increases the exchange rate between the U.S. dollar and foreign currencies, which reduces net exports. Because aggregate expenditure and real GDP decrease as the real interest rate increases, there is a negative relationship between the real interest rate and the quantity of real GDP demanded by households and firms. As we saw in Chapter 9, we express this negative relationship with the *IS* curve.

We can use the *IS–MP* model introduced in Chapter 9 to derive the **aggregate demand (*AD*) curve**, which is a curve that shows the relationship between aggregate expenditure on goods and services by households and firms and the inflation rate. Figure 12.2 shows how we can derive the aggregate demand curve by using the *IS–MP* model and the monetary policy rule.

Aggregate demand (*AD*) curve A curve that shows the relationship between aggregate expenditure on goods and services by households and firms and the inflation rate.

In the figure, short-run equilibrium is initially at point *A* in both panel (a) and panel (b), with real GDP equal to potential GDP, so the output gap equals zero at $\tilde{Y}_1$. The inflation rate, π_1, is equal to the Fed's target rate, π_{Target}. Given the Fed's monetary policy rule, the Fed sets the real interest rate at r_1, so the *MP* curve is MP_1. Now suppose that in panel (b) the inflation rate increases from π_1 to π_2, which is above the Fed's target rate. The monetary policy rule tells us that the Fed will increase the real interest rate as the inflation rate increases. We show the real interest rate increasing from r_1 to r_2 in panel (a). As a result, aggregate expenditure will fall below potential GDP and the output gap moves from $\tilde{Y}_1$ to $\tilde{Y}_2$. The new equilibrium combination of inflation and real GDP demanded is π_2 and $\tilde{Y}_2$, so short-run equilibrium is now at point *B* in both panel (a) and panel (b). Drawing a line connecting points *A* and *B* gives us the aggregate demand curve. Because an increase in the inflation rate leads the Fed to increase the real interest rate, there is an inverse relationship between the inflation rate and the output gap. This relationship is represented by the aggregate demand curve. So, a change in the inflation rate causes a movement along the aggregate demand curve.

The monetary policy rule tells us how much the real interest rate changes as the inflation rate increases, so it is critical for deriving the aggregate demand curve. If the Fed focuses on price stability, it will increase interest rates substantially when inflation rises so aggregate expenditure will decrease substantially. The end result is a relatively flat aggregate demand curve, which shows that aggregate expenditure is very sensitive to changes in the inflation rate. If, however, the Fed is not very concerned about price stability, it will not increase the real interest rate as much when the inflation rate increases, so aggregate expenditure will not decrease as much. The end result in this case is a steep aggregate

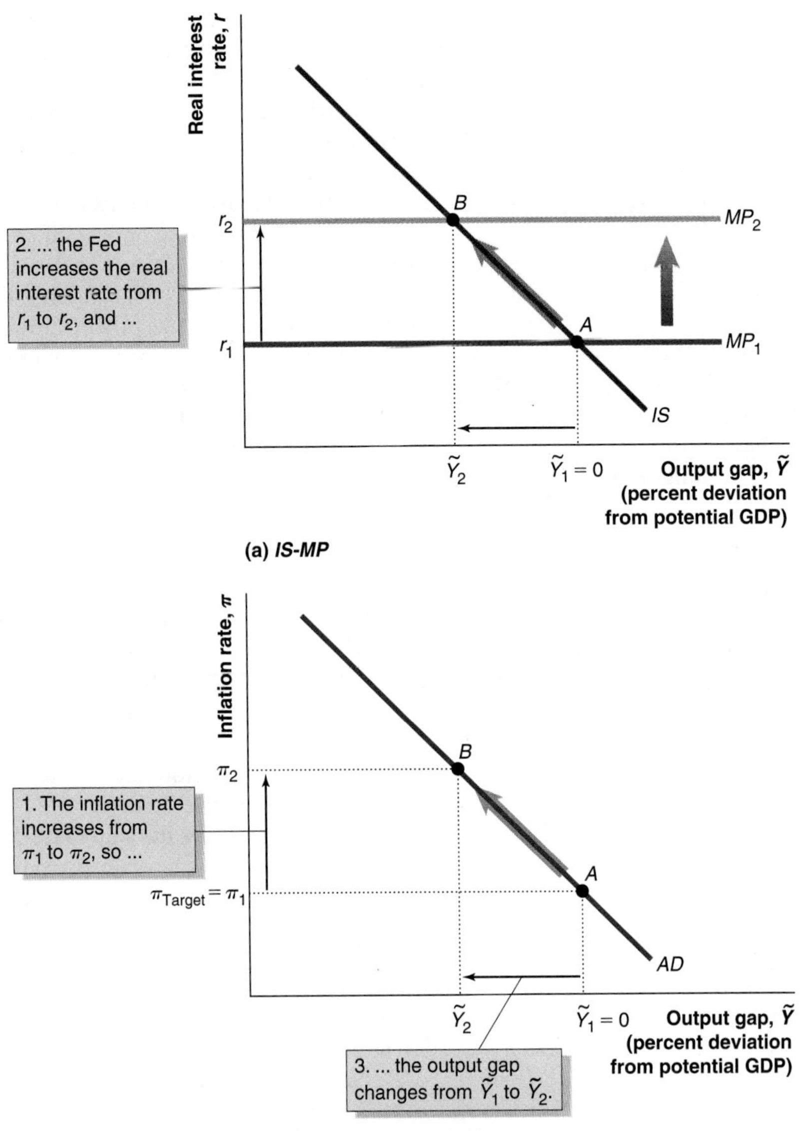

Figure 12.2

Deriving the Aggregate Demand Curve

The aggregate demand curve shows the relationship between aggregate expenditure and the inflation rate, holding the *IS* curve and the monetary policy rule constant. An increase in the inflation rate from π_1 to π_2 in panel (b) causes the Fed to increase the real interest rate, so the *MP* curve shifts from MP_1 to MP_2, causing a movement along the *IS* curve in panel (a). Consumption, investment, and net exports all decline, which reduces real GDP. As a result, the output gap changes from $\tilde{Y}_1$ to $\tilde{Y}_2$, and short-run equilibrium moves from point *A* to point *B* on the *AD* curve. ●

demand curve, which shows that aggregate expenditure is not very sensitive to changes in the inflation rate.

Shifts of the Aggregate Demand Curve

The *AD* curve tells us what happens to the quantity of real GDP demanded if the inflation rate increases, *holding everything else constant.* Therefore, a change in the inflation rate causes a *movement along* a particular *AD* curve. If a factor that would affect the demand for goods and services other than the inflation rate changes, the *AD* curve will *shift* either to the right or to the left.

In deriving the *AD* curve, we assumed that the *IS* curve would remain constant. Anything that causes the *IS* curve to shift to the right will cause the *AD* curve to shift to the right, and anything that causes the *IS* curve to shift to the left will cause the *AD* curve to shift to the left. As we saw in Chapter 9, several factors cause the *IS* curve to shift: changes in autonomous consumption, investment, and government purchases of goods and services, changes in taxes and transfer payments, and changes in net exports. For example, if the government increases spending on infrastructure projects, such as highways and bridges, both the *IS* curve and the *AD* curve would shift to the right. Figure 12.3 shows the effect of an increase in government purchases on the *AD* curve.

In panel (b), the inflation rate equals π_1, and the output gap initially equals $\tilde{Y}_1$, so short-run equilibrium is initially at point *A* on AD_1. Government purchases increase, so in panel (a) the *IS* curve shifts to the right, from IS_1 to IS_2. At the original real interest rate, short-run equilibrium is now at point *B*, and the output gap equals $\tilde{Y}_2$. If the inflation rate remains constant, the new equilibrium combination of the inflation rate and the output gap is π_1 and $\tilde{Y}_2$. Short-run equilibrium is at point *B* in panel (b), which is to the right of the original *AD* curve. Therefore, the *AD* curve must have shifted to the right, from AD_1 to AD_2.

A change in the monetary policy rule will also cause the *AD* curve to shift. There are two key components of the monetary policy rule: the inflation target and the sensitivity of

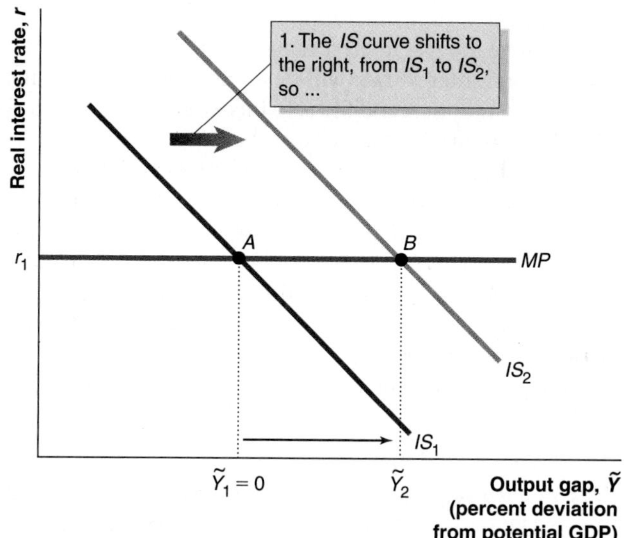

(a) *IS-MP*

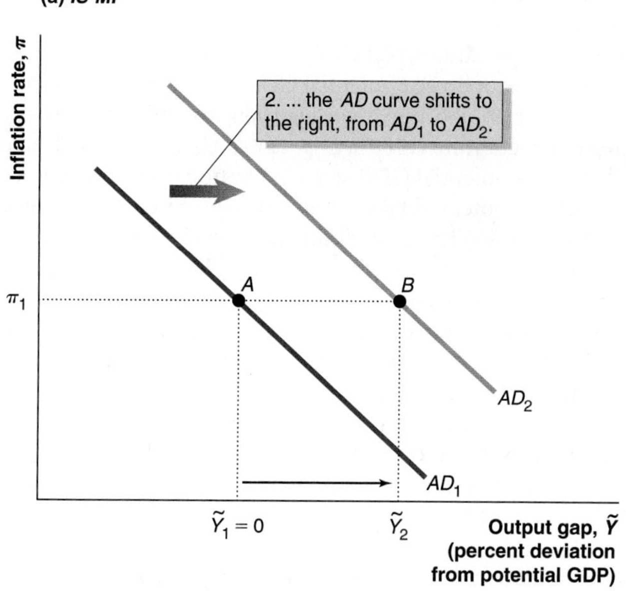

(b) Aggregate demand curve

Figure 12.3

Shifts in the Aggregate Demand Curve: The Case of an Increase in Government Purchases

An increase in government purchases increases aggregate expenditure for any given inflation rate, so the *AD* curve shifts to the right, from AD_1 to AD_2. Any increase in autonomous spending that causes the *IS* curve to shift to the right in panel (a) will also cause the *AD* curve to shift to the right in panel (b). Similarly, any decrease in autonomous spending that causes the *IS* curve to shift to the left will also cause the *AD* curve to shift to the left. ●

the real interest rate to the inflation rate. When either of these two components changes, the *AD* curve will shift. Consider the case when both the target inflation rate and the actual inflation rate equal 2%, so the Fed has no reason to change its target for the real interest rate. Now suppose that the actual inflation rate remains at 2%, but the Fed increases the target inflation rate to 3%. The actual inflation rate is now 1% below the target inflation rate, so the Fed will reduce the real interest rate to increase aggregate expenditure. The increase in aggregate expenditure will shift the *AD* curve to the right.

The Japanese economy has experienced slow growth since the early 1990s. Real GDP in Japan grew at an average annual rate of 4.5% from 1970 to 1991, but it has grown at a rate of less than 1.5% per year since then. Not surprisingly, slow growth has led to low inflation rates. The annual inflation rate in Japan from 1991 to 2010 averaged just 0.2%, and the economy experienced deflation during nine of those years. Some economists have argued that the Bank of Japan has been mistaken in allowing the inflation rate to fall so low. These economists argue that if the Bank of Japan targeted a 2% or 3% rate of inflation, aggregate expenditure would increase, increasing real GDP. This argument is consistent with our discussion of the *AD* curve.

The less the central bank is concerned about deviations of inflation from the target inflation rate, the less sensitive the real interest rate is to the inflation rate. Therefore, for any given inflation rate, the real interest rate will be lower. The lower real interest rate leads households to increase consumption and firms to increase investment, so aggregate expenditure is higher. The decrease in the sensitivity of the real interest rate to the inflation rate will shift the *AD* curve to the right as well.[1] We can think of either an increase in the inflation target or a decrease in the central bank's concern with deviations from this target rate as an expansionary monetary policy that will increase aggregate expenditure, real GDP, and employment. Table 12.1 summarizes the factors that cause the *AD* curve to shift.

We have seen that the *AD* curve builds on the *IS* and *MP* curves from Chapters 9 and 10 and that anything that shifts the *IS* curve shifts the *AD* curve in the same direction. We have also seen that changes in the monetary policy rule will shift the *AD* curve. We can conclude that the aggregate demand curve incorporates the factors underlying the *IS* and *MP* curves in a single curve.

When Are Shifts to the Aggregate Demand Curve Permanent?

In Figure 12.3 on page 453, we used the example of an increase in government purchases to demonstrate a shift to the right of the *AD* curve. This shift is not permanent, and the *AD* curve will eventually shift to the left from AD_2 to AD_1. Why? We know that in long-run equilibrium, aggregate expenditure, real GDP, and potential GDP are all equal. Therefore, aggregate expenditure cannot exceed potential GDP in long-run equilibrium. If point *A* in Figure 12.3 is the long-run equilibrium, then aggregate expenditure equals potential GDP at point *A* and aggregate expenditure is 100% of potential GDP. Suppose that government purchases are initially 20% of potential GDP, so consumption, investment, and net exports are 80% (=100% − 20%) of potential GDP. If government purchases increase from 20% to 25% of potential GDP, and all other expenditures are initially constant, then aggregate expenditure is now 105% (=25% + 80%) of potential GDP. Both the *IS* curve and the *AD* curve shift to the right, and real GDP increases, but this higher real GDP is not a long-run equilibrium because aggregate expenditure cannot remain 105% of potential GDP indefinitely.

There are two ways in which real GDP can return to potential GDP. First, if the increase in government purchases is temporary, government purchases decline back to 20% of potential GDP. The temporary surge in government purchases during wars, such as World War II, is an example of a temporary shift in the *AD* curve. In such cases, aggregate expenditure declines to 100% of potential GDP, and the *AD* curve will shift to

[1]Changes in the responsiveness of the central bank to deviations from the inflation target not only shift the *AD* curve, but also change the slope of the *AD* curve. For simplicity, we focus on the shifts of the *AD* curve.

Table 12.1 **Summary of the Factors That Shift the *AD* Curve**

An increase in . . .	will . . .	so the *AD* curve shifts . . .
aggregate expenditure that is independent of the real interest rate	increase real GDP and the output gap at every inflation rate	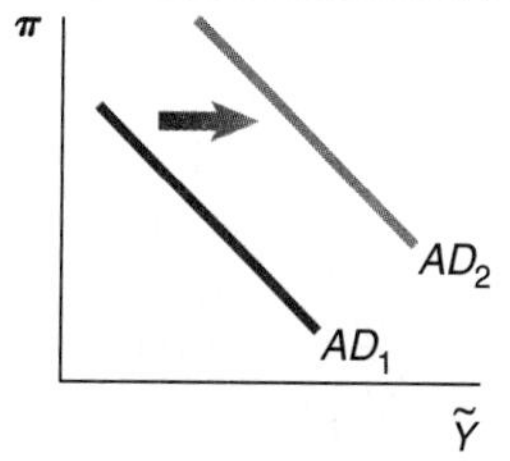 π AD_1 → AD_2 $\tilde{Y}$
the target inflation rate	increase the inflation rate at every level of the output gap	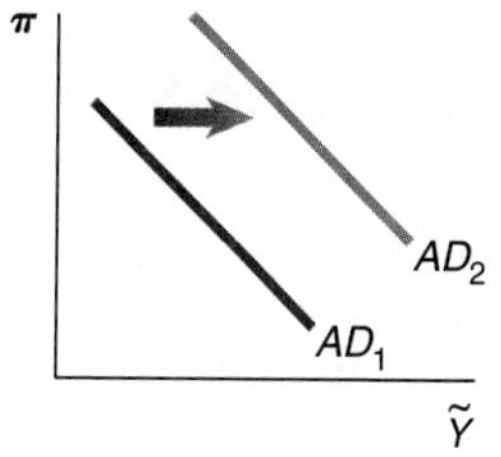 π AD_1 → AD_2 $\tilde{Y}$
the central bank's concern about deviations of inflation from the target inflation rate	decrease the inflation rate at every level of the output gap	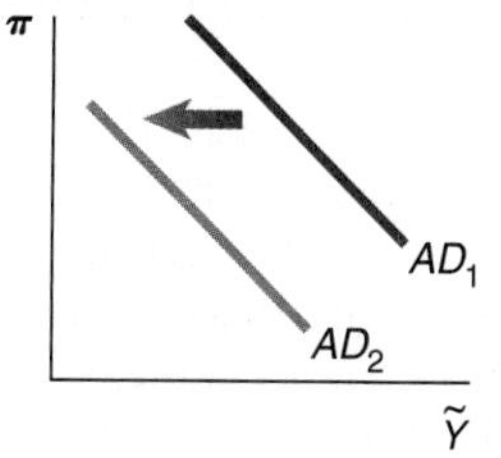 π AD_2 ← AD_1 $\tilde{Y}$

the left, from AD_2 to AD_1, when government purchases decrease. Second, if the increase in government purchases to 25% of potential GDP is permanent, as with a permanent increase in spending on education or highways and bridges, then the sum of consumption, investment, and net exports must decrease to 75% of potential GDP. Our discussion of the loanable funds model in Chapter 3 suggests a mechanism by which this decrease in consumption, investment, and net exports can take place. If the government permanently spends more and financed this spending through deficits, real interest rates would increase, which would cause investment, consumption, and net exports to decrease. If the government chose to finance the increase in government purchases by raising taxes, consumption and investment would decrease. Either way, expenditure by the private sector would decrease in the long run to offset the effect of the increase in government purchases. Irrespective of whether the increase in government purchases is temporary or permanent, the *AD* curve eventually shifts back to its original position. We would reach the same conclusion if consumption, investment, or net exports initially increased to cause the *AD* curve to shift to the right in Figure 12.3. A permanent increase in one component of aggregate expenditure as a share of potential GDP means that one, or some combination, of the other three components of aggregate expenditure must decrease. When this decrease occurs, the *AD* curve shifts back to the left. Therefore, we can conclude that when the economy starts at equilibrium with real GDP equal to potential GDP, changes in autonomous expenditure cause temporary shifts to the *AD* curve.

In contrast to changes in autonomous expenditure, changes in the monetary policy rule cause the *AD* curve to shift permanently. Our example of an increase in the inflation target from 2% to 3% provides an instance. When the central bank announces a higher inflation target, it is announcing that it will accept a higher rate of inflation for any given level of real GDP. For example, when real GDP equals potential GDP, the central bank is willing to accept an inflation rate of 3% rather than 2%. This is also true for any given level of real GDP, so the shift in the *AD* curve is permanent.

When we discuss the complete aggregate demand and aggregate supply model in Section 12.3, it will be important to keep these two results in mind: *Shifts in the* IS *curve temporarily shift the* AD *curve, but changes to the monetary policy rule permanently shift the* AD *curve.* Knowing the difference between permanent and temporary shifts in the *AD* curve helps in understanding how the economy adjusts toward long-run equilibrium. It is also important to note that while the *AD* curve may shift permanently, in the long run, real GDP will always return to its potential level. We will explore the reasons this statement is true in the next section.

12.2

Learning Objective

Explain the relationship between aggregate supply and the Phillips curve.

Aggregate Supply and the Phillips Curve

Aggregate supply (*AS*) curve A curve showing the total quantity of output, or real GDP, that firms are willing and able to supply at a given inflation rate.

We now consider the **aggregate supply (*AS*) curve**, which shows the total quantity of output, or real GDP, that firms are willing and able to supply at a given inflation rate. This definition of the *AS* curve is similar to the definition of the Phillips curve because, in fact, the two curves are the same.[2] As we saw when we first discussed the Phillips curve in Chapter 9, there are three sources of inflationary pressure in the short run: changes in the expected inflation rate, demand shocks, and supply shocks.

The expected inflation rate is important because firms set their prices based on the prices they expect their competitors to charge and the prices they expect to pay their suppliers and employees. If firms expect inflation to increase, they will increase the prices they charge. In this section, we assume that expectations are adaptive in the sense that households and firms expect that the inflation rate from the previous period will persist into the future. For example, if the inflation rate in 2011 is 2%, the expected inflation rate for 2012 will also be 2%. But if the inflation rate rises to 4% in 2012, the expected inflation rate for 2013 will also rise to 4%.

Inflation can occur as a result of a supply shock when, for instance, the price of a key input, such as oil, rises rapidly, and firms pass along some of the price increase to the consumers of final goods and services. An increase in the inflation rate as a result of a supply shock tends to be temporary. For example, a 10% increase in oil prices will increase the inflation rate for a time. But once the economy adjusts to the higher price of oil, the inflation rate will return to its previous level unless oil prices increase again.

Inflation can increase following a demand shock that causes real GDP to increase relative to potential GDP because firms experience capacity constraints as raw materials and labor become harder to find at existing prices. In other words, we would expect a positive relationship between the inflation rate and the output gap. So, just as in Chapter 9, where we drew the Phillips curve as an upward-sloping line, we also draw the aggregate supply curve as an upward-sloping line.

Figure 12.4 shows the aggregate supply curve for an economy. Short-run equilibrium is initially at point *A* with the inflation rate, π_1, equal to the expected inflation rate, π^e, and real GDP equal to potential GDP. If short-run equilibrium moves from point *A* to point *B*, real GDP increases relative to potential GDP, so the output gap changes from $\tilde{Y}_1$ to $\tilde{Y}_2$ and the inflation rate rises from π_1 to π_2. Notice that a change in the output gap causes a *movement along* an aggregate supply curve.

[2]Why two names for the same curve? The traditional name for a curve that relates the inflation rate to the output gap (or to the unemployment rate) is the Phillips curve, which, as explained in Chapter 9, was first derived in the 1950s by the New Zealand economist A. W. H. Phillips. We could have continued to use that name in this chapter, but in the context of a model that includes aggregate demand, it is less confusing to call the curve an aggregate supply curve.

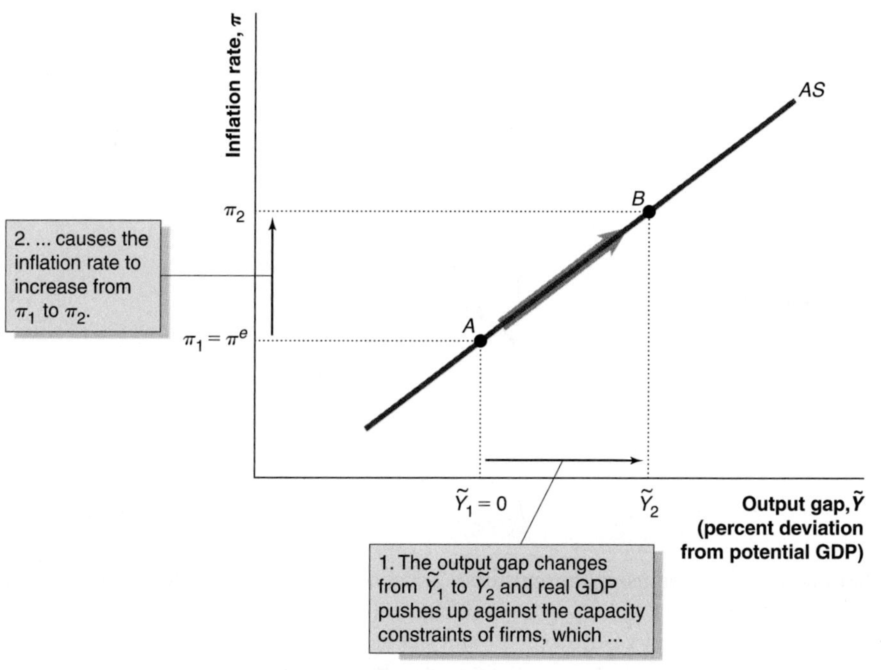
Inflation rate, π
AS
B
A
π_2
$\pi_1 = \pi^e$
2. ... causes the inflation rate to increase from π_1 to π_2.
$\tilde{Y}_1 = 0$
$\tilde{Y}_2$
Output gap, $\tilde{Y}$ (percent deviation from potential GDP)
1. The output gap changes from $\tilde{Y}_1$ to $\tilde{Y}_2$ and real GDP pushes up against the capacity constraints of firms, which ...

Figure 12.4

The Aggregate Supply Curve

The aggregate supply curve is drawn assuming that the expected inflation rate is constant. As aggregate expenditure increases and the output gap changes from $\tilde{Y}_1$ to $\tilde{Y}_2$, real GDP pushes up against the capacity constraints of firms. In response, some firms increase prices, the inflation rate increases from π_1 to π_2, and short-run equilibrium moves from point *A* to point *B* on the *AS* curve. ●

Because the aggregate supply curve is the same as the Phillips curve, we can use the equation for the Phillips curve we developed in Chapter 9 to represent the aggregate supply curve:

$$\pi_t = \pi_t^e + b\tilde{Y}_t - s_t, \tag{12.1}$$

where:

π_t^e = the expected inflation rate
b = the sensitivity of the inflation rate to changes in the output gap
s_t = the effect of supply shocks

A negative sign appears in front of the supply shock term because an increase in oil prices or other negative supply shock increases the inflation rate, and a positive supply shock decreases the inflation rate. We have assumed adaptive expectations, so the expected inflation rate in the current year equals the actual inflation rate in the previous year:

$$\pi_t^e = \pi_{t-1}.$$

We have also assumed that:

$$b > 0$$

because the inflation rate increases as real GDP and the output gap increase.

Shifts in the Aggregate Supply Curve

When we drew the aggregate supply curve in Figure 12.4, we held supply shocks and expected inflation constant. If either of these factors changes, the aggregate supply curve will shift. The experience of the U.S. economy during the 1981–1982 recession provides an example of a shift in the aggregate supply curve. The unemployment rate during the recession of 1981–1982 rose to 10.8%, which is the highest it had been since the Great Depression. There was one positive result from the recession, however: The inflation rate fell dramatically. The

Figure 12.5

A Decrease in Inflationary Expectations and the Aggregate Supply Curve

The expected inflation rate decreases from π_1^e to π_2^e. So, when real GDP equals potential GDP, $\tilde{Y}_1 = 0$, and the value of supply shocks is zero, the inflation rate will decrease from π_1 to π_2. Inflation is now lower for any given level of real GDP, and the *AS* curve shifts down, from AS_1 to AS_2. ●

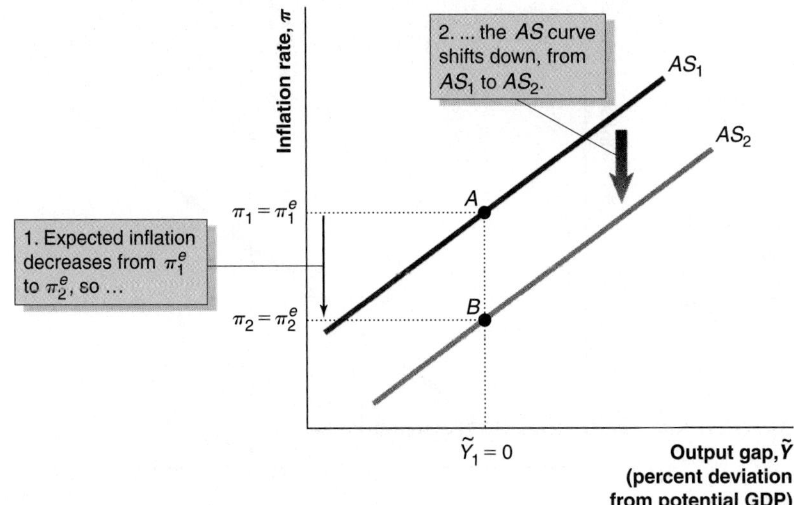

inflation rate, calculated using the consumer price index, fell from 10.8% at the beginning of the 1981–1982 recession to 4.5% by its end. Figure 12.5 illustrates how the severe 1981–1982 recession helped usher in a period of low and stable inflation by reducing the expected inflation rate. The figure shows the effect of a decrease in expected inflation on the aggregate supply curve. A positive supply shock caused by a decrease in oil prices or an increase in productivity growth would have the same effect on the aggregate supply curve.

For simplicity, we assume that the effect of supply shocks is zero. Short-run equilibrium is initially at point *A* on AS_1. Real GDP equals potential GDP, so the output gap is zero, and inflation, π_1, equals expected inflation, π_1^e. Expected inflation decreases to π_2^e, so when real GDP equals potential GDP, $\tilde{Y}_1 = 0$, inflation equals π_2. Short-run equilibrium is at point *B*, which is not on the original *AS* curve. Therefore, the *AS* curve has shifted down, from AS_1 to AS_2. Notice that on AS_2, inflation is now lower for any given level of the output gap, so the economy faces a more favorable trade-off between changes in inflation and changes in the output gap. Table 12.2 summarizes the factors that cause the aggregate supply curve to shift.

Table 12.2 Factors That Shift the Aggregate Supply Curve

An increase in . . .	causes . . .	so the *AS* curve shifts . . .
inflationary expectations	the inflation rate to increase for any given level of the output gap	π, AS_2, AS_1, $\tilde{Y}$
costs of production at every level of output	the inflation rate to increase for any given level of the output gap	π, AS_2, AS_1, $\tilde{Y}$

The Aggregate Demand and Aggregate Supply Model

12.3

Learning Objective

Use the aggregate demand and aggregate supply model to analyze macroeconomic conditions.

The **aggregate demand and aggregate supply (*AD–AS*) model** explains short-run fluctuations in the output gap and in the inflation rate. Unlike the *IS–MP* model from Chapter 9, the *AD–AS* model includes a monetary policy rule so that we can better understand how monetary policy reduces the severity of economic fluctuations. We first discuss how long-run equilibrium is determined in the model and then analyze what factors cause the equilibrium to change.

Aggregate demand and aggregate supply (*AD–AS*) model A model that explains short-run fluctuations in the output gap and the inflation rate.

Equilibrium in the *AD–AS* Model

The long-run equilibrium in the *AD–AS* model is characterized by two conditions—one for real GDP and one for the inflation rate. The economy is in long-run equilibrium when:

1. real GDP equals potential GDP, $\widetilde{Y} = 0$, and
2. the inflation rate equals both the central bank's target inflation rate and the expected inflation rate, $\pi_t = \pi_t^e = \pi_{\text{Target}}$.

Figure 12.6 shows that long-run equilibrium in the *AD–AS* model occurs at point *A*, where the aggregate demand and aggregate supply curves intersect. Point *A* is a long-run equilibrium because real GDP equals potential GDP, so the output gap is zero, and the inflation rate equals both the expected inflation rate and the Fed's target inflation rate.

We are most interested in using the *AD–AS* model to explain how the output gap and the inflation rate respond to shocks—exogenous events that affect the economy, such as a surge in oil prices, a change in the monetary policy rule, or a collapse in stock prices. To accomplish this goal, we first explain how the economy responds to shifts in the aggregate supply curve, and then we discuss how the economy responds to shifts in the aggregate demand curve.

The Effects of a Supply Shock

In 1983, James Hamilton of the University of California, San Diego showed that seven of the eight post-World War II recessions up to that time had been preceded by a large and sudden increase in the price of oil.[3] Since the publication of Hamilton's article, the U.S. economy has experienced three more recessions: 1990–1991, 2001, and 2007–2009. All three recessions were associated with large and sudden increases in the price of oil. For example, the price of oil doubled after Iraq's invasion of Kuwait in August 1990. Many economists believe that the increase in oil prices associated with the invasion was a critical factor in causing the recession.

Many economists are convinced that oil prices play an important role in causing recessions. Many economists also believe that oil price increases play an important role in causing **stagflation**, which is a period of both high inflation and recession, usually resulting from a supply shock. The classic case of stagflation is the severe 1973–1975 global recession. The world economy experienced an oil shock in late 1973, after the Organization of the Petroleum Exporting Countries (OPEC) imposed an oil embargo in response to U.S. and European support of Israel in the 1973 Arab–Israeli War. The price of a barrel of oil rose from \$4.31 during December 1973 to \$10.11 during January 1974—a 135% increase in just one month! Such a large increase in the price of a key input generates inflation as firms try to pass along the higher price of oil to consumers in the form of higher prices for final goods and services. In the United States, real GDP fell from a

Stagflation A combination of high inflation and recession, usually resulting from a supply shock such as an increase in the price of oil.

[3]James Hamilton, "Oil and the Macroeconomy Since World War II," *Journal of Political Economy*, Vol. 91, No. 2, April 1983, pp. 228–248.

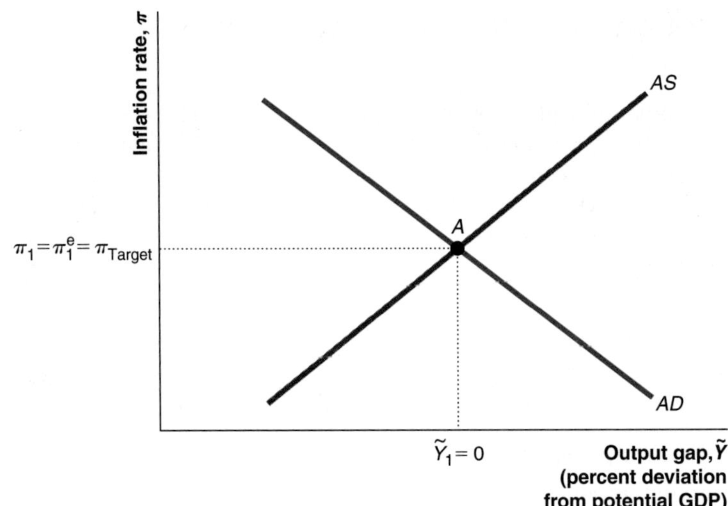

Figure 12.6

Equilibrium in the Aggregate Demand and Aggregate Supply Model

Point *A* represents a long-run equilibrium because real GDP equals potential GDP, and the inflation rate equals both the expected inflation rate and the Fed's target inflation rate. ●

level 4.5% *above* potential GDP during the second quarter of 1973 to a level 4.7% *below* potential GDP during the first quarter of 1975. Inflation rose from 6.6% during the second quarter of 1973 to 12.2% during the fourth quarter of 1974. In contrast to most prior recessions, inflation actually rose substantially during the 1973–1975 recession, so the U.S. economy experienced stagflation.

We can use the *AD–AS* model to show the effects of supply shocks on the economy. Figure 12.7 shows how an economy adjusts to a supply shock. For simplicity, we assume that oil prices increase during the first period and then remain constant—so the supply shock increases inflation during the first period, but not after that. In panel (a), the economy starts off at long-run equilibrium at point *A*, where real GDP equals potential GDP, and the inflation rate, the expected inflation rate, and the target inflation rate are equal. The increase in the price of oil is a negative supply shock, so the inflation rate increases. If the output gap remained at $\tilde{Y}_1 = 0$, the inflation rate would increase to $\pi_1^e - s_1$. However, following its monetary policy rule, the Fed reacts to the supply shock by increasing the real interest rate, which reduces consumption and investment. As a result of this decline in aggregate expenditure, real GDP declines and the output gap changes to $\tilde{Y}_2$, so the inflation rate increases only to π_2 in panel (a). The *AS* curve shifts up from AS_1 to AS_2, and the economy's short-run equilibrium is at point *B*.

Oil prices stop rising after the first period, so the supply shock is now zero, but the *AS* curve does not immediately shift back to AS_1. Because π_2 is greater than π_1, the actual inflation rate is greater than the expected inflation rate. We are assuming that households and firms have adaptive expectations, so the expected inflation rate increases. So, we now have $\pi_2 = \pi_2^e$ when real GDP equals potential GDP. As a result, the *AS* curve in panel (b) shifts down, from AS_2 to AS_3. This shift puts downward pressure on inflation. Following its monetary policy rule, the Fed reduces the real interest rate, so consumption and investment increase, which causes real GDP to increase as well. The new short-run equilibrium is at point *C*, where the output gap is now $\tilde{Y}_3$ and the inflation rate has fallen to π_3. Point *C* is not yet a long-run equilibrium, so the adjustment process continues. Because $\pi_3 < \pi_2^e$ and expectations are adaptive, expected inflation again decreases. As a result, the *AS* curve shifts down from AS_3 back toward the initial *AS* curve, AS_1. This shift allows the Fed to reduce the real interest rate again, so aggregate expenditure and real GDP increase causing the output gap to move closer to 0. This adjustment process continues until eventually the economy is back at the initial long-run equilibrium at point *A*.

We can see from Figure 12.7 that the initial effect of a supply shock is both higher inflation and lower real GDP relative to potential GDP. In other words, our model predicts

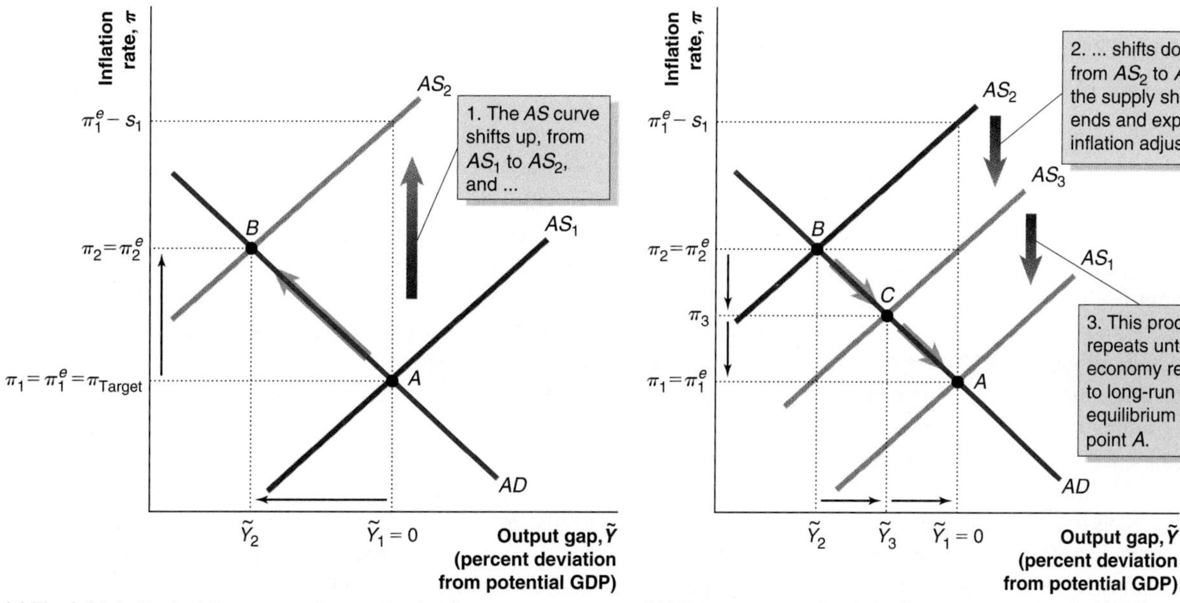

Figure 12.7 The Long-Run and Short-Run Effects of a Supply Shock

In panel (a), a supply shock causes the *AS* curve to shift up from AS_1 to AS_2. Eventually, the expected inflation rate adjusts to the actual inflation rate. In panel (b), the decline in the expected inflation rate causes the *AS* curve to shift back down, and the economy moves back toward potential GDP. Therefore, in response to a supply shock, there is no trade-off between inflation and unemployment in either the short run or the long run. ●

that an increase in oil prices can cause periods of stagflation similar to the 1973–1975 recession. The *AD–AS* model also makes another important point: With higher inflation, real GDP initially decreases, so the unemployment rate initially increases as the inflation rate increases. Therefore, there is no trade-off between inflation and unemployment—even in the short run—in response to a supply shock.

The Effect of a Change in the Monetary Policy Rule

In Chapter 10, we explained how the Fed may have difficulty carrying out an expansionary monetary policy when the short-term nominal interest rate reaches zero. The inability of the Fed to lower interest rates to negative values is called the *zero bound constraint.* In that case, other channels of monetary policy may still operate, such as quantitative easing and the bank lending channel. Changing the target inflation rate provides another possible channel through which the central bank can affect real GDP and employment when facing a zero bound constraint. In their discussion of monetary policy in Japan during the 1990s, Nobel Laureate Paul Krugman of Princeton University and other economists suggested that the Bank of Japan should increase expected inflation by increasing the target inflation rate. We can use the *AD–AS* model to explain how changing the target inflation rate can provide the central bank with another way to affect the economy when facing a zero bound constraint.

Nominal interest rates cannot fall below zero, but real interest rates *can.* Recall that the expression for the expected real interest rate is $r = i - \pi^e$. So, the real interest rate can become negative if the expected inflation rate is greater than the nominal interest rate. For example, suppose that the nominal interest rate is 0%, and expected inflation and target inflation equal 2%. In this case, the expected real interest rate is $-2\% \ (=0\% - 2\%)$. If the Fed announces that it has increased the target inflation rate to 5% and households and

MACRO DATA: ARE OIL SUPPLY SHOCKS REALLY THAT IMPORTANT?

Research by Lutz Kilian of the University of Michigan challenges the view that the OPEC oil embargo and other cost shocks caused the stagflation of the 1970s. Kilian believes that once you measure oil supply shocks correctly, they account for very little of the quarter-to-quarter fluctuation in nominal oil prices. Kilian points out that the prices for many industrial commodities were rising during the early 1970s due to increases in worldwide demand driven by increases in global real GDP prior to the oil embargo. So, Kilian argues that most of the nominal oil price increase during the period was due to *demand* factors rather than supply factors.

Kilian's research also shows that a 10% reduction in oil supply has little effect on either the growth rate of U.S. real GDP or the inflation rate, calculated using the CPI. During the first year following a reduction in the supply of oil, real GDP growth does not respond much. But during the second year, the growth rate of real GDP decreases by up to 2.5 percentage points. The effect on inflation is even smaller. The oil supply shock increases CPI inflation by only about 1 percentage point six to nine months after the shock. These effects are much smaller than macroeconomists had previously believed, and they are too small to have caused the stagflation of the 1970s.

If not oil prices, then what did cause the stagflation of the 1970s? Kilian and Robert Barsky of the University of Michigan argue that "stop-and-go" monetary policy caused the stagflation. According to their view, in 1972 the Fed stimulated the economy, thereby causing both real GDP and the inflation rate to increase. When the Fed became concerned about the rising inflation rate, it increased interest rates in 1973 and inadvertently caused a recession. Inflation is sluggish and adjusts slowly to monetary policy, so the inflation rate continued to increase even as the economy entered a recession. The result was that the economy experienced stagflation.

Athanasios Orphanides, an economist and the current governor of the Central Bank of Cyprus, argues that poor policy decisions due to measurement problems caused the inflation rate to increase. Policymakers receive economic data with a lag, and the initial estimates for key variables such as inflation and the output gap are often incorrect. Orphanides looked at the data available to policymakers *at the time they made their decisions* and found that up to 1.5 percentage points of the increase in the inflation rate during the 1970s were due to incorrect estimates of the inflation rate and up to 5 percentage points of the increase in the inflation rate were due to incorrect estimates of the output gap. We discuss the possibility that monetary policy caused the poor economic performance during the 1970s in greater detail in the next section.

While most economists continue to believe that an oil price shock was the main reason for the stagflation of the mid-1970s, the effect of oil price shocks on the economy remains an active area of macroeconomic research.

Sources: Lutz Kilian, "Exogenous Oil Supply Shocks: How Big Are They and How Much Do They Matter for the U.S. Economy?" *Review of Economics and Statistics*, Vol. 90, No. 2, May 2008, pp. 216–240; Lutz Kilian and Robert Barsky, "Do We Really Know That Oil Caused the Great Stagflation? A Monetary Alternative," in Ben Bernanke and Kenneth Rogoff, eds., *NBER Macroeconomics Annual*, Cambridge, MA: MIT Press, 2001, pp. 137–183; and Athanasios Orphanides, "The Quest for Prosperity Without Inflation," *Journal of Monetary Economics*, Vol. 50, No. 3, April 2003, pp. 633–663.

Test your understanding by doing related problem 3.10 on page 482 at the end of this chapter.

firms believe the Fed will meet its target, the expected real interest rate will decrease to $-5\% (= 0\% - 5\%)$. Therefore, all else being equal, the announcement of a higher inflation target will decrease the expected real interest rate. The lower real interest rate will increase consumption, investment, and net exports, resulting in increases in real GDP and employment.

Figure 12.8 shows how we can use the *AD–AS* model to explain the effect of a change in the monetary policy rule. The economy starts off in long-run equilibrium at point *A*, with real GDP equal to potential GDP and the actual inflation rate, the expected inflation rate, and the initial target inflation rate all equal. Now suppose that the Fed

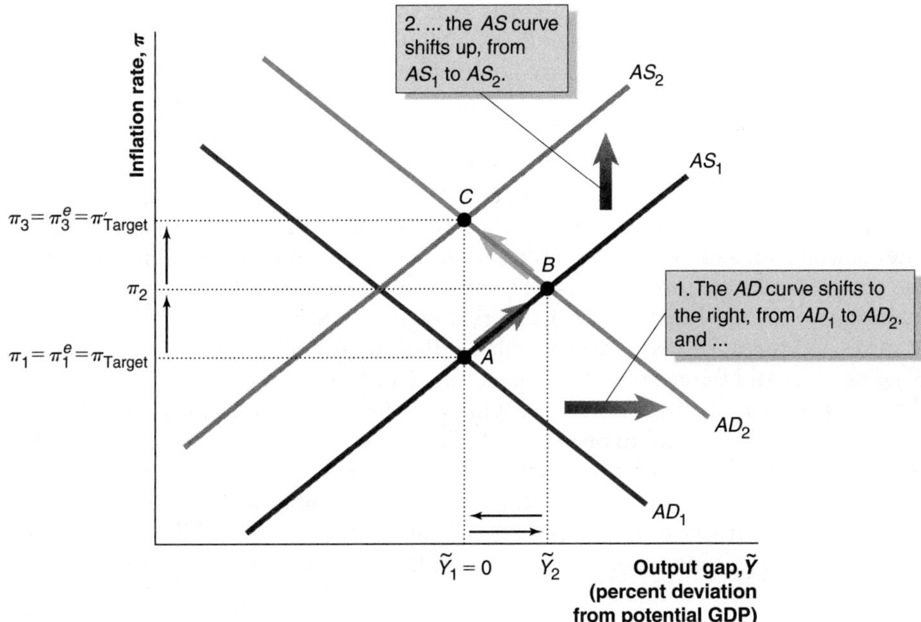

Figure 12.8

The Long-Run and Short-Run Effects of an Increase in the Target Inflation Rate

From an initial long-run equilibrium at point *A*, the Fed decides to increase the target inflation rate by lowering the real interest rate, which shifts the *AD* curve to the right, from AD_1 to AD_2. As a result, the economy moves to a new short-run equilibrium at point *B*, with a higher inflation rate, increased real GDP, and a lower unemployment rate: There is a short-run trade-off between inflation and unemployment. Eventually, the expected inflation rate increases, which causes the *AS* curve to shift up, from AS_1 to AS_2. The economy returns to long-run equilibrium at point *C*, with real GDP equal to potential GDP, so the output gap equals 0. At point *C*, the inflation rate equals the new higher target inflation rate. The result is a higher inflation rate and no change in unemployment. The trade-off between inflation and unemployment disappears in the long run. ●

increases the target inflation rate from π_{Target} to π'_{Target}. The initial interest rate will be too high for the Fed to hit the new higher target inflation rate, so the Fed will have to decrease the real interest rate. The lower real interest rate causes consumption and investment to rise, so the *AD* curve shifts to the right, from AD_1 to AD_2, and real GDP increases, causing the output gap to move to $\tilde{Y}_2$. The economy is now in short-run equilibrium at point *B*. Note that at point *B*, with a higher level of real GDP, the unemployment rate will be lower than it was at point *A*. Point *B* is not a long-run equilibrium, however, because real GDP is above potential GDP and the actual inflation rate, π_2, is greater than the expected inflation rate, π_1^e. Because expectations are adaptive, the expected inflation rate will increase, and the *AS* curve will shift up, from AS_1 to AS_2. As the *AS* curve shifts up, the output gap moves back to zero and the inflation rate increases to the new target inflation rate, π'_{Target}. The economy is in a new long-run equilibrium at point *C*, where the output gap is zero and the inflation rate equals both the expected inflation rate and the target inflation rate.

Figure 12.8 shows that a central bank can temporarily increase real GDP and decrease the unemployment rate by announcing a higher inflation target. The model makes another important point: In the short run, the central bank can achieve a higher level of real GDP and a lower unemployment rate by tolerating a higher inflation rate. However, once the expected inflation rate adjusts, real GDP will return to potential GDP, and the unemployment rate will increase back to its initial level. *As a result, there is no trade-off between the inflation rate and the unemployment rate in the long run. In fact, even to achieve a temporarily higher level of real GDP and a lower unemployment rate, a central bank has to accept a permanently higher inflation rate.* Our discussion of the Phillips curve in Chapter 9 pointed out that Nobel Laureates Milton Friedman and Edmund Phelps independently made this argument in 1968 before most of the increase in the inflation rate resulting from the expansionary monetary policy of the 1960s had actually occurred.

As mentioned earlier, many central banks have either a formal or informal inflation target of about 2% because the costs of inflation are thought to be relatively small when the inflation rate is low and stable. However, Japan's experience of slow growth and low inflation since the 1990s and the slow growth in many countries during and after the

2007–2009 recession led some economists to advocate an increase in the target inflation rate above 2%. We have already seen that a higher inflation target can increase real GDP and employment when the short-term nominal interest rate reaches zero.

More recently, Olivier Blanchard, chief economist of the International Monetary Fund (IMF), along with IMF economists Giovanni Dell'Ariccia and Paolo Mauro, have argued that central banks around the world should permanently increase the target inflation rate from 2% to 4%.[4] Blanchard, Dell'Ariccia, and Mauro believe that the costs of inflation are still low when the inflation rate is 4%, but with a higher expected inflation rate, central banks can cut interest rates more before the interest rate reaches zero and the central banks are forced to resort to nontraditional monetary policy tools such as quantitative easing. Most central bankers disagree with Blanchard, Dell'Ariccia, and Mauro's argument for permanently higher inflation rates. For example, Fed Chairman Ben Bernanke and European Central Bank President Jean-Claude Trichet have suggested that a higher inflation target would be counterproductive because, as we saw in Chapter 6, higher inflation rates tend to be more volatile. When the volatility of the inflation rate increases, it becomes harder to predict, so it is more likely that fluctuations in the inflation rate will cause arbitrary redistributions in wealth. Central bankers may never adopt higher inflation targets, but the fact that economists raised the possibility indicates how the 2007–2009 recession has forced economists to rethink their policy advice.

Making the Connection

The End of Stagflation and the Volcker Recession

Paul Volcker was chairman of the Federal Reserve from August 1979 to August 1987. During his tenure, the United States experienced two recessions. One of these, the severe 1981–1982 recession, became known as the "Volcker Recession" because many commentators have argued that the Federal Reserve deliberately caused the recession. Volcker denies the charge. "We didn't deliberately go out to create a recession. You recognize that there are risks to things happening, but you don't deliberately do it." There is no doubt that Volcker and the Fed took strong action to bring down the actual and expected inflation rates by allowing the nominal federal funds rate to increase to 22% by the end of 1980. The Fed may have taken this unprecedented action to convince the public that it was serious about bringing down the inflation rate. Normally, the inflation rate falls during a recession, but the inflation rate rose during the 1973–1975 and 1980 recessions, remaining above 12% at the end of the 1980 recession. As a result, many people thought the Fed was not serious about keeping inflation low, so the expected inflation rate was also high.

There did not appear to be a short-run trade-off between inflation and unemployment during the 1970s. Such a trade-off, though, assumes that the aggregate supply curve is constant while the aggregate demand curve shifts. Figure 12.7 on page 461 shows that if the aggregate supply curve shifts up, as it did during the 1970s due to an increase in oil prices, the inflation rate increases and real GDP decreases. The decrease in real GDP leads to an increase in unemployment. So, the apparent lack of a short-run trade-off between inflation and unemployment during the 1970s is most likely the result of negative supply shocks during that decade.

The interest rate increases slowed the economy, but Volcker believed that they were necessary. "I . . . felt that in the long run, there wasn't any question that the economy was

---

[4]Olivier Blanchard, Giovanni Dell'Ariccia, and Paolo Mauro, "Rethinking Macroeconomic Policy," IMF Staff Position Note, February 12, 2010.

going to operate more efficiently; productivity would be greater; you would have less instability in the future if you could manage to stabilize prices. . . . I think the evidence is at least consistent with that view."

We can think of Volcker's determination to bring the inflation rate down as a decrease in the inflation target, which will shift the *AD* curve to the left and cause both the inflation rate and real GDP to decrease. The decrease in real GDP will cause the unemployment rate to increase, which is what happened. The inflation rate fell from 10.8% during the first month of the recession in July 1981 to 3.8% during the month after the recession ended in December 1982. In contrast, the unemployment rate rose dramatically during the same period, from 7.2% in July 1981 to 10.8% in December 1982. The inflation rate fell as the unemployment rate rose, so the short-run trade-off between inflation and unemployment had reappeared.

Because the Fed was willing to tolerate such a severe recession, many economists believe that the 1981–1982 recession provided an effective signal of the Fed's determination to bring down the inflation rate. "The markets had incredible confidence in Paul," says William N. Griggs, managing director of Griggs & Santow, a financial advisory firm. "Investors saw him as the one guy with the knowledge, guts and skill to stop inflation and hold the system together." As a result, the expected inflation rate decreased, and the inflation rate remained low for the rest of the 1980s. Since then, it has not been close to the double-digit rates of the stagflation period.

Sources: U.S. Bureau of Economic Analysis; U.S. Bureau of Labor Statistics; Board of Governors of the Federal Reserve System; Leonard Silk, "Volcker on the Crash," *New York Times*, November 8, 1987; and "Paul Volcker Interview," *The First Measured Century*, PBS, 2000, www.pbs.org/fmc/interviews/volcker.htm.

Test your understanding by doing related problem 3.8 on page 482 at the end of this chapter.

The Effect of a Demand Shock

In the mid-1990s, innovations in information and communications technology, such as development of the World Wide Web and the rapid decline in the prices of personal computers, encouraged optimism about the future profits of Internet-based firms. Investors rushed to purchase the stocks of firms such as Amazon, Yahoo, and American Online (AOL). The stocks of many technology companies trade on the NASDAQ stock market, and the NASDAQ stock index soared from 743.58 on January 2, 1995, to 5,048.62 on March 10, 2000—a 579% increase in just five years. The rise was so rapid that the period became known as the *dot-com bubble.* Unfortunately for investors, the expected profits from many Internet firms, such as eToys and Pets.com, failed to materialize, and beginning in the spring of 2000, investors fled Internet stocks. By October 2002, the NASDAQ index had declined to 1,100. The collapse of the dot-com bubble resulted in the Dow Jones Industrial Average and the Standard & Poor's 500 declining sharply as well. The collapse in stock prices had two important effects on the economy: It reduced household wealth, which led households to reduce consumption, and it increased uncertainty about the future, which decreased firms' willingness to invest and further decreased the willingness of households to consume. The decrease in consumption and investment helped contribute to the recession that began in March 2001.

In Figure 12.9, we use the *AD–AS* model to show the effect of a negative demand shock such as a stock market crash. The initial long-run equilibrium occurs at point *A*, where the output gap equals zero and the inflation rate, the expected inflation rate, and the target inflation rate are all equal. The collapse in stock prices causes the *AD* curve to shift to the left, from AD_1 to AD_2, so the economy's equilibrium moves from point *A* to point *B* in panel (a). The economy enters a recession, with real GDP declining,

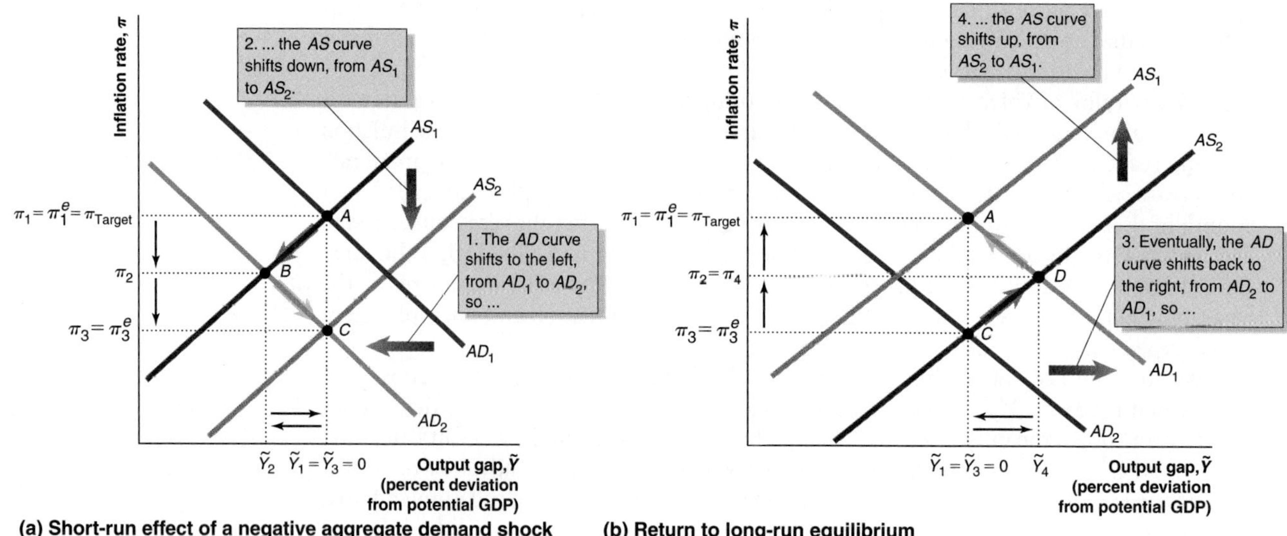

Inflation rate, π
2. ... the AS curve shifts down, from AS_1 to AS_2.
AS_1
AS_2
$\pi_1 = \pi_1^e = \pi_{Target}$
A
B
C
π_2
$\pi_3 = \pi_3^e$
1. The AD curve shifts to the left, from AD_1 to AD_2, so ...
AD_1
AD_2
$\tilde{Y}_2$ $\tilde{Y}_1 = \tilde{Y}_3 = 0$
Output gap, $\tilde{Y}$ (percent deviation from potential GDP)
(a) Short-run effect of a negative aggregate demand shock
4. ... the AS curve shifts up, from AS_2 to AS_1.
$\pi_2 = \pi_4$
D
3. Eventually, the AD curve shifts back to the right, from AD_2 to AD_1, so ...
$\tilde{Y}_1 = \tilde{Y}_3 = 0$ $\tilde{Y}_4$
(b) Return to long-run equilibrium

Figure 12.9 Short-Run and Long-Run Effects of a Negative Demand Shock

Panel (a) shows the effect of a negative demand shock, such as a decrease in stock market wealth, which temporarily shifts the *AD* curve to the left, from AD_1 to AD_2, and the economy's equilibrium is at point *B*. As expected inflation decreases, the *AS* curve shifts down from AS_1 to AS_2, and the economy's equilibrium moves to point *C*. However, eventually the *AD* curve shifts back to the right from AD_2 to AD_1 in panel (b), so the economy's equilibrium is at point *D* and experiences an expansion. Expected inflation adjusts again, so the AS curve shifts up from AS_2 to AS_1, and the economy's equilibrium is at point *A*, which is the long run equilibrium. Therefore, a negative demand shock causes a pattern of recession and expansion. ●

causing the output gap to move from $\tilde{Y}_1$ to $\tilde{Y}_2$. At point *B*, the actual inflation rate, π_2, is less than the expected inflation rate, π_1. Because expectations are adaptive, the expected inflation rate will decrease, and the *AS* curve will shift down, from AS_1 to AS_2. The decrease in the inflation rate allows the Fed to decrease the real interest rate, so consumption and investment increase, increasing real GDP. The new short-run equilibrium is at point *C*.

Point *C* is not a long-run equilibrium because the inflation rate is now less than the Fed's target inflation rate. How does the economy return to long-run equilibrium? Recall that shifts in the *IS* curve cause temporary shifts of the *AD* curve. A decrease in stock prices shifts the *IS* curve, so it causes a temporary shift of the *AD* curve. In the long run, though, the *AD* curve will shift to the right, from AD_2 back to AD_1. Short-run equilibrium moves to point *D* in panel (b). Real GDP increases, moving the output gap from $\tilde{Y}_3$ to $\tilde{Y}_4$; in other words, the economy experiences an expansion as it recovers from the recession caused by the demand shock. The actual inflation rate, π_4, is greater than the expected inflation rate, π_3^e. Because expectations are adaptive, the expected inflation rate increases, and the *AS* curve shifts up, from AS_2 to AS_1. The economy is back in long-run equilibrium at point *A* where the output gap equals zero and the inflation rate, the expected inflation rate, and the target inflation rate are all equal. We can conclude that the collapse in stock prices causes a recession, but the model shows that the economy will eventually adjust, leading to an expansion that restores long-run equilibrium at potential GDP.

Figure 12.9 shows the short-run and long-run effects of a negative demand shock. Demand shocks *temporarily* change real GDP and the output gap. Eventually the economy adjusts to move real GDP back to potential GDP, so the output gap always returns to zero, and the inflation rate returns to the target inflation rate.

Solved Problem 12.3

Applying the *AD–AS* Model to an Increase in Housing Construction

How can we show a positive aggregate demand shock using the *AD–AS* model? In the mid-2000s, the U.S. economy underwent a housing boom. Use the *AD–AS* model to analyze the short-run and long-run effects on real GDP and inflation of the surge in residential construction.

Solving the Problem

Step 1 Review the chapter material. The problem asks you to use the *AD–AS* model to determine the effect of an increase in residential construction on real GDP and inflation, so you may want to review the section "The Effect of a Demand Shock," which begins on page 465.

Step 2 Draw an *AD-AS* graph that shows the initial equilibrium and discuss which curve will shift as a result of the positive demand shock. Your graph should show the initial equilibrium as point *A*, where the aggregate demand and aggregate supply curves intersect:

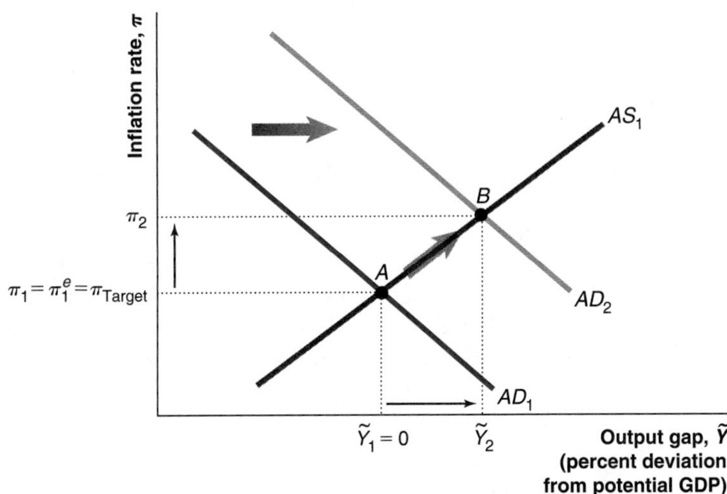

At point *A*, real GDP equals potential GDP, and the inflation rate equals the target inflation rate and the expected inflation rate. So, point *A* is a long-run equilibrium. New residential construction is one of the components of investment, so the housing boom causes aggregate expenditure to increase, and the *AD* curve shifts to the right, from AD_1 to AD_2. Your graph should show that the economy's new short-run equilibrium is at point *B*.

Step 3 Explain the move back to potential GDP. Point *B* is not a long-run equilibrium because the output gap is greater than 0, and the inflation rate is greater than the expected inflation rate. In our earlier examples, we saw that when the actual inflation rate is greater than the expected inflation rate, the expected inflation rate will adjust, shifting the aggregate supply curve, which will return the output gap to 0. Expectations are adaptive, and your graph should show $\pi_2 > \pi_1^e$, so the expected inflation rate will increase. The *AS* curve shifts up, from AS_1 to AS_2. Following its policy rule, the Fed increases the real interest rate as the inflation rate increases, so the output gap moves back to zero. The relative profitability of residential housing is still high so firms still want to produce more housing at any given real interest rate, but now the real interest rate is higher so the output gap is zero. Your graph should show that the economy's new equilibrium is at point *C*.

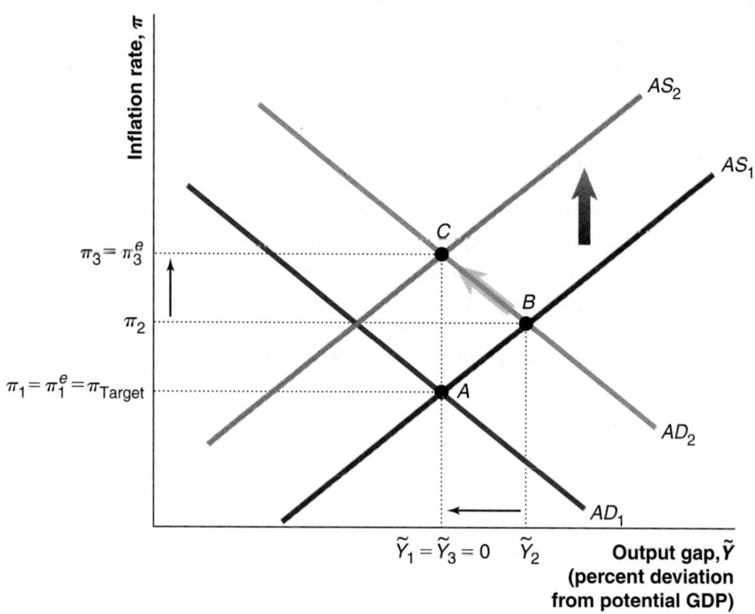

Step 4 Explain how the aggregate demand curve shifts to restore long-run equilibrium. Even though the output gap is 0, point *C* is not a long-run equilibrium because $\pi_3 > \pi_{Target}$. At first, firms wanted to build more residential housing at every given level of the real interest rate. Eventually, the profitability of new residential housing decreases, so the demand shock ends and the AD curve shifts to the left, from AD_2 to AD_1. Therefore, you should draw a new graph and show a new equilibrium at the intersection of AD_1 and AS_2. Now the short-run equilibrium is at point *D*, so real GDP is less than its potential level.

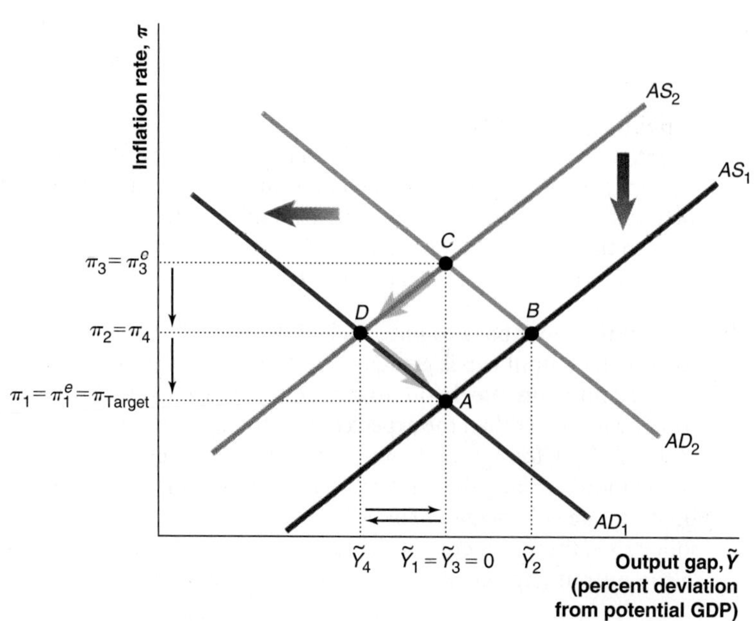

Step 5 Explain the move back toward long-run equilibrium: The aggregate supply curve shifts again. When discussing the economy's adjustment back to potential GDP, we have focused on expected inflation and the aggregate supply curve. Because expectations are adaptive and $\pi_4 < \pi_3^e$, the expected inflation rate decreases, and the *AS* curve shifts down, from AS_2 to AS_1. The economy's equilibrium is now at point *A*, which is the long-run equilibrium: Real GDP equals potential GDP, and the inflation rate equals both the expected inflation rate and the Fed's target inflation rate.

For more practice, do related problem 3.9 on page 482 at the end of this chapter.

Rational Expectations and Policy Ineffectiveness

12.4
Learning Objective
Define rational expectations and explain how it affects policymaking.

In Section 12.3, we saw that by increasing its target for the inflation rate, the Fed can cause real GDP to increase above its potential level temporarily. If the central bank is willing to accept the costs associated with permanently higher inflation, the central bank can increase real GDP and employment temporarily. In arriving at this result, though, we assumed that expectations are adaptive. In our example, expected inflation always lagged behind actual inflation, and expectations only caught up with actual inflation in the new long-run equilibrium. But is the assumption of adaptive expectations the right assumption? Firms have to forecast the inflation rate to determine the prices that maximize profits, so the assumption of adaptive expectations implies that firms are consistently making costly pricing mistakes that reduce profits. Similarly, households have to forecast the inflation rate when deciding where to accept a job offer at a particular annual salary or when calculating the real interest rate they will be paying on a car loan or home mortgage.

Consider a simple example to show the costs a firm may incur from using adaptive expectations. Suppose that the Fed has a target inflation rate of 2%, that the Fed always hits its target for inflation, and that inflation has been 2% for several years. Furthermore, assume that Apple Inc. sets the price of a basic model for the iPad at $500 and wants to keep the real price of the iPad constant in order to maximize profits. That is, the firm wants to increase the price of its product at the same rate as the inflation rate. In 2011, the nominal and real prices of the iPad equaled $500, and inflation in 2011 was 2%—so the firm expects that inflation will be 2% in 2012.

What is the profit-maximizing price for 2012? Based on expected inflation of 2%, Apple should set the price in 2012 at $510. Now suppose that the Fed announces on January 1, 2012, that it will decrease its target for inflation to 0%, so the actual profit-maximizing price turns out to be $500. In this scenario, a firm with adaptive expectations will ignore the new information about the Fed's target inflation rate and continue to expect 2% inflation. If Apple has adaptive expectations, it will set its price too high, so Apple will lose customers to its competitors and fail to maximize profits. Apple would make a costly pricing mistake by ignoring the Fed's announcement that it intended to reduce the target inflation rate.

Pricing mistakes are costly, so households and firms have an incentive to forecast inflation accurately. As a result, many economists argue that it makes sense to assume that households and firms have *rational expectations.* **Rational expectations** is the assumption that people make forecasts of future values of a variable using all available information. In our previous example, if Apple has rational expectations, then it would take into account the Fed's announcement of a new lower target for the inflation rate and following the Fed's announcement, Apple would set the price of the iPad at $500. For Apple, $500 is the profit-maximizing price. In contrast, if Apple had adaptive expectations, then it would set the price of the iPad too high, lose customers, and fail to maximize profits. Rational expectations are consistent with profit maximization, while adaptive expectations may not be. As a result, many economists believe that rational expectations may better describe the way households and firms form expectations than do adaptive expectations.

Rational expectations The assumption that people make forecasts of future values of a variable using all available information; formally, the assumption that expectations equal optimal forecasts, using all available information.

The rational expectations assumption is closely associated with new classical theories of the business cycle that we discussed in Chapter 8. As we discuss next, the assumption of rational expectations led many new classical economists to a surprising conclusion about the effectiveness of monetary policy.

Rational Expectations and Anticipated Policy Changes

Central bank credibility The degree to which households and firms believe the central bank's announcements about future policy.

Suppose that the Fed announces that it will permanently increase its target inflation rate and that households and firms believe the announcement. That is, there is strong **central bank credibility**, which is the degree to which households and firms believe the central bank's announcements about future policy. In this case, we are assuming that the policy is announced and credible, so we can say that the policy change represents an *anticipated policy* change. With adaptive expectations, expectations of inflation adjust slowly because the *actual inflation rate* has to change before the *expected inflation rate* changes. But with rational expectations, expectations of inflation adjust immediately. Refer to Figure 12.8 on page 463 to recall why this difference is important when discussing monetary policy. The increase in the inflation target still shifts the *AD* curve to the right. Because rational individuals take into account all available information, the expected inflation rate increases the moment the central bank announces a higher inflation target. The aggregate supply curve immediately shifts from AS_1 to AS_2, and the economy's equilibrium immediately moves from point *A* to point *C*. As a result, the inflation rate immediately increases from π_1 to π_3. In contrast to the result when expectations are adaptive, the economy's equilibrium never reaches point *B*, at which real GDP is greater than potential GDP. That is, the economy never experiences the temporary expansion. The central bank cannot achieve a temporary increase in real GDP even if it is willing to tolerate permanently higher inflation. *We can conclude that there is no trade-off between inflation and unemployment when expectations are rational and policy changes are anticipated.*

This surprising result is called the *policy ineffectiveness proposition* and was developed by Nobel Laureate Robert Lucas of the University of Chicago, Thomas Sargent of New York University, and Neil Wallace of Pennsylvania State University.[5] According to this proposition, announced and credible changes in monetary policy affect only the inflation rate and do not affect real GDP. Why? When expectations are rational, individuals and firms use all available information, including information about monetary policy rules, to form expectations of the inflation rate. When expected inflation increases, individuals and firms immediately adjust nominal prices. For example, if the Fed announces a 4% inflation target, Apple will increase the nominal price of the iPad by 4%, to $520. As a result, the real price of the iPad will remain unchanged, so monetary policy has no effect on the real price of the iPad. Therefore, the Fed's announced change in the inflation target will not have any effect on the quantity of iPads sold. What is true of Apple's iPad is also true of all other goods and services, so an announced change in the inflation target will not affect real GDP, assuming that there is no cost to adjusting wages and prices.

The policy ineffectiveness proposition led many new classical economists to conclude that monetary policy is ineffective in attempting to offset movements in real GDP over the business cycle. Because households and firms take into account changes in central bank policy when forming their expectations of inflation, there would be no room for announced and credible monetary policy to affect real GDP and employment.

Rational Expectations and Unanticipated Policy Changes

Rational expectations do not imply that all changes in monetary policy are ineffective. For the policy ineffectiveness result to hold, policy changes must be anticipated and credible. If

[5]Robert Lucas, "Some International Evidence on Real GDP-Inflation Tradeoffs," *American Economic Review*, Vol. 63, June 1973, pp. 326–324; and Thomas Sargent and Neil Wallace, "Rational Expectations and the Theory of Economic Policy," *Journal of Monetary Economics*, Vol. 2, April 1976, pp. 169–183.

a policy change is a surprise or if households and firms do not believe that the Fed will actually follow through and change the policy rule, then they will not adjust their actions. In this case, the aggregate supply curve in Figure 12.8 on page 463 will not shift immediately, and the economy's equilibrium will reach point *B*, where real GDP is greater than potential GDP. If the policy change is unannounced or not credible, then the change in the policy has exactly the same result on the economy as it does when we assume that households and firms have adaptive expectations. So, the Fed can temporarily increase real GDP and decrease unemployment if its change in policy is either unanticipated or not credible.

Rational Expectations and Other Demand Shocks

Is there anything special about changes in the monetary policy rule? Not really. If expectations are rational, then any anticipated demand shock should affect only the inflation rate. However, to the extent that households and firms do not anticipate the shock or understand how the shock will affect the economy, demand shocks can still affect real GDP. For example, if the decrease in asset prices we discussed in Figure 12.9 on page 466 had been expected, firms would have expected a lower inflation rate and changed their pricing decisions accordingly. The aggregate supply curve would have immediately adjusted, and real GDP would never have increased, the output gap would have remained 0, and the unemployment rate would never have increased. If households and firms have rational expectations, there is no trade-off between inflation and unemployment in either the short run or the long run when events such as a change in policy or a decrease in asset prices are anticipated. If a demand shock is unanticipated, however, then there is a trade-off between inflation and unemployment in the short run, although not in the long run. Therefore, if households and firms had anticipated the collapse in stock prices in 2000 in the United States or the collapse in real estate prices and stock prices in Japan in the early 1990s, those shocks as they occurred would have had no effect on real GDP and employment.

Are Anticipated and Credible Policy Changes Actually Ineffective?

The assumption of rational expectations is compelling to many economists because it is consistent with the view that households and firms act systematically to achieve goals—maximizing utility in the case of households; maximizing profit in the case of firms. However, not all economists are willing to accept rational expectations or the policy ineffectiveness proposition. Some economists argue that even if expectations are rational, changes in policy can affect real GDP even if the changes are both anticipated and credible. For the policy ineffectiveness proposition to hold, firms must change prices in response to a change in expected inflation. But we saw in Chapter 8 that it can be costly for firms to change prices. If the cost of changing prices is high enough, Apple, for instance, may not adjust the price of its iPads even when its expectations of the inflation rate change. So the cost of changing prices means that prices may not change enough to keep real GDP equal to its potential level. In this case, real GDP and employment may increase even when households and firms have rational expectations.

Another reason some economists doubt the policy ineffectiveness proposition is that the assumption of rational expectations may not be realistic. Rational expectations imply that households and firms know the actual model of how the economy operates, that they have all the relevant information, and that they know how to use that information to make predictions about inflation and other economic variables. Critics of the rational expectations assumption argue that households and firms typically lack the technical sophistication and time to completely analyze all relevant information. Given these constraints, households and firms may disregard information and make decisions according to simple rules of thumb that require less time and effort. For instance, firms may use adaptive expectations and expect the following year's inflation rate to be the same as the current year's inflation rate. Moreover, as we saw in Chapters 10 and 11, when discussing the limitations on monetary and fiscal policy, there is a great deal of uncertainty over the values for key economic parameters, such as the marginal propensity to consume or the multiplier, so it is unlikely that households and firms are using a macroeconomic model capable of yielding optimal forecasts.

The evidence on whether anticipated changes in monetary policy can affect real GDP is mixed. Thomas Sargent of New York University argued that the hyperinflation in Germany at the end of World War I, which we discussed in Chapter 6, ended when the government announced a credible commitment to a lower inflation rate. If expectations of inflation were adaptive, then ending the hyperinflation would have required a severe recession. Germany did not experience a severe recession as the hyperinflation ended, which Sargent interprets as evidence in favor of the rational expectations assumption.

Sargent's research provides some evidence in favor of the policy ineffectiveness proposition. Other studies, however, find that anticipated monetary policy does affect real GDP.[6] As a result, many economists take the view that anticipated changes in monetary policy do affect real GDP, although by less than do unanticipated changes in policy. These economists argue that households and firms do take actions to offset the effects of changes in monetary policy, but because they are not able to calculate exactly what the effects of the changes will be on monetary policy and because it is costly to change prices, real GDP and employment do respond to changes in policy. Economists continue to research how households and firms form their expectations of inflation and the extent to which the assumption of rational expectations matches the actual behavior of households and firms.

12.5

Learning Objective

Discuss the pros and cons of the central bank's operating under policy rules rather than using discretionary policy.

Monetary Policy: Rules Versus Discretion

Central banks are responsible for keeping inflation low and stable, but they are not always successful. The annual inflation rate in the United States measured by the CPI rose steadily from 1.3% in 1963 to 13.5% by 1980. To reduce inflation, the Federal Reserve allowed the federal funds rate to rise to over 20% in mid-1981, which helped cause the severe recession of 1981–1982. Our discussion of rational expectations and the evidence cited by Thomas Sargent and other economists suggests that reducing inflation rates does not have to be so costly.

Reducing inflation was costly in part because during the 1970s the Fed pursued a *discretionary policy*, which means that it conducted monetary policy in any way that it believed would achieve its goals of price stability and high employment. As the Fed switched its focus during those years from containing inflation to stimulating real GDP and employment, the federal funds rate fluctuated widely, as did the unemployment and inflation rates. By the time Paul Volcker became Fed chair in 1979, the Fed had lost credibility because it had allowed the inflation rate to rise. As we have seen, the Fed has difficulty conducting a successful monetary policy if households and firms do not find the Fed's policy announcements to be credible. An alternative to using discretionary policy is a **monetary rule**, which is an attempt by the central bank to follow specific and publicly announced guidelines for monetary policy.

Monetary rule An attempt by the central bank to follow specific and publicly announced guidelines for policy.

The Taylor Rule

Proposals for monetary policy rules take many forms. Some rules place severe restrictions on the central bank's ability to conduct monetary policy, while other rules are more guidelines for good policy than they are formal rules. Nobel Laureate Milton Friedman proposed that the central bank follow a policy rule such that the nominal money supply would

[6]Two classic studies that find that anticipated changes in policy can affect output are: Frederic S. Mishkin, "Does Anticipated Monetary Policy Matter? An Econometric Investigation," *Journal of Political Economy*, Vol. 90, No. 1, February 1982, pp. 22–51 and Robert J. Gordon, "Price Inertia and Policy Effectiveness in the United States, 1890–1980," *Journal of Political Economy*, Vol. 90, No. 6, December 1982, pp. 1087–1117.

grow at a constant rate, regardless of economic conditions.[7] *Currency boards* are monetary policy rules where the central bank maintains a specific value for the exchange rate of the domestic currency against another country's currency or a broad basket of currencies from various countries. The gold standard is a special type of currency board where the central bank commits to maintaining a specific price of gold. No country has ever adopted Friedman's constant money growth rate rule, but the gold standard was very popular during the nineteenth and early twentieth centuries. Hong Kong, Bulgaria, and Lithuania all operate currency boards, and Argentina operated a currency board from 1991–2002. These policy rules strictly limit the central bank's ability to pursue other policy goals because the central bank is mandated by law to keep a constant growth rate of the money supply or stabilize the price of the currency in terms of gold or other currencies. Not all policy rules are this restrictive.

The Fed does not follow an official policy rule. Actual Fed deliberations are complex and incorporate many factors about the economy. John Taylor of Stanford University has summarized these factors in the **Taylor rule** for federal funds rate targeting.[8] The general equation representing the Taylor rule is:

Taylor rule A monetary policy guideline developed by economist John Taylor for determining the target for the federal funds rate.

$$i_{\text{Target}} = r^* + \pi_t + g(\pi_t - \pi_{\text{Target}}) + h\widetilde{Y}_t, \quad (12.2)$$

where:

i_{Target} = target for the nominal federal funds rate
r^* = long-run equilibrium real federal funds rate
π_t = current inflation rate
π_{Target} = target inflation rate
g = how much the nominal target federal funds rate responds to a deviation of inflation from its target
h = how much the nominal target federal funds rate responds to the output gap

Notice that the Taylor rule in Equation (12.2) differs from our earlier monetary policy rule because the Taylor rule explicitly takes into account how the Fed responds to both the inflation rate and to the change in real GDP as measured by the output gap. As a result, the Taylor rule is consistent with the Fed's *dual mandate* of price stability and maximum sustainable employment.

Many economists believe that the Fed's implicit target for inflation is 2% and that the equilibrium real federal funds rate is also 2%. Taylor found that, given these assumptions, the rule in Equation (12.2) does a good job of predicting the Fed's behavior when $g = 0.5$ and $h = 0.5$. Figure 12.10 shows the federal funds rate and the level of the federal funds rate that would have occurred if the Fed had strictly followed the Taylor rule. Because the two lines are close together during most years, the Taylor rule does a reasonable job of explaining Federal Reserve policy. There are, however, some periods when the lines diverge significantly. During the late 1960s and early to mid-1970s, the federal funds rate predicted from the Taylor rule is consistently above the actual federal funds rate. This gap is consistent with the view of most economists that in the face of a worsening inflation rate during those years, the FOMC should have raised the target for the federal funds rate more than it did. Figure 12.10 also indicates that the FOMC lowered the federal funds rate following the severe 1981–1982 recession more slowly than is consistent with the Taylor rule. The figure also indicates that the FOMC kept the target federal funds rate at levels well below those indicated by the Taylor rule during the recovery from the 2001 recession.

---

[7]Milton Friedman, *A Program for Monetary Stability*, New York: Fordham University Press, 1960.
[8]Taylor's original discussion of the rule appeared in John Taylor, "Discretion Versus Policy Rules in Practice," *Carnegie-Rochester Conference Series on Public Policy*, Vol. 39, No. 1, December 1993, pp. 195–214.

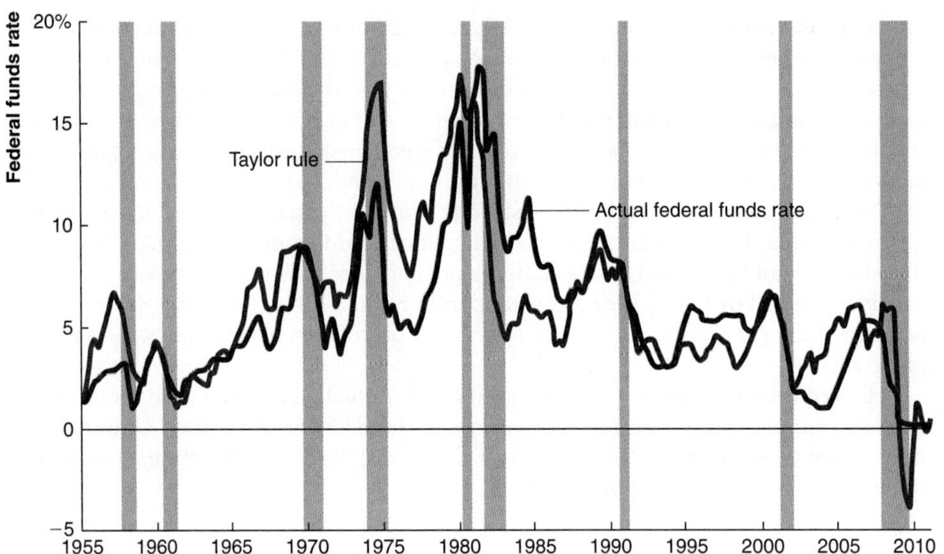

Figure 12.10

The Taylor Rule and Federal Reserve Behavior, 1955–2011

The Taylor rule does a good job of predicting the nominal federal funds rate from the mid-1980s to the end of the 2001 recession. Shaded areas represent recessions as determined by the National Bureau of Economic Research. The inflation rate is calculated as the growth rate of the personal consumption expenditure price index over the previous four quarters.

Sources: U.S. Bureau of Economic Analysis; U.S. Congressional Budget Office; Federal Reserve System; and National Bureau of Economic Analysis. ●

Some economists and policymakers have argued that by keeping the target federal funds at a very low level for an extended period, the Fed helped provide fuel for the housing boom of the mid-2000s. The argument is that a low federal funds rate contributed to low mortgage interest rates, thereby encouraging the housing boom. At the time, Fed Chairman Alan Greenspan argued that low interest rates were needed to guard against the possibility that the economy might lapse into a period of deflation. Current Fed Chairman Ben Bernanke has argued that a global savings glut, rather than Fed policy, was the main reason long-term interest rates were low in the United States during the early 2000s. Finally, notice that the Taylor rule indicates that the federal funds rate should have been negative throughout 2009. This is another indication of the severity of the 2007–2009 recession and helps to explain why the Fed resorted to trying nontraditional monetary policy tools such as quantitative easing.

The United States was not the only country to allow interest rates to persist at low levels with consequences for the housing market. Economists Rudiger Ahrend, Boris Cournede, and Robert Pierce of the Monetary and Fiscal Policy Division of the Organisation for Economic Co-operation and Development (OECD) examined the deviations of short-term nominal interest rates from those suggested by the Taylor rule for countries such as Ireland and Spain.[9] Ahrend and Cournede found that the more the central bank deviated from the nominal interest rate suggested by the Taylor rule, the more the countries' resources flowed into residential and nonresidential investment. These economists believe their research indicates that low nominal interest rates helped contribute to the rapid rise in residential housing during this period. So, to the extent that the collapse in housing markets contributed to the 2007–2009 recession, lax monetary policy may bear part of the blame.

The Taylor Rule and the Real Interest Rate

The Taylor rule applies to the nominal federal funds rate, but real interest rates are far more important for determining the level of economic activity. To see the relationship between the target federal funds rate and the real federal funds rate, consider the Taylor rule

[9]Rudiger Ahrend, Boris Cournede, and Robert Pierce, "Monetary Policy, Market Excesses and Financial Turmoil," Organisation for Economic Co-operation and Development Economics Department Working Paper 597, March 2008.

under the assumption that the Fed has an inflation rate target of 2%, the equilibrium real federal funds rate is 2%, and the values of g and h in Equation (12.2) are both 0.5:

$$i_{\text{Target}} = 2 + \pi_t + 0.5(\pi_t - 2) + 0.5\widetilde{Y}_t = 1 + 1.5\pi_t + 0.5\widetilde{Y}_t. \quad (12.3)$$

According to the Taylor rule, the Fed should increase the target nominal federal funds rate by 1.5 percentage points for each 1-percentage-point increase in inflation. This observation is important because the Fisher relationship tells us that the real interest rate equals the nominal interest rate minus the inflation rate. If inflation increases by 1 percentage point, then the target nominal federal funds rate will increase by 1.5 percentage points, so the real interest rate will increase by 0.5 percentage point. The result is that a higher inflation rate results in a higher real interest rate. The higher real interest rate reduces consumption and investment, which slows the growth of real GDP and lowers the inflation rate. By following this rule, monetary policy helps keep the inflation rate stable.

The Case for Discretion

Economists who believe that policymakers should be allowed discretion argue that simple rules such as the Taylor rule or Friedman's constant money growth rate rule cannot accommodate new and unexpected events. So, policymakers must be free to use all available information in setting monetary policy and not just the information that a simple rule suggests. For example, the Fed cut the target federal funds rate in response to the stock market crash of October 1987, even though the inflation rate and real GDP had not changed. The interest rate cut sent a signal to households and firms that the Fed was determined to prevent the stock market crash from harming the economy. Advocates of discretion argue that the stock market crash was a unique event that no rule could have accounted for, so the proper policy response required the Fed to use discretion.

In addition, rules often assume that key economic values are constant, but this is probably not true in reality. As we saw in Chapter 6, financial innovation and financial crises change the value of the money multiplier. Therefore, if policymakers at the Fed had followed Friedman's constant money growth rate rule, policy might have destabilized the economy. With respect to the Taylor rule, it is possible that the equilibrium real interest rate changes over time in response to technological change and other factors that affect the economy's long-run equilibrium. In those circumstances, strict adherence to the Taylor rule could potentially increase fluctuations in unemployment and inflation.

The Case for Rules

Economists who believe that policymakers should follow a monetary policy rule argue that the period between the mid-1960s and early 1980s, when inflation rose steadily, shows the problems associated with discretionary policy. As we discussed earlier, during this period, the Fed repeatedly switched between the goals of fighting inflation on the one hand and keeping real GDP close to potential GDP on the other hand. The Fed lost credibility with the general public, and both the actual and expected inflation rates increased. Some economists also argue that a policy rule avoids the **time-inconsistency problem**, which is the tendency of policymakers to announce one policy in advance in order to change the expectations of households and firms and then to follow a second policy after households and firms have made economic decisions based on the announced policy. For example, a central bank may announce a target inflation rate of 2% for the next year to get households and firms to make decisions about nominal prices, nominal wages, and nominal interest rates based on an expectation of 2% inflation. Then the central bank announces that it will increase the target inflation rate to 5%, so the real price, real wage, and real interest rate will all be lower than expected.

Time-inconsistency problem The tendency of policymakers to announce one policy in advance in order to change the expectations of households and firms and then to follow a second policy after households and firms have made economic decisions based on the first policy.

Nobel Laureates Finn Kydland of the University of California, Santa Barbara and Edward Prescott of Arizona State University argue that central banks face a time-inconsistency problem.[10] Policymakers have an incentive to promise to achieve low inflation to reduce the expected inflation rate. A lower expected inflation rate results in a lower actual inflation rate as households and firms build the lower expected inflation rate into their pricing decisions. Once households and firms have made their pricing decisions, the central bank has achieved a favorable trade-off between real GDP and inflation. Now the central bank has an incentive to exploit that trade-off by lowering interest rates to increase real GDP and reduce cyclical unemployment. It appears that the central bank can fool households and firms to stimulate the economy. Unfortunately, households and firms are not so easily fooled because they understand that the central bank has an incentive to break a promise to achieve low inflation. As a result, households and firms will expect the central bank to break its promise, so the expected inflation rate and, therefore, the actual inflation rate will remain high. Many economists believe that the time-inconsistency problem explains the poor economic performance of the mid-1960s to the early 1980s.

Advocates of rules argue that following a monetary policy rule provides the central bank with credibility because it is easier for individuals and firms to verify whether it is behaving as promised. Once the central bank achieves credibility, the expected inflation rate will fall, households and firms will build the lower expected inflation rate into their pricing decisions, and inflation will decrease.

Following a rule can also reduce uncertainty about monetary policy and improve economic performance in two other ways. First, when households and firms know how the central bank will respond to changes in the economy, they can more easily plan for the future. Second, rules provide discipline for the central bank, so that it does not constantly switch from trying to fight inflation to trying to keep the output gap close to zero. Uncertainty will still exist with rules because no one can predict shocks, but following a policy rule does eliminate the uncertainty that discretionary monetary policy might create.

Making the Connection

Central Banks Around the World Try Inflation Targeting

In 1989, the Reserve Bank of New Zealand became the first central bank to adopt an explicit inflation target. As of April 2011, a total of 26 central banks had explicit inflation targets, including advanced economies such as Canada and the United Kingdom and emerging markets such as Colombia, Hungary, and South Africa. Inflation targeting has four key elements: (1) an explicit mandate for the central bank to pursue price stability as its sole or primary objective; (2) an explicit target inflation rate, usually between 1% and 3%; (3) accountability for meeting the target rate (for example, the head of New Zealand's central bank can be fired for not meeting the inflation target); and (4) emphasis on the inflation rate over the next several years.

An explicit inflation target acts as a rule to constrain the discretion of the central bank and provide it with credibility as an inflation fighter. Therefore, having an explicit inflation target may be a way to reduce the time-inconsistency problem. However, the central bank retains some discretion in pursuing goals other than price stability because most countries allow the central bank to keep inflation within a specified range. For example, the central bank can increase inflation to the higher end of the range to stimulate the economy, if necessary.

The reason that countries adopt inflation targets is to bring down the inflation rate, but has it worked? The evidence is mixed. Laurence Ball of Johns Hopkins University and Niamh Sheridan of the International Monetary Fund found that inflation did decrease after central banks adopted explicit inflation targets but that the decrease was about the same

---

[10]Finn Kydland and Edward Prescott, "Rules Rather Than Discretion: The Inconsistency of Optimal Plans," *Journal of Political Economy*, Vol. 85, No. 3, June 1977, pp. 473–491.

size as decreases in countries without explicit inflation targets. However, a recent study by economists at the International Monetary Fund found that the surge in oil prices during 2007 caused a smaller increase in the inflation rate in countries that had explicit inflation targets. This connection provides some evidence that explicit inflation targets may help keep actual and expected inflation rates low and stable.

Inflation targeting is still a relatively new strategy, and it is too soon to tell if it will become standard practice for more central banks in the future. However, even countries without explicit inflation targets often have implicit inflation targets and have adopted some of the other features of inflation targeting. For example, Fed Chairman Ben Bernanke has essentially confirmed a target inflation rate of 2% in his public statements. Bernanke was a proponent of inflation targeting during his academic career. Since becoming Chairman of the Fed in 2006, he has adopted some features of inflation targeting. The Fed now makes more of its forecasts of inflation public, and it does a more complete job of explaining the reasoning behind the forecasts. Therefore, the Fed is providing households and firms with information that they can use to determine expected inflation.

Sources: Laurence Ball and Niamh Sheridan, "Does Inflation Targeting Matter?" in Ben S. Bernanke and Michael Woodford, eds., *The Inflation-Targeting Debate*, Chicago: University of Chicago Press, 2005, pp. 249–276; Karl Habermeier, *et al.*, "Inflation Pressures and Monetary Policy Options in Emerging and Developing Countries: A Cross Regional Perspective," International Monetary Fund working paper 09/1, January 2009; Leika Kihara and Stanley White, "Fed and BOJ Chiefs Wary of Inflation Targeting Fixes," *Reuters*, May 26, 2010; and Scott Roger, "Inflation Targeting Turns 20," *Finance and Development*, March 2010, pp. 46–49.

Test your understanding by doing related problem 5.8 on page 484 at the end of this chapter.

Answering the Key Question

Continued from page 448

At the beginning of this chapter we asked the question:

"Did discretionary monetary policy kill the Great Moderation?"

The Great Moderation ended when the collapse of the housing bubble led to the financial crisis and the Great Recession of 2007–2009. In this chapter, we have seen that discretionary monetary policy can lead to poor decisions by the central bank. We have also seen that the federal funds rate was far below the rate suggested by the Taylor rule at exactly the same time that the housing market bubble was developing in the United States. Furthermore, many countries experienced a housing bubble at the same time, and the extent of those bubbles is related to how far central banks in those countries deviated from well-established rules such as the Taylor rule. While this evidence is not conclusive, it does suggest that discretionary monetary policy during the 2001–2006 period contributed to a housing bubble and to the resulting financial crisis that ended the Great Moderation.

Before moving to the next chapter, read *An Inside Look at Policy* on the next page for an analysis of whether households believe the Fed can keep inflation under control.

Has the Fed Successfully Stimulated the Economy?

WALL STREET JOURNAL

Survey Indicates Inflation Expectation Still Muted

U.S. households expect inflation to rise over the short term but remain contained over the longer run, shrugging off higher food and energy prices, in a positive sign for consumer spending patterns. . . .

a If the findings from the Thomson Reuters/University of Michigan Survey of Consumers report are correct, they are also good news for the Federal Reserve. Policymakers are mightily rattled by ebbing core inflation rates. Lifting price pressures has been an express goal of the Federal Reserve's controversial bond buying effort. . . .

The report consisted of recently released data joined with new analysis. The Michigan report repeated that, as of January, consumers expect inflation over the next year will come in at 3.3% as of January, a higher pace than the 3% rate seen over the prior two months and "well above" the 2.2% rate predicted in September. But expectations for the next five years remained stable, indicating "well-anchored expectations, at least at the aggregate level."

b That's the Fed's dream scenario, should it, in fact, play out that way. With core inflation levels — they're stripped of food and energy costs in a bid to smooth volatility — grinding around a very low 1% rate, the Fed wants to see a modest rise. Most policymakers want core inflation back between 1.5% to 2%, a range they consider consistent with price stability. This desire has put the Fed in the very unusual position of seeking to create inflation rather than quell it. Its primary tool to accomplish this agenda is its ongoing effort to buy $600 billion in longer-dated Treasury debt.

The Fed hopes this buying will spur growth and lower unemployment, which should in turn put some upward pressure on inflation. The delicate game for the Fed is that it doesn't want its effort to generate a little inflation to turn into an uncontrolled surge in prices. The Michigan data suggest the public retains confidence the Fed will, over the long run, be able to blunt any unwanted jump in prices.

c The wild card in all of this, aside from the Fed's untested tools to unwind its stimulative actions, is commodity prices. U.S. growth may be underwhelming, but surging activity in many large emerging-market economies is putting significant pressure on food and energy costs. That demand could prove persistent and, over time, price gains in these components could infect core inflation rates in a way the Fed could find difficult to counter. . . .

But since all of this rests on what is expected to happen, risks abound. "If inflation increases are larger and more prolonged than now anticipated, the resulting strain on the already precarious state of consumers' budgets will cause larger, delayed cutbacks in spending," which will wound the recovery effort, the report said.

It could also cause the Fed to tighten policy even in the face of weak growth. Central bankers broadly believe there is no long-run trade-off between growth and inflation, and that sustainable growth is ultimately incompatible with high inflation. . . .

Source: Michael S. Derby, "Survey Indicates Inflation Expectation Still Muted," *Wall Street Journal*, January 24, 2011.

Key Points in the Article

This article discusses consumers' expectations of inflation in the United States. A recent consumer survey showed that consumers expected inflation to rise at the modest rate of 3.3% in 2011 and remain stable for the next five years. This news is good for the Federal Reserve. Since late 2008, the Fed has implemented two rounds of quantitative easing, purchasing assets in an attempt to stimulate the economy and increase consumer spending. The inflation expectations reported in the survey seem to indicate that the Fed's actions to stimulate the economy have been successful and that consumers have faith in the Fed's being able to keep inflation under control.

Analyzing the News

a The consumer survey reported that consumers' expectations of inflation for 2011 were 3.3% in January, 50% higher than only four months earlier. This increase in inflation expectations and the expectation that inflation will remain stable for the next five years is viewed as a positive sign for the Fed and its efforts to stimulate the economy and boost prices. The survey results also indicate that the Fed may find it unnecessary to undertake yet another round of asset purchases to further increase the money supply. The figure below shows data from the Federal Reserve Bank of Cleveland. Although expectations of inflation increased from September 1, 2010 through January 1, 2011, the Fed still predicted inflation below 2% despite the rapid increase in the monetary base in 2008–2009 which we discussed in Chapter 10.

b The Fed implemented asset purchasing programs in an effort to boost the economy during the recession and lift the core inflation rate above its lethargic level of 1%. The survey data show that the Fed has been successful in its effort to create inflation, but the Fed is also concerned that its actions do not over-stimulate the economy and result in a rapid increase in the price level. The survey indicates that the public has confidence in the Fed's ability to control excessive price increases for the long run.

c Despite its apparently successful effort to stimulate the economy and generate a moderate level of inflation, the Fed is concerned about the potential for significant increases in food and energy prices. Substantial increases in these commodity prices could accelerate inflation to unacceptable levels and adversely affect consumer demand, slowing the economic recovery, delaying the tightening of monetary policy, and possibly creating a need for further Fed stimulus.

THINKING CRITICALLY *ABOUT POLICY*

1. If the Fed did choose to implement another new asset purchase program, inflation expectations could further increase, leading to higher nominal interest rates, and a rise in commodity prices. Explain how inflation expectations, nominal interest rates, and commodity prices could increase due to the Fed's implementation of a new asset purchase program. Use *IS-MP* and *AD-AS* graphs to support your answer.
2. The figure shows that despite the rapid increase in the monetary base in 2009 to 2010, analysts at the Federal Reserve expect inflation to remain fairly low and stable for the next ten years. Are the inflation expectations shown in the figure rational or adaptive? Explain why the monetary base can increase dramatically without causing expected inflation to increase as well.

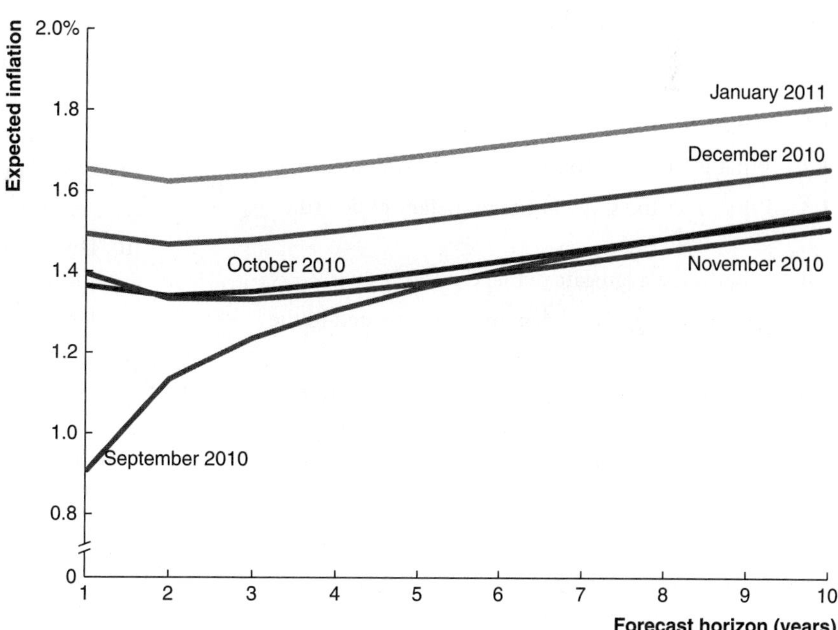

Expected inflation

Source: Federal Reserve Bank of Cleveland. ●

CHAPTER SUMMARY AND PROBLEMS

KEY TERMS

Aggregate demand, p. 449
Aggregate demand (*AD*) curve, p. 451
Aggregate demand and aggregate supply (*AD–AS*) model, p. 459
Aggregate supply, p. 449
Aggregate supply (*AS*) curve, p. 456
Central bank credibility, p. 470
Monetary policy rule, p. 450
Monetary rule, p. 472
Rational expectations, p. 469
Stagflation, p. 459
Taylor rule, p. 473
Time-inconsistency problem, p. 475

12.1 Monetary Policy Rules and Aggregate Demand

Describe monetary policy rules and how they affect aggregate demand.

SUMMARY

Aggregate demand is the level of planned expenditure in the economy, and **aggregate supply** is the total amount of goods and services that firms plan on selling. Economists summarize central bank behavior with a **monetary policy rule**, which describes how the central bank adjusts interest rates in response to changing economic conditions. We can combine the monetary policy rule along with the *IS* curve to obtain an **aggregate demand (*AD*) curve**, which summarizes the information contained in the *IS–MP* graph from that chapter.

Review Questions

1.1 What is a monetary policy rule?

1.2 What is the most common central bank target?

1.3 What does the slope of the monetary policy rule curve indicate?

1.4 What is the aggregate demand curve?

1.5 How is the aggregate demand curve related to the monetary policy rule?

1.6 What factors shift the aggregate demand curve?

1.7 Explain why some shifts of the aggregate demand curve are permanent and some are temporary.

Problems and Applications

1.8 Some central banks have explicit inflation targets. Why isn't the inflation target zero?

1.9 Why doesn't the Fed have an explicit inflation target? Should there be an explicit target?

1.10 Draw a graph of the monetary policy rule and explain how the curve would change if the central bank becomes less tolerant of deviations from the target rate of inflation.

1.11 Consider the following statement: "Because the Fed does not have an explicit inflation target, it does not follow a monetary policy rule." Do you agree with this statement? Briefly explain.

1.12 For each of the following scenarios, state the short-run effect on the *AD* curve.

a. There is an increase in government purchases.
b. Costs of production increase.
c. Investors become more pessimistic.
d. The central bank becomes less tolerant of deviations from the target inflation rate.
e. The price level increases.
f. The target inflation rate increases.

1.13 For each of the scenarios described in problem 1.12, if the *AD* curve shifted, explain whether the shift will be temporary or permanent.

Visit www.myeconlab.com to complete these exercises online and get instant feedback.

12.2 Aggregate Supply and the Phillips Curve
Explain the relationship between aggregate supply and the Phillips curve.

SUMMARY

The **aggregate supply (*AS*) curve** is the Phillips curve from Chapter 9 and shows that inflation depends on expectations, demand shocks, and supply shocks. Expectations are important because households and firms build expected inflation into decisions about prices. Demand factors are important because as production pushes up against capacity constraints, firms find it in their interests to increase prices, and so inflation rises. Supply shocks are important because firms may pass along increases in the cost of production to consumers in the form of higher prices, and so inflation rises.

Review Questions

2.1 What is an aggregate supply curve?

2.2 What demand factors contribute to inflation? How do these factors relate to the aggregate supply curve?

2.3 What cost factors contribute to inflation? How do these factors relate to the aggregate supply curve?

2.4 Explain what factors cause the aggregate supply curve to shift.

Problems and Applications

2.5 For each of the following scenarios, state the short-run effect on the *AS* curve.

a. There is an increase in government spending, which causes demand and real GDP to increase.

b. Nominal wages increase rapidly.

c. Lower inflation is expected in the future.

d. There is a change in technology that lowers the costs of production.

2.6 Write two equations for the *AS* curve. In both cases, assume that expectations are adaptive and that the effect of supply shocks is zero. For the first equation, assume that the inflation rate is very sensitive to changes in the output gap. For the second equation, assume that it is not. Then graph your two curves.

2.7 Some economists argue that the *AS* curve should be drawn as nonlinear, rather than as a straight line—or in other words, b is not constant. Why might inflation react differently to changes in real GDP at low levels of real GDP as compared to at high real GDP? Briefly explain.

2.8 Consider the following statement: "The supply shock inflation parameter, s, must always be positive because supply shocks always push production costs upward." Do you agree with this statement? Briefly explain.

2.9 The Federal Reserve Bank of Cleveland has developed a model of inflation expectations. "According to the latest estimates from the Cleveland Fed model, long-term inflation expectations are still well anchored, a fact that may be important in deciding when to tighten monetary policy." Expected inflation is well anchored when it is stable and does not increase or decrease significantly in response to economic shocks because households and firms expect the Fed will keep the actual inflation rate close to the expected inflation rate. What would happen to the *AS* curve if inflation expectations were not well anchored?

Source: "Inflation Expectations Still Well Anchored, According to Cleveland Fed Researchers," Federal Reserve Bank of Cleveland press release, June 28, 2010.

12.3 The Aggregate Demand and Aggregate Supply Model
Use the aggregate demand and aggregate supply model to analyze macroeconomic conditions.

SUMMARY

We can use the **aggregate demand and aggregate supply (*AD–AS*) model** to show the effect of shocks on real GDP and inflation. Supply shocks, such as oil price increases, may cause inflation and real GDP to move in opposite directions. For example, an increase in oil prices may cause real GDP to decrease at the same time that the inflation rate increases, so **stagflation** results. Demand shocks, such as a collapse in stock prices or a change in the monetary policy rule, cause inflation and real GDP to move in the same direction initially. For example, a decrease in household wealth will cause both real GDP and inflation to decrease.

Review Questions

3.1 What are the long-run equilibrium conditions in the *AD–AS* model?

3.2 What is stagflation, and how does it occur?

3.3 How does the economy readjust to long-run equilibrium after a period of stagflation, assuming that the Fed does not change its monetary policy rule?

3.4 How does the *AD–AS* model explain economic fluctuations?

3.5 How is the *AD–AS* model different from the *IS–MP* model?

Problems and Applications

3.6 Draw a graph of the *AD–AS* model. Label the curves and axes carefully. Then show the effects of the following:

a. a positive demand shock

b. a positive supply shock

How are the effects of these changes on the output gap different from the effects on inflation? If you observed an increase in real GDP so the output gap moved above zero, how could you tell whether *AD* or *AS* had shifted?

3.7 In problem 2.6, you drew two different *AS* supply curves, based on the sensitivity of inflation to the output gap. The following graph shows a curve that is sensitive to inflation changes (AS_1) and a curve that is less sensitive (AS_2):

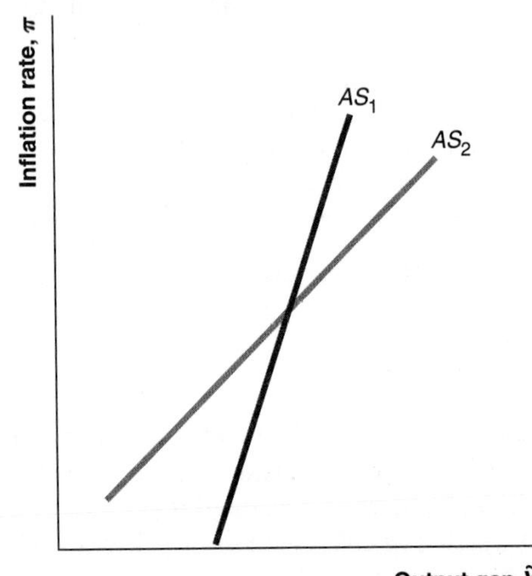

a. Draw an *AD* curve and assume that the equilibrium point represents the long-run equilibrium point.

b. Suppose that a housing boom takes place. Show the effect on *AD* and explain how the short-run inflation and output response are different in the two cases.

3.8 **[Related to the *Making the Connection* on page 464]** Problem 2.9 states that, according to the Cleveland Fed, inflation expectations in 2010 were well anchored. The *Making the Connection* "The End of Stagflation and the Volcker Recession" discusses how the Fed may have induced a recession to reduce both current and expected inflation.

a. Suppose that inflation expectations lose their anchor; in other words, assume that households and firms now expect that inflation will be considerably higher next period. Use the *AD–AS* model to show the short-run effect of this change.

b. What will the Fed have to do to reduce inflation? Carefully analyze using *AD–AS* model.

3.9 **[Related to *Solved Problem 12.3* on page 467]** Even if a family chooses not to sell its home or borrow against its value, the knowledge that the value of the house is increasing makes them feel wealthier. So, a decline in housing prices, such as happened after 2006, has a negative wealth effect. Use the *AD–AS* model to show the short- and long-run effects of a decline in housing prices.

3.10 **[Related to the *Macro Data* feature on page 462]** Real oil prices decreased significantly during the 1990s. The following graph shows the initial equilibrium at point *A* and the shift in aggregate supply due to lower oil prices:

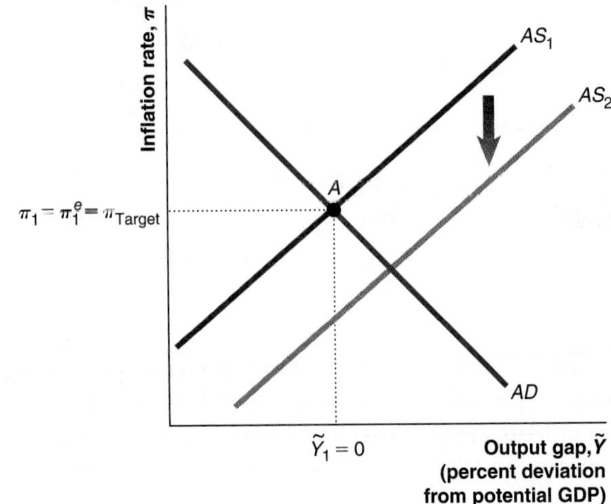

a. Identify the new equilibrium output gap and inflation rate.

b. Assuming that monetary policy does not change, show on the graph how the economy will adjust to the new long-run equilibrium.

3.11 Consider the following statement: "Because most aggregate demand shifts are temporary, they have little lasting effect on the economy, and thus there is no need for monetary or fiscal policy to correct them." Do you agree with this statement? Briefly explain.

3.12 In early 2010, consumer prices in the United Kingdom rose above 3%, even though the economy was growing slowly. An article in the *Economist* commented: "This may not be stagflation, 1970s-style; rather it is slumpflation, given that the economy is bumping along the bottom of the biggest hole dug in GDP since the second world war."

a. What does the article mean by "slumpflation"?

b. Why would we not expect to see rising inflation during a time of slow economic growth?

c. The article also stated that the inflation rate was expected to decline. How would the *AD–AS* model explain this expectation?

Source: "Storm Before the Calm," *Economist*, February 11, 2010.

Rational Expectations and Policy Ineffectiveness

Define rational expectations and explain how it affects policymaking

SUMMARY

Rational expectations exist when households and firms use all available information to forecast economic variables, such as inflation. When expectations are not rational, firms earn lower profits because they make mistakes in setting prices. Therefore, firms devote significant resources to forecasting inflation. If expectations are rational and monetary policy is anticipated, households and firms adjust their pricing decisions as soon as they learn about a change in policy. As a result, monetary policy does not affect real GDP but only affects the inflation rate. Economists call this outcome the *policy ineffectiveness proposition.* This proposition does not apply to unanticipated changes in monetary policy. The proposition may also not hold if it is costly for firms to adjust prices or if households and firms can accurately forecast the effects of changes in monetary policy. **Central bank credibility** is the degree to which households and firms believe the central bank's announcements about future policy.

Review Questions

4.1 What are rational expectations?

4.2 What does it mean to say that a central bank is credible? Are all central banks credible?

4.3 How might rational expectations make monetary policy ineffective?

4.4 Explain why monetary policy might be effective if expectations are rational but a change in policy is a surprise.

4.5 Under what circumstances will demand shocks affect real GDP if expectations are rational?

4.6 Are there reasons to doubt the policy ineffectiveness proposition? Briefly explain.

Problems and Applications

4.7 Suppose that inflation has increased at an annual rate of 2% for several years. Also assume that the central bank's target inflation rate is 2%.

a. If sellers all charge $100 for their products and expectations are adaptive, what price will they charge next year, assuming that the relative demand for their products is unchanged?

b. Suppose that the central bank now announces that its target inflation rate has increased to 5%, and the actual inflation rate also becomes 5%. What price should sellers charge to keep real prices constant? What price will they actually charge if expectations are adaptive?

c. What will be the consequences for the economy of the error in expectations?

4.8 In problem 4.7, what would happen if expectations are rational instead of adaptive?

4.9 Brazil experienced high inflation in the late 1980s and early 1990s. To bring prices under control, the country changed its currency to a new currency unit, the real. Explain why Brazil might need a new currency in order to control prices.

4.10 Consider the following statement: "Rational expectations assumes that all people are completely rational, and because this probably is not true, this theory doesn't help explain price behavior." Do you agree with this statement? Briefly explain.

4.11 Consider the following statement: "Currently, interest rates are very low. Because everyone knows that the Fed will raise rates at some point, the policy will have no effect when it happens." Do you agree with this statement? Briefly explain.

4.12 Deflation can be as great a problem for economies as inflation. Surveying 50 well-known economists in 2010, the *Economist* found that "the rough consensus was that in the near term, as Western economies struggle to recover, the bigger worry there is deflation."

a. Why might falling prices cause problems for an economy?

b. Most central banks in high-income countries have been credibly committed to low inflation rates for some time. Why might this commitment make the task of preventing deflation more difficult?

Source: "A Winding Path to Inflation," *Economist*, June 3, 2010.

12.5 Monetary Policy: Rules Versus Discretion

Discuss the pros and cons of the central bank's operating under policy rules rather than using discretionary policy.

SUMMARY

When using discretionary monetary policy, the central bank adjusts policy as it sees fit to achieve its goals. In a **rules strategy**, the central bank follows specific and publicly announced guidelines for policy. The **Taylor rule** is an often-cited rule in which the Fed sets the target nominal federal funds rate based on the output gap, the target for inflation, the actual inflation rate, and the long-run equilibrium real interest rate. The Taylor rule has become a standard representation of good monetary policy because the Fed's behavior closely approximated the rule during the Great Moderation. Advocates of discretion argue that no central bank can credibly commit itself to a rules strategy. In addition, no rules strategy can anticipate every conceivable economic event, such as the 1987 stock market crash or the 2001 terrorist attacks. Advocates of a rules strategy argue that a discretionary policy suffers from the **time-inconsistency problem**. The only way to solve this problem is for the central bank to commit to a policy rule. Advocates of rules also argue that when the Fed used discretionary policy during the 1970s the result was accelerating inflation.

Review Questions

5.1 Explain the difference between a rules strategy and discretionary policy.

5.2 What is the Taylor rule?

5.3 How might deviation from the Taylor rule have contributed to the 2007–2009 recession?

5.4 If central banks follow the Taylor rule, how does the real interest rate change during the business cycle?

5.5 What are the primary arguments in favor of a rules approach?

5.6 What are the primary arguments in favor of a discretionary approach?

5.7 What is a time-inconsistency problem?

Problems and Applications

5.8 **[Related to the *Making the Connection* on page 476]** Some central banks have explicit inflation targets, while others have implicit targets.

a. In the context of topics discussed in this section, what is the advantage of having an explicit target?

b. What is the advantage of having an implicit target or no target at all?

5.9 **[Related to the *Chapter Opener* on page 448]** Explain how the Fed may have created the Great Moderation. In what way may the Fed have contributed to the end of the Great Moderation?

5.10 A very simple monetary rule might be: "Increase the money supply at the rate of growth of real GDP."

a. What would be the advantages of this monetary rule? What would be the problems?

b. What if the rule said, "Increase the money supply at the rate of growth of real GDP plus 2%?" Then what would be the advantages and problems?

c. What if the rule said, "Increase the money supply at the rate of growth of real GDP plus 2% plus one-half of the output gap?" Then what would be the advantages and problems?

5.11 Consider the following statement: "Because the business cycle is unpredictable and real-time data are usually unobtainable, monetary policy rules probably won't be successful." Do you agree or disagree with this statement? Explain.

5.12 Both Alan Greenspan and Ben Bernanke have claimed that monetary policy was not responsible for the housing bubble. Instead, they blame a change in the relationship between short-term interest rates and long-term mortgage rates. An article in the *Economist* that summarizes their positions states part of the Greenspan explanation as follows: "The rise in desired global saving relative to desired investment caused a global decline in long-term rates, which became delinked from the short-term rates that central bankers control." How would the decoupling of short- and long-term rates create a problem for monetary policy and policy rules?

Source: "It Wasn't Us," *Economist*, March 18, 2010.

DATA EXERCISES

D12.1: Many sources give data on Brazil's inflation rates. Find data for the inflation rate from 1980 to the present. What happened to inflation rates after the country introduced its new currency, the real, in 1994?

D12.2: Use the St. Louis Fed's database (research.stlouisfed.org/fred2/) to find the growth rates of real GDP and potential GDP from 1960 to the present. Can you identify demand and supply shocks in the data?

D12.3: One problem in inflation targeting is choosing what inflation rate to target. The Federal Reserve Bank of San Francisco discusses this problem in "The 'Inflation' in Inflation Targeting" (www.frbsf.org/publications/economics/letter/2010/el2010-17.html). Find data on inflation and core inflation using both the Consumer Price Index and the Personal Consumption Expenditure deflator. Which do you think would make the better inflation target? Why?

D12.4: **[Excel question]** Problem 5.12 suggests that the relationship between short- and long-term interest rates may have weakened during the 1980–2011 period. Find data on short-term rates (such as the 3-month Treasury bill rates) and long-term rates (such as the 30-year mortgage rate) for the past 30 years. (Hint: You can use average monthly data.)

a. What is the correlation between the two rates over the entire period?

b. If you split the data into 5-year periods, does the correlation coefficient change?

CHAPTER 13

Fiscal Policy and the Government Budget in the Long Run

LEARNING OBJECTIVES

After studying this chapter, you should be able to:

- **13.1** Discuss basic facts about the U.S. government's fiscal situation (pages 488–494)
- **13.2** Explain when fiscal policy is sustainable and when it is not sustainable (pages 494–498)
- **13.3** Understand how fiscal policy affects the economy in the long run (pages 498–505)
- **13.4** Explain the fiscal challenges facing the United States (pages 505–511)
- **13A** Derive the conditions for a sustainable fiscal policy (pages 519–520)
- **13B** Derive the equation showing the relationship between budget deficits and private expenditure (page 520)

GOVERNMENT DEBT AROUND THE WORLD

Most developed nations, including Germany, Japan, and the United States, suffer from a long-term fiscal problem: Their national debt is expected to increase rapidly in the near future. The budget deficit measures how much the government borrows in a year, and the national debt is the total amount of bonds and other debt that a government has outstanding. The U.S. Congressional Budget Office forecast that the federal government's budget deficit would be $1.48 trillion in 2011, $1.10 trillion in 2012 and $0.70 trillion in 2013. Economists often measure budget deficits as a fraction of GDP. When the deficit rises above about 3% of GDP, it reaches levels that governments find difficult to sustain in the long run for reasons we will discuss in this chapter. The federal government's budget deficit averaged 2.5% of GDP from 1969 to 2007, which was sustainable. In 2009 and 2010, however, the deficit soared to about 10%, levels previously seen only during

Continued on next page

Key Issue and Question

At the end of Chapter 1, we noted key issues and questions that serve as a framework for the book. Here are the key issue and question for this chapter:

Issue: In 2011, the federal government's budget deficit and the national debt were on course to rise to unsustainable levels.

Question: How should the United States solve its long-run fiscal problem?

Answered on page 511

major wars such as World War I and World War II, and it was not projected to fall back to 3% until 2014. The United States is not alone in running large budget deficits. Economists at the Organisation for Economic Co-operation and Development (OECD), an association of high-income countries, estimated Japan's budget deficit to be over 7% of GDP for both 2011 and 2012. Ireland's deficit in 2010 was 32.3% of GDP—a level rarely seen in a developed country—and is expected to be 9.5% and 7.4% of GDP in 2011 and 2012. Several other member countries of the OECD were facing similarly large government budget deficits.

Where did the large deficits come from? The main cause was the severity of the worldwide recession of 2007–2009. Recessions lead to falling tax revenues as incomes and profits decline and to increasing government expenditures on unemployment benefits and government stimulus programs. In this respect, the budget deficits may have provided a short-run boost to production and employment by increasing aggregate expenditure.

Unfortunately, the deficits have contributed to long-term fiscal problems for many countries. Japan's national debt was 198% of GDP in 2010 and was expected to increase to 210% by 2012. As of mid-2011, the national debt of Portugal, Ireland, Italy, Greece, Spain, and a number of other countries was either above 100% of GDP or soon would be. At these levels of debt, the interest payments the government must make to bondholders rises to levels that squeeze out other spending. The U.S. public debt will rise to "only" about 75% of GDP by 2012, but if current taxing and spending policies remain in place, the debt will exceed 100% of GDP in the decades ahead.

These increases in debt for decades into the future are not primarily the result of the 2007–2009 recession and, in fact, are expected to persist even when most countries have returned to full employment. So what is driving the increase in debt in many countries? Over the long term, the increases in debt are driven by the expected aging of the population and the expected increases in healthcare costs. The percentage of the population over age 65 for the average country in the OECD increased from 8.5% in 1960 to 14.4% in 2009. The increase was less dramatic in the United States, where individuals over age 65 increased from 9.2% of the population in 1960 to 12.8% in 2009. The oldest OECD countries include Japan, where in 2009, 22.0% of the population was over 65, and Italy, where 20.2% was over age 65. As a population ages, there are fewer workers to pay the taxes necessary to support retirement and healthcare programs for the elderly. As a result, unless other government spending decreases or tax rates increase, the budget deficit and the national debt will increase. In addition to the fact that people use more healthcare as they age—healthcare that is typically paid for in large part by the government—healthcare costs are expected to increase more rapidly than incomes.

In the United States, the challenge of dealing with future deficits and rising national debt is so great that a recent survey of economists by the National Association for Business Economics ranked the federal deficit as their biggest long-term concern. How governments choose to deal with these looming fiscal problems will have important consequences for the future of their economies.

AN INSIDE LOOK AT POLICY on page 512 covers discussions among Congress, the deficit commission, and President Obama about cutting the federal budget deficit and addressing the problem of a growing national debt.

Sources: Congressional Budget Office, *Budget and Economic Outlook: Fiscal Years 2011 to 2021*, January 2011; Chris Isidore, "Economists' Biggest Worry: Federal Budget Deficit," CNNMoney.com, February 28, 2011, http://money.cnn.com/2011/02/28/news/economy/economists_federal_deficit_worries/index.htm; Organisation for Economic Co-operation and Development (OECD); Caroline Salas and Scott Lanman, "Bernanke Making Sure Fed Governors Remind Congress Deficit Bigger than QE2," *Bloomberg*, February 10, 2011, www.bloomberg.com/news/2011-02-10/bernanke-making-sure-fed-governors-remind-congress-deficit-bigger-than-qe2.html; and World Bank, World Development Indicators.

In Chapter 10, we discussed how the Federal Reserve uses monetary policy to pursue macroeconomic policy goals. We saw that monetary policy affects only nominal variables such as the inflation rate and leaves real variables such as output and employment unchanged in the long run. By the long run, we mean the period of time where nominal wages and prices are flexible, so real GDP always equals potential GDP. In Chapter 11, we discussed how the government uses fiscal policy such as changes in taxes and government purchases to achieve macroeconomic goals. In this chapter, we explain how fiscal policy affects real variables in the long run.

13.1

Learning Objective

Discuss basic facts about the U.S. government's fiscal situation.

Debt and Deficits in Historical Perspective

To provide context for understanding how fiscal policy affects an economy, it is important to first review some historical facts and key concepts that we first discussed in Chapter 11. **Gross federal debt held by the public** includes the bonds and similar securities issued by the U.S. Treasury (and a small amount of securities issued by federal agencies) not held by the federal government. Figure 11.3 on page 420 showed that the federal debt has tended to increase during wars and decrease during times of peace. The notable exceptions included the Great Depression, the 1980s, and the 2000–2010 period when the national debt rose substantially although the United States was not involved in a major war. There are a number of important issues concerning the effects of the federal debt on the economy. Before we can analyze the key issues connected with the federal debt, though, we need to understand the government's budget constraint.

Gross federal debt held by the public Debt that includes the bonds and other securities issued by the U.S. Treasury (and a small amount of securities issued by federal agencies) not held by the federal government.

The Government Budget Constraint

Households face a budget constraint because the total amount that a household spends cannot exceed the household's income plus the amount the household can borrow. The government faces a similar budget constraint. The government purchases goods and services (G) and makes transfer payments (TR) to households. The government must also make interest payments on existing debt. If i is the nominal interest rate on existing government bonds (B), then interest payments today are:

$$i_t B_{t-1},$$

where t stands for the current year and $t-1$ stands for the previous year. The government can finance these expenditures through tax revenue (T), issuing new government bonds (ΔB), or increasing the monetary base (ΔMB). In Chapter 6, we called increasing the monetary base **seigniorage** because it represents a transfer of wealth from individuals holding currency to the government. The government's budget constraint is then:

Seigniorage The government's profit from issuing fiat money; also called the inflation tax.

$$G_t + TR_t + i_t B_{t-1} = T_t + \Delta B_t + \Delta MB_t.$$

The terms on the left of the equation represent the *uses* of government funds, and the terms on the right side represent the *sources* of government funds. If we move taxes to the left side, we see that:

$$G_t + TR_t - T_t + i_t B_{t-1} = \Delta B_t + \Delta MB_t.$$

The left side of the equation is the **budget deficit**, which is the difference between government expenditure and tax revenue.[1] The right side of the equation tells us that the budget deficit is financed by issuing new government securities and seigniorage. To focus on the government's operations, we define the **primary budget deficit (*PD*)** as:

Budget deficit The difference between government expenditure and tax revenue.

Primary budget deficit (*PD*) The difference between government purchases of goods and services plus transfer payments minus tax revenue.

$$PD_t = G_t + TR_t - T_t.$$

The primary budget deficit is the difference between government purchases of goods and services plus transfer payments minus tax revenue. The primary deficit is the budget deficit excluding interest payments, so we can rewrite the equation for the budget deficit as:

$$PD_t + i_t B_{t-1} = \Delta B_t + \Delta MB_t. \quad (13.1)$$

According to the Congressional Budget Office (CBO), during 2010, federal government expenditures on goods and services plus transfer payments equaled $3,258.9 billion,

[1]In this chapter, a positive number represents a budget deficit and a negative number represents a budget surplus. This is different from earlier chapters where a negative number was a budget deficit and a positive number was a surplus. We make the switch to make the algebra easier to follow.

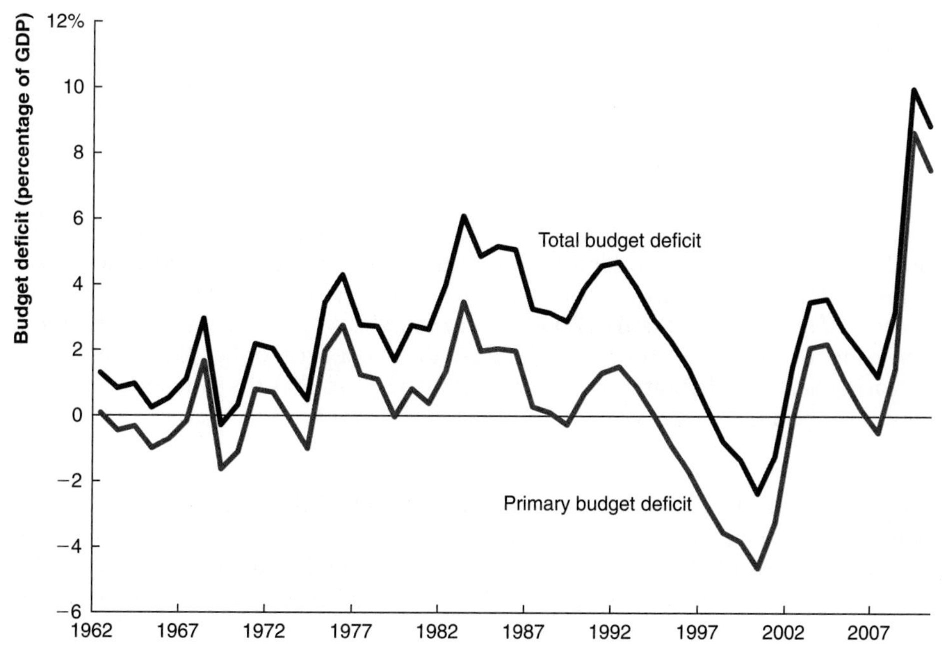

Figure 13.1

The Total Budget Deficit and Primary Budget Deficit for the United States, 1962–2010

Because interest payments are always positive, the primary budget deficit is always less than the total budget deficit. The primary budget deficit was negative, and therefore in surplus, most recently during 2007.

Source: U.S. Bureau of Economic Analysis. ●

and revenues equaled \$2,161.7 billion, so the primary budget deficit equaled \$1,097.2 billion. However, the government also made interest payments of \$196.9 billion, so the total deficit for the year was \$1,294.1 billion. As you can see, the difference between the total and the primary deficits can be hundreds of billions of dollars per year, which is quite substantial. Figure 13.1 shows the total and the primary budget deficits as a percentage of GDP for the United States from 1962 to 2010. The total budget deficit and primary budget deficit track each other closely over time. The primary deficit was last negative—meaning that the primary budget was in surplus—in 2007, while the total budget deficit was last negative (the total budget was in surplus) in 2001.

What Is the Difference Between the Debt and the Deficit?

The debt is the total value of government bonds outstanding, B. When the government runs a budget deficit, it does not have sufficient tax revenue to pay for all its expenditures. To finance the deficit, the U.S. Treasury issues new bonds that are bought by investors, including pension funds, mutual funds, large financial institutions such as Goldman Sachs and Morgan Stanley, foreign governments, and individual investors. Putting aside changes in the monetary base, we can think of the budget deficit as the yearly flow of new government bonds, ΔB. The value of bonds increases, $\Delta B > 0$, when the government runs a budget deficit. The value of bonds decreases, $\Delta B < 0$, when the government runs a budget surplus.

The deficit is a flow variable, and the debt is a stock variable, so you can use the bathtub analogy from Chapter 5 to think about the difference between the deficit and the debt: The level of water in a bathtub (the dollar value of the debt) is a stock variable because we measure it at a point in time, while the water flowing into the tub (a budget deficit, or the dollar value of additional borrowing) and flowing out of the tub (a budget surplus, or the dollar value of the debt repaid) are flow variables that are measured per time period. During years that the government runs budget deficits, more water flows into the bathtub, so the stock of government bonds and the federal debt increases. During years that the government runs budget surpluses, water flows out of the bathtub, so the stock of government bonds and the federal debt decreases.

Whether we care about the deficit, the debt, or both depends on the question we are asking. If we want to know the effect of fiscal policy on the ability of households and firms to borrow to finance consumption, we should look to the yearly budget deficit. Recall from Chapter 3 that the budget deficit affects national saving and the supply of loanable funds. If the government increases the budget deficit, it reduces the pool of national saving available to households and firms to finance consumption and investment. On the other hand, if we want to know whether the government's fiscal policy is sustainable, we need to focus on both the debt and the deficit. There is a limit to how much financial markets will lend to governments, so the debt-to-GDP ratio cannot increase forever. We call a fiscal policy *sustainable* when the debt-to-GDP ratio is constant or decreasing, and we call a fiscal policy *unsustainable* when the debt-to-GDP ratio is increasing. Because the ratio cannot increase forever, a fiscal policy that results in an increasing debt-to GDP ratio must eventually change, so that the ratio either remains constant or begins to decrease.

Gross Federal Debt Versus Debt Held by the Public

Gross federal debt The total dollar value of Treasury bonds and other federal agency bonds plus the dollar value of the small amount of bonds and other securities issued by other federal agencies.

Figure 13.2 shows gross federal debt and gross federal debt held by the public for the United States. **Gross federal debt** is the total dollar value of Treasury bonds plus the dollar value of the small amount of bonds and other securities issued by other federal agencies. As mentioned earlier, gross federal debt held by the public includes just those bonds held outside the federal government. The key to understanding the difference between the two measures is to recognize that the federal government owes some of its debt to itself because some government programs have trust funds that have purchased Treasury bonds. Some government programs, such as Social Security, have specific taxes and fees associated with the program. If the revenues from these taxes and fees exceed what the program pays out that year, the program runs a surplus. Legally, the program must use the surplus to purchase Treasury bonds. The federal government established Social Security in 1935 to provide benefits to retired workers and to the disabled. Workers and firms pay a payroll tax (currently 15.3% up to a wage limit that rises each year) that the Social Security

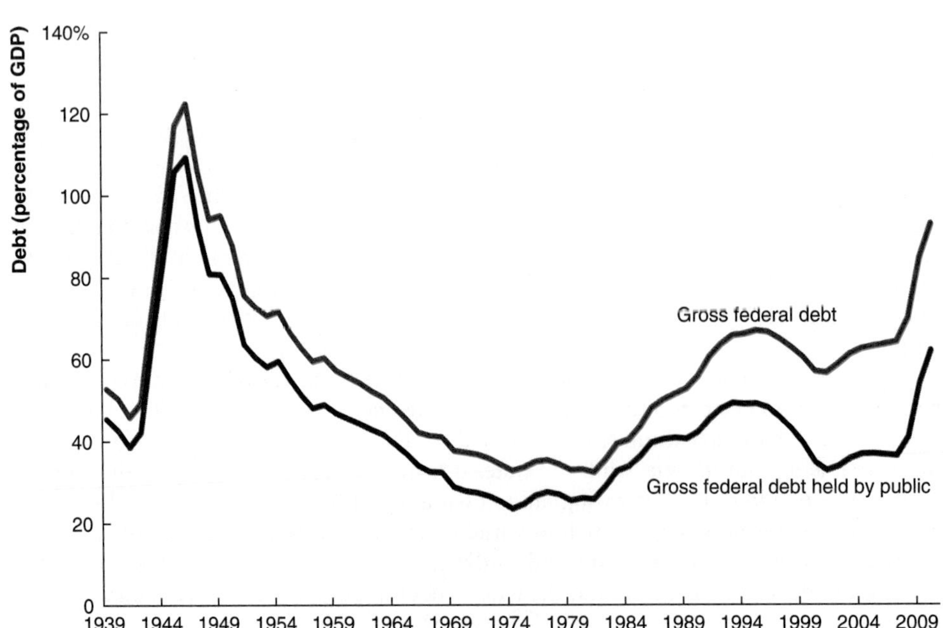

Figure 13.2

Gross Federal Debt and Gross Federal Debt Held by the Public for the United States, 1939–2010

Gross federal debt is greater than debt held by the public, but the two measures of federal debt track each other closely over time. Debt is calculated as the ratio of fiscal year debt to calendar year GDP.

Sources: U.S. Bureau of Economic Analysis and White House Council of Economic Advisers. ●

Table 13.1 Federal Debt Held by Federal Government Trust Funds and by the Federal Reserve, September 30, 2010

Trust funds and the Federal Reserve	Treasury bonds the fund owns (billions of dollars)
Old Age and Survivors (Social Security)	$2,399.1
Federal Employee Retirement Fund	770.1
Department of Defense Military Retirement Fund	282.0
Federal Hospital Insurance	279.5
Federal Disability Insurance	187.2
Other trust funds	620.9
Total Trust Funds	$4,538.8
Federal Reserve	$811.7

Source: U.S. Treasury Department.

Administration uses to pay benefits to retired workers and the disabled.[2] If the Social Security Administration receives $100 billion in payroll tax revenue but pays out just $80 billion in benefits, then it is legally obligated to purchase $20 billion in Treasury bonds. Because the Social Security Administration is part of the federal government, one branch of the federal government (the Treasury) owes a debt to another branch of the federal government (the Social Security Administration).

Gross federal debt at the end of the 2010 fiscal year was $13,561.6 billion. Of that amount, $9,002.8 billion was owned by the public, and $4,538.8 billion was owned by various federal government agencies.[3] The Federal Reserve has also accumulated large holdings of Treasury bonds in the course of conducting monetary policy. Because of the Fed's special status as a public–private agency that is technically independent of the rest of the federal government, the Fed's holdings of Treasury bonds are included with the holdings of the public rather than with the holdings of federal agencies. At the end of fiscal 2010, the Fed held $811.7 billion in Treasury debt. If we subtract the debt held by the Fed from the debt held by the public, we have the *debt held by private investors.* At the end of fiscal 2010, the debt held by private investors was $8,211.1 billion. Table 13.1 shows that the debt held by federal agencies, other than the Fed, was heavily concentrated in just five funds.

When economists evaluate the size of the government's debt, they tend to focus on the gross federal debt held by the public. If the Treasury borrows $20 billion from the Social Security Administration, that borrowing does not affect the funds available to the private sector to finance consumption and investment. As a result, economists usually emphasize the gross federal debt held by the public as the relevant measure when examining the effect of the debt on the current state of the economy. However, the $20 billion that the Social Security Administration loans to the Treasury is not free. Instead, the $20 billion represents a future liability of the federal government because it has promised to pay retirement benefits to the workers who pay Social Security taxes.

[2]Technically, of the 15.3% payroll tax, 12.4% is used to fund Social Security benefits and the other 2.9% is used to fund the Medicare program.

[3]U.S. Treasury, Historical Debt Outstanding—Annual 2000–2010, www.treasurydirect.gov/govt/reports/pd/histdebt/histdebt_histo5.htm.

The Debt-to-GDP Ratio

In this chapter, we emphasize the debt-to-GDP ratio rather than focus on the dollar value of the debt to measure the federal debt because economists believe that the debt-to-GDP ratio does a better job of measuring whether the debt is large or small in determining whether fiscal policy is sustainable. The federal government obtains most of its revenues through taxes, and GDP represents the income potentially available to be taxed. Thinking about the debt of an individual helps us understand why it makes sense to measure debt relative to a nation's income. Is $1 million a high level of debt? It depends. If your income is $50,000 per year, then $1 million in debt is extremely high. However, if you are a rich entrepreneur who earns $50 million per year, then $1 million is probably a low level of debt. It makes sense to measure debt relative to income because income represents your ability to pay the debt.

Figure 13.3 shows the debt of the central government for the United States and several other countries from the Organisation for Economic Co-operation and Development (OECD), which includes 34 advanced economies, including high-income countries such as Germany, Italy, Japan and the United States, as well as emerging economies such as Mexico. Measuring debt as a percentage of GDP, the debt levels for the United States are about average for OECD countries. According to the OECD, the U.S. debt-to-GDP ratio was 61.3% in 2010 and the average for other OECD countries was 51.3%. In contrast, some countries had debt of about 100% of GDP, while Japan's debt was 180% of its GDP. Figure 13.3 shows that the debt-to-GDP ratio is relatively stable for OECD countries, apart from Japan. However, the population is aging in most OECD countries, and expenditures on programs for the elderly will likely cause the debt-to-GDP ratio to increase in the future. Figures 13.1 through 13.3 together suggest that the current level of debt for the U.S. federal government is not high by U.S. historical standards or by the standards of other advanced countries. This situation will change, though, if large deficits in the future cause the debt-to-GDP ratio to continue to increase.

Composition of Federal Government Revenue and Expenditure

The level of debt for the federal government in 2010 was not particularly high relative to U.S. GDP. Nevertheless, the United States does face serious fiscal challenges in the future. To understand these challenges, it is helpful to first understand the composition

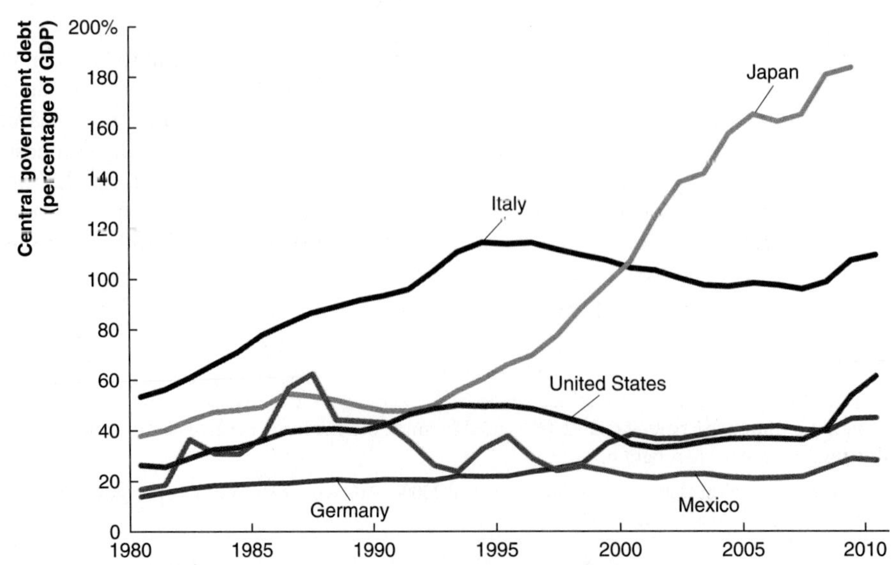

Figure 13.3

Central Government Debt for Countries in the Organisation for Economic Co-operation and Development, 1980–2010

The debt of the central government in the United States is about average for countries in the Organisation for Economic Co-operation and Development.

Source: Organisation for Economic Co-operation and Development. ●

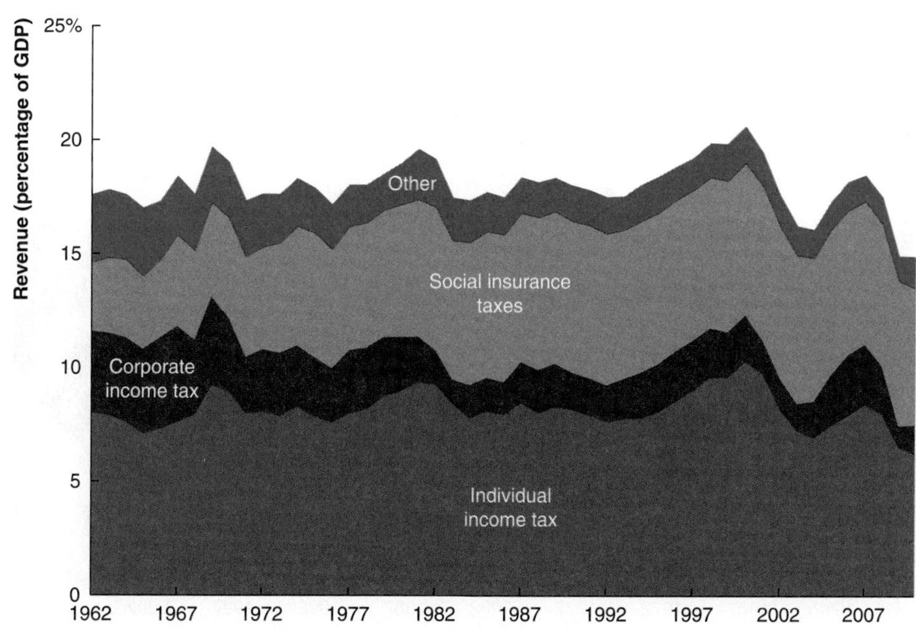

Figure 13.4

Composition of Federal Government Revenue, 1962–2010

Since 1962, corporate income taxes have become relatively less important, while social insurance taxes for Social Security, Medicare, and Medicaid have become more important. Data used for this figure are based on the fiscal year rather than the calendar year. The category "other" includes revenue from tariffs on imports, estate taxes, and excise taxes such as federal gasoline taxes.

Source: U.S. Congressional Budget Office. ●

of federal government expenditure and revenue and how the composition has changed since the 1960s.

Federal Government Revenue As mentioned earlier, the federal government obtains most of its revenue through taxes:

- *Individual income taxes* are the taxes that households pay on their wage and non-wage income.
- *Social insurance taxes* are the *payroll taxes* that households and firms pay to support Social Security and Medicare. *Medicare* is the federal government's program to provide healthcare for the elderly.
- *Corporate income taxes* are taxes that corporations pay on their profits.

Figure 13.4 shows that total federal revenue has averaged about 18% of GDP. The relative importance of the three categories of taxes has changed somewhat between 1962 and 2010. There are year-to-year fluctuations in individual income tax revenue as a percentage of GDP, reflecting the effects of the business cycle and changes in tax law. But there is no long-term trend over the entire period: Individual income tax revenue was 7.8% of GDP in 1962 and 8.1% of GDP in 2008, before falling to 6.2% in 2010 due to the recession of 2007–2009. In contrast, corporate income tax revenue was on a downward trend throughout the time period from 3.6% of GDP in 1962 to 1.3% of GDP in 2010. Revenue from social insurance taxes, on the other hand, doubled from 3.0% to 6.0% of GDP during the same time period.

Seigniorage Tax revenue is by far the most important source of revenue for the federal government, but the government also obtains revenue from seigniorage. When the Federal Reserve increases the monetary base, the purchasing power of previously existing currency decreases, so increasing the monetary base essentially transfers wealth from those who own existing currency to the government. Seigniorage is usually not an important source of revenue; it averaged just 0.2% of GDP from 1990 to 2008 for the United States, while personal income taxes, social insurance taxes, and corporate income taxes combined averaged 18% of GDP.

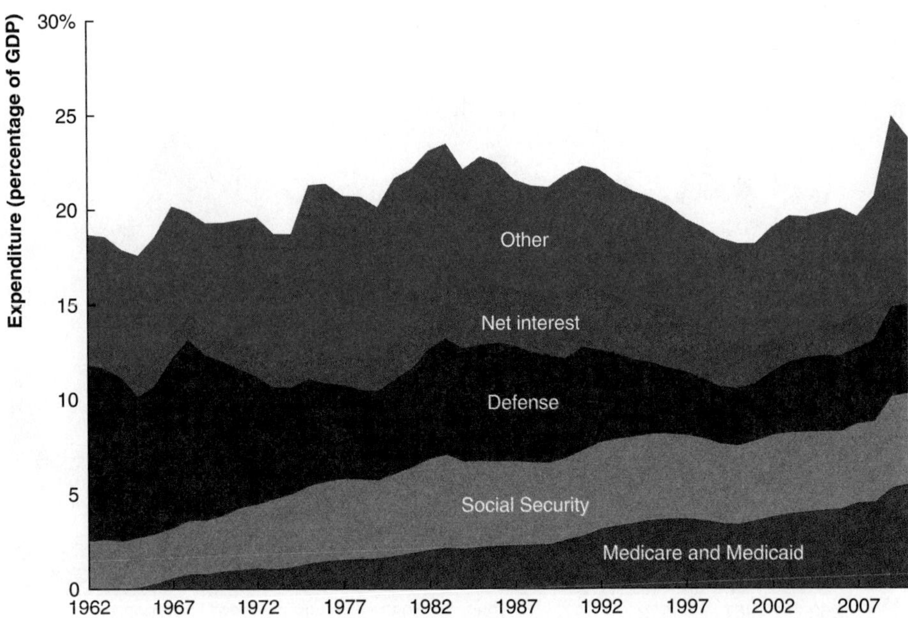

Figure 13.5

Composition of Federal Government Expenditure, 1962–2010

Transfer payments such as Medicare, Medicaid, and Social Security were a much larger percentage of GDP in 2010 than in the 1960s, while defense spending was a much smaller percentage.

Source: U.S. Congressional Budget Office. ●

Federal Government Expenditure

The changing composition of federal government expenditure helps us understand the fiscal challenges the government faces. Figure 13.5 shows federal government expenditure as a percentage of GDP for the United States from 1962 to 2010. Over this period, federal expenditure has averaged 20.5% of GDP. It rose to 25.0% of GDP in 2009, as the government undertook policies to fight the 2007–2009 recession, and remained at 23.8% in 2010. Total federal expenditure was relatively stable, but its composition changed dramatically. In 1962, defense expenditure was 9.3% of GDP, but it decreased to 4.7% in 2010. In contrast, Medicare and Medicaid spending rose from nothing in 1962 (the programs were introduced a few years later) to 5.5% of GDP in 2010, and spending on Social Security rose from 2.5% to 4.8% of GDP during the same time period. In other words, military expenditure has become much less important over time, while spending on transfer payments such as Medicare, Medicaid, and Social Security has become much more important.

13.2

Learning Objective

Explain when fiscal policy is sustainable and when it is not sustainable.

The Sustainability of Fiscal Policy

The previous section showed that federal government debt was not particularly large in 2010 either when viewed historically or in comparison to the debt of other high-income countries. However, according to the CBO, the budget deficit was 10.0% of GDP in 2009 and 8.9% of GDP in 2010 due to the financial crisis and the government's response to the crisis. In addition, as the population of the United States gets older and medical costs continue to rise faster than the inflation rate, the federal government is likely to spend increasing amounts on Medicare and Social Security. In this section, we examine whether the federal government's fiscal policy is sustainable.

The average price level of goods and services is P_t, and real GDP is Y_t, so nominal GDP equals P_tY_t. If we divide Equation (13.1) on page 488 by nominal GDP, we obtain:

$$\frac{PD_t}{P_tY_t} + i_t\frac{B_{t-1}}{P_tY_t} = \frac{\Delta B_t}{P_tY_t} + \frac{\Delta MB_t}{P_tY_t},$$

which is the government's budget constraint with the terms expressed relative to nominal GDP. With a little algebra, we can show that this equation is equivalent to:[4]

$$\Delta\left(\frac{B_t}{P_tY_t}\right) = \frac{PD_t}{P_tY_t} + [i_t - (\pi_t + g_Y)]\frac{B_{t-1}}{P_{t-1}Y_{t-1}} - \frac{\Delta MB_t}{P_tY_t}, \quad (13.2)$$

where π_t is the inflation rate and g_Y is the growth rate of real GDP. Nominal GDP growth equals the inflation rate plus the growth rate of real GDP, or $\pi_t + g_Y$. The debt-to-GDP ratio is stable when the change in the debt-to-GDP ratio, which is the expression on the left side of Equation (13.2), equals zero.

Making the Connection

The European Debt Crisis

The United States was not the only nation to experience an increase in debt during the financial crisis of 2007–2009. During the spring of 2010, many investors became reluctant to buy Greek government bonds because they were afraid that the government might default on the bonds. If the Greek government could not sell new bonds, the ΔB term in Equation (13.2) would become zero. Because Greece uses the euro as its currency, the European Central Bank, rather than the central bank of Greece, controls the Greek monetary base. Therefore, Greece does not have the option of expanding the monetary base to finance a budget deficit and ΔMB is constant. Accordingly, the Greek government was faced with the possibility of either defaulting on the interest payments due on its debt or taking the politically unpopular step of dramatically reducing its primary budget deficit. To help the Greek government and prevent a default, the other countries using the euro and the International Monetary Fund (IMF) put together a bailout package of €110 billion. To receive these funds, the Greek government had to agree to cut spending and increase taxes. European countries and the IMF also put together a €750 billion fund to help other European governments that might have difficulty financing their debts. The goal of the fund was to reassure investors that no country using the euro would default on its debt.

Unfortunately, the sovereign debt crisis that started with Greece during the spring of 2010 spread to Ireland during the fall. Ireland had kept government spending under control, but a collapse in its real estate market similar to the one in the United States greatly weakened Irish banks. In an attempt to calm financial markets and assure the public that Irish banks were safe, the Irish government guaranteed the debt of Irish banks. As a result, the Irish government's budget deficit reached 32% of GDP during 2010. Ireland eventually had to accept a bailout of €85 billion from the European nations and the IMF on November 28, 2010. Despite the bailout, investors were concerned that even with these funds, the Irish government would not be able to make the changes to the budget necessary to stabilize its economy. To make matters worse, the same concerns that forced a bailout of the Irish government led to problems in Spain. Much like Greece, Italy and Portugal had debt problems prior to 2007 that were made worse by the financial crisis. The debt crisis is forcing many countries to reevaluate the benefits of government programs relative to the long-term costs of maintaining those programs.

Sources: "Saving the Euro: Ireland's Woes Are Largely of Its Own Making but German Bungling Has Made Matters Worse," *Economist*, November 18, 2010; "No Easy Exit," *Economist*, December 4, 2010; Stephen Castle, "Economic Divisions in Euro Zone Are Seen as Threat," *New York Times*, November 30, 2010; and "European Sovereign Debt Crisis," *New York Times*, March 11, 2011.

Test your understanding by doing related problem 2.5 on page 515 at the end of this chapter.

[4]We show the full derivation in Appendix 13A at the end of the chapter.

According to Equation (13.2), the debt-to-GDP ratio increases when the primary deficit-to-GDP ratio increases or when seigniorage decreases. The middle term in Equation (13.2) shows the effect of past debt and the growth rate of nominal GDP on the debt-to-GDP ratio. Because the government must pay interest on the debt that it has at the beginning of the year, the higher the nominal interest rate, the larger the interest payments the government must make during the year. Holding everything else constant, these interest payments will increase the debt-to-GDP ratio. And, holding everything else constant, nominal GDP growth will reduce the debt-to-GDP ratio.

It is also useful to remember what the growth rate of nominal GDP is in the long run, when the economy is along the balanced growth path. The quantity theory from Chapter 6 tells us that in the long run, when the growth rate of the money supply increases by one percentage point, the inflation rate also increases by one percentage point. The growth model from Chapter 5 tells us that, in the long run, the growth rate of real GDP equals the growth rate of the labor force plus $\left(\frac{3}{2}\right)g_A$, where g_A is the growth rate of total factor productivity (TFP). So, if either the growth rate of the labor force or TFP growth increases, the debt-to-GDP ratio will decrease.

The effect of an increase in the growth rate of the money supply is more difficult to analyze because the inflation rate also affects the nominal interest rate. When the nominal interest rate is constant, an increase in the growth rate of the money supply increases the inflation rate and reduces the debt-to-GDP ratio. However, the Fisher effect from Chapter 6 tells us that the increase in the inflation rate will lead to a higher nominal interest rate, and that increase will, in turn, raise the debt-to-GDP ratio. So, the net effect of an increase in the growth rate of the money supply is ambiguous and may be zero. This observation raises an important point: It is difficult to finance budget deficits simply by printing more money because nominal interest rates adjust upward, causing interest payments to also increase. This effect is one explanation for the unsustainable hyperinflation in Germany from 1922 to 1923 that we discussed in Chapter 6.

When Is Fiscal Policy Sustainable?

Recall that the real interest rate, r, equals the nominal interest rate minus the inflation rate. So, we can use this relationship to eliminate the nominal interest rate and the inflation rate from Equation (13.2) and rewrite the equation as:

$$\Delta\left(\frac{B_t}{P_tY_t}\right) = \frac{PD_t}{P_tY_t} + (r_t - g_Y)\frac{B_{t-1}}{P_{t-1}Y_{t-1}} - \frac{\Delta MB_t}{P_tY_t}. \tag{13.3}$$

We can use Equation (13.3) to discuss whether a country's debt is sustainable. The debt is sustainable when the debt-to-GDP ratio is either constant or declining. Surprisingly, this is not the same thing as having a primary deficit of zero. To simplify our discussion, we will assume that seigniorage is zero because seigniorage is normally very small. We will also assume that the government's primary deficit is zero, so Equation (13.3) becomes:

$$\Delta\left(\frac{B_t}{P_tY_t}\right) = (r_t - g_Y)\frac{B_{t-1}}{P_{t-1}Y_{t-1}}.$$

Under these conditions, the change in the debt-to-GDP ratio depends only on the real interest rate and the growth rate of real GDP. If:

$$r_t > g_Y,$$

then:

$$\Delta\left(\frac{B_t}{P_tY_t}\right) > 0,$$

so the debt-to-GDP ratio will increase even if the government has a primary deficit of zero. In this case, the government is forced to run a primary surplus just to prevent the debt-to-GDP ratio from rising to higher and higher levels. However, if:

$$r_t < g_Y,$$

then:

$$\Delta\left(\frac{B_t}{P_tY_t}\right) < 0,$$

so the debt-to-GDP ratio will decrease. In this case, it is possible to have a primary deficit greater than zero and still have a sustainable fiscal policy. But if the real interest rate is greater than the growth rate of real GDP, then as we have just seen, even when the primary deficit is zero, fiscal policy is unsustainable.

Consider the United States during 2010. According to the CBO, the debt-to-GDP ratio for the United States was 53.5% during 2009. The average real interest rate that the United States paid on long-term bonds was 1.2%, and the growth rate of real GDP was 2.9% during 2010. Assume that the primary deficit and seigniorage are both zero. Using this information and equation (13.3), we find:

$$\Delta\left(\frac{B_t}{P_tY_t}\right) = (0.012 - 0.029)0.535 = -0.009, \text{or} -0.9\%.$$

That is, if the U.S. government had a primary budget deficit of zero, the debt-to-GDP ratio for the United States would have decreased by 0.9%. However, the U.S. government actually ran a primary deficit during 2010, so the debt-to-GDP ratio actually rose to 62.5% by the end of 2010. The 2.9% growth rate is a bit below the U.S. long-run average, so this calculation suggests that the U.S. government could reduce the debt-to-GDP ratio through economic growth if it found a way to reduce the primary budget deficit to zero.

Solved Problem 13.2

Can Japan Grow Its Way Out of Debt?

In Japan, the government debt reached 226% of GDP during 2010. Economic growth in Japan has averaged just 0.7% per year, and inflation (calculated as the growth rate of the GDP deflator) has averaged –0.7%. The Ministry of Finance reported that the average nominal interest rate that the government paid to borrow for 10 years was 1.2%. Given this information, was Japanese fiscal policy sustainable? If not, what would the primary budget deficit have to be to make fiscal policy sustainable?

Solving the Problem

Step 1 **Review the chapter material.** The problem asks you to determine whether fiscal policy is sustainable, so you may want to review the section "When Is Fiscal Policy Sustainable?" which begins on page 496.

Step 2 **Determine whether Japanese fiscal policy is sustainable.** To determine whether the debt is sustainable, you have to compare the real interest rate with the growth rate of real GDP. You know that the growth rate of real GDP was just 0.7%. You also know that the nominal interest rate was 1.2% and that inflation was –0.7%. Using the the definition of the real interest rate, you can calculate the real interest rate as:

$$r = 1.2 - (-0.7) = 1.9\%.$$

Because:

$$r > g_Y,$$

Japan's debt was not sustainable, so even if the Japanese government had a primary deficit of zero, the debt-to-GDP ratio would continue to increase.

Step 3 **Determine the primary deficit necessary to make the debt stable.** You can use Equation (13.3) from page 496:

$$\Delta\left(\frac{B_t}{P_tY_t}\right) = \frac{PD_t}{P_tY_t} + (r_t - g_Y)\frac{B_{t-1}}{P_{t-1}Y_{t-1}} - \frac{\Delta MB_t}{P_tY_t}.$$

Seigniorage is usually small, so rewrite the preceding equation without seigniorage:

$$\Delta\left(\frac{B_t}{P_tY_t}\right) = \frac{PD_t}{P_tY_t} + (r_t - g_Y)\frac{B_{t-1}}{P_{t-1}Y_{t-1}}.$$

The real interest rate was 1.9%, or 0.019, and the growth rate of real GDP has averaged 0.7%, or 0.007, so plug these values into the preceding equation:

$$\Delta\left(\frac{B_t}{P_tY_t}\right) = \frac{PD_t}{P_tY_t} + (0.019 - 0.007)\frac{B_{t-1}}{P_{t-1}Y_{t-1}}.$$

In 2010, the debt-to-GDP ratio was 226%, or 2.26, so plug this value in for the lagged debt-to-GDP ratio. Furthermore, the debt-to-GDP ratio is sustainable when the ratio is constant, so plug in a value of 0 for the change in the debt-to-GDP ratio on the left side:

$$0 = \frac{PD_t}{P_tY_t} + (0.019 - 0.007)2.26.$$

Now, solve for the primary deficit:

$$\frac{PD_t}{P_tY_t} = -0.027, \text{or} -2.7\%.$$

A negative number means that the Japanese government would have to run a primary surplus of 2.7% of GDP to make the debt sustainable. However, Japan actually had a primary deficit of 5.9% in 2010, so the debt is not sustainable. Unless Japan significantly increases its growth rate in the near future, it will not be able to grow its way out of the debt. Therefore, moving to a sustainable fiscal policy will require a movement from a primary deficit to a primary surplus through a combination of tax increases and spending cuts.

For more practice, do related problem 2.8 on page 515 at the end of this chapter.

13.3

Learning Objective
Understand how fiscal policy affects the economy in the long run.

Effects of Budget Deficits on Investment

In earlier chapters, we discussed how fiscal policy affects consumption, government spending, investment, and trade. In this section, we focus on how budget deficits affect investment.

A Useful Identity

The national income identities that we introduced in Chapter 2 are useful because they must hold, given the definition of the terms. So, the identities act like constraints. Here, we rewrite one of the more useful identities from Chapter 2:

$$Y = C + I + G + NX.$$

When net exports are negative, the economy runs a trade deficit, and when net exports are positive, the economy runs a trade surplus. As shown in appendix 13B, we can modify the preceding equation to become:

$$[(G + TR) - T] = S_{Household} - I - NX, \qquad (13.4)$$

where $S_{Household} = Y + TR - T - C$ and $[(G + TR) - T]$ is the primary budget deficit.

Equation (13.4) tells us that the government's budget deficit is financed by some combination of increased private savings, reduced private investment, and net exports. It might sound strange to say that net exports finance government deficits, but a trade deficit means that a country is borrowing from other countries. We discuss this issue in further detail in Chapter 15. Suppose the government decides to decrease income taxes by \$100 billion. To keep the deficit from increasing, the government could (1) reduce purchases by \$100 billion; or (2) reduce transfer payments, by \$100 billion; or (3) increase other taxes by \$100 billion. The government could pursue one or some combination of the three policy changes, which means the budget deficit would not increase and the private sector would not have to adjust.

If the government does not pursue a policy change, the budget deficit will increase by \$100 billion. The government will have to issue \$100 billion in new Treasury bonds, which requires the private sector to adjust. First, households may increase savings by \$100 billion by purchasing the new bonds. In this case, domestic households could reduce consumption by \$100 billion. In effect, domestic households finance the higher deficit by cutting their own consumption. Second, firms and households could decrease investment by \$100 billion. This decline is called **crowding out**, a reduction in private investment caused by government budget deficits. Third, the trade deficit could increase by \$100 billion. As we will see in Chapter 15, the increased trade deficit would be the equivalent of foreign governments and individuals purchasing \$100 billion in new government bonds. So, the international indebtedness of the government increases. The identity in Equation (13.4) tells us the range of possible responses to a larger budget deficit. However, the identity does not tell us which of the three terms will adjust if the budget deficit increases. For that, we need economic theory.

Crowding out A reduction in private investment caused by government budget deficits.

The Conventional View: Crowding Out Private Investment

The conventional view among economists is that a budget deficit crowds out investment in Equation (13.4). To understand this view, we revisit the loanable funds model from Chapter 3. If the government runs a budget deficit that is not financed through seigniorage, then the government must issue additional government bonds. If the government borrows \$100 billion, then that is \$100 billion that households and firms cannot borrow to finance investment. Figure 13.6 shows that the supply curve for loanable funds shifts to the left, causing the real interest rate to increase and the equilibrium amount of investment to decrease.

The loanable funds model tells us that budget deficits increase long-term real interest rates and reduce investment. The next step in understanding how fiscal policy affects the economy is to think about the effect of the decrease in investment. The easiest way to do this is to recall the bathtub analogy we discussed in connection with the Solow growth model in Chapter 5. In this analogy, the capital stock is the level of water in the bathtub, investment is water flowing into the bathtub, and depreciation is water flowing out of the bathtub. If the government runs a budget deficit, then saving and investment decrease and less water flows into the bathtub. Figure 13.7 shows the effect of the decreased investment with the Solow growth model. The reduced level of saving decreases the saving rate. As a result, the investment curve in the Solow growth model shifts downward and the capital stock decreases over time, so the level of labor productivity decreases. In the end, the economy moves to a balanced growth path with a lower level of potential GDP.

Figure 13.6

The Effect of Government Budget Deficits on Real Interest Rates and Investment

A government budget deficit reduces the supply of loanable funds, so the supply curve shifts to the left, from S_1 to S_2. As a result, the real interest rate increases and the equilibrium amount of investment decreases. ●

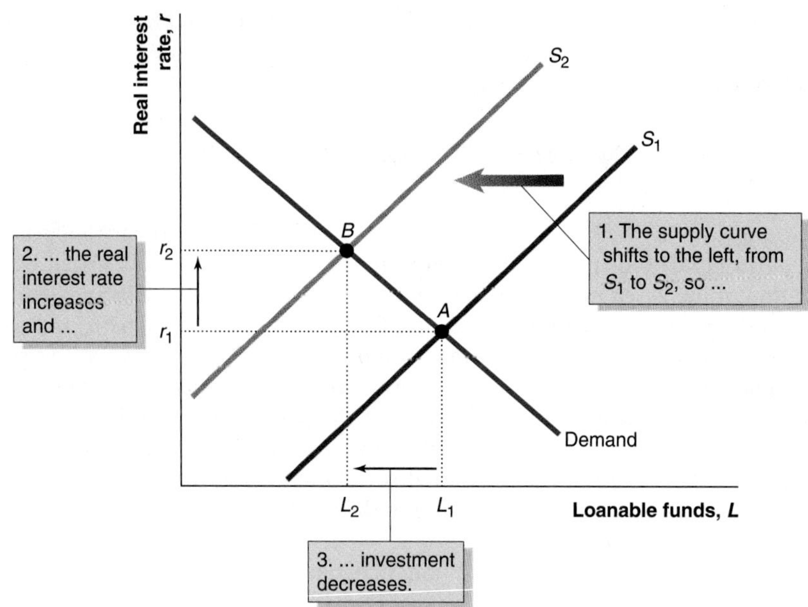

Real interest rate, r
S_2
S_1
1. The supply curve shifts to the left, from S_1 to S_2, so ...
B
A
2. ... the real interest rate increases and ...
r_2
r_1
Demand
L_2
L_1
Loanable funds, L
3. ... investment decreases.

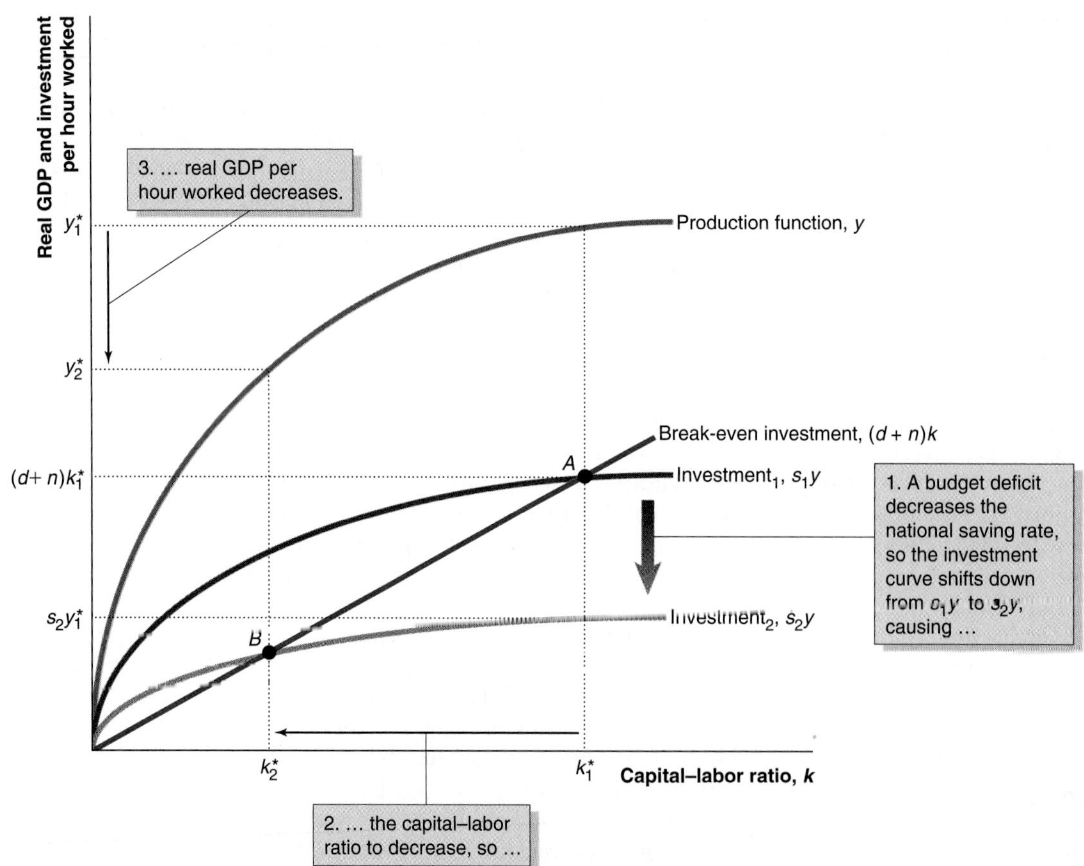

Real GDP and investment per hour worked
3. ... real GDP per hour worked decreases.
y_1^*
Production function, y
y_2^*
Break-even investment, $(d + n)k$
A
$(d+ n)k_1^*$
Investment$_1$, s_1y
1. A budget deficit decreases the national saving rate, so the investment curve shifts down from s_1y to s_2y, causing ...
$s_2y_1^*$
Investment$_2$, s_2y
B
k_2^*
k_1^*
Capital–labor ratio, k
2. ... the capital–labor ratio to decrease, so ...

Figure 13.7 The Long-Run Effect of an Increase in the Budget Deficit

A higher budget deficit reduces national saving, so the saving rate decreases. As a result, the investment curve shifts downward and the economy's steady-state equilibrium moves from point *A* to point *B*. The result is a lower capital-to-labor ratio and lower productivity. The lower productivity leads to a lower level of potential GDP along the balanced growth path. ●

MACRO DATA: DO GOVERNMENT DEFICITS INCREASE REAL INTEREST RATES?

The loanable funds model predicts that budget deficits will lead to higher real interest rates. What is the evidence to support this prediction? Economists William Gale of the Brookings Institution and Peter Orszag, former director of the U.S. Office of Management and Budget, conducted a study in which they found relatively large effects of fiscal policy on long-term real interest rates. Gale and Orszag found that each 1-percentage-point increase in the deficit relative to GDP raises long-term real interest rates by 0.25% to 0.35%. They also found that the increase is between 0.40% and 0.70% when the primary budget deficit increases by 1 percentage point of GDP. Studies using the debt-to-GDP ratio as the measure of fiscal policy often find smaller effects of fiscal policy on real interest rates. Economists Eric Engen of the Board of Governors of the Federal Reserve System and Glenn Hubbard of Columbia University examined the effect of government debt on real interest rates and investment. They found that a 1-percentage-point increase in the debt-to-GDP ratio increases long-term real interest rates by about 0.03%, which is a relatively small amount. The CBO estimates that President Obama's fiscal policy will increase the federal government's debt from 40.8% of GDP during 2008 and to 81.7% of GDP by 2019. This is a 40.9% increase in the debt-to-GDP ratio in just 11 years.

The study by Engen and Hubbard suggests that the forecast increase in the debt-to-GDP ratio will increase long-term real interest rates 1.2 percentage points over what they otherwise would have been. The higher real interest rates should lead to lower investment.

Economists have found a variety of estimates of the effects of fiscal policy on long-term real interest rates. The differences arise because some studies focus on the federal debt, others focus on deficits, and the definitions of *debt* and *deficit* can vary from study to study. In addition, the statistical techniques that economists use can also vary from study to study. As a result, the estimated magnitude of the effect of fiscal policy on long-term real interest rates varies. However, most studies support the conventional view that fiscal policy affects these rates. When fiscal policy leads to higher long-term real interest rates, private investment decreases.

Sources: William Gale and Peter Orszag, "Budget Deficits, National Savings, and Interest Rates," *Brookings Panel on Economic Activity*, Vol. 2004, No. 2, September 2004, pp. 101–187; and Eric Engen and R. Glenn Hubbard, "Federal Government Debt and Interest Rates," in Mark Gertler and Kenneth Rogoff, eds., *National Bureau of Economic Research Macroeconomics Annual*, Cambridge, MA: MIT Press, 2004, pp. 83–160.

Test your understanding by doing related problem 3.13 on page 517 at the end of this chapter.

Solved Problem 13.3

The Effect of a Government Budget Surplus

Suppose that a government runs a budget surplus. Use a graph to show the effects on real interest rates, investment, and potential GDP. Use a second graph to show the effects on the capital stock and labor productivity.

Solving the Problem

Step 1 **Review the chapter material.** This problem asks you to determine the effect of a budget surplus on the economy, so you may want to review the section "The Conventional View: Crowding Out Private Investment," which begins on page 499.

Step 2 **Determine the effect on real interest rates, saving, and investment.** When the government runs a budget surplus, the funds available for investment increase.

So, draw a loanable funds graph with the supply of loanable funds shifting to the right. Your graph should look like this:

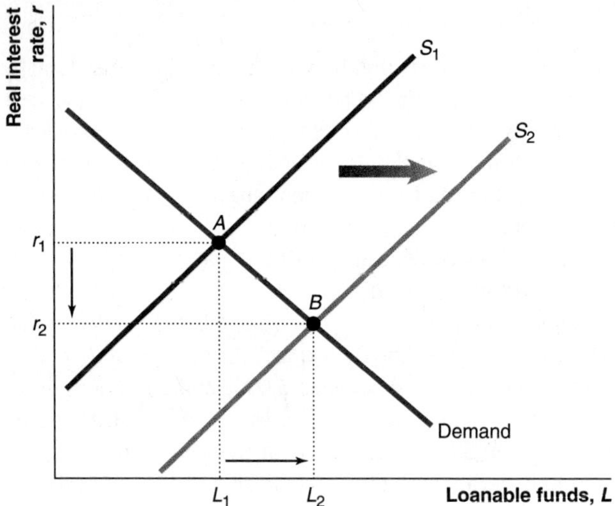

Step 3 Determine the effect on the capital stock and labor productivity. Now you need to think about the effect of more investment in terms of the Solow growth model. The increase saving increases the saving rate so the investment curve shifts upward. As a result, the steady-state capital–labor ratio and level of labor productivity both increase. Your graph showing the effect of the increase in the investment rate using the Solow model should look like this:

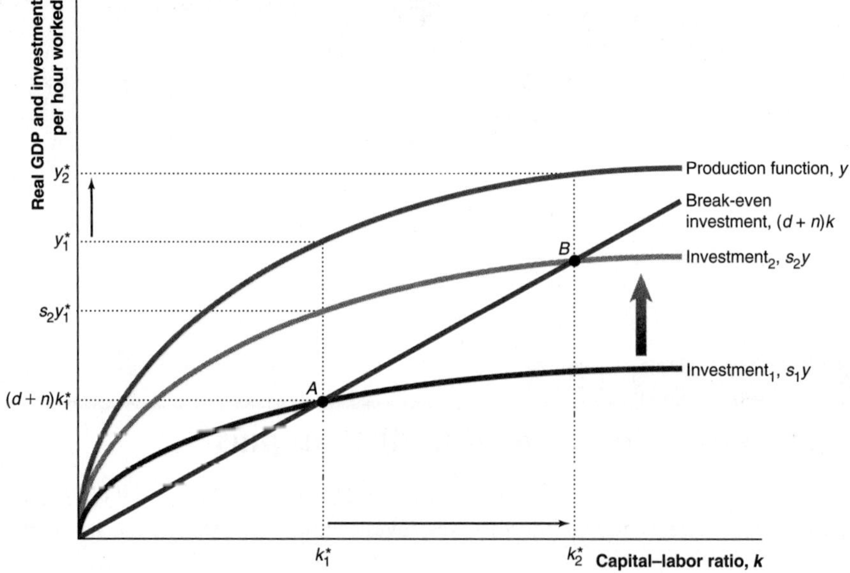

Step 4 Determine the effect on real GDP. Real GDP equals labor productivity multiplied by the number of labor hours worked, so the increase in labor productivity will result in higher real GDP along the new balanced growth path. Because the balanced growth path represents the level of real GDP when labor and capital are fully employed, real GDP equals potential GDP when on the balanced growth path. Therefore, the budget surplus leads to a larger capital stock that increases labor productivity and potential GDP.

For more practice, do related problem 3.10 on page 516 at the end of this chapter.

Table 13.2 The Conventional View of Fiscal Policy and Potential GDP in the Long Run

If the government runs a . . .	the supply of loanable funds to the private sector . . .	so long-term real interest rates . . .	the capital stock . . .	labor productivity and potential GDP . . .
budget deficit	decreases	increase	decreases	decrease.
budget surplus	increases	decrease	increases	increase.

Table 13.2 summarizes the conventional view of the effects of a budget deficit on the economy in the long run.

Ricardian Equivalence

Most economists agree that if government expenditures increase, private investment will decrease. However, not all economists agree that tax cuts will have the same effect. Instead, these economists believe that private saving in Equation (13.4) will adjust. In effect, these economists believe that government budget deficits driven by tax cuts crowd out private consumption rather than private investment.

David Ricardo was a famous nineteenth-century British economist who developed **Ricardian equivalence**, the theory that forward-looking households fully anticipate the taxes implied by government spending, so that changes in lump-sum taxes have no effect on the economy.[5] Lump-sum taxes are independent of the level of income and so do not have the distortionary effects on the decisions to save, invest, and work that changes in marginal tax rates do. According to this view, households consider lifetime disposable income and not just current disposable income when making consumption decisions. Therefore, households increase consumption only when lifetime disposable income increases and reduce consumption only when lifetime disposable income decreases. We consider this type of household behavior more fully in Chapter 14.

Ricardian equivalence The theory that forward-looking households fully anticipate the taxes implied by government spending, so that changes in lump-sum taxes have no effect on the economy.

What does this type of consumption behavior imply about how the economy responds to a tax cut of $100 billion? To keep the analysis simple, assume that the world consists of this year and next year and that the government must eventually pay off its debt. Also assume that the interest rate the government pays to borrow is 0%. This year, the government announces that it will cut taxes by $100 billion. Because the government must pay off the debt next year, it must raise taxes by $100 billion next year. Therefore, the decision by the government to cut taxes today by $100 billion is also a decision to increase taxes next year by $100 billion.

Households are forward-looking in their consumption decisions, so they recognize that their disposable income increases this year by $100 billion but then decreases next year by $100 billion. There is no change in lifetime disposable income for households, so there is no change in consumption. If consumption does not change, how do households alter their behavior in response to the $100 billion tax cut? Disposable income is defined as:

$$Y^D = (Y + TR) - T.$$

Households either consume or save their disposable income, so:

$$Y^D = C + S_{\text{Household}}.$$

Putting these two equations together, we get:

$$(Y + TR) - T = C + S_{\text{Household}}.$$

The tax cut increases disposable income by $100 billion this year on the left side of the equation, but it does not cause consumption to increase because lifetime disposable

[5]David Ricardo actually considered and rejected the idea of Ricardian equivalence. Harvard economist Robert Barro is the most famous modern adherent of Ricardian equivalence. When Barro formulated the argument, he credited Ricardo for first mentioning the idea and so the view has become known as Ricardian equivalence. See Robert J. Barro, "Are Government Bonds Net Wealth?" *Journal of Political Economy*, Vol. 82, No. 6, November–December 1974, pp. 1095–1117.

income has not changed. Therefore, private saving must have increased by $100 billion in response to the tax cut. Ricardian equivalence implies that households use the extra disposable income from the tax cut to purchase government bonds this year and use the revenues from the maturing bonds next year to pay for the higher taxes.

Ricardian equivalence implies that with government purchases and transfer payments *constant*, a change in taxes will not affect consumption. However, a change in fiscal policy that does affect lifetime disposable income may still affect consumption. For example, what happens if the government cut taxes today by $100 billion and at the same time announces that it will cut government expenditures next year by $100 billion? In this case, the government runs a budget deficit of $100 billion this year and then a budget surplus next year of $100 billion, so the government pays off its debt without raising future taxes. Therefore, the tax cut this year does increase lifetime disposable income, so consumption will increase.

Many economists are skeptical about whether Ricardian equivalence accurately describes the behavior of households. First, Ricardian equivalence assumes that households are forward looking in an extreme sense. In the previous example, we assumed that the relevant time frame was just two years. In reality, the government could cut taxes today and then not raise taxes to pay for the debt for 10 or more years. When the tax increase is in the distant future, households may not realize that their taxes will increase, so they may think that their lifetime disposable income has increased. As a result, they may increase consumption. Suppose the tax increase is not even in the current household's lifetime but instead occurs during their children's or grandchildren's lifetime. In this case, the tax cut increases lifetime disposable income for existing households, so current consumption will increase, unless current households take into account the future incomes of their children and grandchildren. Of course, the tax increase in the future reduces lifetime disposable income of future households, but those households do not yet exist, so they cannot reduce consumption in the present.

Second, for Ricardian equivalence to hold, financial markets must work well enough that households can borrow or save as much as they would like at the current interest rates. Suppose the government announces a tax increase this year of $100 billion and a corresponding tax cut of $100 billion next year. Lifetime disposable income has not changed, but current disposable income has decreased by $100 billion. According to Ricardian equivalence, consumption will not change. However, for consumption to remain constant, households must borrow to compensate for the drop in disposable income this year. If some households are not able to borrow enough to keep consumption constant, then the tax increase will cause consumption to decrease.

Third, Ricardian equivalence applies only to lump-sum taxes, while tax changes involve changes in tax rates. Changes in tax rates may affect household behavior. For example, we saw in Chapter 7 that income tax rates affect the decision of individuals to supply labor. As a result, a tax increase today will reduce the quantity of labor supplied and reduce real GDP today. Taxes on capital income will affect the accumulation of the capital stock, which will also affect real GDP. So, tax changes that affect the behavior of households may affect real GDP and consumption.

Foreign-Sector Adjustments

Equation (13.4) shows that the economy can respond in several different ways to a government budget deficit: Private investment spending can decrease, private saving can increase, or the trade deficit can increase. The standard view is that private investment spending decreases, while advocates of Ricardian equivalence believe that private saving will increase in response to a government budget deficit caused by tax cuts. It is also possible that the trade deficit will increase through some combination of an increase in imports and a decrease in exports. We discuss this possibility further in Chapter 15. As we will see in that chapter, running a trade deficit means that a country is accumulating debt or selling off assets to the rest of the world.

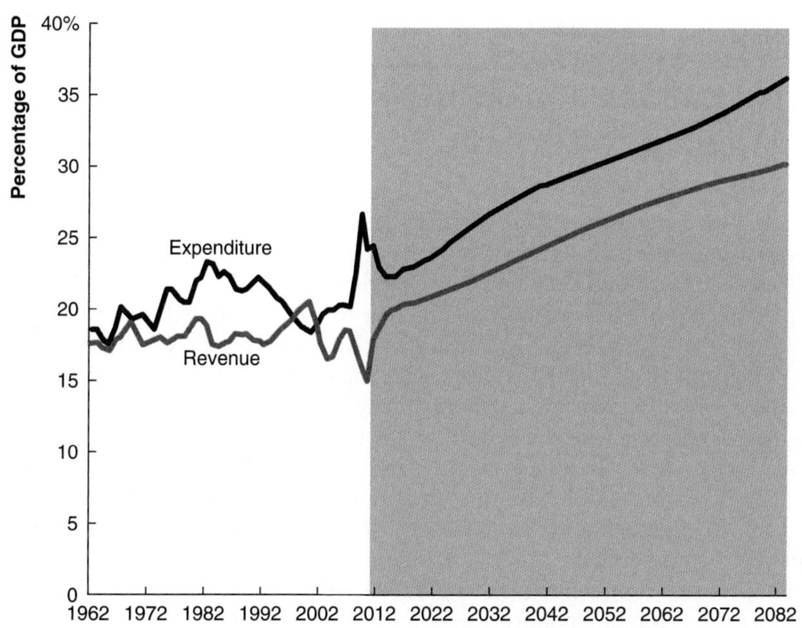

Figure 13.8

Federal Revenue and Expenditure as a Percentage of GDP, 1962–2084

After 2020, federal government expenditure and revenue both begin to rise. However, revenue never catches up to expenditure, so the federal government is expected to run persistent large budget deficits.

Note: The shaded area represents the CBO forecast.

Source: U.S. Congressional Budget Office. ●

The Fiscal Challenges Facing the United States

13.4 Learning Objective

Explain the fiscal challenges facing the United States.

When we discussed the composition of federal government expenditure and revenue in Section 13.1, we saw that transfer programs such as Medicare, Medicaid, and Social Security have been growing in importance. Rising spending on these programs represent the main challenge for fiscal policy in the future. The United States and most industrialized nations will experience similar issues due to the aging of their populations, so our discussion applies to many nations.

Projections of Federal Government Revenue and Expenditure

The CBO is responsible for forecasting federal government revenue and expenditure into the future, which also allows the CBO to forecast the federal budget deficit and the likely path of the debt-to-GDP ratio.[6] Figure 13.8 shows that revenue is expected to increase from 14.9% of GDP in 2010 to 30.3% of GDP in 2084. This change represents a significant increase above the historical average and by itself should lead to lower deficits and a lower debt-to-GDP ratio. However, expenditure is expected to increase from 23.8% of GDP in 2010 to 36.5% of GDP in 2084. So, the CBO forecasts a budget deficit of 6.2% of GDP for 2084, compared to a 2010 budget deficit of 8.9% of GDP. Although the CBO expects smaller budget deficits in the future, it does not expect revenue to rise quickly enough to balance the budget in any year through 2084.

[6]Congressional Budget Office, "The Long-Term Budget Outlook," June 2010. The CBO actually provides two forecasts. The first forecast is the "extended-baseline scenario," in which the CBO assumes that current policies will continue into the future. For example, this scenario assumes that the 2001 and 2003 tax cuts will expire as scheduled in 2012 and that the growth rate of Medicare payments to physicians will follow the current law. Some of these assumptions are unrealistic, so the CBO also provides an "alternative fiscal scenario" forecast that assumes, among other things, that Medicare payments to physicians will grow faster than the current law allows and that the 2001 and 2003 tax cuts are extended. The policy changes in the alternative fiscal scenario have occurred in the past and are expected to occur again in the future. In this chapter, we use the "extended-baseline scenario" forecasts.

Making the Connection

The U.S. National Commission on Fiscal Responsibility and Reform

President Obama created the National Commission on Fiscal Responsibility and Reform to present ideas for reducing the federal budget deficit and put the federal government's debt on a more sustainable path. The CBO expects persistent large budget deficits in the future that will cause gross federal debt held by the public to eventually exceed 100% of U.S. GDP. The gap between projected expenditure and revenue is large enough that Dave Cote, CEO of Honeywell International and a member of the National Commission on Fiscal Responsibility and Reform, asked, "What happens when the bank, in this case foreign countries like China, doesn't want to loan you any more money?" Senator Kent Conrad of North Dakota echoed these sentiments when he said, "If we fail to act now, our country could find itself in a circumstance in which we have to take draconian action at the worst possible time, in the midst of a crisis," which is what recently occurred in Europe with the debt crises in Greece and Ireland. To ensure that the United States does not experience Europe's problem, the commission recommended a number of changes to government expenditure and taxes. The commission's recommendations would reduce, but not eliminate, the budget deficit. If the commission's recommendations were fully implemented *the increase* in the national debt between 2012 and 2020 would be only $4 trillion rather than $8 trillion.

The commission's recommendations were:

1. Raise $1.1 trillion in tax revenues by eliminating or reducing the deduction for home mortgage interest, the deduction for employer healthcare coverage, the tax exemption for municipal bonds, and preferential tax rates for capital gains and dividend income.
2. Increase the federal government tax on gasoline by 15 cents a gallon.
3. Increase federal government taxes on higher-income households to support Social Security by raising or eliminating the income cap on Social Security payments.
4. Cap domestic spending, such as farm subsidies and defense spending.
5. Increase the retirement age from 67 to 69 in the future to reduce Social Security expenditures. The commission would also increase Medicare premiums significantly.

Eliminating the tax deductions and increasing the gasoline tax would allow the government to reduce both corporate and personal income tax rates. As a result, the proposal would have the positive effects on aggregate supply that we discussed in Chapter 11. The commission's recommendations would keep taxes low but cut benefits and harm households that rely on government transfer programs, such as Medicare and Social Security. However, the cut in benefits would not occur until 2050, so current retirees would not be affected.

In December 2010, the commission's recommendations won the votes of 11 of 18 commission members. However, this result was short of the 14 votes required to bring the recommendations to Congress for a vote. Still, the bipartisan support given to the commission's work led both supporters and opponents to believe that it would serve as the basis for future debates on long-term deficit reduction.

Sources: "Deficit Panel: In Members' Words," *Wall Street Journal*, December 1, 2010; Jackie Calmes, "As Final Debt Plan Is Released, Signs That the Fight Is Just Beginning," *New York Times*, December 2, 2010, p. A24; Jackie Calmes, "Panel Seeks Cuts in Social Security and Higher Taxes," *New York Times*, November 11, 2010, p. A1; Lori Montgomery and Brady Dennis, "Deficit Commission Sets Ideology Aside," *Washington Post*, December 2, 2010, p. A1; Damian Paletta and Jonathan Weisman, "Deficit Plan Wins Backers—Bipartisan Support Adds Momentum Despite Sharp Criticism from Left and Right," *Wall Street Journal*, December 2, 2010, p. A1; and "National Commission on Fiscal Responsibility and Reform," *New York Times*, December 3, 2010.

Test your understanding by doing related problem 4.7 on page 518 at the end of this chapter.

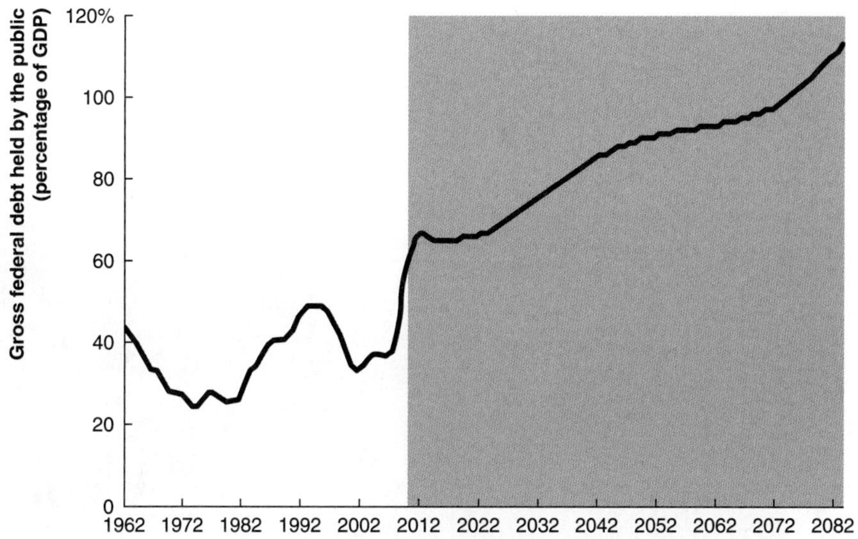

Figure 13.9

Gross Federal Debt as a Percentage of GDP, 1962–2084

The debt-to-GDP ratio is relatively stable until about 2020, and then begins to rise rapidly.

Note: The shaded area represents the CBO forecast.

Source: U.S. Congressional Budget Office. ●

The projected future budget deficits will cause the debt-to-GDP ratio to increase dramatically, as Figure 13.9 shows. Because of the federal government's policies to fight the 2007–2009 recession, the figure shows a jump in the debt-to-GDP ratio from 2009 to 2012, but then the ratio stabilizes until about 2020. After 2020, the ratio begins to increase rapidly as federal government expenditure outpaces revenue. As a result, the debt-to-GDP ratio is forecast to rise from 62.1% in 2010 to 113.0% in 2084. The CBO's forecast tells us that with large projected spending on Social Security and Medicare, the current fiscal policy of the federal government is not sustainable.

Why Does the Debt-to-GDP Ratio Explode?

The debt-to-GDP ratio explodes because government spending on transfer programs such as Medicare, Medicaid, and Social Security outpaces increases in revenue. In addition, the federal government has to pay interest on the new debt it issues, so net interest payments rise dramatically. Figure 13.10 shows the composition of federal government expenditure from 1962 to 2084. "Other primary expenditure" include defense, education, infrastructure, and science. This expenditure is expected to decrease from 12.4% of GDP in 2011 to 6.7% of GDP in 2084. In contrast, spending on Medicare, Medicaid, and Social Security is expected to rise from 10.5% of GDP in 2011 to 24.2% of GDP in 2084. Interest payments are also expected to increase from 1.6% of GDP in 2011 to 5.6% of GDP in 2084. Therefore, the CBO expects that a rising share of the federal government's budget will go to servicing past debt rather than providing goods and services to citizens.

Federal expenditure on all goods and services, transfer programs, and net interest averaged just over 20% of GDP from 1962 to 2010. Figure 13.10 tells us that the CBO forecasts that spending on transfer programs alone will increase by 13.7 percentage points of GDP. Spending on these programs will increase because the population is aging and healthcare costs are expected to rise rapidly. Therefore, given demographic trends, if current transfer programs remain as they are, the government will consume a much larger share of GDP in the future.

Policy Options

What are the consequences of the rising debt-to-GDP ratio? The conventional view is that the expected future budget deficits and increasing debt-to-GDP ratio will crowd out private investment spending and reduce the capital stock. The CBO provides estimates of the

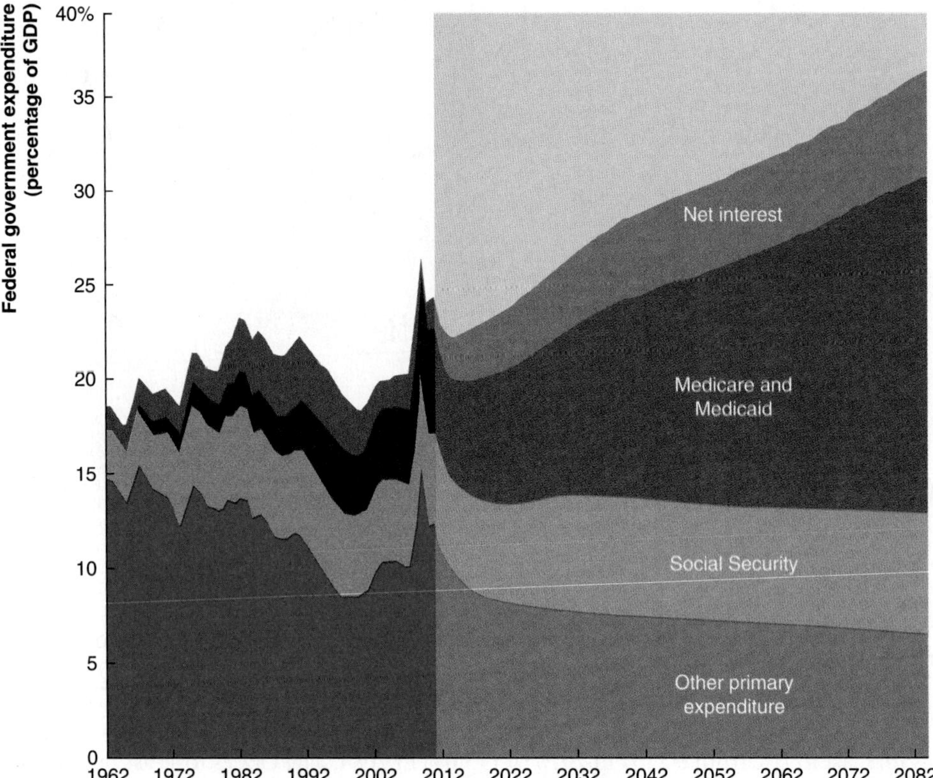

Figure 13.10

Composition of Federal Government Expenditure, 1962–2084

The CBO forecasts that rising spending on Medicare, Medicaid, Social Security, and interest payments will cause federal expenditure to increase to 36.5% of GDP in 2084.

Note: The shaded area represents the CBO forecast.

Source: U.S. Congressional Budget Office. ●

effect of current fiscal policy on GNP, based on the conventional view of deficits. Recall from Chapter 2 that GNP equals GDP plus net factor income from abroad. The CBO focuses on GNP because an increasingly large share of federal debt is owned by foreigners, so part of GDP will be paid to foreigners and will not be available for domestic consumption. According to the CBO, current fiscal policy will reduce real GNP per person by 2.3% in 2035. This amount is relatively modest, and while painful, a decrease in income of this magnitude would not represent a dramatic decrease in material well-being. However, current policy is based on the assumption of higher future taxes, and the CBO's analysis ignores the effects that higher taxes have on the willingness of households to save and invest.[7] As a result, the long-run effects of the current fiscal policy may be much greater than the CBO's analysis indicates.

If the federal government wants to avoid the decrease in income that results from reduction in capital stock, it has several options. We discuss these options for reducing future federal budget deficits in the following sections.

Treasury Bonds or Seigniorage Equation (13.1) on page 488 tells us that the government can finance a budget deficit by issuing new Treasury bonds or through seigniorage.

[7]U.S. Congressional Budget Office, "The Long-Term Budget Outlook," June 2010, p. 20. The CBO's estimates are based on a version of the Solow growth model. However, that model ignores the reaction of financial markets to the government running large budget deficits. If financial markets become concerned about the solvency of the federal government, this could precipitate a financial crisis that adversely affects the economy and limits the ability of the federal government to accumulate more debt.

The CBO's forecasts of the costs of current fiscal policy assume that the federal government finances the budget deficits by issuing new bonds. Can the federal government reduce the costs of its fiscal policy by financing the deficits with seigniorage? No. Seigniorage would require increasing the growth rate of the money supply, which in the long run also increases nominal interest rates through the Fisher effect, as discussed in Chapter 6. So, financing budget deficits by increasing the money supply will cause interest payments to rise more rapidly. The new higher nominal interest rates will increase the budget deficit further, which will require even more seigniorage and an even faster growth rate of the money supply. As the growth rate of the money supply increases, the inflation rate and the risk of hyperinflation also increase. Therefore, it is unlikely that the federal government could sustain the current fiscal policy using seigniorage. In effect, the government would be *monetizing* the budget deficit. As we saw in Chapter 6, countries that rely on monetizing the deficit, such as Germany after World War I, run the risk of experiencing hyperinflation.

Increased Taxes on Labor and Capital Income If the government increases taxes on labor income, this will reduce after-tax income. So, the opportunity cost of leisure will decrease, and the households will supply less labor, as we discussed in Chapter 7. Labor is one of the inputs of the aggregate production function, so the tax increase will decrease potential GDP. The government may consider raising payroll taxes, which are taxes levied on both workers and employers to support specific programs, such as Social Security. The portion of the payroll tax used to fund Social Security has an income cap, although that portion used to fund Medicare does not. So, the federal government could raise a substantial amount of funds by increasing the amount of income subject to the Social Security payroll tax. If the government increases taxes on capital income by raising taxes on dividends and capital gains or by raising the corporate income tax, the after-tax return to capital will decline. As a result, households will save less and investment and the capital stock will decline. Therefore, if the government raises taxes on capital income, potential GDP will decrease. We discuss the effect of taxes on corporate profits in more detail in Chapter 14. Whether the government increases individual income taxes or taxes on corporate profits, the result is likely to be a reduction in potential GDP.

Reduced Primary Expenditure The federal government could reduce expenditure on education, science, and technology. Education expenditure allows individuals to accumulate human capital that makes them more productive and increases total factor productivity. Expenditure on science and technology increases knowledge, which also increases total factor productivity. As we saw in Chapters 4 and 5, when total factor productivity increases, potential GDP also increases. Therefore, cutting these programs may lead to a decrease in potential GDP similar to what would occur if the government increased taxes.

The federal government could also reduce expenditure on infrastructure projects such as roads and bridges. However, this is also likely to lead to lower potential GDP in the future. It is useful to distinguish between private capital, K_{Private}, and government capital, K_{Govt}. Private capital goods are the machines, factories, and office buildings that the private sector uses to produce other goods and services. The private sector is responsible for deciding which and how many private capital goods to produce. However, the government maintains some capital goods, such as roads and bridges. Economists therefore call these capital goods *government capital.* Government capital is also useful for producing goods and services. For example, many firms use highways for transportation of goods and people. Therefore, infrastructure and other public capital is an important factor of production. In fact, we can think of the aggregate production function from Chapter 4 as:

$$Y = AK_{\text{Private}}^{1/3} K_{\text{Govt}}^{\gamma} L^{2/3} = (AK_{\text{Govt}}^{\gamma}) K_{\text{Private}}^{1/3} L^{2/3} = A^{*} K_{\text{Private}}^{1/3} L^{2/3}, \qquad (13.5)$$

where:
Y = real GDP
L = labor input
A = total factor productivity
$A^{*} = AK_{\text{Govt}}^{\gamma}$.

Here we can think of Y as potential GDP because it is the level of GDP that will exist when capital and labor are fully employed. The share of income going to the owners of private capital is one-third, and the share of income going to the owners of labor is two-thirds. The term γ tells us how much potential GDP increases when the public capital stock increases. In Equation (13.5), government capital increases output because it makes capital and labor more productive. For example, more and better roads and bridges allow firms to transport goods and people more quickly, so the productivity of private capital goods increases. Christophe Kamps, a senior economist at the European Central Bank, estimates that in OECD countries a 1% increase in the government capital stock increases real GDP by about 0.22%. In comparison, he finds that increasing the private capital stock by 1% increases real GDP by 0.26%, so government and private capital are about equally productive.[8] The findings of Kamps and other economists suggest that if the government reduces spending on government capital goods to make fiscal policy sustainable, it may also reduce potential GDP.

The government could also reduce spending on national defense. Spending on national defense does not affect total factor productivity, but it does provide other important benefits, such as national security. Even if the federal government reduced defense spending to zero, there would still be a budget deficit, because defense spending was 4.7% of GDP during 2010, while the federal primary budget deficit was 7.5%. Cutting defense spending can reduce, but not eliminate, the deficit.

Reduced Transfer Payments: Medicare, Medicaid, and Social Security Regardless of how the federal government ultimately deals with the looming fiscal challenges, the adjustments are likely to be costly. To maintain the promised expenditure on the elderly and the poor, the federal government will have to take actions that are likely to reduce potential GDP and, therefore, average income. To the extent that the government reduces transfer programs for the elderly and poor, it forces those groups to bear the cost of adjusting fiscal policy. Economic research does provide some guidance on the magnitude of the costs involved. Using economic efficiency as the standard, most economic models imply that reducing government spending is preferable to increasing taxes. Economists Alberto Alesina of Harvard University, Silvia Ardagna of Harvard University, Roberto Perotti of Bocconi University, and Fabio Schiantarelli of Boston College studied the effects of fiscal policy on investment in OECD countries.[9] They found that when transfer payments such as Medicare, Medicaid, and Social Security increase by 1 percentage point of GDP, private investment decreases by 1.3 percentage points of GDP in equilibrium. In addition, increasing taxes on labor by 1 percentage point of GDP to pay for the transfer payments further reduces investment by another 0.7 percentage points of GDP. The CBO forecasts that transfer payments will increase from 8.6% of GDP in 2008 to 24% of GDP in 2084—a 15.4-percentage-point increase. Adjusting current fiscal policy solely by increasing

[8]Christophe Kamps, "New Estimates for Government Net Capital Stocks for 22 OECD Countries, 1960–2001," *International Monetary Fund Staff Papers*, Vol. 53, No. 1, 2006, pp. 120–150.

[9]Alberto Alesina, Silvia Ardagna, Roberto Perotti, and Fabio Schiantarelli, "Fiscal Policy, Profits, and Investment," *American Economic Review*, Vol. 92, No. 3, June 2002, pp. 571–589.

Table 13.3 The Effects of Potential Changes to Fiscal Policy

If the government tries to make the debt sustainable by . . .	then . . .	causing . . .	resulting in . . .
increasing seigniorage	the growth rate of the money supply will have to increase substantially	a rapid increase in inflation	a collapse of the financial system and lower potential GDP.
increasing taxes on labor income	the opportunity cost of leisure will decrease	households to supply less labor	lower potential GDP.
increasing taxes on capital income	the after-tax return to capital goods will decrease	firms and households to accumulate less capital	lower potential GDP.
decreasing expenditure on government capital goods	the government capital stock will decrease	private capital goods to become less productive	lower potential GDP.
decreasing expenditure on transfer programs	the government will not support the elderly and poor as much as projected	some of the elderly and poor to bear the burden of adjusting fiscal policy	lower income and standard of living for the elderly and poor.

taxes on labor would significantly reduce equilibrium investment, the capital-labor ratio, labor productivity, and the standard of living. Economic research indicates that adjusting policy mainly by cutting transfer payments would lead to smaller reductions in potential GDP and, so, would be a more efficient approach. Such reductions, though, would seem inequitable to many people. Any policy changes to address the long-run fiscal challenges facing the United States are likely to take into account both equity and efficiency. Therefore, it seems probable that policymakers will ultimately enact some combination of expenditure reductions and tax increases. Table 13.3 summarizes the effects of potential changes to fiscal policy.

Answering the Key Question

Continued from page 486

At the beginning of this chapter, we asked:

"How should the United States solve its long-run fiscal problem?"

Starting around 2020, the CBO forecasts rapid increases in both federal government expenditure and revenue. Because revenue will lag well behind expenditure, large budget deficits will lead to a rising debt-to-GDP ratio. The CBO forecasts that the debt-to-GDP ratio will rise to such high levels that fiscal policy will become unsustainable. Therefore, the federal government will have to make difficult choices in the future about how to move to a sustainable fiscal policy. Either raising taxes or cutting expenditure seems likely to reduce potential GDP in the future. Using economic efficiency as the standard, current economic research suggests that reducing transfer payments is more efficient than increasing taxes on either individuals or corporations. Equity considerations, however, make it likely that tax increases will play a role in resolving long-run fiscal problems the U.S. faces.

Read an *Inside Look at Policy* on the next page for a discussion of the deficit-reduction options that Congress, President Obama, and the deficit commission are considering.

Senators Display Bipartisan Effort to Reduce Deficit

WASHINGTON POST

More than 60 Senators Call on Obama to Join Deficit-Reduction Talks

More than 60 senators from both parties are calling on President Obama to lead them in developing a comprehensive plan to rein in record budget deficits, a powerful sign of bipartisan willingness to abandon long-held positions on entitlement spending and taxes.

a In a letter sent Friday to the White House, the 64 senators urge Obama "to support a broad approach to solving our current budget problems" along the lines of recommendations issued last year by a presidentially appointed commission. That plan calls for sharp cuts in government spending, elimination or reduction of dozens of popular tax breaks and an overhaul of Social Security that would include raising the retirement age to 69 for today's toddlers. . . .

The letter was drafted by Sens Michael Bennet (D-Colo.) and Mike Johanns (R-Neb.), who said in a conference call Friday with reporters that it took them only a couple of days to convince a super-majority of their colleagues to sign the letter—32 Republicans and 32 Democrats. . . .

"There's no question entitlement reforms and tackling tax reform is going to be tough," Johanns said. . . .

"But we won't have any chance unless the president joins us in this effort," he said. "We feel very very strongly that a crisis looms and that we all have to engage."

b The White House issued a statement Friday agreeing with the letter's goals, but without promising any specific action. . . .

"The president agrees that any serious discussion of how to tackle our long-term fiscal situation needs to include entitlements and tax reform . . ." said White House spokeswoman Amy Brundage. . . .

Obama has declined to endorse the recommendations of his commission, which would reduce deficit spending by more than $4 trillion by the end of the decade. Savings of that magnitude would stabilize the national debt, which has been growing dramatically since the onset of the Great Recession in 2007, and put the nation in a position to begin paying it down.

c While Obama has been slow to embrace the commission's work, it has been kept alive in the Senate, where six members of both parties have been holding increasingly frequent meetings in hopes of coming up with a strategy for advancing the proposal. Friday's letter demonstrates that the so-called Gang of Six talks enjoy broad bipartisan support. . . .

Advocates of a balanced budget called Friday's letter an encouraging sign that momentum is building for serious budget reforms, despite the potential political risk to officeholders.

"This letter is another sign—following the work of the Fiscal Commission, and the ongoing negotiations with the Gang of Six—that members of the Senate appear ready to tackle the serious fiscal challenges facing the country," said Maya MacGuineas, president of the bipartisan Committee for a Responsible Federal Budget, which has encouraged the Gang of Six talks. "No one would have predicted this a year ago, and now look at how many people are signing up to be a part of the solution."

Source: Lori Montgomery, "More than 60 senators call on Obama to join deficit-reduction talks," *Washington Post*, March 18, 2011. From *The Washington Post*, March 18, 2011.

Key Points in the Article

This article discusses a letter sent to the White House, signed by 64 senators, calling on President Obama to support proposals along the lines of those of the White House's deficit commission to cut the federal budget deficit and address the problem of a growing national debt. The letter is an indication that members of the Senate are willing to act in a bipartisan manner to deal with the growing deficit and are open to discussing changes in items previously considered "untouchable," such as entitlement spending and taxes.

Analyzing the News

a Although the severe recession prompted the Obama administration to sign the American Recovery and Reinvestment Act stimulus package in 2009, the resulting increased deficit has many worried about the long-run effects of a rapidly growing federal debt. The deficit reduction plan proposed by the White House's deficit commission in late 2010 would reduce the growth of the federal debt by approximately $4 trillion by 2020, roughly half of the projected $7.7 trillion growth that would occur without the plan. The figure below shows estimates of the yearly and total saving from the deficit commission's proposals. The letter 64 senators sent to the White House endorses many of the commission's proposals.

b The White House issued a statement that agreed with the goals of the senators but stopped short of agreeing to any specific action, including the endorsement of any recommendations of the president's deficit commission, which cover a wide variety of areas. Among those proposals are (1) individual and corporate tax reform, including changes to tax brackets, itemized and mortgage interest deductions, charitable contribution credits, capital gains taxes, and retirement account contributions; (2) a 15-cent-per-gallon increase in gasoline taxes; (3) cuts in Medicare and Medicaid costs; (4) raising the retirement age for Social Security; (5) cutting military spending; (6) freezing salaries for federal workers and members of Congress; and (7) a 15% cut in congressional and White House budgets.

c Despite President Obama's reluctance to commit to any specific recommendations, a bipartisan group of six senators has been holding meetings in an effort to advance the commission's proposals. The letter to the White House indicates that the six senators have broad support in the Senate for these budget reform proposals, and momentum appears to be building even in the face of potential political risk to those endorsing the reforms.

THINKING CRITICALLY *ABOUT POLICY*

1. Suppose that the president agreed with the deficit commission's proposals to reduce the budget deficit, and these recommendations are successfully enacted. Use a graph to show the effects on real interest rates and investment. Use another graph of the Solow model to show the effect on the capital stock and labor productivity. Briefly explain what is happening in each graph.
2. The deficit commission's proposals include tax reform, cuts in Medicare and Medicaid, freezing the salaries of federal workers, and raising the retirement age for Social Security. Explain the potential economic effects of implementing these proposed fiscal policy changes, which are designed to increase tax revenues and decrease expenditure.

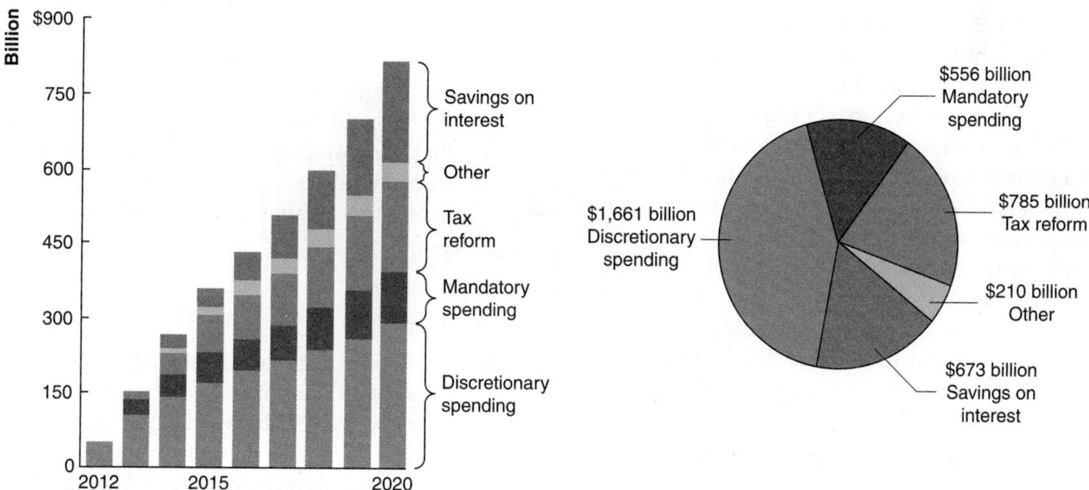

Figure 1 Estimates of the yearly and total savings from the deficit commission's proposals

Figure 2 Total deficit reduction: $3.89 trillion, 2012–2020

Source: National Commission on Fiscal Responsibility and Reform. Figures are from Damian Paletta and Jonathan Weisman, "Deficit Plan Wins Backers," *Wall Street Journal*, December 2, 2010. Reprinted with permission of THE WALL STREET JOURNAL, Copyright © 2010 Dow Jones & Company, Inc. All Rights Reserved Worldwide.

CHAPTER SUMMARY AND PROBLEMS

KEY TERMS

Budget deficit, p. 488
Crowding out, p. 499
Gross federal debt, p. 490
Gross federal debt held by the public, p. 488
Primary budget deficit (*PD*), p. 488
Ricardian equivalence, p. 503
Seigniorage, p. 488

13.1 Debt and Deficits in Historical Perspective

Discuss basic facts about the U.S. government's fiscal situation.

SUMMARY

The government can finance spending through taxes, new bonds, or **seigniorage**, which is the government's profit from issuing fiat money. The difference between all government expenditure and revenue is the **budget deficit**. The difference between government revenue and expenditure on goods and services and transfer payments is the **primary budget deficit**. The government can finance a budget deficit by issuing new bonds or through seigniorage. The stock of outstanding government bonds is the **gross federal debt**. When the budget deficit is positive, the U.S. Treasury issues new bonds, so the government's debt increases. When the government runs a budget surplus, the government's debt decreases. Gross federal debt is the total value of bonds issued by the government, while **gross federal debt held by the public** is the value of bonds held outside the federal government. The two measures of the debt differ because some branches of the federal government, such as the Social Security Administration, own Treasury bonds. Economists prefer to measure the debt and the deficit relative to GDP because GDP is a rough measure of the government's tax base. So, GDP is a measure of the resources that the government could transfer to itself through taxation. Taxes for Medicare, Medicaid, and Social Security have become more important sources of revenue for the federal government, while corporate income taxes have become less important. Similarly, relative to GDP, spending on these transfer programs has increased, while expenditure on other government programs, such as defense, has decreased.

Review Questions

1.1 Define gross federal debt held by the public.

1.2 What is the budget deficit? What is the difference between the budget deficit and the primary budget deficit?

1.3 Use the government's budget constraint to express the budget deficit and the primary budget deficit algebraically.

1.4 What is the difference between the debt and the deficit? Explain in terms of stocks and flows.

1.5 According to the chapter, when is the debt the more useful variable to consider in policymaking? When should policymakers use the deficit instead?

1.6 What is a government trust fund? How is it a liability to the government?

1.7 Why is debt usually measured using the debt-to-GDP ratio rather than the absolute amount of debt?

Problems and Applications

1.8 As stated in the chapter, gross federal debt at the end of the 2010 fiscal year was $13,562 billion. Currently, interest rates are very low, but historically, interest rates on Treasury bonds have been considerably higher. Assume, for simplicity, that the government pays the same interest rate on all outstanding debt. What is the approximate annual interest payment if the interest rate is:

a. 0.5%?

b. 3%?

c. 5%?

1.9 As stated in the chapter, the Congressional Budget Office (CBO) estimates that the federal budget deficit was $1,294 billion in 2010. For each of the interest rates given in problem 1.8, calculate the (hypothetical) primary budget deficit and the difference between the deficit and the primary budget deficit.

1.10 Consider the following statement: "Because the government can always print more money, the size of the budget deficit doesn't matter." Do you agree with this statement? Briefly explain.

1.11 The dollar value of the U.S. public debt is the highest in U.S. history and the highest, in absolute terms, in the world. Is this fact a reason to be concerned about the debt? Briefly explain.

13.2 The Sustainability of Fiscal Policy

Explain when fiscal policy is sustainable and when it is not sustainable.

SUMMARY

A fiscal policy is sustainable if it leads to a constant or decreasing debt-to-GDP ratio. A larger primary deficit and a higher nominal interest rate cause the debt-to-GDP ratio to increase, holding everything else constant. Faster nominal GDP growth and more seigniorage cause the debt-to-GDP ratio to decrease, holding everything else constant. When the economy operates along the balanced growth path, the growth rate of real GDP depends on the growth rate of the labor force and total factor productivity. So, increases in the growth rates of the labor force and total factor productivity cause the debt-to-GDP ratio to decrease, holding everything else constant. When the economy operates along the balanced growth path, the inflation rate equals the growth rate of the money supply minus the growth rate of real GDP, so increases in the money supply growth rate should cause the debt-to-GDP ratio to decrease, holding everything else constant. However, increases in the inflation rate also lead to higher nominal interest rates, and higher nominal interest rates cause the debt-to-GDP to increase. Therefore, it is very difficult to make fiscal policy sustainable by increasing the growth rate of the money supply.

Review Questions

2.1 What does it mean to say that fiscal policy is sustainable?

2.2 Identify each term in Equation (13.3), repeated here:

$$\Delta\left(\frac{B_t}{P_tY_t}\right) = \frac{PD_t}{P_tY_t} + (r_t - g_Y)\frac{B_{t-1}}{P_{t-1}Y_{t-1}} - \frac{\Delta MB_t}{P_tY_t}.$$

2.3 What are the consequences of having a fiscal policy that is not sustainable?

Problems and Applications

2.4 For each of the following scenarios, explain the effect on the debt-to-GDP ratio.

a. The growth rate of the labor force decreases.

b. The nominal interest rate on existing bonds increases.

c. The money supply increases, which causes the rate of inflation to rise.

d. The money supply decreases, but there is no change in the rate of inflation.

2.5 **[Related to the *Making the Connection* on page 495]** On December 7, 2010, Ireland passed a budget designed to help cut the government's budget deficit. A total of €6 billion in savings was expected to come from spending cuts.

a. Can Ireland use changes in the money supply to help with its budget crisis? Briefly explain.

b. Aside from spending cuts, does Ireland have any other alternatives to reduce its deficit?

2.6 Consider the following statement: "The only way for a country with a budget deficit to have sustainable fiscal policy in the long run is to cut government spending." Do you agree with this statement? Briefly explain.

2.7 According to the *Economist*, "It seems certain that the Federal Reserve will continue to accompany fiscal stimulus with the monetary equivalent, in the form of near-zero interest rates and further quantitative easing." How is this monetary policy likely to affect the sustainability of fiscal policy?

Source: "In a Spin," *Economist*, December 29, 2010.

2.8 **[Related to *Solved Problem 13.2* on page 497]** The sustainability of fiscal policy is partly a function of the GDP growth rate. In the wake of the earthquake and related tsunami in March 2011, it appears that Japan's growth rate in the near term may be even lower than the 10-year average of 0.7%.

a. If the growth rate of GDP fell to −0.5%, how would this affect the sustainability of fiscal policy?

b. Based on the growth rate in part (a), calculate the level of the primary deficit required to make fiscal policy sustainable.

c. Historical data suggest that even major catastrophes such as Hurricane Katrina have only a small and short-term effect on economic growth. However, it is certain that the aftermath of the disaster in Japan will require large government expenditure to rebuild infrastructure. How will this affect Japan's deficit and debt in the short run?

2.9 Suppose that a country has a debt-to-GDP ratio of 64%. The growth rate of real GDP is 3%. Assume that seigniorage is zero and the real interest rate is 2%. What primary deficit as a percentage of GDP would be required to make fiscal policy sustainable?

13.3 Effects of Budget Deficits on Investment

Understand how fiscal policy affects the economy in the long run.

SUMMARY

If the government runs a budget deficit, the government can adjust by increasing tax revenue, decreasing expenditure on goods and services, or decreasing expenditure on transfer programs; the private sector can adjust by increasing savings, reducing investment expenditure, or running a trade deficit. **Crowding out** is a decline in private investment that results from the government running a budget deficit. The conventional view is that a budget deficit leads to higher real interest rates that reduce investment. Lower investment causes the capital stock to decrease, labor productivity to decrease, and potential GDP to decrease. **Ricardian equivalence** is the view that, given a path of government expenditure, the timing of lump sum taxes does not cause private-sector consumption or investment to change. In this view, households are forward looking, so consumption changes only if lifetime disposable income changes. The government must eventually balance its budget, so a decision to cut taxes this year is a decision to increase taxes by the same amount in the future. Therefore, lifetime disposable income does not change following a change in lump-sum taxes, so consumption does not change. In the Ricardian equivalence view, a lump-sum tax cut leads to increased private saving. In contrast to the conventional view, this increase in private saving keeps the level of investment constant.

Review Questions

3.1 What is crowding out?

3.2 How can an increase in the government budget deficit lead to a change in the trade deficit?

3.3 Explain how the government can adjust its behavior in response to a decrease in tax revenue.

3.4 How does the debt-to-GDP ratio relate to the real interest rate? Explain.

3.5 How might budget deficits affect long-term economic growth?

3.6 Explain Ricardian equivalence.

3.7 Why are many economists skeptical about the validity of Ricardian equivalence?

Problems and Applications

3.8 **[Related to the *Chapter Opener* on page 486]** The chapter opener suggests that deficits are generally a problem for countries. Based on the models presented in Section 13.3, are there circumstances in which it might be possible that deficits could increase productivity and thus long-run growth?

3.9 Use Equation (13.4), repeated below, to demonstrate how an increase in the budget deficit must increase the trade deficit if neither consumption nor investment changes. What must happen if there is an increase in the budget deficit in a closed economy?

$$[(G + TR) - T] = S_{Household} - I - NX$$

3.10 **[Related to *Solved Problem 13.3* on page 501]** Suppose that the government initially has a balanced budget. Government spending then increases, without an accompanying increase in taxes.

a. Use a graph to show the effects on real interest rates and investment. Use another graph to show the effects on capital stock, labor productivity, and potential GDP.

b. How would your answers in part (a) be different if the increase in government spending resulted in an increase in total factor productivity?

3.11 In early 2011, Congress renewed the tax cuts first passed by the Bush administration in 2001 for a 2-year period. The original tax cuts were set to expire 10 years after they were first passed.

a. Assume the tax cuts were lump sum tax cuts. If Ricardian equivalence holds, what should have been the effect of the original tax cuts?

b. The original tax cuts changed income tax rates so they were not lump sum tax cuts. How does this fact change your answer to part a?

3.12 In December 2010, Ireland passed a budget designed to cut the size of the budget deficit. An article in the *Economist* stated: "'Everybody pays' was the theme of Brian Lenihan, the Irish finance minister, when he presented the toughest budget in Ireland's history on December 7th." Deficit reduction was largely accomplished through spending cuts, including cuts in welfare programs and some government salaries. There was also an increase in some taxes and fees.

a. What is the likely effect of these actions on the loanable funds market?

b. How are the short-run and long-run effects of this deficit reduction likely to be different?

Source: "A Tight Squeeze," *Economist*, December 9, 2010.

3.13 **[Related to the *Macro Data* feature on page 501]** Studies have shown a link between rising debt-to-GDP ratios and real interest rates. Investment is not the only category of spending that might be sensitive to interest rates.

a. How might consumption be affected by rising interest rates due to a government deficit? Will all types of consumption be affected equally?

b. Does the data presented suggest that rising interest rates are currently a significant concern in the United States?

13.4 The Looming Fiscal Challenges Facing the United States

Explain the fiscal challenges facing the United States.

SUMMARY

The CBO forecasts that current U.S. fiscal policy will cause the federal debt held by the public to increase from 62.1% of GDP in 2010 to 113% in 2084. The CBO forecasts that federal revenues will increase from 14.9% of GDP in 2010 to 30.3% of GDP in 2084. Therefore, revenues are expected to increase substantially. However, the CBO also forecasts that government expenditure will increase from 23.8% of GDP in 2010 to 36.5% of GDP in 2084. Expenditure will increase because the aging population and the rapid rise in healthcare prices will cause expenditure on Medicare, Medicaid, and Social Security to increase. The government can make fiscal policy sustainable by increasing taxes, reducing spending, or increasing seigniorage. Higher taxes on labor income will reduce the incentive to work and therefore reduce potential GDP. Higher taxes on corporations will reduce the incentive to accumulate capital and therefore reduce potential GDP. Making fiscal policy sustainable by reducing government expenditure on goods and services would require large cuts in government programs such as education and infrastructure. So, total factor productivity and potential GDP would decrease. Making fiscal policy sustainable through seigniorage would require increasing the growth rate of the money supply so high that hyperinflation might result. Alternatively, the government could reduce spending on Medicare, Medicaid, and Social Security, which would require that the poor and elderly bear the cost of making fiscal policy sustainable. Although cutting spending on transfer programs would likely be the most efficient way of reducing future deficits, equity considerations make it likely that expenditure cuts will be paired with tax increases.

Review Questions

4.1 Explain the reasons for the projected increase in the U.S. budget deficit in coming years.

4.2 Why is the current path of fiscal policy not sustainable?

4.3 List the options for making fiscal policy sustainable.

4.4 State the primary disadvantage of each option you listed in question 4.3.

Problems and Applications

4.5 The budget deficit projections in this chapter include net interest on the debt, which depends on interest rates. Use the loanable funds model to explain what is likely to happen to interest rates and interest payments if the size of the deficit continues to increase.

4.6 The chapter states that "the CBO's analysis ignores the effects that these policies have on the willingness of households to save and invest." How might policies to reduce the deficit change saving and investment?

4.7 **[Related to the *Making the Connection* on page 506]** Evidence suggests that the method of deficit reduction that least reduces economic efficiency may be slower growth in transfer payments, such as Social Security and Medicare.

a. If consumers believe that deficit reduction must occur in this way, how might this change the current behavior of consumers?

b. How might consumer expectations of future Social Security cuts make the process of deficit reduction easier or more difficult?

4.8 Consider the following statement: "Because deficit reduction is costly to the economy, governments should never run budget deficits." Do you agree with this statement? Briefly explain.

4.9 According to Bloomberg.com, "At an Oct. 7 foreign-exchange conference in New York . . . Alan Greenspan called the budget gap 'scary' and said the federal government needs to cut spending on entitlements . . . " Why does former Fed Chairman Alan Greenspan find the budget gap scary?

Source: Vincent Del Guidice, "U.S. Posts Second-Largest Deficit on Record," Bloomberg.com, October 15, 2010.

DATA EXERCISES

D13.1: Information on Ireland's deficit reduction plans can be found in various news sources, such as the *Wall Street Journal*, the *New York Times* and the *Financial Times*. Search for a breakdown of the spending cuts and tax increases. How do you think the deficit reduction plan will affect Ireland's economy? Why do you think these particular choices were made?

D13.2: Countries that want to be part of the euro zone, the part of the European Union that shares a common currency, were required to meet limits on the size of their deficits. Deficits were required to be less than 3% of GDP. Find data for the current deficits of some of the countries using the euro as their currency. (One source for this data is www.oecd.org.) Do most euro-zone countries comply with this deficit limit?

D13.3: The chapter gives a breakdown of the categories of government spending. Government budgets are available on most national government Web sites. How does the breakdown of spending for the United States compare with the breakdown of spending for other industrialized countries? How does the projected U.S. deficit compare with the projected deficits for other countries with aging populations, such as Japan?

D13.4: **[Excel question]** Government debt and deficit data for the United Kingdom can be found at the Office of National Statistics (www.statistics.gov.uk) and downloaded in Excel-compatible format.

a. Find the debt and deficit data from 1948 to the present and download it into a spreadsheet.

b. Graph the data. How do the debt and deficit data compare to the U.S. data presented in the chapter?

APPENDIX

Showing the Conditions for a Sustainable Fiscal Policy

13A Derive the conditions for a sustainable fiscal policy.

To derive Equation (13.2), start with Equation (13.1), divide it by nominal GDP, and move the term representing seigniorage to the left side of the equation to obtain:

$$\frac{PD_t}{P_tY_t} + i_t\frac{B_{t-1}}{P_tY_t} - \frac{\Delta MB_t}{P_tY_t} = \frac{\Delta B_t}{P_tY_t}.$$

Because $\Delta B_t = B_t - B_{t-1}$, we can rewrite the above equation as:

$$\frac{PD_t}{P_tY_t} + i_t\frac{B_{t-1}}{P_tY_t} + \frac{B_{t-1}}{P_tY_t} - \frac{\Delta MB_t}{P_tY_t} = \frac{B_t}{P_tY_t}.$$

Grouping like terms, we obtain:

$$\frac{PD_t}{P_tY_t} + (1 + i_t)\frac{B_{t-1}}{P_tY_t} - \frac{\Delta MB_t}{P_tY_t} = \frac{B_t}{P_tY_t}.$$

We can multiply and divide by last period's nominal GDP and rearrange terms to obtain:

$$\frac{PD_t}{P_tY_t} + (1 + i_t)\frac{B_{t-1}}{P_{t-1}Y_{t-1}}\left(\frac{P_{t-1}Y_{t-1}}{P_tY_t}\right) - \frac{\Delta MB_t}{P_tY_t} = \frac{B_t}{P_tY_t}.$$

The new term in parentheses is the inverse of 1 plus the growth rate of nominal GDP. The growth rate of nominal GDP equals the inflation rate plus the growth rate of real GDP, so we can rewrite the equation as:

$$\frac{PD_t}{P_tY_t} + \left(\frac{1 + i_t}{1 + \pi_t + g_{Y_t}}\right)\frac{B_{t-1}}{P_{t-1}Y_{t-1}} - \frac{\Delta MB_t}{P_tY_t} = \frac{B_t}{P_tY_t}.$$

The ratio $\left(\frac{1 + i_t}{1 + \pi_t + g_{Y_t}}\right) \cong 1 + i_t - \pi_t - g_{Y_t}$, so the above equation becomes:

$$\frac{PD_t}{P_tY_t} + (1 + i_t - \pi_t - g_{Y_t})\frac{B_{t-1}}{P_{t-1}Y_{t-1}} - \frac{\Delta MB_t}{P_tY_t} = \frac{B_t}{P_tY_t}.$$

This expression is just:

$$\frac{PD_t}{P_tY_t} + \frac{B_{t-1}}{P_{t-1}Y_{t-1}} + (i_t - \pi_t - g_{Y_t})\frac{B_{t-1}}{P_{t-1}Y_{t-1}} - \frac{\Delta MB_t}{P_tY_t} = \frac{B_t}{P_tY_t}.$$

Now, just move the $\frac{B_{t-1}}{P_{t-1}Y_{t-1}}$ term to the right side of the equation, and the result is Equation (13.2):

$$\Delta\left(\frac{B_t}{P_tY_t}\right) = \frac{PD_t}{P_tY_t} + [i_t - (\pi_t + g_Y)]\frac{B_{t-1}}{P_{t-1}Y_{t-1}} - \frac{\Delta MB_t}{P_tY_t}.$$

The Fisher relationship tells us that the real interest rate is the nominal interest rate minus inflation, or:

$$r_t = i_t - \pi_t.$$

If we plug the Fisher relationship into Equation (13.2), we get Equation (13.3):

$$\Delta\left(\frac{B_t}{P_tY_t}\right) = \frac{PD_t}{P_tY_t} + [r_t - g_Y]\frac{B_{t-1}}{P_{t-1}Y_{t-1}} - \frac{\Delta MB_t}{P_tY_t}.$$

13B Derive the equation showing the relationship between budget deficits and private expenditure.

We start with the identity from Chapter 2:

$$Y = C + I + G + NX.$$

We add transfer payments to each side and subtract taxes from each side of the equation to obtain:

$$Y + TR - T = C + I + [G + TR - T] + NX.$$

Next, we move consumption to the left side of the equation to obtain:

$$Y + TR - T - C = I + [G + TR - T] + NX.$$

Recall that private savings is:

$$S_{\text{Household}} = Y + TR - T - C.$$

Private savings is therefore just the left side of the previous equation, so:

$$S_{\text{Household}} = I + [(G + TR) - T] + NX.$$

Finally, solve for the government's budget deficit, and the result is Equation (13.4):

$$[(G + TR) - T] = S_{\text{Household}} - I - NX.$$

CHAPTER 14

Consumption and Investment

LEARNING OBJECTIVES

After studying this chapter, you should be able to:

14.1 Discuss the macroeconomic implications of microeconomic decision making by households and firms (pages 522–524)

14.2 Explain the determinants of personal consumption (pages 524–539)

14.3 Explain the determinants of private investment (pages 539–551)

PRESIDENT OBAMA AND CONGRESS AGREE TO A TAX CUT

In November 2010, the U.S. economy was recovering slowly from the 2007–2009 recession, and the unemployment rate was 9.8%, which was actually higher than the 9.5% rate in June 2009, when the recession had ended. Shortly after his inauguration, President Barack Obama had proposed, and Congress had passed, an expansionary fiscal policy in the form of the American Recovery and Reinvestment Act. The act, often referred to as the "stimulus package," was a $814 billion package of government spending increases and tax cuts. The bill proved controversial, and in the fall of 2010, proposals for an additional stimulus package to help spur the recovery did not attract sufficient support in Congress. Congress and the president had a deadline looming, however: On January 1, 2011, tax cuts passed in 2001 and 2003 during the administration of President George W. Bush were set to expire. If the tax cuts expired, the income tax rates of all taxpayers would be raised, potentially causing a significant reduction in consumption spending. In addition, taxes on dividends and capital gains would increase, potentially reducing the willingness of investors to purchase stock, bonds, and other securities.

Continued on next page

Key Issue and Question

At the end of Chapter 1, we noted key issues and questions that serve as a framework for the book. Here are the key issue and question for this chapter:

Issue: Households and firms make decisions about how much to consume and invest based on expectations about the future.

Question: How does government tax policy affect the decisions of households and firms?

Answered on page 551

A prolonged debate arose over how to handle the expiring tax cuts. President Obama initially proposed that the tax cuts be extended only for households earning less than $250,000 per year. In the end, with the deadline looming, a compromise was hammered out, and on December 17, 2010, President Obama signed the Tax Relief, Unemployment Insurance Reauthorization, and Job Creation Act of 2010. The act extended for two more years the tax cuts of 2001 and 2003, provided a one-year reduction of 2 percentage points in the payroll taxes used to fund the Social Security and Medicare programs, and enacted into law various tax incentives for businesses to invest in new capital goods. Tax revenues were projected to be $801 billion below what they would have been had the 2001 and 2003 tax cuts expired and further tax cuts not been passed. In addition, the act provided for $57 billion in extended unemployment insurance benefits. Many economists and policymakers argued that the payroll and personal income tax cuts and increased unemployment insurance benefit payments would encourage households to increase consumption, while the tax incentives to businesses would increase investment. Supporters of the act argued that it would result in an increase in aggregate expenditure, which would increase real GDP and employment. Opponents of the act were skeptical that real GDP and employment would rise significantly, and they pointed out that the falling tax revenue and increased expenditure contained in the act would increase the federal government's budget deficit, which was already near record peacetime levels. A larger budget deficit would necessarily increase the national debt. Furthermore, some critics argued that higher-income households would receive too large a share of the tax cuts.

How much was the bill likely to increase aggregate expenditure? Economists at Deutsche Bank, Goldman Sachs, and JPMorgan Chase forecast that the tax cut package would increase the growth rate of real GDP during 2011 by between 0.5% and 1.0%. The most important provisions in the bill kept tax rates at their 2010 levels for two years or reduced other taxes for just one year. In other words, the tax changes were *temporary* rather than *permanent*. When tax cuts are temporary, households may save rather than spend most of the tax cut, and firms have difficulty making long-term investment decisions. Therefore, the tax package may not have had as much of an effect on consumption and investment as it would have had the changes been permanent. Permanent reductions in taxes, though, would also have resulted in permanent reductions in tax revenues, which, unless the tax cuts were offset by reductions in government spending, would have resulted in higher future budget deficits and higher future levels of the national debt.

AN INSIDE LOOK AT POLICY on page 552 discusses how the extension of tax cuts will affect households and employers.

Sources: David Herszenhorn, "Congress Passes Tax Cut Package for $801 Billion," *New York Times*, December 17, 2010; Janet Hook and John McKinnon, "Congress Passes Tax Deal: Divided Legislature Adopts Sweeping Measure to Avert Increases, Add New Breaks," *Wall Street Journal*, December 17, 2010; and Sudeep Reddy, "The Tax Agreement: Package Would Give Obama a Stealthy Stimulus," *Wall Street Journal*, December 8, 2010.

In Chapters 8–12, we discussed how shocks—unexpected events that have an effect on an important sector of the economy or on the economy as a whole—can cause business cycles. We also discussed the roles that monetary policy and fiscal policy play in responding to these shocks. As we saw, the behavior of consumption and investment is important in explaining how the economy responds both to shocks and to policy. In this chapter, we discuss *consumption* and *investment* in greater detail to have a better understanding of how shocks and policy affect economic activity.

14.1

Learning Objective

Discuss the macroeconomic implications of microeconomic decision making by households and firms.

The Macroeconomic Implications of Microeconomic Decision Making: Intertemporal Choice

The key decisions that affect GDP are made at the microeconomic level—that is, by households and firms. For example, the decision of a household in California to save for retirement rather than purchase a car or the decision of Ford Motor Company to build a new factory in Tennessee rather than wait until next year will, by themselves, not have a large effect on GDP. However, the combined decisions of *all* the households and firms in the economy are critically important for the economy.

Economists assume that households and firms share two important characteristics: First, households and firms act rationally to meet their objectives. Economists assume that the objective of households is to maximize *utility*, or well-being, and that the objective of firms is to maximize profits. Second, households and firms are *forward looking*—that is, they take into account the future when making decisions. The decision of a household to consume or save today is really a decision about when to consume because saving today makes it possible to consume in the future. Households save to accumulate the assets necessary to purchase a house, pay for college, or pay for consumption during retirement. To prepare for retirement, most households save part of their current income by purchasing stocks, shares of mutual funds, or other financial assets. Households hope that these financial assets will appreciate in value and allow them to pay for expenses during retirement. What we expect to happen in the future affects our decisions today. For example, suppose you conclude that the value of your house will increase more rapidly than you had previously expected it to. The fact that you expect to be able to sell your house for a higher price in the future is good news: You will need to save less out of your current income to pay for expenses during retirement. As a result, you may consume more today. This point is very important: *Expectations about the future affect consumption decisions today.*

Expectations about the future are also critical for investment decisions by firms. Capital goods, such as factories, last many years, so a firm must consider the profits to be earned from a factory in the future when deciding whether to invest or not. Many capital goods are expensive. For example, if Ford wants to build a new factory, it has to bear the cost of constructing the building and installing equipment before it will earn any revenue on the cars the factory will produce. If Ford thought that demand for cars was going to decrease in the future, then it would be less likely to build the factory today. So, expectations about future profitability can affect the level of investment—and, therefore, GDP—today.

The Critical Role of the Financial System in Consumption and Investment

The financial system plays a critical role in the ability of households to consume and firms to invest. Some households need to borrow to finance the purchase of a car or a new home or to send children to college. In addition, some firms need to borrow to finance investment projects, such as the purchase of new machinery or the building of a new factory. We saw in Chapter 3 that the financial system is characterized by **asymmetric information**, which is a situation in which one party to an economic transaction has better information than does the other party. When asymmetric information exists, it is costly for lenders to determine which households and firms are likely to repay a loan. For example, someone applying to a bank for a mortgage may know that his or her job is not secure, but the bank does not. Similarly, a firm may know the likelihood of an investment project succeeding, while the bank does not. If a borrower loses her job and is forced to default on her mortgage, or if an investment project fails so the firm cannot repay its loan, the bank suffers an economic loss.

Asymmetric information A situation in which one party to an economic transaction has better information than does the other party.

To minimize the possibility of a default, financial institutions often restrict who they are willing to loan money to and the amount they are willing to lend. One way to restrict loans is to require would-be borrowers to put up a significant portion of their own funds. For example, the bank may require a down payment on a mortgage loan. A family buying a $200,000 house may have to pay $40,000 of its own money and receive a loan for the other $160,000. Because the family has some of its own money at risk, it is less likely to default on the loan. Or the bank may require the borrower to offer collateral—such as another valuable asset—that the borrower will forfeit to the bank if the borrower defaults on the loan. Not every borrower has the resources for a down payment or the ability to post collateral, so these borrowers cannot obtain loans even when they are willing to pay current interest rates. This outcome is called **credit rationing**—the restriction of credit by lenders such that

Credit rationing The restriction of credit by lenders such that borrowers cannot obtain the funds they desire at a given interest rate.

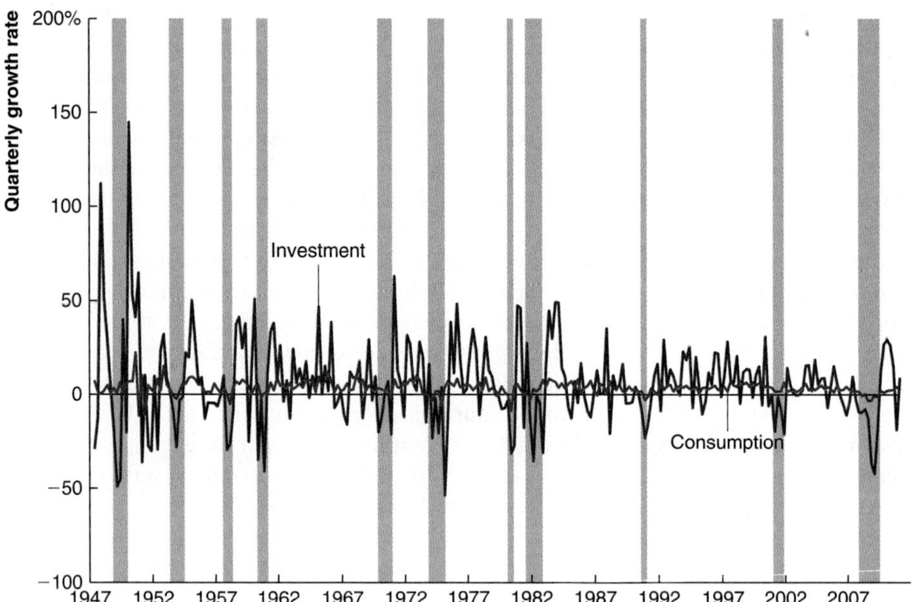

Figure 14.1

Growth Rates for Personal Consumption and Gross Private Investment, 1947–2011

The growth rate of gross private investment is much more volatile than the growth rate of personal consumption. Investment has always decreased during recessions (shaded areas), but consumption has actually increased during some recessions.

Note: The data are quarterly and the growth rates are at an annual rate.

Sources: U.S. Bureau of Economic Analysis; and National Bureau of Economic Research. ●

borrowers cannot obtain the funds they desire at a given interest rate. As we will see in this chapter, credit rationing places important limits on the behavior of households and firms and played a key role in making the 2007–2009 recession particularly severe.

An Important Difference Between Consumption and Investment

Although households and firms are forward looking in their decisions, their behavior can be quite different. In particular, as Figure 14.1 shows, consumption and investment behave differently during recessions. The volatility in the growth rate of investment in the United States is much greater than is the volatility in the growth rate of consumption. For example, during the first quarter of 2009, consumption decreased by 0.5% at an annual rate, but investment decreased by 42.2%! During a typical recession, investment usually decreases much more than consumption. In fact, during some recessions, such as the 2001 recession, consumption has actually risen. To understand how policy affects economic activity, it is important to understand why investment is more volatile than consumption. We focus on consumption in Section 14.2 and investment in Section 14.3.

14.2

Learning Objective

Explain the determinants of personal consumption.

Factors That Determine Consumption

Consumption is less volatile than investment because households tend to smooth consumption over time in response to fluctuations in disposable income. In this section, we discuss the determinants of consumption and explain why it is relatively smooth.

Consumption and GDP

Figure 14.2 shows that, while household consumption averages just over 60% of GDP for all countries for which the World Bank has data, this percentage varies significantly across countries. Household consumption averages nearly 80% of GDP in low-income countries but about 60% in high- and middle-income countries. Consumption in the United States has risen from 62% of GDP in 1967 to over 70% of GDP in 2009. The exact reason for the increase is not yet clear, but developments in financial markets probably played a role as many households experienced increases in wealth that led them to save less of their income and spend more of it. When the stock market boomed during the 1980s and 1990s, many

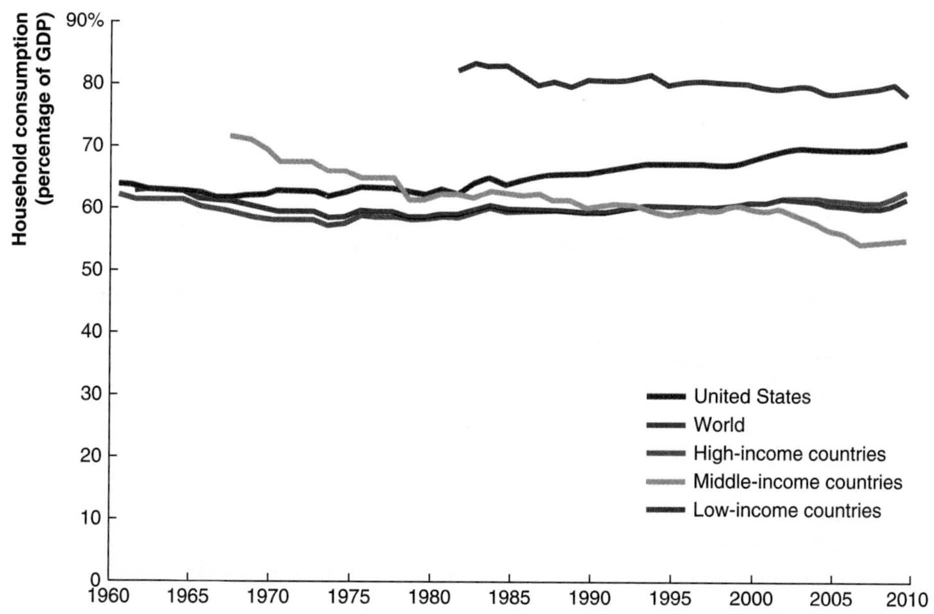

Figure 14.2

Consumption as a Percentage of GDP, 1960–2009

For most countries, consumption is the largest component of GDP.

Source: The World Bank, *World Development Indicators*. ●

households found that they did not need to save as much out of disposable income for retirement. Rising real estate wealth along with increased home ownership rates also played a role. Finally, financial innovations made it easier for households to borrow against the equity in their home and to obtain credit cards. As a result, consumption increased as a percentage of GDP. These trends reversed following the financial crisis, when saving increased while consumption fell as a percentage of GDP.

Some types of consumption are more volatile than others. Figure 14.3 shows the growth rates of expenditure on durable consumption goods, nondurable consumption goods, and services for the United States. The figure shows that expenditure on durable consumption goods such as cars and furniture is quite volatile, but expenditure on nondurable goods

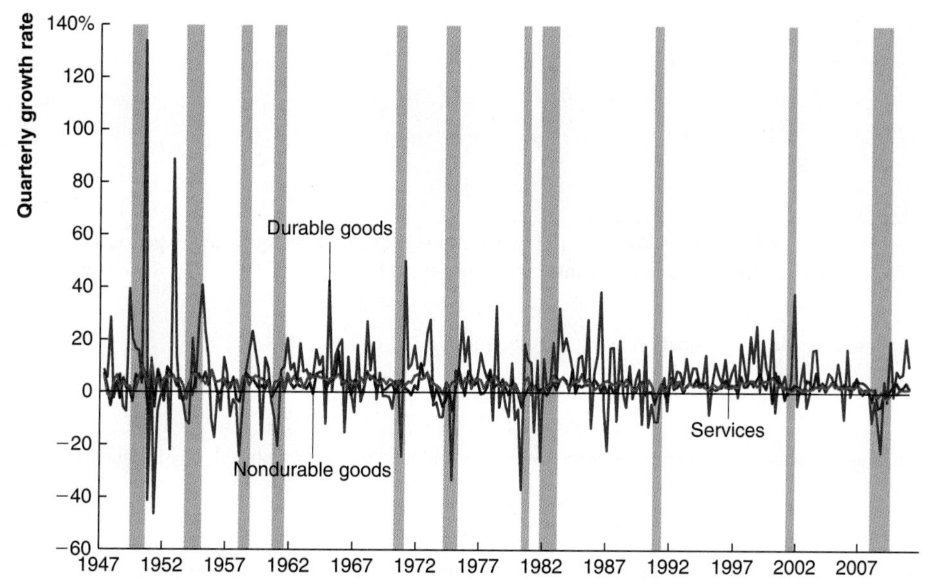

Figure 14.3

Growth Rates in Expenditure on Durable Goods, Nondurable Goods, and Services, 1947–2011

Expenditure on durable consumption goods is much more volatile than expenditure on nondurable goods and services. Shaded areas indicate recessions.

Note: The data are quarterly and the growth rates are at an annual rate.

Sources: U.S. Bureau of Economic Analysis; and National Bureau of Economic Research. ●

such as food and clothing and on services such as health care, is much less volatile. Expenditure on durable goods almost always decreases significantly during recessions, while expenditure on services decreases by much less or even increases. For example, during the 2007–2009 recession, expenditure on durable goods decreased by 11.9%, expenditure on nondurable goods decreased by 3.0%, and expenditure on services decreased by only 0.6%. Why are households more willing to delay purchases of new cars and other durable goods than they are health care and other services? To answer this question, we first need to discuss an important constraint on household consumption.

The Intertemporal Budget Constraint and Consumption Smoothing

Consider the following simple model of consumption in which there are just two time periods (the current year and next year) and there is no government, so taxes and transfer payments are zero and there is no difference between income and disposable income. You seek to maximize utility, or well-being, so the only reason you save is to finance future consumption. We will initially assume that there is no limit on your ability to use financial markets to borrow or to save. Furthermore, we simplify by assuming that you can save or invest as much as you choose at the real interest rate, r.

We call the dollar amount that you consume this year (year 1) C_1, and the amount that you consume next year (year 2) C_2. You receive labor income this year, Y_1, and labor income next year, Y_2. During the first year, the part of your income that you save is S_1. So, for the first year:

$$Y_1 = C_1 + S_1.$$

Therefore, saving during the first year equals:

$$S_1 = Y_1 - C_1.$$

The amount that you save is invested in financial markets this year, earning you a return equal to the real interest rate, r. So, next year, you will have the initial investment plus the interest earned, $(1 + r)S_1$, which you can use for consumption during the second year. Therefore, we can write consumption during year 2 as:

$$C_2 = Y_2 + (1 + r)S_1.$$

We can combine the above equation for saving in the first year with consumption in the second year to get the following expression, which relates lifetime consumption to lifetime income:[1]

$$C_1 + \frac{C_2}{1 + r} = Y_1 + \frac{Y_2}{1 + r}. \qquad (14.1)$$

[1]Here is how we arrived at Equation (14.1): If we substitute the expression for saving in period 1, $S_1 = Y_1 - C_1$, into the expression for consumption in period 2, $C_2 = Y_2 + (1 + r)S_1$, we obtain:

$$C_2 = Y_2 + (1 + r)(Y_1 - C_1).$$

Dividing each side of the equation by $(1 + r)$ produces:

$$\frac{C_2}{(1 + r)} = \frac{Y_2}{(1 + r)} + (Y_1 - C_1).$$

Rearranging terms to put consumption on the left side and income on the right side yields Equation (14.1):

$$C_1 + \frac{C_2}{1 + r} = Y_1 + \frac{Y_2}{1 + r},$$

which is the household's intertemporal budget constraint, which tells us that the present value of lifetime consumption equals the present value of lifetime income.

Equation (14.1) is the **intertemporal budget constraint**, which is a budget constraint that applies to consumption and income in more than one time period. Equation (14.1) tells us that lifetime consumption (the left side) equals lifetime income (the right side)—although in our simple model, "lifetime" is just two years.

Intertemporal budget constraint A budget constraint that applies to consumption and income in more than one time period; it tells us how much a household can consume, given lifetime income.

To understand the intertemporal budget constraint, assume that the real interest rate is zero, so that the sum of your consumption in both years equals the sum of your income from both years. If you prefer to perfectly smooth consumption—that is, equalize your consumption in both years—you will have $C_1 = C_2$. Suppose you work during the first year, so income is positive, $Y_1 = \$60{,}000$, and then you retire during the second year, so income in that year is zero, $Y_2 = 0$. To be able to consume during retirement, you will save \$30,000 during the first year and purchase assets such as stocks or bonds, and then you will sell those assets during the second year to finance your consumption during the second period. If, instead, your income were zero during the first year while you were going to school, $Y_1 = 0$, and \$60,000 in the second year when you worked, $Y_2 = \$60{,}000$, then you would borrow \$30,000 in financial markets during the first year to finance consumption during that period and then repay the loan in the second period. We can use the intertemporal budget constraint to explain why households smooth consumption.

Two Theories of Consumption Smoothing

We can use this simple model to show the effect of changes in current income on consumption. For example, if there are two time periods, and your income increases by \$10,000 in the first year, then you are unlikely to spend all of the \$10,000 the first year. Instead, if you are like most other people, you are likely to spend some of the \$10,000 in the first year and some of it in the second year. Economists call this phenomenon *consumption smoothing*. Nobel Laureate Milton Friedman developed the **permanent-income hypothesis** to explain consumption smoothing.[2] According to this hypothesis, household consumption depends on *permanent income*, and households use financial markets to save and borrow to smooth consumption in response to fluctuations in *transitory income*. Suppose you work for an accounting firm where you receive a salary and are eligible for a bonus for exceptional work. Your salary is **permanent income** because you expect to receive it each year. Your bonus is **transitory income** because you do not expect to receive it each year. You can think of permanent income as average lifetime income and transitory income as a temporary deviation from the lifetime average. Household income is the sum of permanent income, $Y^{\text{Permanent}}$, and transitory income, $Y^{\text{Transitory}}$:

Permanent-income hypothesis The hypothesis that household consumption depends on permanent income and that households use financial markets to save and borrow to smooth consumption in response to fluctuations in transitory income.

Permanent income Income that households expect to receive each year.

Transitory income Income that households do not expect to receive each year.

$$Y = Y^{\text{Permanent}} + Y^{\text{Transitory}}.$$

Milton Friedman argued that the level of consumption depends only on the level of permanent income:

$$C = aY^{\text{Permanent}}, \tag{14.2}$$

where a is a constant and represents the fraction of permanent income that households consume. Friedman argued that if someone experienced an unexpected windfall, such as winning the lottery or receiving a temporary tax cut, the person would view most of this income as transitory. As a result, the person would save most of it and consume very little. Similarly, if the person experienced an unexpected job loss, income would fall temporarily, meaning that transitory income would be negative. In this case, the person would borrow in financial markets to keep consumption at the level indicated by Equation (14.2). In contrast, if the person received a permanent increase in income due to unexpectedly obtaining a better job, consumption would increase significantly. Similarly, if a person accepted a job

[2]Milton Friedman, *A Theory of the Consumption Function, Princeton*, NJ: Princeton University Press, 1957.

Figure 14.4

Consumption, Income, and Saving over the Life Cycle

If a person plans to keep consumption constant over his or her life cycle, the person will borrow when he or she is young and income is low, accumulate assets during peak earning years, and then sell off assets during retirement, when income is zero. ●

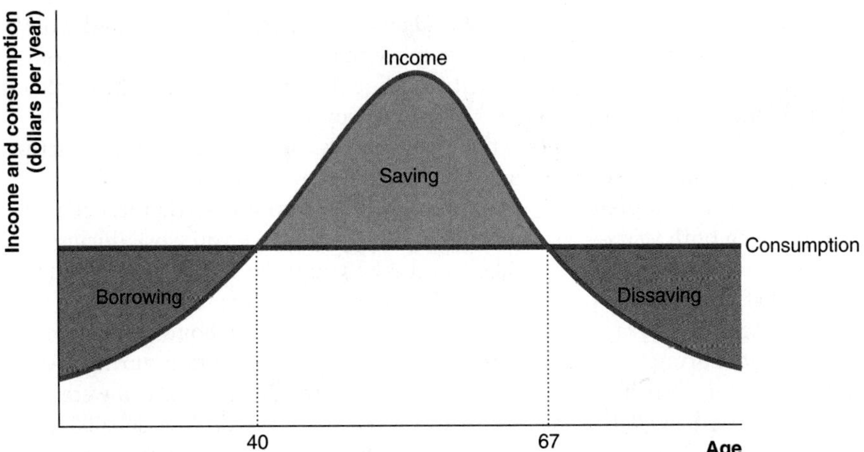

at a lower salary, the person's permanent income would fall, as would his consumption. We can conclude that: *Consumption responds more to changes in permanent income than to changes in transitory income.*

Life-cycle hypothesis The theory that households use financial markets to borrow and save to transfer funds from high-income periods, such as working years, to low-income periods, such as retirement years or periods of unemployment.

Nobel Laureate Franco Modigliani played an important role in developing the *life-cycle hypothesis* as an alternative to the permanent-income hypothesis as an explanation of consumption smoothing. According to the **life-cycle hypothesis**, households use financial markets to borrow and save to transfer funds from high-income periods, such as their working years, to low-income periods, such as their retirement years, periods of unemployment, or years as a student in college. For example, when you retire, your income from employment decreases dramatically because you are no longer working. If you do not want to experience a large decrease in consumption during retirement, then you will have to save during your working years to accumulate assets. When you retire and no longer receive a salary, you can use the income from your assets or sell your assets to finance consumption. In effect, you are saving during the part of your life cycle when income is high to transfer funds to the part of your life cycle when your income is low. Consumption during your retirement will fall by less than your disposable income. In both the permanent-income hypothesis and the life-cycle hypothesis, people give up consumption in the present to save so that they have the resources to finance consumption in the future. In other words, *the goal of saving is to provide for future consumption.*

Figure 14.4 provides an example of the life-cycle hypothesis for a person who wants consumption to be constant over his or her lifetime. The person smooths consumption so that it is constant each year. Initially, income is less than consumption, so the person borrows to finance consumption. As income rises, the person borrows less. After age 40, the person's income is greater than consumption, so the person pays off the debts acquired during the earlier years and begins to save for retirement. After age 67, income falls below consumption, so the person sells off assets—such as stocks and bonds—accumulated during his or her working years to finance consumption.

If a person completely smooths consumption so that it is the same during each year of life, then consumption equals the sum of initial wealth and lifetime income divided by the number of years the person expects to live. If the person earns Y each year and expects to work for B years, then lifetime income is BY. If the person expects to live for N years, then consumption is:

$$C = \frac{\text{Wealth} + BY}{N}.$$

This expression is equivalent to:

$$C = \left(\frac{1}{N}\right)\text{Wealth} + \left(\frac{B}{N}\right)Y, \qquad (14.3)$$

where:

$\left(\frac{1}{N}\right)$ = how much spending increases when wealth increases by \$1

$\left(\frac{B}{N}\right)$ = is the *marginal propensity to consume* out of income.

Marginal propensity to consume (*MPC*) The amount by which consumption increases when disposable income increases by \$1.

The **marginal propensity to consume (*MPC*)** out of income is the amount by which consumption increases when disposable income increases by \$1. For example, if a person expects to live for another 50 years—so that $N = 50$—and work for another 40 years—so that $B = 40$—then the marginal propensity to consume out of income equals $40 \div 50 = 0.8$. As a consequence, the person will consume \$80 per year for each additional \$100 of income. However, it is important to recognize that this is an example of the marginal propensity to consume out of *permanent* increases in income. If an increase in income is *transitory*, then a person's consumption will respond much less. People also use wealth to finance consumption, and if a person expects to live 50 more years, then the marginal propensity to consume out of wealth equals $1 \div 50 = 0.02$, so the person will consume \$2 per year for each additional \$100 in wealth.

Do households really smooth consumption? John Campbell and N. Gregory Mankiw of Harvard University estimated that about one-half of U.S. households make decisions in a manner consistent with the permanent-income hypothesis and the life-cycle hypothesis.[3] Many other economists find strong evidence in favor of consumption smoothing for aggregate consumption.[4] Consumption smoothing is a powerful force that affects a large portion of consumer expenditure in the United States.

Figure 14.3 on page 525 suggests that households more completely smooth expenditure on services and nondurable goods than on durable goods. Because durable goods, such as cars, last many years, households have flexibility about when to replace them. If someone experiences an unexpected decrease in income due to a job loss during a recession, the person is likely to continue driving his or her current car rather than buy a new one. So, expenditures on durable goods decrease during a recession, as households respond to temporarily low income by delaying these purchases. In contrast, nondurable goods, such as food and clothing, are consumed or wear out and must be purchased more frequently. Services, such as health care, are consumed the moment they are purchased, so people have to purchase a service when they need it. Therefore, expenditure on nondurable goods and services tend not to decrease as much during recessions. For these reasons, expenditure on durable goods is more volatile than expenditure on nondurable goods and services, as we saw in Figure 14.3.

Permanent Versus Transitory Changes in Income

The permanent-income hypothesis and the life-cycle hypothesis assume that households prefer to smooth consumption over time. This means that permanent changes in income will have much larger effects on consumption than transitory or one-time changes in

[3] John Campbell and N. Gregory Mankiw, "Consumption, Income, and Interest Rates: Reinterpreting the Time Series Evidence," *National Bureau of Economic Research Macroeconomic Annual*, Vol. 4, 1989, pp. 185–216.

[4] A classic article is: Robert E. Hall, "Intertemporal Substitution in Consumption," *Journal of Political Economy*, Vol. 96, No. 2, April 1988, pp. 339–357.

income. It is easier to illustrate this point using the life-cycle hypothesis, so consider a case in which you are currently 20 years old, your wealth is zero, you will work for 40 years at a constant salary of \$50,000, and you expect to live to age 70. In that case, lifetime income is \$50,000 × 40 years = \$2,000,000, so according to Equation (14.3), consumption is:

$$C = \left(\frac{1}{50}\right)0 + \left(\frac{40}{50}\right)\$50{,}000 = \frac{\$2{,}000{,}000}{50} = \$40{,}000.$$

Therefore, each year you will consume \$40,000 and save \$10,000. Consider the case of a transitory increase in your income to \$60,000 during your first year of work. Your lifetime income is now (\$50,000 × 39 years) + (\$60,000 × 1 year) = \$2.01 million, and you still expect to live to age 70, so:

$$C = 0 + \frac{\$2{,}010{,}000}{50} = \$40{,}200.$$

If you completely smooth consumption, then you consume only an extra \$200 per year. Your marginal propensity to consume out of a transitory increase in income is just:

$$MPC^{\text{Transitory}} = \frac{\Delta C}{\Delta Y} = \frac{\$200}{\$10{,}000} = 0.02.$$

The *MPC* out of transitory changes in income is low because you smooth the \$10,000 increase in income over the 50 additional years you expect to live. In fact, the *MPC* out of a one-time change in income in the formulation is always:

$$MPC^{\text{Transitory}} = \frac{1}{N}.$$

The situation is quite different if your salary permanently increases to \$60,000 per year starting with your first year of work. In this case, your lifetime income is now \$60,000 × 40 years = \$2.4 million, so:

$$C = 0 + \frac{\$2{,}400{,}000}{50} = \$48{,}000.$$

Your consumption increases by \$8,000 per year when the change in income is permanent. As a result, the *MPC* is:

$$MPC^{\text{Permanent}} = \frac{\Delta C}{\Delta Y} = \frac{\$8{,}000}{\$10{,}000} = 0.8.$$

Therefore, the *MPC* is much larger for permanent changes in income. As we will see in the next section, policymakers who want to use changes in taxes to increase consumption need to consider that the *MPC* for permanent income changes is higher than the *MPC* for transitory income changes.

Consumption and the Real Interest Rate

Households use financial markets to smooth consumption by borrowing or by selling financial assets when income is low and by saving when income is high. The real interest rate on financial assets plays an important role in the decisions of households about how much to consume and how much to save. The effect of the real interest rate on consumption is complicated because a change in the real interest rate changes not only the "price" of consumption today but also the incomes of households. As a result, a change in the real interest rate has both a *substitution effect* and an *income effect.*

The real interest rate is the "price" at which an individual trades off current consumption for future consumption. For example, if the real interest rate is 10% and you put $10,000 into your savings account, it will grow to $(1 + 0.10) \times \$10{,}000 = \$11{,}000$ at the end of the year. To get $10,000 worth of consumption this year, you must give up $11,000 of consumption next year. If the real interest rate is 20%, then your saving grows to $(1 + 0.20) \times \$10{,}000 = \$12{,}000$ at the end of the year. To get $10,000 of consumption this year, you must give up $12,000 of consumption next year. The higher the real interest rate, the more "expensive" consumption this year becomes. So, economists think of the real interest rate as *the price of current consumption relative to future consumption.* When the real interest rate increases, individuals reduce current consumption and increase future consumption. This mechanism is the substitution effect.

There is also an income effect associated with a change in the real interest rate. The direction of the income effect depends on whether the individual is a net borrower or lender. If an individual is a lender, an increase in the real interest rate effectively increases his or her income. For example, if you have $1,000 in your savings account and the real interest rate is 10%, then you will have $(1 + 0.10) \times \$1{,}000 = \$1{,}100$ at the end of the year. But if the real interest rate is 20%, then you will have $(1 + 0.20) \times \$1{,}000 = \$1{,}200$ at the end of the year. The extra $100 acts as an increase in your income, which causes you to consume more in the current period. Therefore, the income and substitution effects move in opposite directions for lenders.

The income and substitution effects work in the same direction when someone is a borrower. The increase in the real interest rate causes a decrease in income, so current consumption decreases. To see this effect at work, suppose that instead of saving $1,000, you borrow $1,000. In this case, the increase in the real interest rate from 10% to 20% will cause interest payments to increase, which decreases your wealth by $100. As a result, current consumption decreases. Table 14.1 summarizes the effect of an increase in the real interest rate on consumption.

The substitution effect indicates that higher real interest rates reduce current consumption for both households who are lenders and those who are borrowers, so the substitution effect is negative. The income effect is positive for lenders and negative for borrowers. An increase in the real interest rate will therefore definitely decrease current consumption for households who are borrowers because both the income and substitution effects are negative. The effect on lenders is unclear because the income and substitution effects move in opposite directions.

Whether an increase in the real interest rate increases or decreases current consumption depends partly on whether there are more net borrowers or more net lenders in the economy, and we cannot answer this question with theory alone. For the purposes of our discussion, we will assume that the substitution effect is stronger, so that an increase in the real interest rate will decrease consumption even for households who are lenders. An increase in the real interest rate will therefore lead to a decrease in aggregate consumption and an increase in household saving.

Housing Wealth and Consumption

Our theory of consumption suggests that wealth, in addition to income and interest rates, is also important for consumption. A home is an important asset for many people. However, while the value of a person's home might be important for his or her consumption, it may

Table 14.1 The Effect of the Real Interest Rate on Consumption

	You are a lender	You are a borrower
Substitution effect	Negative	Negative
Income effect	Positive	Negative
Net effect	Unclear	Negative

not be important for aggregate consumption. Many economists have tried to estimate the effect of housing wealth on consumption. For example, the Congressional Budget Office (CBO) estimates that a $1 increase in housing wealth increases consumption by $0.07.[5] However, more recent research by Charles Calomiris of Columbia University and Stanley Longhofer and William Miles of Wichita State University suggests earlier estimates of the wealth effect are too large.[6] Their research shows that a decrease in housing wealth does not change aggregate consumption.

Why would the value of housing have no effect on aggregate consumption? Willem Buiter, chief economist of Citigroup, believes that a decrease in housing prices hurts some households but helps other households.[7] Buiter argues that a decrease in housing prices reduces the wealth of older households and of households planning to purchase and move into houses less expensive than their current house. The decrease in housing wealth should reduce the consumption of these households. However, a decrease in housing prices increases the wealth of both younger households that are more likely to be renters and households planning to purchase and live in houses more expensive than their current house. The decrease in housing prices means these households have to save less from their current income to accumulate the funds necessary to purchase a house. So, wealth and consumption for these households increase. Whether aggregate consumption increases or decreases depends on the mix of households and the marginal propensity to consume out of wealth for each group of households. The collapse in housing prices after 2006 contributed significantly to the 2007–2009 recession, but recent economic research suggests that the effect of the decrease in housing wealth on consumption was likely small. Instead, the effect that the decrease in housing prices had on financial markets and the residential construction industry was probably more important.

How Policy Affects Consumption

Government policy affects consumption by altering disposable income today and in the future. *Disposable income* is total income plus transfer payments minus taxes:

$$Y^D = Y + TR - T.$$

To account for the role of government policy, we simply need to recognize that everything we have discussed so far about the relationship between income and consumption also applies to disposable income and consumption.

To see how government policy can affect consumption, consider the earlier example in which you were 20 years old, expected to work for 40 years, earning $50,000 per year, and to live until age 70. We saw that you would consume $40,000 per year, but that was based on the assumption that you pay no taxes. If you pay $10,000 per year in taxes and receive no transfer payments, then the government takes $10,000 from you each year before you can decide whether to consume or save that income. Therefore, your disposable income is just $40,000 per year, and your lifetime disposable income is $1,600,000. Therefore, your consumption is:

$$C = \left(\frac{1}{N}\right)\text{Wealth} + \left(\frac{B}{N}\right)Y^D = \left(\frac{1}{N}\right)0 + \left(\frac{40}{50}\right)40 = \frac{\$1{,}600{,}000}{50} = \$32{,}000$$

---

[5]Congressional Budget Office, "Housing Wealth and Consumer Spending," January 2007. The CBO considers two estimates—a high estimate of 0.07, which we use, and a low estimate of 0.02. Table 1 of the report discusses recent estimates for the effect which range from a low of 0.017 to a high of 0.21.

[6]Charles Calomiris, Stanley Longhofer, and William Miles, "The (Mythical?) Housing Wealth Effect," National Bureau of Economic Research Working Paper 15075, June 2009.

[7]Willem Buiter, "Housing Wealth Isn't Wealth," National Bureau of Economic Research Working Paper 14204, July 2008.

Table 14.2 Summary of Factors That Affect Household Consumption

If the following occurs . . .	consumption . . .	because . . .
a one-time increase in disposable income	increases	households smooth the one-time increase in income over their entire lifetimes.
a permanent increase in disposable income	increases	households experience a large increase in lifetime income.
a decrease in the real interest rate	increases	borrowers consume more.
an increase in household wealth	increases	households will consume part of the wealth during each time period (college age, working age, retirement age).

If your disposable income is $40,000 per year and you consume $32,000 per year, then you must save $8,000 per year. When taxes were $0 in our previous example, you consumed $40,000 and saved $10,000 per year, so an increase in taxes causes both consumption and saving to decrease. Therefore, a permanent increase in taxes from $0 to $10,000 reduced consumption by $8,000. In the language of the permanent-income hypothesis, the tax increase represents a decrease in permanent income. So, consumption responds significantly. In Solved Problem 14.2, we ask you to determine the effect of a temporary decrease in taxes. Given what you already know about the permanent-income hypothesis, you should be able to predict that the effect of temporary tax cuts is relatively modest.

Table 14.2 summarizes the factors that affect consumption.

Solved Problem 14.2

Effects of a Temporary Tax Cut

During periods of slow economic growth, the government sometimes uses tax rebates to stimulate consumption. For example, the federal government used one-time temporary tax rebates in 2001 and 2008 to try to stimulate consumption. Continue with our previous example where you are 20 years old, you plan to work for 40 years at an after-tax salary of $40,000, and you expect to live to age 70. Assume that your initial wealth is zero. Now suppose the government gives you a one-time tax rebate of $1,000 during your first year of work. Predict the effect of the tax rebate on your consumption.

Solving the Problem

Step 1 **Review the chapter material.** The problem asks you to use the theory of consumption to determine the effect of a one-time tax rebate on consumption, so you may want to review the section "Factors That Determine Consumption," which begins on page 524.

Step 2 **Determine the effect on your lifetime disposable income.** Your lifetime disposable income is now:

$$\$40{,}000 \times 39 \text{ years} + \$41{,}000 \times 1 \text{ year} = \$1{,}601{,}000$$

Step 3 **Apply Equation (14.3) on page 529.** If you smooth consumption completely, then you follow Equation (14.3), so:

$$C = \left(\frac{1}{N}\right)\text{Wealth} + \left(\frac{B}{N}\right)Y^D = \frac{\$1{,}601{,}000}{50} = \$32{,}020.$$

Step 4 **Compare to your earlier level of consumption.** Before the one-time tax rebate, you consumed \$32,000 and saved \$8,000 during the first year. Now you consume \$32,020 and save \$8,980 during the first year because you smooth the entire \$1,000 tax rebate over the entire 50 years that you expect to live. A one-time tax rebate is a transitory increase in disposable income. Given our discussion of the permanent-income hypothesis and consumption smoothing, it should come as no surprise that a one-time tax rebate has a small effect on consumption.

For more practice, do related problem 2.13 on page 555 at the end of this chapter.

Credit Rationing of Households

Our theory of consumption assumes that households can easily access financial markets to borrow and save as necessary to smooth consumption. If households can use financial markets to borrow against future income, then households with low income now that expect higher income in the future can borrow against future income to smooth consumption. For example, students can obtain student loans to finance their education or use credit cards to purchase goods and services even if they do not currently have jobs. As a result, current consumption can exceed current income. However, financial markets do not work perfectly, and households often face constraints on how much they can borrow. Households face these constraints because it is often difficult for banks and other lenders to distinguish between households that are likely to repay loans and those that are likely to default on loans. For example, the members of a household have better information than a bank about their job security, whether a couple is likely to divorce, and other factors that may affect the ability of a household to repay a loan. As a result, there is asymmetric information in financial markets, which makes it risky for banks to make loans to households.

Financial institutions can raise the real interest rate on loans to compensate for this risk, but increasing real interest rates changes the mix of potential borrowers. Some households are safe borrowers because they seek loans only if they are sure they can repay them. Other households are risky borrowers because they are willing to take out loans even if they are not sure that they can repay them. The higher real interest rate means that fewer households can now afford to get loans, and so safe borrowers drop out of the market for loans. Unfortunately, risky borrowers remain, and so the pool of potential borrowers has more risky borrowers relative to safe borrowers than before. The riskiness of loans has increased, which may cause financial institutions to increase the real interest rate again. Of course, this action makes the pool of potential borrowers even riskier.

Financial institutions know asymmetric information exists, so they often require that households have collateral for loans. It is also common for financial institutions to require a household to use some of the household's own funds in addition to borrowed funds for major purchases. For example, many banks and other lenders require that households borrowing money to buy a house or car make a down payment of up to 20% of the purchase price. With a down payment, defaulting on a loan costs the borrower some of his or her own funds. Households are considered credit rationed if they cannot borrow against future income and have to post collateral or cannot obtain loans at all.

The theory of consumption predicts that the *MPC* out of current disposable income is relatively low. In contrast to this theory, if a household is credit rationed, then the *MPC* out of current disposable income is high. Why? If a household is credit rationed, then it would like to consume more but cannot because it cannot borrow money. Therefore, a credit-rationed household is consuming at a lower level than the household would prefer. When the credit-rationed household has an increase in disposable income, it will spend most of the increase in an attempt to reach the preferred level of consumption. If a large number of households face credit rationing, then changes in transitory income, such as the temporary decrease in payroll taxes signed into law in December 2010, can have a large effect on consumption.

How important is credit rationing in practice? Work by economists David Gross of Compass Lexecon and Nicholas Souleles of the University of Pennsylvania support the existence of credit rationing.[8] The consumption-smoothing model assumes that households can borrow as much as they want to smooth consumption. With this assumption, a household should not increase its debt when a credit card company increases the household's credit limit. However, if households are credit rationed, then they will use the increase in the credit limit to increase consumption. In addition, the households most likely to suffer from credit rationing are those currently at their credit limits. Gross and Souleles showed that an increase in credit limits results in an immediate increase in credit card debt. The effect is rather large: A $1,000 increase in a credit limit is associated with an increase in credit card debt of $100 to $140. The results are also large for the aggregate economy. Working with 1995 data, Gross and Souleles estimate that, if every household received a $2,000 increase in the credit limit on each of its credit cards, then consumption would increase by about $40 billion. This change would amount to about 10% of the typical yearly increase in consumption for the economy as a whole. Gross and Souleles also showed that the increase in debt is much larger for households that are already near their credit limits. These results are consistent with the presence of credit rationing.

The work of Gross and Souleles suggests that credit rationing is an important determinant of household consumption. Earlier research also found that credit rationing affects consumption. However, other evidence suggests that the effect of credit rationing on consumption may not be that important. Robert Hall of Stanford University and Frederic Mishkin of Columbia University examined the consumption behavior of households and found that consumption smoothing is a more important determinant than credit rationing.[9] They found that 80% of consumption spending is consistent with the consumption smoothing model, while the remainder is consistent with the presence of credit rationing. Hall and Mishkin's research indicates that consumption smoothing is a more important determinant of aggregate consumption than is credit rationing.

If credit rationing is an important determinant of aggregate consumption, then temporary tax rebates, such as those in the Economic Growth and Tax Relief Reconciliation Act of 2001 and the Economic Stimulus Act of 2008, should boost consumption. The details of the two tax rebates varied, but in each case, some households received a one-time payment of several hundred dollars from the federal government. If households are credit rationed, then their consumption is below what they would prefer. A credit-rationed household should use a tax rebate to increase consumption to the level it would prefer. This effect is more consistent with the consumption smoothing model and the results of Hall and Mishkin than the credit rationing model. So, credit rationing may

[8]David Gross and Nicholas Souleles, "Do Liquidity Constraints and Interest Rates Matter for Consumer Behavior? Evidence from Credit Card Data," *Quarterly Journal of Economics*, Vol. 117, No. 1, February 2002, pp. 149–185.

[9]Robert Hall and Frederic Mishkin, "The Sensitivity of Consumption to Transitory Income: Estimates from Panel Data on Households," *Econometrica*, Vol. 50, No. 2, March 1982, pp. 461–481.

not be a critical determinant of aggregate consumption, but it may be important for individual households.

While credit rationing may not be important during normal times, credit rationing may have played an important role during the 2007–2009 recession. Atif Mian of the University of California at Berkeley and Amir Sufi of the University of Chicago examined the behavior of consumption and consumer credit at the county level in the United States during the 2007–2009 recession.[10] They found that credit card companies continued to increase the credit available to U.S. households during the first part of the recession, so households could still access financial markets to smooth consumption. However, when the financial crisis suddenly worsened in September and October 2008, credit card companies began to reduce borrowing limits. The limits were imposed at precisely the time when home equity was declining and banks were making it more difficult for households to borrow against the equity in their homes. The reduced availability of credit made it difficult for households to find the funds necessary to smooth consumption. In other words, households faced credit rationing and were forced to cut back on the purchases of expensive durable goods such as new cars. Not surprisingly, the Bureau of Economic Analysis reports that spending on consumer durable goods decreased by 12% at an annual rate during the third quarter of 2008 and then by 22.3% during the fourth quarter of 2008. The work of Mian and Sufi indicate that credit rationing may have contributed to the large decrease in spending on consumer durables during the second half of 2008, so credit rationing may help explain why the 2007–2009 recession was so severe.

Making the Connection

The Temporary Cut in Payroll Taxes

The U.S. government levies Social Security payroll taxes in the amount of 12.4% on the first $106,800 of an individual's salary. Half of the tax, 6.2%, is explicitly paid by the employee, and the other half is explicitly paid by the firm. As part of the tax cut package signed into law on December 17, 2010, the government reduced the employee portion of the payroll tax by 2%, to 4.2% for one year. The payroll-tax cut reduced taxes paid and increased disposable income for all individuals who work. For someone earning $70,000 per year, the payroll-tax cut increased disposable income by $1,400, and for someone earning $106,800 the payroll-tax cut increased disposable income by $2,100. The total expected cost to the U.S. government of the payroll-tax cut was $111 billion. Supporters of the payroll-tax cut believed that it would quickly provide an increase in disposable income for 155 million workers, which would lead to increased consumption and increased real GDP. Moreover, supporters argued that because the tax cut would be received disproportionately by low- and middle-income households, the tax cut would increase disposable income for households with higher marginal propensities to consume. Another reason to believe that the payroll-tax cut would increase consumption is the impact it might have on credit-rationed households. Households that are credit rationed consume less than they would prefer, so they are more likely than other consumers to use the tax cut to increase consumption spending when their current disposable incomes increase. Economists at Deutsche Bank predicted the payroll-tax cut would increase the growth rate of real GDP by 0.7% during 2011.

However, our discussion of the permanent-income hypothesis and the life-cycle hypothesis suggests that the effect of the payroll-tax cut is likely to be modest. The payroll-tax cut will last just one year, so it will temporarily increase disposable income. Therefore, it represents a transitory increase in disposable income and, as Solved Problem 14.2 shows,

---

[10]Atif Mian and Amir Sufi, "Household Leverage and the Recession of 2007 to 2009," *IMF Economic Review*, Vol.58, No. 1, August 2010, pp. 74–117.

the cut should have relatively little effect on consumption. The research on the 2001 and 2008 tax rebates also suggests that transitory tax cuts have relatively small effects on consumption. Those two tax rebates were one-time payments to households, but the payroll-tax cut represents a decrease in taxes for each paycheck over an entire year. This difference may be large enough for the payroll-tax cut to significantly increase consumption.

If households do not spend the increase in disposable income, what will they do with it? The experiences with the 2001 and 2008 tax rebates suggest that households will save a large part of the payroll-tax cut. Jimmy Lee, chief executive at Strategic Wealth Associates, recommends that households use a payroll-tax cut to increase their retirement savings. If households follow the advice of wealth managers such as Mr. Lee, then the payroll-tax cut will have a relatively small effect on consumption.

Even the Deutsche Bank economists who predicted that the payroll-tax cut would raise GDP by 0.7% during 2011 based their prediction on the assumption that there would not be offsetting expenditure reductions elsewhere in the federal budget. However, provisions of the American Recovery and Reinvestment Act did begin to expire in 2011. As a result, the pay-roll tax cut may not increase real GDP by as much as the Deutsche Bank economists initially predicted.

Sources: "Factbox: Key Components of U.S. Senate Tax Bill," www.cnbc.com, December 15, 2010; Sudeep Reddy, "The Tax Agreement: Package Would Give Obama a Stealthy Stimulus," *Wall Street Journal*, December 8, 2010; Martin Vaughan, "Payroll Tax Cut: How It Works," *Wall Street Journal*, December 7, 2010; Stephen Ohlemacher, "Does Tax Cut Threaten Social Security? White House Says It Will Not Affect Solvency of Program, but Some Worry," *Houston Chronicle*, December 13, 2010; and U.S. Bureau of Economic Analysis.

Test your understanding by doing related problem 2.17 on page 556 at the end of this chapter.

Precautionary Saving

So far, our discussion of consumption has assumed that households know their future disposable income and can smooth consumption accordingly, so uncertainty about future income does not affect consumption. In fact, of course, households do not know the future and may adjust consumption and savings to protect themselves from unexpected decreases in disposable income. **Precautionary saving** is the extra saving by households to protect themselves from unexpected decreases in future income due to job loss, illness, or disability. In this case, saving acts as insurance to protect households from unexpected events. For example, if the economy starts to perform poorly and households believe that the probability of a job loss has increased, they are likely to increase precautionary savings and reduce consumption.

Precautionary saving
Extra saving by households to protect themselves from unexpected decreases in future income due to job loss, illness, or disability.

One way to think of precautionary savings is to view households as having a desired level of wealth. When wealth is above the desired level, then consumption will exceed disposable income, and wealth will decrease as households draw down their assets to finance consumption. In contrast, if wealth is below the desired level, then consumption will be less than disposable income, and wealth will increase as households save to reach the target. For example, suppose that households prefer to have six months of disposable income in the stock market to protect them from unexpected negative events. If stock prices unexpectedly rise and the household's wealth becomes equal to seven months of disposable income, the household will increase spending on cars or clothes until its wealth decreases to six months of disposable income. If an unexpected event decreases the household's wealth, then the household is likely to decrease consumption to rebuild its wealth.

The theory of consumption emphasizes the importance of future events in determining the level of consumption and savings. Precautionary saving highlights the importance of uncertainty about future events. An increase in uncertainty about the future will increase the desired level of wealth and lead to lower consumption until households have attained the new higher target level of wealth. A decrease in uncertainty about the future will decrease the desired level of wealth and lead to higher spending until households have attained the new lower target level of wealth. Because uncertainty affects consumption when people save for precautionary reasons, uncertainty can affect aggregate consumption and help cause economic fluctuations.

Christopher Carroll of Johns Hopkins University and Andrew Samwick of Dartmouth College have estimated the relative importance of precautionary saving for U.S. households.[11] According to their estimates, reducing uncertainty about future income for all households to the level of the household with the least uncertainty would result in about a 45% decrease in total net worth for households headed by individuals under age 50. In other words, households have accumulated nearly half their net worth to protect themselves from unexpected negative future events. If the estimates of Carroll and Samwick are accurate, then precautionary saving motives can help explain a large component of consumption and saving behavior.

Tax Incentives and Saving

Households save out of disposable income, so an increase in taxes should reduce disposable income and reduce saving. On pages 530–531, we saw that the real interest rate is an important determinant of household saving because the real interest rate determines how much future consumption the household must give up in order to consume today. The higher the real interest rate, the more future consumption is given up, so the more a household will save today to finance consumption in the future. However, what really matters is not the real interest rate but the after-tax real interest rate. Given a real interest rate, taxes on income from saving reduce the after-tax real interest rate and so reduce the incentive to save. An increase in taxes on saving reduces the incentive to save and leads to less saving and more consumption today, while a decrease in taxes on saving increases the incentive to save and leads to more savings and less consumption today.

Two important federal programs reduce taxes on saving, thereby increasing the after-tax real interest rate. First, individual retirement accounts (IRAs) reduce taxes and increase the after-tax real interest rate. A traditional IRA allows an individual to contribute funds to an account without paying taxes until he or she retires and withdraws funds from the account. Because an individual typically does not withdraw funds from the account until many years into the future, the IRA reduces the after-tax real interest rate on saving for retirement. Second, many Americans save for retirement using employer-sponsored 401(k) plans that allow them to invest part of their income in mutual funds that purchase financial assets, such as stocks and bonds. The individuals do not have to pay taxes on the portion of income contributed to a 401(k) account until they withdraw the funds during retirement. So, the 401(k) is also a way to increase the after-tax real interest rates on saving.

Glenn Hubbard of Columbia University and Jonathan Skinner of Dartmouth College surveyed studies of IRAs and 401(k) plans.[12] They noted that part of the problem with assessing the effectiveness of these plans is determining whether they result in net new savings or just cause households to switch savings from financial assets without tax incentives, such as savings accounts in banks, to IRAs and 401(k) plans that do have tax incentives. In addition, if the tax incentives are financed through government budget deficits, then government saving decreases by $1 for every $1 of tax reduction on household saving. Nevertheless, Hubbard and Skinner concluded that the plans do increase national saving. In fact, they argued that in the long run, IRAs increase the private capital stock by $5 for each $1 reduction in government

[11]Christopher Carroll and Andrew Samwick, "How Important Is Precautionary Savings?" *Review of Economics and Statistics*, Vol. 80, No. 3, August 1998, pp. 410–419.

[12]Glenn Hubbard and Jonathan Skinner, "Assessing the Effectiveness of Saving Incentives," *Journal of Economic Perspectives*, Vol. 10, No. 4, Fall 1996, pp. 73–90.

tax revenue and 401(k) plans increase the private capital stock by $17 for each $1 reduction in government tax revenue. These effects of tax incentives are large and suggest that government programs designed to increase saving lead to a significant increase in the private capital stock. The models for the economy in the long run in Chapters 4 and 5 suggest that an increase in the capital stock will increase labor productivity and the standard of living.

Factors That Determine Private Investment

14.3

Learning Objective

Explain the determinants of private investment.

So far in this chapter, we have reviewed the factors that determine consumption. In this section, we consider the factors that determine investment. Investment includes purchases of capital goods, such as new plant and equipment, new residential housing, and inventories. Figure 14.5 shows gross capital formation (a measure of investment) as a percentage of GDP. Investment is a major component of GDP for countries around the world, averaging 22.1% of GDP since 1960. On average, the United States invests 18.6% of GDP, which is substantially less than the average for middle- and high-income countries. In fact, the average low-income country now invests more per year than does the United States.

Investment is a much smaller share of GDP than is consumption for all countries. However, it is still important to understand the determinants of investment. Figure 14.1 on page 524 shows that investment is much more volatile than consumption, and it therefore may contribute significantly to the business cycle. Figure 14.6 shows that some categories of investment are more volatile than others. From the mid-1980s to 2007, economic fluctuations were relatively mild in the United States, prompting economists to call this period the Great Moderation. Before the Great Moderation, spending on residential investment was more volatile than either spending on nonresidential structures or spending on equipment and software. Since the Great Moderation, all three categories of investment have experienced about the same volatility.

The Investment Decisions of Firms

Economists typically assume that firms purchase capital goods to maximize profits. The **desired capital stock** is the level of the capital stock that maximizes a firm's profits. Firms find the desired capital stock by comparing the benefits and costs of purchasing additional capital goods. The benefit is the profit that comes from the goods and services that the capital goods

Desired capital stock The level of capital stock that maximizes a firm's profits.

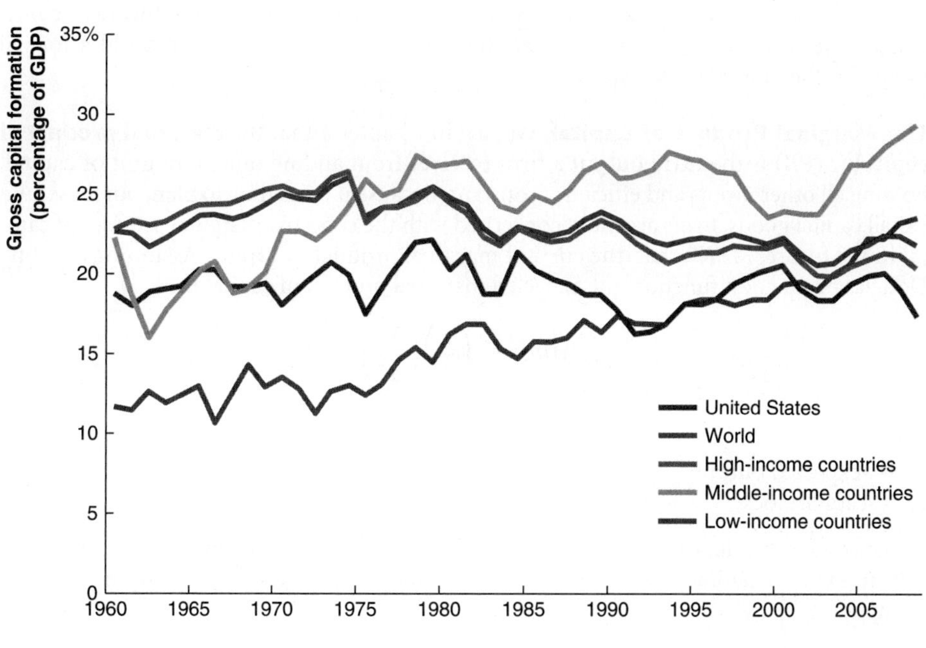

Figure 14.5

Gross Capital Formation Around the World, 1960–2009

Since 1970, the United States has consistently invested a smaller share of GDP than the average global share, which includes the average shares invested in high- and middle-income countries.

Source: The World Bank, *World Development Indicators*.

Figure 14.6

Growth Rates for Types of Investment, 1947–2011

Prior to the Great Moderation, residential investment was the most volatile category of investment. However, since the Great Moderation, all three types of investment have experienced about the same level of volatility. Shaded areas indicate recessions.

Sources: U.S. Bureau of Economic Analysis and National Bureau of Economic Research. ●

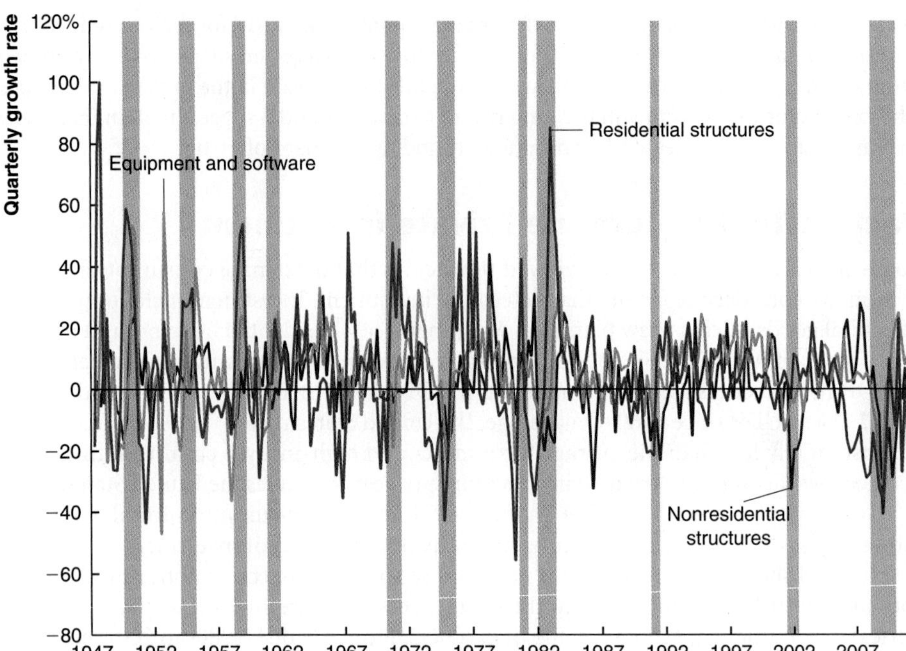

produce. There are three types of costs associated with purchasing capital: (1) the price of the capital goods, (2) the costs of depreciation, and (3) the interest payments to finance the purchase of the capital goods. As we will see next, tax policy affects not only after-tax profits through the corporate income tax but also affects the cost of capital. For example, current government policy allows firms to deduct interest payments and the depreciation of capital goods from their profits before paying taxes. These policies help reduce the cost of capital and encourage greater investment.

We have seen that expectations about the future play an important role in a firm's decision making. It takes time to purchase and install new capital goods, so the benefit to a firm of increasing the capital stock is in the future. In addition, some of the costs of maintaining the capital stock, such as the costs of depreciation, also lie in the future. We now discuss the firm's purchasing decisions in greater detail so that we can build a formal model for the desired capital stock.

Marginal product of capital (*MPK*) The extra output a firm receives from adding one more unit of capital, holding all other inputs and efficiency constant.

The Marginal Product of Capital We saw in Chapter 4 that the **marginal product of capital (*MPK*)** is the extra output a firm receives from adding one more unit of capital, holding all other inputs and efficiency constant. Because it takes time to plan, purchase, and install capital goods, firms are more concerned with the expected marginal product of capital in the future, MPK^e, than the current marginal product of capital. Assuming a Cobb–Douglas production function, the expected marginal product of capital is:

$$MPK^e = \left(\frac{1}{3}\right)\left(\frac{Y^e}{K}\right),$$

where:
$Y^e =$ expected output
$K =$ capital stock

In this example, capital's share of income is one-third, and diminishing marginal returns exist for capital, so as a firm accumulates more capital goods, the marginal product of capital decreases.

What matters to a firm is not the expected marginal product in any one year but the expected marginal product over the entire life of the capital goods. If Ford Motor Company is considering building another automobile factory in the United States that will last for 50 years, then it must consider not only the marginal product of capital this year but also the marginal product of capital for the next 50 years. For example, Ford must consider what will happen to the demand for automobiles if the world price of crude oil increases. It must also try to anticipate the effects of government policy to limit carbon emissions. Restricting carbon emissions may force Ford to adopt a technology that produces fewer carbon emissions but is less efficient at producing automobiles. Ford also has to anticipate the taxes that it will have to pay because the firm is interested in its after-tax profit.

We have emphasized how firms rationally respond to changes based on expectations of future profits. However, John Maynard Keynes in his *General Theory of Employment, Interest, and Money* argued that firms are sometimes overtaken by periods of irrational pessimism and optimism known as **animal spirits** that affect their investment behavior. We can think of animal spirits as changes in the expected marginal product of capital, so when firms are overtaken by irrational optimism, they expect that the marginal product of capital will be higher in the future, and when they are overtaken by irrational pessimism, they expect that the marginal product of capital will be lower in the future. These fluctuations in optimism and pessimism are driven by hopes and fears and not by objective evidence. For example, during the late 1990s, many Internet firms were able to obtain funds in financial markets and undertake investments even though the firms were not yet profitable and had little chance of ever becoming profitable. Therefore, we can say that investment by these firms was driven by animal spirits.

Animal spirits Periods of irrational pessimism and optimism that affect the investment behavior of firms.

The User Cost of Capital The **user cost of capital (uc)** is the expected real cost to a firm of using an additional unit of capital during a period of time. This cost consists of the real price of the capital good, the real interest cost of borrowing to finance the purchase of the capital good, and the depreciation costs associated with actually using the capital good. Most firms are small relative to the market and do not affect the price of capital goods, p_K, or the real interest rate, r. In addition, the depreciation rate, d, is determined by the technology that a firm uses and not how many capital goods the firm purchases. Therefore, the real price of capital goods, the real interest rate, and the rate of depreciation are constants that a firm can take as given.

User cost of capital (uc) The expected real cost to a firm of using an additional unit of capital during a period of time.

The interest cost to a firm equals rp_K and represents the cost to a firm of borrowing funds to purchase a capital good. Even if a firm does not borrow to purchase the capital good, it still pays this cost because a firm could have taken the funds that it used to purchase the capital good and loaned those funds to other firms or households in order to receive interest income. In this case, the interest cost is really an opportunity cost. The capital stock also wears out each period due to normal use, so firms also pay a depreciation cost equal to dp_K. The user cost of capital is the sum of these two costs:

$$uc = rp_K + dp_K = (r + d)p_K.$$

Because a firm is small relative to the market, the user cost of capital does not change as the capital stock changes.

The Desired Capital Stock The desired capital stock (K^*) is the level of the capital stock that maximizes profits. A firm maximizes profits when the expected marginal product of capital equals the user cost of capital. Figure 14.7 shows that the desired capital stock for an individual firm occurs at the intersection of the expected marginal product of capital curve and the user cost of capital curve. The user cost of capital curve is a horizontal line because it is independent of the level of the capital stock. The expected marginal product of capital curve slopes downward due to *diminishing marginal returns.*

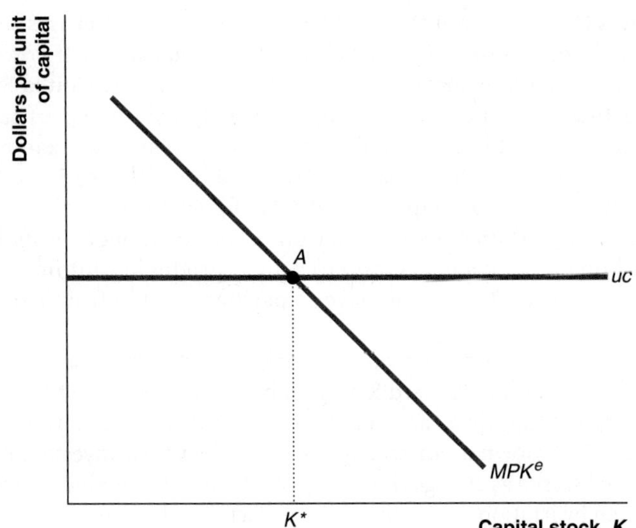

Figure 14.7

The Desired Capital Stock

The desired capital stock for an individual firm occurs where the user cost of capital equals the expected marginal product of capital. ●

Figure 14.7 tells us that the desired capital stock occurs where the expected marginal product of capital equals the user cost of capital:

$$MPK^e = (r + d)p_K. \tag{14.4}$$

Viewed in this way, it is easy to determine what factors cause the desired capital stock to change. Figure 14.8 shows the effect of a decrease in the expected marginal product of capital. If a firm expects that the demand for its product will decrease in the future due to a change in consumer preferences or a change in government policy, then the expected output will decrease from Y_1^e to Y_2^e. The expected marginal product of capital curve will shift to the left, and the desired capital stock will decrease from K_1^* to K_2^*. This example shows how expectations about the future have an important effect on a firm's decision making.

Changes in the user cost of capital also cause the desired capital stock to change. Figure 14.9 shows the effect of an increase in the real interest rate on the user cost of capital and the desired capital stock. The increase in the real interest rate increases the user cost

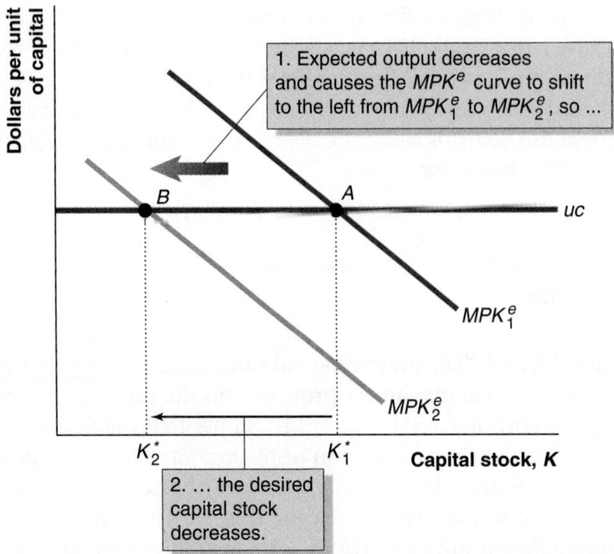

Figure 14.8

A Decrease in the Expected Marginal Product of Capital and the Desired Capital Stock

If a firm expects consumer demand for its product to decrease in the future, then expected output and the expected marginal product of capital will decrease. As a result, the *MPK* curve will shift to the left and the desired capital stock decreases from K_1^* to K_2^*. ●

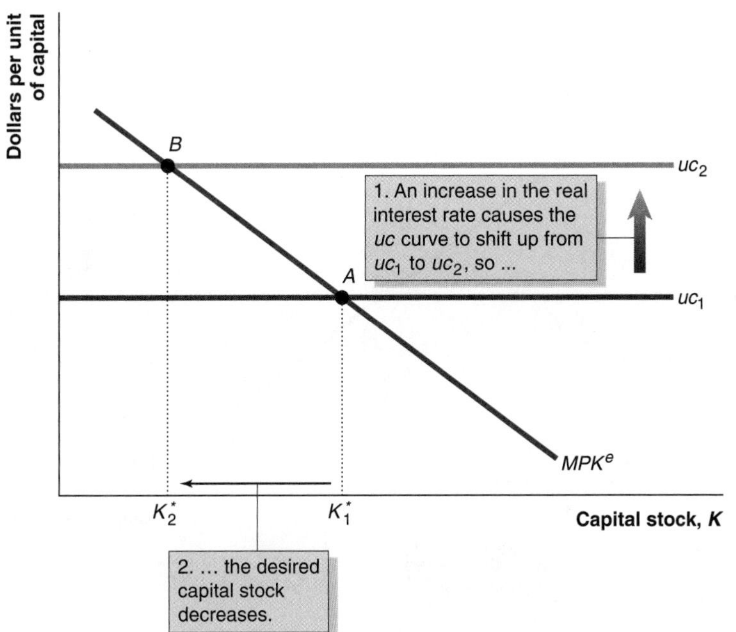

Figure 14.9

An Increase in the User Cost of Capital and the Desired Capital Stock

The increase in the real interest rate increases the user cost of capital, so the *uc* curve shifts up and the desired capital stock decreases from K_1^* to K_2^*. An increase in the user cost of capital due to an increase in either the price of capital or the depreciation rate would have the same effect on the desired capital stock. ●

of capital, so the user cost of capital curve shifts upward. As a result, the desired capital stock decreases. An increase in either the depreciation rate or the real price of capital would have the same effect on the user cost of capital and the desired capital stock.

Corporate Taxes and the Desired Capital Stock

To explain the effect of tax policy on the capital stock, we need to modify our model to allow for the existence of corporate income taxes. After-tax profits, rather than before-tax profits, affect a firm's decision making. For example, if the corporate income tax rate is 30%, the firm retains just 70% of its before-tax profits. Firms purchase capital goods to produce goods and services that generate profits for the owners of the firm. We can think of corporate taxes as reducing the expected marginal product of capital. If the corporate income tax rate is t, then the firm gets to keep $(1 - t)$ of the output from each unit of capital. In our example, $t = 0.30$, so the firm gets to keep $(1 - 0.30) = 0.70$ of output. When accounting for taxes, the expected marginal product of capital is effectively $(1 - t)MPK^e$. Allowing for taxes changes Equation (14.4) to:

$$(1 - t)MPK^e = (r + d)p_K.$$

Rearranging terms, this expression becomes:

$$MPK^e = \frac{(r + d)p_K}{(1 - t)}, \tag{14.5}$$

where the term on the right side is the **tax-adjusted user cost of capital**, which is the after-tax real cost to a firm of purchasing and using an additional unit of capital during a period of time. If the government increases the corporate income tax rate, the tax-adjusted user cost of capital will increase, and the desired capital stock will decrease.

Tax-adjusted user cost of capital The after-tax expected real cost to a firm of purchasing and using an additional unit of capital during a period of time.

Figure 14.10 shows that the increase in the corporate income tax rate causes the after-tax user cost of capital to increase from uc_1 to uc_2. As a result, the desired capital stock decreases from K_1^* to K_2^*.

Table 14.3 on page 545 summarizes the factors that affect the desired capital stock.

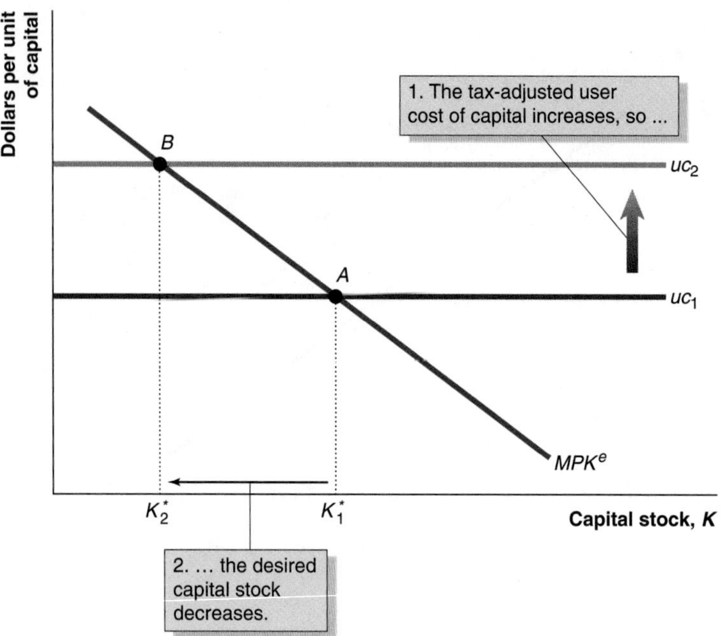

Figure 14.10

An Increase in the Tax-Adjusted User Cost of Capital and the Desired Capital Stock

An increase in the corporate income tax rate causes the after-tax user cost of capital to increase, so the desired capital stock decreases from K_1^* to K_2^*. ●

MACRO DATA: HOW IMPORTANT ARE CORPORATE TAXES FOR INVESTMENT?

The model of investment suggests that corporate taxes may have an important effect on the desired capital stock and, therefore, on aggregate investment. Jason Cummins of Brevan Howard Asset Management LLP, Kevin Hassett of the American Enterprise Institute, and Glenn Hubbard of Columbia University estimated the effect of major tax reforms on investment by firms in 14 countries (Australia, Belgium, Canada, Denmark, France, Germany, Italy, Japan, the Netherlands, Norway, Spain, Sweden, United Kingdom, and the United States). Previous studies had provided varying estimates of the relationship between taxes and investment. However, Cummins, Hassett, and Hubbard focused only on major tax reforms, such as the 1986 Tax Reform Act in the United States, which dramatically decreased the corporate income tax rate from 46% to 34%. They found that in 12 of the 14 countries, a reduction in corporate income taxes significantly increased the level of corporate investment activity.

Cummins, Hassett, and Hubbard also examined changes in corporate income taxes within the United States from 1962 to 1988. During this period, the federal government decreased the corporate income tax rate, in a series of steps, from 52% to 34%. Cummins, Hassett, and Hubbard treated each of these changes as a "natural experiment" to examine the effect of tax changes on investment by firms. They found that after every major tax reform during this period, there was a significant change in investment. For example, the Revenue Act of 1964 reduced the corporate income tax rate from 52% in 1963 to 48% in 1965. As a result, the ratio of equipment investment to the existing stock of equipment increased by 7%. Because the Solow growth model from Chapter 5 tells us that investment is an important determinant of labor productivity and the standard of living, taxes may have important effects on the standard of living.

Sources: Jason Cummins, Kevin Hassett, and Glenn Hubbard, "Tax Reforms and Investment: A Cross-Country Comparison," *Journal of Public Economics*, Vol. 62, No. 1–2, October 1996, pp. 237–273; and Jason Cummins, Kevin Hassett, and Glenn Hubbard, "A Reconsideration of Investment Behavior Using Tax Reforms as Natural Experiments," *Brookings Papers on Economic Activity*, Vol. 25, No. 2, 1994, pp. 1–74.

Test your understanding by doing related problem 3.13 on page 557 at the end of this chapter.

Table 14.3 **Shocks and the Desired Capital Stock**

If there is . . .	then . . .	so, the desired capital stock . . .	Graph of the effect on capital stock . . .
a decrease in expected future output	the marginal product of capital curve shifts to the left	decreases.	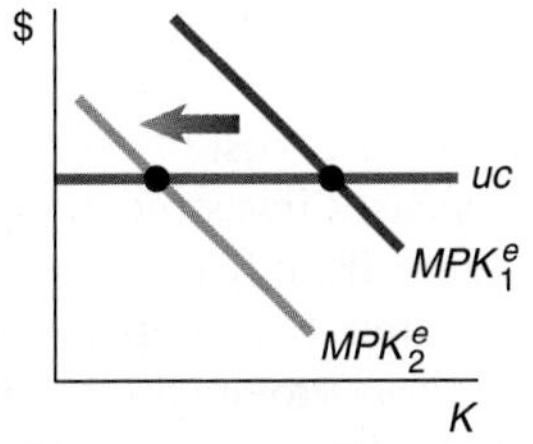 \$; uc; MPK^e_1; MPK^e_2; K
an increase in the real interest rate	the user cost of capital curve shifts up	decreases.	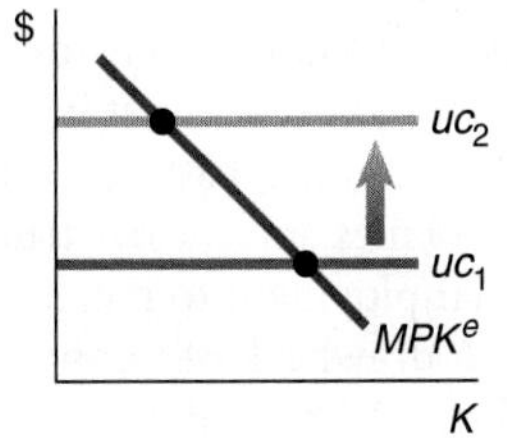 \$; uc_2; uc_1; MPK^e; K
an increase in the depreciation rate	the user cost of capital curve shifts up	decreases.	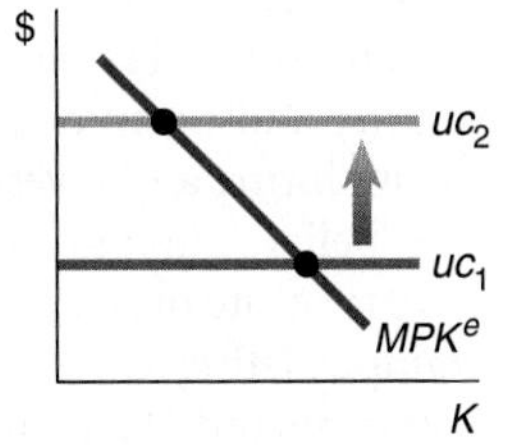 \$; uc_2; uc_1; MPK^e; K
an increase in the real price of capital goods	the user cost of capital curve shifts up	decreases.	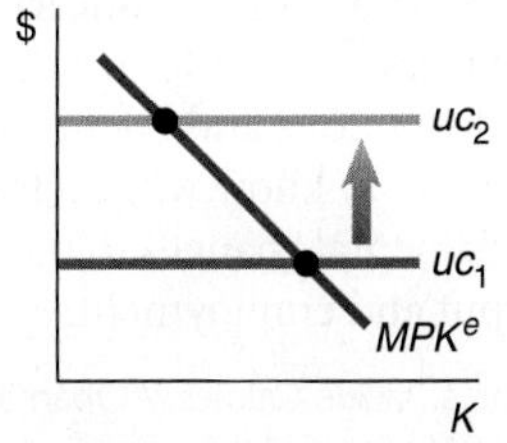 \$; uc_2; uc_1; MPK^e; K
an increase in the corporate income tax rate	the tax-adjusted user cost of capital curve shifts up	decreases.	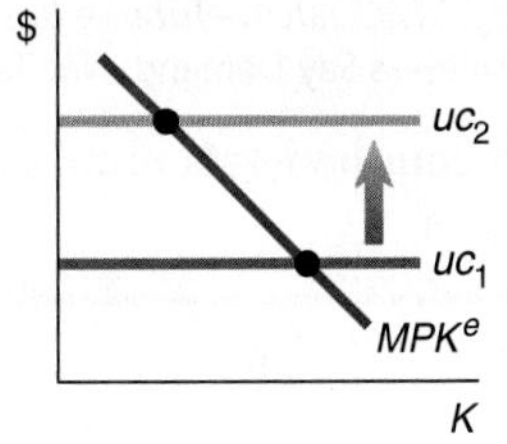 \$; uc_2; uc_1; MPK^e; K

Making the Connection

From Transitory Tax Cuts to Tax Reform

The tax cut package that President Obama signed into law on December 17, 2010, increased from 50% to 100% the fraction of the cost of capital goods that firms can deduct from taxable income in 2011. The model suggests that this policy will decrease the tax-adjusted user cost of capital and increase the desired capital stock. This change should lead to increased investment, higher real GDP, and increased employment during 2011. Initial reactions from firms suggest that this outcome is likely. Cessna is a maker of business jets. Jack Pelton, the company's president and chief executive officer, observed that this change in tax laws provided his company with a "little shot in the arm" that will be helpful to his entire industry. The changes in the new law are likely to help smaller firms as well. Susan Povich, an owner of a small business that transports fresh lobsters from where they are caught in Maine to customers in New York and Washington, DC, said: "The less I pay in taxes the more I invest in my business"—the new tax law will allow her to purchase three rather than just two new lobster trucks in 2011. The extra spending on capital goods such as airplanes and lobster trucks will increase aggregate expenditure, causing both real GDP and employment to increase.

A drawback of temporary tax cuts is that they increase the complexity of the tax code and make firms uncertain about future tax policy. The special tax breaks that President Obama signed into law in December 2010 remain in effect for just a year or two. As recently as the late 1990s, there were only a dozen or so of these temporary tax breaks. By 2011, there were 141. Many economists and business leaders believe that the level of uncertainty and complexity associated with all these temporary provisions discourages firms from hiring and investing. In fact, Tom Duesterberg, president of the Manufacturers Alliance, believes that uncertainty over taxes will provide new and existing firms with an incentive to locate overseas in countries with more stable tax and regulatory environments. For example, Jeffrey Owens, who heads the tax division for the Organisation for Economic Co-operation and Development, points out that very few countries have temporary tax provisions similar to those the United States has enacted or extended.

To deal with the uncertainty in the current U.S. tax system, some economists urge policymakers to consider fundamental tax reform that would eliminate many of the transitory tax deductions and credits while reducing marginal tax rates on households and firms. It is too early to know what reforms, if any, the Obama administration will propose. However, fundamental changes to the tax code could have a substantial effect on investment—and on output and employment.

Sources: Jackie Calmes, "Obama Weighing Broad Overhaul of Income Tax," *New York Times*, December 10, 2010; John McKinnon, Gary Fields, and Laura Saunders, "Transitory Tax Code Puts Nation in a Lasting Bind," *Wall Street Journal*, December 15, 2010; Molly McMillin, "Aviation: Tax Breaks Will Boost Industry," *McClatchy–Tribune Business News*, December 14, 2010; and Daniel Trotta and Kristina Cooke, "Businesses Say Demand, Not Tax Cuts, Drives Growth," www.cnbc.com, December 16, 2010.

Test your understanding by doing related problem 3.14 on page 557 at the end of this chapter.

From the Desired Capital Stock to Investment

Capital goods, such as factories and equipment, produce goods and services that generate profits for firms. A firm that has too little capital stock will not be able to produce enough goods and services to maximize its profits. A firm that has too much capital stock has to spend too much to maintain it and therefore cannot maximize its profits.

It is costly to a firm to adjust its capital stock, which involves purchasing new capital goods or selling unwanted capital goods and also spending time to determine which capital goods to purchase or sell. Firms adjust the capital stock slowly in response to shocks to protect themselves from the negative consequences of building a factory that is too big or building too many factories or too many assembly lines.

Unexpected events that affect the desired capital stock occur frequently. Some events—such as the discovery of a new technology—indicate that future output will increase, thereby increasing the desired capital stock. Other events—such as a large income tax increase—indicate that future profits will decrease, thereby decreasing the desired capital stock. To reduce these costs, firms slowly adjust the capital stock to new information. One way to think of the behavior of firms is to assume that when there is a gap between the desired and actual capital stock, $(K_t^* - K_{t-1})$, a firm eliminates a constant fraction, z, of that stock each period through investment:

$$I_t = z(K_t^* - K_{t-1}) + dK_{t-1}, \tag{14.6}$$

where $0 < z < 1$. If z is 0.10, then firms eliminate 10% of the gap between the actual and the desired capital stock each year; if z is 0.20, then firms eliminate 20% of the gap, and so on. Equation (14.6) tells us that firms set gross investment, or investment before taking into account depreciation, equal to a level high enough to replace the depreciated capital stock, dK_{t-1}, plus a constant fraction of the gap between the desired capital stock next year and this year's capital stock. Any shock that causes the desired capital stock to increase also causes gross investment to increase. For example, an increase in expected output in the future will increase the desired capital stock. As a result, firms will increase investment as they slowly try to accumulate more capital goods or a larger factory.

Solved Problem 14.3

Depreciation, Taxes, and Investment Spending

On December 10, 2010, President Obama signed into law a second stimulus bill formally known as the Tax Relief, Unemployment Insurance Reauthorization, and Job Creation Act of 2010. One of the provisions of the act increased the fraction of investment spending that firms are allowed to depreciate for tax purposes from 50% to 100%. For example, prior to the act, if Ford spent \$100 million to build a new factory, then the company could deduct \$50 million (0.50 × \$100 million) from its taxable income for the year. After the act, Ford could deduct the full \$100 million from its taxable income, thereby increasing its after-tax profit. This provision effectively reduces the tax rate on investment projects for the year 2011. What effect should this provision have on the desired capital stock and the level of investment in 2011? Can we expect this provision to help stimulate the economy in 2011?

Solving the Problem

Step 1 **Review the chapter material.** The problem asks you to use the theory of investment developed in this chapter to determine the effect of a change in the tax treatment of depreciation, so you may want to review the section "Factors That Determine Private Investment," which begins on page 539.

Step 2 **Determine the effect on the desired capital stock.** Allowing firms to deduct 100% of investment spending from taxable income reduces the tax rate on investment projects for the year 2011 from t_1 to t_2. As a result, the tax-adjusted user cost of capital will decrease for 2011 from uc_1 to uc_2. Your graph of the desired capital stock should look like this:

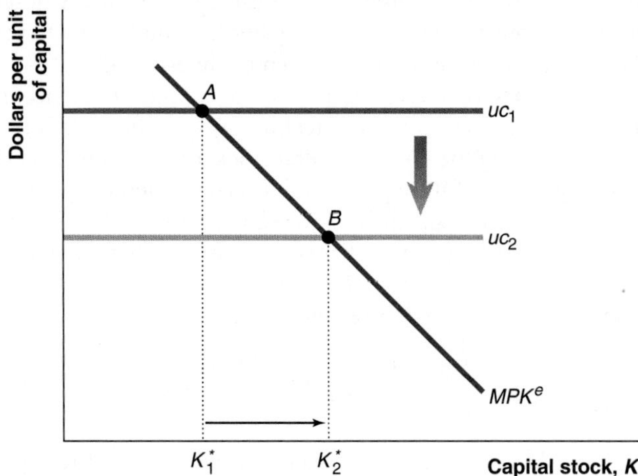

Your graph should show that the tax-adjusted user cost of capital shifts down and that the desired capital stock increases.

Step 3 Determine the effect on investment spending. Equation (14.6) on page 547 tells us how investment spending responds to the desired capital stock, so write Equation (14.6):

$$I_t = z(K_t^* - K_{t-1}) + dK_{t-1}.$$

The increase in the desired capital stock means that the gap between the desired capital stock and yesterday's capital stock, $(K_t^* - K_{t-1})$, has increased. As a result, Equation (14.6) tells us that firms will increase investment spending today to try to increase the capital stock toward the desired level.

The model for investment spending tells us that increasing the amount of investment that firms can deduct from taxable income should lead to an increase in investment spending. This will lead to increased output and employment in 2011 and so should stimulate the economy. Of course, this is just the short-run benefit of the change in tax laws. Allowing firms to increase the amount of investment that is deductible from taxable income will also increase the government's budget deficit, which may decrease potential GDP. Policymakers should weigh any short-run benefits from the change in the tax law against the long-run costs. We discussed these long-run costs in greater detail in Chapter 13.

For more practice, do related problem 3.18 on page 557 at the end of this chapter.

Tobin's *q*: Another Framework for Explaining Investment

Tobin's *q* The ratio of the market value of a firm to the replacement cost of its capital.

Nobel Laureate James Tobin developed a theory of investment that linked the level of investment to the stock market.[13] **Tobin's *q*** is the ratio of the market value of a firm to the replacement cost of its capital and is calculated as:

$$q = \frac{\text{Market value of the firm}}{\text{Replacement cost of capital}}. \quad (14.7)$$

[13]James Tobin, "A General Equilibrium Approach to Monetary Theory," *Journal of Money, Credit, and Banking*, Vol. 1, No. 1, February 1969, pp. 15–29.

In this equation, the market value of the firm equals the price of the firm's stock multiplied by the number of shares of stock. For example, Apple Inc. had about 1 billion shares outstanding, and it traded for about \$320 per share in early 2011, so the market value of Apple was approximately \$320 × 1 billion = \$320 billion. The replacement cost of capital equals what it would cost to purchase the firm's current stock of capital goods. For example, if Apple owns a building that would cost \$100 million to rebuild, then the replacement cost for the building is \$100 million. Apple's stock of capital goods was worth about \$80 billion, so calculating Tobin's q, we get \$320 billion/\$80 billion = 4. That is, the market valued Apple's capital as being four times greater than it would cost Apple to purchase the capital.

If the value of Tobin's q is greater than 1, the market value of a firm is greater than the cost to the firm of acquiring capital. A firm's value of q is a signal from participants in financial markets about whether it is profitable for the firm to acquire more capital goods and use them to expand production. Therefore, you would expect to see the firm increase its capital stock when Tobin's q is greater than 1. In our example, Tobin's q is 4 for Apple, so the market is sending a very strong signal to Apple to invest to acquire more capital goods. Similarly, if Tobin's q is less than 1, the market value of the firm is less than its replacement cost, so the signal from financial markets is that the firm should decrease its capital stock. Therefore, you would expect investment to decrease at a firm with a Tobin's q of less than 1.

The Tobin's q model links investment to fluctuations in the value of the stock market. One of the reasons this link is important is that the price of a share of stock depends on the expected future profits of a firm. If expected future profits increase for any reason, then the price of a share of stock will increase, so the market value of the firm will increase, and Tobin's q will increase. As a result, the firm will increase investment. The emphasis that the Tobin's q model places on expected future profitability is very similar to the emphasis that the previous model places on the expected marginal product of capital.

The price of a share of stock is volatile because expectations about future profitability are also volatile. When expectations about future profits decrease substantially, there is a large decrease in Tobin's q, which then causes firms to substantially decrease investment. Similarly, when expectations about future profits increase, there is a large increase in Tobin's q, and the level of investment. So, if firms' expectations of their future profitability are volatile, investment will also be volatile, as Figure 14.1 on page 524 shows.

Credit Rationing and the Financial Accelerator

The model of investment assumes that firms undertake all profitable investment opportunities. If a firm has enough financial resources on hand, it pays for the investment project with those resources. But if a firm does not have enough of its own resources, it goes to financial markets to borrow the rest. However, just as financial markets do not work perfectly for households, financial markets do not work perfectly for firms. Asymmetric information exists, so some firms may not be able to borrow the funds to finance all profitable investment projects. These firms are credit rationed and cannot pursue some profitable investment projects. For example, a farmer-turned-developer named Mark Wagner wanted to convert his farmland into a housing development. However, before he could build houses, he needed to put in sewer and water lines, construct roads, grade the land, and so on. To pay for these activities, Wagner needed a loan from a bank. Unfortunately, Wagner was unable to obtain a loan from any of the local banks and was quoted as saying "They're not loaning anyone money. They're all gun shy. Find me someone who'll give me \$10 million, and I'll start building again."[14]

Why does credit rationing of firms exist, as in the case of Mark Wagner's residential development firm? Banks and other lenders cannot perfectly observe the financial condition of firms or the willingness of firms to repay loans. However, banks know that, as with households, there are good borrowers and bad borrowers. Increasing the real interest rate on loans to compensate for the risk of lending causes the good borrowers to drop out of

[14]Matt Assad, "Arrested Development," (Allentown, PA) *Morning Call*, May 8, 2010.

the market, while the bad borrowers remain. The pool of potential borrowers therefore becomes riskier. Banks can increase real interest rates to compensate for the risk, but this causes even more good borrowers to withdraw from the market. To protect themselves from making loans to firms that cannot repay them, banks require firms to post collateral for loans or refuse to make loans to certain firms. During recessions, the value of collateral decreases, and corporate profits decrease, so firms do not have the cash flow to finance new investment projects. As a result, firms such as Mark Wagner's lose access to loans. The presence of credit rationing suggests that investment depends on the state of the economy. Federal Reserve Chairman Ben Bernanke, Mark Gertler of New York University, and Simon Gilchrist of Boston University call the dependence of investment on the state of the economy the *financial accelerator.*[15]

Credit rationing and the financial accelerator can help explain why gross private investment is so volatile. A negative demand shock reduces firm's profits. As a result, credit-rationed firms are forced to cut back on investment. The financial accelerator also adds another way for financial markets to affect investment. Suppose that there is a decrease in the price of financial assets. Now credit-rationed firms have less collateral to use for loans. These firms therefore get fewer loans and invest less.

Steven Fazzari and Bruce Petersen of Washington University in St. Louis, and Glenn Hubbard of Columbia University looked for evidence that firms face financing constraints.[16] They showed that from 1970 to 1984, small manufacturing firms with less than $10 million in assets obtained 67% of their long-term debt from banks, while large manufacturing firms with $1 billion or more in assets obtained about 15% of their long-term debt from banks. This difference shows that small manufacturing firms are reliant on banks, while large manufacturing firms can borrow directly from financial markets by issuing corporate bonds. This observation is consistent with the view that there is less information available about small manufacturing firms than exists for large manufacturing firms. Therefore, it is possible that these smaller firms face financing constraints and must rely on bank financing.

To test for the presence of financing constraints, Fazzari, Hubbard, and Petersen divided firms into different categories, based on dividend policy. Firms pay dividends to shareholders out of the firms' profits. Dividends are voluntary payments, so a liquidity-constrained firm is unlikely to make dividend payments because it cannot then use those funds to finance profitable investment projects. Fazzari, Hubbard, and Petersen argued that it is possible to identify which firms face financing constraints based on whether the firms pay dividends. They also showed that profits, or cash flow, affect investment for firms that do not pay dividends, but there is only a weak relationship between cash flow and investment for firms that do pay dividends. Because financing constraints become more binding during recessions, the financial accelerator can worsen economic downturns. As a result, the financial accelerator provides an additional explanation for why investment is as volatile as shown in Figure 14.1 on page 524.

Uncertainty and Irreversible Investment

Federal Reserve Chairman Ben Bernanke has argued that some of the volatility of investment comes from investment projects being irreversible.[17] That is, once an investment project is finished, it is hard for a firm to use the investment for another activity. For

---

[15]Ben Bernanke, Mark Gertler, and Simon Gilchrist, "The Financial Accelerator and the Flight to Quality," *Review of Economics and Statistics*, Vol. 78, No. 1, February 1996, pp. 1–15.

[16]Steven Fazzari, Glenn Hubbard, and Bruce Petersen, "Financing Constraints and Corporate Investment," *Brookings Paper on Economic Activity*, Vol. 1, December 1988, pp. 141–206; and Glenn Hubbard, "Capital Market Imperfections and Investment," *Journal of Economic Literature*, Vol. 36, No. 1, March 1998, pp. 193–225.

[17]Ben Bernanke, "Irreversibility, Uncertainty, and Cyclical Investment," *Quarterly Journal of Economics*, Vol. 98, No. 1, February 1983, pp. 85–106.

example, if Ford Motor Company builds an automobile factory in Tennessee, it is difficult to use that factory to produce other goods. In addition to the irreversible nature of most investment projects, useful information about the profitability of an investment project arrives over time. If the market for automobiles collapses after Ford builds a factory, then the value of the factory will decline sharply.

Ford does not have to build the factory today. Instead, it has the option of waiting until it has acquired more useful information about the profitability of the factory. However, the sooner Ford builds the factory, the sooner the factory will start producing automobiles and potentially start adding to the firm's profits. Firms such as Ford face a trade-off. They trade off the benefit of committing to an investment project and receiving the profits from the investment project against the benefit of waiting to acquire more information so they can pursue an investment project that is better suited to the economic environment.

Suppose there is an increase in uncertainty about the future price of output, the future price of inputs, future interest rates, or regulation. In that case, the value to firms of waiting to acquire additional information also increases. Therefore, a firm will make the decision to delay an investment project so that it can acquire more information. As a result, current investment will decrease. When aggregate shocks such as oil price increases, changes in monetary policy, or changes in housing prices occur, the value of waiting to obtain more information also increases. As a result, most firms change investment, and such changes magnify the initial effect of the shock. The fact that investments are irreversible and can be delayed makes the growth rate of investment prone to wide swings.

Answering the Key Question

Continued from page 521

At the beginning of this chapter, we asked the question:

"How does government tax policy affect the decisions of households and firms?"

Permanent changes in income have larger effects on consumption than transitory changes in income. Therefore, temporary tax cuts and tax rebates are likely to have smaller effects on consumption than are permanent changes in taxes. However, if a large number of households are credit rationed, then even temporary tax cuts can have a large effect on consumption.

Corporate taxes increase the tax-adjusted user cost of capital, which reduces the desired capital stock and investment. Therefore, decreases in corporate taxes can help stimulate the economy during economic downturns because the decreases lead firms to increase their investment in order to increase their capital stock.

Read an *Inside Look at Policy* for a discussion of the features of the 2010 tax bill and how it affects individuals, workers, and firms.

Extension of Tax Cuts to Impact Families, Workers, and Employers

ABC NEWS

What the Tax Cut Extension Means for You

When President Obama officially extended tax cuts enacted by his predecessor in a Rose Garden ceremony today, he ensured the average American will pay about $2,000 less in taxes per year for the next two years.

That figure includes a temporary holiday on the payroll tax, which helps fund Social Security. . . .

The deal . . . will also extend unemployment benefits for the next two years. . . .

While Americans will have less money taken out of their paychecks by Uncle Sam the next two years, the tax compromise will result in lost revenue to the government of between $450 and $600 billion in 2011. That will be added to the nation's $13.8 trillion deficit.

What the Tax Cutting Deal Means for Families, Workers and Employers:

a Families:

- All Bush-era taxes will be extended for two more years for all American families including the wealthy. . . .
- **Impact:** The deal means families making between $40,000 and $50,000 will pay about $1,600 less in taxes per year than if the tax cuts had expired.
- The average U.S. household, with an income of $49,777, will continue to keep its tax cut of $2,142.
- A family with earnings of $311,330, will keep $9,318 as opposed to the $8,012 if the president had had his way.

b Workers:

- 13-month extension of unemployment benefits. The extension is expected to help about 9 million Americans.
- One-year Social Security tax reduction for employees, from 6.2 percent to 4.2 percent for individuals.
- Impact: For example, a worker who makes $40,000 annually would pay $800 less in Social Security taxes and a worker who earns $70,000 would pay $1,400 less.
- Child Tax Credit, Earned Income Tax Credit and the tax credit increases for college tuition (American Opportunity Tax Credit) adopted in 2009 as part of the economic stimulus package will be extended.
- Impact: Families will be allowed to get up to $2,500 per student for tuition credit. . . . And economists say that the reduction of the payroll tax is particularly helpful in stimulating the economy. Every American will pay 2 percent less in tax, on the first $106,000 they make.

c Employers:

- The agreement will also affect businesses and business owners.
  Businesses will be allowed to deduct 100 percent of capital investments in 2011, a doubling from the current write-off figure of 50 percent.
- The agreement also calls for holding the estate tax at 35 percent for two years, with a $5 million floor.
  Moody's projects that the bill will create up to 1.5 million jobs next year, and significantly increase the projected growth of the Gross Domestic Product from nearly 3 percent to almost 4 percent.

"That means we'll be able to create enough jobs to bring unemployment down in a very substantive way," said Mark Zandi, the chief economist at Moody's Analytics.

Of course, the bill will also add $900 billion to the nearly $14 trillion national debt, money that future generations will be responsible for paying back.

Source: Excerpted from "What the Tax Cut Extension Means for You" by Leezel Tanglao and Z. Byron Wolf. *ABC News*, December 17, 2010. Reprinted with permission from *ABC News*.

Key Points in the Article

This article discusses how the extension of tax cuts will affect families, workers, and employers. On December 17, 2010, President Obama signed into law a bill that extended the tax cuts first enacted during the George W. Bush administration in 2001 and 2003. The bill, which extends the tax cuts for two additional years, also includes a one-year reduction of Social Security taxes for employees and an extension of unemployment benefits for the next two years.

Analyzing the News

a The projected cost of the tax cut extension bill is $850 billion. Over half that amount will result from extending the Bush-era tax cuts. As the figure to the right shows, 57% of the cost, or $485 billion, will come from extending the tax cuts to low- and middle-income families. President Obama initially wanted to exclude extending the tax cuts for high-income families, but ended up compromising with congressional Republicans and extended the cuts for all income levels. The inclusion of extending the tax cuts for high-income families, along with changes to estate tax laws, add an additional $139 billion to the overall cost of the bill.

b The tax cut extension bill also includes provisions designed to help workers. Unemployment benefits will be extended an additional 13 months, a move that is expected to assist approximately 9 million people. Social Security taxes are being reduced for one year on the first $106,800 in income from 6.2% to 4.2%, saving a worker who earns $70,000 annually an additional $1,400. In addition to these measures, the increased amounts for the Child Tax Credit, Earned Income Tax Credit, and the American Opportunity Tax Credit, which were a part of the 2009 economic stimulus package, were also extended. As the figure shows, these additional benefits for workers will account for over $200 billion, or 25%, of the total cost of the bill.

c Businesses and business owners will also reap benefits from the bill. The amount that businesses will be allowed to deduct for capital investment will double from 50% in 2010 to 100% in 2011. The cost of this expensing provision is projected at $22 billion, which represents 3% of the total cost of the bill. Moody's Analytics, a credit rating, research, and analysis firm, expects the bill to create 1.5 million new jobs in 2011 and increase projected GDP growth from about 3% to nearly 4%. These benefits do come at a cost, though, as the bill will add close to $900 billion to the already record-high national debt.

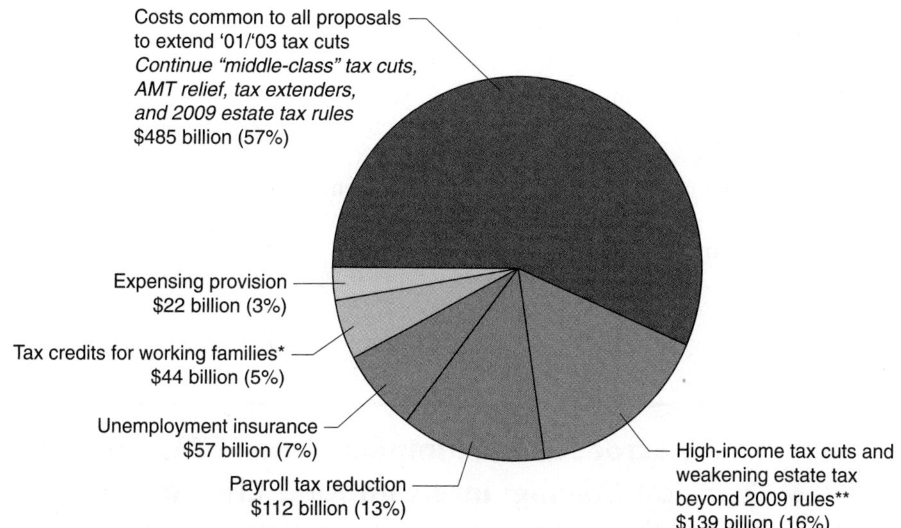

Composition of the Senate Tax Cut-Unemployment Insurance Bill

*Includes two-year extensions of the 2009 improvements to the Child Tax Credit, the Earned Income Tax Credit, and the American Opportunity Tax Credit to help families pay for college.
**The cost shown for the proposal to weaken the estate tax reflects the added cost of this policy relative to maintaining the 2009 estate tax rules.
Percentages may not add to 100 due to rounding.

Sources: Center on Budget and Policy Priorities/cbpp.org; CBPP calculations based on JCT estimates; http://www.cbpp.org/files/12-10-10tax.pdf. Reprinted with permission from the Center on Budget and Policy Priorities. ●

THINKING CRITICALLY *ABOUT POLICY*

1. With the one-year reduction in Social Security taxes, a person earning an annual salary of $70,000 will save an additional $1,400. Using the life-cycle hypothesis, show how this change in income will affect consumption. Assume that wealth is zero, the person will work for 35 years at a constant salary of $70,000, and that the person expects to live for another 55 years. How will your answer change if the reduction in Social Security taxes is made permanent?
2. Many businesses will benefit from the doubling of the capital investment deduction allowance in 2011, as this will act as a de facto corporate tax rate decrease. Use a graph to show the effect of a corporate tax rate decrease on the after-tax user cost of capital and the desired capital stock.

CHAPTER SUMMARY AND PROBLEMS

KEY TERMS

Animal spirits, p. 541
Asymmetric information, p. 523
Credit rationing, p. 523
Desired capital stock, p. 539
Intertemporal budget constraint, p. 527
Life-cycle hypothesis, p. 528
Marginal product of capital (*MPK*), p. 540
Marginal propensity to consume (*MPC*), p. 529
Permanent income, p. 527
Permanent-income hypothesis, p. 527
Precautionary saving, p. 537
Tax-adjusted user cost of capital, p. 543
Tobin's *q*, p. 548
Transitory income, p. 527
User cost of capital (*uc*), p. 541

14.1 The Macroeconomic Implications of Microeconomic Decision Making: Intertemporal Choice

Discuss the macroeconomic implications of microeconomic decision making by households and firms.

SUMMARY

Households maximize welfare, and firms maximize profits. Households and firms are forward looking in their decisions. Households and firms use financial markets to finance consumption and investment. However, financial markets are characterized by **asymmetric information** because financial institutions have less information about the likelihood that a borrower will repay a loan than does the borrower. As a result, financial firms restrict access to loans by requiring large down payments or the posting of collateral. When households and firms are willing to pay the current real interest rate but do not have the necessary down payment or cannot post enough collateral, then **credit rationing** exists. Investment is much more volatile than consumption.

Review Questions

1.1 What do economists assume about how households and firms make decisions and respond to changes in the economy?

1.2 Give some examples of how expectations about the future may affect GDP today.

1.3 What is credit rationing, and how does it affect the choices of consumers and firms?

1.4 How does investment vary over time? How does consumption vary over time? What explains the different patterns of investment and consumption?

Problems and Applications

1.5 During the financial crisis of 2007–2009, credit markets "froze" when financial institutions stopped lending to many consumers and firms because it was difficult to determine who was creditworthy.

a. Did credit rationing occur during 2007–2009? Briefly explain.

b. How did credit rationing during 2007–2009 affect GDP?

1.6 One problem that became clear during the financial crisis of 2007–2009 was that lending standards allowed some borrowers to falsify information about their income and creditworthiness.

a. Explain how this problem of falsifying information relates to asymmetric information.

b. What would you expect to happen to lending standards in the wake of the financial crisis, and how might this affect consumers' ability to allocate spending over time?

1.7 Consider the following statement: "A firm would never increase investment during a recession because current GDP is too low." Do you agree with this statement? Briefly explain.

myeconlab Visit www.myeconlab.com to complete these exercises online and get instant feedback.

14.2 Factors That Determine Consumption
Explain the determinants of personal consumption.

SUMMARY

Spending on consumer durable goods is almost as volatile as spending on investment, but spending on nondurable goods and services is relatively stable. The **intertemporal budget constraint** tells us that the present value of disposable income equals the present value of consumption. If households perfectly smooth consumption, they will keep consumption constant. According to the **permanent-income hypothesis**, household consumption depends on permanent income and households use financial markets to save and borrow to smooth consumption. The **marginal propensity to consume (*MPC*)** is the amount by which consumption increases when disposable income increases. *MPC* out of **permanent income,** such as a salary, is higher than the *MPC* out of **transitory income**, such as a bonus. The **life-cycle hypothesis** suggests that households will borrow early in life when income is low, repay loans and acquire assets as income rises, and then finance consumption during retirement by selling assets. Permanent changes in income have a much larger effect on consumption than do transitory changes in income. As a result, temporary tax cuts and tax rebates have very little effect on consumption. However, when households are credit rationed, transitory changes in income can have large effects on consumption. Households engage in **precautionary saving** to protect themselves from unexpected job losses or illness. The government provides households with tax incentives to save for retirement in the form of individual retirement accounts and 401(k) accounts that allow households to save with pre-tax income. These accounts increase the after-tax rate of return to saving and so encourages the accumulation of savings.

Review Questions

2.1 How does consumption as a percentage of GDP vary among countries?

2.2 What are the three categories of consumption? Which category is the most volatile? Which category is the least volatile?

2.3 Write the equation of the intertemporal budget constraint.

2.4 Explain Milton Friedman's permanent income hypothesis.

2.5 Explain Franco Modigliani's life-cycle hypothesis.

2.6 How are Friedman's and Modigliani's theories of consumption similar? How are these theories different?

2.7 Explain the income and substitution effects of a fall in the real interest rate.

2.8 Explain why the marginal propensity to consume out of transitory income is different from the marginal propensity to consume out of permanent income.

2.9 Why might the intertemporal consumption choices of credit-rationed households be inefficient?

2.10 How does the intertemporal budget constraint change when there are taxes?

2.11 What current government programs encourage saving?

Problems and Applications

2.12 For each of the following scenarios, explain the expected effect on consumption.

a. Housing prices rise.
b. The government increases personal income taxes.
c. Uncertainty about the economy causes the desired level of savings to increase.
d. A tax cut that was expected to be temporary becomes permanent.

2.13 **[Related to *Solved Problem 14.2* on page 533]** Suppose that you expect to work for another 50 years and then live 20 years in retirement. You have no wealth, and there are no taxes. You want to smooth consumption over your lifetime, and you will earn $75,000 per year.

a. Calculate consumption in each period.
b. Now assume that you receive $500,000 in wealth. How will your consumption change?
c. The government decides to tax you $15,000 per year. What is your new level of consumption? [Assume that you still have the wealth received in part (b).]
d. How would your consumption change if the government cut taxes this year from $15,000 to $10,000, but taxes next year and in the future return to $15,000 per year?
e. How would your consumption change if the government permanently decreased taxes from $15,000 to $10,000 per year?

2.14 Some economists advocate a change from an income tax to a consumption tax, such as a national sales tax. A sales tax makes consumption more expensive and so encourages households to save. How would such a change, all other things being equal, affect each of the following?

a. Current consumption
b. Current saving
c. Capital formation
d. Future GDP

2.15 Most students borrow to finance their college educations and repay the loans later. How might the life-cycle hypothesis help to explain this behavior?

2.16 **[Related to the Chapter Opener on page 521]** In late 2010, Congress renewed for a two-year period the tax cuts first passed by the Bush administration. The original Bush tax cuts were set to expire in 2011, 10 years after their original passage.

a. According to the theories of consumption in this chapter, what effect would you expect the original tax cuts to have on consumption?
b. During the debate on the renewal of the tax cuts, many argued that a failure to extend the tax cuts was a bad policy during a recession. Does the analysis presented in this chapter suggest that this argument is correct? Briefly explain.

2.17 **[Related to the *Making the Connection* on page 536]** The United Kingdom has had a value-added tax (VAT) of 17.5% since 1991. The VAT is essentially a national sales tax that some countries levy; a percentage of an item's value is added to the price of most goods. During the recession of 2007–2009, the VAT was temporarily lowered to 15% so the cost of consumption was temporarily reduced. On January 4, 2011, the VAT was permanently increased to 20% so the cost of consumption was permanently increased. Discuss the probable effects of these two tax changes.

14.3 Factors That Determine Private Investment

Explain the determinants of private investment.

SUMMARY

A firm's **desired capital stock** depends on the expected **marginal product of capital** and the **user cost of capital**. Corporate income taxes, depreciation allowances, and the tax treatment of interest payments on debt affect the **tax-adjusted user cost of capital** and provide a mechanism through which tax policy affects the capital stock and investment. A firm's investment spending depends on depreciation and how far the current capital stock is from the desired capital stock. Firms are sometimes overtaken by periods of irrational pessimism and optimism, known as **animal spirits**, that affect their investment behavior. We can think of animal spirits as affecting the expected marginal product of capital. **Tobin's *q*** is the ratio of the market value of a firm to its replacement cost of capital. When Tobin's *q* is greater than 1, it is profitable for the firm to expand, so investment increases; when Tobin's *q* is less than 1, investment decreases. Tobin's *q* helps emphasize the importance of expected future profits for determining the current level of investment.

Due to credit rationing, some firms cannot obtain financing to pursue every profitable investment project. As real GDP increases, firms become better credit risks, so they find it easier to obtain loans, and investment increases, causing real GDP to increase further. As real GDP decreases, firms become worse credit risks, so they find it harder to obtain loans, and investment decreases, causing real GDP to decrease further. Economists call this the financial accelerator, and it helps explain why investment is so volatile. Investment is also volatile because many investment projects, such as new factories, are irreversible in the sense that it is difficult to find alternative uses for a new factory. If uncertainty increases in the economy, then firms have an incentive to wait to acquire additional information about future profits before committing to building a new factory today. As a result, increases in uncertainty can cause investment to decrease.

The importance of expected future profits, the importance of credit rationing and the financial accelerator, and the irreversiblity of investment explain why investment is so volatile.

Review Questions

3.1 What are the three categories of investment?

3.2 How does a firm decide on its desired level of capital investment?

3.3 Why must a firm consider the expected marginal product of capital when choosing the desired capital level?

3.4 What is the user cost of capital?

3.5 How does a firm decide its desired level of the capital stock?

3.6 How do corporate taxes affect the desired level of the capital stock?

3.7 Explain how the desired capital stock determines the level of investment.

3.8 What is Tobin's q, and how does it link financial markets to capital investment?

3.9 Explain how credit rationing, the financial accelerator, and investment are linked.

3.10 Why is investment spending usually irreversible? How does this affect the level of investment when economic conditions are uncertain?

Problems and Applications

3.11 For each of the following scenarios, use a graph to show how the firm's desired capital stock would be likely to change.

a. Technological change increases the productivity of capital.

b. The Fed decreases interest rates (and the inflation rate stays the same).

c. The real price of capital goods decreases.

d. The economy is expected to remain in recession for some time.

3.12 Suppose that the interest rate is 5%, the depreciation rate is 8%, the real price of capital is \$10, and the tax rate is 10%.

a. Calculate the tax-adjusted user cost of capital.

b. Calculate the tax-adjusted user cost of capital if the depreciation rate increases to 10%.

c. Return to the original depreciation rate and calculate the tax-adjusted user cost of capital if the tax rate falls to 6%.

3.13 **[Related to the *Macro Data* feature on page 544]** Cuts in capital gains taxes are often criticized as "tax cuts for the rich" because wealthy individuals are more likely to own financial investments than are poor individuals. How might cuts in capital gains taxes benefit the economy as a whole? (Note: Be sure to distinguish between financial investment and investment in capital goods in your answer.)

3.14 **[Related to the *Making the Connection* on page 546]** If the Obama administration succeeds in passing a tax reform package that eliminates short-lived tax incentives but permanently reduces tax rates on firms, what would be likely to happen to the desired capital stock, investment, and economic growth? Is your answer different for the short run versus the long run?

3.15 The recovery from the 2007–2009 financial crisis and the resulting recession was relatively slow through 2011. While there are many reasons for the slow recovery, how might the high degree of uncertainty about future economic conditions explain the slow recovery?

3.16 In 2009, the market value of most publically traded firms was lower than it was in 2006.

a. Why would the market value of most firms have fallen?

b. Using Tobin's q, what would you expect to have happened to investment during this period?

3.17 During the financial crisis of 2007–2009, it became difficult for firms to get a loan, whether the loan was for short-term funding for business inventories or for larger projects.

a. Explain how this increase in credit rationing affected investment.

b. The Federal Reserve created special funding facilities to improve the liquidity of credit markets during this period. These facilities made it easier for firms and households to borrow in financial markets. What was the Fed trying to avoid?

3.18 **[Related to *Solved Problem 14.3* on page 547]** The following graph shows the marginal product of capital and the user cost of capital. Assume that the economy is currently at point A, with the capital stock equal to K_1^*.

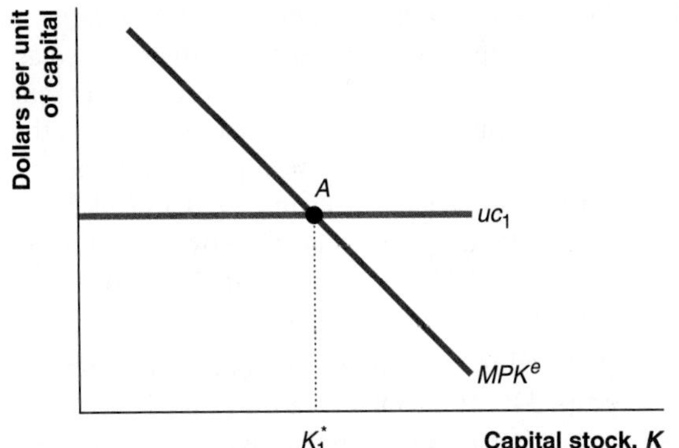

a. Increases in the money supply when the interest rate is near 0% have the effect of lowering real interest rates but not nominal interest rates. All other things being equal, how would you expect asset purchase programs, such as those that the Fed implemented in 2009–2011, to change the user cost of capital? What effect would you expect this change to have on investment and the capital stock in the short run? Show your answer on the graph.

b. Now return to the original graph and suppose that there is an improvement in technology that makes capital more productive. How would the productivity increase change investment and the capital stock in the short run? Revise the graph to support your answer.

3.19 John Maynard Keynes described investors as having "animal spirits," meaning that investors often make decisions based on emotion rather than logic.

a. How might "animal spirits" explain the volatility of investment relative to consumption?

b. Consumers may also be motivated by emotion. Why isn't consumption extremely volatile?

DATA EXERCISES

D14.1: The three categories of consumption behave differently over the business cycle. The volatility of overall consumption across countries may depend on what portion of consumption is accounted for by each category. While it is difficult to easily obtain worldwide data on relative consumption, a *New York Times* article measures per capita spending on a variety of different types of consumption goods in many countries. Go to the *New York Times* site (www.nyt.com) and search for "What Your Global Neighbors Are Buying."

a. What can you observe about buying patterns in different countries?

b. How might these differences in buying patterns affect the volatility of consumption?

D14.2: The Organisation for Economic Co-operation and Development (OECD) collects data for member nations. Go to the OECD site (www.oecd.org) and go to the statistics section. Find data on savings rates for all OECD nations.

a. How do national savings rates differ?

b. What happened to national savings rates during the 2007–2009 financial crisis? How can you explain what happened?

D14.3: Choose a European country and research its value-added tax (VAT) and income tax structure. The VAT is essentially a national sales tax that some countries levy.

a. What percentage of government revenues come from each type of tax?

b. What is the VAT rate? Is it different for different types of goods?

c. How do you think that this tax structure affects consumption, savings, and capital formation?

D14.4: **[Excel question]** Return to the OECD site (www.oecd.org) and enter the statistics section. Find data on corporate tax revenues and on investment. Download the data in Excel format.

a. What is the correlation between investment and corporate tax revenue collected in these countries? Is this what you would expect? Explain.

b. Does this analysis suggest that as tax rates increase, investment falls? If not, how could you improve your model?

CHAPTER 15

The Balance of Payments, Exchange Rates, and Macroeconomic Policy

LEARNING OBJECTIVES

After studying this chapter, you should be able to:

15.1 Explain how to calculate the balance of payments (pages 561–565)

15.2 Explain the relationship between the balance of payments and national income accounting (pages 565–568)

15.3 Distinguish between the nominal and real exchange rates (pages 568–572)

15.4 Explain how exchange rates are determined and how changes in exchange rates affect the prices of imports and exports (pages 572–578)

15.5 Understand the *IS–MP* model of an open economy with a floating exchange rate (pages 578–584)

15.6 Understand the *IS–MP* model of an open economy with a fixed exchange rate (pages 584–589)

15.7 Discuss the problems that the policy trilemma poses for policymakers (pages 589–592)

WHAT IF CHINA STOPS BUYING U.S. TREASURY SECURITIES?

The value of the federal government's debt owned by the public increased from $3.4 trillion at the end of January 2001 to $9.6 trillion at the end of February 2011. This large increase in government debt led Moody's Investors Service and Standard & Poor's, two leading bond rating agencies to announce that U.S. Treasury securities could lose the AAA rating—the highest-quality rating—that they have enjoyed since 1917. The main concern of the rating agencies is that the federal government plans to spend much more than it expects to receive in tax

Continued on next page

Key Issue and Question

At the end of Chapter 1, we noted key issues and questions that serve as a framework for the book. Here are the key issue and question for this chapter:

Issue: Some governments allow the value of their currency to fluctuate in foreign-exchange markets, while other governments fix the value of their currency.

Question: How does the choice of exchange-rate system affect monetary policy and fiscal policy?

Answered on page 593

revenue. The result will be large federal government budget deficits financed by the U.S. Treasury's selling bonds. These deficits will be on top of the increased debt resulting from the large budget deficits incurred during the 2007–2009 financial crisis.

The share of Treasury securities being purchased by foreign financial firms, governments, and individuals has been increasing. Indeed, foreign ownership of U.S. Treasury securities rose from $1.0 trillion in December 2000 to $4.4 trillion in December 2010, or from 29% of publicly held debt to 47%. If we exclude from the totals federal government debt held by the Federal Reserve, then the increase was from 36% to 52%; in other words, by the end of 2010, foreign investors owned more than half of the federal government debt not owned by federal government agencies or by the Federal Reserve. Foreign ownership of the federal government's debt was also highly concentrated, with China, Japan, and the United Kingdom owning the bulk of the foreign-held debt. If in the future, investors, firms, or the governments of these countries became reluctant to purchase U.S. Treasury securities, the resulting decline in demand could increase the interest rates the U.S. Treasury must pay on the money it borrows. Paying higher interest rates will make the federal government's budget deficit worse. Higher interest rates on U.S. Treasury securities will also result in U.S. households and firms facing higher borrowing costs as the interest rates on corporate bonds, mortgage loans, and other forms of borrowing increase. A large enough spike in interest rates could throw the U.S. economy into another recession.

During 2010, there were some signs that the government of China was reevaluating whether to continue purchasing such a large volume of U.S. Treasury securities. During the first six months of 2010, China *reduced* its ownership of Treasury securities by $45 billion. To an extent, China had switched from purchasing U.S. Treasury securities to purchasing other U.S. assets, such as the $1 billion that the China National Offshore Oil Company spent on purchasing one-third of Chesapeake Energy Corp.'s oil and gas fields in Eagle Ford, Texas. The China Investment Corporation, which is a government owned investment fund known as a *sovereign wealth fund*, has also purchased shares of stock in U.S. firms such as Apple Inc., Coca-Cola Company, Johnson & Johnson Health Care Systems Inc., Motorola Solutions Inc., and Visa Inc.

In addition, the government of China announced that it will increase its purchases of European government bonds even as Pacific Investment Management Company (PIMCO), manager of the world's largest bond fund, announced that it was reducing its purchases of European bonds over concerns about possible government defaults. The China Investment Corporation has also been purchasing banks, insurance companies, and other financial firms in Europe, as well as oil and gas companies in Africa and the Middle East and mining companies in Australia and South America.

So far, China has slowly diversified its foreign assets away from Treasury securities and other U.S. assets. The slow pace of change makes it easier for the market for U.S. Treasury securities to adjust to a decline in Chinese demand. However, if China suddenly decided to sell a significant portion of its existing U.S. Treasury securities, the result could be a sharp increase in interest rates in the United States, as well as a decline in the value of the U.S. dollar. Of course, if actions by China forced down the price of U.S. Treasury securities, this would have important consequences for China as well because any securities that China still owned would decrease in value.

The potential effects on U.S. interest rates of the actions of foreign holders of U.S. Treasury securities is just one example of how interconnected countries are financially. The days are long gone when U.S. policymakers could ignore the reactions of foreign governments and foreign investors to U.S. policies.

AN INSIDE LOOK AT POLICY on page 594 discusses the U.S. Treasury Department's revised estimates of foreign holdings of U.S. government debt.

Sources: Liz Alderman, "Beijing, Tendering Financial Support to Europe, Also Helps Itself," *New York Times*, January 7, 2011; Nicole Bullock, Robin Harding, Michael Mackenzie, Richard Milne, and James Politi, "S&P Sounds Alarm on US Debt," *Financial Times*, April 19, 2011; Christopher Leonard, "Moody's Warns U.S., Europe on Rising Costs," *Charleston Gazette*, January 14, 2011; Floyd Norris, "Data Shows Less Buying of U.S. Debt by China," *New York Times*, January 22, 2011; U.S. Treasury, *Treasury Bulletin*, March 2011; David Winning and Jing Yang, "CNOOC Sets Energy Deal in the U.S.," *Wall Street Journal Asia*, February 1, 2011; and Charles Wolf, "China's Next Buying Spree: Foreign Companies," *Wall Street Journal*, January 24, 2011.

The *IS–MP* model that we used in Chapters 9–11 allowed for the possibility that international factors affect the domestic economy but did not explore the channels linking the international and domestic economies. In this chapter, we develop these linkages and explain how international events affect important economic variables such as the exchange rate, net exports, real GDP, and the inflation rate.

The Balance of Payments

15.1

Learning Objective

Explain how to calculate the balance of payments.

When China exports goods to the United States, it receives U.S. dollars in exchange. The Chinese recipients of these dollars have to do something with them. The recipients can use the dollars to purchase U.S. goods and services; purchase U.S. financial assets such as stock in U.S. companies or U.S. Treasury bonds; or exchange the dollars for other currencies. While China exported $376 billion to the United States during 2010, China imported only $113 billion from the United States, so China acquired $263 billion that it either had to use to purchase U.S. assets or exchange for other currencies. This flow of goods, services, currencies, and financial investments is not unique to China and the United States; similar flows occur between many countries. In this section, we explain how to measure the trade and financial flows among nations.

Consumers, firms, and investors in one country routinely interact with consumers, firms, and investors in other countries. A consumer in the United States may use a keyboard assembled in China; a consumer in China may use an iPad designed by Apple in the United States; and a consumer in France may watch a television made in South Korea and wear a sweater made in Italy. A firm in India may sell its technology products in dozens of countries around the world. An investor in London may sell a U.S. Treasury bond to an investor in Mexico City. Nearly all economies are *open economies* and have extensive interactions in trade or finance with other countries. An **open economy** is an economy in which households, firms, and governments borrow, lend, and trade internationally. A **closed economy** is an economy in which households, firms, and governments do not borrow, lend, and trade internationally. No economy today is completely closed, although a few countries, such as North Korea, have very limited economic interactions with other countries.

Open economy An economy in which households, firms, and governments borrow, lend, and trade internationally.

Closed economy An economy in which households, firms, and governments do not borrow, lend, and trade internationally.

One way to measure the importance of trade to an economy is to examine the value of exports and imports relative to GDP. Figure 15.1 shows that trade has been a growing percentage of GDP since 1960. Exports plus imports, a measure of *economic openness*, increased from 24% of world GDP in 1960 to 57% of world GDP in 2007. The global recession and the global financial crisis that reduced incomes worldwide also reduced international trade. From 2007 to 2009, trade decreased for the entire world, from 57% of world GDP to 47%. China experienced a particularly large decrease in trade, from 68% of GDP in 2007 to 49% of GDP in 2009.

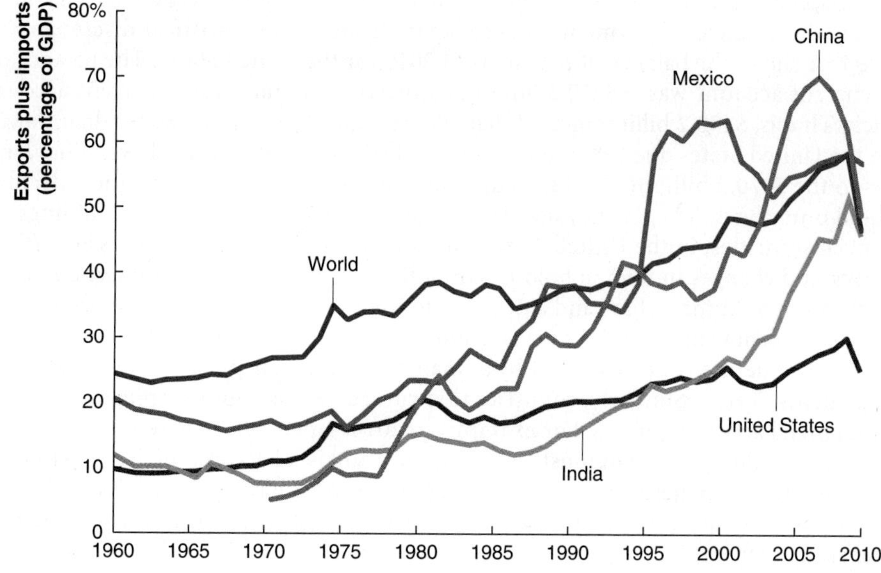

Figure 15.1

Trade as a Percentage of GDP, 1960–2009

Globally, trade has been growing in importance since 1960. Exports plus imports rose from 24% of world GDP in 1960 to 47% of world GDP in 2009. Exports plus imports are generally a smaller percentage of GDP for large economies such as the United States, where trade was just 25% of GDP in 2009.

Source: The World Bank, *World Development Indicators.*

Nominal exchange rate The price of one currency in terms of another currency; also called the *exchange rate*.

Fluctuations in trade can contribute to the severity of business cycles, and one of the key determinants of trade is the exchange rate. Economists define the **nominal exchange rate** as the price of one currency in terms of another currency. For simplicity, the nominal exchange rate is often called the *exchange rate.* An important fact about the international economy is that exchange rates among the major currencies fluctuate. For example, the euro started trading on January 4, 1999, at $1.18 per euro, but the exchange rate was $1.48 per euro on May 3, 2011. This change means the euro purchased more dollars in May 2011 than in January 1999, so the euro became stronger—or *appreciated*—against the U.S. dollar, and the U.S. dollar became weaker—or *depreciated*—against the euro. The euro did not continually appreciate against the dollar. Shortly after the new currency was introduced, the exchange rate for the euro fell and reached a low of $0.83 per euro on October 25, 2000, before rising to $1.60 per euro on April 22, 2008. The fluctuations in the euro affect not only the trade flows between the euro area and the United States but also the financial flows between the two areas.

As Figure 15.1 shows, most countries are open to international trade in goods and services. However, trade is not the only important international transaction. The flow of financial assets, such as stocks and bonds, and real assets, such as the ownership of factories and other capital goods, between countries is at least as important as the flow of goods and services. Just as economists have a system of accounting for measuring economic activity within a country, they also have a system of accounting for measuring economic interactions between countries. Economists call this system the **balance-of-payments accounts**, which is a measure of all flows of private and government funds between a domestic economy and all foreign countries.

Balance-of-payments accounts A measure of all flows of private and government funds between a domestic economy and all foreign countries.

The balance of payments consists of three parts:

1. The **current account** records a country's net exports, net investment income, and net transfers.
2. The **financial account** records purchases of assets a country has made abroad and foreign purchases of assets in the country.
3. The **capital account** records (generally) minor transactions such as migrants' transfers, and sales and purchases of non-produced, non-financial assets, such as a copyrights, patents, trademarks, and rights to natural resources.

Current account The part of the balance of payments that records a country's net exports, net investment income, and net transfers.

Financial account The part of the balance of payments that records purchases of assets a country has made abroad and foreign purchases of assets in the country.

Capital account The part of the balance of payments that records (generally) minor transactions, such as migrants' transfers, and sales and purchases of non-produced, non-financial assets.

The balance of payments accounts are set up so that when one item changes in the accounts, there is an offsetting transaction in another part of the accounts. As a consequence, the balance of payments is zero, apart from minor statistical discrepancies. Table 15.1 shows the balance of payments in 2010 for the United States. The balance on the current account was −$470.2 billion, so the United States ran a current account deficit. That is, $470.2 billion more dollars flowed out of the United States than flowed into the United States due to trade in goods and services and income flows. What happens to the $470.2 billion? The funds did not just disappear. Either foreigners decided to hold onto the dollars, or they decided to purchase assets, such as land, buildings, or financial securities, in the United States. Dollars that are held by foreigners are *official reserves*, and changes in foreign holdings of dollars are *official reserve transactions.* Both a decision to hold the dollars and a decision to use the dollars to purchase assets in the United States show up as positive transactions in the financial account. Therefore, a current account deficit is exactly offset by a financial account surplus, leaving the balance of payments at zero. Similarly, countries that run current account surpluses must also run financial account deficits. For example, in 2010, Japan had a current account surplus of $195 billion, so Japan must also have had a financial account deficit of $195 billion. Therefore, Japanese citizens and governments must have purchased $195 billion more in non-Japanese assets such as U.S. Treasury bonds than non-Japanese citizens purchased in Japan.

Table 15.1 Balance of Payments for the United States, 2010 (billions of dollars)

Current Account		
Exports of goods and services	$1,834.2	
Imports of goods and services	−2,329.9	
Net exports	−495.7	
Income received on investments and labor compensation	662.5	
Income payments on investments and labor compensation	−499.5	
Net factor payments	163	
Net transfers	−137.5	
Balance on current account		−470.2
Financial Account		
Increase in foreign holdings of assets in the United States	1,244.8	
Increase in U.S. holdings of assets in foreign countries	−1,024.7	
Net financial derivatives	15.1	
Balance on financial account		235.2
Capital Account		
Balance on capital account		−0.2
Statistical Discrepancy	−235.2	
Balance of payments		$0.0

Source: U.S. Bureau of Economic Analysis.

Note: For 2010, by chance the balance on the financial account and the statistical discrepancy had the same value but opposite signs. In general, this will not be the case.

The Current Account

The current account for the United States records the following three items:

1. *Net exports*, which are the exports and imports of goods and services between the United States and other countries. For example, in 2010, the United States exported $1,834 billion of goods and services to other countries and imported about $2,330 billion of goods and services from other countries. As a result, net exports were −$496 billion during 2010, so the United States ran a *trade deficit.*
2. *Net factor payments*, which are the income U.S. households and firms receive on investments in other countries and the income foreign households and firms receive on investments in the United States. Many U.S. firms do business overseas through foreign subsidiaries. When these subsidiaries earn a profit or pay dividends, income flows from other countries to the United States. For example, General Electric Co.'s headquarters is in Fairfield, Connecticut, so it is a U.S. company. However, General Electric owns several foreign subsidiaries, including GE Jenbacher GmbH & Co. OHG, a manufacturer of gas engines headquartered in Jenbach, Austria. Part of Jenbacher's profits are paid to General Electric, so net factor payments to the United States increase.
3. *Transfers*, which are the difference between transfer payments made by U.S. residents to residents of other countries and the transfer payments residents of other countries make to residents of the United States. For example, donations by U.S. residents to the victims of the 2011 earthquake in Japan or the 2010 earthquake in Haiti would count as transfers from the United States to the residents of those countries.

If the current account balance is negative, then the country runs a *current account deficit.* A current account deficit indicates that a country is consuming more than its current income. This can happen only if the country borrows from the rest of the world.

The United States had a current account deficit of $470 billion during 2010, so it borrowed from the rest of the world, and some of the borrowing was done by the U.S. government. For example, during 2010, China purchased $256 billion in U.S. Treasury securities, Japan purchased $121 billion, and the United Kingdom purchased $80 billion. A current account surplus indicates that a country is consuming less than its current income. In other words, it is lending to the rest of the world. For example, Japan had a current account surplus of $195 billion during 2010, so Japan was lending to other countries. The $121 billion of U.S. Treasury securities that Japan purchased during the period represents just some of the investments that Japan made.

Table 15.1 shows that two categories of the current account—net exports and net transfers—were negative. However, net income payments for the United States were positive, indicating that U.S. capital and labor abroad earned more than foreign capital and labor in the United States. Recall from Chapter 2 that gross national product (GNP) is larger than gross domestic product (GDP) for the United States. GNP is slightly larger than GDP in this case because net income payments are positive for the United States, although they are small relative to GDP.

Figure 15.2 shows the current account balance for the United States and several other countries. Since the early 1980s, the United States has consistently run large current account deficits. As a result, foreigners have been accumulating Treasury securities and other U.S. assets. China, like many large emerging economies, has run current account surpluses during recent years. Part of the reason for these surpluses is that the domestic financial systems in such economies are not well-developed, which can make investing in them difficult and risky. As a result, funds have flowed from investors in these economies to developed economies such as the United States and Western Europe.

The Financial Account

The financial account records the flow of funds into and out of a country. There is a *capital outflow* from the United States when a U.S. firm builds a factory in another country or when an investor in the United States purchases financial assets, such as the bonds, of foreign firms or governments. For example, if Ford builds a factory in Mexico or if U.S. households use their retirement accounts to purchase stocks and bonds in Mexico, there is a capital outflow from the United States to Mexico. There is a *capital inflow* into the United States when a foreign firm builds a factory in the United States or when a foreign investor

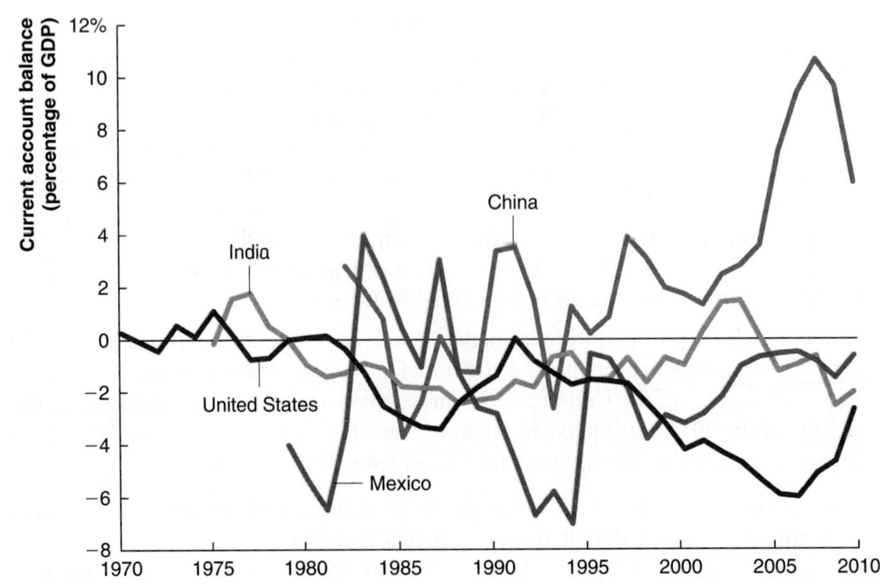

Figure 15.2

Current Account Balance Around the World, 1960–2009

Countries such as India, Mexico, and the United States have run current account deficits, so they have been borrowing from countries that have run large current account surpluses, such as China.

Source: The World Bank, *World Development Indicators*. ●

purchases financial assets. For example, when the Chinese government purchases U.S. Treasury securities or when Toyota builds a factory in Mississippi, there is a financial inflow into the United States. Notice that we are using the word *capital* to refer not only to capital goods, such as factories, but also to financial assets, such as stocks and bonds. When firms build or buy capital goods in foreign countries, they are engaging in *foreign direct investment.* When investors buy stocks or bonds issued in another country, they are engaging in *foreign portfolio investment.* **Net capital outflows** are equal to capital outflows minus capital inflows. In Section 15.2, we will see the important role that capital flows plays in determining exchange rates.

Net capital outflows Capital outflows minus capital inflows.

The Capital Account

The capital account is the third and least quantitatively important part of the balance of payments. This account records generally minor transactions such as (1) migrants' transfers, which consist of goods and financial assets people take with them when they leave or enter a country and (2) sales and purchases of non-produced, non-financial assets, which include copyrights, patents, trademarks, or rights to natural resources. The definitions of the financial account and the capital account are sometimes misunderstood because, prior to 1999, the capital account recorded all the transactions included now in both the financial account and the capital account. In other words, capital account transactions went from being a very important part of the balance of payments to being a relatively unimportant part. Because the balance on what is now called the capital account is so small, for simplicity, we will ignore it in the remainder of the chapter.

The Balance of Payments and National Income Accounting

15.2

Learning Objective

Explain the relationship between the balance of payments and national income accounting.

International financial markets play a critical role in linking economies around the world. From Section 15.1, we know that when we ignore the capital account, the current account balance has the same value as the financial account but with the opposite sign. Bearing in mind that the financial account represents net capital flows, we can write:

$$CA = NCF, \quad (15.1)$$

where *CA* is the current account balance and *NCF* is net capital outflows. If a country has a current account deficit, net capital outflow is also negative. If net capital outflow is negative, then capital is flowing into the country. For example, because the United States ran a current account deficit in 2010, net capital outflows were also negative, so capital was flowing into the United States during 2010.

Equation (15.1) is an identity, which means that, by definition, it must hold true. The equation does not tell us whether an increase in net capital flows causes a current account deficit or whether a current account deficit causes an increase in net capital flows. In other words, the direction of causality is unclear. For example, the United States ran a current account deficit of \$470 billion during 2010, so it also had net capital outflows of −\$470 billion during 2010. There are two equally plausible interpretations for the current account deficit. Either it arises from the desire of the United States to consume more than it produces, *or* it occurs because the United States is a more desirable place to invest than other countries. In the first interpretation, U.S. consumers wanted to consume \$470 billion more in goods and services than the U.S. economy produced. To accomplish this goal, the United States had to borrow from other countries, so capital had to flow to the United States in the amount of \$470 billion. Alternatively, the countries that the United States borrowed from, such as China, have weak financial sectors, leading them to prefer investing in the U.S. economy. As a result, Chinese citizens would like to purchase U.S.

assets, but they must obtain U.S. dollars to acquire the assets. To obtain U.S. dollars, China must sell to the United States more goods and services than the United States sells to China. Economists debate which of these two explanations better accounts for the U.S. current account deficit.

Linking the Balance of Payments to the System of National Accounts

The balance of payments is linked through saving and investment to the national income accounts that we discussed in Chapter 2. In Chapter 3, we explained that the total amount of saving available to firms, households, and governments within a country is:

$$S = S_{Household} + S_{Government} + S_{Foreign},$$

where household saving is:

$$S_{Household} = (Y + TR) - (C + T),$$

and government saving is:

$$S_{Government} = T - (G + TR).$$

Recall from Chapter 2 that we use T for taxes and TR for transfer payments such as unemployment insurance. When government saving is positive, the government runs a budget surplus. When government saving is negative, the government runs a budget deficit.

We link the balance of payments to the national income identities by noting that foreign saving, $S_{Foreign}$, is the flow of funds from foreign countries into the domestic economy. These funds help finance private investment, household consumption, and government budget deficits. In other words, foreign saving is another way of describing net capital inflows, which are the opposite of net capital outflows, *NCF*. So, we can rewrite the equation for national saving as:

$$S = S_{Household} + S_{Government} - NCF.$$

The key to linking the domestic economy with the rest of the world is to recognize that net capital outflows from abroad are one source of funds for domestic borrowing. From the loanable funds model in Chapter 3, we know that gross private domestic investment equals the pool of available saving:

$$I = S,$$

so:

$$I = S_{Household} + S_{Government} - NCF. \tag{15.2}$$

Equation (15.2) tells us that there are three sources of financing gross private investment: household saving, government saving, and net capital outflows from abroad (bearing in mind that a negative capital outflow is a capital inflow). Equation (15.2) links the balance of payments to the national income identities through net capital outflows. Equation (15.1) tells us that net capital outflows is negative when a country runs a current account deficit and positive when a country runs a current account surplus. The large current account deficits that the United States has been running since the early 1980s have helped to finance investment by households and firms, consumption by households, and the budget deficits run by the federal government.

Why Is the United States Called the World's Largest Debtor Nation?

The United States has run current account deficits since the early 1980s. Equation (15.1) tells us that these deficits imply that net capital outflows into the United States have been

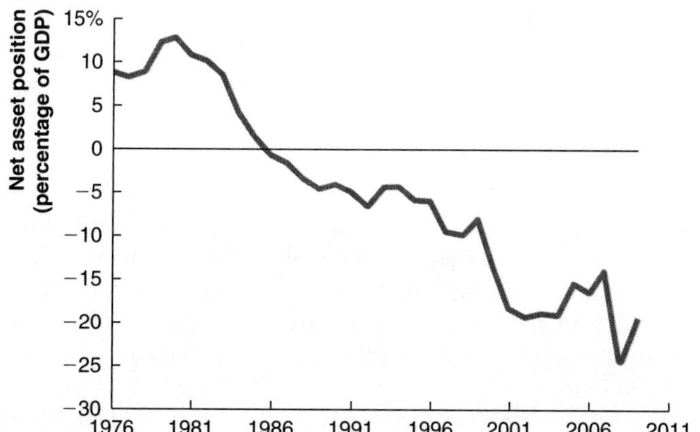

Figure 15.3

The Net Asset Position of the United States, 1976–2009

In 1986, the net asset position of the United States became negative, so the United States became a net debtor country. As of 2009, foreigners owned assets of about 19% of GDP more than U.S. households, firms, and governments owned in other countries.

Source: U.S. Bureau of Economic Analysis. ●

negative during this time period. As a result, capital has been flowing into the United States to finance federal budget deficits as well as consumption and investment by U.S. households and firms. Foreigners have also been purchasing assets such as stocks, bonds, factories, and office buildings in the United States. As a result, foreign ownership of real assets, such as U.S. property, and of financial assets, such as U.S. Treasury securities and shares of U.S. firms have increased dramatically in the past 25 years. Figure 15.3 shows that 1986 marked the year that the United States went from being a net creditor to a net debtor nation. Being a net debtor means that households, firms, and governments in the United States now own fewer assets abroad than households, firms, and governments from other nations own in the United States. In fact, in dollar terms, the United States has become the world's largest debtor nation.

Is there a danger to the United States from being the world's largest debtor nation? What would happen if foreign capital stopped flowing into the United States? The decision by foreigners to make loans to and purchase assets from U.S. citizens is a vote of confidence that the United States is a safe place to invest—that is, investors will be able to obtain their invested funds and returns when needed. If foreigners suddenly decide that the United States is no longer a safe place to invest, they would stop making loans to U.S. firms and households and stop buying U.S. financial or physical capital. Our discussion of the balance of payments tells us that the current account balance would then have to become zero. In 2010, the current account balance was −3.2% of GDP, so net capital outflows were −3.2% of GDP. If net capital outflows suddenly went to zero, then Equation (15.2) tells us that one or more of these three things must happen:

1. Investment would have to decrease, which means the United States would be accumulating fewer of the capital goods required for economic growth.
2. Private saving would have to increase, which means there would be a sudden decrease in household consumption.
3. Government saving would have to increase, which would require some combination of tax increases and cuts in government purchases and transfer payments such as Social Security.

Any combination of these three adjustments would be potentially painful for households and firms in the United States, particularly in the short run when nominal wages and prices are sticky. If these adjustments occur slowly, however, there would be time for nominal wages and prices to adjust without harmful effects on incomes and jobs.

Making the Connection

Multiple Natural Disasters Pose Long-Term Financial Challenges for Japan

On March 11, 2011, a mammoth earthquake and tsunami hit northeastern Japan. The impact of these disasters was magnified when subsequent damage to several nuclear power plants forced the evacuation of thousands of people and caused widespread fears of radiation leaks. As Japan was still reeling from these multiple calamities, financial analysts contemplated the impact on the Japanese and world economies. The impact was quickly registered in financial markets: During March 2011, stocks fell almost 11% in Japan, 5% in Germany, and 4% in France.

The Japanese economy, already burdened with a government debt more than twice the size of the nation's GDP, faced huge additional financing needs as it rebuilt its infrastructure. Moody's Investors Service warned that an erosion of investor confidence in the country's ability to repay its debts would likely increase borrowing costs. "The earthquake may have shifted such a potential tipping point a bit forward, unless Japan's political parties are galvanized by the crisis to also address the country's long-term fiscal challenges," explained Tom Byrne, a Moody's analyst.

Vanessa Rossi, senior research fellow at London-based think tank Chatham House, believed that Japan faced a huge task in rebuilding its infrastructure: "There's enormous damage to infrastructure—installations, power plants, housing, factories, ports, coastline. You couldn't possibly rebuild . . . in the period of 1–2 years. I expect it would be 4–5 years of work." Japan is the second-largest foreign holder of U.S. debt and will likely have to sell some of this debt to cover its rebuilding costs. This will lead to modestly lower bond prices and higher interest rates in the United States, but most economists predicted that the impact on economic growth in the United States would be modest. Patrick O'Keefe, director of economic research at J.H. Cohn, believed that there could even be some reduction, albeit temporary, in energy prices as the Japanese economy slowed and demand for petroleum products fell.

Complicating the task of rebuilding was the relatively low level of insurance coverage in Japan. This could force the government to raise taxes or increase spending. The burden on government could be reduced to the extent that Japanese life insurance and other financial companies might sell assets held abroad to help pay for rebuilding. If spending on rebuilding were large enough, it could result in an increase in the exchange value of the yen, which, in turn, would increase interest rates. This increase would lead to a further slowdown in economic growth.

Sources: David Wessel, "Q&A: Eichengreen on the End of Dollar Dominance," *Wall Street Journal*, March 16, 2011. Kathleen Deveny and Maureen Mackey, "Japan Crisis: Experts Weight Economic Impact," *Fiscal Times*, March 16, 2011; Natsuko Waki, "Analysis: Japan Disaster Costs Seen at Least $180 Billion," *Reuters*, March 14, 2011; and Phil Izzo, "Economists React: If Worst Happens in Japan, All Bets Are Off," *Wall Street Journal*, March 15, 2011.

Test your understanding by doing related problem 2.7 on page 597 at the end of this chapter.

15.3

Learning Objective

Distinguish between the nominal and real exchange rates.

Nominal and Real Exchange Rates

In the previous section, we explored the linkage between the U.S. economy and foreign economies using the balance of payments. In Section 15.4, we explain how exchange rates are determined and how changes in exchange rates affect international trade and financial flows. However, first we need to provide a more complete discussion of exchange rates.

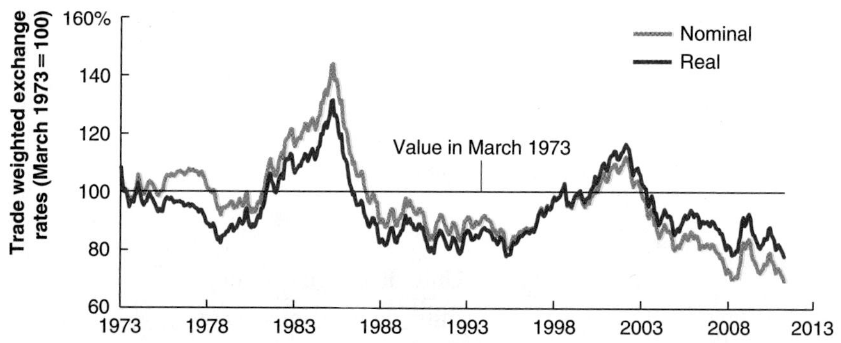

Figure 15.4

The Trade-Weighted Exchange Rate of the U.S. Dollar Against an Index of Major Currencies, 1973–2011

The nominal and real exchange rates for the U.S. dollar have fluctuated widely since the collapse of the Bretton Woods system in 1971.

Source: Board of Governors of the Federal Reserve System. ●

From the end of World War II to 1971, the U.S. dollar operated under the *Bretton Woods system*, in which the value of the U.S. dollar was fixed relative to the price of gold, and the value of other major currencies were fixed relative to the U.S. dollar. During that period, households and firms could purchase assets and conduct international trade with certainty about the relative values of global currencies. However, in 1971, the Bretton Woods system collapsed when the United States suspended the convertibility of the dollar into gold at fixed prices. Recall that the *nominal exchange rate* (also called simply the exchange rate) is the price of one currency in terms of another currency. Figure 15.4 shows the value of the U.S. dollar, as measured against a basket of seven currencies consisting of the euro, the Canadian dollar, the Japanese yen, the British pound, the Swiss franc, the Australian dollar, and the Swedish krona.[1] The index is normalized, so that its value for March 1973 is set to 100. When the index rises above 100, it indicates that the U.S. dollar is stronger than it was in March 1973. When the index falls below 100, it indicates that the U.S. dollar is weaker than it was in March 1973. The U.S. dollar has fluctuated significantly against major world currencies since the collapse of the Bretton Woods system.

Economists call the fluctuations in the value of the exchange rate seen in Figure 15.4 *currency appreciations* and *currency depreciations*. **Currency appreciation** occurs when the market value of a country's currency increases relative to the value of another country's currency. **Currency depreciation** occurs when the market value of a country's currency decreases relative to the value of another country's currency.

Currency appreciation An increase in the market value of one country's currency relative to another country's currency.

Currency depreciation A decrease in the market value of one country's currency relative to another country's currency.

The foreign-exchange value of the U.S. dollar was relatively stable during the 1970s, but then appreciated dramatically against the value of other currencies during the early 1980s, only to depreciate significantly during the late 1980s. The foreign-exchange value of the dollar again depreciated significantly after 2003. Overall, the value of the dollar peaked at 143.9 during March 1985, before hitting a low of 70.1 by May 16, 2011. A dollar in 2011 therefore purchased only about half as much foreign currency as it could in March 1985 and about three-quarters as much as it could in 1973. As we will see, large swings in the exchange rate have important consequences for international trade and financial flows.

A concrete example can help clarify the meaning of the nominal exchange rate. The *Economist* magazine reported on October 14, 2010 that the nominal exchange rate, $E^{\$}$, between the Mexican peso and the U.S. dollar was 12.8 pesos per dollar. We write this example as:

$$E^{\$} = \frac{12.8 \text{ Mexican pesos}}{\$1}.$$

[1]The index compiled by the Federal Reserve Board of Governors weights each currency by the volume of trade that the country does with the United States. Details are available at www.federalreserve.gov/pubs/bulletin/2005/winter05_index.pdf.

This equation tells us that \$1 can purchase 12.8 Mexican pesos. If the value of the nominal exchange rate increased from 12.8 Mexican pesos per U.S. dollar to 15 Mexican pesos per U.S. dollar, then the U.S. dollar can purchase more Mexican pesos. The nominal exchange rate for the U.S. dollar has increased, so it has appreciated against the Mexican peso. Conversely, the nominal exchange rate for the Mexican peso has depreciated against the U.S. dollar, going from \$0.08 per peso to \$0.07 per peso. In general, we can write:

$$E^{\text{Domestic}} = \frac{\text{Units of foreign currency}}{\text{Units of domestic currency}}. \qquad (15.3)$$

The exchange rate is just a price, and you can think of the price of a good such as an iPad as the exchange rate between an iPad and dollars. For example, if the price of an iPad is initially \$500, then each iPad can exchange for \$500. If the price of the iPad increases to \$600, then each iPad can now exchange for \$600 dollars, so the iPad has appreciated against the dollar, while the dollar has depreciated against the iPad.

Real Exchange Rates

Real exchange rate The rate at which goods and services in one country can be exchanged for goods and services in another country.

There is more to the value of a currency than just the nominal exchange rate. The **real exchange rate** is the rate at which goods and services in one country can be exchanged for goods and services in another country. The real exchange rate calculation consists of two steps. First, we use the nominal exchange rate to convert dollars into foreign currencies. This calculation gives us the price of the good in the United States in terms of foreign currencies. Second, we adjust for differences in the prices of the two goods across countries to calculate how many foreign goods a domestic good can purchase.

In Chapter 2, we used the price of a McDonald's Big Mac to illustrate exchange-rate conversions, and we return to that example now. On October 14, 2010, the *Economist* reported that the price of a Big Mac was \$3.71 in the United States and 32.0 Mexican pesos. Furthermore, the nominal exchange rate between Mexican pesos and United States dollars was 12.4 Mexican pesos per U.S. dollar. The real exchange rate tells us how many goods in the foreign country a good in the domestic country can purchase. In this case, we are interested in knowing how many Mexican Big Macs we would need in order to purchase one Big Mac in the United States. The real exchange rate tells us how many goods in the foreign country a good in the domestic country can purchase, so a real exchange rate is expressed in terms of goods rather than currency. The real exchange rate, $e^{\$}$, between the U.S. dollar and the Mexican peso is:

$$\begin{aligned} e^{\$} &= E^{\$}\left(\frac{P_{\text{Big Mac}}^{\text{United States}}}{P_{\text{Big Mac}}^{\text{Mexico}}}\right) \\ &= \left(\frac{12.4 \text{ Mexican pesos}}{\$1}\right)\left(\frac{\$3.71/\text{Big Mac in the United States}}{32.0 \text{ Mexican pesos/Big Mac in Mexico}}\right) \\ &= 1.44 \text{ Big Macs in Mexico per Big Mac in the United States.} \end{aligned}$$

One Big Mac in the United States at current prices and nominal exchange rates can purchase 1.44 Big Macs in Mexico. In general, we can write:

$$e^{\text{Domestic}} = E^{\text{Domestic}}\left(\frac{P^{\text{Domestic}}}{P^{\text{Foreign}}}\right) \qquad (15.4)$$

We used the price of a Big Mac to illustrate the idea of a real exchange rate. However, we use a measure of the aggregate price level in Equation (15.4), so the real exchange rate is in terms of average goods and services. For example, if the real exchange rate between the Mexican peso and U.S. dollar were 2, then this would indicate that the average good or service produced in the United States can purchase two of the average good or service in Mexico.

Figure 15.4 on page 569 shows the real exchange rate for the U.S. dollar from 1973 to 2011 versus the currencies of the major trading partners of the United States. We can see that movements in the real exchange rate largely mirror changes in the nominal exchange rate. As of May 2011, both the real and nominal exchange rates for the U.S. dollar were close to their lowest levels since the end of the Bretton Woods system. The fact that the nominal and real exchange rates have moved together suggests that the relative prices of goods and services between the United States and its major trading partners are fairly stable.

Purchasing Power Parity

Our example for the real exchange rate showed that each Big Mac made in the United States could purchase 1.44 Big Macs in Mexico. Why should a Big Mac in the United States be worth more than a Big Mac in Mexico? It seems more reasonable that one Big Mac made in the United States should be the equivalent of one Big Mac in Mexico. Given the differences in the value of Big Macs between the United States and Mexico, you could take \$3.71 and purchase \$3.71 × 12.4 pesos per dollar = 46.0 pesos in Mexico. Then you could purchase a Big Mac in Mexico for 32.0 pesos and have 14.0 pesos left over. Finally, you could take the Big Mac back to the United States and sell it for \$3.71. At the end of the transactions, you have 14.0 pesos in profit—a profit rate of 30%! When markets work well, everyone sees the same profit opportunities, so the demand for Mexican pesos will increase, and the dollar will depreciate against the Mexican peso until the profit opportunity disappears. In the long run, individuals pursuing profit opportunities should ensure that the one Big Mac in the United States is the equivalent of one Big Mac in Mexico. So, in the long run, you expect that the real exchange rate equals one. Of course, in our example, we ignored barriers to transporting Big Macs to and from the United States. We discuss limitations to our story next.

Purchasing power parity is the theory that, in the long run, nominal exchange rates adjust to equalize the purchasing power of different currencies. Economists believe that this theory holds in the long run because, if it does not, then profit opportunities exist. The price discrepancy between Big Macs in the United States and Mexico is an example of a profit opportunity that arises when the real exchange rate does not equal one. Every day, individuals pursuing these profit opportunities purchase dollars, pesos, and other currencies in foreign-exchange markets. As a result, nominal exchange rates are constantly adjusting to perceived profit opportunities. In the long run, individuals pursuing these profit opportunities should drive the real exchange rate to one. So, purchasing power parity should hold.

Purchasing power parity The theory that, in the long run, nominal exchange rates adjust to equalize the purchasing power of different currencies.

To explore this point further, we can rewrite Equation (15.4) in terms of growth rates to get:

$$\%\text{ change in } e^{\text{Domestic}} = \%\text{ change in } E^{\text{Domestic}} + \%\text{ change in } P^{\text{Domestic}} - \%\text{ change in } P^{\text{Foreign}}. \quad (15.5)$$

If the real exchange rate equals one in the long-run equilibrium, then it is constant:

$$\%\text{change in } e^{\text{Domestic}} = 0,$$

and we have:

$$0 = \%\text{ change in } E^{\text{Domestic}} + \%\text{ change in } P^{\text{Domestic}} - \%\text{ change in } P^{\text{Foreign}}.$$

The inflation rate is the percentage change in a price level, so we can rewrite this equation as:

$$\% \text{ change in } E^{\text{Domestic}} = \pi^{\text{Foreign}} - \pi^{\text{Domestic}}. \quad (15.6)$$

Equation (15.6) tells us that the growth rate of the nominal exchange rate is equal to the difference between the foreign and domestic inflation rates. From Chapter 6, we know that the growth rate of the money supply determines the inflation rate in the long run, so monetary policy will play a critical role in determining the long-run nominal exchange rate. When the domestic inflation rate is lower than the foreign inflation rate, the nominal exchange rate will appreciate, but when the domestic inflation rate is higher than the foreign inflation rate, the nominal exchange rate will depreciate.

Does Purchasing Power Parity Always Hold?

In the previous section, we explain how nominal exchange rates adjust to maintain purchasing power parity, assuming that the real exchange rate is constant. However, for several reasons, purchasing power parity may not hold perfectly in the long run. First, not all goods and services are traded internationally. A Big Mac is perishable and so could not be easily transported from Mexico to the United States, as in our example. Services such as doctor visits are not traded internationally. In these cases individual profit-maximizing behavior will not cause the nominal exchange rate to adjust as predicted by purchasing power parity. Nontradable goods and services are a large component of GDP, so purchasing power parity will not hold exactly in the long run. Second, countries impose barriers to trade such as *tariffs*, taxes on imports, and *quotas*, which are limits on the quantities of goods that can be imported. For example, the U.S. government limits imports of sugar, so the price of sugar in the United States is much higher than the world price. Because of the quota it is not possible for individuals to purchase cheap sugar in the world market and sell it at a profit inside the United States. By legally limiting individual pursuit of profit opportunities, barriers to trade prevent purchasing power parity from holding exactly. Third, products differ across countries as firms adapt products to local tastes. Because the ingredients in Big Macs may vary across countries, U.S. consumers may not be willing to pay $3.71 for a Mexican Big Mac. These differences prevent purchasing power parity from holding perfectly.

15.4

Learning Objective

Explain how exchange rates are determined and how changes in exchange rates affect the prices of imports and exports.

The Foreign-Exchange Market and Exchange Rates

Around the world, approximately $4 trillion worth of trades are made each day in foreign-exchange markets. That amount represents nearly $600 for every person in the world each day. Although the volume of transactions is large, they are concentrated in just a few locations and among just a small number of currencies. The United Kingdom has 37% of all transactions, and the United States has 18% of all transactions, so more than half of all foreign-exchange transactions occur in just two countries. About 85% of all trades involve the U.S. dollar, while 39% involve the euro, 19% involve the yen, and 13% involve the British pound.[2] Foreign-exchange markets are global, and trades occur 24 hours a day, so foreign-exchange markets are usually very close to equilibrium. In this section, we use a simple demand and supply model to explain movements in nominal exchange rates.

Types of Foreign-Exchange Systems

Historically, countries have relied on three major types of foreign-exchange systems: a fixed exchange-rate system, a floating exchange-rate system, and a managed float exchange-rate system.

[2]Bank for International Settlements, "Triennial Central Bank Survey," September 2010.

In a **fixed exchange-rate system**, exchange rates are set at levels determined and maintained by governments. The gold standard, in which countries fix the value of their currencies relative to an ounce of gold, is an example of a fixed exchange-rate system. The Bretton Woods exchange-rate system also acted as a fixed exchange-rate system for the major currencies from the end of World War II to 1971. Another type of fixed exchange-rate system occurs when a country fixes the value of its currency relative to another currency or a group of currencies. Economists call this an *exchange-rate peg* because the value of one currency is pegged to the value of another currency. An extreme version of a fixed exchange-rate system is a currency board. A **currency board** is a fixed exchange-rate system in which the central bank or government maintains complete convertibility of the domestic currency to an anchor currency of another nation. For example, Argentina used a currency board to peg the value of the Argentine peso relative to the U.S. dollar from 1991 to 2002. In this system, individuals could exchange pesos for dollars at a fixed exchange rate.

Fixed exchange-rate system A system in which exchange rates are set at levels determined and maintained by governments.

Currency board A fixed exchange-rate system in which the central bank or government maintains complete convertibility of the domestic currency to an anchor currency of another nation.

The central bank maintains a fixed exchange-rate system by intervening in the market for foreign exchange. Suppose that the Bank of Thailand decides to fix the exchange rate between the baht (Thailand's currency) and the dollar so that $1 is the equivalent of 25 baht. Now suppose that the value of the dollar rises so that $1 now purchases 30 baht. In this case, the Bank of Thailand would sell dollars for baht to increase the supply of dollars and increase the demand for baht in foreign-exchange markets. The end result would be a weaker dollar against the baht, so the value of the dollar would fall back to 25 baht. Now suppose that the value of the dollar falls so that $1 now purchases 20 baht. In this case, the Bank of Thailand would sell baht for dollars to increase the supply of baht and the demand for dollars. The end result would be a stronger dollar against the baht, so the value of the dollar would rise back to 25 baht.

Maintaining a fixed exchange-rate system requires that a country have enough reserves of foreign currencies to maintain the fixed exchange rate. Without the required foreign-exchange reserves, the central bank cannot buy and sell the domestic currency to maintain the fixed exchange rate. For example, Thailand pegged the value of its currency relative to the dollar until 1997 at $1 for 25 baht. Maintaining that fixed exchange rate required the Bank of Thailand to have sufficient U.S. dollar reserves so that if the value of the dollar rose relative to the baht, the Bank of Thailand could sell enough dollars to bring the exchange rate back to $1 for 25 baht.

Speculators buy and sell foreign exchange in an attempt to profit from changes in exchange rates. In May 1997, the Thai baht was hit by large *speculative attacks* because participants in foreign-exchange markets doubted that the Bank of Thailand had enough foreign-exchange reserves to maintain the fixed exchange rate. Speculators began to expect that the Bank of Thailand would be forced to devalue the baht, so these speculators sold the Thai baht in large quantities. Eventually, the Bank of Thailand did not have enough foreign-exchange reserves to maintain the value of the baht, so the Thai government devalued the baht and ended the fixed exchange-rate system on July 2, 1997. The devaluation of the Thai baht led foreign-exchange market participants to doubt the ability of other Asian economies to maintain their fixed exchange-rate systems. The lack of confidence eventually spread to Indonesia, South Korea, and the Philippines. All these countries were eventually forced to devalue their currencies and abandon the fixed exchange-rate systems. The period became known as the *Asian financial crisis* because the currency devaluations were the start of an economic downturn in many Asian countries.

When Thailand and other countries were forced to abandon their fixed exchange-rate system, they moved to a **floating exchange-rate system**, under which the foreign-exchange value of a currency is determined in the foreign-exchange market. In a floating exchange-rate system, the foreign-exchange market sets the price of a currency just as the global market for oil sets the price of oil and local markets for gasoline set the price of gasoline. The

Floating exchange-rate system A system in which the foreign-exchange value of a currency is determined in the foreign-exchange market.

government does not intervene in foreign-exchange markets, so the government does not need foreign-exchange reserves. Once the Thai baht began to float, it did not matter how large the foreign-exchange reserves were at the Bank of Thailand because the bank did not try to maintain a specific exchange rate.

Managed float exchange-rate system An exchange-rate system in which central banks occasionally intervene to affect foreign-exchange values; also called a *dirty float regime*.

Although the Bretton Woods system collapsed in 1971, countries have not let their currencies float completely. Instead, most countries have followed a **managed float exchange-rate system**, under which central banks occasionally intervene to affect foreign-exchange values. This system is also called a *dirty float regime*. Countries intervene in foreign-exchange markets because, as we will see, fluctuations in the nominal exchange rate affect the price of exports and imports and so have important effects on the domestic economy. For example, Figure 15.4 on page 569 shows that the value of the dollar appreciated greatly against other currencies during the early 1980s. In response to this appreciation, the United States and the United Kingdom, France, (then) West Germany, and Japan agreed on September 22, 1985, to depreciate the dollar against other leading currencies. Because the agreement was signed at the Plaza Hotel in New York City, the agreement became known as the Plaza Accord. As you can see in Figure 15.4, the policy was successful for a time, as the U.S. dollar depreciated significantly after the agreement.

Sometimes it is difficult to tell exactly what type of foreign-exchange system a country uses because the country lets the value of its currency fluctuate within a very narrow range. For example, the Chinese government fixed the value of the renminbi until 2005, when it let the renminbi float against the value of a basket of currencies that include the U.S. dollar, euro, Japanese yen, and South Korean won. While the Chinese renminbi does float, the range in which it floats has been small. The renminbi increased in value from 6.83 renminbi per U.S. dollar in June 2010 to 6.58 renminbi per U.S. dollar by January 2011. The fluctuation in the value of the renminbi has been so small that many people argue that the Chinese government has essentially fixed the value of the renminbi against the value of the U.S. dollar.

The Foreign-Exchange Market

The nominal exchange rate for currencies such as the Thai baht, the Mexican peso, and the U.S. dollar are set by the demand and supply for currency in foreign-exchange markets. To understand this market, it helps to have a specific currency in mind, so we will discuss the demand and supply of U.S. dollars. The foreign-exchange market consists of three major types of participants: banks and other financial institutions, customers, and central banks. Banks and other financial institutions are the largest players in foreign-exchange markets and earn profits by purchasing currency when it is cheap and selling it when it is expensive. Customers are mostly large corporations that conduct business across international borders, so they require foreign currency to pay wages to suppliers and workers and to pay interest to bondholders. Individuals also require foreign exchange when they travel abroad or purchase assets in foreign countries. Central banks act on behalf of their governments to buy and sell currency in foreign-exchange markets. For the United States, the Foreign Exchange Desk at the Federal Reserve Bank of New York buys and sells in foreign-exchange markets at the direction of the U.S. Treasury.

Banks and other financial institutions around the world employ currency traders who are linked together by computer. Rather than exchange large amounts of paper currency, traders buy and sell bank deposits in an attempt to profit from changes in exchange rates. A bank buying or selling dollars will actually buy or sell dollar bank deposits. Dollar bank deposits exist not just in banks in the United States but also in banks around the world. Suppose that Credit Lyonnais bank in France wants to sell U.S. dollars and buy Japanese yen. The bank may exchange U.S. dollar deposits that it owns for Japanese yen deposits owned by Deutsche Bank in Germany. Businesses and individuals usually obtain foreign currency from banks in their own country.

The demand side of the foreign-exchange market for the U.S. dollar consists of foreigners who want to purchase U.S. goods, services, and assets. Let's consider the demand for U.S. dollars in exchange for Mexican pesos. In this case, there are three sources of foreign currency demand for the U.S. dollar:

1. Mexican firms and households that want to buy goods and services produced in the United States.
2. Mexican firms and households that want to invest in the United States either through foreign direct investment—buying or building factories or other facilities in the United States—or through foreign portfolio investment—buying stocks and bonds issued in the United States.
3. Currency traders who believe that the value of the dollar in the future will be greater than its value today.

The demand curve for dollars in the foreign-exchange market has the normal downward slope, indicating that when the value of the dollar is high, the quantity demanded of dollars will be low. A Mexican investor is more likely to buy a $1,000 Treasury security when the exchange rate is 10 pesos = $1 and he pays only 10,000 pesos to buy the security than when the exchange rate is 20 pesos = $1 and he must pay 20,000 pesos to buy the security. Similarly, a Mexican firm is more likely to buy $100 million worth of microchips from Intel Corporation when the exchange rate is 10 pesos per dollar and the microchips can be purchased for 1 billion pesos than when the exchange rate is 20 pesos per dollar and the microchips cost 2 billion pesos.

The supply side of the foreign-exchange market for the U.S. dollar consists of domestic firms and households that want to purchase Mexican goods, services, and assets. There are three sources of U.S. dollar supply in exchange for the Mexican peso:

1. U.S. firms and households that want to buy goods and services produced in Mexico.
2. U.S. firms and households that want to invest in Mexico either through buying or building factories or other facilities in Mexico or buying Mexican financial assets such as stocks and bonds.
3. Currency traders who believe that the value of the peso in the future will be greater than its value today.

The supply curve has the normal upward slope. When the value of the dollar is high, the quantity of dollars supplied in exchange for pesos will be high. A U.S. investor will be more likely to buy a 100,000-peso bond issued by the Mexican government when the exchange rate is 20 pesos = $1 and she pays only $5,000 for the bond than when the exchange rate is 10 pesos = $1 and she must pay $10,000 for the bond. If you own a clothing store, you are more likely to purchase 1 million pesos-worth of clothing from Mexico when the exchange rate is 20 pesos = $1 and pay $50,000 than when the exchange rate is 10 pesos = $1 and you must pay $100,000.

Equilibrium in the Foreign-Exchange Market

Figure 15.5 shows the demand and supply of U.S. dollars for Mexican pesos. Our model is for the nominal exchange rate. However, as Equation (15.4) shows us, when price levels are constant, changes in the nominal exchange rate cause the real exchange rate to change. Notice that as we move up the vertical axis in Figure 15.5, the value of the dollar increases relative to the value of the peso. When the exchange rate is 20 pesos per dollar, the dollar is worth twice as much as when the exchange rate is 10 pesos per dollar. As we move up the vertical axis, the dollar appreciates, and the peso depreciates.

As with any other market, equilibrium occurs in the foreign-exchange market where the quantity demanded equals the quantity supplied. In Figure 15.5, the equilibrium exchange rate is 14 pesos = $1. At exchange rates above 14 pesos = $1, there will be a

Figure 15.5

Equilibrium in Foreign-Exchange Markets

The equilibrium nominal exchange rate is 14 pesos per dollar. If the nominal exchange rate is below the equilibrium value, there is a shortage of dollars, so individuals seeking dollars bid up the nominal exchange rate. If the nominal exchange rate is above the equilibrium value, there is a surplus of dollars, so individuals seeking dollars bid down the nominal exchange rate. ●

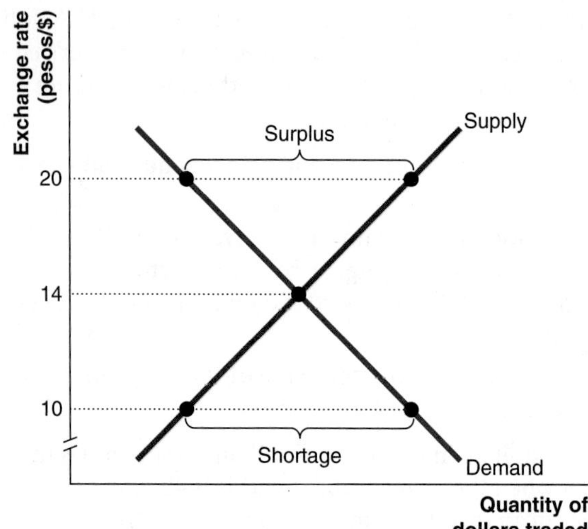

surplus of dollars. Firms and individuals that want to exchange their dollars for pesos will offer to sell their dollars at a lower price, so there is downward pressure on the peso–dollar exchange rate. The surplus and downward pressure will not be eliminated until the exchange rate falls to 14 pesos = \$1. If the exchange rate is below 14 pesos = \$1, there will be a shortage of dollars. Firms and individuals that want to exchange their pesos for dollars will offer to buy dollars at a higher price, so there is upward pressure on the exchange rate. The shortage and upward pressure will not be eliminated until the exchange rate rises to 14 pesos = \$1. Surpluses and shortages in the foreign-exchange market are eliminated very quickly because the volume of trading in major currencies such as the dollar and Mexican peso is very large and because currency traders are linked together electronically. As we mentioned earlier, the foreign-exchange market is huge, and given the volume of trading in those markets, we would expect them to remain close to equilibrium.

Changes in the Equilibrium Exchange Rate

Shifts in the demand and supply curve cause the equilibrium exchange rate to change. Three main factors cause these curves in the foreign-exchange market to shift:

1. Changes in demand for U.S.-produced goods and services and changes in the demand for foreign-produced goods and services.
2. Changes in the desire to invest in the United States and changes in the desire to invest in foreign currencies.
3. Changes in the expectations of currency traders about the likely future value of the dollar and the likely future value of foreign currencies.

Consider how the three factors listed here will affect the demand for U.S. dollars in exchange for Mexican pesos. During an economic expansion in Mexico, the incomes of Mexican households will increase, and the demand by Mexican consumers and firms for U.S. goods and services will increase. At any given exchange rate, the demand for U.S. dollars will increase, and the demand curve will shift to the right. Similarly, if real interest rates in the United States increase, the desirability of investing in U.S. financial assets will increase, and the demand curve for dollars will also shift to the right. Some buyers and sellers in the foreign-exchange market are speculators. If a speculator becomes convinced that the value of the dollar is going to rise relative to the value of the peso, she will sell pesos and buy dollars. If the current exchange rate is 20 pesos = \$1, and the speculator is convinced that it will soon rise to 25 pesos = $1, then she could sell 20 million pesos and receive $1 million (20 million pesos/20 pesos) in return. If the speculator is correct and the value of the dollar rises against the peso to 25 pesos = $1, she will be able to exchange $1 million for 25 million pesos ($1 million × 25 pesos), leaving a profit of 5 million pesos.

The factors that affect the supply curve for dollars are similar to those that affect the demand curve for dollars. An economic expansion in the United States increases the incomes of those in the United States and increases their demand for goods and services, including goods and services made in Mexico. As U.S. consumers and firms increase their spending on Mexican products, they must supply dollars in exchange for pesos, which causes the supply curve for dollars to shift to the right. Similarly, an increase in real interest rates in Mexico will make financial investments in Mexico more attractive to U.S. investors. These higher Mexican interest rates will cause the supply of dollars to shift to the right, as U.S. investors exchange dollars for pesos. Finally, if speculators become convinced that the future value of the peso will be higher relative to the dollar than it is today, the supply curve of dollars will shift to the right, as traders attempt to exchange dollars for pesos.

Solved Problem 15.4

The PIIGS and the Euro

The global financial crisis of 2007–2009 slowed economic growth around the world, which reduced tax revenues and increased government spending on welfare and unemployment benefits for most countries. As a result, many countries were forced to run large budget deficits, so national debts increased substantially, especially for Portugal, Ireland, Italy, Greece, and Spain (PIIGS). From 2007 to 2010, the national debt rose by 21% of GDP for Portugal, 41% for Ireland, 13% for Italy, 42% for Greece, and 22% for Spain. These increases were so large that financial market participants became concerned that one or more of these countries would default on their debts. All of these countries use the euro as their currency. What effect should the increased likelihood of these government's defaulting on their debts have had on the value of the euro relative to the U.S. dollar? Use a graph to support your answer.

Solving the Problem

Step 1 **Review the chapter material.** The problem asks you to determine what should have happened to the nominal exchange rate of the euro as a result of the possibility of governments' defaulting on their debts, so you may want to review the section "Changes in the Equilibrium Exchange Rate," which begins on page 576.

Step 2 **Determine how the demand and supply curves change.** Concern that one or more of these governments will default on their debt makes it less likely that U.S. investors will purchase securities that these governments issue. This change in investor confidence will reduce the demand for the euro in the foreign-exchange market. Similarly, investors who currently own euro-denominated assets will want to sell euros for dollars so that they can invest in the United States. This will increase the supply of euros in the foreign-exchange market.

Step 3 **Use a graph to determine the effect on the value of the euro.** Draw a demand and supply graph for euros. Label the vertical axis "Exchange rate ($/euro)" and label horizontal axis "Quantity of euros traded." Label the initial equilibrium as point *A* and the initial equilibrium exchange rate as E_1. Draw the demand curve shifting to the left, and draw the supply curve shifting to the right. Now label the intersection of the new demand and supply curves as point *B* and the new equilibrium exchange rate as E_2.

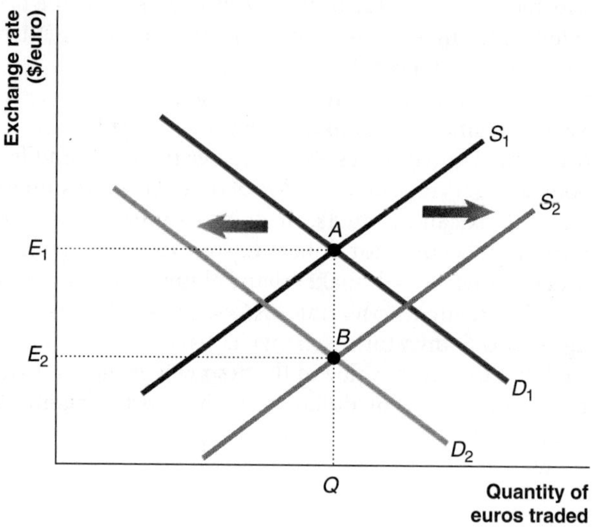

Our model predicts that the nominal exchange rate of the euro should decrease as the foreign-exchange market equilibrium moves from point *A* to point *B*. This change is in fact what happened in foreign-exchange markets: The nominal exchange rate for the euro decreased from $1.60 per euro on April 22, 2008 to $1.20 per euro on June 7, 2010.

For more practice, do related problem 4.7 on page 599 at the end of this chapter.

15.5

Learning Objective

Understand the *IS–MP* model of an open economy with a floating exchange rate.

A Short-Run *IS–MP* Model of an Open Economy with a Floating Exchange Rate

The effect of monetary and fiscal policy on interest rates and economic activity can depend on whether the government has a fixed or floating exchange-rate system. To see how the choice of an exchange-rate system affects monetary and fiscal policy, we need to modify the *IS–MP* model from Chapter 9 to account for the effect of real interest rates on the nominal exchange rate and net exports. Real interest rates affect the nominal exchange rate, net exports, and net capital outflow because real interest rates determine the rate of return on domestic assets. We proceed by first incorporating these effects into the *IS–MP* model from Chapter 9 in the case where a country allows its currency to float.

The *IS* Curve

The *IS* curve from Chapter 9 shows the negative relationship between the real interest rate and expenditures in the market for goods and services. As the real interest rate increases, the cost of borrowing increases, so households and firms borrow less to finance consumption and investment. In Chapter 9, we focused on the effect of real interest rates on consumption and investment. In an open economy, changes in the nominal exchange rate will change net exports. Because net exports are one of the four categories of aggregate expenditure, in this section we take this effect into account by modifying the *IS* curve.

A higher real interest rate should increase the nominal exchange rate and decrease net exports. The higher real interest rate will increase the demand for U.S. assets, so the demand for U.S. dollars increases as investors from outside the United States seek to purchase those assets. The higher demand for U.S. dollars will increase the nominal exchange rate and decrease the price of imports. As a consequence, imports into the United States should increase. The increase in the nominal exchange rates also makes exports from the United States more expensive, so U.S. exports should also decrease. As a result, a higher U.S. real interest rate should reduce net exports and expenditure on goods and services produced within the United States. Similarly, a decrease in the U.S. real interest rate should make exports cheaper and imports more expensive, so a decrease in the real interest rate should increase net exports and expenditure on goods and services produced within the United States. Therefore, explicitly accounting for nominal exchange rates and net exports does not change a basic fact about the *IS* curve: *An increase in the real interest rate will decrease expenditure and output, while a decrease in the real interest rate will increase expenditure and output.* However, the effect of real interest rates on net exports provides us with an additional reason for thinking that real interest rates affect real GDP and the output gap.

When foreign real interest rates increase, foreign investments become more attractive relative to U.S. investments. U.S. and foreign investors will then want to sell U.S. assets and purchase foreign assets. The demand for U.S. assets decreases, and the demand for assets in the rest of the world increases, decreasing the demand for the dollar. The nominal exchange rate for the U.S. dollar decreases, which causes imports into the United States to become more expensive and U.S. exports to become less expensive. Imports then decrease and exports increase. At any given U.S. real interest rate, an increase in foreign real interest rates will increase net exports and real GDP for the United States. Similarly, a decrease in real interest rates in the rest of the world will cause the U.S. dollar to appreciate, so net exports and U.S. real GDP will decrease.

The Monetary Policy Curve

The *MP* curve from Chapter 9 assumed that the central bank does not adjust the real interest rate as the output gap changes. As a result, the *MP* curve from Chapter 9 was horizontal. However, this presentation was a simplification. To better understand how monetary and fiscal policy operate in an open economy, we have to allow for the possibility that the central bank adjusts the real interest rate as the output gap changes. To understand what the new *MP* curve looks like, we need to remember that the Phillips curve from Chapter 9 shows the positive short-run relationship between the inflation rate and the output gap. The Phillips curve reflects the tendency for the inflation rate to increase as the output gap increases. As the output gap increases, the demand for goods and services approaches the capacity of the economy, so firms begin to increase prices, and the inflation rate increases. The central bank is responsible for keeping inflation low and stable, so it will respond to the higher inflation rate by increasing the real interest rate. In fact, many central banks have either an explicit or an implicit inflation target that they try to achieve.

As we saw in Chapter 12, when we take into account the response of central banks to inflation, the *MP* curve should slope upward, which means that central banks tend to increase the real interest rate as the output gap increases. The higher real interest rate makes financial investment in the domestic economy, the United States, more desirable compared to other countries. As a result, capital will flow into the United States, which is equivalent to saying that net capital outflows will decrease. To purchase assets in the United States, investors first have to acquire U.S. dollars, so the demand for U.S. dollars and the nominal exchange rate increase. The increase in the nominal exchange rate will reduce U.S. exports and increase imports into the United States, so net exports decrease. The fact that net exports decrease at the same time that net capital outflows decrease should not be surprising because Equation (15.1) on page 565 tells us that net capital outflows equals the current account balance, and net exports are a large part of the current account balance.

The position of the *MP* curve depends on the central bank's target inflation rate. Figure 15.6 shows the upward-sloping *MP* curve and the effect of changes in the target inflation rate. If the central bank increases the target inflation rate, then it is willing to tolerate a higher equilibrium inflation rate. Therefore, the central bank will decrease the real interest rate at every level of output. For example, if the output gap is $\widetilde{Y}$, the central bank will decrease the

Figure 15.6

The *MP* Curve and Changes in the Target Inflation Rate

The *MP* curve slopes upward to reflect the tendency of central banks to increase real interest rates as output increases. A decrease in the target inflation rate causes the *MP* curve to shift to the left, and an increase in the target inflation rate causes the *MP* curve to shift to the right. ●

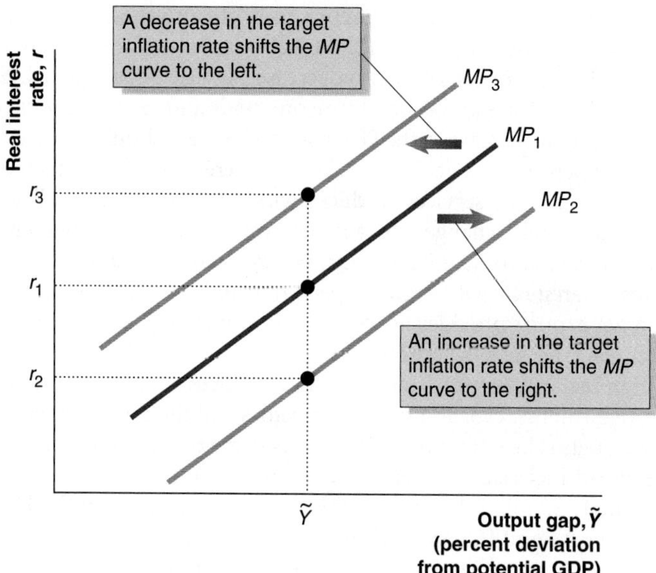

real interest rate from r_1 to r_2. As a result, the *MP* curve will shift to the right, from MP_1 to MP_2. If the central bank decreases the target inflation rate, the central bank wants to decrease the equilibrium inflation rate. For example, if the output gap is $\tilde{Y}$, the central bank will increase the real interest rate from r_1 to r_3. As a result, the *MP* curve will shift to the left, from MP_1 to MP_3.

Our discussion so far makes it clear that real interest rates have important effects on both net exports and net capital outflows. To the extent that monetary policy and fiscal policy also affect real interest rates, these policies will cause changes in net exports and net capital outflows.

Equilibrium with an Open Economy

Figure 15.7 shows equilibrium in the *IS–MP* model when we account for the possibility that monetary policy responds to the level of output and the *MP* curve slopes upward. Equilibrium occurs at point *A*, where the *IS* and *MP* curves intersect. The *IS–MP* graph in panel (a) determines the equilibrium real interest rate. The equilibrium real interest rate then determines net capital outflows in panel (b). Net capital outflows then determine the nominal exchange rate and net exports.

Policy with a Floating Exchange Rate

The effect of monetary and fiscal policy on the economy depends on whether the exchange rate is fixed or floating. The effects of monetary and fiscal policy under a floating exchange-rate system are very similar to the effects in a closed economy where net exports are zero.

Fiscal Policy Figure 15.8 shows the effect of an increase in government purchases of goods and services. An expansionary fiscal policy in the United States shifts the *IS* curve to the right, from IS_1 to IS_2, as shown in panel (a). The increase puts upward pressure on inflation, so the Fed responds by increasing the real interest rate from r_1 to r_2 and the short-run equilibrium moves from point *A* to point *B*. The higher real interest rate makes investment in the United States more attractive, so investors purchase more U.S. assets and net capital outflows decrease from NCF_1 to NCF_2, as shown in panel (b). To purchase U.S. assets, investors need U.S. dollars, so the demand for U.S. dollars increases, causing the dollar to appreciate in value. Because net exports equal net capital outflows, net exports also decrease from NCF_1 to NCF_2.

This example shows that an expansionary fiscal policy leads to a higher real interest rate. In the closed-economy version of the *IS–MP* model, the higher real interest rate reduces private consumption and investment. The open-economy version of the *IS–MP* model shows that expansionary fiscal policy will also reduce net exports due to the appreciation of the

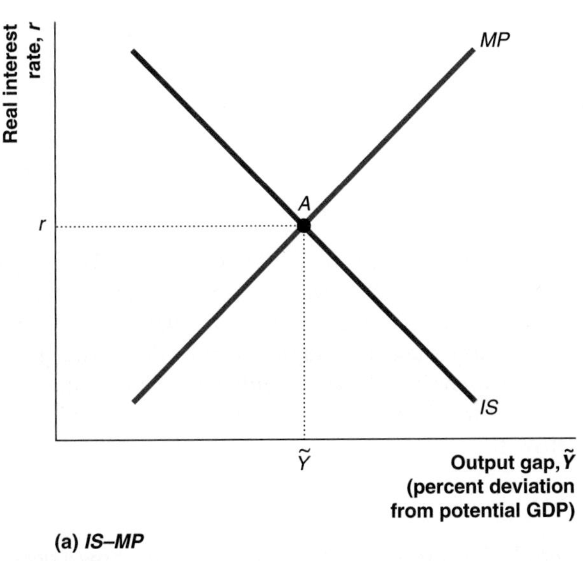

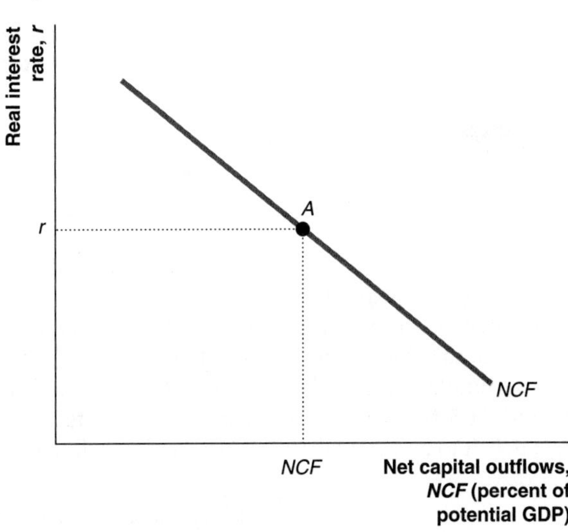

Figure 15.7 Equilibrium in the *IS–MP* Model

Equilibrium occurs in panel (a) where the *IS* and *MP* curves intersect. The *MP* curve slopes upward to allow for the tendency of central banks to increase real interest rates as output increases.

Panel (b) shows that net capital outflows decrease as the real interest rate increases. Because net exports equal net capital outflows, the level of net capital outflows in panel (b) is also the level of net exports. ●

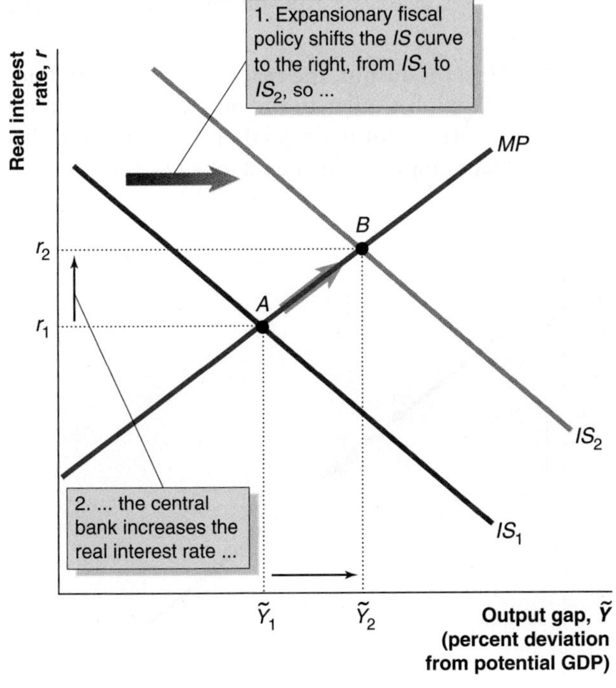

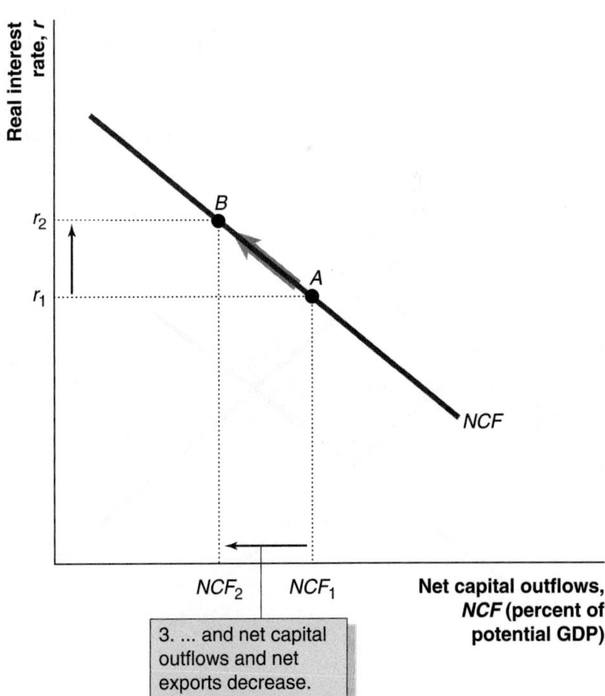

Figure 15.8 An Expansionary Fiscal Policy with Floating Exchange Rates

Under a floating exchange-rate system, an increase in government purchases increases the real interest rate in panel (a). The increase in the real interest rate causes the exchange rate to appreciate, so net capital outflows decrease in panel (b) and net exports also decrease. ●

domestic currency. Therefore, fiscal policy is less effective at increasing real GDP in an open economy with a floating exchange rate than in a closed economy.

Solved Problem 15.5

Explaining the Effect of Deficit Reduction on Exchange Rates

The governments of many industrial economies, such as the United States, experienced large increases in their budget deficits as a result of the 2007–2009 financial crisis. According to the Congressional Budget Office (CBO), the U.S. government ran a budget deficit of $1.4 trillion in 2009 and $1.3 trillion in 2010. The CBO expected the budget deficit to be $1.5 trillion in 2011 and $1.1 trillion in 2012. These are large budget deficits, so the U.S. government will eventually have to decrease government expenditure or increase taxes. Suppose that the U.S. government decides to reduce the budget deficit by decreasing government expenditures. What would be the effect on the U.S. dollar and U.S. net exports? Use a graph to support your answer.

Solving the Problem

Step 1 Review the chapter material. The problem asks you to determine how a decrease in U.S. government expenditures to reduce a budget deficit would affect the U.S. dollar and U.S. net exports, so you may want to review the section "Fiscal Policy," which begins on page 580.

Step 2 Determine how a decrease in the budget deficit affects the *IS–MP* model. A decrease in government expenditure will reduce aggregate expenditure. The *IS* curve shows the relationship between aggregate expenditure and the real interest rate, so if government expenditure decreases, aggregate expenditure also decreases, and the *IS* curve shifts to the left.

Step 3 Use a graph to determine the effect on output, the real interest rate, and net capital outflows. Draw an *IS–MP* graph similar to the one in Figure 15.8 on page 581. Make sure to also draw a graph for net capital outflows and put this graph to the right of the *IS–MP* graph. Your graphs should look like this:

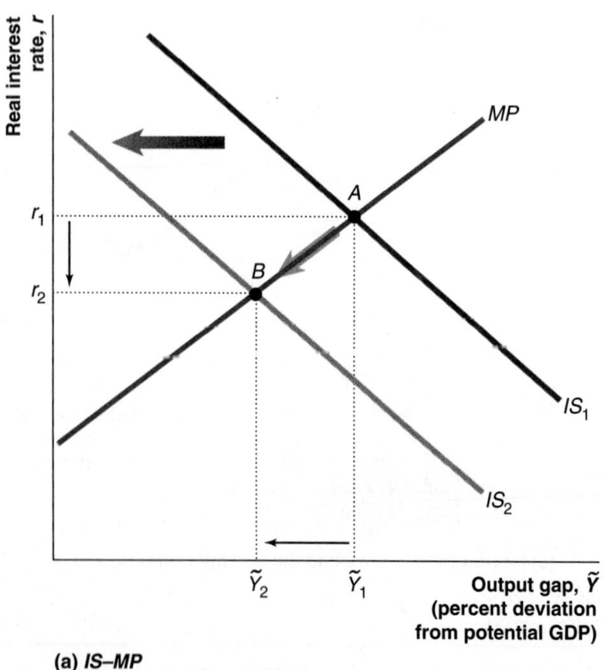

(a) *IS–MP*

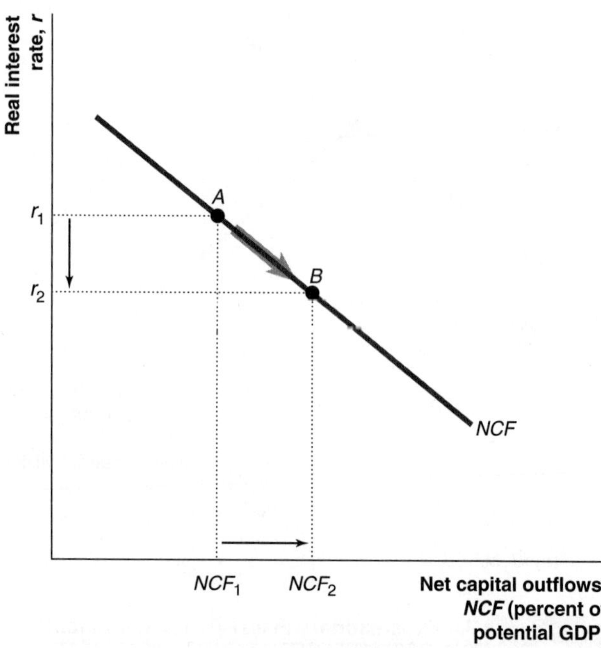

(b) Net capital outflows and the real interest rate

Your *IS–MP* graph should show that the real interest rate decreases when the *IS* curve shifts to the left, from IS_1 to IS_2. The decrease in the real interest rate should also make investments in the United States less desirable to individuals and firms, so your graph for net capital outflows should show an increase in net capital outflows. The output gap also moves from $\tilde{Y}_1$ to $\tilde{Y}_2$.

Step 4 **Determine the effect on exchange rates and net exports.** Net capital outflows have increased, which means investors want to sell U.S. assets and purchase assets outside the United States. As we saw in Section 15.4, this will decrease the demand for U.S. dollars and lead to a depreciation of the dollar. When the U.S. dollar depreciates, exports from the United States become cheaper, and imports into the United States become more expensive. As a result, net exports increase.

For more practice, do related problem 5.6 on page 600 at the end of this chapter.

Monetary Policy Figure 15.9 shows the effect of an expansionary monetary policy, as represented by an increase in the target inflation rate. If the Fed increases its inflation target, then it is willing to tolerate a higher equilibrium inflation rate for any given level of output. As a result, the *MP* curve shifts to the right, from MP_1 to MP_2, as shown in panel (a). This shift decreases the real interest rate, from r_1 to r_2, so the short-run equilibrium moves from point *A* to point *B*. The output gap also moves from $\tilde{Y}_1$ to $\tilde{Y}_2$. The lower real interest rate makes investment in the United States less attractive, so investors purchase fewer U.S. assets and net capital outflows increase from NCF_1 to NCF_2, as shown in panel (b). Because investors purchase fewer U.S. assets, they need fewer U.S. dollars, so the demand

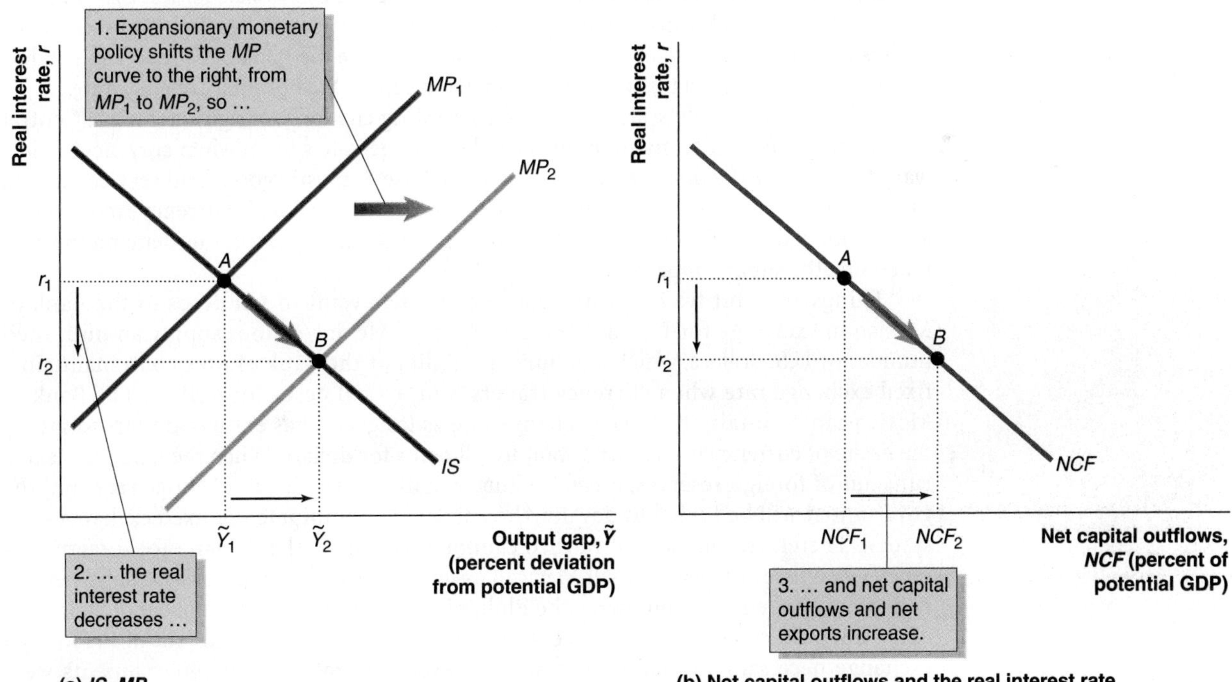

Figure 15.9 An Expansionary Monetary Policy with Floating Exchange Rates

An increase in the inflation target decreases the real interest rate in panel (a). The decrease in the real interest rate causes the exchange rate to depreciate, so net capital outflows increase in panel (b) and net exports also increase. ●

for U.S. dollars decreases, causing the dollar to depreciate in value. Because net exports equal net capital outflows, net exports also increase from NCF_1 to NCF_2.

In a closed-economy version of the *IS–MP* model, an expansionary monetary policy would reduce interest rates, leading to higher consumption and investment. Lower interest rates still lead to higher consumption and investment and a higher output gap in an open-economy version of the model. However, now lower real interest rates also lead to higher net exports, so expansionary monetary policy increases the output gap for a third reason: The lower real interest rates cause the domestic currency to depreciate, so net exports increase.

We also see another important difference between monetary policy and fiscal policy. Expansionary monetary policy reduces real interest rates, depreciates the currency, and increases net exports. In contrast, expansionary fiscal policy increases real interest rates, appreciates the currency, and decreases net exports.

15.6

Learning Objective

Understand the *IS–MP* model of an open economy with a fixed exchange rate.

A Short-Run *IS–MP* Model of an Open Economy with a Fixed Exchange Rate

Under a fixed exchange-rate system, the central bank agrees to buy and sell the domestic currency at a fixed nominal exchange rate. This change in central bank behavior changes the *IS–MP* model in several important ways. Once we understand these changes, we can understand how a fixed exchange-rate system changes the effectiveness of monetary and fiscal policy.

If Mexico decided to fix the exchange rate of the peso at $1 = 14 Mexican pesos, the Bank of Mexico would have to be willing to buy and sell pesos at that exchange rate. This exchange rate means that (1) no currency traders would sell U.S. dollars for less than 14 pesos because the Bank of Mexico is willing to pay 14 pesos for each dollar, and (2) no currency traders would pay more than 14 pesos for a dollar because the Bank of Mexico will sell dollars for 14 pesos each. In this way, the central bank can fix the nominal exchange rate.

Fixed exchange-rate systems pose an interesting challenge for governments. Central banks have no difficulty maintaining a fixed exchange-rate system when currency traders want to purchase the domestic currency to purchase domestic goods and services, assets, or speculate that the domestic currency will appreciate in value. If currency traders want an additional one billion pesos, the Bank of Mexico can always meet this demand through increasing the supply of pesos.

Things are a bit trickier when currency traders want to sell pesos to the Bank of Mexico in exchange for U.S. dollars. The Bank of Mexico cannot supply an unlimited number of U.S. dollars, which can limit the ability of the Bank of Mexico to maintain a fixed exchange rate when currency traders want to sell pesos for dollars. The Bank of Mexico can maintain the fixed exchange rate as long as it has enough dollars to satisfy the desire of currency traders who want to sell pesos for dollars. When the Bank of Mexico runs out of foreign reserves, it can no longer maintain the fixed exchange rate, and the government will be forced to devalue the currency or eliminate the fixed exchange-rate system. Therefore, the Bank of Mexico cannot always meet the demand for foreign currency when investors want to sell Mexican assets to purchase foreign assets. This is essentially what happened to Indonesia, the Philippines, South Korea, and Thailand during the Asian financial crisis of 1997. The central banks in those countries ran out of the foreign exchange necessary to maintain their fixed exchange rates, so the governments were forced to allow their currencies to float.

Central banks can always meet the demand for their domestic currencies, but they are limited in their ability to meet the demand for foreign currencies. This unique feature of fixed exchange-rate systems has important implications for the *MP* curve, which we discuss later.

The *IS* Curve

Under a floating exchange-rate system, an increase in the real interest rate leads to an appreciation of the domestic currency and a decrease in net exports. Therefore, exchange rates and net exports provide a country with an additional mechanism through which an increase in the real interest rate will lead to lower aggregate expenditure and output. Under a fixed exchange-rate system, this mechanism does not exist because the nominal exchange rate is fixed. Therefore, changes in the real interest rate do not affect the nominal exchange rate, so net exports do not change as the real interest rate changes. But the *IS* curve still slopes downward because a higher real interest rate still reduces consumption and investment. In this respect, the *IS* curve under a fixed exchange-rate system is very similar to the *IS* curve for a closed economy.

We now draw the *IS* curve assuming a given fixed exchange rate, which means that the *IS* curve will shift if the government decides to change the fixed exchange rate. Consider what would happen if the government decides to reduce the value of the fixed exchange rate. In that case, exports would become cheaper and imports would become more expensive, so net exports would increase, and the current account deficit would decrease. The increase in net exports would shift the *IS* curve to the right. Similarly, if the government decides to increase the value of the fixed exchange rate, exports would become more expensive, and imports would become cheaper. Net exports would decrease, and the *IS* curve would shift to the left.

The *MP* Curve

As the real interest rate increases, investors want to purchase more domestic assets, which increases the demand for the domestic currency. We have already discussed how the central bank can always supply more of the domestic currency, so it is always able to meet an increase in demand for the domestic currency. Therefore, the *MP* curve will slope upward just as it does under a flexible exchange rate. However, under a fixed exchange-rate system, there is a limit to how low the central bank can set the domestic real interest rate. As the real interest rate decreases, the demand for domestic assets decreases, which causes currency traders to sell the domestic currency for foreign currency. To meet this demand for foreign currency, the central bank needs sufficient foreign-exchange reserves. Unfortunately, as the real interest rate decreases, domestic assets become less and less attractive, so currency traders exchange more and more of the domestic currency for foreign currency. Eventually, the central bank will run out of foreign-exchange reserves, and the fixed exchange-rate system will collapse.

The requirement that the central bank have sufficient foreign-exchange reserves to maintain the fixed exchange-rate system puts a practical limit on how low the domestic real interest rate can fall. The lowest real interest rate that the central bank can set while still maintaining the fixed exchange-rate system is $\bar{r}$. When the real interest rate falls to this level, the central bank cannot lower it any further and still maintain the fixed exchange-rate system, so the *MP* curve becomes horizontal at $\bar{r}$. Panel (a) in Figure 15.10 shows what the *MP* curve looks like under a fixed exchange-rate system. The *MP* curve is horizontal at $\bar{r}$, but becomes upward sloping at higher levels of the real interest rate, just as it does under a floating exchange-rate system. Panel (b) shows how expansionary monetary policy affects the *MP* curve. An increase in the inflation target shifts the *MP* curve to the right, from MP_1 to MP_2, but it can never reduce the real interest rate below $\bar{r}$. Therefore, there is a limit to how much monetary policy can reduce the real interest rate, while maintaining the fixed exchange rate. A decrease in the inflation target shifts the *MP* curve to the left, from MP_1 to MP_3. Regardless of what happens to the *MP* curve, it is always horizontal at $\bar{r}$.

Equilibrium with a Fixed Exchange Rate

Figure 15.11 shows equilibrium in the *IS–MP* model when we account for the shape of the *MP* curve under a fixed exchange-rate system. Equilibrium occurs at point *A*, where the *IS* and *MP*

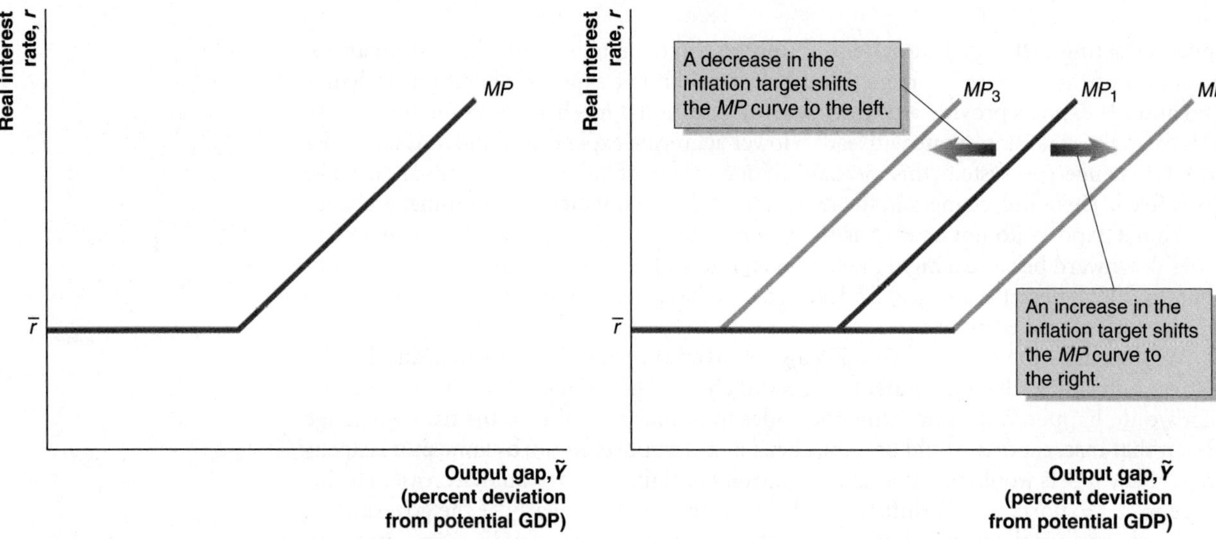

Figure 15.10 The *MP* Curve Under a Fixed Exchange-Rate System

Panel (a) shows the *MP* curve under a fixed exchange-rate system. At low levels of output, the *MP* curve is horizontal but then begins to rise, just like it does under a floating exchange-rate system. Panel (b) shows that an increase in the inflation target shifts the *MP* curve to the right, and a decrease in the inflation target shifts the *MP* curve to the left. ●

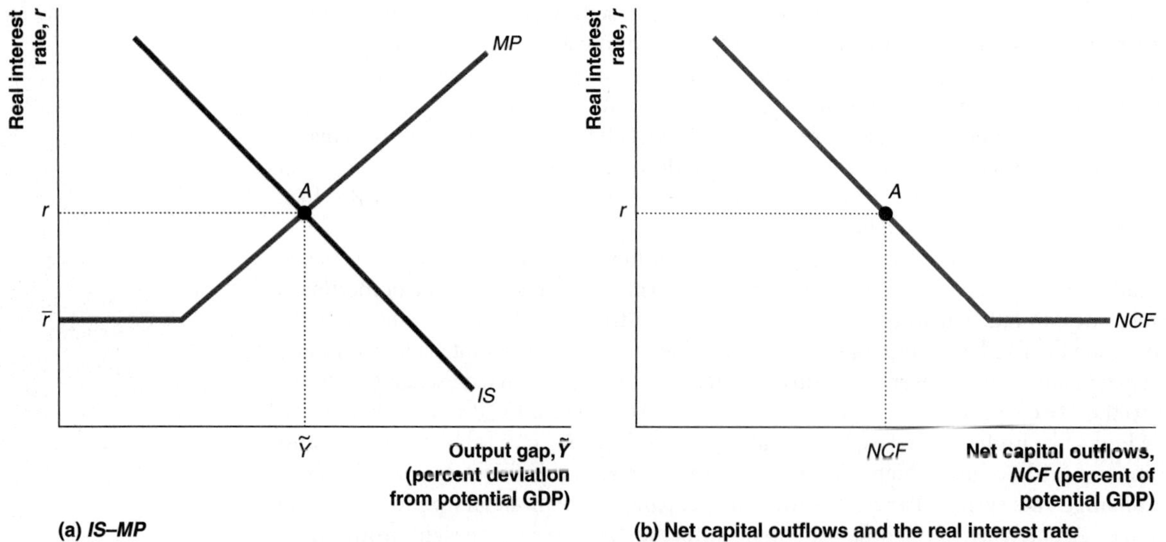

Figure 15.11 Equilibrium in the *IS–MP* Model with a Fixed Exchange Rate

Equilibrium occurs in panel (a), where the *IS* and *MP* curves intersect. The *MP* curve is horizontal when the real interest rate decreases to $\bar{r}$, but it then slopes upward to allow for the tendency of central banks to increase real interest rates as output increases. Panel (b) shows that net capital outflows decrease as the real interest rate increases. If net capital outflows are negative, then the central bank is acquiring foreign-exchange reserves, which makes it easier to maintain the fixed exchange-rate system. However, if net capital outflows are positive, then foreign-exchange reserves are decreasing, which can make it more difficult to maintain the fixed exchange-rate system. ●

curves intersect. The *IS–MP* model in panel (a) determines the equilibrium real interest rate, just as it does under a floating exchange-rate system. The equilibrium real interest rate then determines net capital outflows in panel (b). At high domestic real interest rates, net capital outflows are negative, so investors want to purchase domestic assets. These purchases increase the demand for the domestic currency, so the central bank acquires foreign-exchange reserves as currency traders swap foreign currency for the domestic currency. At low domestic real interest rates, net capital outflows are positive, so investors want to sell domestic assets. These sales decrease the demand for the domestic currency, so the central bank loses foreign-exchange reserves as currency traders swap domestic currency for foreign currency.

Policy with a Fixed Exchange Rate

A fixed exchange-rate system has important implications for the effectiveness of monetary and fiscal policy. We start by discussing fiscal policy.

Fiscal Policy Figure 15.12 shows the effect of an increase in government purchases of goods and services. In panel (a), an expansionary fiscal policy in Mexico shifts the *IS* curve to the right, from IS_1 to IS_2, just as it does under a floating exchange-rate system. The increase in real GDP puts upward pressure on inflation and the Bank of Mexico responds by increasing the real interest rate from r_1 to r_2 as the short-run equilibrium moves from point *A* to point *B*. The higher real interest rate makes investment in Mexico more attractive, so investors purchase more Mexican assets and net capital outflows decrease from NCF_1 to NCF_2, as shown in panel (b). To purchase Mexican assets, investors need Mexican

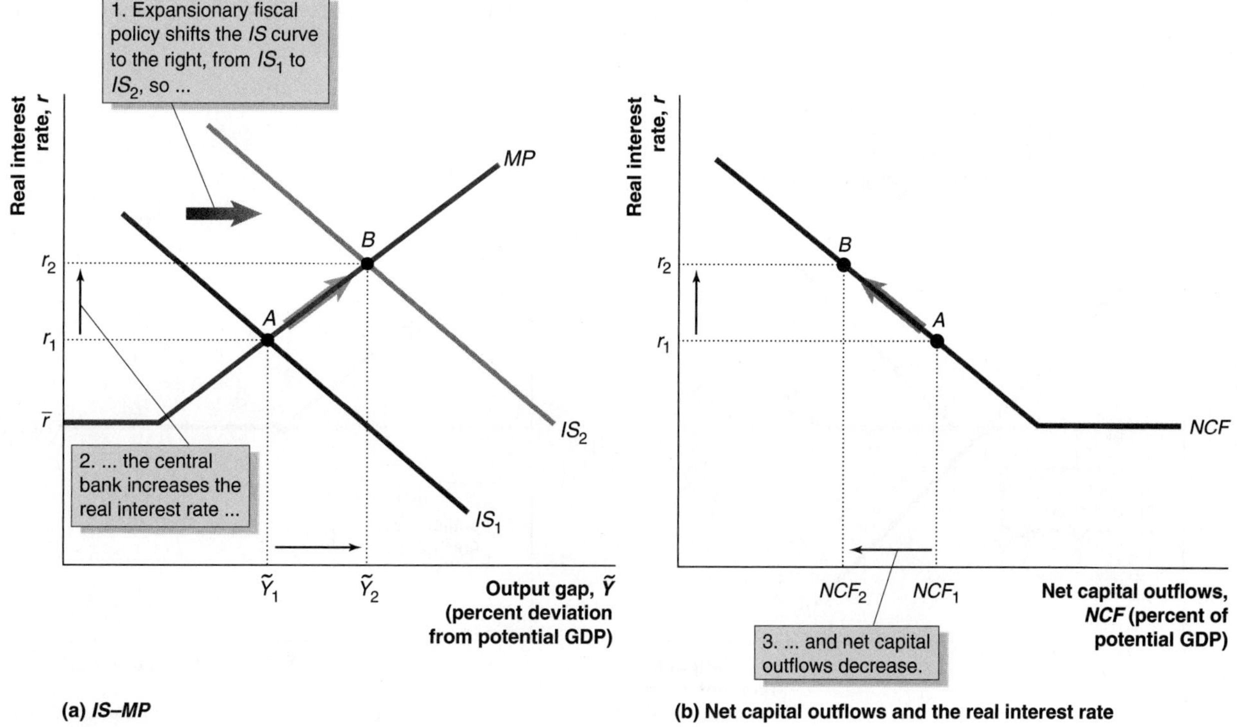

Figure 15.12 **An Expansionary Fiscal Policy with Fixed Exchange Rates**

An increase in government purchases increases the real interest rate in panel (a). The increase in the real interest rate causes net capital outflows to decrease in panel (b), so the central bank acquires foreign-exchange reserves. ●

pesos, so the Bank of Mexico acquires foreign-exchange reserves to help maintain the fixed exchange-rate system. Because expansionary fiscal policy leads to a higher real exchange rate and greater foreign-exchange reserves, a fixed exchange-rate system does not prevent the government from conducting expansionary fiscal policy.

Monetary Policy Figure 15.13 shows the effect of an expansionary monetary policy, as represented by an increase in the inflation target. As long as the initial real interest rate is greater than $\bar{r}$, the central bank can increase the output gap by increasing the target inflation rate to shift the *MP* curve to the right, from MP_1 to MP_2. However, once the *IS* curve intersects the *MP* curve where the real interest rate is $\bar{r}$, the central bank cannot increase real GDP and the output gap and maintain the fixed exchange rate. If the central bank increases the inflation target so that the *MP* curve shifts from MP_1 to MP_2, as shown in panel (a), the *IS* and *MP* curves still intersect at the same point. Therefore, the increase in the inflation target does not increase real GDP and the output gap. Even if the real interest rate is greater than $\bar{r}$, net capital outflows may be positive, so the central bank will lose foreign-exchange reserves. Once the central bank exhausts its foreign-exchange reserves, the government will be forced to abandon the fixed exchange rate or to devalue the currency. A fixed exchange rate clearly puts severe limits on the ability of monetary policy to stimulate the economy. We now discuss the monetary policy of *currency devaluation.*

Devaluing the Currency If a country operates under a fixed exchange-rate system, policymakers have an additional way to affect the economy. The government can decide to maintain a fixed exchange-rate system but with a devalued currency. If the government devalues the currency, then there is a one-time decrease in the nominal exchange rate. The decrease in the nominal exchange rates will make exports cheaper and imports more

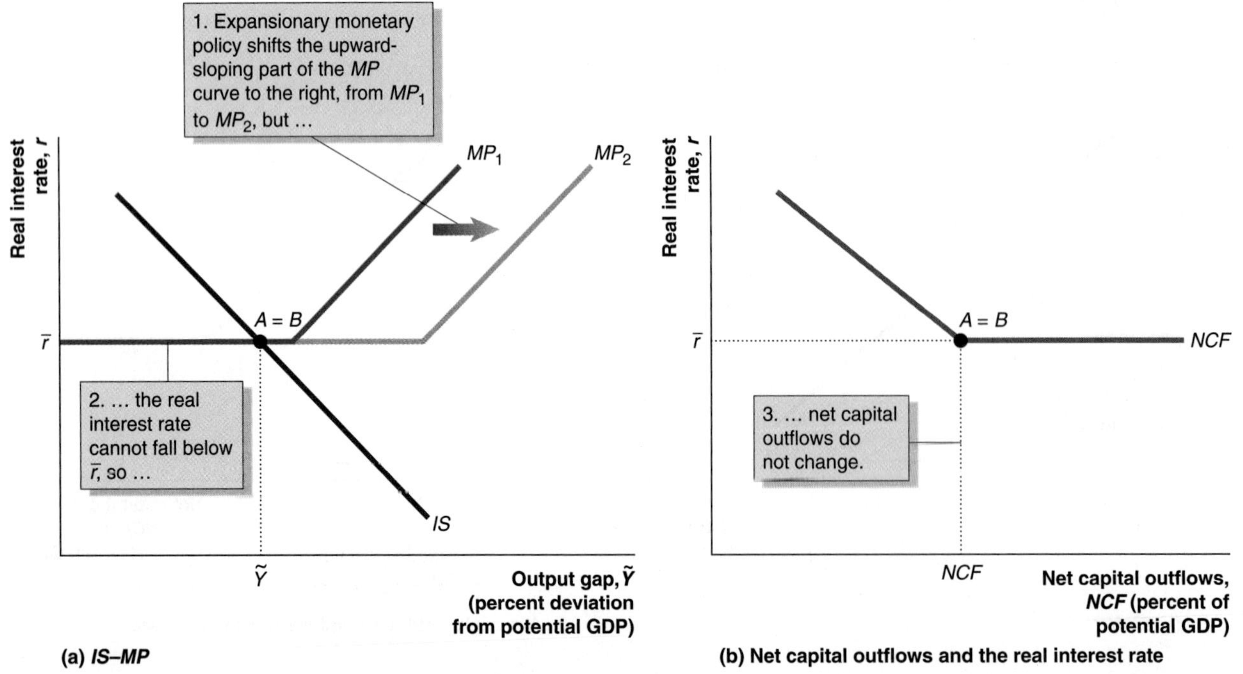

Figure 15.13 An Expansionary Monetary Policy with Fixed Exchange Rates

If the real interest rate is already at the lower bound of $\bar{r}$ in panel (a), then the central bank cannot use an increase in the inflation target to simultaneously increase output and maintain the fixed exchange rate. Therefore, net capital outflows and net exports do not change in panel (b). ●

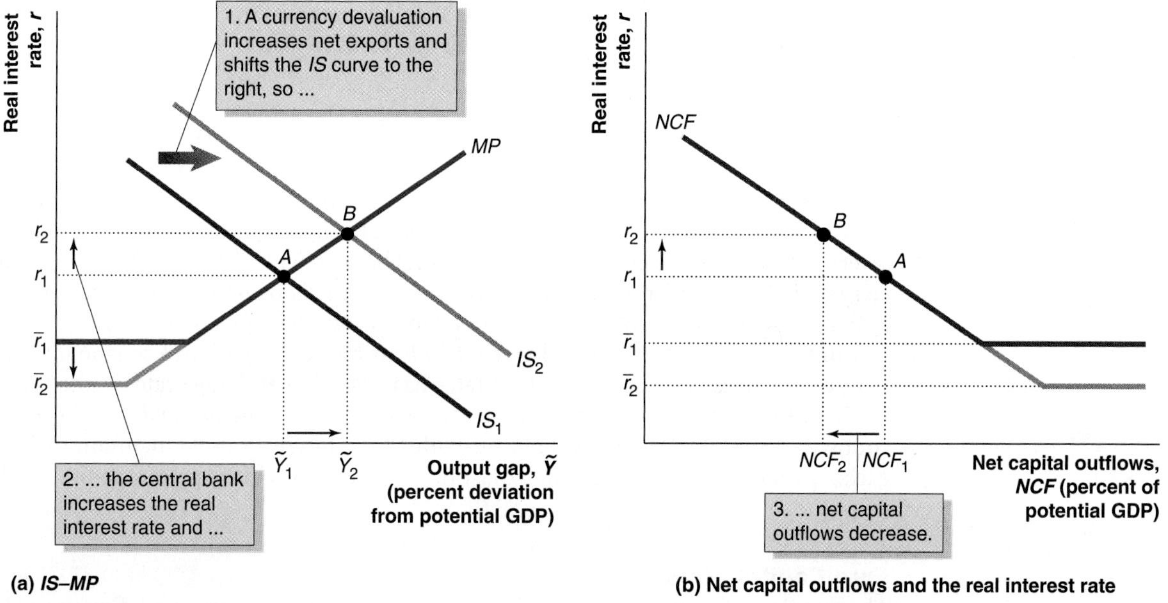

Figure 15.14 A Currency Devaluation

A currency devaluation increases net exports, so the *IS* curve shifts to the right from IS_1 to IS_2 in panel (a). In addition, $\bar{r}$ decreases from $\bar{r}_1$ to $\bar{r}_2$, so the horizontal portion of the *MP* curve shifts down. The increase in the real interest rate causes net capital outflows to decrease in panel (b), so the central bank acquires foreign exchange reserves. ●

expensive, so net exports will increase. Figure 15.14 shows that the increase in net exports will shift the *IS* curve to the right from IS_1 to IS_2, in panel (a). It is possible for the central bank to lower the real interest rate even further while still maintaining the new lower nominal exchange rate so the horizontal portion of the *MP* and *NCF* curves decrease from $\bar{r}_1$ to $\bar{r}_2$. As a result of these changes, the output gap and the real interest rate increase in panel (a). The higher real interest rate causes net capital outflows to decrease in panel (b).

The Policy Trilemma for Economic Policy

15.7 Learning Objective
Discuss the problems that the policy trilemma poses for policymakers.

In an open economy, policymakers generally pursue three goals:

1. Exchange-rate stability
2. Monetary policy independence
3. Free capital flows

Exchange-Rate Stability

All else being equal, exchange-rate stability is desirable because it reduces the uncertainty of conducting buying, selling, and investing across borders. And if exchange rates are stable, households and firms find it easier to make investment and savings decisions. For example, if a U.S. firm knows that the exchange rate between the U.S. dollar and the Mexican peso will always be 12.8 pesos per dollar, then it is easier for the firm to know whether it will be profitable to build a factory in Mexico to export goods to the United States. Uncertainty about the exchange rate makes the U.S. firm less likely to invest in Mexico. It also means that U.S. investors are less willing to purchase Mexican assets, such as stocks and bonds, due to the risk that the exchange rate will change and reduce the rate of return on the investment. Remember that the nominal exchange rate is a price, so the benefits of nominal exchange-rate stability are similar to the benefits of price stability discussed in Chapter 6. Stable nominal exchange rates make it easier for households and firms to plan.

Monetary Policy Independence

If monetary policy can respond to demand and supply shocks, then it is possible for monetary policy to reduce the severity of business cycles. Recall that one of the reasons that economists think that business cycles were so mild from the early 1980s to 2007 was that monetary policy effectively responded to shocks. Effective monetary policy can reduce the severity of business cycles, but it requires central bank independence. In this context, monetary policy independence means the ability of the central bank to use monetary policy to achieve macroeconomic objectives such as stable prices and high employment.

In the United States, the Fed is free to adjust monetary policy to pursue macroeconomic objectives because the United States has a floating exchange rate, so the Fed does not have to adjust nominal interest rates to maintain the value of the dollar. In contrast, countries with fixed exchange rates must adjust the interest rate to maintain their fixed exchange rate, so they cannot also adjust interest rates to achieve price stability and high employment.

Free Capital Flows

The free flow of capital across borders is the third desirable policy goal. Equation (15.2) on page 566 tells us that one way for households and firms to finance gross private investment expenditures is through capital inflows. Capital inflows can also finance government budget deficits so that the domestic government does not have to raise taxes or cut expenditures. Therefore, capital inflows help countries smooth consumption over time.

While access to capital inflows seems desirable, some countries believe that large capital inflows make economic activity more volatile. For example, a large increase in capital outflows will reduce the demand for the domestic currency and lead to a rapid depreciation of the currency. The rapid depreciation of the currency interrupts trade flows and can make critical imports, such as food and fuel, much more expensive for households and firms. As a result, some countries impose capital controls—that is, legal limits or restrictions on the flow of financial capital into and out of a country. Capital controls can limit the destructive swings in the nominal exchange rate by limiting the ability of capital to flow into and out of a country. In the extreme, capital controls may prohibit international transactions in assets such as stocks and bonds, or capital controls may require official government permission to engage in these international transactions. Alternatively, governments may impose taxes on international transactions that make these transactions more costly and, therefore, discourage or limit their volume. In recent years, developing countries such as Brazil (1993–1997), Chile (1991–1998), Colombia (1993–1998), Malaysia (1998–1999), and Thailand (1995–1997) have all used capital controls to restrict short-term capital flows into and out of their countries.

The Policy Trilemma for Economic Policy

Policy trilemma The hypothesis that it is impossible for a country to have exchange-rate stability, monetary policy independence, and free capital flows at the same time.

The hypothesis that it is impossible for a country to have exchange-rate stability, monetary policy independence, and free capital flows at the same time is called the **policy trilemma**. This hypothesis is based on the work of Nobel Laureate Robert Mundell of Columbia University and Marcus Flemming of the International Monetary Fund. If the hypothesis is correct, it is possible to achieve at most two of the policy goals at the same time. Therefore, policymakers must choose which goal they do not wish to pursue. Figure 15.15 shows the policy trilemma. Each side of the triangle indicates one of the desirable policy goals, and each point of the triangle indicates which policy goal is unattainable.

The lower left of the triangle indicates that if policymakers choose to allow free capital flows and have an independent monetary policy, they must let the exchange rate float. The United States currently allows free flow of capital, and the Federal Reserve is free to use

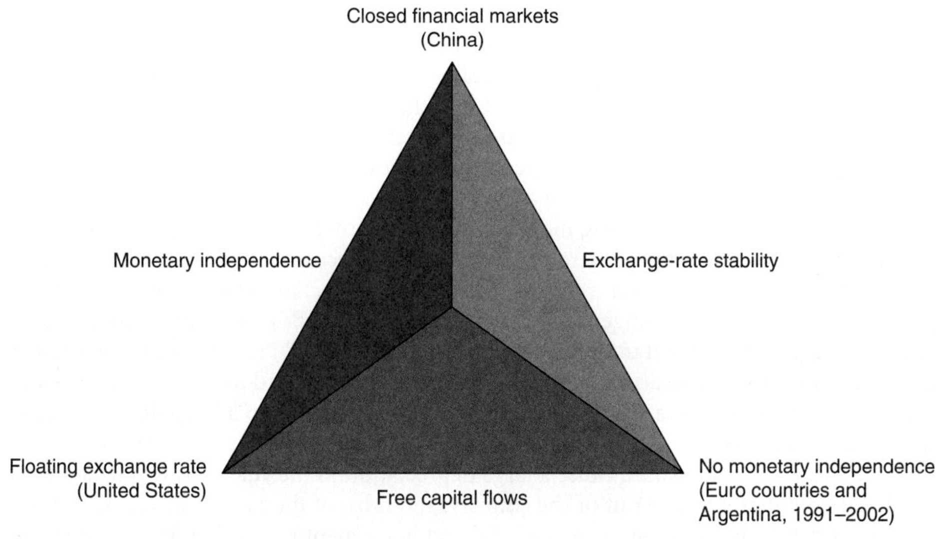

Figure 15.15

The Policy Trilemma

It is impossible for a country to achieve the goals of exchange-rate stability, monetary policy independence, and free capital flows at the same time. At most, a country can achieve two of the three goals, and there is no clear consensus on which two are the best to pursue. ●

monetary policy to pursue macroeconomic objectives such as low inflation and high employment. As a consequence, the United States must let the U.S. dollar float in foreign-exchange markets. Why? Equation (15.6) on page 572 tells us that changes in the nominal exchange rate depend not only on domestic monetary policy but also on monetary policy in other countries. If the Federal Reserve uses monetary policy to keep inflation low, then the U.S. dollar will appreciate or depreciate depending on the monetary policy in other countries. Figure 15.4 on page 569 shows that the United States has, in fact, experienced large fluctuations in the exchange rate. These fluctuations have created exchange-rate risk for U.S. firms and households seeking to invest abroad and for foreign firms and households seeking to invest in the United States. All else being equal, this extra element of risk should reduce the amount of investment.

The lower-right point of the triangle indicates that if policymakers choose to allow free capital flows and achieve exchange-rate stability, then they must give up monetary policy independence. Argentina from 1991 to 2002 maintained a currency board that exchanged Argentine pesos for U.S. dollars at the rate of 1 peso per dollar. Argentina also allowed free capital flows across its borders, so it could not use monetary policy to respond to macroeconomic shocks. Why? Consider what would happen if the Federal Reserve increased interest rates in the United States. The increase would make U.S. assets more attractive relative to Argentine assets, so investors would sell Argentine assets to purchase U.S. assets. This shift would decrease the demand for Argentine pesos, so the peso would depreciate below the official exchange rate to, say, \$0.50 per peso. To maintain the official exchange rate of \$1 per peso, the Argentine currency board would have to use dollars to purchase pesos. Consequently, the supply of pesos in the foreign-exchange market would fall, so the peso would appreciate back to \$1 per peso. If a country such as Argentina wants to keep a fixed exchange rate in addition to free capital flows, the country must use monetary policy to maintain the official exchange rate.

A fixed exchange rate does have some downsides. First, the country loses the ability to use monetary policy to reduce the severity of economic fluctuations. Argentina experienced a series of negative macroeconomic shocks during the 1990s. Because Argentina pegged the value of its currency to the U.S. dollar, Argentina was unable to use monetary policy to reduce the severity of those shocks. Second, maintaining a fixed exchange rate requires that the central bank have enough foreign currency reserves to intervene in foreign-exchange markets as necessary. If the central bank does not have enough foreign currency reserves, then it cannot maintain the official exchange rate and must devalue the currency.

Such a devaluation can occur suddenly and can be very large, leading to disruptions in economic activity. In particular, developing countries often borrow in a foreign currency, such as euros or U.S. dollars, so a devaluation increases the cost of making payments on the debt.

In addition, if investors begin to expect that the central bank will run out of reserves, then investors might start to sell the currency. Even if the central bank initially has enough foreign currency reserves, this type of speculative attack can quickly exhaust those reserves. When the reserves are exhausted, the country has no choice but to devalue its currency. Given the large volume of trading in foreign-exchange markets each day, most countries with fixed exchange rates are vulnerable to this type of speculative attack on the currency.

The top of the triangle indicates that, if policymakers choose monetary policy independence and a stable exchange rate, they must restrict the flow of capital. China maintains an independent monetary policy and has essentially fixed the value of the yuan, also known as the renminbi, relative to foreign currencies, so it has had to restrict capital flows. Why? If China allowed free capital flows, it would be vulnerable to a large drop in the demand for Chinese assets, which would reduce the demand for its currency. This reduction in the demand for yuan would cause a large depreciation in the yuan. However, China restricts capital flows into and out of the country, and most of the foreign investment in the country is in the form of long-term foreign direct investment rather than in short-term financial assets such as stocks and bonds. As a result, the value of the assets that foreigners own in China is relatively stable, so the demand for yuan in foreign-exchange markets is also relatively stable. For example, during 1997, many Asian countries, such as Indonesia, South Korea, and Thailand, experienced dramatic devaluations of their currencies as foreign capital fled those countries. However, China was able to maintain the stability of the yuan partly because the country restricted the outflow of foreign capital.

Answering the Key Question

Continued from page 559

At the beginning of this chapter, we asked:

"How does the choice of exchange-rate system affect monetary policy and fiscal policy?"

Fluctuations in nominal exchange rates, net exports, and net capital outflows can be important sources of economic fluctuations. The choice of exchange-rate system also has important consequences for economic policy. Under a floating exchange-rate system, monetary policy and fiscal policy operate similarly to policy in a closed economy—with one exception. Because monetary policy and fiscal policy affect the real interest rate, these policies also affect the nominal exchange rate and net exports. Under a fixed exchange-rate system, the nominal exchange rate does not fluctuate. However, the desire to fix the nominal exchange rate limits the extent to which expansionary monetary policy can reduce the real interest rate to increase output. If the real interest rate falls too low, the central bank will exhaust its foreign-exchange reserves and will be forced to abandon the fixed exchange-rate system or devalue the currency.

Read *An Inside Look at Policy* for a discussion of revised estimates by the U.S. Treasury Department, which show that U.S. Treasuries held by China and Russia increased substantially by 2011, while the holdings of Canada and the United Kingdom were significantly smaller.

China Owns More U.S. Debt than Previously Thought

FINANCIAL TIMES

China Holds $1,160bn of US Debt

The US Treasury has dramatically revised data on foreign holdings of US government debt, estimating that China owns more Treasuries than previously thought while the UK holds only about half as much.

a The figures released on Monday suggest fears that China has been reducing its US dollar holdings may have been overstated.

Richard Gilhooly, strategist at TD Securities, estimated that the new data means that 42 percent of China's reserves are in Treasuries, compared with his previous estimate of 32 percent.

"The figures definitely suggest that worries about China diversifying away from Treasuries are overblown," he said. "They are still by far the largest [foreign] holder, and if you are worried about concentration among holders, that concern still remains."

The revised figures show that China owned $1,160bn of Treasuries at the end of 2010, compared with a prior estimate of $892bn, published only two weeks ago.

The estimate of UK holdings was slashed to $272bn from $541bn, which suggests that much of the strong foreign buying of Treasury securities over the past year has involved investors using London as a financial centre.

b The revised figures also show a large rise in foreign central-bank holdings of Treasuries at the expense of the private sector.

Foreign central banks held $3,156bn of Treasuries, compared with the previous estimate of $2,800bn.

Overall foreign holdings of Treasuries were revised up to $4,440bn from $4,373bn.

c The new figures could ease concerns about demand for Treasuries once the Federal Reserve stops buying government bonds under its policy of quantitative easing, or QE2, in June.

"The concern that Treasury yields have to rise in order to attract private buying once the Fed ends QE2 may be overstated," said Dominic Konstam, head of interest rate strategy at Deutsche Bank. "The revised data gives us an extra degree of comfort once the Fed stops buying Treasuries."

In other sharp revisions, Canada's holding of Treasuries dropped to $77bn from $135bn, while Russia's rose to $151bn from $106bn.

Japan, the second-largest foreign holder, was relatively steady at $882bn, against a prior figure of $884bn.

Even with the revised numbers, China still owns a little less US government debt than the Fed itself.

The US central bank currently holds $1,205bn in Treasuries and is expected to own $1,600bn by the end of June when QE2 comes to an end.

Source: Michael Mackenzie, "China holds $1,160bn of US debt," *Financial Times,* March 1, 2011. From *The Financial Times*.

Key Points in the Article

This article discusses the U.S. Treasury Department's revised estimates of foreign holdings of U.S. government debt. The data, revised from figures released just two weeks earlier, show that U.S. Treasuries held by China and Russia increased substantially, while the holdings of Canada and the United Kingdom were significantly smaller. The increase in Chinese holdings were almost exactly offset by the decrease in U.K. holdings, suggesting that the original estimates did not take into account Chinese purchases of U.S. Treasuries via London financial centers. The revised data show that as of February 28, 2011, China held $1,160 billion in U.S. government debt, slightly less than the $1,205 billion held by the U.S. Federal Reserve.

Analyzing the News

a During the first half of 2010, data indicated that China was reducing its holdings of U.S. Treasury securities. As the bar graph on this page shows, since 2002, Chinese holdings of U.S. Treasuries rose from just over $100 billion to over $900 billion by 2009. The original estimates from 2010 showed a slight decrease in holdings, causing some concern that the Chinese government had become reluctant to continue purchasing and holding U.S. government debt. The revised figures from February 2011 indicate that this concern may have been exaggerated. The February data report that China's holdings of U.S. Treasury securities totaled $1,160 billion, $268 billion more than reported by the December 2010 data shown in the bar graph.

b According to the revised figures, foreign central banks increased their holdings of U.S. Treasury securities by $356 billion, with overall foreign holdings increasing by $67 billion to $4,440 billion, slightly less than half of the total value of U.S. Treasury securities held by the public. Other recent key buyers of U.S. Treasuries include U.S. households, private pension funds, and commercial banks.

c The Federal Reserve's second round of quantitative easing, dubbed QE2, was scheduled to end in June 2011, at which time the Fed was expected to hold $1,600 billion in U.S. Treasuries. The initial belief that China was reducing its holdings of Treasuries raised concerns that the yield on the Treasury securities would need to rise to attract buyers, especially once the QE2 purchases had ended. The revised data seem to have eased some of these concerns, and indicates that demand remains strong for U.S. Treasury securities.

THINKING CRITICALLY *ABOUT POLICY*

1. Initial data showed that China and other foreign nations were decreasing their holdings of U.S. Treasury securities, but the revised data indicates these holdings are actually increasing. Explain what happens to the U.S. balance of payments and net capital outflow when foreign countries either increase or decrease their purchases of U.S. Treasury securities. How might the original and the revised figures impact interest rates in the United States and the value of the U.S. dollar?
2. The increase in foreign purchases of U.S. Treasury securities over the past few years has helped the U.S. government finance its growing budget deficits and increased spending. What is the effect of increased government expenditures on the U.S. dollar and on U.S. net exports? Illustrate and explain your answer using graphs for *IS-MP* and net capital outflows.

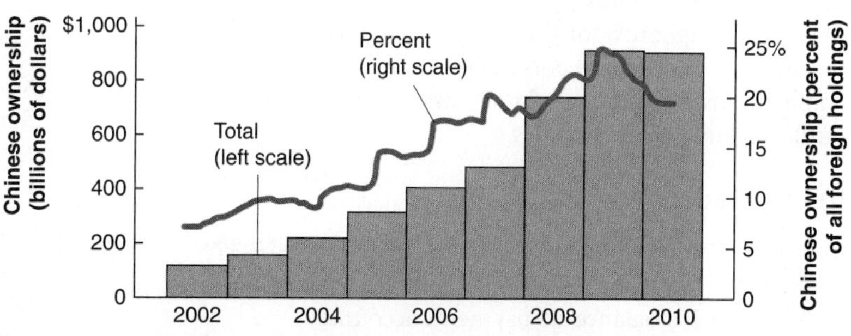

China's revised holdings of U.S. Treasury securities

Sources: Federal Reserve and U.S. Treasury ●

CHAPTER SUMMARY AND PROBLEMS

KEY TERMS

Balance-of-payments accounts, p. 562
Capital account, p. 562
Closed economy, p. 561
Currency appreciation, p. 569
Currency board, p. 573
Currency depreciation, p. 569
Current account, p. 562
Financial account, p. 562
Fixed exchange-rate system, p. 573
Floating exchange-rate system, p. 573
Managed float exchange-rate system, p. 574
Net capital outflows, p. 565
Nominal exchange rate, p. 562
Open economy, p. 561
Policy trilemma, p. 590
Purchasing power parity, p. 571
Real exchange rate, p. 570

15.1 The Balance of Payments

Explain how to calculate the balance of payments.

SUMMARY

In a **closed economy**, households, firms, and governments do not borrow, lend, and trade internationally. In an **open economy**, these activities take place. The **nominal exchange rate** is the price of one currency in terms of another currency. The **balance-of-payments account** is a measure of all flows of private and government funds between domestic and foreign economies. The **financial account** records purchases of assets a country has made abroad and foreign purchases of assets in the country. The **capital account** records only relatively minor transactions, so we tend to ignore it for simplicity. The **current account** records a country's net exports, net investment income, and net transfers. **Net capital outflows** equal capital outflows minus capital inflows.

Review Questions

1.1 Describe how the importance of trade has changed over time as a percentage of GDP.

1.2 What is a balance-of-payments account?

1.3 Describe the components of the current account.

1.4 Describe the components of the capital account.

1.5 Describe the components of the financial account.

Problems and Applications

1.6 Which balance-of-payments account would be associated with each of the following items?

a. An export of goods
b. A purchase of bonds
c. A gift to someone in another country
d. A dividend paid from stock owned in another country

1.7 Balance-of-payments accounting always involves double entries because the inflow of goods and services is always accompanied by financial outflows and vice versa. For each of the following scenarios, show how both sides of the transaction are recorded in the balance of payments.

a. A U.S. tourist goes to Mexico and pays for the trip with funds previously held in a Mexican bank account. (Assume that the value of the trip is $5,000.)
b. The U.S. government gives $1,000,000 in foreign aid to Iraq.
c. Kodak, a U.S. company, sells photographic film in Europe and receives €50,000 in exchange. (Assume that the exchange rate is $1 = €1.)
d. Kodak exchanges the €50,000 received in the previous transaction for dollars at the Federal Reserve Bank of New York.
e. A French investor sells $200,000 worth of stock in a U.S. company and puts the proceeds into a bank in the United States.

1.8 Consider the following statement: "Because the percentage of U.S. GDP accounted for by trade is much less than for many other countries, trade is not very important to the United States." Do you agree with this statement? Briefly explain.

1.9 If every balance-of-payments entry is offset by another (opposite) flow, how is it possible for countries to have balance-of-payments surpluses or deficits? Briefly explain.

Visit www.myeconlab.com to complete these exercises online and get instant feedback.

15.2 The Balance of Payments and National Income Accounting

Explain the relationship between the balance of payments and national income accounting.

SUMMARY

Net capital outflows are a source of funds for domestic spending, so we can link the balance-of-payments to the national income accounts using Equation (15.2) on page 566,

$$I = S_{\text{Household}} + S_{\text{Government}} - NCF,$$

which says that private investment equals private saving plus government saving minus net capital outflows. The United States has run persistent current account deficits since the early 1980s. As a result, the United States became a net debtor nation in 1986, and is now the world's largest debtor nation.

Review Questions

2.1 Explain why the financial account represents the reverse flow of the current account.

2.2 How is the savings–investment relationship affected by capital flows?

2.3 What is a debtor nation? A creditor nation?

Problems and Applications

2.4 Current account deficits are typically viewed as negative factors for a country. However, current account deficits are accompanied by capital inflows. How can capital inflows be beneficial for a country? Explain.

2.5 Suppose that a country with a closed economy has private saving of $5 trillion and a government budget deficit of $3 trillion.

a. What is the equilibrium level of investment?

b. If the economy is open and has net capital inflow of $6 trillion, what is the level of investment?

c. Explain how an open economy can allow a country to run a budget deficit and still have a high level of investment.

2.6 Consider the following statement: "An increase in the current account deficit must be caused by an increase in imports." Do you agree with this statement? Briefly explain.

2.7 **[Related to *Making the Connection* on page 568]** In 2005, Hurricane Katrina hit New Orleans and the Louisiana and Texas coasts, causing damages estimated at around $81 billion, the costliest natural disaster in U.S. history. Federal government agencies spent millions of dollars on aid and rebuilding.

a. What would you expect to happen to the federal budget deficit as a result of this expenditure?

b. What would you expect to happen to net capital outflow for the United States?

c. As discussed in the *Making the Connection*, the magnitude of the cost of the Japanese rebuilding efforts, coupled with the size of the Japanese national debt, could affect the ability of Japan to continue to borrow internationally. Did Hurricane Katrina create similar worries in the United States? Briefly explain.

15.3 Nominal and Real Exchange Rates

Distinguish between the nominal and real exchange rates.

SUMMARY

The nominal exchange rate is the price of one currency in terms of another currency, while the **real exchange rate** is the rate at which goods and services in one country can be exchanged for goods and services in another country. A **currency appreciation** occurs when the value of a currency increases or, in other words, the currency can now buy more of another country's currency; a **currency depreciation** occurs when the value of a currency decreases or in other words the currency now buys less of another country's currency. According to the theory of **purchasing power parity**, the nominal exchange rate will adjust in the long run to equalize the purchasing power of different currencies. For example, one Big Mac in the United States should trade for one Big Mac in Mexico or any other country. The theory also supports Equation (15.6) on page 572:

$$\%\text{ change in } E^{\text{Domestic}} = \pi^{\text{Foreign}} - \pi^{\text{Domestic}},$$

which indicates that in the long run the inflation rate in each of the two countries is the key determinant of the

nominal exchange rate between the two countries. For example, if the inflation rate is higher in the United States than in Mexico, the U.S. dollar will depreciate against the Mexican peso. Similarly, if the inflation rate is lower in the United States, the U.S. dollar will appreciate.

Review Questions

3.1 How was the value of the dollar determined under the Bretton Woods system?

3.2 What term do economists use to describe the value of a currency rising relative to another currency? What term do economists use to describe the value of a currency falling relative to another currency?

3.3 What is the difference between a nominal exchange rate and a real exchange rate?

3.4 What is purchasing power parity?

3.5 Why doesn't purchasing power parity always hold?

Problems and Applications

3.6 If the euro appreciates, how will this affect your purchases of U.S. and German goods? Explain.

3.7 Suppose that you are planning to study abroad in Mexico for a semester. In planning for your trip, you calculate what you spend in a semester in the United States. Then you check to see what the current exchange rate is.

a. If you spend $2,000 per semester on food, entertainment, and other incidental expenses in Mexico, and if the current exchange rate is $1 = 12 pesos, how many pesos do you need if your expenses are identical?

b. Assuming that you consume the same amount of food and other goods no matter where you are in Mexico, do you think that this method will correctly calculate the number of pesos you need for your trip? Briefly explain.

3.8 In each of the following cases, calculate the nominal exchange rate assuming purchasing power parity holds.

a. A bottle of wine sells for $16 in the United States and €10 in France.

b. A book sells for $10 in the United States and ¥950 in Japan.

c. A shirt sells for $45 in the United States and £30 in the United Kingdom.

3.9 If you were an importer or exporter, why might you prefer an exchange-rate system like Bretton Woods to the current system?

3.10 Suppose that the inflation rate in the United States is 5%, and the inflation rate in the United Kingdom is 8%. Use purchasing power parity to explain what is likely to happen to the value of the British pound (relative to the dollar).

15.4 The Foreign-Exchange Market and Exchange Rates

Explain how exchange rates are determined and how changes in exchange rates affect the prices of imports and exports.

SUMMARY

Most foreign-exchange transactions happen in either the United Kingdom or the United States and involve major currencies such as the U.S. dollar, the euro, the yen, or the British pound. The market is global and operates 24 hours a day, with over $4 trillion of transactions in a single day. Therefore, the market is highly liquid and likely to be close to equilibrium. Currencies can trade under two basic types of systems. Under a **fixed exchange-rate system**, the exchange rate is set by the government, and the central bank agrees to buy and sell the domestic currency to ensure that the fixed exchange rate prevails in the market. A **currency board** is an extreme version of the fixed exchange-rate system where the government maintains complete convertibility of the domestic currency into the anchor currency of another nation. Argentina operated a form of a currency board from 1991 to 2002, using the U.S. dollar as the anchor currency. Under a **floating exchange-rate system**, the government allows the value of its currency to fluctuate with demand and supply conditions in the foreign-exchange market. Most countries have adopted a **managed float exchange-rate system**, under which the government intervenes in the foreign-exchange market only rarely. The demand for the domestic currency in foreign-exchange markets is driven by foreign households and firms that want to purchase domestic goods and services or purchase domestic assets. Currency traders also purchase the domestic currency when they believe that the currency will appreciate in value in the future. The supply of the domestic currency in foreign-exchange markets is driven by domestic firms and households wanting to purchase foreign goods and services or purchase foreign assets. Currency traders also sell the domestic currency when they believe it will depreciate in value in the future.

Review Questions

4.1 What is a fixed exchange-rate system?

4.2 Give two examples of fixed exchange-rate systems and how they work.

4.3 Why would a country want to have a currency board?

4.4 What is a floating exchange-rate system? What is a managed float?

4.5 In a foreign-exchange market, who are the demanders of currency? In a foreign-exchange market, who are the suppliers of currency?

4.6 What factors shift the demand for a currency? What factors shift the supply of a currency?

Problems and Applications

4.7 **[Related to *Solved Problem 15.4* on page 577]** Use a graph of the foreign-exchange market to explain the likely effect of the March 2011 tsunami in Japan on the relative value of the dollar and the yen.

4.8 The graph below shows the market for yuan:

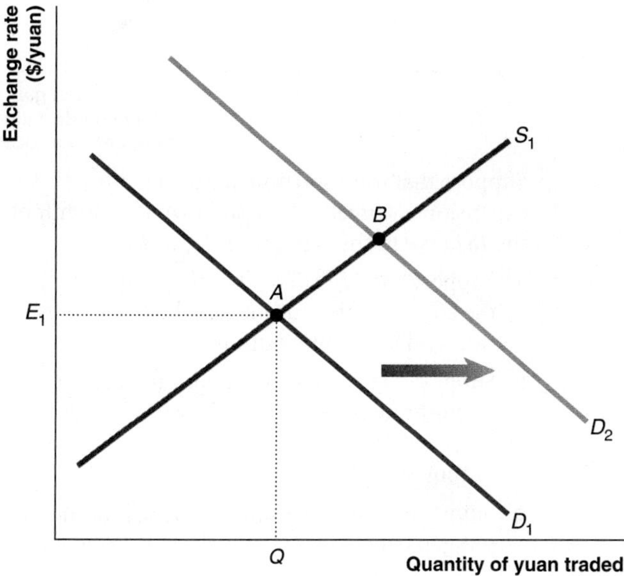

Suppose that the market for yuan and dollars is in equilibrium at point *A*. An increase in demand for Chinese exports causes the demand for yuan to shift to the right.

a. If the Chinese central bank wants to keep the exchange rate fixed at E_1, what must it do? Explain and demonstrate on the graph.

b. What consequences might the central bank's actions have for the Chinese economy?

4.9 Draw a graph of the market for euros in terms of U.S. dollars. Then show and explain the effect of each of the following changes:

a. There is an increase in demand for U.S. exports.

b. Stock markets in Europe are perceived to be less risky than those in other parts of the world.

c. Economic growth in Europe slows relative to that in the United States.

d. It is believed that the value of the euro will increase in the future.

4.10 During the 1990s, strong U.S. economic growth contributed to the rise of stock markets' values, making financial investment more attractive. At the same time, income growth spurred the demand for imports.

a. How would these factors change the value of the dollar?

b. How would these factors change the trade deficit?

4.11 Some countries with fixed exchange rates have attempted to overvalue their currencies; that is, they have tried to keep the exchange rate above the market rate.

a. How can a country overvalue its currency?

b. Why would a country want to maintain an overvalued currency?

c. Why is it difficult to maintain an overvalued currency for a long period of time? Briefly explain.

15.5 A Short-Run *IS–MP* Model of an Open Economy with a Floating Exchange Rate

Understand the *IS–MP* model of an open economy with a floating exchange rate.

SUMMARY

In a closed economy, the *IS* curve slopes downward because an increase in the real interest rate reduces both consumption and investment expenditures. In an open economy, an increase in the domestic real interest rate also decreases net exports, so there is an additional reason for the downward slope of the *IS* curve. An increase in the domestic real interest rate makes domestic assets more attractive to financial market participants, so net capital outflows decrease. To purchase these assets, currency traders need to purchase the domestic currency, so the demand for the domestic currency increases and the currency appreciates. When the domestic currency appreciates, the price of imports decreases, and the price of exports increases, so net exports decrease. The *MP* curve slopes upward because an increase in output leads to higher inflation, and the central bank responds by increasing the real interest rate. Under a floating exchange rate, expansionary fiscal policy increases output, raises real interest rates, causes an appreciation of the domestic currency, and, so, crowds out net exports. Expansionary monetary policy leads to higher output, lower real interest rates, and a depreciation of the domestic currency. As a consequence, net exports rise.

Review Questions

5.1 How do imports and exports relate to the *IS* curve under a floating exchange-rate system?

5.2 How does a central bank's inflation rate target relate to the shape and position of the *MP* curve under a floating exchange-rate system?

5.3 What are the effects on interest rates and output of expansionary fiscal policy in an open economy?

5.4 What are the effects on interest rates and output of expansionary monetary policy in an open economy?

Problems and Applications

5.5 For each of the following cases, use the *IS–MP* model and the *NCF* curve to explain the effect on the output gap, the real interest rate, and net capital flows, assuming that exchange rates are flexible.

a. Consumers decide to spend more and save less.

b. There is an increase in demand for exports, so net exports increase.

c. Monetary authorities contract the money supply.

d. Expected profits from newly built factories in the domestic economy increase.

5.6 **[Related to *Solved Problem 15.5* on page 582]** The graph below shows the *IS–MP* model. Suppose that the economy is currently in equilibrium at point *A*.

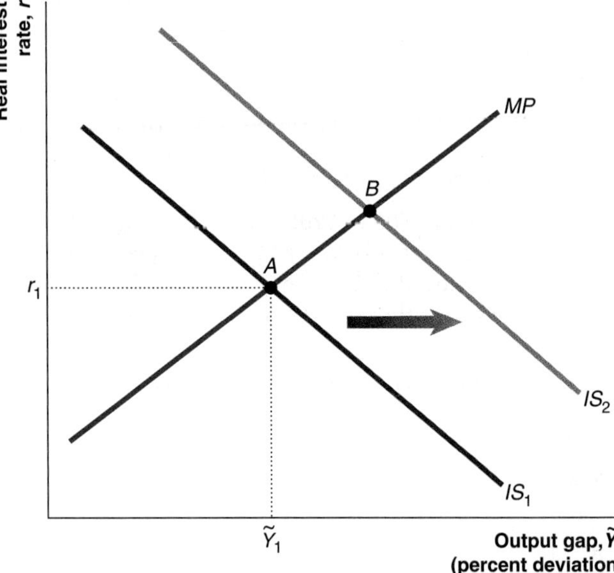

Suppose that the government pursues an expansionary fiscal policy, as shown by the shift of the *IS* curve to the right, from IS_1 to IS_2.

a. Suppose the *MP* curve does not shift. What are the effects on the output gap, the real interest rate, and net capital outflows?

b. Suppose the Fed changes policy to keep the real interest rate constant at its initial value. What are the effects on the output gap, and net capital outflows?

c. Suppose the Fed changes policy to keep the output gap constant at its initial value. What are the effects on the real interest rate and net capital outflows?

5.7 Consider the following statement: "Because monetary policy is more effective in an open economy, it is always a better choice than fiscal policy." Do you agree with this statement? Briefly explain.

5.8 In early April 2011, the European Central Bank (ECB) was expected to raise interest rates, while other major central banks held target interest rates constant.

a. What effect would a rise in European interest rates be expected to have on output in Europe? What effect would it have on net capital flows?

b. How would this rise in European interest rates affect the value of the euro relative to the value of the dollar?

15.6 A Short-Run *IS–MP* Model of an Open Economy with a Fixed Exchange Rate

Understand the *IS–MP* model of an open economy with a fixed exchange rate.

SUMMARY

The central bank can always supply more of the domestic currency, so it faces no difficulty in maintaining the fixed exchange rate as domestic real interest rates increase and domestic assets become more attractive. However, the central bank cannot always supply foreign currency, which limits the ability of the central bank to maintain a fixed exchange-rate system when domestic real interest rates are decreasing and domestic assets become less attractive. A government must have sufficient foreign-exchange reserves to meet the desire of currency traders to sell the domestic currency for foreign currencies. When these foreign-exchange reserves are exhausted, the government has to devalue the currency or abandon the fixed exchange-rate system entirely. Therefore, under a fixed exchange-rate system, there is a limit to how low the domestic real interest rate can go before the government exhausts its foreign-exchange reserves. As a result, the *MP* curve is horizontal at this lower bound for the domestic real interest rate. Expansionary fiscal policies are still effective under fixed exchange-rate systems because such policies lead to higher real interest rates. However, expansionary monetary policy leads to lower domestic real interest rates, so there is a limit to how much the central bank can stimulate the economy while maintaining the fixed exchange-rate system.

Review Questions

6.1 How do imports and exports relate to the *IS* curve under a fixed exchange-rate system?

6.2 How does a central bank's inflation rate target relate to the shape and position of the *MP* curve under a fixed exchange-rate system?

6.3 What are the effects on interest rates and output of expansionary fiscal policy in an open economy with fixed exchange rates?

6.4 What are the effects on interest rates and output of expansionary monetary policy in an open economy with fixed exchange rates?

Problems and Applications

6.5 Repeat problem 5.5, but now assume that the exchange rate is fixed. How are your answers different?

6.6 The International Monetary Fund (IMF) makes loans of currency reserves to countries which are running out of reserves.

a. How would a loan of currency reserves help a country maintain a fixed exchange rate?

b. The IMF makes loans only when it believes that currency problems are temporary. Why would a country have temporary currency problems, and what must happen to the exchange rate if these problems persist?

6.7 A currency devaluation has similar effects to an expansionary fiscal policy.

a. Use the *IS–MP* model to show the effect of a currency devaluation.

b. Why don't countries with fixed exchange rates use devaluation as a common policy tool?

6.8 **[Related to the *Chapter Opener* on page 559]** Unlike countries with currency problems, China has used a fixed exchange rate to keep the value of its currency below its market level.

a. Why is it easier for a country to undervalue a currency than to overvalue it?

b. Why does China's exchange-rate policy affect its purchase of U.S. Treasury securities?

c. What is likely to happen to China's imports, exports, and purchases of U.S. securities if the exchange rate is allowed to float?

15.7 The Policy Trilemma for Economic Policy

Discuss the problems that the policy trilemma poses for policymakers.

SUMMARY

The hypothesis that it is impossible for a country to have exchange-rate stability, monetary policy independence, and free capital flows at the same time is called the **policy trilemma**. At most, a country can achieve two of the three goals. Exchange rate stability reduces the uncertainty of international transactions. Monetary policy independence allows the central bank to use monetary policy to pursue macroeconomic objectives. Free capital flows means that households, firms and the government can borrow and lend across international borders.

Review Questions

7.1 Why is exchange-rate stability important?

7.2 What are the benefits of monetary policy independence?

7.3 Why are free capital flows desirable?

7.4 What is the policy trilemma?

7.5 A fixed exchange rate creates exchange-rate stability. What is the primary disadvantage of a fixed exchange rate?

7.6 Why would a country want to institute capital controls?

Problems and Applications

7.7 Because the Fed is not constrained by a fixed exchange rate, it is free to set monetary policy without concerns about the effect on the value of the dollar.

a. How would the Fed's actions during the 2007–2009 financial crisis have been constrained if the exchange rate had been fixed?

b. The value of the dollar actually increased at some points during the 2007–2009 recession. Is this increase the result you would have expected? If not, how can you explain this increase ?

7.8 Suppose that a country has a fixed exchange rate and no capital controls. Due to a political crisis, projections for economic growth in coming years are revised sharply downward. As a result of the new projections, savers wish to purchase financial assets in other countries.

a. What is the likely effect of having savers purchase foreign assets on the ability of the country to maintain its exchange rate?

b. How would the situation be different if there were a flexible exchange rate?

c. Would capital controls be desirable in this situation? What if there were a flexible rate?

7.9 Capital flows can cause problems for exchange-rate stability.

a. Why do countries allow the free movement of capital?

b. Are some countries more likely to allow the free movement of capital than other countries? Briefly explain.

7.10 The United States has chosen to have free capital mobility and monetary policy independence. Does this mean that the value of the dollar is not stable? Briefly explain.

7.11 China has chosen to have exchange-rate stability and monetary policy independence, although the yuan may be allowed to float freely in the near future.

a. What are the advantages to China having a fixed exchange-rate system and monetary policy independence?

b. When a country, such as China, prevents the free flow of capital then it must impose capital controls to prevent capital from suddenly leaving a country. Is this the case in China? If not, explain why China has capital controls.

7.12 In the wake of the Japanese earthquake and tsunami in March 2011, the value of the yen increased sharply. According to the *Economist*: "The Bank of Japan tried to counteract that process, easing monetary policy in a bid both to support the markets and to prevent rapid yen strengthening from damaging the prospects of exporters."

a. What dilemmas do Japanese monetary authorities face in this situation?

b. At the same time, the values of both U.S. and Japanese bonds rose. Why do you think this happened at the same time that the yen was strengthening?

Source: "Aftershocks," *Economist*, March 17, 2011.

DATA EXERCISES

D15.1: The trade-weighted value of the dollar (that is, the trade-weighted exchange index) can be found in the St. Louis Fed's database (research.stlouisfed.org).

a. How has the value of the dollar changed over the past decade?

b. Would you characterize the exchange rate as stable or unstable? Briefly explain.

c. What impact would you expect the changes in the value of the dollar to have on U.S. trade?

D15.2: Return to the St. Louis Fed database (research.stlouisfed.org), and consider data on the current account. How do current account movements correspond with the exchange-rate movements you studied in the exercise D15.1?

D15.3: The U.S. Treasury publishes data on capital flows. Treasury International Capital Flows can be found at www.treasury.gov/resource-center/data-chart-center/tic/Pages/index.aspx. Go to U.S. Transactions in long-term securities.

a. Look at recent net purchases of long-term securities. How have purchases of securities changed?

b. Return to the previous page and look at gross purchases of long-term securities. Which countries hold the most U.S. securities? How have foreign holdings of U.S. securities changed over time?

D15.4: **[Excel question]** The Bank for International Settlements (BIS) publishes data on real and nominal effective exchange rates (www.bis.org/statistics/eer/index.htm). This index attempts to measure competitiveness.

a. Find and download the real and nominal effective exchange rate for the Chinese yuan for the past five years.

b. Plot the two series against each other.

c. The nominal effective exchange rate of the yuan changes little because it is a fixed rate. How is the real effective exchange rate different from this? What accounts for these differences? (Hint: It may be helpful to read the BIS explanation of its indexes of competitiveness.)

Glossary

Actual real interest rate: The nominal interest rate minus the actual inflation rate. *(p. 202)*

Adaptive expectations: The assumption that people make forecasts of future values of a variable using only past values of the variable. *(p. 332)*

Adverse selection: The situation where one party to a transaction takes advantage of knowing more than the other party. *(p. 68)*

Aggregate demand: The level of planned aggregate expenditure in the economy. *(p. 449)*

Aggregate demand (*AD*) curve: A curve that shows the relationship between aggregate expenditure on goods and services by households and firms and the inflation rate. *(p. 451)*

Aggregate demand and aggregate supply (*AD–AS*) model: A model that explains short-run fluctuations in the output gap and the inflation rate. *(p. 459)*

Aggregate production function: An equation that shows the relationship between the inputs employed by firms and the maximum output firms can produce with those inputs. *(p. 107)*

Aggregate supply: The total quantity of goods and services that firms are willing to supply. *(p. 449)*

Aggregate supply (*AS*) curve: A curve showing the total quantity of output, or real GDP, that firms are willing and able to supply at a given inflation rate. *(p. 456)*

Animal spirits: Periods of irrational pessimism and optimism that affect the investment behavior of firms. *(p. 541)*

Asset: Anything of value owned by a person or a firm. *(p. 61)*

Asymmetric information: A situation in which one party to an economic transaction has better information than does the other party. *(pp. 68, 383,* and *523)*

Automatic stabilizers: Taxes, transfer payments, or government expenditure that automatically increase or decrease along with the business cycle. *(p. 414)*

Balanced growth: A situation in which the capital–labor ratio and real GDP per hour worked grow at the same rate. *(p. 168)*

Balance-of-payments accounts: A measure of all flows of private and government funds between a domestic economy and all foreign countries. *(p. 562)*

Bank panic: A situation in which many banks simultaneously experience runs. *(p. 69)*

Bank run: The process by which depositors who have lost confidence in a bank simultaneously withdraw enough funds to force the bank to close. *(pp. 69* and *365)*

Board of Governors: The governing board of the Federal Reserve System, consisting of seven members appointed by the president of the United States. *(p. 366)*

Bond: A financial security issued by a corporation or government that represents a promise to repay a fixed amount of funds. *(p. 61)*

Bubble: A situation in which the price of an asset rises significantly above the asset's fundamental value; an unsustainable increase in the price of a class of assets. *(p. 66)*

Budget deficit: The situation in which the government's expenditure is greater than its tax revenue. *(pp. 414* and *488)*

Budget surplus: The situation in which the government's expenditure is less than its tax revenue. *(p. 414)*

Business cycle: Alternating periods of economic expansion and economic recession. *(pp. 2* and *273)*

Capital: Goods, such as machine tools, computers, factories, and office buildings, that are used to produce other goods and services. *(p. 27)*

Capital account: The part of the balance of payments that records (generally) minor transactions, such as migrants' transfers, and sales and purchases of non-produced, nonfinancial assets. *(p. 562)*

Capital–labor ratio: The dollar value of capital goods per unit of labor; measured as either the dollar value of capital divided by the total number of hours worked, or as the dollar value of capital divided by the total number of workers. *(p. 123)*

Central bank credibility: The degree to which households and firms believe the central bank's announcements about future policy. *(p. 470)*

Classical dichotomy: The assertion that in the long run, nominal variables, such as the money supply or the price level, do not affect real variables, such as the levels of employment or real GDP. *(p. 256)*

Classical economics: The perspective that business cycles can be explained using equilibrium analysis. *(p. 273)*

Closed economy: An economy in which households, firms, and governments do not borrow, lend, and trade internationally. *(p. 561)*

Cobb–Douglas production function: A production function that takes the form $Y = AK^{\alpha}L^{1-\alpha}$. *(p. 108)*

Coincident indicators: Economic variables that tend to rise and fall at the same time as real GDP. *(p. 288)*

Commodity money: A good used as money that has value independent of its use as money. *(p. 190)*

Constant returns to scale: A property of a production function such that if all inputs increase by the same percentage, real GDP increases by the same percentage. *(p. 107)*

Consumer price index (CPI): An average of the prices of the goods and services purchased by the typical urban family of four. *(p. 42)*

Consumption: The purchase of new goods and services by households. *(p. 29)*

Countercyclical variable: An economic variable that moves in the opposite direction as real GDP—decreasing during expansions and increasing during recessions. *(p. 288)*

Credit rationing: The restriction of credit by lenders such that borrowers cannot obtain the funds they desire at a given interest rate. *(p. 523)*

Crowding out: The reduction in private investment that results from an increase in government purchases. *(pp. 79, 434, and 499)*

Currency appreciation: An increase in the market value of one country's currency relative to another country's currency. *(p. 569)*

Currency board: A fixed exchange-rate system in which the central bank or government maintains complete convertibility of the domestic currency to an anchor currency of another nation. *(p. 573)*

Currency depreciation: A decrease in the market value of one country's currency relative to another country's currency. *(p. 569)*

Current account: The part of the balance of payments that records a country's net exports, net investment income, and net transfers. *(p. 562)*

Cyclical unemployment: Unemployment caused by a recession; measured as the difference between the actual level of unemployment and the level of unemployment when the unemployment rate equals the natural rate of unemployment. *(p. 243)*

Cyclical unemployment rate: The difference between the actual unemployment rate and the natural unemployment rate. *(p. 284)*

Cyclically adjusted budget deficit or surplus: The deficit or surplus in the federal government's budget if real GDP equaled potential GDP; also called the full-employment budget deficit or surplus. *(p. 417)*

Default risk: The risk that a borrower will fail to make payments of interest or principal. *(p. 314)*

Deflation: A sustained decrease in the price level. *(p. 7)*

Depreciation: The reduction in the capital stock that occurs either because capital goods become worn out by use or because they become obsolete. *(p. 154)*

Desired capital stock: The level of capital stock that maximizes a firm's profits. *(p. 539)*

Discount rate: The interest rate that the Federal Reserve charges on discount loans. *(p. 372)*

Discretionary fiscal policy: Government policy that involves deliberate changes in taxes, transfer payments, or government purchases to achieve macroeconomic policy objectives. *(p. 414)*

Disposable income: National income plus transfer payments minus personal tax payments. *(p. 410)*

Efficiency wage: A higher-than-market wage that a firm pays to motivate workers to be more productive. *(p. 254)*

Endogenous growth theory: A theory of economic growth that tries to explain the growth rate of total factor productivity. *(p. 182)*

Endogenous variable: A variable that is explained by an economic model. *(p. 14)*

Exogenous variable: A variable that is taken as given and is not explained by an economic model. *(p. 14)*

Expansion: The period of a business cycle during which real GDP and employment are increasing. *(p. 273)*

Expected real interest rate: The nominal interest rate minus the expected inflation rate. *(p. 202)*

Factor of production: Any input used to produce goods and services. *(p. 27)*

Federal funds rate: The interest rate that banks charge each other on short-term loans. *(p. 367)*

Federal Open Market Committee (FOMC): The 12-member Federal Reserve committee that directs open market operations. *(p. 367)*

Federal Reserve: The central bank of the United States; usually referred to as "the Fed." *(pp. 44 and 365)*

Federal Reserve System: The central bank of the United States; commonly referred to as "the Fed." *(p. 365)*

Fiat money: Money, such as paper currency, that has no value apart from its use as money. *(p. 191)*

Final good or service: A good or service purchased by a final user. *(p. 25)*

Financial account: The part of the balance of payments that records purchases of assets a country has made abroad and foreign purchases of assets in the country. *(p. 562)*

Financial asset: A financial claim. *(p. 61)*

Financial intermediary: An institution, such as a commercial bank, that borrows funds from savers to lend to borrowers. *(p. 61)*

Financial market: A place or channel for buying or selling stocks, bonds, or other financial securities. *(p. 61)*

Financial system: The financial intermediaries and financial markets that together facilitate the flow of funds from lenders to borrowers. *(pp. 27* and *60)*

Fiscal policy: Changes in government taxes, purchases of goods and services, and transfer payments intended to achieve macroeconomic policy objectives. *(pp. 9* and *408)*

Fisher effect: The assertion by Irving Fisher that the nominal interest rate rises or falls point-for-point with changes in the expected inflation rate. *(p. 203)*

Fisher equation: The equation stating that the nominal interest rate is the sum of the expected real interest rate and the expected inflation rate. *(p. 203)*

Fixed exchange-rate system: A system in which exchange rates are set at levels determined and maintained by governments. *(p. 573)*

Floating exchange-rate system: A system in which the foreign-exchange value of a currency is determined in the foreign-exchange market. *(p. 573)*

Frictional unemployment: Short-term unemployment that arises from the process of matching the job skills of workers to the requirements of jobs. *(p. 240)*

GDP deflator: A measure of the price level, calculated by dividing nominal GDP by real GDP and multiplying by 100; also called the GDP implicit price deflator. *(p. 35)*

Government purchases: Spending by federal, state, and local governments on newly produced goods and services. *(p. 30)*

Gross domestic product (GDP): The market value of all final goods and services produced in a country during a period of time. *(p. 25)*

Gross federal debt: The total dollar value of Treasury bonds and other federal agency bonds plus the dollar value of the small amount of bonds and other securities issued by other federal agencies. *(p. 490)*

Gross federal debt held by the public: Debt that includes the bonds and other securities issued by the U.S. Treasury (and a small amount of securities issued by federal agencies) not held by the federal government; also called national debt. *(pp. 419* and *488)*

Gross national product (GNP): The value of final goods and services produced by residents of a country, even if the production takes place outside that country. *(p. 33)*

Human capital: The accumulated knowledge and skills that workers acquire from education and training or from life experiences. *(p. 165)*

Hyperinflation: Extremely high rates of inflation, exceeding 50% or more per month. *(p. 191)*

Impact lag: The period of time between a policy change and the effect of that policy change. *(p. 386)*

Implementation lag: The period of time between when policymakers recognize that a shock has occurred and when they adjust policy to the shock. *(p. 386)*

Inflation rate: The percentage increase in the price level from one year to the next. *(p. 7)*

Interest rate: The cost of borrowing funds, usually expressed as a percentage of the amount borrowed. *(p. 45)*

Interest-rate risk: The risk that the price of a financial asset will fluctuate in response to changes in market interest rates. *(p. 92)*

Intermediate good or service: A good or service that is an input into another good or service, such as a tire on a truck. *(p. 25)*

Intertemporal budget constraint: A budget constraint that applies to consumption and income in more than one time period; it tells us how much a household can consume, given lifetime income. *(p. 527)*

Investment: Spending by firms on new factories, office buildings, machinery, and additions to inventories, plus spending by households and firms on new houses. *(p. 29)*

***IS* curve:** A curve in the *IS–MP* model that shows the combination of the real interest rate and aggregate output that represents equilibrium in the market for goods and services. *(p. 304)*

***IS–LM* model:** A macroeconomic model that assumes that the central bank targets the money supply. *(p. 353)*

***IS–MP* model:** A macroeconomic model consisting of an *IS* curve, which represents equilibrium in the goods market; an *MP* curve, which represents monetary policy; and a Phillips curve, which represents the short-run relationship between the output gap (which is the percentage difference between actual and potential real GDP) and the inflation rate. *(p. 304)*

Keynesian economics: The perspective that business cycles represent disequilibrium or nonmarket-clearing behavior. *(p. 273)*

Labor force: The sum of employed and unemployed workers in the economy. *(pp. 6* and *47)*

Labor productivity: The quantity of goods and services that can be produced by one worker or by one hour of work. *(p. 2)*

Lagging indicators: Economic variables that tend to rise and fall after real GDP. *(p. 289)*

Leading indicators: Economic variables that tend to rise and fall in advance of real GDP. *(p. 288)*

Life-cycle hypothesis: The theory that households use financial markets to borrow and save to transfer funds from high-income periods, such as working years, to low-income periods, such as retirement years or periods of unemployment. *(p. 528)*

Liquidity: The ease with which an asset can be exchanged for cash. *(p. 66)*

***LM* curve:** A curve that shows the combinations of the real interest rate and output that result in equilibrium in the market for money. *(p. 353)*

Long-run economic growth: The process by which increasing productivity raises the average standard of living. *(p. 2)*

M1: A narrower measure of the money supply: The sum of currency in circulation, checking account deposits, and holdings of traveler's checks. *(p. 193)*

M2: A broader measure of the money supply: All the assets that are included in M1, as well as time deposits with a value of less than $100,000, savings accounts, money market deposit accounts at banks, and noninstitutional money market mutual fund shares. *(p. 193)*

Macroeconomic shock: An unexpected exogenous event that has a significant effect on an important sector of the economy or on the economy as a whole. *(p. 274)*

Macroeconomics: The study of the economy as a whole, including topics such as inflation, unemployment, and economic growth. *(p. 2)*

Managed float exchange-rate system: An exchange-rate system in which central banks occasionally intervene to affect foreign-exchange values; also called a *dirty float regime*. *(p. 574)*

Marginal product of capital (*MPK*): The extra output a firm receives from adding one more unit of capital, holding all other inputs and efficiency constant. *(pp. 109* and *540)*

Marginal product of labor (*MPL*): The extra output a firm receives from adding one more unit of labor, holding all other inputs and efficiency constant. *(pp. 111* and *233)*

Marginal propensity to consume (*MPC*): The slope of the consumption function: The amount by which consumption increases when disposable income increases by $1. *(pp. 306* and *529)*

Medium of exchange: Something that is generally accepted as payment for goods and services; a function of money. *(p. 190)*

Menu costs: The costs to firms of changing prices due to reprinting price lists, informing customers, and angering customers; costs related to expected inflation. *(pp. 207* and *275)*

Microeconomics: The study of how households and firms make choices, how they interact in markets, and how the government attempts to influence their choices. *(p. 2)*

Monetary base (or high-powered money): The sum of currency in circulation and bank reserves. *(p. 195)*

Monetary policy: The actions that central banks take to manage the money supply and interest rates to pursue macroeconomic policy objectives. *(pp. 9* and *365)*

Monetary policy rule: A rule or formula that a central bank uses to set interest rates in response to changing economic conditions; the rule is publicly announced. *(pp. 450* and *472)*

Money multiplier: The number indicating how much the money supply increases when the monetary base increases by $1. *(p. 195)*

Moral hazard: Actions people take after they have entered into a transaction that make the other party to the transaction worse off; in financial markets, the problem investors experience in verifying that borrowers are using their funds as intended. *(pp. 68* and *393)*

***MP* curve:** A curve in the *IS–MP* model that represents Federal Reserve monetary policy. *(p. 304)*

Multiplier: The change in equilibrium GDP divided by the change in autonomous expenditure. *(p. 308)*

Multiplier effect: A series of induced increases (or decreases) in consumption spending that results from an initial increase (or decrease) in autonomous expenditure; this effect amplifies the effect of economic shocks on real GDP. *(pp. 290* and *308)*

National income accounting: The rules used in calculating GDP and related measures of total production and total income. *(p. 26)*

Natural rate of unemployment: The normal rate of unemployment, consisting of frictional unemployment plus structural unemployment. *(p. 243)*

Net capital outflows: Capital outflows minus capital inflows. *(p. 565)*

Net exports: The value of all exports minus the value of all imports. *(p. 33)*

Nominal exchange rate: The price of one currency in terms of another currency; also called the *exchange rate*. *(p. 562)*

Nominal GDP: The value of final goods and services calculated using current-year prices. *(p. 33)*

Nominal interest rate: The stated interest rate on a loan. *(p. 45)*

Normative analysis: Analysis concerned with what ought to be. *(p. 14)*

Okun's law: A statistical relationship discovered by Arthur Okun between the cyclical unemployment rate and the output gap. *(p. 284)*

Open economy: An economy in which households, firms, and governments borrow, lend, and trade internationally. *(p. 561)*

Open market operations: The Federal Reserve's purchases and sales of securities, usually U.S. Treasury securities, in financial markets. *(pp. 195* and *367)*

Output gap: The percentage deviation of actual real GDP from potential GDP. *(p. 282)*

Permanent income: Income that households expect to receive each year. *(p. 527)*

Permanent-income hypothesis: The hypothesis that household consumption depends on permanent income and that households use financial markets to save and borrow to smooth consumption in response to fluctuations in transitory income. *(p. 527)*

Personal consumption expenditures (PCE) price index: A price index similar to the GDP deflator, except that it includes only the prices of goods from the consumption category of GDP. *(p. 44)*

Phillips curve: A curve that represents the short-run relationship between the output gap (or the unemployment rate) and the inflation rate. *(p. 304)*

Policy trilemma: The hypothesis that it is impossible for a country to have exchange-rate stability, monetary policy independence, and free capital flows at the same time. *(p. 590)*

Positive analysis: Analysis concerned with what is. *(p. 14)*

Potential GDP: The level of real GDP attained when firms are producing at capacity and labor is fully employed. *(p. 273)*

Precautionary saving: Extra saving by households to protect themselves from unexpected decreases in future income due to job loss, illness, or disability. *(p. 537)*

Present value: The value today of funds that will be received in the future. *(p. 85)*

Primary budget deficit (*PD*): The difference between government purchases of goods and services plus transfer payments minus tax revenue. *(p. 488)*

Procyclical variable: An economic variable that moves in the same direction as real GDP—increasing during expansions and decreasing during recessions. *(p. 288)*

Profit: Total revenue minus total cost. *(p. 116)*

Purchasing power parity: The theory that, in the long run, nominal exchange rates adjust to equalize the purchasing power of different currencies. *(p. 571)*

Quantitative easing: A central bank policy that attempts to stimulate the economy by buying long-term securities. *(p. 384)*

Quantity equation (or equation of exchange): An identity that states that the money supply multiplied by the velocity of money equals the price level multiplied by real GDP. *(p. 197)*

Quantity theory of money: A theory about the connection between money and prices that assumes that the velocity of money is constant. *(p. 198)*

Rational expectations: The assumption that people make forecasts of future values of a variable using all available information; formally, the assumption that expectations equal optimal forecasts, using all available information. *(p. 469)*

Real exchange rate: The rate at which goods and services in one country can be exchanged for goods and services in another country. *(p. 570)*

Real GDP: The value of final goods and services calculated using base-year prices. *(p. 33)*

Real gross domestic product (GDP): The value of final goods and services, adjusted for changes in the price level. *(p. 4)*

Real interest rate: The nominal interest rate adjusted for the effects of inflation. *(p. 46)*

Recession: The period of a business cycle during which real GDP and employment are decreasing. *(p. 273)*

Recognition lag: The period of time between when a shock occurs and when policymakers recognize that the shock has occurred. *(p. 386)*

Reserve requirements: Regulations that require banks to hold a fraction of checking account deposits as vault cash or deposits with the Fed. *(p. 372)*

Reserves: A bank asset consisting of vault cash plus bank deposits with the Federal Reserve. *(p. 195)*

Ricardian equivalence: The theory that forward-looking households fully anticipate the taxes implied by government spending, so that changes in lump-sum taxes have no effect on the economy. *(p. 503)*

Risk: The degree of uncertainty in the return on an asset. *(p. 66)*

Risk structure of interest rates: The relationship among interest rates on bonds that have different characteristics but the same maturity. *(pp. 90* and *313)*

Securitization: The process of converting loans and other financial assets that are not tradable into securities. *(p. 67)*

Seigniorage: The government's profit from issuing fiat money; also called inflation tax. *(pp. 206* and *488)*

Shoe-leather costs: The costs of inflation to households and firms from holding less money and making more frequent trips to the bank; costs related to expected inflation. *(p. 207)*

Stagflation: A combination of high inflation and recession, usually resulting from a supply shock such as an increase in the price of oil. *(pp. 331* and *459)*

Standard of deferred payment: An asset that facilitates transactions over time; a function of money. *(p. 191)*

Steady state: An equilibrium in the Solow growth model in which the capital–labor ratio and real GDP per hour worked are constant but capital, labor, and output are growing. *(p. 154)*

Stock: A financial security that represents a legal claim on a share in the profits and assets of a firm. *(p. 61)*

Store of value: The accumulation of wealth by holding dollars or other assets that can be used to buy goods and services in the future; a function of money. *(p. 190)*

Structural unemployment: Unemployment that arises from a persistent mismatch between the job skills or attributes of workers and the requirements of jobs. *(p. 241)*

Tax wedge: The difference between the before-tax and after-tax return to an economic activity. *(p. 431)*

Tax-adjusted user cost of capital: The after-tax expected real cost to a firm of purchasing and using an additional unit of capital during a period of time. *(p. 543)*

Taylor rule: A monetary policy guideline developed by economist John Taylor for determining the target for the federal funds rate. *(p. 473)*

Term premium: The additional interest investors require in order to be willing to buy a long-term bond rather than a comparable sequence of short-term bonds. *(pp. 92* and *313)*

Term structure of interest rates: The relationship among the interest rates on bonds that are otherwise similar but that have different maturities. *(pp. 90* and *313)*

Time-inconsistency problem: The tendency of policymakers to announce one policy in advance in order to change the expectations of households and firms and then to follow a second policy after households and firms have made economic decisions based on the first policy. *(p. 475)*

Tobin's *q*: The ratio of the market value of a firm to the replacement cost of its capital. *(p. 548)*

Too-big-to-fail policy: A policy in which the federal government does not allow large financial firms to fail for fear of damaging the financial system. *(p. 393)*

Total factor productivity (*TFP*): An index of the overall level of efficiency of transforming capital and labor into real GDP. *(p. 108)*

Transfer payments: Payments by the government to individuals for which the government does not receive a good or service in return. *(p. 31)*

Transitory income: Income that households do not expect to receive each year. *(p. 527)*

Unemployment insurance: A government program that allows workers to receive benefits for a period of time after losing their jobs. *(p. 241)*

Unemployment rate: The percentage of the labor force that is unemployed. *(pp. 6 and 47)*

Unit of account: A way of measuring value in an economy in terms of money; a function of money. *(p. 190)*

User cost of capital (*uc*): The expected real cost to a firm of using an additional unit of capital during a period of time. *(p. 541)*

Velocity of money: The average number of times each dollar in the money supply is used to purchase goods and services included in GDP. *(p. 198)*

Index

THE PEARSON SERIES IN ECONOMICS

Abel/Bernanke/Croushore
*Macroeconomics**

Bade/Parkin
*Foundations of Economics**

Berck/Helfand
The Economics of the Environment

Bierman/Fernandez
Game Theory with Economic Applications

Blanchard
*Macroeconomics**

Blau/Ferber/Winkler
The Economics of Women, Men and Work

Boardman/Greenberg/Vining/Weimer
Cost-Benefit Analysis

Boyer
Principles of Transportation Economics

Branson
Macroeconomic Theory and Policy

Brock/Adams
The Structure of American Industry

Bruce
Public Finance and the American Economy

Carlton/Perloff
Modern Industrial Organization

Case/Fair/Oster
*Principles of Economics**

Caves/Frankel/Jones
World Trade and Payments: An Introduction

Chapman
Environmental Economics: Theory, Application, and Policy

Cooter/Ulen
Law & Economics

Downs
An Economic Theory of Democracy

Ehrenberg/Smith
Modern Labor Economics

Ekelund/Ressler/Tollison
*Economics**

Farnham
Economics for Managers

Folland/Goodman/Stano
The Economics of Health and Health Care

Fort
Sports Economics

Froyen
Macroeconomics

Fusfeld
The Age of the Economist

Gerber
*International Economics**

Gordon
*Macroeconomics**

Greene
Econometric Analysis

Gregory
Essentials of Economics

Gregory/Stuart
Russian and Soviet Economic Performance and Structure

Hartwick/Olewiler
The Economics of Natural Resource Use

Heilbroner/Milberg
The Making of the Economic Society

Heyne/Boettke/Prychitko
The Economic Way of Thinking

Hoffman/Averett
Women and the Economy: Family, Work, and Pay

Holt
Markets, Games and Strategic Behavior

Hubbard/O'Brien
*Economics**

*Money, Banking, and the Financial System**

Hubbard/O'Brien/Rafferty
*Macroeconomics**

Hughes/Cain
American Economic History

Husted/Melvin
International Economics

Jehle/Reny
Advanced Microeconomic Theory

Johnson-Lans
A Health Economics Primer

Keat/Young
Managerial Economics

Klein
Mathematical Methods for Economics

Krugman/Obstfeld/Melitz
*International Economics: Theory & Policy**

Laidler
The Demand for Money

Leeds/von Allmen
The Economics of Sports

Leeds/von Allmen/Schiming
*Economics**

Lipsey/Ragan/Storer
*Economics**

Lynn
Economic Development: Theory and Practice for a Divided World

Miller
*Economics Today**

Understanding Modern Economics

Miller/Benjamin
The Economics of Macro Issues

Miller/Benjamin/North
The Economics of Public Issues

Mills/Hamilton
Urban Economics

Mishkin
*The Economics of Money, Banking, and Financial Markets**

*The Economics of Money, Banking, and Financial Markets, Business School Edition**

*Macroeconomics: Policy and Practice**

Murray
Econometrics: A Modern Introduction

Nafziger
The Economics of Developing Countries

O'Sullivan/Sheffrin/Perez
*Economics: Principles, Applications and Tools**

Parkin
*Economics**

Perloff
*Microeconomics**

*Microeconomics: Theory and Applications with Calculus**

Perman/Common/McGilvray/Ma
Natural Resources and Environmental Economics

Phelps
Health Economics

Pindyck/Rubinfeld
*Microeconomics**

Riddell/Shackelford/Stamos/ Schneider
Economics: A Tool for Critically Understanding Society

Ritter/Silber/Udell
*Principles of Money, Banking & Financial Markets**

Roberts
The Choice: A Fable of Free Trade and Protection

Rohlf
Introduction to Economic Reasoning

Ruffin/Gregory
Principles of Economics

Sargent
Rational Expectations and Inflation

Sawyer/Sprinkle
International Economics

Scherer
Industry Structure, Strategy, and Public Policy

Schiller
The Economics of Poverty and Discrimination

Sherman
Market Regulation

Silberberg
Principles of Microeconomics

Stock/Watson
Introduction to Econometrics

Introduction to Econometrics, Brief Edition

Studenmund
Using Econometrics: A Practical Guide

Tietenberg/Lewis
Environmental and Natural Resource Economics

Environmental Economics and Policy

Todaro/Smith
Economic Development

Waldman
Microeconomics

Waldman/Jensen
Industrial Organization: Theory and Practice

Weil
Economic Growth

Williamson
Macroeconomics

* denotes myeconlab titles

Key Symbols and Abbreviations

π_t: Current inflation rate
π_t^e: Expected inflation rate
α: Capital's share in national income
$1 - \alpha$: Labor's share in national income
A: Index of how efficiently the economy transforms capital and labor into real GDP; total factor productivity
AD: Aggregate demand curve
AE: Aggregate expenditure
AS: Aggregate supply curve
B: U.S. Treasury bonds
C: Personal consumption expenditures
C: Currency in circulation
CA: Current account balance
CPI: Consumer price index
D: Checking account deposits
d: Depreciation rate
DP: Default-risk premium
ER: Excess reserves
f: Rate of job finding
G: Government purchases
g_A: Growth rate of total factor productivity
g_K: Growth rate of the capital stock
g_L: Growth rate of labor hours
I: Investment or gross private domestic investment
i: Nominal interest rate
i: Investment per hour worked
i_{Target}: Target for the nominal federal funds rate
i_{LT}: Long-term nominal interest rate
IS curve: Equilibrium in the goods market; shows the equilibrium combinations of the real interest rate and real GDP (or the output gap)
K: Quantity of capital goods available to firms, or the capital stock
k: Capital per hour worked, or the capital–labor ratio
k^*: Steady-state capital–labor ratio
L: Quantity of labor
LM curve: Equilibrium in the market for money; shows the equilibrium combinations of the real interest rate and the output gap
M: Money supply
MB: Monetary base
m: Money multiplier
M1: A narrower measure of the money supply
M2: A broader measure of the money supply
M: Sum of currency in circulation, *C*, and checking account deposits, *D*
MP curve: Monetary policy curve
MPC: Marginal propensity to consume
MPK: Marginal product of capital
MPL: Marginal product of labor
NCF: Net capital outflows
NX: Net exports of goods and services
P: Price level
PCE: Personal consumption expenditures price index
r: Real interest rate, or real rental price of capital
r^*: Long-run equilibrium real federal funds rate
rr_D: Required reserve ratio
R: Nominal rental cost of capital
R: Bank reserves
RR: Required bank reserves
s: Rate of job separation
s: Saving rate
$S_{Foreign}$: Saving from the foreign sector
$S_{Government}$: Saving from the government
$S_{Household}$: Saving from households
s_t: Effects of a supply shock
sy: Investment per hour worked
T: Taxes
TR: Transfer payments
TSE: Term structure effect
U_t: Current unemployment rate
U^N: Natural rate of unemployment
W: Nominal wage
w: Real wage
Y: Real GDP; also total income
y: Real GDP per hour worked
$\tilde{Y}$: Output gap
Y^D: Disposable income

Equations

Actual real interest rate: Actual $r = i - \pi$	Chapter 6, page 202
Aggregate Expenditure (*AE*): $C + I + G + NX$	Chapter 9, page 304
Basic growth accounting equation: $g_Y = g_A + \left(\frac{1}{3}\right)g_K + \left(\frac{2}{3}\right)g_L$	Chapter 4, page 121
Break-even investment: Depreciation + Dilution $= dk + nk = (d + n)k$	Chapter 5, page 154
Budget deficit: $PD_t + i_tB_{t-1} = \Delta B_t + \Delta MB_t$	Chapter 13, page 488
Budget deficits and private behavior: $[(G + TR) - T] = S_{Household} - I - NX$	Chapter 13, page 499
Capital–labor ratio: $k = \frac{K}{L}$	Chapter 4, page 123
Cobb–Douglas production function (real GDP): $Y = AK^{\alpha}L^{1-\alpha}$	Chapter 4, page 108
Cobb–Douglas production function (U.S. data): $Y = AK^{\frac{1}{3}}L^{\frac{2}{3}}$	Chapter 4, page 108
Cobb–Douglas production function (real GDP per hour worked): $y = Ak^{\frac{1}{3}}$	Chapter 4, page 123
Consumption function: $C = \overline{C} + MPC \times Y^D$	Chapter 9, page 305
Current account and net capital outflows: $CA = NCF$	Chapter 15, page 565
Expenditure multiplier: $\frac{\Delta Y}{\Delta \text{ Autonomous expenditure}} = \frac{1}{(1 - MPC)}$	Chapter 9, page 308
Expected inflation rate: $\pi^e = i - r$	Chapter 2, page 46 Chapter 2, page 46
Expected real interest rate: Expected $r = i - \pi^e$	Chapter 6, page 202
GDP: GNP + Net factor payments	Chapter 2, page 33
Inflation rate: Inflation rate $= \pi_{t+1} = \frac{P_{t+1} - P_t}{P_t} \times 100$	Chapter 2, page 36
Investment per hour worked: $i = sy$	Chapter 5, page 153
Investment and sources of funds: $I = S_{Household} + S_{Government} - NCF$	Chapter 15, page 566
Fiscal Policy sustainability 1: $\Delta\left(\frac{B_t}{P_tY_t}\right) = \frac{PD_t}{P_tY_t} + [i_t - (\pi_t + g_Y)]\frac{B_{t-1}}{P_{t-1}Y_{t-1}} - \frac{\Delta MB_t}{P_tY_t}$	Chapter 13, page 495
Fiscal Policy sustainability 2: $\Delta\left(\frac{B_t}{P_tY_t}\right) = \frac{PD_t}{P_tY_t} + (r_t - g_Y)\frac{B_{t-1}}{P_{t-1}Y_{t-1}} - \frac{\Delta MB_t}{P_tY_t}$	Chapter 13, page 496
Government budget constraint: $G_t + TR_t + i_tB_{t-1} = T_t + \Delta B_t + \Delta MB_t$	Chapter 13, page 488
GDP deflator: GDP deflator $= \frac{\text{Nominal GDP}}{\text{Real GDP}} \times 100$	Chapter 2, page 35
Growth accounting equation for real GDP (absolute): $g_Y = g_A + \left(\frac{1}{3}\right)g_K + \left(\frac{2}{3}\right)g_L$	Chapter 4, page 121
Growth accounting equation for real GDP (relative share): $1 = \left(\frac{g_A}{g_Y}\right) + \left(\frac{1}{3}\right)\left(\frac{g_K}{g_Y}\right) + \left(\frac{2}{3}\right)\left(\frac{g_L}{g_Y}\right)$	Chapter 4, page 122